THE EARTH AND ITS PEOPLES

A GLOBAL HISTORY

THE EARTH AND ITS PEOPLES

A GLOBAL HISTORY

BRIEF SECOND EDITION

Richard W. Bulliet
Columbia University

Pamela Kyle Crossley
Dartmouth College

Daniel R. Headrick
Roosevelt University

Steven W. Hirsch
Tufts University

Lyman L. Johnson
University of North Carolina–Charlotte

David Northrup
Boston College

Houghton Mifflin Company   Boston   New York

Editor-in-chief: Jean L. Woy
Senior sponsoring editor: Nancy Blaine
Senior project editor: Carol Newman
Editorial assistant: Reba Frederics
Senior designer: Henry Rachlin
Senior production/design coordinator: Jill Haber
Manufacturing manager: Florence Cadran
Senior marketing manager: Sandra McGuire

Cover image: *Basket Ferry, Hida Province, Japan.* Print by Kago Watashi/Superstock.

Printed in the U.S.A.

Library of Congress Catalog Card Number: 2001097076

ISBN: 0-618-21463-1

1 2 3 4 5 6 7 8 9-DC-06 05 04 03 02

BRIEF CONTENTS

CONTENTS

PART FOUR

INTERREGIONAL PATTERNS OF CULTURE AND CONTACT, 1200–1550

259

PART FIVE

THE GLOBE ENCOMPASSED, 1500–1800

361

PART SIX

REVOLUTIONS RESHAPE
THE WORLD,
1750–1870
441

MAPS

ENVIRONMENT AND TECHNOLOGY

SOCIETY AND CULTURE

PREFACE

When we, the authors of *The Earth and Its Peoples,* received our first copies of its first edition in 1997, we breathed a collective sigh of deep relief. Merging six perspectives on world history into a single integrated global history had not been easy, nor had it been painless. But we had accomplished it.

Fortunately, none of us then realized how much we would have to rethink and reengineer to produce a second edition. As classroom teachers around the country used our book, they spotted many opportunities, both great and small, for improvement. These responses became our mandate for preparing a second edition, and our relief on accomplishing that task was no less heartfelt than it had been four years earlier.

But what of the Brief Edition that had succeeded and been based on our first edition? No one believed that minor amendments here and there would suffice. Thus we decided that nothing short of a completely new abridgement would do. And our heightened awareness of the needs of instructors and students steeled our determination to put full authorial effort into the job.

The Brief Edition is designed for a range of instructor choices. For those instructors who choose to assign a large amount of supplementary reading, the briefer narrative will provide the backbone of the story. The shorter narrative accommodates the needs of a quarter semester world history survey. It is also perfect for those instructors who prefer to assign less reading to students in general. The Brief Edition is produced in two formats: A complete edition covers the entire chronology from prehistory to the present, and a two-volume edition can be used for the two-semester survey. Volume I covers the period from prehistory to 1550 and Volume II covers 1500 to the present. There is a brief introduction to Volume II that orients students to the general political and social climate of the world at 1500.

Our overall goal, however, remains unchanged: to produce a textbook that not only speaks for the past, but speaks to today's student and today's teacher. Students and instructors alike should take away from this text a broad vision of human societies beginning as sparse and disconnected communities reacting creatively to local circumstances; experiencing ever more intensive stages of contact, interpenetration, and cultural expansion and amalgamation; and arriving at a twenty-first century world situation in which people increasingly visualize a single global community.

Process, not progress, is the keynote of this book: a steady process of change over time, at first differently experienced in various regions, but eventually interconnecting peoples and traditions from all parts of the globe. Students should come away from this book with a sense that the problems and promises of their world are rooted in a past in which people of every sort, in every part of the world, confronted problems of a similar character and coped with them as best they could. We believe our efforts will help students see where their world has come from and learn thereby something useful for their own lives.

CENTRAL THEMES

We have subtitled *The Earth and Its Peoples* "A Global History" because the book explores the common challenges and experiences that unite the human past. Although the dispersal of early humans to every liveable environment resulted in a myriad different economic, social, political, and cultural systems, all societies displayed analogous patterns in meeting their needs and exploiting their environments. Our challenge was to select the particular data and episodes that would best illuminate these global patterns of human experience.

To meet this challenge, we adopted two themes to serve as the spinal cord of our history: "technology and the environment," and "authority and diversity." The former represents the commonplace material bases of all human societies at all times. It grants no special favor to any cultural group even as it embraces subjects of the broadest topical, chronological, and geographical range. The latter expresses the reality that every human society has constructed or inherited structures of authority, whether political, religious, or cultural, but simultaneously recognizes that alternative lifestyles and visions of societal organization continually manifest themselves both within and in dialogue with every structure of authority.

With respect to "technology and the environment," it is vital for students to understand that technology, in the broad sense of experience-based knowledge of the physical world, underlies all human activity. Writing is a technology, but so is oral transmission from generation to generation of lore about medicinal or poisonous plants. The magnetic compass is a navigational technology, but so is a Polynesian mariner's hard-won knowledge of winds, currents, and tides that made possible the settlement of the Pacific islands.

All technological development, moreover, has come about in interaction with environments, both physical and human, and has, in turn, affected those environments. The story of how humanity has changed the face of the globe is an integral part of this central theme.

Yet technology and the environment do not by themselves explain or underlie all important episodes of human change and experience. In keeping with the theme of "authority and diversity," discussions of politics, culture, and society interweave with our presentation of the material base of human society to reveal additional historical patterns. Thus when narrating the histories of empires, we describe a range of human experiences within and beyond the imperial frontiers without assuming that the imperial institutions are a more fit topic for discussion than the economic and social organization of pastoral nomads or the life patterns of peasant women. And when religious and cultural traditions occupy our narrative, our primary concern is to complement descriptive presentation with commentary on cultural alternatives within the societies in question.

CHANGES IN THE SECOND EDITION

While an entirely fresh abridgment, based on the second edition of the comprehensive version of *The Earth and Its Peoples,* is the hallmark of this second edition, the adoption of a full color format not only brightens the page but makes maps clearer and more effective. The opening pages of each part have similarly been reconceived to give students an instant geographic and chronological overview of what is to come. The timelines and world maps that now accompany the part-opening essay unify content while focusing student attention on broad themes and historical benchmarks. Consolidated timelines within each chapter enable students to see at a glance the sorts of comparisons being made in the text.

Guides to pronunciation of uncommon words and foreign terms, previously at the back of the book, have been moved to the bottom of each page. In the area of study aids, the key terms boldfaced in the text and listed at the end of each chapter are now defined in the glossary at the end of the book. In addition, two-to-four focus questions have been placed at the end of the vignette opening each chapter to draw student attention to the main themes of the chapter.

We believe that these unobtrusive changes will improve student understanding of the main narratives and make it easier to grasp the main points of each chapter, as well as to review for examinations.

ORGANIZATION

The Earth and Its Peoples, Brief Edition uses eight broad chronological divisions to define its conceptual scheme of global historical development. In **Part I: The Emergence of Human Communities, to 1500 B.C.E.,** we examine important patterns of human communal organization. Small, dispersed human communities living by foraging spread to most parts of the world over tens of thousands of years. They responded to enormously diverse environmental conditions, at different times and in different ways discovering how to cultivate plants and utilize the products of domestic animals. On the basis of these new modes of sustenance, population grows, permanent towns appear, and political and religious authority, based on collection and control of agricultural surpluses, spreads over extensive areas.

Part II: The Formation of New Cultural Communities, 1000 B.C.E.–550 C.E., introduces the concept of a "cultural community," in the sense of a coherent pattern of activities and symbols pertaining to a specific human community. While all human communities develop distinctive cultures, including those discussed in Part I, historical development in this stage of global history prolonged and magnified the impact of some cultures more than others. In the geographically contiguous African-Eurasian land mass, the cultures that proved to have the most enduring influence traced their roots to the second and first millennia B.C.E.

Part III: Growth and Interaction of Cultural Communities, 300 B.C.E.–1500 C.E., deals with early episodes of technological, social, and cultural exchange and interaction on a continental scale both within and beyond the framework of imperial expansion. These are so different from earlier interactions arising from more limited conquests or extensions of political boundaries that they constitute a distinct era in world history, an era that set the world on the path of increasing global interaction and interdependence that it has been following ever since.

In **Part IV: Interregional Patterns of Culture and Contact, 1200–1550,** we take a look at the world during three centuries that saw both intensified cultural and commercial contact and increasingly confident self-definition of cultural communities in Europe, Asia, and Africa. The Mongol conquest of a vast empire extending from the Pacific Ocean to eastern Europe greatly stimulated trade and interaction. In the West, strengthened European kingdoms began maritime expansion in the Atlantic, forging direct ties with sub-Saharan Africa and laying the base for expanded global contacts after 1500.

Part V: The Globe Encompassed, 1500–1800, treats a period dominated by the global effects of European expansion and continued economic growth. European ships took over, expanded, and extended the maritime trade of the Indian Ocean, coastal Africa, and the Asian rim of the Pacific Ocean. This maritime commercial enterprise had its counterpart in European colonial empires in the Americas and a new Atlantic trading system. The contrasting capacities and fortunes of traditional land empires and new maritime empires, along with the exchange of domestic plants and animals between the hemispheres, underline the technological and environmental dimensions of this first era of complete global interaction.

In **Part VI: Revolutions Reshape the World, 1750–1870,** the word revolution is used in several senses: in the political sense of governmental overthrow, as in France and the Americas; in the metaphorical sense of radical transformative change, as in the Industrial Revolution; and in the broadest sense of a perception of a profound change in circumstances and worldview. Technology and environment lie at the core of these developments. With the rapid ascendancy of the Western belief that science and technology could overcome all challenges, environmental or otherwise, technology became not only an instrument of transformation but also an instrument of domination, to the point of threatening the integrity and autonomy of cultural traditions in nonindustrial lands.

Part VII: Global Dominance and Diversity, 1850–1949, examines the development of a world arena in which people conceived of events on a global scale. Imperialism, world war, international economic connections, and world-encompassing ideological tendencies, like nationalism and socialism, present the picture of a globe becoming increasingly interconnected. European dominance took on a worldwide dimension, seeming at times to threaten the diversity of human cultural experience with permanent subordination to European values and philosophies, while at other times triggering strong political or cultural resistance. The accelerating pace of technological change deepened other sorts of cleavages as well.

For **Part VIII: The Perils and Promises of a Global Community, 1945–2001,** we decided to divide the last half of the twentieth century into three time periods: 1945–1975, 1975–1991, and 1991–2001. Nevertheless, there is a good deal of continuity from chapter to chapter. The challenges of the Cold War and post-colonial nation building dominate the period and involve global economic, technological, and political forces that become increasingly important factors in all aspects of human life. Technology plays a central role in this part both because of its integral role in the growth of a global community and because its many benefits in improving the quality of life seem clouded by real and potential negative impacts on the environment.

SUPPLEMENTS

We have assembled an array of on-line supplements to aid students in learning and instructors in teaching. The web site, which features an *Instructor's Resource Manual*, web activities, and the ACE self-testing quiz program, in addition to our *Computerized Test Bank,* provides a tightly integrated program for teaching and learning.

New to the book-specific web site is the *Instructor's Resource Manual,* thoroughly revised by John Reisbord (Ph.D. Northwestern University), which provides useful teaching strategies for the global history course and tips for getting the most out of the text. Each chapter contains instructional objectives, a detailed chapter outline, discussion questions, in-depth learning projects, and audiovisual resources.

Students visiting our web site can access our ACE practice quizzes, which feature 10–20 multiple-choice questions per chapter. In addition to reinforcing important chapter material, the program provides useful feedback for every option so that students can note what material they need to review further. New to our student site are web activities, also created by John Reisbord, which are designed to encourage further critical thinking. Students can explore themes and issues covered in the text in more depth by using information on select sites to answer questions posed in the exercises.

Our *Computerized Test Bank*, prepared by Jane Scimeca of Brookdale Community College, offers 14 to 16 key-term identifications, 4 to 6 essay questions with answer guidelines, 24–26 multiple-choice questions, and 2 to 3 history and geography exercises.

The GeoQuest World CD-ROM, features thirty interactive maps that demonstrate for students the connection between history and geography from ancient times to the present. Each map is accompanied by exercises with answers and essay questions. Four different types of interactivity allow students to move at their own pace through each section.

ACKNOWLEDGMENTS

We have benefited from the critical readings of many colleagues. Our sincere thanks go in particular to the following instructors: Henry Abramson, Florida Atlantic University; Paul V. Adams, Shippensburg University/University of San Carlos; Maria S. Arbelaez, University of Nebraska at Omaha; William J. Astore, United States Air Force Academy; Fritz Blackwell, Washington State University; Corinne Blake, Rowan University; Thomas Borstelmann, Cornell University; Byron Cannon, University of Utah; David A. Chappell, University of Hawaii; Nancy Clark, California Polytechnic State University at San Luis Obispo; Aaron Cohen, California State University, Sacramento; Lee Congdon, James Madison University; James Coolsen, Shippensburg University; Bruce Cruikshank, Hastings College; Linda T. Darling, University of Arizona; Susan Deans-Smith, University of Texas at Austin; Gregory C. Ference, Salisbury State University; Alan Fisher, Michigan State University; Donald M. Fisher, Niagara County Community College; Cathy A. Frierson, University of New Hampshire; Rosanna Gatens, Belmont University; Lorne E. Glaim, Pacific Union College; Matthew S. Gordon, Miami University; Steve Gosch, University of Wisconsin at Eau Claire; Kolleen M. Guy, University of Texas at San Antonio; James R. Hansen, Auburn University; Randolph C. Head, University of California at Riverside; David Hertzel, Southwestern Oklahoma State University; Richard J. Hoffman, San Francisco State University; Catherine M. Jones, North Georgia College and State University; Joy Kammerling, Eastern Illinois University; Carol A. Keller, San Antonio College; Jonathan Lee, San Antonio College; Miriam R. Levin, Case Western Reserve University; Richard Lewis, St. Cloud State University; James E. Lindsay, Colorado State University; Charles W. McClellan, Radford University; Andrea McElderry, University of Louisville; Stephen L. McFarland, Auburn University; Gregory McMahon, University of New Hampshire; Mark McLeod, University of Delaware; Stephen S. Michot, Mississippi County Community College; Shawn W. Miller, Brigham Young University; Stephen Morillo, Wabash College; Kalala Joseph Ngalamulume, Central Washington University; Patricia O'Neill, Central Oregon Community College; Chandrika Paul, Shippensburg University; John R. Pavia, Ithaca College; Thomas Earl Porter, North Carolina A&T State University; Jean H. Quataert, SUNY at Binghamton; William Reddy, Duke University; Thomas Reeves, Roxbury

Community College; Dennis Reinhartz, University of Texas at Arlington; Richard Rice, University of Tennessee at Chattanooga; Jane Scimeca, Brookdale Community College; William Schell, Murray State University; Alyssa Goldstein Sepinwall, California State University at San Marcos; Deborah Shackleton, United States Air Force Academy; Anita Shelton, Eastern Illinois University; Jeffrey M. Shumway, Brigham Young University; David R. Smith, California State Polytechnic University at Pomona; Linda Smith, Samford University; Mary Frances Smith, Ohio University; George E. Snow, Shippensburg University; Charlotte D. Staelin, Washington College; Paul D. Steeves, Stetson University; Robert Shannon Sumner, State University of West Georgia; Yi Sun, University of San Diego; Willard Sunderland, University of Cincinnati; Thaddeus Sunseri, Colorado State University; Sara W. Tucker, Washburn University; John M. VanderLippe, SUNY at New Paltz; Mary A. Watrous-Schlesinger, Washington State University; James A. Wood, North Carolina A&T State University; Eric Van Young, University of California at San Diego; and Alex Zukas, National University, San Diego.

We also want to extend our collective thanks to Lynda Schaffer for her early conceptual contributions as well as to the history departments of Shippensburg University, the United States Air Force Academy, and the State University of New York at New Paltz for arranging reviewer conferences that provided crucial feedback for our revision of the book. Individually, Richard W. Bulliet thanks Jack Garraty and Isser Woloch for first involving him in world history; Pamela Kyle Crossley wishes to thank Gene Garthwaite, Charles Wood, and David Morgan; Steven W. Hirsch extends his gratitude to Dennis Trout and Peter L. D. Reid; Lyman L. Johnson extends his to Kenneth J. Andrien, Richard Boyer, Grant D. Hones, William M. Ringle, Hendrik Kraay, Daniel Dupre, and Steven W. Usselman; and David Northrup thanks Allen Howard and Prasanan Parthasarathi. Lyman Johnson also thanks the members of the Department of History of North Carolina A&T University for their many helpful and pertinent suggestions.

The three people who kept us on course in preparing the second edition deserve our special thanks: Jean L. Woy, Editor-in-Chief for History, Political Science, and Economics; Nancy Blaine, Senior Sponsoring Editor; and Annette Fantasia, Editorial Assistant. We also had the pleasure of working again with several people who helped so much with the first and second editions, including Carol Newman, Senior Project Editor; Reba Frederics, Editorial Assistant, Charlotte Miller, Art Editor; Carole Frolich, Photo Researcher; Jill Haber, Senior Production/Design Coordinator; and Florence Cadran, Manufacturing Manager.

We thank also the many students whose questions and concerns, expressed directly or through their instructors, shaped much of this revision. We continue to welcome all our readers' suggestions, queries, and criticisms. Please contact us at our respective institutions or at this e-mail address: history@hmco.com.

ABOUT THE AUTHORS

Richard W. Bulliet Professor of Middle Eastern History at Columbia University, Richard W. Bulliet received his Ph.D. from Harvard University. He has written scholarly works on a number of topics: the social history of medieval Iran (*The Patricians of Nishapur*), the historical competition between pack camels and wheeled transport (*The Camel and the Wheel*), the process of conversion to Islam (*Conversion to Islam in the Medieval Period*), and the overall course of Islamic social history (*Islam: The View from the Edge*). He is the editor of the *Columbia History of the Twentieth Century*. He has published four novels, co-edited *The Encyclopedia of the Modern Middle East*, and hosted an educational television series on the Middle East. He was awarded a fellowship by the John Simon Guggenheim Memorial Foundation.

Pamela Kyle Crossley Pamela Kyle Crossley received her Ph.D. in Modern Chinese History from Yale University. She is Professor of History, Rosenwald Research Professor in the Arts and Sciences, and Chair of Asian and Middle Eastern Studies at Dartmouth College. Her books include *A Translucent Mirror: History and Identity in Qing Imperial Ideology, The Manchus*, and *Orphan Warriors: Three Manchu Generations and the End of the Qing World*. Her research, which concentrates on the cultural history of China, Inner Asia, and Central Asia, has most recently been supported by the John Simon Guggenheim Memorial Foundation and the National Endowment for the Humanities.

Daniel R. Headrick Daniel R. Headrick received his Ph.D. in History from Princeton University. Professor of History and Social Science at Roosevelt University in Chicago, he is the author of several books on the history of technology, imperialism, and international relations, including *The Tools of Empire: Technology and European Imperialism in the Nineteenth Century, The Tentacles of Progress: Technology Transfer in the Age of Imperialism, The Invisible Weapon: Telecommunications and International Politics*, and *When Information Came of Age: Technologies of Knowledge in the Age of Reason and Revolution, 1700–1850*. His articles have appeared in the *Journal of World History* and the *Journal of Modern History*, and he has been awarded fellowships by the National Endowment for the Humanities, the John Simon Guggenheim Memorial Foundation, and the Alfred P. Sloan Foundation.

Steven W. Hirsch Steven W. Hirsch holds a Ph.D. in Classics from Stanford University and is currently Associate Professor of Classics and History at Tufts University. He has received grants from the National Endowment for the Humanities and the Massachusetts Foundation for Humanities and Public Policy. His research and publications include *The Friendship of the Barbarians: Xenophon and the Persian Empire*, as well as articles and reviews in the *Classical Journal*, the *American Journal of Philology*, and the *Journal of Interdisciplinary History*.

Lyman L. Johnson Professor of History at the University of North Carolina at Charlotte, Lyman L. Johnson earned his Ph.D. in Latin American History from the University of Connecticut. A two-time Senior Fulbright-Hays Lecturer, he also has received fellowships from the Tinker Foundation, the Social Science Research Council, the National Endowment for the Humanities, and the American Philosophical Society. His recent books include *The Faces of Honor* (with Sonya Lipsett-Rivera), *The Problem of Order in Changing Societies, Essays on the Price History of Eighteenth-Century Latin America* (with Enrique Tandeter), and *Colonial Latin America* (with Mark A. Burkholder). He also has published in journals, including the *Hispanic American Historical Review*, the *Journal of Latin American Studies*, the *International Review of Social History, Social History*, and *Desarrollo Económico*. He recently served as president of the Conference on Latin American History.

David Northrup Professor of History at Boston College, David Northrup earned his Ph.D. in African and European History from the University of California at Los Angeles. He has published scholarly volumes on precolonial Nigeria, on precolonial and colonial Congo, on the Atlantic slave trade, and on Asian, African, and Pacific Islander indentured labor in the nineteenth century. His recent work appeared in the *Oxford History of the British Empire, Revue française d'histoire d'outre-mer, Slavery and Abolition*, and the *Journal of World History*. He is vice president of the World History Association and has received research support from the Fulbright-Hays Commission, the National Endowment for the Humanities, and the Social Science Research Council.

NOTE ON SPELLING AND USAGE

Where necessary for clarity, dates are followed by the letters C.E. or B.C.E. The abbreviation C.E. stands for "Common Era" and is equivalent to A.D. (*anno Domini*, Latin for "in the year of the Lord"). The abbreviation B.C.E stands for "before the Common Era" and means the same as B.C. ("before Christ"). In keeping with our goal of approaching world history without special concentration on one culture or another, we chose these neutral abbreviations as appropriate to our enterprise. Because many readers will be more familiar with English than with metric measurements, however, units of measure are generally given in the English system, with metric equivalents following in parentheses.

In general, Chinese has been romanized according to the *pinyin* method. Exceptions include proper names well established in English (e.g., Canton, Chiang Kai-shek) and a few English words borrowed from Chinese (e.g., kowtow). Spellings of Arabic, Ottoman Turkish, Persian, Mongolian, Manchu, Japanese, and Korean names and terms avoid special diacritical marks for letters that are pronounced only slightly differently in English. An apostrophe is used to indicate when two Chinese syllables are pronounced separately (e.g., Chang'an).

For words transliterated from languages that use the Arabic script—Arabic, Ottoman Turkish, Perisan, Urdu—the apostrophe indicating separately pronounced syllables may represent either of two special consonants, the *hamza* or the *ain*. Because most English-speakers do not hear the distinction between these two, they have not been distinguished in transliteration and are not indicated when they occur at the beginning or end of a word. As with Chinese, some words and commonly used place-names from these languages are given familiar English spellings (e.g., Quran instead of Qur'an, Cairo instead of al-Qahira). Arabic romanization has normally been used for terms relating to Islam, even where the context justifies slightly different Turkish or Persian forms, again for ease of comprehension.

There is an ongoing debate about how best to render Amerindian words in English. It has been common for authors writing in English to follow Mexican usage for Nahuatl and Yucatec Maya words and place-names. In this style, for example, the capital of the Aztec state is spelled Tenochtitlán, and the important late Maya city-state is spelled Chichén Itzá. Although these forms are still common even in the specialist literature, we have chosen to follow the scholarship that sees these accents as unnecessary. The exceptions are modern place-names, such as Mérida and Yucatán, which are accented. A similar problem exists for the spelling of Quechua and Aymara words from the Andean region of South America. Although there is significant disagreement among scholars, we follow the emerging consensus and use the spellings khipu (not quipu), Tiwanaku (not Tiahuanaco), and Wari (not Huari). However, we keep Inca (not Inka) and Cuzco (not Cusco), since these spellings are expected by most of our potential readers and we hope to avoid confusion.

THE EARTH AND ITS PEOPLES

A GLOBAL HISTORY

PART ONE

THE EMERGENCE OF HUMAN COMMUNITIES,
TO 1500 B.C.E.

CHAPTER 1
FROM THE ORIGINS OF AGRICULTURE TO THE FIRST RIVER-VALLEY
CIVILIZATIONS, 8000–1500 B.C.E.

CHAPTER 2
THE LATE BRONZE AGE IN THE EASTERN HEMISPHERE, 2200–500 B.C.E.

Around 10,000 years ago, some human groups, living as foragers in different parts of the world, began to cultivate plants, domesticate animals, and make pottery vessels for storage. One consequence of this shift to agriculture was the emergence of permanent settlements—at first small villages but eventually larger towns as well.

The earliest complex societies arose in the great river valleys of Asia and Africa: around 3100 B.C.E. in the valley between the Tigris and Euphrates Rivers in Mesopotamia and along the Nile River in Egypt, somewhat later in the valley of the Indus River in Pakistan and on the floodplain of the Yellow River in China. In these arid regions, agriculture depended on irrigation with river water, and centers of political power arose to organize the massive human labor required to dig and maintain channels to carry water to the fields and dikes to protect lives and property from river floodings.

Kings and priests dominated these early societies. Kings controlled the military forces; priests managed the temples and the wealth of the gods. Within the urban centers—in the midst of palaces, temples, fortification walls, and other monumental buildings— lived administrators, soldiers, priests, merchants, craftsmen, and others with specialized skills. The production of surplus food grown on rural estates by a dependent peasantry sustained the activities of these groups. Professional scribes kept administrative and financial records and preserved their civilization's religious and scientific knowledge.

Over time, certain centers extended their influence and came to dominate broad expanses of territory. The rulers of these early empires were motivated primarily by the need to secure access to vital raw materials—especially tin and copper, from which to make bronze. A similar motive accounts for the development of long-distance trade and diplomatic relations between major powers. Fueling long-distance trade was the desire for bronze, which had both practical and symbolic importance. From bronze, artisans made weapons, tools and utensils, and ritual objects. Ownership of bronze items was a sign of wealth and power. Trade and diplomacy contributed to the spread of culture and technology from the core river-valley areas to neighboring regions, such as Nubia and the Aegean.

	8000 B.C.E.	7000 B.C.E.	6000 B.C.E.	5000 B.C.E.
Americas		• 7000 Incipient plant domestication in Peru		• 5000 Beans and squash domestication in Mesoamerica
Europe	Spread of Indo-European languages		• 6000 Farming in southern Europe	
Africa	• 8000 Farming in eastern Sahara			• 5500 Farming in Egypt
Middle East	• 8000 Domestication of plants and animals in Fertile Crescent			• 5000 Irrigation in Mesopotamia
Asia and Oceania			• 6500 Rice cultivation in China	• 5000 Farming in India

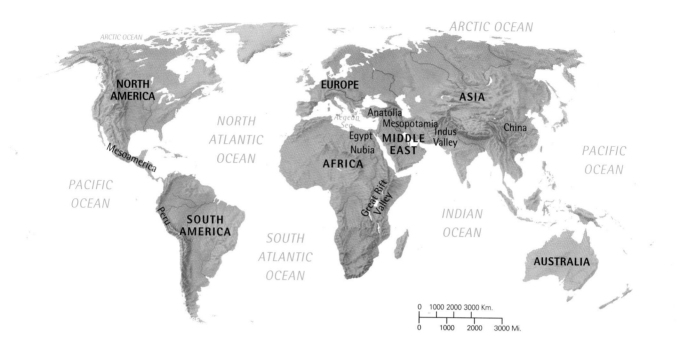

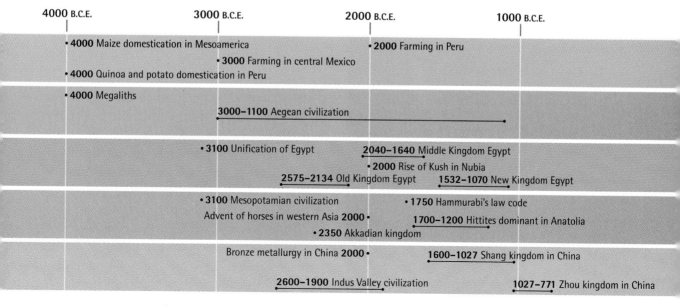

4000 B.C.E.   3000 B.C.E.   2000 B.C.E.   1000 B.C.E.

• 4000 Maize domestication in Mesoamerica   • 2000 Farming in Peru
          • 3000 Farming in central Mexico
• 4000 Quinoa and potato domestication in Peru

• 4000 Megaliths

3000–1100 Aegean civilization

• 3100 Unification of Egypt   2040–1640 Middle Kingdom Egypt
          • 2000 Rise of Kush in Nubia
          2575–2134 Old Kingdom Egypt   1532–1070 New Kingdom Egypt

• 3100 Mesopotamian civilization   • 1750 Hammurabi's law code
          Advent of horses in western Asia 2000 •   1700–1200 Hittites dominant in Anatolia
          • 2350 Akkadian kingdom

Bronze metallurgy in China 2000 •   1600–1027 Shang kingdom in China

          2600–1900 Indus Valley civilization   1027–771 Zhou kingdom in China

1

FROM THE ORIGINS OF AGRICULTURE TO THE FIRST RIVER-VALLEY CIVILIZATIONS,

8000–1500 B.C.E.

Before Civilization • Mesopotamia • Egypt •
• The Indus Valley Civilization
ENVIRONMENT AND TECHNOLOGY: Environmental Stress in the Indus Valley

Some five thousand years ago in Mesopotamia (present-day Iraq), people living in Sumer, the world's first urban civilization, cherished the story of Gilgamesh, superhero king of the city of Uruk. The goddess of creation, it recounted, fashioned the wild man Enkidu°:

> There was virtue in him of the god of war, of Ninurta himself. His body was rough, he had long hair like a woman's; it waved like the hair of Nisaba, the goddess of corn. His body was covered with matted hair like Samuqan's, the god of cattle. He was innocent of mankind; he knew nothing of the cultivated land. Enkidu ate grass in the hills with the gazelle and jostled with the wild beasts at the water-holes; he had joy of the water with the herds of wild game.

When Gilgamesh learns of Enkidu from a hunter, he sends a temple prostitute to tame him. After her seduction causes the wild beasts to shun him, she says:

> Come with me. I will take you to strong-walled Uruk, to the blessed temple of Ishtar and of Anu, of love and of heaven . . . there all the people are dressed in their gorgeous robes, every day is holiday, the young men and the girls are wonderful to see. How sweet they smell! . . . O Enkidu, you who live life, I will show you Gilgamesh.[1]

She clothes Enkidu and teaches him to eat cooked food, drink beer, and bathe and oil his body. Her words and actions signal the principal traits of civilized life in Sumer, just as the divine comparisons of the wild Enkidu show Sumer's dependence on grain and livestock.

The Sumerians, like other peoples, equated civilization with their own way of life. But lifestyles varied. Given the ambiguity of the term *civilization*, therefore, the common understanding that the first civilizations arose in

Enkidu (EN-kee-doo)

Mesopotamia and Egypt sometime before 3000 B.C.E. needs examination.

Scholars agree that settled agricultural life and certain political, social, economic, and technological traits are indicators of **civilization,** if not of every civilization. These traits include (1) cities as administrative centers, (2) a political system based on defined territory rather than kinship, (3) many people engaged in specialized, non-food-producing activities, (4) status distinctions based largely on accumulation of wealth, (5) monumental building, (6) a system for keeping permanent records, (7) long-distance trade, and (8) sophisticated interest in science and art.

The earliest societies exhibiting these traits appeared in the floodplains of great rivers: the Tigris° and Euphrates° in Iraq, the Indus in Pakistan, the Yellow (Huang He°) in China, and the Nile in Egypt (see Map 1.1). Periodic flooding fertilized the land with silt and provided water for agriculture but also threatened lives and property. To control the floods, the peoples living near the rivers created new technologies and forms of political and social organization.

In this chapter, we describe the origins of domestication among the scattered groups of foragers living at the end of the last Ice Age and the slow development of farming and herding societies. We then trace the rise of complex societies in Mesopotamia, Egypt, and the Indus River Valley from approximately 3500 to 1500 B.C.E. (China, developing slightly later, is discussed in Chapter 2). This story roughly coincides with the origins of writing, allowing us to document aspects of human life not revealed by archaeological evidence alone.

As you read this chapter, ask yourself the following questions:

- How did plant and animal domestication set the scene for the emergence of civilization?
- Why did the earliest civilizations arise in river valleys?
- How did the organization of labor shape political and social structures?
- How did metallurgy, writing, and monumental construction contribute to the power and wealth of elite groups?
- How do religious beliefs reflect interaction with the environment?

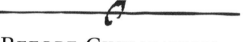

BEFORE CIVILIZATION

Evidence of human artistic creativity first came to the light in 1940 near Lascaux in southwestern France with the discovery of a vast underground cavern. The cavern walls were covered with paintings of animals, including many that had been extinct for thousands of years. Similar cave paintings have been found in Spain and elsewhere in southern France.

To even the most skeptical person, these artistic troves reveal rich imaginations and sophisticated skills, qualities also apparent in the stone tools and evidence of complex social relations uncovered from prehistoric sites. The production of such artworks and tools over wide areas and long periods of time demonstrates that skills and ideas were not simply individual but were deliberately passed along within societies. These learned patterns of action and expression constitute **culture.** Culture includes material objects, such as dwellings, clothing, tools, and crafts, along with nonmaterial values, beliefs, and languages. Although it is true that some animals also learn new ways, their activities are determined primarily by inherited instincts. Only human communities trace profound cultural developments over time. The development, transmission, and transformation of cultural practices and events are the subject of **history.**

Tigris (TIE-gris)   **Euphrates** (you-FRAY-teez)
Huang He (hwang huh)

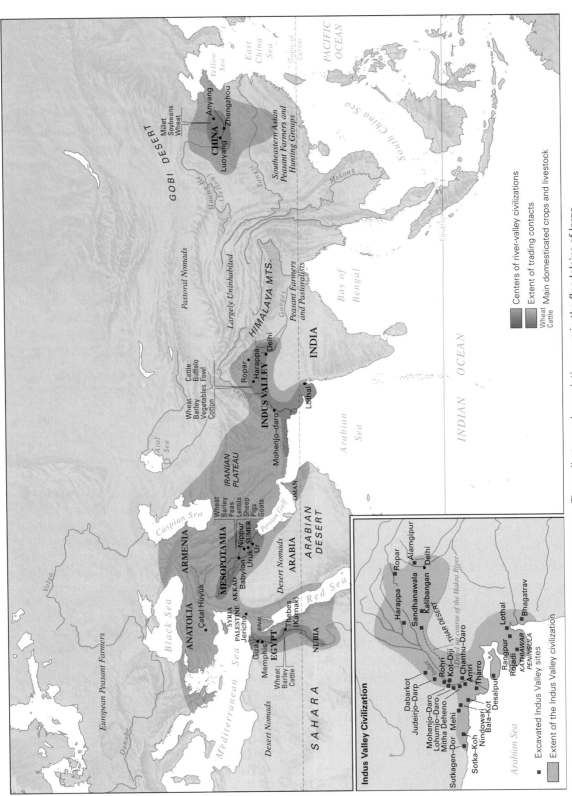

Map 1.1 River-Valley Civilizations, 3500–1500 B.C.E. The earliest complex societies arose in the floodplains of large rivers: in the fourth millennium B.C.E. in the valley of the Tigris and Euphrates Rivers in Mesopotamia and the Nile River in Egypt, in the third millennium B.C.E. in the valley of the Indus River in Pakistan, and in the second millennium B.C.E. in the valley of the Yellow River in China.

CHRONOLOGY

	Mesopotamia	Egypt	Indus Valley
3500 B.C.E.			
3000 B.C.E.	**3000–2350** B.C.E. Early Dynastic (Sumerian)	**3100–2575** B.C.E. Early Dynastic	
2500 B.C.E.		**2575–2134** B.C.E. Old Kingdom	**2600** B.C.E. Beginning of Indus Valley civilization
2000 B.C.E.	**2350–2230** B.C.E. Akkadian (Semitic) **2112–2004** B.C.E. Third Dynasty of Ur (Sumerian) **1900–1600** B.C.E. Old Babylonian (Semitic)	**2134–2040** B.C.E. First Intermediate Period **2040–1640** B.C.E. Middle Kingdom	**1900** B.C.E. End of Indus Valley civilization
1500 B.C.E.	**1500–1150** B.C.E. Kassite	**1640–1532** B.C.E. Second Intermediate Period **1532–1070** B.C.E. New Kingdom	

Food Gathering and Stone Technology

Stone toolmaking, the first recognizable cultural activity, first appeared around 2 million years ago. The **Stone Age,** which lasted from then until around 4,000 years ago, can be a misleading label. Stone tools abound at archaeological sites, but not all tools were of stone. They were made as well of bone, skin, and wood, materials that survive poorly. In addition, this period encompasses many cultures and subperiods. Among the major subdivisions, the **Paleolithic°** (Old Stone Age) lasted until 10,000 years ago, about 3,000 years after the end of the last Ice Age, long periods when glaciers covered much of North America, Europe, and Asia. The **Neolithic°** (New Stone Age), which is associated with the origins of agriculture, followed.

Fossilized animal bones bearing the marks of butchering tools testify to the scavenging and hunting activities of Stone Age peoples, but anthropologists do not believe that early humans lived primarily on meat. Modern **foragers** (hunting and food-gathering peoples) in the Kalahari Desert of southern Africa and Ituri Forest of central Africa derive the bulk of their day-to-day nourishment from wild vegetable foods. They eat meat at feasts. Stone Age peoples probably did the same, even though the tools and equipment for gathering and processing vegetable foods have left few archaeological traces.

Like modern foragers, ancient humans would have used skins and mats woven from leaves for collecting fruits, berries, and wild seeds, and they would have dug up edible roots with wooden sticks. Archaeologists suspect that the doughnut-shaped stones often found at Stone Age sites served as weights to make wooden digging sticks more effective.

Paleolithic (pay-lee-oh-LITH-ik)
Neolithic (nee-oh-LITH-ik)

Cooking makes both meat and vegetables tastier and easier to digest, something early humans may have discovered inadvertently after wildfires. Humans may have begun setting fires deliberately 1 million to 1.5 million years ago, but proof of cooking does not appear until some 12,500 years ago, when clay cooking pots came into use in East Asia.

Studies of present-day foragers also indicate that Ice Age women probably did most of the gathering and cooking, which they could do while caring for small children. Women past child-bearing age would have been the most knowledgeable and productive food gatherers. Men, with stronger arms and shoulders, would have been better suited for hunting, particularly for large animals. Some early cave art suggests male hunting activities.

The same studies, along with archaeological evidence from Ice Age campsites, indicate that early foragers lived in groups that were big enough to defend themselves from predators and divide responsibility for food collection and preparation, but small enough not to exhaust the food resources within walking distance. Even bands of around fifty men, women, and children would have moved regularly to follow migrating animals or collect seasonally ripening plants in different places.

In regions with severe climates or lacking in natural shelters like caves, people built huts of branches, stones, bones, skins, and leaves as seasonal camps. Animal skins served as clothing, with the earliest evidence of woven cloth appearing about 26,000 years ago. Groups living in the African grasslands and other game-rich areas probably spent only three to five hours a day securing food, clothing, and shelter. This would have left a great deal of time for artistic endeavors, tool-making, and social life.

The foundations of what later ages called science, art, and religion also date to the Stone Age. Gatherers learned which local plants were edible and when they ripened, as well as which natural substances were effective for medicine, consciousness altering, dyeing, and other purposes. Hunters learned the habits of game animals. People experimented with techniques of using plant and animal materials for clothing, twine, and construction. Knowledge of the environment included identifying which minerals made good paints and which

stones made good tools. All of these aspects of culture were passed orally from generation to generation.

Early music and dance have left no traces, but visual artwork has survived abundantly. Cave paintings appear as early as 32,000 years ago in Europe and North Africa and somewhat later in other parts of the world. Because many feature food animals like wild oxen, reindeer, and horses, some scholars believe the art records hunting scenes or played a magical and religious role in hunting. A newly discovered cave at Vallon Pont-d'Arc° in southern France, however, features rhinoceros, panthers, bears, owls, and a hyena, which probably were not hunted for food. Other drawings include people dressed in animal skins and smeared with paint and stencils of human hands. Some scholars suspect that other marks in cave paintings and on bones may represent efforts at counting or writing.

Some cave art suggests that Stone Age people had well-developed religions, but without written texts, it is hard to know what they believed. Some graves from about 100,000 years ago contain stone implements, food, clothing, and red-ochre powder, indicating that early people revered their leaders enough to honor them in death and may have believed in an afterlife.

The Agricultural Revolutions

Around 10,000 years ago, some human groups began to meet their food needs by raising domesticated plants and animals. Gradually over the next millennium, most people became food producers, although hunting and gathering continued in some places.

The term *Neolithic Revolution* commonly given to the changeover from food gathering to food producing can be misleading. *Neolithic* means "new stone," but the new tool designs that accompanied the beginnings of agriculture did not define it. Nor was the "revolution" a single event. The changeover occurred in different parts of the world at different times. The term **Agricultural Revolutions** is more precise because it emphasizes the central role of food production and signals that

Vallon Pont-d'Arc (vah-LON pon-DAHRK)

the changeover occurred several times. The adoption of agriculture often included the domestication of animals for food.

Food gathering gave way to food production over hundreds of generations. The process may have begun when forager bands, returning year after year to the same seasonal camps, scattered seeds and cleared away weeds to encourage the growth of foods they liked. Such semicultivation could have supplemented food gathering without the permanent settlement of the group. Families choosing to concentrate their energies on food production, however, would have had to settle permanently near their fields.

Specialized stone tools first alerted archaeologists to new food-producing practices: polished or ground stone heads to work the soil, sharp stone chips embedded in bone or wooden handles to cut grasses, and stone mortars to pulverize grain. Early farmers used fire to clear fields of shrubs and trees and discovered that ashes were a natural fertilizer. After the burn-off, farmers used blades and axes to keep the land clear.

Selection of the highest-yielding strains of wild plants led to the development of domesticated varieties over time. As the principal gatherers of wild plant foods, women probably played a major role in this transition to plant cultivation, but the task of clearing fields probably fell to the men.

In the Middle East, the region with the earliest evidence of agriculture, human selection had transformed certain wild grasses into higher-yielding domesticated grains, now known as emmer wheat and barley, by 8000 B.C.E. Farmers there also discovered that alternating the cultivation of grains and pulses (plants yielding edible seeds such as lentils and peas) helped maintain fertility.

Plants domesticated in the Middle East spread to adjacent lands, but in many parts of the world, agriculture arose independently. Exchanges of crops and techniques occurred between regions, but societies that had already turned to farming borrowed new plants, animals, and farming techniques more readily than foraging groups did.

The eastern Sahara, which went through a wet period after 8000 B.C.E., preserves the oldest traces of food production in northern Africa. As in the Middle East, emmer wheat and barley became the principal crops and sheep, goats, and cattle the

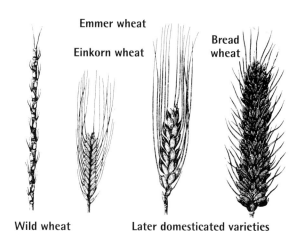

Domestication of Wheat Through selection of the largest seeds of this wild grass, early farmers in the Middle East were able to develop varieties with larger edible kernels. Bread wheat was grown in the Nile Valley by 5000 B.C.E. (From Iris Barn, Discovering Archaeology, © 1981)

main domestic animals. When drier conditions returned around 5000 B.C.E., many Saharan farmers moved to the Nile Valley, where the river's annual flood provided water for crops.

In Greece, wheat and barley cultivation, beginning as early as 6000 B.C.E., combined local experiments with Middle Eastern borrowings. Shortly after 4000 B.C.E., farming developed in the light-soiled plains of Central Europe and along the Danube River. As forests receded because of climate changes and human clearing efforts, agriculture spread to other parts of Europe over the next millennium.

Early farmers in Europe and elsewhere practiced shifting cultivation, also known as swidden agriculture. After a few growing seasons, farmers left the fields fallow (abandoned to natural vegetation) and cleared new fields nearby. Between 4000 and 3000 B.C.E., for example, communities of from forty to sixty people in the Danube Valley supported themselves on about 500 acres (200 hectares) of farmland, cultivating a third or less each year while leaving the rest fallow to regain its fertility. From around 2600 B.C.E., people in Central Europe began using ox-drawn wooden plows to till heavier and richer soils.

Although the lands around the Mediterranean

seem to have shared a complex of crops and farming techniques, geographical barriers blocked the spread elsewhere. Rainfall patterns south of the Sahara favored locally domesticated grains—sorghums, millets, and (in Ethiopia) teff—over wheat and barley. Middle Eastern grains did not grow at all in the humidity of equatorial West Africa; there, yams became an early domestic crop.

Domestic rice originated in southern China, the northern half of Southeast Asia, or northern India, possibly as early as 10,000 B.C.E. but more likely closer to 5000 B.C.E. The warm, wet climate of southern China particularly favored rice. Indian farmers cultivated hyacinth beans, green grams, and black grams along with rice by about 2000 B.C.E.

In the Americas a decline of game animals in the Tehuacán° Valley of Mexico after 8000 B.C.E. increased people's dependence on wild plants. Agriculture based on maize° (corn) developed there about 3000 B.C.E. and gradually spread. At about the same time, the inhabitants of Peru developed a food production pattern based on potatoes and quinoa°, a protein-rich seed grain. People in the more tropical parts of Mesoamerica cultivated tomatoes, peppers, squash, and potatoes. In South America's tropical forests, the root crop manioc became the staple food after 1500 B.C.E. Manioc and maize then spread to the Caribbean islands.

The domestication of animals expanded rapidly during these same millennia. The first domesticated animal, the dog, may have helped hunters track game well before the Neolithic period. Later, animals initially provided meat but eventually supplied milk, wool, and energy as well.

Refuse dumped outside Middle East villages show a gradual decline in the number of wild gazelle bones after 7000 B.C.E. This probably reflects the depletion of wild game through overhunting by local farmers. Meat eating, however, did not decline. Sheep and goat bones gradually replaced gazelle bones. Possibly wild sheep and goats learned to graze around agricultural villages to take advantage of the suppression of predators by humans. The tamer animals may gradually have accepted human control and thus become themselves a ready supply of food. The bones of tame animals initially differ so little from those of their wild ancestors that the early stages of domestication are hard to date. However, selective breeding for characteristics like a wooly coat and high milk production eventually yielded distinct breeds of domestic sheep and goats.

Elsewhere, other wild species were evolving domestic forms during the centuries before 3000 B.C.E.: cattle in northern Africa or the Middle East, donkeys in northern Africa, water buffalo in China, humped-back Zebu° cattle in India, horses and two-humped camels in Central Asia, one-humped camels in Arabia, chickens in Southeast Asia, and pigs in several places. Like domestic plant species, varieties of domesticated animals spread from one region to another. The Zebu cattle originally domesticated in India, for example, became important in sub-Saharan Africa about 2,000 years ago.

Once cattle and water buffalo had become sufficiently tame to be yoked to plows, long after their initial domestication, they became essential to the agricultural cycle of grain farmers. In addition, animal droppings provided valuable fertilizer. Wool and milk production also followed initial domestication by a substantial period.

In the Americas, domestic llamas provided meat, transport, and wool, while guinea pigs and turkeys provided meat. Dogs assisted hunters and also provided meat. Some scholars believe that no other American species could have been domesticated, but this cannot be proven. Domestic species could not be borrowed from elsewhere, however, because of the geographical isolation of the Americas.

Pastoralism, a way of life dependent on large herds of grazing livestock, came to predominate in arid regions. As the Sahara approached its maximum dryness around 2500 B.C.E., pastoralists replaced farmers who migrated southward (see Chapter 6). Moving herds to new pastures and watering places throughout the year made pastoralists almost as mobile as foragers and discouraged accumulation of bulky possessions and substantial dwellings. Like modern pastoralists, early cattle keepers probably relied more heavily on milk than meat since killing animals diminished the size of

---

Tehuacán (teh-wah-KAHN)   maize (mayz)
quinoa (kee-NOH-uh)

Zebu (ZEE-boo)

their herds. During wet seasons, they may also have engaged in semicultivation or bartered meat and skins for plant foods with nearby farming communities.

Why did the Agricultural Revolutions occur? Some theories assume that growing crops had obvious advantages. Grain, for example, provided both a dietary staple and the makings of beer. Beer drinking appears frequently in ancient Middle Eastern art and can be dated to as early as 3500 B.C.E. Most researchers today, however, believe that climate change drove people to abandon hunting and gathering in favor of pastoralism and agriculture. So great was the global warming that ended the last Ice Age that geologists gave the era since about 9000 B.C.E. a new name: the **Holocene°**. Scientists have also found evidence that temperate lands were exceptionally warm between 6000 and 2000 B.C.E., when people in many parts of the world adopted agriculture. The precise nature of the climatic crisis probably varied. In the Middle East, shortages of wild food caused by dryness or population growth may have stimulated food production. Elsewhere, a warmer, wetter climate could have turned grasslands into forest and thereby reduced supplies of game and wild grains.

In many drier parts of the world where wild food remained abundant, agriculture did not arise. The inhabitants of Australia relied exclusively on foraging until recent centuries, as did some peoples on the other continents. Amerindians in the arid grasslands from Alaska to the Gulf of Mexico hunted bison, and salmon fishing sustained groups in the Pacific Northwest. Fish, shellfish, and aquatic animals permitted food gatherers east of the Mississippi River to become increasingly sedentary. In the equatorial rain forest and in the southern part of Africa, conditions also favored retention of older ways.

Whatever the causes, the gradual adoption of food production transformed most parts of the world. A hundred thousand years ago, world population, mostly living in the temperate and tropical regions of Africa and Eurasia, did not exceed 2 million. The population may have fallen still lower during the last glacial epoch, between 32,000 and 13,000 years ago. Agriculture supported a gradual population increase, perhaps to 10 million by 5000 B.C.E., and then a mushrooming to between 50 million and 100 million by 1000 B.C.E.[2]

Life in Neolithic Communities

Evidence that an ecological crisis may have triggered the transition to food production has prompted reexamination of the assumption that farmers enjoyed a better life than foragers did. Early farmers probably had to work much harder and for much longer periods than food gatherers. Long days spent clearing and cultivating the land yielded meager harvests. Guarding herds from predators, guiding them to fresh pastures, and tending to their needs imposed similar burdens.

Although early farmers commanded a more reliable food supply, their diet contained less variety and nutrition than that of foragers. Skeletons show that Neolithic farmers were shorter on average than earlier foragers. Death from contagious diseases ravaged farming settlements contaminated by human waste, infested by disease-bearing vermin and insects, and inhabited by domesticated animals—especially pigs and cattle—whose diseases could infect people.

A dependable supply of food that could be stored between harvests to see people through nonproductive seasons, droughts, and other calamities proved decisive in the long run, however. Over several millennia, farmers came to outnumber nonfarmers, permanent settlements generated cultural changes, and specialized crafts appeared in fledgling towns.

Some researchers envision violent struggles between farmers and foragers. Others see a more peaceful transition. Violence may well have accompanied land clearance that constrained the foragers' food supplies. And farmers probably fought for control of the best land. In most cases, however, farmers seem to have displaced foragers by gradual infiltration rather than conquest.

The archaeologist Colin Renfrew maintains that over a few centuries, farming populations in Europe could have increased by a factor of fifty to one hundred just on the basis of the dependability of their food supply. In his view, as population

---

Holocene (HAWL-oh-seen)

densities rose, individuals with fields farthest away from their native village formed new settlements, leading to a steady, nonviolent expansion of agriculture consistent with the archaeological record. An expansion by only 12 to 19 miles (20 to 30 kilometers) in a generation could have brought farming to every corner of Europe between 6500 and 3500 B.C.E.[3] Yet it would have happened so gradually as to minimize sharp conflicts with foragers, who would simply have stayed clear of the agricultural frontier or gradually adopted agriculture themselves. Studies that map similar genetic changes in the population also suggest a gradual spread of agricultural people across Europe from southeast to northwest.[4]

Like forager bands, kinship and marriage bound farming communities together. Nuclear family size (parents and their children) may not have risen, but kinship relations traced back over more generations brought distant cousins into a common kin network. This encouraged the holding of land by large kinship units known as lineages° or clans.

Because each person has two parents, four grandparents, eight great-grandparents, and so on, each individual has a bewildering number of ancestors. Some societies trace descent equally through both parents, but most give greater importance to descent through either the mother (matrilineal° societies) or the father (patrilineal° societies).

Some scholars believe descent through women and perhaps rule by women prevailed in early times. The traditions of Kikuyu° farmers on Mount Kenya in East Africa, for example, relate that women ruled until the Kikuyu men conspired to get all the women pregnant at once and then overthrew them while they were unable to fight back. No specific evidence can prove or disprove legends such as this, but it is important not to confuse tracing descent through women (matrilineality) with rule by women (matriarchy°).

Religiously, kinship led to reverence for departed ancestors. Old persons often received elaborate burials. A plastered skull from Jericho° in the

Jordan Valley of modern Israel may be evidence of early ancestor reverence or worship at the dawn of agriculture.

The religions of foragers tended to center on sacred groves, springs, and wild animals. In contrast, the rituals of farmers often centered on the Earth Mother, a deity believed to be the source of new life, an all-powerful (and usually male) Sky God, and divinities representing fire, wind, and rain.

Assemblages of **megaliths** (meaning "big stones") seem to relate to religious beliefs. One complex built in the Egyptian desert before 5000 B.C.E. includes stone burial chambers, a calendar circle, and pairs of upright stones that frame the rising sun on the summer solstice. Stonehenge, a famous megalithic site in England constructed about 2000 B.C.E., marked the position of the sun and other celestial bodies at key points in the year. In the Middle East, the Americas, and other parts of the world, giant earth burial mounds may have served similar ritual and symbolic functions.

In some parts of the world, a few Neolithic villages grew into towns, which served as centers of trade and specialized crafts. Two towns in the Middle East, Jericho on the west bank of the Jordan River and Çatal Hüyük° in central Anatolia (modern Turkey), have been extensively excavated (Map 1.1 shows their location). Jericho revealed an elaborate early agricultural settlement. The round mud-brick dwelling characteristic of Jericho around 8000 B.C.E. may have imitated the shape of the tents of foragers who once had camped near Jericho's natural spring. A millennium later, rectangular rooms with finely plastered walls and floors and wide doorways opened onto central courtyards. Surrounding the 10-acre (4-hectare) settlement a massive stone wall protected against attacks.

The ruins of Çatal Hüyük, an even larger Neolithic town, date to between 7000 and 5000 B.C.E. and cover 32 acres (13 hectares). Its residents lived in plastered mud-brick rooms with elaborate decorations, but Çatal Hüyük had no wall. Instead, the outer walls of its houses formed a continuous barrier without doors or large windows. Residents en-

---

lineage (LIN-ee-ij)   matrilineal (mat-ruh-LIN-ee-uhl)
patrilineal (pat-ruh-LIN-ee-uhl)   Kikuyu (Ki-KOO-yoo)
matriarchy (MAY-tree-ahr-key)   Jericho (JER-ih-koe)

Çatal Hüyük (cha-TAHL hoo-YOOK)

tered their houses by climbing down ladders through a hole in the roof.

Long-distance trade at Çatal Hüyük featured obsidian, a hard volcanic rock that artisans chipped, ground, and polished into tools, weapons, mirrors, and ornaments. Other residents made fine pottery, wove baskets and woolen cloth, made stone and shell beads, and worked leather and wood. House sizes varied, but nothing indicates that Çatal Hüyük had a dominant class or a centralized political structure.

Representational art at Çatal Hüyük makes it clear that hunting retained a powerful hold on people's minds. Wall paintings of hunting scenes closely resemble earlier cave paintings. Many depict men and women adorned with leopard skins. Men were buried with weapons rather than with farm tools, and bones from rubbish heaps prove that wild game featured prominently in their diet.

Yet Çatal Hüyük's economy rested on agriculture. The surrounding fields produced barley and emmer wheat, as well as legumes° and other vegetables. Pigs were kept along with goats and sheep. Nevertheless, foragers' foods, such as acorns and wild grains, had not yet disappeared.

Çatal Hüyük had one religious shrine for every two houses. At least forty rooms contained shrines with depictions of horned wild bulls, female breasts, goddesses, leopards, and handprints. Rituals involved burning dishes of grain, legumes, and meat but not sacrifice of live animals. Statues of plump female deities far outnumber statues of male deities, suggesting that the inhabitants venerated a goddess as their principal deity. The large number of females who were buried elaborately in shrine rooms may have been priestesses of this cult. The site's principal excavator maintains that although male priests existed, "it seems extremely likely that the cult of the goddess was administered mainly by women."[5]

Metalworking became a specialized occupation in the late Neolithic period. At Çatal Hüyük, objects of copper and lead, which occur naturally in fairly pure form, date to about 6400 B.C.E. Silver and gold also appear at early dates in various parts of the world. Because of their rarity and their soft-

Neolithic Goddess   Many versions of a well-nourished and pregnant female figure were found at Çatal Hüyük. Here she is supported by twin leopards whose tails curve over her shoulders. To those who inhabited the city some 8,000 years ago the figure likely represented fertility and power over nature.   (C. M. Dixon)

ness, these metals did not replace stone tools and weapons. The discovery of decorative and ceremonial objects of metal in graves indicates that they became symbols of status and power.

Towns, specialized crafts, and religious shrines forced the farmers to produce extra food for nonfarmers like priests and artisans. The building of permanent houses, walls, and towers, not to mention megalithic monuments, also called for added labor. Stonehenge, for example, took some 30,000 person-hours to build. Whether these tasks were performed freely or coerced is unknown.

---

legume (LEG-yoom)

MESOPOTAMIA

Because of the unpredictable nature of the Tigris and Euphrates Rivers, the peoples of ancient Mesopotamia saw themselves at the mercy of gods, who embodied the forces of nature. The Babylonian Creation Myth (**Babylon** was the most important city in southern Mesopotamia in the second and first millennia B.C.E.) climaxes in a cosmic battle between Marduk, the chief god of Babylon, and Tiamat°, a female figure who personifies the salt sea. Marduk cuts up Tiamat and from her body fashions the earth and sky. He then creates the divisions of time, the celestial bodies, rivers, and weather phenomena. From the blood of a defeated rebel god, he creates human beings. Myths of this sort explained to the ancient inhabitants of Mesopotamia the environment in which they were living.

Settled Agriculture in an Unstable Landscape

Mesopotamia means "land between the rivers" in Greek. It reflects the centrality of the Euphrates and Tigris Rivers to the way of life in this region (see Map 1.1). The plain alongside and between the rivers, which originate in the mountains of eastern Anatolia (modern Turkey) and empty into the Persian Gulf, gains fertility from the silt deposited by river floods over many millennia.

Today mostly in Iraq, the Mesopotamian plain gives way to mountains in the north and east: an arc extending from northern Syria through southeastern Anatolia to the Zagros° Mountains that separate the plain from the Iranian Plateau. To the west and southwest lie the Syrian and Arabian deserts, to the southeast the Persian Gulf. Floods caused by snow melting in the northern mountains can be sudden and violent. They come inconveniently in the spring when crops, planted in winter to avoid the torrid summer temperatures, are ripening. Floods sometimes cause the rivers to change course, abruptly cutting off fields and towns from water and river communication.

Although the first domestication of plants and animals around 8000 B.C.E. occurred nearby, in the "Fertile Crescent" region of northern Syria and southeastern Anatolia, agriculture did not reach Mesopotamia until approximately 5000 B.C.E. "Dry" (unirrigated) farming requires at least 8 inches (20 centimeters) of rain a year. The hot, arid climate of southern Mesopotamia calls for irrigation, the artificial provision of water to crops. Initially, people probably channeled floodwater into nearby fields, but shortly after 3000 B.C.E., they learned to construct canals to supply water as needed and carry it to more distant fields.

Ox-drawn plows, developed by around 4000 B.C.E., cut a furrow in the earth into which carefully measured amounts of seed dropped from an attached funnel. Farmers favored barley as a cereal crop because it could tolerate the Mesopotamian climate and withstand the toxic effects of salt drawn to the surface of the soil by evaporation. Fields stood fallow (unplanted) every other year to replenish the nutrients in the soil. Date palms provided food, fiber, and wood. Garden plots produced vegetables. Reeds growing along the rivers and in the marshy southern delta yielded raw material for mats, baskets, huts, and boats. Fish was a dietary staple. Herds of sheep and goats, which grazed on fallow land or the nearby desert, provided wool, milk, and meat. Donkeys, originally domesticated in northeast Africa, joined cattle as beasts of burden in the third millennium B.C.E., as did camels from Arabia and horses from the mountains in the second millennium B.C.E.

The written record begins with the **Sumerians** and marks the division, by some definitions, between prehistory and history. Archaeological evidence places the Sumerians in southern Mesopotamia at least by 5000 B.C.E. and perhaps even earlier. They created the framework of civilization in Mesopotamia during a long period of dominance in the third millennium B.C.E. Other peoples lived in Mesopotamia as well. As early as 2900 B.C.E., personal names recorded in inscriptions from the more northerly cities reveal a non-Sumerian

---

Tiamat (TIE-ah-mat)   Zagros (ZAG-ruhs)

Semitic° language. (*Semitic* refers to a family of languages spoken in parts of western Asia and northern Africa. They include the Hebrew, Aramaic°, and Phoenician° of the ancient world and the Arabic of today.) Possibly the descendants of nomads from the desert west of Mesopotamia, these Semites seem to have lived in peace with the Sumerians, adopting their culture and sometimes achieving positions of wealth and power.

By 2000 B.C.E., the Semitic peoples had become politically dominant. From this time on, Akkadian°, a Semitic language, took precedence over Sumerian, although the Sumerian cultural legacy survived in translation. The Sumerian-Akkadian dictionaries compiled at the time to facilitate translations from Sumerian allow us today to read the language, which has no known relatives. The characteristics and adventures of the Semitic gods also indicate cultural borrowing. This cultural synthesis parallels a biological merging of Sumerians and Semites through intermarriage. Though other ethnic groups, including Kassites° from the eastern mountains and Elamites° and Persians from farther south in Iran, played roles in Mesopotamian history, the Sumerian/Semitic cultural heritage remained fundamentally unaltered until the arrival of Greeks in the late fourth century B.C.E.

Cities, Kings, and Trade

Mesopotamian farmers usually lived in villages. A group of families, totaling a few hundred persons perhaps, could protect one another, work together at key times in the agricultural cycle, and share tools, barns, and threshing floors. Village society also provided companionship and a pool of potential marriage partners.

Occasionally, as a particularly successful village grew, small satellite villages developed nearby and eventually merged with the main village to form an urban center. Cities depended on agriculture and therefore on the villages. Many early Mesopotamian city dwellers went out each day to labor in nearby fields. Other city dwellers, however, depended for food on the surplus food production of the villagers. Some specialized in crafts—for example, pottery, artwork, and forging weapons, tools, and other objects out of metal. Others served the gods or carried out administrative duties. Mesopotamian cities controlled the agricultural land and collected crop surpluses from villages in their vicinity. In return, the city provided rural districts with military protection against bandits and raiders and a market where villagers could acquire manufactured goods produced by urban specialists.

The term **city-state** refers to a self-governing urban center and the agricultural territories it controlled. Stretches of uncultivated land, either desert or swamp, served as buffers between the many small city-states of early Mesopotamia. Nevertheless, disputes over land, water rights, and movable property often sparked hostilities between neighboring cities and the building of protective walls of sun-dried bricks. At other times, cities cooperated, sharing water and allowing traders safe passage through their territories.

Mesopotamians opened new land to agriculture by building and maintaining irrigation networks. Canals brought water from river to field; drainage ditches carried the water back to the river before evaporation could draw harmful salt and minerals to the surface. Weirs (partial dams) raised the water level of the river so that water could flow by gravity into the canals. Dikes along the riverbanks protected against floods. The silt carried by floods clogged the canals, which required frequent dredging. In some places, levers with counterweights lifted buckets of irrigation water out of a river or canal.

Successful operation of such sophisticated irrigation systems depended on leaders compelling or persuading large numbers of people to work together. Other projects called for similar cooperation: harvesting, sheep shearing, building of fortifications and large public buildings, and warfare. Two centers of power, the temple and the palace of the king, have left written records, but details of governmental life remain scanty, as are the hints at some sort of citizens' assembly that may have evolved from traditional village councils.

One or more temples, centrally located, housed

Semitic (suh-MIT-ik)   **Aramaic** (ar-uh-MAY-ik)
Phoenician (fi-NEE-shuhn)   **Akkadian** (uh-KAY-dee-uhn)
Kassite (KAS-ite)   **Elamite** (EE-luh-mite)

each city-state's deity or deities and their associated cults—sets of religious rituals. Temples owned agricultural lands and stored the gifts that worshipers donated. The central location of the temple buildings confirms the importance of cults. Head priests, who controlled each shrine and managed its wealth, played prominent political and economic roles.

In the third millennium B.C.E., Sumerian documents show the emergence of a *lugal*° or "big man"—what we would call a king. An increase in warfare as ever-larger communities quarreled over land, water, and raw materials may have prompted this development, but details are lacking. According to one theory, communities chose certain men to lead their armies in time of war, and these individuals found ways to prolong their authority in peacetime and assume judicial and ritual functions. Although the lugal's position was not hereditary, it often passed from a father to a capable son.

The location of the temple in the city's heart and the less prominent siting of the king's palace symbolize the later emergence of royalty. The king's power grew at the expense of the priesthood, however, because the army backed him. The priests and temples retained influence because of their wealth and religious mystique, but they gradually became dependent on the palace. Some Mesopotamian kings claimed divinity, but this concept did not take root. Normally the king portrayed himself as the deity's earthly representative.

By the late third millennium B.C.E., kings assumed responsibility for the upkeep and building of temples and the proper performance of ritual. Other royal responsibilities included maintaining city walls and defenses, extending and repairing irrigation channels, guarding property rights, warding off foreign attacks, and establishing justice.

The *Epic of Gilgamesh* referred to at the beginning of this chapter shows both the ambition and the value to the community of the kings. Gilgamesh, who is probably based on a historical king of Uruk, stirs resentment by demanding sexual favors from new brides, but the community relies on his immense strength, wisdom, and courage. In quest of everlasting glory, Gilgamesh walls the

city magnificently, stamping his name on every brick. His journey to the faraway Cedar Mountains reflects the king's role in accessing valuable resources.

A few city-states became powerful enough to dominate their neighbors. Sargon°, ruler of Akkad° around 2350 B.C.E., pioneered in uniting many cities under one king and capital. His title, King of Sumer and Akkad, symbolized this claim to universal dominion. Sargon and the four family members who succeeded him over 120 years secured their power in several ways. They razed the walls of conquered cities and installed governors backed by garrisons of Akkadian troops. They gave soldiers land to ensure their loyalty. Being of Semitic stock, they adapted the cuneiform° system of writing used for Sumerian (discussed later in the chapter) to express their own language. Their administration featured a uniform system of weights and measures and standardized formats for official documents. These measures facilitated assessment and collection of taxes, recruitment of soldiers, and organization of labor projects.

For reasons that remain obscure, the Akkadian state fell around 2230 B.C.E. The Sumerian language and culture revived in the cities of the southern plain under the Third Dynasty of Ur (2112–2004 B.C.E.), a five-king dynasty that maintained itself for a century through campaigns of conquest and prudent marriage alliances. The Akkadian state had controlled more territory, but tighter government control based on a rapidly expanding bureaucracy and obsessive recordkeeping now secured Ur's dominance. Messengers and well-maintained road stations speeded up communications; and an official calendar, standardized weights and measures, and uniform writing practices improved central administration. To protect against nomadic Semitic Amorites° from the northwest, the kings erected a wall 125 miles (201 kilometers) long. Eventually, however, nomad incursions combined with an Elamite attack from the southeast toppled the Third Dynasty of Ur.

The Amorites founded a new city at Babylon, not far from Akkad. Toward the end of a long reign,

---

lugal (LOO-guhl)

Sargon (SAHR-gone)   Akkad (AH-kahd)
cuneiform (kyoo-NEE-uh-form)   Amorite (AM-uh-rite)

Hammurabi° (r. 1792–1750 B.C.E.) initiated a series of aggressive military campaigns, and Babylon became the capital of what historians have named the "Old Babylonian" state, which eventually stretched beyond Sumer and Akkad into the north and northwest, from 1800 to 1600 B.C.E. Hammurabi's famous Law Code, inscribed on a polished black stone pillar, provided judges with a lengthy set of examples illustrating the principles to be used in deciding cases. Some examples call for severe physical punishments to compensate for crimes. These Amorite notions of justice differed from the monetary penalties prescribed in earlier codes from Ur.

Conquest gave some Mesopotamian city-states access to vital resources. Trade offered an alternative, and long-distance commerce flourished in most periods. Evidence of seagoing vessels appears as early as the fifth millennium B.C.E. Wood, metals, and stone came from foreign lands in exchange for wool, cloth, barley, and vegetable oil. Cedar forests in Lebanon and Syria yielded wood, Anatolia produced silver, Egypt gold, and the eastern Mediterranean and Oman (on the Arabian peninsula) copper. Tin, which in alloy with copper made bronze, came from Afghanistan (in south-central Asia), and chlorite, a greenish, easily carved stone, from the Iranian plateau. Jewelers and stone-carvers used black diorite from the Persian Gulf, blue lapis lazuli° from Afghanistan, and reddish carnelian° from Pakistan.

Most merchants worked for the palace or the temple in the third millennium B.C.E. They alone commanded the financial resources and organizational skills needed for acquiring, transporting, and protecting valuable commodities. Merchants exchanged surpluses from the royal or temple farmlands for raw materials and luxury goods. In the second millennium B.C.E., independent merchants and merchant guilds gained increasing influence.

Sources do not reveal whether the most important commercial transactions took place in the area just inside the city gates or in the vicinity of the docks. Wherever they occurred, coined money played no role. Coins—stamped metal pieces of state-guaranteed value—first appeared in the sixth century B.C.E. and did not reach Mesopotamia until several centuries later. For most of Mesopotamian history, items that could not be bartered—traded for one another—had their value calculated in relation to fixed weights of precious metal, primarily silver, or measures of grain.

Mesopotamian Society

Urbanized civilizations foster social division, that is, obvious variation in the status and privileges of different groups according to wealth, social function, and legal and political rights. Urbanization, specialization of function, centralization of power, and use of written records enabled certain groups to amass unprecedented wealth. Temple leaders and the kings controlled large agricultural estates, and the palace administration collected taxes from subjects. How elite individuals acquired large private landholdings is unknown since land was rarely put up for sale. In some cases, however, debtors lost their land to creditors, or soldiers and priests received land in return for their services.

The Law Code of Hammurabi in the eighteenth century B.C.E. reflects social divisions that may have been valid for other places and times despite inevitable fluctuations. It identifies three classes: (1) the free landowning class—royalty, high-ranking officials, warriors, priests, merchants, and some artisans and shopkeepers; (2) the class of dependent farmers and artisans, whose legal attachment to royal, temple, or private estates made them the primary rural work force; and (3) the class of slaves, primarily employed in domestic service. Penalties prescribed in the Law Code depend on the class of the offender. The lower orders received the most severe punishments. Slaves, many of them prisoners of war from the mountains and others, insolvent debtors, played a lesser economic role than they would in the later societies of Greece and Rome (see Chapters 4 and 5). Identified by a distinctive hair style rather than chains or brands, they would have a barber shave off the telltale mark if they were lucky enough to regain their freedom. Because commodities such as food and oil were distributed to all people in proportion to their age,

---

Hammurabi (HAM-uh-rah-bee)
lapis lazuli (LAP-is LAZ-uh-lee)
carnelian (kahr-NEEL-yuhn)

gender, and task, documents do not always distinguish between slaves or dependent workers and free laborers. In the Old Babylonian period, the class of people who were not dependent on the temple or palace grew, the amount of land and other property in private hands increased, and free laborers became more common.

The daily lives of ordinary Mesopotamians, especially those in villages or on large estates, left few archaeological or literary traces. Peasants built with mud brick and reeds, which quickly disintegrate, and they had few metal possessions. Being illiterate, they left no written record of their lives. Male domination of the position of **scribe**—an administrator or scholar charged by the temple or palace with reading and writing tasks—further complicates efforts to reconstruct the lives of women. For the most part, their writings reflect elite male activities. Archaeology only partially fills this gap.

Anthropologists theorize that women lost social standing and freedom with the spread of agriculture. In hunting and gathering societies, they believe, women's foraging provided most of the community's food. But in Mesopotamia, food production depended on the heavy physical labor of plowing, harvesting, and digging irrigation channels, jobs usually performed by men. Since food surpluses made larger families possible, bearing and raising children became the primary occupation of many women, leaving them little time to acquire the specialized skills of a scribe or artisan.

Women could own property, maintain control of their dowry, and even engage in trade, but men monopolized political life. Some women worked outside the household in textile factories and breweries or as prostitutes, tavern keepers, bakers, or fortune-tellers. Home tasks for nonelite women probably included helping with farming, growing vegetables, cooking, cleaning, fetching water, tending the household fire, and weaving baskets and textiles.

The standing of women seems to have declined further in the second millennium B.C.E., perhaps because of the rise of an urbanized middle class and an increase in private wealth. Husbands gained authority in the household and benefited from marriage and divorce laws. A man normally took just one wife, but he could obtain a second if the first gave him no children. In later Mesopotamian history, kings and rich men had several wives. Marriage alliances arranged between families made women instruments for preserving and enhancing family wealth. Alternatively, a family might decide to avoid a daughter's marriage, with the resulting loss of a dowry, by dedicating her to temple service as "god's bride." Constraints on women's lives that eventually became part of Islamic tradition, such as remaining at home and wearing veils in public, may date back to the second millennium B.C.E. (see Chapter 8).

Gods, Priests, and Temples

The Sumerian gods embodied the forces of nature: Anu the sky, Enlil the air, Enki the water, Utu the sun, Nanna the moon. The goddess Inanna governed sexual attraction and violence. When the Semitic peoples became dominant, they equated their deities with those of the Sumerians. The Sumerian gods Nanna and Utu, for example, became the Semitic Sin and Shamash, while the goddess Inanna became Ishtar. The Semitic gods took over the myths and many of the rituals of their Sumerian predecessors.

People imagined their gods as anthropomorphic°, that is, like humans in form and conduct. The gods had bodies and senses, sought nourishment from sacrifice, enjoyed the worship and obedience of humanity, and experienced the human emotions of lust, love, hate, anger, and envy. Religious beliefs instilled fear of the gods, who could alter the landscape, and a desire to appease them.

Public, state-organized religion stands out in the archaeological record. Cities built temples and showed devotion to the divinity or divinities who protected the community. All the peoples of Sumer regarded Nippur (see Map 1.1) as a religious center because of its temple to the air god Enlil. As with other temples, they considered it the god's residence and believed the cult statue in its interior shrine embodied his life-force. Priests attended this divine image, trying to anticipate and meet its every need in a daily cycle of waking, bathing, dressing, feeding, moving around, entertaining,

---

anthropomorphic (an-thruh-puh-MORE-fik)

soothing, and revering. These rituals reflected the message of the Babylonian Creation Myth that humankind existed only to serve the gods. Several thousand priests may have staffed a large temple like that of the god Marduk at Babylon.

Priests passed their office and sacred lore to their sons, and their families lived on rations of food from the deity's estates. The amount an individual received depended on his rank within a complicated hierarchy of status and specialized function. The high priest performed the central acts in the great rituals. Certain priests pleasured the gods with music. Others exorcised evil spirits. Still others interpreted dreams and divined the future by examining the organs of sacrificed animals, reading patterns in rising incense smoke, or casting dice.

A high wall surrounded the temple precinct, which contained the shrine of the chief deity; open plazas; chapels for lesser gods; housing, dining facilities, and offices for priests and other temple staff; and buildings for crafts, storage, and other services. The compound focused on the **ziggurat°**, a multistory, mud-brick, pyramid-shaped tower approached by ramps and stairs. Scholars are still debating the ziggurat's function and symbolic meaning.

Scholars similarly debate whether common people had much access to temple buildings or how religious practices and beliefs affected their everyday lives. Individuals placed votive statues in the sanctuaries in the belief that these miniature replicas of themselves could continually seek the deity's favor. The survival of many **amulets** (small charms meant to protect the bearer from evil) and representations of a host of demons suggests widespread belief in magic—the use of special words and rituals to manipulate the forces of nature. They believed, for example, that a demon caused headaches and could be driven out of the ailing body. Lamashtu, the demon who caused miscarriages, could be frightened off if a pregnant woman wore an amulet with the likeness of the hideous but beneficent demon Pazuzu. A god or goddess might also be persuaded to reveal the future in return for a gift or sacrifice.

Elite and common folk came together in great festivals such as the twelve-day New Year's festival held each spring in Babylon as the new grain was beginning to sprout in the fields. In the early days of the festival, in conjunction with rituals of purification and invocations of Marduk, a priest read to the god's image the text of the Babylonian Creation Epic. Many subsequent activities in the temple courtyard and streets reenacted the events of the myth. Following their belief that time moved in a circular path through a cycle of birth, growth, maturity, and death, they hoped through this ritual to persuade the gods to grant a renewal of time and life at winter's end.

Technology and Science

The term *technology* comes from the Greek word *techne*, meaning "skill" or "specialized knowledge." It normally refers to the tools and processes by which humans manipulate the physical world. However, many scholars also use it more broadly for any specialized knowledge used to transform the natural environment and human society. Ancient Mesopotamian irrigation techniques that expanded agricultural production fit the first definition, priestly belief in their ability to enhance prosperity through prayers and rituals the second.

Writing, which first appeared in Mesopotamia before 3300 B.C.E., partakes more of the second definition than the first. The earliest inscribed tablets, found in the chief temple at Uruk, date from a time when the temple was the community's most important economic institution. The most plausible current theory maintains that writing originated from a system of tokens used to keep track of property—sheep, cattle, wagon wheels—as wealth accumulated and the volume and complexity of commerce strained people's memories. The shape and number of tokens inserted in clay "envelopes" (balls of clay) indicated the contents of a shipment or storeroom, and pictures of the tokens incised on the outside of the envelope reminded the reader of what was inside.

Eventually people realized that the incised pictures, the first written symbols, provided an adequate record of the transaction and made the tokens inside the envelope redundant. Each early

---

ziggurat (ZIG-uh-rat)

Mesopotamian Cylinder Seal   Seals indicated the identity of an individual and were impressed into wet clay or wax to "sign" legal documents or to mark ownership of an object. This seal, produced in the period of the Akkadian Empire, depicts Ea (second from right), the god of underground waters, symbolized by the stream with fish emanating from his shoulders; Ishtar, whose attributes of fertility and war are indicated by the date cluster in her hand and the pointed weapons showing above her wings; and the sun-god Shamash, cutting his way out of the mountains with a jagged knife, an evocation of sunrise.   (Courtesy of the Trustees of the British Museum)

symbol represented a thing, but it could also stand for the sound of the word for that thing when that sound was a syllable of a longer word. For example, the symbols *shu* for "hand" and *mu* for "water" could be combined to form *shumu*, the word for "name."

The usual method of writing involved pressing the point of a sharpened reed into a moist clay tablet. Because the reed made wedge-shaped impressions, the early pictures, which were more or less realistic, evolved into stylized combinations of strokes and wedges, a system known as **cuneiform** (Latin for "wedge-shaped") writing. Mastering cuneiform, which in any particular period involved several hundred signs, as compared to the twenty-five or so in an alphabetic system, required years of practice. In the "tablet-house" attached to a temple or palace, students learned writing and mathematics under a stern headmaster and endured bullying by older student tutors called "big brothers." The prestige and regular employment that went

with their position may have made scribes reluctant to simplify the cuneiform system. In the Old Babylonian period, the growth of private commerce brought an increase in the number of people who could read and write, but literacy remained a rare accomplishment.

Developed originally for the Sumerian language, cuneiform—a system of writing rather than a language—later served to express the Akkadian language of the Mesopotamian Semites as well as other languages of western Asia such as Hittite, Elamite, and Persian. The remains of the ancient city of Ebla° in northern Syria illustrate the Mesopotamian influence on other parts of western Asia. Ebla's buildings and artifacts follow Mesopotamian models, and thousands of tablets inscribed with cuneiform symbols bear messages in both Sumerian and the local Semitic dialect. The

---

Ebla (EH-bluh)

high point of Ebla's wealth and power occurred from 2400 to 2250 B.C.E., roughly contemporary with the Akkadian Empire. Ebla then controlled extensive territory and derived wealth from agriculture, manufacture of woolen cloth, and trade with Mesopotamia and the Mediterranean coast.

Economic concerns predominate in the earliest Sumerian documents, but cuneiform came to have wide-ranging uses beyond the recordkeeping that apparently inspired its invention. Legal acts that had formerly been validated by the recitation of oral formulas and performance of symbolic acts came to be accompanied by written documents marked with the seals of the participants. Cuneiform similarly served political, literary, religious, and scientific purposes.

In the physical realm, irrigation, the basis of Mesopotamian agriculture, required the construction and maintenance of canals, weirs, and dikes. Cattle drew carts and sledges in some locations. In the south, where numerous water channels cut up the landscape, boats and barges predominated. In northern Mesopotamia, donkeys served as pack animals for overland caravans in the centuries before the advent of the camel around 1200 B.C.E.

To improve on stone tools, the Mesopotamians imported ores containing copper, tin, and arsenic. From these they made bronze, a form of copper alloyed with either of the other two elements. Craftsmen poured molten bronze into molds shaped like weapons or tools. The cooled metal took a sharper edge than stone, was less likely to break, and was more easily repaired. Yet stone implements remained in use among poor people who could not afford bronze.

Clay, Mesopotamia's most abundant resource, went into the making of mud bricks. Whether dried in the sun or baked in an oven for greater durability, these constituted the main building material. Construction of city walls, temples, and palaces required practical knowledge of architecture and engineering. For example, the reed mats that Mesopotamian builders laid between the mud-brick layers of ziggurats served the same stabilizing purpose as girders in modern high-rise construction. Abundance of good clay also made pottery the most common material for dishes and storage vessels. By 4000 B.C.E., potters had begun to use a revolving platform called a potter's wheel.

Spun by hands or feet, the potter's wheel made possible rapid manufacture in precise and complex shapes.

Military technology changed as armies evolved from militias called up for short periods in the earliest periods to well-trained and well-paid full-time soldiers by the late third and second millennia B.C.E. In the early second millennium B.C.E., horses appeared in western Asia, and the horse-drawn chariot, a technically complicated device, came into vogue. Infantry found themselves at the mercy of swift chariots carrying a driver and an archer who could easily overtake them. Using increasingly effective siege machinery, Mesopotamian soldiers learned to climb over, undermine, or knock down the walls protecting the cities of their enemies.

In another area where the Mesopotamians sought to gain control of their physical environment, they used a base-60 number system (the origin of the seconds and minutes we use today) in which numbers were expressed as fractions or multiples of 60 (in contrast to our base-10 system). Such advances in mathematics along with careful observation of the skies made the Mesopotamians sophisticated practitioners of astronomy. Mesopotamian priests compiled lists of omens or unusual sightings on earth and in the heavens, together with a record of the events that coincided with them. They consulted these texts at critical times, for they believed that the recurrence of such phenomena could provide clues to future developments. The underlying premise was that the elements of the material universe, from the microcosmic to the macrocosmic, were interconnected in mysterious but undeniable ways.

EGYPT

No other place exhibits the impact of the natural environment on the history and culture of a society better than ancient Egypt. Though located at the intersection of Asia and Africa, Egypt was less a crossroads than an isolated land protected by surrounding barriers of desert and a harborless, marshy seacoast. Where Mesopotamia was open to migration or invasion and was dependent on imported resources, Egypt's natural isolation and material self-sufficiency fostered a unique culture that for long periods had relatively little to do with other civilizations.

The Land of Egypt: "Gift of the Nile"

The world's longest river, the Nile flows northward from Lake Victoria and draws water from several large tributaries in the highlands of tropical Africa. Carving a narrow valley between a chain of hills on either side, it terminates at the Mediterranean Sea (see Map 1.2). Though bordered mostly by desert, the banks of the river support lush vegetation. About 100 miles (160 kilometers) from the Mediterranean, the river divides into channels to form a triangular delta. Most of Egypt's population lives on the twisting, green ribbon of land along the river or in the Nile Delta. Bleak deserts of mountains, rocks, and dunes occupy the remaining 90 percent of the country. The ancient Egyptians distinguished between the low-lying, life-sustaining "Black Land" with its dark soil and the elevated, deadly "Red Land" of the desert. The fifth-century B.C.E. Greek traveler Herodotus° demonstrated insight when he called Egypt the "gift of the Nile."

Travel and communication centered on the river, with the most important cities located upstream away from the Mediterranean. Because the river flows from south to north, the Egyptians called the southern part of the country "Upper Egypt" and the northern delta "Lower Egypt." The First Cataract of the Nile, the northernmost of a series of impassable rocks and rapids below Aswan° (about 500 miles [800 kilometers] south of the Mediterranean) formed Egypt's southern boundary in most periods, but Egyptian control sometimes extended farther south into what they called "Kush" (later Nubia, today part of southern Egypt and northern Sudan). The Egyptians also settled certain large oases, green and habitable "islands" in the midst of the desert, which lay west of the river.

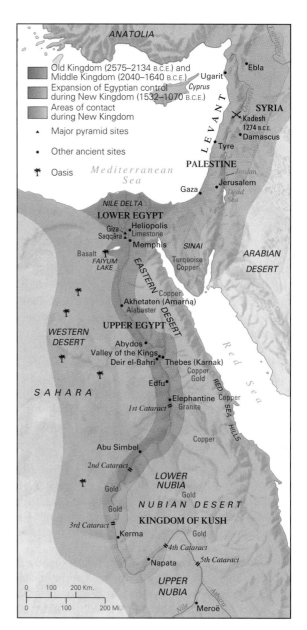

Map 1.2   Ancient Egypt   The Nile River, flowing south to north, carved out of the surrounding desert a narrow green valley that became heavily settled in antiquity.

Herodotus (he-ROD-uh-tuhs)   **Aswan** (AS-wahn)

The hot, sunny climate favored agriculture. Though rain rarely falls south of the delta, the river provides water to irrigation channels that carry water out into the valley and increase the area suitable for planting. In one large depression west of the Nile, drainage techniques reduced the size of Lake Faiyum° and allowed land to be reclaimed for agriculture.

Each September, the river overflowed its banks, spreading water into the bordering valley. Unlike the Mesopotamians, the Egyptians needed no dams or weirs to raise the level of the river and divert water into channels. Moreover, the Nile, unlike the Tigris and Euphrates, flooded at the best time for grain agriculture. When the flood receded and its waters drained back into the river, the land had a fertile new layer of mineral-rich silt, and farmers could easily plant their crops in the moist soil. The Egyptians' many creation myths commonly featured the emergence of a life-supporting mound of earth from a primeval swamp.

The level of the flood's crest determined the abundance of the following harvest. "Nilometers," stone staircases with incised units of height along the river's edge, recorded each flood. Too much water washed out the dikes protecting inhabited areas and caused much damage. Too little water left fertile land unirrigated and hence uncultivable, plunging the country into famine. The ebb and flow of successful and failed regimes seems linked to the cycle of floods. Nevertheless, remarkable stability characterized most eras, and Egyptians viewed the universe as an orderly and beneficent place.

Egypt's other natural resources offered further advantages. Papyrus reeds growing in marshy areas yielded fibers that made good sails, ropes, and a kind of paper. The wild animals and birds of the marshes and desert fringe and the abundant river fish attracted hunters and fishermen. Building stone could be quarried and floated downstream from a number of locations in southern Egypt. Clay for mud bricks and pottery could be found almost everywhere. Copper and turquoise deposits in the Sinai desert to the east and gold from Nubia to the south were within reach, and the state organized armed expeditions and forced labor to exploit these resources. Thus, Egypt was substantially more self-sufficient than Mesopotamia.

The farming villages that appeared in Egypt as early as 5500 B.C.E. relied on domesticated plant and animal species that had emerged several millennia earlier in western Asia. Egypt's emergence as a focal point of civilization, however, stemmed at least partially from a gradual change in climate from the fifth to the third millennium B.C.E. Before that time, the Sahara, today the world's largest desert, had a relatively mild and wet climate. Its lakes and grasslands supported a variety of plant and animal species as well as populations of hunter-gatherers (see Chapter 6). As the climate changed and the Sahara began to dry up, displaced groups migrated into the then marshy Nile Valley, where they developed a sedentary way of life.

Divine Kingship

The increasing population called for greater complexity in political organization, including a form of local kingship. Later generations of Egyptians saw the unification of such smaller units into a single state by Menes°, a ruler from the south, as a pivotal event. Scholars question whether this event, dated to around 3100 B.C.E., took place at the hands of a historical or mythical figure, but many authorities equate Menes with Narmer, a historical ruler who is shown on a decorated slate palette exulting over defeated enemies. Later kings of Egypt bore the title "Ruler of the Two Lands"—Upper and Lower Egypt—and wore two crowns symbolizing the unification of the country. Unlike Mesopotamia, Egypt discovered unity early in its history.

Following the practice of Manetho, an Egyptian priest from the fourth century B.C.E., historians divide Egyptian history into thirty dynasties (sequences of kings from the same family). The rise and fall of dynasties often reflects the dominance of one or another part of the country. Scholars also divide Egyptian history into "Old," "Middle," and "New Kingdoms," each a period of centralized

---

Faiyum (fie-YOOM)

Menes (MEH-neez)

political power and brilliant cultural achievement. "Intermediate Periods" signal political fragmentation and cultural decline. Although experts debate the specific dates, the chronology (on page 7) reflects current opinion.

The Egyptian state centered on the king, often known by the New Kingdom term **pharaoh,** from an Egyptian phrase meaning "palace." From the Old Kingdom on, if not earlier, Egyptians considered the king a god on earth, the incarnation of Horus and the son of the sun-god Re°. In this role he maintained **ma'at°,** the divinely authorized order of the universe. As a link between the people and the gods, his benevolent rule ensured the welfare and prosperity of the country. The Egyptians' conception of a divine king, the source of law and justice, may explain the apparent absence in Egypt of an impersonal code of law comparable to Hammurabi's Code in Mesopotamia.

So much depended on the kings that their deaths evoked elaborate efforts to ensure the well-being of their spirits on their journey to rejoin the gods. Carrying out funerary rites, constructing royal tombs, and sustaining the kings' spirits in the afterlife by perpetual offerings in adjoining funerary chapels demanded massive resources. Flat-topped, rectangular tombs made of mud brick sufficed for the earliest rulers, but around 2630 B.C.E., Djoser°, a Third Dynasty king, ordered the construction of a stepped **pyramid—**a series of stone platforms laid one on top of the other—at Saqqara°, near Memphis. Rulers of the Fourth Dynasty filled in the steps of Djoser's tomb to create the smooth-sided, limestone pyramids that most often symbolize ancient Egypt. Between 2550 and 2490 B.C.E., the pharaohs Khufu° and Khefren° erected huge pyramids at Giza, several miles north of Saqqara, the largest stone structures ever built. Khufu's pyramid originally reached a height of 480 feet (146 meters).

Egyptians accomplished this construction with stone tools (bronze was still expensive and rare) and no machinery other than simple levers, pulleys, and rollers. Calculations of the human muscle power needed to build a pyramid within a ruler's lifetime indicate that large numbers of people must have been pressed into service for part of each year, probably during the flood season, when no agricultural work could be done. The Egyptian masses probably considered this demand for labor a kind of religious service that would help ensure prosperity. Most of Egypt's surplus resources went into constructing these artificial mountains of stone. The age of the great pyramids lasted about a century, though construction of pyramids on a smaller scale continued for two millennia.

Administration and Communication

Ruling dynasties usually placed their capitals in the area of their original power base. **Memphis,** near today's Cairo at the apex of the Nile delta, held this central position during the Old Kingdom; but **Thebes,** far to the south, often supplanted it during the Middle and New Kingdom periods (see Map 1.2). A complex bureaucracy kept detailed records of the country's resources. Beginning at the village level and progressing to the district level and finally to the central government based in the capital, bureaucrats kept track of land, labor, products, and people, extracting as taxes a substantial portion—as much as 50 percent—of the annual revenues of the country. This income supported the palace, bureaucracy, and army; paid for building and maintaining temples; and made possible great monuments celebrating the king's grandeur. The government maintained a monopoly over key sectors of the economy and controlled long-distance trade. The urban middle-class traders who increasingly managed the commerce of Mesopotamia had no parallel in Egypt.

Literacy according to a writing system developed before the Early Dynastic period marked the administrative class. **Hieroglyphics°,** the earliest form of this system, featured picture symbols standing for words, syllables, or individual sounds. We can read ancient Egyptian writing today only because of the discovery in the early nineteenth century C.E. of the Rosetta Stone, an inscription from the second century B.C.E. that gave hieroglyphic and Greek versions of the same text.

Re (ray)   ma'at (muh-AHT)   Djoser (JO-sur)
Saqqara (suh-KAHR-uh)   Khufu (KOO-foo)
Khefren (KEF-ren)

hieroglyphics (high-ruh-GLIF-iks)

Hieroglyphic writing long continued in use on monuments and ornamental inscriptions. By 2500 B.C.E., however, administrators and copyists had developed a cursive script, in which the original pictorial nature of the symbol was less apparent, for their everyday needs. They wrote with ink on a writing material called **papyrus°**, made from the stems of the papyrus reed that grew in the Nile marshes. Papyrus makers laid the stems out in a vertical and horizontal grid pattern, moistened them, and then pounded them with a soft mallet until they adhered into a sheet of writing material. A uniquely Egyptian product, papyrus served scribes throughout the ancient world and was exported in large quantities. The word *paper* comes from Greek and Roman words for papyrus.

Apart from administrative recordkeeping, Egyptian literary compositions included tales of adventure and magic, love poetry, religious hymns, and instruction manuals on technical subjects. Scribes in workshops attached to the temples made copies of traditional texts.

Strong monarchs appointed and promoted officials on the basis of merit and accomplishment, giving them grants of land cultivated by dependent peasants. Low-level officials worked in villages and district capitals; high-ranking officials served in the royal capital. During the Old Kingdom, the tombs of officials lay near the monumental tomb of the king so they could serve him in death as they had in life.

Egyptian history exhibits a recurring tension between the centralizing power of the monarchy and the decentralizing tendencies of the bureaucracy. The shift of officials' tombs from the vicinity of the royal tomb to home districts where they spent much of their time and exercised power more or less independently signaled the breakdown of centralized power in the late Old Kingdom and First Intermediate Period. Inheritance of administrative posts similarly indicated a decline in centralized power. The early monarchs of the Middle Kingdom restored centralized power by reducing the power and prerogatives of the old elite and creating a new middle class of administrators.

The common observation that Egypt was a land of villages without real cities stems from its capitals being primarily extensions of the palace and central administration. Compared to Mesopotamia, a far larger percentage of the Egyptian population lived in farming villages, and Egypt's wealth derived to a higher degree from cultivating the land. The towns and cities that did exist unfortunately lie buried beneath modern urban sites since Egypt has too little land in its cultivable region to afford abandonment of a large area.

Egypt largely stuck to itself during the Old and Middle Kingdoms, all foreigners being technically regarded as enemies. When necessary, local militia units backed up a small standing army of professional soldiers. Nomadic groups in the eastern and western deserts and Libyans to the northwest posed a nuisance more than a real danger. The king maintained limited contact with other advanced civilizations in the region. Egypt's interests abroad focused on maintaining access to resources rather than on acquiring territory. Trade with the Levant° coast (modern Israel, Lebanon, and Syria) brought in cedar wood in return for grain, papyrus, and gold.

Egypt's strongest interests involved goods from the south. Nubia contained gold mines (in Chapter 2 we examine the rise in Nubia of a civilization influenced by Egypt but also vital, original, and long lasting), and the southern course of the Nile offered access to sub-Saharan Africa. In the Old Kingdom, Egyptian noblemen living at Aswan on the southern border led donkey caravans south in search of gold, incense, and products from tropical Africa such as ivory, ebony, and exotic animals. Forts along the border protected Egypt from attack. In the early second millennium B.C.E., Egyptian forces invaded Nubia and extended the Egyptian border as far as the Third Cataract of the Nile, taking possession of the gold fields.

The People of Egypt

The estimated million to a million and half inhabitants of Egypt included various physical types, ranging from dark-skinned people related to the populations of sub-Saharan Africa to lighter-skinned people akin to the populations of North Africa and western Asia who spoke Berber and

---

Semitic languages, respectively. Though Egypt experienced no migrations or invasions on a scale common in Mesopotamian history, settlers periodically trickled into the Nile Valley and mixed with the local people.

Egypt had less pronounced social divisions than Mesopotamia, where a formal class structure emerged. The king and high-ranking officials enjoyed status, wealth, and power. Below them came lower-level officials, local leaders, priests and other professionals, artisans, and well-to-do farmers. Peasants, at the bottom, constituted the vast majority of the population.

Peasants lived in rural villages and devoted themselves to the seasonally changing tasks of agriculture: plowing, sowing, tending emerging shoots, reaping, threshing, and storing. They maintained irrigation channels, basins, and dikes. Fish and meat from domesticated animals—cattle, sheep, goats, and poultry—supplemented a diet based on wheat or barley, beer, and vegetables. Villages probably shared implements, work animals, and storage facilities and helped one another at peak times in the agricultural cycle and in building projects. Festivals to the local gods and other public celebrations occasionally brought feasting and ceremonies into their lives; labor conscripted for pyramid construction and other state projects brought hardship. If the burden of taxation or compulsory service proved too great, flight into the desert usually offered the only escape.

This account of village life depends on guesswork and bits and pieces of archaeological and literary evidence. Tomb paintings of the elite sometimes depict the lives of common folk. The artists employed conventions to indicate status: obesity for the rich and comfortable, baldness and deformity for the working classes. Egyptian poets frequently employed metaphors of farming and hunting, and papyrus documents preserved in the hot, dry sands tell of property transactions and legal disputes among ordinary people.

Slavery existed on a limited scale and was of little economic significance. Prisoners of war, condemned criminals, and debtors could be found on country estates or in the households of the king and wealthy families. But humane treatment softened the burden of slavery, as did the possibility of being freed.

Scarceness of sources also clouds the experiences of women. What is known about the lives of elite women derives from the possibly distorted impressions of male artists and scribes. Tomb paintings, rendered with dignity and affection, show women of the royal family and elite classes accompanying their husbands and engaging in domestic activities. Subordination to men is evident. The convention of depicting men with a dark red and women with a yellow flesh tone implies that elite women stayed indoors, away from the searing sun. In the beautiful love poetry of the New Kingdom, lovers address each other in terms of apparent equality and express emotions akin to our own ideal of romantic love. Whether this poetry represents the attitudes prevalent in other periods or among nonelite groups remains unknown.

Legal documents show that Egyptian women could own property, inherit from their parents, and will their property to whomever they wished. Marriage, usually monogamous, arose from a couple's decision to establish a household together rather than through legal or religious ceremony. Either party could dissolve the relationship, and the woman retained rights over her dowry in case of divorce. At certain times, queens and queen-mothers played significant behind-the-scenes roles in the politics of the royal court, and priestesses sometimes supervised the cults of female deities. In general, the limited evidence suggests that women in ancient Egypt enjoyed greater respect and more legal rights and social freedom than women in Mesopotamia and other ancient societies.

Belief and Knowledge

Egyptian religion evoked the landscape of the Nile Valley and the vision of cosmic order that this environment fostered. The sun rose every day into a clear and cloudless sky, and the river flooded on schedule every year, ensuring a bounteous harvest. Recurrent cycles and periodic renewal seemed a part of the natural world. Egyptians imagined the sky to be a great ocean surrounding the inhabited world. The sun-god Re traversed its waters in a boat by day, then returned through the Underworld at night, fighting off the attacks of demonic serpents so that he could be born anew each morning. In one especially popular story, Osiris°, a god who once ruled the land of Egypt, dies at the hand of his jealous brother Seth, who scatters his dismembered remains. Isis, Osiris's sister and wife, finds and reassembles the pieces, while Horus, his son, takes revenge on Seth. Restored to life and installed as king of the Underworld, Osiris represented hope for a new life in a world beyond this one.

The king, represented as Horus and as the son of Re, fit into the pattern of the dead returning to life and the sun-god renewing life. As Egypt's chief priest, he intervened with the gods on behalf of his land and people. When a particular town became the capital of a ruling dynasty, the chief god of that town gained prominence throughout the land. Thus, did Ptah° of Memphis, Re of Heliopolis°, and Amon° of Thebes become gods of all Egypt, serving to unify the country and strengthen the monarchy.

Egyptian rulers zealously built new temples, refurbished old ones, and made lavish gifts to the gods, at the same time overseeing construction of their own tombs. Thus, much of the country's wealth went for religious purposes in the ceaseless effort to win the gods' favor, maintain the continuity of divine kingship, and ensure the renewal of life-giving forces.

Some deities normally appear with animal heads; others always take human form. Few myths about the origins and adventures of the gods have survived, but there must have been a rich oral tradition. Many towns had temples in which locally prominent deities were thought to reside. Such local deities could be viewed as manifestations of the great gods, and gods could merge to form hybrids, such as Amon-Re. Ordinary believers were excluded from cult activities in the inner reaches of the temples, where priests served the daily needs of the deity by attending to his or her statue. Food offered to the image was later distributed to temple staff. As in Mesopotamia, some temples possessed extensive landholdings worked by dependent peasants, and the priests who administered the deity's wealth played an influential role locally and sometimes throughout the land.

During great festivals, the priests paraded a boat-shaped litter carrying the shrouded statue and cult items of the deity around the town. This brought large numbers of people into contact with the deity in an outpouring of devotion and celebration. Little is known about the day-to-day beliefs and practices of the common people, however. At home, family members revered and made small offerings to Bes, the grotesque god of marriage and domestic happiness, to local deities, and to the family's ancestors. They relied on amulets and depictions of demonic figures to ward off evil forces. In later times, Greeks and Romans commented on the Egyptian devotion to magic.

Egyptians believed in the afterlife. They prepared extensively for a safe passage and a comfortable existence once they arrived. Hazards abounded on the soul's journey after death. The Egyptian Book of the Dead, present in many excavated tombs, contained rituals and spells to protect the journeying spirit. The weighing of the deceased's heart (believed to be the source of personality, intellect, and emotion) in the presence of the judges of the Underworld presented the ultimate challenge—the one that determined whether the deceased had led a good life and deserved to reach the blessed destination.

The Egyptian obsession with the afterlife produced concerns about the physical condition of the dead body and a perfection of mummification techniques for preserving it. The idea probably derived from the slow decomposition of bodies buried in hot, dry sand on the edge of the desert, an early practice. The elite classes spent the most on mummification. Specialists removed vital organs for preservation and storage in stone jars laid out around the corpse and filled the body cavities with various packing materials. After immersing the cadaver for long periods in dehydrating and preserving chemicals, they wrapped it in linen. They then placed the **mummy** in one or more decorated wooden caskets with a tomb.

Building tombs at the edge of the desert left the lowlands free for farming. Pictures and samples of food and objects from everyday life accompanied the mummy to provide whatever he or she might need in the next life. Much of what is now known about ancient Egyptian life comes from examining utilitarian and luxury household objects

---

Osiris (oh-SIGH-ris) **Ptah** (puh-TAH)
Heliopolis (he-lee-OP-uh-lis) **Amon** (AH-muhn)

Painted Wooden Models from the Tomb of an Egyptian Nobleman, ca. 2000 B.C.E.   Meketre,
seated at right, oversees inspection of his cattle with the help of herdsmen and other servants.
(Giraudon/Art Resource, NY)

found in tombs. Small figurines called shawabtis°
represented the servants whom the deceased
might need or the laborers he might send as substitutes if asked to provide compulsory labor. The
elite classes ordered chapels attached to their
tombs and left endowments to subsidize the daily
attendance of a priest and offerings of foodstuffs to
sustain their spirits for eternity.

The form of the tomb also reflected wealth and
status. Simple pit graves or small mud-brick chambers sufficed for the common people. Members
of the privileged classes built larger tombs and
covered the walls with pictures and inscriptions.
Kings erected pyramids and other grand edifices,
employing trickery to hide the sealed chamber con-

taining the body and treasures, as well as curses and
other magical precautions to foil tomb robbers.
Rarely did they succeed, however. Archaeologists
have seldom discovered an undisturbed royal tomb.

The ancient Egyptians explored many areas of
knowledge and developed advantageous technologies. They learned about chemistry through developing the mummification process, which also
provided opportunities to learn about human
anatomy. Egyptian doctors served in royal courts
throughout western Asia because of their relatively
advanced medical knowledge and techniques.

The endless cycle of flooding and irrigation
spurred the development of mathematics for de-
termining the dimensions of fields and calculating
the quantity of agricultural produce owed to the
state. Through careful observation of the stars,

---

shawabtis (shuh-WAB-tees)

they constructed the most accurate calendar in the world, and they knew that when the star Sirius appeared on the horizon shortly before sunrise, the Nile flood surge was imminent.

For pyramids, temple complexes, and other monumental building projects, vast quantities of earth had to be moved and the construction site made level. Large stones had to be quarried, dragged on rollers, floated downstream on barges, lifted into place along ramps of packed earth, carved to the exact size needed, and then made smooth. Long underground passageways connected mortuary temples by the river with tombs near the desert's edge. More practically, several Egyptian kings dredged a canal more than 50 miles (80 kilometers) long to connect the Nile Valley to the Red Sea and expedite the transport of goods.

Besides river barges for transporting building stones, the Nile carried lightweight ships equipped with sails and oars. These sometimes ventured into the Mediterranean and Red Seas. Canals and flooded basins limited the use of carts and sledges, but archaeologists have discovered an 8-mile (13-kilometer) road made of slabs of sandstone and limestone connecting a rock quarry with Faiyum Lake. The oldest known paved road in the world, it dates to the second half of the third millennium B.C.E.

THE INDUS VALLEY CIVILIZATION

Civilization developed almost as early in South Asia as in Mesopotamia and Egypt. Just as each Middle Eastern civilization centered on a great river valley, so civilization in the Indian subcontinent originated on a fertile floodplain. In the valley of the Indus River, settled farming created the agricultural surplus essential to urbanized society.

Natural Environment

A plain of more than 1 million acres (400,000 hectares) stretches between the mountains of western Pakistan and the Thar° Desert to the east in the central portion of the Indus Valley, the province of Sind° in modern Pakistan (see Map 1.1). Silt carried downstream and deposited on the land by the Indus River over many centuries elevates the riverbed and its banks above the level of the plain. Twice a year, the river overflows and inundates surrounding land as far as 10 miles (16 kilometers) distant. Snowmelt from the Pamir° and Himalaya° mountains feeds the flood in March and April. In August, seasonal winds called monsoons (see Chapter 13) bring rains from the southwest that feed a second flood. Though extremely dry for the rest of the year, Sind's floods make two crops a year possible. In ancient times, the Hakra° River (sometimes referred to as the Saraswati), which has since dried up, ran parallel to the Indus about 25 miles (40 kilometers) to the east and supplied water to a second cultivable area.

Adjacent regions shared distinctive cultural traits with this core area. In Punjab (literally "five waters"), to the northeast, five rivers converge to feed the main stream of the Indus. Closer to the northern mountains, the Punjab receives more rainfall but less floodwater than Sind. Culturally similar settlements extend from the Punjab as far east as Delhi° in northwest India. Settlement also extended through the Indus delta in southern Sind down into India's hook-shaped Kathiawar° Peninsula, an area of alluvial plains and coastal marshes. The Indus Valley Civilization, as scholars labeled this area of cultural homogeneity when they first discovered it eighty years ago, covered an area roughly equivalent to modern France.

Material Culture

Although archaeologists have located several hundred communities that flourished from approximately 2600 to 1900 B.C.E., the remains of two urban sites, known by the modern names **Harappa** and **Mohenjo-Daro°**, best typify the Indus Valley Civilization. Unfortunately,

---

Thar (tahr) **Sind** (sinned) **Pamir** (pah-MEER)
Himalaya (him-uh-LAY-uh) **Hakra** (HAK-ruh)
Delhi (DEL-ee) **Kathiawar** (kah-tee-uh-WAHR)
Mohenjo-Daro (moe-hen-joe–DAHR-oh)

the high water table at these sites makes excavation of the earliest levels of settlement nearly impossible.

Scholars once believed that the people who created this civilization spoke Dravidian° languages related to those spoken today in southern India. Invaders from the northwest speaking Indo-European languages, they thought, conquered these people around 1500 B.C.E., causing some of them to migrate to the southeast. Skeletal evidence, however, indicates that the population of the Indus Valley has remained stable from ancient times to the present. Settled agriculture in this region seems to date back to at least 5000 B.C.E. Archaeological investigations have not yet revealed the relations between the Indus Valley Civilization and earlier cultural complexes in the Indus Valley and the hilly lands to the west or the forces that gave rise to the urbanization, population increase, and technological advances that occurred in the mid-third millennium B.C.E. Nevertheless, the case for continuity with earlier cultures seems stronger than the case for a sudden transformation due to the arrival of new peoples.

The writing system of the Indus Valley people contained more than four hundred signs to represent syllables and words. Archaeologists have recovered thousands of inscribed seal stones and copper tablets. The inscriptions are so brief, however, that no one has yet deciphered them, though some scholars believe they represent an early Dravidian language.

Harappa, 3½ miles (5.6 kilometers) in circumference, may have housed a population of 35,000 and Mohenjo-Daro several times that. These cities show marked similarities in planning and construction: high, thick, encircling walls of brick; streets laid out in a rectangular grid; and covered drainpipes to carry away waste. The consistent width of streets and length of city blocks, and the uniformity of the mud bricks used in construction, suggest a strong central authority, located possibly in the citadel—an elevated, enclosed compound containing large buildings. Scholars think the well-ventilated structures near the citadel stored grain for local use and for export. The presence of barracks may point to some regimentation of skilled artisans.

Though it is presumed that these urban centers controlled the surrounding farmlands, different centers may have served different functions, which might account for their locations. Mohenjo-Daro seems to dominate the great floodplain of the Indus. Harappa, which is nearly 500 miles (805 kilometers) to the north, sits in the zone where farmlands give way to pasturelands. No settlements have been found west of Harappa, which may have served as a gateway for copper, tin, precious stones, and other resources coming from the northwest. Coastal towns to the south engaged in seaborne trade with Sumer and lands around the Persian Gulf, as well as fishing and gathering highly prized seashells.

While published accounts of the Indus Valley civilization tend to treat Mohenjo-Daro and Harappa, the most extensively excavated sites, as the norm, most people surely lived in smaller settlements, which exhibit the same artifacts and the same standardization of styles and shapes as the large cities. Some scholars attribute this standardization to extensive exchange of goods within the zone of Indus Valley civilization rather than to a strong and authoritarian central government.

Metal appears more frequently in Indus Valley sites than in Mesopotamia or Egypt. Tools and other useful objects outweigh in importance the decorative objects—jewelry and the like—so often found in those other regions. Largely the possessions of elite groups in the Middle East, metal goods belonged to a broad cross-section of the population in the Indus Valley.

Technologically, the Indus Valley people showed skill in irrigation, used the potter's wheel, and fired bricks to rocky hardness in kilns for use in the foundations of large public buildings (sun-dried bricks exposed to floodwaters would have dissolved quickly). Smiths worked with various metals—gold, silver, copper, and tin. The varying ratios of tin to copper in their bronze objects suggest awareness of the hardness of different mixtures. They used less tin, a relative scarce metal, in objects that did not require maximum hardness, like knives, and more tin in things like axes that had to be harder.

Archaeological finds point to widespread trad-

Dravidian (druh-VID-ee-uhn)

ing contacts. Mountain passes through the northwest granted access to the valuable resources of eastern Iran and Afghanistan, as well as to ore deposits in western India. These resources included metals (such as copper and tin), precious stones (lapis lazuli, jade, and turquoise), building stone, and timber. Rivers provided thoroughfares for transporting goods within the zone of Indus Valley culture. The undeciphered writing on the many seal stones, some scholars feel, may represent the names of merchants who stamped their wares.

Inhabitants of the Indus Valley and of Mesopotamia obtained raw materials from some of the same sources. The discovery of Indus Valley seal stones in the Tigris-Euphrates Valley indicates that merchants from the former region may have acted as middlemen in long-distance trade, obtaining raw materials from the northwest and shipping them to the Persian Gulf.

We know little about the political, social, economic, and religious structures of Indus Valley society. Efforts to link artifacts and images to cultural features characteristic of later periods of Indian history (see Chapter 6), including sociopolitical institutions (a system of hereditary occupational groups, the predominant role of priests), architectural forms (bathing tanks like those later found in Hindu temples, private interior courtyards in houses), and religious beliefs and practices (depictions of gods and sacred animals on the seal stones, a cult of the mother-goddess), remain speculative. Further knowledge on these matters awaits additional archaeological finds and deciphering the Indus Valley script.

Transformation of the Indus Valley Civilization

The Indus Valley cities were abandoned sometime after 1900 B.C.E. Archaeologists once thought that invaders destroyed them, but they now believe this civilization suffered "systems failure"—a breakdown of the fragile interrelationship of political, social, and economic systems that sustained order and prosperity. The precipitating cause may have been one or more natural disasters, such as an earthquake or massive flooding. Gradual ecological changes may also have played a role as the Hakra river system dried

up, and salinization (an increase in the amount of plant-inhibiting salt in the soil) and erosion increased (see Environment and Technology: Environmental Stress in the Indus Valley).

Towns left dry by a change of riverbed, seaports removed from the coast by silt deposited in deltas, and regions suffering loss of fertile soil would have necessitated the relocation of populations and a change in the livelihood of those who remained. The causes, patterns, and pace of change probably varied, with urbanization persisting longer in some regions than in others. The urban centers eventually succumbed, however, and village-based farming and herding took their place. As the interaction between regions lessened, regional variation replaced the standardization of technology and style of the previous era.

Historians can do little more than speculate about the causes behind the changes and the experiences of the people who lived in the Indus Valley around 1900 B.C.E. Two tendencies bear remembering, however. In most cases like this, the majority of the population adjusts to the new circumstances. But members of the political and social elite, who depend on urban centers and complex political and economic structures, lose the source of their authority and merge with the population as a whole.

CONCLUSION

Tens of thousands of years elapsed between the first appearance of the earliest ancestors of humankind and the agricultural revolutions that made possible the transition to civilization. Domesticated plants and animals contributed to the settling down of wandering groups of foragers and, in time, produced sufficient surplus food to relieve a small minority of people from the labor of tilling fields and watching flocks. Some of these people availed themselves of this opportunity to advance already existing skills—painting, stone-working, weaving, building—to higher levels requiring more specialized techniques. Others specialized in warfare, administration, religious ceremonies, and accumulation of knowledge. Thus did humanity

Environmental Stress in the Indus Valley

Vulnerability to environmental change characterizes the arid or semiarid river valleys discussed in this chapter. Debates about the possible impact of such changes on the Indus Valley Civilization highlight some of the significant factors as well as the difficulties of verifying and interpreting long-ago changes.

An earlier generation of scholars believed the Indus Valley was considerably wetter during the height of that civilization than it is now. They cited the enormous quantities of timber needed to bake the millions of bricks used in the cities (see photo), human settlement remains on land now unfit for agriculture, and depictions of jungle and marsh animals on carved seals. Assuming that the population growth, prosperity, and complexity of the Indus Valley Civilization in the third millennium B.C.E. required wet conditions, this approach concludes that a drier climate caused its decline in the early second millennium.

Other experts doubt such a radical climatic change, presenting alternative estimates of timber consumption and evidence of barley cultivation, a grain that tolerates dry conditions. Recent studies of the stabilization of sand dunes, a sign of heavy rainfall, and of the sediments deposited by rivers and winds strengthen the model of third millennium wetness and early-to-mid-second-millennium dryness, which continues today.

Scholars agree, however, that earthquakes caused shifts in the courses of rivers. Satellite photographs and on-the-ground inspections reveal old riverbeds, in particular a second major river system, the Hakra, that once ran parallel to the Indus some distance to the east. Lined with towns and fields, the Hakra appears to have been a second axis of this civilization. Either the Sutlej, which now feeds into the Indus, or the Yamuna, which now pours into the Ganges, flowed into the Hakra before undergoing a change of course. The drying of the Hakra meant loss of arable land, abandonment of cities and villages, migration of populations, shifts in the trade, and increased competition for shrinking resources.

Mud-Brick Fortification Wall of the Citadel at Harappa
Built upon a high platform, this massive and towering construction required large numbers of bricks and extensive labor resources. *The Cambridge History of India: The Indus Civilization,* 3d ed. (1968), by Sir Mortimer Wheeler. With permission of the Syndics of the Cambridge University Press.

The Indus itself, in its lower reaches, has shifted 100 miles (161 kilometers) to the west since the Greek conqueror Alexander the Great arrived in the late fourth century B.C.E., and its mouth has migrated 50 miles (80 kilometers) southward because of silt deposited by floods. Similar shifts may have occurred in the third and second millennia B.C.E.

An authoritative study concludes: "It is obvious that ecological stresses, caused both climatically and technically, played an important role in the life and decay" of the Indus civilization.

Source: Quotation from D. P. Agarwal and R. K. Sood in Gregory L. Possehl, ed., *Harappan Civilization: A Contemporary Perspective* (Warminster, England: Aris and Phillips, 1982), 229.

pass from the prehistoric era to the era of civilized history.

The first civilizations developed high levels of political centralization, urbanization, and technology because their situations in river valleys too arid to support agriculture through rainfall forced communities to work together on constructing and maintaining canals, dams, weirs, and dikes. Crops harvested from irrigated fields not only fed the farming populations of Mesopotamia, Egypt, and the Indus Valley, but produced enough surplus to support artisans with specialized expertise in engineering, mathematics, and metallurgy.

Unpredictable and violent floods constantly threatened communities in the Tigris-Euphrates Basin, but the opportune and gradual Nile floods usually brought joy and satisfaction to those in Egypt. Relationships with nature stamped the worldview of both peoples. Mesopotamians tried to appease their harsh deities in order to survive in an unpredictable world. Egyptians trusted in and nurtured the supernatural powers they believed guaranteed orderliness and prosperity.

In both Egypt and Mesopotamia, kingship emerged as the dominant political form. The Egyptian king's divine origins and symbolic association with the forces of renewal made him central to the welfare of the entire country and gave him a religious monopoly superseding the authority of the temples and priests. Egyptian monarchs lavished much of the country's wealth on their tombs, believing that a proper burial would ensure the continuity of kingship and the attendant blessings that it brought to the land and people. Mesopotamian rulers, who were not normally regarded as divine, built new cities, towering walls, splendid palaces, and religious edifices as lasting testaments to their power.

Both cultures revered a hierarchy of gods, ranging from protective demons and local deities to gods of the state, whose importance rose or fell with the power of the political centers with which they were associated. Cheered by the stability of their environment, Egyptians conceived a positive notion of the gods' designs for humankind. They believed that despite hazards, the righteous spirit could journey to the next world and look forward to a blessed existence. In contrast, terrifying visions of the afterlife torment Gilgamesh, the Mesopotamian hero: disembodied spirits of the dead stumbling around in the darkness of the Underworld for all eternity, eating dust and clay, and slaving for the heartless gods of that realm.

Cultural continuity marked both Egypt and Mesopotamia despite substantial ethnic diversity. Immigrants assimilated to the dominant language, belief system, and lifestyles of the civilization. Culture, not physical appearance, served as the criterion of personal identification. Reduced freedom and legal privilege for Mesopotamian women in the second millennium B.C.E. may relate to a high degree of urbanization and class stratification. In contrast, Egyptian pictorial documents, love poems, and legal records indicate an attitude of respect and a higher degree of equality for women in the valley of the Nile.

In the second millennium B.C.E., as the societies of Mesopotamia and Egypt consolidated their cultural achievements and entered new phases of political expansion, and as the Indus Valley centers went into irreversible decline, a new and distinctive civilization, based on exploiting the agricultural potential of a floodplain, emerged in the valley of the Yellow River in eastern China. We turn to that area in Chapter 2.

■ Key Terms

civilization	scribe
culture	ziggurat
history	amulet
Stone Age	cuneiform
Paleolithic	pharaoh
Neolithic	ma'at
foragers	pyramid
Agricultural Revolutions	Memphis
Holocene	Thebes
megalith	hieroglyphics
Babylon	papyrus
Sumerians	mummy
Semitic	Harappa
city-state	Mohenjo-Daro
Hammurabi	

■ Suggested Reading

Reliable textbooks are Brian Fagan's *People of the Earth: An Introduction to World Prehistory*, 9th ed. (1997), and Bernard G. Campbell, *Humankind Emerging*, 6th ed. (1992). Fagan also has written *World Prehistory: A Brief Introduction*, 4th ed. (1998).

Ann Sieveking, *The Cave Artists* (1979), Mario Ruspoli, *The Cave Art of Lascaux* (1986), and N. K. Sanders, *Prehistoric Art in Europe* (1968) provide overviews of major European sites.

For ideas on the transition to food production, see Jared Diamond, *Guns, Germs, and Steel: The Fates of Human Societies* (1997), and Allen W. Johnson and Timothy Earle, *The Evolution of Human Societies: From Foraging Group to Agrarian State* (1987). Jean-Pierre Mohen, *The World of Megaliths* (1990), analyzes early monumental architecture. James Mellaart, the principal excavator of Çatal Hüyük, discusses his work for the general reader in *Çatal Hüyük: A Neolithic Town in Anatolia* (1967).

Jack M. Sasson, ed., *Civilizations of the Ancient Near East*, 4 vols. (1993), contains up-to-date articles and a bibliography on a wide range of topics. An excellent starting point for geography, chronology, and basic institutions and cultural concepts in ancient western Asia is Michael Roaf, *Cultural Atlas of Mesopotamia and the Ancient Near East* (1990). Amelie Kuhrt, *The Ancient Near East, c. 3000–330 B.C.*, 2 vols. (1995), is the best and most up-to-date introduction to the historical development of western Asia and Egypt, offering a clear and concise historical outline and a balanced presentation of continuing controversies. Other general historical introductions can be found in A. Bernard Knapp, *The History and Culture of Ancient Western Asia and Egypt* (1988); Hans J. Nissen, *The Early History of the Ancient Near East, 9000–2000 B.C.* (1988); H. W. F. Saggs, *Civilization Before Greece and Rome* (1989); and Georges Roux, *Ancient Iraq*, 3d ed. (1992). Joan Oates, *Babylon* (1979), focuses on the most important of all the Mesopotamian cities. J. N. Postgate, *Early Mesopotamia: Society and Economy at the Dawn of History* (1992), offers deep insights into political, social, and economic dynamics. Daniel C. Snell, *Life in the Ancient Near East 3100–322 B.C.E.* (1997), emphasizes social and economic matters for advanced students. Stephanie Dalley, ed., *The Legacy of Mesopotamia* (1998), explores Mesopotamian interactions with other parts of the ancient world.

David Ferry's *Gilgamesh: A New Rendering in English Verse* (1992) is an attractive translation. The evolving mentality of Mesopotamian religion comes through in Thorkild Jacobsen, *The Treasures of Darkness: A History of Mesopotamian Religion* (1976). Stephanie Dalley, *Myths from Mesopotamia* (1989), Henrietta McCall, *Mesopotamian Myths* (1990), and Jeremy Black and Anthony Green, *Gods, Demons and Symbols of Ancient Mesopotamia* (1992), cover myth, religion, and religious symbolism. Pierre Amiet, *Art of the Ancient Near East* (1980), introduces various arts with good illustrations. Dominique Collon, *First Impressions: Cylinder Seals in the Ancient Near East* (1988), reveals much about art and daily life.

C. B. F. Walker, *Cuneiform* (1987), is a concise guide to the Mesopotamian writing system. James B. Pritchard, *Ancient Near Eastern Texts Relating to the Old Testament*, 3d ed. (1969), contains translated documents and texts from western Asia and Egypt. For women's matters, see Barbara Lesko, "Women of Egypt and the Ancient Near East," in *Becoming Visible: Women in European History*, 2d ed., ed. Renata Bridenthal, Claudia Koonz, and Susan Stuard (1994), and Guity Nashat, "Women in the Ancient Middle East," in *Restoring Women to History* (1988). Harvey Weiss, ed., *Ebla to Damascus: Art and Archaeology of Ancient Syria* (1985), and Giovanni Pettinato, *Ebla: A New Look at History* (1991), discuss Syria's relationship with Mesopotamia.

A lavishly illustrated introduction to ancient Egyptian civilization is David P. Silverman, ed., *Ancient Egypt* (1997). John Baines and Jaromir Malek, *Atlas of Ancient Egypt* (1980), and T. G. H. James, *Ancient Egypt: The Land and Its Legacy* (1988), are organized around the sites of ancient Egypt and provide general introductions. Historical treatments include B. G. Trigger, B. J. Kemp, D. O'Connor, and A. B. Lloyd, *Ancient Egypt: A Social History* (1983); Barry J. Kemp, *Ancient Egypt: Anatomy of a Civilization* (1989); and Nicholas-Cristophe Grimal, *A History of Ancient Egypt* (1992). John Romer, *People of the Nile: Everyday Life in Ancient Egypt* (1982); Miriam Stead, *Egyptian Life* (1986); and Eugen Strouhal, *Life of the Ancient Egyptians* (1992), emphasize social history. For women, see the chapter by Lesko cited above; Barbara Watterson, *Women in Ancient Egypt* (1991); Gay Robins, *Women in Ancient Egypt* (1993); and the articles and museum exhibition catalogue in Anne K. Capel and Glenn E. Markoe, eds., *Mistress of the House, Mistress of Heaven: Women in Ancient Egypt* (1996).

Stephen Quirke, *Ancient Egyptian Religion* (1990), is a highly regarded treatment of a complex subject. George Hart, *Egyptian Myths* (1990), presents evidence for what must have been a thriving oral tradition. Pritchard's collection, cited above, and Miriam Lichtheim, *Ancient*

Egyptian Literature: A Book of Readings, Vol. 1, *The Old and Middle Kingdoms* (1973), provide translated texts and documents. William Stevenson Smith, *The Art and Architecture of Ancient Egypt* (1998), and Gay Robins, *The Art of Ancient Egypt* (1997), cover the visual record.

For the Indus Valley civilization, see the brief treatment by Stanley Wolpert, *A New History of India,* 3d ed. (1989). Jonathan Mark Kenoyer, *Ancient Cities of the Indus Valley Civilization* (1998), supersedes the occasionally still useful works of Mortimer Wheeler, *Civilizations of the Indus Valley and Beyond* (1966) and *The Indus Civilization,* 3d ed. (1968). Gregory L. Poschl has edited two collections of articles: *Ancient Cities of the Indus* (1979) and *Harappan Civilization: A Contemporary Perspective* (1982).

■ Notes

1. N. K. Sandars, *The Epic of Gilgamesh* (Baltimore: Penguin Books, 1960), 61–63.
2. Colin McEvedy and Richard Jones, *Atlas of World Population History* (New York: Penguin Books, 1978), 13–15.
3. Colin Renfrew, *Archaeology and Language: The Puzzle of Indo-European Origins* (Cambridge: Cambridge University Press, 1988), 125, 150.
4. Luigi Cavalli-Sforza, L. Luca, Paolo Menozzi, and Alberto Piazza, *The History and Geography of Human Genes* (Princeton, NJ: Princeton University Press, 1994).
5. James Mellaart, *Çatal Hüyük: A Neolithic Town in Anatolia* (New York: McGraw-Hill, 1967), 202.

2

THE LATE BRONZE AGE IN THE EASTERN HEMISPHERE, 2200–500 B.C.E.

**Early China • The Cosmopolitan Middle East • Nubia •
The Aegean World • The Fall of Late Bronze Age Civilizations •**
ENVIRONMENT AND TECHNOLOGY: **Chinese and Mesopotamian Divination**

round 1460 B.C.E., Queen Hatshepsut° of Egypt sent a naval expedition to the fabled land of "Punt°." Historians believe Punt was the northern coastal region of modern Somalia. Myrrh° (the fragrant, hardened sap of a local tree) from Punt usually passed through multiple intermediaries, thus raising its price. Hatshepsut hoped to bypass the middlemen and establish direct trade between Punt and Egypt.

The mortuary temple of Hatshepsut at Deir el-Bahri°, near Thebes, preserves a written and pictorial record of this expedition. Besides bringing back myrrh and exotic goods like ebony, ivory, live monkeys, and panther skins, the ships carried young myrrh trees, probably to produce at home this precious substance, which the Egyptians burned in religious rites. The temple inscriptions term these treasures tribute from

the people of Punt to their Egyptian overlord. In fact, Egyptian emissaries must have traded for them. Hatshepsut displayed them to emphasize her unprecedented accomplishments, but Egypt never actually controlled Punt.

The Punt reveals a historical pattern of the second millennium B.C.E. Major centers sought resources, through trade or conquest, because power, wealth, and legitimacy depended on such commodities. In northeastern Africa, the eastern Mediterranean, western Asia, and East Asia, regions and states, large and small, interconnected in complex webs of political relationships and economic activities. Embassies, treaties, trade agreements, political marriages, and scribal use of common languages and writing systems linked heterogeneous peoples. Long-distance trade, particularly in metals, supported the power and prosperity of the ruling classes and facilitated the flow of ideas and technologies, including concepts of kingship, administrative practices, writing systems, religious

---

Hatshepsut (hat-SHEP-soot) **Punt** (poont) **myrrh** (murr)
Deir el-Bahri (DIRE uhl–BAH-ree)

beliefs and rituals, artistic tastes, metallurgical skills, and transportation techniques. The Late Bronze Age was a cosmopolitan and comfortable era, a time of stability, prosperity, technological progress, and cultural accomplishment.

The spread of ideas and technologies sparked political changes across the Eastern Hemisphere (Asia, Africa, and Europe). Ancient civilizations in Egypt and southern Mesopotamia (introduced in Chapter 1) continued to flourish while new centers of power formed involving peoples who would take center stage in the first millennium B.C.E.: Assyrians in northern Mesopotamia, Nubians in northeastern Africa, Greeks in the eastern Mediterranean, and the Shang and Zhou in northeastern China.

As you read this chapter, ask yourself the following questions:

- Why were raw materials important to the ruling elites?
- How did the civilizations of the Late Bronze Age communicate, exchange goods, and settle differences?
- How did the ancient centers affect the culture and technology of the new civilizations?

Early China

On the eastern edge of Eurasia, Neolithic cultures from as early as 8000 B.C.E. evolved in the second millennium into a more complex civilization. Under the Shang and Zhou monarchs, many of the institutions and values of classical Chinese civilization emerged and spread south and west. As elsewhere, the rise of cities, specialization of labor, bureaucratic government, writing, and other advanced technologies resulted from exploiting a great river system—the Yellow River (Huang He) and its tributaries—to support intensive agricul-

ture. Although archaeology has revealed some movement of goods and ideas between western and eastern Asia, developments in the east were largely independent of the complex societies in the Middle East and the Indus Valley.

Geography and Resources

Natural barriers isolate China from the rest of the Eastern Hemisphere: the Himalaya° mountains on the southwest; the Pamir° and Tian° Mountains and Takla Makan° Desert on the west; the Gobi° Desert and the treeless plains of the Mongolian Steppe on the northwest (see Map 2.1). To the east lies the Pacific Ocean. Despite some flow of goods, people, and ideas between China, India, and Central Asia, China's development was in many respects distinctive.

Although mountains made overland travel, transport, and communications difficult and slow, the river systems of eastern China—the Yellow and Yangzi° Rivers with their tributaries—facilitate east-west movement. These eastern river valleys, where clustered populations practiced intensive agriculture, differed from Mongolia's steppes, Xinjiang's° deserts and oases, and Tibet's high plateau, where populations were sparse and livelihoods took different forms. East Asia also encompasses diverse climate zones, from the dry, subarctic reaches of Manchuria in the north to the lush, subtropical forests of the south, each with distinctive varieties of plant and animal life.

Within the eastern agricultural zone, north and south differ considerably. The monsoons that affect India and Southeast Asia (see Chapter 1) drench southern China with heavy rainfall in summer, the best time for agriculture. Precipitation in northern China is meager and more erratic. Consequently, north and south exhibit different patterns of land use, crop selection, and agricultural organization. As in Mesopotamia, the Indus Valley, and southern Greece (see below), technological and social developments in China unfolded in relatively

---

Himalaya (HIM-uh-LAY-uh)   **Pamir** (pah-MEER)
Tian (tee-en)   **Takla Makan** (TAH-kluh muh-KAHN)
Gobi (GO-bee)   **Yangzi** (yang-zuh)   **Xinjiang** (shin-jyahng)

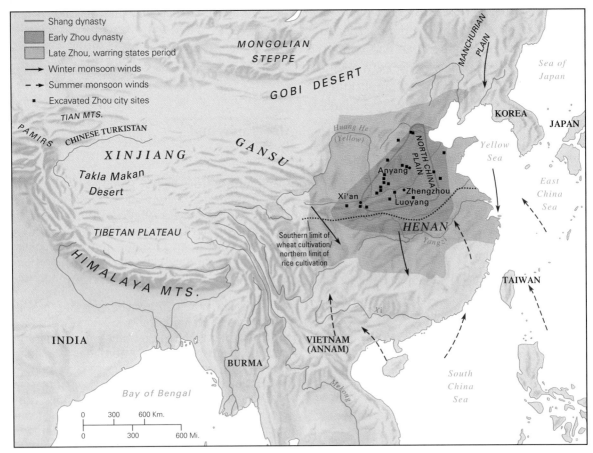

Map 2.1   China in the Shang and Zhou Periods, 1750–221 B.C.E.   The Shang dynasty arose in the second millennium B.C.E. in the floodplain of the Yellow River. While southern China benefits from monsoon rains, northern China relies on irrigation. As population increased, the Han Chinese migrated from their eastern homeland to other parts of China, carrying their technologies and cultural practices. Other ethnic groups predominated in outlying regions. The nomadic peoples of the northwest constantly challenged Chinese authority.

adverse conditions. China's early history centers on the northern plains, a demanding environment that stimulated important technologies and political traditions, as well as philosophical and religious viewpoints that become hallmarks of Chinese civilization. In the third century C.E., the political and intellectual center moved south because of gradual population migration.

The eastern river valleys and North China Plain contained timber, stone, and ore deposits and, above all, potentially productive land. Over centuries, dust blowing from Central Asia had built

up a thick mantle of yellowish-brown soil called **loess**° (silt suspended in water gives the Yellow River its hue and name). Although it is extremely fertile and soft enough to be worked with wooden digging sticks, its lack of compactness accounts for the severe damage that earthquakes cause in this region.

Agriculture there demanded immense human labor. In some areas, forests had to be cleared. Recurrent floods on the Yellow River necessitated

---

loess (less)

CHRONOLOGY

	China	Western Asia and Southeastern Europe	Northeastern Africa
2500 B.C.E.	**8000–2000 B.C.E.** Neolithic cultures	**2500 B.C.E.** Bronze metallurgy	**2040–1640 B.C.E.** Middle Kingdom in Egypt
2000 B.C.E.	**2000 B.C.E.** Bronze metallurgy **1750–1027 B.C.E.** Shang dynasty	**ca. 2000 B.C.E.** Early Minoan civilization on Crete **2000 B.C.E.** Horses in use in western Asia **1700–1200 B.C.E.** Hittites dominant in Anatolia **1600 B.C.E.** Rise of Mycenaean civilization in Greece	**1750 B.C.E.** Rise of kingdom of Kush
1500 B.C.E.		**1460 B.C.E.** Kassites assume control of southern Mesopotamia **1450 B.C.E.** Destruction of Minoan palaces in Crete	**1532 B.C.E.** Beginning of New Kingdom in Egypt **1500 B.C.E.** Egyptian conquest of Nubia; bronze metallurgy **1470 B.C.E.** Queen Hatshepsut of Egypt dispatches expedition to Punt **1353 B.C.E.** Akhenaten launches reforms in Egypt **1285 B.C.E.** Pharoah Ramesses II battles Hittites at Kadesh
1000 B.C.E.	**1027–221 B.C.E.** Zhou dynasty **600 B.C.E.** Iron metallurgy	**1200–1150 B.C.E.** Destruction of Late Bronze Age centers in Anatolia, Syria, and Greece **1000 B.C.E.** Iron metallurgy	**1200–1150 B.C.E.** Peoples of the Sea attack **1070 B.C.E.** End of New Kingdom in Egypt **1000 B.C.E.** Iron metallurgy

construction of earthen dikes and overflow channels. Prolonged droughts called for digging catch basins (reservoirs) to store river water and rainfall. As the population grew, people built retaining walls to partition the hillsides into tiers of flat, fertile terraces.

The staple crops in the north were millet, a native Chinese grain, and wheat, which spread to East Asia from the Middle East. Rice, which requires a higher temperature, prospered in the south. Rice cultivation in the Yangzi River Valley and the south demanded much labor, but the effort was worthwhile: rice feeds more people per cultivated acre than any other grain.

Irrigation requires that rice paddies be absolutely flat and surrounded by water channels. Seedlings sprout in a nursery, are transplanted individually to the paddy, and are then flooded. Flooding eliminates weeds and supports microscopic organisms that keep the soil fertile. When the crop ripens, the paddy is drained, the rice stalks harvested with a sickle, and the edible kernels separated out. Spectacular yields reward this effort.

The Shang Periods

Pottery styles and burial practices differ among China's several Neolithic cultural complexes. These early populations grew millet, raised pigs and chickens, and used stone tools. They made pottery on a wheel. They pioneered silk production, first raising silkworms on mulberry leaves and then unraveling their cocoons. Buildings had earthen walls made by hammering soil into temporary wooden frames until it became hard as cement. Bronze was in use by 2000 B.C.E., roughly a millennium after its advent in the Middle East.

Later generations related tales of the ancient Xia° kings, said to have ruled the core region of the Yellow River Valley. Some archaeologists identify these semi-legendary Xia with the Neolithic Longshan cultural complex in the centuries before and after 2000 B.C.E. Chinese history proper, however, begins with the Shang° clans, whose rise in the

early second millennium B.C.E. coincides with the earliest writing.

The dominant warrior aristocracy of the Shang reveled in warfare, hunting (for recreation and practicing war skills), exchanging gifts, feasting, and wine drinking. From their Yellow River homeland in the present-day province of Henan°, the **Shang** expanded northward into Mongolia, westward as far as Gansu°, and southward into the Yangzi River Valley between approximately 1750 and 1027 B.C.E. The last and most important of their several capitals was near modern Anyang° (see Map 2.1).

The royal court ruled the Shang core area directly. Aristocrats served as generals, ambassadors, supervisors of public works, and governors of outlying provinces. In the most distant regions, native rulers acknowledged ties of allegiance to the Shang king, who traveled often to the courts of his subordinates to reinforce their loyalty.

Frequent military expeditions provided the warrior aristocracy with plunder and an arena for accomplishment while periodically rolling back the nomadic peoples of the steppe and desert regions to the north and west, whom the Chinese called "barbarians." (The word *barbarian* reflects the language and view of Chinese sources. Modern readers should be wary of the Chinese claim that these nomads were culturally backward and morally inferior to the Chinese.) Large numbers of war prisoners from these campaigns labored in the Shang capital as slaves.

Far-reaching networks of trade brought to the Shang core area such valued commodities as jade, ivory, and mother of pearl (a hard, shiny substance from the interior of mollusk shells) used for jewelry, carved figurines, and decorative inlays. Some evidence suggests that Shang China may also have exchanged goods and ideas with the distant civilization of Mesopotamia.

The ideology of Shang rule presented the kings as indispensable intermediaries between their people and the gods. The royal family and aristocracy worshiped the spirits of their male ancestors, whom they believed were intensely interested in

---

Xia (shah)   Shang (shahng)

Henan (heh-nahn)   Gansu (gahn-soo)
Anyang (ahn-yahng)

the fortunes of their descendants and had special influence with the gods. Before taking any action, the kings used **divination** to ascertain the will of the gods (see Environment and Technology: Chinese and Mesopotamian Divination), and they courted divine favor with sacrifices to their gods and ancestors. Royal burials also entailed sacrifices, both animal and human, including noble courtiers, women, servants, soldiers, and prisoners of war.

Although copper and tin, the principal ingredients of bronze, were not plentiful in northern China, bronze weapons and ritual objects symbolized authority and nobility. The relatively modest tomb of one queen contained 450 bronze ritual vessels, bells, weapons, and mirrors, along with numerous objects made from jade, bone, ivory, and stone; 7,000 cowrie shells; 16 sacrificed men, women, and children; and 6 dogs. Finding and mining copper and tin deposits, refining the ores into metal, transporting the ingots to the capital, and casting and forging weapons and beautifully decorated objects constituted major state functions.

The foundries were placed outside the walls of the main cities. After mixing the copper and tin in the right proportions, the artisans poured the molten bronze into clay molds. Separate hardened pieces might later be joined together. Their products, whether weapons, chariot fittings, and musical instruments, or vessels for liquids and solids used in religious ceremonies, were often decorated with designs of real or imaginary animals.

Among other technological advances, the horse-drawn chariot, which the Shang adopted from Central Asia, proved a formidable instrument of war, and the domesticated water buffalo provided additional animal power. Improved engineering techniques and effective labor organization favored the construction of cities, massive defensive walls of pounded earth, and monumental royal tombs.

The form of writing developed in this era facilitated effective administration. It combined pictograms (pictures representing objects and concepts) and symbols representing the sounds of syllables in a system that required scribes to memorize hundreds of signs. Mastering this system took time; hence, writing became the preserve of the elite class. Although the shapes and pronunciations of signs evolved over time, the fundamental principles of this system still prevail. By contrast, ancient writing systems like Mesopotamian cuneiform and Egyptian hieroglyphics, also difficult to learn and the preserve of scribal elites, eventually gave way to simpler alphabetic approaches.

The Zhou Period

Shang domination lasted more than six centuries. In the eleventh century B.C.E., Wu, the ruler of **Zhou°**, a dependent state in the valley of the Wei° River, defeated the last Shang king. The Zhou line of kings (ca. 1027–221 B.C.E.) proved the longest lasting and most revered of all Chinese dynasties. As the Semitic peoples in Mesopotamia had adopted and adapted the Sumerian legacy (see Chapter 1), the Zhou preserved the essentials of Shang culture and added new ideological and technological elements.

Zhou propagandists skillfully constructed the positive image of their masters and propagated a new ideology of kingship to justify their seizure of power. They called the chief deity "Heaven" and the monarch "Son of Heaven." He ruled with the "**Mandate of Heaven.**" The new theory proclaimed the ruler the choice of the supreme deity and declared that he would retain this backing as long as he remained a wise, principled, and energetic guardian of his people. Prosperity and stability proved divine favor. If the ruler misbehaved, as the last Shang ruler had, his right to rule could be withdrawn. Corruption, violence, arrogance, and insurrection, such as occurred under the last Shang king, signified royal misbehavior and divine displeasure. The new dynasty thus validated its overthrow of the Shang and proclaimed that the moral order of the universe supported their just rule.

Although elements of Shang ritual continued, divination declined, as did extravagant and bloody sacrifices and burials. The priestly power of the ruling class, the sole contact with the ancestral spirits under the Shang, largely disappeared. This separation of religion from government gave rise to important secular philosophies in the Zhou period. The bronze vessels that had been sacred implements in the Shang period became family treasures.

Zhou (joe)   **Wei** (way)

Chinese and Mesopotamian Divination

Many ancient peoples, including the Chinese and Mesopotamians, believed the gods controlled the forces of nature and shaped destinies. They practiced various techniques of divination to discover the signs of divine intention concealed in natural phenomena. They sought to communicate with the gods and thereby anticipate, and even influence, the future.

The Chinese elite sought guidance from shamans, including the Shang monarch himself, who claimed the ability to contact ancestors and other higher powers. Chinese shamans divined by oracle bones. The shaman touched the heated point of a stick to a tortoise shell or an animal's shoulder blade, sometimes prepared with small drilled indentations. The shell or bone would crack, and the shaman would "read" the crack as a message from the spirit world.

Tens of thousands of oracle bones survive. They tell us about Shang life because the shaman's questions and answers were subsequently inscribed on their back side. The proper performance of ritual, the outcome of wars or hunts, the prospects for rainfall or harvest, and the meaning of strange occurrences are typical topics.

In Mesopotamia in the third and second millennia B.C.E., divination concentrated on close inspection of the form, size, and markings of the organs of sacrificed animals. Archaeologists have found models of sheep's livers accompanied by written explanations of what various features signified. Other techniques of divination included following smoke from burning incense and examining the patterns of oil thrown on water.

From about 2000 B.C.E., Mesopotamian diviners also used the movements of the sun, moon, planets, stars, and constellations to foretell the future. In the centuries after 1000 B.C.E., celestial divination acquired such great importance that specialists maintained precise records of astronomical events. Calculating the movements of celestial bodies required sophisticated mathematics, the best in the ancient Middle East. A place-value system, in which a number stands for its value multiplied by the value of the column it is in (such as our ones, tens, and hundreds columns), made possible complex operations with large numbers and small fractions.

The astrological division of the sky into the twelve signs of the zodiac and the charting of planetary positions to predict an individual's destiny developed out of Mesopotamian scrutiny of the movements of celestial bodies. Horoscopes—charts with calculations and predictions based on date of birth—appear shortly before 400 B.C.E. In the Hellenistic period (323–30 B.C.E.), Greek migrants to western Asia built on this Mesopotamian foundation and greatly advanced the study of astrology.

Chinese Divination Shell After inscribing questions on a bone or shell, the diviner applied a red-hot point and interpreted the resulting cracks as a divine response. (Institute of History and Philology, Academia Sinica)

The eleventh through ninth centuries B.C.E., sometimes called the Western Zhou era, saw a sophisticated administration develop. Zhou capital cities featured foundations and walls constructed of pounded earth. Major buildings faced south, reflecting an already ancient concern to orient structures in harmonious relationship with the terrain; the forces of wind, water, and sunlight; and the invisible energy perceived to flow through nature. Imperial officials, including the king, personified morality, fairness, and concern for the general welfare.

Decentralized like the Shang, the Zhou kings used members and allies of the royal family to rule more than a hundred largely autonomous subject territories. Elaborate court ceremonies, embellished by music and dance, impressed on observers the glory of Zhou rule and reinforced the bonds between rulers and ruled.

Around 800 B.C.E., Zhou power began to wane. Proud and ambitious local rulers operated ever more independently and waged war on one another while nomadic peoples attacked the northwest frontiers (see Map 2.1). The ensuing Eastern Zhou era saw members of the Zhou lineage relocate, in 771 B.C.E., to a more secure capital near Luoyang°. They retained the imperial title but received only token recognition from the real power brokers, who competed fiercely as power shifted back and forth among numerous small and independent states. Historians conventionally subdivide the Eastern Zhou. The years between 771 and 481 B.C.E. are the "Spring and Autumn Period," named for a collection of chronicles that give annual entries for those two seasons. The period from 480 B.C.E. to 221 B.C.E. is called the "Warring States Period."

Cities, some of them quite large, were a feature of the Eastern Zhou era. Long walls of pounded earth, precursors of the Great Wall of China, protected the competing kingdoms from predatory neighbors and northern nomads. By 600 B.C.E., iron tools and weapons began to replace bronze. Ironworking probably came from the northwest no-

madic peoples. Subsequently, metalworkers in southern China, where bronze was rare, pioneered new techniques, such as introducing carbon into the smelting process to produce hard-edged steel. Nomads also passed on the practice of fighting from horseback.

Using expanded bureaucracies, governments compiled law codes, taxed peasants directly, imposed standardized money, and managed large-scale public works projects. An authoritarian philosophy that came to be called **Legalism** justified state control of wealth and demands for obedience. Legalist thinkers deemed human nature essentially wicked, arguing that people behave properly only when compelled by a ruler's strict laws and harsh punishments. Every aspect of human society therefore ought to be controlled and personal freedom sacrificed to state policies.

The governments of the major Zhou states thus took over many of the traditional functions of the aristocracy. To retain influence, aristocrats sought positions advising the rulers. One who lived through the political flux and social change of this anxious time was Kongzi (551–479 B.C.E.), known in the West by the Latin form of his name, **Confucius,** who came from a small state in Shandong. His administrative career was not outstanding, but his advocacy of duty and public service, initially aimed at fellow aristocrats, was to become a central influence in Chinese thought.

Rooted in earlier Chinese beliefs, Confucius's teachings borrowed from folk religion and the rites of the Zhou royal family, such as veneration of ancestors and elders and worship of the deity Heaven. Assuming that hierarchy is innate in the order of the universe and that the patterns of human society should echo and harmonize with the cycles of nature, Confucius taught that maintaining the social order depended on each person playing a particular role and observing proper conduct and ceremonial behavior. The family paralleled the state. The father sits atop the family hierarchy with his sons, wives, and daughters ranked by age below him. Similarly the ruler presides over the state hierarchy; the public officials are the sons, and the common people the women.

Social ideas implied broad moral abstractions. Confucius expanded a traditional term for feelings

---

Luoyang (LWOE-yahng)

Women Beating Chimes   This scene, from a bronze vessel of the Zhou era, highlights the role of music in festivals, religious rituals, and court ceremonies. During the Eastern Zhou period, small states adopted distinctive musical scales and instrumental ensembles as marks of independence. (Courtesy, Imperial Palace Museum, Beijing)

between family members (*ren*) into a universal ideal of benevolence, which he believed was the foundation of moral government. Government exists, he said, to serve the people, and the administrator or ruler commands respect and authority through fairness and integrity. Confucian teachings emphasized benevolence, avoidance of violence, justice, rationalism, loyalty, and dignity. They sought to affirm and maintain the political and social order by improving it.

Although Confucius had little influence in his own time, his ideas inspired his influential follower Mencius (Mengzi, 371–289 B.C.E.) to oppose despotism and the authoritarian ideology of the Legalists. By the birth of the empire in 221 B.C.E., Confucianism had become the dominant political philosophy (see Chapter 5).

A school of thought known as **Daoism°** also developed in the Warring States Period. According to tradition, Laozi sought to stop warfare by urging humanity to follow the *Dao,* or "path." Daoists accept the world as they find it, avoiding futile struggles and adhering to the "path" of nature. They prefer to avoid violence, but when it is unavoidable and they are forced to act, they use it minimally. Rather than fight the current of a stream, said the Daoists, the wise man allows the waters to flow around him. Aware that the world is always chang-

ing and lacks absolute morality or meaning, the Daoists taught that the individual's fundamental understanding of the "path" was all that mattered.

Subsequent centuries saw great elaboration of the original Daoist philosophy and its incorporation of popular beliefs, magic, and mysticism. Daoism represents an important stream of thought throughout Chinese history. By idealizing individuals who find their own "path" to right conduct, it offered an alternative to the Confucian emphasis on hierarchy and duty and the Legalist approval of force.

Social organization also changed in this period. The clan-based relations of the Shang and early Zhou periods gave way to the three-generation family of grandparents, parents, and children as the fundamental social unit. The concept of private property accompanied this change. Land belonged to the men of the family and was divided equally among the sons when the father died.

Although little is known about women's affairs in the earliest periods, some scholars believe that women may have acted as shamans, entering into trances to communicate with supernatural forces, making requests on behalf of their communities, and receiving predictions of the future. By the Zhou period when written records begin to tell us more, they show women in subordinate positions in the strongly patriarchal family.

Confucian thought codified this male-female

Daoism (DOW-ism)

hierarchy. Men alone could conduct rituals and make offerings to the ancestors, though women could help maintain household ancestral shrines. Fathers wielded authority over women and children, arranged marriages, and could sell the labor of family members. Though limited to one wife, a man could have low-status concubines as additional sexual partners. Among the elite, marriages confirmed political alliances, and the groom's family commonly offered a substantial "bride-gift" to the bride's family. A man whose wife died had a duty to remarry in order to produce male heirs and maintain the cult of the ancestors.

The opposition of **yin** and **yang,** the complementary roles of male and female in nature, symbolized gender differences. The male principle (yin) equated with the sun: active, bright, and shining. The female principle (yang) echoed the moon: passive, shaded, and reflective. Male toughness balanced female gentleness, male action and initiative female endurance and need for completion, male leadership female supportiveness. In its earliest form, yin and yang alternated and were equal, like day and night, creating balance in the world.

The classical Chinese patterns of family, property, and bureaucracy took shape during the centuries of Zhou rule and competition among smaller states. What remained was for a strong central power to unify the Chinese lands. The state of Qin°, whose aggressive and disciplined policies gave it ascendancy over the other warring states by the third century B.C.E., achieved this outcome (see Chapter 5).

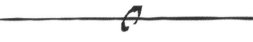

THE COSMOPOLITAN MIDDLE EAST

Mesopotamia and Egypt succumbed to outside invaders in the seventeenth century B.C.E. (see Chapter 1). Eventually, the outsiders were either ejected or assimilated, and political equilibrium was reestablished. Between 1500 and 1200 B.C.E., large territorial states dominated the Middle East (see Map 2.2), controlling smaller city-states, kingdoms, and kinship groups while they competed and sometimes fought one another for control of valuable commodities and trade routes.

Historians have called the region's Late Bronze Age a "cosmopolitan" era, meaning a time of widely shared cultures and lifestyles. Diplomatic relations and commercial contacts fostered flows of goods and ideas that conferred a relatively high living standard and similar possessions and values on elite groups everywhere. The majority—peasants and villagers—may have seen some improvement in their standard of living, but they benefited less from the increasing contacts and trade.

Western Asia

By 1500 B.C.E., Mesopotamia was divided into two distinct political zones. Assyria dominated the north. In the south, the dynasty of Hammurabi in the eighteenth and seventeenth centuries B.C.E. propelled the city of Babylon to political and cultural ascendancy (see Map 2.2). By 1460 B.C.E , however, an inflow of Kassites° from the Zagros Mountains to the east, who spoke a non-Semitic language, had established a Kassite dynasty in Babylon. Kassite names reflect their native language, but otherwise they embraced Babylonian language and culture and intermarried with the native population. During 250 years in power, the Kassite lords of Babylonia contented themselves with defending their core area and trading for vital raw materials and did not pursue territorial conquest.

The Assyrians of the north had more expansionist designs. In the twentieth century B.C.E., the city of Ashur, the leading urban center on the northern Tigris, anchored a busy trade that crossed the northern Mesopotamian plain and ascended the Anatolian Plateau. Representatives of Assyrian merchant families maintained settlements outside the walls of important Anatolian cities. They imported textiles and tin, used since roughly 2500 B.C.E. in bronze casting, to exchange for Anatolian silver. In the eighteenth century B.C.E., an Assyrian dynasty gained control of Mari°, a key city-state on

---

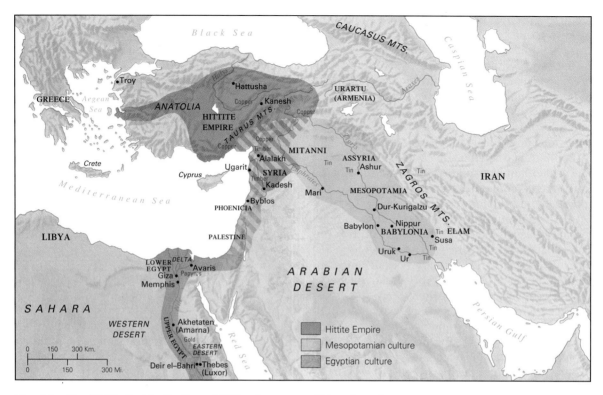

Map 2.2   The Middle East in the Second Millennium B.C.E.   Although warfare was not uncommon, treaties, diplomatic missions, and correspondence in Akkadian cuneiform fostered cooperative relationships between states. Extensive networks of exchange centered on the trade in metals. Peripheral regions, such as Nubia and the Aegean lands, were drawn into the network.

the upper Euphrates River. Although this "Old Assyrian" kingdom soon declined, its history testifies to the importance of controlling the trade routes between Mesopotamia, Anatolia, and the Syria-Palestine coast. After 1400 B.C.E., a resurgent "Middle Assyrian" kingdom again engaged in economic expansion and campaigns of conquest.

On the periphery of Mesopotamia, Elam in southwest Iran and Mitanni° in the plain lying between the upper Euphrates and Tigris Rivers showed similar ambition. From around 1700 to 1200 B.C.E., the **Hittites°**, a more formidable people who spoke an Indo-European language, dominated Anatolia from their capital at Hattusha°, near present-day Ankara°. Using horse-drawn war

chariots and exploiting Anatolia's rich deposits of copper, silver, and iron, the Hittites participated heavily in international commerce. Hittite kings promulgated standardized laws, granted land in return for labor and military service, and employed artists and craftsmen to build and decorate their palaces and temples.

Mesopotamian political and cultural concepts originating from the Sumerian core area in southern Mesopotamia diffused across much of western Asia during the second millennium B.C.E. Akkadian°, the language of international diplomacy, used the cuneiform system of writing, which was also employed for Elamite°, Hittite, and other languages. Many peoples adopted Mesopotamian myths and legends and imitated Mesopotamian

---

Mitanni (mih-TAH-nee)   Hittite (HIT-ite)
Hattusha (haht-tush-SHAH)   Ankara (ANG-kuh-ruh)

Akkadian (uh-KAY-dee-uhn)   Elamite (ee-luh-mite)

art and architecture. Newcomers who had learned and improved on the lessons of Mesopotamian civilization often put pressure on the old core area. The small, fractious city-states of the third millennium B.C.E. had competed with their neighbors in southern Mesopotamia. Now, substantially larger states interacted politically, militarily, and economically in a geopolitical sphere encompassing all of western Asia.

New Kingdom Egypt

The Middle Kingdom declined in the seventeenth century B.C.E. as high-level officials ceased to cooperate and new groups migrated into the Nile Valley. Political fragmentation, economic decline, and cultural disruption culminated round 1640 B.C.E. in the unprecedented establishment of foreign rule by the Hyksos°, or "Princes of Foreign Lands."

The precise identity of the Hyksos and the circumstances of their ascent to power are unknown. But peoples speaking Semitic languages from the region that today encompasses Israel, Palestine, Jordan, Lebanon, and Syria had been migrating into the eastern Nile Delta for centuries. Other peoples may have joined them and established control in the delta and then throughout the middle of the country (see Map 2.2) in the way the Amorites and Kassites first settled in and then took over Babylonia. The Hyksos intermarried with Egyptians, used their language, and maintained their institutions and culture. Whereas outsiders were easily assimilated in Mesopotamia, the Egyptians, with their strong ethnic identity and political tradition, continued to call the Hyksos "foreigners."

Just as the princes of Thebes reunified Egypt and established the Middle Kingdom a half millennium earlier, native Theban kings, Kamose° and Ahmose°, fought for three decades to expel the Hyksos. Their triumph inaugurated the New Kingdom, which lasted from about 1532 to 1070 B.C.E.

Hyksos domination had shaken Egyptian pride and erased the isolationist mind-set of earlier eras. Aggressive and expansionist, New Kingdom Egypt engaged in frequent campaigns of conquest, extending control northward into Syria-Palestine and southward into Nubia. Egypt thereby won access to valuable commodities such as timber, gold, and copper (bronze metallurgy took hold in Egypt around 1500 B.C.E.), not to mention taxes and tribute (compulsory payments from a subject state to a conqueror). Newly conquered territories also buffered Egypt against foreign attack. The pharaohs imposed direct control over Nubia and pressed the native population to adopt Egyptian language and culture. In the Syria-Palestine region, however, they relied on strategically placed forts, Egyptian garrisons, and collaboration with local rulers to maintain control.

New Kingdom Egypt participated in the network of diplomatic and commercial relations that linked the states of western Asia. Soldiers, administrators, diplomats, and merchants returning to Egypt from assignments abroad exposed their countrymen to exotic fruits and vegetables, new musical instruments, and technologies like improved potter's wheels, looms, and the war chariot.

At least one woman held the throne of New Kingdom Egypt. **Hatshepsut**, the queen of Pharaoh Tuthmosis° II, is the era's one known female pharaoh. At first as regent for her young stepson after Tuthmosis's death, she soon claimed the royal title for herself (r. 1473–1458 B.C.E.). Inscriptions at her mortuary temple at Deir el-Bahri often used the male pronouns, and drawings show her wearing the long, conical beard symbolic of kingship. Her naval expedition to Punt described at the beginning of this chapter opened direct trade between Egypt and the land of myrrh and possibly bolstered her claim to the throne. After her death, discontent at having endured a female ruler caused her picture to be defaced and her name erased wherever it appeared.

Another ruler who departed from traditional ways ascended the throne as Amenhotep° IV, but he began to refer to himself as **Akhenaten°** (r. 1353–1335 B.C.E.), meaning "beneficial to the

---

Hyksos (HICK-soes)   Kamose (KAH-mose)
Ahmose (AH-mose)

Tuthmosis (tuth-MOE-sis)
Amenhotep (ah-muhn-HOE-tep)
Akhenaten (ahk-NAH-ten)

Aten°" (the disk of the sun). His devotion to Aten as the supreme deity involved more than a name change. He closed temples to other gods, challenging the age-old supremacy of Amon° as chief god and the power and influence of Amon's priests.

Some scholars have gone so far as to credit Akhenaten with inventing monotheism—the belief in one exclusive god. It is likely, however, that Akhenaten's motives were at least partly political: to reassert the king's superiority over the priests and to renew belief in the king's divinity. Worship of Aten was actually confined to the royal family; the common people continued to revere the divine ruler.

Akhenaten built a new capital at modern-day Amarna°, halfway between Memphis and Thebes. He transplanted thousands of Egyptians to do the work and serve the ruling elite. Amarna artworks show a new style of realism: the king, his wife, Nefertiti°, and their daughters are depicted in fluid, natural poses. The discovery at Amarna of nearly 400 letters between the Egyptian government and rulers elsewhere illumines the diplomatic and commercial currents of this so-called Amarna period. To Milkilu, prince of Gezer, the Pharaoh writes: "Behold, I am sending to thee Hanya, the commissioner of the archers, together with goods, in order to procure fine concubines (i.e.) weaving women: silver, gold, linen garments, turquoise, all sorts of precious stones, chairs of ebony, as well as every good thing, totalling 160 deben. . . . So send me very fine concubines in whom there is no blemish."[1]

Government officials, priests, and others whose privileges and wealth were linked to traditional ways resented Akhenaten's reforms. Upon his death, the temples reopened, Amon resumed his primacy in the pantheon, and the priesthood claimed new authority. The boy-king Tutankhamun° (r. 1333–1323), one of Akhenaten's immediate successors—and famous solely because his tomb survived unrobbed until 1922—reveals in his name (meaning "beautiful in life is Amon") and in his insignificant reign the ultimate failure of Akhenaten's revolution.

The Ramessides, the dynasty established a short time later by the general Haremhab, renewed the policy of conquest and expansion that Akhenaten had neglected. The greatest monarch of this line, **Ramesses° II**—sometimes called Ramesses the Great—ruled for sixty-six years (r. 1290–1224 B.C.E.). Living into his nineties, he had 200 wives and fathered 160 children. His monumental building projects stamped his mark in all parts of Egypt. Many of his sons were buried in a recently discovered network of more than a hundred corridors and chambers carved into a hillside in the Valley of the Kings.

Commerce and Diplomacy

Early in his reign, Ramesses II fought a major battle against the Hittites at Kadesh in northern Syria (1285 B.C.E.). Egyptian scribes presented this encounter as a great victory, but other evidence suggests a draw. In subsequent years, Egyptian and Hittite diplomats negotiated a series of territorial agreements, and Ramesses married a Hittite princess. At issue was control of Syria-Palestine. Strategically placed between the great regional powers and at the end of the east-west land route across Asia, the inland cities of Syria-Palestine, such as Mari on the upper Euphrates and Alalakh° in western Syria, afforded meeting places to merchants from different lands. The coastal ports, particularly Ugarit° on the Syrian coast and the up-and-coming Phoenician towns of the Lebanese seaboard, served as transshipment points for products traded across the Mediterranean Sea.

In the eastern Mediterranean, northeast Africa, and western Asia, access to metals was vital for any state with pretensions to power. Commerce in metals energized long-distance trade. We have mentioned the Assyrian traffic in silver from Anatolia, and later in this chapter we discuss the Egyptian passion for Nubian gold. The sources of the most utilitarian metals—copper and tin to make bronze—lay in different directions. Copper came from Anatolia and Cyprus; tin came from Afghan-

---

Aten (AHT-n) Amon (AH-muhn)
Amarna (uh-MAHR-nuh) Nefertiti (nef-uhr-TEE-tee)
Tutankhamun (toot-ahng-KAH-muhn)

Ramesses (ram-ih-SEEZ) Alalakh (UH-luh-luhk)
Ugarit (OO-guh-reet)

istan and possibly the British Isles. Both had to be carried long distances and pass through numerous hands before reaching their final destinations.

New modes of transportation expedited communications and commerce. Horses arrived in western Asia around 2000 B.C.E. Domesticated by nomadic peoples in Central Asia, they reached Mesopotamia through the Zagros mountains. Egypt had horses by about 1500 B.C.E. The speed of travel and communication that horses made possible contributed to the creation of large territorial states and empires. Soldiers and government agents could now cover great distances quickly, and swift, maneuverable horse-drawn chariots dominated battlefields. The team of driver and archer could ride forward and unleash a volley of arrows or trample terrified foot soldiers.

Sometime after 1500 B.C.E in Syria-Palestine, but not for another thousand years in Egypt, nomads began to make common use of camels, although the animal may have been domesticated a millennium or more earlier in southern Arabia. Thanks to their strength and capacity to go long distances without water, camels were able to travel across barren terrain. Their physical qualities eventually led to the emergence of a new kind of desert nomad and the creation of cross-desert trade routes (see Chapter 6).

NUBIA

Since the first century B.C.E. the name *Nubia* has designated a thousand-mile (1,600-kilometer) stretch of the Nile Valley lying between Aswan° and Khartoum° and straddling the southern part of modern Egypt and the northern part of Sudan. The ancient Egyptians called it Ta-sety, meaning "Land of the Bow," after the favorite weapon of its warriors. Nubia is the only continuously inhabited territorial link between sub-Saharan Africa (the lands south of the Sahara Desert) and North Africa. An age-old corridor for trade between tropical Africa and the Mediterranean, it was also richly endowed

with natural resources: gold, copper, and semi-precious stones like diorite.

Nubia's geographical location and natural wealth, along with Egypt's quest for Nubian gold, explain the early rise there of a civilization with a complex political organization, social stratification, metallurgy, monumental architecture, and writing. Nubia traditionally was considered a periphery, or outlying region, of Egypt, and its culture was regarded as stemming from Egypt. Scholars today, however, emphasize the interactions between Egypt and Nubia and the mutually beneficial borrowings and syntheses that took place.

Early Cultures and Egyptian Domination

The Nubian Nile flows through rocky desert, grassland, and fertile plain. River irrigation was essential in the torrid, nearly rainless climate. Six cataracts, stretches of rapids formed by large boulders, obstructed boat traffic. Commerce and travel depended on boats covering shorter distances between the cataracts and caravan tracks bypassing them.

In the fourth millennium B.C.E., bands of people in northern Nubia made the transition from seminomadic hunting and gathering to settled life based on grain agriculture and cattle herding. Although the deserts bordering the Nile had not yet become completely barren, Nubia even then served as a corridor for long-distance commerce. Egyptian craftsmen of that period worked in ivory and in ebony brought from tropical Africa through Nubia.

Old Kingdom Egyptian accounts of trade missions to southern lands document Nubia's entry into history around 2300 B.C.E. Aswan, just north of the First Cataract, marked the southern limit of Egyptian control whence Egyptian noblemen led donkey caravans south in quest of gold, incense, ebony, ivory, slaves, and exotic animals. Successful traders undertook delicate negotiations with local Nubian chiefs to arrange protection; their substantial profits justified the dangers.

During the Middle Kingdom (ca. 2040–1640 B.C.E.), Egypt acted more aggressively. Pharaohs sought to control the gold mines east of the Nile directly and cut out the Nubian chiefs, whose

Aswan (AS-wahn)   Khartoum (kahr-TOOM)

Wall Painting of Nubians Arriving in Egypt with Rings and Bags of Gold, Fourteenth Century B.C.E. This image from the tomb of an Egyptian administrator in Nubia depicts Nubian cultural traits, such as haircuts, animal skins, and feathered headdress, in Egyptian artistic style. Skin colors show diversity of population.

demands inflated the cost of tropical goods. They placed Egyptian garrisons in a string of mud-brick forts on islands and riverbanks south of the Second Cataract to protect the southern frontier and regulate the flow of commerce. The Egyptian soldiers remained aloof from the generally peaceful local population, which continued its age-old farming and herding practices.

Farther south, where the Nile makes a great U-shaped turn in the fertile plain of the Dongola Reach, politics took a more dynamic turn. Beginning around 1750 B.C.E., the kings of the state that the Egyptians called **Kush** marshaled a labor force to build monumental walls and mud-brick buildings at Kerma, which became one of the earliest urbanized centers in tropical Africa. The dozens, sometimes hundreds, of servants and wives sacrificed for burial with the kings, along with rich objects found in their tombs, testify to the wealth and power of Kush and a belief in some sort of afterlife. Kushite craftsmen excelled in metalworking, for

weapons and jewelry, and their pottery surpassed anything produced in Egypt.

During the expansionist New Kingdom (ca. 1532–1070 B.C.E.), the Egyptians penetrated more deeply into Nubia. They destroyed Kush and its capital and extended their frontier to the Fourth Cataract. A high-ranking Egyptian official called "Overseer of Southern Lands" or "King's Son of Kush" ruled Nubia from a new administrative center at Napata°, near Gebel Barkal°, the "Holy Mountain," believed to be the abode of a local god. Recognized as the prime source of gold in the west Asian trading world, Egypt exploited the mines of Nubia at considerable human cost. Native workers succumbed to the brutal desert while the army suffered attacks from desert nomads.

Five hundred years of Egyptian domination imprinted Egyptian culture on the Nubia population. Hostage children from elite families grew up

Napata (na-PAY-tuh)　**Gebel Barkal** (JEB-uhl BAHR-kahl)

at the Egyptian royal court and absorbed Egyptian language, culture, and religion while guaranteeing the obedient behavior of their relatives at home. Other Nubians served as archers in the Egyptian army. The manufactured goods they brought back to Nubia have been found in their graves. Nubian towns followed Egyptian models. Stone temples honored Egyptian gods. The popular depiction of Amon with a ram's head may represent the chief Egyptian god and a Nubian ram deity in combination.

The Kingdom of Meroë

Egypt's authority in Nubia collapsed with the onset of Egyptian weakness after 1200 B.C.E. Between the eighth and fourth centuries B.C.E., Napata, the former Egyptian headquarters, served as capital of a powerful native kingdom. Then, from the fourth century B.C.E. to the fourth century C.E., its center of gravity shifted southward to the site of **Meroë**°, near the Sixth Cataract.

From around 712 to 660 B.C.E., the kings of Nubia ruled all of Egypt as the Twenty-Fifth Dynasty. They adopted the royal titles, costumes, and burial practices dictated by age-old Egyptian custom, but they kept their Nubian names and were depicted with Nubian physical features suggesting peoples of sub-Saharan Africa. Building on a monumental scale for the first time in centuries and reinvigorating Egyptian art, architecture, and religion by drawing selectively on practices and styles of previous periods, they presided over a period of cultural renaissance. The kings resided at Memphis, the Old Kingdom capital, while Thebes, the New Kingdom capital, housed a celibate female member of the king's family who was titled "God's Wife of Amon."

Problems arose beginning in 701 B.C.E. when Egypt offered help to local rulers in Palestine who were struggling against the Assyrian Empire. The Assyrians invaded Egypt and drove the Nubian monarchs back to their southern domain by 660 B.C.E. Napata again became the chief royal residence and religious center of the kingdom. Egyp-

tian cultural influences remained strong, with hieroglyphs the medium of written communication and modestly sized sandstone pyramids marking the subterranean burial chambers of mummified royalty.

The southward shift to Meroë in the fourth century B.C.E. facilitated the agriculture and trade on which the Nubian kingdom depended, but it also furthered a displacement of Egyptian by sub-Saharan Africa cultural patterns. Egyptian hieroglyphs gave way to a new set of symbols, still essentially undeciphered, for writing Meroitic. Worship of Amon and Isis, an Egyptian goddess representing fertility and sexuality, continued, but Nubian deities like the lion god Apedemak now shared the stage. Meroitic art combined Egyptian, Greco-Roman, and indigenous traditions.

Royal women played important roles in Meroitic politics, another reflection, perhaps, of the influence of sub-Saharan Africa. In the Nubian matrilineal system, the king was succeeded by his sister's son. Nubian queens sometimes ruled by themselves and sometimes in partnership with husbands. Greek, Roman, and biblical sources mention a Nubian queen named Candace. Since these sources relate to different times, *Candace* was probably a recurrent title rather than a proper name. At least seven queens ruled Nubia between 284 B.C.E. and 115 C.E. The scant details of their reigns cite their roles in warfare, diplomacy, and the building of temples and pyramid tombs.

A huge city for its time, Meroë occupied more than a square mile overlooking fertile grasslands and converging trade routes. Precious rainfall collected in great reservoirs. Craftsmen excelled in smelting iron, which after 1000 B.C.E. had replaced bronze as the primary metal for tools and weapons. An avenue of stone rams led to the Temple of Amon while palaces, temples, and administrative buildings filled the enclosed "royal city." A professional class of officials, priests, and army officers attended the ruler, who may have been regarded as divine.

Nomads from the western desert, made more mobile by the adoption of camels from Arabia, may have overrun Meroë in the early fourth century C.E. But long-distance commerce affected the Nubian kingdom's fall as it had its rise. The shift of profitable commerce with Rome to a Red Sea maritime

Meroë (MER-oh-ee)

route and the rising kingdom of Aksum° (in present-day Ethiopia) played a significant role in Meroë's decline and fall.

THE AEGEAN WORLD

In the lands of the Aegean Sea, a gulf of the eastern Mediterranean, the emergence of Minoan° civilization on Crete and Mycenaean° civilization in Greece parallel the rise of Nubian civilization. As the latter drew from the already ancient civilization of Egypt, so the former benefited from the fertilizing influence of older centers.

The rocky, arid terrain of southern Greece and the Aegean islands permits the growing of grain, grapevines, and olive trees on small plains separating ranges of hills. Flocks of sheep and goats graze the slopes. Sharply indented coastlines, natural harbors, and small islands lying within sight of one another made ships the preferred mode of transport. With few ore deposits and little timber at home, Aegean seafarers imported these commodities, as well as food, for a flourishing population. The rise and fall of these societies therefore depended on their commercial and political relations with other peoples.

The Minoan Civilization of Crete

The first civilization in Europe to have complex political and social structures and advanced technologies like those found in western Asia and northeastern Africa appeared by 2000 B.C.E. on the island of Crete. Centralized government, monumental architecture, bronze metallurgy, and written records distinguished this civilization, which archaeologists labeled **Minoan,** after Greek legends about King Minos. Tradition claimed that Minos ruled a vast naval empire and kept the monstrous Minotaur° (a creature half-man and half-bull) beneath his palace in a maze-like labyrinth built by the inventor Daedalus°. Thus did later Greeks recollect a time when Crete was home to many ships and skillful craftsmen.

The ethnicity of the Minoans is uncertain since their writings have not been translated. But archaeologists have uncovered sprawling palaces at Cnossus°, Phaistos°, and Mallia°, and Cretan pottery and crafts found elsewhere testify to widespread trade in the Mediterranean and Middle East. Egyptian, Syrian, and Mesopotamian influences show up in Minoan palace design, centralized government, and writing technique. Their kings, however, unlike their Middle Eastern counterparts, did not authorize grandiose self-portraits, perhaps because of a different conception of authority.

Statuettes of women with elaborate headdresses and serpents coiling around their limbs possibly represent fertility goddesses, but colorful **frescoes** (paintings done on moist plaster) on palace walls also portray groups of women in frilly, layered skirts engaged in conversation or watching rituals or entertainments. Pictures of young acrobats vaulting over the horns and back of an onrushing bull could record a religious activity or a mere sport. Scenes of servants carrying jars and fishermen throwing nets and hooks from boats suggest a joyful attitude toward work, but this could say more about the tastes of the elite classes than the reality of daily toil. Plants with swaying leaves and octopuses whose tentacles wind around the surface of the vase typify the stylized designs painted on pottery and reflect a delight in the beauty and order of nature.

Around 1450 B.C.E. destruction engulfed the palaces (except Cnossus), the houses of the elite, and even peasant villages. Because Mycenaean Greeks took over at Cnossus, most historians consider them the likely culprits.

The Rise of Mycenaean Civilization

Most historians believe that speakers of an Indo-European language ancestral to Greek migrated into the Greek peninsula

---

Aksum (Ahk-soom)   Minoan (mih-NO-uhn)
Mycenaean (my-suh-NEE-uhn)   Minotaur (MIN-uh-tor)

Daedalus (DED-ih-luhs)   Cnossus (NOSS-suhs)
Phaistos (FIE-stuhs)   Mallia (mahl-YAH)

around 2000 B.C.E., although some argue for a much earlier date. Through intermarriage and an assimilation of languages and cultural traditions, a mixed population of natives and newcomers gave birth to the first Greek culture. For centuries, farmers and shepherds lived in essentially Stone Age conditions, wringing a bare living from the land. Then, sometime around 1600 B.C.E., Greek life changed relatively suddenly.

More than a century ago, a German businessman, Heinrich Schliemann, set out to prove that the *Iliad* and the *Odyssey* were true. These epic compositions attributed to the poet Homer, who probably lived shortly before 700 B.C.E., named Agamemnon° as king of **Mycenae°** in southern Greece. In 1876, Schliemann stunned the scholarly world by discovering at Mycenae a circle of graves at the base of deep, rectangular shafts. These **shaft graves,** containing the bodies of men, women, and children along with weapons, utensils, and gold jewelry and ornaments, indicated an unsuspected level of wealth, authority, and capacity to mobilize human labor. Subsequent excavations uncovered a large palace complex, massive walls, more shaft graves, and other evidence of a rich and technologically advanced Mycenaean civilization that lasted from around 1600 to 1150 B.C.E.

Mycenae's sudden rise, paralleled at other Greek sites, stirred memories of Greek legends concerning immigrants from Phoenicia (modern Lebanon) and Egypt, but archaeology provided no confirmation. Another legend held that King Minos of Crete demanded from the Greek city of Athens an annual tribute of ten maidens and ten young men. The Athenian hero Theseus° went to Crete, entered the labyrinth, and slew the Minotaur, thereby liberating his people.

Cretan political control of the Greek mainland cannot be demonstrated archaeologically, but Mycenaean civilization, named for its first excavated city, certainly borrowed from the Minoans the idea of the palace, the centralized economy, and the administrative bureaucracy, as well as the Minoan writing system. Minoan culture also supplied styles and techniques of architecture, pottery making, and fresco and vase painting. Economi-

cally, most historians look to the profits from trade and piracy, and perhaps also pay and booty brought back by mercenaries (soldiers who served for pay in foreign lands), to explain Mycenaean prosperity.

Since Schliemann's day, excavations at Tiryns°, about 10 miles (16 kilometers) from Mycenae; Pylos°, in the southwest; Athens and Thebes in central Greece; and Iolcus° in northern Greece have revealed a common pattern of citadels located on hilltops surrounded by high, thick fortification walls made of stones so large that Greek legends attributed them to the one-eyed giant Cyclopes°. The fortified enclosure provided a refuge for the entire community in time of danger and contained the palace and administrative complex: a large central hall with an open hearth and columned porch surrounded by courtyards; living quarters for the royal family, courtiers, and servants; and offices, storerooms, and workshops. Frescoes brightly painted on palace walls depicted scenes of war, the hunt, and daily life, as well as decorative motifs from nature.

The tombs of the rulers and leading families— shaft graves at first and later grand beehive shapes made of stone and covered with earthen mounds— lay nearby. Large houses just outside the walls housed the aristocracy, while peasants lived on the lower slopes and in the plain below, close to the land they worked.

Over four thousand baked clay tablets written in a script now called **Linear B** tell us more about Mycenaean life. Pictorial signs represent the syllables of what is recognizably an early form of Greek. Earlier writings from Crete use the same system, referred to as Linear A, but still cannot be read. Knowledge of this unwieldy writing system was probably confined to palace administrators since the tablets consist mostly of inventories: chariot wheels stored in the palace, rations paid to textile workers, gifts to particular deities, or ships stationed along the coasts. The palace bureaucracy kept exhaustive records of people, animals, and goods and thereby exercised great control over the economy. In certain regions, such as the territory

---

Agamemnon (ag-uh-MEM-non)   **Mycenae** (my-SEE-nee)
Theseus (THEE-see-uhs)

Tiryns (TEER-inz)   **Pylos** (PIE-lohs)   **Iolcus** (YOL-kuhs)
Cyclopes (sigh-KLOE-pees)

controlled by Pylos in the southwest, well-organized grain production supported large populations. (Archaeologists can roughly estimate population sizes through tabulating the number of broken pottery pieces from a given period visible on the ground.)

Certain activities, such as wool production, seem to have been state monopolies. Scribes kept track of the flocks in the field, the sheared wool, the distribution of wool to spinners and weavers, and the production, storage, and disbursal of finished cloth.

Yet the tablets say almost nothing about individual personalities—not even the name of a single Mycenaean king—and very little about political and legal practices, social structures, gender relations, and religious beliefs. Their silence extends to particular historical events and relations with other Mycenaean centers or peoples overseas.

In Homer's *Iliad*, Agamemnon, the king of Mycenae, commands a great expedition of Greeks from different regions against the city of **Troy** in northwest Anatolia. This political cooperation seems to correspond to the similarity in the shapes, decorative styles, and production techniques typical of the buildings, tombs, utensils, tools, clothing, and works of art at Mycenaean sites. Yet the plot of the *Iliad* revolves around Agamemnon's difficulties in asserting control over other leaders, such as the indomitable warrior Achilles°. Archaeological remains and the Linear B tablets strongly suggest the independence of centers like Mycenae and Pylos. Extensive contacts and commerce among the Greek kingdoms might therefore explain their cultural uniformity better than political unity.

Overseas Commerce, Settlement, and Aggression

Minoan and Mycenaean trade relied on seafaring. The characteristics of Aegean vessels are known to us through wall paintings from Egypt and the island of Thera and through excavation of sunken vessels preserved by the sandy seafloor. Freighters relied on wind and sail. Warships could lower their mast and resort to oars. Sailors preferred to keep land in sight and sail during daylight hours. Their light wooden vessels had little decking and storage area, so the crews beached their shallow-keeled ship at night and slept ashore.

Cretan and Greek pottery and craft goods are found not only in the Aegean area but elsewhere around the Mediterranean and Middle East. At certain sites where the quantity and range of artifacts suggest Aegean settlement, the oldest materials are Minoan; then Minoan and Mycenaean objects are found together; and eventually Cretan goods disappear. Such evidence indicates that Cretan merchants pioneered trade routes and established trading posts and then admitted Greek traders, who eventually supplanted them by the fifteenth century B.C.E.

Aegean pots found abundantly throughout the Mediterranean and Middle East once contained wine or olive oil. Other possible exports include weapons and other manufactures, along with slaves and mercenaries. Minoan and Mycenaean sailors may also have profited from carrying goods for other peoples.

As for imports, amber (a hard, translucent, yellowish-brown fossil resin used for jewelry) from northern Europe and ivory carved in Syria turn up at Aegean sites, and large populations in southwest Greece and elsewhere probably consumed imported grain. Above all, the Aegean lands lacked metals—both the gold prized by rulers and the copper and tin needed to make bronze. Sunken ships carrying copper ingots have been found on the floor of the Mediterranean. Scholars believe they carried metals from the island of Cyprus, in the northeast corner of the Mediterranean (see Map 2.2). As in early China, the elite classes monopolized possession of metal goods and accorded them symbolic importance. The bronze tripods heaped in the storerooms of the epic Greek heroes bring to mind the bronze vessels buried in Shang tombs.

Trade and piracy can be closely linked. Tough, warlike, and acquisitive, Mycenaean sailors traded with strong peoples and stole from those who were too weak to resist. This may have led to run-ins

Achilles (uh-KIL-eez)

Fresco from the Aegean Island of Thera, ca. 1600 B.C.E.   This picture, originally painted on wet plaster, depicts people watching from town walls a fleet's arrival. Legend credits the Minoan civilization of Crete with great naval power, and the fresco reveals the contemporary appearance and design of ships. In the seventeenth century B.C.E., a massive volcanic explosion devastated Thera and disrupted Aegean society, inspiring, perhaps the myth of Atlantis sinking beneath the sea. (Archaeological Receipts Fund, Athens)

with the Hittite kings of Anatolia in the fourteenth and thirteenth centuries B.C.E. Documents found in the archives at Hattusha, the Hittite capital, refer to the king and land of Ahhijawa°, most likely a Hittite rendering of *Achaeans*°, the term Homer used for the Greeks.

They portray the Ahhijawa as aggressive and prone to take advantage of Hittite preoccupation or weakness. Homer's *Iliad*, the tale of the Achaeans' ten-year siege of Troy, a city on the fringes of Hittite territory and controlling the sea route between the Mediterranean and Black Seas, should be read in the context of Mycenaean belligerence and opportunism. Archaeology has confirmed a destruction at Troy around 1200 B.C.E.

Ahhijawa (uh-key-YAW-wuh)   Achaeans (uh-KEY-uhns)

THE FALL OF LATE BRONZE AGE CIVILIZATIONS

Hittite-Ahhijawa friction and the Greek attack on Troy typify the troubles that culminated in the destruction of many of the old centers of the Middle East and Mediterranean around 1200 B.C.E. Large numbers of people were on the move in this period for unknown reasons. Migrants swarming into one region dislodged other peoples, who then joined the tide of refugees.

Around 1200 B.C.E., unidentified invaders destroyed Hattusha, and the Hittite kingdom in

Anatolia came crashing down. The destructive tide moved south into Syria. The great coastal city of Ugarit was swept away. Around 1220 B.C.E., Pharaoh Merneptah, the son and successor of Ramesses II, repulsed an assault on the Nile Delta. His official account identifies the attackers as "Libyans and Northerners coming from all lands." Thirty years later, Ramesses III checked an invasion of Palestine by "Peoples of the Sea." He claimed a great victory, but one group of invaders, the Philistines, occupied the coast of Palestine. Barely able to survive, Egypt surrendered its territories in Syria-Palestine and lost contact with the rest of western Asia. Nubia also fell away, providing an opportunity for a new native kingdom centered on Napata.

Egyptian inscriptions list the Ekwesh° among the invaders. If that word means Achaeans, then it would appear that Greeks marauding abroad just as their Mycenaean civilization was collapsing at home participated in the destructions of the first half of the twelfth century B.C.E. Some Mycenaean construction of more extensive fortifications and more secure water supplies suggests that some rulers saw trouble coming, but their efforts were in vain. Nearly every palace was destroyed, though the raging fires preserved the Linear B tablets by baking them hard, like pottery.

The archaeological record contains no trace of the foreign invaders whom scholars used to charge with the destruction. Greek legends portray this as a time of internal dynastic struggles and wars between rival kingdoms. One compelling explanation combines external and internal factors. Observing that the collapse of Mycenaean civilization roughly coincided with the fall of other civilizations, it proposes that Mycenaean leaders whose wealth and power depended on trade and imports may have been weakened by the annihilation of major trading partners and disruption of routes. Thus, competition for resources could have stirred internal unrest and ultimately political disintegration.

The political and economic domination of the ruling class ended with the destruction of the palaces. The centralized control revealed in the Linear B tablets disappeared. Writing, a purely administrative technique, was forgotten. Archaeological surface surveys indicate depopulation in some regions and inflows of people to other regions that had escaped destruction. Yet Greek language persisted, and a millennium later, people still worshipped gods mentioned in the Linear B tablets. People also continued to make their customary vessels and implements, though artistry and technical skills declined in an impoverished society. The cultural uniformity of the Mycenaean era gave way to regional variations in shapes, styles, and techniques, reflecting the increased isolation of different parts of Greece from one another.

Thus perished the cosmopolitan world of the Late Bronze Age in the Mediterranean and Middle East. External violence and internal weaknesses shattered the fragile infrastructure of civilization. Societies that had long prospered through complex links of trade, diplomacy, and shared technologies now entered a centuries-long "Dark Age" of poverty, isolation, and loss of knowledge.

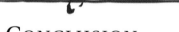

CONCLUSION

The societies described in this chapter prized access to metals, above all, copper and tin alloyed into bronze. Production and ownership of bronze tools, weapons, and luxury and ceremonial items underlay the wealth and power of the elite classes.

Bronze metallurgy began at different times: in western Asia around 2500 B.C.E., in East Asia around 2000, and in northeastern Africa around 1500. The Bronze Age also ended at different times. The transition to iron as the primary metal came around 1000 B.C.E. in the eastern Mediterranean, northeastern Africa, and western Asia and about 500 years later in East Asia.

Political, military, and economic strategies often reflected the demand for bronze. In early China, the state largely controlled prospecting, mining, refining, alloying, and manufacturing. In western Asia, long-distance trade networks facilitated acquisition of metals. Cities sprang up and

---

Ekwesh (ECK-wesh)

prospered along these routes. Military and diplomatic activity commonly focused on commercial crossroad areas, such as Syria-Palestine, over which the Egyptians and Hittites came to blows.

The uses to which bronze was put also varied, though it was rarely used by common people. Bronze weapons with hard, sharp edges enabled the warriors of the Mycenaean and Shang ruling classes, as well as the royal armies of Egypt and Mesopotamia, to dominate the peasant masses. Homer describes Greek aristocrats hoarding bronze weapons and utensils in heavy-gated storerooms and ritually exchanging them to create bonds of friendship and obligation. In Shang China, bronze vessels played a vital role in the rituals for communing with the ancestors.

Between 2200 and 500 B.C.E., complex societies arose in China, Syria-Palestine, Anatolia, Nubia, and the Aegean. Many new civilizations drew on the cultures of ancient centers in Mesopotamia and Egypt. Those centers did not remain static. In an increasingly competitive and interconnected world, travel, transport, and communication accelerated. Akkadian cuneiform writing spread throughout western Asia, and horses hastened communication between central governments and outlying areas.

In the eastern Mediterranean and western Asia, interdependence promoted prosperity, development, and the spread of ideas and technologies. But interdependence also spelled weakness during the migrations and invasions around 1200 B.C.E. Trade disruption reduced access to metals and other valuable commodities, undermining the ruling classes as invaders and wandering displaced peoples toppled unwieldy bureaucracies.

East Asia suffered no parallel fall. China was far away and not tightly linked by trade relations to the eastern Mediterranean and western Asia. The Zhou replaced the Shang, but continuity prevailed in political, religious, and cultural traditions. By contrast, destruction was so great in the eastern Mediterranean and western Asia that the old centers failed to survive or were severely wounded. Within a few centuries, new peoples would come to the fore, in particular, the Assyrians, Phoenicians, and Israelites, whose story unfolds in the next chapter.

■ Key Terms

loess	Akhenaten
Shang	Ramesses II
divination	Kush
Zhou	Meroë
Mandate of Heaven	Minoan
Legalism	frescoes
Confucius	Mycenae
Daoism	shaft graves
yin/yang	Linear B
Hittites	Troy
Hatshepsut	

■ Suggested Reading

Caroline Blunden and Mark Elvin, *Cultural Atlas of China* (1983), contains geographic, ethnographic, and historical information about China through the ages. Edward L. Shaughnessy and Michael Loewe, eds., *The Cambridge History of Ancient China* (1998), Jessica Rawson, *Ancient China: Art and Archaeology* (1980), and Kwang-chih Chang, *The Archaeology of Ancient China*, 4th ed. (1986), thoroughly cover the archaeology and early history. W. Thomas Chase, *Ancient Chinese Bronze Art: Casting the Precious Sacral Vessel* (1991), discusses metallurgical techniques and the significance of bronze vessels. Robert Temple, *The Genius of China: 3,000 Years of Science, Discovery, and Invention* (1986), explores technological history under such broad headings as agriculture, engineering, and medicine. Sharon L. Sievers, in *Restoring Women to History* (1988), and Patricia Ebrey, "Women, Marriage, and the Family in Chinese History," in *Heritage of China: Contemporary Perspectives on Chinese Civilization*, ed. Paul S. Ropp (1990), present the limited evidence on women in early China. Michael Loewe and Carmen Blacker, *Oracles and Divination* (1981), covers divinatory practices in China and elsewhere. Simon Leys, *The Analects of Confucius* (1997), translates and comments on a fundamental text. Benjamin I. Schwartz, *The World of Thought in Ancient China* (1985), broadly introduces ethical and spiritual concepts.

In addition to the Suggested Reading for Chapter 1, see Miriam Lichtheim, *Ancient Egyptian Literature: A Book of Readings*, vol. 2, *The New Kingdom* (1973); Donald B. Redford, *Egypt, Canaan, and Israel in Ancient Times* (1992), which explores the relations of Egypt with the

Syria-Palestine region; and H. W. F. Saggs, *Babylonians* (1995). On the Hittites, see O. R. Gurney, *The Hittites*, 2d ed., rev. (1990), and J. G. Macqueen, *The Hittites and Their Contemporaries in Asia Minor* (1975). Tamsyn Barton, *Ancient Astrology* (1994), describes early astrology in Mesopotamia and Egypt.

Bruce G. Trigger's pioneering work, *Nubia Under the Pharaohs* (1976), is now updated by David O'Connor, *Ancient Nubia: Egypt's Rival in Africa* (1993); Joyce L. Haynes, *Nubia: Ancient Kingdoms of Africa* (1992); Karl-Heinz Priese, *The Gold of Meroë* (1993); P. L. Shinnie, *Ancient Nubia* (1996); and Derek A. Welsby, *The Kingdom of Kush: The Napatan and Meroitic Empires* (1996), all reflect new interest in Nubian art and artifacts. John H. Taylor, *Egypt and Nubia* (1991), emphasizes the interaction of Egyptian and Nubian cultures.

R. A. Higgins, *The Archaeology of Minoan Crete* (1973) and *Minoan and Mycenaean Art,* new rev. ed. (1997); J. Walter Graham, *The Palaces of Crete* (1987); O. Krzyszkowska and L. Nixon, *Minoan Society* (1983); and N. Marinatos, *Minoan Religion* (1993), examine the ar-

chaeological evidence for the Minoan civilization. The brief discussion of M. I. Finley, *Early Greece: The Bronze and Archaic Ages* (1970), and the much fuller accounts of Emily Vermeule, *Greece in the Bronze Age* (1972), and J. T. Hooker, *Mycenaean Greece* (1976), rely primarily on archaeological evidence. On the Linear B tablets, see John Chadwick, *Linear B and Related Scripts* (1987) and *The Mycenaean World* (1976). J. V. Luce, *Homer and the Heroic Age* (1975), and Carol G. Thomas, *Myth Becomes History: Pre-Classical Greece* (1993), examine the value for historians of the Homeric poems. For the disruptions and destructions of the Late Bronze Age in the eastern Mediterranean, see N. K. Sandars, *The Sea Peoples: Warriors of the Ancient Mediterranean* (1978), and Trude Dothan and Moshe Dothan, *People of the Sea: The Search for the Philistines* (1992).

■ **Note**

1. W. F. Albright in James B. Pritchard, ed., *Ancient Near Eastern Texts Relating to the Old Testament,* 3rd ed. (Princeton: Princeton University Press, 1969).

THE FORMATION OF
NEW CULTURAL COMMUNITIES,
1000 B.C.E.–550 C.E.

he fourteen centuries from 1000 b.c.e. to 400 c.e. mark a new chapter in the story of humanity. Important changes in the ways of life established in the river-valley civilizations in the two previous millennia occurred, and the scale of human institutions and activities increased.

The political and social structure of the earliest river-valley centers reflected the importance of irrigation for agriculture. Powerful kings, hereditary priesthoods, dependent laborers, limited availability of metals, and very restricted literacy are hallmarks of the complex

societies described in Part One. In the first millennium B.C.E. new centers arose, in lands watered by rainfall and worked by a free peasantry, on the shores of the Mediterranean, in Iran, India, Southeast Asia, and in Central and South America. Shaped by the natural environments in which they arose, they developed new patterns of political and social organization and economic activity, and moved in new intellectual, artistic, and spiritual directions, though under the influence of the older centers.

The rulers of the empires of this era took steps intended to control and tax their subjects:

they constructed extensive networks of roads and promoted urbanization. These measures brought incidental benefits: more rapid communication, the transport of trade goods over greater distances, and the broad diffusion of religious ideas, artistic styles, and technologies. Large cultural zones unified by common traditions emerged. A number of these cultural traditions— Hellenistic, Roman, Chavín, Olmec—were to exercise substantial influence on subsequent ages. The influence of some—Hindu and Chinese—persists into our own time.

The expansion of agriculture and trade and improvements in technology led to population increases, the spread of cities, and the growth of a comfortable middle class. In many parts of the world iron replaced bronze as the preferred metal for weapons, tools, and utensils. People using iron tools cleared extensive forests around the Mediterranean, in India, and in eastern China. Iron weapons gave an advantage to the armies of Assyria, Greece, Rome, and imperial China. Metal, still an important item of long-distance trade, was available to more people than it had been in the preceding age. Metal coinage, which originated in Anatolia, was adopted by many peoples. Metal coins facilitated commercial transactions and the acquisition of wealth.

New systems of writing also developed. Because they were more easily and rapidly learned, writing moved out of the control of specialists. The vast majority of people remained illiterate, but writing became an increasingly important medium for preserving and transmitting cultural knowledge. The spread of literacy gave birth to new ways of thinking, new genres of literature, and new types of scientific endeavor.

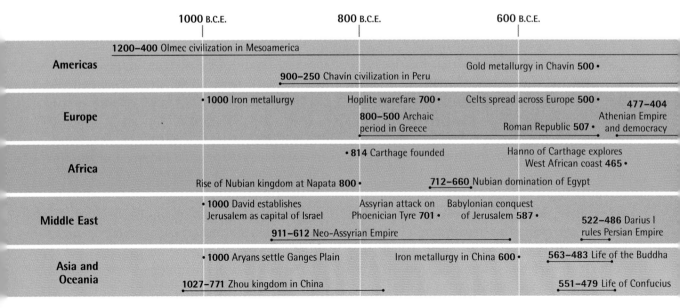

	1000 B.C.E.	800 B.C.E.	600 B.C.E.
Americas	1200–400 Olmec civilization in Mesoamerica	900–250 Chavin civilization in Peru	Gold metallurgy in Chavin 500 •
Europe	• 1000 Iron metallurgy	Hoplite warefare 700 • • 800–500 Archaic period in Greece	Celts spread across Europe 500 • Roman Republic 507 • 477–404 Athenian Empire and democracy
Africa	Rise of Nubian kingdom at Napata 800 •	• 814 Carthage founded 712–660 Nubian domination of Egypt	Hanno of Carthage explores West African coast 465 •
Middle East	• 1000 David establishes Jerusalem as capital of Israel 911–612 Neo-Assyrian Empire	Assyrian attack on Phoenician Tyre 701 •	Babylonian conquest of Jerusalem 587 • 522–486 Darius I rules Persian Empire
Asia and Oceania	• 1000 Aryans settle Ganges Plain 1027–771 Zhou kingdom in China	Iron metallurgy in China 600 •	563–483 Life of the Buddha 551–479 Life of Confucius

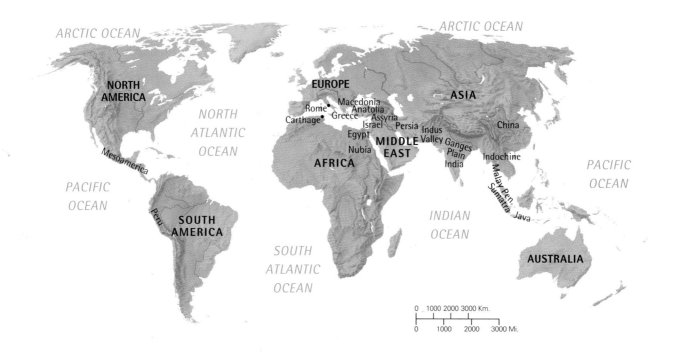

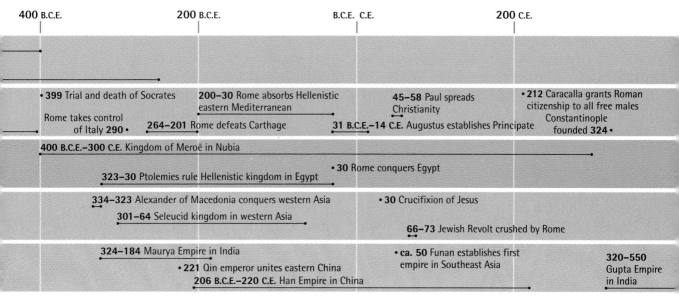

400 B.C.E.	200 B.C.E.	B.C.E. C.E.	200 C.E.

• **399** Trial and death of Socrates

200–30 Rome absorbs Hellenistic eastern Mediterranean

45–58 Paul spreads Christianity

• **212** Caracalla grants Roman citizenship to all free males

Rome takes control of Italy **290** •

264–201 Rome defeats Carthage

31 B.C.E.–14 C.E. Augustus establishes Principate

Constantinople founded **324** •

400 B.C.E.–300 C.E. Kingdom of Meroë in Nubia

323–30 Ptolemies rule Hellenistic kingdom in Egypt

• **30** Rome conquers Egypt

334–323 Alexander of Macedonia conquers western Asia

301–64 Seleucid kingdom in western Asia

• **30** Crucifixion of Jesus

66–73 Jewish Revolt crushed by Rome

324–184 Maurya Empire in India

• **221** Qin emperor unites eastern China

206 B.C.E.–220 C.E. Han Empire in China

• **ca. 50** Funan establishes first empire in Southeast Asia

320–550 Gupta Empire in India

New Civilizations in the Americas and Western Eurasia,

1200–250 B.C.E.

**First Civilizations of the Americas • Celtic Europe • The Assyrian
Empire • Israel • Phoenicia and the Mediterranean • Failure
and Transformation**

SOCIETY AND CULTURE: Mass Deportation in the Neo-Assyrian Empire

*A*ncient peoples enjoyed stories about their origins. Although these stories were not always historically correct, they show how people thought about themselves. The origins story concerning the city of Carthage in present-day Tunisia, which long dominated the western Mediterranean, held that Dido, a queen from the Phoenician city-state of Tyre° in southern Lebanon, fled in 814 B.C.E. with her supporters to North Africa after her brother murdered her husband, the king of Tyre. The refugees persuaded the local population to give them as much land as a cow's hide could cover. By cutting the hide into narrow strips, they marked out a substantial piece of territory: Kart Khadasht, the "New City" (*Carthago* on the tongues of their Roman enemies). Faith-

ful to her dead husband's memory, Dido later committed suicide rather than marry a local chieftain.

Migration and resettlement characterized the first millennium B.C.E., known as the Early Iron Age, in the Mediterranean lands and western Asia. Some populations fled invaders. Some conquered peoples were forcibly transplanted by conquerors. Still others settled in distant lands because of political, military, or economic pressures.

This same period saw the earliest complex societies arise in the Western Hemisphere: the Olmec° people in east-central Mexico and the Chavín° civilization in western Peru. Their cultural and technological traditions decisively influenced later societies in the Americas. Although

---

Tyre (tire)

Olmec (OHL-meck)   **Chavín** (cha-BEAN)

Olmec Head   Giant heads sculpted from basalt distinguish the Olmec culture. The largest of the sixteen so far discovered is approximately 11 feet (3.4 meters) tall. Archaeologists believe the heads are portraits of individual rulers, warriors, or ballplayers.   (Georg Gerster/Photo Researchers, Inc.)

Western Hemisphere developments were sometimes analogous to earlier stages of cultural and technological development in the Eastern Hemisphere, they did not necessarily run in parallel.

This chapter begins with the first complex societies in the Americas and then shifts to the Celtic peoples of Europe; the Assyrians of northern Mesopotamia; the Israelites; and the Phoenicians of Lebanon, Syria, and the western Mediterranean (mainly Carthage) in the late second and early first millennia B.C.E. Following the decline of the centers that dominated the third and second millennia B.C.E., these four societies formed new political, cultural, and commercial centers.

By the end of the second millennium B.C.E., much of the Eastern Hemisphere had entered the **Iron Age**. Iron offered several advantages over bronze for weapons and tools. Iron ore was

abundant and did not have to be alloyed with scarce tin. Once perfected, ironware proved harder and sharper than bronze. Some scholars believe disruptions in copper and tin shipments accompanying the troubles beginning around 1200 B.C.E. forced metalworkers to experiment with iron residue found in slag dumps, a by-product of bronze production. Iron smelting requires a higher temperature than bronze, and hardness depends on the presence of carbon during forging. As techniques improved, however, the superiority of iron became widely recognized, though use of bronze continued.

As you read this chapter, ask yourself the following questions:

• What environmental, technological, political, and cultural factors influenced the institutions and values of these societies?

• Why did peoples seek new homes, and what were the consequences?

• Why did certain cultures perish while others survived?

• Why did the Eastern and Western Hemispheres differ in the chronology and sequencing of societal and technological developments?

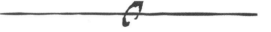

FIRST CIVILIZATIONS OF THE AMERICAS

Humans reached the Western Hemisphere through a series of migrations from Asia. Some scholars date the earliest migration to 35,000–25,000 B.C.E.; others favor the period 20,000–13,000 B.C.E. By either theory, peoples in the Western Hemisphere lived in isolation from the rest of the world for at least fifteen thousand years, which partially explains the distinctiveness of their cultures. While civilizations in Asia, Africa, and Europe exchanged technological innovations, societies in the Americas faced the challenges of the natural environment on their own.

Over thousands of years, the human population increased and dispersed throughout the hemisphere, encountering environments ranging from frozen polar regions, tropical rain forests, and high mountains to deserts, woodlands, and prairies. Cultures marked by complex social stratification and urbanization developed in Mesoamerica (Mexico and northern Central America) and the Andes mountains of South America. Well before 1000 B.C.E., plant domestication of new plant varieties, trade, and the deployment of new technologies enabled their cultural elites to concentrate political and religious authority, organize large-scale irrigation and drainage works, clear forests, and construct terraced fields on hillsides. These transformed environments supported urban centers dominated by monumental religious structures and housing for the elite. By 1000 B.C.E., the major urban centers of Mesoamerica and the Andes had begun to project political and cultural power afar; they had become civilizations. The most important of these civilizations, the Olmec and Chavín, left cultural legacies in Mesoamerica and the Andes, respectively, that persisted for more than a thousand years.

The Mesoamerican Olmecs, 1200–400 B.C.E.

Within Mesoamerica, a region of great geographic and climatic diversity, Amerindian peoples exploited the indigenous plants and animals in different ecological niches, as well as minerals like obsidian, quartz, and jade. Contacts across environmental boundaries encouraged trade and cultural exchange, which combined with increasing population and agricultural productivity to foster urbanization and powerful political and religious forces. Although none of Mesoamerica's militarily powerful civilizations could unify the region politically, they all shared fundamental elements of material culture, technology, religion, political organization, art, architecture, and sport.

Olmec civilization flourished between 1200 and 400 B.C.E. (see Map 3.1). The most influential in early Mesoamerica, it centered near the tropical Atlantic coast of the states of Veracruz and Tabasco in today's Mexico. Smaller sites recently excavated indicate that Olmec cultural influence reached the Pacific coast of Central America and Mexico's Central Plateau.

Between 900 and 600 B.C.E., La Venta° replaced San Lorenzo as the most flourishing Olmec center, only to be superseded by Tres Zapotes°. When San Lorenzo and La Venta were in turn abandoned, their monuments were defaced or buried and their buildings destroyed. Archaeologists take this as evidence of internal upheaval or invasion by neighboring peoples.

The domestication by 3500 B.C.E. of the staples of the Mesoamerican diet—corn, beans, and squash—enabled farmers to produce dependable surpluses and thus permitted the first stages of craft specialization and social stratification, and ultimately the emergence of the Olmec cities. Emerging religious and political elites organized the population to dig irrigation and drainage canals, grow crops on raised fields, and build the large-scale religious and civic buildings characteristic of Olmec civilization.

Artificial platforms and mounds of packed earth dominated Olmec cities and framed the collective ritual and political activities that attracted the rural population at ceremonial times. Most raised platforms served religious purposes; some also supported elite residences. Urban complexes were aligned according to certain stars, reflecting belief in the significance of astronomical events. Since the centers had few permanent residences, their construction reflects the ability of the Olmec elite to recruit thousands of laborers from a broad region. Skilled artisans who lived in the urban core produced high-quality crafts, including carved jade figurines, necklaces, and ceremonial knives and axes. Archaeology indicates as well the presence of merchants who traded with distant peoples for obsidian, jade, and pottery.

What little is known about Olmec political structure suggests a form of kingship that com-

---

La Venta (LA BEN-tah)
Tres Zapotes (TRACE zah-POE-tace)

CHRONOLOGY

	Israel	Phoenicia/Carthage	Mesopotamia	Americas
1200 B.C.E.	**1250–1200 B.C.E.** Israelite occupation of Canaan			**1200–900 B.C.E.** Rise of Olmec civilization, centered on San Lorenzo
1000 B.C.E.	**1000 B.C.E.** David establishes Jerusalem as capital	**969 B.C.E.** Hiram of Tyre comes to power		
	960 B.C.E. Solomon builds First Temple			
900 B.C.E.	**920 B.C.E.** Division into two kingdoms		**911 B.C.E.** Rise of Neo-Assyrian Empire	**900–600 B.C.E.** La Venta, the dominant Olmec center
800 B.C.E.		**814 B.C.E.** Foundation of Carthage		**900–250 B.C.E.** Chavín civilization in the Andes
			744–727 B.C.E. Reforms of Tiglathpileser	
700 B.C.E.	**721 B.C.E.** Assyrian conquest of northern kingdom	**701 B.C.E.** Assyrian humiliation of Tyre		
			668–627 B.C.E. Reign of Ashurbanipal	
			626–539 B.C.E. Neo-Babylonian kingdom	
600 B.C.E.			**612 B.C.E.** Fall of Assyria	**600–400 B.C.E.** Ascendancy of Tres Zapotes and Olmec decline
	587 B.C.E. Neo-Babylonian capture of Jerusalem	**ca. 550–300 B.C.E.** Rivalry of Carthaginians and Greeks in western Mediterranean		

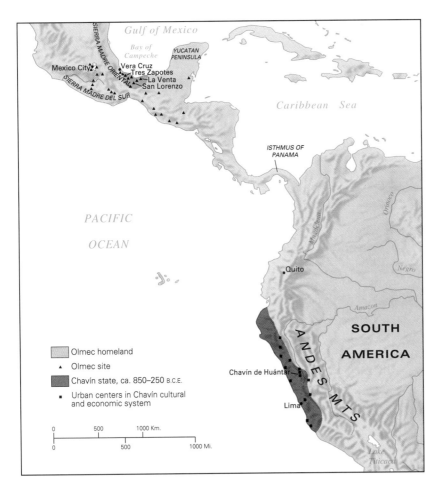

Map 3.1   Olmec and Chavín Civilizations   The regions of Mesoamerica (most of modern Mexico and Central America) and the Andean highlands of South America have hosted impressive civilizations since early times. The civilizations of the Olmec and Chavín were the originating civilizations of these two regions, providing the foundations of architecture, city planning, and religion.

bined religious and secular roles with the building of urban centers. Although no Olmec empire arose, Olmec products and images, such as the jaguar god carved in jade, spread as far as central Mexico. The best-known Olmec monuments are carved stone heads as much as 11 feet (3.4 meters) high, each unique and indicating a distinctive personality. Archaeologists consider these memorials to rulers. The Olmec elite dominated this complex society through religious rituals, control of finely crafted objects, and awe-inspiring architecture.

Most Olmec deities had dual (male and female) natures. Some blended human and animal characteristics. Images of jaguars or men being transformed into jaguars were common. The shamans and healers who organized religious affairs also developed a form of writing and pro-

duced a calendar charting the cycle of the year based on observation of the stars. The Olmec probably invented the ritual ball game that became an enduring part of Mesoamerican ceremonial life.

Early South American Civilization: Chavín, 900–250 B.C.E.

Geography influenced the development of human society in the Andes. Diverse environments—a mountainous core, arid coastal plain, and dense interior jungles—challenged human populations to develop specialized regional production and the complex social institutions and cultural standards needed for interregional exchanges and shared labor responsibilities.

These environmental adaptations became enduring features of Andean civilization.

Complex urban society in South America (see Map 3.1) began with the **Chavín** civilization, with its capital at Chavín de Huántar°, 10,300 feet (3,139 meters) up in the eastern range of the Andes north of the modern city of Lima. Between 900 and 250 B.C.E., roughly coinciding with Olmec civilization, Chavín dominated the political and economic life of a densely populated region encompassing large areas of the Peruvian coastal plain and Andean foothills. Trade routes connecting the coast with populous mountain valleys converged at Chavín de Huántar, giving its rulers advantages over rivals in both ecological zones.

The capital's huge size and the dispersal of Chavín pottery, religious motifs, and architectural forms over a wide area suggest some degree of political integration and trade dependency, possibly enforced militarily. Most scholars believe, however, that Chavín's influence, like Olmec influence, depended more on an appealing system of religious beliefs and rituals, as indicated by findings of jaguar deity images, Chavín's most potent religious symbol, over a broad area.

Chavín depended on earlier developments in agriculture and trade. The abundance of fish and mollusks along the Peruvian coast and the introduction of maize cultivation from the north made the development of cities possible in the centuries before its rise. Chavín's trade linked the coastal economy with the producers of quinoa (a local grain), potatoes, and llamas in the high mountain valleys and, to a lesser extent, with Amazonian producers of coca and fruits.

Reciprocal labor obligations that permitted the construction and maintenance of roads, bridges, temples, palaces, and large irrigation and drainage projects developed along with trade, as did textile production. The precise nature of labor obligations at Chavín is unknown, but in later times, the clan served this purpose, its members claiming descent from a common ancestor and holding land communally. Like brothers and sisters, clan members were obligated to help each other. Clan-based organization of labor and distribution of goods influenced every level of Andean society.

Increasing use of **llamas** to move goods from one ecological zone to another promoted specialization of production and trade. Domesticated in the mountainous interior of Peru as the only beasts of burden in the Americas, llamas helped integrate the Andean region. Their importance to Chavín's development resembles that of the camels in the evolution of trans-Saharan trade (see Chapter 6). Llamas provided meat and wool and accelerated commercial exchange by replacing human porters on trade routes. A single driver could control ten to thirty animals, each carrying up to 70 pounds (32 kilograms); human porters carried about 50 pounds (22.5 kilograms) each.

Chavín's architecture featured multilevel platforms made of packed earth or rubble faced with cut stone or adobe (sun-dried brick made of clay and straw). Atop the platforms, small buildings, usually decorated with relief carvings of serpents, condors, jaguars, or humans, hosted rituals or served as elite residences. The largest platform at Chavín de Huántar measured 250 feet (76 meters) on each side and rose to a height of 50 feet (15 meters). The one-third of its interior that is hollow contains narrow galleries and small rooms that may have housed royal burials.

Metallurgy developed in the Andean region and from there reached Mesoamerica. Excavations at Chavín de Huántar and smaller centers have unearthed three-dimensional ornaments made of a gold-silver alloy, a clear advance over earlier technologies. Textile manufacture and design similarly improved as Chavín rose. High-quality cloth, probably used only by the elite or in religious rituals, added to Chavín's prestige and projection of its power. Textiles, like sculpture and pottery, commonly depicted a jaguar-man reminiscent of the common Olmec symbol.

As Chavín flourished, class distinctions increased. Scholars believe that Chavín's politics featured both local chiefs and a more powerful chief or king, as well as a priestly class. Some graves have yielded high-quality textiles, gold crowns, breastplates, and jewelry, clearly distinguishing them from common burials. These objects, along with an abundance of fine pottery and the building and

---

Chavín de Huántar (cha-BEAN day WAHN-tar)

decorative skills evident in the monumental architecture, prove the presence of master artisans as well.

Destruction did not accompany Chavín's eclipse as it had the Olmec centers. But unrest throughout the region around 200 B.C.E. may have disrupted Chavín's trade and thereby undermined the governing elite's authority. Chavín's collapse remains a mystery, but its technologies, material culture, statecraft, architecture, and urban planning influenced the Andean region for centuries.

CELTIC EUROPE

Around 500 B.C.E., Celtic peoples spread across a substantial portion of Europe and, by coming into contact with the literate societies of the Mediterranean, entered the historical record. Information about the early **Celts°** comes from the archaeological record, Greek and Roman travelers and conquerors, and Celtic literature from Wales and Ireland preserved orally by bards (singers of ballads) and until written down during the European Middle Ages.

The Spread of the Celts

Celtic designates a branch of the Indo-European language family that corresponds to an archaeological cultural complex dating to the early first millennium B.C.E. in parts of present-day Germany, Austria, and the Czech Republic. The early Celts lived in or near hill-forts—lofty natural locations defended by earthwork fortifications. New styles of manufacture and art that appeared around 500 B.C.E. suggest trade with the Mediterranean lands.

These new cultural features coincided with a rapid expansion of Celtic groups to the west—Celts occupied nearly all of France and much of Britain and Ireland, and in combination with indigenous peoples created the Celtiberian culture of northern Spain—and to the east and south. They overran

northern Italy in the fifth century B.C.E. and made destructive raids into central Greece. One group, the Galatians, even reached central Anatolia (modern Turkey). By 300 B.C.E., Celts were found north of the Alps from present-day Hungary to Spain and Ireland. Place names preserve their memory: rivers (Danube, Rhine, Seine, Thames, and Shannon), countries (Belgium), regions (Bohemia, Aquitaine), and towns (Paris, Bologna, Leiden). Grouped into hundreds of small, loosely organized kinship groups, they shared elements of language and culture but created no Celtic state.

Greek and Roman sources describe burly men with shaggy mustaches; loud, deep voices; and long red hair, often kept stiff and upright by a cement-like solution of lime. Trousers, usually an indication of horse riding, and twisted gold collars added to their exotic image, as did warriors who fought naked and made the heads of slain enemies into trophies. The same sources characterize the Celts as fond of war, courageous, childishly impulsive, emotional, fond of boasting and exaggeration, quick-witted, and eager to learn.

The Roman military commander Gaius Julius Caesar composed a detailed account of his conquest of Gaul (present-day France) between 58 and 51 B.C.E. Celtic groups in Gaul had once been ruled by kings, but those whom Caesar encountered periodically chose public officials, perhaps under Greek and Roman influence.

Celtic society encompassed an elite class of warriors, professional groups of priests and bards, and a mass of commoners. Warriors monopolized power and wealth in the form of sheep, cattle, and land worked by commoners. Welsh and Irish legends, which reflect a political and social development less complex than what Caesar encountered in France, describe warriors raiding one another's flocks, reveling in drunken feasts, and contesting with each other in strength and wit. Warriors sometimes fought to the death at banquets to claim the choicest meat, known as the "hero's portion."

Druids, the Celtic priests, formed a well-organized fraternity that performed religious, judicial, and educational functions. Trainees spent years learning prayers, rituals, legal precedents, and other traditions. Not being restricted by boundaries between kin groups, Druids could sometimes

Celts (kelts)

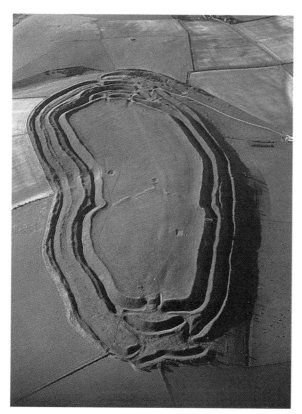

Celtic Hill-Fort in England   Sites like these, hundreds of which have been found across Europe, served as centers for governing, manufacturing, mustering armies, storing food and trade goods, and seeking refuge. Ditches and earthwork walls added to the natural defensive position of the hill. The so-called Gallic Wall, made of earth, stone, and timber, had both the strength and flexibility to absorb a pounding from siege engines.   (Royal Commission for Historic Monuments)

avert warfare or serve as judges in intergroup disputes. In the first century C.E., Roman governors in Celtic areas set about eradicating the Druids. They claimed to be offended by ritual human sacrifices, but preventing Druids from stirring opposition to Roman rule concerned them as well.

Celtic farmers cultivating the heavy but fertile soils of continental Europe supported large populations, and Celtic metalworking surpassed that of the Mediterranean peoples. Navigable rivers facilitated extensive trade, and groups along the Atlantic coast of France braved the ocean in well-built ships. By the first century B.C.E., some hill-forts were evolving into urban centers.

Women's lives focused on child rearing, food production, and some crafts. Although they were better off than their sisters in the Middle East or the Mediterranean, enjoying freer sexual relations, for example, they still lacked equality with men. Celtic women appear strong and proud in Greek and Roman sources, while Welsh and Irish tales portray women sitting at banquet with their husbands, engaging in witty conversation, and often providing ingenious solutions to problems. Both husband and wife contributed property to a marriage, and each inherited the estate of the other.

Tombs of elite women have yielded rich collections of clothing, jewelry, and furniture for use in the next world, and marriages among elites confirmed group alliances. The Roman invaders of Celtic Britain in the first century C.E. sometimes confronted Celtic peoples headed by queens, though some scholars deem this an abnormal circumstance prompted by the Roman invasion.

Belief and Knowledge

Sources name more than four hundred gods and goddesses, mostly associated with particular places or kinship groups. More widely revered deities include Lug°, the god of light, crafts, and inventions; the horse goddess Epona°; and the horned god Cernunnos°. "The Mothers," three goddesses shown holding symbols of abundance, seem to reflect some kind of fertility cult. Halloween and May Day preserve the respective ancient Celtic holidays of Samhain and Beltaine, which marked key moments in the agricultural cycle.

The early Celts worshipped wherever they sensed divinity—at springs, groves, and hilltops—rather than solely in temples. At the sources of the Seine and Marne Rivers in France, archaeologists have discovered masses of wooden statues identified as Celtic thrown into the water by worshippers.

Elite graves containing wagons filled with

Lug (loog)   **Epona** (eh-POH-nuh)
Cernunnos (KURN-you-nuhs)

extensive grave goods suggest belief in some sort of afterlife. In Irish and Welsh legends, heroes and divinities pass from the natural to the supernatural world with relative ease compared with other mythologies, and magical occurrences abound. Belief in reincarnation—the rebirth of a soul in a new body—lowered the barrier separating life from death that other peoples in Europe and western Asia considered unbridgeable.

Roman invasions from the second century B.C.E. to the first century C.E. curtailed the evolution of Celtic society in Spain, southern Britain, France, and Central Europe. The conquered peoples generally adopted Roman ways (see Chapter 5), including Latin speech, the ancestor of French and Spanish. From the third century C.E. on, Germanic invaders diminished the Celts still further. English, a Germanic tongue with negligible Celtic influence, became the language of Britain. Only on the coastal fringes of Europe—in Brittany (northwest France), Wales, Scotland, and Ireland—did Celtic peoples maintain their language, art, and culture into modern times.

THE ASSYRIAN EMPIRE

Far to the south and east of the Celtic lands, the peoples of western Asia also experienced momentous changes in the first millennium B.C.E., chiefly at the hands of the powerful and aggressive **Neo-Assyrian Empire** (911–612 B.C.E.). Although earlier regional powers are sometimes called *empires*, the Assyrians of this era were the first to rule over far-flung lands and diverse peoples.

Living in northern Mesopotamia, a hillier, rainier, and cooler region than Sumer and Akkad to the south, Assyrian peasant farmers routinely confronted raiders, whether mountaineers to the east and north or nomads from the arid west. They thus provided a solid military base for a revival of Assyrian power in the ninth century B.C.E. Initially designed for self-defense and reestablishment of old claims, Assyrian aggression spurred ceaseless campaigning along long-distance trade routes: westward across the steppe and desert to the

Mediterranean, north into mountainous Urartu° (modern Armenia), east across the Zagros range onto the Iranian Plateau, and south along the Tigris River to Babylonia.

In the eighteenth century B.C.E., Assyria's kings had controlled the upper Euphrates region, and Assyrian merchants had established trading settlements alongside major cities in Syria and Anatolia (see Chapter 2). Now, enriched by booty, tribute, and access to resources like iron and silver, their control of international commerce resumed.

Driven by pride, greed, and religious conviction, the Assyrians defeated every rival: Elam (southwest Iran), Urartu, Babylon, and Egypt. Their empire extended from Syria-Palestine and Egypt in the west, across Anatolia, Armenia, and Mesopotamia, and into western Iran. Greater in extent than any previous state, the empire oppressed its subjugated peoples to enrich the imperial center.

God and King

The king was literally and symbolically the center of the Assyrian universe. Chosen by the gods, the land was his, and the people, even high-ranking officials, were his servants. A king normally named one of his sons as successor, a choice then confirmed by divine oracles and the Assyrian elite. The high priest anointed the new king's head in the ancient city of **Ashur** and conferred on him a crown and scepter. The kings were buried in Ashur.

Every day, messengers and spies brought the king information from every corner of the empire. He made decisions, appointed officials, and heard complaints. He dictated correspondence to scribes and received foreign envoys and high-ranking government figures. As military leader, he planned campaign strategy, inspected troops, and commanded important operations.

Beyond these many responsibilities, the king supervised the state religion, devoting much time to public and private rituals and oversight of the temples. He made no state decisions without consulting the gods through elaborate rituals of divination. All state actions were carried out in the

---

Urartu (ur-RAHR-too)

name of Ashur, the chief god, and deemed in accord with his wishes. Assyrian victories proved Ashur's superiority over the gods of the conquered peoples.

Relentless government propaganda secured popular support for military campaigns that mostly benefited the king and nobility. Royal inscriptions posted throughout the empire cataloged victories, extolled the charisma and will of the king, and promised ruthless punishment for those who resisted him. Relief sculptures depicting hunts, battles, sieges, executions, and deportations covered the walls of the royal palaces at Kalhu° and Nineveh° and reinforced the message. Looming over most scenes was the godlike king: larger than life, muscular and fierce, inspiring awe in every court visitor.

Conquest and Control

Military organization and technology underlay the Assyrians' conquests. Early Assyrian armies consisted of two groups: men who served in return for grants of land and peasants and slaves contributed by large landowners. Later, Tiglathpileser° (r. 744–727 B.C.E.) added a core of professional soldiers drawn from both Assyrians and subject peoples. At its peak, the Assyrian state could mobilize a half-million troops, including light-armed bowmen and slingers, armored spearmen, cavalry equipped with bow or spear, and four-man chariots.

Iron weapons and speedy, mobile cavalry gave Assyrian soldiers an advantage over many opponents. Assyrian engineers developed machinery and tactics for besieging fortified towns. They tunneled under the walls, built mobile towers for archers, and applied battering rams to weak points. Fortified cities like Babylon, Thebes in Egypt, Tyre in Phoenicia, and Susa in Elam succumbed to these tactics. Couriers and signal fires provided long-distance communications while a network of spies gathered intelligence.

Terror tactics—swift and harsh retribution and brutal punishments—discouraged rebellion. **Mass deportation**—forcibly uprooting entire communities and resettling them elsewhere—broke the spirit of rebellious peoples and warned others not to resist (see Society and Culture: Mass Deportation in the Neo-Assyrian Empire). Deportation also shifted human resources from the periphery to the center, where the deportees labored on royal and noble estates, constructed palaces and cities, and opened new lands to agriculture. Deported craftsmen and soldiers could be assigned to the army.

Vast distances and diverse landscapes populated by peoples who differed in language, customs, religion, and political organization posed enormous problems of organization and communication. The Assyrians never found a successful way of governing nomadic and sedentary kinship groups, temple-states, city-states, and subject kingdoms in a single empire. Control was tight and effective close to the core area but declined with distance. The need to reimpose control on territories previously subdued prompted many military campaigns.

Provincial officials oversaw tribute and tax payment, maintained law and order, raised troops, undertook public works, and provisioned armies and administrators who were crossing their territory. They and the local elite classes faced frequent inspections by royal overseers.

Courtiers, supervisors, scribes, and servants staffed the palace and central government offices. High-ranking officials, with courts of their own and estates worked by peasants tied to the land, were themselves bound to the monarchy by oaths of obedience, fear of punishment, and expectation of land grants or share of booty and taxes as rewards for loyalty and performance. Oaths, fears, and rewards similarly bound the professional class of priests, diviners, scribes, doctors, and artisans.

Plunder and tribute defrayed the cost of military campaigns. Wealth from the periphery flowed to the center, where the king and nobility grew rich. Proud kings embellished the ancestral capital and religious center at Ashur and built new royal cities. Dur Sharrukin, the "Fortress of Sargon," took a mere ten years to build, an indicator of the size of the labor force drawn from prisoners of war and Assyrian citizens who owed periodic service to the state. Although the core area benefited most, the infrastructure of the provinces may have received

---

Kalhu (KAL-oo)   **Nineveh** (NIN-uh-vuh)
Tiglathpileser (TIG-lath-pih-LEE-zuhr)

Mass Deportation in the Neo-Assyrian Empire

The Assyrian mentality appears in the unprecedented scale of their resort to mass deportation, a tactic previously used in Sumer, Babylon, Urartu, Egypt, and the Hittite Empire. Surviving documents record the relocation of over 1 million people, and historians estimate the true figure exceeds 4 million.

The following entries from a set of inscriptions recording the year-by-year achievements of King Sargon II (r. 721–705 B.C.E.) reveal the fate of the people and territory of the northern Israelite kingdom and several coastal cities.

[First Year] I besieged and conquered Samaria [the capital of the northern Israelite kingdom], led away as booty 27,290 inhabitants of it. I formed from among them a contingent of 50 chariots and made the remaining inhabitants resume their social positions. I installed over them an officer of mine and imposed upon them the tribute of the former king. . . . [Seventh Year] Upon a trust-inspiring oracle given by my lord Ashur, I crushed the tribes of Tamud, Ibadidi, Marsimanu, and Haiapa, the Arabs who live, far away, in the desert [and] who know neither overseers nor officials and who had not yet brought their tribute to any. I deported their survivors and settled them in Samaria. . . . [Eleventh Year] I besieged and conquered the cities Ashdod, Gath, Asdudimmu; I declared his [the ruler of Ashdod's] images, his wife, his children, all the possessions and treasures of his palace as well as the inhabitants of his country as booty. I reorganized the administration of these cities and settled therein people from the regions of the East which I had conquered personally. I installed an officer of mine over them and declared them Assyrian citizens and they pulled the straps of my yoke.

Notice the variety of uses to which deportees were put. Some were drafted into the Assyrian military. Others worked in construction and agriculture. The specific numbers suggest careful recordkeeping, though they may exaggerate. The documents do not tell us why some people were deported and others permitted to stay. The Assyrians may have chosen to remove members of the elite who provided leadership and individuals with useful skills. Though technically considered "booty," conquered peoples were subject to the same obligations as other Assyrian citizens.

In this document, the king orchestrates an exchange of populations. Deportation rendered both groups in such exchanges docile and even loyal to the interests of the Assyrian state, because submission alone protected them in an often hostile new environment. Despite their numerical and geographical precision, these documents conceal the human experience of the deportees.

What would have been the psychological and emotional impacts of being forcibly removed from the familiar landscape, monuments, climate, and people of one's homeland and resettled in an alien environment? How might the deportees' culture have changed to adapt to the new circumstances?

Source: Transcriptions recording the year-by-year achievements of King Sargon II: James B. Pritchard, ed., *The Ancient Near East: An Anthology of Texts and Pictures* (Princeton, NJ: Princeton University Press, 1958), 195–197. Copyright © 1958 by Princeton University Press. Reprinted with permission of Princeton University Press.

Wall Relief from the Palace of Sennacherib at Nineveh   Against a backdrop of wooded hills representing the landscape of Assyria, workers haul a huge stone sculpture from the riverbank to the palace under the watchful eyes of officials and soldiers. They accomplish this task with simple equipment—a lever, a sledge, and thick ropes—and a lot of muscle power.   (Courtesy of the Trustees of the British Museum)

some royal investment. Cities and merchant classes prospered from thriving long-distance commerce, and some subject populations were surprisingly loyal to their Assyrian rulers.

Assyrian Society and Culture

The royal deeds and victories and government operations dominate the sources, but some information pertains to the lives and activities of the millions of subjects. In the core area, people belonged to the same three classes that had existed in Hammurabi's Babylon a millennium before (see Chapter 2): (1) free, landowning citizens, (2) farmers and artisans attached to royal or noble estates, and (3) slaves. Slaves—bankrupt debtors and prisoners of war—enjoyed legal rights and could rise to positions of influence.

The government saw all subjects, both native Assyrian and non-Assyrian, as entitled to equal legal protection and owing the same labor and military obligations. Over time, the inflow of deportees and other outsiders changed the ethnic makeup of the core area.

The vast majority of subjects worked on the land, supporting those engaged in specialized activities in towns and cities—soldiers, government officials, religious experts, merchants—as well as artisans and shopkeepers who dealt in locally consumed goods like pottery, tools, and clothing. Although most trade was local, the state encouraged long-distance trade. Imported goods such as metals, fine textiles, dyes, gems, and ivory earned customs revenues and pleased consumers among the royal family and elite classes. Coinage not yet being known, silver served as a medium of exchange by weight.

Building on knowledge of their Mesopotamian ancestors (see Environment and Technology: Chinese and Mesopotamian Divination, in Chapter 2), Assyrian scholars compiled and preserved lists of such things as plant and animal names, geographic terms, and astronomical occurrences, and they made original contributions in mathematics and astronomy. Their assumption that gods or demons caused disease obstructed understanding of illness, but in addition to exorcists trained to expel demons from sick people, some physicians experimented with practical medicines and surgical treatments.

Some urban temples may have had libraries. At Nineveh, archaeologists uncovered more than 25,000 tablets or fragments of tablets. This **Library of Ashurbanipal,** built by one of the last Assyrian kings, Ashurbanipal° (r. 668–627 B.C.E.), contained official documents as well as literary and scientific texts, some brought to the capital from elsewhere and others copied at the king's command. The "House of Knowledge" referred to in some of the documents may have been an academy of learned men attracted to the court by Ashurbanipal's fascination with the scientific and literary heritage of Mesopotamia. Much of what we know about Mesopotamian art, literature, and science and about earlier historical eras comes to us from excavations of Assyrian sites.

ISRAEL

On the western edge of the Assyrian Empire, bordering the "Upper Sea," as they called the Mediterranean, lived a people who probably counted for little in Assyrian eyes but who were to play an important role in world history. Ancient Israel experienced two grand and interconnected dramas that played out between 2000 and 500 B.C.E.: (1) a loose collection of nomadic kinship groups and caravan drivers settled as farmers, developed complex political and social institutions, and became integrated into the commercial and diplomatic networks of the Middle East; and (2)

their austere worship of a desert god generated a unique concept of deity from which evolved the ethical and intellectual traditions and the distinctive way of life of the Jewish people.

Both the land and the people at the heart of this story have gone by various names: Canaan, Israel, Palestine, Hebrews, Israelites, and Jews. For consistency, the people are referred to here as *Israelites* and the land they occupied in antiquity as **Israel.**

Geographically, Israel links Anatolia, Egypt, Arabia, and Mesopotamia and thus enjoys a prominence in both ancient and modern times out of all proportion to its size and economic potential. Its natural resources are few. The Negev Desert and the wasteland of Sinai lie to the south. Non-Israelites, notably the Philistines, held the fertile coastal plain throughout much of the biblical period. At the center are the rock-strewn hills of the Shephelah°. Galilee to the north, by the sea of the same name, offered grassy hills, small plains, and relatively fertile land. The Jordan River flanking Israel on the east flowed into the Dead Sea, so named because its high salt content is toxic to life.

Origins, Exodus, and Settlement

Some information about ancient Israel comes from archaeological excavations and references in contemporary documents such as the royal annals of Egypt and Assyria. However, the fundamental source is the collection of writings preserved in the **Hebrew Bible** (called the Old Testament by Christians). The Hebrew Bible contains materials that originated with different groups, who employed distinctive vocabularies and advocated particular interpretations of past events. Long transmitted orally, traditions about the Israelites' early days began to be written down in the tenth century using an alphabet borrowed from the nearby Phoenicians. The text we use today dates from the fifth century B.C.E., with a few later additions, and reflects the views of the priests who controlled the Temple in Jerusalem. Historians disagree about how closely this document follows Israelite history. In the absence of alternative narratives, however, it

---

Ashurbanipal (ah-shur-BAH-nuh-pahl)   **Shephelah** (sheh-FEH-luh)

provides a historical base to be used critically and checked against archaeological discoveries.

The Hebrew language of the Bible reflects Israelite speech prior to about 500 B.C.E. A Semitic language closely related to Aramaic, which succeeded it in Israel, and Phoenician to the north, its more distant relations include Arabic and the Akkadian spoken by the Assyrians. These linguistic relations probably parallel the Israelites' ethnic relations with neighboring peoples.

Unique as the primary source of the Judeo-Christian tradition central to Western civilization, the history of the Israelites nevertheless reflects a familiar pattern in the ancient Middle East: nomadic pastoralists from the desert margins raiding the villages of settled peoples and eventually settling down as farmers. The Hebrew Bible tells the story of the family of Abraham. Born in the city of Ur in southern Mesopotamia, probably in the twentieth century B.C.E., Abraham rejected the traditional idol worship and emigrated with his family and livestock (sheep, cattle, donkeys) across the Syrian desert. The Bible relates that the land of Israel, his destination, had been promised to him and his descendants as part of a covenant, or pact, with the Israelite god, Yahweh.

These "recollections" of Abraham's journey may compress the experiences of generations of pastoralists migrating from grazing lands between the upper reaches of the Tigris and Euphrates Rivers to the Mediterranean coast. The actions of Abraham's group recall common patterns of pastoral life. During the dry season, they camped by a well or waterhole. The rest of the year, they shifted their flocks and herds, which provided milk, meat, and wool, from one grazing area to another in an established sequence. The friction between pastoral Israelites and their settled neighbors, a common phenomenon in the region, comes through in such biblical stories as the slaying of Adam's shepherd son, Abel, by his farmer brother, Cain, and Yahweh's destruction of the wicked cities of Sodom and Gomorrah°.

Isaac succeeded his father, Abraham, as leader, and his son Jacob succeeded him. In the next generation, discord among the offspring of Jacob's several wives led to his sons' selling their brother Joseph as a slave to merchants heading for Egypt. Through luck and ability, Joseph became a high official at Pharaoh's court, which put him in a position to help his family when drought struck Israel and forced them to migrate to Egypt with their flocks. Egyptians feared and despised the Israelite herders, eventually treating them as slaves and putting them to work on Pharaoh's building projects.

This account given in the Hebrew Bible skips over the centuries (1700–1500 B.C.E.) of Hyksos domination of Egypt. Since the Hyksos are thought to have spoken a Semitic language and to have infiltrated the Nile Delta from the northeast (see Chapter 2), the Israelite migration to Egypt and later enslavement may have been connected to their rise and fall. In addition, although Egyptian sources do not mention Israelite slaves, they do complain about Apiru°, a derogatory term applied to caravan drivers, outcasts, bandits, and other marginal groups. The word seems to designate a class of people rather than a particular ethnic group, but some scholars believe that *Apiru* and *Hebrew* may be the same. The period of Israelite slavery also coincides with the ambitious building programs launched by Sethos I and Ramesses II between 1400 and 1200 B.C.E.

Moses, an Israelite with connections to the Egyptian royal family, reportedly led the Israelite slaves out of captivity. Folktale motifs like the ten plagues that Yahweh inflicted on Egypt to persuade Pharaoh to release the Israelites and the miraculous parting of the Red Sea that enabled the refugees to escape embellish this narrative in the biblical book of Exodus. Yet this does not remove the possibility that oral tradition preserved memories of a real Israelite emigration followed by years living as nomads in Sinai.

During their reported forty years in the desert, the Israelites became the "Chosen People" of their stern and warlike god, Yahweh, and promised to worship him exclusively. Tablets brought down by Moses from the top of Mount Sinai confirmed this pact. The Ten Commandments inscribed on them established the basic tenets of Jewish belief and practice. They prohibit murder, adultery, theft, lying, and envy and command respect for parents

---

Gomorrah (guh-MORE-uh)

Apiru (uh-PEE-roo)

and relaxation from work on the Sabbath, the seventh day of the week.

The biblical narrative tells how Joshua, Moses's successor, led the Israelites from the east side of the Jordan River into the land of Canaan (modern Israel and Palestine), during which invasion they attacked and destroyed Jericho and other Canaanite cities. Archaeology confirms the destruction of some Canaanite towns between 1250 and 1200 B.C.E., though they do not always match those in the Bible. When lowland sites were resettled and new ones established in the hill country a short time later, rainwater cisterns carved into nonporous rock and hillside terraces expanded the cultivable area. The material goods of the new settlers continued Canaanite designs but exhibit cruder craftsmanship.

Most scholars doubt the conquest of Canaan by a unified Israelite army. They attribute the decline of cities to disruption throughout the region and see the Israelite migrants, along with other loosely organized groups and refugees from the Canaanite cities, as taking advantage of a time of troubles.

As in other historical situations, this mix of peoples invented a common ancestry, calling themselves the "Children of Israel." Twelve "tribes," supposedly descended from the sons of Jacob and Joseph, installed themselves in different parts of the country, each tribe led by one or more chiefs. Such leaders usually had limited power. Mostly they mediated disputes and saw to the welfare and protection of the group. Certain personalities, famed for daring in war or genius in arbitration, were called "Judges" and, like the Celtic Druids, enjoyed a special standing that transcended tribal boundaries. The tribes also shared access to a shrine in the hill country at Shiloh. It housed the Ark of the Covenant, a sacred chest containing the tablets Yahweh had given to Moses.

Rise of the Monarchy

The time of troubles that struck the eastern Mediterranean around 1200 B.C.E. (see Chapter 2) also brought the Philistines to Israel. Possibly related to the pre-Greek population of the Aegean Sea region or to the "Sea Peoples" who attacked Egypt, the Philistines occupied the coastal plain and fought many battles with the Israelites. The biblical tales of the long-haired strongman Samson, who toppled a Philistine temple, and the youth David, whose slingshot felled the towering warrior Goliath, memorialized this conflict.

A religious leader named Samuel recognized the need for a stronger central authority and anointed Saul as Israel's first king around 1020 B.C.E. Saul had mixed success. When he perished in battle, the throne passed to David (r. ca. 1000–960 B.C.E.).

Gifted as a musician, warrior, and leader, David completed the transition from tribal confederacy to unified monarchy and strengthened royal authority by turning the captured hill city of Jerusalem, which lay outside tribal boundaries, into his capital. Soon after, the Ark was transferred to Jerusalem, making it a religious as well as political center. To calm blood feuds, David designated "cities of refuge"—places to which those guilty of certain crimes could flee. He ordered a census to improve tax collection and established a standing army, whose soldiers were paid by and loyal to the king. These innovations enabled David to win battles and expand Israel's borders.

David's son Solomon (r. ca. 960–920 B.C.E.) ruled at the peak of Israelite grandeur. Solomon's political and commercial alliances included joining with Hiram, the king of Tyre in Phoenicia, to commission a maritime expedition into the Red Sea that brought gold, ivory, jewels, sandalwood, and exotic animals from distant Ophir, and receiving a visit from the queen of Sheba, who brought gold, precious stones, and spices. The latter legend probably reflects real trade relations with Saba (biblical Sheba) in south Arabia (present-day Yemen) or the Horn of Africa (present-day Somalia). Such wealth supported a lavish court life, sizable bureaucracy, and intimidating chariot army. Solomon also undertook ambitious building projects employing slaves and compulsory labor by citizens. The **First Temple**, built in Jerusalem, further linked religious and royal authority. The new central shrine with its impressive rituals competed effectively with non-Israelite cults.

The Temple priests became a powerful and wealthy class by sacrificing animals to Yahweh on behalf of the community in return for a percentage

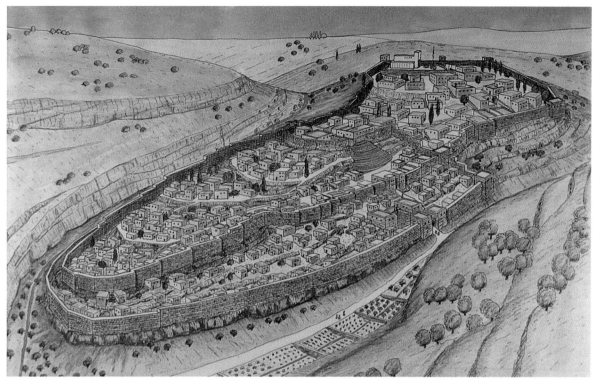

Artist's Rendering of Solomon's Jerusalem Strategically located on a high plateau amid the lands occupied by Israelite tribes, Jerusalem overlooks the central hills and the Judaean desert. King David captured the city around 1000 B.C.E. and made it his capital (the City of David is at left, the citadel and palace complex at center). His son Solomon built the First Temple for the worship of the Israelite god, Yahweh. The Neo-Babylonians destroyed Solomon's Temple (at upper right) during their sack of the city in 587 B.C.E. The modest structure built soon after to take its place was replaced by the magnificent Second Temple, erected by King Herod in the last decades of the first century B.C.E. The Romans destroyed it in 70 C.E. (Ritmeyer Archaeological Design, London)

of the annual harvest. Jerusalem's growth, expanding commerce, and the increasing prestige of the Temple hierarchy affected Israelite society. A gap between urban and rural, rich and poor, polarized a people who previously had been relatively united.

Israelite families recognized the authority of the eldest male, several generations inhabiting the "house of the father," as it was called. At marriage, usually arranged between families, the groom gave a substantial gift to the bride's father. Her entire family participated in the ceremony weighing the silver or gold. The wife brought a dowry, which often included a slave girl who attended her for life.

Male heirs being of paramount importance, firstborn sons received a double share of inheritance. With monogamy the norm, a couple with no son could adopt one, or the husband could have one with the wife's slave attendant. If a man died childless, his brother was expected to marry his widow and sire an heir.

Israelite women helped sustain the family with goods and services and thus enjoyed relative equality with their husbands in family and village life. Legally, however, they could not inherit or initiate divorce. Extramarital relations, permitted to men, incurred a death sentence. Working-class women joined in agricultural or pastoral tasks while keeping house and raising children. With urbanization, some women worked outside the home as cooks, bakers, perfumers, wet nurses (recent mothers, still producing milk, hired to provide nourishment to another person's child), prostitutes, and singers of laments at funerals. Deborah the Judge, who led troops in battle against the Canaanites, illustrates the heights women occasionally reached. Those known collectively as "wise women" appear to have composed sacred texts in poetry and prose. Unfortunately, the male bias of the Hebrew Bible and a decline in women's status with the urbanization of the monarchy period prevents a balanced assessment of women's lives.

Fragmentation and Dispersal

After Solomon died around 920 B.C.E., resentment over royal demands and neglect of tribal rights split the monarchy in two: Israel in the north, with its capital at Samaria, and Judah around Jerusalem. The two sometimes fought and sometimes allied together.

Monotheism, the absolute belief in Yahweh as the one and only god, now crystallized, but religious leaders still contended with cults professing polytheism, the belief in multiple gods. The ecstatic rituals of the Canaanite storm god Baal and the fertility goddess Astarte° attracted many Israelites. Prophets claiming revelations from Yahweh condemned foreign ritual and accused the monarchs and aristocracy of corruption, impiety, and neglect of the poor.

Israel allied with several small states of Syria to oppose the Neo-Assyrian Empire, but to no avail. In 721 B.C.E., the Assyrians destroyed the northern kingdom of Israel and deported much of its population (see Society and Culture: Mass Deportation in the Neo-Assyrian Empire), replacing them with settlers who changed the area's ethnic, cultural, and religious character and thus removed it from the mainstream of Jewish history. The kingdom of Judah survived another century, sometimes rebelling, sometimes paying tribute to the Assyrians

or the Neo-Babylonian kingdom (626–539 B.C.E.) that succeeded them. When the Neo-Babylonian monarch Nebuchadnezzar° captured Jerusalem in 587 B.C.E., he destroyed the Temple and deported to Babylon the royal family, the aristocracy, and many skilled workers such as blacksmiths and scribes.

The deportees prospered so well in their new home "by the waters of Babylon" that half a century later, most of their descendants refused the offer of the Persian monarch Cyrus (see Chapter 4) to return to their homeland. Thus originated the Jewish **Diaspora**—Greek for "dispersal" or "scattering"—which continues to this day. To maintain their religion and culture outside the homeland, the Diaspora communities developed institutions like the synagogue (Greek for "bringing together"), a communal meeting place that came to serve religious, educational, and social functions.

Several groups of Babylonian *Jews*—as we call these people who survived Israel's period of independence—eventually returned to Judah, but met a cold reception from the local population. Persevering, they rebuilt the Temple in modest form and drafted the Deuteronomic° Code (*deuteronomic* is Greek for "second code of laws")—new laws and rules of conduct. The fifth century B.C.E. also saw the compilation of much of the Hebrew Bible in roughly its present form.

Their identity sharpened by loss of independence and the hardship of exile, the Jews confirmed their unyielding monotheism and lived by a rigid set of rules. Dietary restrictions forbade consumption of pork and shellfish and the eating of meat and dairy products in the same meal. Women had to take ritual baths to remove the impurity of menstruation. Venerating the Sabbath on the example of Yahweh, whom the Bible says rested after creating the world in six days (this is the origin of the concept of the weekend), meant refraining from work and combat. These strictures and others, like a ban on marrying non-Jews, tended to isolate the Jews socially, but they also fostered a powerful sense of community and a belief in divine protection.

Astarte (uh-STAHR-tee)

Nebuchadnezzar (NAB-oo-kuhd-nez-uhr)
Deuteronomic (doo-tuhr-uh-NAHM-ik)

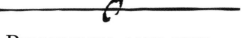

PHOENICIA AND THE MEDITERRANEAN

The ancient inhabitants of present-day Syria, Lebanon, and Israel (sometimes called the Levant or Syria-Palestine) are commonly designated **Phoenicians°**, though they referred to themselves by the ethnic designation "Can'ani"—Canaanites. Despite the sparse written record and archaeological evidence complicated by migrations and invasions, enough of their history survives to reveal major transformations.

Destruction struck many settlements in Syria-Palestine during the period of upheaval and population migration in western Asia and the eastern Mediterranean around 1200 B.C.E. (see Chapter 2). Nomadic pastoralists known as Aramaeans appeared along Syria's eastern desert fringe; farther south, the Israelites entered Canaan, and the Philistines, the first people in the region to use iron, settled the coast of present-day Israel.

The Phoenician City-States

By 1100 B.C.E. Canaanite territory had shrunk to a narrow strip of present-day Lebanon between the mountains and the sea. New political forms, manufactures, and seaborne commerce flourished in this land that the Greeks of the early first millennium B.C.E. called Phoenicia. Their word *Phoinikes°* may mean "red men" and relate to Canaanite skin color, or it may refer to the highly valued purple dye they extracted from the murex snail.

Rivers and rocky spurs sliced the Lebanese coastal plain into a series of small city-states: Aradus, Byblos°, Berytus°, Sidon, Sarepta°, and Tyre. Trade in raw materials, foodstuffs, cedar and pine products, metals, papyrus, wine, spices, salted fish, incense, textiles, carved ivory, and glass

brought wealth to these states and gave them a voice in international politics.

Using earlier Canaanite models, the Phoenicians developed the first alphabetic writing system in which each of the two dozen or so symbols stood for a consonant or vowel sound. In the more cumbersome cuneiform and hieroglyphic systems, hundreds of signs represent specific syllables or words. Ironically, few Phoenician writings survive from this period, perhaps because the scribes used perishable papyrus. Some reports in Greek and Roman sources, however, seem to be of Phoenician origin.

In the second millennium B.C.E., Byblos stood out as a distribution center for cedar from the slopes of Mount Lebanon and papyrus from Egypt. Our word *bible* comes from the Greek word *biblion*, meaning "book written on papyrus from Byblos." By the early first millennium, Tyre in the south surpassed Byblos. King Hiram took the throne in 969 B.C.E. and led Tyre's rise, providing his Israelite friend King Solomon with skilled Phoenician craftsmen and Lebanese cedar wood for building the Temple in Jerusalem. In return, Tyre gained access to silver, food, and trade routes to the east and south. In the ninth century B.C.E., Tyre took control of nearby Sidon and monopolized Mediterranean coastal trade.

Its location on an island just offshore made Tyre practically impregnable. A canal connected its two harbors, one facing north, the other south. Many of its 30,000 or more citizens lived in mainland suburbs, the island being occupied by a large marketplace, a palace complex with treasury and archives, and temples to the gods Melqart° and Astarte. That the mainland also supplied Tyre's food and freshwater was its one strategic weakness.

Aside from a list of kings and scanty evidence suggesting political domination by merchant families, as little is known about Tyre's internal affairs as about the other Phoenician cities. Assyrian aggression in the ninth through seventh centuries B.C.E., followed in the sixth century by Neo-Babylonian and later Persian expansion (see Chapter 4), tested the well-developed diplomatic skills

---

Phoenician (fi-NEE-shunn)   Phoinikes (FOY-nee-kes)
Byblos (BIB-loss)   Berytus (buh-RIE-tuhs)
Sarepta (suh-REP-tuh)

Melqart (MEL-kahrt)

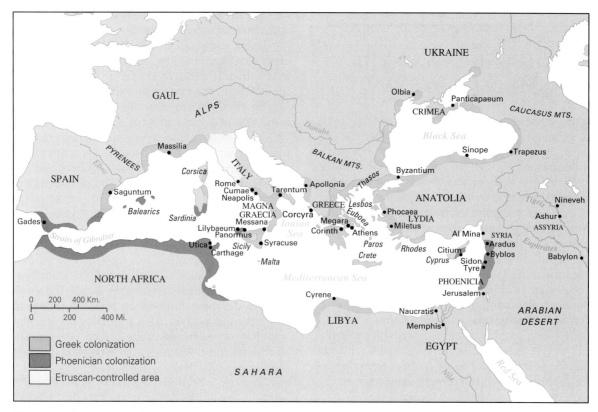

Map 3.2   Colonization of the Mediterranean   In the ninth century B.C.E., Phoenicians searching for raw materials and trading opportunities sailed from Lebanon to explore the western Mediterranean. They planted colonies on the North Africa coast, in southern and eastern Spain, and on the islands of Sicily and Sardinia.

of the Phoenician city-states. They preserved their autonomy by playing the great powers off against one another when possible and accepting a subordinate relationship to a distant master when necessary.

Expansion into the Mediterranean

In the ninth century, Tyre began to interest itself in westward expansion, establishing colonies on the copper-rich and commercially strategic island of Cyprus 100 miles (161 kilometers) from the Syrian coast (see Map 3.2). In his *Iliad* and *Odyssey*, Homer (ca. 700 B.C.E.) mentions Phoenician merchants sailing the Aegean Sea. Within a century or

so, a string of settlements in the western Mediterranean made up three legs of a "Phoenician triangle": (1) the North African coast from western Libya and Tunisia to Morocco; (2) the south and southeastern coast of Spain, including Gades (modern Cadiz) on the Strait of Gibraltar controlling passage between the Mediterranean and the Atlantic Ocean; and (3) the islands of Sardinia, Sicily, and Malta off the Italian coast. Colonies situated on promontories or offshore islands, in imitation of Tyre, provided strongpoints for a Phoenician trading network that spanned the entire Mediterranean.

While state enterprise and private initiative made Tyrian expansion possible, Assyrian invasions and lack of arable land probably made it necessary. New colonies took excess population and provided trading partners and new sources of goods. Until 701 B.C.E., Tyre maintained its autonomy by paying the Assyrians tribute, but it finally fell to an Assyrian army that stripped it of territory and population, allowing Sidon to become Phoenicia's leading city in the sixth and fifth centuries.

In the western Mediterranean, the Phoenicians clashed often with the Greeks, who were also exploring for resources while colonizing southern Italy and Sicily. Phoenicians occupied the western end of Sicily, the focal point of their rivalry, and the Greeks the eastern and central sectors. Surviving stories narrate many atrocities, massacres, enslavements, and deportations from the centuries of savage struggle for control of Sicily. The high level of brutality suggests that each side felt its survival was at stake. Although the Greek colonies did survive, the Phoenician colony of Carthage in Tunisia eventually led a Phoenician to dominance over all of Sicily by the mid-third century B.C.E.

Carthage's Commercial Empire

Historians know more about Carthage and the other Phoenician colonies in the west than they do about the Phoenician homeland. Their knowledge comes from the accounts of their enemies, but the Greek and Roman historians seem to draw on Phoenician sources for stories like that of Dido's founding of Carthage related at the beginning of this chapter.

Archaeological excavation has roughly confirmed the city's traditional foundation date of 814 B.C.E. Just outside the present-day city of Tunis, **Carthage** controlled the middle portion of the Mediterranean, where Europe comes closest to Africa, and quickly achieved dominance over other Phoenician colonies in the west.

The crowded heart of the city, on a narrow promontory jutting out into the sea, stretched between Byrsa°, the original fortified hilltop citadel, and a double harbor. The inner harbor, with naval command headquarters on an island in its center, could accommodate up to 220 warships. A watch-

tower commanded the surrounding area, and high walls screened it from outside observers. Commercial docks and shipyards lined the outer harbor. A huge iron chain closed the harbor mouth during attacks.

Government offices ringed a large central square where magistrates heard legal cases in the open air. The inner city was a maze of narrow, winding streets, multistory apartment buildings, and sacred enclosures. Farther out, the villas of the wealthy dotted the fields and vegetable gardens of the sprawling suburb of Megara. A wall 22 miles (35 kilometers) long enclosed this entire urban complex. At its most critical point—the 2½-mile-wide (4-kilometer-wide) isthmus connecting the promontory to the mainland—the wall exceeded 40 feet in height (13 meters) and 30 feet in thickness (10 meters) and had high watchtowers.

Providing food, water, and sanitation for a population of roughly 400,000—Carthage was then one of the world's largest cities—must have posed a technological challenge. Besides the descendants of Phoenician immigrants, indigenous peoples from whom today's Berbers are descended and immigrants from other Mediterranean lands and sub-Saharan Africa constituted a diverse population. Dido's legendary reluctance to marry a local chief did not prevent other Phoenicians from intermarrying locally.

Each year two "judges"—the word is related to the Hebrew word for the Israelites' early leaders—elected from upper-class families implemented state policies and sat as judges. Members of the leading merchant families, serving for life, made up the Senate, the power center that set policies and regulated state affairs. An inner circle of thirty or so senators made the most crucial decisions. When leading senators and officials disagreed or wanted to stir popular enthusiasm for some venture, they convened a popular Assembly to elect officials or vote on issues, but this seldom occurred.

The limited information available on internal Carthaginian affairs does not indicate the sorts of social and political unrest that later plagued Greece and Rome (see Chapters 4 and 5), but this is not certain. Economically successful and socially ambitious individuals seeking to push their way into the circle of politically influential citizens

Byrsa (BURR-suh)

could gain acceptance from a merchant elite more readily than from a hereditary nobility. Sharing the riches of empire with the masses may also have protected the elite from unrest.

Carthaginian power rested on its navy, which with expert navigators and citizen oarsmen dominated the western Mediterranean for centuries. Phoenician coastal towns provided a chain of friendly ports throughout the western Mediterranean. The Carthaginian fleet of fast, maneuverable galleys—oared warships—had sturdy pointed bows that could ram enemy vessels and pierce their hulls below the water line, while marines (shipboard soldiers) on deck cast projectiles at them. Innovations in the placement of benches and oars made room for 30, 50, and eventually as many as 170 rowers. Phoenician and Greek technological advances set a common standard for Mediterranean warships.

Carthaginian foreign policy concentrated on protecting sea-lanes, acquiring raw materials, and fostering trade. Foreign merchants could sail to Carthage on business, but if they tried to trade independently in the western Mediterranean, they risked their ships being sunk. Treaties with other states formally recognized this maritime commercial monopoly.

Few Carthaginian commodities show up in archaeological excavations. Some goods, like foodstuffs, animal skins, and slaves, might have left no trace; and raw metals like silver, lead, iron, and tin might not be identifiable as Carthaginian; but it would seem that the manufactured goods that Carthaginian merchants traded were crafted elsewhere, brought to Carthage, and reexported at a profit.

Carthage may also have been in contact with Africans south of the Sahara desert. A Carthaginian captain named Hanno boasted of sailing through the Strait of Gibraltar and down Africa's Atlantic coast in the fifth century B.C.E. (see Map 3.2). His reports of small coastal settlements and interior explorations include fanciful-sounding descriptions of ferocious savages, drums in the night, and rivers of fire. Since Hanno's topographic descriptions and distances do not correspond to the actual geography of West Africa, some scholars dismiss his report as fiction. Others believe he misstated distances and exaggerated dangers to deter other explorers from retracing his route and gaining a trade advantage. Other Carthaginians who passed through the Strait of Gibraltar explored the Atlantic coast of Spain and France and developed trade with the "Tin Islands" (probably Cornwall in southwest Britain). As a component of bronze, tin remained a valuable commodity during the Iron Age.

War and Religion

Carthage did not rule a large amount of territory directly. A belt of fertile land in northeastern Tunisia, owned by Carthaginians but worked by native peasants and imported slaves, provided a secure food supply. Unlike the Assyrians, the Carthaginians ruled most of their "empire" indirectly and allowed other Phoenician communities in the western Mediterranean to remain independent. These communities nevertheless looked to Carthage for military protection and followed its lead in foreign policy. Carthaginian governors and garrisons maintained direct control in Sardinia and southern Spain, presumably to guarantee their agricultural, metal, and manpower resources.

As citizens of a merchant state, Carthaginians were not required to serve in the military. Carthage had few potential enemies close to home since the indigenous North African population lacked political and military sophistication. Operations overseas during a series of fierce and destructive wars with Greeks and Romans from the fifth through third centuries B.C.E. prompted the employment of mercenaries—Numidians from North Africa, Iberians from Spain, Gauls from France, and various peoples from Italy. Professional Carthaginian officers commanded these well-paid soldiers.

In keeping with the secondary role that warfare played, the civilian leaders controlled the military command. The Senate hired generals and determined their term of service. This encouraged professionalism within a class of officers who studied war and gained skills through their periods of command. Unlike the kings of Assyria and other states of the ancient Middle East, Carthaginian officials seldom led military campaigns.

Carthaginian religion, a subject of fascination for Greek and Roman writers, featured powerful and capricious entities—principally Baal Hammon, a

The Tophet of Carthage   The cremated remains of sacrificed children, buried here between the seventh and second centuries B.C.E., confirm ancient assertions that the Carthaginians sacrificed children to their gods at times of crisis. One or more infants and occasionally older children lie beneath these stone markers bearing magical signs, symbols of divinities, and family names. (Martha Cooper/Peter Arnold, Inc.)

male storm god, and Tanit°, a female fertility figure—reminiscent of those of Mesopotamia (see Chapter 1). During crises, the Carthaginian elite sacrificed their own male children to appease these gods. Excavations at Carthage and other Phoenician towns in the west have turned up **tophets**°—walled enclosures where thousands of small, sealed urns containing the burned bones of children lay buried. Although some scholars regard these as resting places of infants born prematurely or taken by childhood illnesses, most see them as evidence of child sacrifice on a more or less regular basis.

Presumably the Carthaginians sacrificed their children to win the favor of the gods on the eve of decisive battles and at other crucial times. This elite practice seems to have become more common and to have involved broader elements of the population in the fourth and third centuries, however.

Plutarch, a Greek who lived around 100 C.E., long after the demise of Carthage, wrote the following on the basis of earlier sources:

> The Carthaginians are a hard and gloomy people, submissive to their rulers and harsh to their subjects, running to extremes of cowardice in times of fear and of cruelty in times of anger; they keep obstinately to their decisions, are austere, and care little for amusement or the graces of life.[1]

We should not take Greek and Roman opinions on this subject at face value. Such reports do illustrate, however, the cultural barriers separating the Carthaginians from their foes and contributing to the misunderstandings and prejudice that beset encounters between these ancient Mediterranean

---

Tanit (TAH-nit)   tophet (TOE-fet)

peoples. In Chapter 5, we follow the protracted and bloody struggle between Rome and Carthage for control of the western Mediterranean.

FAILURE AND TRANSFORMATION

The extension of Assyrian power over the entire Middle East caused the stories of Mesopotamia, Israel, and Phoenicia to converge. Assyrian invasion destroyed the northern kingdom of Israel and put relentless pressure on the southern kingdom of Judah. Assyrian threats and demands for tribute spurred the Phoenicians to colonize and exploit the western Mediterranean. Tyre's fall in 701 B.C.E. accelerated the decline of the Phoenician homeland, allowing the western colonies, especially Carthage, to flourish.

Even Egypt, previously impregnable behind its desert barriers, fell to Assyrian invasion in the mid-seventh century B.C.E. Thebes, its ancient capital, never recovered. With the birthplace of Mesopotamian civilization in the southern plains of Sumer and Akkad reduced to a protectorate, venerable Babylon endured alternate destruction and rebuilding at Assyrian hands. Close to home, the Assyrians destroyed their rivals Urartu and Elam.

By the mid-seventh century B.C.E., Assyria stood unchallenged in western Asia. But the arms race with Urartu, the frequent expensive campaigns, and the protection of lengthy borders had sapped Assyrian resources. Brutality and exploitation had aroused the hatred of conquered peoples. In addition, population changes in the homeland and in the ethnic composition of the army had reduced popular commitment to the Assyrian state.

A resurgent Babylonia under the Neo-Babylonian, or Chaldaean, dynasty (the Chaldaeans had infiltrated southern Mesopotamia around 1000 B.C.E.) and the kingdom of the Medes, an Iranian people who by the seventh century B.C.E. were extending their control eastward across the Iranian Plateau, spearheaded resistance to Assyria. In a series of at-

tacks on the Assyrian homeland, they succeeded in destroying the chief Assyrian cities by 612 B.C.E. Assyria's stunningly rapid fall resulted in the depopulation of northern Mesopotamia. Two centuries later, when a corps of Greek mercenaries passed by mounds that concealed the ruins of the Assyrian capitals, the Athenian chronicler Xenophon° had no idea their empire had ever existed.

The Medes took over in the north, but the **Neo-Babylonian kingdom** (626–539 B.C.E.) benefited most. Kings Nabopolassar° (r. 625–605 B.C.E.) and Nebuchadnezzar (r. 604–562 B.C.E.) took over much of the old empire. Enlarged and adorned, the city of Babylon became the greatest metropolis in the world. Old cults revived with new temples and festivals, and the related pursuits of mathematics, astronomy, and astrology reached new heights.

CONCLUSION

This chapter depicts the first millennium B.C.E. traces on five continents. In the Eastern Hemisphere, Assyria, Israel, and Phoenicia continue, but also differ significantly from, the cultural patterns of Mesopotamia and Egypt. Far from the ancient river valley centers, the Celts build a society in response to the terrain, resources, and climate of temperate Europe. Mediterranean trade links the two regions and provides a mechanism for limited cultural exchange. Still farther away, the Olmec and Chavín civilizations develop, respectively, in Mexico and the Andes without contact with the Eastern Hemisphere.

Why did similar political, technological, and cultural developments occur later in the Western than in the Eastern Hemisphere? Recent scholarship highlights environmental differences.

The Eastern Hemisphere seems to have possessed more wild plant and animal species suitable for domestication. In addition, the east-west axis

---

Xenophon (ZEN-uh-fuhn)
Nabopolassar (NAB-oh-poe-lass-uhr)

of the Eurasian landmass favored the spread of domestication of plants and animals along climatically similar latitudes. Population growth accompanied agriculture, leading to complex political and social institutions, division of economic tasks, and improved technologies.

In contrast, the north-south axis of North and South America, and the scarceness of species that could be domesticated slowed the spread of agriculture and the development of complex societies. The Western Hemisphere's physical barriers—mountains, deserts, and dense forests—slowed development still further, impeding the interregional exchange of technologies like metallurgy.

This comparison suggests that sequences of technological development differed from the Western Hemisphere to the Eastern Hemisphere. Without large draft animals, wheeled vehicles, or metal implements, the Olmec and Chavín peoples nevertheless created sophisticated political, social, and economic institutions rivaling those in the Eastern Hemisphere in the third and second millennia B.C.E.

Population movement, another thread running through this chapter, sparked profound changes in Europe, North Africa, and western Asia. The Assyrians exemplify forced relocation, deporting large numbers of captives from conquered territories to their northern Mesopotamian homeland. Phoenician colonization of North Africa, Spain, and several Mediterranean islands exemplifies a different pattern: citizens leaving overpopulated homelands to found new settlements and transplant their cultures. The Israelites who settled in Canaan and the Celts who spread across Europe experienced political, social, and cultural transformations as they settled in new regions.

Diasporas proved fertile sources of innovation and means of cultural preservation. Although Carthage fell to Rome, the Jews and Celts survive into our own time. Ironically, the Assyrians, the most powerful society of all, suffered total eclipse. Sticking by choice to their homeland, their culture died when their state was toppled in the late seventh century B.C.E. The Neo-Babylonian kingdom built on the ashes of the Neo-Assyrian Empire would bring to an end the cultural legacy of early Mesopotamia.

■ Key Terms

Iron Age	Israel
Olmec	Hebrew Bible
Chavín	First Temple
llama	monotheism
Celts	Diaspora
Druids	Phoenicians
Neo-Assyrian Empire	Carthage
Ashur	tophet
mass deportation	Neo-Babylonian kingdom
Library of Ashurbanipal	

■ Suggested Reading

Jared Diamond, *Guns, Germs, and Steel: The Fates of Human Societies* (1997), asks why technological development took different paths in the Eastern and Western Hemispheres.

In *Prehistory of the Americas* (1987), Stuart Fiedel introduces the early history of the Western Hemisphere. *Early Man in the New World*, ed. Richard Shutler, Jr. (1983), is also useful. *Atlas of Ancient America* (1986), by Michael Coe, Elizabeth P. Benson, and Dean R. Snow, offers maps and information. George Kubler, *The Art and Architecture of Ancient America: The Mexican, Maya, and Andean Peoples* (1984), is a dated but essential tool.

Jacques Soustelle, *The Olmecs: The Oldest Civilization in Mexico* (1984), and, more reliably, Michael Coe, *The Olmec World* (1996), cover early Central America. Richard W. Keatinge, ed., *Peruvian Prehistory* (1988), introduces Andean scholarship. Richard L. Burger, *Chavín and the Origins of Andean Civilization* (1992), is recent and useful.

Simon James, *The World of the Celts* (1993), provides a good concise introduction. Also useful are Peter Ellis, *The Celtic Empire: The First Millennium of Celtic History, c. 1000 B.C.–51 A.D.* (1990); T. G. E. Powell, *The Celts* (1980); and Barry Cunliffe, *The Celtic World* (1979). Miranda J. Green, *The Celtic World* (1995), contains many articles on aspects of Celtic civilization. On Celtic religion and mythology, see James MacKillop, *Dictionary of Celtic Mythology* (1998); Proinsias Mac Cana, *Celtic Mythology* (1983); and Miranda Green, *The Gods of the Celts* (1986) and *Celtic Myths* (1993). Peter Ellis, *Celtic Women: Women in Celtic Society and Literature* (1996), collects and evaluates the evidence. For art, see Ruth and Vincent

Megaw, *Celtic Art: From Its Beginnings to the Book of Kells* (1989), and I. M. Stead, *Celtic Art* (1985). Patrick K. Ford, *The Mabinogi and Other Medieval Welsh Tales* (1977), and Jeffrey Gantz, *Early Irish Myths and Sagas* (1981), present translations and brief discussions.

Jack M. Sasson, ed., *Civilizations of the Ancient Near East*, 4 vols. (1995), is essential, containing nearly two hundred expert articles and bibliographies covering the entire ancient period. Barbara Lesko, ed., *Women's Earliest Records: From Ancient Egypt and Western Asia* (1989), is a collection of papers. John Boardman, I. E. S. Edwards, N. G. L. Hammond, and E. Sollberger, *The Cambridge Ancient History*, 2d ed., vols. 3.1–3.3 (1982–1991), provides extremely detailed coverage of the entire Mediterranean and western Asia.

For general history and cultural information about the Neo-Assyrian Empire and its historical context, see Michael Roaf, *Cultural Atlas of Mesopotamia and the Ancient Near East* (1990); Amelie Kuhrt, *The Ancient Near East, c. 3000–300 B.C.* (1995); H. W. F. Saggs, *Civilization Before Greece and Rome* (1989); and A. Bernard Knapp, *The History and Culture of Ancient Western Asia and Egypt* (1988). H. W. F. Saggs, *Babylonians* (1995), details the fate of the old southern Mesopotamia centers under northern domination. For translated primary texts dealing with Assyria and other parts of western Asia, see James B. Pritchard, ed., *Ancient Near Eastern Texts Relating to the Old Testament*, 3d ed. (1969).

Jeremy Black and Anthony Green, *Gods, Demons and Symbols of Ancient Mesopotamia: An Illustrated Dictionary* (1992), is valuable for religious concepts, institutions, and mythology. Julian Reade, *Assyrian Sculpture* (1983), succinctly introduces the relief sculptures from the Assyrian palaces. J. E. Curtis and J. E. Reade, eds., *Art and Empire: Treasures from Assyria in the British Museum* (1995), and Andre Parrot, *The Arts of Assyria* (1961), cover all artistic media.

Michael Grant, *The History of Israel* (1984); J. Maxwell Miller and John H. Hayes, *A History of Ancient Israel and Judah* (1986); and J. Alberto Soggin, *A History of Israel: From the Beginnings to the Bar Kochba Revolt*, A.D. 135 (1984), provide general accounts of ancient Israel. Ammon Ben-Tor, *The Archaeology of Ancient Israel* (1991), and Amihai Mazar, *Archaeology of the Land of the Bible, 10,000–586 B.C.E.* (1990), and Hershel Shanks, *Jerusalem,*

an Archaeological Biography (1995), review archaeological discoveries in Israel. For social and economic issues, see Shunya Bendor, *The Social Structure of Ancient Israel: The Institution of the Family (beit 'ab) from the Settlement to the End of the Monarchy* (1996), and Moses Aberbach, *Labor, Crafts and Commerce in Ancient Israel* (1994). Carol Meyers, *Discovering Eve: Ancient Israelite Women in Context* (1998), sifts literary and archaeological evidence for a balanced assessment of the position of women before the monarchy. For the Philistines, see Trude Dothan, *The Philistines and Their Material Culture* (1982).

Donald Harden, *The Phoenicians* (1962), and Gerhard Herm, *The Phoenicians: The Purple Empire of the Ancient World* (1975), introduce the Phoenicians and their homeland. Maria Eugenia Aubet, *The Phoenicians and the West: Politics, Colonies and Trade* (1993), explores the dynamics of Phoenician expansion. Lionel Casson, *The Ancient Mariners: Seafarers and Sea Fighters of the Mediterranean in Ancient Times*, 2d ed. (1991), discusses the design of warships and merchant vessels. For Carthage, see Serge Lancel, *Carthage: A History* (1995), and David Soren, Aicha Ben Abed Ben Khader, and Hedi Slim, *Carthage: Uncovering the Mysteries and Splendors of Ancient Tunisia* (1990). Aicha Ben Abed Ben Khader and David Soren, *Carthage: A Mosaic of Ancient Tunisia* (1987), includes articles by American and Tunisian scholars along with an exhibition catalogue. R. C. C. Law, "North Africa in the Period of Phoenician and Greek Colonization, c. 800 to 323 B.C.," Chapter 2 in *The Cambridge History of Africa*, vol. 2 (1978), places Carthage in an African perspective.

Elizabeth Wayland Barber, *Women's Work: The First 20,000 Years: Women, Cloth, and Society in Early Times* (1994), details textile manufacture in antiquity, with emphasis on the role of women. I. Irving Ziderman, "Seashells and Ancient Purple Dyeing," *Biblical Archaeologist* 53 (June 1990): 98–101, summarizes Phoenician purple-dyeing technology.

■ Note

1. Plutarch, *Moralia*, 799 D, trans. B. H. Warmington *Carthage* (Harmondsworth, England: Penguin 1960), 163.

4

GREECE AND IRAN,

1000–30 B.C.E.

INDIA,

1500 B.C.E.–550 C.E.

Ancient Iran • The Rise of the Greeks • The Struggle of Persia and Greece • The Hellenistic Synthesis • Foundations of Indian Civilization • Imperial Expansion and Collapse
THE ENVIRONMENT AND TECHNOLOGY: Indian Mathematics

he Greek historian Herodotus° (ca. 485–425 B.C.E.) relates that the Persian king Darius° I, whose empire stretched from eastern Europe to northwest India, questioned some Greek and Indian sages. Under what circumstances, he asked the Greeks, would they eat their deceased fathers' bodies? The Greeks, who practiced cremation, recoiled in revulsion. Darius then asked the Indians whether they would ever burn the bodies of their dead parents. This similarly repelled them because they practiced ritual eating of the bodies of the dead. Herodotus argues from this that every people has practices they regard as "natural" and superior. But it also illustrates the difficulty of relying on ancient sources that are sometimes accurate, as Herodotus is about Greek funerary

customs, and sometimes wildly inaccurate, as are his views on Indian rituals.

Peoples and cultural systems that previously had little direct contact confronted each other within the Persian Empire, in that empire's struggle with the Greeks and eventual fall to Alexander the Great, and under the Hellenistic Greek rulers who succeeded Alexander from Greece to the frontiers of India. This cross-cultural interaction both alarmed and stimulated the peoples involved, in some instances giving rise to new cultural syntheses.

This chapter first recounts the experiences of the Persians and Greeks in the first millennium B.C.E. and then describes the related but strikingly different culture of India. Historians traditionally consider the rivalry of Greeks and Persians the first act of an age-long drama: the

Herodotus (heh-ROD-uh-tuhs)   Darius (duh-RIE-us)

clash of East and West, of fundamentally different ways of life destined to collide. Some regard America's confrontation with hostile states and terrorist organizations in the Islamic world as a contemporary manifestation of this conflict.

Ironically, Greeks and Persians, and many Indian peoples as well, had more in common than they realized. They spoke related languages belonging to the Indo-European family, and they inherited fundamental cultural traits, forms of social organization, and religious outlooks from their shared past.

As you read this chapter, ask yourself the following questions:

- How did geography, environment, and contacts with other peoples shape the institutions and values of Persians, Greeks, and Indians?

- What brought the Greek city-states and the Persian Empire into conflict, and what determined the outcome of their rivalry?

- How did domination by the Persian Empire and the Greek kingdoms that succeeded it influence—culturally, economically, and politically—the lands and peoples of the eastern Mediterranean and western and southern Asia?

- How did religious traditions with distinctive conceptions of space, time, divinity, and the life cycle shape South Asian culture?

ANCIENT IRAN

Iran, the "land of the Aryans," links western Asia and southern and Central Asia. In the sixth century B.C.E., the Persians of southwest Iran created the largest empire the world had yet seen. Heirs to the legacy of Mesopotamia, they introduced distinctly Iranian elements and developed new forms of political and economic organization.

Scant written evidence from within the Per-

sian Empire forces us to rely on works by Greeks—ignorant outsiders at best, usually hostile, and interested primarily in events affecting them. This leaves us largely uninformed about developments in the central and eastern portions of the Persian Empire, though archaeology and close analysis of the few writings from within the empire can supplement and help correct the Greek perspective.

Geography and Resources

The Zagros Mountains bound Iran on the west, the Caucasus° Mountains and Caspian Sea on the northwest and north, the mountains of Afghanistan (ancient Arachosia) and the desert of Baluchistan° (ancient Gedrosia) on the east and southeast, and the Persian Gulf to the southwest. The northeast lies open to attacks or population movements from Central Asia.

Winter rain and snow on the high mountains encircling the country feed streams that flow away from the central plateau into rivers that drain into seas or terminate in interior salt lakes and marshes. Exploiting limited water resources holds the key to survival on the arid interior plateau. Lacking a great river like the Nile, Indus, or Tigris-Euphrates, ancient Iran had a sparse population, most numerous in the moister north and west and decreasing toward the arid south and east. The Great Salt Desert, covering much of eastern Iran and Baluchistan, does not support life. Mountain barriers separated scattered settlements on the narrow plains along the Persian Gulf from the interior plateau.

In the first millennium B.C.E., irrigation made possible an expansion of agriculture from the mountain valleys to the bordering plains. Irrigation specialists laid out underground irrigation channels that prevented evaporation and used gravity to deliver water to the fields. Constructing these channels and the vertical shafts that gave access to them demanded labor cooperation. Local leaders probably supervised the network in each district and expanded it when strong central authorities made possible large-scale labor organization. Royal authority and prosperity went hand in hand. Even so, human survival depended on a

---

Caucasus (KAW-kuh-suhs)   **Baluchistan** (buh-loo-chi-STAN)

CHRONOLOGY

	Greece and the Hellenistic World	Persian Empire	India
1500 B.C.E.			**ca. 1500 B.C.E.** Migration of Indo-European peoples into northwest India
	1150–800 B.C.E. Greece's "Dark Age"		
1000 B.C.E.		**ca. 1000 B.C.E.** Persians settle in southwest Iran	**ca. 1000 B.C.E.** Indo-European groups move into the Ganges Plain
800 B.C.E.	**ca. 800 B.C.E.** Resumption of Greek contact with eastern Mediterranean **800–480 B.C.E.** Greece's Archaic Period **ca. 750–550 B.C.E.** Era of colonization **ca. 700 B.C.E.** Beginning of hoplite warfare **ca. 650–500 B.C.E.** Era of tyrants		
600 B.C.E.	**594 B.C.E.** Solon reforms laws at Athens **546–510 B.C.E.** Pisistratus and sons hold tyranny at Athens	**550–530 B.C.E.** Reign of Cyrus **522–486 B.C.E.** Reign of Darius **530–522 B.C.E.** Reign of Cambyses; conquest of Egypt	
500 B.C.E.	**490 B.C.E.** Athenians check Persians at Marathon **477 B.C.E.** Athens becomes leader of Delian League **461–429 B.C.E.** Pericles dominant at Athens; Athenian democracy **431–404 B.C.E.** Peloponnesian War	**480–479 B.C.E.** Xerxes' invasion of Greece	**ca. 500 B.C.E.** Siddhartha Gautama founds Buddhism; Mahavira founds Jainism
400 B.C.E.	**399 B.C.E.** Trial and execution of Socrates **338 B.C.E.** Philip II of Macedon takes control of Greece	**387 B.C.E.** King's Peace makes Persia arbiter of Greek affairs **334–323 B.C.E.** Alexander the Great defeats Persia and creates empire	

CHRONOLOGY *(continued)*

	Greece and the Hellenistic World	Persian Empire	India
300 B.C.E.	**317 B.C.E.** End of democracy in Athens **ca. 300 B.C.E.** Foundation of the Museum and start of lighthouse construction **200 B.C.E.** First Roman intervention in the Hellenistic East	**323–30 B.C.E.** Hellenistic period	**324 B.C.E.** Chandra Gupta founds Mauryan Empire
100 B.C.E.			**184 B.C.E.** Fall of Mauryan Empire
1 C.E.	**30 B.C.E.** Roman annexation of Egypt, the last Hellenistic kingdom		
500 C.E.			**320 C.E.** Chandra Gupta establishes Gupta Empire **550 C.E.** Collapse of Gupta Empire **606–647 C.E.** Reign of Harsha Vardhana

delicate ecological balance. A buildup of salt in the soil, a falling water table, or the collapse or silting up of an underground channel sometimes forced the abandonment of settlements.

The mountains yielded copper, tin, iron, gold, and silver, all exploited on a limited scale in antiquity, as well as wood for fuel, construction, and crafts, the hillsides being more heavily wooded then than now. With little agricultural surplus, export goods consisted largely of minerals and crafted goods such as textiles and metalwork.

The Rise of the Persian Empire

In discussions of ancient history, the term *Iranian* describes a group of peoples speaking related languages and sharing certain cultural characteristics. They lived in a broad area of western and Central Asia comprising not only the modern state of Iran but also Turkmenistan, Uzbekistan, Afghanistan, and Pakistan. One group, the Medes (Mada

in Iranian),* instituted a complex political order in northwestern Iran in the late second millennium B.C.E., influenced in part by the ancient centers in Mesopotamia and Urartu (modern Armenia and northeast Turkey). The Medes played a major role in destroying the Assyrian Empire in the late seventh century B.C.E. and extended their control westward across Assyria into Anatolia (modern Turkey). They also projected power southeastward toward the Persian Gulf, a region settled by another Iranian people, the Persians (Parsa).

The Persian rulers, called Achaemenids° because of an ancestor named Achaemenes, cemented relations with the Median court through marriage. **Cyrus** (Kurush), the son of a Persian chieftain and a Median princess, united the Persian tribes and overthrew the Median monarch around 550 B.C.E. The differences between these

---
*Familiar Greek names of Iranian groups and individuals are followed by the original Iranian names in parentheses.
Achaemenid (a-KEY-muh-nid)

two peoples being slight—notably in dialect and costume—Cyrus placed both Medes and Persians in positions of responsibility and retained the framework of Median rule. The Greeks could not readily tell the two apart.

Patriarchal family organization among the Medes and Persians, like that among most other Indo-European peoples, gave the male head of the household authority over family members. The warrior class dominated the other two social and occupational classes, the priests and peasants. Noble warriors, the king the most illustrious among them, owned land and took pleasure in hunting, fighting, and gardening. The priests, or Magi (*magush*), supervised sacrifices and other rituals. Village-based farmers and shepherds made up the third class.

Over the course of two decades, Cyrus (r. 550–530 B.C.E.) redrew the map of western Asia. In 546 B.C.E., he won a cavalry battle outside Sardis, the capital of Lydia in western Anatolia, reportedly because the smell of his camels caused a panic among his opponents' horses. All Anatolia, including the Greek city-states on the western coast, came under Persian control. In 539 B.C.E., he swept into Mesopotamia, where the Neo-Babylonian dynasty had ruled since the collapse of Assyrian power (see Chapter 3). Cyrus allied with disaffected elements within Babylon, who surrendered the city to him. A skillful propagandist, Cyrus respected the Babylonian priesthood and had his son crowned king in accordance with local tradition.

Cyrus died in 530 B.C.E. while campaigning against nomadic Iranians in the northeast. His son Cambyses° (Kambujiya, r. 530–522 B.C.E.) set his sights on Egypt. Defeating the Egyptians in a series of bloody battles, the Persians sent exploratory expeditions south to Nubia and west to Libya. Greek sources depict Cambyses as a cruel and impious madman, but contemporary Egyptian documents reflect a practical outlook. Like his father, he cultivated local priests and notables and respected their traditions.

When Cambyses died in 522 B.C.E., **Darius I** (Darayavaush) seized the throne, crushing chal-

lengers with skill, energy, and ruthlessness. The Medes now played lesser roles; most important posts went to leading Persian nobles. Darius (r. 522–486 B.C.E.) extended Persian control eastward to the Indus Valley and westward into Europe, bridging the Danube River and chasing the nomadic Scythians° north of the Black Sea. He erected a string of forts in Thrace (modern-day northeast Greece and Bulgaria). In maritime matters, Darius dispatched a fleet to explore the route from the Indus Delta to the Red Sea and completed a canal linking the Red Sea with the Nile.

Imperial Organization and Ideology

The empire of Darius I, the largest the world had yet seen, stretched from eastern Europe to Pakistan, from southern Russia to Sudan. It encompassed myriad ethnic groups and every form of social and political organization, from nomads to subordinate kingdoms to city-states. Darius created an organizational structure that survived the remaining two centuries of the empire's existence.

He placed each of the empire's twenty provinces under a Persian **satrap°**, or governor, usually a relative or connection by marriage. The satrap's court mirrored the royal court on a smaller scale. Governorships frequently became hereditary, so that satraps' families lived in the province governed by their head, acquired knowledge about local conditions, and formed connections with the local elite. The farther a province was from the empire's center, the more autonomy the satrap had since slow communications usually made contact with the central administration difficult.

Darius prescribed how much precious metal each province owed annually to the central treasury. The satrap collected and sent it. Some went for necessary expenditures, but most was hoarded. This increasingly took precious metal out of circulation, forcing up the price of gold and silver and making it hard for provinces to meet their quotas. Evidence from Babylonia shows increasing taxes

---

Cambyses (kam-BIE-sees)

Scythian (SITH-ee-uhn)   **satrap** (SAY-trap)

and official corruption causing gradual economic decline by the fourth century B.C.E.

Royal roads, well maintained and patrolled, connected outlying provinces to the imperial center. Way stations sheltered important travelers and couriers. Garrisons controlled movements at strategic points: mountain passes, river crossings, and important urban centers. The ancient Elamite capital of Susa, in southwest Iran, served as the imperial administrative center. Greeks and others went there with requests and messages for the king. It took at least three months to make the journey to Susa. For Greek ambassadors, the time spent traveling, waiting for an audience, and returning home could take a year or more.

The king lived and traveled with numerous wives and children. Information about the royal women comes from foreign sources and is thus suspect. The Book of Esther in the Hebrew Bible tells how King Ahasuerus° (Xerxes) picked the Jewish woman Esther as a wife, putting her in a position to save the Jewish people from a plot to massacre them. Greek sources depict royal women as pawns in power struggles—Darius married a daughter of Cyrus, and later the conqueror Alexander the Great married a daughter of the last Persian king—and as intriguers, poisoning rival wives and plotting their sons' paths to the throne.

The king's entourage also included (1) sons of Persian aristocrats, who were educated at court and also served as hostages for their parents' loyalty; (2) noblemen who attended the king when not on other assignments; (3) administrative officers and employees of the treasury, secretariat, and archives; (4) the royal bodyguard; and (5) courtiers and slaves. Long gone were the simple days when the king hunted and caroused with his warrior companions. Inspired by Mesopotamian conceptions of monarchy, the Persian king became an aloof figure of majesty and splendor: "The Great King, King of Kings, King in Persia, King of countries." He referred to everyone, even the Persian nobility, as "my slaves," and anyone who approached him had to bow down before him.

The king owned vast tracts of land throughout the empire, some of which he gave to his supporters. Donations called "bow land," "horse land," and "chariot land" in Babylonian documents obliged the recipient to provide military service. The *paradayadam* (meaning "walled enclosure"—the term has come into English as *paradise*), consisting of gardens or orchards belonging to the king or high nobility, symbolized the prosperity of the king and his servants.

The Persepolis Treasury and Fortification Texts, inscribed in Elamite cuneiform on baked clay tablets, show government officials distributing food and other goods to workers of various nationalities, some of them prisoners of war working on construction projects, irrigation networks, or royal estates. Women received less than men of equivalent status, but pregnant women and new mothers received more. Skilled workers of either sex received more than the unskilled.

Tradition remembered Darius as issuing the "laws of the King," appointing royal judges throughout the empire, and encouraging the codification of the laws of subject peoples. As master of a decentralized empire, he allowed each people its own traditions and ordinances.

Scribes from Elam and Mesopotamia served the kings in the central administration. Sometimes, however, the kings returned to their homeland of Fars, to **Persepolis** (Parsa), a ceremonial capital begun by Darius and completed by his son Xerxes°. The palaces, audience halls, treasury buildings, and barracks built on an artificial platform took inspiration from Mesopotamia, where the Assyrian kings had created fortress-cities to advertise their power.

The relief sculptures on the foundations, walls, and stairwells at Persepolis feature representatives of the peoples of the empire—recognizable by distinctive hair styles, beards, dress, hats, and footwear—bringing gifts to the king. These images did not depict a real ceremony but rather advertised the vast extent, abundant resources, and cooperative spirit of the empire. One scene shows erect subjects effortlessly shouldering a giant platform bearing Darius's throne. Similar scenes from the Assyrian empire show the subjects staggering

---

Ahasuerus (uh-HAZZ-yoo-ear-uhs)

Xerxes (ZERK-sees)

View of the East Front of the Audience Hall at Persepolis, ca. 500 B.C.E.   To the right lies the Gateway of Xerxes. Built in the Persian homeland by Darius I and his son Xerxes, Persepolis was reserved for special ceremonies: coronations, royal weddings, funerals, and the New Year festival. The stone foundations, walls, and stairways bear sculpted images of members of the court and embassies bringing gifts, offering a vision of imperial grandeur and harmony.   (Courtesy of the Oriental Institute, University of Chicago)

under the weight. Persepolis probably served as a setting for New Year's festivals, coronations, marriages, and funerals. Tombs cut into the cliffs at nearby Naqsh-i Rustam° sheltered the remains of Darius and his successors.

Several dozen inscriptions cut into cliff faces provide other perspectives on the imperial ideology. At Naqsh-i Rustam, Darius claims:

> Ahuramazda° [the chief Persian deity], when he saw this earth in commotion, thereafter bestowed it upon me, made me king. . . . By the favor of Ahuramazda I put it down in its place. . . . I am of such a sort that I am a friend to right, I am not a friend to wrong. It is not my desire that the weak man should have wrong done to him by the mighty; nor is that my desire, that the

mighty man should have wrong done to him by the weak.[1]

Since the religion of **Zoroastrianism**° recognized Ahuramazda as god, it seems certain that Darius and his successors were Zoroastrians.

Questions surround the origins of Zoroastrianism. Worshippers believe that Zarathushtra (Zoroaster in Greek) wrote hymns called Gathas, the dialect and physical setting of which indicate an origin in eastern Iran. Scholarly guesses place Zarathushtra's life sometime between 1700 and 500 B.C.E. Ahuramazda, "the wise lord," created the world, according to Zarathushtra. Angra Mainyu°, "the hostile spirit," and a host of demons threaten it. In this dualist universe, the struggle between good and evil plays out over 12,000 years. At the

---

Naqsh-i Rustam (NUHK-shee ROOS-tuhm)
Ahuramazda (ah-HOOR-uh-MAZZ-duh)

Zoroastrianism (zo-ro-ASS-tree-uh-niz-uhm)
Angra Mainyu (ANG-ruh MINE-yoo)

end of time, good will prevail, and the world will return to the pure state of creation. In the meantime, humanity participates in this cosmic struggle, and individuals reap rewards or torments in the afterlife according to their actions.

The Persians also drew on pre-Zoroastrian moral and metaphysical concepts. Alive to the beauties of nature, they venerated water, which they kept pure, and fire, which burned continuously at altars. Bodily purity, a matter of intense concern, ceased with death. Zoroastrians exposed corpses to carrion-eating birds and the elements to avoid sullying the earth through burial or fire through cremation. Some earlier gods, such as Mithra, a sun deity and defender of oaths and compacts, retained divine status despite Zarathushtra's focus on one god. The Persians honored promises and telling the truth. Darius's inscriptions castigate evildoers as followers of "the Lie."

Zoroastrianism preached belief in one supreme deity, maintained high ethical standards, and promised salvation. Expanding with the advance of the Persian Empire, it may have influenced Judaism and thus, indirectly, Christianity. God and the devil, heaven and hell, reward and punishment, the Messiah and the end of time: all appear in this belief system. Yet the Islamic conquest of Iran in the seventh century C.E. (see Chapter 7) triggered the faith's decline in Iran. Only tiny communities survive there now. Larger communities, called Parsees, live in South Asia.

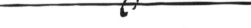

THE RISE OF THE GREEKS

The cultural features that emerged in resource-poor Greece in the first millennium B.C.E. depended on access to foreign markets and sources of raw materials. Greek merchants and mercenaries brought home not only raw materials and crafted goods but also ideas. Population pressure, poverty, war, and political crises prompted Greeks to venture throughout the Mediterranean and western Asia, carrying with them their language and culture and exerting influence on other societies. Greek identity and interest in geography,

ethnography, and history grew from experience with non-Greek practices and beliefs, as well as a two-century-long rivalry with the Persian Empire.

Geography and Resources

Bounded by the Atlantic, the Alps, the Syrian desert, and the Sahara, the lands of the Mediterranean climatic zone share seasonal weather patterns and many plants and animals. In summer, a stalled weather front near the entrance of the Mediterranean holds up storms from the Atlantic and allows winds from the Sahara to flow over the region. In winter, the front dissolves, and ocean storms roll in, bringing waves, wind, and cold. Such similarities facilitated migration within the zone since people did not have to change familiar practices and occupations.

Greek civilization arose around the Aegean Sea: the Greek mainland, the Aegean islands, and Anatolia's western coast (see Map 4.1). As we saw in Chapter 2, small plains between low mountain ranges characterize southern Greece, a land with no navigable rivers. The islands dotting the Aegean, inhabited from early times, made sailing from Greece to Ionia (western Anatolia) comparatively easy. From about 1000 B.C.E., Greeks began to settle Ionia, where rivers with broad, fertile plains made for a comfortable life. These coastal Greeks maintained closer contact with Greeks across the Aegean than with the peoples of Anatolia's rugged interior. The sea served as a connector, not a barrier.

Mainland farmers depended on rainfall to water their crops. In the south, limited land, thin topsoil, and sparse rainfall supported only small populations. Farmers planted the plains with barley, which is hardier than wheat, and the edges of the plains with olive trees. Grapevines grew on the terraced lower slopes of the foothills. Sheep and goats grazed the hillsides. Northern Greece, with more rainfall and broader plains, supported herds of cattle and horses. Resources included abundant building stone, including fine marble, but few metal deposits or forests.

The difficulty and expense of overland transport, the availability of good anchorages, and the need to import metals, timber, and grain drew the

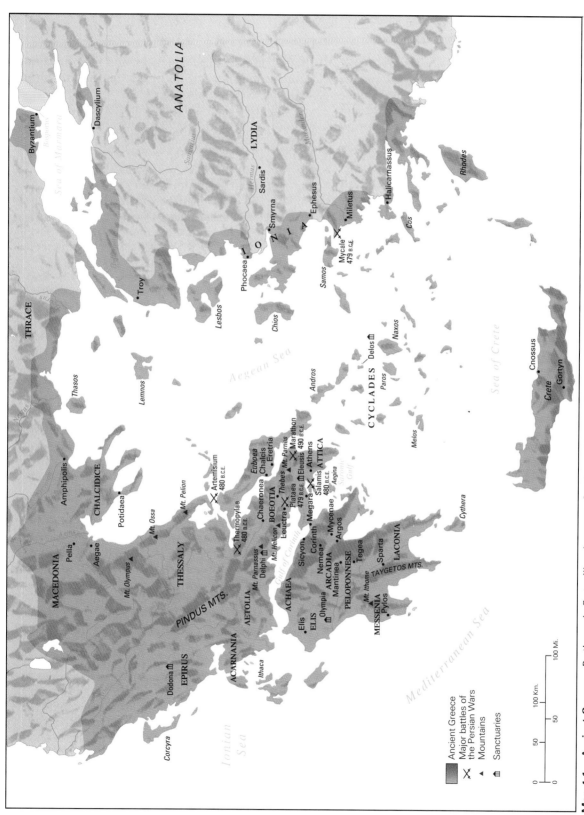

Map 4.1 Ancient Greece By the early first millennium B.C.E., Greek-speaking peoples were dispersed throughout the Aegean region, occupying the Greek mainland, most of the islands, and the western coast of Anatolia. Seafaring and trade with other lands in the Mediterranean suited a geography with many islands and a rugged mainland poorly suited to extensive agriculture.

Greeks to the sea. They obtained timber from the northern Aegean, gold and iron from Anatolia, copper from Cyprus, tin from the western Mediterranean, and grain from the Black Sea, Egypt, and Sicily. Though never comfortable with "the wine-dark sea," as Homer called it, the Greeks relied on it, their small, frail ships hugging the coastline or island hopping where possible.

The Emergence of the Polis

After the destruction of the Mycenaean palace-states (see Chapter 2), Greece lapsed into a "Dark Age" (ca. 1150–800 B.C.E.), a time of depopulation, poverty, and backwardness that has left few archaeological traces. Decline of trade and lack of access to resources lay behind the poverty of the Dark Age. Within Greece, regional distinctiveness in pottery and crafts indicates declining interconnections.

By reestablishing contact between the Aegean and the Middle East, Phoenician traders (see Chapter 3) gave Greek civilization a push that inaugurated the Archaic period of Greek history (ca. 800–480 B.C.E.). Greek ships reappeared in Mediterranean waters looking for raw materials, trade opportunities, and fertile farmland.

Lifelike human and animal figures and imaginative mythical beasts on painted Greek pottery signal new ideas from the east, as does a writing system of Phoenician inspiration. The Phoenicians used twenty-two symbols to represent consonants, leaving most vowel sounds unwritten. The Greek vowels use symbols for Phoenician consonants that do not appear in Greek, thus completing the first true alphabet. Cuneiform or hieroglyphics, systems where several hundred symbols stood for syllables rather than letters, took years of training and remained the preserve of an elite scribal class. By contrast, the alphabetic symbols made literacy easier to acquire.

Whether first used for economic purposes, as some have argued, or for preserving oral poetry, the Greek alphabet facilitated new forms of literature, law codes, religious dedications, and epitaphs. Yet Greek culture continued to center on storytelling, rituals, and performances. Theatrical drama, philosophical dialogues, and political and courtroom oratory demonstrate the dynamic interaction of speaking and writing.

Population grew rapidly during the Archaic period. Cemeteries around Athens show a five- or sevenfold increase during the eighth century B.C.E. Herding gave way to intensive farming on the previously uncultivated margins of the plains. Increasing population and prosperity stimulated the importation of food and raw materials, a merging of villages into urban centers, and specialization of labor. Freed from farming by rising surpluses, some people developed skills in crafts, commerce, and religion.

The Greek **polis°,** or city-state, ranging in size from a few thousand souls to several hundred thousand in the case of Athens, consisted of an urban center and the surrounding countryside. Typically, a fortified hilltop, the *acropolis* ("top of the city"), offered refuge in emergencies. The town spread around its base. In the open area around government buildings and markets called an *agora* ("gathering place"), citizens debated the decisions of leaders and organized for war. Walls surrounded the urban center, but population growth prompted construction beyond them. Food came from surrounding farms, though many living within the walls worked nearby fields. Unlike the dependent rural workers of Mesopotamia, Greek farmers enjoyed full citizenship.

Frequent city-state conflicts led, by the early seventh century B.C.E., to a kind of warfare based on **hoplites**—heavily armored infantrymen who fought in close formation. Protected by helmet, breastplate, and leg guards, each hoplite brandished a thrusting spear while guarding his left side and the right side of the hoplite beside him with a round shield, keeping a sword in reserve. Victory depended on maintaining one's battleline while breaking open the enemy's. The losers suffered most of their casualties while fleeing.

Private citizens, mostly farmers called up for brief periods, rather than professional soldiers served as hoplites. Special training counted less than strength for bearing weapons and armor and courage to stand one's ground. When an army ap-

polis (POE-lis)

Painted Cup of Arcesilas of Cyrene   The ruler of this Greek community in North Africa supervises the weighing and export of silphium, a valuable medicinal plant.   (Bibliothèque nationale de France)

proached, the farmers of the community under attack mustered to defend their land and buildings. The clash of hoplite lines resulted in quick decisions. Battles rarely lasted more than a few hours, with the survivors promptly returning home to their farms.

As population growth strained the agricultural resources of the small plains, many communities sent excess population abroad to establish independent colonies. Sources tell of people chosen by lot to be colonists and forbidden to return on pain of death. Volunteers, however, sought adventure or escape from poverty. Colonists sought the approval of the god Apollo at his sanctuary at Delphi and then departed by sea carrying a fire from the communal hearth of the mother city, a symbol of the kinship and religious ties that would connect the two communities. The "founder," a prominent member of the mother city, chose a hill or other

natural refuge, assigned parcels of land, and drafted laws. Sometimes colonists intermarried with local inhabitants; alternatively, they drove them away or reduced them to semi-servility.

From the mid-eighth through the mid-sixth centuries B.C.E., colonists spread Greek culture to the northern Aegean area, the Libyan coast of North Africa, and around the Black Sea, with southern Italy and Sicily becoming heavily Greek. Establishing new homes, farms, and communities posed many challenges, but the similarity in climate and ecology helped the Greek settlers transplant their way of life.

Greeks called themselves *Hellenes*° (the Romans later used *Graeci*) to distinguish themselves from *barbaroi* (literally "non-Greek speakers," whence the English word *barbarian*). Interaction

---

Hellenes (HELL-leans)

with new peoples and exposure to their cultures made the Greeks aware of their unity of language, religion, and lifestyle. It also introduced them to new ideas and technologies. Developments in the colonial world traveled back to the Greek homeland: urban planning, forms of political organization, and new intellectual currents.

Coinage, invented in the early sixth century B.C.E. in Lydia (western Anatolia), spread throughout the Greek world and beyond. Scarcity, durability, divisibility, and ease of use made silver, gold, and copper appropriate for minting into metal pieces of state-guaranteed weight and purity. (Societies in other parts of the world used items with similar qualities, including beads, hard-shelled beans, and cowrie shells.) Coinage made weighing quantities of metal obsolete and fostered quicker trading transactions, better recordkeeping, and easier wealth storage. Trade grew, as did the total wealth of communities, but different weight standards used by different states often confused exchanges of currencies.

Colonization relieved pressures within the Archaic Greek world but did not eliminate political instability. At some point, councils representing the noble families superseded the Dark Age kings depicted in Homer's *Iliad* and *Odyssey*. This aristocracy derived wealth and power from land ownership. The peasants who farmed these lands kept only a portion of their harvest. Debt slaves, people who lost their freedom when they could not repay money or seed borrowed from the lord, also worked the land. Free peasants owned small farms and joined urban-based craftsmen and merchants as part of a "middle class."

Tyrants—individuals who seized power in violation of normal political institutions—gained control of many city-states in the mid-seventh and sixth centuries B.C.E. Often disgruntled aristocrats with middle-class backing, such tyrants appealed to hoplite soldiers, whose numbers increased with growing prosperity and lower prices for weaponry. The tyrants granted these supporters political rights.

Some tyrants passed their positions on to sons, but communities eventually expelled the tyrant families and opted for oligarchy°, where a group of the wealthiest men held power, or **democracy,** where all free, adult males shared power. The absence of a professional military class made this broadening of the political system possible.

The Greeks worshipped several sky gods—Zeus who sent storms and lightning, Poseidon who controlled the sea and earthquakes—before entering the Greek peninsula at the end of the third millennium B.C.E. The *Iliad* and *Odyssey*, which schoolboys memorized and performers recited, gave personalities to these deities. Homer portrayed them as anthropomorphic°, or humanlike in appearance (though taller, more beautiful, and more powerful, with a supernatural radiance), with humanlike emotions of love, anger, and jealousy. More than anything else, immortality distinguished gods from humans.

State religious ceremonies conferred civic identity. **Sacrifice,** the central ritual, took place at altars in front of temples where the gods were thought to reside. Gifts as humble as a small cake or a cup of wine poured on the ground accompanied prayers for favor and protection. In grander sacrifices, people would kill one or more animals, spray the altar with its blood, and burn parts of its body so that the aroma would ascend to the gods.

Oracles situated at sacred sites responded to human pleas for information, advice, or prediction. At Delphi in central Greece, the most honored site, the god Apollo spoke through his priestess, the Pythia°. The male priests who administered the sanctuary interpreted her obscure utterances. Our dependence on literary texts expressing the values of an educated, urban elite limits our knowledge of fertility cults, based usually on female deities, that appealed to the agricultural majority of the population.

New Intellectual Currents

Prosperity, new technologies, and social and political development led to innovations in intellectual and artistic outlook, including a growing emphasis on the individual. In early Greek communities, the family enveloped the individual, and

---

oligarchy (OLL-ih-gahr-key)

anthropomorphic (an-thruh-puh-MORE-fik)
Pythia (PITH-ee-uh)

Vase Painting Depicting a Sacrifice to the God Apollo, ca. 440 B.C.E.   Sacrifice created a relationship between human worshipers and deities and gave hope of divine favor. The statue of Apollo, at the far right, stands on a pedestal and bears a characteristic bow and laurel branch while the sacrificer places bones wrapped in fat on an altar. The worshipers, with garlands in their hair, will feast on the meat the boy carries. (Museum für Vor-und. Frühgeschichte, Frankfurt)

land belonged collectively to the family, including ancestors and descendants. Ripped from this communal network and forced to resettle elsewhere, colonists became models of individualism, as did the tyrant who seized power for himself alone. The concept of humanism—a valuing of the uniqueness, talents, and rights of the individual—remains a central tenet of Western civilization.

In the new lyric poetry, short verses deal with personal subjects drawn from the poet's experience. Archilochus°, a soldier and poet living in the first half of the seventh century B.C.E., wrote:

> Some barbarian is waving my shield, since I was obliged to
> leave that perfectly good piece of equipment behind
> under a bush. But I got away, so what does it matter?
> Let the shield go; I can buy another one equally good.[2]

Here Archilochus pokes fun at the heroic ideal that scorned soldiers who ran from the enemy. In challenging traditional values and expressing personal feelings, lyric poets pointed toward the modern Western conception of poetry.

In religion, thinkers now known as pre-Socratic philosophers called into question Homer's representations of the gods. Xenophanes°, living in the sixth century B.C.E., protested:

Archilochus (ahr-KIL-uh-kuhs)
Xenophanes (zeh-NOFF-eh-nees)

But if cattle and horses or lions had hands, or were able to draw with their hands and do the works that men can do, horses would draw the forms of the gods like horses, and cattle like cattle, and they would make their bodies such as they each had themselves.[3]

The term *pre-Socratic* refers to philosophers before Plato, a student of Socrates, who in the later fifth century B.C.E. shifted the focus of philosophy to ethical questions. They rejected traditional explanations of the origins and nature of the world and sought more rational answers: How was the world created? What is it made of? Why does it change? Some postulated that earth, air, fire, and water, the primal elements, combine or dissolve to form the substances found in nature. One taught that microscopic atoms (from a Greek word meaning "indivisible") move through the void of space, colliding randomly and combining in various ways to form the natural world. This intuition coincidentally resembles modern atomic theory. Most pre-Socratics came from Ionia and southern Italy, where Greeks lived close to non-Greeks. Encountering peoples with different ideas may have stimulated some of their thoughts.

Also in Ionia in the sixth century B.C.E., men later referred to as logographers ("writers of prose accounts") gathered information on ethnography (the physical characteristics and cultural practices of a people), Mediterranean geography, the foundation of cities, and the origins of famous families. They called their accumulation of information *historia,* "investigation/research." **Herodotus** (ca. 485–425 B.C.E.), from Halicarnassus in southwest Anatolia, published his *Histories*. Its early parts contain geographic and ethnographic reports, legends, folktales, and marvels. Later parts focus on the Persian-Greek wars of the previous generation. He opens his work as follows:

> I, Herodotus of Halicarnassus, am here setting forth my history, that time may not draw the color from what man has brought into being, nor those great and wonderful deeds, manifested by both Greeks and barbarians, fail of their report, and, together with all this, the reason why they fought one another.[4]

His search for causes reveals the thinking of a true historian. Thus did *historia* begin to narrow and acquire the modern meaning of *history*, with Herodotus gaining the nickname Father of History.

Athens and Sparta

Athens and Sparta, the preeminent city-states of the late Archaic and Classical periods, differed in character despite environmental and cultural similarities. The Spartans' ancestors migrated into the Peloponnese°, the southernmost part of Greece, around 1000 B.C.E. Their community resembled others until the seventh century B.C.E., when the population increases and shortage of farmland that affected all communities prompted them to react differently. Instead of sending out colonies, the Spartans invaded the fertile plain of Messenia to the west (see Map 4.1). The resulting takeover, aided perhaps by hoplite tactics, saw the Messenians reduced to the status of helots°, the most abused and exploited population on the Greek mainland.

The Sparta state quickly turned into a military camp, always prepared for a helot uprising. The state divided Messenia and Laconia, the Spartan homeland, into several thousand lots, each assigned to a Spartan citizen. Helots worked the land and turned over part of their harvest to their Spartan masters. Freed from farming, the Spartans devoted their lives to military affairs.

The Spartan army outclassed all others since it did not rely on militias summoned only during crises. The Spartans paid a price, however. Taken from their families and put into barracks at age seven, boys underwent a severe regimen of discipline, beatings, and deprivation. The demands of the state consumed a Spartan male's whole life.

The economic, political, and cultural revival of the Archaic Greek world passed Sparta by: no poets or artists, no precious metals or coinage, no commerce or other activities that could introduce inequality. The fifth-century B.C.E. historian Thucydides°, a native of Athens, remarked that in his day, Sparta looked like a large village and that no future observer of the site would be able to guess its power.

Other Greeks admired Spartan courage, commitment, and martial skills but abhorred their arrogance, ignorance, and cruelty. The Spartan Council of Elders and two kings, who commanded in battle, practiced a cautious and isolationist foreign policy. Reluctant to venture far for fear of a helot uprising, they worked for peace through the Peloponnesian League, a system of alliances with their neighbors.

Athens, by comparison, possessed an unusually large and populous territory: the fertile plains of Attica with their groves of olive trees. By the fifth century B.C.E., it numbered approximately 300,000 people. Villages and a few larger towns dotted the peninsula where the urban center stood beside the sheer-sided Acropolis some 5 miles (8 kilometers) from the sea.

Abundant land lessened the initial stresses of the Archaic period. Nevertheless, in 594 B.C.E., to avoid civil war, the Athenians conferred lawgiving powers on Solon, an aristocrat with ties to the merchant community. He divided the citizens into four classes based on the yield of their farms. The top three classes could hold state offices. The lowest class, with little or no property, held no offices but could participate in meetings of the Assembly. Although a far cry from democracy, this linkage between rights, privileges, and wealth broke the power of a dominant cluster of aristocratic families

---

Peloponnese (PELL-eh-puh-neze)   helot (HELL-ut)   Thucydides (thoo-SID-ih-dees)

and favored social and political mobility. By abolishing debt slavery, Solon also guaranteed the freedom of Athenian citizens.

Despite Solon's efforts, in 546 B.C.E. an aristocrat named Pisistratus° seized power. Most Athenians still lived in villages, identified primarily with their district, and accepted the leadership of landlords who lived in sturdy manor houses. So the tyrant Pisistratus turned to the urban population as opposed to the villagers loyal to the landlords. He undertook building projects, including a Temple of Athena on the Acropolis, and instituted or expanded popular urban festivals: the City Dionysia°, later famous for dramatic performances, and the Panathenaea°, a religious procession combined with athletic and poetic competitions.

With Spartan assistance, the Athenians expelled Pisistratus's sons, who had inherited his position. In the 460s and 450s B.C.E., **Pericles°** led a democratic movement to transfer all power to popular organs of government: the Assembly, Council of 500, and People's Courts. Henceforward, Athenians of moderate or slender means could hold office and participate in politics. Selected by lot for even the highest positions, officials now received pay for their services so they could afford to leave their other occupations. Some key offices—managing public money, commanding military forces—were filled by elections that took into account the candidates' abilities.

The Assembly of all citizens held open debates several times a month; anyone could speak to the issues of the day. Members of the Council of 500 took turns presiding and representing the Athenian state. Through effective political organizing, Pericles dominated Athenian politics from 461 B.C.E. until his death in 429 B.C.E.

Athens's economic position paralleled its political evolution. From the time of Pisistratus, Athenian pottery becomes increasingly prominent at archaeological sites around the Mediterranean. These pots often contained olive oil, Athens's chief export, but elegant painted vases were themselves luxury commodities. Trade-related increases in the size and prosperity of the middle class help explain the growth of Athenian democracy.

THE STRUGGLE OF PERSIA AND GREECE

The Persian-Greek wars dominated Greek life in the fifth and fourth centuries B.C.E. Persians probably considered developments farther east more important. Nevertheless, in the end, the encounter profoundly affected the history of the eastern Mediterranean and western Asia.

Early Encounters

Cyrus's conquest of Lydia in 546 B.C.E. led to the subjugation of the Ionian Greek cities. Some groups and individuals collaborated with the Persian government, but in 499 B.C.E., Greeks and other subject peoples on the western frontier staged the Ionian Revolt. The Persians needed five years and massive infusions of troops and resources to stamp out the insurrection.

This failed revolt led to the **Persian Wars**: two Persian attacks on Greece in the early fifth century B.C.E. In 490 B.C.E., Darius dispatched a naval fleet to punish Eretria° and Athens, two mainland Greek states allied with the Ionian rebels. Disloyal citizens betrayed Eretria to the Persians, who marched the survivors off to exile. In this, as in many other things, the Persians copied their Assyrian predecessors, although they did not boast of mass deportations. Athens would probably have suffered a similar fate if its hoplites had not defeated the lighter-armed Persian troops in a sharp engagement at Marathon, 26 miles (42 kilometers) from Athens.

Xerxes (Khshayarsha, r. 486–465 B.C.E.) succeeded his father in 486 B.C.E. and soon turned his attention to the troublesome Greeks. In 480 B.C.E., he gathered a huge invasion force, including

Pisistratus (pie-SIS-truh-tuhs)
Dionysia (die-uh-NIZ-ee-uh)
Panathenaea (pan-ath-uh-NEE-uh)
Pericles (PER-eh-kleez)

Eretria (er-EH-tree-uh)

contingents from all over the Persian Empire and a large fleet. Crossing the Hellespont (the narrow strait separating Europe and Asia) and traversing Thrace, the Persian throng descended into central and southern Greece. Xerxes sent messengers ahead demanding of the city-states "earth and water"—tokens of submission.

Many city-states complied. But in southern Greece the Spartans formed an alliance that historians call the Hellenic League. At the pass of Thermopylae° in central Greece, three hundred Spartans and their king fought to the last man to buy time for their fellows to escape, and the Persians sacked Athens in 480 B.C.E. Then the outnumbered Athenians lured the Persian navy into narrow waters at nearby Salamis°, where numbers lost their advantage, and administered a devastating defeat. A rout of the Persian army at Plataea the following spring relieved the immediate threat.

Athens's stubborn refusal to submit and the effectiveness of the Athenian navy earned the city great respect. Naval strategies dominated the next phase of the war designed to liberate Greek states still under Persian control. This gave Athens priority over land-based, isolationist Sparta. The Delian League, formed in 477 B.C.E., brought the Greek states together. In less than twenty years, League forces led by Athenian generals swept the Persians from the eastern Mediterranean and freed all Greek communities except those in distant Cyprus.

The Height of Athenian Power

Scholars date the Classical period of Greek history (480–323 B.C.E.) to this defense of the Greek homeland. Ironically, Athens exploited its crucial role in these events to become an imperial power. Some Greek allies contributed money instead of troops, and the Athenians used the money to strengthen their navy. They treated other members of the Delian League as subjects and demanded annual contributions. States attempting to leave the League were brought back by force, stripped of their defenses, and rendered subordinate to Athens.

Athenian naval technology transformed Greek warfare and brought power and wealth to Athens itself. Unlike commercial ships with stable, round-bodied hulls propelled by a square sail, military vessels relied on large numbers of rowers. Having little deck room or storage space, these ships hugged the coastline and put ashore nightly to replenish food supplies and let the crew sleep. Fifty-oared ships had dominated naval warfare until the late sixth century B.C.E., when sleek, fast **triremes**° powered by 170 rowers brought an end to crude engagements in which warriors cleared the enemy's decks with spears and arrows before boarding and fighting hand to hand.

Approximately 115 by 15 feet (35 by 6 meters) in size, the trireme positioned rowers on three levels with oars of different lengths to avoid interference. The fragile vessels could achieve up to 7 knots in short bursts. Athenian crews, by constant practice, became the best in the eastern Mediterranean. They disabled enemy vessels by sheering off their oars, smashing their hulls below the water line with an iron-tipped prow, or forcing collisions by running around them in ever-tighter circles.

The primacy of the fleet contributed to a democratic system in which each male citizen had, at least in principle, an equal voice. The middle or upper class produced hoplites, who bought their own armor and weapons. Rowers came from the lower classes, but they insisted on full rights as protectors of the community.

Athenian maritime power reached farther than any citizen militia. Victors in Greek wars seldom occupied enemy lands permanently (the exception being Sparta's takeover of Messenia). Booty with minor adjustments to boundary lines sufficed. But Athens could exert continual domination and readily did so to promote its commerce. Athens's port, Piraeus°, became the most important commercial center in the eastern Mediterranean.

Annual dues from subject states subsidized the increasingly expensive Athenian democracy and paid the construction costs of the Parthenon, a majestic temple to Athena on the Acropolis. The Athenian leader Pericles gained extraordinary popularity this way since many Athenians worked to

Thermopylae (thuhr-MOP-uh-lee)
Salamis (SAH-lah-miss)

trireme (TRY-reem)   **Piraeus** (pih-RAY-uhs)

construct and decorate this and other monuments. When political enemies protested Pericles' use of Delian League funds for construction, he replied: "They [Athens's subjects] do not give us a single horse, nor a soldier, nor a ship. All they supply is money. . . . It is no more than fair that after Athens has been equipped with all she needs to carry on the war, she should apply the surplus to public works, which, once completed, will bring her glory for all time."[5]

The proceeds of empire indirectly subsidized the festivals at which the dramatic tragedies of Aeschylus, Sophocles, and Euripides and the comedies of Aristophanes° were performed. The brightest and most creative artists and thinkers flocked to Athens. Traveling teachers called Sophists ("wise men") provided instruction in logic and public speaking to fee-paying pupils. The new discipline of rhetoric—the crafting of attractive and persuasive arguments—gave those with training and quick wits a great advantage in politics and the courts. Greeks became connoisseurs of oratory, eagerly listening for each innovation yet so aware of the power of words that *sophist* came to mean one who uses cleverness to manipulate reality.

These intellectual currents came together in 399 B.C.E. when the philosopher **Socrates** (ca. 470–399 B.C.E.) went on trial charged with corrupting the youth of Athens and not believing in the city's gods. A sculptor by trade, Socrates spent his time conversing with young men who enjoyed hearing him deflate the pretensions of those who thought themselves wise. He wryly commented that he knew one more thing than everyone else: that he knew nothing.

At his trial, Socrates easily disposed of the actual charges, because he was a deeply religious man, and the families of the young men he associated with supported him. He argued that the real basis of the prosecution was twofold: (1) blame for attempts by several of his aristocratic students to overthrow the Athenian democracy and (2) blame for the controversial teachings of the Sophists, which many believed undermined morality and religious tradition. In Athenian trials, juries of hundreds of citizens decided guilt and punishment, often spurred by emotion more than legal principles.

Convicted by a close vote, Socrates maintained his innocence and said he should be rewarded for his services instead. This led the jury to condemn him to death by drinking hemlock. Socrates' disciples considered him a martyr, and smart young men like Plato withdrew from public life and dedicated themselves to philosophical pursuits.

Socrates himself wrote nothing, preferring to converse with people he met in the street. His disciple Plato (ca. 428–347 B.C.E.) may represent the first truly literate generation. He learned from books and habitually wrote down his thoughts. On the outskirts of Athens, Plato founded the Academy, a school where young men could pursue higher education. Yet even Plato reflected the oral culture of his upbringing by writing dialogues—an oral form—in which his protagonist, Socrates, uses the "Socratic method" of question and answer to reach a deeper understanding of values like justice, excellence, and wisdom. Plato refused to write down the most advanced teachings of the Academy. Higher reality, he believed, appeared only in pale reflection in the sensible world and could be grasped only by "initiates" who had completed the earlier stages.

Inequality in Classical Greece

The Athenian democracy that historically underlies modern traditions of democracy included only a small percentage of Attica's population: true citizens—free adult males of pure Athenian ancestry. Excluding women, children, slaves, and foreigners, this group amounted to 30,000 or 40,000 people out of approximately 300,000. Equally exclusive practices probably existed in less well-known Greek democracies.

Slaves, mostly foreigners, constituted perhaps one-third of the population of Attica in the fifth and fourth centuries B.C.E. The average Athenian family owned one or more. Slaves ran the shop or worked the farm while the master attended meetings of the Assembly or served on a board overseeing the day-to-day activities of the state. As "living pieces of property," slaves did any work, submitted to any sexual acts, and suffered any punishments their owners ordained, though some communities prohibited arbitrarily killing slaves. Overall, Greece

---

Aristophanes (ar-uh-STOFF-uh-neze)

saw few of the extremes of cruelty and abuse inflicted on slaves in other places and times.

Farms being small, most slaves performed domestic service rather than field labor, often working with the master or mistress on the same tasks. Daily contact fostered relationships between owners and slaves that made it hard for owners to act inhumanely. Still, Greek thinkers justified slavery by arguing that *barbaroi* (non-Greeks) lacked the capacity to reason and thus were better off under Greek owners. The stigma attached to slavery was so great that most Athenians refused to work as wage laborers because following an employer's orders resembled being his slave.

The position of women varied. Spartan women, who were expected to bear and raise strong children, exercised regularly and enjoyed a level of public visibility and outspokenness that shocked other Greeks. At the opposite extreme, Athenians confined and oppressed women. Ironically, the exploitation of women in Athens reflects the high degree of freedom that Athenian men enjoyed in the democratic state.

Inequality marked Athenian marriages. A man of thirty, reasonably educated, a war veteran, experienced in business and politics, commonly married, after negotiating with her parents, a teenaged woman with no formal education and minimal training in weaving, cooking, and household management. Coming into the home of a husband she hardly knew, the wife had no political rights and limited legal protection. Given the differences in age, social experience, and authority, the relationship between husband and wife resembled that of father and daughter.

The function of marriage was to produce children, preferably male. The ancients were sufficiently ashamed of infanticide—the killing through exposure of unwanted children—to say little about it. But it is likely that more girls than boys were abandoned.

The husband spent his day outdoors attending to work or political responsibilities; he dined with male friends at night. The wife stayed home to cook, clean, raise the children, and supervise the servants. The closest relationship in the family was likely to be between the wife and her slave attendant, a woman of roughly the same age. The servant could be sent on errands. The wife stayed

home, except to attend funerals and certain festivals or make discreet visits to female relatives. Greek men claimed that confinement to the home stifled female promiscuity and prevented illegitimate births that could threaten family property and erode regulation of citizenship rights. Athenian law allowed a husband to kill an adulterer caught in the act with his wife.

Without documents written by women, we cannot tell how Athenian women felt about their situation. Women's festivals, such as the Thesmophoria°, provided a rare opportunity for women to get out. During this three-day festival, the women of Athens lived together and managed their own affairs in a great encampment, carrying out mysterious rituals meant to enhance the fertility of the land. Bold and self-assertive women appeared on the Athenian stage: the defiant Antigone° of Sophocles' play, who buried her brother despite the king's prohibition; and the wives in Aristophanes' comedy *Lysistrata*°, who withheld sex from their husbands until the men ended a war. Although imagined by men and probably reflecting a fear of strong women, these characters must partly reflect the playwrights' mothers, sisters, and wives.

To find his intellectual and emotional "equal," men often looked to other men. Bisexuality arose as much from the social structure as from biological inclinations. An older man commonly admired, pursued, and mentored a youth, thus making bisexuality part of the youth's education and initiation into the adult male community. Though commonplace among the intellectual groups that loom large in the written sources, the frequency of bisexuality and the confinement of women among the Athenian masses remain uncertain.

Failure of the City-State and Triumph of the Macedonians

Athens's rise to empire led in 431 B.C.E. to the outbreak of the **Peloponnesian War,** a struggle for survival between Athenian and Spartan alliances that encompassed most of the Greek world. To insulate themselves from attack by land, in midcen-

Thesmophoria (thes-moe-FOE-ree-uh)
Antigone (ar-TIG-uh-nee)   **Lysistrata** (lis-uh-STRAH-tuh)

tury the Athenians had built three long walls connecting the city with the port of Piraeus and the adjacent shoreline. As long as Athens controlled the sea-lanes and could provision itself, a land-based siege could not starve it into submission.

At the start of the war, Pericles broke precedent by refusing to engage the Spartan-led armies that invaded Attica each year. He knew that the enemy hoplites must soon return to their farms. Thus, instead of culminating in a short, decisive battle, the Peloponnesian War dragged on for nearly three decades, with great loss of life and resources. It sapped the morale of all Greece and ended only with the defeat of Athens in a naval battle in 404 B.C.E. The Persian Empire had bankrolled the construction of ships by the Spartan alliance, so Sparta was able to take the conflict into Athens's own element, the sea.

The victorious Spartans, who had entered the war championing "the freedom of the Greeks," took over Athens's overseas empire until their increasingly high-handed behavior aroused the opposition of other city-states. Indeed, the fourth century B.C.E. was a time of nearly continuous skirmishing among Greek states. The independent polis that lent glory to Greek culture also fostered rivalries and fears among neighbors.

The Persians recouped old losses. By the King's Peace of 387 B.C.E., encompassing most of the war-weary Greek states, all of western Asia, including the Ionian Greek communities, went to Persia. The Persian king guaranteed a status quo that kept the Greeks divided and weak until rebellions in Egypt, Cyprus, and Phoenicia, combined with trouble from some western satraps, diverted his attention from thoughts of another Greek invasion.

Meanwhile, in northern Greece Philip II (r. 359–336 B.C.E.) was transforming his previously backward kingdom of Macedonia into a premier military power. (Although southern Greeks long doubted the "Greekness" of the rough and rowdy Macedonians, modern scholarship considers their language and culture Greek at base, though influenced by non-Greek neighbors.) Philip improved the traditional hoplite formation. He increased its striking power and mobility by equipping his soldiers with longer thrusting spears and lighter armor. Using horses bred on Macedonia's broad grassy plains, he experimented with coordinating

infantry and cavalry. Finally, his engineers developed new siege weapons, including the first catapults—machines using the power of twisted cords that, when relaxed, hurled arrows or stones great distances.

In 338 B.C.E., Philip defeated a southern coalition and established the Confederacy of Corinth to control the Greek city-states. Appointed military commander of all the Greeks, he planned a campaign against Persia and established a bridgehead on the Asiatic side of the Hellespont. This seems to reflect the advice of Greek thinkers who urged an anti-Persian crusade to unify their quarrelsome countrymen.

An assassin cut short Philip's ambitions in 336 B.C.E. **Alexander** (356–323 B.C.E.), his son, crossed into Asia in 334 B.C.E., vowing revenge for Xerxes' invasion a century and half earlier. He defeated the Persians in three pitched battles—against the western satraps at the Granicus River in northwest Anatolia and against King Darius III (r. 336–330 B.C.E.) himself at Issus in southeast Anatolia and at Gaugamela°, north of Babylon.

Alexander the Great, as he came to be called, maintained the Persian administrative system but replaced Persian officials with Macedonians and Greeks. To control strategic points, he settled wounded and aged ex-soldiers in a series of Greek-style cities, beginning with Alexandria in Egypt. After Gaugamela (331 B.C.E.), he experimented with leaving cooperative Persian officials in place, also admitting some Persians and other Iranians into his army and court circle. Adopting elements of Persian dress and court ceremonials, he married several Iranian women who had royal or aristocratic connections and pressed his leading comrades to do the same.

In opting for unexpected policies that the Macedonian nobility fiercely resented, Alexander probably acted from both pragmatic and idealistic motives. His Asian campaign began with visions of glory, booty, and revenge. But the farther east he traveled, the more he saw himself as the legitimate successor of the Persian king (a claim facilitated by the death of Darius III). Alexander may have recognized that he had responsibilities to all the peoples who fell under his control and that controlling so

---

Gaugamela (GAW-guh-mee-luh)

vast an empire would require the cooperation of local leaders. In this, he followed the example of the Achaemenids.

THE HELLENISTIC SYNTHESIS

When he died suddenly in 323 B.C.E. at the age of thirty-two, Alexander had no plans for the succession. A half-century of chaos followed as the most ambitious and ruthless of his generals struggled to succeed him. When the dust cleared, they had broken the empire into three major kingdoms, each ruled by a Macedonian dynasty: the Seleucid°, Ptolemaic°, and Antigonid° kingdoms (see Map 4.2). A rough balance of power prevented any of the three from gaining the upper hand and enabled smaller states to survive by playing off the great powers.

Historians call the epoch following Alexander's conquests the **Hellenistic Age** (323–30 B.C.E.) because large parts of northeastern Africa and western Asia became "Hellenized"—that is, influenced by Greek culture. This era of large kingdoms containing ethnically mixed populations, great cities, powerful rulers, pervasive bureaucracies, and vast disparities in wealth differed profoundly from the Archaic and Classical ages with their small, homogeneous, independent city-states. The Hellenistic world more closely resembled our own in its long-distance trade and communications, new institutions like libraries and universities, new kinds of scholarship and science, and sophisticated tastes in art and literature.

The Seleucids, who ruled the bulk of Alexander's empire, faced the greatest challenges. The Indus Valley and Afghanistan soon split off, and over the course of the third and second centuries B.C.E., Iran fell to the Parthians (see Chapter 6). Mesopotamia, Syria, and parts of Anatolia thus constituted the Seleucid core; the kings ruled from Antioch in Syria. Like the Persians before them,

they governed many different ethnic groups organized under various political and social forms. In the farming villages, where most of the population resided, the Seleucids maintained an administration modeled on the Persian system. They also continued Alexander's policy of founding Greek-style cities to serve as administrative centers and attract colonists from Greece. The Seleucids desperately needed Greek soldiers, engineers, and administrators.

The dynasty of the **Ptolemies**° ruled Egypt and sometimes laid claim to Palestine. Since most Egyptians belonged to one ethnic group and lived in villages alongside the Nile, the Ptolemies took over much of the administrative structure of the pharaohs. Vast revenues poured into the royal treasury from rents (the king owned most of the land), taxes, and royal monopolies on olive oil, salt, papyrus, and other key commodities.

The Ptolemies ruled from **Alexandria.** Memphis and Thebes, the capitals of ancient Egypt, had been located upriver. Alexandria, situated near the mouth of the westernmost branch of the Nile, linked Egypt with the Mediterranean world. In the language of the Ptolemaic bureaucracy, Alexandria was technically "beside Egypt" rather than in it, as if to emphasize the gulf between rulers and subjects.

Like the Seleucids, the Ptolemies encouraged Greek immigration. In return for collaboration in the military or civil administration, the immigrants received land and a privileged position in the new society. But the Ptolemies did not plant Greek-style cities throughout the Egyptian countryside and made no effort to force the Greek language or customs on the Egyptian population. So separate was the ruling class from the subject population that only the last Ptolemy, Queen Cleopatra (r. 51–30 B.C.E.), bothered to learn the Egyptian language. The advent of new masters brought few changes to the Egyptian peasants. Nevertheless, from the early second century B.C.E., native insurrections in the countryside, though quickly stamped out by government forces and Greek and Hellenized settlers, indicate growing resentment of Greek exploitation and arrogance.

In Europe, the Antigonid dynasty ruled the

Seleucid (sih-LOO-sid)   **Ptolemaic** (tawl-uh-MAY-ik)
Antigonid (an-TIG-uh-nid)

Ptolemies (TAWL-uh-meze)

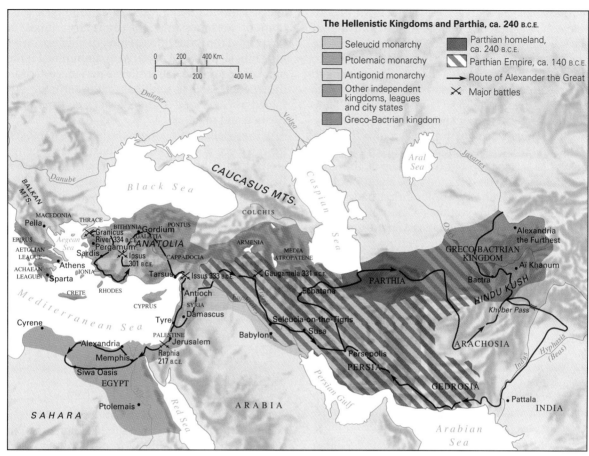

Map 4.2   Hellenistic Civilization   After the death of Alexander the Great in 323 B.C.E., his vast empire soon split apart into a number of large and small political entities. A Macedonian dynasty was established on each continent: the Antigonids ruled the Macedonian homeland and tried with varying success to extend their control over southern Greece; the Ptolemies ruled Egypt; and the Seleucids inherited the majority of Alexander's conquests in Asia, though they lost control of the eastern portions because of the rise of the Parthians of Iran in the second century B.C.E. This period saw Greeks migrating in large numbers from their overcrowded homeland to serve as a privileged class of soldiers and administrators on the new frontiers, where they replicated the lifestyle of the city-state.

Macedonian homeland and parts of northern Greece. Compact and ethnically homogeneous, the Antigonid kingdom experienced little of the hostility that the Seleucid and Ptolemaic rulers faced. Macedonian garrisons gave the Antigonids a toehold in central and southern Greece, and the shadow of Macedonian intervention always threatened the south. The southern states responded by joining confederations, such as the Achaean°

League in the Peloponnese, in which the member states maintained local autonomy but pooled resources and military power.

Athens and Sparta stood apart from these confederations. Never abandoning their myth of invincibility, the Spartans made a number of heroic but futile stands against Macedonian armies. Athens, now cherished for the artistic and literary accomplishments of the fifth century B.C.E., pursued a policy of neutrality. The city became a large museum, filled with the relics and memories of a

Achaean (uh-KEY-uhn)

glorious past, as well as a university town that attracted the children of the well-to-do from all over the Mediterranean and western Asia.

Alexandria, the greatest Hellenistic city, with a population of nearly half a million, had at its heart the royal compound, containing the palace and administrative buildings. The magnificent Mausoleum of Alexander enshrined the body that the first Ptolemy had stolen during its return to Macedonia for burial. He had hoped by this to gain legitimacy as a ruler through the luster of the great conqueror, who was declared to be a god.

The famed Library of Alexandria had several hundred thousand volumes. The Museum, or "House of the Muses" (divinities who presided over the arts and sciences), supported the work of the greatest poets, philosophers, doctors, and scientists. A great lighthouse—a multistory tower with a fiery beacon visible at a distance of 30 miles (48 kilometers)—guided seafarers to two harbors serving the commerce of the Mediterranean, the Red Sea, and the Indian Ocean.

Alexandrian Greeks enjoyed citizenship in a polis, complete with Assembly, Council, and officials overseeing local affairs. They took advantage of Greek-style amenities and institutions: public baths and shaded arcades, theaters featuring revivals of ancient plays, and concert halls for musical performances and demonstrations of oratory. Young men of the privileged classes took classes at gymnasiums where athletics and fitness combined with music and literature in the curriculum. Jews had their own civic corporation, officials, and courts and predominated in two of the five main residential districts. The sights, sounds, and smells of Syria, Anatolia, and the Egyptian countryside lent distinctiveness to other quarters.

In all the Hellenistic states, ambitious members of the indigenous populations learned the Greek language and adopted elements of the Greek lifestyle, because doing so helped them become part of a privileged and wealthy ruling class. Language and customs more than physical traits made a person a Greek. The Hellenistic Age saw a spontaneous synthesis of Greek and indigenous ways. Egyptians migrated to Alexandria, and Greeks and Egyptians intermarried in the villages. Greeks living amid the monuments and descendants of the ancient civilizations of Egypt and western Asia

learned the mathematical and astronomical wisdom of Mesopotamia, the mortuary rituals of Egypt, and the attractions of foreign religions. With little official planning or blessing, stemming for the most part from the day-to-day experiences of ordinary people, a great multicultural experiment unfolded as Greek and Middle Eastern cultural traits clashed and merged.

The Hellenistic kingdom farthest removed from Greece and Macedonia flourished in the region of Bactria in northern Afghanistan. Despite being cut off from the other Hellenistic kingdoms by the rise of Parthian power in Persia, Bactria played an important role in transmitting Greek artistic forms to India. We now turn to India as a land of great diversity, many of whose peoples shared with the Greeks and the Iranians a heritage of Indo-European language and culture.

FOUNDATIONS OF INDIAN CIVILIZATION

India is called a *subcontinent* because it is a large—roughly 2,000 miles (3,200 kilometers) in both length and breadth—and physically isolated landmass within the continent of Asia. The Himalayas°, the world's highest mountains, form a barrier to the north; the Indian Ocean bounds it on the east, south, and west (see Map 4.3). The one frontier easily accessible to invaders and migrating peoples lies to the northwest. But people using this corridor must cross over the mountain barrier of the Hindu Kush and the Thar° Desert east of the Indus River.

The Indian Subcontinent

This region of the modern states of Pakistan, Nepal, Bhutan, Bangladesh, India, and the adjacent island of Sri Lanka divides into three topographical zones. The mountainous northern zone takes in the heavily forested foothills and high meadows on

---

Himalayas (him-uh-LAY-uhs)   **Thar** (tahr)

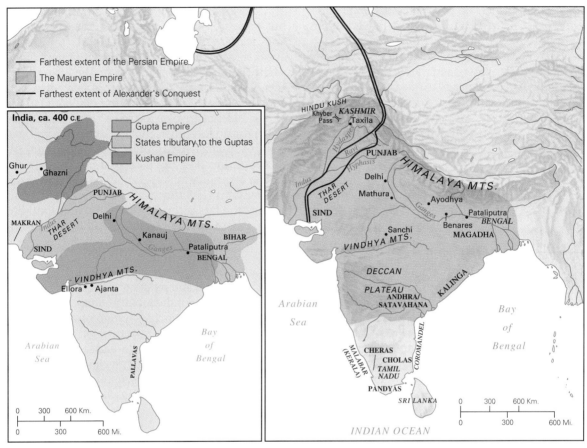

Map 4.3   Ancient India   Mountains and ocean largely separate the Indian subcontinent from the rest of Asia. Migrations and invasions usually came through the Khyber Pass in the northwest.

the edge of the Hindu Kush and Himalaya ranges. Next come the great basins of the Indus and Ganges Rivers. Originating in the mountainous borderlands of Tibet, these rivers flood annually, leaving layers of silt that over time have created large alluvial plains. The Vindhya range and the Deccan°, an arid, rocky plateau reminiscent of the American Southwest, separate northern India from the third zone, the peninsula proper. The tropical coastal strip of Kerala (Malabar) in the west, the Coromandel Coast in the east with its web of rivers descending from the Deccan, the flatlands of Tamil Nadu on the southern tip of the peninsula, and the island of Sri Lanka often have

followed paths of political and cultural development separate from those of northern India.

The mountainous northern rim shelters the subcontinent from cold Arctic winds and gives it a subtropical climate. The **monsoon** (seasonal wind) comes annually when the Indian Ocean lags behind the Asian landmass in heating and cooling with the changing seasons. The temperature difference between water and land acts like a bellows, producing a great wind over the ocean. The southwest monsoon begins in June, picks up moisture from the Indian Ocean, and delivers heavy precipitation to the Ganges Basin and the rain-forest belt on India's western coast. The moist, flat Ganges Delta (modern Bengal) favors rice production. Elsewhere, wheat, barley, and millet predominate.

Deccan (de-KAN)

Indus Valley farmers, in contrast, see little precipitation (see Chapter 1) and therefore rely on extensive irrigation.

Indian Ocean mariners learned to ride the monsoon winds across open waters from northeast to southwest in January and to make the return voyage in July. Ships ventured across the Arabian Sea to the Persian Gulf, the southern coast of Arabia, and East Africa, and east across the Bay of Bengal to Indochina and Indonesia (see Chapter 6).

The Vedic Age, 1500–500 B.C.E.

Many features of later Indian civilization surely date back to the Indus Valley civilization of the third and early second millennia B.C.E. (see Chapter 1). Since the writing from that period remains undeciphered, however, the earliest textual knowledge about Indian roots comes from the period 1500 to 500 B.C.E., called the "Vedic Age" after religious texts known as the *Vedas.* Most historians believe that nomads speaking an Indo-European language called Vedic Sanskrit migrated into northwest India at the beginning of the period. Some argue for a much earlier Indo-European presence in this region deriving from the spread of agriculture.

After the collapse of the Indus Valley civilization, the central authority presumed to have organized large-scale irrigation disappeared. The region became home to bands of Vedic-speaking cattle herders who also engaged in farming. Like other Indo-European peoples—Celts, Greeks, Iranians, Romans—patriarchal traditions made the father dominant in the family just as the king ruled the group as a whole. Warriors boasted of their martial skill and courage, relished combat, feasted on beef, and filled their leisure time with chariot racing and gambling.

After 1000 B.C.E., some groups pushed eastward into the Ganges Plain. Iron tools—harder than bronze and able to hold a sharper edge—allowed settlers to fell trees and work the newly cleared land with ox-drawn plows. The fertile plain, watered by the annual monsoon, sustained two or three crops a year. As in Greece at roughly the same time, the use of iron tools must have led to a population increase.

Stories about this era, written down much later but preserved by oral recitation, speak of rivalry and warfare between two peoples: the Aryas, speakers of Vedic Sanskrit and practitioners of the sacrificial religion prescribed in the Vedas, and the Dasas, indigenous speakers of Dravidian languages, whose religion, it is pointedly noted in the Vedas, did not involve sacrifice to or worship of the Vedic gods. Some scholars argue that the real process by which Arya groups became dominant in the north involved the absorption of some Dasas into Arya populations and a merging of elites from both groups. For the most part, however, Aryas pushed the Dasas south into central and southern India, where their descendants still live. Indo-European languages descended from those of the Aryas predominate in northern India today, while Dravidian languages prevail in the south.

The cultural and religious differences between the Aryas and the indigenous peoples contributed to sharp social divisions. A system of **varnas,** literally "colors" but usually translated as "castes," indicated something akin to classes. Individuals belonged by birth to one of four classes: *Brahmins,* the group comprising priests and scholars; *Kshatriyas°,* warriors and the king; *Vaishyas°,* all other Aryas; and *Shudras°,* non-Aryas who were servants and slaves of the other three varnas. The designation *Shudra* originally may have signified Dasa. Indeed, the term *dasa* came to mean "slave." Eventually a fifth group emerged: the Untouchables. Excluded from the caste system and shunned by the other castes, they worked in demeaning or polluting trades such as tanning, which involved touching dead animals, and sweeping away ashes after cremations.

According to one creation myth, a primordial man named Purusha allowed himself to be sacrificed. From his mouth sprang the varna of Brahmin priests. From his arms came the Kshatriya warriors; from his thighs the Vaishya merchants, artisans, and peasants; and from his feet the Shudra workers.

Within the broad varna divisions, the popula-

Kshatriya (kshuh-TREE-yuh)   **Vaishya** (VIESH-yuh)
Shudra (SHOOD-ra)

tion further divided into numerous smaller groups, called **jatis,** or castes. Each jati had its proper occupation, duties, and rituals. Members of a given jati lived and married within the group and ate only with fellow jati members. Elaborate rules governed interactions between groups. Members of higher-status groups feared pollution from contacting lower-caste individuals and had to undergo rituals of purification to remove any taint.

The caste system became connected to a belief in reincarnation. The Brahmin priests taught that every living creature had an immortal essence: the *atman*, or "self." Separated from the body at death, the atman returned in the body of an insect, an animal, or a human depending on the **karma,** or deeds, of the atman in its previous incarnations. People of exemplary goodness returned in a higher caste. Those who misbehaved fell to a lower caste or even a lower life form. The underlying message ran: You are where you deserve to be, and the only way to improve your lot in the next incarnation is to accept your current station and its attendant duties.

Many of the Vedic deities, mostly male, were associated with the heavens. Indra, like Zeus a god of war and master of the thunderbolt, commanded the greatest devotion and represented the chieftains who led their warriors into battle. Agni, the fire god, consumed the sacrifice and bridged the spheres of gods and humans. Vedic religion centered on sacrifice, the dedication to a god of a valued possession, often a living creature. The offerings invigorated the gods and thereby sustained their creative powers and promoted stability in the world.

Brahmin priests alone knew the rituals and prayers. The *Rig Veda,* a collection of more than a thousand poetic hymns to various deities, and the *Brahmanas,* detailed prose descriptions and explanations of ritual procedures, all in the Sanskrit language of the Arya upper classes, passed orally from one generation of priests to the next. The Brahmins may have opposed the introduction of writing. This would explain why this technology did not spread in India until the Gupta period (320–550 C.E.). The priests' "knowledge" (the term *veda* means just that) earned them rewards for officiating at sacrifices and gave them social and political

power as the intermediaries between gods and humans.

As elsewhere in the ancient world, the lives of Indian women left few traces. Limited evidence indicates that in the Vedic period, women studied sacred lore, composed religious hymns, and participated in sacrifices. They could own property and usually did not marry until their middle or late teens. A number of strong and resourceful women appear in the *Mahabharata* epic. In the *Ramayana* epic, on the other hand, we see the familiar motif of the hero Rama rescuing his wife Sita after she has been abducted.

The internal divisions of Indian society, the complex hierarchy of groups, and the claims of some to superior virtue and purity provided each individual with a clear identity and role and offered the benefits of group solidarity and support. Sometimes groups even upgraded their status within the system, which was not entirely static and provided mechanisms for releasing social tensions. Many of these features persisted into modern times.

Challenges to the Old Order: Jainism and Buddhism

After 700 B.C.E., reactions against Brahmin power and privilege emerged. People who objected to the rigid social hierarchy could always retreat to the forest. Despite extensive clearing for agriculture, forest covered much of ancient India. Never far away, these wild places symbolized freedom from societal constraints.

Individuals who wandered in the forest sometimes attracted followers. Questioning priestly power and the necessity of sacrifices, they offered alternate paths to salvation: individual pursuit of insight into the nature of the self and the universe through physical and mental discipline (*yoga*), which included dietary restrictions, and meditation. They taught that by distancing oneself from desire for the things of this world, one could achieve **moksha,** or liberation, "a deep, dreamless sleep" that released one from endless reincarnations through union with the divine force of the universe. The Upanishads, which continue the explanations of ritual begun in the Brahmanas, also reflect this questioning of Vedic ritualism.

Jainism° and Buddhism challenged not only Vedic ritualism, but the authority of the Vedic priests themselves. *Jainism* took its name from the teacher Mahavira (540–468 B.C.E.), known to his followers as Jina, "the Conqueror." Mahavira respected the life force so much that he commanded strict nonviolence. Jains wore masks to avoid inadvertently inhaling small insects and before sitting down brushed off the seat. Some practiced extreme asceticism including nudity and eventually starved themselves to death. Less zealous Jains engaged in commerce in cities since agricultural work inevitably involved killing.

Buddhism, a far more successful movement, stemmed from the life of Siddhartha Gautama (563–483 B.C.E.), known as the **Buddha,** "the Enlightened One," about whom myriad legends have arisen. From a Kshatriya family in what is now Nepal, he enjoyed the princely lifestyle that was his birthright until he experienced a change of heart and gave up family and privilege to become a wandering ascetic. After six years, he decided that asceticism was no more likely to produce spiritual insight than his earlier luxurious life, so he opted for a "Middle Path." Sitting under a tree in a deer park near Benares on the Ganges River, he gained a sudden and profound insight, which he set forth as "Four Noble Truths": (1) life is suffering, (2) suffering arises from desire, (3) the solution to suffering lies in curbing desire, and (4) desire can be curbed if a person follows the "Eightfold Path" of right views, aspirations, speech, conduct, livelihood, effort, mindfulness, and meditation. Rising up, the Buddha preached his First Sermon, a central text of Buddhism, and set into motion the "Wheel of the Law." He soon attracted followers, some of whom took vows of celibacy, nonviolence, and poverty.

At first, Buddhism centered on the individual. It denied the usefulness of the gods to a person seeking enlightenment. What mattered was living moderately to minimize desire and suffering, and searching for spiritual truth through self-discipline and meditation. One should seek *nirvana*, literally "snuffing out the flame," a release from the cycle of reincarnations and enjoyment of perpetual tranquility. The Upanishadic tradition emphasized the

Jainism (JINE-iz-uhm)

Sculpture of the Buddha, Second or Third Century C.E. This depiction, showing the effects of a fast, comes from Gandhara in the northwest and displays the realism of Greek art introduced by Greek settlements established by Alexander the Great.   (Robert Fisher)

eternal survival of the atman, the "self" or nonmaterial essence of the individual. Buddhism, on the other hand, regarded the individual as a composite of features such as breath and wind, but without a soul.

At his death, Buddha left no final instructions, urging his disciples to "be their own lamp." His followers spread his philosophy throughout India and into Central, Southeast, and East Asia. Its wide appeal subverted its individualistic and atheistic underpinnings. Buddhist monasteries with hierarchies of monks and nuns came into being.

Worshipers erected *stupas* (large earthen mounds symbolizing the universe) over relics of the cremated founder and other holy men and walked around them in a clockwise direction. Believers began to worship the Buddha himself as a god. Many Buddhists also revered *bodhisattvas*°, men and women who had achieved enlightenment and were on the threshold of nirvana but chose rebirth into mortal bodies to help others along the path to salvation.

Early representations show the Buddha only indirectly, through symbols such as his footprints, begging bowl, or the tree under which he achieved enlightenment, as if to emphasize his achievement of a state of nonexistence. From the second century C.E., however, statues of the Buddha and bodhisattvas proliferated, sculpted in styles that showed the influence of the Greek settlements established in Bactria (northern Afghanistan) by Alexander the Great. A schism emerged within Buddhism. Devotees of **Mahayana**° ("Great Vehicle") **Buddhism** embraced the popular new features. Practitioners of **Theravada**° ("Teachings of the Elders") **Buddhism** followed most of the original teachings of the founder.

The Rise of Hinduism

Challenged by the new religious movements, Vedic religion evolved by the fourth century C.E. into **Hinduism,** the dominant religion in South Asia today. (The term *Hinduism* originated with Islamic invaders in the eleventh century C.E. as a label for the diverse practices they encountered: "what the Indians do.") Though based on the Vedic religion of northern India, Hinduism incorporated Dravidian cultural elements from the south, such as intense devotion to a deity and the prominence of goddesses.

Brahmin priests survived the transition with their social status and influence intact, but sacrifice lost its central place. Opportunities for individual worshipers to have direct contact with deities

increased. Hinduism emphasized the worshiper's personal devotion to a particular deity, usually Vishnu or Shiva, or Devi ("the Goddess"). The goddess is of Dravidian origin, and her incorporation into the cult shows how Arya and indigenous cultures fused to form Hindu civilization. Vishnu, who has a clear Aryan pedigree, remains more popular in northern India, and Shiva is dominant in the south. These deities appear in many guises, bear various cult names, and give rise to a complex symbolism of stories, companion animals, birds, and objects.

Vishnu, the preserver, benevolently helps his devotees in time of need. Hindus believe that whenever demonic forces threaten the cosmic order, an *avatara*, or incarnation of Vishnu, appears on earth. His avatars include the legendary hero Rama, the cowherd god Krishna, and the Buddha (a clear attempt to co-opt the rival religion's founder). Shiva, who lives in ascetic isolation on Mount Kailasa in the Himalayas, represents a cyclical process of creation and destruction that is symbolized in statues showing him dancing. Devi can manifest herself as a full-bodied mother goddess representing fertility and procreation, as Shiva's loving wife, Parvati, or as the frightening deity who, under the name Kali or Durga, lets loose violence and destruction.

The multiplicity of gods (330 million according to one tradition), sects, and local practices within Hinduism reflects the ethnic, linguistic, and cultural diversity of India. Yet within this variety, there is unity. A worshiper's devotion to one god or goddess does not entail denial of the other main deities or the host of lesser divinities and spirits. Ultimately, all are manifestations of a single divine force pervading the universe. This underlying unity appears in the way various manifestations of Devi represent different female potentials, in composite statues—half Shiva, half Vishnu—signifying complementary aspects of one cosmic principle, and in sacred texts like the Bhagavad-Gita in which the warrior Arjuna sees the god Krishna truly after thinking that he was merely his chariot driver:

> It was a multiform, wondrous vision,
> with countless mouths and eyes
> and celestial ornaments.

---

bodhisattva (boe-dih-SUT-vuh)
Mahayana (mah-huh-YAH-nuh)
Theravada (there-eh-VAH-duh)

Hindu Temple at Khajuraho This sandstone temple of the Hindu deity Shiva, representing the celestial mountain of the gods, was erected at Khajuraho, in central India, around 1000 C.E. following the architectural symbolism of the Gupta period. Worshipers made their way through several rooms to the image of the deity, located in the innermost "womb-chamber" beneath the tallest tower. (Jean-Louis Nou)

Everywhere was boundless divinity
containing all astonishing things,
wearing divine garlands and garments,
anointed with divine perfume.
If the light of a thousand suns
were to rise in the sky at once,
it would be like the light
of that great spirit.
Arjuna saw all the universe
in its many ways and parts,
standing as one in the body
of the god of gods.[6]

Hindus may approach god and obtain divine favor through special knowledge of sacred truths, mental and physical discipline, or extraordinary devotion to the deity. Worship centers on temples, which range from humble shrines to richly decorated stone edifices built under royal patronage. Statues beckon the deity to take up temporary residence within the image and be available to eager worshipers. *Puja*, or service to the deity, can include bathing, clothing, or feeding the statue. Glimpsing the divine image conveys potent blessings.

Sacred places where a worshiper can directly sense and benefit from divine power dot the Indian subcontinent. Mystery and sanctity surround certain mountains, caves, trees, plants, and rocks. *Tirthayatra*, the term for a pilgrimage site, means "journey to a river crossing," illustrating the association of Hindu sacred places with flowing water. The Ganges River is especially sacred. Millions of worshipers travel each year to bathe and receive the restorative and purifying power of its waters.

Pilgrimage to shrines fosters contact and exchange of ideas among people from different parts of India, helping to create a broad Hindu identity and the concept of India as a single civilization.

Religious duties depend on social standing and gender as well as stage of life. Young men from the three highest classes (Brahmin, Kshatriya, and Vaishya) undergo ritual rebirth through the ceremony of the sacred thread, marking attainment of manhood and readiness to receive religious knowledge. The life cycle then passes through four stages: (1) student of the sacred texts, (2) married householder with children and material goods, (3) forest dweller meditating on the meaning of existence after the birth of his grandchildren, and (4) wandering ascetic awaiting death. Such a life fulfills first his duties to society and then his duties to himself, leaving him disconnected from the world and prepared for moksha (liberation).

Hinduism responded to the needs of people for personal deities with whom they could establish direct connections. The austerity of early Buddhism, its denial of the importance of gods, and its demand that individuals find their own path to enlightenment may have required too much of ordinary people. What eventually made Mahayana Buddhism popular—gods, saints, and myths—also made it more easily absorbed into the social and cultural fabric of Hinduism.

IMPERIAL EXPANSION AND COLLAPSE

Political unity has rarely lasted in India. The varied terrain—mountains, foothills, plains, forests, steppes, deserts—favors different forms of organization and economic activity. Peoples occupying topographically diverse zones may also differ in language and cultural practices. Caste and family have generated the strongest feeling of personal identity, allegiance to a higher political authority being a secondary concern.

Nevertheless, two empires arose in the Ganges Plain: the Mauryan Empire of the fourth to second centuries B.C.E. and the Gupta Empire of the fourth to sixth centuries C.E.

The Mauryan Empire, 324–184 B.C.E.

Among the many kinship groups and independent states that dotted the north Indian landscape, the kingdom of Magadha, in the modern Indian state of Bihar, began to play an influential role around 600 B.C.E. thanks to wealth based on agriculture, iron mines, and strategic location astride the trade routes of the eastern Ganges Basin. In the late fourth century B.C.E., Chandragupta Maurya°, a man of Vaishya or Shudra origins, took control of Magadha and founded the **Mauryan Empire.** Greek tradition claimed that Alexander the Great met an Indian native named "Sandracottus," an apparent corruption of "Chandragupta," when his armies reached the Punjab (northern Pakistan) in 326 B.C.E., implying that he might have served as a role model for the new ruler.

Greek rule in the Punjab collapsed after Alexander's death, allowing Chandragupta (r. 324–301 B.C.E.) and his successors Bindusara (r. 301–269 B.C.E.) and Ashoka (r. 269–232 B.C.E.) to extend Mauryan control over the entire subcontinent except for its southern tip.

Tradition holds that Kautilya, a crafty elderly Brahmin, guided Chandragupta and wrote a treatise on government, the *Arthashastra*. Although recent studies have shown that the existing form of the *Arthashastra* dates only to the third century C.E., its core may well go back to Kautilya. This pragmatic guide to political success advocates the so-called *mandala* (circle) theory of foreign policy: "My enemy's enemy is my friend." It also lists schemes for enforcing and increasing tax collection and prescribes the use of spies to keep watch on one's subjects.

A quarter of all agricultural output went in taxes to support the Mauryan government. Relatives and associates of the king governed districts based on ethnic boundaries. The imperial army—with infantry, cavalry, chariot, and elephant

---

Maurya (MORE-yuh)

divisions—secured central authority, which also controlled mining, shipbuilding, and arms making. Standard coinage fostered support for the government and promoted trade.

The Mauryan kings ruled from Pataliputra (modern Patna), where five tributaries join the Ganges. Descriptions by foreign visitors testify to the international connections of the Indian monarchs. Surrounded by a timber wall and moat, the city extended along the river for 8 miles (13 kilometers). Six governing committees oversaw manufacturing, trade, sales, taxes, the welfare of foreigners, and the registration of births and deaths.

Ashoka, Chandragupta's grandson, began his reign by extending the boundaries of the empire. After killing, wounding, or deporting thousands of people during his conquest of Kalinga (modern Orissa, a coastal region southeast of Magadha), remorse overcame him and he converted to Buddhism, thereafter preaching nonviolence, morality, moderation, and religious tolerance in both government and private life.

Ashoka publicized this program through edicts inscribed on great rocks and polished sandstone, the earliest decipherable Indian texts:

> For . . . many hundreds of years the sacrificial slaughter of animals, violence toward creatures, unfilial conduct toward kinsmen, improper conduct toward Brahmins and ascetics [have increased]. Now with the practice of morality by King [Ashoka], the sound of war drums has become the call to morality. . . . You [government officials] are appointed to rule over thousands of human beings in the expectation that you will win the affection of all men. All men are my children. Just as I desire that my children will fare well and be happy in this world and the next, I desire the same for all men. . . . King [Ashoka] . . . desires that there should be the growth of the essential spirit of morality or holiness among all sects. . . . There should not be glorification of one's own sect and denunciation of the sect of others for little or no reason. For all the sects are worthy of reverence for one reason or another.[7]

Despite his commitment to employ peaceful means whenever possible, Ashoka reminded po-

tential transgressors that "the king, remorseful as he is, has the strength to punish the wrongdoers who do not repent."

Commerce and Culture in an Era of Political Fragmentation

The Mauryan Empire prospered for a time after Ashoka's death in 232 B.C.E. Then, weakened by dynastic disputes, it collapsed under attacks from the northwest in 184 B.C.E. Five hundred years passed before another state succeeded in extending control over northern India. Despite the political fragmentation, however, economic, cultural, and intellectual development continued. The roads and towns of the Mauryans fostered commerce within the subcontinent, while land and sea routes linked India to China, Southeast Asia, Central Asia, the Middle East, East Africa, and the lands of the Mediterranean. Guilds of merchants and artisans regulated the lives of their members and had an important voice in local affairs. They patronized culture and endowed religious sects, particularly Buddhism and Jainism, with temples and monuments.

During the last centuries B.C.E. and the first centuries C.E., the greatest Indian epics, the *Ramayana* and the *Mahabharata*, based on centuries-old oral predecessors, achieved their final form. They place the events they describe in the distant past, but their proud kings, beautiful queens, family wars, heroic conduct, and chivalric values seem to reflect the late Vedic period, when Aryan warrior societies moved onto the Ganges Plain.

The *Ramayana* relates the exploits of Rama, a heroic prince who came to be considered an incarnation of Vishnu. When the chief of the demons kidnaps his wife, Sita, he destroys the demons with the help of his brother and a troop of monkeys. The vast **Mahabharata**—eight times the length of the *Iliad* and *Odyssey* combined—tells how two sets of cousins, the Pandavas and Kauravas, quarreled over succession to the throne and fought a cataclysmic battle at Kurukshetra. The battle is so destructive on both sides that Yudhishthira, the eldest of the Pandava brothers and their leader, accepts the fruits of victory only reluctantly because the battle losses were so great.

The ***Bhagavad-Gita*** is a self-contained (and perhaps originally separate) episode set in the battle. The hero Arjuna shrinks from fighting his kinsmen until his charioteer, the god Krishna, tutors him on the necessity of fulfilling his duty as a warrior. Death means nothing in a universe of endless reincarnation. The Bhagavad-Gita resolves the tension in Indian civilization between duty to society and duty to one's soul. Dutiful action taken without regard for personal benefit serves society and may earn release from the cycle of rebirths.

Science and technology flourished in this era as well. Indian doctors applied herbal remedies and served in the courts of western and southern Asia. In linguistics, Panini (late fourth century B.C.E.) undertook a detailed analysis of Sanskrit word forms and grammar. This led to the standardization of Sanskrit, which arrested its natural development and turned it into a formal, literary language. Prakrits—popular dialects—emerged to become the ancestors of the modern languages of northern and central India.

Historians of southern India consider the period from the third century B.C.E. to the third century C.E., dominated by three often feuding **Tamil kingdoms**—the Cholas, Pandyas, and Cheras—a "classical" period for Tamil art and literature. Patronized by the Pandya kings and guided by an academy of five hundred authors, Tamil writers composed grammatical treatises, collections of ethical proverbs, epics, and short poems about love, war, wealth, and the beauty of nature while performers excelled in music, dance, and drama.

The Gupta Empire, 320–550 C.E.

Like its Mauryan predecessor, the **Gupta Empire** grew from the kingdom of Magadha and had its capital at Pataliputra. Its founder called himself Chandra Gupta (r. 320–335 C.E.), borrowing the name of the Mauryan founder. Though they never controlled as much land as the Mauryans, the Gupta monarchs took the title "Great King of Kings."

Trade, agriculture, and iron mining brought prosperity to the Guptas as they had to the Mau-

ryans, and the kings followed similar methods of taxation and administration. In addition to a 25 percent tax on agriculture, users of the irrigation network paid fees, and some commodities were subject to special taxes. The state maintained monopolies over mining and salt production, exploited state-owned farmlands, and required subjects to work a specified number of days on maintaining roads, wells, and irrigation works.

The Gupta administration and intelligence network were smaller and less pervasive than those of the Mauryans. A powerful army maintained tight control of the empire's core, but provincial governors had a freer hand, which they sometimes used to exploit the populace. Governorships often passed from father to son within high-ranking military or administrative families. The most distant areas, controlled by kinship groups or subordinate kings, made annual donations of tribute. Garrisons stationed at frontier points kept trade routes open and ensured the collection of customs duties.

A constant round of solemn rituals, dramatic ceremonies, and cultural events in Pataliputra demonstrated to visitors from remote areas the benefits of belonging to the empire. Modern historians call such a regime a **theater-state.** Ruler and subjects in a theater-state have an economic relationship. The former accumulates luxury goods and profits from trade and redistributes them to dependents through gifts and other means. Subordinate princes gained prestige by emulating the center and maintained close ties through visits, gifts, and marriages with the Gupta family. Gupta patronage also supported the Indian mathematicians who invented the concept of zero and developed the so-called Arabic numerals and place-value notation (see Environment and Technology: Indian Mathematics).

The moist climate of the Ganges Plain does not favor the preservation of buildings and artifacts, so archaeology has little to say about the Gupta era. However, a Chinese Buddhist monk named Faxian°, who made a pilgrimage to the homeland of his faith around 400 C.E., penned a description of the Gupta kingdom:

Faxian (fah-shee-en)

Indian Mathematics

The Arabic numerals used in most parts of the world today developed in India. Place-value notation, which depended on the ingenious invention of a sign for zero, put Indian mathematics far ahead of the clumsy Egyptian, Greek, and Roman numerical systems. Its use has spread more widely than the alphabet derived from the Phoenicians, forming, in a sense, the only truly global language.

When fully developed, Indian arithmetic notation employed a base 10 system. Single digits, tens, hundreds, and so forth each had a column, with the zero sign indicating the absence of units in a given column. Very large numbers can thus be expressed simply, and calculations that the Romans with their inconvenient numerals had to do mentally or on a counting board become relatively easy.

Property deeds incised in the Sanskrit language on copper plates (see below) and given by kings or wealthy individuals to religious institutions show the numerals 1 to 9 in use in early India. The earliest dates to 595 C.E. Some evidence suggests that the place-value system and zero sign existed in the fifth century, but the earliest document showing them comes from the eighth century.

Other peoples recognized the new system's superiority, and it spread to the Middle East, Southeast Asia,

and East Asia by the seventh century, sometimes using indigenous symbols. Gerbert of Aurillac, a French monk, learned the mathematics of the Arabs in Spain between 967 and 970. In 999, he became Pope Sylvester II and helped popularize the "Arabic" system.

A mechanical calculating device based on the Roman counting board but bearing counters marked with variants of the Indian numeral shapes furthered the spread of the new practice. The counters could turn sideways or upside down so the shapes varied considerably. By the twelfth century, standard forms appeared similar to those in use today, and the counting board, which signified zero by an empty column, gave way to the written zero sign.

Indian cosmology may have led to the invention of the system. Indians conceived of immense spans of time—trillions of years (far exceeding current estimates of 15 to 20 billion years for the age of the universe)—during which innumerable universes came into being and passed away. In one myth, Vishnu creates and destroys worlds with every breath as he slumbers on the coils of a serpent at the bottom of the ocean. Our world, the Indians thought, passed through a series of epochs lasting more than 4 million years—a brief and insignificant moment in the sweep of time. The Indian number system allowed the expression of such vast concepts.

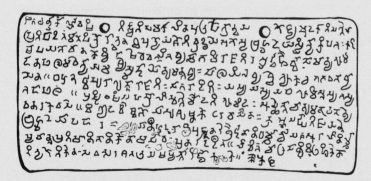

Copper Plate with Indian Numerals
This property deed from western India shows an early form of the symbols for numbers that spread throughout the world.   (Facsimile by Georges Ifrah. Reproduced by permission of Georges Ifrah.)

The cities and towns of this country are the greatest of all in the Middle Kingdom. The inhabitants are rich and prosperous, and vie with one another in the practice of benevolence and righteousness. . . . The heads of the Vaishya families in them establish in the cities houses for dispensing charity and medicines. All the poor and destitute in the country, orphans, widowers, and childless men, maimed people and cripples, and all who are diseased, go to those houses, and are provided with every kind of help.[8]

At this time, the civil disabilities of women, which had always existed as custom, hardened into law with the emergence of law books like *The Laws of Manu*. Indian women lost the right to own or inherit property, and girls married at increasingly early ages, sometimes at six or seven. The husband could thus ensure his wife's virginity, and, by bringing her up in his own household, he could train her to suit his purposes. As in Confucian China, a woman owed obedience to her father, then her husband, and finally her sons (see Chapter 2). In certain parts of India, a practice called *sati*° required a widow to cremate herself on her husband's funeral pyre. Widows who refused to follow this custom could not remarry and suffered social rejection.

Entry into a Jainist or Buddhist religious community offered some women an escape from male control. Women from powerful families and courtesans trained in poetry and music, as well as sexual technique, sometimes enjoyed high social standing and gave money for Buddhist stupas and other shrines.

The Gupta monarchs sought sanctity through reviving Vedic practices. The influence of Brahmin priests gained renewed prominence. Yet the kings also patronized Buddhist and Jain endeavors. Buddhist monasteries with hundreds, even thousands, of monks and nuns flourished in the cities. Northern India drew Buddhist pilgrims from Southeast and East Asia to the birthplace of their faith.

The classic form of the Hindu temple, evolved during the Gupta era, symbolizes the sacred mountain or palace where the gods reside. Sitting atop a raised platform surmounted by high towers, it mirrored the order of the universe. From an exterior courtyard, worshipers approached the central shrine containing the statue of the deity. In rich temples, painted or sculpted gods and mythical events covered the walls. Frescoes and statues also adorned cave temples carved into cliffs.

The vibrant commerce of the period of fragmentation continued under the Guptas. Coins served as the medium of exchange, and artisan guilds influenced the economic, political, and religious life of towns. The Guptas sought control of the ports on the Arabian Sea but saw trade with the weakening Roman Empire decline. Trade with Southeast and East Asia increased, however. Merchants from eastern and southern India voyaged to the Malay° Peninsula and the islands of Indonesia to exchange cotton cloth, ivory, metalwork, and exotic animals for Chinese silk or Indonesian spices. The overland Silk Road from China brought further trade but was vulnerable to disruption by Central Asian nomads (see Chapter 6).

The Gupta empire collapsed around 550 C.E. under the pressure of nomadic invaders from the northwest. In the early seventh century, Harsha Vardhana (r. 606–647), the ruler of the region around Delhi, briefly restored imperial power. An account of his reign by a courtier named Bana shows him to be a fervent Buddhist, poet, patron of artists, and dynamic warrior. After Harsha's death, northern India reverted to political fragmentation and remained divided until the Muslim invasions of the eleventh and twelfth centuries (see Chapter 13).

CONCLUSION

Greece, Iran, and India represent three ways in which societies with shared Indo-European linguistic and religious roots adapted to different geographical environments and indigenous cultures. Although scholars can easily trace resemblances among gods, customs, and philosophical outlooks in these areas, the peoples themselves had no sense of kinship with one another. Only

sati (suh-TEE)

Malay (muh-LAY)

Wall Painting from the Caves at Ajanta, Fifth or Sixth Century C.E.   Kings and patrons financed the construction and decoration of Buddhist, Hindu, and Jain religious shrines. At Ajanta, in central India, twenty-nine caves contain paintings and sculptures illustrating religious and secular scenes. This segment depicts, at left, a princess and her attendants in a garden and, at right, a royal couple in the harem. While representing scenes from the earlier life of the Buddha, the artists give glimpses of life in their own times.   (Jean-Louis Nou)

briefly, under Alexander the Great, did they come into direct contact in meaningful ways, and the resulting Hellenistic culture touched all three regions.

While some technologies, such as coinage, took hold in all areas, and trade flourished, both overland and across the Mediterranean Sea and Indian Ocean, local circumstances dictated political and social formations. The ancient cultural centers of Egypt and Mesopotamia influenced the Greeks and the Persians, while India saw a synthe-

sis of the cultures and social systems of the Aryan peoples and their Dravidian precursors.

In comparing the histories of these regions, the question arises of the degree to which different states and societies follow similar paths because of shared heritages, as opposed to responding similarly but independently to analogous challenges. We will explore this subject in the next chapter through a comparison of Rome and China under the Han Dynasty.

■ Key Terms

Cyrus	Alexandria
Darius I	monsoon
satrap	Vedas
Persepolis	varnas
Zoroastrianism	jatis
polis	karma
hoplite	moksha
tyrant	Buddha
democracy	Mahayana Buddhism
sacrifice	Theravada Buddhism
Herodotus	Hinduism
Pericles	Mauryan Empire
Persian Wars	Ashoka
triremes	*Mahabharata*
Socrates	*Bhagavad-Gita*
Peloponnesian War	Tamil kingdoms
Alexander	Gupta Empire
Hellenistic Age	theater-state
Ptolemies	

■ Suggested Reading

J. M. Cook's *The Persian Empire* (1983) provides the most accessible treatment. Josef Wiesehofer, *Ancient Persia: From 550 B.C. to 650 A.D.* (1996); Richard N. Frye, *The History of Ancient Iran* (1984); and volume 2 of *The Cambridge History of Iran*, ed. Ilya Gershevitch (1985), give the interpretations of Iranian specialists and include good bibliographies. John Curtis, *Ancient Persia* (1989), emphasizes the archaeological record. Maria Brosius, *Women in Ancient Persia, 559–331 B.C.* (1996), draws together scattered evidence. Vesta Sarkhosh Curtis, *Persian Myths* (1993), concisely introduces Iranian myths and legends, with illustrations.

The Cambridge Ancient History, 3d ed., vols. 3–7 (1970–), treats the history of this period fully. Sarah B. Pomeroy, Stanley M. Burstein, Walter Donlan, and Jennifer Tolbert Roberts, *Ancient Greece: A Political, Social, and Cultural History* (1999), offers a fine one-volume treatment. Frank J. Frost, *Greek Society*, 3d ed. (1987), covers social history. Peter Levi, *Atlas of the Greek World* (1980), contains maps and pictures. For essays by contemporary experts on every aspect of Greco-Roman civilization with up-to-date bibliographies, see Michael Grant and Rachel Kitzinger, eds., *Civilization of the Ancient Mediterranean* (1987).

Consult Michael Crawford and David Whitehead, eds., *Archaic and Classical Greece: A Selection of Ancient Sources in Translation* (1983), for translated documents. David G. Rice and John E. Stambaugh, eds., *Sources for the Study of Greek Religion* (1979); Mary R. Lefkowitz and Maureen B. Fant, eds., *Women's Life in Greece and Rome: A Source Book in Translation* (1982); Thomas Wiedemann, ed., *Greek and Roman Slavery* (1981); and Michael Gagarin and Paul Woodruff, *Early Greek Political Thought from Homer to the Sophists* (1995), are specialized collections.

Victor Davis Hanson, *The Other Greeks: The Family Farm and the Agrarian Roots of Western Civilization* (1995); Eric A. Havelock, *The Muse Learns to Write: Reflections on Orality and Literacy from Antiquity to the Present* (1986); Elaine Fantham, Helene Peet Foley, Natalie Boymel Kampen, Sarah B. Pomeroy, and H. Alan Shapiro, *Women in the Classical World* (1994); Cynthia Patterson, *The Family in Greek History* (1998); Yvon Garlan, *Slavery in Ancient Greece* (1988); Walter Burkert, *Greek Religion* (1985); Victor Davis Hanson, *The Western Way of War: Infantry Battle in Classical Greece* (1989); Lionel Casson, *The Ancient Mariners: Seafarers and Sea Fighters of the Mediterranean in Ancient Times*, 2d ed. (1991); Michail Yu Treister, *The Role of Metals in Ancient Greek History* (1996); Joint Association of Classical Teachers, *The World of Athens: An Introduction to Classical Athenian Culture* (1984); N. G. L. Hammond, *The Macedonian State: The Origins, Institutions and History* (1989); Joseph Roisman, ed., *Alexander the Great: Ancient and Modern Perspectives* (1995); and William R. Biers, *The Archaeology of Greece: An Introduction* (1990) explore specific aspects of Greek culture and society. For the Hellenistic world, see F. W. Walbank, *The Hellenistic World*, rev. ed. (1993), and Michael Grant, *From Alexander to Cleopatra: The Hellenistic World* (1982).

Karl J. Schmidt, *An Atlas and Survey of South Asian History* (1995), provides a good starting point with maps and facing text illustrating diverse features of Indian civilization. Concise histories include Stanley Wolpert, *A New History of India*, 3d ed. (1989), and Romila Thapar, *A History of India*, vol. 1 (1966). D. D. Kosambi, *Ancient India: A History of Its Culture and Civilization* (1965), and Paul Masson-Oursel, *Ancient India and Indian Civilization* (1998), offer fuller presentations.

Translations of primary texts with an emphasis on religion take up Ainslie T. Embree's *Sources of Indian Tradition*, vol. 1, 2d ed. (1988). Barbara Stoler Miller, *The Bhagavad-Gita: Krishna's Counsel in Time of War* (1986), is a readable translation. R. K. Narayan's *The Mahabharata: A Shortened Modern Prose Version of the Indian Epic* (1978) abbreviates this huge epic. For a classic

Sanskrit text on state building, see T. N. Ramaswamy, *Essentials of Indian Statecraft: Kautilya's Arthasastra for Contemporary Readers* (1962). Romila Thapar, *Asoka and the Decline of the Mauryas* (1963), covers the most important Maurya king.

David R. Kinsley, *Hinduism: A Cultural Perspective* (1982), and David G. Mandelbaum, *Society in India,* 2 vols. (1970), provide insights into religion and social status. Jacob Pandian, *The Making of India and Indian Tradition* (1995), gives attention to southern India in analyzing the diversity of contemporary India. Stephanie W. Jamison, *Sacrificed Wife/Sacrificer's Wife: Women, Ritual, and Hospitality in Ancient India* (1996), deals with the roles of early Indian women. Stella Kramrisch, *The Hindu Temple*, 2 vols. (1946), and Surinder M. Bhardwaj, *Hindu Places of Pilgrimage in India: A Study in Cultural Geography* (1973), examine elements of Hindu worship.

For special topics, see Georges Ifrah, *From One to Zero: A Universal History of Numbers* (1985); Jean W. Sedlar, *India and the Greek World: A Study in the Transmission of Culture* (1980); and Liu Hsin-ju, *Ancient India and Ancient China: Trade and Religious Exchanges, A.D. 1–600* (1994).

■ Notes

1. Quoted in Roland G. Kent, *Old Persian: Grammar, Texts, Lexicon,* 2d ed. (New Haven, CT: American Oriental Society, 1953), 138, 140.
2. Richmond Lattimore, *Greek Lyrics*, 2d ed. (Chicago: University of Chicago Press, 1960), 2.
3. G. S. Kirk and J. E. Raven, *The Presocratic Philosophers: A Critical History with a Selection of Texts* (Cambridge, England: Cambridge University Press, 1957), 169.
4. Herodotus, *The History,* trans. David Grene (Chicago: University of Chicago Press, 1988), 33. (Herodotus 1.1)
5. Plutarch, *Pericles* 12, trans. Ian Scott-Kilvert, *The Rise and Fall of Athens: Nine Greek Lives by Plutarch* (Harmondsworth: Penguin Books, 1960), 178.
6. Barbara Stoller Miller, *The Bhagavad-Gita: Krishna's Counsel in Time of War* (New York: Bantam, 1986), 98–99.
7. B. G. Gokhale, *Asoka Maurya,* (New York: Twayne, 1966), 152–153, 156–157, 160.
8. James Legge, *The Travels of Fa-hien: Fa-hien's Record of Buddhistic Kingdoms* (New Delhi: Oriental Publishers, 1971), 77–79.

5

AN AGE OF EMPIRES: ROME AND HAN CHINA, 753 B.C.E.–330 C.E.

**Rome's Creation of a Mediterranean Empire, 753 B.C.E.–330 C.E. •
The Origins of Imperial China, 221 B.C.E.–220 C.E. •
Imperial Parallels**
SOCIETY AND CULTURE: Slavery in Rome and China

*A*ccording to Chinese sources, in the year 166 C.E., a group of travelers identifying themselves as delegates from Andun, the king of distant Da Qin, arrived at the court of the Chinese emperor Huan, one of the Han rulers. Andun was Marcus Aurelius Antoninus, the emperor of Rome.

These first known "Romans" to reach China probably hailed from one of Rome's eastern provinces, perhaps Egypt or Syria, and may have stretched the truth in claiming to be representatives of the Roman emperor. The Chinese officials had had no direct contact with the Roman Empire, however, and so the travelers, probably merchants hoping to trade for highly prized Chinese silk, easily got away with the imposture.

Direct or regular contact between the empires never developed, but the episode reveals that in the early centuries C.E., Rome and China dimly recognized each other's existence across the far-flung trading networks that spanned the Eastern Hemisphere. Both states, moreover, emerged from the last centuries B.C.E. and the first centuries C.E. as a new kind of empire, both qualitatively and quantitatively.

The Roman Empire encompassed the lands surrounding the Mediterranean Sea and substantial portions of inland Europe and the Middle East. The Han Empire, named for China's ruling family, stretched from the Pacific Ocean to the oases of Central Asia. The largest empires the world had yet seen, they nevertheless managed to centralize control, achieve unprecedented stability and longevity, and assert dominance over the many cultures and peoples within their borders.

Since neither empire influenced the other, what caused them to arise and flourish at the same time? Some stress supposedly common factors, such as climate change or challenges from

Central Asian nomads, but no theory has won the general support of scholars.

As you read this chapter, ask yourself the following questions:

- How did the Roman and Han Empires come into being?
- What fostered their stability or instability?
- What benefits and liabilities did they confer on rulers and subjects?

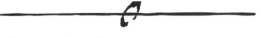

ROME'S CREATION OF A MEDITERRANEAN EMPIRE, 753 B.C.E.–330 C.E.

The boot-shaped Italian peninsula, with the large island of Sicily, constitutes a bridge almost linking Europe and Africa (see Map 5.1). Rome too lay at a crossroads, being situated at the midpoint of the peninsula, about 15 miles (24 kilometers) from its western coast, where a north-south road intersected an east-west river route. The Tiber River on one side and a double ring of seven hills on the other afforded natural protection to the site.

The Apennine mountains form Italy's spine, separating the eastern and western coastal plains, and the arc of the Alps shields it on the north. Navigable rivers and passes through the Apennines, and even through the snowcapped Alps, eased travel by merchants and armies. The Mediterranean climate afforded a long growing season and favorable conditions for a wide variety of crops. Hillside forests, today largely gone, provided timber for construction and fuel. Iron and other metals came from the region of Etruria in the northwest.

Although hills account for 75 percent of Italy's land area, the coastal plains and river valleys provide arable land, with fertile volcanic soil capable of supporting a much larger population than that of Greece. While expanding within Italy, the Roman state effectively tapped these human resources.

A Republic of Farmers

According to legend, Romulus, cast adrift on the Tiber River as a baby and nursed by a she-wolf, founded Rome in 753 B.C.E. Archaeological research, however, has revealed occupation on the Palatine Hill, one of the city's seven hills, dating to 1000 B.C.E. Several hilltop communities merged shortly before 600 B.C.E., forming an urban nucleus made possible by the draining of a swamp on the site of the future Roman Forum (civic center).

The Latin speech and cultural patterns of the inhabitants of the site resembled those of most of the other peoples of the peninsula. However, tradition remembered Etruscan immigrants arriving in the seventh century B.C.E, and Rome came to pride itself on offering hospitality to exiles and outcasts.

Agriculture anchored the economy of early Rome, and land constituted wealth. Landownership brought social status and political privilege while buttressing fundamental values. Most early Romans cultivated their own small plots of land, but a few families managed to acquire large tracts of land. The heads of these wealthy families served in the Senate, a "Council of Elders" that dominated the politics of the Roman state. Their families constituted the senatorial class.

Tradition maintains that seven kings ruled Rome between 753 and 507 B.C.E., Romulus being the first and the tyrannical Tarquinius Superbus the last. In 507 B.C.E., members of the senatorial class, led by Brutus "the Liberator," deposed Tarquinius Superbus and instituted a *res publica*, a "public possession," or republic.

Far from being a democracy, the **Roman Republic,** which lasted from 507 to 31 B.C.E., vested power in several assemblies. Male citizens could attend their sessions, but the votes of the wealthy counted for more than the votes of the poor. The hierarchy of state officials, elected for one year, culminated in two consuls, who presided over the Senate and other assemblies and commanded the army on campaigns.

Technically an advisory council, first to the kings and later to the annually changing Republican officials, the **Roman Senate** increasingly made policy and governed. Senators nominated their sons for public offices and filled senatorial vacan-

CHRONOLOGY

	Rome	China
1000 B.C.E.	**1000 B.C.E.** First settlement on site of Rome	
500 B.C.E.	**507 B.C.E.** Establishment of the Republic	
		480–221 B.C.E. Warring States Period
300 B.C.E.		
	264–202 B.C.E. Wars against Carthage guarantee Roman control of western Mediterranean	**221 B.C.E.** Qin emperor unites eastern China
		206 B.C.E. Han dynasty succeeds Qin
200 B.C.E.	**200–146 B.C.E.** Wars against Hellenistic kingdoms lead to control of eastern Mediterranean	
		140–87 B.C.E. Emperor Wu expands the Han Empire
100 B.C.E.		
	88–31 B.C.E. Civil wars and failure of the Republic	
	31 B.C.E.–14 C.E. Augustus establishes the Principate	
50 C.E.	**45–58 C.E.** Paul spreads Christianity in the eastern Mediterranean	**23 C.E.** Han capital transferred from Chang'an to Luoyang
200 C.E.		**220 C.E.** Fall of Han Empire
	235–284 C.E. Third-century crisis	
300 C.E.		
	324 C.E. Constantine moves capital to Constantinople	

cies with former officials. This self-perpetuating body, whose members served for life, brought together wealth, influence, and political and military experience.

Roman families consisted of several generations as well as domestic slaves. The oldest living male, the *paterfamilias*, exercised absolute authority over every family member. This *auctoritas*, enjoyed by important male members of the society as a whole, enabled a man to inspire and demand obedience from his inferiors.

Complex ties of obligation, such as the **patron/**

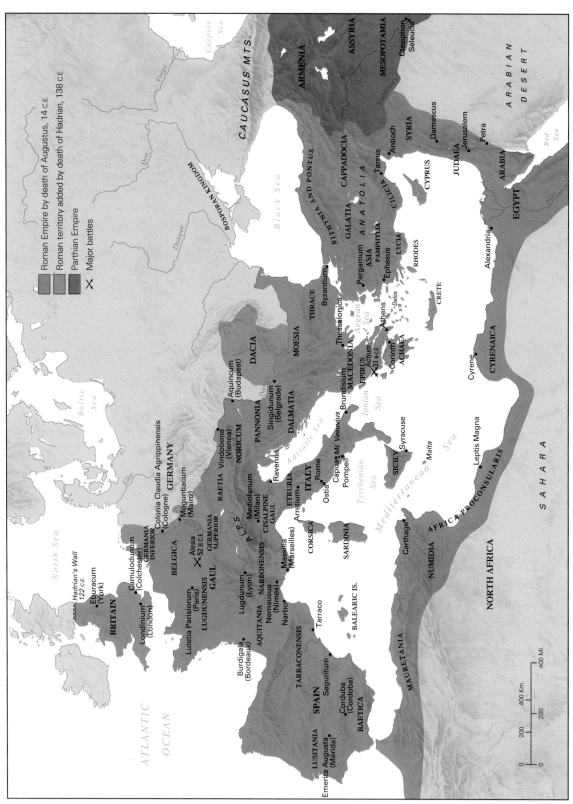

Map 5.1 The Roman Empire   The Roman Empire came to encompass all the lands surrounding the Mediterranean Sea, as well as parts of interior Europe. When Augustus died in 14 C.E., he left instructions to his successors not to expand beyond the limits he had set, but Claudius nevertheless invaded southern Britain in the mid–first century, and the soldier-emperor Trajan added Romania early in the second century.

Roman Empire by death of Augustus, 14 C.E.

Roman territory added by death of Hadrian, 138 C.E.

Parthian Empire

X Major battles

client relationship, bound together individuals and families. *Clients* sought the help and protection of *patrons*, men of wealth and influence. A senator might have dozens or even hundreds of clients, whom he provided legal advice and representation, physical protection, and monetary loans in tough times. In turn, the client followed his patron out to battle, supported him in the political arena, worked on his land, and even contributed to his daughter's dowry. Throngs of clients awaited their patrons in the morning and accompanied them to the Forum for the day's business. Especially large retinues brought great prestige. Middle-class clients of the aristocracy might be patrons to poorer men. Rome thus accepted and institutionalized inequality and made of it a system of mutual benefits and obligations.

Roman women played no public role and hence appear infrequently in sources. Nearly all information pertains to those in the upper classes. In early Rome, a woman never ceased to be a child in the eyes of the law. She started out under the absolute authority of her paterfamilias. When she married, she came under the jurisdiction of the paterfamilias of her husband's family. Unable to own property or represent herself in legal proceedings, she had to depend on a male guardian to advocate her interests.

Despite the limitations, Roman women seem less constrained than their Greek counterparts (see Chapter 4). Over time, they gained greater personal protection and economic freedom. Some took advantage of a form of marriage that left a woman under the jurisdiction of her father and independent after his death. Many stories involve strong women who greatly influenced their husbands or sons and thereby helped shape Roman history. Roman poets expressed love for women who appeared educated and outspoken, and the careers of the early emperors abound with tales of self-assured and assertive queen-mothers and consorts.

Like other Italian peoples, Romans believed in invisible, shapeless forces known as *numina*. Vesta, the living, pulsating energy of fire, dwelled in the hearth. Janus guarded the door. The Penates watched over food stored in the cupboard. Other deities resided in hills, caves, grottoes, and springs. Small offerings of cakes and liquids supplicated the favor of these spirits. Certain gods operated in larger spheres—for example, Jupiter, the god of the sky, and Mars, initially a god of agriculture as well as war.

The Romans strove to maintain the *pax deorum* ("peace of the gods"), a covenant between the gods and the Roman state. Boards of priests drawn from the aristocracy performed sacrifices and other rituals to win the gods' favor. In return, the Roman state counted on the gods for success in its undertakings. When the Romans encountered the Greeks of southern Italy (see Chapter 4), they equated their major deities with gods from the Greek pantheon, such as Zeus (Jupiter) and Ares (Mars), and took over the myths attached to them.

Expansion in Italy and the Mediterranean

The fledgling Roman Republic of 500 B.C.E. did not stand out among the city-states of Latium, a region of central Italy. Three and a half centuries later, Rome commanded a huge empire encompassing virtually all the Mediterranean lands. Expansion began slowly but picked up momentum, peaking in the third and second centuries B.C.E.

Some scholars ascribe Rome's success to the greed and aggressiveness of a people fond of war. Others observe that the structure of the Roman state encouraged recourse to war, because the two consuls had only one year in office in which to gain military glory. The Romans invariably claimed they were only defending themselves. Possibly fear drove the Romans to expand their territory in order to provide a buffer against attack: each new conquest became vulnerable, and a sense of insecurity led to further expansion.

Ongoing friction between the pastoral hill peoples of the Apennines, who depended on herding, and the farmers of the coastal plains sparked Rome's conquest of Italy. In the fifth century B.C.E., Rome achieved leadership within a league of central Italian cities organized for defense against the hill peoples. In the fourth century B.C.E., the Romans occasionally defended the wealthy and sophisticated cities of Campania, the region on the Bay of Naples possessing the richest farmland in the peninsula. By 290 B.C.E., after three wars with the peoples of Samnium in central Italy, the

Romans had extended their "protection" over nearly the entire peninsula.

The Romans consolidated their hold over Italy by granting the political, legal, and economic privileges of citizenship to conquered populations. In this, they contrasted with the Greeks, who did not share citizenship with outsiders (see Chapter 4). The Romans co-opted the most influential elements within the conquered communities and made Rome's interests their interests. Rome demanded that its Italian subjects provide soldiers. A seemingly inexhaustible reservoir of manpower bolstered military success. Rome could endure higher casualties than the enemy and prevail by sheer numbers.

Between 264 and 202 B.C.E., Rome fought two protracted wars against the Carthaginians, those energetic descendants of the Phoenicians who had settled in Tunisia and dominated the commerce of the western Mediterranean (see Chapter 3). The Roman state emerged as the master of the western Mediterranean and acquired its first overseas provinces in Sicily, Sardinia, and Spain (see Map 5.1). Between 200 and 146 B.C.E., a series of wars pitted the Roman state against the major Hellenistic kingdoms in the eastern Mediterranean (see Chapter 4). Reluctant to occupy such distant territories, the Romans withdrew their troops at the conclusion of several wars. But when the settlements they imposed failed to take root, a frustrated Roman government took over direct administration of these turbulent lands. The conquest of the Celtic peoples of Gaul (modern France; see Chapter 3) by Rome's most brilliant general, Gaius Julius Caesar, between 59 and 51 B.C.E., led to the first territorial acquisitions in Europe's heartland.

The Romans resisted extending to distant provinces the governing system and privileges of citizenship they employed in Italy. Indigenous elite groups willing to collaborate with Rome enjoyed considerable autonomy, including responsibility for local administration and tax collection. Every year a senator, usually someone who had held high office, served as governor in each province. Accompanied by a surprisingly small retinue of friends and relations who served as advisers and deputies, the governor defended the province against outside attack and internal disruption, oversaw the collection of taxes, and judged legal cases.

Over time, this system proved inadequate. Officials chosen through political connections often lacked competence, and the one-year period of service gave them little time to gain experience. A few governors extorted huge sums of money from the provincial populace. Rome still depended on the institutions and attitudes of a city-state to govern an ever-growing empire.

The Failure of the Republic

The frequent wars and territorial expansion of the third and second centuries B.C.E. set off changes in the Italian landscape. Peasant farmers spent long periods of time away from home on military service, while most of the wealth generated by conquest and empire ended up helping the upper classes purchase Italian land. Investors easily acquired the property of absent soldier-farmers by purchase, deception, or intimidation. The small self-sufficient farms of the Italian countryside, whose peasant owners provided the backbone of the Roman legions (units of 6,000 soldiers), gave way to *latifundia*, literally "broad estates," or ranches.

The new owners had ample space to graze herds of cattle or grow grapes for wine in the place of less profitable wheat. Thus, much of Italy, especially in the cities, became dependent on expensive imported grain. Meanwhile, cheap slave labor provided by war prisoners made it hard for peasants who had lost their farms to find work in the countryside (see Society and Culture: Slavery in Rome and China). They moved to Rome and other cities, but found no work there either and ended up living in poverty. The growing urban masses, idle and prone to riot, would play a major role in the political struggles of the late Republic.

The decline of peasant farmers in Italy produced a shortage of men who owned the minimum amount of property required for military service. During a war that the Romans fought in North Africa at the end of the second century B.C.E., Gaius Marius—a "new man" as the Romans labeled politically active individuals from outside the traditional ruling class—achieved political prominence by enlisting in the legions poor, propertyless men to whom he promised farms upon retirement from military service. These grateful troops helped Mar-

Base and Lower Registers of Trajan's Column   The Roman emperor Trajan erected this soaring (125-foot, 38-meter) marble column in Rome in the early second century C.E. to commemorate his conquest of Dacia (modern Romania). The relief carving, which snakes around the column for 656 feet (200 meters), provides detailed pictures of the uniforms, weaponry, equipment, procedures, rituals, and conduct of the Roman army in the field.   (Scala/Art Resource, New York)

ius get elected to an unprecedented (and illegal) six consulships.

Between 88 and 31 B.C.E., several ambitious individuals—Sulla, Pompey, Julius Caesar, Mark Antony, and Octavian—commanded armies that were more loyal to them than to the state. Their use of Roman troops to increase their personal power led to civil wars between military factions. The generals who seized Rome on several occasions executed their political opponents and exercised dictatorial control.

Julius Caesar's grandnephew and heir, Octavian (63 B.C.E.–14 C.E.), eliminated all rivals by 31

B.C.E. and set about refashioning the Roman system of government while retaining the offices, honors, and social prerogatives of the senatorial class. A dictator in fact, he never called himself king or emperor, claiming merely to be *princeps*, "first among equals," hence the term **Roman Principate** for the period following the Roman Republic. ***Augustus,*** a title Octavian received from the Senate, implied prosperity and piety and became the name by which he is known to posterity. Augustus's ruthlessness, patience, and intuitive grasp of psychology enabled him to manipulate each group in society. When he died in 14 C.E., after forty-five years of carefully veiled rule, scarcely anyone could remember the Republic. During his reign, the empire expanded into Egypt and parts of the Middle East and Central Europe, leaving only the southern half of Britain and modern Romania to be added later.

So popular was Augustus that four members of his family succeeded to the position of "emperor" (as we call it) despite serious personal and political shortcomings. After the mid–first century C.E., other families obtained the post. In theory, the Senate affirmed the early emperors; in reality, the armies chose them. By the second century C.E., the so-called Good Emperors instituted a new mechanism of succession: each designated as his successor a mature man of proven ability whom he adopted as his son and with whom he shared offices and privileges.

Augustus had allied himself with the ***equites,*** the class of well-to-do Italian merchants and landowners second in wealth and social status only to the senatorial class. These competent and self-assured individuals became the core of a new civil service. At last Rome had an administrative bureaucracy capable of managing a large empire with considerable honesty, consistency, and efficiency.

An Urban Empire

Calling the Roman Empire of the first three centuries C.E. an "urban" empire does not mean that most people lived in cities and towns. Perhaps 80 percent of the empire's 50 to 60 million people lived in agricultural villages or on isolated farms. The network of towns and cities served as administrative centers,

SOCIETY & CULTURE

Slavery in Rome and China

Although slaves existed in most ancient societies, slave labor became the indispensable foundation of the Roman economy. The frequent wars of the second century B.C.E. caused large numbers of prisoners to become slaves. Such slaves were sold cheaply, and landowners and manufacturers could work them longer and harder than hired laborers. Such harshness periodically resulted in slave revolts.

The following excerpt, from a manual on agriculture, gives advice about controlling and exploiting slaves:

When the head of a household arrives at his estate, after he has prayed to the family god, he must go round his farm on a tour of inspection on the very same day, if that is possible.

... On the next day after that he must call in his manager. ... If the work doesn't seem to him to be sufficient, and the manager starts to say how hard he tried, but the slaves weren't any good, and the weather was awful, and the slaves ran away, and he was required to carry out some public works, then when he has finished mentioning these and all sorts of other excuses, you must draw his attention to your calculation of the labor employed and time taken. ... There are all sorts of jobs that can be done in rainy weather—washing wine-jars, coating them with pitch, cleaning the house, storing grain, shifting muck, digging a manure pit, cleaning seed, mending ropes or making new ones. ... The head of the household ... should sell any old oxen, cattle or sheep that are not up to standard, wool and hides, an old cart or old tools, an old slave, a sick slave—anything else that is surplus to requirements. (Cato the Elder, *Concerning Agriculture*, bk. 2, second century B.C.E.)

Cato, a noted defender of traditional Roman ways and author of the excerpt, equated slaves as property with animals and tools. His calculations of productivity ignored the slaves' feelings. Cato's famously stern manner and hard-edged traditionalism reflect a point of view that Roman society found acceptable. In reality, Roman masters treated slaves in varying ways. Cato also indicates passive-resistant tactics by slaves: feigning ignorance and stupidity, claiming illness, and running away.

Slavery counted for less in ancient China. During the Warring States Period, dependent peasants and slaves both worked the estates of the landowning aristocracy. The Qin government sought to abolish slavery, but it persisted into the Han period. Nevertheless, it involved only a small fraction of the population and played little role in the economy. The relatives of

however, with corresponding benefits for the urban populace.

Numerous towns had several thousand inhabitants. A handful of major cities—Alexandria in Egypt, Antioch in Syria, and Carthage—had populations of several hundred thousand. Rome itself had approximately a million residents. The largest cities put huge strains on the government's technical ability to provide food and water and remove sewage.

At Rome, the upper classes lived in elegant hillside townhouses. The house centered around an *atrium*, a rectangular courtyard with an open skylight in the ceiling to let in light and rainwater for drinking and washing. A dining room for dinner and drinking parties, an interior garden, a kitchen, and perhaps a private bath surrounded the atrium with bedrooms on an upper level. Pebble mosaics decorated the floors and frescoes of mythological scenes or outdoor vistas on the walls and ceilings,

criminals could be seized and enslaved, and poor families sometimes sold unwanted children into slavery. Slaves generally performed domestic tasks, whether they belonged to the state or to individuals.

Wang Ziyuan of Shu Commandery went to the Jian River on business, and went up to the home of the widow Yang Hui, who had a male slave named Bianliao. Wang Ziyuan requested him to go and buy some wine. Picking up a big stick, Bianliao climbed to the top of the grave mound and said: "When my master bought me, Bianliao, he only contracted for me to care for the grave and did not contract for me to buy wine for some other gentleman."

Wang Ziyuan was furious and said to the widow: "Wouldn't you prefer to sell this slave?" . . . Wang Ziyuan immediately settled on the sale contract. . . .

The slave again said: "Enter in the contract everything you wish to order me to do. I, Bianliao, will not do anything not in the contract."

Wang Ziyuan said: "Agreed."

The text of the contract said: ". . . The slave shall obey orders about all kinds of work and may not argue. He shall rise at dawn and do an early sweeping. After eating he shall wash up. Ordinarily he should pound the grain mortar, tie up broom straws, carve bowls and bore wells, scoop out ditches, tie up fallen fences, hoe the garden, trim up paths and dike up plots of land, cut big flails, bend bamboos to make rakes, and scrape and fix the well pulley . . . [the list of tasks continues for two-and-a-half pages]. . . ."

The reading of the text of the contract came to an end. The slave was speechless and his lips were tied. Wildly he beat his head on the ground, and beat himself with his hands. He said: "If it is to be exactly as master Wang says, I would rather return soon along the yellow-soil road, with the grave worms boring through my head. Had I known before I would have bought the wine for master Wang." (Wang Bao, first century B.C.E.)

This story shows that Chinese slaves could be forced to work hard and engaged in many of the same menial tasks as their Roman counterparts. However, it is hard to imagine a Roman slave daring to refuse a request and argue publicly with a nobleman. It also appears that slaves in China had some legal protections provided by contracts specifying and limiting what could be demanded of them.

Why might slavery have been less important in Han China than in the Roman Empire? Why would the treatment of slaves have been less harsh in China than in Rome?

Source: Thomas Wiedemann, *Greek and Roman Slavery* (Baltimore: Johns Hopkins University Press, 1981), 139–141, 183–184; C. Martin Wilbur, *Slavery in China During the Former Han Dynasty, 206 B.C.–A.D. 25* (Chicago: Field Museum of Natural History, 1943), 383, 388.

giving a sense of openness in the absence of windows. The typical aristocrat also owned a number of villas in the countryside as retreats from the pressures of city life.

The poor inhabited crowded slums in the low-lying parts of the city. Damp, dark, and smelly, with few furnishings, their wooden tenements suffered from frequent fires. Fortunately, Romans could spend the day outdoors for much of the year.

Other cities and towns, including the ramshackle settlements that sprang up beside frontier forts, mirrored the capital city in political organization, physical layout, and appearance. A town council and two annually elected officials drawn from prosperous members of the community maintained law and order and collected both urban and rural taxes. In return for the privilege of running local affairs and in appreciation of the state's protection of their wealth and position, this "municipal aristocracy" served Rome loyally. In

Sign for a Roman Shop   The woman behind the counter is selling fruit to one customer while two men are taking game hanging from a rack. The snail and two monkeys to the right may represent the name of the establishment. Towns served as markets where farmers exchanged their surplus products for crafted goods. Local commerce in agricultural products must have played a major economic role, but it has left few archaeological traces.   (Archivo Fotografico della Soprintendenza Archeologica di Ostia)

striving to imitate Roman senators, they lavishly endowed their cities and towns, which had little revenue of their own, with attractive elements of Roman urban life: a forum, government buildings, temples, gardens, baths, theaters, amphitheaters, and games and public entertainments of all sorts. These amenities made the situation of the urban poor superior to that of the rural poor. Poor people in a city could pass time at the baths, seek refuge from the elements under the colonnades, and attend the games.

Hard work and drudgery marked life in the countryside, relieved only by occasional festive days and the everyday pleasures of sex, family, and social exchange. Rural people had to fend for themselves in dealing with bandits, wild animals, and other hazards. People outside urban centers had little direct contact with the government beyond an occasional run-in with bullying soldiers and the dreaded arrival of the tax collector.

The concentration of ownership reversed temporarily during the civil wars that ended the Republic; it resumed under the emperors. But the end of new conquests reduced the number of slaves and forced landowners to find new labor. Landlords turned to tenant farmers, whom they allowed to live on and cultivate plots of land in return for a portion of their crop. The landowners themselves still lived in cities and hired foremen to manage their estates. Thus, wealth based on rural productivity became concentrated in the cities.

Some urban dwellers became rich from manufacture and trade. The ***pax romana*** ("Roman peace"), the safety and stability guaranteed by Roman might, favored commerce. Grain, meat, and vegetables usually could be exchanged only locally because transportation was costly and many products spoiled quickly. The city of Rome, however, depended on grain shipments from Sicily and Egypt to feed its huge population. Special naval squadrons performed this task.

Some exporters dealt in glass, metalwork, delicate pottery, and other fine manufactures. The centers of production, first located in Italy, moved into the provinces as knowledge of the necessary skills spread. Roman armies on the frontiers provided a large market, and their presence promoted the prosperity of border provinces. Other merchants traded in luxury items from beyond the empire's boundaries, especially Chinese silks, Indian spices, and Arabian incense. The tax revenues of rich provinces like Gaul (France) and Egypt flowed to Rome to support the emperor and the central government, and to the frontier provinces to subsidize the armies.

Romanization, the spread of the Latin language and Roman way of life, proved an enduring consequence of empire among the diverse peoples in the western provinces. Hellenism dominated the eastern Mediterranean (see Chapter 4). Portuguese, Spanish, French, Italian, and Romanian evolved from the Latin language, proving that the language of the conquerors spread among the common people as well as the elite.

The Roman government did not force Romanization. The inhabitants of the provinces themselves chose Latin and adopted cultural practices like wearing the *toga* (the traditional cloak worn by Roman male citizens). Making this choice brought advantages, as do learning English and wearing a suit and tie today in some developing nations. Latin facilitated dealings with the administration and helped merchants get contracts to supply the military. Many also must have been drawn by the aura of success surrounding the language and culture of a people who had created so vast an empire.

As towns sprang up and acquired the Roman urban amenities, they attracted ambitious members of the indigenous populations. The empire gradually and reluctantly extended Roman citizenship, with its attendant privileges, legal protections, and certain tax exemptions, to people living outside Italy. Completing a twenty-six-year term of service in the native military units that backed up the Roman legions earned soldiers citizenship that could pass to their descendants. Emperors granted citizenship to individuals or entire communities as rewards for service. Then in 212 C.E., the emperor Caracalla granted citizenship to all free, adult, male inhabitants of the empire.

The gradual extension of citizenship mirrored the empire's transformation from an Italian dominion over the Mediterranean lands into a commonwealth of peoples. As early as the first century C.E., some of the leading literary and intellectual figures came from the provinces. By the second century, even the emperors hailed from Spain, Gaul, and North Africa.

The Rise of Christianity

The Jewish homeland of Judaea (see Chapter 3), roughly equivalent to present-day Israel, came under direct Roman rule in 6 C.E. Over the next half-century, Roman governors insensitive to the Jewish belief in one god managed to increase tensions. Various kinds of opposition to Roman rule sprang up. Many Jews anticipated the arrival of the Messiah, the "Anointed One," presumed to be a military leader who would liberate the Jewish people and drive the Romans out.

It is in this context that we must see the career of **Jesus,** a young carpenter from the Galilee region in northern Israel. In place of what he considered excessive concern with money and power among Jewish leaders and perfunctory religious observance by mainstream Jews, Jesus prescribed a return to the personal faith and spirituality of an earlier age. He eventually attracted the attention of the Jewish authorities in Jerusalem, who regarded popular reformers as potential troublemakers. They turned him over to the Roman governor, Pontius Pilate. Jesus was imprisoned, condemned, and executed by crucifixion, a punishment usually reserved for common criminals. His followers, the Apostles, subsequently sought to spread his teachings and their belief that he had been resurrected (returned from death to life) among their fellow Jews.

Paul, a Jew from the Greek city of Tarsus in southern Anatolia, converted to the new creed and between 45 and 58 C.E. devoted himself to spreading the word. Traveling throughout Syria-Palestine, Anatolia, and Greece, he found most Jews unwilling to accept his claim that Jesus was the Messiah and had ushered in a new age. Frustrated, Paul redirected his efforts toward non-Jews (sometimes called "gentiles") who were also experiencing a spiritual hunger. He set up a string of Christian (from the Greek term *christos*, meaning "anointed one," given to Jesus by his followers) communities in the eastern Mediterranean.

Paul's career exemplifies the cosmopolitan nature of the Roman Empire in this era. Speaking both Greek and Aramaic, he moved comfortably between the Greco-Roman and Jewish worlds. He used Roman roads, depended on the peace guaranteed by Roman arms, called on his Roman citizenship to protect him from local authorities, and moved from city to city in his quest for converts.

In 66 C.E., tensions in Roman Judaea erupted in a revolt that lasted until 73. The Jerusalem-based Christian community, which focused on converting Jews, fell victim to the Roman reconquest. This cleared the field for Paul's non-Jewish converts, and Christianity began to diverge more and more from its Jewish roots.

The sect grew slowly but steadily. Many early converts came from disenfranchised groups: women, slaves, and the urban poor. They hoped to receive a respect not accorded them in the larger society and to obtain positions of responsibility when the early Christian communities elected their leaders. However, as the religious movement grew and prospered, it developed a hierarchy of priests and bishops and engaged in bitter disputes over theological doctrine (see Chapter 8).

As monotheists forbidden to worship other gods, early Christians met persecution from Roman officials who took their refusal to worship the emperor as a sign of disloyalty. Nevertheless, despite mob attacks and occasional government attempts at suppression, or perhaps because of them, the Christian movement continued to attract converts. By the late third century C.E., adherents to Christianity were a sizable minority within the empire and included many educated and prosperous people holding local and imperial posts.

By the Greek Classical period, a number of "mystery" cults had gained popularity by claiming to provide secret information about the nature of life and death and promising a blessed afterlife to their adherents. In the Hellenistic and Roman periods, belief systems making similar promises arose in the eastern Mediterranean and spread throughout the Greco-Roman lands, presumably responding to a spiritual and intellectual hunger not satisfied by paganism. These included the cults of the mother-goddess Cybele in Anatolia, the Egyptian goddess Isis, and the Iranian sun-god Mithra. We shall see how the ultimate victory of Christianity over these rivals arose from historical circumstances as much as from spiritual appeal.

Technology and Transformation

The ease and safety of travel brought by Roman arms and engineering helped the early Christians spread their faith. Surviving remnants of roads, fortification walls, aqueducts, and buildings testify to the Romans' engineering expertise. Some of the best engineers served with the army, building bridges, siege works, and siege weapons. In peacetime, soldiers often worked on construction projects. **Aqueducts**—long elevated or underground conduits—used gravity to carry water from a source to an urban center. The Romans pioneered the use of arches, which allow the even distribution of great weights without thick supporting walls. The invention of concrete—a mixture of lime powder, sand, and water that could be poured into molds—enabled the construction of vast vaulted and domed interior spaces, in contrast to the rectilinear post-and-lintel designs employed by the Greeks and Egyptians.

Defending borders that stretched for thousands of miles posed a great administrative challenge. In a document released after his death, Augustus advised against expanding the empire because the costs of administration and defense would exceed any increase in revenues. His successors' reorganization and redeployment of the Roman army reflect the shift from an offensive to a defensive strategy. Mountains, deserts, and seas protected the empire at most points. But the lengthy Rhine/Danube frontier in Germany and Central Europe was vulnerable and thus guarded by forts with relatively small garrisons intended to repel raiders. On more desolate frontiers in Britain and North Africa, the Romans built long walls to keep out the peoples who lived beyond.

Most of Rome's neighbors lacked sufficient technology and military organization to pose a serious threat. The one exception lay on the eastern frontier, where the Parthian kingdom controlled the lands that are today Iran and Iraq. Rome and Parthia fought exhaustingly for centuries, with neither side gaining significant territory.

The Roman state prospered for two and a half centuries after Augustus stabilized the political situation and instituted a program of reforms. In the third century C.E., cracks in the edifice became visible. Historians call the period from 235 to 284 C.E.

the **third-century crisis,** a time when political, military, and economic problems nearly destroyed the empire. A frequent change of rulers marked the crisis. Twenty or more men claimed the office of emperor during this period. Most reigned for only a few months or years before being overthrown by a rival or killed by their own troops. Germanic peoples on the Rhine/Danube frontier took advantage of the disorders to raid deep into the empire. For the first time in centuries, Roman cities built protective walls. Some regions, feeling a lack of imperial protection, turned to anyone who promised to put their interests first.

Political and military emergencies devastated the empire's economy. Buying the loyalty of the army and paying to defend the increasingly permeable frontiers drained the treasury. The resultant demands for more tax revenues from the provinces, as well as the interruption of commerce by fighting, eroded urban prosperity. Shortsighted emperors, desperate for cash, secretly reduced the amount of precious metal in Roman coins and pocketed the excess. But the public quickly caught on, and the devalued coinage became less and less acceptable in the marketplace. Indeed, the empire reverted to a barter economy, which curtailed large-scale and long-distance commerce even more.

The municipal aristocracy, once the empire's most vital and public-spirited class, suffered heavily. As town councilors, its members had to make up any shortfall in taxes owed to the state. As the decline in trade eroded their wealth, which often derived from manufacture and commerce, many evaded their civic duties and even went into hiding.

Population shifted out of the cities and into the countryside. Many people sought employment and protection from raiders *and* government officials on the estates of wealthy and powerful country landowners. This process lay the foundation for the social and economic structures of the European Middle Ages—a period of roughly seven hundred years in which wealthy rural lords dominated a peasant population tied to the land (see Chapter 8).

Just when things looked bleakest, one man pulled the empire back from the brink. Diocletian, like several other emperors, hailed from one of the eastern European provinces most vulnerable to invasion. A commoner by birth, he rose through the ranks of the army and gained power in 284. He was

so successful that he ruled for over twenty years and died in bed.

To halt inflation (the process by which prices rise as money becomes worth less), Diocletian issued an edict specifying the maximum prices for various commodities and services. To ensure an adequate labor supply in vital services, he froze people in their professions and made them train their sons to succeed them. This unprecedented regulation of prices and vocations had unforeseen consequences. A "black market" arose among buyers and sellers who chose to ignore the price controls. More broadly, many imperial citizens began to see the government as an oppressive entity that no longer deserved their loyalty.

When Diocletian resigned in 305, the old divisiveness reemerged as various claimants battled for the throne. By 324, a general named **Constantine** (r. 306–337) had reunited the empire under his sole rule. In 312, Constantine won a key battle at the Milvian Bridge over the Tiber River near Rome. He later claimed that before this battle, he had seen in the sky a cross (the sign of the Christian God) superimposed on the sun. Believing that the Christian God had helped him achieve the victory, Constantine converted to Christianity. Throughout his reign, he supported the Christian church, although he tolerated other beliefs as well. Historians disagree about whether Constantine's conversion resulted from spiritual motives or from a pragmatic desire to unify the empire under a single religion. Regardless of the reason, large numbers of people now converted, because they saw that Christians had advantages over non-Christians in seeking offices and favors.

Constantine also transferred the capital in 324 from Rome to Byzantium, an ancient Greek city on the Bosporus° strait leading from the Mediterranean into the Black Sea. Renamed Constantinople° ("City of Constantine"), it represented a concentration of attention on the threatened imperial borders in eastern Europe (see Map 5.1). The cities and middle classes of the eastern provinces had better withstood the third-century crisis than those in the west. In addition, more educated

---

Bosporus (BAHS-puhr-uhs)
Constantinople (cahn-stan-tih-NO-pul)

people and more Christians lived in the east (see Chapter 8).

Some see the conversion of Constantine and the transfer of the imperial capital as events marking the end of Roman history. But many of the important changes that culminated during Constantine's reign had their roots in the previous two centuries, and the Roman Empire as a whole survived for at least another century. Moreover, the eastern, or Byzantine, portion of it (discussed in Chapter 8) survived Constantine by more than a thousand years. Nevertheless, the Roman Empire of the fourth century differed fundamentally from what had existed before, a fact that justifies seeing Constantine's reign as the beginning of a new epoch in the West.

THE ORIGINS OF IMPERIAL CHINA, 221 B.C.E.–220 C.E.

A fragmentation seemingly dictated by geography characterized the early history of China (see Chapter 2). The Shang (ca. 1750–1027 B.C.E.) and Zhou (1027–221 B.C.E.) wielded authority over a relatively compact zone in northeastern China. The last few centuries of nominal Zhou rule—the Warring States Period—saw rivalry among a group of small states, a situation reminiscent of the contemporary Greek city-states (see Chapter 4). As in Greece, competition and conflict fostered many elements of a national culture.

In the second half of the third century B.C.E. the Qin° state in the Wei° Valley conquered its rivals and created China's first empire (221–206 B.C.E.). But it barely survived the death of its founder, Shi Huangdi. Power passed to a new dynasty, the Han, which ruled China from 206 B.C.E. to 220 C.E. (see Map 5.2). The imperial tradition of political and cultural unity thus begun lasted into the twentieth century and still has meaning for China today.

Resources and Population

An imperial state controlling lands of great diversity in topography, climate, plant and animal life, and human population faced greater obstacles to long-distance communications and a uniform way of life than did the Roman Empire. Rome's territories were roughly similar in climate and agriculture, and Rome benefited from an internal sea—the Mediterranean—that facilitated rapid and inexpensive transport. What resources, technologies, institutions, and values made the Chinese empire possible?

Agriculture produced the wealth and taxes that supported the institutions of imperial China. The main tax, a percentage of the annual harvest, funded government activities ranging from the luxurious lifestyle of the royal court to the military garrisons on the frontiers. The imperial capitals, first Chang'an° and later Luoyang°, housed large populations that had to be fed. As intensive agriculture spread in the Yangzi River Valley, the need to transport southern crops to the north spurred the construction of canals to connect the Yangzi with the Yellow River. The government also stored surplus grain during prosperous times for sale at reasonable prices during shortages.

To assess its labor resources, the government periodically conducted a census. Results survive for the years 2 C.E. and 140 C.E. The earlier survey indicates approximately 12 million households and 60 million people; the later, not quite 10 million households and 49 million people. Then as now, the vast majority of the population lived in the eastern river valley regions that supported intensive agriculture. The early demographic center in the Yellow River Valley and North China Plain had begun to shift south to the Yangzi River Valley by early Han times.

In the intervals between seasonal agricultural tasks, able-bodied men donated one month of labor to public building projects—palaces, temples, fortifications, and roads—or to transporting goods, excavating and maintaining canals, cultivating imperial estates, or mining. The state also required two years of military service. On the frontiers, con-

---

Qin (chin)   **Wei** (way)

Chang'an (chahng-ahn)
Luoyang (LWOE-yahng)

Terracotta Soldiers from the Tomb of Shi Huangdi, "First Emperor" of China   Thousands of these life-size, baked-clay figures, each with distinctive features, have been unearthed. This buried model army reflects the power and totalitarian rule of the Qin Empire.   (© 1995 Dennis Cox / ChinaStock)

scripted young Chinese men built walls and forts, kept an eye on barbarian neighbors, fought when necessary, and grew crops to support themselves. Registers of land and households enabled imperial officials to keep track of money and services due. Like the Romans, the Chinese governments depended on a large population of free peasants to contribute taxes and services to the state.

Throughout the Han period, the Han Chinese gradually expanded into the territory of other ethnic groups. Population growth in the core regions and a shortage of good land spurred the pioneers onward. Sometimes the government organized new settlements—at militarily strategic sites, for example, and on the frontiers. Neighboring kingdoms also invited Chinese settlers so they could exploit their skills and learn their technologies.

Han people preferred regions suitable to the agriculture they had practiced in the eastern river valleys. On the northern frontier, they pushed back nomadic populations. They also expanded into the tropical forests of southern China and settled in the western oasis. Places not suitable for their preferred kind of agriculture, particularly the steppe and deserts, did not attract them.

Hierarchy, Obedience, and Belief

The Han Chinese brought with them their social organization, values, language, and other cultural practices. The Chinese family, the basic social unit, included not only the living generations but also the previous generations—

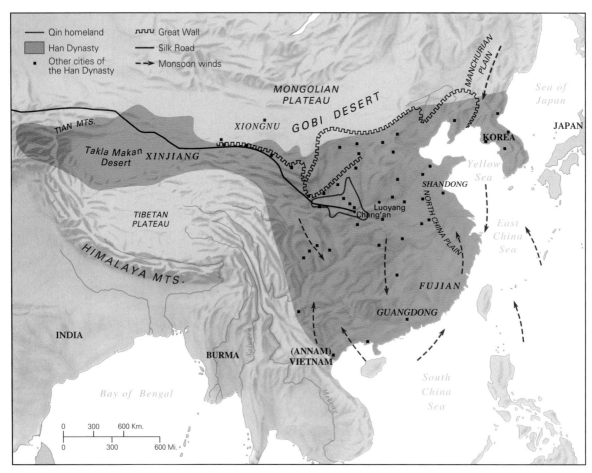

Map 5.2   Han China   The Qin and Han rulers of northeast China extended their control over all of eastern China and extensive territories to the west. Walls in the north and northwest, built to check nomadic raiders, eventually joined to form the precursor of today's Great Wall. The Silk Road carried China's main export to Central and Western Asia and the Mediterranean lands.

the ancestors. The Chinese believed their ancestors maintained an ongoing interest in the fortunes of the family and therefore consulted, appeased, and venerated their ancestors to maintain their favor. Viewed as a living, self-renewing organism, the family required sons to perpetuate itself and ensure the immortality offered by the ancestor cult.

The doctrine of Confucius (Kongzi), which had its origins in the sixth century B.C.E. (see Chapter 2), became a fundamental source of values in the imperial period. Confucianism considered hierarchy a natural social phenomenon and assigned tasks and rules of conduct to each person. Absolute au-

thority rested with the father, who presided over the rituals that linked living family members to the ancestors. People saw themselves as having responsibilities within the domestic hierarchy according to gender, age, and family relationship rather than as individual agents. The same concepts operated in society as a whole. Peasants, soldiers, administrators, and rulers all contributed distinctively to the welfare of society. Confucianism optimistically maintained that education, imitation of role models, and self-improvement could guide people to the right path. Because the state mirrored the family, the basic family values of loy-

Tax Collection in the Han Empire This stamped brick, found in a tomb in western China, depicts, at center, a stooped peasant pouring grain into a basket. The tax collector, seated and wearing fine clothing, clutches bamboo slips on which he keeps his records. A number of pictorial elements—positioning in the composition, posture, clothing, and vehicles—contrast the wealth, comfort, and superior social status of the government official with the poverty, toil, and low status of the peasant. (Chinese Cultural Center of San Francisco)

alty, obedience to authority, respect for elders and ancestors, and concern for honor and appropriate conduct carried over into relations between individuals and the state.

Contemporary written sources say little about the experiences of women. Confucian ethics stressed the impropriety of women participating in public life. Traditional wisdom about the appropriate female conduct appears in a story of the mother of the Confucian philosopher Mencius (Mengzi):

> A woman's duties are to cook the five grains, heat the wine, look after her parents-in-law, make clothes, and that is all! . . . [She] has no ambition to manage affairs outside the house. . . . She must follow the "three submissions." When she is young, she must submit to her parents. After her marriage, she must submit to her husband. When she is widowed, she must submit to her son.[1]

This ideal, perpetuated by males of the upper classes who composed most of the surviving texts, placed women under considerable pressure to conform. Women of the lower classes, less affected by Confucian ways of thinking, may have been less constrained than their more "privileged" counterparts.

After her parents arranged her marriage, a young bride went to live with her husband's family, who saw her as a stranger until she proved herself. Ability and force of personality (as well as the capacity to produce sons) could make a difference, but dissension between the wife and her mother-in-law and sisters-in-law grew out of their competition for influence with husbands, sons, and brothers and for a larger share of the economic resources held in common by the family.

Like the early Romans, the Chinese believed that divinity resided within nature rather than outside and above it. They worshiped and tried to appease the forces of nature. The state maintained shrines to the lords of rain and winds, as well as to certain great rivers and high mountains. Gathering at mounds or altars dedicated to local earth spirits, people sacrificed sheep and pigs and beat drums to promote fertility. Unusual natural phenomena like eclipses or heavy rains prompted them to tie a red cord around the sacred spot, symbolically restraining the deity. A belief that supernatural forces, bringing good and evil fortune, flowed through the landscape led experts in *feng shui*, "earth divination," to determine the most favorable location and orientation for buildings and graves. The faithful adapted their lives to the complex rhythms of nature.

Some people sought to cheat death by taking life-enhancing drugs or building ostentatious tombs, flanked by towers or covered by mounds of earth, and filling them with what they believed they would need for a blessed afterlife. The objects in these tombs provide a wealth of knowledge about Han society.

The First Chinese Empire

In the second half of the third century B.C.E., the state of the **Qin** suddenly burst forth and took over the other "warring states" one by one. By 221 B.C.E., the first emperor had united the northern plain and the Yangzi River Valley under one rule, marking the creation of China and the inauguration of the imperial age. The name "China" may derive from "Qin."

The Qin ruler, entitled **Shi Huangdi** ("First Emperor"), and his adviser Li Si were able and ruthless men who exploited the exhaustion resulting from centuries of interstate rivalry. The Qin homeland in the valley of the Wei, a tributary of the Yellow River, provided a large pool of sturdy peasants to serve in the army but was less urbanized and commercialized than the kingdoms farther east. Mobilizing manpower for irrigation and flood-control works had strengthened the authority of the Qin king at the expense of the nobles and taught his administrators organizational skills.

Shi Huangdi and Li Si created a totalitarian structure that subordinated the individual to the needs of the state. They cracked down on Confucianism, regarding its demands for benevolent and nonviolent conduct from rulers as a check on the absolute power they sought. They favored instead a philosophy known as Legalism (see Chapter 2). Its major proponent, Li Si himself, considered the will of the ruler supreme. Discipline and obedience maintained through the rigid application of rewards and punishments defined the lives of his subjects.

The new regime sought to eliminate the land-owning aristocracy of the conquered states and the system supporting their wealth and power. It abolished primogeniture—the eldest son's inheritance of a family's lands—because it allowed a few individuals to accumulate vast estates. Estates had to be broken up and passed on to several heirs.

Slaves (see Society and Culture: Slavery in Rome and China) and peasant serfs, who owed the landlord a substantial portion of their harvest, worked the lands of the aristocracy. The Qin abolished slavery and established a free peasantry who owed taxes and labor, as well as military service, to the state.

During the Warring States Period, the small states had emphasized their independence through differing symbolic practices. For example, each state had its own forms of music, with different scales, systems of notation, and instruments. The Qin imposed standard weights, measures, and coinage, a uniform law code, a common system of writing, and even regulations governing the axle length of carts so as to standardize road and street widths.

Thousands of miles of roads, comparable in scale to the roads of the Roman Empire, connected the parts of the empire and helped move Qin armies quickly. The Qin also built canals to connect the northern and southern river systems. The 20-mile-long (32.2-kilometer-long) Magic Canal, which ingeniously linked two rivers that flowed in opposite directions with strong currents, is still in use. The frontier walls of the old states were gradually combined into a continuous barricade, the precursor of the Great Wall (see Chapter 10), to protect cultivated lands from raids by northern nomads. Shi Huangdi's financial exploitation and demands for forced labor led, after his death in 210 B.C.E., to rebellions that ended the dynasty.

The Long Reign of the Han

When the dust cleared, Liu Bang, possibly a peasant by background, had outlasted his rivals and established a new dynasty, the **Han** (206 B.C.E.–220 C.E.). Rejecting the excesses and mistakes of the Qin, he restored the institutions of a venerable past. Yet the Han administration retained much of the structure and Legalist ideology put in place by the Qin, though with less fanatical zeal. A form of Confucianism revised to address the circumstances of a large, centralized political entity tempered the Legalist methods. This Confucianism emphasized the benevolence of government and the appropriateness of particular rituals and behaviors in a manifestly hierarchical society. The Han administration became the standard for later ages, and the Chinese people today refer to themselves ethnically as Han.

After eighty years of imperial consolidation, Emperor Wu (r. 140–87 B.C.E.) launched a period of military expansion, south into Fujian, Guangdong, and present-day north Vietnam and north into Manchuria and present-day North Korea. Han armies went west, to inner Mongolia and Xinjiang°, to secure the lucrative Silk Road (see Chapter 6). However, controlling the newly acquired territories proved expensive, so Wu's successors curtailed further expansion.

The Han Empire endured, with a brief interruption between 9 and 23 C.E., for more than four hundred years. **Chang'an,** in the Wei Valley, an ancient seat of power from which the Zhou and Qin dynasties had emerged, served as the capital from 202 B.C.E. to 8 C.E.—the period of the Early, or Western, Han. From 23 to 220 C.E., the Later, or Eastern, Han established its base in the more centrally located Luoyang.

A wall of pounded earth and brick 15 miles (24 kilometers) in circumference surrounded Chang'an, which had a population of 246,000 in 2 C.E. Contemporaries described it as a bustling place, filled with courtiers, officials, soldiers, merchants, craftsmen, and foreign visitors. Broad thoroughfares running north and south intersected others running east and west. High walls protected and restricted access to the imperial palaces, administrative offices, barracks, and storehouses. Temples and marketplaces were scattered about the civic center. Chang'an became a model of urban planning, its main features being imitated throughout the Han Empire.

Living in multistory houses, wearing fine silks, and traveling about the capital in ornate horse-drawn carriages, well-to-do officials and merchants devoted their leisure time to art and literature, occult religious practices, elegant banquets, and various entertainments: music and dance, juggling and acrobatics, dog and horse races, cock and tiger fights. In contrast, the common people inhabited a sprawling warren of alleys, living in dwellings packed "as closely as the teeth of a comb," as one poet put it.

As in the Zhou monarchy (see Chapter 2), people thought the emperor, the "Son of Heaven," enjoyed the Mandate of Heaven. He stood at the center of government and society like a father wielding authority in a family and linking the living generations with the ancestors. He brought the support of powerful imperial ancestors and guaranteed the harmonious interaction of heaven and earth. More than his Roman counterpart, he was regarded as a divinity on earth. His word was law. Failure to govern well, however, could lose him the backing of Heaven. Given their belief that events in Heaven, the natural world, and human society corresponded, his subjects might regard floods, droughts, and earthquakes as both the consequences and symptoms of ethical failure and mismanagement. Successful revolutions thus proved to many that Heaven had withdrawn its support from an unworthy ruler.

Secluded within the palace compound, surrounded by his many wives and children, servants, courtiers, and officials, the emperor presided over an unceasing round of pomp and ritual emphasizing the worship of Heaven and imperial ancestors, as well as the practical business of government. When the emperor died, his chief widow chose his heir from the male members of the ruling clan, thus making the royal compound a hive of intrigue.

A prime minister, a civil service director, and nine ministers charged with military, economic, legal, and religious responsibilities ran the central government. As in imperial Rome, the Han depended on local officials for the day-to-day administration of the vast empire. Local people collected taxes and dispatched revenues to the central government, oversaw conscription for the army and labor projects, provided local protection, and settled disputes. The remote central government rarely impinged on the lives of most citizens, who normally contacted only local officials. Who, then, were the local officials?

The Han period saw the rise of a class that scholars call the **gentry.** To weaken the rural aristocrats, the Qin and Han emperors allied themselves with the class next in wealth below them. These moderately prosperous landowners, usually men with education and valued expertise, resemble the Roman equites favored by Augustus and his successors. The local officials who came from this class became a privileged and respected group within Chinese society and made the government more efficient and responsive.

Xinjiang (SHIN-jyahng)

The new gentry class, with imperial support, adopted a version of Confucianism that provided a system for training officials to be intellectually capable and morally worthy of their roles and set forth a code of conduct for measuring their performance. Chinese tradition speaks of an imperial university, located outside Chang'an and said to have 30,000 students, as well as provincial centers of learning. (Some scholars doubt that such a complex institution existed this early.)

From these centers, students entered government service, receiving distinctive emblems and privileges, including preferential legal treatment and exemption from military service, as they advanced in rank. In theory, young men from any class could rise in the state hierarchy. In practice, sons of the gentry had an advantage, because they received better training in the Confucian classics. Gradually, the gentry became a new aristocracy of sorts, banding together in cliques and family alliances that worked to advance the careers of group members.

Daoism, which originated in the Warring States Period (see Chapter 2), took deeper root among the common people in the Han period. With its emphasis on the *Dao*, or "path," of nature, its valuing of harmony with the cycles and patterns of the natural world, and its search for enlightenment through solitary contemplation and physical and mental discipline rather than education, Daoism called into question age-old beliefs and values and rejected the hierarchy, rules, and rituals of Confucianism. It urged passive acceptance of the disorder of the world, denial of ambition, contentment with simple pleasures, and trust in one's own instincts.

Technology and Trade

Chinese tradition seems to recognize the importance of technology for the success and spread of Chinese civilization. It credits the legendary first five emperors with the introduction of major new technologies.

The advent of bronze tools around 1500 B.C.E. helped open land for agriculture on the North China Plain. A millennium later, iron arrived. The Qin took full advantage of iron technology. Chinese metalworkers used more advanced techniques than those elsewhere in the hemisphere. Whereas Roman blacksmiths produced wrought-iron tools and weapons by hammering heated iron, the Chinese mastered the technique of liquefying iron and pouring it into molds. The resulting cast-iron and steel tools and weapons had a higher carbon content and were harder and more durable.

In the succeeding centuries, crossbows and cavalry helped the Chinese military to beat off the attacks of nomads. The watermill, which harnessed the power of running water to turn a grindstone, appeared in China long before it did in Europe. Horse collar and breast strap harnessing that did not constrict the animal's neck allowed horses in China to pull heavier loads than European horses could.

The Han rulers continued the Qin road-building program. Besides using the roads to move troops and supplies, the government created a network of official couriers using horses, boats, and even footpaths, and it provided food and shelter at relay stations. Canal construction too continued, and river navigation improved.

The population growth and increasing trade that resulted gave rise to local market centers. Some of these became county seats from which imperial officials operated. Estimates of the proportion of the population living in Han towns and cities range from 10 percent, a number roughly comparable to Europe, to 30 percent.

Silk dominated China's export trade. Silk cocoons are secreted onto the leaves of mulberry trees by silkworms. The Chinese understood this and kept it a closely guarded secret, which gave them a monopoly on the manufacture of silk. Carried through the Central Asian oases to the Middle East, India, and the Mediterranean, and passing through the hands of middlemen who added their own fees to the price, this beautiful textile may have increased in value a hundred-fold by the end of its journey. Controlling the Silk Road and its profits justified periodic military campaigns into Central Asia and the installation there of garrisons and Chinese colonies.

The Decline of the Han Empire

For the Han, as for the Romans, maintaining frontier security, particularly in the north and northwest, posed a serious challenge. In the end, non-Chinese peoples raiding across the frontier or moving into imperial territory brought the empire down.

The different ways of life of farmers, who usually accepted Han rule, and herders, who preferred their own kings, gave rise to insulting stereotypes on both sides. The settled Chinese thought of nomads as "barbarians"—rough, uncivilized people—a viewpoint much like that of the Romans who looked down on the Germanic peoples on their frontiers.

Often, the closeness of herding and farming populations led to commercial exchange. The nomads sought agricultural products and crafted goods, while the settled peoples bought horses and other herd animals and animal products. Sometimes, however, nomad raiders seized what they wanted from farming settlements. Tough and warlike because of their way of life, mounted nomads struck swiftly and as swiftly disappeared.

Although nomadic groups tended to be small and inclined to fight one another, circumstances and a charismatic leader could bring them together from time to time. In the Han period, the **Xiongnu°,** a great confederacy of Turkic peoples, threatened the empire, though they were usually contained on the frontier by cavalry forces created to match the nomads' mobility. This strategy made access to good horses and pastureland a state priority. Other strategies included maintaining garrisons and colonies of soldier-farmers on the frontier, settling compliant nomads within the borders to serve as a buffer, bribing nomad chiefs to promote disunity, and paying protection money. The "tributary system," in which nomad rulers accepted Chinese supremacy and exchanged tribute payments for marriages to Chinese princesses, receptions at court, and imperial gifts worth more than the tribute, often worked well.

Yet military vigilance burdened Han finances and made the economic troubles of later Han times worse. Despite measures to suppress the aristocracy and turn land over to a free peasantry, by the end of the first century, B.C.E. nobles and successful merchants again acquired control of huge estates, and many peasants sought their protection against the exactions of the imperial gov-

ernment. This trend spread over the next two centuries. As strongmen largely independent of imperial control emerged, the central government lost tax revenues and manpower. Military conscription broke down, forcing the government to hire more and more foreign soldiers and officers. These served for pay, but their loyalty was weak.

The Han regime fell in 220 C.E. for several reasons: factional intrigues within the ruling clan, official corruption and inefficiency, uprisings of desperate and hungry peasants, the spread of banditry, unsuccessful reform movements, attacks by nomads, and the ambitions of rural warlords. China entered a period of political fragmentation and economic and cultural regression that lasted until the rise of the Sui° and Tang° dynasties in the late sixth and early seventh centuries C.E., a story that we take up in Chapter 9.

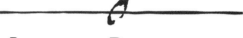

IMPERIAL PARALLELS

The similarities between the Han and Roman empires begin with the family, comprising in both cultures the living generations who obeyed an all-powerful patriarch. Strong loyalties and obligations bound the family members. Obedience, respect for superiors, piety, and a strong sense of duty and honor—family values that individuals carried into the wider social and political world—created a pervasive social cohesion.

Agriculture provided the fundamental economic activity and source of wealth for both. Government revenues derived primarily from taxes on the annual harvest. Both empires depended on a free peasantry for military service and compulsory labor. Conflicts over landownership and land use prompted political and social turmoil in both territories. Autocratic rulers secured their positions by seizing some of the aristocrats' lands and reallocating them to small farmers (while keeping extensive tracts for themselves). They pretended that these revolutionary changes simply restored venerable institutions. The later reversal of this process, as wealthy noblemen once again acquired estates

---

Xiongnu (SHE-OONG-noo)

Sui (sway)   **Tang** (tahng)

and turned peasants into tenant farmers, signaled the erosion of state authority.

Spreading from ethnically homogeneous cores, both empires encompassed diverse ecosystems, populations, and ways of life, and the cultural unity they fostered has persisted, at least in part, to the present day. The skills of Roman and Chinese farmers produced high yields that led to population growth. This pressure caused Italian and Han settlers to move from the core areas into new regions, bringing along their languages, beliefs, customs, and technologies. Many people in the conquered lands adopted the culture of the rulers to attach themselves to a "winning cause."

In order to administer far-flung territories in an era when a man on horseback provided the fastest communication, the central governments delegated considerable autonomy to local officials. These elites identified their own interests with those of the state they served. Thus developed a kind of civil service, staffed by educated and capable members of a prosperous middle class.

Roads built for moving troops became the highways of commerce and the thoroughfares by which imperial culture spread. A network of cities and towns provided each empire with local administrative centers while fostering commerce and radiating imperial culture into the surrounding countryside.

Cities and towns modeled themselves on the capital cities—Rome and Chang'an. Travelers could find in outlying regions the same types of buildings and urban amenities that they knew from the capital, though on a smaller scale. People living in urban centers enjoyed the advantages of empire most. The majority of the population, however, resided in the countryside.

The Roman and Han empires faced similar defense problems: long borders far from the capital and aggressive neighbors. The staggering cost of building walls and maintaining frontier forts and garrisons eventually eroded economic prosperity. Rough neighbors acquired the skills that had given the empires an initial advantage and thereby closed the technology gap. Increasingly beholden to the military, governments demanded more taxes and services from the hard-pressed civilians. This cost them the loyalty of many people, some of whom sought protection on the estates of powerful landowners. Eventually, borders were overrun and the central governments collapsed. Ironically, the new immigrants who took control respected the imperial culture so deeply that they maintained it to the best of their abilities.

The respective ends of the two empires had different long-term consequences, however. The Chinese imperial model revived in subsequent eras, but the lands of the Roman Empire never again achieved such unification. Several interrelated factors help to account for the different outcomes.

First, these cultures assessed the obligations of the individual to the state differently. In China, the individual was deeply embedded in the larger social group. Family hierarchy, unquestioning obedience, and solemn rituals of deference to elders and ancestors served as the model for society and the state. Respect for authority still remains a deep-seated habit. Qin Legalism made the word of the emperor law, and Confucianism sanctified hierarchy and governed the conduct of professionals and public officials. Although the Roman family had its own hierarchy and traditions of obedience, the family did not serve as the model for society and state. Rome also lacked a philosophy like Confucianism that could perpetuate its political organization and social code.

Economic and social mobility, which enable some people to rise dramatically in wealth and status, tend to enhance the significance of the individual. Ancient China presented few opportunities for individuals to improve their economic status. The government frequently disparaged and constrained the merchant class. The more important role of commerce in the Roman Empire, and the resulting economic mobility, heightened Roman awareness of individual rights.

Although Roman emperors tried to create an ideology to bolster their position, persistent Republican traditions and ambiguities about the imperial office deliberately cultivated by Augustus hampered this effort. Consequently, the dynastic principle remained weak, the cult of the emperor lacked spiritual content, and the army or the Senate chose the emperors. This contrasts sharply with the Chinese belief in the emperor as the Son of Heaven with privileged access to the power of the royal ancestors. Thus, Rome's fall left to later ages no compelling basis for reviving the position of emperor or imperial territorial claims.

Finally, weight must be given to new belief systems that took root in each empire. In insisting on monotheism and one doctrine of truth, Christianity negated the emperor's pretensions to divinity and would not compromise with pagan beliefs. Christianity's spread, and the collapse of the western half of the empire in the fifth century C.E. (see Chapter 8), constituted an irreversible break with the past. In contrast, Buddhism, which came to China in the early centuries C.E. and flourished in the post-Han era (see Chapter 9), accommodated traditional Chinese values and beliefs more easily.

CONCLUSION

Both the Roman Empire and the first Chinese empire arose from relatively small states. Discipline and military toughness enabled them to subdue other small quarreling neighbors. Ultimately, they unified widespread territories under strong central governments.

The Qin Empire could emerge during the reign of a single ruler because many elements of unification were already present. The Shang and Zhou states had controlled large core areas in the North China Plain. The "First Emperor" drew on the preexisting concept of the Mandate of Heaven, which claimed divine backing for the ruler as the Son of Heaven, and the Legalist ideology justified authoritarian measures. Although resistance to the harshness of the new order soon brought down the Qin dynasty, its Han successors moderated and built on Qin institutions to create a durable imperial regime.

The early Roman state enjoyed no similar precedents. The Roman Empire grew more slowly, with solutions evolving by trial and error. The Republican form of government, appropriate for an Italian city-state, proved inadequate to the demands of empire, and Rome's military success led to social and economic disruption and acute political conflict. Out of this crisis emerged the institutions of the Principate, which persevered for several centuries. Even so, the Roman emperors never developed an effective ideology of rule.

In both empires, professional armies maintained order and defended the frontiers. Educated civil servants kept records and collected taxes to support the military and government. Roads, cities, standardized systems of money and measurement, and widely understood languages facilitated travel, commerce, and communication. The culture of the imperial center spread, and this shared culture, as well as shared self-interest, bonded local elites to the empire's ruling class.

For long periods, these stabilizing forces, bringing peace, prosperity, and improved standards of living, outweighed the weaknesses inherent in the two systems. Over time, however, the costs of defending lengthy frontiers drained imperial treasuries and increased taxation. As hard-pressed subjects sought the protection of rural landowners, cities shrank, commerce declined, and the central government found fewer ways of compelling tax payment and fewer recruits for the army.

In the end, both empires succumbed to external pressures and internal divisions. In China, however, the imperial tradition and the class structure and value system that maintained it lived on (see Chapters 2 and 9). In Europe, North Africa, and the Middle East, the Roman Empire passed into history. In the next chapter, we will look at some of the forces leading these areas in different directions.

■ Key Terms

Roman Republic	aqueducts
Roman Senate	third-century crisis
patron/client relationship	Constantine
Roman Principate	Qin
Augustus	Shi Huangdi
equites	Han
pax romana	Chang'an
Romanization	gentry
Jesus	Xiongnu
Paul	

■ Suggested Reading

Tim Cornell and John Matthews, *Atlas of the Roman World* (1982), offers a general introduction, pictures, and maps. Michael Grant and Rachel Kitzinger, eds., *Civilization of the Ancient Mediterranean,* 3 vols. (1988), contains essays with bibliographies by specialists on different aspects of the Greek and Roman worlds. Michael Grant, *History of Rome* (1978), is a good survey. Naphtali Lewis and Meyer Reinhold, eds., *Roman Civilization,* 2 vols. (1951), contains ancient sources in translation.

For Roman institutions, attitudes, and values, see J. A. Crook, *Law and Life of Rome: 90 B.C.–A.D. 212* (1967). Michael Crawford, *The Roman Republic,* 2d ed. (1993), and Chester G. Starr, *The Roman Empire, 27 B.C.–A.D. 476: A Study in Survival* (1982), discuss the state during the Republic and Principate. Fergus Millar, *The Emperor in the Roman World (31 B.C.–A.D. 337)* (1977), studies the position of the princeps.

For Roman military matters, see W. V. Harris, *War and Imperialism in Republican Rome* (1979), and Stephen L. Dyson, *The Creation of the Roman Frontier* (1985). For military technology, see M. C. Bishop, *Roman Military Equipment: From the Punic Wars to the Fall of Rome* (1993). David Macaulay, *City: A Story of Roman Planning and Construction* (1974), and K. D. White, *Greek and Roman Technology* (1984), reveal the wonders of Roman engineering. For urban life, see John E. Stambaugh, *The Ancient Roman City* (1988).

Kevin Greene, *The Archaeology of the Roman Economy* (1986), deals with social and economic history. Suzanne Dickson, *The Roman Family* (1992), Lionel Casson, *Everyday Life in Ancient Rome* (1998), and U. E. Paoli, *Rome: Its People, Life and Customs* (1983), look at social life. Jo-Ann Shelton, ed., *As the Romans Did: A Sourcebook in Roman Social History* (1998), offers translated sources. Elaine Fantham, Helene Peet Foley, Natalie Boymel Kampen, Sarah B. Pomeroy, and H. Alan Shapiro, *Women in the Classical World: Image and Text* (1994), provides an up-to-date discussion. Mary R. Lefkowitz and Maureen B. Fant, eds., *Women's Life in Greece and Rome: A Source Book in Translation* (1982), and Thomas Wiedemann, ed., *Greek and Roman Slavery* (1981), offer translated sources on these topics.

John Boardman, Jasper Griffin, and Oswyn Murray, eds., *The Roman World* (1988), contains chapters on Roman intellectual and literary achievements. Ronald Mellor, ed., *The Historians of Ancient Rome* (1998), provides context for reading historical sources. Michael von Albrecht, *History of Roman Literature: From Livius Andronicus to Boethius: With Special Regard to Its Influence on World Literature* (1997), and Nancy H. Ramage and Andrew Ramage, *The Cambridge Illustrated History of Roman Art* (1991), survey Roman creativity. R. M. Ogilvie, *The Romans and Their Gods in the Age of Augustus* (1969), introduces public and private religion. R. A. Markus, *Christianity in the Roman World* (1974), investigates the rise of Christianity.

For the geography and demography of China, see the well-illustrated *Cultural Atlas of China* (1983), by Caroline Blunden and Mark Elvin. Basic surveys include Jacques Gernet, *A History of Chinese Civilization* (1982), and John K. Fairbank, *China: A New History* (1992). For greater depth on the ancient period, see Edward L. Shaughnessy and Michael Loewe, eds., *The Cambridge History of Ancient China* (1998); Denis Twitchett and Michael Loewe, eds., *The Cambridge History of China,* vol. 1, *The Ch'in and Han Empires, 221 B.C.–A.D. 220* (1986); Michele Pirazzoli-t'Serstevens, *The Han Dynasty* (1982); and Kwang-chih Chang, *The Archaeology of Ancient China,* 4th ed. (1986). W. de Bary, W. Chan, and B. Watson, eds., have assembled sources in translation in *Sources of Chinese Tradition* (1960). Sima Qian, *Historical Records* (1994), translated by Raymond Dawson, provides a readable selection of varied material pertaining to the Qin dynasty compiled by the premier historian of the Han period.

For social history, see Michael Loewe, *Everyday Life in Early Imperial China During the Han Period, 202 B.C.–A.D. 220* (1988), and Barbara N. Ramusack and Sharon L. Sievers, eds., *Restoring Women to History. Women in Asia* (1999). For economic history and foreign relations, see Hsin-ju Liu, *Ancient India and Ancient China: Trade and Religious Exchanges, A.D. 1–600* (1994), and Ying-shih Yu, *Trade and Expansion in Han China* (1967). For scientific and technological achievements, see Robert Temple, *The Genius of China: 3,000 Years of Science, Discovery, and Invention* (1986).

Benjamin I. Schwartz addresses intellectual history in *The World of Thought in Ancient China* (1985). Spiritual matters are taken up by Laurence G. Thompson, *Chinese Religion: An Introduction,* 3d ed. (1979). For art, see Michael Sullivan, *A Short History of Chinese Art,* rev. ed. (1970), and Jessica Rawson, *Ancient China: Art and Archaeology* (1980).

For a stimulating comparison of the Roman and Han Empires that emphasizes their differences, see the first chapter of S. A. M. Adshead, *China in World History,* 2d ed. (1995).

■ Note

1. Patricia Buckley Ebrey, ed., *Chinese Civilization and Society: A Sourcebook* (New York: Free Press, 1981), 33–34.

PART
THREE

GROWTH AND INTERACTION OF CULTURAL COMMUNITIES,
300 B.C.E.–1500 C.E.

I n 300 B.C.E., societies still had only limited contacts beyond their frontiers. Fifteen centuries later, by 1200 C.E., this situation had changed dramatically. Trade, folk migrations, and religious missionary work had created a world of pervasive interconnections among peoples. Three long-distance trade routes fostered the exchange of products and technologies: the Silk Road across Central Asia, trans-Saharan caravan routes linking northern and sub-Saharan Africa, and a variety of maritime routes connecting the coastal lands of the Indian Ocean.

In Africa, the spread of the Bantu peoples from West Africa brought iron implements and new techniques of food production to most of sub-Saharan Africa and helped foster a distinctive African cultural pattern. In the Middle East, the Arabs of the Arabian peninsula, under the inspiration of the Prophet Muhammad, conquered an empire that stretched from Spain to India, implanting their faith, their cultural values, and an urban-based style of life.

In Asia, Buddhism drew on the energies of missionaries and pilgrims as it spread by land

and sea from India to Sri Lanka, Tibet, Southeast Asia, China, Korea, and Japan. In each of these lands, the new faith interacted with older philosophies and religious outlooks to produce distinctive patterns of social interaction. At about the same time, the expansion of the Tang Empire resulted in the dissemination of Chinese culture and technologies throughout Central and East Asia.

In Europe, monks and missionaries labored to convert the Celtic, Germanic, and Slavic peoples to Christianity. Christian beliefs became wedded to new political and social structures: a struggle between royal and church authority in western Europe; a combining of religious and imperial authority in the Byzantine East; and distinctive Christian kingdoms in Armenia, Kievan Russia, and Ethiopia. The Crusades opened new contacts between western Europe and lands to the east after centuries of near isolation.

Unexplored seas still separated the Eastern and Western Hemispheres, but the development of urban, agricultural civilizations in the Andes, the Yucatán lowlands, and the central plateau of Mexico climaxed during this period in the Aztec and Inca Empires and, somewhat earlier, in the flourishing of the Maya. All of the aspects of long-distance cultural exchange and interaction that mark this era in Eurasia and Africa have their counterparts in the Western Hemisphere.

	300 B.C.E.	B.C.E. C.E.	300 C.E.
Americas	• **300** Migrants from Mesoamerica bring irrigation farming to Arizona	• **100** Teotihuacan founded	**250–900** Classic period of Maya civilization / **200–700** Moche culture in coastal Peru
Europe		• **146** Rome destroys Carthage, begins direct control of territories ouside Europe	Council of Nicaea **325** • / Reign of Roman emperor Diocletian **284–305** / Fall of Roman Empire in West **476** •
Africa	**500 B.C.E.–1000 C.E.** Bantu migrations	Bananas and yams reach Africa from Southeast Asia **ca. 100** •	First Christian bishop in Ethiopia **ca. 330** • / • **ca. 300** Camel use spreads in southern Sahara
Middle East	• **300** Petra flourishes as caravan city in Jordan / **248 B.C.E–226 C.E** Kingdom of Parthia in Iran		• **276** Prophet Mani martyred / **226–650** Sasanid Empire in Iraq and Iran
Asia and Oceania	• **128** Chinese general Zhang Jian explores Silk Road / **206 B.C.E–220 C.E** Han Empire in China	• **ca. 100** Stirrup developed in Afghanistan	**200–400** Rice introduced to Japan from Korea

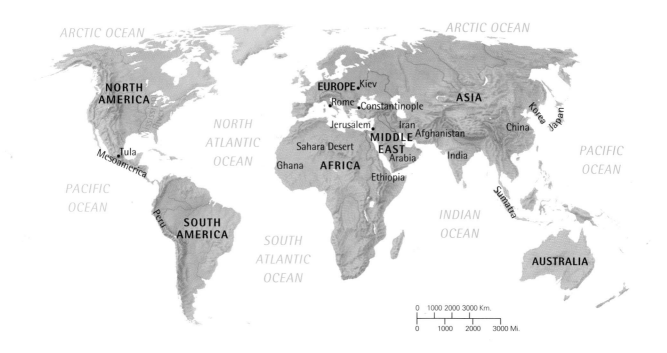

ARCTIC OCEAN

ARCTIC OCEAN

NORTH
AMERICA

EUROPE • Kiev

Rome • Constantinople

ASIA

Korea Japan

NORTH
ATLANTIC
OCEAN

Jerusalem • Iran Afghanistan

China

PACIFIC
OCEAN

Tula
Mesoamerica

Sahara Desert

MIDDLE
EAST

Arabia

India

PACIFIC
OCEAN

Ghana

AFRICA

Ethiopia

SOUTH
AMERICA

Peru

SOUTH
ATLANTIC
OCEAN

INDIAN
OCEAN

Sumatra

AUSTRALIA

0 1000 2000 3000 Km.

0 1000 2000 3000 Mi.

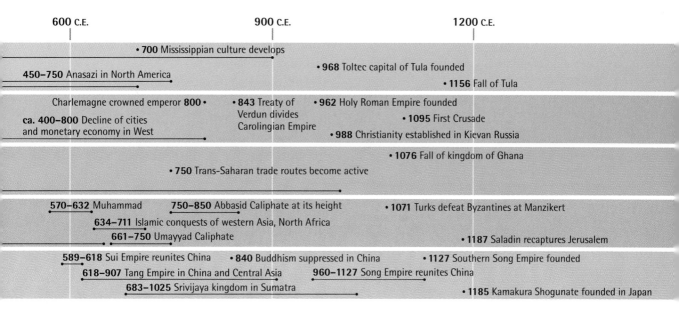

| 600 C.E. | 900 C.E. | 1200 C.E. |

• 700 Mississippian culture develops

• 968 Toltec capital of Tula founded

450–750 Anasazi in North America

• 1156 Fall of Tula

Charlemagne crowned emperor 800 •

• 843 Treaty of
Verdun divides
Carolingian Empire

• 962 Holy Roman Empire founded

ca. 400–800 Decline of cities
and monetary economy in West

• 1095 First Crusade

• 988 Christianity established in Kievan Russia

• 1076 Fall of kingdom of Ghana

• 750 Trans-Saharan trade routes become active

570–632 Muhammad

750–850 Abbasid Caliphate at its height

• 1071 Turks defeat Byzantines at Manzikert

634–711 Islamic conquests of western Asia, North Africa

661–750 Umayyad Caliphate

• 1187 Saladin recaptures Jerusalem

589–618 Sui Empire reunites China

• 840 Buddhism suppressed in China

• 1127 Southern Song Empire founded

618–907 Tang Empire in China and Central Asia

960–1127 Song Empire reunites China

683–1025 Srivijaya kingdom in Sumatra

• 1185 Kamakura Shogunate founded in Japan

6

NETWORKS OF COMMUNICATION AND EXCHANGE, 300 B.C.E.–1100 C.E.

The Silk Road • The Indian Ocean and Southeast Asia • Routes Across the Sahara • Sub-Saharan Africa • The Spread of Ideas
ENVIRONMENT AND TECHNOLOGY: Camel Saddles

round the year 800 C.E., a Chinese poet named Po Zhuyi° nostalgically wrote:

Iranian whirling girl, Iranian whirling girl—
Her heart answers to the strings,
Her hands answer to the drums.
At the sound of the strings and drums, she raises
    her arms,
Like whirling snowflakes tossed about, she turns
    in her twirling dance.
Iranian whirling girl,
You came from Sogdiana°.
In vain did you labor to come east more than ten
    thousand tricents.
For in the central plains there were already some
    who could do the Iranian whirl,
And in a contest of wonderful abilities, you would
    not be their equal.[1]

The western part of Central Asia, the region around Samarkand° and Bukhara° known in the eighth century C.E. as Sogdiana, was 2,500 miles (4,000 kilometers) from the Chinese capital of Chang'an°. Caravans took more than four months to trek across the mostly unsettled deserts, mountains, and grasslands.

The Silk Road connecting China and the Middle East across Central Asia fostered the exchange of agricultural goods, manufactured products, and ideas. But musicians and dancing girls traveled too, as did camel pullers, merchants, monks, and pilgrims. The Silk Road was not just a means of bringing peoples and parts of the world into contact; it was a social system. This and similar trading networks that have had

---

Po Zhuyi (boh joo-yee) **Sogdiana** (sog-dee-A-nuh)

Samarkand (SAM-mar-kand) **Bukhara** (boo-CAR-ruh)
Chang'an (chahng-ahn)

a deep impact on world history deserve special scrutiny.

With every expansion of territory, the growing wealth of temples, kings, and emperors enticed traders to venture ever farther afield for precious goods. For the most part, their customers were wealthy elites. But the knowledge of new products, agricultural and industrial processes, and foreign ideas and customs these long-distance traders brought with them sometimes affected an entire society.

Travelers and traders seldom owned much land or wielded political power. Socially isolated (sometimes by law) and secretive because any talk about markets, products, routes, and travel conditions could help their competitors, they nevertheless contributed more to drawing the world together than did all but a few kings and emperors.

This chapter examines the social systems and historical impact of exchange networks that developed between 300 B.C.E. and 1100 C.E. in Europe, Asia, and Africa. The Silk Road, the Indian Ocean maritime system, and the trans-Saharan caravan routes in Africa illustrate the nature of long-distance trade in this era.

Trading networks were not the only medium for the spread of new ideas, products, and customs, however. Chapter 5 discussed the migration into the Roman Empire of peoples speaking Germanic languages and the beginning of Christian missionary activity in Europe. This chapter compares the development of the Saharan trading system of northern Africa with the simultaneous folk migrations of Bantu-speaking peoples within sub-Saharan Africa. It also discusses the spread of Buddhism in Asia and Christianity in Africa.

As you read this chapter, ask yourself the following questions:

- What role does technology play in long-distance trade?
- How does geography affect trade patterns?
- How do human groups affect communication between regions?
- Why do some goods and ideas travel more easily than others?

THE SILK ROAD

Archaeology and linguistic studies show that the peoples of Central Asia engaged in long-distance movement and exchange from at least 1500 B.C.E. In Roman times, the imagination of Europeans became captivated by the idea of the **Silk Road.** A trade route linking the lands of the Mediterranean with China by way of Mesopotamia, Iran, and Central Asia, the Silk Road experienced several periods of heavy use (see Map 6.1). The first extended from approximately 100 B.C.E. to 907 C.E., when the collapse of the Tang° Empire in China led to disruption at its eastern end (see Chapter 9). Another period of heavy use began in the thirteenth century C.E. and lasted until the seventeenth century (see Chapter 11).

Origins and Operations

The Seleucid kings who succeeded to the eastern parts of Alexander the Great's empire in the third century B.C.E. focused their energies on Mesopotamia and Syria, allowing an Iranian nomadic leader to establish an independent kingdom in northeastern Iran. The **Parthians,** named after their homeland east of the Caspian Sea, had become a major force by 247 B.C.E. They left few written sources, and recurring wars between the Parthians and the Seleucids, and later between the Parthians and the Romans, prevented travelers from the Mediterranean region from gaining firm

---

Tang (tahng)

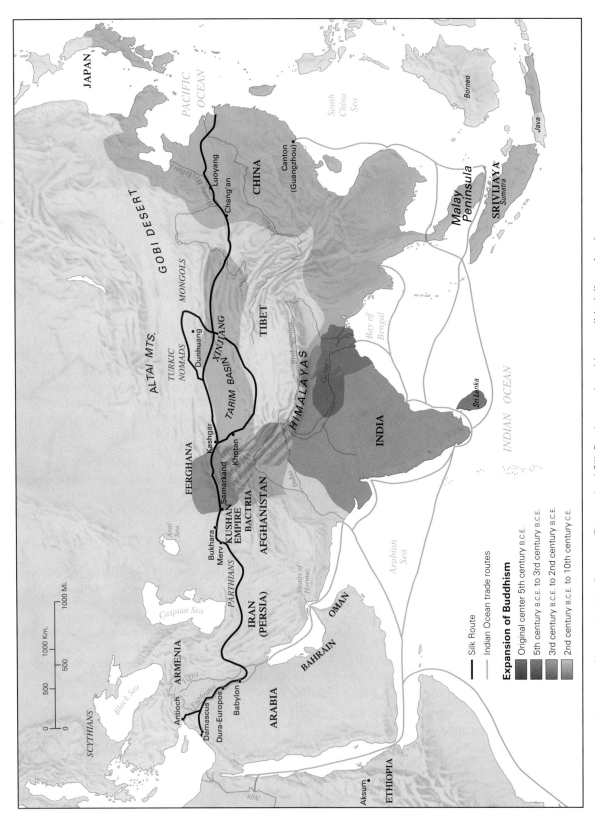

Map. 6.1 Asian Trade and Communication Routes The overland Silk Road was vulnerable to political disruption, but was much shorter than the maritime route from the South China Sea to the Red Sea, and ships were more expensive than pack animals. Moreover, China's political centers were in the north.

CHRONOLOGY

	Silk Road	Indian Ocean Trade	Saharan Trade
300 B.C.E.			**500 B.C.E.–ca. 1000 C.E.** Bantu migrations
	247 B.C.E. Parthian rule begins in Iran		
	128 B.C.E. General Zhang Jian reaches Ferghana		**ca. 200 B.C.E.** Camel nomads in southern Sahara
1 C.E.	**100 B.C.E.–300 C.E.** Kushans rule northern Afghanistan and Sogdiana	**1st cent. C.E.** *Periplus of the Erythraean Sea*; Indonesian migration to Madagascar	**46 B.C.E.** First mention of camels in northern Sahara
300 C.E.			**ca. 300** Beginning of camel nomadism in northern Sahara
	ca. 400 Buddhist pilgrim Faxian travels Silk Road		**6th cent.** Kingdom of Ghana begins
600 C.E.			
	ca. 630 Buddhist pilgrim Xuanzang travels Silk Road	**683–1025** Srivijaya trading kingdom in Southeast Asia	**639–42** Arabs conquer Egypt
		711 Arabs conquer lower Indus Valley partially by sea	**711** Berbers and Arabs conquer Spain
			740 Berber revolts; independent states in North Africa; trade develops across Sahara
900 C.E.	**907** Collapse of Tang Empire	**ca. 900** Arab and Persian merchants in Canton	
			1076 Almoravids defeat ruler of Ghana

knowledge of the Parthian kingdom. It seems likely, however, that their place of origin on the threshold of Central Asia and the lifestyle they had in common with nomadic pastoral groups farther to the east helped foster the Silk Road.

In 128 B.C.E., a Chinese general named Zhang Jian° made his first exploratory journey westward across the dangerous deserts of Central Asia on behalf of Emperor Wu of the Han dynasty. After crossing the broad and desolate Tarim Basin north of Tibet, he reached the fertile valley of Ferghana° and for the first time encountered westward-flowing rivers. There he found horse breeders whose animals far outclassed any horses he had seen.

Zhang Jian (jahng jee-en)

Ferghana (fer-GAH-nuh)

Later Chinese historians looked on General Zhang, who led eighteen expeditions, as the originator of overland trade with the western lands, and they credited him with personally introducing a whole garden of new plants and trees. Zhang's own account, however, proves that the people of Ferghana were already receiving goods from China, though probably by way of India.

Long-distance travel was much more familiar to the Central Asians than to the Chinese. Kin to the trouser-wearing, horse-riding Parthians in language and customs, the populations of Ferghana and neighboring regions included many nomads. But their migrations following their herds had had little to do with trade. The Silk Road involved, on the eastern end, Chinese eagerness for western products, especially horses, and on the western end, the organized Parthian state controlling the flourishing markets of Mesopotamia and culturally linked to the pastoralists of Central Asia. In between were caravan cities to support the traders and camel- and horse-breeding nomads to supply them with livestock.

Once the route was fully functioning, around 100 B.C.E., Greeks could buy Chinese silk from Parthian traders in Mesopotamian border entrepôts. Yet caravans also bought and sold goods along the way in prosperous Central Asian trading cities like Samarkand and Bukhara. These cities grew and flourished, often under the rule of local princes.

General Zhang seems definitely to have brought to China two plants: alfalfa and wine grapes. The former provided the best fodder for the growing Chinese herds of Ferghana horses. In addition, Chinese farmers adopted pistachios, walnuts, pomegranates, sesame, coriander, spinach, and other new crops. Chinese artisans and physicians used other trade products, such as jasmine oil, oak galls (used in tanning animal hides, dyeing, and ink making), sal ammoniac (for medicines), copper oxides, zinc, and precious stones.

Caravan traders going from east to west carried from China new fruits such as peaches and apricots, which the Romans attributed mistakenly to the eastern lands of Persia and Armenia, respectively. They also carried cinnamon, ginger, and other spices that could not be grown in the West. Manufactured goods—particularly silk, pottery,

Iranian Musicians from Silk Road   This three-color glazed pottery figurine, 23 inches (58.4 centimeters) high, comes from a northern Chinese tomb of the Tang era (sixth to ninth centuries C.E.). The musicians playing Iranian instruments confirm the migration of Iranian culture across the Silk Road. At the same time, dishes decorated by the Chinese three-color glaze technique were in vogue in northern Iran.   (The National Museum of Chinese History)

and paper—were eventually adopted or imitated in western lands, starting with Iran.

The Impact of the Silk Road

As trade became a more important part of Central Asian life, the Iranian-speaking peoples settled increasingly in trading cities and surrounding farm villages. This allowed nomads originally from the

Altai Mountains farther east to spread across the steppes and become the dominant pastoral group. These peoples spoke Turkic languages unrelated to the Iranian tongues and are well in evidence by the sixth century C.E. The prosperity that trade created affected not only the ethnic mix of the region but also cultural values. The nomads continued to live in the round, portable felt huts called yurts that can still be seen occasionally in Central Asia, but prosperous merchants and landholders built stately homes decorated with brightly colored wall paintings. The paintings show these merchants and landholders wearing Chinese silks and Iranian brocades and riding on richly outfitted horses and camels. They also give evidence of an avid interest in Buddhism, which competed with Christianity, Manichaeism, Zoroastrianism, and eventually Islam in a lively and inquiring intellectual milieu.

Religion (discussed later in this chapter) exemplifies the impact of foreign customs and beliefs on the Central Asian peoples, but Central Asian practices also affected surrounding areas. For example, Central Asian military techniques had a profound impact on both East and West. Chariot warfare and the use of mounted bowmen originated in Central Asia and spread eastward and westward through military campaigns and folk migrations that began in the second millennium B.C.E. and recurred throughout the period of the Silk Road.

Evidence of the **stirrup,** one of the most important inventions, comes first from the Kushan people who ruled northern Afghanistan in approximately the first century C.E. At first a solid bar, then a loop of leather to support the rider's big toe, and finally a device of leather and metal or wood supporting the instep, the stirrup gave riders far greater stability in the saddle, which in all likelihood was an earlier Central Asian invention.

Using stirrups, a mounted warrior could supplement his bow and arrow with a long lance and charge his enemy at a gallop without fear that the impact of his attack would push him off his mount. Far to the west, the stirrup made possible the armored knights who dominated the battlefields of Europe (see Chapter 8), and it contributed to the superiority of the Tang cavalry in China (see Chapter 9).

THE INDIAN OCEAN AND SOUTHEAST ASIA

A multilingual, multiethnic society of seafarers established the **Indian Ocean Maritime System,** a trade network across the Indian Ocean and the South China Sea. These people left few records and seldom played a visible part in the rise and fall of kingdoms and empires, but they forged increasingly strong economic and social ties between the coastal lands of East Africa, southern Arabia, the Persian Gulf, India, Southeast Asia, and southern China.

This trade took place in three distinct regions: (1) In the South China Sea, Chinese and Malays (including Indonesians) dominated trade. (2) From the east coast of India to the islands of Southeast Asia, Indians and Malays were the main traders. (3) From the west coast of India to the Persian Gulf and the east coast of Africa, merchants and sailors were predominantly Persians and Arabs. However, Chinese and Malay sailors could and did voyage to East Africa, and Arab and Persian traders reached southern China.

From the time of Herodotus in the fifth century B.C.E., Greek writers regaled their readers with stories of marvelous voyages down the Red Sea into the Indian Ocean and around Africa from the west. Most often, they attributed such trips to the Phoenicians, the most fearless of Mediterranean seafarers. But occasionally a Greek appears. One such was Hippalus, a Greek ship's pilot who was said to have discovered the seasonal monsoon winds that facilitate sailing across the Indian Ocean.

The regular seasonal alternation of steady winds could not have remained unnoticed for thousands of years, waiting for an alert Greek to happen along. The great voyages and discoveries made before written records became common should surely be attributed to the peoples who lived around the Indian Ocean rather than to interlopers from the Mediterranean Sea. The story of Hippalus resembles the Chinese story of General Zhang Jian, whose role in opening trade with

Indian Ocean Sailing Vessel   Ships like this one, in a rock carving on the Buddhist temple of Borobodur in Java, probably carried colonists from Indonesia to Madagascar.   (Allen Eaton/Ancient Art & Architecture)

Central Asia overshadows the anonymous contributions made by the indigenous peoples.

Mediterranean sailors of the time of Alexander used square sails and long banks of oars to maneuver among the sea's many islands and small harbors. Indian Ocean vessels relied on roughly triangular lateen sails and normally did without oars in running before the wind on long ocean stretches. Mediterranean shipbuilders nailed their vessels together. The planks of Indian Ocean ships were pierced, tied together with palm fiber, and caulked with bitumen. Mediterranean sailors rarely ventured out of sight of land. Indian Ocean sailors, thanks to the monsoon winds, could cover long reaches entirely at sea.

The world of the Indian Ocean developed differently from the world of the Mediterranean Sea, where the Phoenicians and Greeks established colonies that maintained contact with their home cities (see Chapters 3 and 4). The traders of the Indian Ocean, where distances were greater and contacts less frequent, seldom retained political ties with their homelands. The colonies they established were sometimes socially distinctive but rarely independent of the local political powers. War, so common in the Mediterranean, seldom beset the Indian Ocean maritime system prior to the arrival of European explorers at the end of the fifteenth century C.E.

Origins of Contact and Trade

By 2000 B.C.E., Sumerian records indicate regular trade between Mesopotamia, the islands of the Persian Gulf, Oman, and the Indus Valley. However, this early trading contact eastward broke off, and later Mesopotamian trade references mention East Africa more often than India.

A similarly early chapter in Indian Ocean history concerns migrations from Southeast Asia to Madagascar, the world's fourth largest island, situated off the southeastern coast of Africa. Some 2,000 years ago, people from one of the many Indonesian islands of Southeast Asia established themselves in that forested, mountainous land some 6,000 miles (9,500 kilometers) from home. They could not possibly have carried enough supplies for a direct voyage across the Indian Ocean, so their route must have touched the coasts of India and southern Arabia. No remains of their journeys have been discovered, however.

Apparently, the sailing canoes of these people plied the seas along the increasingly familiar route for several hundred years. Settlers farmed the new land and entered into relations with Africans, who found their way across the 250-mile-wide (400-kilometer-wide) Mozambique° Channel around the fifth century C.E. Descendants of the seafarers preserved the language of their homeland and some of its culture, such as the cultivation of bananas, yams, and other native Southeast Asian plants. These food crops spread to mainland Africa. But gradually the memory of their distant origins faded, not to be recovered until modern times, when scholars established the linguistic link between the two lands.

The Impact of Indian Ocean Trade

The only extensive written account of trade in the Indian Ocean before the rise of Islam in the seventh century C.E. is an anonymous work by a Greco-Egyptian of the first century C.E. *The Periplus of the Erythraean° Sea* (that is, the Red Sea) describes ports of call along the Red Sea and down the East African coast to somewhere south of the island of Zanzibar. Then it describes the ports of southern Arabia and the Persian Gulf before continuing eastward to India, mentioning ports all the way around the subconti-

Mozambique (moe-zam-BEEK)
Erythraean (eh-RITH-ree-an)

nent to the mouth of the Ganges River. Although the geographer Ptolemy, who lived slightly later, had heard of ports as far away as Southeast Asia, the author of the *Periplus* had obviously voyaged to the places he mentions. What he describes is unquestionably a trading *system* and is clear evidence of the steady growth of interconnections during the preceding centuries.

The demand for products from the coastal lands inspired mariners to persist in their long ocean voyages. Africa produced exotic animals, wood, and ivory. However, since ivory also came from India, Mesopotamia, and North Africa, the extent of African ivory exports cannot be determined. The highlands of northern Somalia and southern Arabia grew the scrubby trees whose aromatic resins were valued as frankincense and myrrh. Pearls abounded in the Persian Gulf, and evidence of ancient copper mines has been found in Oman in southeastern Arabia. India shipped spices and manufactured goods, and more spices came from Southeast Asia, along with manufactured items, particularly pottery, obtained in trade with China. In sum, the Indian Ocean trading region was one with a great variety of highly valued products. Given the long distances and the comparative lack of islands, however, the volume of trade there was undoubtedly much lower than in the Mediterranean Sea.

Furthermore, the culture of the Indian Ocean ports was often isolated from the hinterlands, particularly in the west. The coasts of the Arabian peninsula, the African side of the Red Sea, southern Iran, and northern India (today Pakistan) were mostly barren desert. Ports in all these areas tended to be small, and many suffered from meager supplies of fresh water. Farther south in India, the monsoon provided ample water, but steep mountains cut off the coastal plain from the interior of the country. Thus, few ports between Zanzibar and Sri Lanka had substantial inland populations within easy reach. The head of the Persian Gulf was one exception: shipborne trade was possible as far north as Babylon and, from the eighth century C.E., nearby Baghdad.

By contrast, eastern India, the Malay Peninsula, and Indonesia afforded more hospitable and densely populated shores with easier access to inland populations. Although the fishers, sailors, and traders of the western Indian Ocean system supplied a long series of kingdoms and empires, none of these consumer societies became primarily maritime in orientation, as the Greeks and Phoenicians did in the Mediterranean. In the east, in contrast, seaborne trade and influence seem to have been important even to the earliest states of Southeast Asia, as we shall see.

In coastal areas throughout the Indian Ocean system, small groups of seafarers sometimes had a significant social impact despite their usual lack of political power. Women seldom accompanied their menfolk on long sea voyages, so sailors and merchants often married local women in port cities. The families thus established were bilingual and bicultural. As in many other situations in world history, women played a crucial, though not well-documented role, as mediators between cultures. Not only did they raise their children to be more cosmopolitan than children from inland regions, but they introduced their menfolk to customs and attitudes that they carried with them when they returned to sea. As a consequence, the designation of specific seafarers as Persian, Arab, Indian, or Malay often conceals mixed heritages and a rich cultural diversity.

Southeast Asia

The Malay Peninsula and the islands of Indonesia figured large in the Indian Ocean system because they channeled trade into one of two routes, across the narrowest part of the peninsula or through the strait that separated it from Sumatra. Natural resources enhanced this importance. Tropical temperatures and monsoon rains give Southeast Asia several growing cycles each year and thus the ability to support a large human population, particularly on the floodplains of rivers flowing into the South China Sea. Southeast Asian plant and animal species that spread to other regions include wet rice (rice cultivated in deliberately flooded fields), soybeans, sugar cane, yams, bananas, coconuts, cocoyams, chickens, and pigs.

Historians believe that the **Malay peoples,** who became the dominant population, migrated from southern China in several waves beginning around 3000 B.C.E. and in some cases merged with the in-

digenous peoples. By the first millennium B.C.E., Southeast Asia seafarers had developed impressive navigational skills. They could ride the monsoon winds and interpret the patterns of swells, winds, clouds, and bird and sea life. Over several thousand years, groups of Malay peoples in large double-outrigger canoes settled thousands of islands spread across the Pacific and Indian Oceans.

Sizable states emerged in the early centuries C.E. in response to two powerful forces: commerce and Hindu/Buddhist culture. In part to satisfy a fast-growing demand for silk in the Roman Empire, a route developed across the South China Sea, by land over the narrow Isthmus of Kra on the Malay Peninsula, and across the Bay of Bengal to India. Merchants extended this exchange network to include goods from Southeast Asia, such as aromatic woods, resins, and cinnamon, pepper, cloves, nutmeg, and other spices.

Commerce brought Indian merchants and sailors into the ports of Southeast Asia and made Southeast Asia a way station for Buddhist missionaries and pilgrims traveling to and from the birthplace of their faith. Indian cosmology, rituals, art, and statecraft enhanced the legitimacy of local rulers who adopted them. Sanskrit terms such as *maharaja°* (great king) came into use along with Indian ceremonial and artistic styles and the use of scribes.

The first major Southeast Asian center, called **Funan** by Chinese visitors, flourished in southern Vietnam between the first and sixth centuries C.E. Funan dominated the Isthmus of Kra, which merchants preferred because it saved them a dangerous thousand-mile (sixteen-hundred-kilometer) voyage around the Malay Peninsula.

By the sixth century, however, merchants had shifted to an all-sea route around the peninsula. A new center of power, **Srivijaya°**—Sanskrit for "Great Conquest"—dominated the southerly route by 683 C.E. Srivijaya, with its capital at modern-day Palembang on Sumatra, had a good natural harbor on a broad and navigable river and a productive agricultural hinterland. It controlled the southern part

---

maharaja (mah-huh-RAH-juh)
Srivijava (sree-vih-JUH-yuh)

of the Malay Peninsula, Sumatra, and parts of Java and Borneo.

The king with his clerks, scribes, judges, and tax collectors controlled the rich agricultural zone around the capital directly. Local rulers bound to the center by oaths of loyalty, court ceremonies, and shares in trading profits dominated the Sumatran uplands, which produced valuable forest products. Sea nomads—pirates who fought for the king as long as he paid them—gave Srivijaya control of rival river ports.

The kings of Srivijaya who constructed and maintained this complex network of social, political, and economic relationships deployed diplomatic and even theatrical talents to hold their state together. A **theater-state,** Srivijaya overawed its dependents by its sheer splendor and ability to attract labor, talent, and luxury products. One tradition maintains that the Srivijayan monarch deposited bricks of gold in the river to appease the local gods. Another describes a hillside covered with silver and gold images of the Buddha.

The kings built and patronized Buddhist monasteries and schools. In central Java, local dynasties allied with Srivijaya built magnificent temple complexes like that of **Borobodur,** built between 770 C.E. and 825 C.E. The largest human construction in the Southern Hemisphere, its ten tiers of volcanic stone present a Buddhist allegory for the progressive stages of enlightenment. Sculptured reliefs depicting Buddhist legends provide modern viewers with glimpses of daily life in early Java.

The Southeast Asian kingdoms were not just passive recipients of Indian culture. They synthesized it with indigenous beliefs, values, and institutions. Moreover, they trained their own people in the new ways, so that the bureaucracy contained both foreign experts and native disciples. The process amounted to a cultural dialogue between India and Southeast Asia, with both partners as active participants.

But the system the Srivijayan kings erected depended on international trade. Change in trade patterns probably contributed to its decline in the eleventh century, even though the immediate cause was a destructive raid in 1025 C.E. on the Srivijayan capital by forces from southeast India. The leading role then passed to new, vigorous kingdoms on the eastern end of Java, but the maritime realm of Southeast Asia remained prosperous and connected to the international network of trade.

ROUTES ACROSS THE SAHARA

The windswept Sahara, a desert stretching from the Red Sea to the Atlantic Ocean and broken only by the Nile River, isolates sub-Saharan Africa from the Mediterranean world (see Map 6.2). The current dryness of the Sahara dates only to about 2500 B.C.E., however. The period of drying out that preceded that date lasted twenty-five centuries and encompassed several cultural changes. During that time, travel between a slowly shrinking number of grassy areas was comparatively easy. However, by 300 B.C.E., scarcity of water was restricting travel to a few difficult routes initially known only to desert nomads. Trade over **trans-Saharan caravan routes,** at first only a trickle, eventually expanded into a significant stream.

Early Saharan Cultures

Sprawling sand dunes, sandy plains, and vast expanses of exposed rock make up most of the great desert. Stark and rugged mountain and highland areas separate its northern and southern portions. The cliffs and caves of these highlands, the last spots where water and grassland could be found as the climate changed, preserve rock paintings and engravings that constitute the primary evidence for early Saharan history.

Though dating is difficult, what appear to be the earliest images, left by hunters in obviously much wetter times, include elephants, giraffes, rhinoceros, crocodiles, and other animals that have long been extinct in the region. Overlaps in the artwork indicate that the hunting societies were gradually joined by new cultures based on cattle breeding and well adapted to the sparse grazing that remained. Cattle domestication probably originated in western Asia and reached Africa before the Sahara became completely dry. How-

Cattle Herders in Saharan Rock Art These paintings represent the most artistically accomplished type of Saharan art. Herding societies of modern times living in the Sahel region south of the Sahara strongly resemble the society depicted here. (Henri Lhote)

ever, the beautiful paintings of cattle and detailed scenes of daily life found in the Sahara depict pastoral societies that bear little similarity to any in Asia. The people seem physically akin to today's West Africans, and the customs depicted, such as dancing and wearing masks, as well as the breeds of cattle, strongly suggest later societies to the south of the Sahara. These factors support the hypothesis that some southern cultural patterns originated in the Sahara.

Overlaps in artwork also show that horse herders succeeded the cattle herders. The rock art changes dramatically in style, from the superb realism of the cattle pictures to sketchier images that are often strongly geometric. Moreover, the horses are frequently shown drawing light chariots. According to the most common theory, intrepid charioteers from the Mediterranean shore drove their flimsy vehicles across the desert and established societies in the few remaining green areas of the central Saharan highlands. Some scholars suggest possible chariot routes that refugees from the collapse of the Mycenaean and Minoan civilizations

of Greece and Crete (see Chapter 2) might have followed deep into the desert around the twelfth century B.C.E. However, no archaeological evidence of actual chariot use in the Sahara has ever been discovered, and it is difficult to imagine large numbers of refugees from the politically chaotic Mediterranean region trekking and driving chariots into a waterless, trackless desert in search of a new homeland somewhere to the south.

As with the cattle herders, therefore, the identity of the Saharan horse breeders, and the source of their passion for drawing chariots, remain a mystery. Only with the coming of the camel is it possible to make firm connections with the Saharan nomads of today through the depiction of objects and geometric patterns still used by the veiled, blue-robed Tuareg° people of the highlands in southern Algeria, Niger, and Mali.

Some historians maintain that the Romans inaugurated an important trans-Saharan trade, but they lack archaeological evidence. More plausibly,

Tuareg (TWAH-reg)

Saharan trade relates to the spread of camel domestication. Supporting evidence comes from rock art, where overlaps of images imply that camel riders in desert costume constituted the latest Saharan population. The camel-oriented images are decidedly the crudest found in the region.

Latin texts from 46 B.C.E. first mention camels in North Africa. The camel is not native to Africa, so it must have reached the Sahara from Arabia, probably through Egypt in the first millennium B.C.E. From the upper Nile region, they could have been adopted by peoples farther and farther to the west, from one central Saharan highland to the next, only much later spreading northward and coming to the attention of the Romans.

Camel herding made it easier for people to move away from the Saharan highlands and roam the deep desert. Through contacts made by far-ranging camel herders, the people north of the Sahara finally gained access to the camel, though they exploited it primarily as a work animal, even developing harnesses for attaching camels to plows and carts. These practices, entirely unknown in the southern Sahara, persist in Tunisia° today (see Environment and Technology: Camel Saddles).

Trade Across the Sahara

Linkage between two different trading systems, one in the south and the other in the north, developed slowly. Southern traders concentrated on supplying salt from large deposits in the southern desert to the peoples of sub-Saharan Africa. Traders from the equatorial forest zone brought forest products, such as kola nuts and palm oil, to trading centers near the desert's southern fringe. Each received from the other, or from the farming peoples of the **Sahel**°—literally "the coast" in Arabic, the southern borderlands of the Sahara (see Map 6.2)—the products they needed in their homelands. Middlemen who were native to the Sahel played an important role in this trade, but precise historical details are lacking.

In the north, Roman colonists supplied Italy with agricultural products, primarily wheat and olives. Surviving mosaic pavements depicting scenes from daily life show that people living on the farms and in the towns of the interior consumed Roman manufactured goods and shared Roman styles. This northern pattern began to change in the third century C.E. with the decline of the Roman Empire, the abandonment of many Roman farms, the growth of nomadism, and a lessening of trade across the Mediterranean. After the Arabs invaded North Africa in the middle of the seventh century C.E., the direction of trade shifted to the Middle East, the center of Arab rule. Since the Arab conquests were inspired by the new religion of Islam (see Chapter 7), and the Christian lands of Europe constituted enemy territory, trans-Mediterranean trade diminished still further. The Arabs, many of them from camel-breeding societies in their homeland, felt a cultural kinship with those Berber speakers who had taken up camel pastoralism during the preceding centuries, and they related better to the peoples of the interior than previous conquerors had.

A series of Berber revolts against Arab rule from 740 onward led to the appearance of several small principalities on the northern fringe of the Sahara. The Islamic beliefs of their rulers, which differed somewhat from those of the Arab rulers to the east, may have interfered with their east-west overland trade and led them to look for new possibilities elsewhere. It appears that these city-states, Sijilmasa° and Tahert°, developed the first significant and regular trading contact with the south in the ninth century. Most of their populations being Berber, they probably already knew that nomads speaking closely related languages inhabited the central and southern reaches of the desert.

Once traders looked south, they discovered that the southern nomads received gold dust in exchange for salt. The gold came from deposits along the Niger and other West African rivers (see Map 6.2). The people who panned for the gold did not value it nearly as highly as did the traders from

---

Tunisia (too-NEE-zhee-uh)
Sahel (SAH-hel)

Sijilmasa (sih-jil-MAS-suh)
Tahert (TAH-hert)

Camel Saddles

As seemingly simple a technology as saddle design can indicate a society's economic structure. The South Arabian saddle was good for riding, and baggage could easily be tied to the wooden arches at its front. It was militarily inefficient, however, because the rider knelt on the cushion behind the camel's hump, which made it difficult to use weapons.

The North Arabian saddle was a significant improvement that came into use in the first centuries B.C.E. A solid wooden framework made tying on cargo easy, and prominent front and back arches and placement over the camel's hump gave warriors a solid seat and the advantage of height over cavalry. Arabs in northern Arabia took control of caravan trading by using these saddles.

The best riding saddles come from the southern Sahara, indicating that travel and war took priority there over trade. These excellent war saddles could not be used for baggage because they did not offer a convenient place to tie bundles.

Camel Saddles   The militarily inefficient south Arabian saddle (above) seats the rider behind the animal's hump atop its hindquarters. The rider controls his mount by tapping its neck with a long camelstick. The Tuareg saddle (below) seats the rider over the animal's withers, leaving his hands free to wield a sword and letting him control his mount with his toes.   (above: Private collection; below: Fred Bavendam/Peter Arnold, Inc.)

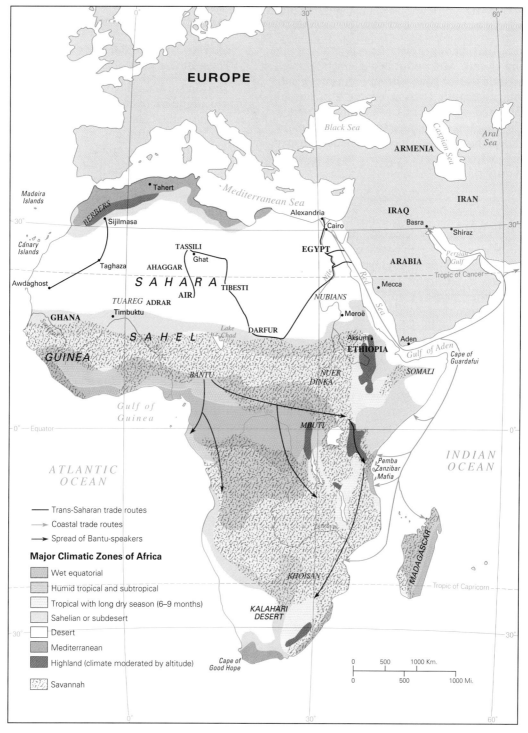

Map. 6.2 Africa and the Trans–Saharan Trade Routes   The Sahara and the surrounding oceans isolated most of Africa from foreign contact before 1000 C.E. The Nile Valley, a few trading points on the east coast, and limited transdesert trade provided exceptions to this rule; but the dominant forms of sub-Saharan African culture originated far to the west, north of the Gulf of Guinea.

Sijilmasa. They readily provided the nomads of the southern desert, who controlled the salt sources but had little use for gold, with products not available from the south, such as copper and certain manufactured goods. Thus, everyone benefited from the creation of the new trade link. Sijilmasa and Tahert became wealthy cities, the former minting gold coins that circulated as far away as Egypt and Syria.

The Kingdom of Ghana

The earliest known sub-Saharan beneficiary of the new exchange system, the kingdom of **Ghana°,** first appears in an Arabic text of the late eighth century as the "land of gold." Yet until the mid-eleventh century, few details survive about this realm, established by the Soninke° people and covering parts of Mali, Mauritania, and Senegal. Then the Arab geographer al-Bakri (d. 1094) described it as follows:

> The city of Ghana consists of two towns situated on a plain. One of these towns is inhabited by Muslims. It is large and possesses a dozen mosques, one being for the Friday prayer, and each having imams [prayer leaders], muezzins [people to make the call to prayer], and salaried reciters of the Quran. There are jurisconsults [legal specialists] and scholars. Around the town are sweet wells, which they use for drinking and for cultivating vegetables. The royal city, called al-Ghaba ["the grove"], is six miles away, and the area between the two towns is covered with habitations. Their houses are constructed of stone and acacia wood. The king has a palace with conical huts, surrounded by a fence like a wall. In the king's town, not far from the royal court, is a mosque for the use of Muslims who visit the king on missions. . . . The interpreters of the king are Muslims, as are his treasurer and the majority of his ministers.
>
> Their religion is paganism, and the worship of idols. . . . Around the royal town are domed dwellings, woods and copses where live their

sorcerers, those in charge of their religious cults. There are also their idols and their kings' tombs.[2]

The king of Ghana required the sons of vassal kings to attend his court. He meted out justice and controlled trade, collecting taxes on the salt and copper coming from the north. His large army of bowmen and cavalry made Ghana the dominant power in the entire region. By the end of the tenth century, the king's sway extended even to Awdaghost°, the Arab and Berber trade entrepôt that had grown up in the desert at the southern end of the track to Sijilmasa.

After 1076, Ghana fell prey to a new state formed by Muslim desert nomads known as Almoravids°. Later Muslim historians assert that many people in Ghana converted to Islam during the decade of nomad domination before the Almoravids withdrew to concentrate on Morocco and Spain. Although Ghana regained its independence, many former provinces had fallen away, and it never recovered its greatness.

Prior to the arrival of the religiously zealous Almoravids, the traders who had reached Ghana from the north had not been overly insistent on propagating Islam. Over the three centuries separating al-Bakri's account in the eleventh century from the earliest mention of Ghana, Muslims had come to hold high economic positions, and the kings tolerated their religious practices. But in general, the people of Ghana had not converted to Islam. General adoption of the Islamic religion, with consequent impact on the way of life of the Sahel peoples, came under later kingdoms.

SUB-SAHARAN AFRICA

The Indian Ocean network and, somewhat later, trade across the Sahara provided **sub-Saharan Africa,** the portion of Africa south of the Sahara, with a few external contacts. The most important African network of cultural exchange from 300 B.C.E. to 1100 C.E., however, arose within sub-

---

Ghana (GAH-nuh)
Soninke (soh-NIN-kay)

Awdaghost (OW-duh-gost)
Almoravid (al-moe-RAH-vid)

Saharan Africa. These exchanges led to enduring characteristics of African culture.

A Challenging Geography

Many geographic obstacles impede access to and movement within sub-Saharan Africa (see Map 6.2). The Sahara, the Atlantic and Indian Oceans, and the Red Sea bound the region. With the exception of the Nile, a ribbon of green traversing the Sahara from south to north, the major river systems empty into either the Atlantic, in the case of the Senegal, Niger, and Zaire°, or the Mozambique Channel of the Indian Ocean, in the case of the Zambezi. Rapids limit the use of these rivers for navigation.

Stretching over 50 degrees of latitude, sub-Saharan Africa encompasses dramatically different environments. A 4,000-mile (6,500-kilometer) trek from the southern edge of the Sahara to the Cape of Good Hope would take a traveler from the flat, semiarid **steppes** of the Sahel region to tropical **savanna** covered by long grasses and scattered forest, next to **tropical rain forest** on the lower Niger and in the Zaire Basin. The rain forest then gives way to another broad expanse of savanna, followed by more steppe and desert, and finally a region of temperate highlands at the southern extremity, located as far south of the equator as Greece and Sicily are to its north. East-west travel is comparatively easy in the steppe and savanna regions but difficult in the equatorial rain-forest belt and across the mountains and deep rift valleys that abut the rain forest to the east and separate East from West Africa.

The Development of Cultural Unity

Cultural heritages shared by the educated elites within each region—heritages that some anthropologists call **"great traditions"**—typically include a written language, common legal and belief systems, ethical codes, and other intellectual traditions. They loom large in written records as traditions that rise above the diversity of local customs and beliefs commonly distinguished as **"small traditions."**

By the year 1 C.E., sub-Saharan Africa had become a distinct cultural region, though one not shaped by imperial conquest or characterized by a shared elite culture, that is, a "great tradition." The cultural unity of sub-Saharan Africa rested on similar characteristics shared to varying degrees by many popular cultures, or "small traditions." These had developed during sub-Saharan Africa's long period of isolation from the rest of the world and had been refined, renewed, and interwoven by repeated episodes of migration and social interaction. Historians know little about this complex prehistory. Thus, to a greater degree than in other regions, they call on anthropological descriptions, oral history, and comparatively late records of various "small traditions" to reconstruct the broad outlines of cultural formation.

Sub-Saharan Africa's cultural unity is less immediately apparent than its diversity. By one estimate, Africa is home to 2,000 distinct languages, many corresponding to social and belief systems endowed with distinctive rituals and cosmologies. There are also numerous food production systems, ranging from hunting and gathering—very differently carried out by the Mbuti° Pygmies of the equatorial rain forest and the Khoisan° peoples of the southwestern deserts—to the cultivation of bananas, yams, and other root crops in forest clearings and of sorghum and other grains in the savanna lands. Pastoral societies display a similar diversity.

Sub-Saharan Africa covered a larger and more diverse area than any other cultural region of the first millennium C.E. and had a lower overall population density. Thus, societies and polities had room to form and reform, and a substantial amount of space separated groups. The contacts that did occur did not last long enough to produce rigid cultural uniformity.

In addition, external conquerors could not penetrate the region's natural barriers and impose a uniform culture for centuries. The Egyptians occupied Nubia, but the Nile cataracts and the vast swampland in the Nile's upper reaches blocked

---

Zaire (zah-EER)

Mbuti (m-BOO-tee)
Khoisan (KOI-sahn)

movement farther south. The Romans sent expeditions against people living in the Libyan Sahara but could not incorporate them into the Roman world. Indeed, not until the nineteenth century did outsiders gain control of the continent and begin the process of establishing an elite culture: that of western Europe.

African Cultural Characteristics

Outside visitors who got to know the sub-Saharan region well in the nineteenth and twentieth centuries observed broad commonalities underlying African life and culture. African kingdoms varied, but kingship displayed common features, most notably the ritual isolation of the king himself (see Society and Culture: Personal Styles of Rule in India and Mali in Chapter 13). Even societies too small to organize themselves into kingdoms had social categories: age groupings, fixed kinship divisions, distinct gender roles and relations, and occupational groupings. Although not hierarchical, these filled a role similar to the divisions between noble, commoner, and slave prevalent where kings ruled. In agriculture, the common technique was cultivation by hoe and digging stick.

Africans played many musical instruments, yet common features, particularly in rhythm, made African music as a whole distinctive. Music played an important role in social rituals, as did dancing and wearing masks. Such indications of underlying cultural unity have led modern observers to identify a common African quality throughout most of the region, although most sub-Saharan Africans themselves did not perceive it. An eminent Belgian anthropologist, Jacques Maquet, has called this quality "Africanity."

Some historians hypothesize that this cultural unity emanated from the peoples who once occupied the southern Sahara. In Paleolithic times, periods of dryness alternated with periods of wetness as the ice ages that locked up much of the world's fresh water in glaciers and icecaps came and went. As European glaciers receded with the waning of the last ice age, a storm belt brought increased wetness to the Saharan region. Rushing rivers scoured deep canyons. Now filled with fine sand, those canyons are easily visible on flights over the south-

ern parts of the desert. As the glaciers receded farther, the storm belt moved northward to Europe, and dryness set in after 5000 B.C.E. As a consequence, runs the hypothesis, the region's population migrated south, becoming increasingly concentrated in the Sahel, which may have been the initial incubation center for pan-African cultural patterns.

Continuing dryness and the resulting population pressure drove some people out of this core into more sparsely settled lands to the east, west, and south. Farther east, migration away from the desert contributed to the settling of the Nile Valley and the emergence of the Old Kingdom of Egypt (see Chapter 1).

The Advent of Iron and the Bantu Migrations

Archaeology confirms that agriculture had become common between the equator and the Sahara by the early second millennium B.C.E. It then spread southward, displacing hunting and gathering as a way of life. Moreover, botanical evidence indicates that banana trees, probably introduced to southeastern Africa from Southeast Asia, made their way north and west, retracing the presumed migrations of the first agriculturists.

Archaeology has also uncovered traces of copper mining in the Sahara from the early first millennium B.C.E., in the Niger Valley somewhat later, and in the Central African copper belt between 400 and 900 C.E. Gold was mined in Zimbabwe by the eighth and ninth centuries C.E. Most important of all, iron smelting began in northern sub-Saharan Africa in the early first millennium C.E. and from there spread southward, becoming firmly established in southern Africa by the year 800.

Many historians believe that the secret of smelting iron, which requires very high temperatures, was discovered only once, by the Hittites of Anatolia (modern Turkey) around 1500 B.C.E. (see Chapter 2); but how iron smelting reached sub-Saharan Africa remains unclear. The earliest evidence of ironworking from the kingdom of Meroë, on the upper Nile and in cultural contact with Egypt, is no earlier than the evidence from West Africa (northern Nigeria). Even less plausible than the Nile Valley is the idea of a spread southward from Phoenician settlements in North Africa, since archaeological evidence has not substantiated vague Greek and Latin accounts of Phoenician excursions to the south.

Some historians suggest that Africans discovered for themselves how to smelt iron. They might have done so while firing pottery in kilns. No firm evidence exists to prove or disprove this theory.

Linguistic analysis provides the strongest evidence of extensive contacts among sub-Saharan Africans in the first millennium C.E. and offers suggestions about the spread of iron. More than three hundred languages spoken south of the equator belong to the branch of the Niger-Congo family known as **Bantu,** after the word meaning "people" in most of the languages.

The distribution of the Bantu languages both north and south of the equator is consistent with a divergence beginning in the first millennium B.C.E. By comparing core words common to most of the languages, linguists have drawn some conclusions about the original Bantu speakers, whom they call "proto-Bantu." They engaged in fishing, using canoes, nets, lines, and hooks. They lived in permanent villages on the edge of the rain forest, where they grew yams and grains and harvested wild palms from which they pressed oil. They possessed domesticated goats, dogs, and perhaps other animals. They made pottery and cloth. Linguists surmise that the proto-Bantu homeland was near the modern boundary of Nigeria and Cameroon. Although dates for their dispersal are scarce, Bantu-speaking people appear in East Africa by the eighth century C.E.

Because the presumed home of the proto-Bantu lies near the known sites of early iron smelting, migration by Bantu speakers seems a likely mechanism for the southward spread of iron. The migrants probably used iron axes and hoes to hack out forest clearings and plant crops. According to this scenario, they established an economic basis for new societies that were able to sustain much denser populations than could earlier societies dependent on hunting and gathering. Thus, the period from 500 B.C.E. to 1000 C.E. saw a massive transfer of Bantu traditions and practices southward, eastward, and westward and their transformation into Pan-African traditions and practices.

THE SPREAD OF IDEAS

Ideas, like social customs, religious attitudes, and artistic styles, can spread along trade routes and through folk migrations. In both cases, documenting the dissemination of ideas, particularly in preliterate societies, poses a difficult historical problem.

The Spread of Buddhism

Buddhism grew to become, with Christianity and Islam, one of the most popular and widespread religions in the world (see Chapter 7). In all three cases, the religious ideas spread without dependency on a single ethnic or kinship group.

King Ashoka, the Maurya ruler of India, and Kanishka, the greatest king of the Kushans of northern Afghanistan, promoted Buddhism between the third century B.C.E. and the second century C.E. However, monks, missionaries, and pilgrims who crisscrossed India, followed the Silk Road, or took ship on the Indian Ocean brought the Buddha's teachings to Southeast Asia, China, Korea, and ultimately Japan (see Map 6.1).

The Chinese pilgrims Faxian° (died between 418 and 423 C.E.) and Xuanzang° (600–664 C.E.) left written accounts of their travels. Both followed the Silk Road, from which Buddhism had arrived in China. Along the way they encountered Buddhist communities and monasteries that previous generations of missionaries and pilgrims had established.

Faxian began his trip in the company of a Chinese envoy to an unspecified ruler or people in Central Asia. After traveling from one Buddhist site to another across Afghanistan and India, he reached Sri Lanka, a Buddhist land where he lived for two years. Then he embarked for China on a merchant ship with two hundred men aboard. A storm drove the ship to Java, which, being a Hindu land, he did not describe. After five months ashore,

Faxian (fah-shee-en)
Xuanzang (shoo-wen-zahng)

Faxian finally reached China on another ship. The narrative of Xuanzang's journey two centuries later is quite similar, though he returned to China the way he had come, along the Silk Road.

Less reliable accounts make reference to missionaries traveling to Syria, Egypt, and Macedonia, as well as to Southeast Asia. One of Ashoka's sons allegedly led a band of missionaries to Sri Lanka. Later, his sister brought a company of nuns along with a branch of the sacred Bo tree under which the Buddha received enlightenment. According to Buddhist tradition, she accomplished her journey by air. At the same time, there are reports of other monks traveling to Burma, Thailand, and Sumatra. Ashoka's missionaries may also have reached Tibet by way of trade routes across the Himalayas. A firmer tradition maintains that in 622 C.E., a minister of the Tibetan king traveled to India to study Buddhism and on his return introduced writing to his homeland.

The different lands that received the story and teachings of the Buddha preserved or adapted them in different ways. Theravada Buddhism, "Teachings of the Elder," centered in Sri Lanka. Holding closely to the Buddha's earliest teachings, it maintained that the goal of religion, available only to monks, is *nirvana,* the total absence of suffering and the end of the cycle of rebirth (see Chapter 4). This teaching contrasted with Mahayana, or "Great Vehicle" Buddhism, which stressed the goal of becoming a *bodhisattva,* a person who attains nirvana but chooses to remain in human company to help and guide others.

An offshoot of Mahayana Buddhism stressing ritual prayer and personal guidance by "perfected ones" became dominant in Tibet after the eighth century C.E. In China, another offshoot, Chan (called Zen in its Japanese form), focused on meditation and sudden enlightenment. It became one of the dominant sects in China, Korea, and Japan (see Chapter 9).

The Spread of Christianity

The post-Roman development of Christianity in Europe is discussed in Chapter 8. The Christian faith enjoyed an earlier spread in Asia and Africa before its confrontation with Islam (described in

Chapter 7). Jerusalem in Palestine, Antioch in Syria, and Alexandria in Egypt became centers of Christian authority soon after the crucifixion of Jesus, but the spread of Christianity to Armenia and Ethiopia illustrates the connections between religion, trade, and imperial politics.

Situated in eastern Anatolia (modern Turkey), **Armenia** served recurrently as a battleground between Iranian states to the south and east and Mediterranean states to the west. Each imperial power wanted to control this region so close to the frontier where Silk Road traders met their Mediterranean counterparts. In Parthian times, Armenia's kings favored Zoroastrianism. Armenian not being a written language, Christianity was known to "only those who were to some degree acquainted with Greek or Syriac learning" and thus able to obtain "some partial inkling of it."[3]

The invention of an Armenian alphabet in the early fifth century opened the way to a wider spread of Christianity. The Iranians did not give up domination easily, but the Armenian Apostolic Church had become the center of Armenian cultural life within a century.

Far to the south, Christians similarly sought to outflank Iran. The Christian emperors in Constantinople (see Chapter 8) sent missionaries along the Red Sea trade route to seek converts in Yemen and **Ethiopia.** In the fourth century C.E., a Syrian philosopher, traveling with two young relatives, sailed to India. On the way back, the ship docked at a Red Sea port occupied by Ethiopians from the prosperous kingdom of Aksum. Being then at odds with the Romans, the Ethiopians killed everyone on board except two boys: Aedisius, who later narrated this story, and Frumentius. Impressed by their learning, the king made the former his cupbearer and the latter his treasurer and secretary.

When the king died, his wife urged Frumentius to govern Aksum on her behalf and that of her infant son, Ezana. As regent, Frumentius sought out Roman Christians among the merchants who visited the country and helped them establish Christian communities. When he became king, Ezana, who may have become a Christian, permitted Aedisius and Frumentius to return to Syria. The patriarch of Alexandria, on learning about the progress of Christianity in Aksum, elevated Frumentius to the rank of bishop, though he had not previously

Stele of Aksum   This 70-foot (21-meter) stone is the tallest remnant of a field of stelae, or standing stones, marking the tombs of Aksumite kings. The carvings of doors, windows, and beam ends imitate common features of Aksumite architecture, suggesting that each stele symbolized a multistory royal palace. The largest stelae date from the fourth century C.E.   (J. Allan Cash)

been a clergyman, and sent him back to Ethiopia as the first leader of its church.

The patriarch of Alexandria continues today to appoint the head of the Ethiopian Church, but the spread of Christianity into Nubia, the land south of Egypt along the Nile River, proceeded from Ethiopia rather than Egypt. Politically and economically, Ethiopia became a power at the western end of the Indian Ocean trading system, occasionally even extending its influence across the Red Sea and asserting itself in Yemen (see Map 6.2).

Ethiopian Christianity developed its own unique features. One popular belief, perhaps deriving from the Ethiopian Jewish community, was that the Ark of the Covenant, the most sacred object of the ancient Hebrews (see Chapter 3), had been transferred from Jerusalem to the Ethiopian church of Our Lady of Zion. Another tradition maintains that Christ miraculously dried up a lake to serve as the site for this church, which became the place of coronation for Ethiopia's rulers.

CONCLUSION

Exchange within early long-distance trading systems differed in many ways from the ebb and flow of culture, language, and custom that folk migrations brought about. New technologies and agricultural products worked great changes on the landscape and in people's lives, but nothing akin to the Africanity observed south of the Sahara can be attributed to the societies involved in the Silk Road, Indian Ocean, or trans-Saharan exchanges. The peoples directly involved in these complex social systems of travel and trade were few in comparison with the populations their routes brought into contact, and their lifestyles as pastoral nomads or seafarers isolated them still further. The Bantu, if current theories are correct, brought with them metallurgical skills and agricultural practices that permitted much denser habitation in the lands they spread to. Moreover, they settled among and merged with the previous inhabitants, becoming not just the bearers of new technologies but their primary beneficiaries as well.

The most obvious exception to this generalization lies in the intangible area of ideas. Christianity, Buddhism, and Islam all developed local customs and understandings as they spread, despite the overall doctrinal unity of each. As "great traditions," these religions linked priests, monks, nuns, and religious scholars across the vast distances. The masses of believers, however, seldom considered their faith in such broad contexts. Missionary religions imported through long-distance trading networks merged with myriad "small traditions" to provide for the social and spiritual needs of peoples living in many lands under widely varying circumstances.

■ ■ ■ ■ ■ ■ ■

■ Key Terms

Silk Road	Ghana
Parthians	sub-Saharan Africa
stirrup	steppes
Indian Ocean Maritime System	savanna
Malay peoples	tropical rain forest
Funan	great traditions
Srivijaya	small traditions
theater-state	Bantu
Borobodur	Armenia
trans-Saharan caravan routes	Ethiopia
Sahel	

■ Suggested Reading

For broad and suggestive overviews on cross-cultural exchange, see Philip D. Curtin, *Cross-Cultural Trade in World History* (1985), and C. G. F. Simkin, *The Traditional Trade of Asia* (1968).

Readable overviews of the Silk Road include Luce Boulnois, *The Silk Road* (1966), and Irene M. Franck and David M. Brownstone, *The Silk Road: A History* (1986). For products traded across Central Asia based on an eighth-century Japanese collection, see Ryoichi Hayashi, *The Silk Road and the Shoso-in* (1975). Xinru Liu, *Silk and Religion* (1996), covers one specific product. Owen Lattimore gives a first-person account of traveling by camel caravan in *The Desert Road to Turkestan* (1928). More generally on Central Asia, see Denis Sinor, *Inner Asia, History-Civilization-Languages: A Syllabus* (1987), and Karl Jettmar, *Art of the Steppes,* rev. ed. (1967). Richard Foltz, *Religions of the Silk Road* (1999), is an excellent brief introduction.

For a readable but sketchy historical overview, see August Toussaint, *History of the Indian Ocean* (1966). Alan Villiers recounts what it was like to sail traditional trading vessels called dhows between East Africa and the Persian Gulf in *Sons of Sinbad* (1940).

On a more scholarly plane, see K. N. Chaudhuri's *Trade and Civilization in the Indian Ocean: An Economic History from the Rise of Islam to 1750* (1985). Archaeologist Pierre Vérin treats the special problem of Madagascar in *The History of Civilisation in North Madagascar* (1986). For Rome and India, see E. H. Warmington's *The Commerce Between the Roman Empire and India* (1974); J. Innes Miller's *The Spice Trade of the Roman Empire, 29 B.C. to A.D. 641* (1969); and Vimala Begley and Richard Daniel De Puma's edited collection of articles, *Rome and India: The Ancient Sea Trade* (1991), along with the primary source *The Periplus Maris Arythraei: Text with Introduction, Translation, and Commentary* (1989), edited and translated by Lionel Casson. George F. Hourani's brief *Arab Seafaring in the Indian Ocean in Ancient and Early Medieval Times* (1975) covers materials in Arabic sources.

Nicholas Tarling, ed., *The Cambridge History of Southeast Asia*, vol. 1 (1992); D. R. SarDeSai, *Southeast Asia: Past and Present*, 3d ed. (1994); and Milton E. Osborne, *Southeast Asia: An Introductory History* (1995), provide general accounts of Southeast Asian history. Lynda Shaffer, *Maritime Southeast Asia to 1500* (1996), focuses on the world historical context. Also useful is Kenneth R. Hall, *Maritime Trade and State Development in Early Southeast Asia* (1985).

For art, see M. C. S. Diskul, *The Art of Srivijaya* (1980); Maud Girard-Geslan et al., *Art of Southeast Asia* (1998); and Daigoro Chihara, *Hindu-Buddhist Architecture in Southeast Asia* (1996).

Richard W. Bulliet's *The Camel and the Wheel* (1975) deals with camel use in the Middle East, along the Silk Road, and in North Africa and the Sahara. For a well-illustrated account of Saharan rock art, see Henri Lhote, *The Search for the Tassili Frescoes: The Story of the Prehistoric Rock-Paintings of the Sahara* (1959). Additional views on Saharan trade and politics appear in E. Ann McDougall, "The Sahara Reconsidered: Pastoralism, Politics and Salt from the Ninth Through the Twelfth Centuries," *History in Africa 12* (1983): 263–286, and Nehemia Levtzion, *Ancient Ghana and Mali*, 2d ed. (1980). For translated texts, see J. F. P. Hopkins and Nehemia Levtzion, eds., *Corpus of Early Arabic Sources for West African History* (1981).

J. F. A. Ajayi and Michael Crowder, *A History of West Africa*, vol. 1 (1976), and G. Mokhtar, ed., *General History of Africa II: Ancient Civilizations of Africa* (1981), contain many articles by numerous authors, the latter work specifically treating ironworking and the Bantu migrations. On African cultural unity, see Jacques Maquet, *Africanity: The Cultural Unity of Black Africa* (1972).

Of special importance on Christianity in Asia and Africa is Garth Fowden, *Empire to Commonwealth: Consequences of Monotheism in Late Antiquity* (1993).

For specific topics treated in this chapter, see Stuart Munro-Hay, *Aksum: An African Civilisation of Late Antiquity* (1991); Xinru Liu, *Ancient India and Ancient China: Trade and Religious Exchanges, A.D. 1–600* (1998); Rolf A. Stein, *Tibetan Civilization* (1972); Tilak Hettiarachchy, *History of Kingship in Ceylon up to the Fourth Century A.D.* (1972); and Yoneo Ishii, *Sangha, State, and Society: Thai Buddhism in History* (1986). The Chinese travelers' accounts cited are Fa-hsien [Faxian], *The Travels of Fahsien (399–414 A.D.), or, Record of the Buddhistic Kingdoms,* trans. H. A. Giles (1923; reprint, 1981), and Hiuen Tsiang [Xuanzang], *Si-Yu-Ki: Buddhist Records of the Western World,* trans. Samuel Beal (1884; reprint, 1981).

■ Notes

1. Victor H. Mair, ed., *The Columbia Anthology of Traditional Chinese Literature* (New York: Columbia University Press, 1994) p. 485; translated by Victor H. Mair.
2. J. F. A. Ajayi and Michael Crowder, eds., *History of West Africa,* vol. 1 (New York: Columbia University Press, 1976), 120–121.
3. Pawstos Busand, *Epic Histories* (late fifth century), quoted in Garth Fowden, *Empire to Commonwealth* Princeton NJ: Princeton University Press, (1993), 105.

The Sasanid Empire and the Rise of Islam,

200–1200

–f

The Sasanid Empire, 224–651 • **The Origins of Islam** • **The Rise and Fall of the Caliphate, 632–1258** • **Islamic Civilization**
SOCIETY AND CULTURE: **The Fraternity of Beggars**

he story is told that in the early days of Islam, at the time of the Prophet Muhammad's last pilgrimage to Mecca in 630, a dispute over distribution of booty arose between his daughter's husband, Ali, who was also Muhammad's first cousin, and some troops Ali commanded. Muhammad quelled the grumbling and later on the same journey, at a place named Ghadir al-Khumm°, drew his followers together, took Ali's hand, and declared: "Am I not nearer to the believers than their own selves? Whomever I am nearest to, so likewise is Ali. O God, be the friend of him who is his friend, and the foe of him who is his foe."

Written narrations of Muhammad's praise of Ali date to well over a century after the event. By that time, Ali had served as leader of Muhammad's community for a brief time and then been defeated in a civil war and assassinated. Subsequently, his son Husain and his family died in battle while trying to claim leadership as the Prophet's grandson.

Out of these events grew a division in the Islamic community: some believers, called **Shi'ites°**, from the Arabic term *Shi'at Ali,* meaning "Party of Ali," thought that religious leadership rightfully belonged to Ali and his descendants; others, eventually called **Sunnis°,** followers of the sunna, or "tradition" of the community, felt that the community should choose its leaders more broadly. Sunnis and Shi'ites agreed that Muhammad commended Ali at Ghadir al-Khumm. But the Sunnis thought that his remarks related only to the distribution of the booty, and the Shi'ites

---

Ghadir al-Khumm (ga-DEER al-KUM)

Shi'ite (SHE-ite)   **Sunni** (SUN-nee)

understood them to be Muhammad's formal and public declaration of Ali's special and elevated position and, hence, his right to rule.

Shi'ite rulers rarely achieved power, but those who ruled from Cairo between 969 and 1171 made the commemoration of Ghadir al-Khumm a major festival. At the beginning of every year, Shi'ites also engaged in public mourning over the deaths of Husain and his family. Sunni rulers, in contrast, sometimes ordered that Ali be cursed in public prayers.

Muhammad's Arab followers conquered an enormous territory in the seventh century and created in the name of Islam an empire that encompassed many peoples speaking many languages and worshiping in many ways. Its immediate forerunners, the realms of the Byzantine emperors (see Chapter 8) and Iran's Sasanid° shahs, closely linked religion with imperial politics.

Although urbanism, science, manufacturing, trade, and architecture flourished in the lands of Islam while medieval Europe was enduring hardship and economic contraction, religion shaped both societies. Just as the medieval Christian calendar revolved around Easter and Christmas, Islamic fasts and pilgrimages and political religious observances like Ghadir al-Khumm marked the yearly cycle in the lands of Muhammad's followers.

As you read this chapter, ask yourself the following questions:

- How did social and political developments under the Sasanid Empire pave the way for the spread of Islam?

- How did the Arab conquests grow out of the career of Muhammad?

- Why did the caliphate break up?

- What was the relationship between urbanization and the development of Islamic culture?

THE SASANID EMPIRE, 224–651

The rise in the third century of a new Iranian state, the **Sasanid Empire,** continued the old rivalry between Rome and the Parthians along the Euphrates frontier. However, behind this facade of continuity, a social and economic transformation took place that set the stage for a new and powerful religio-political movement: Islam.

Politics and Society

Ardashir, a descendant of Sasan, defeated the Parthians around 224 and established the Sasanid kingdom. To their west, the new rulers confronted the Romans, whom historians refer to as the Byzantines after about 330. Along their desert Euphrates frontier, the Sasanids subsidized nomadic Arab chieftains to protect their empire from invasion (the Byzantines did the same with Arabs on their desert Jordanian frontier). Arab pastoralists farther to the south remained isolated and independent. The rival empires launched numerous attacks on each other across that frontier between the 340s and 628. In times of peace, however, exchange between the empires flourished, allowing goods transported over the Silk Road to enter the zone of Mediterranean trade.

The Arab pastoralists inhabiting the desert between Syria and Mesopotamia supplied camels and guides and played a significant role as merchants and organizers of caravans. The militarily efficient North Arabian camel saddle (see Chapter 6, Environment and Technology: Camel Saddles), developed around the third century B.C.E., provided another key to Arab prosperity. The Arabs used it to take control of the caravan trade in their territories and became so important as suppliers of

Sasanid (suh-SAH-nid)

animal power even in agricultural districts that wheeled vehicles—mostly ox carts and horse-drawn chariots—entirely disappeared by the sixth century C.E.

The mountains and plateaus of Iran proper formed the Sasanids' political hinterland, often ruled by the cousins of the shah (king) or powerful nobles. Cities there were small walled communities that served more as military strongpoints than as centers of population and production. Society revolved around a local aristocracy who lived on rural estates and cultivated the arts of hunting and war just like the noble warriors described in the sagas of ancient kings and heroes sung at their banquets.

Despite the dominance of powerful aristocratic families, long-lasting political fragmentation of the medieval European variety did not develop. Also, although many nomads lived in the mountains and desert regions, no folk migration arose comparable to that of the Germanic peoples of the Late Roman Empire. The Sasanid and Byzantine Empires successfully maintained central control of imperial finances and military power and found effective ways of integrating frontier peoples as mercenaries or caravaneers.

The Silk Road brought new products to Mesopotamia, some of which became part of the agricultural landscape. Sasanid farmers pioneered in planting cotton, sugar cane, rice, citrus trees, eggplants, and other crops adopted from India and China. Although the acreage devoted to new crops increased slowly, these products became important consumption and trade items during the succeeding Islamic period.

Religion and Empire

The Sasanids established their Zoroastrian faith (see Chapter 4), which the Parthians had not particularly stressed, as a state religion similar to Christianity in the Byzantine Empire (see Chapter 8). The proclamation of Christianity and Zoroastrianism as official faiths marked the fresh emergence of religion as an instrument of politics both within and between the empires, setting a precedent for the subsequent rise of Islam as the focus of a political empire.

Both Zoroastrianism and Christianity practiced intolerance. A late-third-century inscription in Iran boasts of the persecutions of Christians, Jews, and Buddhists carried out by the Zoroastrian high priest. Yet sizable Christian and Jewish communities remained, especially in Mesopotamia. From the fourth century onward, councils of Christian bishops declared many theological beliefs heretical—so unacceptable that they were un-Christian.

Christians became pawns in the political rivalry with the Byzantines, sometimes persecuted and sometimes patronized by the Sasanid kings. In 431, a council of bishops called by the Byzantine emperor declared the Nestorian Christians heretics for overemphasizing the humanness of Christ. The Nestorians believed that human characteristics and divinity coexisted in Jesus and that Mary was not the mother of God, as many other Christians maintained, but the mother of the human Jesus. After the bishops' ruling, the Nestorians sought refuge under the Sasanid shah and eventually spread their missionary activities across Central Asia.

In the third century, a preacher named Mani founded a new religion in Mesopotamia: Manichaeism. He preached a dualist faith—a struggle between Good and Evil—theologically derived from Zoroastrianism. Although at first Mani enjoyed the favor of the shah, he was martyred in 276 with many of his followers. Yet his religion survived and spread widely. Nestorian missionaries in Central Asia competed with Manichaean missionaries for converts. In later centuries, the term *Manichaean* was applied to all sorts of beliefs in a cosmic struggle between Good and Evil.

The Arabs became enmeshed in this web of religious conflict. The border protectors subsidized by the Byzantines adopted a Monophysite theology, which emphasized Christ's divine nature; the allies of the Sasanids, the Nestorian faith. Through them, knowledge of Christianity penetrated deeper into the Arabian peninsula during the fifth and sixth centuries.

Religion penetrated all aspects of community life. Most subjects of the Byzantine emperors and Sasanid shahs identified themselves first and foremost as members of a religious community. Their schools and law courts were religious. They looked

CHRONOLOGY

	The Arab Lands	Iran and Central Asia
200		**224–651** Sasanid Empire
600	**570–632** Life of the Prophet Muhammad	
	634 Conquests of Iraq and Syria commence	
	639–42 Conquest of Egypt by Arabs	
	656–61 Ali caliph; first civil war	
700	**661–750** Umayyad Caliphate rules from Damascus	
	711 Berbers and Arabs invade Spain from North Africa	**711** Arabs capture Sind in India
	740 Berber revolts in North Africa; Kharijite states founded	**747** Abbasid revolt begins in Khurasan
	750 Beginning of Abbasid Caliphate	
	755 Umayyad state established in Spain	
	776–809 Caliphate of Harun al-Rashid	
800	**835–92** Abbasid capital moved from Baghdad to Samarra	**875** Independent Samanid state founded in Bukhara
900	**909** Fatimids seize North Africa, found Shi'ite Caliphate	
	929 Abd al-Rahman III declares himself caliph in Cordoba	
	945 Shi'ite Buyids take control in Baghdad	**945** Buyids from northern Iran take control of Abbasid Caliphate
	969 Fatimids conquer Egypt	
1000	**1055** Seljuk Turks take control in Baghdad	**1036** Beginning of Turkish Seljuk rule in Khurasan
	1099 First Crusade captures Jerusalem	
	1171 Fall of Fatimid Egypt	
	1187 Saladin recaptures Jerusalem	
	1250 Mamluks control Egypt	
	1258 Mongols sack Baghdad and end Abbasid Caliphate	
	1260 Mamluks defeat Mongols at Ain Jalut	

on priests, monks, rabbis, and mobads (their Zoroastrian equivalents) as moral guides in daily life. Most books discussed religious subjects. And in some areas, religious leaders represented their flocks even in secular matters such as tax collection.

THE ORIGINS OF ISLAM

The Arabs who lived beyond the frontiers of the Sasanid Empire seldom interested the Sasanid rulers. But it was precisely in the interior of Arabia, far from the gaze and political reach of the Sasanid and Byzantine Empires, that the religion of Islam took form and inspired a movement that would humble the proud emperors.

The Arabian Peninsula Before Muhammad

Throughout history, most of the people living on the Arabian peninsula have lived in settled communities rather than as pastoral nomads. The highlands of Yemen, fertile and abundantly watered by the spring monsoon, and the interior mountains farther east in southern Arabia support farming and village life. Small inlets along the coast favored occasional fishing or trading communities. However, the enormous sea of sand known as the "Empty Quarter" isolated these southern regions from the Arabian interior. In the seventh century, most people in southern Arabia knew more about Africa, India, and the Persian Gulf than about the forbidding interior and the scattered camel- and sheep-herding nomads who lived there.

Exceptions to this pattern mostly involved caravan trading. Several kingdoms rose and fell in Yemen, leaving stone ruins and enigmatic inscriptions to testify to their bygone prosperity. From these commercial entrepôts came the aromatic resins frankincense and myrrh. Nomads derived income from providing camels, guides, and safe passage to merchants wanting to transport incense northward, where the fragrant substances had long

been burned in religious rituals. Return caravans brought manufactured products from Mesopotamia and the Mediterranean.

Just as the Silk Road enabled small towns in Central Asia to become major trading centers, so the trans-Arabian trade gave rise to desert caravan cities. The earliest and most prosperous, Petra in southern Jordan and Palmyra° in northern Syria, were swallowed up by Rome. This, coupled with early Christian distaste for incense, which seemed too much a feature of pagan worship, contributed to a slackening of trade in Sasanid times. Nevertheless, trade across the desert did not lapse altogether. Camels, leather, and gold and other minerals mined in the mountains of western Arabia took the place of frankincense and myrrh as exports. This reduced trade kept alive the relations between the Arabs and the settled farming regions to the north, and it familiarized the Arabs who accompanied the caravans with the cultures and lifestyles of the Sasanid and Byzantine Empires.

In the desert, Semitic polytheism, with its worship of natural forces and celestial bodies, began to encounter other religions. Christianity, as practiced by Arabs in Jordan and southern Mesopotamia, and Judaism, possibly carried by refugees from the Roman expulsion of the Jews from their homeland in the first century C.E., made inroads on polytheism.

Mecca, a late-blooming caravan city, lies in a barren mountain valley halfway between Yemen and Syria along the Red Sea coast of Arabia (see Map 7.1). A nomadic kin group known as the Quraysh° settled in Mecca in the fifth century and assumed control of this trade. Mecca rapidly achieved a measure of prosperity, partly because it was too far from Byzantine Syria, Sasanid Iraq, and Ethiopian-controlled Yemen for them to attack it.

A cubical shrine called the Ka'ba°, containing idols, a holy well called Zamzam, and a sacred precinct surrounding the two wherein killing was prohibited contributed to the emergence of Mecca as a pilgrimage site. Some Meccans associated the shrine with stories known to Jews and Christians. They regarded Abraham (Ibrahim in Arabic) as the

---

Palmyra (pal-MY-ruh)   **Quraysh** (koo-RYYSH)
Ka'ba (KAH-buh)

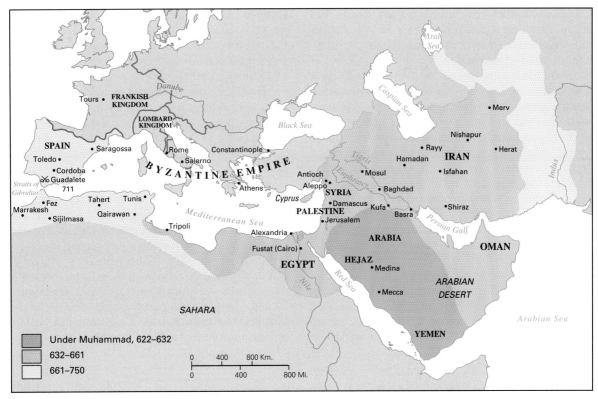

Map. 7.1   Early Expansion of Muslim Rule   Arab conquests of the first Islamic century brought vast territory under Muslim rule, but conversion to Islam proceeded slowly. In most areas outside the Arabian peninsula, the only region where Arabic was then spoken, conversion did not accelerate until the third century after the conquest.

builder of the Ka'ba, and they identified a site outside Mecca as the location where God asked Abraham to sacrifice his son. The son was not Isaac (Ishaq in Arabic), the son of Sarah, but Ishmael (Isma'il in Arabic), the son of Hagar, cited in the Bible as the forefather of the Arabs.

Muhammad in Mecca

Born in Mecca in 570, **Muhammad** grew up an orphan in the house of his uncle. He engaged in trade and married a Quraysh widow named Khadija°, whose caravan interests he superintended. Their son died in childhood, but several

Khadija (kah-DEE-juh)

daughters survived. Around 610, Muhammad began meditating at night in the mountainous terrain around Mecca. During one night vigil, known to later tradition as the "Night of Power and Excellence," a being whom Muhammad later understood to be the angel Gabriel (Jibra'il in Arabic) spoke to him:

> Proclaim! In the name of your Lord who created.
> Created man from a clot of congealed blood.
> Proclaim! And your Lord is the Most Bountiful.
> He who has taught by the pen.
> Taught man that which he knew not.[1]

For three years, he shared this and subsequent revelations only with close friends and family members. This period culminated in Muhammad's conviction that he was hearing the words of God

(Allah° in Arabic). Khadija, his uncle's son Ali, his friend Abu Bakr°, and others close to him shared this conviction. The revelations continued until Muhammad's death in 632.

Like most other people of the time, including Christians and Jews, the Arabs believed in unseen spirits: gods, desert spirits called *jinns,* demonic *shaitans,* and so forth. They further believed that certain individuals had contact with the spirit world, notably seers and poets, who were thought to be possessed by a jinn. Therefore, when Muhammad began to recite his rhymed revelations in public, many people believed he was inspired by an unseen spirit even if it was not, as Muhammad asserted, the one true god.

Muhammad's earliest revelations called on people to witness that one god had created the universe and everything in it, including themselves. At the end of time, their souls would be judged, with their sins balanced against their good deeds. The blameless would go to paradise; the sinful would taste hellfire:

> By the night as it conceals the light;
> By the day as it appears in glory;
> By the mystery of the creation of male and
>   female;
> Verily, the ends ye strive for are diverse.
> So he who gives in charity and fears God,
> And in all sincerity testifies to the best,
> We will indeed make smooth for him the path
>   to Bliss.
> But he who is a greedy miser and thinks himself
>   self-sufficient,
> And gives the lie to the best,
> We will indeed make smooth for him the path
>   to misery.[2]

The revelation called all people to submit to God and accept Muhammad as the last of his messengers. Doing so made one a **muslim,** meaning one who makes "submission," **Islam,** to the will of God.

Because earlier messengers mentioned in the revelations included Noah, Moses, and Jesus, Muhammad's hearers felt that his message resembled the Judaism and Christianity they were already somewhat familiar with. Yet his revelations charged the Jews and Christians with being negligent in preserving God's revealed word. Thus, even though they identified Abraham/Ibrahim, whom Muslims consider the first Muslim, as the builder of the Ka'ba, which superseded Jerusalem as the focus of Muslim prayer in 624, Muhammad's followers considered his revelation more perfect than the Bible because it had not gone through an editing process.

Some non-Muslim scholars maintain that Muhammad's revelations appealed especially to people distressed over wealth replacing kinship as the most important aspect of social relations. They see verses criticizing taking pride in money and neglecting obligations to orphans and other powerless people as conveying a message of social reform. Other scholars, along with most Muslims, put less emphasis on a social message and stress the power and beauty of Muhammad's revelations. Forceful rhetoric and poetic vision, coming in the Muslim view directly from God, go far to explain Muhammad's early success.

The Formation of the Umma

Mecca's leaders feared that accepting Muhammad as the sole agent of the one true God would threaten their power and prosperity. They pressured his kin to disavow him and persecuted the weakest of his followers. Stymied by this hostility, Muhammad and his followers fled Mecca in 622 to take up residence in the agricultural community of **Medina** 215 miles (346 kilometers) to the north. This hijra° marks the beginning of the Muslim calendar.

Prior to the hijra, Medinan representatives had met with Muhammad and agreed to accept and protect him and his followers because they saw him as an inspired leader who could calm their perpetual feuding. Together, the Meccan migrants and major groups in Medina bound themselves into a single **umma°,** a community defined solely by acceptance of Islam and of Muhammad as the "Messenger of God," his most common title. Three Jewish kin groups chose to retain their own faith, thus contributing to the Muslims' changing the di-

---

Allah (AH-luh) **Abu Bakr** (ah-boo BAK-uhr)

hijra (HIJ-ruh) **umma** (UM-muh)

rection of their prayer toward the Ka'ba, now thought of as the "House of God."

During the last decade of his life, Muhammad took active responsibility for his umma. Having left their Meccan kin groups, the Meccan immigrants in Medina felt vulnerable. Fresh revelations provided a framework for regulating social and legal affairs and stirred the Muslims to fight against the still-unbelieving city of Mecca. Sporadic war, largely conducted by raiding and negotiation with desert nomads, sapped Mecca's strength and convinced many Meccans that God favored Muhammad. In 630, Mecca surrendered. Muhammad and his followers made the pilgrimage to the Ka'ba unhindered.

Muhammad did not return to Mecca again. Medina had grown into a bustling city-state. The Jews he had expelled or eliminated for alleged disloyalty during the war. Delegations from all over Arabia came to meet Muhammad, and he sent emissaries back with them to teach about Islam and collect their alms. Muhammad's mission to bring God's message to humanity had brought him unchallenged control of a state that was coming to dominate the Arabian peninsula. But the supremacy of the Medinan state, unlike preceding short-lived nomadic kingdoms, depended not on kinship but on a common faith in a single god.

In 632, after a brief illness, Muhammad died. Within twenty-four hours, a group of Medinan leaders, along with three of Muhammad's close friends, determined that Abu Bakr, one of the earliest believers and the father of Muhammad's favorite wife, A'isha°, should succeed him. They called him the *khalifa°*, or "successor," the English version of which is *caliph*. But calling Abu Bakr a successor did not clarify his powers. Everyone knew that neither Abu Bakr nor anyone else could receive revelations, and they also knew that Muhammad's revelations made no provision for succession or for any government purpose beyond maintaining the umma. Indeed, some people thought the world would soon end because God's last messenger was dead.

Abu Bakr continued and confirmed Muhammad's religious practices, notably the so-called Five Pillars of Islam: (1) avowal that there is only one god and Muhammad is his messenger, (2) prayer five times a day, (3) fasting during the lunar month of Ramadan, (4) paying alms, and (5) making the pilgrimage to Mecca at least once during one's lifetime. He also reestablished and expanded Muslim authority over Arabia's nomadic and settled communities. After Muhammad's death, some had abandoned their allegiance to Medina or followed various would-be prophets. Muslim armies fought hard to confirm the authority of the newborn **caliphate.** In the process, some fighting spilled over into non-Arab areas in Iraq.

Abu Bakr ordered those who had acted as secretaries for Muhammad to organize the Prophet's revelations into a book. Hitherto written haphazardly on pieces of leather or bone, the verses of revelation became a single document gathered into chapters. This resulting book, which acquired its final form around the year 650, was called the **Quran°,** or the Recitation. Muslims regard it not as the words of Muhammad but as the unalterable word of God. As such, it compares not so much to the Bible, a book written by many hands over many centuries, as to the person of Jesus Christ, whom Christians consider a human manifestation of God.

Although united in its acceptance of God's will, the umma soon disagreed over the succession to the caliphate. The first civil war in Islam followed the assassination of the third caliph, Uthman°, in 656. His assassins, rebels from the army, nominated to succeed him Ali, Muhammad's first cousin and the husband of his daughter Fatima. Ali had been passed over three times previously even though many people considered him to be the Prophet's natural heir. He and his supporters felt that Muhammad had indicated as much at Ghadir al-Khumm.

When Ali accepted the nomination to be caliph, two of Muhammad's close companions and A'isha challenged him. Ali defeated them in the Battle of the Camel (656), so called because the fighting raged around the camel on which A'isha was seated in an enclosed woman's saddle.

After the battle, the governor of Syria, Mu'awiya°, a kinsman of the slain Uthman from

---

A'isha (AH-ee-shah)   khalifa (kah-LEE-fuh)

Quran (kuh-RAHN)   Uthman (ooth-MAHN)
Mu'awiya (moo-AH-we-yuh)

the Umayya clan of the Quraysh, renewed the challenge. Inconclusive battle gave way to arbitration. The arbitrators decided that Uthman, whom his assassins considered corrupt, had not deserved death and that Ali had erred in accepting the nomination. Ali rejected the arbitrators' findings, but before he could resume fighting, one of his own supporters killed him for agreeing to the arbitration. Mu'awiya then offered Ali's son Hasan a dignified retirement and thus emerged as caliph in 661.

Mu'awiya chose his own son, Yazid, to succeed him, thereby instituting the **Umayyad° Caliphate.** When Hasan's brother Husayn revolted in 680 to reestablish the right of Ali's family to rule, Yazid ordered Husayn and his family killed. Sympathy for Husayn's martyrdom helped transform Shi'ism from a political movement into a religious sect.

Several variations in Shi'ite belief developed, but Shi'ites have always agreed that Ali was the rightful successor to Muhammad and that God's choice as Imam, leader of the Muslim community, has always been one or another of Ali's descendants. They see the office of caliph as more secular than religious. Because the Shi'ites seldom held power, their religious feelings came to focus on outpourings of sympathy for Husayn and other martyrs and on messianic dreams that one of their Imams some day would triumph.

Those Muslims who supported the first three caliphs gradually came to be called "People of Tradition and Community"—in Arabic, *Ahl al-Sunna wa'l-Jama'a,* or Sunnis for short. Sunnis consider the caliphs to be Imams. As for Ali's followers who had abhorred his acceptance of arbitration, they evolved into small and rebellious Kharijite sects (from *kharaja,* meaning "to secede or rebel") claiming righteousness for themselves alone. These three divisions of Islam, the last now quite minor, still survive. Today the umma approaches 1 billion people.

THE RISE AND FALL OF THE CALIPHATE, 632–1258

The Islamic caliphate built on the conquests the Arabs carried out after Muhammad's death gave birth to a dynamic and creative religious society. By the late 800s, however, one piece after another of this huge realm had broken away. Yet the idea of a caliphate, however unrealistic it became, remained a touchstone of Sunni belief in the unity of the umma.

Islam never granted a single person the power to define true belief, expel heretics, and discipline clergy. Thus, the caliphs, unlike Christian popes and patriarchs, had little basis for reestablishing their originally universal authority once they lost political and military power.

The Islamic Conquests, 634–711

Arab conquests outside Arabia began under the second caliph, Umar (r. 634–644), possibly prompted by earlier forays into Iraq. Arab armies had wrenched Syria (636) and Egypt (639–642) away from the Byzantine Empire and defeated the last Sasanid shah, Yazdigird III (r. 632–651) (see Map 7.1). After a decade-long lull, expansion began again. Tunisia fell and became the governing center from which was organized, in 711, the conquest of Spain by an Arab-led army mostly composed of Algerian and Moroccan Berbers. In the same year, Sind, the southern Indus Valley and westernmost region of India, succumbed to partially seaborne invaders from Iraq. The Muslim dominion remained roughly stable for the next three centuries. In the eleventh century, conquest began anew in India, Anatolia, and sub-Saharan Africa. Islam also expanded peacefully by trade in these and other areas.

The speed and political cohesiveness of the Arab campaigns distinguishes them from the piecemeal incursions of the Germanic peoples into the Roman Empire (see Chapter 5). The close Meccan companions of the Prophet, men of political

---

Umayyad (oo-MY-ad)

and economic sophistication inspired by their experience of his charisma, guided the conquests. The social structure and hardy nature of Arab society lent itself to flexible military operations, and the authority of Medina, reconfirmed during the caliphate of Abu Bakr, ensured obedience.

The decision made during Umar's caliphate to prohibit Arabs from taking over conquered territory for their own use proved important. Umar tied army service, with its regular pay and occasional windfalls of booty, to residence in large military camps: two in Iraq, one in Egypt, and one in Tunisia. East of Iraq, Arabs settled in small garrison towns at strategic locations and in one large garrison at Marv in present-day Turkmenistan. Down to the early eighth century, this policy kept the armies together and ready for action and preserved life virtually unchanged in the countryside, where some three-fourths of the population lived. Most people who became subjects of the caliphate by conquest probably never saw an Arab, and only a tiny proportion in Syria and Iraq understood the Arabic language.

The million or so Arabs who participated in the conquests constituted a small, self-isolated ruling minority living on the taxes paid by a vastly larger non-Arab, non-Muslim subject population. The Arabs had little material incentive to encourage conversion, and there is no evidence of coherent missionary efforts to spread Islam during the conquest period.

The Umayyad and Early Abbasid Caliphates, 661–850

The Umayyad caliphs presided over an ethnically defined Arab realm rather than a religious empire. Ruling from Damascus, their armies consisted almost entirely of Muslim Arabs. They adopted and adapted the administrative practices of their Sasanid and Byzantine predecessors, as had the caliphs who preceded them. Only gradually did they replace non-Muslim secretaries and tax officials with Muslims and introduce Arabic as the language of government. The introduction of distinctively Muslim silver and gold coins early in the eighth century symbolized the new order. From that time on, silver dirhams and gold dinars bearing Arabic religious phrases circulated in monetary exchanges from Morocco to the frontiers of China.

The Umayyad dynasty fell in 750 after a decade of growing unrest in many quarters. Converts to Islam, by that date no more than 10 percent of the indigenous population, were numerically significant because of the comparatively small number of Arab warriors. They resented not achieving equal status with the Arabs. The Arabs of Iraq and elsewhere envied the Syrian Arab influence in caliphal affairs. Pious Muslims looked askance at the secular and even irreligious behavior of the caliphs. And Shi'ites and Kharijites attacked the Umayyad family's legitimacy as rulers, launching a number of rebellions.

In 747, a rebellion in the region of Khurasan° in northeastern Iran, Afghanistan, and Turkmenistan overthrew the last Umayyad caliph, though one family member escaped to Spain and set up an Umayyad state there in 755. Many Shi'ites supported the rebellion thinking they were fighting for the family of Ali. As it turned out, the family of Abbas, one of Muhammad's uncles, controlled the secret organization that coordinated the revolt. Upon victory, they established the **Abbasid° Caliphate.** Some of the Abbasid caliphs who ruled after 750 befriended their relatives in Ali's family, and one even flirted with transferring the caliphate to them. The Abbasid family, however, held on to the caliphate until 1258, when Mongol invaders killed the last of them in Baghdad (see Chapter 13).

At its outset, the Abbasid dynasty made a fine show of leadership and concern for Islam. Theology and religious law became preoccupations at court and among a growing community of scholars, along with interpretation of the Quran, collecting the sayings of the Prophet, and Arabic grammar. Some caliphs fought on the Byzantine frontier to extend Islam. Others sponsored ambitious projects to translate the great works of Greek, Persian, and Indian thought into Arabic.

At the same time, the new dynasty, with its roots among the semi-Persianized Arabs of Khurasan, gradually adopted the ceremonies and customs of the Sasanid shahs. Government grew increasingly complex in Baghdad, the newly built

Khurasan (kor-uh-SAHN)   Abbasid (ah-BASS-id)

capital city on the Tigris River. As more and more non-Arabs converted to Islam, the ruling elite became more cosmopolitan. Greek, Iranian, Central Asian, and African cultural currents met in the capital and gave rise to an abundance of literary works, a process facilitated by the introduction of paper-making from China. Arab poets neglected the traditional odes extolling life in the desert and wrote instead wine songs (despite Islam's prohibition of alcohol) or poems in praise of their patrons.

The translation of Aristotle into Arabic, the founding of the main currents of theology and law, and the splendor of the Abbasid court—reflected in stories of *The Arabian Nights* set in the time of the caliph Harun al-Rashid° (r. 776–809)—in some respects warrant calling the early Abbasid period a "golden age." Yet the refinement of Baghdad culture only slowly made its way into the provinces. Egypt remained predominantly Christian and Coptic speaking in the early Abbasid period. Iran never adopted Arabic as a spoken tongue. And Berber-speaking North Africa freed itself almost entirely of caliphal rule: Morocco and Algeria through Kharijite revolts in 740, Tunisia after 800 by agreeing to pay regular tribute to Baghdad.

Gradual conversion to Islam among the conquered population grew strong only in the second quarter of the ninth century. Social discrimination against non-Arab converts gradually faded, and the Arabs themselves—at least those living in cosmopolitan urban settings—lost their previously strong attachment to kinship and ethnic identity.

Political Fragmentation, 850–1050

Abbasid decline became evident in the second half of the ninth century as conversion to Islam accelerated (see Map 7.2). No government ruling an empire stretching almost a quarter of the way around the world could hold power easily. Caravans traveled only 20 miles (32 kilometers) a day, and the couriers of the caliphal post system usually did not exceed 100 miles (160 kilometers) a day. News of frontier revolts took weeks to reach Baghdad. Military responses might take months. Administrators struggled to centralize tax payments, often made in grain or other produce rather than cash, and ensure that provincial governors forwarded the proper amounts to Baghdad.

The first Arab garrisons had been strung like beads across territory populated mostly by non-Muslims; revolts against Arab rule had been a concern. Members of the Muslim umma had had every reason to cling together, despite the long distances. But with the massive conversion of the population to Islam, the idea that Islam might disappear faded. Muslims became the overwhelming majority and gradually realized that a highly centralized empire with a rich and splendid capital did not necessarily serve the interests of all the people.

Eighth-century revolts had often targeted Arab or Muslim domination. By the middle of the ninth century, this type of rebellion gave way to movements within the Islamic community that concentrated on seizure of territory and formation of a principality. None of the states carved out of the Abbasid Caliphate after 850 repudiated or even threatened Islam. They did, however, prevent tax revenues from flowing to Baghdad, thereby increasing local prosperity. Local Muslim communities either supported such rebels or remained neutral.

Increasingly starved for funds by breakaway provinces and by a fall in revenues from Iraq itself, the caliphate experienced a crisis in the late ninth century. Distrusting generals and troops from outlying areas, the caliphs purchased Turkic slaves, **mamluks°,** from Central Asia and established them as a standing army. Well trained and hardy, the Turks proved an effective but expensive military force. When the government could not pay them, the mamluks took it on themselves to seat and unseat caliphs, a process made easier by the construction of a new capital at Samarra, north of Baghdad on the Tigris River.

The Turks dominated Samarra without interference from an unruly Baghdad populace that regarded them as rude and highhanded. However, the money and effort that went into the huge city, which was occupied only from 835 to 892, sapped the caliphs' financial strength and deflected labor from more productive pursuits.

Harun al-Rashid (hah-ROON al–rah-SHEED)

mamluk (MAM-luke)

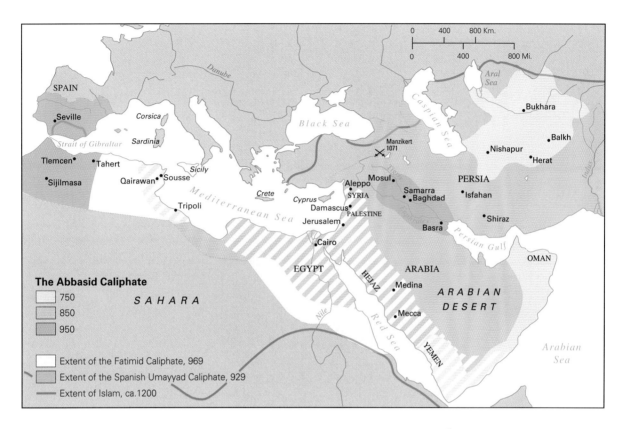

Map. 7.2 Rise and Fall of the Abbasid Caliphate   Although Abbasid rulers occupied the caliphal seat in Iraq from 750 to 1258, when Mongol armies destroyed Baghdad, real political power waned sharply and steadily after 850. The rival caliphates of the Fatimids (909–1171) and Spanish Umayyads (929–976) were comparatively short-lived.

In 945, after several attempts at finding a strongman to reform government administration and restore military power, the Abbasid Caliphate fell under the control of mountain warriors from the province of Daylam in northern Iran. Led by the Shi'ite Buyid° family, they conquered western Iran as well as Iraq. Each Buyid commander ruled his own principality. After almost two centuries of glory, the sun began to set on Baghdad. The Abbasid caliph remained, but the Buyid princes controlled him. Being Shi'ites, the Buyids had no special reverence for the Sunni caliph. According to their particular Shi'ite sect, the twelfth and last divinely appointed Imam had disappeared around

873 and would return as a messiah only at the end of the world. Thus, they had no Shi'ite Imam to defer to and retained the caliph only to help control their predominantly Sunni subjects.

Dynamic growth in outlying provinces paralleled the caliphate's gradual loss of temporal power. In the east, in 875, the dynasty of the Samanids°, one of several Iranian families to achieve independence, established a glittering court in Bukhara, a major city on the Silk Road (see Map 7.2). Samanid princes patronized literature and learning, but the language they favored was Persian written in Arabic letters. For the first time, a non-Arabic literature rose to challenge the emi-

---

Buyid (BOO-yid)   **Samanid** (sah-MAN-id)

Mosque and Minaret at Samarra   A unique spiral minaret 171 feet (52 meters) high marks the ruins of Samarra, an Abbasid capital begun in 835 on the east bank of the Tigris River 65 miles (104 kilometers) north of Baghdad. The caliph returned to Baghdad in 892 because of severe friction between the people of Baghdad and Turkish mamluks.   (Creswell Photographic Archive, Ashmolean Museum, Oxford, neg. C270)

nence of Arabic within the Islamic world. The new Persian poetry and prose foreshadowed the world of today, in which Iran sharply distinguishes itself from the Arab world.

In Egypt, a Shi'ite ruler established himself as a rival caliph in 969, culminating a sixty-year struggle by his family, the Fatimids°, to extend their power beyond an initial base in Tunisia. His governing complex outside Fustat° was named Cairo. For the first time, Egypt became a major cultural, intellectual, and political center of Islam (see Map 7.2). The al-Azhar Mosque built at this time remains

a paramount religious and educational center to this day. Shi'ite religious influence in Sunni Egypt remained slight despite two centuries of Fatimid rule. Nevertheless, the abundance of Fatimid gold coinage, derived from West African sources, made them an economic power in the Mediterranean.

Cut off from the rest of the Islamic world by the Strait of Gibraltar and, from 740 onward, by independent city-states in Morocco and Algeria, Umayyad Spain developed a distinctive Islamic culture blending Roman, Germanic, and Jewish traditions with those of the Arabs and Berbers (see Map 7.1). Historians disagree on how rapidly and completely the Spanish population converted to Islam. If we assume a process similar to that in the eastern

---

Fatimid (FAT-uh-mid)   **Fustat** (fuss-TAHT)

regions, it seems likely that the most rapid surge in Islamization occurred in the mid-tenth century.

As in the east, governing cities symbolized the Islamic presence in al-Andalus, as the Muslims called their Iberian territories. Cordoba, Seville, Toledo, and other cities grew substantially, becoming larger and richer than comparable cities in neighboring France. Converts to Islam and their descendants, unconverted Arabic-speaking Christians, and Jews joined with the comparatively few descendants of Arab settlers to create new architectural and literary styles. In the countryside, where the Berbers preferred to settle, a fusion of preexisting agricultural technologies with new crops, notably citrus fruits, and irrigation techniques from the east gave Spain the most diverse and sophisticated agricultural economy in Europe.

The rulers of al-Andalus took the title *caliph* only in 929, when Abd al-Rahman° III (r. 912–961) did so in response to a similar declaration by the newly established (909) Fatimid ruler in Tunisia. By the century's end, however, this caliphate encountered challenges from breakaway movements that eventually splintered al-Andalus into a number of small states. But political decay did not impede cultural growth. Some of the greatest writers and thinkers in Jewish history worked in Muslim Spain in the eleventh and twelfth centuries, sometimes writing in Arabic, sometimes in Hebrew. At the same time, Islamic thought in Spain attained its loftiest peaks in Ibn Hazm's treatises on love and other subjects, the philosophical writings of Ibn Rushd° (known in Latin as Averroës°) and Ibn Tufayl°, and the mystic speculations of Ibn al-Arabi.°

The Samanids, Fatimids, and Spanish Umayyads represent the political diversity and awakening of local awareness that coincided with Abbasid decline. Yet drawing and redrawing political boundaries did not result in the rigid division of the Islamic world into kingdoms, as was then occurring in Europe. Religious and cultural developments, particularly the rise in cities of a social group of religious scholars known as the **ulama**°—

Abd al-Rahman (AHB-d al–ruh-MAHN)
Ibn Rushd (IB-uhn RUSHED)   **Averroës** (uh-VERR-oh-eez)
Ibn Tufayl (IB-uhn too-FILE)
Ibn al-Arabi (IB-uhn ahl-AH-rah-bee)
ulama (oo-leh-MAH)

Arabic for "people with (religious) knowledge"—worked against any permanent division of the Islamic umma.

Assault from Within and Without, 1050–1258

The role that Turkish mamluks played in the decline of Abbasid power established an enduring stereotype of the Turk as a ferocious warrior little interested in religion or urban sophistication. This image gained strength in the 1030s when the Seljuk° family established a Turkish Muslim state based on nomadic power. Taking the Arabic title *Sultan,* meaning "power," and the revived Persian title *Shahan-shah*°, the Seljuk ruler Tughril° Beg created a kingdom that stretched from northern Afghanistan to Baghdad, which he occupied in 1055. After a century under the thumb of the Shi'ite Buyids, the Abbasid caliph breathed more easily under the slightly lighter thumb of the Sunni Turks. The Seljuks pressed on into Syria and Anatolia, administering a lethal blow to Byzantine power at the Battle of Manzikert° in 1071. The Byzantine army fell back on Constantinople, leaving Anatolia open to Turkish occupation.

Under Turkish rule, cities shrank as pastoralists overran their agricultural hinterlands, already short on labor because of migration to the cities. Irrigation works suffered from lack of maintenance in the unsettled countryside. Tax revenues fell. Twelfth-century Seljuk princes contesting for power fought over cities, but few Turks participated in urban cultural and religious life. The gulf between a religiously based urban society and the culture and personnel of the government deepened. When factional riots broke out between Sunnis and Shi'ites, or between rival schools of Sunni law, rulers remained aloof, even as destruction and loss of life mounted. Similarly, when princes fought for the title *sultan,* religious leaders advised citizens to remain neutral.

By the early twelfth century, unrepaired damage from floods, fires, and civil disorder had re-

---

Seljuk (sel-JOOK)   **Shahan-shah** (SHAH-han–SHAH)
Tughril (TUUG-ruhl)   **Manzikert** (MANZ-ih-kuhrt)

duced old Baghdad on the west side of the Tigris to ruins. The caliphs took advantage of fighting among the Seljuks to regain some power locally and built a wall around the palace precinct on the east side of the river. Nevertheless, the heart of the city died, not to regain prosperity until the twentieth century. The withering of Baghdad reflected a broader environmental problem: the collapse of the canal system on which agriculture in the Tigris and Euphrates valley depended. For millennia a center of world civilization, Mesopotamia underwent substantial population loss.

The Turks alone cannot be blamed for the demographic and economic misfortunes of Iran and Iraq. Too-robust urbanization had strained food resources, and political fragmentation had dissipated revenues. The growing practice of using land grants to pay soldiers and courtiers also played a role. When absentee grant holders used agents to collect taxes, the agents tended to gouge villagers and take little interest in improving production, all of which weakened the agricultural base of the economy.

The Seljuk Empire was beset by internal quarrels when the first crusading armies of Christians reached the Holy Land. The First Crusade captured Jerusalem in 1099 (see Chapter 8). Although charged with the stuff of romance, the Crusades had little lasting impact on the Islamic lands. The crusader principalities of Edessa, Anitoch, Tripoli, and Jerusalem simply became pawns in the shifting pattern of politics already in place. Newly arrived knights eagerly attacked the Muslim enemy, whom they called Saracens°. But veteran crusaders, including the religious orders of the Knights of the Temple (Templars) and the Knights of the Hospital of St. John (Hospitallers), recognized that diplomacy and seeking partners of convenience among rival Muslim princes offered a sounder strategy.

The Muslims finally unified to face the European enemy in the mid-twelfth century. Nur al-Din ibn Zangi° established a strong state based in Damascus and sent an army to terminate the Fatimid Caliphate in Egypt. A nephew of the Kurdish commander of that expedition, Salah-al-Din, known in the West as Saladin, took advantage of Nur al-Din's timely death to seize power and unify Egypt and Syria. The Fatimid dynasty fell in 1171. In 1187, Saladin recaptured Jerusalem from the Europeans.

Saladin's descendants fought off subsequent Crusades. After one such battle, however, in 1250, Turkish mamluk troops seized control of the government, ending Saladin's dynasty. In 1260, these mamluks rode east to confront a new invading force. At the Battle of Ain Jalut° (Spring of Goliath) in Syria, they met and defeated an army of Mongols from Central Asia, thus stemming an invasion that had begun several decades before and legitimizing their claim to dominion over Egypt and Syria.

The Mongol invasions shocked the world of Islam (see Chapters 13 and 14), especially their destruction of the Abbasid Caliphate in Baghdad in 1258 and their imposition of non-Muslim rule from Iraq eastward for much of the thirteenth century. Although the Mongols left few ethnic or linguistic traces in these lands, their initial destruction of cities, their diversion of trans-Asian trade to the north of the traditional Silk Road, and their casual disregard for urban and religious life, even after their conversion to Islam, hastened currents of change already under way.

ISLAMIC CIVILIZATION

Though complex and unsettled in its political dimension, life in the ever-expanding Islamic world underwent a fruitful evolution in law, social structure, and religious expression. Religious conversion and urbanization reinforced each other to create a distinct Islamic civilization. The immense geographical and human diversity of the Muslim lands allowed many "small traditions" to coexist with the developing "great tradition" of Islam.

Saracen (SAR-uh-suhn)
Nur al-Din ibn Zangi (NOOR-al-DEEN ib-uhn ZAN-gee)

Ain Jalut (ine jah-LOOT)

Scholarly Life in Medieval Islam   Books being scarce and expensive, teachers dictated to their students, as shown on the right. Notice that the student is writing on a single sheet of paper while the scholar in the center holds an entire book. On the left, an author presents his work to a wealthy patron.   (Bibliothèque nationale de France)

Law and Dogma

The Shari'a, the law of Islam, provides the foundation of Islamic civilization. Yet aside from certain Quranic verses conveying specific divine ordinances—most pertaining to personal and family matters—Islam had no legal system at the time of Muhammad. Arab custom and the Prophet's own authority offered the only guidance. After Muhammad died, the umma tried to follow his example. This became harder and harder to do, however, as those who knew Muhammad best died, and many Arabs found themselves living in far-off lands. Non-Arab converts to Islam, who at first tried to follow Arab customs they had little familiarity with, had an even harder time.

Islam slowly developed laws to govern social and religious life. The full sense of Islamic civilization, however, goes well beyond the basic Five Pillars mentioned earlier. Some Muslim thinkers felt that the reasoned consideration of a mature man—women had little voice in religious matters—offered the best resolution of issues not covered by Quranic revelation. Others argued that the sunna, or tradition, of the Prophet was the best guide. To understand that sunna they collected and studied the thousands of reports, called **hadith°,** purporting to convey the precise words or deeds of Muhammad. It gradually became customary to precede each hadith with a statement indicating whom the speaker had heard it from, whom that person had heard it from, and so on, back to the Prophet personally.

Many hadith dealt with ritual matters, such as how to wash before prayer. Others provided answers to legal questions not covered by Quranic revelation or suggested principles for deciding

---

hadith (hah-DEETH)

such matters. By the eleventh century, most legal thinkers had accepted the idea that Muhammad's personal behavior provided the best model for Muslim behavior and that the hadith constituted the most authoritative basis for Islamic law after the Quran itself.

Yet the hadith themselves posed a problem because the tens of thousands of anecdotes included not only genuine reports about the Prophet but also invented ones, politically motivated ones, and stories derived from non-Muslim religious traditions. Only a specialist could hope to separate a sound from a weak tradition. As the hadith grew in importance, so did the branch of learning devoted to their analysis. Scholars discarded thousands for having weak chains of authority. The most reliable they collected into books that gradually achieved authoritative status. Sunnis placed six books in this category; Shi'ites, four. The Shari'a grew over centuries, incorporating the ideas of many legal scholars, as well as the implications of thousands of hadith.

The Shari'a embodies a vision of an umma in which all Muslims subscribe to the same moral values. In this vision, political or ethnic divisions lose importance, for the Shari'a expects every Muslim ruler to abide by and enforce the religious law. In practice, this expectation often lost out in the hurly-burly of political life. Even so, it proved an important basis for an urban lifestyle that varied surprisingly little from Morocco to India.

Converts and Cities

Conversion to Islam, more the outcome of people leaning about the new rulers' religion than an escape from the tax on non-Muslims, as some scholars have suggested, helped spur urbanization. Conversion did not require extensive knowledge of the faith. To become a Muslim, a person recited, in the presence of a Muslim, the profession of faith in Arabic: "There is no God but God, and Muhammad is the Messenger of God."

Few converts knew Arabic, and fewer could read the Quran. Many converts knew no more of the Quran than the verses necessary for their daily prayers. Muhammad had established no priesthood to define and spread the faith. Thus, new converts, whether Arab or non-Arab, faced the problem of finding out for themselves what Islam was about and how they should act as Muslims.

Spending time with Muslims, learning their language, and imitating their behavior proved the best way to solve this problem. In many areas, this meant migration to an Arab governing center. The alternative, to convert to Islam but remain in one's home community, posed a problem. Even before the emergence of Islam, religion had become the main component of social identity in the Middle East. Converts to Islam thus encountered discrimination if they went on living within their Christian, Jewish, or Zoroastrian communities. Again, migration afforded a solution that the economic opportunities opened up by tax revenues flowing into the Arab governing centers made more attractive.

The Arab military settlements of Kufa and Basra in Iraq blossomed into cities and became important centers for Muslim cultural activities. But as conversion rapidly spread in the mid-ninth century, urbanization also increased in other regions, most visibly in Iran, where most cities previously had been quite small. Nishapur in the northeast grew from fewer than 10,000 pre-Islamic inhabitants to between 100,000 and 200,000 by the year 1000. Other Iranian cities experienced similar growth. In Iraq, Baghdad and Mosul joined Kufa and Basra as major cities. In Syria, Aleppo and Damascus flourished under Muslim rule. New districts added to Fustat—the final one in 969 named Cairo—created one of the largest and greatest of the Islamic cities. The primarily Christian patriarchal cities of Jerusalem, Antioch, and Alexandria, not being Muslim governing centers, shrank and stagnated.

The cities became heavily Muslim before the countryside. Muhammad and his first followers had lived in a commercial city, and Islam acquired a peculiarly urban character very different from that of medieval European Christianity. Mosques in large cities served as both ritual centers and places for learning and social activities.

Islam colored all aspects of urban social life (see Society and Culture: The Fraternity of Beggars). Without religious officials to instruct them, the new Muslims imitated Arab dress and customs and emulated people they regarded as particularly pious. Inevitably, in the absence of a central reli-

The Fraternity of Beggars

Beggars, tricksters, and street performers belonged to a single loose fraternity: Banu Sasan, or Tribe of Sasan. Tales of their tricks and exploits amused staid, pious Muslims, who often encountered them in cities and on their scholarly travels. Beggars and scholars constituted mobile elements of the population. These descriptive verses come from a tenth-century poet who studied beggars' jargon and way of life.

We are the beggars' brotherhood, and no one can deny us our lofty pride . . .

And of our number is the feigned madman and mad woman, with metal charms strung from their [sic] necks.

And the ones with ornaments drooping from their ears, and with collars of leather or brass round their necks . . .

And the one who simulates a festering internal wound, and the people with false bandages round their heads and sickly, jaundiced faces.

And the one who slashes himself, alleging that he has been mutilated by assailants, or the one who darkens his skin artificially pretending that he has been beaten up and wounded . . .

And the one who practices as a manipulator and quack dentist, or who escapes from chains wound round his body, or the one who uses almost invisible silk thread mysteriously to draw off rings . . .

And of our number are those who claim to be refugees from the Byzantine frontier regions, those who go round begging on pretext of having left behind captive families . . .

And the one who feigns an internal discharge, or who showers the passers-by with his urine, or who farts in the mosque and makes a nuisance of himself, thus wheedling money out of people . . .

And of our number are the ones who purvey objects of veneration made from clay, and those who have their beards smeared with red dye.

And the one who brings up secret writing by immersing it in what looks like water, and the one who similarly brings up the writing by exposing it to burning embers.

How do the beggars' practices reflect social values? How is the cosmopolitanism of Islamic society visible in these verses?

Source: Excerpts from Clifford Edmund Bosworth, *The Mediaeval Islamic Underworld: The Banu Sasan in Arabic Society and Literature* (Leiden: E. I. Brill, 1976), 191–199. Copyright © 1976. With kind permission of Koninklijke Brill N.V. Leiden, the Netherlands.

gious authority comparable to a pope, local variations developed in the way people practiced Islam and in the hadith they attributed to the Prophet. This gave the rapidly growing religion the flexibility to accommodate many different social situations. Since the profession of faith called only for the acknowledgment of God's unity and Muhammad's prophethood, Islam escaped most of the severe conflicts over heresy that beset Christianity at a comparable stage of development.

By the tenth century, urban growth was affecting the countryside by expanding the consumer market. Citrus fruits, rice, and sugar cane increased in acreage and spread to new areas. Cotton became a major crop in Iran and elsewhere and supplied a diverse and profitable textile industry. Irrigation works expanded. Diet diversified. Abundant coinage made for a lively economy. Intercity and long-distance trade flourished, providing regular links between isolated districts and integrating the pastoral nomads who provided pack animals into the region's economy. Manufacturing expanded as well, particularly the production of cloth, metal goods, and pottery. The urban economy grew under the strong influence of Islamic ethics and law, overseen by a religiously sanctioned market inspector.

Building on Hellenistic traditions and their own observations and experience, Muslim doctors and astronomers developed skills and theories far in advance of their European counterparts. The mathematician and physicist Ibn al-Haytham°, working in Egypt in the eleventh century, wrote more than a hundred works. Among other things, he determined that the Milky Way lies far beyond earth's atmosphere, proved that light travels from a seen object to the eye and not the reverse, and explained why the sun and moon appear larger on the horizon than overhead.

Islam, Women, and Slaves

Women seldom traveled. Those living in rural areas worked in the fields and tended animals. Urban women, particularly members of the elite, lived in seclusion and did not leave their homes without covering themselves completely. Seclusion of women in their houses and veiling in public already existed in Byzantine and Sasanid times. Through interpretation of specific verses from the Quran, these practices now became fixtures of Muslim social life. Women sometimes studied and became literate, but they did so away from the gaze of men who were not related to them. Although women played influential roles within the family, any public role had to be indirect, through their husbands. Only slave women could perform before unrelated men as musicians and dancers. A man could have sexual relations with as many slave concubines as he pleased, in addition to marrying as many as four wives.

In some ways, Muslim women fared better legally under Islamic law than did Christian and Jewish women under the practices of Christianity and Judaism. Muslim women could own property and retain it in marriage. They could remarry if their husbands divorced them, and they received a cash payment upon divorce. Although a man could divorce his wife without stating a cause, a woman

could initiate divorce under specified conditions. Women could practice birth control. They could testify in court, although their testimony counted as half that of a man's. And they could go on pilgrimage. Nevertheless, a misogynistic tone sometimes appears in Islamic writings. One saying attributed to the Prophet observed: "I was raised up to heaven and saw that most of its denizens were poor people; I was raised into the hellfire and saw that most of its denizens were women."[3]

In the absence of writings by women about women from this period, the status of women must be deduced from the writings of men. The Prophet's wife A'isha, the daughter of Abu Bakr, provides an example of how Muslim men appraised women in society. Only eighteen years old when Muhammad died, A'isha lived for another fifty years. Early reports stress her status as Muhammad's favorite, the only virgin he married and the only wife to see the angel Gabriel. These reports emanate from A'isha herself, who was an abundant source of hadith.

A'isha became especially known for two episodes. As a fourteen year old, she became separated from a caravan and rejoined it only after traveling through the night with a man who found her alone in the desert. Gossips accused her of being untrue to the Prophet, but a revelation from God proved her innocence. The other event was her participation in the Battle of the Camel, fought to derail Ali's caliphate. These two episodes came to epitomize what Muslim men feared most about women: sexual infidelity and meddling in politics. Even though the earliest literature dealing with A'isha stresses her position as Muhammad's favorite, his first wife, Khadija, and his daughter, Fatima, Ali's wife, eventually surpassed A'isha as ideal women. Both appear as model wives and mothers with no suspicion of sexual irregularity or political manipulation.

As the seclusion of women became commonplace in urban Muslim society, some writers extolled homosexual relationships, partly because a male lover could appear in public or go on a journey. Although Islam deplored homosexuality, one ruler wrote a book advising his son to follow moderation in all things and thus share his affections equally between men and women. Another ruler

---

Ibn al-Haytham (IB-uhn al–HY-tham)

Women Playing Chess in Muslim Spain   As shown in this thirteenth-century miniature, women in their own quarters, without men present, wore whatever clothes and jewels they liked. Notice the henna decorating the hands of the woman in the middle. The woman on the left, probably a slave, plays an oud.   (Institute Amatller d'Art Hispanic. © Patrimonio Nacional, Madrid)

and his slaveboy became models of perfect love in the verses of mystic poets.

Islam allowed slavery but forbade Muslims from enslaving other Muslims or so-called People of the Book—Jews, Christians, and Zoroastrians, who revered holy books respected by the Muslims—living under Muslim protection. Being enslaved as a prisoner of war constituted an exception. Later centuries saw a constant flow of slaves into Islamic territory from Africa and Central Asia. A hereditary slave society, however, did not develop. Usually slaves converted to Islam, and many masters then freed them as an act of piety. The offspring of slave women and Muslim men were born free.

The Recentering of Islam

Early Islam centered on the caliphate, the political expression of the unity of the umma. No formal organization or hierarchy, however, directed the process of conversion. Thus, there emerged a multitude of local Islamic communities so disconnected from each other that numerous competing interpretations of the developing religion arose. Inevitably, the centrality of the caliphate diminished (see Map 7.2). The appearance of rival caliphates in Tunisia and Cordoba accentuated the problem of decentralization just as Abbasid temporal power waned.

The rise of the ulama as community leaders did not prevent the growing fragmentation because the ulama themselves divided into contentious factions. During the twelfth century, however, factionalism began to abate, and new socioreligious institutions emerged to provide the umma with a different sort of religious center. These new developments stemmed in part from an exodus of religious scholars from Iran in response to the economic and political disintegration of the late eleventh and twelfth centuries.

The flow of Iranians to the Arab lands and newly conquered territories in India and Anatolia increased after the Mongol invasion. Fully versed in Arabic as well as their native Persian, immigrant scholars met a warm reception. They brought with them a view of religion developed in Iran's urban centers. A type of religious college, the madrasa°, gained sudden popularity outside Iran, where madrasas had been known since the tenth century. Scores of madrasas, many founded by local rulers, appeared throughout the Islamic world.

madrasa (MAH-dras-uh)

Quran Page Printed from a Woodblock Printing from woodblocks or tin plates existed in Islamic lands between approximately 800 and 1400. Most prints were narrow amulets designed to be rolled and worn around the neck in cylindrical cases. Less valued than handwritten amulets, many prints came from Banu Sasan conmen. Why block-printing had so little effect on society in general and eventually disappeared is unknown. (Cambridge University Library)

given to ecstatic and poetic utterances and wonderworking. They attracted disciples but did not try to organize them. The growth of brotherhoods, a less ecstatic form of Sufism, set a tone for society in general. It soon became common for most Muslim men, particularly in the cities, to belong to at least one brotherhood.

A sense of the social climate the Sufi brotherhoods fostered can be gained from a twelfth-century manual:

> Every limb has its own special ethics. . . . The ethics of the tongue. The tongue should always be busy in reciting God's names (*dhikr*) and in saying good things of the brethren, praying for them, and giving them counsel. . . . The ethics of hearing. One should not listen to indecencies and slander. . . . The ethics of sight. One should lower one's eyes in order not to see forbidden things. . . . The ethics of the hands: to give charity and serve the brethren and not use them in acts of disobedience.[4]

Special dispensations allowed people who merely wanted to emulate the Sufis and enjoy their company to follow less demanding rules:

> It is allowed by way of dispensation to possess an estate or to rely on a regular income. The Sufis' rule in this matter is that one should not use all of it for himself, but should dedicate this to public charities and should take from it only enough for one year for himself and his family. . . .
>
> There is a dispensation allowing one to be occupied in business; this dispensation is granted to him who has to support a family. But this should not keep him away from the regular performance of prayers. . . .
>
> There is a dispensation allowing one to watch all kinds of amusement. This is, however, limited by the rule: What you are forbidden from doing, you are also forbidden from watching.[5]

Some Sufi brotherhoods spread in the countryside. Local shrines and pilgrimages to the tombs of Muhammad's descendants and saintly Sufis became popular. The pilgrimage to Mecca, too, received new prominence as a religious duty. The end of the Abbasid Caliphate enhanced the religious centrality of Mecca, which eventually became an important center of madrasa education.

Iranians also contributed in the twelfth and thirteenth centuries to the growth of mystic groups known as *Sufi* brotherhoods. The doctrines and rituals of certain Sufis spread from city to city, giving rise to the first geographically extensive Islamic religious organizations. Sufi doctrines varied, but a quest for a sense of union with God through rituals and training provided a common denominator. Sufism had begun in early Islamic times and had doubtless benefited from the ideas and beliefs of converts to Islam from religions with mystic traditions.

The early Sufis had been saintly individuals

CONCLUSION

With the way paved by the state religions of the Sasanid and Byzantine Empires, Islam culminated a transition from identity based on ethnicity and localism to identity based on religion. The concept of the umma united all Muslims in a universal community embracing enormous diversity of language, appearance, and social custom. Although Muslim communities adapted to local "small traditions," by the twelfth century a religious scholar could travel anywhere in the Islamic world and blend easily into the local Muslim community.

By the ninth century, the forces of conversion and urbanization fostered social and religious experimentation in urban settings. From the eleventh century onward, political disruption and the spread of pastoral nomadism slowed this early economic and technological dynamism. The Muslim community then turned to new religious institutions, such as the madrasas and Sufi brotherhoods, to create the flexible and durable community structures that carried Islam into new regions and protected ordinary believers from capricious political rule.

■ Key Terms

Shi'ites	umma
Sunnis	caliphate
Sasanid Empire	Quran
Mecca	Umayyad Caliphate
Muhammad	Abbasid Caliphate
muslim	mamluks
Islam	ulama
Medina	hadith

■ Suggested Reading

For Sasanid history, see Richard N. Frye's *The Heritage of Persia* (1963; reprint, 1993). Ehsan Yarshater, ed., *The Cambridge History of Iran*, vol. 3 (pts. 1–2), *The Seleucid,*

Parthian and Sasanian Periods (1983), contains up-to-date articles on Iranian history just prior to Islam.

Ira M. Lapidus, *A History of Islamic Societies* (1988), focuses on social developments and includes the histories of Islam in India, Southeast Asia, sub-Saharan Africa, and other parts of the world. Marshall G. S. Hodgson, *The Venture of Islam*, 3 vols. (1974), critiques traditional ways of studying the Islamic Middle East while offering alternative interpretation. Bernard Lewis's *The Middle East: A Brief History of the Last 2,000 Years* (1995) provides a lively narration from the time of Christ.

For a shorter survey, see J. J. Saunders, *History of Medieval Islam* (1965; reprint, 1990). Richard W. Bulliet, *Islam: The View from the Edge* (1993), offers, in brief form, an approach that concentrates on the lives of converts to Islam and local religious notables.

Muslims regard the Quran as untranslatable because they consider the Arabic in which it is couched to be inseparable from God's message. Most "interpretations" in English adhere reasonably closely to the Arabic text. Arthur J. Arberry, *The Koran Interpreted* (1955; reprint, 1986), tries to capture the poetic quality of Quranic language.

Martin Lings, *Muhammad: His Life Based on the Earliest Sources*, rev. ed. (1991), offers a readable biography reflecting Muslim viewpoints. The standard Western treatments include W. Montgomery Watt's *Muhammad at Mecca* (1953) and *Muhammad at Medina* (1956; reprint, 1981), and their one-volume summary, *Muhammad, Prophet and Statesman* (1974). Michael A. Cook, *Muhammad* (1983), intelligently discusses historiographical problems and source difficulties. Karen Armstrong's *Muhammad: A Biography of the Prophet* (1993) achieves a sympathetic balance.

Articles in Michael Gervers and Ramzi Jibran Bikhazi, eds., *Conversion and Continuity: Indigenous Christian Communities in Islamic Lands, Eighth to Eighteenth Centuries* (1990), detail Christian responses to Islam. For a Zoroastrian perspective, see Jamsheed K. Choksy, *Conflict and Cooperation: Zoroastrian Subalterns and Muslim Elites in Medieval Iranian Society* (1997). Jacob Lassner summarizes S. D. Goitein's definitive multivolume study of the Jews of medieval Egypt in *A Mediterranean Society: An Abridgement in One Volume* (1999). On the process of conversion, see the work in quantitative history of Richard W. Bulliet, *Conversion to Islam in the Medieval Period* (1979).

The History of al-Tabari (1985–1997), in thirty-eight volumes under the general editorship of Ehsan Yarshater, translates the most important chronicle of early Islamic history. Later primary sources include Usamah ibn

Munqidh, *An Arab-Syrian Gentleman and Warrior in the Period of the Crusades,* trans. Philip Hitti (1929; reprint, 2001), and Ibn Battuta, *Travels in Asia and Africa, 1325–1354,* trans. H. A. R. Gibb (1929; reprint, 1983). The latter author has been well studied by Ross E. Dunn, *The Adventures of Ibn Battuta: A Muslim Traveler of the Fourteenth Century* (1986; reprint, 1989).

Roy P. Mottahedeh, *Loyalty and Leadership in an Early Islamic Society* (1980), Richard W. Bulliet, *The Patricians of Nishapur* (1972), and Ira Marvin Lapidus, *Muslim Cities in the Later Middle Ages* (1984), discuss social history in tenth-century Iran, eleventh-century Iran, and fourteenth-century Syria, respectively. Jonathan Berkey, *The Transmission of Knowledge in Medieval Cairo: A Social History of Islamic Education* (1992), and Michael Chamberlain, *Knowledge and Social Practice in Medieval Damascus, 1190–1350* (1994), put forward competing assessments of education and the ulama.

Ahmad Y. al-Hassan and Donald R. Hill, *Islamic Technology: An Illustrated History* (1986), introduces a little-studied field. For a more crafts-oriented look, see Hans E. Wulff, *The Traditional Crafts of Persia: Their Development, Technology, and Influence on Eastern and Western Civilizations* (1966).

Denise Spellberg, *Politics, Gender, and the Islamic Past: The Legacy of A'isha bint Abi Bakr* (1994), provides path-breaking guidance on women's history. Basim Musallam, *Sex and Society in Islamic Civilization* (1983), treats the social, medical, and legal history of birth control. On race and slavery, see Bernard Lewis, *Race and Slavery in the Middle East: A Historical Enquiry* (1992).

Islamic law is well covered in Noel J. Coulson *A History of Islamic Law* (1979). For Sufism, see Annemarie Schimmel, *Mystical Dimensions of Islam* (1975).

Two religious texts available in translation are Abu Hamid al-Ghazali, *The Faith and Practice of al-Ghazali,* trans. W. Montgomery Watt (1967; reprint, 1982), and Abu al-Najib al-Suhrawardi, *A Sufi Rule for Novices,* trans. Menaham Milson (1975).

■ Notes

1. Quran. Sura 96, verses 1–5.
2. Quran. Sura 92, verses 1–10.
3. Richard W. Bulliet, *Islam: The View from the Edge* (New York: Columbia University Press, 1994), 87.
4. Abu Najib al-Suhrawardi, *A Sufi Rule for Novices,* trans. Menaham Milson (Cambridge, MA: Harvard University Press, 1975), 45–58.
5. Ibid., 73–82.

8

CHRISTIAN EUROPE EMERGES,

300–1200

— ₡ —

Early Medieval Europe, 300–1000 • The Western Church •
The Byzantine Empire, 300–1200 • Kievan Russia, 900–1200 •
Western Europe Revives, 1000–1200
ENVIRONMENT AND TECHNOLOGY: Castles and Fortifications

hristmas Day in the year 800 found Charles, king of the Franks, in Rome instead of at his palace in northeastern France. At six-foot-three, Charles towered over the average man of his time. His royal career had been equally gargantuan. Crowned king in his mid-twenties in 768, he had crisscrossed Europe for three decades, waging war on Muslim invaders from Spain, Avar invaders from Hungary, and myriad German princes.

Charles had subdued many enemies and become protector of the papacy. So it is hard to believe the eyewitness report of his secretary and biographer that Charles was surprised when Pope Leo III stepped forward as the king rose from his prayers and placed a new crown on his head. "Life and victory to Charles the August, crowned by God the great and pacific Emperor of the Romans," proclaimed the pope.[1] Then, amid the cheers of the crowd, he humbly knelt before the new emperor.

Charlemagne° (from Latin *Carolus magnus,* "Charles the Great") was the first to bear the title *emperor* in western Europe for over three hundred years. Rome's decline and Charlemagne's rise marked a shift of focus for Europe—away from the Mediterranean and toward the north and west. The world of Charlemagne, dominated by the Germanic peoples of the north, opened an era in European history in which German custom and Christian piety transformed the Roman heritage to create a new civilization. Irish monks replaced Greek philosophers as the leading intellectuals. Roads were neglected, and trade languished. This era is commonly called early **"medieval,"** literally "middle age," because

Charlemagne (SHAHR-leh-mane)

it comes between the era of Greco-Roman civilization and the intellectual, artistic, and economic changes of the Renaissance in the fourteenth century.

The imperial title did not long survive Charlemagne. His realm fell apart under less able successors; even during his lifetime, he had acknowledged a rival emperor in the East, where Rome's political and legal heritage continued in the Eastern Roman, or **Byzantine Empire.** Western Europeans lived amid the ruins of empire. The Byzantines maintained and reinterpreted Roman traditions for centuries. The authority of the Byzantine emperors blended with the influence of the Christian church to form a cultural synthesis that helped shape the emerging kingdom of **Kievan Russia.**

As you read this chapter, ask yourself the following questions:

- What role did Christianity play in reshaping European society in east and west?
- What institutions underlay the economy and social structure of medieval western Europe?
- Did Kievan Russia more closely resemble western Europe or the Byzantine Empire?
- How did Mediterranean trade and the Crusades help revive western Europe?

EARLY MEDIEVAL EUROPE, 300–1000

The emperor Constantine (r. 306–337) reunited the Roman Empire under his sole rule (see Chapter 5), but the union did not last. Division between east and west became permanent in 395. Germanic peoples fleeing the Huns, a new invader from Asia, put pressure on both halves. Byzantine armies could defend the comparatively short Danube River frontier, but the Roman legions in the West could not hold. Gaul, Britain, Spain, and North Africa fell to various Germanic peoples in the early fifth century. Visigoths sacked Rome itself in 410, and the last Roman emperor was deposed in 476.

The disappearance of the legal framework that had persisted to the final days of the Western Roman Empire and the rise of various kings, nobles, and chieftains changed the political landscape of western Europe. In region after region, the family-based traditions of the Germanic peoples supplanted the edicts of the Roman emperors.

Fear and physical insecurity led communities to seek the protection of local strongmen. In places where looters and pillagers might appear at any moment, a local lord with a castle where peasants could take refuge counted for more than a distant king. Dependency of weak people on strong people became a hallmark of the post-Roman period in western Europe.

From Roman Empire to Germanic Kingdoms

Rome's decline signaled the end of an era in which the interrelated societies and economies of the eastern Mediterranean Sea—Egypt, Syria, Anatolia, and Tunisia—cooperated fruitfully under Roman rule. Rome itself lay at the western fringe of this region, far from the great Eastern cities of Athens, Antioch, Damascus, Jerusalem, and Alexandria. The emperors Diocletian and Constantine concerned themselves most with preserving power in the heavily populated and prosperous East.

Left on its own, the Western Roman Empire fragmented into a handful of kingdoms under Germanic rulers. The Franks held much of Gaul; the Visigoths ruled in Spain; Saxons and Angles took over Britain (see Map 8.1). In the sixth century, Lombards ruled northern Italy, although the Byzantines kept footholds in the south and around Ravenna along the east coast. Rome proper lost political importance but retained prominence as the seat of the most influential Western churchman, the bishop of Rome. Local noble families com-

CHRONOLOGY

	Western Europe	Eastern Europe
300		**325** Constantine convenes Council of Nicaea; Arian heresy condemned
		392 Emperor Theodosius bans paganism in Byzantine Empire
500	**476** Deposing of the last Roman emperor in the West	**527–565** Justinian and Theodora rule Byzantine Empire; imperial edicts collected in single law code
	ca. 547 Death of Saint Benedict	
		634–650 Muslims conquer Byzantine provinces of Syria, Egypt, and Tunisia
800	**711** Muslim conquest of Spain **732** Battle of Tours	
	800 Coronation of Charlemagne **843** Treaty of Verdun divides Carolingian Empire among Charlemagne's grandsons	
	910 Monastery of Cluny founded **962** Beginning of Holy Roman Empire	**882** Varangians take control of Kiev
1000		**980** Vladimir becomes grand prince of Kievan Russia
	1054 Formal schism between Latin and Orthodox Churches **1066** Normans under William the Conqueror invade England **1077** Climax of investiture controversy **1095** Pope Urban II preaches First Crusade	**1081–1118** Alexius Comnenus rules Byzantine Empire, calls for western military aid against Muslims
1200		**1204** Western knights sack Constantinople in Fourth Crusade **1237–1240** Mongol invasion of Kievan Russia

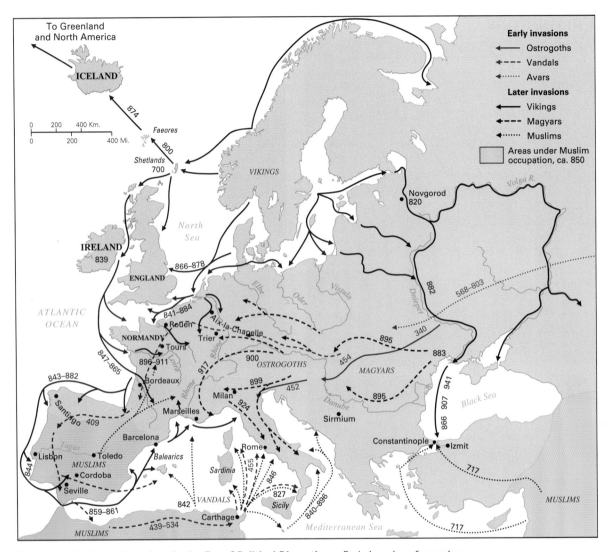

Map. 8.1   Raids and Invasions in the Era of Political Disruption   Early invasions focused on the primary centers of Roman imperial authority: Rome, Milan, Carthage, and Constantinople. Later invasions reflect the shift of power to northern Europe. Viking activity along the rivers of eastern Europe opened up trade routes to Byzantium and Iran.

peted for control of this position, which over several centuries acquired the title of *pope* along with supreme power in the Western church.

The educated few, increasingly restricted to Christian priests and monks, retained a somewhat simplified form of Latin. But the vulgar Latin of the uneducated masses rapidly evolved into Romance dialects—Portuguese, Spanish, French, Italian—

except in northern and northeastern Europe, where Latin gave way to Germanic and Scandinavian dialects. Thus, Europe divided roughly into three linguistic zones: (1) countries in the west and south speaking Romance languages, (2) countries in the north and center speaking Germanic and Scandinavian languages, and (3) countries in the east speaking the Slavic languages of peoples who moved westward on the heels of the Germanic folk migrations.

In 711, a frontier raiding party of Arabs and Berbers, acting under the authority of the Muslim ruler in Damascus, in Syria, crossed the Strait of Gibraltar and overturned the kingdom of the Visigoths in Spain (see Chapter 7). The disunited Europeans could not stop them from consolidating their hold on the Iberian Peninsula. After pushing the remaining Christian chieftains into the Pyrenees mountains, the Muslims moved on to France. They conquered much of the southern coast and penetrated as far north as Tours, less than 150 miles (240 kilometers) from the English Channel, before Charlemagne's grandfather, Charles Martel, stopped their most advanced raiding party in 732.

Military effectiveness keyed the rise of the Carolingian° family (from Latin *Carolus*, "Charles") as protectors of the Frankish kings, then as kings themselves, and finally, under Charlemagne, as emperors. At the peak of Charlemagne's power, the Carolingian Empire encompassed all of Gaul and parts of Germany and Italy, with the pope ruling part of the latter. When Charlemagne's son, Louis the Pious, died, the Treaty of Verdun (843) split the empire into eastern, middle, and western portions, each ruled by one of Louis's sons. The three regions never reunited, but the Carolingian economic system based on landed wealth and a brief intellectual revival sponsored personally by Charlemagne (though he was illiterate) provided a common heritage.

A new threat appeared in 793 when the Vikings, sea raiders from Scandinavia, attacked and plundered a monastery on the English coast. Local sources from France, the British Isles, and Muslim Spain attest to widespread dread of Viking warriors descending from multi-oared dragon-prowed boats to pillage monasteries, villages, and towns. In the ninth century, raiders from Denmark and Norway harried the British and French coasts, while Swedish Varangians° pursued raiding and trading interests, and eventually the building of kingdoms, along the rivers of eastern Europe and Russia, as we shall see. Although many Viking raiders sought booty and slaves, in the 800s and 900s Viking captains organized the settlement of Iceland, Greenland, and, around the year 1000, Vinland on the eastern coast of Canada.

Vikings long settled in Normandy (in northwestern France) organized the most important and ambitious expeditions in terms of numbers of men and horses and long-lasting impact. William the Conqueror, the duke of Normandy, invaded England in 1066 and brought Anglo-Saxon domination of the island to an end. Other Normans (from "North men") attacked Muslim Sicily in the 1060s and, after thirty years of fighting, permanently severed it from the Muslim world.

A Self-Sufficient Economy

Archaeology and records kept by Christian monasteries and nunneries reveal a profound economic transformation beneath the political jumble of newly arising Germanic kingdoms. The urban-based civilization of the Romans withered and shrank. Cities lost population, in some cases becoming villages. Roman roads fell into disuse and disrepair. Small thatched houses sprang up beside abandoned villas, and public buildings made of marble became dilapidated in the absence of the laborers, money, and civic leadership needed to maintain them. Purchases paid for in coin largely gave way to the bartering of goods and services.

Trade languished. Egyptian wheat that had once fed the multitudes of Rome now went to Constantinople°. In 439, an invasion by Germanic Vandals from Spain cut off Tunisia, another of Rome's breadbaskets. Although occasional shipments from Egypt and Syria continued to reach western ports, most of western Europe had to rely on meager local resources. These resources, however, underwent a redistribution.

Roman centralization had channeled the wealth and production of the empire toward the capital, from which Roman culture radiated to the provinces. As Germanic and other territorial lords replaced Roman governors, local self-sufficiency became more important, and the decline of literacy and other aspects of Roman civilized life made

---

Carolingian (kah-roe-LIN-gee-uhn)
Varangians (va-RAN-gee-anz)

Constantinople (cahn-stan-tih-NO-pul)

room for new trends. These trends reflected local folk cultures, the "small traditions" of the various Germanic and Celtic peoples.

The diet in the northern countries featured beer, lard or butter, and bread made of barley, rye, or wheat, all supplemented by pork from herds of swine fed on forest acorns and beechnuts and by game from the same forests. The Roman diet based on wheat, wine, and olive oil persisted in the south. Nutritionally, the average western European of the ninth century probably did better than his or her descendants three hundred years later, when population was increasing and the nobility monopolized the forests.

In both north and south, self-sufficient farming estates known as **manors** became the primary centers of agricultural production. Wealthy Romans had commonly owned country houses situated on their lands. From the fourth century onward, political insecurity prompted common farmers to give their lands to large landowners in return for political and physical protection. The warfare and instability of the post-Roman centuries made unprotected country houses especially vulnerable to pillaging and encouraged the fortification of manors. Isolated by poor communications and lack of organized government, landowners depended on their own resources for survival. Many became warriors or maintained a force of armed men. Others swore allegiance to landowners who had the armed force to protect them.

A well-appointed manor possessed fields, gardens, grazing lands, fish ponds, a mill, a church, workshops for making implements, and a village where the farmers dependent on the lord of the manor lived. Protection, ranging from a ditch and wooden stockade to a stone wall surrounding a fortified keep (a stone building), varied with local conditions. Fortification tended to increase down to the twelfth century (see Environment and Technology: Castles and Fortifications).

Manor life reflected one's personal status. The lord and his family exercised almost unlimited power over the **serfs**—agricultural workers who belonged to the manor—who tilled their fields and owed other dues and obligations. Serfs could not leave the manor where they were born and attach themselves to another lord. Particular conditions varied from region to region. Most peasants in England, France, and western Germany were unfree serfs in the tenth and eleventh centuries, whereas in Bordeaux°, Saxony, and a few other regions, free peasantry survived based on the egalitarian social structure of the Germanic peoples during their period of migration. Outright slavery, the mainstay of the Roman economy (see Chapter 5), diminished as more and more peasants became serfs in return for a lord's protection.

Early Medieval Society

Europe's reversion to a self-sufficient economy limited the freedom and potential for personal achievement of most people. But an emerging class of nobles reaped great benefits. During the Germanic migrations, and continuing later among the Vikings of Scandinavia, men regularly answered the call to arms issued by war chiefs, to whom they swore allegiance. All warriors shared in the booty gained from raiding. But as settlement enhanced the importance of agricultural tasks, laying down the plow and picking up the sword at the chieftain's call became harder.

Those who, out of loyalty or desire for adventure, continued to join the war parties included a growing number of horsemen. The mounted warrior became the mainstay of the Carolingian army. At first, fighting from horseback did not make a person either a nobleman or a landowner. By the tenth century, however, nearly constant warfare to protect land rights or support the claims of a superior lord brought about the gradual transformation of the mounted warrior into the noble knight, a transformation that led to landholding becoming almost inseparable from military service.

In trying to understand long-standing traditions of landholding and obligation, lawyers in the sixteenth century and later simplified thousands of individual agreements into a neat system they called "feudalism." It became common to refer to medieval European as a "feudal society" in which kings and lords gave land to **"vassals"** in return for sworn military support. (Recent historians have

Bordeaux (bore-DOE)

Castles and Fortifications

The word *castle* brings to mind the great stone fortresses that climaxed a long evolution. The Romans built square army camps surrounded by stockades to protect their frontiers. Upon breaching those frontiers, the new rulers of Europe, each with far fewer men than a Roman legion, turned to smaller fortifications: either a ringwork (a circular wooden stockade surrounding a group of wooden buildings) or, more often, a motte-and-bailey—the motte an artificial mound with a trench around it and a wooden tower of some sort on top, the bailey a courtyard or enclosed area with a wooden stockade at the foot of the mound. Archaeologists have identified over 200 ringworks and 1,050 mottes in Britain, Wales, and Scotland alone, but wood construction has caused most of their buildings to perish.

As security needs increased, some lords and rulers built a fortified stone building, called a keep, within the bailey or atop the motte. Castle Acre in England began as a country house surrounded by a fairly weak ringwork. In the mid-twelfth century, the mound was raised and the house redesigned as a keep within a smaller, more imposing ringwork. The builders doubled the thickness of the house walls and buried much of the first floor to strengthen the house's foundation. The final twelfth-century version of the keep, looking more like today's image of a castle, was taller, smaller, and surrounded by a still more formidable wall.

Stone walls steadily replaced wooden stockades. Wood served for most interior buildings, except for the keep, and for drawbridges, stairways, and other parts of the fortification. Further advances in castle design featured towers along the walls from which archers shooting through arrow slits could flank enemies attacking the walls; heavily fortified gateways; and a barbican, or fortified gateway, on the far side of the bridge over a moat.

Source: John R. Kenyon, *Medieval Fortifications* (Leicester, England: Leicester University Press, 1990). Used with permission of Girando/ Art Resource, NY.

Remains of a Motte and Bailey Castle   The immense stone castles of the Crusader era originated in this simple combination of an artificial hill and surrounding earthen rampart. (Aerofilms Limited)

discovered this oversimplification by analyzing original records.) Relations between landholders and serfs and between lords and vassals varied according to place and time, though military security concerned most parts of Europe.

The German foes of the Roman legions had equipped themselves with a helmet, a shield, and a sword, spear, or throwing ax. Some rode horses, but most fought on foot. The rise of the mounted warrior depended on the use of stirrups. Before the invention of the stirrup by Central Asian pastoralists in approximately the first century C.E., horsemen had gripped their mounts with their legs and fought with bow and arrow, throwing javelin, stabbing spear, and sword. Stirrups allowed the rider to stand in the saddle and absorb the impact of his lance as it struck his enemy at full gallop. This type of warfare required heavy grain-fed horses rather than the small grass-fed animals of the Central Asian pastoralists. Thus, agricultural Europe rather than the grassy steppes produced the charges of armored knights that came to dominate the battlefield.

By the eleventh century, the knight had emerged as the central figure in medieval warfare. He wore an open-faced helmet and a long linen shirt, or hauberk°, studded with small metal disks. A century later, knightly equipment commonly included a visored helmet that covered the head and neck and a hauberk of chain mail.

Each increase in armor for knight and horse entailed a greater financial outlay. With land the basis of all wealth, nobody could serve as a knight who did not enjoy financial support from land revenues. Accordingly, kings began to reward armed service with grants of land from their own property. Nobles with extensive properties did the same to build their own military retinues.

A grant of land in return for a pledge to provide specified military service was often called a **fief.** At first, kings granted fiefs on a temporary basis, but by the tenth century, most fiefs could be inherited as long as the specified military service continued to be provided. Although patterns varied greatly, the association of landholding with military service lent a distinctive cast to medieval European history.

Kings depended on their vassals, noble follow-ers whose services a king or some other noble might be able to command for only part of the year. Vassals who held land from several different lords could swear loyalty to each one. Moreover, the allegiance that a vassal owed to one lord could entail military service to that lord's master in time of need.

A typical medieval realm—actual practices varied between and within realms—consisted of certain lands directly owned by a king or a count and administered by his royal officers. The king's or count's major vassals held and administered other lands, often the greater portion, in return for military service. These vassals, in turn, granted land to their own vassals.

Because direct royal government was quite limited, a lord's manor provided governance and justice. The king had few financial resources and seldom exercised legal jurisdiction at a local level. Members of the clergy, as well as the extensive agricultural lands owned by monasteries and nunneries, fell under the supervision and legal jurisdiction of the church, which further limited the reach and authority of the monarch.

Noblewomen became enmeshed in this tangle of obligations as heiresses and as candidates for marriage. A man who married the widow or daughter of a lord with no sons could gain for himself control of that lord's property. Marriage alliances affected entire kingdoms. Noble daughters and sons had little to say in marriage matters, for issues of land, power, and military service took precedence over personal preferences. Noblemen guarded the women in their families as closely as their other valuables.

Nevertheless, women could own land. Some noblewomen administered their husband's lands when they were away at war. Nonnoble women usually worked alongside their menfolk, performing agricultural tasks such as raking and stacking hay, shearing sheep, and picking vegetables. As artisans, women spun, wove, and sewed clothing. The Bayeux° Tapestry, a piece of embroidery 230 feet (70 meters) long and 20 inches (51 centimeters) wide depicting in continuous sequence of images William the Conqueror's invasion of England in 1066, was designed and executed entirely by women.

---

hauberk (HAW-berk)

Bayeux (bay-YUH)

Noblewoman Directing Construction of a Church   This picture of Berthe, wife of Girat de Rouissillion, acting as mistress of the works comes from a tenth-century manuscript but shows a scene from the ninth century. Wheelbarrows rarely appear in medieval building scenes.   (Copyright Bibliothèque royale Albert Ier, Bruxelles, Ms. 6, fol. 554 verso)

THE WESTERN CHURCH

The Christian church claimed jurisdiction over large segments of Europe's population. Just as the growing Christian populations in eastern Europe followed the patriarch of Constantinople, the pope commanded similar authority over church affairs in western Europe. There, missionaries added territory to Christendom with forays into the British Isles and the lands of the Germans.

Regional disagreements over church regulations, shortages of educated and trained clergy, difficult communications, political disorder, and the general insecurity of the period posed formidable obstacles to unifying church standards and practices. Clerics in some parts of western Europe issued prohibitions against the worship of rivers, trees, and mountains as late as the eleventh century. Church problems included lingering paganism and lax enforcement of prohibitions against married clergy, nepotism (giving preferment to one's close kin), and simony (selling ecclesiastical appointments, often to people who were not members of the clergy). The persistence of the **papacy**— the office of the pope—in asserting its legal jurisdiction over clergy, combating heretical beliefs, and calling on secular rulers to recognize the pope's authority constituted a rare force for unity and order in a time of disunity and chaos.

The Structure of Christian Faith

From the fourth century onward, divisions on matters of doctrine endangered the Christian church. Jesus's disciples had established Christian communities, or patriarchates°, in Jerusalem, Antioch, Alexandria, and Rome. Most Christians recognized the patriarchs who headed these communities as paramount leaders. In the fourth century, the emperor Constantine made his capital city, Constantinople, a fifth patriarchate. The patriarchs appointed bishops throughout the regions that recognized their authority, and each bishop consecrated priests within his area of jurisdiction, called a diocese. Church rules set by the patriarch or by councils of bishops guided priests in serving the needs of ordinary believers.

Priests commemorated Christ's sacrifice on the cross in the consumption of bread and wine in the mass, or church service, and performed rituals related to birth, marriage, and death. But church leaders differed on the precise form of rituals and on which should be considered sacred mysteries, or sacraments. Before baptism became standardized as a ritual for newborns, for example, it was sometimes postponed until late in life so that the person baptized could benefit from the forgiveness of sin that it conveyed.

The church hierarchy strove for consistency in Christian belief throughout the Christian community, but disagreement arose here as well. One area of disagreement centered on Jesus's relationship to God the Father and to the Holy Spirit. Christians generally agreed that these together formed a divine Trinity in which three aspects or manifestations of God somehow came together. But they did not all understand the Trinity in the same way. They also disagreed on whether Mary was the mother of God, or the mother of a man named Jesus, and on whether images of God or Jesus or Mary, called icons, were proper objects to pray before because they stimulated pious thoughts, or whether praying before them too closely resembled praying to pagan statues.

Disagreements like these led to charges and countercharges of heresy, beliefs or practices so unacceptable as to be un-Christian. Charges of heresy touched ordinary people, even when they involved hard-to-understand theological issues, because they involved the issue of salvation. They also threatened the unity of the Christian church at a time of rapidly increasing political fragmentation.

The most severe disagreements arose in North Africa and the lands of the eastern Mediterranean and resulted in **schism**°—a formal division resulting from disagreements about doctrine. Monophysite° doctrine, for example, emphasized the divinity of Jesus Christ and minimized his human characteristics. It persists to this day in Egyptian, Ethiopian, and Armenian Christian churches.

Commonly a council of bishops deliberated and declared a particular doctrine true or false. In the East, the Byzantine emperor claimed the authority to call such conferences. In the West, the pope took the lead after the tenth century, when Roman nobles lost control of the papacy and it became a more powerful international office. Schismatics—believers in heretical ideas—sometimes called conferences of their own. Councils of bishops set rules, called canons, to regulate the priests and lay people (men and women who were not members of the clergy) under their jurisdiction.

The doctrine of Arianism°, which was widespread among the Germanic peoples, threatened church unity in western Europe most dangerously. Although the Council of Nicaea° called by the emperor Constantine in 325 declared heretical the teaching of the Alexandrian bishop Arius that Jesus was a creation of God the Father and a lesser sort of divinity, it did not quickly disappear.

Politics and the Church

In politically fragmented western Europe, the pope needed allies. He found them in rulers like Charlemagne, who upheld papal rights in return for legitimization of his rule. Not until 962, however, with the papal coronation of a "Holy Roman Em-

---

patriarchate (PAY-tree-ar-kayt)

schism (SKIZ-uhm)   Monophysite (muh-NAH-fi-site)
Arianism (AIR-ree-uh-niz-uhm)   Nicaea (neye-SEE-uh)

peror" (Charlemagne never held this title), did a secular political authority come into being that claimed to represent general Christian interests. Essentially a loose confederation of German princes who named one of their own to the highest office, the **Holy Roman Empire** had little influence west of the Rhine River.

Although the pope crowned the early Holy Roman Emperors, this did not signify political superiority. The Canon Law of the church accorded the pope exclusive legal jurisdiction over all clergy and church property wherever located. But bishops who held land as vassals owed military support or other services and dues to kings and princes. The secular rulers argued that they should have the power to appoint those bishops because that was the only way to guarantee fulfillment of their duties as vassals. The popes disagreed.

In the eleventh century, this conflict over the control of ecclesiastical appointments came to a head. Hildebrand°, an Italian monk, capped a career of reforming and reorganizing church finances by being named Pope Gregory VII in 1073. His personal notion of the papacy (preserved among his letters) represented an extreme position, stating among other claims, that

§ The pope can be judged by no one;
§ The Roman church has never erred and never will err till the end of time;
§ The pope alone can depose and restore bishops;
§ He alone can call general councils and authorize canon law;
§ He can depose emperors;
§ He can absolve subjects from their allegiance;
§ All princes should kiss his feet.[2]

Such claims antagonized lords and monarchs, who had become accustomed to *investing,* that is, conferring a ring and a staff as symbols of authority on bishops and abbots in their domains. Historians apply the term **investiture controversy** to the struggle to control ecclesiastical appointments; the term also refers to the broader conflict of popes versus emperors and kings. When Holy Roman Emperor Henry IV defied Gregory's reforms, Gregory excommunicated him in 1076, thereby cutting him off from church rituals. Stung by the resulting decline in his influence, Henry stood barefoot in the snow for three days outside a castle in northern Italy waiting for Gregory, a guest there, to receive him. Henry's formal act of penance induced Gregory to forgive him and restore him to the church. The reconciliation, an apparent victory for the pope, did not last. In 1078, Gregory declared Henry deposed. The emperor then forced the pope to flee from Rome to Salerno, where Gregory died two years later.

Nevertheless, the reforming legacy of Gregory VII survived. The struggle between the popes and emperors continued until 1122, when a compromise was reached at Worms, a town in Germany. In the Concordat of Worms, Emperor Henry V renounced his right to choose bishops and abbots or bestow spiritual symbols on them. In return, Pope Calixtus II permitted the emperor to invest papally appointed bishops and abbots with any lay rights or obligations before their spiritual consecration.

Assertions of royal authority triggered other conflicts as well. Though barely twenty years old when he became king of England in 1154, Henry II, a great-grandson of William the Conqueror, instituted reforms designed to strengthen the power of the Crown and weaken the nobility. He appointed traveling justices to enforce his laws. He made juries, a holdover from traditional Germanic law, into powerful legal instruments. He established the principle that criminal acts violated the "king's peace" and should be tried and punished in accordance with charges brought by the Crown instead of in response to charges brought by victims.

Henry had a harder time controlling the church. His closest friend and chancellor, or chief administrator, Thomas à Becket (ca. 1118–1170), lived the grand and luxurious life of a courtier. In 1162, Henry persuaded Becket to become a priest and assume the position of archbishop of Canterbury, the highest church office in England. Becket agreed but cautioned that as an official of the church, he would act solely in the interest of the church when it came into conflict with the Crown. Later, when Henry sought to try clerics accused of crimes in royal instead of ecclesiastical courts,

---

Hildebrand (HILL-de-brand)

Archbishop Becket, now leading an austere and pious life, resisted.

In 1170, four of Henry's knights, knowing that the king desired Becket's death, murdered the archbishop in Canterbury Cathedral. Their crime backfired. An outpouring of sympathy caused Canterbury to become a major pilgrimage center, and in 1173 the pope declared the martyred Becket a saint. Henry, his authority badly damaged, allowed himself to be publicly whipped in penance twice for the crime.

The investiture controversy and Henry II's conflict with Thomas à Becket yielded no clear victor. Three legal traditions competed in Western Europe: (1) feudal law, with roots in Germanic custom; (2) canon, or church, law based on Roman precedent in its visualizing a single hierarchical legal institution with jurisdiction over all of Western Christendom; and (3) Roman law, a compilation of Roman imperial decrees that after centuries of disregard began to be studied anew at the fledgling University of Bologna°, in Italy, around 1088. These conflicting legal theories and jurisdictions set the region apart from the Byzantine Empire, Russia, and the Muslim states that succeeded the Byzantines in Syria, Egypt, and Tunisia (see Chapter 7).

Monasticism

The origins of **monasticism** lay in the eastern lands of the Roman Empire. Pre-Christian practices such as celibacy, continual devotion to prayer, and living apart from society (alone or in small groups) came together in Christian form in Egypt. A fourth-century account portrays Anthony, the most important hermit monk, as a pious desert hermit continually tempted by Satan. On one occasion, "when he was weaving palm leaves . . . that he might make baskets to give as gifts to people who were continually coming to visit him . . . he saw an animal which had the following form: from its head to its side it was like a man, and its legs and feet were those of an ass."[3] As was his custom, Anthony prayed to God upon seeing this sight, and Satan left him alone.

The most important form of monasticism in

Bologna (boe-LOAN-yuh)

Illuminated Manuscript from Monastic Library   This page from the Book of Kells, written around 800 in Ireland, contains the Greek letters chi and rho, or CR, a monogram for Jesus Christ. The intricate interwoven forms that fill the background derive from pagan design traditions that featured intertangled dragons, snakes, and other beasts. (Trinity College Library, Dublin, Ms. 58, fol. 84v)

western Europe involved groups of monks or nuns living together in a single community. Benedict of Nursia (ca. 480–547), in Italy, began his pious career as a hermit in a cave but eventually organized several monasteries, each headed by an abbot. The rule he wrote to govern the monks' behavior, known as the Rule of Benedict, emphasizes celibacy, poverty, and obedience to the abbot. Those who lived by this or any other rule became *regular clergy*, in contrast to *secular clergy*, priests who followed no code of regulations. The Rule of Benedict provided the starting point for most forms of western European monastic life and remains in force today in Benedictine monasteries.

Monastic life removed thousands of pious

men and women from towns and villages and thus reinforced the separation of religious affairs from ordinary politics and economics. Monasteries followed Jesus's axiom that one should "render unto Caesar what is Caesar's and unto God what is God's" better than the many town-based bishops, who behaved like lords.

Monasteries preserved literacy and learning in the centuries following the decline of the Western Empire, although a few rulers, like Charlemagne, encouraged scholarship at court. Many illiterate lay nobles interested themselves only in warfare and hunting. Monks (but seldom nuns) saw copying manuscripts and even writing books as a religious calling. Without the monks of the ninth century, most ancient Latin works would have disappeared.

Monasteries and nunneries served other functions as well. A few planted Christianity in new lands, as Irish monks did in parts of Germany. Most serviced the needs of travelers, organized agricultural production on their lands, and took in abandoned infants. Nunneries provided refuge for widows and other women who lacked male protection in the harsh medieval world or who desired a spiritual life. These religious houses presented problems of oversight to the church, however. A bishop might have authority over an abbot or abbess (head of a nunnery), but he could not exercise constant vigilance over what went on behind monastery walls.

An influential movement of reform arose within the monastic establishment itself at the Benedictine abbey of Cluny° in eastern France. Founded in 910 by William the Pious, the first duke of Aquitaine, who completely freed it of lay authority. Cluny gained similar freedom from the local bishop a century later. Its abbots pursued a vigorous campaign, in alliance with reforming popes like Gregory VII, to improve monastic discipline and administration. A magnificent new abbey church, designed in the Romanesque° style with small arched windows and heavy stone walls, symbolized Cluny's claims to eminence. With later additions, it became the largest church in the world.

At the peak of Cluny's influence, nearly a thousand Benedictine abbeys and priories (lower-level monastic houses) in various countries accepted the authority of the abbot of Cluny. The Benedictine Rule had presumed that each monastery would be independent; the Cluniac reformers stipulated that every abbot and every prior (head of a priory) be appointed by the abbot of Cluny and have personal experience of the religious life of Cluny. The Cluniac movement set the pattern for the monasteries, cathedral clergy, and preaching friars that would dominate ecclesiastical life in the thirteenth century.

THE BYZANTINE EMPIRE, 300–1200

The Byzantine emperors represented a continuation of Roman imperial rule and tradition almost entirely absent in the West. They inherited Roman law intact and, exercising an authority known as *caesaropapism*, combining both the imperial ("Caesar") and the papal, made a comfortable transition into the role of all-powerful Christian monarchs. The Byzantine drama, however, played on a smaller and steadily shrinking stage. Territorial losses and almost constant military pressure from north and south deprived the empire of long periods of peace.

Church and State   In 324, in the nineteenth year of his reign, Constantine led a procession marking out the expanded limits of the city he had selected as his new capital: the millennium-old Greek city of Byzantium, located on a long, narrow inlet at the entrance to the Bosporus strait. In the forum of the new Constantinople, he erected a 120-foot-tall (36-meter) column topped with a statue of Apollo, and he retained the old Roman title *pontifex maximus*° (chief priest). Nevertheless, he

---

Cluny (KLOO-nee)   **Romanesque** (roe-man-ESK)

pontifex maximus (PAHN-tih-fex MAX-ih-muhs)

leaned toward Christianity, if not embracing it fully at that time, and he studded the city with churches.

The Byzantine emperor appointed the patriarch of Constantinople and involved himself in doctrinal disputes over which beliefs constituted heresy. In 325, Constantine called hundreds of bishops to a council at the city of Nicaea (modern Iznik in northwestern Turkey) and persuaded them to reject the Arian doctrine that Jesus was of lesser importance than God the Father. Nevertheless, disputes over theology and quarrels among the patriarchs of Constantinople, Alexandria, and Antioch continued to tear at the Byzantine Empire. The literature of the period is devoted largely to religious concerns, which deeply permeated society. A fourth-century bishop reported, "Everything is full of those who are speaking of unintelligible things . . . . I wish to know the price of bread; one answers, 'The Father is greater than the Son.' I inquire whether my bath is ready; one says, 'The Son has been made out of nothing.'"[4]

In the Byzantine world, in contrast with the West, polytheism died fairly quickly, surviving longest among the country folk (Latin *pagani*, whence the word *pagan* for people who believe in strange gods). The emperor Julian (r. 361–363) tried in vain to restore the old polytheism. When a blind Christian called Julian an apostate (a renegade from Christianity), the emperor said, "You are blind, and your God will not cure you," to which the Christian replied, "I thank God for my blindness, since it prevents me from beholding your impiety." In 392, the emperor Theodosius banned all pagan ceremonies. The following year, he terminated the Olympic Games.

Having a single ruler endowed with supreme legal and religious authority prevented the breakup of the Eastern Empire into petty principalities, but it did not guarantee peace or prosperity. A new Iranian empire ruled by the Sasanid family (see Chapter 7) threatened from the east in the fourth century. From the north came Germanic Goths and the nomadic Huns of Central Asia. Bribes, diplomacy, and occasional military victories persuaded the Goths and Huns to settle peacefully or move on and attack western Europe. War with the Sasanids, however, recurred for almost three hundred years. Finally, a new enemy appeared from the Arabian peninsula: followers of the Arab prophet Muhammad, who between 634 and 650 destroyed the Sasanid Empire and captured Egypt, Syria, and Tunisia. By the end of the twelfth century, at least two-thirds of the Christians in the former Byzantine territories had adopted the Muslim faith.

The loss of these populous and prosperous provinces permanently reduced the power of the empire and set it on a downward path. Although it survived until 1453, its later emperors faced Muslim enemies to the south and newly arriving Slavic and Turkic peoples to the north. At the same time, relations with the popes and princes of western Europe steadily worsened. In the mid-ninth century, the patriarchs of Constantinople had challenged the territorial jurisdiction of the popes of Rome and some of the practices of the Latin Church. These arguments worsened over time and in 1054 culminated in a formal schism between the Latin Church and the Orthodox Church, a break that has been only partially mended. This ill will did not prevent Eastern and Western Christians from cooperating in some measure during the crusading era of the twelfth century. But it contributed to the decision by the leaders of the Fourth Crusade (see below) to sack Constantinople in 1204 and establish Latin principalities on Byzantine territory.

Society and Urban Life

The maintenance of imperial authority and the accompanying urban prosperity in the eastern provinces of the old Roman Empire initially saved Byzantium from the population losses and economic collapse suffered in the West from the third century on. Nevertheless, a similar though less pronounced transformation set in around the seventh century, possibly sparked by the loss of Egypt and Syria to the Muslims. Narrative histories tell us little, but saints' lives show a transition from stories about educated saints hailing from cities to stories about saints originating as peasants. In many areas, barter replaced money transactions, cities declined in population and prosperity, and the traditional class of local urban notables nearly disappeared.

The disappearance of that class left a social gap between the high-ranking aristocrats at the imperial court and the rural landowners and peasants. By the end of the eleventh century, a family-based military aristocracy somewhat similar to the landed nobility of western Europe had emerged. Of Byzantine emperor Alexius Comnenus° (r. 1081–1118), it was said, "He considered himself not a ruler, but a lord, conceiving and calling the empire his own house."

The situation of women changed too. Earlier Roman family structure had granted women comparative freedom in public. Now the family became a more rigid unit, and women increasingly found themselves confined to the home. When they went out, they concealed their faces behind veils. The only men they socialized with were family members. Paradoxically, however, women ruled the Byzantine Empire with their husbands from 1028 to 1056.

Although no connection between these changes and the parallel seclusion of women in neighboring Islamic countries has materialized, the two developments may be linked despite the differences in religion. By comparison with Christianity in western Europe, Byzantine Christianity manifested less interest in, or felt less need for, the provision of refuge for women in nunneries. This too finds its parallel in the development of Islam.

Economically, the Byzantine emperors continued a Late Roman inclination to set prices, order grain shipments to the capital city, and monopolize trade in luxury goods like Tyrian purple cloth. Such government intervention may have slowed technological development and economic innovation. So long as merchants and pilgrims hastened to Constantinople from all points of the compass, aristocrats could buy rare and costly goods. But other Byzantine cities suffered declines. In the countryside, Byzantine farmers continued to use light scratch plows and creaky oxcarts long after farmers in western Europe had adopted heavy plows and efficiently harnessed horses.

Because Byzantium's Roman inheritance was so much richer than western Europe's, few people recognized the slow deterioration that began in the seventh century. Gradually, however, pilgrims and visitors from the West saw the reality beyond the awe-inspiring, incense-filled domes of cathedrals and beneath the glitter and silken garments of

Alexius Comnenus (uh-LEX-see-uhs kom-NAY-nuhs)

Byzantine Church from a Twelfth-Century Manuscript
The upper portion shows the church facade and domes. The lower portion shows the interior with a picture or mosaic of Christ enthroned at the altar end.   (Bibliothèque nationale de France)

the royal court. An eleventh-century French visitor wrote:

> The city itself [Constantinople] is squalid and fetid and in many places harmed by permanent darkness, for the wealthy overshadow the streets with buildings and leave these dirty, dark places to the poor and to travelers; there murders and robberies and other crimes which love the darkness are committed. Moreover, since people live lawlessly in this city, which has as many lords as rich men and almost as many thieves as poor men, a criminal knows neither fear nor shame, because crime is not punished by law and never entirely comes to light. In every respect she exceeds moderation; for, just as she surpasses other cities in wealth, so too, does she surpass them in vice.[5]

Anna Comnena, the brilliant daughter of Emperor Alexius Comnenus, expressed the view from the other side. She described the Western knights of the First Crusade (1096–1099) as uncouth barbarians, albeit sometimes gifted with an impressive manliness. She even turned her scorn on a prominent churchman and philosopher who happened to be from Italy: "Italos . . . was unable with his barbaric, stupid temperament to grasp the profound truths of philosophy; even in the act of learning he utterly rejected the teacher's guiding hand, and full of temerity and barbaric folly, [believed] even before study that he excelled all others."[6]

By the time of the **Crusades,** western Europe was visibly forging ahead of Byzantium. With their most valuable provinces gone, their army played only a supporting role in the conquest of the Holy Land. Their maritime commerce depended on ships from Genoa, Venice, and Pisa. From the sack of Constantinople during the Fourth Crusade in 1204 to its fall in 1453, vestiges of the legendary Byzantine pomp and political intrigue remained. But this heir to the Roman Empire amounted to little more than a small, weak principality centered on a shrunken, looted, and dilapidated Constantinople and a few outlying cities.

Cultural Achievements

Several emperors ordered collections of laws and edicts to be made, the most famous and complete collection being the *Corpus Juris Civilis (Body of Civil Law)* compiled in Latin by seventeen legal scholars at the behest of the emperor Justinian (r. 527–565). In the late eleventh century, the University of Bologna in Italy took this collection as the basis for *civil* law (as opposed to *canon* and *feudal* law). Many modern principles of law thus derive from Roman models, which accounts for the many Latin expressions in legal use today.

Architectural tradition represented by Hagia Sophia°, the great domed cathedral of Constantinople, also dates to the reign of Justinian and his influential wife, the empress Theodora. Domed buildings, which required careful calculation of the stress of the stone dome's weight, were compara-

tively rare in the western lands of the Roman Empire. But they evolved splendidly in Byzantium, creating enormous spaces with an aesthetic appeal completely different from that of the long, lofty naves of Western cathedrals. The great architects of the Italian Renaissance (in the fifteenth and sixteenth centuries) had Byzantine models in mind when they turned their hand to designing domes for Catholic churches.

Other important Byzantine achievements date to the empire's long period of political decline. In the ninth century, two brothers named Cyril and Methodius embarked on a highly successful mission to the Slavs of Moravia (part of the modern Czech Republic). They preached in the local language, and their followers perfected a writing system, called Cyrillic°, that came to be used by Slavic Christians adhering to the Orthodox—that is, Byzantine—rite.

KIEVAN RUSSIA, 900–1200

After the fall of Byzantium, Russia became the paramount center of Orthodox Christianity and heir to the Byzantine imperial tradition. The territory between the Black and Caspian Seas in the south and the Baltic and White Seas in the north divides into a series of east-west zones. Frozen tundra in the far north gives way to a cold forest zone, then a more temperate forest, then a mix of forest and steppe grasslands, and finally just grassland. Several navigable rivers run from north to south across these zones.

Early historical sources reflect repeated linguistic and territorial changes, seemingly under pressure from poorly understood population migrations. Most of the Germanic peoples, along with some Iranian and west Slavic peoples, migrated westward in Roman times. The peoples who remained spoke eastern Slavic languages, except in the far north and south: Finns and related peoples lived in the former region, Turkic speakers in the latter.

Forest dwellers, farmers, and steppe nomads complemented each other economically. Nomads

---

Hagia Sophia (AH-yah SOH-fee-uh)

Cyrillic (sih-RIL-ik)

traded animals for the farmers' grain; and honey, wax, and furs from the forest became important exchange items. Traders could travel east and west by steppe caravan (see Chapters 6 and 11), or they could move north and south on the Volga, Dnieper°, and Don Rivers.

Scandinavians, relatives of the Vikings who are called Varangians in early sources, dominated the river trade. They exchanged forest products and slaves for manufactured goods and Muslim silver coins at markets controlled by the Khazar Turks, whose powerful kingdom centered around the mouth of the Volga River.

The Rise of the Kievan State

Historians debate the early meaning of the word *Rus* (from which *Russia* is derived), but at some point it came to refer to societies of western Slavs ruled by Varangians. The Varangian princes and their *druzhina* (military retainers) lived in cities, unlike western European lords, while the Slavs farmed. The princes occupied themselves in trade and fending off enemies. The Rus of the city of Kiev° controlled trade on the Dnieper River and dealt more with Byzantium than the Muslim world because the Dnieper flows into the Black Sea. The Rus of Novgorod° played the same role on the Volga. The semi-legendary account of the Kievan Rus conversion to Christianity must be seen against this background.

In 980, Vladimir° I, a former ruler of Novgorod, returned from exile to Kiev with a band of Varangians and made himself the grand prince of Kievan Russia. Although his grandmother Olga had been a Christian, Vladimir built a temple on Kiev's heights and placed there the statues of the six gods his Slavic subjects worshipped. The earliest Russian chronicle reports that Vladimir and his advisers decided against Islam as the official religion because of its ban on alcohol, rejected Judaism (the religion to which the Khazars had converted) because they thought that a truly powerful god would not have let the ancient Jewish kingdom be destroyed, and even spoke with German emissaries advocating Latin Christianity. Eventually, Vladimir chose Orthodox Christianity as the religion of the Kievan state because of the magnificence of Constantinople. After visiting Byzantine churches, his agents reported: "We knew not whether we were in heaven or on earth, for on earth there is no such splendor of [*sic*] such beauty, and we are at a loss how to describe it. We know only that God dwells there among men, and their service is finer than the ceremonies of other nations."[7]

After choosing a reluctant bride from the Byzantine imperial family, Vladimir converted to Orthodox Christianity, probably in the year 988, and opened his lands to Orthodox clerics and missionaries. The patriarch of Constantinople appointed a metropolitan (chief bishop) at Kiev to govern ecclesiastical affairs. Churches arose in Kiev, one of them atop the ruins of Vladimir's earlier pagan temple. Writing was introduced, using the Cyrillic alphabet devised earlier for the western Slavs. This extension of Orthodox Christendom northward provided a barrier against the eastward expansion of Latin Christianity. Kiev became firmly oriented toward trade with Byzantium and turned its back on the Muslim world, though the Volga trade continued through Novgorod.

Struggles within the ruling family and with other enemies, most notably the steppe peoples of the south, marked the later political history of Kievan Russia. But down to the time of the Mongols in the thirteenth century (see Chapter 11), the state retained its identity and served as an instrument for the Christianization of the eastern Slavs.

Society and Culture

In Kievan Russia, political power derived from trade rather than landholding, so the manorial agricultural system of western Europe never developed. Farmers practiced shifting cultivation of their own lands. They would burn a section of forest and then lightly scratch the ash-strewn surface with a plow. When fertility waned, they would move to another section of forest. Poor land and a short growing season in the most northerly latitudes made food scarce. Living on their own estates, the druzhina evolved from infantry into cavalry and focused their efforts more on horse breeding than agriculture.

Dnieper (d-NYEP-er)   **Kiev** (KEE-yev)
Novgorod (NOHV-goh-rod)   **Vladimir** (VLAD-ih-mir)

Large cities like Kiev and Novgorod may have reached 30,000 or 50,000 people—roughly the size of contemporary London or Paris but far smaller than Constantinople or major Muslim metropolises like Baghdad and Nishapur. Many cities amounted to little more than fortified trading posts. They nevertheless served as centers for the development of crafts, some, such as glassmaking, based on skills imported from Byzantium. Artisans enjoyed a higher status in society than peasant farmers. Construction relied on wood from the forests, although Christianity brought with it the building of stone cathedrals and churches on the Byzantine model.

Christianity penetrated the general population slowly. Several pagan uprisings occurred in the eleventh century, particularly in times of famine. Passive resistance led some groups to reject Christian burial and persist in cremating the dead and keeping the bones of the deceased in urns. Women continued to use pagan designs on their clothing and bracelets, and as late as the twelfth century they turned to pagan priests for charms to cure sick children. Traditional Slavic marriage practices involving casual and polygamous relations particularly scandalized the clergy.

Eventually, Christianity triumphed, and with success came increasing church engagement in political and economic affairs. In the twelfth century, Christian clergy became involved in government administration, some of them collecting fees and taxes related to trade. Direct and indirect revenue from trade provided the rulers with the money they needed to pay their soldiers. The rule of law also spread as Kievan Russia experienced its peak of culture and prosperity in the century before the Mongol onslaught.

Western Europe Revives, 1000–1200

Between 1000 and 1200, western Europe slowly emerged from nearly seven centuries of subsistence economy—one in which most people who worked on the land could meet only their basic needs for food, clothing, and shelter. Population and agricultural production climbed, and a growing food surplus found its way to town markets, speeding the return of a money-based economy and providing support for larger numbers of craftspeople, construction workers, and traders.

Historians have attributed western Europe's revival to population growth spurred by new technologies and to the appearance in Italy and Flanders (modern Belgium and Holland) of self-governing cities devoted primarily to trade and seafaring. For kings, the changes facilitated improvements in central administration, greater control over vassals, and consolidation of realms on the way to becoming strong national kingdoms.

The Role of Technology

A lack of concrete evidence confirming the spread of technological innovations frustrates efforts to relate the exact course of Europe's revival to technological change. Nevertheless, most historians agree that technology played a significant role in the near doubling of the population of western Europe between 1000 and 1200. The population of England seems to have risen from 1.1 million in 1086 to 1.9 million in 1200, and the population of the territory of modern France seems to have risen from 5.2 million to 9.2 million over the same period.

An example that illustrates the difficulty of drawing historical conclusions from scattered evidence of technological change concerns a new type of plow and the use of efficient draft harnesses for pulling wagons. The Roman plow, which farmers in southern Europe continued to use, merely scratched the soil. The new plow had a coulter (blade), which made a vertical cut in the soil, and a moldboard, which lifted and turned the cut layer of soil. The new plow could bite through the heavy, wet soil of the northern river valleys. Combined with the new harness, this favored the emergence of the horse as western Europe's primary work animal, replacing the ox in many areas.

A mystery surrounds the adoption of harnesses that did not strangle a horse pulling a heavy load, as the old-style harnesses derived from the yoke tended to do. The **horse collar,** which lowers the point of traction from the animal's neck to its shoulders, first appears around 800 in a miniature painting, and it is shown clearly as a harness for plow horses in the Bayeux Tapestry, embroidered after 1066. The breast-strap harness, which is less well adapted for the heaviest work but was preferred in southern Europe, seems to have appeared around the year 500. In both cases, linguists have tried to trace key technical terms to Chinese or Turko-Mongol words and have argued for technological diffusion across Eurasia. Yet third-century Roman farmers in Tunisia and Libya used both types of efficient harness to hitch horses and camels to plows and carts. This technology, which is still employed in Tunisia, appears clearly on Roman bas-reliefs and lamps, but there is no more evidence of its movement northward into Europe than there is of similar harnessing moving across Asia. Thus, the question of whether efficient harnessing began in 500 or in 800, or was known even earlier but not extensively used, cannot easily be resolved.

Hinging on this problem is the question of when and why landowners in northern Europe began to use teams of horses to pull plows through moist, fertile river valley soils that were too heavy for teams of oxen. Stronger and faster than oxen, horses increased the productivity of these and other lands by reducing the time needed for plowing. This undoubtedly contributed to a greater agricultural surplus, but the breeding of larger horses for knightly warfare may have been as important a factor as the new technology in starting the move away from oxen.

Cities and the Rebirth of Trade

Independent cities governed and defended by communes of leading citizens appeared first in Italy and Flanders and then elsewhere. Lacking extensive farmlands, these cities turned to manufacturing and trade. Equally important, they won for themselves a legally independent position between the jurisdiction of the church and that of the secular lord and therefore could frame their laws specifically to favor manufacturing and trade. These laws made serfs free, so these cities attracted many migrants from the countryside. Cities in Italy that had shrunk within walls built by the Romans now pressed against those walls, forcing the construc-

tion of new ones. Pisa built a new wall in 1000 and expanded it in 1156. Other twelfth-century cities that built new walls include Florence, Brescia°, Pavia, and Siena°.

Venice grew up on a group of islands at the northern end of the Adriatic Sea that had been largely uninhabited in Roman times. In the eleventh century, it became the dominant seapower in the Adriatic. With its rivals Pisa and Genoa on the western side of Italy, Venice competed for leadership in the trade with Muslim ports in North Africa and the eastern Mediterranean. A somewhat later merchant's list mentions some three thousand "spices" (including dyestuffs, textile fibers, and raw materials) being traded, among them alum (for dyeing), eleven types; wax, eleven types; cotton, eight types; indigo, four types; ginger, five types; paper, four types; and sugar, fifteen types; along with cloves, caraway, tamarind, and fresh oranges.

Ghent, Bruges°, and Ypres° in Flanders rivaled the Italian cities in prosperity, trade, and industry. Enjoying comparable independence based on privileges gained by their communes from the counts of Flanders, these cities centralized the wool trade of the North Sea, transforming raw wool from England into woolen cloth that reached a very wide market.

More abundant coinage also signaled the upturn in economic activity. In the ninth and tenth centuries, most gold coins had come from Muslim lands and Byzantium. Being worth too much for most trading purposes, they seldom reached Germany, France, and England. The widely imitated Carolingian silver penny sufficed. With the economic revival of the twelfth century, minting of silver coins began in Scandinavia, Poland, and other outlying regions. In the following century, the reinvigoration of Mediterranean trade made possible a new and abundant gold coinage.

The Crusades

The Crusades, a series of Christian military campaigns against Muslims in the eastern Mediterranean, dominated the politics of Europe from 1100 to 1200 (see Map 8.2).

Brescia (BREH-shee-uh)   **Siena** (see-EN-uh)
Bruges (broozh)   **Ypres** (EEP-r)

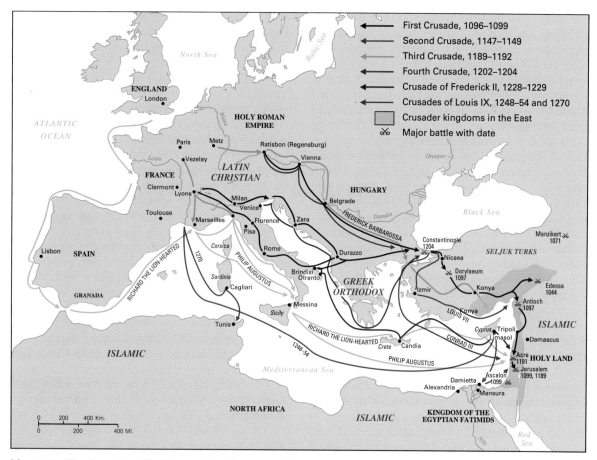

Map. 8.2   The Crusades   The first two Crusades proceeded overland through Byzantine territory. The Third Crusade included contingents under the French and English kings, Philip Augustus and Richard the Lion-Hearted, that traveled by sea, and a contingent under the Holy Roman Emperor Frederick Barbarossa that took the overland route. Frederick died in southern Anatolia. Later Crusades were mostly seaborne, with Sicily, Crete, and Cyprus playing important roles.

They culminated in several social and economic currents of the eleventh century. First, reforming leaders of the Latin Church interested in softening the warlike tone of society popularized the Truce of God. This movement limited fighting between Christian lords by specifying times of truce, such as during Lent (the forty days before Easter) and on the Sunday sabbath. Crusading warfare approved by the church thus appealed to knights. Second, ambitious rulers were looking for new lands to conquer, an objective best represented by the Norman invasions of England and Sicily. Knights, particularly younger sons in areas where the oldest

son inherited everything, needed land to maintain their noble status. Third, Italian merchants wanted to increase trade in the eastern Mediterranean and acquire trading posts in Muslim territory.

Several factors focused attention on the Holy Land, which had been under Muslim rule for four centuries. **Pilgrimages** played an important role in European religious life. Pilgrims traveled in special costume under royal protection, some actually being tramps, thieves, beggars, peddlers, and merchants using pilgrimage as a safe way of traveling. Genuinely pious pilgrims often journeyed to visit the old churches and sacred relics preserved in

Armored Knights in Battle   This painting, made around 1135, shows the armament of knights at the time of the Crusades. Chain mail, a helmet, and a shield carried on the left side protect the rider. The lance carried underarm and the sword are the primary weapons. Notice that riders about to make contact with lances have their legs straight and braced in the stirrups while riders with swords and in flight have bent legs.   (Pierpont Morgan Library/Art Resource, NY)

Others heard of the war conducted by seafaring Normans against the Muslims in Sicily, whom they finally defeated in the 1090s after thirty years of fighting.

The tales of pilgrims returning from the East further induced both churchmen and nobles to consider the Muslims a proper target for Christian militancy. Muslim rulers, who had controlled Jerusalem, Antioch, and Alexandria ever since the seventh century, generally tolerated and protected Christian pilgrims. But that changed after 1071 when a Turkish army defeated the Byzantine emperor at the Battle of Manzikert and opened the way for Turkish nomads to spread throughout Anatolia (see Chapter 7). Growing Muslim power threatened ancient centers of Christianity previously under Byzantine control.

From time to time, the Byzantine emperor Alexius Comnenus suggested to the pope and western European rulers that they help him confront the Muslim threat. In 1095, at the Council of Clermont, Pope Urban II responded. He addressed a huge crowd of people gathered in a field and called on them, as Christians, to stop fighting one another and go to the Holy Land to fight Muslims.

"God wills it!" exclaimed voices in the crowd. People cut cloth into crosses and sewed them on their shirts to symbolize their willingness to march on Jerusalem. Thus began the holy war now known as the First Crusade, a word taken from Latin *crux* for "cross." People at the time, however, spoke not of a "crusade" but of *peregrinatio,* a "pilgrimage." Urban promised to free crusaders who had committed sins from their normal penance, or acts of atonement, the usual reward for peaceful pilgrims to Jerusalem.

The three Crusades of the eleventh and twelfth centuries contributed to ending western Europe's long isolation. Sicily, seized from the Muslims, yielded Arabic translations of Greek philosophical and scientific works and equally important original works by Arabs and Iranians. Spain yielded an even greater bounty to translators who worked in both the Christian and the Muslim kingdoms. Later, Greece was ransacked for ancient manuscripts after the Venetians persuaded the leaders of the Fourth Crusade in 1204 to satisfy their financial debts by capturing Constantinople and occupying, for a century, most of the shrunken Byzantine Empire.

Rome, Constantinople, and Jerusalem to fulfill a vow or atone for a sin.

Knights who followed a popular pilgrimage route across northern Spain to pray at the shrine of Santiago de Compostela learned of the expanding efforts of Christian kings to dislodge the Muslims.

Generations passed before all these works were translated into Latin and studied, but they eventually transformed the thought of the western Europeans, who previously had had little familiarity with Greek writings except through Latin intermediaries.

CONCLUSION

The collapse of imperial Rome was not unique. China's Han dynasty (see Chapter 5) and the Abbasid Caliphate (Chapter 7) both dissolved into successor states. Although western Europe endured chaos, disunity, and economic regression, the cultural vitality that emerged from the centuries of disorder bears comparison with other instances. The Tang Empire, which emerged in China in the seventh century C.E. (Chapter 9), had a distinctive and lively culture based only in part on survivals from the Han era. In the Middle East, the emergence of a distinctive society based on the Islamic religion largely followed the collapse of the central Islamic state in the tenth century (Chapter 7). The dynamic development of Islam after this political collapse parallels the overwhelming influence gained by Christianity in western Europe by the end of the twelfth century.

In contrast, the Byzantine Empire built on Roman practices in an economic and political environment that was both more prosperous and more peaceful than that of western Europe. Furthermore, Byzantine society became deeply Christian well before a comparable degree of Christianization had been reached in western Europe. Yet despite their success in transmitting their versions of Christianity and imperial rule to Kievan Russia, the Byzantines failed to demonstrate the dynamism and ferment that characterized both the Europeans to their west and the Muslims to their south.

■ Key Terms

Charlemagne	papacy
medieval	schism
Byzantine Empire	Holy Roman Empire
Kievan Russia	investiture controversy
manors	monasticism
serfs	Crusades
vassals	horse collar
fief	pilgrimages

■ Suggested Reading

Roger Collins's *Early Medieval Europe, 300–1000* (1991) surveys institutional and political developments. For the later part of the period, see Susan Reynolds, *Kingdoms and Communities in Western Europe, 900–1300*, 2d ed. (1997). Georges Duby, *The Early Growth of the European Economy* (1974), reviews economic and social history reflecting up-to-date historical methods. Jacques Le Goff, *Medieval Civilization, 400–1500* (1989), stresses questions of social structure. Richard W. Southern, *Western Society and the Church in the Middle Ages* (1970), concentrates on church matters, and his *The Making of the Middle Ages* (1953) gives a memorable impression of the period based on specific lives and events. Archibald R. Lewis, *Naval Power and Trade in the Mediterranean, A.D. 500–1100* (1951), focuses on the ebb and flow of power between Christians and Muslims. Susan Reynolds makes the case for avoiding the term *feudalism* in *Fiefs and Vassals* (1994).

More specialized economic and technological studies include Lynn White, Jr., *Medieval Technology and Social Change* (1962), and C. M. Cipolla, *Money, Prices and Civilization in the Mediterranean World, Fifth to Seventeenth Century* (1956), and his more general history, *Before the Industrial Revolution: European Society and Economy, 1000–1700* (1980). J. C. Russell, *The Control of Late Ancient and Medieval Population* (1985), analyzes demographic history and the problems of data. Georges Duby, *Rural Economy and Country Life in the Medieval West* (1990), includes translated documents.

On France, see Pierre Riché, *Daily Life in the World of Charlemagne* (1978), and Georges Duby, *The Chivalrous Society* (1977); on England, Dorothy Whitelock, *The Beginnings of English Society* (1952), and Doris Mary Stenton, *English Society in the Early Middle Ages (1066–1307)* (1951); on Italy, Edward Burman, *Emperor to Emperor:*

Italy Before the Renaissance (1991); on Germany and the Holy Roman Empire, Timothy Reuter, *Germany in the Early Middle Ages, c. 80–1056* (1991); on Spain, Bernard F. Reilly, *The Medieval Spains* (1993); and on Viking Scandinavia, Gwyn Jones, *A History of the Vikings* (1984).

Amy Keller, *Eleanor of Aquitaine and the Four Kings* (1950), tells the story of an extraordinary woman. Dhuoda, *Handbook for William: A Carolingian Woman's Counsel for Her Son,* translated by Carol Neel (1991), offers a firsthand look at a Carolingian noblewoman. More general works include Margaret Wade's *A Small Sound of the Trumpet: Women in Medieval Life* (1986), and Bonnie S. Anderson and Judith P. Zinsser's *A History of Their Own: Women in Europe from Prehistory to the Present* (1989). In the area of religion, Caroline Bynum's *Jesus as Mother: Studies in the Spirituality of the High Middle Ages* (1982) illustrates new views about women.

Hans Eberhard Mayer's *The Crusades* (1988) and Jonathan Riley-Smith's *The Crusades: A Short History* (1987) briefly narrate the crusading era. For a longer account with a Byzantine viewpoint, see Steven Runciman, *A History of the Crusades,* 3 vols. (1987). Benjamin Z. Kedar, *Crusade and Mission: European Approaches Toward the Muslims* (1988), explains the religious issues underlying the conflict.

Henri Pirenne, *Medieval Cities: Their Origins and the Revival of Trade* (1952), and Robert S. Lopez, *The Commercial Revolution of the Middle Ages, 950–1350* (1971), masterfully discuss the revival of trade. Lopez and Irving W. Raymond compile and translate primary documents in *Medieval Trade in the Mediterranean World: Illustrative Documents with Introductions and Notes* (1990).

Standard Byzantine histories include Georgij A. Ostrogorsky, *History of the Byzantine State* (1969), Alexander Aleksandrovich Vasiliev, *History of the Byzantine Empire,* 2 vols. (1952), and Warren Treadgold, *A History of Byzantine State and Society* (1997). Cyril Mango's *Byzantium: The Empire of New Rome* (1980) emphasizes cultural matters. For later Byzantine history, see A. P. Kazhdan and Ann Wharton Epstein in *Change in Byzantine Culture in the Eleventh and Twelfth Centuries* (1985), which stresses social and economic issues. On Kievan Russia, see Janet Martin's *Medieval Russia, 980–1584* (1995).

■ Notes

1. Lewis G. M. Thorpe, *Two Lives of Charlemagne* (Harmondsworth: Penguin, 1969).
2. R. W. Southern, *Western Society and the Church in the Middle Ages* (Harmondsworth: Penguin, 1970), 102.
3. Anne Fremantle, *A Treasury of Early Christianity* (New York: New American Library of World Literature, 1960), 400–401.
4. A. A. Vasiliev, *History of the Byzantine Empire, 324–1453,* vol. 1 (Madison: University of Wisconsin Press, 1978), 79–80.
5. A. P. Kazhdan and Ann Wharton Epstein, *Change in Byzantine Culture in the Eleventh and Twelfth Centuries* (Berkeley: University of California Press, 1985), 255.
6. Ibid., 248.
7. S. A. Zenkovsky, ed., *Medieval Russia's Epics, Chronicles, and Tales* (New York: New American Library, 1974), 67.

9

CENTRAL AND EASTERN ASIA,

400–1200

—𝒜—

The Sui and Tang Empires, 581–755 • **Fractured Power in Central Asia and China, to 907** • **The Emergence of East Asia, to 1200**
ENVIRONMENT AND TECHNOLOGY: **Writing in East Asia, 400–1200**

n the warfare that resulted from Han disintegration in 220 C.E. and the subsequent competition among the small kingdoms that divided its territory, infectious diseases spread from one army to another and among the civilian population. The scholar Ge Hong° (281–361 C.E.) described epidemics—probably smallpox—and the circumstances of their spread: "Because the epidemic was introduced . . . when Chinese armies attacked the barbarians . . . it was given the name of 'Barbarian pox.'"[1] As refugees fled south of the Yellow River, they carried the deadly infection with them.

Remarkable discoveries and inventions accompanied the social dislocation and disease of the third to sixth centuries. Ge Hong, a Daoist and alchemist, sought the elixir of life (a formula for immortality). Although alchemists failed in this quest, their investigations increased knowledge of physiology and permitted the refinement and use of stimulants such as ephedrine. Daoists also made advances in metallurgy, pharmacology, and mathematics. Ge Hong himself passed on knowledge of hallucinogenic drugs, the prevention of rabies, and magnetism, among other things.

With China's reunification in the late sixth century, the new knowledge spread over recentralized networks of trade, travel, and education. Under the Sui° and then the Tang° rulers, scientific and cultural influences spread throughout Central Asia and East Asia.

Several smaller empires followed the fall of the Tang Empire in 907. Many of them preserved and added to the cultural, scientific, and politi-

---

Ge Hong (guh hoong)

Sui (sway) **Tang** (tahng)

cal heritage of the Tang. Song° China excelled in science, mathematics, and engineering, Korea in printing and textiles, Japan in metallurgy and ceramics. This specialization and diversification of knowledge fostered new technologies, economic growth, and brilliant achievements in philosophy and the arts.

As you read, ask yourself the following questions:

- On what were new relationships among East Asian societies based after the fall of the Tang?
- Why does Buddhism play different political roles in Tang China, Tibet, Korea, and Japan after the ninth century?
- What accounts for the scientific and economic advancement of Song China?

THE SUI AND TANG EMPIRES, 581–755

The brief Sui Empire and its long-lived successor, the Tang, sprang from the political diversity of the period of disunion. The fall of the Han Empire left a power vacuum in which many small kingdoms explored various political styles. Some favored the Chinese style, with an emperor, a bureaucracy using the Chinese language exclusively, and a Confucian state philosophy (see Chapter 2). Others reflected Tibetan, Turkic, or other regional cultures and depended on Buddhism to legitimate their rule.

Reunification Under the Sui and Tang

In less than forty years, the Sui rulers reunified China. They reestablished Confucianism as the governing philosophy and passed it on to the Tang. But Buddhism exerted a

Song (soong)

strong political influence too, and other religious and philosophical beliefs, including Daoism, Nestorian Christianity, and Islam, became popular.

The Sui rulers called their new capital Chang'an° in honor of the old Han capital nearby in the Wei° River Valley (modern Shaanxi province). To facilitate communication and trade with growing population centers to the south, they built the 1,100-mile **Grand Canal,** linking the Yellow River with the Yangzi° River. The Sui also improved the Great Wall, constructed irrigation systems in the increasingly populated Yangzi River Valley, and waged war against Korea and Vietnam.

Such intense military expansion and public works required levels of organization and resources—people, livestock, wood, iron, staple crops—that the Sui could not sustain. Overextension weakened Sui authority and prompted the transition to the Tang.

In 618, the powerful Li family ended Sui rule and created the **Tang Empire** (Map 9.1). The Tang expanded primarily westward into Central Asia, under the brilliant emperor **Li Shimin°** (r. 627–649). They avoided overcentralization by allowing local nobles, gentry, officials, and religious establishments to exercise significant power.

As descendants of both the Turkic elites that built small states in northern China after the Han and Chinese officials and settlers intermarried with the Turks, the Tang emperors and nobility appreciated Central Asian culture as well as Chinese traditions. In warfare, for instance, the Tang combined Chinese weapons—the crossbow and armored infantrymen—with Central Asian expertise in horsemanship and the use of iron stirrups. From about 650 to about 750, this combination made the Tang armies the most formidable in the world.

Buddhism and the Tang Empire

The Central Asian heritage of the Tang rulers showed in their political use of Buddhism, a religion that charged kings and emperors with the spiritual function of bringing humankind into the

Chang'an (chahng-ahn)   Wei (way)   Yangzi (yahng-zeh)
Li Shimin (lee shir-meen)

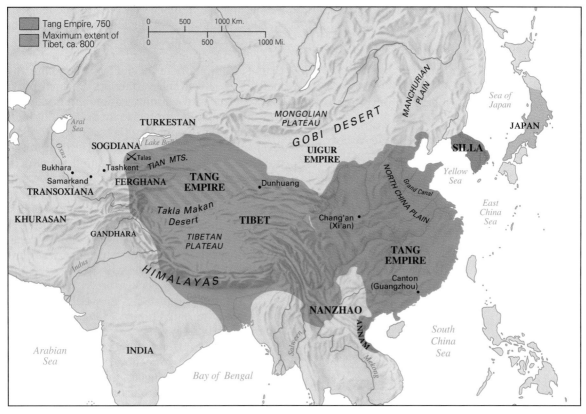

Map 9.1 The Tang Empire in Central and Eastern Asia, 750 For over a century, the Tang Empire controlled China and much of Central Asia. Defeat in 751 at the hands of Arabs, Turks, and Tibetans at the Talas River ended Tang westward expansion. To the east, the Tang dominated Annam, and Japan and the Silla kingdom in Korea were leading tributary states.

Buddhist realm. Protecting spirits were to help the ruler govern and prevent harm from coming to his people. State cults based on Buddhism flourished in Central Asia and north China after the fall of the Han.

In Central and East Asia, Mahayana°, or "Great Vehicle," Buddhism predominated. Mahayana fostered faith in enlightened beings—bodhisattvas—who postpone nirvana (see Chapter 2) to help others achieve enlightenment. This permitted the absorption of local gods and goddesses into Mahayana sainthood. Mahayana also encouraged translating Buddhist scripture into local languages, and it accepted religious practices not based on written texts. The tremendous reach of Mahayana

views, which proved so adaptable to different societies and classes of people, invigorated travel, language learning, and cultural exchange.

Early Tang princes competing for political influence enlisted monastic leaders to pray for them, preach on their behalf, counsel aristocrats to support them, and—perhaps most important—contribute monastic wealth to their war chests. In return, the monasteries received tax exemptions, land privileges, and gifts.

As the Tang Empire expanded westward, contacts with Central Asia and India increased, and so did the complexity of Buddhist influence throughout China. Chang'an, the Tang capital, became the center of a continent-wide system of communication. Central Asians, Tibetans, Vietnamese, Japanese, and Koreans regularly visited the capital and

---

Mahayana (mah-HAH-YAH-nah)

CHRONOLOGY

	Central Asia	China	Northeast Asia	Japan
200		220–589 China disunited		
	552 Turkic Empire founded			
600		581–618 Sui unification		
		618 Tang Empire founded		
		627–649 Li Shimin reign		645–655 Taika era
		690–705 Wu Zhao reign	668 Silla victory in Korea	
	744 Uigur Empire founded			710–784 Nara as capital
	751 Battle of Talas River	755–757 An Lushan rebellion		752 "Eye-opening" ceremony
800				794–1185 Heian era
	ca. 850 Buddhist political power secured in Tibet	840 Suppression of Buddhism		
		879–881 Huang Chao rebellion		
		907 End of Tang	916 Liao Empire founded	
		938 Liao capital at Beijing	918 Koryo founded	ca. 950–1180 Fujiwara influence
		960 Song Empire founded		
1000				ca. 1000 *The Tale of Genji*
		1127–1279 Southern Song period	1115 Jin Empire founded	1185 Kamakura shogunate founded

took away with them the most recent ideas and styles. Thus, the Mahayana network connecting Central Asia and China intersected with a vigorous commercial world where material goods and cultural influences mixed. Regional variety coexisted with shared knowledge of Buddhism, Confucianism, and other philosophies and written Chinese with regional commitments to other languages and writing systems. Textiles reflected Persian, Korean, and Vietnamese styles, and influences from every part of Asia appeared in sports, music, and painting. Many historians characterize the Tang Empire as "cosmopolitan" because of its breadth and diversity.

Iron Stirrups   This bas-relief from the tomb of Li Shimin depicts the type of horse on which the Tang armies conquered China and Central Asia. Saddles with high supports in front and back, breastplates, and cruppers point to the importance of high speeds and quick maneuvering. Iron stirrups, used generally in Central Asia from the time of the Huns (fifth century), could support the weight of shielded and well-armed soldiers rising in the saddle to shoot arrows or use lances.   (University of Pennsylvania Museum, neg. #S8-62844)

To Chang'an by Land and Sea

Well-maintained roads and water transport, including the Grand Canal, connected Chang'an, the capital and hub of Tang communications, to the coastal towns of south China, most importantly Canton (Guangzhou°). Chang'an became the center of what is often called the **tributary system,** dating from Han times, by which independent countries acknowledged the Chinese emperor's supremacy by sending regular embassies to the capital to pay tribute (see Chapter 5).

During the Tang period, Chang'an had something over a million people, a minority of whom lived in the central city. Most people lived in the suburbs that extended beyond the main gates. Many dwelled in towns that had special responsibilities like maintaining the imperial tombs or operating the imperial resort, where aristocrats relaxed in sunken tile tubs while the steamy waters of the natural springs swirled around them.

Special compounds in Chang'an, including living accommodations and general stores, serviced foreign merchants, students, and ambassadors. Restaurants, inns, temples, mosques, and street stalls along the main streets kept busy every evening. At curfew, generally between eight and ten o'clock, commoners returned to their neighborhoods, which were enclosed by brick walls and wooden gates that guards locked until dawn to control crime.

Of the many routes converging on Chang'an, the Grand Canal commanded special importance with its own army patrols, boat design, canal towns, and maintenance budget. It contributed to the economic and cultural development of eastern China. After the Tang, Chinese rulers established capitals farther to the east largely because of the economic and political effects of the Grand Canal.

The Tang consolidated Chinese control of the southern coastal region, thus increasing access to the Indian Ocean and helping Islamic and Jewish influences to spread. The uncle of Muhammad is credited with erecting the Red Mosque at Canton in the mid-seventh century. By the end of the Tang period, West Asians in Chang'an probably numbered over 100,000.

Chinese seamen excelled in compass design and the design of very large oceangoing vessels. The government built grain transport vessels for the Chinese coastal cities and the Grand Canal. But commercial ships, built to sail from south China to the Philippines and Southeast Asia, carried twice as much as contemporary Byzantine and Abbasid vessels.

The sea route between West Asia and Canton

Guangzhou (gwahng-jo)

also brought **bubonic plague** to East Asia in the fifth century. References to plague in Canton and south China date to the early 600s. The pestilence found a hospitable environment in parts of southwestern China and lingered there long after its disappearance in West Asia and Europe. The disease followed trade and embassy routes to Korea, Japan, and Tibet, where initial outbreaks followed the establishment of diplomatic ties in the seventh century. Unlike their contemporaries in Europe and West Asia, city dwellers in East Asia learned to control its spread, but the disease persisted in isolated rural areas.

Tang Integration

Influences from Central Asia and the Islamic world introduced lively new animal motifs to ceramics, painting, and silk designs. Life-size sculpture also became common. In north China, clothing styles changed. Working people switched from robes to the pants favored by horse-riding Turks from Central Asia. Inexpensive cotton, imported from Central Asia, gradually replaced hemp in clothes worn by commoners. The Tang court promoted polo playing, a Central Asian pastime, and followed the Central Asian tradition of allowing noblewomen to compete. Various stringed instruments reached China across the Silk Road, along with Central Asian folk melodies. Grape wine, tea, sugar, and spices transformed the Chinese diet.

Such changes reflected new economic and trade relationships with South Asia, West Asia, and northeastern Africa. Silk had dominated the caravan trade across Central Asia in Han times. Now China's monopoly on silk disappeared as several centers in West Asia learned to compete. However, western Asia lost its monopoly in cotton: by the end of the Tang, China had begun to produce its own. This process of import substitution—the domestic production and sale of previously imported goods—also affected tea and sugar.

By about the year 1000, the magnitude of exports from Tang territories, facilitated by China's excellent transportation systems, dwarfed the burgeoning trade between Europe, West Asia, and South Asia. Anecdotal accounts claimed that ships carrying Chinese exports outnumbered those laden with South Asian, West Asian, European, or African

goods by a hundred to one. Regardless of the exact figures, Tang exports unbalanced the commerce of both Central Asia and the Indian Ocean.

China remained the source of superior silks. Tang factories created more and more complex styles, partly to counter foreign competition. China became the sole supplier of porcelain—a fine, durable ceramic made from a special clay—to West Asia. As travel across Central Asia, Southeast Asia, and the Indian Ocean increased, the economies of ports and oases involved in the trade—even distant ones—became increasingly commercialized, creating special needs for new instruments of credit and finance.

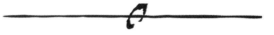

FRACTURED POWER IN CENTRAL ASIA AND CHINA, TO 907

Between 600 and 750, the Uigurs° and Tibetans built states to rival the Tang Empire, reaching some degree of political accommodation by the end of the period. By the mid-800s, all three empires were experiencing political decay and military decline. The problems of one aggravated those of the others, since governmental collapse allowed soldiers, criminals, and freebooters to roam without hindrance into neighboring territories.

Centralization and integration being deepest in Tang territory, the impact fell most heavily there. Nothing remained of Tang power but pretense by the early 800s. In the provinces, military governors suppressed the rebellion of the Sogdian general An Lushan°, which raged from 755 to 757, and then seized power for themselves. Farmers felt helpless before local bosses with private armies. Eunuchs controlled Chang'an and the Tang court and publicly executed bureaucrats who opposed them.

The nomads of Central Asia survived the social disorder and agricultural losses best. The caravan cities, which had prospered from overland trade, had as much to lose as China itself, but the

Uigur (WEE-ger)   **An Lushan** (ahn loo-shahn)

economies of Central Asia and East Asia proved resilient. The strongest backlashes were cultural, particularly in China, where disillusionment with Central Asian neighbors and social anxieties fueled a powerful reaction against "foreign" cultures.

Reaction and Repression

After two centuries of widespread Buddhist influence, members of the imperial family began to distrust the monasteries and blame the Buddhist clergy for political upheavals. In 840 (a year of disintegration on many fronts), the government moved to crush the monasteries. The Tang elites strongly reasserted Confucian ideology instead, particularly the rationalist "neo-Confucian" school.

Even Chinese gentry living in safe and prosperous localities associated Buddhism with social ills. People who worried about "barbarians" ruining their society pointed to Buddhism as evidence of the foreign evil since it had such strong roots in Central Asia and Tibet. They claimed that eradicating Buddhist influence would restore the ancient values of hierarchy and social harmony. Because Buddhism shunned earthly ties, monks and nuns severed relations with the secular world in search of enlightenment. They paid no taxes, served in no army. They deprived their families of advantageous marriage alliances and denied descendants to their ancestors. The Confucian elites saw all this as threatening to the family and to the family estates that underlay the Tang economic and political structure.

The tax exemption of monasteries allowed them to purchase land and precious objects and employ large numbers of serfs. Wealthy believers gave the monasteries large tracts of land. Poor people flocked to the monasteries and nunneries to work as artisans, field hands, cooks, housekeepers, and guards. Some eventually converted to Buddhism and took up the monastic life. Others came as beggars and then began to study the religion. By the ninth century, hundreds of thousands of people had entered monasteries and nunneries.

The Tang elites saw Buddhism as undermining the Confucian idea of the family as the model for the state as well as women's roles in politics. Wu Zhao°, a woman who had married into the imperial family, seized control of the government in 690, declared herself emperor, and reigned until 705. She based her legitimacy on the claim of being a bodhisattva, and she favored Buddhists and Daoists over Confucianists.

Later Confucian writers expressed contempt for Emperor Wu and other powerful women, such as the concubine Yang Guifei°. Bo Zhuyi°, in his poem "Everlasting Remorse," lamented the influence of women at the Tang court, which had caused "the hearts of fathers and mothers everywhere not to value the birth of boys, but the birth of girls."[2] Confucian elites heaped every possible charge on prominent women who offended them, blaming Yang Guifei for the An Lushan rebellion and accusing Emperor Wu of grotesque tortures and murders, including tossing the dismembered but still living bodies of enemies into wine vats and cauldrons.

Serious historians dismiss the stories about Wu Zhao as stereotypical characterizations of "evil" rulers. In fact, she seems to have ruled effectively and was not deposed until extreme old age (eighty-plus in 705) incapacitated her. Nevertheless, since Confucian historians commonly describe unorthodox rulers and all powerful women as evil, the true facts about Wu will never be known.

The dissolution of the monasteries caused an incalculable loss in cultural artifacts. Some sculptures and grottoes survived in defaced form. Wooden temples and facades sheltering great stone carvings burned to the ground. Monasteries became legal again in later times, but Buddhism never recovered the social, political, and cultural influence of early Tang times.

The End of the Tang Empire

The Tang order succumbed to the very forces that were essential to its creation and maintenance. The campaigns of expansion in the seventh century left the empire dependent on local military commanders and a complex tax collection system. The battle of Talas River halted the drive westward across Central Asia. Such reverses led to military demoralization and underfunding. Suppressing the

---

Wu Zhao (woo jow)

Yang Guifei (yahng gway-fay)   **Bo Zhuyi** (baw joo-ee)

An Lushan rebellion a few years later gave provincial military governors new powers and independence.

Despite the continuing prosperity, political disintegration and the elite's sense of cultural decay created an unsettled environment that encouraged aspiring dictators. A disgruntled member of the gentry, Huang Chao, led the most devastating uprising between 879 and 881. Despite imposing ruthless and violent control over the villages it controlled, it attracted hundreds of thousands of poor farmers and tenants who could not protect themselves from local bosses, sought escape from oppressive landlords or taxes, or simply did not know what else to do in the deepening chaos. The new hatred of "barbarians" spurred the rebels to murder thousands of foreign residents in Canton and Peking.

Local bosses finally wiped out the rebels using the same violent tactics, but Tang society did not find peace. Refugees, the urban homeless, and migrant workers became permanent fixtures. Residents of northern China fled to the southern frontiers as groups from Central Asia moved into the north.

The smaller states that succeeded the Tang Empire in 907 each controlled considerable territory, and some of them had lasting historical influence. But none could integrate the economic and cultural interests of vastly disparate territories or transmit goods and knowledge across huge distances. East Asia fragmented and lost its communication with Europe and the Islamic world. Important artistic styles, technical advances, and philosophical developments emerged in East Asia, but the brilliant cosmopolitanism of the Tang disappeared for centuries.

Monument to an Early Turk   The Turks originated in the northern part of present-day Mongolia. The flat steppes suited the Turks and their herds. Steppe geography allowed constant communication from eastern Iran to western China. This monument to an unknown Turkic leader, probably of the late 500s, surveys lands similar to those of the Silk Road.   (Sergei I. Vainshtein, Institute of Ethnography, Moscow)

The Uigur and Tibetan Empires in Central Asia

The original homeland of the Turks lay in the northern part of modern Mongolia. After the fall of the Han Empire, Turkic peoples began moving south and west through Mongolia, and then on to Central Asia, on the long migration that eventually brought them to Anatolia (modern Turkey). Various Turkic groups controlled Central Asia during the period of fragmentation between the Han and Tang Empires, but in 552 a unified Turkic Empire arose, only to split internally a century later. This fissure helped the Tang Empire under Li Shimin to establish control over Central Asia. Yet within a century, a new Turkic group, the **Uigurs,** had taken much of Central Asia.

Under the Uigurs, caravan cities like Bukhara, Samarkand, and Tashkent (see Map 9.1) displayed a literate culture with strong ties to both the Islamic world and China. The Uigurs excelled as merchants and as scribes able to transact business in many languages. They adapted the Sogdians' syllabic script, related to the Syriac script used in West Asia, to writing Turkic. This made possible several innovations in Uigur government, such as changing from a tax paid in kind (with products or services) to a money tax and, later, the minting of coins. Their flourishing urban culture embraced the Buddhist classics, religious art derived from northern India, and a mixture of East Asian and Islamic styles.

Unified Uigur power collapsed after half a century, leaving only Tibet as a Central Asian rival to the Tang. A large, stable empire critically positioned where China, Southeast Asia, South Asia, and Central Asia meet, Tibet experienced a variety of cultural influences. In the seventh century, Chinese Buddhists on pilgrimage to India advanced contacts between India and Tibet. The Tibetans derived their alphabet from India, as well as a variety of artistic and architectural styles. Mathematics, astronomy, divination, the cultivation of grains, and the use of millstones came from India and China, knowledge of Islam and the monarchical traditions of Iran and Rome from Central Asia and the Middle East. The Tibetan royal family favored Greek medicine transmitted through Iran.

Under Li Shimin, cautious friendliness prevailed between the empires. A Tang princess, called Kongjo by the Tibetans, came to Tibet to marry the Tibetan king and thereby forge an alliance in 634. She brought with her Mahayana Buddhism, which combined with the native religion to create a local religious style. Tibet sent ambassadors to join Koreans, Japanese, and other peoples as students in the Tang imperial capital.

Regular contact and Buddhist influences consolidated the Tang-Tibet relationship for a time. The Tibetan kings encouraged Buddhist religious establishments and prided themselves on being cultural intermediaries between India and China. Tibet also excelled at war. Horses and armor, borrowed from the Turks, raised Tibetan forces to a level that startled even the Tang. By the late 600s, the Tang emperor and the Tibetan king were rivals for religious leadership and political dominance in Central Asia, and Tibetan power reached into what are now Qinghai°, Sichuan°, and Xinjiang° provinces in China. Tensions grew, and peace returned only after the Tang defeat on the Talas River in 751.

Yet political differences remained. Although a new king in Tibet decided to follow the Tang lead and eradicate the political and social influence of the monasteries in the 800s, monks assassinated him, and control of the Tibetan royal family passed into the hands of religious leaders. In ensuing years, monastic domination isolated Tibet from surrounding regions.

THE EMERGENCE OF EAST ASIA, TO 1200

In the aftermath of the Tang, new states emerged and competed to inherit its legacy. The Liao° Empire of the Kitan° people established their rule in the north, at what is now Beijing°, immediately after the overthrow of the last Tang emperor. Soon after, the Minyak people (closely related to the Tibetans) established a large empire in western China and called themselves "Tangguts°" to show their connection with the former empire. In 960, the **Song Empire** arose in central China.

While these empires competed, the earlier relationship between East Asia and Central Asia ended. Sea connections among East Asia, West Asia, and Southeast Asia continued, however, and the Song developed advanced seafaring and sailing technologies. The Song elite, like their late Tang predecessors, rejected "barbaric" or "foreign" influences while struggling under enormous military demands. Meanwhile, Korea and Japan strengthened political and cultural ties with China, and some Southeast Asian states, relieved of any Tang military threat, entered into friendly relations with the Song court. The allied societies of East Asia formed a Confucian region actively exchanging goods, resources, and knowledge.

The Liao and Jin Challenge

The Liao and other northern empires included many nomads. Their rulers acknowledged the economic and social differences between peoples and made no attempt to create a single elite culture. They encouraged Chinese elites to use their own language, study their own classics, and see the emperor through Confucian eyes, and they encouraged other peoples to use their own languages and see the emperor as a champion of

---

Qinghai (CHING-hie) Sichuan (SUH-chwahn)
Xinjiang (shin-jee-yahng)

Liao (lee-OW) Kitan (kee-tan) Beijing (bay-jeeng)
Tanggut (TAHNG-gut)

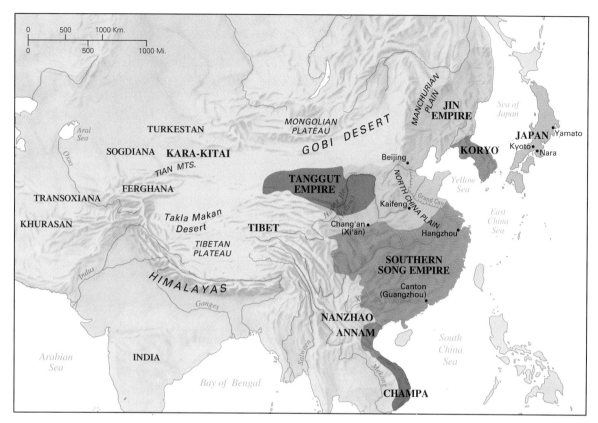

Map 9.2   Jin and Southern Song Empires, c. 1200   After 1127, Song abandoned its northern territories to Jin. The Southern Song continued the policy of annual payments—to Jin rather than Liao—and maintained high military preparedness to prevent further invasions.

Buddhism or as a nomadic leader. As a consequence, Buddhism far outweighed Confucianism in the northern states, where rulers depended on their roles as bodhisattvas or as Buddhist kings to legitimate power.

The Liao Empire of the Kitan people ruled an expanse from Siberia to Central Asia and thus connected China with societies to the north and west. Variations on the Kitan name became the name for China in these distant regions: "Kitai" for the Mongols, "Khitai" for the Russians, and "Cathay" for those, like the contemporaries of Marco Polo, who reached China from Europe.

Liao rule lasted from 916 to 1121. Relics of the Liao period can today be seen in Beijing, one of its capitals. In ceramics, painting, horsemanship, reli-

gion, and some forms of architecture, Liao made a lasting contribution to Asian civilization.

Superb horsemen and archers, the Kitans adapted siege machines from China and Central Asia and challenged the Song. In 1005, the Song agreed to a truce that included enormous annual payments in cash and silk to the Liao to forestall further war. Liao and Song worked out an efficient and sophisticated diplomatic system. But the economically burdensome relations with the Liao eventually led the Song into a secret alliance with the Jurchens of northeastern Asia, also chafing under Liao rule. In 1125 the Jurchens destroyed the Liao capital in Mongolia, proclaimed their own empire—the Jin—and turned against the Song (Map 9.2).

The Jurchens were hunters and fishers and semiagricultural, but they had learned the Kitan military arts and political organization. They became formidable enemies of the Song Empire, mounting an all-out campaign in 1127. They laid siege to the Song capital, Kaifeng°, and captured the Song emperor. Within a few years the Song withdrew south of the Yellow River, leaving central as well as northern China in Jurchen control. The Song also made annual payments to the Jin Empire to avoid open warfare. Historians generally refer to this period as the "Southern Song" (1127–1279).

Song Industries

China in this period did not have access to the Tang's far-flung networks of communication. Many of the advances in technology, medicine, astronomy, and mathematics for which Song is famous derived from information that had come to China in Tang times, sometimes from very distant places. Song had the motivation and resources to adapt Tang information and technology to meet practical, sometimes urgent, Song requirements, particularly in warfare and colonization and in the development of new methods for managing economic and social changes.

The arts of measurement and observation absorbed Chinese scholars, as they did the Indian and West Asian mathematicians and astronomers who had migrated to the Tang Empire, bringing their knowledge with them. Song mathematicians innovated the use of fractions, first employing them to describe the phases of the moon. From lunar observations, Song astronomers constructed a precise calendar and alone among the world's astronomers noted the explosion of the Crab Nebula in 1054. Chinese scholars used their work in astronomy and mathematics to make significant contributions to timekeeping and the development of the compass.

In 1088, the engineer Su Song constructed a gigantic mechanical celestial clock. Escapement mechanisms for controlling the revolving wheels in water-powered clocks had appeared under the Tang, as had the application of water wheels to

weaving and threshing. But this knowledge had not been widely applied. Su Song adapted the escapement and water wheel to his clock, which featured the first known chain-drive mechanism. The clock told the time of day and the day of the month, and it indicated the movement of the moon and certain stars and planets across the night sky. An observation deck and a mechanically rotated armillary sphere crowned the 80-foot (24-meter) structure. The clock exemplified the Song ability to integrate observational astronomy, applied mathematics, and engineering.

Familiarity with celestial coordinates, particularly the Pole Star, refined the design of compasses. Long known in China, the magnetic compass shrank in size in Song times, and it gained a fixed stem and sometimes even a small protective case with a glass covering for the needle. These changes made the compass suitable for seafaring, a use first attested in 1090. The Chinese compass and the Greek astrolabe, introduced later, improved navigation throughout Southeast Asia and the Indian Ocean.

Development of the seaworthy compass coincided with new techniques in building **junks.** A stern-mounted rudder improved the steering of the large ships in uneasy seas, and watertight bulkheads helped keep them afloat in emergencies. The merchants of the Persian Gulf quickly adopted these features.

Military pressure from the Liao and Jin Empires helped feed the technological explosion. Although less than half the size of the Tang Empire, the Song fielded an army four times as large—about 1.25 million men (roughly the size of the present-day army of the United States of America). For leadership, the Song employed men educated especially for the task, examined on military subjects, and paid regular salaries.

Because of the military importance of iron and steel, the Song and their northern rivals fought over the iron ore and coal regions of north China. The volume of Song mining and iron production, which again became a government monopoly in the eleventh century, soared. By the end of that century, cast-iron production reached about 125,000 tons (113,700 metric tons), putting it on a par with the output of eighteenth-century Britain.

Kaifeng (kie-fuhng)

Engineers became skilled at high-temperature metallurgy. They produced steel weapons of unprecedented strength through the use of enormous bellows, often driven by water wheels, to superheat the molten ore. Impervious to fire or concussion, iron buttressed Song defensive works, featured in mass-produced body armor (in small, medium, and large sizes), and provided the material of bridges and small buildings. Mass-production techniques in use in China for nearly two thousand years for bronze and ceramics were adapted to iron casting and assembly.

To counter cavalry assaults, the Song experimented with **gunpowder,** which they used to propel a cluster of flaming arrows. During the wars against the Jurchens in the 1100s, the Song introduced a new and terrifying weapon. Shells launched from Song fortifications exploded in the midst of the enemy, blowing out shards of iron and dismembering men and horses. But the short range of the shells limited them to defensive uses, and they made no major impact on the overall conduct of war.

Economy and Society

Despite the continuous military threats and the vigor of Song responses, Song elite culture idealized civil pursuits. Socially, the civil man outranked the military man. Private academies, designed to train students for the official examinations and develop intellectual interests, became influential in culture and politics. The neo-Confucianism of the late Tang became more sophisticated, more idealistic, and much more pervasive during the Song. But popular Buddhist sects persisted, and elites elaborated on and adopted some Tang era folk practices derived from India and Tibet. The best known, Chan Buddhism (in Japan known as **Zen,** in Korea as **Son**), asserted that mental discipline alone could win salvation.

Meditation offered scholars relief from preparation for civil service examinations, the examination system dating from the Tang period. Dramatically different from the Han policy of hiring and promoting on the basis of recommendations, Song-style examinations persisted for nearly a thousand years. A large bureaucracy oversaw their design and administration. Test questions, which changed each time the examinations were given, often related to economic management or foreign policy.

The examinations had social implications, for hereditary class distinctions meant less than they had in Tang times. The new system recruited the most talented men, both prestigious and humble in origin, for government service. Men from wealthy families, however, succeeded most often. The tests required memorization of classics believed to date from the time of Confucius. Preparation consumed so much time that peasant boys, who worked in the fields, could rarely compete.

Success in the examinations brought good marriage prospects, the chance for a high salary, and enormous prestige. Failure could bankrupt a family and ruin a man socially and psychologically. This put great pressure on candidates who spent days at a time in tiny, dim, airless examination cells, attempting to produce—in beautiful calligraphy—their answers to questions.

Changes in printing, from woodblock to an early form of movable type, allowed cheaper printing of many kinds of informative books and test materials. The Song government realized that the examination system indoctrinated millions of ambitious young men—many times the number who eventually would pass the tests. The advancement of printing thus aided the ideological goals of the government and the personal goals of the candidates. Mass-production of authorized preparation books appeared by the year 1000. Although a man had to be literate to buy even the cheap preparation books, and basic education was still not common, access to the examinations for people of limited means did increase, and a moderate number of candidates entered the bureaucracy without noble, gentry, or elite backgrounds.

Printing changed country life as well, offering advice on planting and irrigation techniques, harvesting, tree cultivation, threshing, and weaving. Landlords frequently gathered their tenants and workers to show them illustrated texts and explain their meaning. This dissemination of knowledge, along with new technologies, furthered the development of new agricultural land south of the Yangzi River. Iron agricultural implements such as plows and rakes, first used in the Tang, were adapted to wet-rice cultivation as the population moved south. Landowners and village leaders learned from books how to fight the mosquitoes that carried malaria. Control of the disease allowed more immigration by northerners and a sharp increase in population.

The profitability of farming stimulated the production of books on the subject. Commercial agriculture interested the sons of the gentry. Still a frontier for Chinese settlers under the Tang, the south saw an increasing concentration of landownership in the hands of a few wealthy families who claimed extensive tracts in advance of later colonists. In the settlement process, the indigenous inhabitants of the region, related to the modern populations of Malaysia, Thailand, and Laos, retreated into the mountains or southward toward Vietnam.

During the 1100s, the total population of the Chinese territories, spurred by prosperity, rose above 100 million. An increasing proportion lived in large towns and cities, though the leading Song cities had under a million inhabitants apiece. This still put them among the largest cities in the world.

In the Song capitals, multistory wooden apartment houses and narrow streets—sometimes only 4 or 5 feet (1.2 to 1.5 meters) wide—clogged by peddlers or families spending time outdoors created a crush that demanded expertise in waste management, water supply, and firefighting. Controlling urban rodent and insect infestations improved health and usually kept the bubonic plague isolated to a few rural areas.

In Hangzhou°, in particular, engineers channeled the currents of the nearby river to produce a steady flow of water and air through the city, flushing away waste and disease. Turkic, Arab, and European travelers, sensitive to urban crowding in their own societies, expressed amazement at the way Hangzhou sheltered its densely packed population from danger, while restaurants, parks, bookstores, wine shops, tea houses, and theaters gave beauty and pleasure to the inhabitants.

The idea of credit, originating in the robust long-distance trade of the Tang period, spread widely under the Song. Intercity or interregional credit—what the Song called "flying money"—depended on the acceptance of guarantees that the paper could be redeemed for coinage at another location. The public accepted the practice because credit networks tended to be managed by families, so that usually brothers and cousins were honoring each other's certificates.

"Flying money" certificates differed from government-issued paper money, which the Song pioneered. In some years, military expenditures consumed 80 percent of the government budget. The state responded to this financial pressure by distributing paper money. But this made inflation so severe that by the beginning of the 1100s, paper money traded for only 1 percent of its face value. Eventually, the government withdrew the paper money and instead imposed new taxes, sold monopolies, and offered financial incentives to merchants.

Rapid economic growth undermined the government monopolies and strict regulation that had become traditional. Hard-pressed for the revenue needed to maintain the army, canals, roads, waterworks, and other state functions, the government sold some functions, such as tax collection, to privateers, who made their profit by collecting the maximum amount and sending an agreed-on smaller amount to the government. This meant exorbitant rates for services and much heavier tax burdens on the common people. But economic privatization also created opportunities for individuals with capital to engage in businesses that previously had been state monopolies.

Now, merchants and artisans as well as gentry and officials could make fortunes. Urban life reflected the elite's growing taste for fine fabrics, porcelain, exotic foods, large houses, and exquisite paintings and books. With land no longer the only source of wealth, the traditional social hierarchy common to an agricultural economy weakened, while cities, commerce, consumption, and the use of money and credit boomed. Because the government and traditional elites did not control much of the new commercial and industrial activities, historians often describe Song China as "modern."

For women, the Song era initiated a long period of cultural subordination, legal disenfranchisement, and social restriction. This fit with the backlash against Buddhism and revival of Confucianism that began under the Tang and intensified under the Song. It also related closely to the eco-

---

Hangzhou (hahng-jo)

Going up the River Song cities hummed with commercial and industrial activity, much of it concentrated on the rivers and canals linking the capital, Kaifeng, to the provinces. This detail from *Going Upriver at the Qingming [Spring] Festival* shows a tiny portion of the scroll painting's panorama. Painted by Zhang Zeduan sometime before 1125, its depiction of daily life makes it an important source of information on working people. Before open shop fronts and tea houses, a camel caravan departs, donkey carts are unloaded, a scholar rides loftily (if gingerly) on horseback, and women of wealth go by in closed sedan chairs. (The Palace Museum, Beijing)

nomic and status concerns of the gentry and the rising merchant classes.

Merchants spent long periods away from home, and many maintained more than one household. Frequently, they depended on wives to manage their homes and even their businesses in their absence. As women took on responsibility for the management of their husbands' property, they steadily lost the right to control property of their own. Laws changed in the Song period. A woman's property automatically passed to her husband, and women could not remarry if their husbands divorced them or died.

Absolute subordination of women to men proved compatible with Confucianism, and it became fashionable to educate girls just enough to read simple versions of Confucian philosophy, edited to emphasize the lowly role of women. Modest education made these young women more marketable as companions for the sons of other gentry or noble families and more desirable as mothers to the sons of aspiring families. Only occasionally did women of extremely high station and unusual personal determination, such as the poet

Li Qingzhao (1083–1141), manage to acquire extensive education and freedom to pursue the literary arts.

Female footbinding, first in evidence among slave dancers at the Tang court but not widespread before the Song, forced the toes under and toward the heel, so that the bones eventually broke and the woman could not walk on her own. In noble and gentry families, footbinding began when girls were between ages five and seven. In less wealthy families, girls worked until they were older, so footbinding began only in a girl's teens.

Many literate men condemned the maiming of innocent girls and the general uselessness of footbinding. Nevertheless, bound feet became a status symbol. By 1200, a woman with unbound feet had become undesirable in elite circles, and mothers of elite status, or aspiring to it, almost without exception bound their daughters' feet. They knew that girls with unbound feet faced rejection by society, prospective husbands, and ultimately their own families. Footbinding did not occur among working women and the native peoples of the south. Women in these classes and cultures enjoyed

The Players Women, often enslaved, entertained at Chinese courts from early times. Tang art often depicts women with slender figures, but Tang taste also admired more robust physiques. Song women, usually pale with willowy figures, appear as here with bound feet. The practice appeared in Tang times but was not widespread until the Song, when the image of weak, housebound women unable to work became a status symbol and pushed aside the earlier enthusiasm for healthy women who participated in family businesses. (The Palace Museum, Beijing)

considerably more economic independence than did elite women.

Essential Partners: Korea, Japan, and Vietnam

Korea, Japan, and Vietnam, like Song China, depended overwhelmingly on agriculture. The cultivation of rice, an increasingly widespread crop, fit well with Confucian social ideas. Tending the young rice plants, irrigating the rice paddies, and managing the harvest required coordination among many village and kin groups and rewarded hierarchy, obedience, and self-discipline. Confucianism also justified using agricultural profits to support the education, safety, and comfort of the literate elite.

Political ideologies in Korea, Japan, and Vietnam varied somewhat from the Song, which asserted Confucian predominance over all other philosophies, particularly Buddhism. These three East Asian neighbors had first centralized power under a ruling house in the early Tang period, and their state ideologies continued to resemble that of the early Tang, when Buddhism and Confucianism were compatible.

Government service in Korea, Japan, and Vietnam did not rest on an elaborate examination and never called for the esoteric knowledge of Confucian texts. Landowning and agriculture remained the major sources of income and did not face challenges from huge cities or the rise of a large merchant class.

Nevertheless, men in Korea, Japan, and Vietnam prized literacy in classical Chinese and a good knowledge of Confucian texts. Popular education and indoctrination by the elite increasingly instilled the Confucian emphasis on hierarchy and harmony into the minds of ordinary people. Since Han times, Confucianism had spread through East Asia with the spread of the Chinese writing system. The elite in every country learned to read Chinese and the Confucian classics, and the Chinese characters contributed to locally invented writing systems (see Environment and Technology: Writing in East Asia, 400–1200).

Those developments came too slow for the East Asian societies to record their earliest histories. Our first knowledge of Korea, Japan, and Vietnam comes from early Chinese officials and travelers. When the Qin Empire established its first colony in Korea in the third century B.C.E., Chinese bureaucrats began documenting Korean history. Han writers noted the horse breeding, strong hereditary elites, and **shamanism** (belief in the ability of certain individuals to contact the ancestors and the invisible spirit world) of Korea's small kingdoms. But Korea quickly absorbed Confucianism and Buddhism, both of which they transmitted to Japan.

Korea's hereditary elites remained strong and in the early 500s made inherited status—the "bone ranks"—permanent in Silla°, the leading Korean state. In 668, with Tang encouragement, Silla conquered its neighbors and took control of much of the Korean peninsula. But Silla proved unable to

Silla (SILL-ah or SHILL-ah)

Writing in East Asia, 400–1200

An ideographic writing system that originated in China became a communications tool throughout East Asia. Variations on this system, based more on depictions of meanings than representations of sound, spread widely by the time of the Sui and Tang Empires. Many East Asian peoples adapted ideographic techniques to writing languages unrelated to Chinese in grammar or sound.

The Vietnamese, Koreans, and Japanese often simplified Chinese characters and associated them with the sounds of local languages. For instance, the Chinese character *an,* meaning "peace" (Fig. 1), was pronounced "an" in Japanese and was familiar as a Chinese character to Confucian scholars in Japan's Heian (hay-ahn) period. However, nonscholars simplified the character and used it to write the Japanese sound "a" (Fig. 2). A set of more than thirty of these syllabic symbols adapted from Chinese characters could represent the inflected forms of any Japanese word. Murasaki Shikibu used such a syllabic system when she wrote *The Tale of Genji.*

In Vietnam and later in northern Asia, phonetic and ideographic elements combined in new ways. The apparent circles in some *chu nom* writing from Vietnam (Fig. 3) derive from the Chinese character for "mouth" and indicate a primary sound association for the word. The Kitans, who spoke a language related to Mongolian, developed an ideographic system of their own, inspired by Chinese characters. The Chinese character *wang* (Fig. 4), meaning "king, prince, ruler," was changed to represent the Kitan word for "emperor" by adding an upward stroke representing a "superior" ruler (Fig. 5). Because the system was ideographic, we do not know the pronunciation of this Kitan word. The Kitan character for "God" or "Heaven" adds a top stroke representing the "supreme" ruler or power to the character meaning "ruler" (Fig. 6). Though inspired by Chinese characters, Kitan writings could not be read by anyone who was not specifically educated in them.

The Kitans developed another system to represent the sounds and grammar of their language. They used small, simplified elements arranged within an imaginary frame to indicate the sounds in any word. This idea might have come from the phonetic script used by the Uigurs. Here (Fig. 7) we see the word for horse in a Kitan inscription. Fitting sound elements within a frame also occurred later in *hangul,* the Korean phonetic system introduced in the 1400s. Here (Fig. 8) we see the two words making up the country name "Korea."

The Chinese writing system served the needs of the Chinese elite well. But peoples speaking unrelated languages continually experimented with the Chinese invention to produce new ways of expressing themselves. Some of the resulting sound-based writing systems remain in common use; others are still being deciphered.

安　あ　哿呷　王　主　王　刘朼　한국

Figure 1　Figure 2　Figure 3　Figure 4　Figure 5　Figure 6　Figure 7　Figure 8

maintain its position without Tang support. After the fall of the Tang in the early 900s, the ruling house of **Koryo°**, from which the modern name "Korea" derives, united the peninsula. At constant threat from the Liao and then the Jin, Koryo pursued amicable relations with Song China. The Koryo kings supported Buddhism and made superb printed editions of Buddhist texts.

Woodblock printing exemplifies the technological exchanges that Korea enjoyed with China. The oldest surviving woodblock print in Chinese characters comes from Korea in the mid-700s. Commonly used during the Tang period, woodblock printing required time-consuming work by skilled artisans who carved hundreds of characters to produce a single printed page. Koreans developed their own advances in printing. By Song times, Korean experiments with **movable type** reached China, where further improvements led to metal or porcelain type from which texts could be cheaply printed.

Japan's earliest history, like Korea's, comes from Chinese records. The first description, dating from the fourth century, tells of an island at the eastern edge of the world, divided into hundreds of small countries and ruled over by a shamaness named Himiko or Pimiko. This account shows the Japanese terrain, mountainous with small pockets and stretches of land suitable for agriculture, influencing the social and political structures of the early period. The unification of central Japan came in the fourth or fifth century C.E. How it occurred remains a question, but horse-riding warriors from Korea may have united the small countries of Japan under a central government at Yamato, on the central plain of Honshu island.

In the mid-600s, the rulers based at Yamato implemented the **Taika°** and other reforms, giving the Yamato regime key features of Tang government, known through embassies to Chang'an: a legal code, an official variety of Confucianism, and a strong state interest in Buddhism. Within a century, a complex system of law stipulated a centralized government, and a massive history in the Confucian style appeared. The Japanese mastered Chinese building techniques so well that **Nara°**

and Kyoto, Japan's early capitals, provide invaluable evidence of the wooden architecture that vanished from China. During the eighth century, Japan in some ways surpassed China in Buddhist studies. In 752, dignitaries from all over Mahayana Buddhist Asia gathered at the enormous Todaiji temple, near Nara, to celebrate the "eye-opening" of the "Great Buddha" statue.

All things Chinese did not come to Japan, however. Although the Japanese adopted Chinese building styles and some street plans, constant warfare did not plague central Japan in the seventh and eighth centuries as it did China, so Japanese cities were built without walls. Also, the Confucian Mandate of Heaven, which justified dynastic changes, played no role in legitimating Japanese government. The *tenno*—often called "emperor" in English—belonged to a family believed to have ruled Japan since the beginning of known history. The dynasty never changed. The royal family endured because the emperors seldom wielded political power. A prime minister and the leaders of the native religion, in later times called Shinto—the "way of the gods"—exercised real control.

In 794, the central government moved to Kyoto, usually called by its ancient name, Heian. Legally centralized government lasted there until 1185, although power became decentralized toward the end. Members of the **Fujiwara°** family, an ancient family of priests, bureaucrats, and warriors, controlled power and protected the emperor. The Fujiwara elevated men of Confucian learning over the generally illiterate warriors. Noblemen of the Fujiwara period read the Chinese classics, appreciated painting and poetry, and refined their sense of wardrobe and interior decoration.

Pursuit of an aesthetic way of life prompted the Fujiwara nobles to entrust responsibility for local government, policing, and tax collection to their warriors. Though often of humble origins, a small number of warriors had achieved wealth and power by the late 1000s. By the mid-1100s, the nobility had lost control, and civil war between rival warrior clans engulfed the capital.

A literary epic, the *Tale of the Heike*, later cele-

Koryo (KAW-ree-oh) Taika (TIE-kah) Nara (NAH-rah)

Fujiwara (foo-jee-WAH-rah)

brated a new elite culture based on military values. The standing of the Fujiwara family fell as nobles and the emperor hurried to accommodate the new warlords. The new warrior class (in later times called *samurai*) eventually absorbed some of the Fujiwara aristocratic values, but the age of the civil elite had ended. In 1185, the **Kamakura° Shogunate,** the first of three decentralized military regimes, established itself in eastern Honshu, far from the old religious and political center at Kyoto.

Vietnam had had contact with empires based in China since the third century B.C.E., but not until Tang times did the relationship become close enough for economic and cultural assimilation. The rice-based agriculture of Vietnam made the region well suited for integration with southern China. As in southern China, the wet climate and hilly terrain of Vietnam demanded expertise in irrigation.

The ancestors of the Vietnamese may have preceded the Chinese in using draft animals in farming, working with metal, and making certain kinds of pots. But in Tang and Song times, the elites of "Annam°"—as the Chinese called early Vietnam—adopted Confucian bureaucratic training, Mahayana Buddhism, and other Chinese cultural traits. Annamese elites continued to rule in the Tang style after that dynasty's fall. Annam assumed the name Dai Viet° in 936 and maintained good relations with Song China as an independent country.

Champa, located largely in what is now southern Vietnam, rivaled the Dai Viet state. The cultures of India and Malaya strongly influenced Champa through the networks of trade and communication that encompassed the Indian Ocean. Although hostile to one another during the period of Tang domination in the north, Champa and Dai Viet both cooperated with the Song, the former as a voluntary tributary state. **Champa rice** (originally from India), a fast-maturing variety, came to the Song from Champa as a tribute gift and contributed to the advancement and specialization of Song agriculture.

All the East Asian societies shared a Confucian interest in hierarchy, but practices relating to gen-

der differed. Footbinding did not spread. In Korea, strong family alliances that functioned like political and economic organizations allowed women a role in negotiating and disposing of property. Before Confucianism, Annamese women enjoyed higher status than women in China, perhaps because of the need for both women and men to participate in wet-rice cultivation. Women in south and southeastern China may have enjoyed similar high status before the growth of northern Chinese influence. The Trung sisters of Vietnam, who lived in the second century C.E. and led local farmers in resistance against the Han Empire, still serve as national symbols in Vietnam and as local heroes in southern China. They recall a time when women played visible and active roles in community and political life.

All the East Asian neighbors believed in limited education for women, as Confucianism prescribed. The hero of a Japanese novel, *The Tale of Genji,* written around the year 1000 by the noblewoman Murasaki Shikibu, accurately and ironically remarks: "Women should have a general knowledge of several subjects, but it gives a bad impression if they show themselves to be attached to a particular branch of learning."[3] Fujiwara noblewomen lived in near-total isolation, generally spending their leisure time studying Buddhism. To communicate with their families or among themselves, they depended on writing. The simplified syllabic script that they used represented the Japanese language in its fully inflected form (the Chinese classical script used by Fujiwara men could not do so). Loneliness, free time, and a ready instrument for expression produced an outpouring of poetry, diaries, and storytelling by women of the Fujiwara era. Their best-known achievement, however, remains Murasaki's portrait of Fujiwara court culture.

CONCLUSION

The Tang Empire put into place a solid system of travel, trade, and communications that allowed cultural and economic influences to move quickly from central Asia to Japan. Diversity within the

---

Kamakura (kah-mah-KOO-rah)   **Annam** (ahn-nahm)
Dai Viet (die vee-yet)

empire produced great wealth and new ideas. But tensions among rival groups weakened the political structure and led to great violence and misery.

The post-Tang fragmentation permitted regional cultures to emerge. They experimented with and often improved on Tang military, architectural, and scientific technologies. In northern and Central Asia, these refinements included state ideologies based on Buddhism, bureaucratic practices based on Chinese traditions, and military techniques combining nomadic horsemanship and strategies with Chinese armaments and weapons. In Song China, the spread of Tang technological knowledge resulted in the privatization of commerce, major advances in technology and industry, increased productivity in agriculture, and deeper exploration of ideas relating to time, cosmology, and mathematics. China, however, was not self-reliant. Like its East Asian neighbors Korea, Japan, and Vietnam, it was enriched by the sharing of technological advances.

The brilliant achievements of the Song period came from mutually reinforcing developments in economy and technology. Avoiding the Tang's distortion of trade relations and inhibition of innovation and competition, the Song economy, though much smaller than its predecessor, showed great productivity, circulating goods and money throughout East Asia and stimulating the economies of neighbors. All of the East Asian societies made advances in agricultural technology and productivity. All raised their literacy rates after the improvement of printing. In terms of industrial specialization, Song China dominated military technology and engineering, Japan developed advanced techniques in steel making, and Korea excelled in textiles and agriculture. In the long run, Song China could not maintain the equilibrium necessary to sustain its own prosperity and that of the region. Constant military challenges from the north eventually overwhelmed Song finances, and the need for steel from Japan caused a drain of copper coinage.

The potential of any of the East Asian societies to adjust their mutual relationships and deepen their involvement in Pacific trade will never be known. In the thirteenth century, the societies of continental eastern Asia were destroyed—and the region was united again—by the forces of the Mongol Empire.

■ Key Terms

Grand Canal	gunpowder
Tang Empire	Zen
Li Shimin	shamanism
tributary system	Koryo
bubonic plague	movable type
Uigurs	Kamakura shogunate
Song Empire	Champa rice
junks	

■ Suggested Reading

René Grousset's *The Empire of the Steppes: A History of Central Asia* (1988) is a classic text that can be profitably supplemented by Denis Sinor, ed., *The Cambridge History of Early Inner Asia* (1990). On the transport technologies of Central Asia, see Richard Bulliet, *The Camel and the Wheel* (1975). Francesca Bray, *The Rice Economies: Technology and Development in Asian Societies* (1994), furnishes an important discussion of comparative economy, technology, and society.

Arthur Wright, *The Sui Dynasty* (1978), offers a readable narrative of sixth-century China. For a variety of enduring essays, see Arthur F. Wright and David Twitchett, eds., *Perspectives on the T'ang* (1973). On Tang contacts with other cultures, see Edward Schaeffer, *The Golden Peaches of Samarkand* (1963), *The Vermilion Bird* (1967), and *Pacing the Void* (1977). Christopher I. Beckwith, *The Tibetan Empire in Central Asia* (1987), and Rolf Stein, *Tibetan Civilization* (1972), introduce medieval Tibet. On the Uigurs, see Colin MacKarras, *The Uighur Empire* (1968).

Karl Wittfogel and Chia-sheng Feng, *History of Chinese Society: Liao* (1949), is a classic text on the post-Tang empires of Central and northern Asia, which are poorly covered in English. On the Jurchen Jin, see Jin-sheng Tao, *The Jurchens in Twelfth Century China* (1976); on the Tangguts, see Ruth Dunnell, *The State of High and White: Buddhism and the State in Eleventh-Century Xia* (1996).

Joseph Needham's monumental work covering Song technology is introduced in his *Science in Traditional China* (1981). Mark Elvin, *The Pattern of the Chinese Past* (1973), presents a classic thesis on Song advancement (and Ming backwardness). Joel Mokyr, *The Lever of Riches* (1990), puts China in comparative context. On the poet Li Qingzhao, see Hu Pin-ch'ing, *Li Ch'ing-chao* (1966). For neo-Confucianism and Buddhism, see W. T. de Bary, W-T. Chan, and B. Watson, comps., *Sources of*

Chinese Tradition, vol. 1 (1964). On social and economic history, see Miyazaki Ichisada, *China's Examination Hell* (1971); Richard von Glahn, *The Land of Streams and Grottoes* (1987); and Patricia Ebery, *The Inner Quarters: Marriage and the Lives of Chinese Women in the Sung Period* (1993).

For Korean history, see Andrew C. Nahm, *Introduction to Korean History and Culture* (1993), and Ki-Baik Kim, *A New History of Korea* (1984). Paul H. Varley, *Japanese Culture* (1984), introduces Japanese history well. David John Lu, *Sources of Japanese History,* vol. 1 (1974), and R. Tsunoda, W. T. de Bary, and D. Keene, comps., *Sources of Japanese Tradition,* vol. 1 (1964), contain translated sources. Ivan Morris, *The World of the Shining Prince: Court Life in Ancient Japan* (1979), describes the literature and culture of Fujiwara Japan. For Vietnam, see Keith Weller Taylor, *The Birth of Vietnam* (1983).

■ Notes

1. The edited quotation is from William H. McNeill, *Plagues and Peoples* (Garden City, NY: Anchor Press, 1976), 118. McNeill, following his translator, mistakes Ge Hong as "Ho Kung" (pinyin romanization "He Gong").
2. Quoted in David Lattimore, "Allusion in T'ang Poetry," in *Perspectives on the T'ang,* ed. Arthur F. Wright and David Twitchett (New Haven, CT: Yale University Press, 1973), 436.
3. Quoted in Ivan Morris, *The World of the Shining Prince: Court Life in Ancient Japan* (New York: Penguin Books, 1979), 221–222.

10

Peoples and Civilizations of the Americas, 200–1500

Classic-Era Culture and Society in Mesoamerica, 200–900 • The
Postclassic Period in Mesoamerica, 900–1500 • Northern Peoples •
Andean Civilizations, 200–1500
ENVIRONMENT AND TECHNOLOGY: Inca Roads

n late August 682 C.E., the Maya°
princess Lady Wac-Chanil-Ahau°
walked down the steep steps from her
family's residence and mounted a sedan chair
decorated with rich textiles and animal skins.
Leaving the urban center of Dos Pilas°, her military escort spread through the fields and woods
to prevent an ambush. Her destination? The
Maya city of Naranjo°, where she was to marry a
powerful nobleman and thereby reestablish the
royal dynasty that had fallen when Caracol defeated Naranjo. Lady Wac-Chanil-Ahau's passage to Naranjo symbolized her father's quest for
a military alliance to resist Caracol.

Smoking Squirrel, the son of Lady Wac-
Chanil-Ahau, ascended the throne of Naranjo as
a five-year-old in 693 C.E. During his long reign,

he proved a careful diplomat, formidable warrior, and prodigious builder. He expanded and
beautified his capital and, mindful of his
mother's Dos Pilas lineage, erected numerous
stelae (carved stone monuments) that celebrated her life.[1]

Warfare and dynastic crisis, caused by population increase and scarcity of resources, convulsed the world of Wac-Chanil-Ahau. Caracol's
defeat of the city-states of Tikal and Naranjo
undermined long-standing commercial and political relations in southern Mesoamerica. The
dynasty created by the heirs of Lady Wac-
Chanil-Ahau eventually challenged Caracol. Yet
despite a shared culture and religion, the Maya
city-states remained divided by dynastic ambition and competition for resources.

The Amerindian[2] hereditary elites organized
their societies to meet these challenges, even as
their ambitions ignited new conflicts. No single

Maya (MY-ah) **Wac-Chanil-Ahau** (wac-cha-NEEL-ah-HOW)
Dos Pilas (dohs PEE-las) **Naranjo** (na-ROHN-hoe)

set of political institutions or technologies worked in every environment, so American cultures varied widely. Productive and diversified agriculture and cities that rivaled the Chinese and Roman capitals in size and beauty developed in Mesoamerica (Mexico and northern Central America) and the Andean region of South America. In the rest of the hemisphere, indigenous peoples maintained a wide variety of settlement patterns, political forms, and cultural traditions based on combinations of hunting and agriculture.

As you read this chapter, ask yourself the following questions:

- What environmental differences influenced the Mesoamerican, Andean, and northern peoples?
- What technologies developed to meet environmental challenges?
- What similarities and differences marked the civilizations of Mesoamerica and the Andean region?
- How did religious belief and practice affect political life?

CLASSIC-ERA CULTURE AND SOCIETY IN MESO-AMERICA, 200–900

Between 200 and 900 C.E., the peoples of Meso-america created a civilization based on similarities in material culture, religious beliefs and practices, and social structures, despite differences in language and the absence of regional political integration. Building on the achievements of the Olmecs and others (see Chapter 3), the peoples then living in Central America and south and central Mexico developed new political institutions,

made great strides in astronomy and mathematics, and improved agricultural productivity. During the classic period, population grew, a greater variety of products were traded over longer distances, social hierarchies became more complex, and great cities served as governing and religious centers.

The platforms and pyramids devoted to religious functions that still dominated the cities featured more impressive and diversified architecture. Large full-time urban populations, divided into classes, served hereditary political and religious elites who also controlled the nearby towns and countryside.

The agricultural foundation of Mesoamerican civilization had been developed centuries earlier. The major agricultural technologies—irrigation, wetland drainage, and hillside terracing—preceded the cities built after 200 C.E. by more than a thousand years. What made the achievements of the classic era possible was the extended reach and power of religious and political leaders. The impressive architecture and great size of Teotihuacan° and the great Maya cities illustrate both Meso-american aesthetic achievements and the development of powerful political institutions.

Teotihuacan

At the height of its power, from 450 to 600 C.E., **Teotihuacan** (100 B.C.E.–750 C.E.), located about 30 miles (48 kilometers) northeast of modern Mexico City (see Map 10.1), housed between 125,000 and 200,000 inhabitants. The largest city in the Americas, it outshone all but a few contemporary European and Asian cities.

Enormous pyramids dedicated to the sun and moon and more than twenty smaller temples devoted to other gods flanked a central avenue. Among the man-gods worshiped, Quetzalcoatl°, the feathered serpent, was considered the originator of agriculture and the arts. Like the Olmecs, people of Teotihuacan practiced human sacrifice as a sacred duty toward the gods and a necessity for the well-being of human society. The excavation of

---

Teotihuacan (teh-o-tee-WAH-kahn)
Quetzalcoatl (kate-zahl-CO-ah-tal)

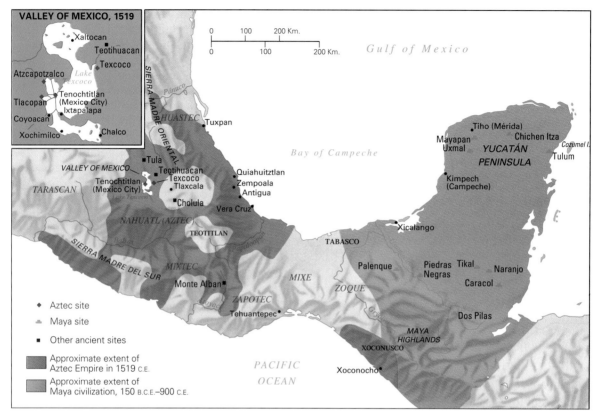

Map 10.1 Major Mesoamerican Civilizations, 1000 B.C.E.–1519 C.E. From their island capital of Tenochtitlan, the Aztecs militarily and commercially dominated a large region. Aztec achievements built on the legacy of earlier civilizations such as the Olmecs and Maya.

the temple of Quetzalcoatl uncovered scores of sacrificial victims.

The urban population had grown rapidly from the forced relocation of villagers in the region. More than two-thirds of the city's residents continued to farm, walking from their city homes to the fields. The elite used the city's growing labor resources to expand agriculture, draining swamps, building irrigation works, and cutting terraces into hillsides. They also expanded **chinampas°**, sometimes called "floating gardens." These narrow artificial islands, anchored by trees and created by heaping lake muck and waste material on beds of reeds, permitted year-round agriculture

because the subsurface irrigation resisted frost and thus helped greatly to sustain the region's growing population.

The housing of commoners changed as the population grew. Apartment-like stone buildings housed, among other people, the craftsmen who produced goods for export. Teotihuacan pottery has turned up throughout central Mexico and even in the Maya region of Guatemala. More than 2 percent of the urban population crafted similarly widespread obsidian tools and weapons.

The city's role as a religious center signified divine approval of the increasingly prosperous elite. Members of this elite controlled the state bureaucracy, tax collection, and commerce. Their diet and style of dress reflected their prestige, and they lived in separate aristocratic compounds. Temple and

chinampas (chee-NAM-pahs)

CHRONOLOGY

	Mesoamerica	Northern Peoples	Andes
100	**100** Teotihuacan founded	**100–400** Hopewell culture in Ohio River Valley	
	250 Maya early classic period begins		**200–700** Moche culture of Peruvian coast
400			
			500–1000 Tiwanaku and Wari control Peruvian highlands
700		**700–1200** Anasazi culture	
	ca. 750 Teotihuacan destroyed		
	800–900 Maya centers abandoned, end of classic period	**919** Pueblo Bonito founded	
	968 Toltec capital of Tula founded		
1000			
		1050–1250 Cahokia reaches peak power	
		1150 Collapse of Anasazi centers begins	
	1156 Tula destroyed		**1200** Chimú begins military expansion
1300			
	1325 Aztec capital Tenochtitlan founded		**1438** Inca expansion begins
			1465 Inca conquer Chimú
1500		**1500** Mississippian culture declines	**1500–1525** Inca conquer Ecuador
	1502 Moctezuma II crowned Aztec ruler		

palace murals confirm the central position and great prestige of the priestly class. Pilgrims came to Teotihuacan from as far away as Oaxaca and Veracruz. Some became permanent residents.

Unlike other classic-period societies, the people of Teotihuacan did not have a single ruler. The deeds of the rulers do not feature in public art, nor were they represented by statues as in other Mesoamerican civilizations. Some scholars see alliances of elite families or weak kings dominated by powerful families as Teotihuacan's governing authority.

Historians debate the role of the military at Teotihuacan. The absence of walls or other defensive structures before 500 C.E. suggests relative peace during its early development. However, archaeology indicates that the city created a powerful military to protect long-distance trade and compel peasants to hand over their surplus production. The discovery of representations of soldiers in typical Teotihuacan dress in the Maya region of Guatemala may indicate the military being used to expand trade. Unlike later postclassic civilizations, however, Teotihuacan was not an imperial state controlled by a military elite.

Although the reason for the collapse of Teotihuacan about 650 C.E. remains a mystery, evidence of weakness appears as early as 500 C.E., when the urban population declined to about forty thousand and the city began to build defensive walls. These fortifications and pictorial evidence from murals point to violent decades toward the end. Indications of conflict within the ruling elite and of mismanagement of resources has challenged earlier theories of conquest by a rival city nearby or by nomadic peoples from the north. Class conflict and the breakdown of public order may explain the destruction of the most important temples in the city center, the defacing of religious images, and the burning of elite palaces. Regardless of the causes, the eclipse of Teotihuacan reverberated throughout Mexico and into Central America.

The Maya

Contemporary with Teotihuacan, the **Maya** developed a civilization in the region that today includes Guatemala, Honduras, Belize, and southern Mexico (see Map 10.1). The difficulties of a tropical climate and fragile soils make the cultural and architectural achievements of the Maya all the more remarkable. Although they shared a single culture, they never unified politically. Instead, rival kingdoms led by hereditary rulers competed for regional dominance.

Today, Maya farmers prepare their fields by cutting down small trees and brush and burning the dead vegetation to fertilize the land. This swidden agriculture produces high yields for a few years, but it exhausts the soil's nutrients, eventually forcing a move to fresh land. The high population levels of the Maya classic period (250–900 C.E.) required more intensive forms of agriculture. Maya living near the major urban centers achieved high agricultural yields by draining swamps and building elevated fields. They used irrigation in areas with long dry seasons, and they terraced hillsides in the cooler highlands. Nearly every household planted a garden to provide condiments and fruits. The Maya also practiced forest management, favoring the growth of useful trees and shrubs and promoting the conservation of deer and other animals hunted for food.

During the classic period, city-states proliferated, the most powerful controlling groups of smaller dependent cities. Religious temples and rituals linked the power of kings to the gods. Unlike earlier sites, these cities had dense central precincts dominated by monumental architecture, commonly aligned with the movements of the sun and Venus. High pyramids and elaborately decorated palaces, often built on high ground or constructed mounds, surrounded open plazas, an awesome prospect for the masses drawn in for religious and political rituals.

Bas-reliefs and bright paint covered nearly all public buildings. Common motifs included religious allegories, the genealogies of rulers, and important historical events. Carved altars and stone monoliths arose near major temples. Masses of men and women aided only by levers and stone tools cut and carried construction materials and lifted them into place.

The Maya cosmos consisted of three layers connected along a vertical axis that traced the course of the sun. The earthly arena of human existence came between the heavens, conceptualized as a sky-monster, and a dark underworld. A sacred tree rose through the layers, its roots in the underworld and its branches in the heavens. The temple precincts of Maya cities physically represented this cosmology: the pyramids as sacred mountains reaching to the heavens, their doorways as portals to the underworld.

Rulers and other members of the elite decorated their bodies with paint and tattoos and wore elaborate costumes of textiles, animal skins, and feathers to project both secular power and divine sanction. Kings communicated directly with the supernatural residents of the other worlds and with deified royal ancestors through bloodletting rituals and hallucinogenic trances. Scenes of rulers drawing blood from lips, ears, and penises are common in frescoes and on painted pottery.

Warfare in particular was infused with religious meaning and elaborate ritual. Scenes of battle and the torture and sacrifice of captives appear frequently. Days of fasting, sacred ritual, and purification rites preceded battle. The king, his kinsmen, and other ranking nobles fought personally,

The Great Plaza at Tikal   Maya centers provided a dramatic setting for the rituals that dominated public life. Construction of Tikal began before 150 B.C.E.; abandonment occurred around 900 C.E. The Great Plaza included a ball court and residences for the elite.   (Martha Cooper/Peter Arnold, Inc.)

with the goal of taking captives. Elite captives nearly always became sacrificial victims; commoners usually became slaves.

Two women are known to have ruled Maya kingdoms, though women from ruling lineages played other political and religious roles. The consorts of male rulers participated in bloodletting rituals and in other public ceremonies. Their noble blood helped legitimate their husbands' rule. Though generally patrilineal (tracing descent in the male line), some male rulers traced their lineages bilaterally (in both the male and the female lines). Like Lady Wac-Chanil-Ahau's son Smoking Squirrel, some rulers emphasized the female line if it held higher status. As for women of the lower classes, scholars believe that they played a central

role in the household economy, maintaining garden plots, weaving, and managing family life.

Building on Olmec precedents, the Maya advanced the development of the calendar, mathematics, and writing. The complexity of their calendric system, with each day marked by three separate dating systems, reflects their interest in time and the cosmos. One calendar, shared by other Mesoamerican peoples, tracked the ritual cycle (260 days divided into 13 months of 20 days), another the solar calendar (365 days divided into 18 months of 20 days, plus 5 "unfavorable days" at the end of the year). The concurrence of these two calendars every 52 years was considered especially ominous. Alone among Mesoamerican peoples, the Maya also maintained a continuous "long count" calendar, which began at a fixed date in the past that scholars have identified as 3114 B.C.E., a date probably associated with creation.

Their system of mathematics, which underlay the calendar, incorporated the concept of the zero and place value, but it had limited notational signs. Maya writing used hieroglyphs that signified whole words or concepts as well as phonetic cues or syllables. Aspects of public life, religious belief, and the biographies of rulers and their ancestors were recorded in deerskin and bark-paper books, on pottery, and on the stone columns and monumental buildings of the urban centers.

Abandonment or destruction befell many of the major urban centers between 800 and 900 C.E., although a small number survived for centuries. In some areas, decades of urban population decline and increased warfare preceded the collapse. Some experts maintain that the destruction of Teotihuacan after 650 C.E. disrupted trade, thus undermining the legitimacy of Maya rulers who used trade goods in rituals. Others suggest that population pressure led to environmental degradation and declining agricultural productivity. This, in turn, might have caused social conflict and warfare as desperate elites sought additional agricultural land through conquest. Epidemic disease and pestilence may have contributed as well.

THE POSTCLASSIC PERIOD IN MESOAMERICA, 900–1500

The collapse of Teotihuacan and many of the major Maya centers occurred over more than a century and a half, making the division between classic and postclassic periods somewhat arbitrary. In fact, some important classic-period civilizations survived unscathed; and essential cultural characteristics in religious belief and practice, architecture, urban planning, and social organization carried over to the postclassic.

Important differences exist nevertheless. The population of Mesoamerica apparently expanded during the postclassic period, causing an intensification of agricultural practices and increased warfare. The governing elites of the major postclassic states—the Toltecs and the Aztecs—increased the size of their armies and developing political institutions that facilitated control of large and culturally diverse territories gained through conquest.

The Toltecs

Scholars speculate that the **Toltecs°**, little known before their arrival in central Mexico, originated as a satellite population protecting the northern frontier of Teotihuacan from nomad raids. After migrating south, they created an important postclassic civilization on the cultural legacy of Teotihuacan. Memories of their military achievements and the violent imagery of their political and religious rituals dominated the Mesoamerican imagination in the late postclassic period. In the fourteenth century, the Aztecs and their contemporaries erroneously believed that the Toltecs created nearly all of the Mesoamerica's cultural monuments. One Aztec source declared:

> In truth [the Toltecs] invented all the precious and marvelous things. . . . All that now exists was their discovery. . . . And these Toltecs were very wise; they were thinkers, for they originated the year count, the day count. All their discoveries formed the book for interpreting dreams. . . . And so wise were they [that] they understood the stars which were in the heavens.[3]

Actually, the most important Toltec innovations came in politics and war. The Toltecs created the first conquest state as they extended their political influence from north of modern Mexico City to Central America. Established about 968 C.E., Tula°, the Toltec capital, followed the grand style (see Map 10.1). Its public architecture featured colonnaded patios and numerous temples. Though never as large as Teotihuacan, Tula dominated central Mexico. Nearly all its public buildings and temples carried representations of warriors and scenes suggesting human sacri-

---

Toltec (TOLL-tek)   **Tula** (TOO-la)

The Mesoamerican Ball Game   From Guatemala to Arizona, archaeologists have found evidence of a game played with a solid rubber ball on slope-sided courts shaped like a capital T. The Maya associated the game with a creation myth and thus gave it deep religious meaning. Sometimes players were sacrificed. This scene from a ceramic jar shows players wearing elaborate ritual clothing—including heavy protective pads around the chest and waist—playing with a ball much larger than the ball actually used. Some representations show balls drawn to suggest a human head.   (Dallas Art Museum/Justin Kerr)

fice, reflecting an increasingly warlike and violent worldview.

Two chieftains or kings apparently ruled the Toltec state together, a system that may eventually have sapped Toltec power and opened Tula to destruction. Sometime after 1000 C.E., a struggle between elite groups identified with rival religious cults undermined the Toltec state. According to later Aztec legends, Topiltzin°—one of the two rulers and a priest of the cult of Quetzalcoatl—and his followers bitterly accepted exile in the east, "the land of the rising sun." These legendary events coincided with growing Toltec influence among the Maya of the Yucatán Peninsula. One text relates the following:

> Thereupon he [Topiltzin] looked toward Tula, and then wept. . . . And when he had done these things . . . he went to reach the seacoast. Then he fashioned a raft of serpents. When he had arranged the raft, he placed himself as if it were his boat. Then he set off across the sea.[4]

Toltec decline set in after the exile of Topiltzin, and around 1156 C.E. northern invaders overcame Tula itself. This destruction triggered a centuries-long process of cultural and political assimilation to produce a new political order based on the Toltec heritage. Like Semitic peoples of the third millennium B.C.E. interacting with Sumerian culture (see Chapter 1), the new Mesoamerican elites came in part from the invading cultures. The Aztecs of the Valley of Mexico became the most important of these late postclassic peoples.

The Aztecs

The Mexica°, more commonly known as the **Aztecs,** pushed into central Mexico from the north after Tula's fall. Originally based on clans, they began to adopt the political and social practices of predecessors who had developed both agriculture and cities. Serving first as serfs and mercenaries for more powerful neighbors, the Aztecs gained strength and relocated to some small islands near the shore of Lake Texcoco. They began to build their twin capitals, **Tenochtitlan°** and Tlatelolco (modern Mexico City), around 1325 C.E.

Topiltzin (tow-PEELT-zeen)

Mexica (meh-SHE-ca)   Tenochtitlan (teh-noch-TIT-lan)

The increased economic independence and greater political security they gained by seizing control of additional agricultural land along the lakeshore eased the introduction of a monarchical system similar to that of more powerful neighboring states. Clans persisted down to the Spanish conquest, but power increasingly flowed to hereditary aristocrats and monarchs, though the latter had neither absolute power nor succession based on primogeniture. A council of powerful aristocrats selected new rulers from male members of the ruling lineage. Once selected, the ruler renegotiated the submission of tribute-paying dependencies and demonstrated his divine mandate by new conquests. War took on religious meaning, providing the ruler with legitimacy and increasing the prestige of successful warriors.

As kinship-based clans lost influence, social divisions sharpened. Conquest allowed the warrior elite to seize land and peasant labor as spoils of war (see Map 10.1). The royal family and highest-ranking aristocrats came to own extensive estates cultivated by slaves and landless commoners. The lower classes received some rewards from imperial expansion but lost most of their influence over decisions. Hereditary nobles monopolized the highest social ranks, although some commoners gained status through success on the battlefield or by entering the priesthood.

Urban space in Tenochtitlan and Tlatelolco continued to recognize the clans, whose members maintained a common ritual life and accepted responsibilities like caring for the sick and elderly. Clan members also fought as military units. However, their control over common agricultural land and fishing and hunting rights declined. By 1500 C.E., great inequalities in wealth and privilege characterized Aztec society.

Elaborate ceremonies distinguished kings and aristocrats from commoners. One Spaniard who witnessed the conquest of the Aztec Empire remembered his first meeting with the Aztec ruler Moctezuma° II (r. 1502–1520): "Many great lords walked before the great Montezuma [Moctezuma II], sweeping the ground on which he was to tread

and laying down cloaks so that his feet should not touch the earth. Not one of these chieftains dared look him in the face."[5]

Commoners lived in small dwellings and ate a limited diet of staples. Nobles lived in well-constructed two-story houses and dined on meat and other dishes flavored by condiments and expensive imports like chocolate brought from Maya country to the south. Rich dress and jewelry also set apart the elite, who practiced polygamy while the commoners were monogamous.

The Aztec state fed an urban population of approximately 150,000 by efficiently organizing the clans and additional laborers sent by defeated peoples to expand agricultural land. Land reclamation centered on a dike more than 5½ miles (9 kilometers) long by 23 feet (7 meters) wide that separated the freshwater and saltwater parts of Lake Texcoco. The dike, whose construction consumed 4 million person-days, made possible greater irrigation and more chinampas. Aztec chinampas contributed maize, fruits, and vegetables to the markets of Tenochtitlan. The imposition of a **tribute system** on conquered peoples helped relieve the capital's population pressure. Unlike Tang China, where tribute had a largely symbolic character (see Chapter 9), one-quarter of Tenochtitlan food requirements came from maize, beans, and other foods sent by nearby political dependencies. The Aztecs also demanded cotton cloth, military equipment, luxury goods like jade and feathers, and sacrificial victims.

A specialized class of merchants controlled long-distance trade. In the absence of draft animals and wheeled vehicles, lightweight and valuable products like gold, jewels, feathered garments, cacao, and animal skins dominated this commerce. Merchants also provided political and military intelligence. Operating beyond the reach of Aztec military power, merchant expeditions carried arms and often used them. Although some merchants became wealthy and powerful, none could enter the ranks of the high nobility.

Mesoamerican commerce took place without money or credit, but cacao, quills filled with gold, and cotton cloth provided standard units of value in barter transactions. Aztec expansion integrated producers and consumers in the central Mexi-

---

Moctezuma (mock-teh-ZU-ma)

can economy so that the markets of Tenochtitlan and Tlatelolco offered goods from as far away as Central America and what is now the southwestern border of the United States. Hernán Cortés (1485–1547), the Spanish adventurer who conquered the Aztecs, admired the abundance of the Aztec marketplace:

> One square in particular is twice as big as that of Salamanca and completely surrounded by arcades where there are daily more than sixty thousand folk buying and selling. Every kind of merchandise such as may be met with in every land is for sale. . . . There is nothing to be found in all the land which is not sold in these markets, for over and above what I have mentioned there are so many and such various things that on account of their very number . . . I cannot detail them.[6]

The combined population of Tenochtitlan and Tlatelolco and the cities and hamlets of the surrounding lakeshore totaled approximately 500,000 by 1500 C.E. In the island capital, canals and streets intersected at right angles. Three causeways connected the city to the lakeshore.

Religious rituals dominated public life. The Aztecs worshiped numerous gods, most of them having both male and female natures. As the Aztec state grew in power and wealth, the cult of Huitzilopochtli°, the southern hummingbird, grew in importance. Although originally associated with war, Huitzilopochtli eventually symbolized the sun, worshiped as a divinity throughout Mesoamerica. To bring the sun's warmth to the world, Huitzilopochtli required a daily diet of human hearts. Twin temples devoted to Huitzilopochtli and Tlaloc, the rain god—the two symbolizing war and agriculture as the bases of the Aztec system—dominated Tenochtitlan.

Sacrificial victims included war captives, the most preferred, but also criminals, slaves, and people provided as tribute by dependent regions. The Aztecs and other societies of the late postclassic period transformed the Mesoamerican tradition of human sacrifice by increasing its scale. The numbers sacrificed reached into the thousands every year. Some scholars have emphasized the politically intimidating nature of this rising tide, noting that sacrifices took place before large crowds that included leaders from enemy and subject states, as well as the masses of Aztec society.

NORTHERN PEOPLES

By the end of the classic period in Mesoamerica, around 900 C.E., improved agricultural productivity and population growth had fostered settled life and complex social and political structures in the southwestern desert region and along the Ohio and Mississippi river valleys of what is now the United States. In the Ohio Valley, Amerindian peoples who lived by hunting and gathering and harvesting of locally domesticated seed crops developed large villages with monumental earthworks.

Growing populations cultivating maize, a staple introduced from Mesoamerica, undertook large-scale irrigation projects in the southwestern desert and the eastern river valleys. However, the two regions evolved different political traditions. The Anasazi° and their neighbors in the southwest maintained a relatively egalitarian social structure and retained collective forms of political organization based on kinship and age. The mound builders of the eastern river valleys evolved more hierarchical political institutions: a hereditary chief wielded both secular and religious authority over his political center and subordinate groups of small towns.

Southwestern Desert Cultures

Immigrants from Mexico brought irrigation agriculture to Arizona around 300 B.C.E. With two harvests per year, the population grew, and settled vil-

---

Huitzilopochtli (wheat-zeel-oh-POSHT-lee)

Anasazi (ah-nah-SAH-zee)

Mesa Verde Cliff Dwelling Located in southern Colorado, the Anasazi cliff dwellings of Mesa Verde hosted a population of about 7,000 in 1250 C.E. Increased warfare in the region probably prompted the construction of housing complexes and religious buildings in large caves. (David Muench Photography)

lage life soon appeared. The Hohokam of the Salt and Gila river valleys show the strongest Mexican influence, with platform mounds and ball courts similar to those of Mesoamerica. Hohokam pottery, clay figurines, cast copper bells, and turquoise mosaics also reflect Mexican influence. By 1000 C.E., the Hohokam had constructed an elaborate irrigation system that included one canal more than 18 miles (30 kilometers) in length. Hohokam agricultural and ceramic technology gradually spread, but it was the Anasazi to the north who left the most vivid legacy.

Archaeologists use **Anasazi,** a Navajo word meaning "ancient ones," to identify a number of dispersed though similar desert cultures located in the Four Corners region of Arizona, New Mexico, Colorado, and Utah. Between 450 and 750 C.E. the Anasazi lived in large villages and grew maize, beans, and squash. Their cultural life centered on underground buildings called kivas, which they may have used for weaving cotton and making pottery with geometric patterns. After 900 C.E., they began to construct large multistory residential and ritual centers.

Chaco Canyon in northwestern New Mexico sheltered one of the largest communities: eight large towns in the canyon itself and four more on surrounding mesas, suggesting a regional population of approximately fifteen thousand. Many smaller villages were located nearby. Each town contained hundreds of rooms arranged in tiers around a central plaza. At Pueblo Bonito, the largest town, a four-story block of residences and storage spaces contained more than 650 rooms. Pueblo Bonito had thirty-eight kivas, including a great kiva more than 65 feet (19 meters) in diameter. Social life and craft activities took place in small, open plazas or common rooms. Hunting, trade, and maintenance of irrigation works often drew men away from the village. Besides food preparation and child care, women shared in agricultural tasks and many crafts. The practice of modern Pueblos, cultural descendants of the Anasazi, suggests that houses and furnishings may have belonged to women formed into extended families with their mothers and sisters.

Pueblo Bonito and its nearest neighbors exerted some kind of political or religious dominance over a large region. The Chaco Canyon culture may have originated as a colonial appendage of Mesoamerica, but archaeological evidence is scarce. Merchants from Chaco provided Toltec-period peoples in northern Mexico with turquoise in exchange for shell jewelry, copper bells, macaws, and trumpets. But these exchanges occurred late in Chaco's development. More important signs of Mesoamerican influence, such as pyramid-shaped mounds, ball courts, and class distinctions signaled by burials or residences, do not appear at Chaco. Instead, it appears that the Chaco Canyon culture developed from earlier societies in the region.

Drought probably forced the abandonment of Chaco Canyon in the twelfth century. Nevertheless, the Anasazi continued in the Four Corners region for more than a century. Anasazi settlements on the Colorado Plateau and in Arizona used large natural caves high above valley floors. Such hard-to-reach locations suggest increased warfare, probably provoked by population pressure on limited arable land. The Pueblo peoples of the Rio Grande Valley and Arizona still live in multistory villages and worship in kivas.

Mound Builders: The Adena, Hopewell, and Mississippian Cultures

The Adena people of the Ohio River Valley, who lived from hunting and gathering supplemented by harvests of locally domesticated seed crops, constructed large villages with monumental earthworks from about 500 B.C.E. Most Adena mounds contained burials with contents indicative of a hierarchical society. The elite owned rare and valuable goods such as mica from North Carolina and copper from the Great Lakes region.

Around 100 C.E., the Adena culture blended into a successor culture now called Hopewell, also centered in the Ohio River Valley but spreading as far as Wisconsin, New York, Louisiana, and Florida. Hopewell people shared the sustenance patterns of the Adena but had a political system based on **chiefdoms**—territories with as many as 10,000 people ruled by a chief, a hereditary leader with both religious and secular responsibilities. Chiefs organized rituals of feasting and gift giving that established bonds among diverse kinship groups and guaranteed access to specialized crops and craft goods. They also managed long-distance trade, which provided luxury goods and additional food supplies.

The largest Hopewell towns in the Ohio River Valley served as ceremonial and political centers and had several thousand inhabitants. Large mounds housing elite burials and serving as platforms for temples and the chief's residence dominated these centers. Elite burial vaults containing valuable goods like river pearls and copper jewelry sometimes entomb women and retainers apparently sacrificed to accompany a dead chief into the afterlife. The abandonment of major Hopewell sites around 400 C.E. has no clear environmental or political explanation.

Hopewell technology and mound building continued in smaller centers linked to the development of Mississippian culture (700–1500 C.E.). Maize, beans, and squash suggest to some a Mississippian cultural link to Mesoamerica, but these plants and related technologies probably arrived by way of intervening cultures.

The urbanized Mississippian chiefdoms

resulted from the accumulated effects of small increases in agricultural productivity, the adoption of the bow and arrow, and the expansion of trade networks. The largest towns shared a common urban plan based on a central plaza surrounded by large platform mounds. People bartered essential commodities, such as flint used for weapons and tools, in these centers.

The Mississippian culture culminated in the great urban site of Cahokia, located near East St. Louis, Illinois. North America's largest mound, a terraced structure 100 feet (30 meters) high and 1,037 by 790 feet (316 by 241 meters) at the base, stands at its center, an area of elite housing and temples ringed by areas where commoners lived. At its height in about 1200 C.E., Cahokia had a population of about 30,000—as large as the great Maya city Tikal.

Cahokia controlled surrounding agricultural lands and a number of secondary towns ruled by subchiefs. One burial containing more than fifty young women and retainers sacrificed to accompany a ruler after death suggests the exalted position of Cahokia's chiefs. Nothing links the decline and eventual abandonment of Cahokia (1250 C.E.) to military defeat or civil war, although climate changes and population pressures may have undermined its vitality. After the decline of Cahokia, smaller Mississippian centers flourished in the southeast until the arrival of Europeans.

ANDEAN CIVILIZATIONS, 200–1500

Much of the Andean region's mountainous zone seems too high for agriculture and human habitation, and the arid plain of its Pacific coastland poses difficult challenges to cultivation. To the east of the Andes Mountains, the hot, humid Amazon headwaters also would seem to discourage the organization of complex societies. Yet the Amerindian peoples of the region developed some of the most socially complex and politically advanced societies of the Western Hemisphere.

Cultural Response to Environmental Challenge

People living in the high mountain valleys and on the dry coastal plain overcame the environmental challenges through effective organization of labor using a recordkeeping system more limited than those of Mesoamerica. A system of knotted colored cords, **khipus°,** helped administrators record population counts and tribute obligations. Large-scale drainage and irrigation works and the terracing of hillsides to control erosion and provide additional farmland increased agricultural production. People worked collectively on road building, urban construction, and even textile production.

The clan, or **ayllu°,** provided the foundation for Andean achievement. Members of an ayllu claiming descent from a common ancestor, though not necessarily related in fact, held land communally. Ayllu members thought of each other as brothers and sisters with obligations to help each other in tasks beyond the ability of a single household. These reciprocal obligations provided the model for the organization of labor and the distribution of goods at every level of Andean society. Just as individuals and families provided labor to kinsmen, members of an ayllu provided labor and goods to their hereditary chief.

When territorial states ruled by hereditary aristocracies and kings developed after 1000 B.C.E., these obligations grew in scale. The **mit'a°** required ayllu members to work the fields and care for the herds of llamas and alpacas owned by religious establishments, the royal court, and the aristocracy. Each allyu met a yearly quota of workers for specific tasks. Mit'a laborers built and maintained roads, bridges, temples, palaces, and large irrigation and drainage projects. They produced textiles and goods essential to ritual life such as beer made from maize and coca (dried leaves chewed as a stimulant and now also a source of cocaine).

Jobs divided along gender lines, but the work of men and women was interdependent. Men hunted and served as soldiers and administrators. Women had responsibilities in textile production,

---

khipus (KEY-pooz)   **ayllu** (aye-YOU)   **mit'a** (MEET-ah)

agriculture, and the home. One early Spanish commentator remarked:

> [Women] did not just perform domestic tasks, but also [labored] in the fields, in the cultivation of their lands, in building houses, and carrying burdens. . . . And more than once I heard that while women were carrying these burdens, they would feel labor pains, and giving birth, they would go to a place where there was water and wash the baby and themselves. Putting the baby on top of the load they were carrying, they would then continue walking as before they gave birth.[7]

Because the region's mountain ranges created a multitude of small ecological areas with specialized resources, each community sought to control a variety of environments to gain access to essential goods. Coastal regions produced maize, fish, and cotton. Mountain valleys contributed quinoa (the local grain), potatoes, and other tubers. Higher elevations contributed the wool and meat of llamas and alpacas. The Amazonian region provided coca and fruits. Colonists sent to exploit these ecological niches remained linked to their original region and ayllu by marriage and ritual. Historians commonly refer to this system of controlled exchange across ecological boundaries as vertical integration, or verticality.

Both Mesoamerica and the Andes region developed integrated political and economic systems long before 1500. However, the unique environmental challenges of the Andean region led to distinctive highland and coastal cultures. Here, more than in Mesoamerica, geography influenced regional cultural integration and state formation.

Moche and Chimú

Around 200 C.E., some four centuries after the collapse of Chavín (see Chapter 3), the **Moche**° achieved dominance of the north coastal region of Peru. They did not establish a centralized state, but they did deploy military forces, and major urban centers like Cerro Blanco

Moche (MO-che)

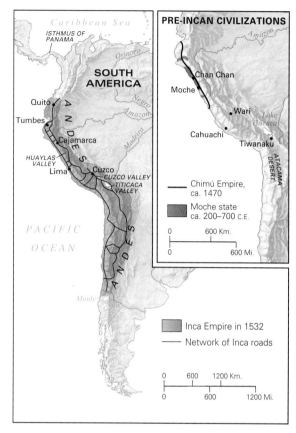

Map 10.2   Andean Civilizations, 200 B.C.E.–1532 C.E.
Andean peoples made complex social and technological adaptations to environmental challenges posed by an arid coastal plain and high interior mountain ranges. In 1532, the Inca Empire's territory stretched from modern Chile in the south to Colombia in the north.

near the modern Peruvian city of Trujillo (see Map 10.2) established hegemony over smaller towns and villages.

The Moche cultivated maize, quinoa, beans, manioc, and sweet potatoes with the aid of massive irrigation works. At higher elevations, they produced coca, used ritually. Complex networks of canals and aqueducts connecting fields with water sources as far away as 75 miles (121 kilometers) depended on mit'a labor imposed on Moche commoners and subject peoples. Large herds of alpacas and llamas transported goods across difficult terrain. Their wool, along with cotton,

Moche Portrait Vase The Moche of ancient Peru produced representations of gods and spirits, scenes of daily life, and portrait vases of important people. This man wears a headdress adorned by two birds and seashells. The stains next to the eyes of the birds represent tears. (Museo de Arquelolgica y antropologia, Lima/Lee Bolton Picture Library)

provided raw material textile production, and their meat was an important dietary element.

Murals and decorated ceramics show Moche society to be stratified and theocratic. Labor organization helped to promote class divisions. Wealth and power, along with political control, lay with the priests and military leaders, a situation reinforced by military conquest of neighboring regions. The elite literally lived above the commoners, having their residences on large platforms at Moche ceremonial centers. Their rich clothing, including tall headdresses, confirmed their divine status and set them further apart from commoners. Gold and gold alloy jewelry signified social position: gold plates suspended from the noses concealed the lower portion of the faces, and large gold plugs decorated the ears.

One tomb of a warrior-priest buried from the Lambeyeque Valley contained a treasure that in-

cluded gold, silver, and copper jewelry; textiles; feather ornaments; and shells. Two women and three men accompanied him in death. Each retainer had one foot amputated to ensure continued subservience and dependence in the afterlife.

Commoners lived by subsistence farming and labored for their ayllu and the elite. Agriculture, the care of llama herds, and the household economy involved both men and women. They lived in one-room buildings clustered in the outlying areas of cities and in surrounding agricultural zones.

Moche textiles, ceramics, and metallurgy give evidence of numerous skilled artisans. As in Chavín, women played a major role in textile production; even elite women devoted time to weaving. Moche craftsmen produced highly individualized portrait vases, ceramics decorated with line drawings representing myths and rituals, and vessels depicting explicit sexual acts. Their metalwork included gold and silver objects devoted to religious and decorative functions or to elite adornment, as well as heavy copper and copper alloy tools for agricultural and military purposes.

The archaeological record shows that the rapid decline of the major centers coincided with a succession of natural disasters in the sixth century and the rise of a new military power in the Andean highlands. When an earthquake altered the course of the Moche River, major flooding caused serious damage, and a thirty-year period of drought expanded the area of coastal sand dunes, which then blew over cultivated fields, overwhelming the irrigation system. As the land dried, periodic heavy rains caused erosion that further damaged the economy. Religious and political leaders whose privileges stemmed from a presumed ability to control natural forces through rituals lost credibility. Despite massive efforts to maintain irrigation and the construction of new urban centers in less vulnerable valleys to the north, Moche civilization never recovered. In the eighth century, a new military power, the **Wari°,** put pressure on trade routes linking the coastal region with the highlands and thus contributed to the disappearance of the Moche.

At the end of the Moche period, the **Chimú°** developed a more powerful coastal civilization

Wari (WAH-ree)   **Chimú** (chee-MOO)

centered on Chan Chan, a capital built around 800 C.E. near the earlier Moche cultural center. Chimú expanded aggressively after 1200 C.E. and at the apex of its power controlled 625 miles (1,000 kilometers) of the Peruvian coast.

Within Chan Chan was a series of walled compounds, each one containing a burial pyramid. Scholars believe that each Chimú ruler built his own walled compound in Chan Chan and was buried there beneath a pyramid. Sacrifices and rich grave goods accompanied each royal burial. As with the Moche, Chimú's rulers separated themselves from the masses and demonstrated divine favor through consumption of rare and beautiful textiles, ceramics, and precious metals. The Chimú dynasty may have practiced split inheritance, the goods and lands of the deceased ruler going to secondary heirs or for religious sacrifices. The heir who inherited the throne therefore had to construct his own residence compound and undertake new conquests to fund his household. After the Inca conquered the northern coast in 1465, they borrowed from the rituals and court customs of Chimú.

Tiwanaku and Wari

After 500 C.E., two powerful civilizations developed in the Andean highlands. At nearly 13,000 feet (3,962 meters) on the high, treeless plain near Lake Titicaca in modern Bolivia stand the ruins of **Tiwanaku**° (see Map 10.2). Initial occupation may have occurred as early as 400 B.C.E., but significant urbanization began only after 200 C.E. Modern excavations provide the outline of vast drainage projects that reclaimed nearly 200,000 acres (8,000 hectares) of rich lakeside marshes for agriculture. This system of raised fields and ditches permitted intensive cultivation similar to that achieved through chinampas in Mesoamerica. Fish and llamas added protein to a diet largely dependent on potatoes and grains. Llamas also serviced long-distance trade that brought in corn, coca, tropical fruits, and medicinal plants.

Tiwanaku's construction featured high-quality stone masonry. An organized workforce—probably

thousands of laborers over a period of years—moved large stones and quarried blocks many miles to construct a terraced pyramid, walled enclosures, and a reservoir. With copper alloy tools their only metallic resource, Tiwanaku's artisans cut stone so precisely that little mortar was needed to fit the blocks. They also produced gigantic human statuary; the largest example, a stern figure with a military bearing, was cut from a single stone 24 feet (7 meters) high.

Evidence of daily life is scarce, but Tiwanaku clearly had a stratified society ruled by a hereditary elite. Most women and men devoted their time to agriculture and the care of llamas, though construction and pottery required specialized artisans. Tiwanaku ceramics found in distant places suggest a specialized merchant class as well.

Many scholars portray Tiwanaku as the capital of a vast empire, a precursor to the later Inca state. The elite certainly controlled a large, disciplined labor force in the surrounding region, and conquests and the establishment of colonies provided the highland capital with products from ecologically distinct zones. Tiwanaku influence also extended eastward to the jungles and southward to the coastal regions and oases of the Atacama Desert in Chile. But archaeological evidence suggests that in comparison with contemporary Teotihuacan in central Mexico, Tiwanaku had a relatively small full-time population of around 30,000, and it served as a ceremonial and political center for a large regional population more than as a metropolis.

The contemporary site of Wari about 450 miles (751 kilometers) to the northwest, near the modern Peruvian city of Ayacucho, had cultural and technological links, but the exact relationship remains unclear. Wari may have begun as a dependency of Tiwanaku, or they may have been joint capitals of a single empire. Each had a unique cultural signature.

Wari exceeded Tiwanaku in size, measuring nearly 4 square miles (10 square kilometers). A massive wall surrounded the city center, which included a large temple and numerous multifamily housing blocks. Housing for commoners sprawled across a suburban zone. Unlike most other urban centers in the Andes, Wari had no central planning. The small scale of its monumental architecture and the near absence of cut stone masonry in

---

Tiwanaku (tee-wah-NA-coo)

public and private buildings distinguish Wari from Tiwanaku. Wari ceramic style also differs, the difference enabling experts to trace Wari's expansion, at a time of increasing warfare throughout the Andes, to the coastal area earlier controlled by the Moche and to the northern highlands. Wari roads maintained communications with remote fortified dependencies. Perhaps as a consequence of military conflict, both Tiwanaku and Wari declined to insignificance by about 1000 C.E.

The Inca

In little more than one hundred years, the **Inca** developed a vast imperial state, which they called "Land of Four Corners." By 1525, the empire had a population of more than 6 million inhabitants and stretched from the Maule River in Chile to northern Ecuador, from the Pacific coast across the Andes to the upper Amazon and, in the south, into Argentina (see Map 10.2). In the early fifteenth century, the Inca competed for power locally in the southern highlands, an area of limited significance after the collapse of Wari. Centered in the valley of Cuzco, the Inca were initially organized as a chiefdom based on reciprocal gift giving and the redistribution of food and textiles. Strong leaders consolidated political authority in the 1430s and undertook a campaign of military expansion.

The Inca state incorporated traditional Andean social customs and economic practices. Tiwanaku had used colonists to provide resources from ecologically distinct zones. The Inca built on this by using their large, professional military to conquer distant territories and by increasing the scale of forced exchanges.

Like earlier highland civilizations, the Inca were pastoralists, their prosperity and military strength depending on vast herds of llamas and alpacas. Both men and women cared for these herds—the women weaving woolen cloth, the men driving animals in long-distance trade. This pastoral background led the Inca to believe that the gods and their ruler shared the obligations of the shepherd to his flock, an idea reminiscent of the Old Testament image conveyed by the lines, "The Lord is my Shepherd."

Cuzco, the imperial capital, and the provincial cities, the royal court, the imperial armies, and the state's religious cults all rested on the efforts of mit'a laborers. The mit'a system also provided the bare necessities for the old, weak, and ill of Inca society. Each ayllu contributed approximately one-seventh of its adult male population to meet these collective obligations. These draft laborers served as soldiers, construction workers, craftsmen, and runners to carry messages along post roads. They also drained swamps, terraced mountainsides, filled in valley floors, built and maintained irrigation works, and built storage facilities and roads. Inca laborers constructed 13,000 miles (20,930 kilometers) of road, facilitating military troop movements, administration, and trade (see Environment and Technology: Inca Roads).

Imperial administration incorporated existing political structures and established elite groups. The hereditary chiefs of ayllus carried out administrative and judicial functions. As the Inca expanded, they generally left local rulers in place. This risked rebellion, but the Inca controlled these risks through a thinly veiled system of hostage taking and the use of military garrisons. Rulers of defeated regions sent their heirs to live at the Inca court in Cuzco, and representations of important local gods were brought to Cuzco to join the imperial pantheon.

Conquests magnified the authority of the Inca ruler and led to the creation of an imperial bureaucracy drawn from his kinsmen. The royal family claimed descent from the sun, the primary Inca god. Members of the royal family lived in palaces maintained by armies of servants. Political and religious rituals dominated the lives of the ruler and his family and helped legitimize their authority. Each new ruler began his reign with conquest because extending imperial boundaries by warfare constituted an imperial duty.

At the height of Inca power in 1530, Cuzco had a population of fewer than 30,000, a fifth that of Tenochtitlan at the same time. Nevertheless, Cuzco contains impressive buildings constructed of carefully cut stones fitted together without mortar. Laid out in the shape of a giant puma (a mountain lion), the city's center contained the palaces each ruler built on ascending the throne, as well as the major temples. The Temple of the Sun had an interior

Inca Roads

From the time of Chavín (900–250 B.C.E.), Andean peoples built roads to facilitate trade across ecological boundaries and to project political power over conquered peoples. In the fifteenth and sixteenth centuries, the Inca extended and improved the road networks constructed in earlier eras. Inca collection and redistribution of tribute paid in food, textiles, and chicha (corn liquor) depended on roads.

Two roads connected Cuzco, the Inca capital in southern Peru, to Quito, Ecuador, in the north and Chile farther south. One ran along the flat and arid coastal plain, the other through the mountainous interior. Shorter east-west roads connected coastal and interior cities. Administrative centers sited along these routes expedited communication with the capital. Rest stops at convenient distances provided shelter and food to traveling officials and couriers. Warehouses built along the roads provided food and military supplies for passing Inca armies and supplied local laborers working in construction projects or cultivating the ruler's fields.

Routes had level roadbeds wherever possible and avoided natural obstacles to reduce travel time. Mit'a laborers recruited from nearby towns and villages built and maintained the roads. Stone or packed earth surfaces, often with stone or adobe walls alongside, kept soldiers or pack trains of llamas from straying into the fields. In mountainous terrain, some roads were little more than improved paths, but in flat country, three or four people could walk abreast. Damage caused by rain runoff or other drainage problems called for quick repair.

The Inca road builders excelled in the mountains. They built suspension bridges across high gorges and cut roadbeds into the face of cliffs. A Spanish priest living in Peru in the seventeenth century commented that the Inca roads "were magnificent constructions, which could be compared favorably with the most superb roads of the Romans."

Source: Quotation from Father Bernabe Cobo, *History of the Inca Empire: An Account of the Indians' Customs and Origin Together with a Treatise on Inca Legends, History, and Social Institutions* (Austin: University of Texas Press, 1983), 223.

Inca Road This paved, walled road is still used in Peru. (Loren McIntyre/ Woodfin Camp & Associates)

lined with sheets of gold and a patio decorated with golden representations of llamas and corn. The ruler made every effort to awe and intimidate visitors and residents with a nearly continuous series of rituals, feasts, and sacrifices. Sacrifices of textiles, animals, and other goods sent as tribute dominated the city's calendar. The destruction of these valuable commodities and a small number of human sacrifices conveyed an impression of splendor and sumptuous abundance that appeared to validate the ruler's descent from the sun.

We know that astronomical observation occupied the priestly class, as in Mesoamerica, but the Inca calendar is unknown. Non-oral communication involved the khipus borrowed from earlier Andean civilizations. Inca weaving and metallurgy, building on earlier regional developments, excelled that of Mesoamerica. Inca craftsmen produced tools and weapons of copper and bronze along with decorative objects of gold and silver. Inca women produced textiles of extraordinary beauty from cotton and llama and alpaca wool.

The Inca did not introduce new technologies, but they increased economic output and added to the region's prosperity. Ruling large populations in environmentally distinct regions allowed the Inca to multiply exchanges between ecological niches. But imperial economic and political expansion reduced equality and diminished local autonomy. The imperial elite lived in richly decorated palaces in Cuzco and other urban centers, increasingly cut off from the masses. The royal court held members of the provincial nobility at arm's length, and commoners faced execution if they looked directly at the ruler's face.

After only a century of regional dominance, the Inca Empire faced a crisis in 1525. The death of the Inca ruler Huayna Capac at the conclusion of the conquest of Ecuador initiated a bloody struggle for the throne. Powerful factions coalesced around two sons whose rivalry compelled both the military and the Inca elite to choose sides. The resulting civil war weakened imperial institutions and ignited the resentments of conquered peoples spread over more than 3,000 miles (4,830 kilometers) of mountainous terrain. On the eve of the arrival of Europeans, this violent conflict undermined the institutions and economy of Andean civilization.

CONCLUSION

The indigenous societies of the Western Hemisphere developed unique technologies and cultural forms in mountainous regions, tropical rain forests, deserts, woodlands, and arctic regions. In Mesoamerica, North America, and the Andean region, the natural environment powerfully influenced cultural development. The Maya of southern Mexico developed agricultural technologies that compensated for the tropical cycle of heavy rains followed by long dry periods. On the Peruvian coast, the Moche used systems of trade and mutual labor obligation to meet the challenge of an arid climate and mountainous terrain. The mound builders of North America expanded agricultural production by using the floodplains of the Ohio and Mississippi Rivers. Across the Americas, hunting and gathering peoples and urbanized agricultural societies alike developed religious and aesthetic traditions, suitable technologies, and effective social institutions in response to local conditions. These cultural traditions proved very durable.

The Aztec and Inca Empires culminated a long developmental process that began before 1000 B.C.E. Each empire controlled extensive and diverse territories with ethnically and environmentally diverse populations that numbered in the millions. The capital cities of Tenochtitlan and Cuzco displayed some of the finest achievements of Amerindian technology, art, and architecture. Both states grew through conquest and depended on the tribute of subject peoples. In both traditions, religion met spiritual needs while also organizing collective life and legitimizing the authority of powerful hereditary rulers.

Yet the empires differed significantly. Elementary markets developed in Mesoamerica to distribute specialized regional production, although the forced payment of goods as tribute remained important. In the Andes, allocation of goods involved reciprocal labor obligations and managed exchange relationships. The Aztecs forced defeated peoples to provide food, textiles, and sacrificial captives as tribute, but they left local hereditary elites in place. The Incas created a more centralized administrative structure managed by a trained bureaucracy.

As the Western Hemisphere's long isolation drew to a close in the late fifteenth century, powerful neighbors or internal revolts shook both empires. In earlier periods, similar challenges had contributed to the decline of great civilizations in both Mesoamerica and the Andean region. Long periods of adjustment and the creation of new institutions followed the collapse of powers such as the Toltecs in Mesoamerica and Tiwanaku in the Andes. The arrival of Europeans would transform this cycle of crisis and adjustment, and the future of Amerindian peoples would become linked to the cultures of the Old World.

■ Key Terms

Teotihuacan	khipu
chinampas	ayllu
Maya	mit'a
Toltecs	Moche
Aztecs	Wari
Tenochtitlan	Chimú
tribute system	Tiwanaku
Anasazi	Inca
chiefdoms	

■ Suggested Reading

In *Prehistory of the Americas* (1987), Stuart Fiedel summarizes the early history of the Western Hemisphere. Alvin M. Josephy, Jr., in *The Indian Heritage of America* (1968), also provides a good introduction. *Canada's First Nations* (1992), by Olive Patricia Dickason, traces Canada's Amerindian peoples to the modern era. *Early Man in the New World*, edited by Richard Shutler, Jr. (1983), complements these works. *Atlas of Ancient America* (1986), by Michael Coe, Elizabeth P. Benson, and Dean R. Snow, contains useful maps and information.

George Kubler, *The Art and Architecture of Ancient America* (1962), is valuable though dated.

Eric Wolf provides an enduring synthesis of Mesoamerican history in *Sons of the Shaking Earth* (1959). For recent research on Teotihuacan, see Esther Pasztori, *Teotihuacan* (1997). Linda Schele and David Freidel summarize recent research on the classic-period Maya in *A Forest of Kings* (1990). The best summary of Aztec history is Nigel Davies, *The Aztec Empire: The Toltec Resurgence* (1987). Jacques Soustelle, *Daily Life of the Aztecs*, translated by Patrick O'Brian (1961), is a good introduction. Though controversial, Inga Clendinnen's *Aztecs* (1991) makes an important contribution.

Chaco and Hohokam (1991), edited by Patricia L. Crown and W. James Judge, summarizes research issues. Robert Silverberg, *Mound Builders of Ancient America* (1968), supplies a good introduction.

For an introduction to early Andean societies, see Karen Olsen Bruhns, *Ancient South America* (1994). For the Moche, see Garth Bawden, *The Moche* (1996). *The History of the Incas* (1970), by Alfred Metraux, offers a dated but useful summary. The best recent synthesis is María Rostworowski de Diez Canseco, *History of the Inca Realm*, trans. Harry B. Iceland (1999). John Murra, *The Economic Organization of the Inca State* (1980), and Irene Silverblatt, *Moon, Sun, and Witches: Gender Ideologies and Class in Inca and Colonial Peru* (1987), offer challenging views of pre-Columbian Peru. Frederick Katz, *The Ancient Civilizations of the Americas* (1972), offers a useful comparative perspective.

■ Notes

1. This summary follows closely the narrative offered by Linda Schele and David Freidel in *A Forest of Kings: The Untold Story of the Ancient Maya* (New York: Morrow, 1990), 182–186.

2. Before 1492, the inhabitants of the Western Hemisphere had no single name for themselves, no sense that physical similarities created a shared identity. Identity derived from kin groups, language, cultural practices, and political structures. Conquest and the occupation by Europeans after 1492 imposed on America's original inhabitants a racial consciousness and racial identity. All collective terms for these first American peoples reflect this history. *Indians, Native Americans, Amerindians, First Peoples,* and *Indigenous Peoples* find common usage. This book uses the names of individual cultures and states wherever possible. It tries to reserve *Amerindian* and other

terms that suggest transcultural identity and experience for the period after 1492.

3. From the Florentine Codex, quoted in Inga Clendinnen, *Aztecs* (Cambridge: Cambridge University Press, 1991), 213.

4. Quoted in Nigel Davies, *The Toltec Heritage: From the Fall of Tula to the Rise of Tenochtitlán* (Norman: University of Oklahoma Press, 1980), 3.

5. Bernal Díaz del Castillo, *The Conquest of New Spain*, trans. J. M. Cohen (London: Penguin Books, 1963), 217.

6. Hernando Cortés, *Five Letters, 1519–1526,* trans. J. Bayard Morris (New York: Norton, 1991), 87.

7. Quoted in Irene Silverblatt, *Moon, Sun, and Witches: Gender Ideologies and Class in Inca and Colonial Peru* (Princeton, NJ: Princeton University Press, 1987), 10.

PART FOUR

INTERREGIONAL PATTERNS OF CULTURE AND CONTACT, 1200–1550

In Eurasia, overland trade along the Silk Road, which had begun before the Roman and Han Empires, reached its peak during the era of the Mongol empires. Beginning in 1206 with the rise of Genghis Khan, the Mongols linked Europe, the Middle East, Russia, Central Asia, and East Asia with threads of conquest and trade. In the century and a half of Mongol domination, some communities in Eurasia thrived on the continental connections that the Mongols' hold on the overland routes made possible, while others groaned under the tax burdens and phys-ical devastation of Mongol rule. But whether for good or ill, Mongol power was based on the skills, strategies, and technologies of the over-land trade and life on the steppes.

The impact of the Mongols was also felt by societies that remained outside Mongol rule. In Europe, Southeast Asia, and Japan, the Mongol challenge stimulated societies that had already begun to urbanize, develop new industries, and undertake political centralization, and it accel-erated many of these changes.

By 1500, Mongol dominance was past, and

new powers were emerging. A new Chinese empire, the Ming, was expanding its influence in Southeast Asia. The Ottomans had captured Constantinople and overthrown the Byzantine Empire. And Christians had defeated Muslims in Spain and were laying the foundations of a new overseas empire. With the fall of the Mongol Empire, Central Asia was no longer a major crossroads of trade.

As the great overland trade of Eurasia faded, merchants, soldiers, and explorers took to the seas. The most spectacular of the early state-sponsored long-distance ocean voyages were undertaken by the Chinese admiral Zheng He. Polynesian colonization of the central and Pacific islands continued, as did Amerindian colonization in the Caribbean Sea. By 1500 the navigator Christopher Columbus, sailing for Spain, had reached the Americas, and the Portuguese had sailed around the world. In earlier centuries travelers had considered a journey between Europe and East Asia as crossing the whole world. But new kinds of ships and better knowledge of the size of the globe as well as its shorelines made sub-Saharan Africa, the Indian Ocean, Asia, Europe, and finally the Americas accessible to each other with unexpected ease.

The great overland routes of Eurasia had generated massive wealth in East Asia and growing hunger for commerce in Europe. These factors animated the development of the sea trade, too. Exposure to the achievements, wealth, and resources of societies in the Americas, sub-Saharan Africa, and Asia excited the interest of the emerging European monarchies in further development and control of the seas.

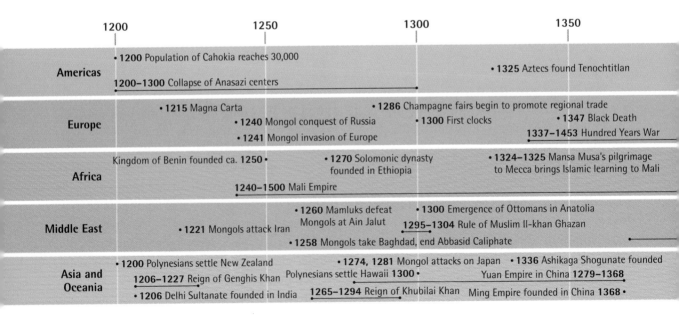

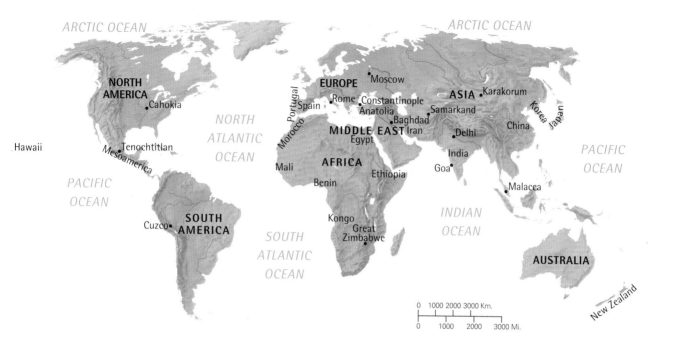

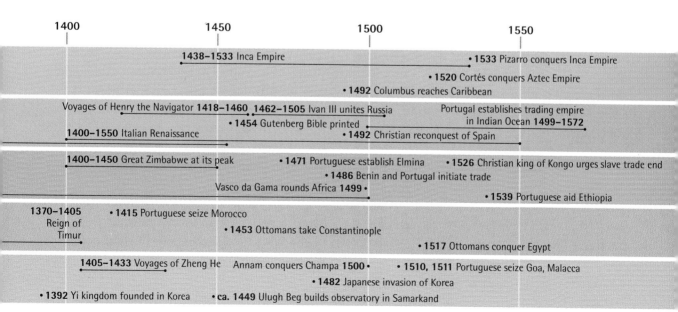

1400

1450

1500

1550

1438–1533 Inca Empire   •1533 Pizarro conquers Inca Empire

•1520 Cortés conquers Aztec Empire

•1492 Columbus reaches Caribbean

Voyages of Henry the Navigator 1418–1460   1462–1505 Ivan III unites Russia   Portugal establishes trading empire in Indian Ocean 1499–1572

•1454 Gutenberg Bible printed

1400–1550 Italian Renaissance   •1492 Christian reconquest of Spain

1400–1450 Great Zimbabwe at its peak   •1471 Portuguese establish Elmina   •1526 Christian king of Kongo urges slave trade end

•1486 Benin and Portugal initiate trade

Vasco da Gama rounds Africa 1499 •

•1539 Portuguese aid Ethiopia

1370–1405 Reign of Timur   •1415 Portuguese seize Morocco

•1453 Ottomans take Constantinople

•1517 Ottomans conquer Egypt

1405–1433 Voyages of Zheng He   Annam conquers Champa 1500 •   •1510, 1511 Portuguese seize Goa, Malacca

•1482 Japanese invasion of Korea

•1392 Yi kingdom founded in Korea   •ca. 1449 Ulugh Beg builds observatory in Samarkand

11

WESTERN EURASIA,
1200–1500

—*Ⴊ*—

The Rise of the Mongols, 1200–1260 • The Fall and Rise of Islam,
1260–1500 • Regional Definition in Response to the Mongols
SOCIETY AND CULTURE: Dueling Pieties

hen the Mongol leader Temüjin°
was a boy, a rival group murdered his
father. Temüjin's mother tried to
shelter him (and protect him from dogs, which
he feared), but she could not find a safe haven.
At age fifteen, Temüjin sought refuge with
Toghoril°, leader of the Keraits°. Among Mongolia's many warring confederations, the Keraits
spoke Turkic and had a strong interest in both
Christianity and Buddhism. Temüjin learned
the charisma of personal strength, courage, and
intelligence; the importance of religious tolerance; the necessity to show no mercy to determined enemies; and the versatility of the
cultural and economic institutions of Central
Asia, all lessons he would one day employ in
building an empire.

In 1206, the **Mongols** and their allies acknowledged Temüjin as **Genghis Khan°**, or
supreme leader. He counted among his advisers
adherents of all the major religions of the Middle
East and East Asia, as well as speakers of many of
the region's languages. They helped him rule the
diverse civilizations of Eurasia more effectively.
His deathbed speech, which cannot be literally
true even though a contemporary recorded it,
captures the strategy behind Mongol success: "If
you want to retain your possessions and conquer
your enemies, you must make your subjects submit willingly and unite your diverse energies to a
single end."[1]

Scholars today recognize the importance of
Temüjin and his successors for the development
of the later medieval world, but the common
view remains that one expressed in European

Temüjin (TEM-uh-jin)   Toghoril (TOE-hoe-rill)
Keraits (keh-rates)

Genghis Khan (GENG-iz KAHN)

and Asian sources of the time: the Mongols stand for death, gore, suffering, and conflagration. The Mongol conquests certainly involved bloody encounters and unprecedented levels of slaughter in many areas. The rapid movement of Mongol soldiers, their equipment, and their captives also accelerated the spread of virulent diseases, including the plague.

But Mongol rule also provided advantages. By 1250, the Mongol Empire stretched from Poland to Siberia (see Map 11.1). Its tremendous extent promoted the movement of people and ideas from one end of Eurasia to the other. Specialized skills developed in different parts of the world spread rapidly throughout the Mongol domains. Trade routes improved, markets expanded, the demand for products grew, and the Silk Road revived.

Although the period from 1200 to about 1350 is considered the age of Mongol domination, the Mongols themselves are only one part of the story. The Mongols had limited economic and strategic interest in the areas they controlled. They usually permitted local cultures to survive and continue to develop. Mongol unification of large territories and local reactions against their domination helped regions find definition. Thus, although the Mongols did stimulate economic and cultural exchange among widely separated regions, China, Russia, and Iran reacted by refining their sense of difference and their search for self-rule.

As you read this chapter, ask yourself the following questions:

- What accounts for the magnitude and speed of the Mongol conquests?
- What benefits resulted from the integration of Eurasia?

- What was the impact of the Il-khan conversion to Islam?
- How did Mongol rule affect Russia, Central Asia, and the Middle East?

THE RISE OF THE MONGOLS, 1200–1260

The environment, economic life, cultural institutions, and political traditions of the **steppes** (dry, high plains) and deserts of Central Asia contributed to the expansion and contraction of empires. The Mongol empire owes its origin at least as much to these long-term trends as to any special abilities of Genghis Khan and his followers.

Animal Husbandry   In nomadic societies, men and boys tended the herds in the pastures. More technical tasks—breeding, birthing, shearing, milking, and the processing of pelts—fell to the women, who worked together in teams and passed their knowledge from older to younger members of the community.   (Ulan Bator Fine Arts Museum)

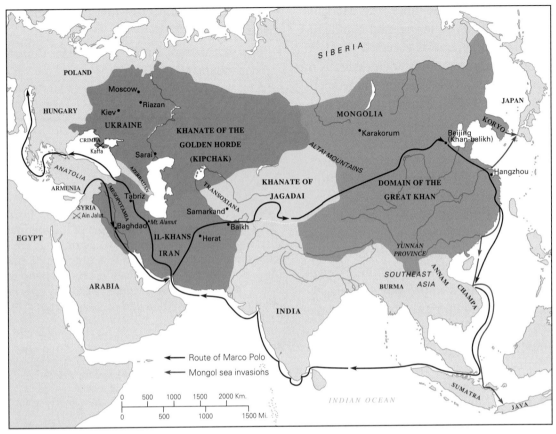

Map 11.1 The Mongol Domains in Eurasia in 1300   After the death of Genghis Khan in 1227, his sons and grandsons divided his empire. Son Ögödei succeeded Genghis as Great Khan. Grandson Khubilai expanded the Domain of the Great Khan into eastern China by 1279. Grandson Hülegü became the first Il-khan in the Middle East. Grandson Batu founded the Khanate of the Golden Horde in southern Russia. Son Jagadai ruled the Jagadai Khanate in Central Asia.

Nomadism in Central Asia

Nomadism arises from scarcity of resources. Nomadic groups have by far the lowest rates of population density. They move continually to find pastures and water for their livestock, frequently coming into contact with other nomadic groups seeking the same resources. These encounters commonly result in warfare, alliance, or both. In times of drought, conflicts increase. Small groups disappear, alliances grow, and people leave groups that have grown too large. Historians believe this sort of environmental stress afflicted northern Eurasia around 1000 C.E. and contributed to the dislocations and conflicts from which the Mongol

empire emerged. Rain inundated some agricultural lands in this period, but northern Eurasia became unusually dry, setting nomadic peoples on a southward move.

Superb riders, herdsmen, hunters, and warriors, like all other steppe nomads, the Mongols followed the ancient tradition of putting their infants on goats to accustom them to riding. Pressure to make movements efficiently and accurately made centralized decision making a necessity, and the independence of individual Mongols and their families made decision making public, with many voices being heard. Even during a military campaign, nomad warriors moved with their families and possessions. If they disagreed with a decision,

CHRONOLOGY

	Central Asia	Middle East	Russia
1200	**1206** Temüjin chosen Genghis Khan of the Mongols **1227** Death of Genghis Khan **1227–1241** Reign of Great Khan Ögödei	**1221–1223** First Mongol attacks in Iran **1250** Mamluk regime controls Egypt and Syria **1258** Mongols sack Baghdad and kill the caliph **1260** Mamluks defeat Il-khans at Ain Jalut	**1221–1223** First Mongol attacks on Russia **1240** Mongols sack Kiev **1242** Alexander Nevskii defeats Teutonic Knights **1260** War between Il-khans and Golden Horde
1300		**1295** Il-khan Ghazan converts to Islam **1349** End of Il-khan rule **ca. 1350** Egypt infected by plague	**1346** Plague outbreak at Kaffa
1400	**1370–1405** Reign of Timur	**1453** Ottomans capture Constantinople	**1462–1505** Ivan III unites Russia under rule of Moscow, throws off Mongol rule (1480)

they could strike off on their own. Central Asian political structures accommodated the conflicting centralizing and decentralizing forces of nomadic life. A council of the leaders of powerful families ratified the decisions of the leader—the *khan*—although they also recognized hierarchical authority.

Many men and women captured during warfare or raids became slaves and did menial work in camps. Some individuals entered into slavery willingly, in order to avoid starvation. Slaves also served as currency. Weak groups secured land rights and protection from strong groups by providing

them with slaves, livestock, weapons, silk, or cash. Many powerful groups (such as the one to which Genghis Khan's father belonged) found they could live almost entirely off tribute, so they spent less time and fewer resources on herding and more on the warfare designed to secure greater tribute.

Federations arose, based on growing wealth and more numerous alliances among groups, almost always expressed in arranged marriages between the leading families. Children became pawns of diplomacy: their marriages were arranged in childhood—in Temüjin's case, at the age of eight.

Women from prestigious families could wield power in negotiation and management, and could suffer assassination or execution just like the men.

Long-distance, seasonal movements created channels for trade and communication. This favored cultural diversity and helped Manichaeism, Judaism, Christianity, Buddhism, and Islam spread across Central Asia. Within a single family were commonly included believers in two or more religions, in combination with traditional shamanism (ancient practices by which special individuals visited and influenced the supernatural world). This plurality of religious practice reflects the nomads' disassociation of rulership from religion.

Ancient beliefs included the idea of world rulership by a khan, who, with the aid of his shamans, would speak to and for an ultimate god, represented as Sky or Heaven. This universal ruler, as the speaker for Heaven, would transcend particular cultures and dominate them all. The words attributed to Genghis on his deathbed reflect this belief.

Self-sufficiency dictated a diet that nomads could provide for themselves—primarily meat and milk—and wearing clothes made from felt (from wool), leather, and furs. Women oversaw the breeding and birthing of livestock and the preparation of furs.

Nomads, however, never lived completely independent of the settled regions. They needed iron for bridles, stirrups, wagons, and weapons. With no mines of their own, they acquired iron implements in trade and reworked them to suit their purposes. As early as the 600s, the Turks had large ironworking stations south of Mount Altai in western Mongolia. Neighboring agricultural states tried to limit the export of iron but never succeeded. In fact, Central Asians improved certain sedentary technologies, such as iron forging, and exported them back to the agricultural regions. The Mongols revered iron and the secrets of ironworking. Temüjin, Genghis Khan's personal name, means "blacksmith," and several of his prominent followers were sons of blacksmiths.

Central Asian nomads also traded wool, leather, and horses for wood, cotton and cotton seed, silk, vegetables, and grain. Appreciating the value of permanent settlements for growing grain and cotton, as well as for the working of iron, many nomads established villages at strategic points, often with the help of migrants from the agricultural regions. The frontier regions east of the Caspian Sea and in northern China thus became economically and culturally pluralistic.

Despite their interdependence, nomads and farmers often came into conflict. When farming societies needed land, their soldiers tried to seize additional territory. When nomads needed agricultural goods or slaves, they resorted to raiding or invasion. Warfare tended to break out when normal trade relations between the two became disrupted.

The Mongol Conquests

Shortly after his acclamation in 1206, Genghis set out to convince the kingdoms of Eurasia to pay him tribute. Two decades of Mongol aggression followed. The earliest campaigns targeted Central Asia, the Middle East, and Russia.

Genghis Khan died in 1227, possibly of alcoholism. His son and successor, the Great Khan Ögödei°, continued to assault China. He destroyed the Tanggut and then the Jin Empires and put their territories under Mongol governors (see Chapter 12). In 1236, Genghis's grandson Batu° (d. 1255) attacked Russian territories, and took control of all the towns along the Volga° River (see Map 11.1). Within five years, he conquered Moscow and Kievan Russia, Poland, and Hungary. Europe would have suffered grave damage in 1241 had the Mongol forces not lifted their attack because of the death of the Great Khan Ögödei and the need to return to the Mongol capital at Karakorum for the election of a new Great Khan. With Genghis's grandson Güyük° installed, Mongol pressure on the Middle East intensified. It climaxed in 1258 with the sacking of Baghdad and the murder of the last Abbasid caliph (see Chapter 7).

The Mongols did not outnumber their enemies, but they combined extraordinary abilities on horseback and superior bows. The Mongol bow could shoot one-third farther (and was signifi-

Ögödei (ERG-uh-day) **Batu** (BAH-too)
Volga (VOHL-gah) **Güyük** (gi-yik)

cantly more difficult to pull) than Middle Eastern and European bows of the period. The bow's composite structure and a jade thumb ring that allowed the archer's hand to withstand the tremendous tension of the drawn bowstring also gave the Mongols an advantage.

Mounted Mongol archers rarely expended the five dozen or more arrows they carried in their quivers. As the battle opened, they shot a volley of arrows from a distance to decimate enemy marksmen. Then they galloped nearly without challenge into sword, lance, javelin, and mace combat against the enemy's infantry. The Mongol cavalry met its match only at the Battle of Ain Jalut°, where it confronted Mamluk forces, whose war techniques reflected the same traditions.

They adapted their techniques to penetrate fortifications, first firing a volley of flaming arrows and then hurling enormous projectiles—frequently on fire—from catapults. The first Mongol catapults, taken from the Chinese, transported easily but had short ranges and poor accuracy. From the defeated Khwarazmshahs° in Central Asia, the Mongols adapted a catapult design that was half again as powerful as the Chinese catapult. They used this improved weapon against the cities of Iran and Iraq.

Cities under Mongol attack faced immediate slaughter if they opened their gates to fight or slow starvation followed by slaughter if they did not. Alternatively, the Mongols offered food, shelter, and protection in return for surrender. The bloodletting the Mongols inflicted on cities such as Balkh° (in present-day northern Afghanistan) gave staggering force to these appeals. Throughout the Middle East, the Mongols found populations willing to acknowledge their overlordship. With the capture of each city, the "Mongol" armies swelled in number. The conquest in the Middle East involved a small Mongol elite overseeing armies of recently recruited Turks, Iranians, and Arabs.

The Mongols quickly learned about the rivalries among neighboring groups and found ways to take advantage of them. In their campaigns against cities in Central Asia, the Mongols ex-

Celebrating Battle   The Mongols gained fame for their mobility and the unusual distance and accuracy their archers could attain. This detail from a painted bowl of the early Il-khan period illustrates the military skills of shooting from horseback, as well as the violence of the battlefield. But it carefully avoids a fact of war in the thirteenth-century Middle East: the slaughter, starvation, and enslavement of civilians.   (Courtesy of the Freer Gallery of Art, Smithsonian Institution, Washington, DC.)

ploited Muslim resentments against nonbelievers. In the Middle East, the Mongols exploited Christian resentment of Muslim rule, sometimes forcing the conversion of mosques into churches. When Hülegü° captured Baghdad in 1258, he agreed to the requests of his Christian wife that Christians be sought out and put in prominent posts.

Overland Trade and the Plague

The cosmopolitan nature of the Mongol conquests underscores the Mongol role in transmitting military technology and related scientific knowledge across Eurasia. Civil technologies and artistic styles spread as well. Silk affords a good example. Like their aristocratic predecessors in Central Asia,

---

Ain Jalut (ine jah-LOOT)
Khwarazmshah (hwa-RAZZ-um-shah)   **Balkh** (bahlk)

Hülegü (HOO-luh-goo)

Passport   The Mongol Empire that united Eurasia in the mid-1200s provided good roads and protection for the movement of products, merchants, and diplomats. Individuals traveling from one culture area to another encountered new languages, laws, and customs. The *paisa* (from a Chinese word for "card" or "sign"), with its inscription in Mongolian, proclaimed to all that the traveler had the ruler's permission to travel. Europeans later borrowed the practice, making it the ancestor of the modern passport.   (The Metropolitan Museum of Art, purchase bequest of Dorothy Graham Bennett, 1993 [1993.256]. Photograph 1997 The Metropolitan Museum of Art)

Mongol nobles had the exclusive right to wear silk, almost all of it brought from China. Eurasian commercial integration under Mongol rule brought new styles and huge quantities of silk westward, not just for clothing but also for wall hangings and furnishings. Abundant silk transformed the daily life of the elite and urban groups in the Middle East and Europe and fostered a mixing and merging of artistic motifs from Japan and Tibet to England and Morocco.

Mongol control and tax policies favored overland commerce, but the traders came from all over Eurasia. Merchants mixed with ambassadors, scholars, and missionaries over the long routes to the Mongol courts. The resulting travel literature provides vivid insights into the Eurasian world of the thirteenth century. Some narratives, such as that of the Venetian traveler Marco Polo° (1254–1324), freely mixed the fantastic with the factual. These books convey an image of the inexhaustible wealth of the Mongols, and of Asia generally, creating in Europeans an ambition to find easier routes to Asia.

These travel accounts have mesmerized readers for centuries, but many people had similar experiences. In the towns they visited in Central Asia or China, they regularly encountered other Europeans: sometimes travelers, sometimes captives, all part of a steady flow of people across Eurasia. Technical knowledge, whether of pharmacology, engineering, mathematics, or financial management, flowed abundantly between China and Iran.

Mongol competition could also encourage contacts. The wish of the Mongols in the Middle East (in the Il-khan Empire) to drive the Mongols of Russia out of the Caucasus in the 1260s helped spark a half-century of complex diplomacy in which Muslims often allied themselves with European rulers—sometimes against Christians, sometimes against the Mongols. Similarly, when the Mongols in Russia granted a trade charter to merchants from Genoa, the Mongols in the Middle East granted similar privileges to Venice.

Exchange also held great dangers. Europe had been free of **bubonic plague** since about 700. The Middle East had seen no plague since about the year 1200. In southwestern China, however, plague had festered in Yunnan province since the early Tang period. In the mid-thirteenth century, Mongol troops established a garrison in Yunnan whose military and supply traffic provided the means for flea-infested rats carrying plague to reach central China, northwestern China, and Central Asia. Marmots and other desert rodents along the routes became infected and passed the disease to dogs and people. The caravan traffic infected the oasis towns when rats and fleas disembarked from overloaded camels, covered wagons, and the wagon-mounted felt tents of the nomads. Plague incapacitated the

---

Marco Polo (mar-koe POE-loe)

Mongols themselves during their assault on the city of Kaffa° in Crimea° in 1346. They withdrew, but the plague infiltrated Crimea. From Kaffa, rats infected by fleas repeatedly reached Europe and Egypt by ship.

Typhus, influenza, and smallpox traveled with the plague. The combination of these and other diseases created what is often called the "great pandemic" of 1347–1352. The human and cultural damage far exceeded any of the direct consequences of the Mongol conquests. It was not the Mongol invaders who brought the disease westward. Rather, it came with the trade they encouraged. Peace and profit, not conquest, gave rise to the great pandemic.

THE FALL AND RISE OF ISLAM, 1260–1500

By 1260 the **Il-khan°** Empire, established by Genghis's grandson Hülegü, controlled parts of Armenia and all of Azerbaijan, Mesopotamia, and Iran. The Mongols who had conquered southern Russia settled north of the Caspian Sea and established the capital of their Khanate of the **Golden Horde** (also called the Kipchak° Khanate) at Sarai° on the Volga River. There, they formed a close relationship with the indigenous Muslim Turkic nomads.

Mongol Rivalry

Some members of the Mongol imperial family had already professed Islam before the Mongol assault on the Middle East, and Mongols had frequently relied on Central Asian Muslims as advance men and intermediaries. Indeed, certain of the Il-khans showed the Muslims favor, and Hülegü himself, though a Buddhist, had a trusted Shi'ite adviser and granted privileges to the Shi'ites. As a whole, however, the Mongols under Hülegü's command came only slowly to Islam.

Tensions between individual Mongols and Muslims paralleled tensions between Muslim principles and Mongol culture. Many Muslims could not forgive the murder of the last Abbasid caliph. In accordance with Mongol customs for the execution of high-born persons, the caliph had been rolled in a rug and trampled to death by horses to prevent his blood from spilling on the ground. The Mongols considered the elimination of the supreme religious leader of the Muslims necessary for their control of the region.

The passage of time did little to reconcile Islamic doctrines with Mongol ways. Muslims abhorred the Mongols' worship of idols, a fundamental part of shamanism. Furthermore, the shamanic method of slaughtering livestock avoided the spilling of blood, while Islamic purity laws required the draining of blood from the carcass for the meat to be *halal*°, or permitted. Litigation on this and related matters flooded the Il-khanid law courts.

Islam became a point of tension between the two empires when Batu's successor as leader of the Golden Horde declared himself a Muslim, announced his intention of avenging the murder of the caliph, and laid claim to the Caucasus—the region between the Black and Caspian Seas—which was—also claimed by the Il-khans. Through the Caucasus, the Golden Horde could gain direct access to Il-khan territories, and particularly to the Il-khan capital at Tabriz° (see Map 11.2).

The conflict initiated conflict between Mongol domains, and the fact that the Golden Horde embraced Islam led some European leaders to believe they could enlist the non-Muslim Il-khans in a campaign to drive the Muslims out of contested religious sites in Syria, Lebanon, and Palestine. This resulted in a brief diplomatic correspondence between the Il-khan court and Pope Nicholas IV (r. 1288–1292) and an exchange of ambassadors that sent two Christian Turks, Markuz° and Rabban

---

Kaffa (KAH-fah)   **Crimea** (cry-MEE-ah)   **Il-khan** (IL-con)
Kipchak (KIP-chahk)   **Sarai** (sah-RYE)

halal (haa-LAAL)   **Tabriz** (ta-BREEZE)

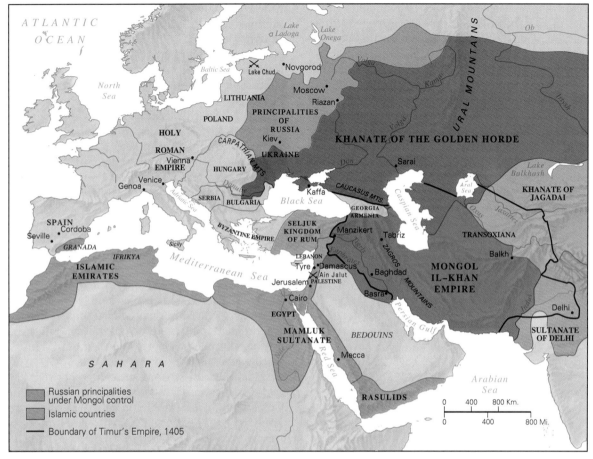

Map 11.2 **Western Eurasia in the 1300s** During the conflict between the Il-khans and the Golden Horde in the 1260s, European leaders hoped to ally themselves with the Il-khans against Muslim defenders in Palestine. Ghazan's conversion to Islam in 1295 dashed these hopes, but the powerful alliance between the Mamluks and the Golden Horde kept the Il-khans from advancing west.

Sauma°, on a remarkable tour of western Europe as Il-khan ambassadors in the late 1200s.

For their part, the Il-khans attempted to get help from the Europeans in ejecting the Golden Horde from the Caucasus. Many Christian crusaders enlisted in the Il-khan effort, and the pope later excommunicated some for doing so. The Golden Horde responded by seeking an alliance with the Muslim Mamluks in Egypt against both the crusaders and the Il-khans. These complications effectively extended the life of the Crusader

kingdoms in Palestine and Syria; the Mamluks did not finish ejecting the crusaders until the fifteenth century.

Before the Europeans could realize their plan of allying with the Mongols, the new Il-khan ruler, Ghazan° (1271–1304), declared himself a Muslim in 1295. His prime minister and confidant, **Rashid al-Din°**, a convert from Judaism to Shi'ite Islam, had convinced the Il-khan to convert, though the Il-khans eventually opted for the Sunni form of the religion. In the following decades, the Il-khans and

Markuz (MARK-uhz)   Rabban Sauma (rah-bahn SAU-ma)   Ghazan (gaz-zan)   Rashid al-Din (ra-SHEED ad-DEEN)

the Golden Horde both promoted Islam throughout their domains.

Islam and the State

Taxation provided the most efficient means for achieving the Il-khan goal of extracting maximum wealth from their domain. **Tax farming,** their preferred method, had developed earlier in the Middle East. The government sold tax-collecting contracts to small corporations, mostly owned by merchants who might also work together to finance caravans, small industries, or military expeditions. The corporations that agreed to generate the most revenue for the government won the contracts. They could use whatever methods they chose and could keep anything over the contracted amount.

In the short term, the state's cost of collecting taxes fell, and the state received large amounts of grain, cash, and silk. But over the long term, the exorbitant rates the tax farmers charged drove many landowners into debt and servitude and prevented the reinvestment necessary to maintain productivity. Payments of taxes in kind drove the price of grain so high that the government had difficulty procuring supplies for the soldiers' granaries and had to appropriate land to grow its own grain. This land, like religious land grants, paid no taxes, so the tax base shrank even as the demands of the army and the Mongol nobility for revenue continued to grow.

Economic woes abounded when Ghazan became Il-khan in 1295 and converted to Islam. Citing the humane values of Islam, he announced his intention to reduce the government's tax demands. He also looked abroad for new methods of economic management. He believed he found one in the Chinese practice of using paper money, and he ordered the use of paper money in his domain. But the peoples of the Middle East had no previous exposure to paper money and no confidence in its value. The economy quickly sank into a depression that lasted until after the end of the Il-khan period in 1349.

After Ghazan, the Il-khan regime experienced the same slow decline of Mongol regimes elsewhere. Paying high taxes to support the Mongol military elite caused widespread popular unrest and resentment among local elites. Mongol nobles in the Middle East competed fiercely among themselves for the decreasing revenues, and fighting among Mongol factions destabilized the government. The fragmentation of Il-khan power aroused the expansive ambitions of the Mongols north of the Caspian. In the mid-fourteenth century, Mongols from the khanate of the Golden Horde moved through the Caucasus into the western regions of the Il-khan Empire and soon into the Il-khan's central territory, Azerbaijan. These Mongols from Russia participated in the dismemberment of the Il-khan Empire and briefly occupied its major cities.

Meanwhile, a new power emerged in Central Asia where the descendants of Genghis's son Jagadai (d. 1242) held sway. Under the leader **Timur°,** known to Europeans as Tamerlane, the Jagadai° Khanate (see Map 11.1) drew on the political traditions of the Mongols and on Islam. The campaigns of Timur in western Eurasia exceeded in brutality the earlier Mongol campaigns. By the late fourteenth century, he had subdued much of the Middle East, but he died in 1405 before he could march on China. The Timurids (descendants of Timur) held the Middle East together long enough to deepen and consolidate Sunni Islamic influence, and they laid the groundwork for the later establishment in India of a Muslim Mongol-Turkic regime, the Mughals, in the sixteenth century. But Central Asia never regained the glory of Timurid times.

Art and Science in Islamic Eurasia

Thanks partly to the wide-ranging cultural exchange fostered by the Mongols, the Il-khans and Timurids presided over a brilliant period in Islamic civilization. Many of the intellectual developments of the era directly affected Europe. Others had an indirect but equally important influence. The sharing of artistic trends and political ideas between Iran and China, which had begun prior to the Mongols in exchanges along the Silk Road, created the

---

Timur (tee-MOOR)   **Jagadai** (jahg-ah-die)

illusion in European eyes that east of the Mediterranean lay an "Orient" of uniform tastes and political cultures. Although Timur died before he could reunite Iran and China, his forcible concentration of scholars, artists, and craftsmen in his capital, Samarkand, fostered advancement in some specific activities under his descendants.

The historian Juvaini°, the eminent literary figure who noted Genghis Khan's deathbed speech, came from the city of Balkh, which the Mongols devastated in 1221. His family switched their allegiance to the Mongols, and both Juvaini and his older brother assumed high government posts. The Il-khan Hülegü, seeing an opportunity to both immortalize and justify the Mongol conquest of the Middle East, enthusiastically supported Juvaini's historical projects. This resulted in the first comprehensive narrative of the rise of the Mongols under Genghis Khan.

Juvaini's work and methods—he often criticized the Mongols—inspired Rashid al-Din, the prime minister of Ghazan, to attempt the first history of the world, including the earliest known general history of Europe, based on information from European monks. Rich illustrations accompanied many copies of Rashid al-Din's work. Pictures adapted from European paintings portrayed European persons and events, and pictures adapted from Chinese paintings depicted Chinese persons and events. Chinese principles of watercolor composition and portraiture thus became familiar in Iran.

Rashid al-Din himself had converted from Judaism to Islam. He traveled widely in Mongol service and became aware of many cultures and points of view. He kept in constant touch with Mongol officials in Central Asia and China through personal attendance upon them and letters explaining his ideas on economic management. This advice helps explain how similar financial and monetary reforms evolved at roughly the same time in Iran, Russia, and China. Rashid advocated conducting government in accord with the moral principles of the majority of the population, and he convinced Ghazan to convert to Islam.

Under the Timurids, the tradition of the Il-khan historians continued. Timur himself met with the greatest historian of the age, **Ibn Khaldun°** (1332–1406), a Tunisian. In a scene reminiscent of Ghazan answering Rashid al-Din's questions on the history of the Mongols, Timur and Ibn Khaldun sat in Damascus, exchanging historical, philosophical, and geographical viewpoints. Like Genghis, Timur saw himself as a world conqueror. At their capitals of Samarkand and Herat (in modern-day Afghanistan), later Timurid rulers sponsored historical writing in both Persian and Turkish. Miniature painting also flourished as artists illustrated these works and volumes of poetry.

Juvaini had accompanied Hülegü in 1256 in the campaigns against the Assassins, a Shi'ite religious sect derived from the Fatimid dynasty in Egypt (see Chapter 7), and he worked to preserve the historical archives the Assassins maintained at Alamut° in the mountains of northern Iran. A multitalented Shi'ite named **Nasir al-Din Tusi°** may have joined Hülegü's entourage as an adviser at Alamut.

Nasir al-Din interested himself in history, poetry, ethics, and religion, but made his most outstanding contributions in mathematics and cosmology. Drawing on the work of a poet and mathematician of the Seljuk° period, Omar Khayyam° (1038?–1131), he laid the foundations for complex algebra and trigonometry. His work had considerable impact. A group of his followers, working at their observatory at Maragha°, an academy near the Il-khan capital of Tabriz, used it to solve a fundamental problem in classical cosmology.

Islamic scholars had preserved and elaborated on the insights of the Greeks in astronomy and mathematics and adopted the cosmological model of Ptolemy°, which assumed a universe with the earth at its center surrounded by the sun, moon, and planets traveling in concentric circular orbits. Astronomers knew the flaws in Ptolemy's model.

Juvaini (joo-VINE-nee)

Ibn Khaldun (ee-bin kal-DOON)   Alamut (ah-lah-moot)
Nasir al-Din Tusi (nah-SEER ad-DEEN TOO-see)
Seljuk (SEL-jook)   Omar Khayyam (oh-mar kie-YAM)
Maragha (mah-rah-gah)   Ptolemy (TOHL-uh-mee)

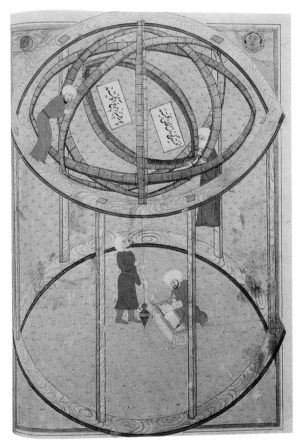

Astronomy and Engineering   Throughout Eurasia, observational astronomy went hand in hand not only with mathematics and calendrical science but also with engineering, as the construction of platforms, architecture for solar measurement, and armillary spheres became more sophisticated. Publication of instruction manuals helped refine the science and the technology. This manual in Persian (completed in the 1500s but illustrating activities that occurred in the Il-khan period) provides instruction on the establishment of a plumb line for an enormous outdoor armillary sphere.   (Istanbul University Library)

The motions of the five visible planets did not coincide with predictions based on circular orbits. Since Ptolemy's time, astronomers and mathematicians had sought a mathematically consistent explanation for the actual movement of the planets that they observed.

Nasir al-Din proposed such a model based on the idea of small circles rotating within a large circle, changing vectors in such a way as to account for the movements observed from the earth. A student of Nasir al-Din reconciled the model with the ancient Greek idea of epicycles (small circles rotating around a larger circle) to explain the movement of the moon around the earth, and here occurred the breakthrough that changed cosmological thought. The mathematical tables and geometric models devised by this student somehow became known to Nicholas Copernicus (1473–1543), a Polish monk and astronomer. Copernicus adopted the lunar model as his own, virtually without revision. He then proposed the model of lunar movement developed under the Il-khans as the proper model for planetary movement as well—but with the planets circling the sun.

Perhaps because the Central Asian nomads depended on the stars to guide their migrations, Central Asian empires—particularly the Uigurs° and the Seljuks—had excelled in their sponsorship of observational astronomy and the making of calendars. Under the Il-khans, the astronomers of Maragha excelled in predicting lunar and solar eclipses. Astrolabes, armillary spheres, three-dimensional quadrants, and other instruments acquired a new precision.

The Il-khan astronomers collected astronomical data from all parts of the Islamic world, as well as from China. Their remarkably accurate eclipse predictions and tables reached the hostile Mamluk lands in Arabic translation. Byzantine monks took them to Constantinople and translated them into Greek. Christian scholars working in Muslim Spain translated them into Latin. In India, the sultan of Delhi ordered them translated into Sanskrit. The Great Khan Khubilai° (see Chapter 12) summoned a team of Iranians to Beijing to build an observatory for him. And the Timurids themselves continued to sponsor large observatories. Indeed, the Timurid ruler Ulugh Beg° (1394–1449) practiced astronomy and actively participated in the construction of a great observatory at Samarkand.

The Timurids also supported another major advance in mathematics. Ghiyas al-Din Jamshid

---

Uigur (WEE-ger)   **Khubilai** (KOO-bih-lie)
Ulugh Beg (OO-look bek)

al-Kashi°, in his studies of Chinese calendars, noted that Chinese astronomers had long used a unit for the measurement of new moons that was calculated as 1/10,000th of a day. This seems to have inspired al-Kashi's use of the decimal fraction, by which quantities less than 1 could be represented by the manipulation of a marker to show place. This enabled al-Kashi to propose a far more precise calculation for *pi* (π) than had been achieved since the value had first been established in classical times. This innovation arrived in Europe by way of Constantinople, where a Greek translation of al-Kashi's work appeared in the fifteenth century.

REGIONAL DEFINITION IN RESPONSE TO THE MONGOLS

Cities and rural areas in the Middle East and elsewhere experienced different fates under Mongol rule. Safe, reliable overland trade throughout Eurasia stimulated many of the commercial cities of Iran and Iraq. But the countryside, subjected to extensive damage in the conquest, sporadically continuing violence, and crushing taxes, suffered terribly. Although from the time of Ghazan the Il-khans moved away from maximum extraction from the rural sector toward a more constructive and protective policy, the change came too late to stop the decline in population and deterioration of agriculture.

In the cultural area, the Il-khans and Timurids favored Persian as a written language, particularly for poetry, epic writing, and songs. Similarly, both showed a strong interest in popular religious practices, especially the mystical form of Islam known as Sufism°.

Ghiyas al-Din Jamshid al-Kashi (gee-YASS ad-DIN jamsheed al-KAH-shee) **Sufism** (SOO-fiz-uhm)

Russia and Rule from Afar

Kievan Russia first encountered the Mongols in 1223 when the latter defeated a combined Russian and Kipchak (a Turkic people) army in southeastern Russia. An onslaught led by Batu followed in the late 1230s, culminating in the Mongol capture and pillage of the town of Riazan°. Unlike others who invaded Russia before and after, the Mongols campaigned effectively in the winter, though their cavalry found the springtime mud difficult to manage. The Russian princes failed to unite against the invaders, and in 1240 the central town of Kiev° fell. The princes of Hungary acknowledged Batu's supremacy shortly afterward, and the entire region came under Mongol domination.

The Golden Horde established by Batu and his descendants consisted of a collection of small khanates, many of which survived when others died out at the end of the 1300s. The White Horde, for instance, ruled much of southeastern Russia until the 1480s, and the khan of Crimea succumbed to Russian invasion only in 1783.

The Mongols generally placed their capitals at the ends of caravan routes, but in Russia only the region at the mouth of the Volga River could be connected to this network. Thus, the Mongols of the Golden Horde settled well to the south and west of their Russian domains, first at (Old) Sarai just north of the Caspian Sea (see Map 11.1). As part of their rule-from-afar, the Mongols granted great privileges to the Orthodox Church, which then helped to reconcile the Russian people to their distant Mongol masters. Old Church Slavonic, an ecclesiastical language, revived; but Russian became the dominant written language of Russia. Russian scholars shunned the Greek language even though the Golden Horde permitted renewed contacts with Constantinople. The Golden Horde enlisted Russian princes to act as their agents (primarily as tax collectors and census takers) and frequently as ambassadors to the court of the Great Khans at Karakorum in Mongolia.

Extraction of wealth became the Mongols' primary concern in Russia, as in their other domains.

Riazan (ree-AH-zahn) **Kiev** (kee-yef)

The flow of silver and gold into Mongol hands starved the local economy of currency. Like the Il-khans, the khans of the Golden Horde attempted to introduce paper money as a response to the currency shortage. This left such a vivid memory that the Russian word for money (*denga*°) comes from the Mongolian word for the stamp (*tamga*°) used to create paper currency.

Alexander Nevskii° (ca. 1220–1263), the prince of Novgorod, aided in the Mongol conquest by persuading many of the Russian princes that it would be better to submit than to resist them. In return, the Mongols favored both Novgorod (under Alexander's rule) and the emerging town of Moscow (under the rule of Alexander's brother Daniel). These towns eclipsed devastated Kiev as political, cultural, and economic centers. This, in turn, encouraged people to move northward, away from the Mongol pasture lands in the southwest, and led to the opening of new agricultural land far north of the Caspian Sea. During the 1300s, Moscow emerged as the new center of Russia, and control of Moscow became equivalent to control of the entire country (see Map 11.2).

Russia preserved reminders of the Mongol presence for many years. Some regions of southern Russia, particularly Crimea, remained breeding grounds for the bubonic plague. In the late Kievan period (1000–1230), Ukraine° had been a fertile and well-populated region. Under the Mongols, Ukraine suffered a severe loss of population. The Mongols crossed the region repeatedly in their campaigns against eastern Europe and raided it continually to punish villages that were slow to pay their taxes.

Historians debate the effect of Mongol domination on the shaping of Russia. For some, the pillaging of Riazan, like the capture of Balkh, typified the Mongol conquests, which effectively isolated Russia and parts of eastern Europe from developments in early modern Europe. These historians refer to the "Mongol yoke" and hypothesize a sluggish economy and a dormant culture under the Mongols.

Other historians point out that decline had

Transformation of the Kremlin   Like many peoples of northern medieval Europe, the Russians of the Kievan period built in wood. But the fortification of important political centers, which were vulnerable to assault, called for stone. In the 1300s, the city of Moscow emerged as a leading political center, and its old palace, the Kremlin, was gradually transformed from a wooden to a stone structure. This contemporary drawing illustrates this process. (Novosti)

struck the Kievan economy before the Mongols arrived and that the Kievan princes had already ceased to mint money. In addition, although the Mongols made heavy demands and their internationally oriented monetary measures did not always work, the Russian territories regularly paid their taxes in silver. These tax payments suggest regular surpluses in income and an economy capable of regular conversion of goods to cash. Increases in the tax burden stemmed not from the Mongols but from their tax collectors, Russian princes who often exempted their own lands and shifted the additional burden to the peasants.

denga (DENG-ah)   *tamga* (TAHM-gah)
Nevskii (nih-EFF-skee)   **Ukraine** (you-CRANE)

Historians who are skeptical of the hypothesized cultural isolation of Russia, point out that before the Mongol invasion, Russia labored under Byzantine domination. The Orthodox Church, which did not encourage relations of any sort with western Europe, would have isolated Russia from outside influences with or without the influence of the Mongols.

It does not appear that the Mongols destroyed the traditional forms of elite participation in government or significantly changed the structure of local government. At the regional level, the princely families continued to battle among themselves for dominance. The Mongols merely added a new player to those struggles.

Ivan° III, the prince of Moscow (r. 1462–1505), established himself as an autocratic ruler in the late 1400s. Before Ivan, the title **tsar** (from "caesar") applied only to the foreign rulers (whether the emperors of Byzantium or the Turkic khans of the steppe) who dominated the disunited Russian principalities. After throwing off Mongol dominion in 1480, Russian leaders adopted the title *tsar* to show that Russia should be ruled by Russians and not from afar.

While in Russia, the Mongols ended the dominance of Kiev and encouraged the rise of Moscow. In the Middle East, the Mongols ended the political and cultural dominance of Baghdad and encouraged the emergence of new centers of power and commerce. Like the Mongols who first occupied Iran, the Mongols in Russia had little interest in the dominant religious system. The distance between the Mongols and the Russian people prevented the Mongols from attempting to become patrons of the local religion. Not only did the Russian Orthodox religious hierarchy survive, but the Russian Orthodox Church developed a strong association with Russian identity and aspirations to independence. Also, in Russia as elsewhere, Mongol domination encouraged centralization. In its aftermath, Russia's strongest leaders and its most centralized political system emerged.

Social Change and Centralization in Europe and Anatolia

Parallel to the division of the western part of the Mongol Empire between the Golden Horde and the Il-khans, a cleavage between the political forces of the papacy and those of Frederick II of the Hohenstaufen family, who was the Holy Roman Emperor and hereditary ruler of the German territories, buffeted Europe at the same time. Raised in Sicily, Frederick (r. 1212–1250) appreciated Muslim culture. When the pope threatened him with excommunication unless he participated in the Crusades in Palestine and Syria, Frederick conspired with the Mamluk rulers of Egypt and Syria to present the illusion of retaking Jerusalem.

The conflict between pope and emperor left the kingdoms of eastern Europe, particularly Hungary and Poland, to deal with the onslaught of the Golden Horde on their own. Many eastern European princes capitulated and went to (Old) Sarai to declare themselves slaves of Batu. The Teutonic° Knights, however, resisted.

Like the Knights Templar in the Middle East (see Chapter 7), the Teutonic Knights had a crusading goal: to Christianize the Slavic and Kipchak populations of northern Europe, whose territories they colonized with thousands of German-speaking settlers. Alexander Nevskii, the prince of Novgorod, led the Mongol campaigns against the Teutonic Knights and their Finnish allies, who in 1242 lost so many of their number through the ice at Lake Chud (see Map 11.2) that their power broke and the northern Crusades virtually ceased.

Alexander Nevskii's role in this campaign makes it clear that the "Mongol" armies the Europeans encountered were barely Mongol at all. Mongols held most command positions; one of them—Sübüdei, who was Batu's chief general in western Eurasia—is considered by historians a military genius. But Mongol recruitment and conscription created an international force of Mongols, Turks, Chinese, Iranians, Europeans, and at least one Englishman, who went to the Middle East a crusader but ended up joining the Mongols and serving in their campaigns in Hungary.

Ivan (ee-VAHN)

Teutonic (two-TOHN-ik)

When the Danube River froze in 1241, Sübüdei's troops rode across it and inflicted a series of defeats on the eastern European kingdoms. Mongols appeared at the outskirts of Vienna and at the foot of the Alps, apparently menacing northern Italy and possibly Venice. Poles, Hungarians, Austrians, and Bohemians struggled frantically to mount some resistance while the rest of Europe panicked.

Rumors and fanciful histories described the Mongols as cannibalistic with bodies that were part dog. Some theorized that they came from Hell or from the caves where Alexander the Great confined the monsters of antiquity. People in Germany believed them to be the lost tribes of Israel, a rumor that led to lynchings of Jews in the eastern German territories for being in secret alliance with the invaders. Recently Christianized Kipchaks in Hungary suffered as well under accusations of aiding the Mongols. The king of France resigned himself to defeat, accepting it as God's will, while the pope, despite his unhappiness with Frederick II, authorized a crusade against the Mongols and added to the daily liturgy a line begging God for deliverance.

Suddenly the prayers seemed answered. Before the Europeans could mount a united force to repel the Mongols, Sübüdei's forces withdrew in December 1241. The Great Khan Ögödei had died, and the Mongol princes returned to Mongolia to participate in the election of a new Great Khan.

Several European leaders responded to the retreat by sending peaceful emissaries to the Il-khan in Iran, hoping through him to reach the Great Khan in Mongolia. The Mongol rulers received merchants and craftsmen favorably, but they welcomed ambassadors from kings or from the Vatican only if they brought messages of submission from their lords (see Society and Culture: Dueling Pieties).

European embassies to the Golden Horde and to the Great Khan in Mongolia proliferated. As Europeans learned the Mongol trade routes and the internal structure of Mongol rule, their terror gave way to awe of, and eventual idealization of, their wealth and power. The Europeans gained for the first time a systematic knowledge of Eurasian geography, cultural patterns, natural resources,

and commerce. They learned about diplomatic passports, coal and how to mine it, movable type, high-temperature metallurgy, efficient enumeration and higher mathematics, gunpowder, and, in the fourteenth century, the casting and use of bronze cannon. Nevertheless, the terror created by the Mongol invasions, combined with other factors, such as the outbreak of bubonic plague in the late 1340s (see Chapter 14), ignited a storm of religious questioning and anxiety, especially in the most imperiled regions of eastern and Central Europe.

In the fourteenth century, several regions, most notably Lithuania° (see Map 11.2) , escaped the Mongol grip. In the mid-thirteenth century, just as Russia fell to the Mongols and eastern Europe was first invaded, Lithuania had experienced an unprecedented centralization and military strengthening. Like Alexander Nevskii, the Lithuanian leaders struck a deal with the Mongols to maintain their independence. In the late 1300s, Lithuania capitalized on its privileged position to dominate its neighbors, particularly Poland, and ended all hopes of the Teutonic Knights regaining power.

In the Balkans, independent and well-organized kingdoms separated themselves from the chaos of the Byzantine Empire and thrived until the Turkic Ottomans conquered them in the 1500s and 1600s. In the history of the Mongol period, Eastern Europe, the Balkans, and Anatolia (then under the control of the Byzantine Empire) experienced parallel developments under the shadow of Mongol dominion.

Communications between the Il-khans and Constantinople gave Europe a second doorway (Spain provided the first) to the scientific and philosophical achievements of Islamic culture. Because direct Il-khan conquests did not extend into Anatolia, the Byzantine Empire survived, and Anatolia became a haven for Turkic groups pushed eastward by the Mongols.

The ancestors of the **Ottomans** had come to Anatolia in the same wave of Turkic migrations

---

Lithuania (lith-oo-WAY-nee-ah)

SOCIETY & CULTURE

Dueling Pieties

Written communication between Europe and the Mongols survives as a result of a complex process. Europeans wrote to the Mongols in Latin, which was normally translated into Persian when the parties reached the Il-khan territories. On route to the Mongol capital at Karakorum, a means had to be found to translate the Persian into Mongolian. Translation could be done orally if the ambassadors received an audience with the Great Khan or his representatives. For messages going from east to west, the process was reversed.

The messages were not complicated, but each side found the other's ideas so bizarre that they suspected mistakes in translation. This passage in a letter from Pope Innocent IV to the Great Khan in 1245 is typical. (Innocent did not know that there was no one to receive the letter, for Ögödei had died in 1241 and Güyük had not yet been installed as the next Great Khan.)

It is not without cause that we are driven to express in strong terms our amazement that you, according to what we have heard, have invaded many countries belonging both to Christians and to others and are laying them waste in a horrible desolation, and with a fury still unabated you do not cease from breaking the bond of natural ties, sparing neither sex nor age, you rage against all indiscriminately with the sword of chastisement.

Like popes before and after him, Innocent explained that he was sending monks to convert the Great Khan to Christianity, to baptize him, and to make him not a waster of the Christian lands but their protector. Group after group of Christian missionaries tried to convert the Mongols; all were disappointed.

When Güyük became Great Khan in 1246, he answered Innocent's letter. He expressed befuddlement at the idea that he should be chastised for

---

as the Seljuks (see Chapter 7). The Il-khans' quarrels with the Golden Horde enabled the Ottomans to maintain their independence. By 1400, strengthened by Muslim warriors who desired to fight on the frontier against the Christians, the Ottomans had come into direct conflict with the Byzantines. After building a territorial base in the Balkans, in 1453, the Ottomans conquered Constantinople and killed the last of the Byzantine emperors. This stunned Christians of eastern Europe and Russia, who for centuries yearned to regain Constantinople, now popularly called Istanbul, for Christendom.

Stabilization of Mamluk Rule in Egypt

The **Mamluks°** (see Chapter 7) provide the best example of a government that became stronger and more centralized through its resistance to the Mongol advance, most notably its defeat of a Mongol army in 1260. The Mamluks retained control of their base in Egypt and their lands in Syria (see Map 11.2). This same strength manifested itself later in the defeat and destruction of the Crusader kingdoms and the ruthless suppression of the violent Assassin sect in northern Syria. Religiously legit-

---

Mamluk (MAM-look)

invading Christian lands and at the suggestion that he himself should be baptized. Güyük questioned Innocent's arrogance in presuming to know God's intentions:

Though you also say that I should become a trembling Christian, worship God, and be an ascetic, how do you know whom God absolves, or in truth to whom He shows mercy? How do you know that such words as you speak are with God's approval? From the rising of the sun to its setting, all the lands have been made subject to me. Who could do this contrary to the command of God?

The Great Khans shared the traditional Central Asian belief that Heaven shows its will in the unfolding of history, that victors are necessarily the messengers of Heaven's will, and that the supreme victor is the supreme messenger. As often as the popes warned the Great Khans to be baptized and submit to the guidance of Rome, the Great Khans responded with the simple message that they were not about to submit to the church and that all Europe had best submit to the Great Khans—or suffer the consequences.

Güyük sternly closed his letter to Innocent:

If you do not observe God's command, and if you ignore my command, I shall know you as my enemy. Likewise I shall make you understand. If you do otherwise, God knows what I know.

In 1254, the Great Khan Möngke (MERNG-keh), the last to rule the united Mongol Empire in Eurasia, used similarly ringing rhetoric on Louis IX of France:

If, when you hear and understand the decree of the eternal God, you are still unwilling to pay attention and believe it, saying "Our country is far away, our mountains are mighty, our sea is vast," and in this confidence you bring an army against us—we know what we can do: He who made what was difficult easy and what was far away near, the eternal God, He knows.

What did the popes regard as the primary evidence that the Mongols were evil? What did the Mongols see as the basic test of their supreme righteousness?

Source: Adapted from Christopher Dawson, ed., *Mission to Asia*, Medieval Academy Reprints for Teaching Series (Toronto: University of Toronto Press, 1981), 75, 85–86, 204. Archaic language has been amended to make the quotations more readable.

---

imized by a puppet Abbasid caliph in Cairo, the Mamluks became the bulwark of Sunni Islam in the Middle East.

The Mamluks, who ruled until their conquest by the Ottomans in 1517 and continued to be a dominant elite in Egypt until the end of the eighteenth century, had a cosmopolitan and practical outlook. They enjoyed friendly relations with the Hohenstaufen family and sent the Syrian diarist and judge Jamal al-Din Muhammad ibn Salim° as ambassador to Frederick II's son Manfred in Italy. Links with the Golden Horde, established during the conflict with the Il-khans, kept a steady stream of people and goods moving by ship between Cairo and the port of Kaffa in Crimea.

From the late 1300s to the very end of the 1700s, the Mamluks and their successors continued to import soldiers from Crimea, and, with them, the plague. At the height of the fourteenth-century plague pandemic, around 1350, Egypt may have lost a third of its population. The plague spread swiftly through the coastal towns of Lebanon, Palestine, and Syria, but the epidemic there quickly subsided. Egypt, however, suffered repeated reinfection into the modern period.

---

ibn Salim (ee-bin sah-LEEM)

CONCLUSION

Basic features of nomadic society afforded the Mongols the military capabilities and the organizational habits to begin their conquests in Central Asia. They were ready to adopt any useful technologies and to incorporate men from anywhere into their forces. The decentralized structure of the Mongol Empire facilitated even more innovation, because the regional khans felt free to forge their own relationships with local elites, cultures, and economies.

The Il-khans' involvement in Iranian society eventually led them to convert to Islam. In Russia, however, the Mongols remained aloof from Russian society, both physically and politically, and never developed an interest in or identification with the local culture. These seemingly opposite results of Mongol rule actually reflect a common policy of allowing local populations to continue their traditional religious practices.

The Mongols also fostered the development of local languages by weakening traditional elites. During the Il-khan period, Persian gained preeminence as a literary language in Iran. Russian similarly emerged as a literary language in Russia. Both had previously taken second place to foreign, classical languages, Arabic in Iran and Greek in Russia. The effects of the bubonic plague in Europe paralleled the effects of Mongol domination in Iran and Russia. Traditional elites weakened, and Latin lost ground to local vernacular languages.

Comparison of the experiences of the Mongol domains to the Mongol peripheries helps to explain the full impact of the Mongol conquests. The directly controlled domains frequently gained local definition and cultural coherence under the Mongols, and many sectors of the economy benefited from their participation in the Eurasian trade system. But in general, their century or so of subjugation left them drained of wealth, and sometimes demographically depressed, and deprived them of the technological stimulation they might have gained had the Mongols not imposed on them nearly a century of peace.

The peripheries, in contrast, frequently integrated themselves with the Mongol trade networks and enjoyed a flow of information, experience, and often wealth (as in the cases of Genoa and Venice) that aided in their growth. Under military pressure from the Mongols, they often tightened and strengthened their leadership (as in the cases of Lithuania and the Mamluks), or they explored new working alliances (as between the Mamluks and the Holy Roman Emperor).

■ Key Terms

Mongols	tax farming
Genghis Khan	Timur
steppes	Ibn Khaldun
nomadism	Nasir al-Din Tusi
bubonic plague	Alexander Nevskii
Il-khan	tsar
Golden Horde	Ottomans
Rashid al-Din	Mamluks

■ Suggested Reading

For an accessible introduction, see David Morgan's *The Mongols* (1986). A more specialized study is Thomas T. Allsen, *Mongol Imperialism: The Policies of the Grand Qan Möngke in China, Russia, and the Islamic Lands, 1251–1259* (1987). René Grousset's classic *The Empire of the Steppes: A History of Central Asia* (1970; reprint, 1988) remains useful. Sechin Jagchid and Paul Hyer, *Mongolia's Culture and Society* (1979), and Larry Moses and Stephen A. Halkovic, Jr., *Introduction to Mongolian History and Culture* (1985), link early and modern Mongol history and culture. Tim Severin's *In Search of Chinggis Khan* (1992) retraces Genghis's paths of conquest. William H. McNeill's *Plagues and Peoples* (1976) outlines the demographic effects of the Mongol conquests, while Joel Mokyr discusses the technological effects in *The Lever of Riches: Technological Creativity and Economic Progress* (1990). For a thesis of global development connecting commercial development in Europe to the Eurasian trade routes of the Mongol era, see Janet L. Abu-Lughod, *Before European Hegemony: The World System A.D. 1250–1350* (1989).

S. A. M. Adshead, *Central Asia in World History* (1993) provides an overview of the history of Central Asia when it first came under the rule of the Jagadai Khanate. For a recent scholarly study of Timur, see Beatrice Manz, *The Rise and Rule of Tamerlane* (1989).

The only "primary" document relating to Genghis Khan, *Secret History of the Mongols,* has been reconstructed in Mongolian from Chinese script and made available in scholarly editions by Igor de Rachewilz and Francis Woodman Cleaves, among others. Paul Kahn produced a readable prose English paraphrase of the work in 1984. For a version by a modern Mongol author, see *The History and the Life of Chinggis Khan: The Secret History of the Mongols, Translated and Annotated by Urgunge Onon* (1990). Recent good biographies of Genghis Khan include Leo de Hartog, *Genghis Khan, Conqueror of the World* (1989); Michel Hoang, *Genghis Khan,* trans. Ingrid Canfield (1991); and Paul Ratchnevsky, *Genghis Khan: His Life and Legacy,* trans. and ed. Thomas Nivison Haining (1992).

The best single single-volume work on the Mongols in Russia is Charles Halperin, *Russia and the Golden Horde: The Mongol Impact on Medieval Russian History* (1987). For more detail, see John Lister Illingworth Fennell, *The Crisis of Medieval Russia, 1200–1304* (1983), and Devin DeWeese, *Islamization and Native Religion in the Golden Horde* (1994).

David Morgan, cited above, covers the Il-khans best in the relevant chapters of his *The Mongols* (1986). Among the works of the great Il-khan historians are 'Ala al-Din 'Ata Malek Joveyni, *The History of the World-Conqueror,* translated by John Andrew Boyle (1958); a small portion of Rashid al-Din's work is translated by David Talbot Rice, *The Illustrations to the World History of Rashid al-Din,* edited by Basil Gray (1976); and *The Successors of Genghis Khan,* translated by John Andrew Boyle (1971). For the account of an important traveler, see C. Defremery and B. R. Sanguinetti, eds., *The Travels of Ibn Battuta, A.D. 1325–1354,* translated by H. A. R. Gibb (1994), and Ross E. Dunn, *The Adventures of Ibn Battuta, a Muslim Traveler of the 14th Century* (1986).

James Chambers, *The Devil's Horsemen: The Mongol Invasion of Europe* (1979), provides a lively narration. Travelers from Europe to the Mongol courts whose accounts are available include Marco Polo, and the Franciscan friars John of Plano Carpini and William of Rubruck. Christopher Dawson, ed., *Mission to Asia* (1955; reprint, 1981), compiles such accounts, but see also Frances Wood, *Did Marco Polo Really Go to China?* (1995). Morris Rossabi, *Visitor from Xanadu* (1992), relates the travels in Europe of Rabban Sauma, a Christian Turk.

◼ Note

1. Quotation adapted from Desmond Martin, *Chingis Khan and His Conquest of North China* (Baltimore: The Johns Hopkins University Press, 1950), 303.

12

EASTERN EURASIA,
1200–1500

Mongol Domination in Eastern Eurasia, 1200–1368 • The Early
Ming Empire, 1368–1500 • Centralization and Militarism in
East Asia, 1200–1500
ENVIRONMENT AND TECHNOLOGY: From Gunpowder to Guns

After the Mongols conquered northern China in the 1230s, Great Khan Ögödei° told his newly recruited Confucian adviser, Yelu Chucai°, that he planned to turn the heavily populated North China Plain into a pasture for livestock. Yelu reacted calmly but argued that taxing the existing cities and villages would bring greater wealth. The Great Khan decided on the gentler approach, though he chose the oppressive tax farming system already in use in the Il-khan Empire rather than the fixed-rate method traditional to China.

The Chinese suffered under this system during the early years, but rule by the Mongols also brought benefits. They secured routes of transport and communication, and they forced the exchange of experts and advisers between east-ern and western Eurasia. Information, ideas, and skills spread as a result.

Different regions experienced Mongol domination differently. China and in some ways Korea gained new unity and definition but suffered great losses of agricultural wealth and population. Japan and northern Vietnam (then called Annam) shared—in very different ways—the complex effects of being at the margins of the Mongol Empire. Song° China and Korea resisted the Mongols for decades; Japan and northern Vietnam weathered attacks but remained unconquered. Warfare engulfed eastern Asia through nearly the entire thirteenth century, a far longer period than in the west.

The military technologies that the Mongols appropriated, refined, and carried westward—

Ögödei (ERG-uh-day)   Yelu Chucai (yay-loo CHOO-tsye)   Song (soong)

gunpowder, metal casting, and the building of wagons and bridges—helped foster large-scale trade in iron ore, sulfur, coal, and copper in eastern Eurasia. China and Korea benefited from such technological developments, though their societies struggled for decades to recover from the social impact of the Mongol century.

As you read this chapter, ask yourself the following questions:

- How did Mongol rule affect Chinese government, economy, and culture?
- What stimulated economic growth in the early Ming period?
- What impact did the Mongol period have on state formation in Korea, Japan, and Vietnam?

MONGOL DOMINATION IN EASTERN EURASIA, 1200–1368

The Mongol conquest of southern China in 1279 ended the prolonged struggle of the Southern Song Empire (1127–1279) against northern invaders—a struggle that had produced a new centralization of government and many technological advances. After destroying the Tanggut and Jin Empires in northern China, Genghis's grandson Khubilai° established a new empire based in China, the Yuan°. Integrating Korea into his empire and maintaining close relations with the Il-khans, Khubilai created a system that allowed technologies improved in the Song period to spread throughout Eurasia, while technologies and sciences of the Islamic world became more accessible in China than at any other time since the Tang° Empire (618–906).

The Mongol Conquests, 1206–1279

Nine years after Temüjin° became Genghis Khan, supreme leader of the Mongols, he led the attack on the Jin capital at Beijing°. The first Mongol invasions of Russia and the Middle East (see Chapter 11) coincided with the extensive campaigns against the Tanggut and Jin Empires in the early 1220s. Genghis died in 1227, but the conquest of China continued under his son Ögödei. By 1234, the Mongols controlled most of northern China and were threatening the Southern Song.

Although the Mongols initially launched their campaigns to convince the rulers to render tribute, Ögödei desired to rule territories. He established his imperial capital at Karakorum°. Between 1240 and 1260, it attracted merchants, ambassadors, missionaries, and adventurers from all over Eurasia. The European missionary Giovanni di Piano Carpini (John of Plano Carpini), who visited in 1246, found it isolated but well populated and cosmopolitan.

The Mongol Empire remained united until about 1265. During that period, the Great Khan in Mongolia, chosen in gatherings of Mongol aristocrats that took years to conclude, exercised authority over the khans of the Golden Horde, the khans of the Jagadai domains in Central Asia, and the Il-khans in the Middle East. The widow of the deceased Great Khan sometimes governed during the deliberations. After Ögödei's death in 1241, the Mongol Empire began to disintegrate. When Khubilai declared himself Great Khan in 1265, the descendants of Jagadai and other lineages refused to accept him. The ensuing fighting destroyed Karakorum, so Khubilai created a new capital at what is now **Beijing.** In 1271, he declared himself founder of the **Yuan Empire.**

Jagadai's descendants continued to dominate Central Asia, where they nursed a hatred of Khubilai and the Yuan Empire. The political prestige of the Jagadai Khanate and the ability of the Jagadai Mongols to defend themselves prevented Yuan absorption of Central Asia. Jagadai independence

---

Khubilai (KOO-bih-lie)   **Yuan** (yu-wenn)   **Tang** (tahng)

Temüjin (TEM-uh-jin)   **Beijing** (bay-JING)
Karakorum (kah-rah-KOR-um)

also contributed to the strengthening of Central Asian ties to Islam and to Turkic language and culture. The rise of Timur (r. 1370–1405) in the later fourteenth century (Timur's empire is described in Chapter 11) depended on these Islamic and Turkic links, and the enmity between the Jagadai khans and the Yuan Empire may have inspired his unfulfilled wish to conquer China.

After the Yuan Empire destroyed the Southern Song in 1279, Mongol troops crossed south of the Red River and attacked Annam (now northern Vietnam). They occupied Hanoi three times and then withdrew after arranging for the payment of tribute. In 1283, Kubilai's forces invaded Champa in what is now southern Vietnam and made it a tribute nation as well. Ten years later, a combined Mongol, Uigur, and Chinese force, numbering perhaps 40,000, set out for Java from China's southeast coast, but an internal dispute and squandered resources kept them from conquering the island. In Southeast Asia, as in eastern Europe, Mongol war techniques reached their limit.

Drawing a lesson from contacts with Islamic and Christian hierarchies in the Middle East and Russia, the Mongols cultivated religious leaders in eastern Eurasia. In China, Buddhist and Daoist leaders visited the Great Khan and came away believing that they had all but convinced him to accept their beliefs. But only the religious leaders of Tibet succeeded in gaining influence over the Mongol rulers. The Tibetan idea of a militant universal ruler, bringing the whole world under control of the Buddha and thus pushing it nearer to salvation, agreed with the ancient idea of universal rulership in Central Asia.

The Great Khan personally oversaw the governance of Tibet and reinforced the dominance of Lamaism, a Tibetan variant of Buddhism. A **lama**° taught special techniques for contacting the deities. Tibetan Buddhism became increasingly familiar to Mongol nobles during the 1200s and 1300s.

The Yuan Empire, 1279–1368

Khubilai Khan appreciated the Chinese traditions of imperial rule. He gave his oldest son a Chinese name and had Confucianists participate in the boy's education. In public announcements and the crafting of laws, he took Confucian conventions into consideration. Beijing, his capital after 1265, occupied a critical spot on the overland trade routes of the Mongol world: the eastern terminus of the caravan routes that began near Tabriz, the Ilkhan capital, and Sarai, the Golden Horde capital. An imperial horseback courier system, utilizing hundreds of stations and protected trails, maintained close communications.

Called Great Capital (Dadu) or City of the Khan (*khan-balikh*°, Marco Polo's "Cambaluc"), Khubilai's capital featured massive mud walls of rammed earth, a tiny portion of which can still be seen. Khubilai's engineers widened the streets and developed linked lakes and artificial islands at the city's northwest edge to form a closed imperial complex. As a summer retreat, Khubilai maintained the palace and parks at Shangdu°, now in Inner Mongolia. This was "Xanadu°" celebrated by the English poet Samuel Taylor Coleridge; its "stately pleasure dome" was the hunting preserve where Khubilai and his courtiers practiced riding and shooting.

"China" as we think of it today did not exist before the Mongols. The Tanggut and Jin Empires controlled the north. The Southern Song ruled south of the Yellow River. The state of Nanzhao occupied part of the southwest. These states had different languages, writing systems, forms of government, and elite cultures. The Great Khans destroyed all these regional regimes and encouraged the restoration or preservation of many features of Chinese government and society, thereby reuniting China in a permanent fashion.

The Mongols also introduced their own practices and large numbers of immigrant professionals. As in the Middle East, they concentrated on counting the population and collecting taxes. In the early period, tax farming in the Middle Eastern

---

lama (LAH-mah)

khan-balikh (kahn-BAL-ik)   **Shangdu** (shahng-DOO)
Xanadu (ZAH-nah-doo)

CHRONOLOGY

	Central Asia and Mongolia	China and Southeast Asia	Korea and Japan
1200	**1206** Temüjin chosen Genghis Khan of the Mongols **1227** Death of Genghis Khan **1265** Khubilai becomes last Great Khan; destruction of Karakorum	**1234** Mongols conquer northern China **1271** Founding of Yuan Empire **1279** Mongol conquest of Southern Song **1283** Yuan invades Annam **1293** Yuan attacks Java	**1258** Mongols conquer Koryo rulers in Korea **1274, 1281** Mongols attack Japan
1300		**1368** Ming Empire founded	**1333–1338** End of Kamakura Shogunate in Japan, beginning of Ashikaga
1400	**1405** Death of Timur	**1403–1424** Reign of Yongle **1405–1433** Voyages of Zheng He **1449** Mongol attack on Beijing **1471–1500** Annam conquers Champa	**1392** Founding of Yi kingdom in Korea

style replaced direct taxation. Persian, Arab, Uigur, and Turkic administrators came to China to staff the offices of taxation and finance. The Yuan appointed Muslim scholars to the offices of calendar making and astronomy.

By law, Mongols had the highest social ranking. Below them came Central Asians and Middle Easterners, northern Chinese, and finally southern Chinese. This apparent racial ranking also reflected a hierarchy of functions, the Mongols being the empire's warriors, the Central Asians and Middle Easterners its census takers, tax collectors, and calendar managers. The northern Chinese had come under Mongol control almost two generations before the southern Chinese and thus outranked them. The southern Chinese, the last to be conquered, had the strongest attachment to Confucian principles.

Despite Khubilai's attempts to include "Confucians" (now a formal and hereditary status) in government, their comparatively low status and philosophical objections to the conquest helped weaken their position in comparison with pre-Mongol times. The Confucians criticized the elevation of merchants; the Yuan gave privileges to merchants—mostly from Central Asia, the Middle East, or northern China. The Confucians regarded doctors as at best technicians and at worst heretical practitioners of Daoist mysticism; the Yuan encouraged medicine and began the long process of integrating Chinese medical and herbal knowledge with other Eurasian practices.

For purposes of census taking and administration, the Mongols organized China into provinces and put these larger units under provincial governors, tax collectors, and garrison commanders.

The creation of the provinces—a strong assertion of Mongol ownership—marked a radical change and increased central control.

The impact of Mongol rule on the economy is difficult to assess because the scarce contemporary records and the hostility of later Chinese writers obscure economic matters. Nevertheless, many cities seem to have prospered: in north China by being on the caravan routes; in the interior by being on the Grand Canal, which with reunification fulfilled its original purpose of revitalizing trade between north and south China; and along the coast through maritime grain shipments from south China. The reintegration of East Asia (though not Japan) with the overland Eurasian trade further stimulated the urban economies.

The privileges and prestige that merchants enjoyed changed urban life and the economy of China. The old Chinese elites competed for a limited number of government posts, so the great families who had previously spent their fortunes on educating sons for government service needed other outlets. Many gentry families chose commerce, despite their sense of a loss of prestige.

Corporations—groups of individual investors who behaved as single commercial and legal units and shared the risk of doing business—handled most commercial activities, from the financing of caravans, to tax farming, to lending money to the Mongol aristocracy. They developed from caravan-financing groups in Central Asia and the Middle East. Central Asians and Middle Easterners headed most corporations in the early Yuan period, but Chinese bought shares, so most corporations soon had mixed membership, or even complete Chinese ownership.

Credit became a great issue, partly because Mongol conquests damaged the agricultural base from which taxes were drawn and partly because the Mongol aristocracy absorbed more wealth than it generated. The imperial government issued paper money, as had earlier Chinese governments on a smaller scale, to address its economic shortages; but the massive quantity of unsecured notes they issued failed to earn the people's trust.

The improved stability of copper coins partially offset the failure of the paper currency. During the Song, exports of copper coins to Japan had caused a severe coin shortage in China. The short-age raised the coins' value and distorted the ratio of copper to silver. By cutting off trade with Japan, the Mongols unintentionally stabilized the value of copper coins.

The financial and commercial life of Yuan China inspired the gentry to move to cities from their traditional homes in the countryside. Cities began to cater to the tastes of merchants instead of the traditional scholars. Specialized shops selling clothing, grape wine, furniture, and properly butchered meats (reflecting customers' religious convictions) became common. Teahouses thrived, particularly those featuring sing-song girls, drum singers, operas, and other arts previously considered coarse. The rise of literature written in the style of everyday speech and the increasing influence of the northern, Mongolian-influenced Chinese language that in the West is often called Mandarin resulted in lasting linguistic change.

In the countryside, where 90 percent of the people lived, **cottage industries** linked to the urban economies continued to advance. The cultivation of mulberry trees and cotton and the construction of dams, water wheels, and irrigation systems—the Mongols favored Middle Eastern irrigation techniques—became common features of village technology. Important treatises on planting, harvesting, threshing, and butchering were published. Villagers continued to worship as local gods technological innovators such as Huang Dao Po°, who in the Yuan period brought her special knowledge of cotton growing, spinning, and weaving from her native Hainan Island to the fertile Yangzi Delta.

Overall, however, farmers and other rural villagers did poorly during the Yuan period. After the initial conquests, the Mongol princes evicted many farmers and subjected the rest to the brutality of the tax farmers, their agents, and their enforcers. By the end of the 1200s, the Mongol government in China, as in Iran, lightened these burdens and moved to protect and encourage farmers, but the change came too late. Servitude or homelessness had overtaken many farmers, and flooding, particularly of the Yellow River, reached disastrous levels because of neglect of dams and dikes.

Rural hardship had a demographic impact. If

Huang Dao Po (hwahng DOW poh)

Song records before the Mongol conquest and the Ming census taken after their overthrow are reliable (each may exaggerate in one direction or another), China may have lost as much as 40 percent of its population in the eighty years of Mongol rule. Many localities in northern China may have lost as much as five-sixths of their populations.

Privations in the countryside, possibly exacerbated by the traditional practice of female infanticide, were not the sole cause. The continuous warfare of the 1220s, resulting from effective resistance by the Southern Song, constituted another, and the massive, continuous southward movement of people fleeing the Mongols and the Yellow River flooding was a third. The last might explain why losses in the north exceeded those in the south and why the population along the Yangzi River markedly increased.

The bubonic plague and its attendant diseases, spread by the constant population movements, may have had a greater impact. The Mongol opening of Yunnan° to a government based in China exposed the lowlands to plague (see Map 12.1). Cities managed these outbreaks better than rural areas did as the epidemic moved from south to north in the 1300s.

Scientific Exchange

Khubilai in China kept in constant contact with his brother Hülegü° in Iran, as did their primary advisers. The two empires shared similar economic and financial policies, as well as a devotion to engineering, astronomy, and mathematics. Il-khan science and technology reached China and Korea. Muslims from the Middle East oversaw most of the weapons manufacture and engineering projects for Khubilai's armies.

From China, the Il-khans imported scholars and texts that helped them understand Chinese technological advances. These included the use of sighting tubes for isolating astronomical objects, stabilized on sling-shot-shaped equatorial mounts; mechanically driven armillary spheres; and new techniques for measuring the movement of the moon. Khubilai commissioned a team of Iranians

to come to Beijing to construct an observatory and an institute for astronomical studies similar to the Il-khans' facility at Maragha. For the remainder of the imperial period in China, maintaining and staffing the observatory became a state responsibility.

In mathematics, the Yuan Empire promoted an integration of Chinese skills with new ideas from the Middle East. The Chinese had contributed the concept of fractions to Middle Eastern mathematics, and Middle Easterners brought the latest developments in algebra and trigonometry. Chinese mathematicians were encouraged to develop and publish their treatises.

Muslim doctors and Persian medical texts—particularly in anatomy, pharmacology, and ophthalmology—circulated in China during the Yuan. The Yuan emperors—particularly Khubilai, who suffered from alcoholism and gout—gave doctors an influential position. The introduction of new seeds and formulas from the Middle East stimulated experimentation and publication in the traditional Chinese study of herbs, drugs, and potions.

Dispersal of the Mongols

In the 1340s, power contests among the Mongol princes shredded the political fabric of the Yuan Empire. By the 1360s, local rebellions by farmers and feuds among the Mongols engulfed the land. Amid the chaos, a charismatic Chinese leader, Zhu Yuanzhang°, mounted a campaign that destroyed the Yuan Empire and in 1368 brought China under control of his new empire, the Ming. Many Mongols—as well as the Muslims, Jews, and Christians who had come with them—remained in China, some as farmers or shepherds, some as high-ranking scholars and officials. Most of their descendants took Chinese names and became part of the diverse cultural world of China.

Mongol power in Eurasia survived the fall of the Yuan. New Mongol leaders prevented Ming armies from controlling Mongolia and Turkestan, and Timur held much of Central Asia and Iran. The reconcentration of Mongols on the steppes

---

Yunnan (YOON-nahn) **Hülegü** (HE-luh-gee)

Zhu Yuanzhang (JOO yuwen-JAHNG)

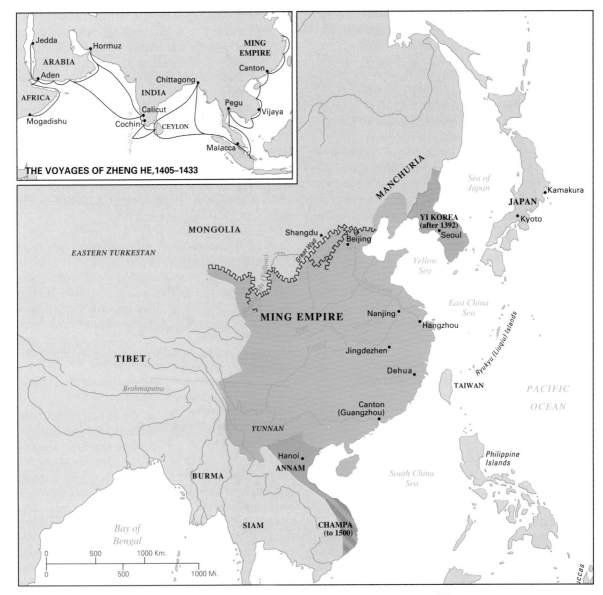

THE VOYAGES OF ZHENG HE, 1405–1433

Map 12.1 The Ming Empire and Its Allies, 1368–1500 The Ming Empire controlled China but had a hostile relationship with peoples in Mongolia and Central Asia.

fostered Mongol unity. Islam united some Mongol groups; Tibetan Buddhism, others.

Since the 600s, a steady influx of Chinese and Korean settlers had worked to develop the agriculture and towns of **Manchuria** (see Map 12.1), a comparatively well-populated region of northeastern Asia, whose indigenous population shared lin-

guistic and cultural traits with the Tungus people in the extreme northeast. Manchuria became the Mongols' steppingstone to Korea. Using Mongolian terms and Mongol organizational institutions, the dominant indigenous people—the Jurchens, who had once ruled the area as part of the Jin Empire—made gains in economic and military power.

In the late 1400s, the Jurchens challenged the **Ming Empire** for control of Manchuria. The growing disorder hindered overland Eurasian trade, which remained an important economic resource in Central Asia.

The Mongols controlling Central Asia continued as superb mounted warriors and posed a persistent threat to agricultural areas. This frustrated the Ming objective of dominating all the Mongols and making them participate in the tributary system. The Mongols did participate, but only to the extent needed to facilitate their trade. Otherwise, they were hostile. Ming attempts to suppress a Mongol resurgence led, in the mid-1400s, to a disastrous war in which the Mongols captured the Ming emperor and in 1449 attacked Beijing.

The Early Ming Empire, 1368–1500

After the fall of the Yuan, interest in war technology waned, while population growth reduced the need for mechanization in agriculture and some manufacturing. Eastern Eurasia became a wealthy and culturally brilliant region. But the absence of technologically innovative, ambitious rivals on the northern frontier contributed to a slowdown in technological change.

Ming China on a Mongol Foundation

During the Yuan Empire's chaotic last decades, Zhu Yuanzhang, who had been a monk, a soldier, and a bandit, vanquished his rivals in rebellion and assumed imperial power under the name Hongwu (r. 1368–1398). Zhu attributed his dedication to rebellion to the deaths of his parents and other family members from famine and disease, which he blamed on Mongol misrule. He also shared a radical Buddhist belief in a coming age of salvation. As Emperor Hongwu, he ruled a highly centralized, militarily formidable empire.

With strong nationalist passions, the Ming sited their capital at Nanjing° ("southern capital") on the Yangzi River, turning away from the Mongols' Beijing ("northern capital") (see Map 12.1). Buttressing their aggressive intimidation of the remaining Mongols and the other peoples of Central and Southeast Asia, they used Confucianism to depict the Ming emperor as the champion of civilization and virtue, justified in making war on uncivilized "barbarians."

Hongwu moved to choke off the close relations with Central Asia and the Middle East that had been part of the Mongol trade system. He imposed strict limits on imports and closed much of the border to foreigners. He also ordered all tax and commercial payments to be made in silver instead of paper money. These early practices proved economically unhealthy and did not last, but they demonstrate an anti-Mongol ideology. The Ming government resembled the Yuan nevertheless. Ming rulers retained the provincial structure and continued to observe hereditary professional categories. They also retained Muslims for making calendars and running their new observatory at Nanjing (a replica of Khubilai's at Beijing) and continued to use the calendar promulgated by the Mongols.

Ming continuities with the Yuan became more evident after an imperial prince seized power through a coup d'état to rule as the emperor **Yongle**° (r. 1403–1424). He returned the capital to Beijing, enlarging and improving Khubilai's imperial complex. The central part of this complex, the **Forbidden City,** acquired its present character, with moats, outer vermilion walls, golden roofs, and alabaster bridges. Yongle intended this combination fortress, religious site, bureaucratic center, and imperial residential park to overshadow the imperial architecture at Nanjing. It survives today as China's most imposing traditional architectural complex.

Yongle also restored commercial links with the Middle East. Because the hostile Mongols still controlled much of the caravan route, Yongle looked for a maritime connection. In Southeast Asia, Annam became a Ming province as the early emperors continued the Mongol program of aggression.

Nanjing (nahn-JING) **Yongle** (yoong-LAW)

Forbidden Spaces   Khubilai Khan determined the general shape of the imperial complex at Beijing and the set of artificial lakes at its northwest corner in the late 1200s. The architectural style dates to the Yongle period (1403–1424) of the Ming. In addition to gold-tiled roofs and vermilion walls, the Forbidden City features marble-paved courtyards and three large central palaces, all set on a north-south axis designed to give it supernatural protection.   (Reproduced by permission of the Commercial Press [Hong Kong] Limited, from The Forbidden City)

This helped inspire the naval expeditions of the trusted imperial eunuch **Zheng He°** from 1405 to 1433.

Exchange of seafaring knowledge between China and the peoples of Southeast Asia had persisted for centuries. Tens of thousands of Chinese had settled throughout Southeast Asia, in the regions ringing the Indian Ocean, almost certainly in some parts of coastal Australia, and possibly in

some sites in eastern Africa. In one sense, Zheng He merely retraced routes that the Chinese had long known about. But with the emperor as his sponsor and an enormous budget, this superb sea captain rightly saw his exploits as measurably increasing the glory of Emperor Yongle, whom he served unflinchingly.

A Muslim whose father and grandfather had made the pilgrimage to Mecca, Zheng He had a good knowledge of the Middle East, and his religion helped relations with the states of the Indian subcontinent, where he directed his first three voy-

---

Zheng He (jehng huh)

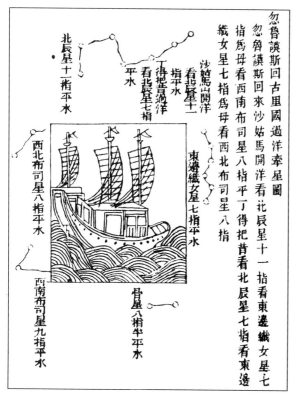

西北布司星八指平水

西南布司星九指半水

骨星八指半水

北辰星十一指平水

看起屋星七指

西南布司星八指平水

看北長星七指

得把背星過洋

東邊織女星七指平水

沙姑馬開洋

織女星七指平水

指為母看西南布司星八指平丁得把背看北辰星七指看東邊

忽魯謨斯回來沙姑馬開洋看北辰星十一指看東邊織女星七

忽魯謨斯回古里國過洋牽星圖

How to Navigate   This manual, which details Zheng He's well-established and tested navigational techniques, underscores his mission to carry out political and, if possible, economic mandates.   (From Wubei zhi [records of military preparations], 1621)

Sporadic embassies reached Beijing from rulers in India, the Middle East, Africa, and Southeast Asia. During one such visit, the ruler of Brunei° died and received a grand burial at the Chinese capital. Many expeditions brought exotic animals for the Ming imperial zoo. The Chinese court especially loved the giraffe.

The expeditions that began in 1405 continued sporadically until the 1430s, after the death of both Yongle and Zheng He. Long before the Europeans undertook voyages of similar ambition, the Chinese fleets, involving ships of unprecedented size, surveyed nearly the entire Indian Ocean and left a documented record. Having accomplished long-distance navigation far in advance of the Europeans, why did the Chinese not develop seafaring for commercial and military gain?

Technology cannot answer this question. The designs of the enormous junks and the compasses that Zheng He used were not new, nor were his navigation techniques and geographical concepts. Most dated from the Song period. Any empire based in China since the eleventh century could have undertaken similar voyages. But neither the Song nor the Yuan had considered it worth the trouble.

The expectations of new commercial opportunities and awing the overseas Chinese and foreign nations into immediate submission to Yongle fell short of realization. In the meantime, Japanese coastal piracy intensified, and Mongol threats in the north and west grew. The human and financial demands of fortifying the north, remodeling and strengthening Beijing, and outfitting military expeditions against the Mongols distracted a government that had outgrown its enthusiasm for maritime empire.

What people at the time understood Zheng He's voyages to be explains them best: the personal project of Emperor Yongle. This ruler, who vaulted to power through a coup d'état, always sought to prove his worthiness. In Beijing, he built the Forbidden City. He sponsored gigantic encyclopedia projects designed to collect and organize all known knowledge and literature. He campaigned effectively in Mongolia and northeastern Asia. The

ages. Subsequent expeditions reached Hormuz on the Persian Gulf, sailed the southern coast of Arabia and the Horn of Africa (modern Somalia), and possibly reached as far south as the Strait of Madagascar (see Map 12.1).

Zheng He's early voyages aimed at visiting Chinese merchant communities in Southeast Asia, affirming their allegiance to the Ming Empire, and demanding taxes. When a community on Sumatra resisted, he ordered the men slaughtered to set an example. His voyages also publicized the reversal of Hongwu's opposition to foreign trade and sought commercial relationships with the Middle East and possibly with Africa.

Trade with these regions did not increase significantly, but the expeditions added some fifty new tributary states to the Ming imperial universe.

Brunei (broo-NIE)

inspiration for the voyages may have been Khubilai Khan, who sent enormous fleets against Japan and Southeast Asia. Indeed, Yongle so emulated Khubilai that his political enemies spread the rumor that he was a Mongol.

Ending the voyages did not represent a Chinese turning away from the sea, only a lack of interest by later Ming emperors in centralizing the organization of voyages, funding them with government money, and turning them to military uses. As a large, complex, and constantly challenged land-based empire, the Ming saw little reason to try imposing and sustaining rule over distant and far-flung colonies. Regardless of the expeditions mounted by Europeans before 1500, there is no reason to consider the cessation of the voyages a major miscalculation by the Ming emperors.

Technology and Population

The economy of Ming China fueled the enrichment of East Asia and attracted ambitious Europeans. Innovation continued in all areas of the Ming economy but became less frequent and less important than under the Song, particularly in agriculture. Agricultural productivity peaked around the mid-1400s and remained level for more than a century.

The slowing of technological development seems to have occurred first in mining and metallurgy, during the Yuan period. The Mongol conquest brought peace to China, and peace removed the constant pressure to manufacture weapons. The techniques for making high-quality bronze and steel notably diminished. Central Asian and Middle Eastern technicians rather than Chinese cast the instruments for Khubilai's observatory at Beijing. The failure to preserve Song knowledge of high-temperature metallurgy remains puzzling.

While Chinese metallurgy stagnated, Japan made dramatic advances and quickly surpassed China in the production of extremely high-quality steel swords. Copper, iron, and steel had become expensive in China (remember that the early Ming government preferred metal coins to paper money)—so expensive that farm implements and well caps made of these materials became prohibi-tive to manufacture. Shipbuilding also declined sharply, particularly after the death of Emperor Yongle in 1424, and few advances occurred in printing, timekeeping, and agricultural technology. Mechanization of weaving saw new techniques through the fifteenth century, but rarely after 1500.

Shifts in the career patterns of educated men contributed to the technological slowdown. Under the Yuan, when few government posts were open to Chinese, wealthy families had turned to commerce, investing in trading ventures and agriculture. The Ming government reactivated the examination system, employed large numbers of educated men in government, and deprived the commercial economy of some of its best educated, most ambitious men.

A labor glut may also have lowered incentives for mechanization. At the end of the Yuan period in 1368, the population had fallen to perhaps 60 million. By 1400, it numbered nearly 100 million, reflecting a boom to which the economy may have adjusted awkwardly. Rapid population growth shifted economic emphasis away from commercial agriculture, the area of many Song period innovations, to the production of staples: wheat, millet, and barley in the north and rice in the south. Staple crops, though necessary to feed the population, did not offer the profit margins of specialized commercial crops and did not provide farmers with money for capital improvements.

Materials for building machines became scarce. The Ming government attempted to limit mining, partly to reinforce the value of metal coins and partly to control and tax the industry. Farmers had difficulty obtaining iron and bronze, while deforestation in southern and central China, caused by the needs of a growing population, made wood expensive as well. Farmers who could not acquire plows did not need draft animals or harnesses and could not grow crops that required deep planting.

In warfare, the Ming faced few technological challenges. The Mongols whom the Ming confronted in the north fought on horseback with simple weapons. The Ming fought back with arrows, scattershot mortars, and explosive canisters. They used cannons, which they knew about from contacts with the Middle East and later with Europeans, but only selectively in small numbers (see Environment and Technology: From Gunpowder to Guns).

Fear of **technology transfer**—whether from the state to the people or from China to foreign nations—seems evident in the behavior of the Ming government. Encyclopedias of practical knowledge from the early Ming period had their chapters on gunpowder and guns censored. Shipyards and ports shut down to avoid contact with Japanese pirates and prevent Chinese from migrating to Southeast Asia. As printing techniques stagnated, buyers of printed editions of rare Tang or Song books looked to Korean suppliers. When superior steel was needed, supplies came from Japan. New crops, such as sweet potatoes, became available but not widely adopted.

The early Ming technology gap with Korea and Japan foreshadowed the disparities between China and Europe that were to attract the attention of historians looking at the later Ming period. For the first time, Korea moved ahead of China in the design and production of firearms and ships and in the sciences of weather prediction and calendar making. Japan surpassed China in mining and metallurgy and in the manufacture of novel household goods. Nevertheless, it is important to remember that the issue is not "advancement" or "development." Ming China lagged in technological innovation, but it led the world in the generation of wealth; wealth fueled innovation by Korean and Japanese merchants who hoped to tap the China market.

The Ming Achievement

The early Ming period—the late 1300s and the 1400s—was one of cultural brilliance. The wealth and the consumerism of the time led to achievements in literature, the decorative arts, and painting. The Yuan period interest in plain writing came to fruition in some of the world's earliest novels. One of the most famous, *Water Margin,* came from the raucous drum song performances of the Yuan period (and was loosely related to Chinese opera). A group of dashing Chinese bandits struggle against Mongol rule, much as Robin Hood and his Merry Men legendarily resisted Norman rule in Eng-

land. The fictional work distorts many of the original stories, and many authors had a hand in its final commission to paper and print.

Romance of the Three Kingdoms, based on a much older series of stories that in some ways resemble the Arthurian legends, is attributed to one of the authors of *Water Margin,* Luo Guanzhong°. It describes the attempts of an upright but doomed war leader and his talented followers to restore the Han Empire of ancient times and resist the power of the cynical but brilliant villain, Cao Cao. *Romance of the Three Kingdoms* and *Water Margin* expressed much of the militant but joyous pro-China sentiment of the early Ming and remain among the most appreciated Chinese fictional works.

Early Ming advances in porcelain making gained particular renown. The imperial ceramic works at Jingdezhen° introduced not only technological improvements but superior ways of organizing and rationalizing labor. Ming patterns—most famously the blue-on-white widely recognized as "Ming ware"—developed in the 1400s from Indian, Central Asian, and Middle Eastern motifs. With porcelain among the most prized commercial products of Eurasia, the Ming industrial organizers evidently responded effectively to increased international demand. Other Ming goods in high demand included furniture, lacquered screens, and silk, all eagerly transported by both Chinese and foreign merchants throughout Southeast Asia and the Pacific, India, the Middle East, and East Africa.

Centralization and Militarism in East Asia, 1200–1500

As in western Eurasia, in eastern Eurasia areas at the margins of the Mongol advance tended to centralize their government and develop a sense of

---

Luo Guanzhong (law gwahb-joong)
Jingdezhen (JING-deh-JUHN)

From Gunpowder to Guns

Gunpowder had a variety of uses long before guns appeared. Chinese and Korean engineers used it to excavate mines, canals, and irrigation works. Alchemists in China sought to paralyze enemies and expel evil spirits with noxious gas pellets compounded from similar formulas. These successfully reduced disease-carrying insects and helped the colonization of malarial regions. The fireworks the Mongols displayed on ceremonial occasions delighted European visitors to Karakorum who saw them for the first time.

Anecdotal evidence in Chinese records credits a Sogdian Buddhist monk of the 500s with the invention of gunpowder. The monk described the wondrous alchemical transformation produced by a combination of charcoal and saltpeter. In this connection, he also mentioned sulfur. Naphtha distillation, too, seems to have been a skill first developed in Central Asia, for some of the earliest devices for distilling naphtha found in the Gandhara region (in modern Pakistan) indicate that that process may have also originated in the same area.

By the eleventh century, the Chinese had flame-throwers powered by the slow igniting of naphtha, sulfur, or gunpowder in a long tube. They used these weapons to intimidate and injure foot soldiers and horses, to fire thatched roofs in hostile villages, and occasionally to burn the rigging of enemy ships.

Fighting the Mongols, the Song learned to enrich saltpeter to increase the nitrate level in gunpowder and thereby produce explosions that could destroy bridges and buildings. Launched from catapults, canisters filled with explosive could rupture fortifications, inflict mass casualties, and destroy ships.

The Song also experimented with metal gun barrels from which to fire projectiles propelled by the explosion of gunpowder. Special wagons carried these broad, squat gun barrels to their emplacements. Firing the gun projected saltpeter mixed with scattershot minerals from the mouths of the barrels. The Chinese and then the Koreans applied gunpowder to shooting masses of arrows—sometimes flaming—at enemy fortifications. The Mongols used this Song expertise to invent cannon.

In 1280, after conquering the Southern Song, the Yuan devised a projectile that completely filled the mouth of the barrel and thus concentrated the explosive force. They used cast bronze barrels and iron cannonballs. The new weapon shot farther and more accurately than the earlier Song devices. Its ability to smash through brick, wood, and flesh without suffering destruction itself was unprecedented.

Knowledge of cannons moved westward across Eurasia. By the end of the thirteenth century, more accurate, more mobile cannon appeared in the Middle East. By 1327, Europe was producing small, squat cannon called "bombards."

Launching Flaming Arrows Song soldiers used gunpowder to launch flaming arrows. (British Library)

local solidarity. The Mongols conquered Korea after a difficult war, and Korean elites associated closely with the leaders of the Yuan Empire. Japan and Annam escaped Mongol conquest.

Korea suffered socially and economically from Mongol rule but, like China, emerged from the experience with a revitalized interest in its own language and history. Korean merchants continued the international connections established in the Mongol period, and Korean armies established a new kingdom and fended off pirates. Japan and Annam, in contrast, changed under the Mongol threat and responded to the fall of the Yuan Empire with more effective and expansive regimes.

Korea from the Mongols to the Yi, 1231–1500

During the 1200s, the battle against the Southern Song led the Mongols to seek greater control of the coasts of East Asia. They hoped to find new launching sites for naval expeditions against the south and for strategic points to choke off Song sea trade. Korea offered such possibilities.

When the Mongols attacked in 1231, the leader of a prominent Korean family assumed the role of military commander and protector of the king (not unlike the shoguns of Japan). Under this leader, a defensive war that lasted for over twenty years left a ravaged countryside, exhausted Korean armies, and burned treasures, including the renowned nine-story pagoda at Hwangnyong-sa° and the wooden printing blocks of the *Tripitaka*°, a ninth-century masterpiece of printing art. The commander's underlings killed him in 1258, and soon afterward, the Koryo° king surrendered to the Mongols and linked his family to the Great Khan by marriage.

By the mid-1300s, the Koryo kings were mostly Mongol by descent and employed the Mongolian language, dress, and customs. Many lived in Beijing. The kings, their families, and their entourages traveled often between China and Korea, thus exposing Korea to the current philosophical and artistic styles of Yuan China: neo-Confucianism, Chan Buddhism (in Korea, called *Sŏn*), and light green celadon ceramics.

Korea had been somewhat isolated since the tenth century. Under the Mongols, cotton growing began in southern Korea, gunpowder came into use, and the art of calendar making, including eclipse prediction and vector calculation, stimulated astronomical observation and mathematics. Korean celestial clocks built for the royal observatory at Seoul reflect Central Asian and Islamic influences, only superficially resembling Chinese celestial clocks. New avenues of advancement opened for Korean scholars willing to learn Mongolian, landowners willing to open their lands to falconry and grazing, and merchants servicing the new royal traffic to Beijing. These developments contributed to the rise of a new landed and educated class.

When the Yuan Empire fell in 1368, the Koryo ruling family remained loyal to the Mongols and had to be forced to recognize the new Ming Empire. But within a generation, Koryo collapsed, to be succeeded by the **Yi**° kingdom in 1392. Korea's new royal family, the Yi, sought to reestablish a local identity. Like Russia and China after the Mongols, the Yi regime publicly rejected the period of Mongol domination. Yet the Yi government continued to administer Mongol-style land surveys, taxation in kind, and military garrison techniques.

Like the Ming Empire, the Yi kingdom revived the study of the Confucian classics, an activity that required knowledge of Chinese and showed the dedication of the state to learning. This revival may have led to a key technological breakthrough in printing technology.

Koreans had begun using Chinese woodblock printing in the 700s. This technology worked well in China, where a large number of men wanted copies of a comparatively small number of texts. But in Korea, the comparatively few literate men had interests in a wide range of texts. Movable wooden or ceramic type appeared in Korea in the early thirteenth century and may have been invented there. But the texts were frequently

Hwanghnyong-sa (hwahng-NEEYAHNG-sah)
Tripitaka (tri-PIH-tah-kah)   **Koryo** (KAW-ree-oh)

Yi (YEE)

Movable Type The improvement of cast bronze tiles, each showing a single character, superseded the casting or carving of whole pages. In Korea, where this set originated, superior stability in fitting the movable type into the frame gave a more pleasing appearance. All parts of East Asia eventually adopted this technique of printing for cheap, popular books. (Courtesy, Yushin Yoo)

inaccurate and difficult to read. In the 1400s, Yi printers, working directly with the king, developed a reliable device to anchor the pieces of type to the printing plate: they replaced the old beeswax adhesive with solid copper frames. The legibility of the printed page improved, and high-volume, accurate production became possible. Combined with the phonetic *han'gul*° writing system, this printing technology laid the foundation for a high literacy rate in Korea.

Building on Eurasian knowledge imported by the Mongols, the Yi Koreans used the astronomical arts of the Koryo period to develop a meteorological science of their own. Redesigned and newly invented instruments to measure wind speed and rainfall, the first of their kind, augmented the as-

han'gul (HAHN-goor)

tronomical clock and armillary spheres of the royal observatory at Seoul. A local calendar based on minute comparisons with the calendrical systems of China and the Islamic world was perfected. Interest in commercial agriculture sparked improvements in the production and use of fertilizer, the transplanting of seedlings in rice paddies, and the engineering of reservoirs (of which there were thousands in Yi times), all disseminated through the powerful new publishing abilities of the Yi government.

Yi agriculture developed so well that the growing of cash crops became common—roughly the reverse of developments in Ming China. **Cotton,** the primary cash crop, enjoyed such high value that the state accepted it for tax payments. The large and frequently mobilized Yi army used cotton uniforms, and it became the favored fabric of the Korean civil elite. With cotton gins and spinning wheels often powered by water, Korea advanced more rapidly than China in mechanization and came to export considerable amounts of cotton to China and Japan.

The Yi rulers launched military campaigns toward the north, where Jurchens and other northeastern peoples threatened control of the Yalu River, and against the coastal pirates who had previously operated freely and driven harassed farmers inland. Although both the Yuan and Ming withheld the formula for gunpowder from the Korean government, Korean officials acquired the information by subterfuge. By the later 1300s, they had mounted cannon on patrol ships and used gunpowder-driven arrow launchers against enemy personnel and the rigging of enemy ships. Combined with skills in armoring ships, these techniques made the small Yi navy a formidable defense force.

Political Transformation in Japan, 1274–1500

Having conquered Korea in the mid-thirteenth century, the Mongols looked toward Japan as a target easily accessible by sea from Korea's southern tip and a possible base for controlling China's southern coast. The Mongols launched their first expedition against Japan in 1274. The invading force included not only Mongol cavalry but also light catapults and incendiary and explosive projectiles of Chinese manufacture. Korean ship captains and archers joined the force, as did Jurchens and other peoples from northeastern Asia, many of whom were excellent archers and experienced sailors. With 30,000 combatants and the latest military techniques, the expedition presented a clear threat to Japanese independence. Defeat came from the weather in Hakata° Bay on the north side of Kyushu° Island (see Map 12.2). Although the Mongol forces landed and decimated the mounted Japanese warriors, a storm prevented the establishment of a beachhead. The Mongols returned to their ships and sailed back to Korea.

The Mongol invasion deeply impressed Japan's leaders and hastened social and political changes already under way. Under the Kamakura° Shogunate established in 1185—another powerful family actually exercised control—the shogun, or military leader, distributed land and privileges to his followers, who paid him tribute and supplied him with soldiers. This stable but decentralized system depended on the balancing of power among regional warlords. Little connected the lords in the north and east of Japan's main island to those in the south and west beyond their declared devotion to the emperor and the shogun. The alien, terrifying, and prolonged nature of the Mongol threat united them.

After the initial foray in 1274, Khubilai sent envoys to Japan demanding submission. Japanese leaders executed them and began preparing for war. Previously, ambitious local commanders had frequently ignored the civil code that limited their power. Now the shogun took steps to centralize his military government and strengthen his midlevel military officials, thus increasing the influence of warlords from the south and west of Honshu (Japan's main island) and from the island of Kyushu, where invasion seems most likely.

Military planners studied Mongol tactics and retrained and outfitted Japanese warriors for defense against advanced weaponry. Farm laborers drafted from all over the country constructed defensive fortifications at Hakata and other points

---

Hakata (HAH-kah-tah)   **Kyushu** (KYOO-shoo)
Kamakura (kah-mah-KOO-rah)

Map 12.2   Korea and Japan, 1200–1500   The proximity of Korea and northern China to Japan gave the Mongols the opportunity for launching their enormous fleets. The Kamakura Shogunate controlled most of the three islands (Honshu, Shikoku, and Kyushu) of central Japan.

along the Honshu and Kyushu coasts. This effort demanded, for the first time, a national system to move resources toward western points rather than toward the imperial or shogunal centers to the east.

The Mongols attacked again in 1281. They brought 140,000 warriors, including Mongols, Chinese, Koreans, and Jurchens, as well as thousands of horses, in hundreds of ships. However, the Japanese had built a wall cutting off Hakata Bay from the mainland. The wall deprived the Mongol forces of a reliable landing point. Japanese swordsmen rowed out to board the Mongol ships lingering offshore. Their superb steel swords shocked the invaders. After months of standoff, a typhoon struck and sank perhaps half the Mongol ships. The remainder sailed away, never again to harass Japan. The Japanese gave thanks to the "wind of the Gods"—*kamikaze°*—for driving away the Mongols.

Nevertheless, the Mongol threat continued to influence Japanese development. Prior to his death in 1294, Khubilai had in mind a third invasion. His successors did not carry through with it, but the shoguns did not know that the Mongols had given up the idea of conquering Japan. Their planning for coastal defense, which continued well into the fourteenth century, helped consolidate the social position of Japan's warrior elite and stimulated the development of a national infrastructure for trade and communication. But the Kamakura shogunate, based on regionally collected and regionally dispersed revenues, had too small a central treasury to pay for centralized road and defense systems.

At least one member of the imperial family, which for centuries had lived in seclusion without exercising real political power, saw opportunities in the weakening of the shoguns. Between 1333 and 1338, the emperor Go-Daigo tried to reclaim power from the shoguns and thereby ignited a civil war that destroyed the Kamakura system. In 1338, with the Mongol threat waning, a new shogunate, the **Ashikaga°**, arose at the imperial center of Kyoto.

Provincial warlords enjoyed renewed independence under the Ashikaga Shogunate. Around their imposing castles, they sponsored the development of market towns, religious institutions, and schools. The application of technologies imported in earlier periods, including water wheels, improved plows, and Champa rice, which matures faster than plain rice, increased agricultural productivity. Growing wealth and relative peace stimulated artistic creativity, mostly reflecting the Zen Buddhist beliefs of the warrior elite. In the simple elegance of architecture and gardens, in the contemplative landscapes of artists like Sesshu Toyo, and in the eerie, stylized performances of the No theater, the unified aesthetic code of Zen became established in the Ashikaga era.

Despite the technological advancement, artistic productivity, and rapid urbanization of this period, competition among the warlords and their followers led to regional wars. By the later 1400s,

Painting by Sesshu Sesshu Toyo (1420–1506) created a distinctive style in ink painting that contrasted with the Chinese styles that predominated earlier in Japan. As a youth, he traveled to China, where he first learned his techniques. A market for his art developed among the merchant communities of the Ashikaga period and spread to other urban elites. (Collection of the Tokyo National Museum)

these conflicts resulted in the near destruction of the warlords. The great Onin War in 1477 left Kyoto devastated and the Ashikaga Shogunate a central government in name only. Ambitious but low-ranking warriors, some with links to trade with the continent, began to scramble for control of the provinces.

After the fall of the Yuan in 1368, trade among China, Korea, and the islands of Japan and Okinawa resumed. Japan exported copper, sulfur, and

---

kamikaze (KUM-i-kuh-zee) **Ashikaga** (ah-shee-KAH-gah)

other raw materials to China and Korea, partly to support their firearms industries. Other exports included folding fans, invented in Japan during the period of isolation, and swords. From China, Japan imported primarily books and porcelain. Japan's volatile political environment gave rise to partnerships between warlords and local merchants. Everyone worked to strengthen his own town and treasury through overseas commerce or, sometimes, through piracy.

The Emergence of Vietnam, 1200–1500

The states of Annam (northern Vietnam) and **Champa** (southern Vietnam) related uneasily before the Mongol invasions. Annam (once called Dai Viet) had close relations with empires in China and had been subject to the Tang. Chinese political ideas, social philosophies, dress, religion, and language heavily influenced its official culture. Champa related more closely to the trading networks of the Indian Ocean, its official culture reflecting a strong influence from Indian religion, language, architecture, and dress. During the Song period, Annam being neither formally subject to China nor particularly threatening, Champa had entered into a trade and tribute relationship with China that spread fast-ripening Champa rice throughout East Asia.

The Mongols exacted submission and tribute from both Annam and Champa, but after the fall of the Yuan, the old conflicts resurfaced, leading to war between Annam and Champa by 1400. With Annam's army concentrated on its southern border, Ming troops from the north occupied Hanoi and installed a puppet government. The puppet government lasted almost thirty years before Annam regained independence and resumed a tributary status.

As with Lithuania, the Ottomans, Egypt, and Korea, Annam's struggle against a greater empire inspired expansionist dreams when the Ming turned to meet Mongol challenges in the mid-1400s. In a series of ruthless campaigns, Annamese armies defeated the forces of Champa. By 1500, Champa had disappeared, and the ancestor of the modern state of Vietnam had been born.

The new state, still called Annam, reinforced its centralization with Confucian bureaucratic government and an examination system. But its practices differed from the Chinese: the Vietnamese legal code preserved group landowning and decision making within the villages, and it preserved women's property rights. Both developments probably had roots in an early rural culture based on the growing of rice in wet paddies, but by this time, the Annamese considered them distinctive features of their own culture.

Conclusion

The effects of the Mongol period in eastern Eurasia differed from region to region. In China, the Mongols destroyed the empires that had divided the region. They consolidated China geographically and afforded access to scientific, commercial, and cultural influences from Central Asia and the Middle East. Though merchants, artists, and some officials flourished under the Yuan, the farming majority suffered. By the time the Mongol rulers recognized the negative impact of their taxation policies, rebellions, infighting among Mongol princes, and floods were ravaging the country.

But the Mongol impact lasted longer than the Yuan Empire. The Ming pursued many projects inspired by the Mongols, including completion of the Forbidden City and conquests in Southeast Asia. They also reacted to the period of Mongol domination by sponsoring cultural and commercial measures intended to limit or purge foreign influences and restoring what they saw as the classical civilization of China.

With the Ming established in 1368, the population began a rapid recovery. For decades, this swelled tax revenues, fed hungry labor markets, and allowed the recovery of profitable farmland.

The reversal of the isolationist economic policies of the Hongwu period stimulated Ming industries, particularly procelain, which brought prosperity to China's ports, water transport systems, and industrial centers. Demand grew, labor remained cheap, credit was ample, and the currency was stable.

The concentrations of wealth created huge markets into which merchants from all parts of China tapped, as well as ambitious and technologically innovative manufacturers in Korea and Japan. It simply happened that the powerful economic engine of the Ming did not promote technological innovation in China itself.

The connections forged between Korea and China under the Yuan fostered commercial growth. Innovations in printing and the Korean writing system accelerated the spread of knowledge, including Yi programs to establish an extensive literature on Korean history. Koreans used the sciences and technologies acquired under Mongol domination to minimize vulnerability to floods and droughts while maximizing exploitation of cash crops. The Yi state, and its many military enterprises, stimulated industries associated with cotton, mining, and forestry.

The prolonged threat of Mongol invasion challenged Japan's decentralized system of military rule, the shogunate. Warrior elites gained in status, and regional balances of power changed. When the threat ended, the reestablishment of trade with China provided a strong economic stimulus and spurred advances in metallurgy and ceramics. The wealth of the Ashikaga period, based on increasing agricultural productivity as well as overseas trade, accelerated urbanization and produced a brilliant period in the arts.

In Vietnam, Mongol attacks threatened both Annam and Champa. Ming China subjugated Annam in the late 1300s, but this fueled a strong movement for ending Chinese interference. When Ming preoccupation with Mongol enemies in the north allowed, Annam threw off Ming control and obliterated Champa's independence. A united Vietnam thus benefited, like certain other peripheral states throughout Eurasia, from a birth of independence, and increased national consciousness stimulated by resistance to Mongol domination.

■ Key Terms

Beijing	Forbidden City
Yuan Empire	Zheng He
lama	technology transfer
Khubilai Khan	Yi
cottage industries	cotton
Manchuria	*kamikaze*
Ming Empire	Ashikaga
Yongle	Champa

■ Suggested Reading

See Chapter 11 for general works on the Mongols. For China, see Morris Rossabi's *Khubilai Khan: His Life and Times* (1988). Mark Elvin, *The Pattern of the Chinese Past* (1973); Joel Mokyr, *The Lever of Riches: Technological Creativity and Economic Progress* (1990); and Joseph Needham, *Science in Traditional China* (1981) discuss economy and technology in Yuan and Ming China. Andre Gunder Frank, *ReORIENT: Global Economy in the Asian Age* (1998), analyzes Ming economic achievement.

The Cambridge History of China, vol. 8, *The Ming Dynasty 1368–1644, part 2*, edited by Denis Twitchett and Frederick W. Mote (1998), gives needed coverage of the early Ming period. See also Albert Chan, *The Glory and Fall of the Ming Dynasty* (1982), and Edward L. Farmer, *Early Ming Government: The Evolution of Dual Capitals* (1976).

On early Ming literature, see Lo Kuan-chung, *Three Kingdoms: A Historical Novel Attributed to Luo Guanzhong*, translated and annotated by Moss Roberts (1991); Pearl Buck's translation of *Water Margin*, entitled *All Men Are Brothers*, 2 vols. (1933), and a later translation by J. H. Jackson, *Water Margin, Written by Shih Nai-an* (1937); Richard Gregg Irwin, *The Evolution of a Chinese Novel: Shui-hu-chuan* (1953); Ellen Widmer, *The Margins of Utopia: Shui-hu hou-chuan and the Literature of Ming Loyalism* (1987); and Shelley Hsüeh-lun Chang, *History and Legend: Ideas and Images in the Ming Historical Novels* (1990).

On Ming painting, see James Cahill, *Parting at the Shore: Chinese Painting of the Early and Middle Ming Dynasty* (1978), and selected essays in Paul S. Ropp, ed., *Heritage of China* (1990).

The classic interpretation of the Zheng He expeditions in Joseph R. Levenson, ed., *European Expansion and the Counter-Example of Asia, 1300–1600* (1967), is updated in Philip Snow, *The Star Raft* (1988). For a livelier account, see Louise Levathes, *When China Ruled the Seas* (1993).

General histories of Korea include Andrew C. Nahm, *Introduction to Korean History and Culture* (1993); Ki-Baik Lee, *A New History of Korea* (1984); and William E. Henthorn, *Korea: The Mongol Invasions* (1963). On technology, see Joseph Needham et al., *The Hall of Heavenly Records: Korean Astronomical Instruments and Clocks, 1380–1780* (1986).

For Japan, see John W. Hall and Toyoda Takeshi, eds., *Japan in the Muromachi Age* (1977), and H. Paul Varley, trans., *The Onin War: History of Its Origins and Background with a Selective Translation of the Chronicle of Onin* (1967). On the Mongol invasion, see Yamada Nakaba, *Ghenko, the Mongol Invasion of Japan, with an Introduction by Lord Armstrong* (1916), and the novel *Fûtô* by Inoue Yasushi, translated by James T. Araki as *Wind and Waves* (1989). Donald Keene, *No: The Classical Theatre of Japan* (1966), and Ueda Makoto, trans., *The Old Pine Tree and Other Noh Plays* (1962), offer accounts of No theater and Zen aesthetics.

13

TROPICAL AFRICA AND ASIA,

1200–1500

**Tropical Lands and Peoples • New Islamic Empires •
Indian Ocean Trade • Social and Cultural Change**
SOCIETY AND CULTURE: Personal Styles of Rule in India and Mali

ultan Abu Bakr° customarily offered hospitality to distinguished visitors to his city of Mogadishu, an Indian Ocean port on the northeast coast of Africa. In 1331, he provided food and lodging for Muhammad ibn Abdullah **Ibn Battuta**° (1304–1369), a young Muslim scholar from Morocco who had set out to explore the Islamic world. With a pilgrimage to Mecca and travel throughout the Middle East behind him, Ibn Battuta was touring the trading cities of the Red Sea and East Africa. Subsequent travels took him to Central Asia and India, China and Southeast Asia, Muslim Spain, and sub-Saharan West Africa. Recounting some 75,000 miles (120,000 kilometers) of travel over twenty-nine years, Ibn Battuta's journal provides invaluable information on these lands.

Hospitality being considered a noble virtue among Muslims, regardless of physical and cultural differences, the reception at Mogadishu mirrored that at other cities. Ibn Battuta noted that Sultan Abu Bakr had skin darker than his own and spoke a different native language (Somali), but as brothers in faith, they prayed together at Friday services, where the sultan greeted his foreign guest in Arabic, the common language of the Islamic world: "You are heartily welcome, and you have honored our land and given us pleasure." When Sultan Abu Bakr and his jurists heard and decided cases after the mosque service, they used the religious law familiar in all Muslim lands.

Islam aside, the most basic links among the diverse peoples of Africa and southern Asia derived from the tropical environment itself. A network of overland and maritime routes joined their lands (see Chapter 6), providing avenues

Abu Bakr (a-BOO BAK-uhr)
Ibn Battuta (IB-uhn ba-TOO-tuh)

for the spread of beliefs and technologies, as well as goods. Ibn Battuta sailed with merchants down the coast of East Africa and joined trading caravans across the Sahara to West Africa. His path to India followed overland trade routes, and a merchant ship carried him on to China.

As you read this chapter, ask yourself the following questions:

- How did environmental differences shape cultural differences in tropical Africa and Asia?

- How did cultural and ecological differences promote trade in specialized goods from one place to another?

- How did trade and other contacts promote state growth and the spread of Islam?

TROPICAL LANDS AND PEOPLES

To obtain food, the people who inhabited the tropical regions of Africa and Asia used methods that generations of experimentation had proved successful, whether at the desert's edge, in grasslands, or in tropical rain forests. Much of their success lay in learning how to blend human activities with the natural order, but their ability to modify the environment to suit their needs appeared in irrigation works and mining.

The Tropical Environment

Because of the angle of earth's axis, the sun's rays warm the **tropics** year-round. The equator marks the center of the tropical zone, and the Tropic of Cancer and Tropic of Capricorn mark its outer limits. As Map 13.1 shows, Africa lies almost entirely within the tropics, as do southern Arabia, most of India, and all of the Southeast Asian mainland and islands.

Lacking the hot and cold seasons of temperate lands, the rainy and dry seasons of the Afro-Asian tropics derive from wind patterns across the surrounding oceans. Winds from a permanent high-pressure air mass over the South Atlantic deliver heavy rainfall to the western coast of Africa during much of the year. However, in December and January, large high-pressure zones over northern Africa and Arabia produce a southward movement of dry air that limits the inland penetration of the moist ocean winds.

In the lands around the Indian Ocean, the rainy and dry seasons reflect the influence of alternating winds known as **monsoons.** A gigantic high-pressure zone over the Himalaya° Mountains that peaks from December to March produces southern Asia's dry season through a strong southward air movement (the northeast monsoon) in the western Indian Ocean. Between April and August, a low-pressure zone over India creates a northward movement of air from across the ocean (the southwest monsoon) that brings southern Asia the heavy rains of its wet season.

Areas with the heaviest rainfall—the broad belt along the equator in coastal West Africa and west-central Africa, parts of coastal India, and Southeast Asia—have dense rain forests. Lighter rains produce other forest patterns. The English word *jungle* comes from an Indian word for the tangled undergrowth in the forests that once covered most of India.

Some other parts of the tropics rarely see rain at all. The world's largest desert, the Sahara, stretches across northern Africa and continues eastward across Arabia, southern Iran and Pakistan, and northwest India. Another desert occupies southwestern Africa. Most of tropical India and Africa falls between the deserts and rain forests and experiences moderate rainy seasons. These lands range from fairly wet woodlands to the much drier grasslands characteristic of much of East Africa.

Altitude produces other climatic variations. Thin atmospheres at high altitudes hold less heat than atmospheres at lower elevations. Snow covers some of the volcanic mountains of eastern Africa all

---

Himalaya (him-uh-LAY-uh)

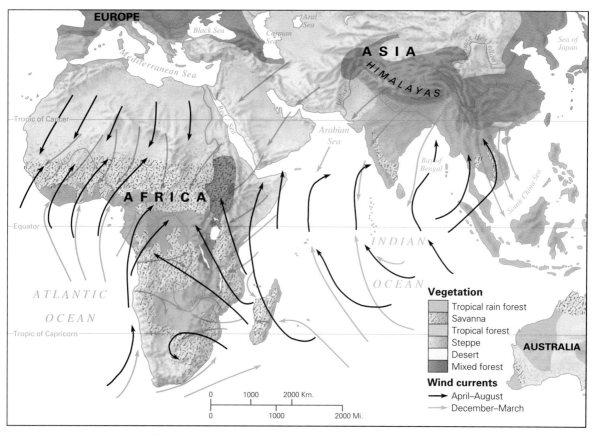

Map 13.1 Africa and the Indian Ocean Basin: Physical Characteristics Seasonal wind patterns control rainfall in the tropics and produce the different tropical vegetation zones to which human societies have adapted over thousands of years. The wind patterns also dominated sea travel in the Indian Ocean.

or part of the year. The snowcapped Himalayas that form India's northern frontier rise so high that they block cold air from moving south and thus give northern India a more tropical climate than its latitude would suggest. The plateaus of inland Africa and the Deccan° Plateau of central India also enjoy cooler temperatures than the coastal plains.

Human Ecosystems

Thinkers in temperate lands once imagined surviving in the tropics to be simply a matter of picking wild fruit off trees. A careful observer touring the tropics in 1200 would have noticed, however, many differences in societies deriving from their particular ecosystems—that is, from how human groups used the plants, animals, and other resources of their physical environments.

Domesticated plants and animals had become commonplace long before 1200, but people in some environments continued to rely primarily on hunting, fishing, and gathering. For Pygmy° hunters in the dense forests of Central Africa, small size permitted pursuit of prey through dense undergrowth. Hunting also prevailed in the upper altitudes of the Himalayas and in some desert environments. A Portuguese expedition led by Vasco

---

Deccan (de-KAN)

Pygmy (PIG-mee)

CHRONOLOGY

	Tropical Africa	Tropical Asia
1200		**1206** Delhi Sultanate founded in India
	1230s Mali Empire founded	
	1270 Solomonic dynasty in Ethiopia founded	**1298** Delhi Sultanate annexes Gujarat
1300		
	1324–1325 Mansa Musa's pilgrimage to Mecca	
		1398 Timur sacks Delhi; Delhi Sultanate declines
1400	**1400s** Great Zimbabwe at its peak	
	1433 Tuareg retake Timbuktu; Mali declines	
1500		**1500** Port of Malacca at its peak

da Gama visited the arid coast of southwestern Africa in 1497 and saw there a healthy group of people feeding themselves on "the flesh of seals, whales, and gazelles, and the roots of wild plants." Fishing, which was common along all the major lakes and rivers as well as in the oceans, might be combined with farming. The ocean fishermen of East Africa, Southeast Asia, and coastal India had boating skills that often led to engagement in ocean trade.

Herding provided sustenance in areas too arid for agriculture. Pastoralists consumed milk from their herds and traded hides and meat to farmers in return for grain and vegetables. The world's largest concentration of pastoralists inhabited the arid and semiarid lands of northeastern Africa and Arabia. Like Ibn Battuta's host at Mogadishu, some Somalis lived in towns, but most grazed goats and camels in the desert hinterland of the Horn of Africa. The western Sahara sustained herds of sheep and camels belonging to the Tuareg°, whose intimate knowledge of the desert made them invaluable as guides to caravans, such as the one Ibn Battuta joined on the two-month journey across the desert. Along the Sahara's southern edge the

cattle-herding Fulani° people gradually extended their range during this period. By 1500, they had spread throughout the western and central Sudan. A few weeks after encountering the hunter-gatherers of southwest Africa, Vasco da Gama's expedition bartered for meat with a pastoral people possessing fat cattle and sheep.

The density of agricultural populations reflected the adequacy of rainfall and soils. South and Southeast Asia were generally wetter than tropical Africa, making intensive cultivation possible. High yields supported dense populations. In 1200, over 100 million people lived in South and Southeast Asia, more than four-fifths of them on the fertile Indian mainland. Though a little less than the population of China, this was triple the number of people living in all of Africa and nearly double those in Europe.

India's lush vegetation led one Middle Eastern writer to call it "the most agreeable abode on earth. Its delightful plains resemble the garden of Paradise."[1] Rice cultivation dominated in the fertile Ganges plain of northeast India, mainland Southeast Asia, and southern China. In drier areas, farmers grew grains—wheat, sorghum, millet, and ensete—and legumes such as peas and beans

---

Tuareg (TWAH-reg)

Fulani (foo-LAH-nee)

whose ripening cycles matched the pattern of the rainy and dry seasons. Tubers and tree crops characterized farming in rain-forest clearings.

The spread of farming, including the movement to Africa of Asian crops like yams, cocoyams, and bananas, did not necessarily change the natural environment. In most of sub-Saharan Africa and much of Southeast Asia, extensive rather than intensive cultivation prevailed. Instead of enriching fields with manure and vegetable compost so they could be cultivated year after year, farmers abandoned fields when the natural fertility of the soil fell and cleared new fields. Ashes from the brush, grasses, and tree limbs they cut down and burned boosted the new fields' fertility. Shifting to new land every few years made efficient use of labor in areas with comparatively poor soils.

Water Systems and Irrigation

Though the inland delta of the Niger River received naturally fertilizing annual floods and could grow rice for sale to the trading cities along the Niger bend, many tropical farmers had to move the water to their crops. Conserving some of the monsoon rainfall for use during the dry season helped in Vietnam, Java, Malaya, and Burma, which had terraced hillsides with special water-control systems for growing rice. North and south India also had water-storage dams and irrigation canals. In this time period, villagers in southeast India built stone and earthen dams across rivers to store water for gradual release through elaborate irrigation canals. Extended over many generations, these canals irrigated a wide area.

As had been true since the days of the first river-valley civilizations (see Chapter 1), governments built and controlled the largest irrigation systems. The **Delhi° Sultanate** (1206–1526) in northern India acquired extensive new water-control systems. Ibn Battuta admired a large reservoir constructed in the first quarter of the thirteenth century that supplied the city of Delhi with water. Farmers planted sugar cane, cucumbers, and melons along the reservoir's rim as the water level fell during the dry season. In the fourteenth century, the Delhi sultan built in the Ganges plain a network of irrigation canals that remained unsurpassed until the nineteenth century. Such systems made it possible to grow crops throughout the year.

Since the tenth century, the Indian Ocean island of Ceylon (modern Sri Lanka°) had been home to the world's greatest concentration of irrigation reservoirs and canals. These facilities supported the large population of the Sinhalese° kingdom in arid northern Ceylon. In Southeast Asia, another impressive system of reservoirs and canals served Cambodia's capital city, Angkor°.

Between 1250 and 1400, however, the irrigation complex in Ceylon fell into ruin when invaders from south India disrupted the Sinhalese government. Malaria spread by mosquitoes breeding in the irrigation canals ravaged the population. In the fifteenth century, the great Cambodian system fell into ruin when the government that maintained it collapsed. Neither system was ever rebuilt.

The vulnerability of complex irrigation systems built by powerful governments contrasts with village-based irrigation systems. Invasion and natural calamity might damage the latter, but they usually bounced back because they depended on local initiative and simpler technologies.

Mineral Resources

The most productive metal trade in the tropics, iron-working, provided the hoes, axes, and knives farmers used to clear and cultivate their fields. Between 1200 and 1500, the rain forests of coastal West Africa and Southeast Asia opened up for farming. Iron also supplied spear and arrow points, needles, and nails. Indian metalsmiths became known for forging strong and beautiful swords. In Africa, many people attributed magical powers to iron smelters and blacksmiths.

Copper and its alloys had special importance in the Copperbelt of southeastern Africa during the fourteenth and fifteenth centuries. Smelters cast the metal into large X-shaped ingots (metal cast-

---

Delhi (DEL-ee)

Sri Lanka (sree LAHNG-kuh)   Sinhalese (sin-huh-LEEZ)
Angkor (ANG-kor)

ings). Local coppersmiths worked these into wire and decorative objects. In the western Sudan, Ibn Battuta described a mining town that produced two sizes of copper bars that served as currency in place of coins. Some coppersmiths in West Africa cast copper and brass (an alloy of copper and zinc) statues and heads that now rank as masterpieces of world art. They utilized the "lost-wax" method, in which molten metal melts a thin layer of wax sandwiched between clay forms, replacing the "lost" wax with hard metal.

African gold moved in quantity across the Sahara and into the Indian Ocean and Red Sea trades. Some came from stream beds along the upper Niger River and farther south in modern Ghana°. In the hills south of the Zambezi° River (in modern Zimbabwe°), archaeologists have discovered thousands of mine shafts, dating from 1200, that were sunk up to 100 feet (30 meters) into the ground to get at gold ores. Although panning for gold remained important in the streams descending from the mountains of northern India, the gold and silver mines in India seem to have been exhausted by this period. Thus, Indians imported from Southeast Asia and Africa considerable quantities of gold for jewelry and temple decoration.

The· labors and skills of ordinary people— farmers, fishermen, herders, metalworkers, and others—made possible the rise of powerful states and commercial systems. Caravans could not have crossed the Sahara without desert dwellers serving as guides. The seafaring skills of coastal fishermen underlay the trade of the Indian Ocean. Farmers produced the taxes that supported the city-based empires of Delhi and Mali.

King and Queen of Ife   This copper-alloy work shows the royal couple of the kingdom of Ife, the oldest and most sacred of the Yoruba kingdoms of southwestern Nigeria. The casting dates to between 1100 and 1500, except for the reconstruction of the male's face, the original of which shattered in 1957 when the road builder who found it accidentally struck it with his pick.   (Andre Held, Switzerland)

NEW ISLAMIC EMPIRES

The empires of Mali in West Africa and Delhi in northern India, the largest and richest tropical states of the period between 1200 and 1500, both

Ghana (GAH-nuh)   Zambezi (zam-BEE-zee)
Zimbabwe (zim-BAHB-way)

utilized administrative and military systems introduced from the Islamic heartland. Yet **Mali,** an indigenous African dynasty that had earlier adopted Islam through the peaceful influence of Muslim merchants and scholars, differed in many ways from the Delhi Sultanate founded and ruled by invading Turkish and Afghan Muslims. The wealth of Mali depended on trans-Saharan trade, but long-distance trade played only a minor role in Delhi.

Mali in the Western Sudan

Muslim rule beginning in the seventh century (see Chapter 7) greatly stimulated increased trade along the routes that crossed the Sahara. In the centuries that followed, the faith of Muhammad gradually spread to the lands south of the desert, which the Arabs called the *bilad al-sudan*°, "land of the blacks."

Muslim Berbers invading out of the desert in 1076 caused the collapse of Ghana, the empire that preceded Mali in the western Sudan (see Chapter 6), but their conquest did little to spread Islam. To the east, the Muslim attacks that destroyed the Christian Nubian kingdoms on the upper Nile in the late thirteenth century opened that area to Muslim influences, but Christian Ethiopia successfully withstood Muslim advances. Instead, Islam's spread south of the Sahara usually followed a pattern of gradual and peaceful conversion. The expansion of commercial contacts in the western Sudan and on the East African coast greatly promoted the conversion process. Most Africans found meaning and benefit in the teachings of Islam and found it suited their interests. Takrur° in the far western Sudan became the first sub-Saharan African state to adopt the new faith around 1030.

Shortly after 1200, Takrur expanded under King Sumanguru° only to suffer a major defeat some forty years later at the hands of Sundiata°, the upstart leader of the Malinke° people. Though both leaders professed Islam, Malinke legends recall their battles as clashes between powerful magicians, suggesting how much old and new beliefs mingled. Sumanguru could reportedly appear and disappear at will, assume dozens of shapes, and catch arrows in midflight. Sundiata defeated Sumanguru's much larger forces through superior military maneuvers and by successfully wounding his adversary with a special arrow that robbed him of his magical powers. This victory was followed by others that created Sundiata's Mali empire.

Mali, the empire that grew from Sundiata's victories, depended on a well-developed agricultural base and control of the regional and trans-Saharan trade routes, as had Ghana before it. Mali, however, controlled a greater area than Ghana, including not only the core trading area of the upper Niger but the gold fields of the Niger headwaters to the southwest as well. Moreover, its rulers fostered the spread of Islam among the empire's political and trading elites. Control of the gold and copper trades and contacts with North African Muslim traders gave Mali unprecedented prosperity.

Under the ruler **Mansa Kankan Musa**° (r. 1312–1337), the empire's reputation for wealth spread far and wide. Mansa Musa's pilgrimage to Mecca in 1324–1325 fulfilled his personal duty as a Muslim and at the same time put on display his exceptional wealth. He traveled with a large entourage. Besides his senior wife and five hundred of her ladies in waiting and their slaves, one account says there were also 60,000 porters and a vast caravan of camels carrying supplies and provisions. For purchases and gifts, he brought along eighty packages of gold, each weighing 122 ounces (3.8 kilograms). In addition, five hundred slaves each carried a golden staff. Mansa Musa dispersed so many gifts when he passed through Cairo that the value of gold was depressed for years.

On his return from this pilgrimage, Mansa Musa built new mosques and opened Quran schools in the cities along the Niger bend. Ibn Battuta, who visited Mali from 1352 to 1354 during the reign of Mansa Musa's successor, Mansa Suleiman° (r. 1341–1360), lauded the Malians for their faithful recitation of prayers and their zeal in teaching children the Quran.

He also reported that "complete and general safety" prevailed in the vast territories ruled by Suleiman and that foreign travelers had no reason to fear being robbed or having their goods confiscated if they died. (For Ibn Battuta's account of the sultan's court and his subjects' respect, see Society and Culture: Personal Styles of Rule in India and Mali.)

Two centuries after its founding, Mali began to disintegrate. Mansa Suleiman's successors could

---

bilad al-sudan (bih-LAD uhs-soo-DAN)
Takrur (TAHK-roor)   **Sumanguru** (soo-muhn-GOO-roo)
Sundiata (soon-JAH-tuh)   **Malinke** (muh-LING-kay)

Mansa Kankan Musa (MAHN-suh KAHN-kahn MOO-suh)
Mansa Suleiman (MAHN-suh SOO-lay-mahn)

Sankore Mosque, Timbuktu
The wall and tower at the left and center represent traditional styles of construction in clay in a region with little building stone. A major emporium for trade at the southern edge of the Sahara, Timbuktu also served as an Islamic religious and educational center during its heyday in the fourteenth through sixteenth centuries. (Aldona Sabalis/ Photo Researchers, Inc.)

not prevent rebellions breaking out among the diverse peoples subjected to Malinke rule. Other groups attacked from without. The desert Tuareg retook their city of Timbuktu° in 1433. By 1500, the rulers of Mali had dominion over little more than the Malinke heartland.

The cities of the upper Niger survived Mali's collapse, but some trade and intellectual life moved east to the central Sudan. Shortly after 1450, the rulers of several Hausa city-states officially adopted Islam. These states took on importance as manufacturing and trading centers, becoming famous for cotton textiles and leatherworking. The central Sudanic state of Kanem-Bornu° also expanded in the late fifteenth century from the ancient kingdom of Kanem, whose rulers had accepted Islam in about 1085. At its peak around 1250, Kanem had absorbed the state of Bornu south and west of Lake Chad and gained control of routes crossing the central Sahara. As Kanem-Bornu's armies conquered new territories, they also spread the rule of Islam.

Timbuktu (tim-buk-TOO)
Kanem-Bornu (KAH-nuhm-BOR-noo)

The Delhi Sultanate in India

Having long ago lost the defensive unity of the Gupta Empire (see Chapter 4), the divided states of northwest India fell prey to raids by Afghan warlords from the early eleventh century. In the last decades of the twelfth century, a Turkish dynasty armed with powerful crossbows captured the northern Indian cities of Lahore and Delhi. One partisan Muslim chronicler wrote: "The city [Delhi] and its vicinity was freed from idols and idol-worship, and in the sanctuaries of the images of the [Hindu] Gods, mosques were raised by the worshippers of one God."[2] Turkish adventurers from Central Asia flocked to join the invading armies, overwhelming the small Indian states, which were often at war with one another.

Between 1206 and 1236, the Muslim invaders extended their rule over the Hindu princes and chiefs in much of northern India. Sultan Iltutmish° (r. 1211–1236) consolidated the conquest in a series of military expeditions that made his realm the largest in India (see Map 13.2). He also secured

Iltutmish (il-TOOT-mish)

Personal Styles of Rule in India and Mali

Ibn Battuta vividly described the rulers of the Muslim states he visited. His account of Sultan Muhammad ibn Tughluq of Delhi reflects the familiarity he acquired during a long stay in India in the 1340s.

Muhammad is a man who, above all others, is fond of making presents and shedding blood. There may always be seen at his gate some poor person becoming rich, or some living one condemned to death. His generous and brave actions, and his cruel and violent deeds, have obtained notoriety among the people. In spite of this, he is the most humble of men, and the one who exhibits the greatest equity. The ceremonies of religion are dear to his ears, and he is very severe in respect of prayer and the punishment which follows its neglect.

One of the most serious charges against this Sultan is that he forced all the inhabitants of Delhi to leave their homes. [After] the people of Delhi wrote letters full of insults and invectives against [him,] the Sultan . . . decided to ruin Delhi, so he purchased all the houses and inns from the inhabitants, paid them the price, and then ordered them to remove to Daulatabad. . . .

The greater part of the inhabitants departed, but [h]is slaves found two men in the streets: one was paralyzed, the other blind. They were brought before the sovereign, who ordered the paralytic to be shot away from a *manjanik* [catapult], and the blind man to be dragged from Delhi to Daulatabad, a journey of forty days' distance. The poor wretch fell to pieces during the journey, and only one of his legs reached Daulatabad.

In contrast, Ibn Battuta describes Mansa Suleiman of Mali, whom he visited in 1353, in remote and impersonal terms that accord with African political traditions.

On certain days the sultan holds audiences in the palace yard, where there is a platform under a tree . . . carpeted with silk, [over which] is raised the official recognition of the Delhi Sultanate as a Muslim state by the caliph of Baghdad. Although pillaging continued, especially on the frontiers, the incorporation of north India into the Islamic world marked the beginning of the invaders' transformation from brutal conquerors to somewhat more benign rulers. Muslim commanders extended protection to the conquered, freeing them from persecution in return for payment of a special tax. Yet Hindus never forgot the intolerance and destruction of their first contacts with the invaders.

Iltutmish astonished his ministers by passing over his weak and pleasure-seeking sons and designating as his heir his beloved and talented daughter Raziya°. When they questioned the unprecedented idea of a woman ruling a Muslim state, he said, "My sons are devoted to the pleasures of youth: no one of them is qualified to be king. . . . There is no one more competent to guide the State than my daughter." In the event, her brother—who delighted in riding his elephant through the bazaar, showering the crowds with coins—ruled ineptly for seven months before the ministers relented and put Raziya on the throne.

Raziya (rah-ZEE-uh)

umbrella, . . . surmounted by a bird in gold, about the size of a falcon. The sultan comes out of a door in a corner of the palace, carrying a bow in his hand and a quiver on his back. On his head he has a golden skull-cap, bound with a gold band which has narrow ends shaped like knives, more than a span in length. His usual dress is a velvety red tunic, made of the European fabrics called mutanfas. The sultan is preceded by his musicians, who carry gold and silver [two-stringed guitars], and behind him come three hundred armed slaves. He walks in a leisurely fashion, affecting a very slow movement, and even stops and looks round the assembly, then ascends [the platform] in the sedate manner of a preacher ascending a mosque-pulpit. As he takes his seat, the drums, trumpets, and bugles are sounded. Three slaves go at a run to summon the sovereign's deputy and the military commanders, who enter and sit down. . . .

The blacks are of all people the most submissive to their king and the most abject in their behavior before him. They swear by his name, saying *Mansa Suleiman ki* [by Mansa Suleiman's law]. If he summons any of them while he is holding an audience in his pavilion, the person summoned takes off his clothes and puts on worn garments, removes his turban and dons a dirty skullcap and enters with his garments and trousers raised knee-high. He goes forward in an attitude of humility and dejection, and knocks the ground hard with his elbows, then stands with bowed head and bent back listening to what he says. If anyone addresses the king and receives a reply from him, he uncovers his back and throws dust over his head and back, for all the world like a bather splashing himself with water. I used to wonder how it was that they did not blind themselves.

How can the kind and cruel sides of Sultan Muhammad be reconciled? What role would Islam have played in his generosity? Could cruelty have brought any benefits to the ruler of a conquest state? How did Mansa Suleiman's ritual appearances serve to enhance his majesty? What attitudes toward Suleiman do his subjects' actions suggest? How different were the ruling styles of Muhammad and Suleiman?

Source: The first excerpt is from Henry M. Elliot, *The History of India as Told by Its Own Historians* (London: Trübner and Co., 1869–1871) 3:609–614. The second excerpt is adapted from H. A. R. Gibb, ed., *Selections from the Travels of Ibn Battuta in Asia and Africa* (London: Cambridge University Press, 1929), pp. 326–327. Copyright © 1929. Reprinted with permission of the Cambridge University Press.

A chronicler who knew her explained why this able ruler lasted less than four years (r. 1236–1240):

> Sultan Raziya was a great monarch. She was wise, just, and generous, a benefactor to her kingdom, a dispenser of justice, the protector of her subjects, and the leader of her armies. She was endowed with all the qualities befitting a king, but that she was not born of the right sex, and so in the estimation of men all these virtues were worthless. May God have mercy upon her![3]

Doing her best to prove herself a proper king, Raziya dressed like a man and led her troops atop an elephant. In the end, however, the Turkish chiefs imprisoned her, and a robber killed her during an escape attempt.

After a half-century of stagnation and rebellion, the ruthless but efficient policies of Sultan Ala-ud-din Khalji° (r. 1296–1316) increased his control over the empire's outlying provinces. Successful frontier raids and high taxes kept his treasury full, wage and price controls in Delhi kept down the cost of maintaining a large army, and a

---

Ala-ud-din Khalji (uh-LAH-uh-DEEN KAL-jee)

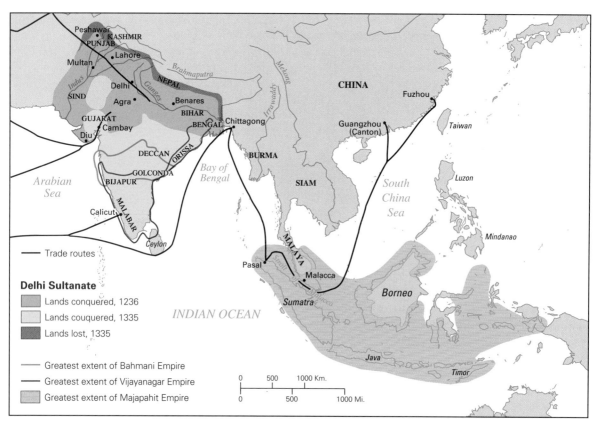

Map 13.2   South and Southeast Asia, 1200–1500   The rise of new empires and the expansion of maritime trade reshaped the lives of many tropical Asians.

network of spies stifled intrigue. When a Mongol threat from Central Asia eased, Ala-ud-din's forces extended the sultanate's southern flank, seizing the rich trading state of **Gujarat°** in 1298, and then drove southward, briefly seizing the southern tip of the Indian peninsula.

When Ibn Battuta visited Delhi, Sultan Muhammad ibn Tughluq° (r. 1325–1351) received him in his celebrated Hall of a Thousand Pillars. The world traveler praised the sultan's piety and generosity, but also recounted his cruelties (see Society and Culture: Personal Styles of Rule in India and Mali). The sultan enlarged the sultanate to its greatest extent at the expense of the independent Indian states but balanced his aggressive policy with religious toleration. He even attended Hindu

religious festivals. However, his successor, Firuz Shah° (r. 1351–1388), alienated powerful Hindus by taxing the Brahmins, preferring to cultivate good relations with the Muslim elite. Muslim chroniclers praised him for constructing forty mosques, thirty colleges, and a hundred hospitals.

A small minority in a giant land, the Turkish rulers relied on terror to keep their subjects submissive, on harsh military reprisals to put down rebellion, and on pillage and high taxes to sustain the ruling elite in luxury and power. Though little different from most other large states of this time (including Mali) in being more a burden than a benefit to most of its subjects, the sultanate never lost the disadvantage of foreign origins and alien religious identity. Nevertheless, over time, the sul-

---

Gujarat (goo-juh-RAHT)   **Tughluq** (toog-LOOK)   **Firuz Shah** (fuh-ROOZ shah)

tans did incorporate some Hindus into their administrations, and some members of the ruling elite also married women from prominent Hindu families, though the brides had to become Muslim.

Personal and religious rivalries within the Muslim elite, along with Hindu discontent, threatened the Delhi Sultanate whenever it showed weakness and finally hastened its end. In the mid-fourteenth century, Muslim nobles challenged the sultan's dominion and established the independent Bahmani° kingdom (1347–1482) on the Deccan Plateau. Defending against the southward push of Bahmani armies, the Hindu states of South India united to form the Vijayanagar° Empire (1336–1565), which at its height controlled the rich trading ports on both coasts of south India and held Ceylon as a tributary state.

The elites of Vijayanagar and the Bahmani state turned a blind eye to religious differences when doing so favored their interests. Bahmani rulers sought to balance Muslim domination with the practical policies of incorporating the Hindu leaders into the government, marrying Hindu wives, and appointing Brahmins to high offices. Vijayanagar rulers hired Muslim horsemen and archers to strengthen their military forces and formed an alliance with the Muslim-ruled state of Gujarat.

By 1351, when all of south India had cast off Delhi's rule, much of north India rose in rebellion. In the east, Bengal broke away from the sultanate in 1338, becoming a center of the mystical Sufi tradition of Islam (see Chapter 7). In the west, Gujarat regained its independence by 1390. The weakening of Delhi's central authority tempted fresh Mongol interest in the area. In 1398, the Turko-Mongol leader Timur (see Chapter 11) captured the city of Delhi. When his armies withdrew the next year with vast quantities of loot and tens of thousands of captives, the largest city in southern Asia lay empty and in ruins. The Delhi Sultanate never recovered.

For all its shortcomings, the Delhi Sultanate triggered the development of centralized political authority in India. Prime ministers and provincial governors serving under the sultans established a bureaucracy, improved food production, promoted trade, and put in circulation a common currency. Despite the many conflicts that Muslim conquest and rule provoked, Islam gradually acquired a permanent place in South Asia.

ℓ

INDIAN OCEAN TRADE

The maritime network that stretched across the Indian Ocean from the Islamic heartlands of Iran and Arabia to Southeast Asia connected with routes reaching into Europe, Africa, and China. The Indian Ocean routes also facilitated the spread of Islam.

Monsoon Mariners

Between 1200 and 1500, the volume of trade in the Indian Ocean increased, stimulated by and contributing to the prosperity of Islamic and Mongol empires in Asia, cities in Europe, and new kingdoms in Africa and Southeast Asia. The demand for luxuries—precious metals and jewels, rare spices, fine textiles, and other manufactures—rose. Larger ships made shipments of bulk cargoes of ordinary cotton textiles, pepper, food grains (rice, wheat, barley), timber, horses, and other goods profitable. When the collapse of the Mongol Empire in the fourteenth century disrupted overland routes across Central Asia, the Indian Ocean assumed greater strategic importance in tying together the peoples of Eurasia and Africa.

Some goods were transported from one end of this trading network to the other, but few ships or crews made a complete circuit. Instead, the Indian Ocean trade divided into two legs: from the Middle East across the Arabian Sea to India and from India across the Bay of Bengal to Southeast Asia (see Map 13.2).

Shipyards in ports on the Malabar coast (southwestern India) built large numbers of **dhows°,** the characteristic cargo and passenger ships of the Arabian Sea. They grew from an average capacity of

---

Bahmani (bah MAHN-ee)
Vijayanagar (vee-juh-yah-NAH-gar)

dhow (dow)

100 tons in 1200 to 400 tons in 1500. On a typical expedition, a dhow might sail west from India to Arabia and Africa on the northeast monsoon winds (December to March) and return on the southwest monsoons (April to August). Small dhows kept the coast in sight. Relying on the stars to guide them, skilled pilots steered large vessels by the quicker route straight across the water. A large dhow could sail from the Red Sea to mainland Southeast Asia in from two to four months, but few did so. Eastbound cargoes and passengers from dhows reaching India were likely to be transferred to junks, which dominated the eastern half of the Indian Ocean and the South China Sea.

The largest, most technologically advanced, and most seaworthy vessels of this time, junks first appeared in China and spread with Chinese influence. Enormous nails held together hulls of heavy spruce or fir planks, in contrast with dhows, whose planks were sewn together with palm fiber. Below the deck, watertight compartments minimized flooding in case of damage to the ship's hull. According to Ibn Battuta, the largest junks had twelve sails made of bamboo and carried a crew of a thousand men, including four hundred soldiers. A large junk might accommodate a hundred passenger cabins and a cargo of over 1,000 tons. Junks dominated China's foreign shipping to Southeast Asia and India, but the Chinese did not control all of the junks that plied these waters. During the fifteenth century, similar vessels came out of shipyards in Bengal and Southeast Asia to be sailed by local crews.

Decentralized and cooperative commercial interests, rather than political authorities, connected the several regions that participated in the Indian Ocean trade. The **Swahili° Coast** supplied gold from inland areas of eastern Africa. Ports around the Arabian peninsula supplied horses and goods from the northern parts of the Middle East, the Mediterranean, and eastern Europe. Merchants in the cities of coastal India received goods from east and west, sold some locally, passed others along, and added Indian goods to the trade. The Strait of Malacca°, between the eastern end of the Indian Ocean and the South China Sea, provided a meeting point for trade from Southeast Asia, China, and the Indian Ocean. In each region, certain ports functioned as giant emporia, consolidating goods from smaller ports and inland areas for transport across the seas.

Africa: The Swahili Coast and Zimbabwe

Trade expanded steadily along the East African coast from about 1250, giving rise to between thirty and forty separate city-states by 1500. After 1200, masonry buildings as much as four stories high replaced mud and thatch dwellings, and archaeological findings include imported glass beads, Chinese porcelain, and other exotic goods. Coastal and island peoples shared a common culture and a language built on African grammar and vocabulary but enriched with many Arabic and Persian terms and written in Arabic script. In time, these people became known as "Swahili," from the Arabic name *sawahil° al-sudan,* meaning "shores of the blacks."

Sometime after Ibn Battuta's visit to Mogadishu in 1331, the more southerly city of Kilwa surpassed it as the Swahili Coast's most important commercial center. Ibn Battuta declared Kilwa "one of the most beautiful and well-constructed towns in the world." He noted its inhabitants' dark skins and Muslim piety, and he praised their ruler for the traditional Muslim virtues of humility and generosity.

What attracted the Arab and Iranian merchants whom oral traditions associate with the Swahili Coast's commercial expansion? By the late fifteenth century, Kilwa was annually exporting a ton of gold mined by inland Africans much farther south. Much of it came from or passed through a powerful state on the plateau south of the Zambezi River. At its peak in about 1400, its capital city, now known as **Great Zimbabwe,** occupied 193 acres (78 hectares) and had some 18,000 inhabitants.

Between about 1250 and 1450, local African craftsmen built stone structures for Great Zimbabwe's rulers, priests, and wealthy citizens. The largest structure, an enclosure the size and shape

Royal Enclosure, Great Zimbabwe   The rulers who lived here prospered from Great Zimbabwe's trade. The narrow corridor between two high walls through which visitors entered created an awe-inspiring effect.   (Courtesy of the Department of Information, Rhodesia)

of a large football stadium with drystone walls 17 feet (5 meters) thick and 32 feet (10 meters) high, served as the king's court. A large conical stone tower was among the many buildings inside the walls.

As in Mali, mixed farming and cattle herding provided the economic basis of the Great Zimbabwe state, but long-distance trade brought added wealth. Trade began regionally with copper ingots from the upper Zambezi Valley, salt, and local manufactures. Gold exports to the coast expanded in the fourteenth and fifteenth centuries and brought Zimbabwe to its peak. However, historians suspect that the city's residents depleted nearby forests for firewood while their cattle overgrazed surrounding grasslands. The resulting ecological crisis hastened the empire's decline in the fifteenth century.

Arabia: Aden and the Red Sea

The city of **Aden°** near the southwestern tip of the Arabian peninsula had a double advantage in the Indian Ocean trade. Monsoon winds brought enough rainfall to supply drinking water to a large population and grow grain for export, and its location made it a convenient stopover for trade with India, the Persian Gulf, East Africa, and Egypt. Aden's merchants dealt in cotton cloth and beads from India; spices from Southeast Asia; horses from Arabia and Ethiopia; pearls from the Red Sea; manufactured luxuries from Cairo; slaves, gold, and ivory from Ethiopia; and grain, opium, and dyes from Aden's own hinterland.

After visiting Mecca in 1331, Ibn Battuta sailed down the Red Sea to Aden, probably wedged in among bales of trade goods. His comments on the

Aden (AY-den)

wealth of Aden's leading merchants include a story about the slave of one merchant who bought a ram for the fabulous sum of 400 dinars in order to keep the slave of another merchant from buying it. Instead of punishing the slave for extravagance, the master freed him as a reward for outdoing his rival. Ninety years later, a Chinese Muslim visitor, Ma Huan, found "the country . . . rich, and the people numerous," living in stone residences several stories high.

Common commercial interests generally promoted good relations among the different religions and cultures of this region. For example, in the mid-thirteenth century, a wealthy Jew from Aden named Yosef settled in Christian Ethiopia, where he acted as an adviser. South Arabia had been trading with neighboring parts of Africa since before the times of King Solomon of Israel. The dynasty that ruled Ethiopia after 1270 claimed descent from Solomon and from the South Arabian princess Sheba. Solomonic Ethiopia's consolidation accompanied a great increase in trade through the Red Sea port of Zeila°, including slaves, amber, and animal pelts, which went to Aden and on to other destinations.

Friction sometimes arose, however. In the fourteenth century, the Sunni Muslim king of Yemen sent materials for building a large mosque in Zeila, but the local Somalis (who were Shi'ite Muslims) threw the stones into the sea. This resulted in a year-long embargo of Zeila ships in Aden. In the late fifteenth century, Ethiopia's territorial expansion and efforts to increase control over the trade provoked conflicts with Muslims who ruled the coastal states of the Red Sea.

India: Gujarat and the Malabar Coast

The state of Gujarat in western India prospered from the expanding trade of the Arabian Sea and the rise of the Delhi Sultanate. Blessed with a rich agricultural hinterland and a long coastline, Gujarat attracted new trade after the Mongol destruction of Baghdad in 1258 disrupted the northern land routes. After the initial violence of its forced incorporation into the Delhi Sultanate in 1298, Gu-

jarat prospered from increased trade with Delhi's ruling class despite occasional military crackdowns. Independent again after 1390, the Muslim rulers of Gujarat extended their control over neighboring Hindu states and regained their preeminent position in the Indian Ocean trade.

Gujaratis exported cotton textiles and indigo to the Middle East and Europe, in return for gold and silver. They also shipped cotton cloth, carnelian beads, and foodstuffs to the Swahili Coast in exchange for ebony, slaves, ivory, and gold. During the fifteenth century, traders expanded eastward to the Strait of Malacca. These Gujarati merchants helped spread the Islamic faith among East Indian traders, some of whom even imported specially carved gravestones from Gujarat.

Unlike Kilwa and Aden, Gujarat manufactured goods for trade. According to the thirteenth-century Venetian traveler Marco Polo, Gujarat's leatherworkers dressed enough skins in a year to fill several ships to Arabia and other places. They made sleeping mats for export to the Middle East "in red and blue leather, exquisitely inlaid with figures of birds and beasts, and skillfully embroidered with gold and silver wire," as well as leather cushions embroidered in gold. Later observers compared the Gujarati city of Cambay with cities in Flanders and northern Italy (see Chapter 14) in the scale, artisanry, and diversity of its textile industries. Cotton, linen, and silk cloth, along with carpets and quilts, found a large market in Europe, Africa, the Middle East, and Southeast Asia. Cambay also produced polished gemstones, gold jewelry, carved ivory, stone beads, and both natural and artificial pearls. At the height of its prosperity in the fifteenth century, its well-laid-out streets and open places boasted fine stone houses with tiled roofs. Although Muslim residents controlled most Gujarati overseas trade, its Hindu merchant caste profited so much from related commercial activities that their wealth and luxurious lives became the envy of other Indians.

More southerly cities on the Malabar Coast duplicated Gujarat's success. Calicut° and other coastal cities prospered from locally made cotton textiles and locally grown grains and spices, and served as clearing-houses for the long-distance

---

Zeila (ZEYE-luh)

Calicut (KAL-ih-cut)

trade of the Indian Ocean. The Zamorin° (ruler) of Calicut presided over a loose federation of its Hindu rulers that united the coastal region. As in eastern Africa and Arabia, rulers generally tolerated religious and ethnic groups who contributed to commercial profits. Most trading activity lay in the hands of Muslims, many originally from Iran and Arabia, who intermarried with local Indian Muslims. Jewish merchants also operated from Malabar's trading cities.

Southeast Asia: The Rise of Malacca

At the eastern end of the Indian Ocean, the Strait of Malacca between the Malay Peninsula and the island of Sumatra provided the principal passage into the South China Sea (see Map 13.2). As trade increased in the fourteenth and fifteenth centuries, this commercial choke point became the site of political rivalry. The mainland kingdom of Siam controlled most of the upper Malay Peninsula, while the Java-based kingdom of Majapahit° extended its dominion over the lower Malay Peninsula and much of Sumatra. Majapahit, however, could not suppress a nest of Chinese pirates based at the Sumatran city of Palembang° who preyed on ships sailing through the strait. In 1407, a fleet sent from China smashed the pirates' power and took their chief back home for trial.

Majapahit, weakened by internal struggles, could not take advantage of China's intervention, making the chief beneficiary the newer port of **Malacca** (or Melaka), which dominated the narrowest part of the strait. Under a prince from Palembang, Malacca had grown from an obscure fishing village into an important port through a series of astute alliances. Nominally subject to the king of Siam, Malacca also secured an alliance with China that was sealed by the visit of the imperial fleet in 1407. The conversion of an early ruler from Hinduism to Islam helped promote trade with Muslim merchants from Gujarat and elsewhere. Merchants also appreciated Malacca's security and low taxes.

Malacca served not just as a meeting point but also as an emporium for Southeast Asian products: rubies and musk from Burma, tin from Malaya, gold from Sumatra, cloves and nutmeg from the Moluccas (or Spice Islands, as Europeans later dubbed them). Shortly after 1500, when Malacca was at its height, one resident counted eighty-four languages spoken among the merchants gathered there, who came from as far away as Turkey, Ethiopia, and the Swahili Coast. Four officials administered the foreign merchant communities: one for the Gujaratis, one for other Indians and Burmese, one for Southeast Asians, and one for the Chinese and Japanese. Malacca's wealth and its cosmopolitan residents set the standard for luxury in Malaya for centuries to come.

SOCIAL AND CULTURAL CHANGE

State growth, commercial expansion, and the spread of Islam between 1200 and 1500 led to many changes in the social and cultural life of tropical peoples. The political and commercial elites grew in size and power, as did the number of slaves they owned. The spread of Muslim practices and beliefs affected social and cultural life—witness words of Arabic origin like *Sahara, Sudan, Swahili,* and *monsoon*—yet local traditions remained important.

Architecture, Learning, and Religion

Social and cultural changes typically affected cities more than rural areas. As Ibn Battuta and other travelers observed, wealthy merchants and ruling elites spent lavishly on mansions, palaces, and places of worship. Most places of worship surviving from this period blend older traditions and new influences. African Muslims produced Middle Eastern mosque designs in local building materials: sun-baked clay and wood in the western Sudan and coral stone on the Swahili Coast. Hindu temple architecture influenced

---

Zamorin (ZAH-much-ruhn)
Majapahit (mah-jah-PAH-hit)   Palembang (pah-lem-BONG)

mosque designs in Gujarat, which sometimes incorporated pieces of older structures. The congregational mosque at Cambay, built in 1325 with the traditional Islamic courtyard, cloisters, and porches, utilized pillars, porches, and arches taken from sacked Hindu and Jain° temples. The congregational mosque erected at the Gujarati capital of Ahmadabad° in 1423 had the open courtyard typical of mosques everywhere, but the surrounding verandas incorporated many typical Gujarati details and architectural conventions.

In Africa, King Lalibela° of Ethiopia constructed his capital, Lalibela, during the first third of the thirteenth century and ordered eleven churches to be carved out of solid rock, each commemorating a sacred Christian site in Jerusalem. These structures carried on an old Ethiopian tradition of rock sculpture, though on a far grander scale.

Mosques, churches, and temples were centers of education as well as prayer. Muslims promoted literacy among their sons (and sometimes their daughters) so that they could read sacred texts. Ibn Battuta reported seeing several boys in Mali wearing chains until they completed memorizing passages of the Quran. Literacy and Islam spread together in sub-Saharan Africa where Christian Ethiopia had previously been the only literate society. In time, scholars adapted the Arabic alphabet to write local languages.

Islam affected literacy less in India, which had a long literate heritage. Arabic served primarily for religious purposes, while Persian became the language of high culture used at court. Eventually **Urdu**° arose, a Persian-influenced literary form of Hindi written in Arabic characters. Muslims also introduced papermaking in India.

Advanced Muslim scholars studied Islamic law, theology, and administration, as well as works on mathematics, medicine, science, and philosophy, partly derived from ancient Greek writings. In sixteenth-century **Timbuktu,** over 150 schools taught the Quran while leading clerics taught advanced classes in mosques or homes. Books imported from North Africa brought high prices.

Al-Hajj Ahmed, a scholar who died in Timbuktu in 1536, possessed some seven hundred volumes, an unusually large library for that time. In Southeast Asia, Malacca became a center of Islamic learning from which scholars spread Islam throughout the region. Other important centers of learning developed in Muslim India, particularly in Delhi, the capital.

Even in lands seized by conquest, Muslim rulers seldom required conversion. Example and persuasion by merchants and Sufis proved more effective. Many Muslims worked hard to persuade others of Islam's superiority. Muslim domination of long-distance trade assisted the adoption of Islam. Commercial transactions could take place across religious boundaries, but the common code of morality and law that Islam provided encouraged trust and drew many local merchants to Islam. From the major trading centers along the Swahili Coast, in the Sudan, in coastal India, and in Southeast Asia, Islam's influence spread along regional trade routes.

Marriage also played a role. Single Muslim men traveling to and settling in tropical Africa and Asia often married local women. Their children grew up in the Islamic faith. Some wealthy men had dozens of children from up to four wives and additional slave concubines. Servants and slaves in such households normally professed Islam.

In India, Muslim invasions eliminated the last strongholds of long-declining Buddhism, including, in 1196, the great Buddhist center of study at Nalanda° in Bihar°. Its manuscripts were burned and thousands of monks killed or driven into exile in Nepal and Tibet. With Buddhism reduced to a minor faith in the land of its birth, Islam emerged as India's second most important religion. Hinduism still prevailed in 1500, but Islam displaced Hinduism in most of maritime Southeast Asia.

Islam also spread among rural peoples, such as the pastoral Fulani of West Africa and Somali of northeastern Africa and various pastoralists in northwest India. In Bengal, Muslim religious figures oversaw the conversion of jungle into farmland and thereby gained many converts.

Jain (jine) **Ahmadabad** (AH-muhd-ah-bahd)
Lalibela (LAH-lee-BEL-uh) **Urdu** (ER-doo)

Nalanda (nuh-LAN-duh) **Bihar** (bee-HAHR)

Church of Saint George, Ethiopia King Lalibela (r. ca. 1180–1220) had churches carved out of solid volcanic rock in his new capital (also named Lalibela). The church of Saint George, excavated to a depth of 40 feet (13 meters) and hollowed out inside, has the shape of a Greek cross. (S. Sassoon/ Robert Harding Picture Library)

The spread of Islam did not mean simply the replacement of one set of beliefs by another. Islam adapted to the cultures of the regions it penetrated, developing African, Indian, and Indonesian varieties.

Social and Gender Distinctions

A growth in slavery accompanied the rising prosperity of the elites. Military campaigns in India, according to Islamic sources, reduced hundreds of thousands of Hindu "infidels" to slavery. Delhi overflowed with slaves. Sultan Ala ud-Din owned 50,000 and Firuz Shah 180,000, including 12,000 skilled artisans. Sultan Tughluq sent 100 male slaves and 100 female slaves as a gift to the emperor of China in return for a similar gift.

Mali and Bornu sent slaves across the Sahara to North Africa, including beautiful maidens and eunuchs (castrated males). The expanding Ethiopian Empire regularly sent captives for sale to Aden traders at Zeila. According to modern estimates, Saharan and Red Sea traders sold about 2.5 million enslaved Africans between 1200 and 1500. African slaves from the Swahili Coast played conspicuous roles in the navies, armies, and administrations of some Indian states, especially in the fifteenth century. A few African slaves even reached China, where a source from about 1225 says rich families preferred gatekeepers with bodies "black as lacquer."

With "free" labor abundant and cheap, few slaves worked as farmers. In some places, hereditary castes of slaves dominated certain trades and military units. Indeed, the earliest rulers of the Delhi Sultanate rose from military slavery. A slave general in the western Sudan named Askia Muhammad seized control of the Songhai Empire (Mali's successor) in 1493. Less fortunate slaves, like the men and women who mined copper in Mali, did hard menial work.

Wealthy households used many slave servants. Eunuchs guarded the harems of wealthy Muslims, but women predominated as household slaves, serving also as entertainers and concubines. Some rich men aspired to having a concubine from every part of the world. One of Firuz Shah's nobles reportedly had two thousand harem slaves, including women from Turkey and China.

Sultan Ala ud-Din's campaigns against Gujarat at the end of the thirteenth century yielded a booty of twenty thousand maidens in addition to innumerable younger children of both sexes. The supply of captives became so great that the lowest grade of horse sold for five times as much as an ordinary female slave, although beautiful young virgins commanded far higher prices.

Hindu legal digests and commentaries suggest that the position of Hindu women may have improved somewhat compared to earlier periods. The ancient practice of sati°—that is, of an upper-caste widow throwing herself on her husband's funeral pyre—remained a meritorious act strongly approved by social custom. But Ibn Battuta makes it clear that sati was strictly optional. Since the Hindu commentaries devote considerable attention to the rights of widows without sons to inherit their husbands' estates, one may even conclude that sati was exceptional.

Indian parents still gave their daughters in marriage before the age of puberty, but consummation of the marriage took place only when the young woman was ready. Wives faced far stricter rules of fidelity and chastity than their husbands and could be abandoned for any serious breach. But other offenses against law and custom usually brought lighter penalties than for men. A woman's male master—father, husband, or owner—determined her status. Women seldom played active roles in commerce, administration, or religion.

Besides child rearing, women involved themselves with food preparation and, when not prohibited by religious restrictions, brewing. In many parts of Africa, women commonly made beer from grains or bananas. These mildly alcoholic beverages played an important part in male rituals of hospitality and relaxation.

Throughout tropical Africa and Asia, women did much of the farm work. They also toted home heavy loads of food, firewood, and water for cooking balanced on their heads. Other common female activities included making clay pots for

Indian Woman Spinning, ca. 1500 This drawing of a Muslim woman by an Indian artist betrays Persian stylistic influence. The spinning wheel, which the Muslim invaders introduced, made this traditional woman's task much easier. Men then wove the spun threads into the cotton textiles for which India was celebrated. (British Library, Oriental and Indian Office Library, Or 3299, f. 151)

cooking and storage and making clothing. In India, the spinning wheel, introduced by the Muslim invaders, greatly reduced the cost of making thread for weaving. Women typically spun at home, leaving weaving to men. In West Africa, women often sold agricultural products, pottery, and other craftwork in the markets.

Adopting Islam did not necessarily mean accepting the social customs of the Arab world. In Mali's capital, Ibn Battuta was appalled that Muslim women both free and slave did not completely cover their bodies and veil their faces when appearing in public. He considered their nakedness an offense to women's (and men's) modesty. In another part of Mali, he berated a Muslim merchant from Morocco for permitting his wife to sit on a couch and chat with her male friend. The husband replied, "The association of women with men is agreeable to us and part of good manners, to which no suspicion attaches." Ibn Battuta refused to visit the merchant again.

sati (suh-TEE)

CONCLUSION

Tropical Africa and Asia contained 40 percent of the world's population and over a quarter of its habitable land. Between 1200 and 1500, commercial, political, and cultural currents drew the region's peoples closer together. The Indian Ocean became the world's most important and richest trading area. The Delhi Sultanate brought the greatest political unity to India since the decline of the Guptas. Mali extended the political and trading role pioneered by Ghana in the western Sudan. Trade and empire followed closely the enlargement of Islam's presence and the accompanying diversification of Islamic customs.

Yet many social and cultural practices remained stable. Most tropical Africans and Asians never ventured far outside the rural communities where their families had lived for generations. Their lives followed the pattern of the seasons, the cycle of religious rituals and festivals, and the stages from childhood to elder status. Most people engaged in farming, herding, and fishing. Village communities proved remarkably hardy. They might be ravaged by natural disaster or pillaged by advancing armies, but over time most recovered. Empires and kingdoms rose and fell, but the villages endured.

In comparison, social, political, and environmental changes taking place in the Latin West, described in the next chapter, had great implications for tropical peoples after 1500.

■ Key Terms

Ibn Battuta	**dhows**
tropics	**Swahili Coast**
monsoons	**Great Zimbabwe**
Delhi Sultanate	**Aden**
Mali	**Malacca**
Mansa Kankan Musa	**Urdu**
Gujarat	**Timbuktu**

■ Suggested Reading

Patricia Risso, *Merchants and Faith: Muslim Commerce and Culture in the Indian Ocean* (1995), briefly introduces the Indian Ocean trading system. Janet Abu-Lughod, *Before European Hegemony: The World System, A.D. 1250–1350* (1989), provides a more extensive and speculative view that may usefully be read with K. N. Chaudhuri, *Asia Before Europe: Economy and Civilization of the Indian Ocean from the Rise of Islam to 1750* (1991). For Islam's influences in tropical Asia and Africa, see Ira Lapidus, *A History of Islamic Societies* (1988), part II, and for commercial relations, Philip D. Curtin, *Cross-Cultural Trade in World History* (1984).

Greater detail on Southeast Asia is contained in Nicholas Tarling, ed., *The Cambridge History of Southeast Asia,* vol. 1 (1992); John F. Cady, *Southeast Asia: Its Historical Development* (1964); and G. Coedes, *The Indianized States of Southeast Asia,* ed. Walter F. Vella (1968). R. C. Majumdar, ed., *The History and Culture of the Indian People,* vol. 4, *The Delhi Sultanate,* 2d ed. (1967), covers India at length. Stanley Wolpert, *A New History of India,* 6th ed. (1999), offers a briefer account, and David Ludden, *A Peasant History of South India* (1985), approaches it from an intriguing perspective. For advanced topics, see Tapan Raychaudhuri and Irfan Habib, eds., *The Cambridge Economic History of India,* vol. 1, *c. 1200–c. 1750* (1982).

Africa in this period is well served by the later parts of Graham Connah's *African Civilizations: Precolonial Cities and States in Tropical Africa: An Archaeological Perspective* (1987), which covers Africa in general. For studies of greater depth, see D. T. Niane, ed., *UNESCO General History of Africa,* vol. 4, *Africa from the Twelfth to the Sixteenth Century* (1984), and Roland Oliver, ed., *The Cambridge History of Africa,* vol. 3, *c. 1050 to c. 1600* (1977).

Salim Kidwai, "Sultans, Eunuchs and Domestics: New Forms of Bondage in Medieval India," in *Chains of Servitude: Bondage and Slavery in India,* edited by Utsa Patnaik and Manjari Dingwaney (1985), and the first two chapters of Paul E. Lovejoy, *Transformations in Slavery: A History of Slavery in Africa* (1983), give good treatments of slavery and the slave trade.

Along with H. A. R. Gibb's three-volume translation of *The Travels of Ibn Battuta, A.D. 1325–1354* (1958–1971), see Ross E. Dunn, *The Adventures of Ibn Battuta: A Muslim of the Fourteenth Century* (1986). For annotated selections, see Said Hamdun and Noël King, *Ibn Battuta in Black Africa* (1995).

The most accessible survey of Indian Ocean sea travel is George F. Hourani, *Arab Seafaring,* expanded ed. (1995).

For a Muslim Chinese traveler's observations, see Ma Huan, *Ying-yai Sheng-lan, "The Overall Survey of the Ocean's Shore" [1433]*, translated and edited by J. V. G. Mills (1970). Another valuable contemporary account is G. R. Tibbetts, *Arab Navigation in the Indian Ocean Before the Coming of the Portuguese, Being a Translation of the Kitab al-Fawa'id . . . of Ahmad b. Majidal-Najdi* (1981).

■ **Notes**

1. Tarikh-i-Wassaf, in Henry M. Elliot, *The History of India as Told by Its Own Historians,* ed. John Dowson (London: Trübner and Co., 1869–1871), 2:28.
2. Hasan Nizami, Taju-l Ma-asir, in ibid., 2:219.
3. Minhaju-s Siraj, Tabakat-i Nasiri, in ibid., 2:332–333.

14

THE LATIN WEST,
1200–1500

*Rural Growth and Crisis • Urban Revival • Learning, Literature,
and the Renaissance • Political and Military Transformations*
SOCIETY AND CULTURE: **Blaming the Black Death on the Jews,
Strasbourg, 1349**

n the summer of 1454, a year after the Ottoman Turks captured the Greek Christian city of Constantinople, Aeneas Sylvius Piccolomini°, destined in four years to become pope, expressed doubts as to whether anyone could persuade the rulers of Christian Europe to take up arms together against the Muslims: "Christendom has no head whom all will obey—neither the pope nor the emperor receives his due." The Christian states thought more of fighting each other. French and English armies had been battling for over a century. The German emperor presided over dozens of states but did not really control them. The numerous kingdoms and principalities of Spain and Italy could not unite. With only slight exaggeration, Aeneas Sylvius moaned, "Every city has its own king, and there are as many princes as there are households."

He attributed this lack of unity to European preoccupation with personal welfare and mate-

rial gain. Both pessimism about human nature and materialism had increased during the previous century, after a devastating plague had carried off a third of western Europe's population.

Yet despite all these divisions, disasters, and wars, historians now see the period from 1200 to 1500 (Europe's Later Middle Ages) as a time of unusual progress. Prosperous cities adorned with splendid architecture, institutions of higher learning, and cultural achievements counterbalanced the avarice and greed that Aeneas Sylvius lamented. Frequent wars caused havoc and destruction, but also promoted the development of military technology and more unified monarchies.

Although their Muslim and Byzantine neighbors commonly called western Europeans "Franks," they ordinarily referred to themselves as "Latins," underscoring their allegiance to Roman Catholicism and the Latin language used in its rituals. Some common elements promoted the **Latin West's** vigorous revival: competition, the pursuit of success, and the effective use of borrowed technology and learning.

Aeneas Sylvius Piccolomini (uh-NEE-uhs SIL-vee-uhs
pee-kuh-lo-MEE-nee)

As you read this chapter, ask yourself the following questions:

- How well did western Europeans deal with their natural environment?

- How did warfare help rulers in the Latin West acquire the skills, weapons, and determination to challenge other parts of the world?

- How did technology promote excellence in business, learning, and architecture in the Latin West?

- How much did the region's achievements depend on its own people and how much on things borrowed from Muslim and Byzantine neighbors?

RURAL GROWTH AND CRISIS

Between 1200 and 1500, the Latin West brought more land under cultivation using new farming techniques and made greater use of machinery and mechanical forms of energy. Yet for the nine out of ten people who lived in the countryside, hard labor brought meager returns, and famine, epidemics, and war struck often. After the devastation of the Black Death between 1347 and 1351, social changes speeded up by peasant revolts released many persons from serfdom and brought some improvements to rural life.

Peasants, Population, and Plague

In 1200, most western Europeans lived as serfs tilling the soil on large estates owned by the nobility and the church (see Chapter 8). They owed their lord both a share of their harvests and numerous labor services. As a consequence of the inefficiency of farming practices and their obligations to landowners, peasants received meager returns for their hard work. Even with numerous religious holidays, peasants labored some 54 hours a week in their fields, more than half the time in support of the local nobility. Each noble household typically lived from the labor of fifteen to thirty peasant families. The standard of life in the lord's stone castle or manor house contrasted sharply with the peasant's one-room thatched cottage containing little furniture and no luxuries.

Scenes of rural life show both men and women at work in the fields, but equality of labor did not mean equality in decision making at home. In the peasant's hut as elsewhere in medieval Europe, women were subordinate to men. The influential theologian Thomas Aquinas° (1225–1274) spoke for his age when he argued that although both men and women were created in God's image, there was a sense in which "the image of God is found in man, and not in woman: for man is the beginning and end of woman; as God is the beginning and end of every creature."[1]

Rural poverty resulted from rapid population growth as well as inefficient farming methods and social inequality. In 1200, China's population may have exceeded Europe's by two to one; by 1300, the population of each was about 80 million. China's population fell because of the Mongol conquest (see Chapter 12) while Europe's more than doubled between 1100 and 1445. Some historians believe the reviving economy stimulated the increase. Others argue that severe epidemics were few, and warmer-than-usual temperatures reduced mortality from starvation and exposure.

More people required more productive farming and new agricultural settlements. One widespread new technique, the **three-field system,** replaced the custom of leaving half the land fallow (uncultivated) every year to regain its fertility. Farmers grew crops on two-thirds of their land each year and planted the third field in oats. The oats restored nitrogen to the depleted soil and produced feed for plow horses. In much of Europe, however, farmers continued to let half of their land lie fallow and use oxen (less efficient but cheaper than horses) to pull their plows.

Population growth also encouraged new agricultural settlements. In the twelfth and thirteenth centuries, large numbers of Germans migrated into

---

Aquinas (uh-KWY-nuhs)

CHRONOLOGY

	Technology and Environment	Culture	Politics and Society
1200	**1200s** Use of crossbows and longbows becomes widespread; windmills in increased use		**1200s** Champagne fairs **1204** Fourth Crusade launched **1215** Magna Carta issued
		1210s Religious orders founded: Teutonic Knights, Franciscans, Dominicans **1225–1274** Thomas Aquinas, monk and philosopher **1265–1321** Dante Alighieri, poet **ca. 1267–1337** Giotto, painter	
1300	**1300** First mechanical clocks in the West	**1300–1500** Rise of universities **1304–1374** Francesco Petrarch, humanist writer **1313–1375** Giovanni Boccaccio, humanist writer	
	1315–1317 Great Famine	**ca. 1340–1400** Geoffrey Chaucer, poet	**1337** Start of Hundred Years War
	1347–1351 Black Death **ca. 1350** Growing deforestation		**1381** Wat Tyler's Rebellion
		1389–1464 Cosimo de' Medici, banker	
1400	**1400s** Large cannon in use in warfare; hand-held firearms become prominent	**ca. 1390–1441** Jan van Eyck, painter	**1415** Portuguese take Ceuta
			1431 Joan of Arc burned as witch
		1449–1492 Lorenzo de' Medici, art patron	
	ca. 1450 First printing with movable type in the West **1454** Gutenberg Bible printed	**1452–1519** Leonardo da Vinci, artist	**1453** End of Hundred Years War; Turks take Constantinople
		ca. 1466–1536 Erasmus of Rotterdam, humanist **1472–1564** Michelangelo, artist	**1469** Marriage of Ferdinand of Aragon and Isabella of Castile
		1492 Expulsion of Jews from Spain	**1492** Fall of Muslim state of Granada

the fertile lands east of the Elbe River and into the eastern Baltic states. Knights belonging to Latin Christian religious orders slaughtered or drove away native inhabitants who had not yet adopted Christianity. During the thirteenth century, the Order of Teutonic Knights conquered, resettled, and administered a vast area along the Baltic that later became Prussia (see Map 14.2 on page 337). Other Latin Christians founded new settlements on lands conquered from the Muslims and Byzantines in southern Europe and on Celtic lands in the British Isles.

Draining swamps and clearing forests also

brought new land under cultivation. But as population continued to rise, some people had to farm lands that had poor soils or were vulnerable to flooding, frost, or drought. Average crop yields fell accordingly after 1250, and more people lived at the edge of starvation. According to one historian, "By 1300, almost every child born in western Europe faced the probability of extreme hunger at least once or twice during his expected 30 to 35 years of life."[2] One unusually cold spell produced the Great Famine of 1315–1317, which affected much of Europe.

The **Black Death** reversed the population growth. This terrible plague originated in China and spread across Central Asia with the Mongol armies (see Chapter 11). In 1346, the Mongols attacked the city of Kaffa° on the Black Sea; a year later, Genoese° traders in Kaffa carried the disease to Italy and southern France. For two years, the Black Death spread across Europe, in some places carrying off two-thirds of the population. Average losses in western Europe amounted to one in three.

Victims developed boils the size of eggs in their groins and armpits, black blotches on their skin, foul body odors, and severe pain. In most cases, death came within a few days. Town officials closed their gates to people from infected areas and burned the victims' possessions. Such measures helped to spare some communities but could not halt the advance of the disease (see Map 14.1). Bubonic plague, the primary form of the Black Death, spreads from person to person and through the bites of fleas infesting the fur of certain rats. Although medieval doctors did not associate the disease with rats, eliminating the rats that thrived on urban refuse would have been difficult.

The plague left a psychological mark, bringing home to people how sudden and unexpected death could be. Some people became more religious, giving money to the church or hitting themselves with iron-tipped whips to atone for their sins. Others chose reckless enjoyment, spending their money on fancy clothes, feasts, and drinking. Whatever their mood, most people soon resumed their daily routines.

Periodic returns of plague made recovery from population losses slow and uneven. Europe's population in 1400 equaled that in 1200. Not until after 1500 did it rise above its preplague level.

Social Rebellion

In addition to its demographic and psychological effects, the Black Death triggered social changes in western Europe. Skilled and manual laborers who survived demanded higher pay for their services. At first, authorities tried to freeze wages at the old levels. Seeing this as a plot by the rich, peasants rose up against wealthy nobles and churchmen. During a widespread revolt in France in 1358, known as the Jacquerie, peasants looted castles and killed dozens of persons. In a large revolt led by Wat Tyler in 1381, English peasants invaded London, calling for an end to serfdom and obligations to landowners. Demonstrators murdered the archbishop of Canterbury and many royal officials. Authorities put down these rebellions with even greater bloodshed and cruelty, but they could not stave off the higher wages and other social changes the rebels demanded.

Serfdom practically disappeared in western Europe as peasants bought their freedom or ran away. Many free persons earning higher wages saved their money and bought land. Some English landowners who could no longer afford to hire enough fieldworkers began pasturing sheep for their wool. Others grew crops that required less care or made greater use of draft animals and labor-saving tools. Because the plague had not killed wild and domesticated animals, survivors had abundant meat and leather for shoes. Thus, the welfare of the rural masses generally improved after the Black Death, though the gap between rich and poor remained wide.

In urban areas, employers raised wages to attract workers. Guilds (see below) shortened the period of apprenticeship. Competition within crafts also became more common. Although the overall economy shrank with the decline in population, per capita production actually rose.

Mills and Mines

Mining, metalworking, and the use of mechanical energy expanded so greatly in the centuries before 1500 that some histo-

---

Kaffa (KAH-fah)   Genoese (JEN-oh-eez)

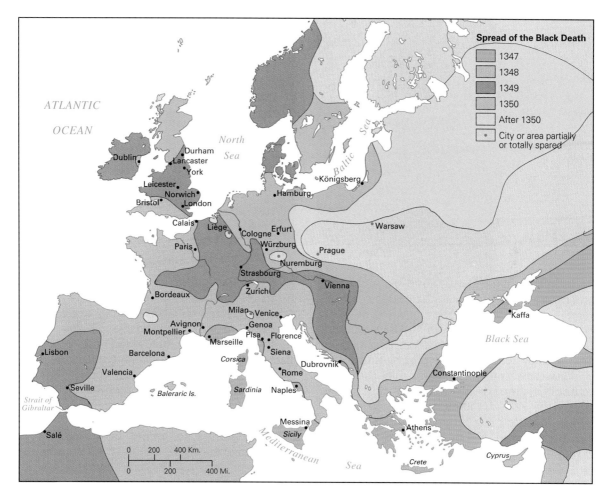

Map 14.1   The Black Death in Fourteenth-Century Europe   Spreading from southwestern China along the routes opened by Mongol expansion, the plague reached the Black Sea port of Kaffa in 1346. This map documents its deadly progress year by year across the face of Europe.

rians speak of an "industrial revolution" in medieval Europe. That may be too strong a term, but the landscape fairly bristled with mechanical devices. Mills powered by water or wind ground grain, sawed logs, crushed olives, tanned leather, and made paper.

In 1086, 5,600 watermills flanked England's many rivers. After 1200, mills spread rapidly across the western European mainland. By the early fourteenth century, entrepreneurs had crammed 68 watermills into a one-mile section of the Seine° River in Paris. Less efficient **water wheels** de-

pended on the flow of a river passing beneath them. Greater efficiency came from channeling water to fall over the top of the wheel so that gravity added force to the water's flow. Dams ensured a steady flow of water throughout the year. Some watermills in France and England even harnessed the power of ocean tides.

Windmills multiplied in comparatively dry lands like Spain and in northern Europe, where ice made water wheels useless in winter. Designs for watermills dated back to Roman times, and the Islamic world, which inherited Hellenistic technologies, knew both water wheels and windmills.

Seine (sen)

Floating Watermills on the Grand Pont Bridge in Paris The current of the Seine River flowing beneath the mills turn the water wheels. The mills float to allow for changes in water level. Gears translate the vertical motion of the wheels into the horizontal motion of the millstones shown in the windows above them. (Bibliothèque Nationale de France)

But people in the medieval Latin West used these devices on a much larger scale than did people elsewhere.

Owners invested heavily in building mills, but since nature furnished the energy to run them for free, they returned great profits. Individuals or monasteries constructed some mills, but most were built by groups of investors. Rich millers often aroused the jealousy of their neighbors. In his *Canterbury Tales*, the English poet Geoffrey Chaucer (c. 1340–1400) captured their unsavory reputation by portraying a miller as "a master-hand at stealing grain" by pushing down on the balance scale with his thumb.[3]

Waterpower aided the great expansion of iron making. Water powered the stamping mills that broke up the iron, the trip hammers that pounded it, and the bellows (first documented in the West in 1323) that raised temperatures to the point where the iron was liquid enough to be poured into molds. Blast furnaces producing high-quality iron are documented from 1380. Finished products ranged from armor to nails, from horseshoes to hoes.

Demand stimulated iron mining in many parts of Europe. In addition, new silver, lead, and copper mines in Austria and Hungary supplied metal for coins, church bells, cannons, and statues. Techniques of deep mining developed in Central Europe spread west in the latter part of the fifteenth century. A building boom stimulated stone quarrying in France during the eleventh, twelfth, and thirteenth centuries.

Industrial growth changed the landscape. Towns grew outward and new ones were founded, dams and canals changed the flow of rivers, and quarries and mines scarred the hillsides. Urban tanneries (factories that cured and processed leather), the runoff from slaughterhouses, and human waste polluted streams. England's Parliament enacted the first recorded antipollution law in 1388, but enforcement proved difficult.

Deforestation accelerated. Trees provided timber for buildings and ships. Tanneries stripped bark to make acid for tanning leather. Many forests gave way to farmland. The glass and iron industries used great quantities of charcoal, made by controlled burning of oak or other hardwood, to produce the high temperatures required. A single iron furnace could consume all the trees within five-eighths of a mile (1 kilometer) in just forty days. Consequently, the later Middle Ages saw the end of many of western Europe's once-dense forests, except in places where powerful landowners established hunting preserves.

URBAN REVIVAL

In the tenth century, no town in the Latin West could compete in size, wealth, or comfort with the cities of Byzantium and Islam. Yet by the later

Middle Ages, the Mediterranean, Baltic, and Atlantic coasts boasted wealthy port cities, as did some major rivers draining into these seas. Some Byzantine and Muslim cities still exceeded those of the West in size, but not in commercial, cultural, and administrative dynamism, as marked by impressive new churches, guild halls, and residences.

Trading Cities

Most urban growth after 1200 resulted from manufacturing and trade, both between cities and their hinterlands and over long distances. Northern Italy particularly benefited from maritime trade with the port cities of the eastern Mediterranean and, through them, the markets of the Indian Ocean and East Asia. In northern Europe, commercial cities in the County of Flanders (roughly today's Belgium) and around the Baltic Sea profited from regional networks and from overland and sea routes to the Mediterranean.

A Venetian-inspired assault in 1204 against the city of Constantinople, misleadingly named the "Fourth Crusade," temporarily eliminated Byzantine control of the passage between the Mediterranean and the Black Sea and thereby allowed Venice to seize Crete and expand its trading colonies around the Black Sea. Another boon to Italian trade came from the westward expansion of the Mongol Empire, which opened trade routes from the Mediterranean to China (see Chapter 11).

A young merchant named Marco Polo set out from Venice in 1271 and reached the Mongol court in China after a long trek across Central Asia. He served the emperor Khubilai Khan for many years as an ambassador and governor of a Chinese province. Some scholars question Marco's later account of these adventures and a treacherous return voyage through the Indian Ocean that returned him to Venice in 1295, after an absence of twenty-four years. Similar reports of the riches of the East came from other European travelers.

When Mongol decline interrupted the caravan trade in the fourteenth century, Venetian merchants purchased eastern silks and spices brought by other middlemen to Constantinople, Damascus, and Cairo. Three times a year, Venice dispatched convoys of two or three galleys, with sixty oarsmen each, capable of bringing back 2,000 tons

of goods. Other merchants explored new overland or sea routes.

The sea trade of Genoa on northern Italy's west coast probably equaled that of Venice. Genoese merchants established colonies in the western and eastern Mediterranean and around the Black Sea. In northern Europe, an association of trading cities known as the **Hanseatic° League** traded extensively in the Baltic, including the coasts of Prussia, newly conquered by German knights. Their merchants ranged eastward to Novgorod in Russia and westward across the North Sea to London.

In the late thirteenth century, Genoese galleys from the Mediterranean and Hanseatic ships from the Baltic converged on the trading and manufacturing cities in Flanders. Artisans in the Flemish towns of Bruges°, Ghent°, and Ypres° transformed raw wool from England into a fine cloth that was softer and smoother than the coarse "homespuns" from simple village looms. Dyed in vivid hues, these Flemish textiles appealed to wealthy Europeans, who also appreciated fine textiles from Asia.

Along the overland route connecting Flanders and northern Italy, important trading fairs developed in the Champagne° region of Burgundy. The Champagne fairs began as regional markets, exchanging manufactured goods, livestock, and farm produce once or twice a year. When the king of France gained control of Champagne at the end of the twelfth century, royal guarantees of safe conduct to merchants turned these markets into international fairs that were important for currency exchange and other financial transactions as well. A century later, fifteen Italian cities had permanent consulates in Champagne to represent the interests of their citizens. During the fourteenth century, the large volume of trade made it cheaper to ship Flemish woolens to Italy by sea than to pack them overland on animal backs. Champagne's fairs consequently lost some international trade while remaining important as a regional market.

In the late thirteenth century, the English monarchy raised taxes on exports of raw wool, making cloth manufacture in England more profitable than in Flanders. Flemish specialists crossed

---

Hanseatic (han-see-AT-ik)   **Bruges** (broozh)
Ghent (gent [hard *g* as in *get*])   **Ypres** (EE-pruh)
Champagne (sham-PAIN)

Flemish Weavers, Ypres The city of Ypres in Flanders (now northern Belgium) flourished as a textile center in the thirteenth century. This fourteenth-century drawing shows a man and a woman weaving cloth while a child makes thread on a spinning wheel. (Stedelijke Openbare Bibliotheek, Ypres)

the English Channel and introduced the spinning wheel and other devices to England. Annual raw wool exports fell from 35,000 sacks of wool at the beginning of the fourteenth century to 8,000 in the mid-fifteenth century, while English wool cloth production rose from 4,000 pieces just before 1350 to 54,000 a century later.

Florence also replaced Flemish imports with its own woolens industry financed by local banking families. In 1338, Florence manufactured 80,000 pieces of cloth, while importing only 10,000. These changes in the textile industry show how competition promoted the spread of manufacturing and encouraged new specialties.

The growing textile industries used the power of wind and water channeled through gears, pulleys, and belts to drive all sorts of machinery. Flemish mills cleaned and thickened woven cloth by beating it in water, a process known as fulling. Other mills produced paper, starting in southern Europe in the thirteenth century. Unlike the Chinese and Muslim papermakers, who had pursued the craft for centuries, the Europeans introduced machines to do the heavy work.

In the fifteenth century, Venice surpassed its European rivals in the volume of its trade in the Mediterranean as well as across the Alps into Central Europe. Its craftspeople manufactured luxury goods once obtainable only from eastern sources,

notably silk and cotton textiles, glassware and mirrors, jewelry, and paper. Exports of Italian and northern European woolens to the eastern Mediterranean also rose. In the space of a few centuries, western European cities had used the eastern trade to increase their prosperity and then reduce their dependence on eastern goods.

Civic Life

Most northern Italian and German cities were independent states, much like the port cities of the Indian Ocean basin (see Chapter 13). Other European cities held royal charters exempting them from the authority of local nobles. Their autonomy enabled them to adapt to changing market conditions more quickly than cities controlled by imperial authorities, as in China and the Islamic world. Since anyone who lived in a chartered city for over a year could claim freedom, urban life promoted social mobility.

Europe's Jews mostly lived in cities. Spain had the largest communities because of the tolerance of earlier Muslim rulers. Commercial cities elsewhere welcomed Jews with manufacturing and business skills. Despite official protection by certain Christian princes and kings, Jews endured violent religious persecutions or expulsions in times of crisis, such as during the Black Death (see Society and

Culture: Blaming the Black Death on the Jews, Strasbourg, 1349). In 1492, the Spanish monarchs expelled all Jews in the name of religious and ethnic purity. Only the papal city of Rome left its Jews undisturbed throughout the centuries before 1500.

Within most towns and cities, powerful associations known as guilds dominated civic life. **Guilds** brought together craft specialists, such as silversmiths, or merchants working in a particular trade, to regulate business practices and set prices. Guilds also trained apprentices and promoted members' interests with the city government. By denying membership to outsiders and Jews, guilds protected the interests of families that already belonged. Guilds also perpetuated male dominance of most skilled jobs.

Nevertheless, in a few places, women could join guilds either on their own or as the wives, widows, or daughters of male guild members. Large numbers of poor women also toiled in nonguild jobs in urban textile industries and in the food and beverage trades, generally receiving lower wages than men.

Some women advanced socially through marriage to wealthy men. One of Chaucer's *Canterbury Tales* concerns a woman from Bath, a city in southern England, who became wealthy by marrying a succession of old men for their money (and then two other husbands for love), "aside from other company in youth." She was also a skilled weaver, Chaucer says: "In making cloth she showed so great a bent, / She bettered those of Ypres and of Ghent."

By the fifteenth century, a new class of wealthy merchant-bankers was operating on a vast scale and specializing in money changing and loans and making investments on behalf of other parties. Merchants great and small used their services. They also handled the financial transactions of ecclesiastical and secular officials and arranged for the transmission to the pope of funds known as Peter's pence, a collection taken up annually in every church in the Latin West. Princes and kings supported their wars and lavish courts with credit. Some merchant-bankers even developed their own news services, gathering information on any topic that could affect business.

Florentine financiers invented checking accounts, organized private shareholding companies (the forerunners of modern corporations), and im-

proved bookkeeping techniques. In the fifteenth century, the Medici° family of Florence operated banks in Italy, Flanders, and London. Medicis also controlled the government of Florence and commissioned art works. The Fuggers° of Augsburg, who had ten times the Medici bank's lending capital, topped Europe's banking fraternity by 1500. Beginning as cloth merchants under Jacob "the Rich" (1459–1525), the family's many activities included the trade in Hungarian copper, essential for casting cannon.

Since Latin Christians generally considered charging interest (usury) sinful, Jews predominated in money lending. Christian bankers devised ways to profit from loans indirectly in order to get around the condemnation of usury. Some borrowers repaid loans in a different currency at a rate of exchange favorable to the lender. Others added to their repayment a "gift" in thanks to the lender. For example, in 1501, church officials agreed to repay a Fugger loan of 6,000 gold ducats in five months along with a "gift" of 400 ducats, amounting to an effective interest rate of 16 percent a year. In fact, the return was less since the church failed to repay the loan on time.

Yet most residents of western European cities lived in poverty and squalor rather than wealth. European cities generally lacked civic amenities, such as public baths and water supply systems, that had existed in the cities of Western antiquity and still survived in cities of the Islamic Middle East.

Gothic Cathedrals

Master builders and associated craftsmen counted among the skilled people in greatest demand. Though cities competed with one another in the magnificence of their guild halls, town halls, and other structures, **Gothic cathedrals,** first appearing about 1140 in France, cost the most and brought the greatest prestige. The pointed, or Gothic, arch, replacing the older round, or Roman, arch proved a hallmark of the new design. External (flying) buttresses stabilizing the high, thin stone columns below the arches constituted another distinctive feature. This method of construction enabled master builders to push the Gothic cathedrals to great heights and fill the

Medici (MED-ih-chee)   **Fuggers** (FOOG-uhrz)

SOCIETY & CULTURE

Blaming the Black Death on the Jews, Strasbourg, 1349

This selection from the official chronicles of the upper-Rhineland towns reflects the prejudice against Jews that was common in the Latin West.

In the year 1349 there occurred the greatest epidemic that ever happened. Death went from one end of the earth to the other, on that side and this side of the [Mediterranean] sea.... This epidemic also came to Strasbourg in the summer of [that] year, and ... about sixteen thousand people died.

In the matter of this plague the Jews throughout the world were reviled and accused in all lands of having caused it through the poison which they are said to have put into the water and the wells—that is what they were accused of—and for this reason the Jews were burnt all the way from the Mediterranean into Germany, but not in Avignon, for the pope protected them there.

... The deputies of the city of Strasbourg were asked what they were going to do with their Jews. They answered and said that they knew no evil of them. [The town council was deposed. A new council gave in to the mob and arrested the Jews.]

On Saturday—that was St. Valentine's Day—they burnt the Jews on a wooden platform in their cemetery. There were about two thousand people of them. Those who wanted to baptize themselves were spared. Many small children were taken out of the fire and baptized against the will of their fathers and mothers. And everything that was owed to the Jews was cancelled, and the Jews had to surrender all pledges and notes that they had taken for debts. The council, however, took the cash that the Jews possessed and divided it among the working-men proportionately. The money was indeed the thing that killed the Jews. If they had been poor and if the feudal lords had not been in debt to them, they would not have been burnt.

To what extent was the massacre of the Strasbourg Jews due to fear of the plague, to prejudice, and to greed? Why did some officials try to protect them?

Source: Jacob R. Marcus, ed., *The Jew in the Medieval World: A Source Book, 315–1791* (1938; reprint, Westport, CT: Greenwood, 1975), 45–47. Reprinted with permission of the Hebrew Union College Press, Cincinnati.

---

outside walls with giant windows depicting religious scenes in brilliantly colored stained glass. During the next four centuries, interior heights soared ever higher, towers and spires pierced the heavens, and walls became dazzling curtains of stained glass.

The men who designed and built the cathedrals had little or no formal education and limited understanding of the mathematical principles of modern civil engineering. Master masons sometimes miscalculated, causing parts of some overly ambitious cathedrals to collapse. The record-high choir vault of Beauvais Cathedral, for instance—154 feet (47 meters) in height—came tumbling down in 1284. But as builders gained experience and invented novel solutions to their problems,

success rose from the rubble of their mistakes. The cathedral spire in Strasbourg reached 466 feet (142 meters) into the air—as high as a forty-story building. Such heights were unsurpassed until the twentieth century.

LEARNING, LITERATURE, AND THE RENAISSANCE

Throughout the Middle Ages, people in the Latin West lived amid reminders of the achievements of the Romans. They wrote and worshiped in a ver-

Strasbourg Cathedral   Work on this Gothic cathedral ceased in 1439 with only one of two spires completed. This engraving of the tallest masonry structure of medieval Europe dates to 1630.   (Courtesy of the Trustees of the British Museum)

in northern Italy and later spread to northern Europe. Some Italian authors saw the Italian Renaissance as a sharp break with an age of darkness. Others see this era as the high noon of a day that had been dawning for several centuries.

Universities and Scholarship

Before 1100, Byzantine and Islamic scholarship generally surpassed scholarship in Latin Europe. When Latin Christians wrested southern Italy from the Byzantines and Sicily and Toledo from the Muslims in the eleventh century, they acquired many manuscripts of Greek and Arabic works. These included works by Plato and Aristotle° and Greek treatises on medicine, mathematics, and geography, as well as scientific and philosophical writings by Muslim writers. Latin translations of the Iranian philosopher Ibn Sina° (980–1037), known in the West as Avicenna°, had great influence because of their sophisticated blend of Aristotelian and Islamic philosophy. Jewish scholars contributed significantly to the translation and explication of Arabic and other manuscripts.

The thirteenth century saw the foundation of two new religious orders, the Dominicans and the Franciscans, some of whose most talented members taught in the independent colleges that arose after 1200. Some scholars believe that the colleges established in Paris and Oxford patterned themselves on similarly endowed places of study then spreading in the Islamic world—*madrasas,* which provided subsidized housing for poor students and paid the salaries of their teachers. The Latin West, however, innovated the idea of **universities,** degree-granting corporations specializing in multidisciplinary research and advanced teaching.

Between 1300 and 1500, sixty universities joined the twenty established before that time. Students banded together to start some of them; guilds of professors founded others. Teaching guilds, like the guilds overseeing manufacturing and commerce, set standards for the profession, trained apprentices and masters, and defended their professional interests.

sion of their language, traveled their roads, and obeyed some of their laws. The vestments and robes of popes, kings, and emperors followed the designs of Roman officials. Yet the learning of Greco-Roman antiquity virtually disappeared with the rise of the biblical world described in the Hebrew and Christian scriptures.

A small revival of learning associated with the court of Charlemagne in the ninth century was followed by a larger renaissance (rebirth) in the twelfth century. Cities became centers of intellectual and artistic life. The universities established across the Latin West after 1200 contributed to this cultural revival. In the mid-fourteenth century, the pace of intellectual and artistic life quickened in what is often called the **Renaissance,** which began

---

Aristotle (AR-ih-stah-tahl)   **Ibn Sina** (IB-uhn SEE-nah)
Avicenna (av-uh-SEN-uh)

Universities set the curriculum for each discipline and instituted final examinations for degrees. Students who passed the exams that ended their apprenticeship received a "license" to teach. Students who completed longer training and defended a masterwork of scholarship became "masters" and "doctors." The University of Paris gradually absorbed the city's various colleges, but the colleges of Oxford and Cambridge remained independent, self-governing organizations.

Since all universities used Latin, students and masters could move freely across political and linguistic lines, seeking the courses they wanted and the most interesting professors. Some universities offered specialized training. Legal training centered on Bologna°; Montpellier and Salerno focused on medicine; Paris and Oxford excelled in theology.

The prominence of theology stemmed from many students aspiring to ecclesiastical careers, but scholars also saw theology as "queen of the sciences"—the central discipline encompassing all knowledge. Hence, thirteenth-century theologians sought to synthesize the rediscovered philosophical works of Aristotle and the commentaries of Avicenna with the Bible's revealed truth. These efforts to synthesize reason and faith were known as **scholasticism°**.

Thomas Aquinas, a brilliant Dominican priest who taught theology at the University of Paris, wrote the most notable scholastic work, the *Summa Theologica°*, between 1267 and 1273. Although his exposition of Christian belief organized on Aristotelian principles came to be accepted as a masterly demonstration of the reasonableness of Christianity, scholasticism upset many traditional thinkers. Some church authorities tried to ban Aristotle from the curriculum. In addition, rivalry between the leading Dominican and Franciscan theological scholars continued over the next two centuries. However, the considerable freedom of medieval universities from both secular and religious authorities enabled the new ideas to prevail over the fears of church administrators.

Humanists and Printers

Dante Alighieri° (1265–1321) completed a long, elegant poem, the *Divine Comedy,* shortly before his death. This supreme expression of medieval preoccupations tells the allegorical story of Dante's journey through the nine circles of hell and the seven terraces of purgatory, followed by his entry into Paradise. The Roman poet Virgil guides him through hell and purgatory; Beatrice, a woman he had loved from afar since childhood and whose death inspired the poem, guides him to Paradise.

The *Divine Comedy* foreshadows the literary fashions of the later Italian Renaissance. Like Dante, later Italian writers made use of Greco-Roman classical themes and mythology and sometimes courted a broader audience by writing not in Latin but in their local language (Dante used the vernacular spoken in Tuscany°.)

The poet Geoffrey Chaucer, many of whose works show the influence of Dante, wrote in vernacular English. The *Canterbury Tales,* a lengthy poem written in the last dozen years of his life, contains often humorous and earthy tales told by fictional pilgrims on their way to the shrine of Thomas à Becket in Canterbury (see Chapter 8). They present a vivid cross-section of medieval people and attitudes.

Dante influenced a literary movement of the **humanists** that began in his native Florence in the mid-fourteenth century. The term refers to their interest in grammar, rhetoric, poetry, history, and moral philosophy (ethics)—subjects known collectively as the humanities, an ancient discipline. With the brash exaggeration characteristic of new intellectual fashions, humanist writers like the poet Francesco Petrarch° (1304–1374) and the poet and storyteller Giovanni Boccaccio° (1313–1375) proclaimed a revival of the classical Greco-Roman tradition they felt had for centuries lain under the rubble of the Middle Ages.

This idea of a rebirth of learning dismisses too readily the monastic and university scholars who for centuries had been recovering all sorts of

Bologna (buh-LOHN-yuh)
scholasticism (skoh-LAS-tih-sizm)
Summa Theologica (SOOM-uh thee-uh-LOH-jih-kuh)

Dante Alighieri (DAHN-tay ah-lee-GYEH-ree)
Tuscany (TUS-kuh-nee)
Francesco Petrarch (fran-CHES-koh PAY-trahrk)
Giovanni Boccaccio (jo-VAH-nee boh-KAH-chee-oh)

Greco-Roman learning and writers like Dante (whom the humanists revered) who anticipated humanist interests by a generation. Yet the humanists had a great impact as educators, advisers, and reformers. Their greatest influence came in reforming secondary education. They introduced a curriculum centered on the languages and literature of Greco-Roman antiquity, which they felt provided intellectual discipline, moral lessons, and refined tastes. This curriculum dominated European secondary schools well into the twentieth century. The universities felt the humanist influence less, mostly after 1500. Theology, law, medicine, and branches of philosophy other than ethics remained prominent in university education during this period.

Many humanists tried to duplicate the elegance of classical Latin and (to a lesser extent) Greek, which they revered as the pinnacle of learning, beauty, and wisdom. Boccaccio gained fame with his vernacular writings, which resemble Dante's, and especially for the *Decameron,* an earthy work that has much in common with Chaucer's boisterous tales. Under Petrarch's influence, however, Boccaccio turned to writing in classical Latin.

As humanist scholars mastered Latin and Greek, they turned their language skills to restoring the original texts of Greco-Roman writers and of the Bible. By comparing different manuscripts, they eliminated errors introduced by generations of copyists. To aid in this task, Pope Nicholas V (r. 1447–1455) created the Vatican Library, buying scrolls of Greco-Roman writings and paying to have accurate copies and translations made. Working independently, the Dutch scholar Erasmus° of Rotterdam (ca. 1466–1536) produced a critical edition of the New Testament in Greek. Erasmus corrected many errors and mistranslations in the Latin text that had been in general use throughout the Middle Ages. Later, this humanist priest and theologian wrote—in classical Latin—influential moral guides, including the *Enchiridion militis christiani* (*The Manual of the Christian Knight,* 1503) and *The Education of a Christian Prince* (1515).

The influence of the humanists grew after 1450 as the new technology of printing made their critical editions of ancient texts, literary works, and moral guides more available. The Chinese and the Arabs used carved wood blocks for printing (see Chapters 7 and 9), and block-printed playing cards circulated in Europe before 1450, when three improvements revolutionized printing: (1) movable pieces of type consisting of individual letters, (2) new ink suitable for printing on paper, and (3) the **printing press,** a mechanical device that pressed inked type onto sheets of paper.

Johann Gutenberg° (ca. 1394–1468) of Mainz led the way. The Gutenberg Bible of 1454, the first book in the West printed from movable type, exhibited a beauty and craftsmanship that bore witness to the printer's years of experimentation. Humanists worked closely with the printers, who spread the new techniques to Italy and France. Erasmus did editing and proofreading for the Italian scholar-printer Aldo Manuzio (1449–1515) in Venice. Manuzio's press published many critical editions of classical Latin and Greek texts.

By 1500, at least 10 million printed volumes flowed from presses in 238 European towns, launching a revolution that affected students, scholars, and a growing literate population. These readers consumed unorthodox political and religious tracts along with ancient texts.

Renaissance Artists

Although the artists of the fourteenth and fifteenth centuries continued to depict biblical subjects, the Greco-Roman revival led some, especially in Italy, to portray ancient deities and myths. Another popular trend involved scenes of daily life.

Neither theme was entirely new, however. Renaissance art, like Renaissance scholarship, owed a debt to earlier generations. Italian painters of the fifteenth century credited the Florentine painter Giotto° (ca. 1267–1337) with singlehandedly reviving the "lost art of painting." In religious scenes, Giotto replaced the stiff, staring figures of the Byzantine style, which were intended to overawe viewers, with more natural and human portraits

Erasmus (uh-RAZ-muhs)

Johann Gutenberg (yoh-HAHN GOO-ten-burg)
Giotto (JAW-toh)

A French Printshop, 1537   A workman operates the "press," a screw device that presses the paper to the inked type. Other employees examine the printed sheets, each of which holds eight pages. When folded and sewn together, several sheets make a book.   (Giraudon/Art Resource, NY)

with whose emotions of grief and love viewers could identify. Rather than floating on backgrounds of gold leaf, his saints inhabit earthly landscapes.

North of the Alps, the Flemish painter Jan van Eyck° (ca. 1390–1441) mixed his pigments with linseed oil in place of the egg yolk of earlier centuries. Oil paints dried more slowly and gave pictures a superior luster. Italian painters quickly copied van Eyck's technique, though his own masterfully realistic paintings on religious and domestic themes remained distinctive.

Leonardo da Vinci° (1452–1519) used oil paints for his *Mona Lisa*. Renaissance artists like Leonardo worked in many media, including bronze sculp-

tures and frescos (painting on wet plaster) like *The Last Supper*. His notebooks contain imaginative designs for airplanes, submarines, and tanks. Leonardo's younger contemporary Michelangelo° (1472–1564) painted frescoes of biblical scenes on the ceiling of the Sistine Chapel in the Vatican, sculpted statues of David and Moses, and designed the dome for a new Saint Peter's Basilica in Rome.

The patronage of wealthy and educated merchants and prelates underlay the artistic blossoming in the cities of northern Italy and Flanders. The Florentine banker Cosimo de' Medici (1389–1464) and his grandson Lorenzo (1449–1492), known as "the Magnificent," spent immense sums on paintings, sculpture, and public buildings. In Rome, the papacy° launched a building program that culminated in the construction of the new Saint Peter's Basilica and a residence for the pope.

These scholarly and artistic achievements exemplify the innovation and striving for excellence of the Late Middle Ages. The new literary themes and artistic styles of this period had lasting influence on Western culture. But the innovations in the organization of universities, in printing, and in oil painting had wider implications, for they were later adopted by cultures all over the world.

POLITICAL AND MILITARY TRANSFORMATIONS

Stronger and more unified states and armies developed in western Europe in parallel with the economic and cultural revivals (see Map 14.2). Through the prolonged struggle of the Hundred Years War, French and English monarchs forged closer ties with the nobility, the church, and the merchants. Crusades against Muslim states brought consolidation to Spain and Portugal. In Italy and Germany, however, political power remained in the hands of small states and loose alliances.

Jan van Eyck (yahn vahn-IKE)
Leonardo da Vinci (lay-own-AHR-doh dah-VIN-chee)

Michelangelo (my-kuhl-AN-juh-low)
papacy (PAY-puh-see)

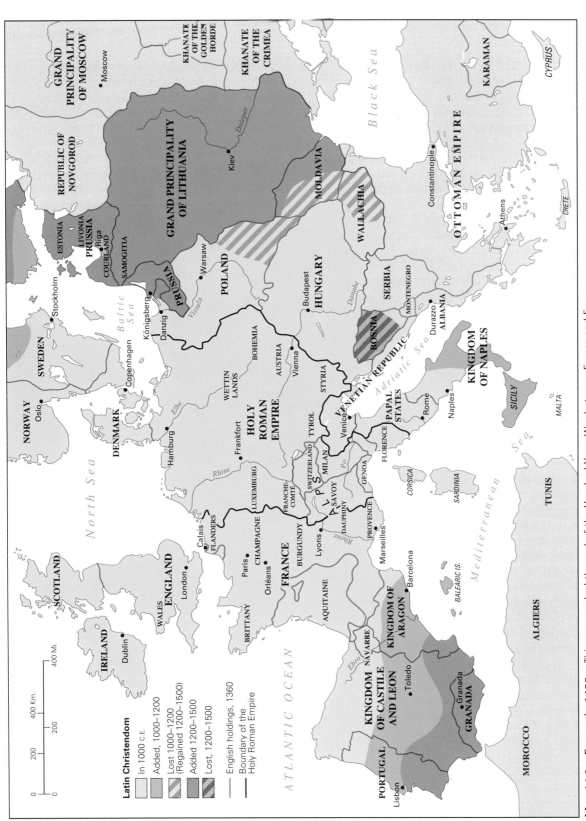

Map 14.2 Europe in 1453 This year marked the end of the Hundred Years War between France and England and the fall of the Byzantine capital city of Constantinople to the Ottoman Turks. Christian conquests in southern Italy and the Iberian Peninsula and the conversion of Lithuania offset Muslim advances into southeastern Europe.

Latin Christendom

In 1000 C.E.

Added, 1000–1200

Lost 1000–1200 (Regained 1200–1500)

Added 1200–1500

Lost, 1200–1500

English holdings, 1360

Boundary of the Holy Roman Empire

0   200   400 Km.

0   200   400 Mi.

Monarchs, Nobles, and the Church

Thirteenth-century states continued early medieval state structures (see Chapter 8). Hereditary monarchs topped the political pyramid, but modest treasuries and the rights of nobles and the church limited their powers. Powerful noblemen who controlled vast estates had an important voice in matters of state. The church guarded closely its traditional rights and independence. Towns, too, had acquired rights and privileges. Towns in Flanders, the Hanseatic League, and Italy approached independence from royal interference.

In theory the ruler's noble vassals owed military service in time of war. In practice, vassals sought to limit the monarch's power.

In the year 1200, knights still formed the backbone of western European armies, but changes in weaponry brought this into question. Improved crossbows could shoot metal-tipped arrows with enough force to pierce helmets and light body armor. Professional crossbowmen, hired for wages, became increasingly common and much feared. Indeed, a church council in 1139 outlawed the crossbow—ineffectively—as being too deadly for use against Christians. The arrival in Europe of firearms based on the Chinese invention of gunpowder (see Chapter 12) further transformed the medieval army.

The church also resisted royal control. In 1302, the outraged Pope Boniface VIII (r. 1294–1303) asserted that divine law made the papacy superior to "every human creature," including monarchs. Issuing his own claim of superiority, King Philip "the Fair" of France (r. 1285–1314) sent an army to arrest the pope, a chastisement that hastened Pope Boniface's death. Philip then engineered the election of a French pope, who established a new papal residence at Avignon° in southern France in 1309.

A succession of French-dominated popes residing in Avignon improved church discipline but at the price of compromising their neutrality in the eyes of other rulers. The **Great Western Schism** between 1378 and 1415 saw rival papal claimants at Avignon and Rome vying for Christian loyalties. The papacy eventually regained its independence and returned to Rome, but the long crisis broke the pope's ability to challenge the rising power of monarchs like Philip, who had used the dispute to persuade his nobles to grant him a new tax.

The English monarchy wielded more centralized power as a result of consolidation that took place after the Norman conquest of 1066. The Anglo-Norman kings also extended their realm by assaults on their Celtic neighbors. Between 1200 and 1400, they incorporated Wales and reasserted control over most of Ireland. Nevertheless, under King John (r. 1199–1216), royal power suffered a severe setback. Forced to acknowledge the pope as his overlord in 1213, he lost his bid to reassert claims to Aquitaine in southern France the following year and then yielded to his nobles by signing the Magna Carta in 1215. This "Great Charter" affirmed that monarchs were subject to established law, confirmed the independence of the church and the city of London, and guaranteed the nobles' hereditary rights.

The Hundred Years War

The conflict between the king of France and his vassals known as the **Hundred Years War** (1337–1453) affords a key example of the transformation in politics and war. These vassals included the kings of England (for lands that belonged to their Norman ancestors), the counts of prosperous and independent-minded Flanders, and the dukes of Brittany and Burgundy. In typical fashion, the conflict grew out of a marriage alliance.

Marriage between Princess Isabella of France and King Edward II of England (r. 1307–1327) should have ensured the king's loyalty, as a vassal, to the French monarchy. However, when the next generation of the French ruling house produced no other sons, Isabella's son, King Edward III of England (r. 1327–1377), laid claim to the French throne in 1337. French courts instead awarded the throne to a more distant (and more French) cousin. Edward decided to fight for his rights.

The new military technology shaped the conflict. Early in the war, hired Italian crossbowmen reinforced the French cavalry, but the English longbow proved superior. Adopted from the Welsh, the 6-foot (1.8-meter) longbow could shoot farther and more rapidly than the crossbow. Its arrows could not pierce armor, but concentrated volleys found gaps in the knights' defenses or struck their less-protected horses. Heavier and more encompassing armor provided a defense but limited a knight's movements. Once pulled off his steed by a foot soldier armed with a pike (hooked pole), he could not get up.

Later in the Hundred Years War, firearms gained prominence. The first cannons scared the horses with smoke and noise but did little damage. As they grew larger, however, they proved effective in battering the walls of castles and towns. The first artillery use against the French, at the Battle of Agincourt (1415), gave the English an important victory.

Faced with a young French peasant woman called Joan of Arc, subsequent English gains stalled. Acting, she believed, on God's instructions, she put on armor and rallied the French troops to defeat the English in 1429. Shortly afterward, she fell into English hands; she was tried by English churchmen and burned at the stake as a witch in 1431.

In the final battles, French cannon demolished the walls of once-secure castles held by the English and their allies. The truce that ended the struggle in 1453 left the French monarchy in firm control.

New Monarchies in France and England

The war proved a watershed in the rise of **new monarchies** in France and England, centralized states with fixed "national" boundaries and stronger representative institutions. English monarchs after 1453 consolidated control over territory within the British Isles, though the Scots defended their independence. The French monarchs also turned to consolidating control over powerful noble families, especially those headed by women. Mary of Burgundy (1457–1482) was forced to surrender most of her family's vast holdings to the king. Then in 1491, Anne of Brittany's forced marriage to the king led to the eventual incorporation of her duchy° into France.

Military technology undermined the nobility. Smaller, more mobile cannon developed in the late fifteenth century pounded castle walls. Improvements in hand-held firearms, able by the late fifteenth century to pierce the heaviest armor, ended the domination of the armored knight. Armies now depended less on knights and more on bowmen, pikemen, musketeers, and artillery men.

The new monarchies needed a way to finance their full-time armies. Some nobles agreed to money payments in place of military service and to additional taxes in time of war. For example, in 1439 and 1445, Charles VII of France (r. 1422–1461) successfully levied a new tax on his vassals' land. This not only paid the costs of the war with England but provided the monarchy a financial base for the next 350 years.

Merchants' taxes also provided revenues. Taxes on the English wool trade, begun by King Edward III, paid most of the costs of the Hundred Years War. Some rulers taxed Jewish merchants or extorted large contributions from wealthy towns. Individual merchants sometimes curried royal favor with loans. The fifteenth-century French merchant Jacques Coeur° gained many social and financial benefits for himself and his family by lending money to French courtiers, but his debtors accused him of murder and had his fortune confiscated.

The church provided a third source of revenue through voluntary contributions to support a war. English and French monarchs won the right to appoint important church officials in their realms in the fifteenth century. They subsequently used state power to enforce religious orthodoxy more vigorously than the popes had been able to do. But reformers complained that the church's spiritual mission became subordinate to political and economic concerns.

The shift in power to the monarchs and away from the nobility and the church did not deprive nobles of their social position and roles as government officials and military officers. Moreover, the kings of England and France in 1500 had to deal with representative institutions that had not existed in 1200. The English Parliament proved a permanent check on royal power: the House of Lords contained the great nobles and church officials; the House of Commons represented the towns and the leading citizens of the counties. In France, the Estates General, a similar but less effective representative body, represented the church, the nobles, and the towns.

---

duchy (DUTCH-ee)

Coeur (cur)

Iberian Unification

Spain and Portugal's **reconquest of Iberia** from Muslim rule expanded the boundaries of Latin Christianity. The knights who pushed the borders of their kingdoms southward furthered both Christianity and their own interests. The spoils of victory included irrigated farmland, rich cities, and ports on the Mediterranean Sea and Atlantic Ocean. Serving God, growing rich, and living off the labor of others became a way of life for the Iberian nobility.

The reconquest proceeded over several centuries. Toledo fell and became a Christian outpost in 1085. English crusaders bound for the Holy Land helped take Lisbon in 1147. It displaced the older city of Oporto (meaning "the port"), from which Portugal took its name, as both capital and the kingdom's leading city. A Christian victory in 1212 broke the back of Muslim power; the reconquest accelerated. Within decades, Portuguese and Castilian forces captured the prosperous cities of Cordova (1236) and Seville (1248) and drove the Muslims from the southwestern region known as Algarve° ("the west" in Arabic). Only the small kingdom of Granada hugging the Mediterranean coast remained in Muslim hands.

By incorporating Algarve in 1249, Portugal attained its modern territorial limits. After a pause to colonize, Christianize, and consolidate this land, Portugal took the crusade to North Africa. In 1415, Portuguese knights seized the port of Ceuta° in Morocco, where they learned more about the Saharan caravan trade in gold and slaves (see Chapter 13). During the next few decades, Portuguese mariners sailed down the Atlantic coast of Africa seeking rumored African Christian allies and access to this trade (see Chapter 15).

Elsewhere in Iberia, the reconquest continued. Spain came into being when the marriage of Princess Isabella of Castile and Prince Ferdinand of Aragon in 1469 led to the union of their kingdoms when they inherited their respective thrones a decade later. Their conquest of Granada in 1492 secured the final piece of Muslim territory for the new kingdom.

Ferdinand and Isabella sponsored the first voyage of Christopher Columbus in 1492 (see Chapter 15). In a third momentous event of that year, the monarchs manifested their crusading mentality by ordering all Jews expelled from their kingdoms. Attempts to convert or expel the remaining Muslims led to a revolt at the end of 1499 that lasted until 1501. The Spanish rulers expelled the last Muslims in 1502. Portugal expelled the Jews in 1496, including 100,000 refugees from Spain.

CONCLUSION

Ecologically, the peoples of Latin Europe harnessed the power of wind and water and mined and refined their mineral wealth at the cost of localized pollution and deforestation. However, inability to improve food production and distribution in response to population growth created a demographic crisis that climaxed with the Black Death that devastated Europe in the mid-fourteenth century.

Politically, basic features of the modern European state began to emerge. Frequent wars caused kingdoms of moderate size to develop exceptional military strength. The ruling class saw economic strength as the twin of political power and promoted the welfare of cities specializing in trade, manufacturing, and finance, the profits of which they taxed.

Culturally, autonomous universities and printing supported the advance of knowledge. Art and architecture reached unsurpassed peaks in the Renaissance. Late medieval society displayed a fundamental fascination with tools and techniques. New inventions and improved versions of old ones underlay the new dynamism in commerce, warfare, industry, and navigation.

Ironically, many of the tools that the Latin West would use to challenge Eastern supremacy—printing, firearms, and navigational devices—originally came from the East. However, western European success depended as much on strong motives for expansion. From the eleventh century onward, population pressure, religious zeal, economic enterprise, and intellectual curiosity drove an expansion of territory and resources that took the crusaders to

---

Algarve (ahl-GAHRV) **Ceuta** (say-OO-tuh)

the Holy Land, merchants to the eastern Mediterranean and Black Seas, the English into Wales and Ireland, German settlers across the Elbe River, and Iberian Christians into the Muslim south. The early voyages into the Atlantic, discussed in the next chapter, extended these activities.

■ Key Terms

Latin West	universities
three-field system	scholasticism
Black Death	humanists (Renaissance)
water wheel	printing press
Hanseatic League	Great Western Schism
guilds	Hundred Years War
Gothic cathedrals	new monarchies
Renaissance (European)	reconquest of Iberia

■ Suggested Reading

Robert Fossier, ed., *The Cambridge Illustrated History of the Middle Ages,* vol. 3, *1250–1520* (1986), provides a fine guide to the Latin West. Denys Hay, *Europe in the Fourteenth and Fifteenth Centuries,* 2d ed. (1989), is comprehensive and up-to-date. For economic matters, see Robert S. Lopez, *The Commercial Revolution of the Middle Ages, 950–1350* (1976), and Harry A. Miskimin, *The Economy of Early Renaissance Europe, 1300–1460* (1975).

James Bruce Ross and Mary Martin McLaughlin, eds., *The Portable Medieval Reader* (1977) and *The Portable Renaissance Reader* (1977), provide excerpts from primary sources. *The Notebooks of Leonardo da Vinci,* edited by Pamela Taylor (1960), show this versatile genius at work.

For technological change, see Arnold Pacey, *The Maze of Ingenuity: Ideas and Idealism in the Development of Technology* (1974); Jean Gimpel, *The Medieval Machine: The Industrial Revolution of the Middle Ages* (1977); and William H. McNeill, *The Pursuit of Power: Technology, Armed Force, and Society Since A.D. 1000* (1982). On the environment, see Roland Bechmann, *Trees and Man: The Forest in the Middle Ages* (1990).

Olef Pedersen, *The First Universities:* Studium Generale *and the Origins of University Education in Europe* (1998), and Johan Huizinga, *The Waning of the Middle Ages* (1924), discuss intellectual currents. For the Renaissance, see Lisa Jardine, *Worldly Goods: A New History of the Renaissance* (1996), and John R. Hale, *The Civilization of Europe in the Renaissance* (1995).

Georges Duby, *Rural Economy and Country Life in the Medieval West* (1990), covers social history in the earlier centuries. George Huppert, *After the Black Death: A Social History of Early Modern Europe* (1986), takes the analysis past 1500. Eileen Power, *Medieval People,* new ed. (1997), and Frances Gies and Joseph Gies, *Women in the Middle Ages* (1978), highlight individual lives. Mary Erler and Maryanne Kowaleski, eds., *Women and Power in the Middle Ages* (1988), contains more systematic essays. Vita Sackville-West, *Saint Joan of Arc* (1926; reprint, 1991), introduces this extraordinary person.

Christopher Alland, *The Hundred Years War: England and France at War, ca. 1300–ca. 1450* (1988), covers key events. Joseph F. O'Callaghan, *A History of Medieval Spain* (1975), provides good one-volume coverage. Jocelyn N. Hillgarth, *The Spanish Kingdoms,* 2 vols. (1976, 1978), offers more detail. For a popular account, see Barbara W. Tuchman, *A Distant Mirror: The Calamitous Fourteenth Century* (1978). P. Ziegler, *The Black Death* (1969), supplies a thorough introduction.

On the Latin West's expansion, see Robert Bartlett, *The Making of Europe: Conquest, Colonization, and Cultural Change* (1993); J. R. S. Phillips, *The Medieval Expansion of Europe,* new ed. (1998); and P. E. Russell, *Portugal, Spain and the African Atlantic, 1343–1492* (1998).

Francis C. Oakley, *The Western Church in the Later Middle Ages* (1985), summarizes modern scholarship. Kenneth R. Stow, *Alienated Minority: The Jews of Medieval Latin Europe* (1992), provides a survey through the fourteenth century. On the Latin West's external ties, see Khalil I. Semaan, ed., *Islam and the Medieval West: Aspects of Intercultural Relations* (1980).

■ Notes

1. Quoted in Marina Warner, *Alone of All Her Sex: The Myth and Cult of the Virgin Mary* (New York: Random House, 1983), 179.
2. Harry Miskimin, *The Economy of the Early Renaissance, 1300–1460* (Englewood Cliffs, NJ: Prentice Hall, 1969), 26–27.
3. Quotations here and later in the chapter are from Geoffrey Chaucer, *The Canterbury Tales,* trans. Nevill Coghill (New York: Penguin Books, 1952), 25, 29, 32.

15

THE MARITIME REVOLUTION,

TO 1550

Global Maritime Expansion Before 1450 • Iberian Expansion,
1400–1550 • Encounters with Europe, 1450–1550
SOCIETY AND CULTURE: European Male Sexual Dominance Overseas

n 1511, the young Ferdinand Magellan sailed from Europe around the southern tip of Africa and eastward across the Indian Ocean as a member of the first Portuguese expedition to explore the East Indies (maritime Southeast Asia). Eight years later, in the service of Spain, he headed an expedition that sought to reach the East Indies by sailing westward from Europe. By the middle of 1521, Magellan's expedition had sailed across the Atlantic, rounded the southern tip of South America, and crossed the Pacific Ocean—but at a high price.

One of the five ships wrecked on a reef; the captain of another deserted and sailed back to Spain. The passage across the Pacific took much longer than anticipated. Dozens of sailors died of starvation and disease. In the Philippines, Magellan himself was killed on April 27, 1521, while aiding a local king who had promised to become a Christian. Magellan's successor met the same fate a few days later.

The expedition's survivors consolidated their resources by burning the least seaworthy of their remaining three ships and transferring the men and supplies to the smaller *Victoria*, which continued westward across the Indian Ocean, around Africa, and back to Europe. Magellan's flagship, the *Trinidad*, tried unsuccessfully to recross the Pacific to Central America. The *Victoria*'s return to Spain on September 8, 1522, confirmed Europe's ability and determination to master the oceans. The Portuguese crown had backed a century of daring and dangerous voyages to open routes to Africa, Brazil, and the Indian Ocean. Since 1492, Spain had opened contacts with the American continents. Now the broad Pacific Ocean had been crossed.

Before 1500, powerful states and the rich trading networks of Asia had led the way in overland and maritime expansion. The Iberians set out on their voyages of exploration to reach Eastern markets, and their success began a new era in which the West gradually became the world's center of power, wealth, and innovation.

As you read this chapter, ask yourself the following questions:

- Why did Portugal and Spain undertake voyages of exploration?

- Why do the voyages of Magellan and other Iberians mark a turning point in world history?

- What were the consequences for the different peoples of the world of the contacts resulting from these voyages?

◌

GLOBAL MARITIME EXPANSION BEFORE 1450

By 1450, mariners had discovered and settled most of the islands of the Pacific, the Atlantic, and the Indian Oceans, and a great trading system united the peoples around the Indian Ocean. But we know of no individual crossing the Pacific in either direction. Even the narrower Atlantic formed a barrier that kept the peoples of the Americas, Europe, and Africa in ignorance of each other's existence. The inhabitants of Australia were also completely cut off from contact with the rest of humanity. All this was about to change.

The Pacific Ocean

The vast distances that Polynesian peoples voyaged out of sight of land across the Pacific Ocean are one of the most impressive feats in maritime history before 1450 (see Map 15.1 on page 346). Though they left no written records, over several thousand years mariners from the Malay° Peninsula of Southeast Asia explored and settled the island chains of the East Indies and continued on to New Guinea and the smaller islands of Melanesia°. Beginning some time before the Common Era (C.E.), a wave of expansion from the area of Fiji brought the first humans to the islands of the central Pacific known as Polynesia. Their sailing canoes reached the easternmost Marquesas° Islands about 400 C.E.; Easter Island, 2,200 miles (3,540 kilometers) off the coast of South America, a century later; and the Hawaiian Islands by 500 C.E. Settlement in New Zealand began about 1200. Between 1100 and 1300, new voyages northward from Tahiti brought more Polynesian settlers to Hawaii.

Historians have puzzled over how the Polynesians reached the eastern Pacific islands without compasses to plot their way, particularly in view of the difficulties Magellan's flagship encountered sailing eastward across the Pacific. In 1947, explorer Thor Heyerdahl° argued that Easter Island and Hawaii were settled from the Americas and sought to prove his theory by sailing his balsawood raft *Kon Tiki* westward from Peru.

Although some Amerindian voyagers did use ocean currents to travel northward from Peru to Mexico between 300 and 900 C.E., there is now considerable evidence that planned expansion by Polynesian mariners accomplished the settlement of the islands of the eastern Pacific. The languages of the islanders relate closely to the languages of the western Pacific and ultimately to those of Malaya. In addition, accidental voyages could not have brought sufficient numbers of men and women for founding a new colony along with all the plants and domesticated animals common to other Polynesian islands.

In 1976, a Polynesian crew led by anthropologist Ben Finney used traditional navigational methods to sail the *Hokulea,* a 62-foot-long (19-meter-long) double canoe, from Hawaii south to Tahiti. Some old oceangoing canoes, using inverted triangular sails and steered by paddles (not by a rudder) measured 120 feet (37 meters) long. The Hokulea's crew navigated using only their observation of the currents, stars, and evidence of land.

The Indian Ocean

While Polynesian mariners settled the Pacific islands, other Malayo-Indonesians sailed westward across the Indian Ocean and colonized the large island of Madagascar off the southeastern coast of Africa. These voyages continued through the fifteenth century.

Malay (May-LAY)   **Melanesia** (mel-uh-NEE-zhuh)

Marquesas (mar-KAY-suhs)   **Heyerdahl** (HIGH-uhr-dahl)

To this day, the inhabitants of Madagascar speak Malayo-Polynesian languages. However, part of the island's population is descended from Africans who crossed the 600 miles (1,000 kilometers) from the mainland to Madagascar, most likely in the centuries just before 1500.

The rise of Islam gave Indian Ocean trade an important boost. The great Muslim cities of the Middle East provided a demand for valuable commodities, and networks of Muslim traders tied the region together (see Chapter 13). The Indian Ocean traders operated largely independent of the empires and states that they served, but in East Asia, China's early Ming emperors took an active interest in these wealthy ports of trade, sending Admiral **Zheng He**° on a series of expeditions (see Chapter 12).

The first Ming fleet in 1405 consisted of sixty-two specially built "treasure ships," large Chinese junks each about 300 feet long by 150 feet wide (90 by 45 meters). Most of the one hundred smaller accompanying vessels exceeded in size the flagship in which Columbus later sailed across the Atlantic. Each treasure ship had nine masts, twelve sails, many decks, and a carrying capacity of 3,000 tons (six times the capacity of Columbus's entire fleet). One expedition carried over 27,000 individuals, including infantry and cavalry troops. Although the ships carried small cannon, highly accurate crossbows dominated most Chinese sea battles.

One Chinese-Arabic interpreter kept a journal recording the customs, dress, and beliefs of the people visited, along with the trade, towns, and animals of their countries. Among his observations were these: exotic animals such as the black panther of Malaya and the tapir of Sumatra; beliefs in legendary "corpse-headed barbarians" whose heads left their bodies at night and caused infants to die; the division of coastal Indians into five classes, which correspond to the four Hindu varnas and a separate Muslim class; and the fact that traders in the Indian port of Calicut° could perform error-free calculations by counting on their fingers and toes rather than using the Chinese abacus. After his return, the interpreter went on tour in China, telling of these exotic places and "how far the majestic virtue of [China's] imperial dynasty extended."[1]

Interest in new contacts was not confined to the Chinese side. In 1415–1416, at least three trading cities on the Swahili° Coast of East Africa sent delegations to China. Although no record of African and Chinese reactions to one another survives, China's lavish gifts to local rulers stimulated the Swahili market for silk and porcelain.

The Atlantic Ocean

The Vikings, northern European raiders and pirates, used their small, open ships to attack coastal European settlements for several centuries. They also discovered and settled one island after another in the North Atlantic. Like the Polynesians, the Vikings had neither maps nor navigational devices. They found their way using their knowledge of the heavens and the seas.

The Vikings first settled Iceland in 770. From there, some moved on to Greenland in 982, and one group sighted North America in 986. Fifteen years later, Leif Ericsson established a short-lived Viking settlement on the island of Newfoundland, which he called Vinland. When the climate turned colder after 1200, the northern settlements in Greenland went into decline. Vinland became a mysterious place mentioned in Norse sagas.

Some southern Europeans also explored the Atlantic. In 1291, two Vivaldo brothers from Genoa set out to sail around Africa to India. They were never heard of again. Other Genoese and Portuguese expeditions into the Atlantic in the fourteenth century discovered (and settled) the islands of Madeira°, the Azores°, and the Canaries.

Mention also occurs of African voyages of exploration in the Atlantic. The Syrian geographer al-Umari (1301–1349) relates that when Mansa Kankan Musa°, the ruler of the West African empire of Mali, passed through Egypt on his lavish pilgrimage to Mecca in 1324, he told of voyages to cross the Atlantic undertaken by his predecessor, Mansa Muhammad. Muhammad had sent out four hundred vessels with men and supplies, telling them, "Do not return until you have reached the

---

Zheng He (jung huh)   **Calicut** (KAL-ih-kut)

Swahili (swah-HEE-lee)   **Madeira** (muh-DEER-uh)
Azores (A-zorz)
Mansa Kankan Musa (MAHN-suh KAHN-kahn MOO-suh)

CHRONOLOGY

	Pacific Ocean	Atlantic Ocean	Indian Ocean
Pre-1400	**400–1300** Polynesian settlement of Pacific islands	**770–1200** Viking voyages **1300s** Settlement of Madeira, Azores, Canaries **Early 1300s** Mali voyages	
1400 to 1500		**1418–1460** Voyages of Henry the Navigator **1440s** Slaves from West Africa **1482** Portuguese at Gold Coast and Kongo **1486** Portuguese at Benin **1488** Bartolomeu Dias reaches Indian Ocean **1492** Columbus reaches Caribbean **1493** Columbus returns to Caribbean (second voyage) **1498** Columbus reaches mainland of South America (third voyage) **1492–1500** Spanish conquer Hispaniola	**1405–1433** Voyages of Zheng He **1498** Vasco da Gama reaches India
1500 to 1550		**1500** Cabral reaches Brazil **1513** Ponce de León explores Florida	**1505** Portuguese bombard Swahili Coast cities **1510** Portuguese take Goa **1511** Portuguese take Malacca **1515** Portuguese take Hormuz
	1519–1522 Magellan expedition	**1519–1520** Cortés conquers Aztec Empire **1531–1533** Pizarro conquers Inca Empire	**1535** Portuguese take Diu **1538** Portuguese defeat Ottoman fleet **1539** Portuguese aid Ethiopia

other side of the ocean or if you have exhausted your food or water." After a long time, one canoe returned, reporting the others had been swept away by a "violent current in the middle of the sea." Muhammad himself then set out at the head of a second, even larger, expedition, from which no one returned.

On the other side of the Atlantic, Amerindian voyagers from South America colonized the West Indies. By the year 1000, Amerindians known as the **Arawak°** had moved from the small islands of the Lesser Antilles (Barbados, Martinique,

Arawak (AR-uh-wahk)

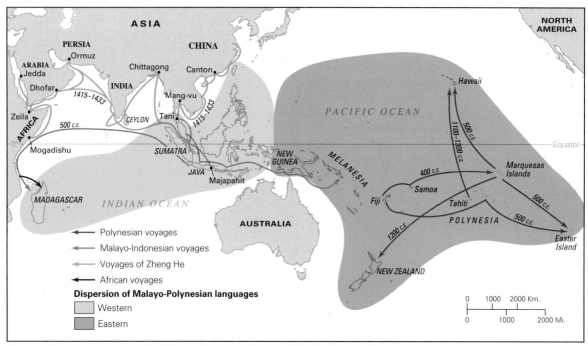

Map 15.1 Exploration and Settlement in the Indian and Pacific Oceans Before 1500 Over many centuries, mariners originating in Southeast Asia gradually colonized the islands of the Pacific and Indian Oceans. The Chinese voyages led by Zheng He in the fifteenth century were lavish official expeditions.

Guadaloupe) into the Greater Antilles (Cuba, Hispaniola, Jamaica, and Puerto Rico), as well as into the Bahamas. Another people, the Carib, followed their route. By the late fifteenth century, they had overrun most Arawak settlements in the Lesser Antilles and were raiding parts of the Greater Antilles. From the West Indies, Arawak and Carib also undertook voyages to the North American mainland.

IBERIAN EXPANSION, 1400–1550

The preceding survey shows that maritime exploration occurred in many parts of the world before 1450. The sea voyages sponsored by the Iberian kingdoms of Portugal and Spain attract special interest because they began a maritime revolution that profoundly altered the course of world history. The Portuguese and Spanish expeditions ended the isolation of the Americas and increased global interaction. The influence in world affairs of the Iberians and other Europeans who followed them overseas rose steadily after 1500.

Iberian overseas expansion arose from two related phenomena. First, Iberian rulers had strong economic, religious, and political motives to expand their contacts and increase their dominance. Second, improvements in maritime and military technologies gave them the means to master treacherous and unfamiliar ocean environments, seize control of existing maritime trade routes, and conquer new lands.

Background to Iberian Expansion

In many ways, these voyages continued four trends evident in the Latin West from about the year 1000:

Polynesian Canoes
Sailing canoes such as these, shown in an eighteenth-century painting, made long voyages of exploration and settlement. A large platform connects two canoes at the left, providing more room for the expedition. A sail supplements the paddlers. ("Tereoboo, King of Owyhee, bringing presents to Captain Cook," D. L. Ref. p. xx 2f. 35. Courtesy, The Dixon Library, State Library of New South Wales)

(1) the revival of urban life and trade, (2) a struggle with Islamic powers for dominance of the Mediterranean that mixed religious motives with the desire for trade with distant lands, (3) growing intellectual curiosity about the outside world, and (4) a peculiarly European alliance between merchants and rulers.

The city-states of northern Italy took the lead in all of these developments. By 1450, they had well-established trade links to northern Europe, the Indian Ocean, and the Black Sea, and their merchant princes had sponsored an intellectual and artistic Renaissance. But the Italian states did not take the lead in exploring the Atlantic, even after the expansion of the Ottoman Empire in the fourteenth and fifteenth centuries disrupted their trade to the East (see Chapter 19), because Venice and Genoa preferred to continue the lucrative alliances with Muslims that had given their merchants privileged positions and because Mediterranean ships were ill suited to the more violent weather of the Atlantic. However, many individual Italians played leading roles in Atlantic exploration.

By contrast, the Iberian kingdoms had engaged in anti-Muslim warfare since the eighth century, when Muslim forces overran most of the peninsula. By about 1250, the Iberian kingdoms of Portugal, Castile, and Aragon had conquered all the Muslim lands in Iberia except the southern kingdom of Granada, which finally fell to the united kingdom of Castile and Aragon in 1492 (see Chapter 14). These territories gradually amalgamated to form Spain, sixteenth-century Europe's most powerful state.

Christian militancy continued to drive Portugal and Spain in their overseas ventures. But the Iberian rulers and their adventurous subjects also sought material returns. Their small share of the Mediterranean trade made them more willing than the Italians to take risks to find new routes to Africa and Asia through the Atlantic. Moreover, both kingdoms participated in the shipbuilding changes and the gunpowder revolution under way in Atlantic Europe. Though not centers of Renaissance learning, both states had exceptional rulers who appreciated new geographical knowledge.

Portuguese Voyages

When the Muslim government of Morocco in northwestern Africa weakened in the fifteenth century, the Portuguese went on the attack, beginning with the city of Ceuta° in 1415. This assault combined aspects of a religious crusade, a plundering expedition, and a military tournament in which young Portuguese knights displayed their bravery. Despite the capture of several more ports along Morocco's Atlantic coast, the Portuguese could not

---

Ceuta (say-OO-tuh)

Chinese Junk This modern drawing compares one of Zheng He's ships with one of Vasco da Gama's. Watertight interior bulkheads made junks the most seaworthy large ships of the fifteenth century. Sails were made of pleated bamboo matting. A stern rudder provided steering. European ships had greater speed and maneuverability. (Dugald Stermer)

push inland and gain access to the gold trade they learned about, so they sought more direct contact with the gold producers by sailing down the African coast.

Young Prince Henry (1394–1460), third son of the king of Portugal, led the attack on Ceuta. Because he devoted the rest of his life to promoting exploration, he is known as **Henry the Navigator.** His official biographer emphasized his desire to convert Africans to Christianity, make contact with Christian rulers believed to exist in Africa, and launch joint crusades with them against the Ottomans. Profit also figured in his dreams. His initial explorations focused on Africa. His ships established permanent contact with the islands of Madeira in 1418 and the Azores in 1439. Only later did reaching India become a goal.

"The Navigator" himself never ventured farther from home than North Africa. Instead, he founded a sort of research institute at Sagres° for studying navigation and collecting information about new lands. His staff drew on the pioneering efforts of Italian merchants, especially the

Genoese, who had learned some of the secrets of the trans-Saharan trade, and of fourteenth-century Jewish cartographers who used information from Arab and European sources to produce remarkably accurate sea charts and maps of distant places. They also studied and improved navigational instruments that had come into Europe from China and the Islamic world: the magnetic compass, first developed in China, and the astrolabe, an instrument of Arab or Greek invention that enabled mariners to determine their latitude by measuring the position of the sun or the stars.

The Portuguese developed a new type of long-distance sailing vessel, the **caravel°.** The many-oared galleys of the Mediterranean could not carry enough food and water for long ocean voyages. The three-masted ships of the North Atlantic, powered by square sails, could not sail at much of an angle against the wind. The caravel, which was only one-fifth the size of the largest European ships and the large Chinese junks, could enter shallow coastal waters and explore upriver, yet it had the strength to weather ocean storms. When equipped with lateen sails, caravels had great maneuverability and could sail deeply into the wind; when sporting square Atlantic sails, they had great speed. The addition of small cannon made them good fighting ships as well. The caravels' economy, speed, agility, and power justified a contemporary's claim that they were "the best ships that sailed the seas."[2]

Pioneering captains had to overcome crews' fears that the South Atlantic waters were boiling hot and contained ocean currents that would prevent their ever returning home. It took Prince Henry from 1420 to 1434 to coax an expedition to venture beyond southern Morocco in northwest Africa (see Map 15.2). The next stretch of coast, 800 miles (1,300 kilometers) of desert, offered little of interest to the explorers. Finally in 1444, the mariners reached the Senegal River and the populous, well-watered lands below the Sahara beginning at what they named Cape Verde (Green Cape) because of its vegetation.

In the years that followed, Henry's explorers learned how to return speedily to Portugal. Instead of battling the prevailing northeast trade winds and currents back up the coast, they discovered that by sailing northwest into the Atlantic to the latitude of the Azores, ships could pick up prevailing westerly winds that would blow them back to Portugal. The knowledge that ocean winds tend to form large circular patterns helped explorers discover many other ocean routes.

To pay for the research, ships, and expeditions, Prince Henry drew partly on the income of the Order of Christ, a military religious order of which he was the governor. The Order of Christ had been founded to inherit the Portuguese properties and the crusading tradition of the Order of Knights Templar (see Chapter 7), which had disbanded in 1314. The Order of Christ received the exclusive right to promote Christianity in all the lands that were discovered, and the Portuguese emblazoned their ships' sails with the crusaders' red cross.

The first financial returns came from selling into slavery Africans captured in raids on the northwest coast of Africa and the Canary Islands during the 1440s. The Portuguese had captured or purchased eighty thousand Africans by the end of the century. However, gold quickly became more important than slavery. By 1457, enough African gold was coming back to Portugal for the kingdom to issue a new gold coin called the cruzado (crusade), another reminder of how deeply the Portuguese entwined religious and secular motives.

By the time Prince Henry died in 1460, his explorers had established a base of operations in the uninhabited Cape Verde Islands and explored 600 miles (950 kilometers) of coast beyond Cape Verde, as far as what they named Sierra Leone° (Lion Mountain). From there, they knew the coast of Africa curved sharply toward the east. After spending four decades covering the 1,500 miles (2,400 kilometers) from Lisbon to Sierra Leone, Portuguese explorers traveled the remaining 4,000 miles (6,400 kilometers) to the continent's southern tip in only three decades.

Royal sponsorship continued, but private commercial participation sped the progress. In 1469, a Lisbon merchant named Fernão Gomes purchased from the Crown the privilege of exploring 350 miles (550 kilometers) of new coast a year for five years and a monopoly on any resulting trade. Gomes discovered the uninhabited island of São Tomé° on the equator; in the next century, it became a major source of sugar produced with African slave labor. He also explored what later Europeans called the **Gold Coast,** which became the headquarters of Portugal's West African trade.

The expectation of finding a passage around Africa to the Indian Ocean spurred the final thrust down the African coast. **Bartolomeu Dias** rounded the southern tip of Africa (in 1488) and entered the Indian Ocean. In 1497–1498, **Vasco da Gama** led a Portuguese expedition around Africa to India. In 1500, ships in an expedition under Pedro Alvares Cabral°, while swinging wide to the west in the South Atlantic to catch the winds that would sweep them around southern Africa and on to India, came on the eastern coast of South America, laying the basis for Portugal's later claim to Brazil.

Spanish Voyages

Spain's early discoveries owed more to haste and blind luck than to careful planning. Only in the last decade of the fifteenth century did the Spanish monarchs turn their

---

Sierra Leone (see-ER-uh lee-OWN)
São Tomé (sow toh-MAY)   Cabral (kah-BRAHL)

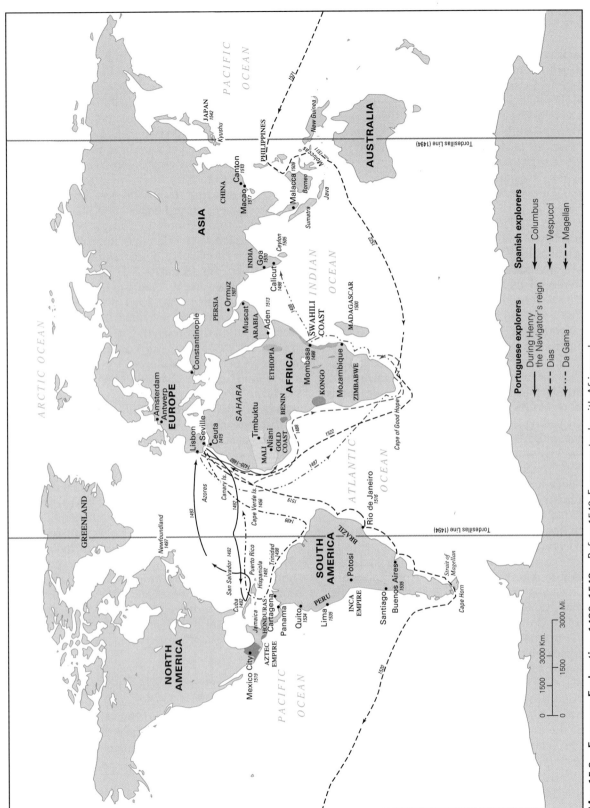

Map 15.2 European Exploration, 1420–1542 Before 1540, European trade with Africa and Asia exceeded that with the Americas. After the conquest of the Aztec and Inca Empires, transatlantic trade increased. Notice the Tordesillas line that theoretically separated Spanish and Portuguese spheres of activity.

attention from reconquest and organization of previously Muslim territories to overseas exploration. By this time, the Portuguese had already found their route to the Indian Ocean.

The leader of their overseas mission would be **Christopher Columbus** (1451–1506), a Genoese mariner. His three voyages between 1492 and 1498 would reveal the existence of vast and unexpected lands across the Atlantic. But this momentous discovery fell disappointingly short of Columbus's intention of finding a new route to the Indian Ocean even shorter than that of the Portuguese.

As a younger man, Columbus had gained considerable experience while participating in Portuguese explorations along the African coast, but he dreamed of a shorter way to the riches of the East. By his reckoning (based on a serious misreading of a ninth-century Arab authority), a mere 2,400 nautical miles (4,450 kilometers) separated the Canary Islands from Japan. The actual distance was five times greater.

Portuguese authorities twice rejected his plan to reach the East by sailing west, first in 1485 following a careful study and again in 1488 after Dias had established the feasibility of the African route. Columbus received more sympathy, but initially no support, from Queen Isabella of Castile. A Castilian commission appointed by Isabella studied the proposal for four years and concluded that a westward sea route to the Indies rested on questionable geographical assumptions. Nevertheless, Columbus's persistence finally won over the queen and her husband, King Ferdinand of Aragon. In 1492, elated perhaps by finally expelling the Muslims from Granada, they agreed to fund a modest expedition.

Columbus recorded in his log that the *Santa María*, the *Santa Clara* (nicknamed the *Niña*), and a vessel now known only by its nickname, the *Pinta*, with a mostly Spanish crew of ninety men "departed Friday the third day of August of the year 1492," toward "the regions of India." Their mission, the royal contract stated, was "to discover and acquire certain islands and mainland in the Ocean Sea." Columbus carried letters of introduction from the Spanish sovereigns to Eastern rulers, including one to the "Grand Khan" (meaning the Chinese emperor). An Arabic-speaking Jewish convert to Christianity had the job of communicating with the peoples of eastern Asia.

Unfavorable headwinds had discouraged other attempts to explore the Atlantic west of the Azores. But on earlier voyages along the African coast, Columbus had learned about winds blowing westward at the latitude of the Canaries. After reaching the Canaries, he replaced the *Niña*'s lateen sails with square sails, for he knew that from then on, speed would be more important than maneuverability since his supplies would last for only a fixed number of days.

In October, the expedition encountered the islands of the Caribbean. Columbus called the inhabitants "Indians" because he believed he had reached the East Indies. A second voyage in 1493 did nothing to change his mind. On a third voyage in 1498, two months after Vasco da Gama reached India, Columbus sighted the mainland of South America, which he insisted was part of Asia. But by then, other Europeans had become convinced that his discoveries were of lands previously unknown to the Old World (Europe, Asia, and Africa). Amerigo Vespucci's explorations, first on behalf of Spain and then for Portugal, led mapmakers to name the new continents "America," after him.

To prevent disputes about exploiting these new lands and spreading Christianity among their peoples, Spain and Portugal agreed to split the world between them. The Treaty of Tordesillas°, negotiated by the pope in 1494, drew an imaginary north-south line down the middle of the Atlantic Ocean. Lands east of the line in Africa and southern Asia could be claimed by Portugal; lands to the west in the Americas belonged to Spain. Cabral's discovery of Brazil, however, gave Portugal a valid claim to the part of South America that bulged east of the line.

But if the Tordesillas line were extended around the earth, where would Spain's and Portugal's spheres of influence divide in the East? Given European ignorance of the earth's true size in 1494, no one knew whether the Moluccas°, the source of the valuable spices of the East Indies, belonged to Portugal or Spain. The missing information concerned

---

Tordesillas (tor-duh-SEE-yuhs)
Moluccas (muh-LOO-kuhz)

the size of the Pacific Ocean, which a Spanish adventurer named Vasco Núñez de Balboa° had spotted in 1513 when he crossed the isthmus (a narrow neck of land) of Panama from the east. The 1519 expedition of **Ferdinand Magellan** (ca. 1480–1521) sought to complete Columbus's interrupted westward voyage by sailing around the Americas and across the Pacific. The Moluccas turned out to lie well within Portugal's sphere, as Spain formally acknowledged in 1529.

Magellan's voyage laid the basis for Spanish colonization of the Philippine Islands after 1564. It also gave Magellan credit, despite his death, for being the first person to encircle the globe, for a decade earlier, he had sailed from Europe to the East Indies on an expedition sponsored by his native Portugal.

Columbus and those who followed in his path laid the basis for the colonial empires of Spain and other European nations. In turn, these empires promoted, among the four Atlantic continents, a new trading network whose importance rivaled and eventually surpassed that of the Indian Ocean. Of more immediate importance, Portugal's entry into the Indian Ocean led quickly to a major European presence and profit. Both the eastward and the westward voyages of exploration marked a tremendous expansion of Europe's role in world history.

ENCOUNTERS WITH EUROPE, 1450–1550

The ways in which Africans, Asians, and Amerindians perceived their European visitors and interacted with them influenced their future relations. Some welcomed the Europeans as potential allies; others viewed them as rivals or enemies. In general, Africans and Asians readily recognized the benefits and dangers of European contact. However, the long isolation of the Amerindians added to the strangeness of their encounter with the Spanish and made them more

Balboa (bal-BOH-uh)

vulnerable to the unfamiliar diseases they inadvertently introduced.

Western Africa

Many Africans welcomed trade with the Portuguese, which gave them new markets for their exports and access to imports cheaper than those coming by caravan across the Sahara. Miners in the hinterland of the Gold Coast, which the Portuguese first visited in 1471, had long sold their gold to merchants from trading cities along the southern edge of the Sahara for transshipment to North Africa. Recognizing the possibility of more favorable trading terms, coastal Africans negotiated with the royal representative of Portugal, who arrived in 1482 seeking permission to erect a trading fort.

The Portuguese noble in charge and his officers (likely including the young Christopher Columbus, who had entered Portuguese service in 1476) strove to make a proper impression. They dressed in their best clothes, erected a fancy reception platform, celebrated a Catholic Mass, and signaled the start of negotiations with trumpets, tambourines, and drums. The African king, Caramansa, staged his entrance with equal ceremony, arriving with a large retinue of attendants and musicians. Through an African interpreter, the two leaders exchanged flowery speeches pledging goodwill and mutual benefit. Caramansa then gave permission for a small trading fort, assured, he said, by the appearance of these royal delegates that they were honorable persons, unlike the "few, foul, and vile" Portuguese visitors of the previous decade.

Neither side made a show of force, but Caramansa warned that if the Portuguese failed to be peaceful and honest traders, he and his people would move away and deprive their post of food and trade. Trade at the post of Saint George of the Mine (later called Elmina) enriched both sides. The Portuguese crown was soon purchasing gold amounting to one-tenth of the world's production at the time. In return, Africans received shiploads of goods brought by the Portuguese from Asia, Europe, and other parts of Africa.

Early contacts involved a mixture of commercial, military, and religious interests. Some African rulers quickly saw the value of European firearms.

Afro-Portuguese Ivory   An ivory carver from the kingdom of Benin probably made this saltcellar. Intended for a European market, it depicts a Portuguese ship on the cover and Portuguese nobles around the base.   (Courtesy of the Trustees of the British Museum)

Coastal rulers also proved willing to test the value of Christian practices, which the Portuguese eagerly promoted. The rulers of Benin and Kongo, the largest coastal kingdoms, invited Portuguese missionaries and soldiers to accompany them into battle to test the Christians' religion along with their muskets.

The kingdom of Benin in the Niger Delta, near the peak of its power after a century of aggressive expansion, had a large capital city, also known as Benin. Its *oba* (king) responded to a Portuguese visit in 1486 by sending an ambassador to Portugal to learn more about their homeland. Then he established a royal monopoly on Portuguese trade, selling pepper and ivory tusks (to be taken back to Portugal) as well as stone beads, textiles, and prisoners of war (to be resold at Elmina). In return, Portuguese merchants provided Benin with copper and brass, fine textiles, glass beads, and a horse for the king's royal procession. In the early six-

teenth century, as the demand for slaves for the Portuguese sugar plantations on the nearby island of São Tomé grew, the oba first raised the price of slaves and then imposed restrictions on their sale.

Efforts to spread Catholicism ultimately failed. Early kings showed some interest, but after 1538, the rulers declined to receive further missionaries. They also closed the market in male slaves for the rest of the sixteenth century. Both steps illustrate their power to control how much interaction they wanted.

Farther south, on the lower Congo River, the *manikongo*° (king) of Kongo also sent delegates to Portugal, established a royal monopoly on trade, and expressed interest in missionary teachings. But here the royal family made Catholicism the kingdom's official faith. Lacking ivory and pepper, Kongo sold more and more slaves to acquire the goods brought by the Portuguese and pay missionary expenses.

Soon the royal trade monopoly broke down. In 1526, the Christian manikongo, Afonso I (r. 1506–ca. 1540), wrote to his royal "brother," the king of Portugal, begging for his help in stopping the slave trade because unauthorized Kongolese were kidnapping and selling people, even members of good families. Afonso's appeal that contacts be limited to "some priests and a few people to teach in the schools, and no other goods except wine and flour for the holy sacrament" received no reply. After 1540, the major part of the slave trade from this part of Africa moved farther south.

Eastern Africa

As Vasco da Gama sailed up the eastern coast of Africa in 1498, most rulers of the coastal trading states received him coolly. Visitors who painted crusader crosses on their sails raised their suspicions. The ruler of Malindi, however, saw in the Portuguese an ally who could help him expand Malindi's trade, and he provided da Gama with a pilot to guide him to India. The suspicions of most rulers came to fruition seven years later when a Portuguese war fleet bombarded and looted most of the coastal cities in the name of Christ and commerce. It spared Malindi.

manikongo (mah-NEE-KONG-goh)

Christian Ethiopia also saw benefits in allying with the Portuguese. In the fourteenth and fifteenth centuries, Ethiopian conflicts with Muslim states along the Red Sea increased. After the Ottoman Turks conquered Egypt and launched a fleet in the Indian Ocean to counter the Portuguese in 1517, the warlord of the Muslim state of Adal attacked Ethiopia. A decisive victory in 1529 put the Christian kingdom in jeopardy, making Portuguese support a crucial matter.

For decades, delegations from Portugal and Ethiopia had talked of a Christian alliance. Queen Helena of Ethiopia, who acted as regent for her young sons after her husband's death in 1478, sent a letter in 1509 to "our very dear and well-beloved brother," the king of Portugal, along with a gift of two tiny crucifixes said to be made of wood from the cross Christ was crucified on. She proposed to combine her land army and Portugal's fleet against the Turks. At her death in 1522, no alliance had come into being, but the worsening situation brought renewed Ethiopian appeals.

Finally, a small Portuguese force commanded by Vasco da Gama's son Christopher reached Ethiopia in 1539. With Portuguese help, another queen rallied the desperate Ethiopians. Muslim foes captured Christopher da Gama and tortured him to death but lost heart when their leader fell in battle. Portuguese aid helped save the Ethiopian kingdom from extinction, but Ethiopia's refusal to transfer their Christian affiliation from the patriarch of Alexandria to the pope prevented a permanent alliance.

As these examples illustrate, African encounters with the Portuguese before 1550 varied considerably. Africans and Portuguese might become royal brothers, bitter opponents, or partners in a mutually profitable trade, but Europeans were still a minor presence in most of Africa in 1550. The Indian Ocean trade by then was occupying most of their attention.

Indian Ocean States

Vasco da Gama's arrival on the Malabar Coast of India in May 1498 did not impress the citizens of Calicut. The Chinese fleets of gigantic junks that had called at Calicut sixty-five years earlier dwarfed his four small ships, which were no larger than many of the dhows° already filling the harbor. The *samorin* (ruler) of Calicut and his Muslim officials showed mild interest, but the gifts da Gama brought evoked derisive laughter: twelve pieces of striped cloth, four scarlet hoods, six hats, and six wash basins. When da Gama defended his gifts as those of an explorer, not a merchant, the samorin cut him short, asking whether he had come to discover men or stones: "If he had come to discover men, as he said, why had he brought nothing?"

Coastal rulers soon discovered that the Portuguese had no intention of remaining poor competitors in the Indian Ocean trade. Upon da Gama's return to Portugal in 1499, the jubilant King Manuel styled himself "Lord of the Conquest, Navigation, and Commerce of Ethiopia, Arabia, Persia, and India." Previously, the Indian Ocean had been an open sea, used by merchants (and pirates) of all the surrounding coasts. Now the Portuguese crown intended to make it Portugal's sea, which others might use only on Portuguese terms.

Portugal's hope of controlling the Indian Ocean stemmed from the superiority of its ships and weapons over the smaller and lightly armed merchant dhows. In 1505, the Portuguese fleet of 81 ships and some 7,000 men bombarded Swahili Coast cities. Goa, on the west coast of India, fell to a well-armed fleet in 1510, becoming the base from which the Portuguese menaced the trading cities of Gujarat° to the north and Calicut and other Malabar Coast cities to the south. The port of Hormuz, controlling the entry to the Persian Gulf, fell in 1515. Aden, at the entrance to the Red Sea, preserved its independence, but the capture of the Gujarati port of Diu in 1535 consolidated Portuguese dominance of the western Indian Ocean.

Farther east, the independent city of Malacca° on the strait separating the Malay Peninsula and Sumatra became the focus of their attention. During the fifteenth century, Malacca had become the main entrepôt° (a place where goods are stored or deposited and from which they are distributed) for the trade from China, Japan, India, the Southeast Asian mainland, and the Moluccas. The city's

---

dhow (dow)   Gujarat (goo-juh-RAHT)
Malacca (muh-LAH-kuh)   entrepôt (ON-truh-poh)

100,000 residents spoke eighty-four different languages, according to a Portuguese source, and included merchants from Cairo, Ethiopia, and the Swahili Coast. Many non-Muslim residents supported letting the Portuguese join this cosmopolitan trading community, perhaps to offset the growing solidarity of Muslim traders. In 1511, however, the Portuguese seized Malacca with a force of a thousand fighting men, including three hundred recruited in southern India.

On the China coast, local officials and merchants persuaded the imperial government to allow the Portuguese to establish a trading post at Macao° in 1557. Subsequently, Portuguese ships nearly monopolized trade between China and Japan.

Control of the major port cities enabled the Portuguese to enforce their demands that all spices be carried in Portuguese ships, as well as all goods on the major ocean routes such as between Goa and Macao. The Portuguese also tried to control and tax other Indian Ocean trade. Merchant ships entering and leaving their ports had to carry a Portuguese passport and pay customs duties. Portuguese patrols seized vessels that did not comply, confiscated their cargoes, and either killed the captain and crew or sentenced them to forced labor.

Reactions to this power grab varied. Like the emperors of China, the Mughal° emperors of India largely ignored Portugal's maritime intrusions (see Chapters 12 and 19). The Ottomans confronted the Christian intruders more aggressively. They supported Egypt's defensive efforts from 1501 to 1509 and then sent their own fleet into the Indian Ocean in 1538. However, Ottoman galleys proved no match for the faster, better-armed Portuguese vessels in the open ocean. They retained their advantage only in the Red Sea and Persian Gulf, where they controlled many ports.

Smaller trading states could not challenge the Portuguese. Mutual rivalry kept them from forming a common front. Some cooperated with the Portuguese to safeguard their prosperity and security. Others engaged in evasion and resistance.

When the merchants of Calicut put up sustained resistance, the Portuguese embargoed all trade with Aden, Calicut's principal trading partner, and centered their trade on the port of Cochin,

which had once been a dependency of Calicut. Some Calicut merchants evaded their patrols, but Calicut's importance shrank as Cochin gradually became the major pepper-exporting port on the Malabar Coast.

Farther north, Gujarat initially resisted Portuguese attempts at monopoly and in 1509 joined Egypt's futile effort to sweep the Portuguese from the Arabian Sea. But in 1535, with his state weakened by Mughal attacks, the ruler allowed the Portuguese to build a fort at Diu in return for their support. Once established, the Portuguese gradually extended their control. By midcentury, they were licensing and taxing all Gujarati ships. Even after the Mughals took control of Gujarat in 1572, the Mughal emperor, Akbar, permitted the Portuguese to continue their maritime monopoly in return for allowing one pilgrim ship a year to sail to Mecca without paying a fee.

The Portuguese never gained complete control of the Indian Ocean trade, but their domination of key ports and trade routes brought them considerable profit in the form of spices and other luxury goods. The Portuguese broke the trading monopoly of Venice and Genoa by selling pepper for less than what they charged for shipments obtained through Egyptian middlemen.

The Americas

In the Americas, the Spanish established a vast territorial empire, in contrast to the trading empire of the Portuguese. The Spanish kingdoms drew on somewhat greater resources, but the Spanish and Portuguese monarchies had similar motives for expansion and used identical ships and weapons. The isolation of the Amerindian peoples provided a key difference. The first European settlers in the Caribbean resorted to conquest and plunder rather than trade. They later extended this practice to the more powerful Amerindian kingdoms on the American mainland. After 1518, deadly epidemics among the Amerindians weakened their ability to resist.

The Arawak whom Columbus first encountered on Hispaniola (modern Haiti and the Dominican Republic) in the Greater Antilles and the Bahamas to the north cultivated maize (corn), cassava (a tuber), sweet potatoes, and hot peppers, as well as cotton

---

Macao (muh-COW)   **Mughal** (MOO-gahl)

Arawak Women Making Tortillas This sixteenth-century woodcut depicts techniques of food preparation in the West Indies. The woman at the left grinds cornmeal on a metate. The woman in the center pats cornmeal dough flat and fries the tortillas. The third woman serves tortillas with a bowl of stew. (Courtesy of the John Carter Brown Library at Brown University)

and tobacco. They mined and worked gold, but they did not trade gold, nor did they have iron. They extended a cautious welcome to Columbus but told him exaggerated stories about gold in other places to persuade him to move on.

Columbus brought with him several hundred settlers from southern Iberia, as well as missionaries, on his second trip to Hispaniola in 1493. The settlers stole gold ornaments, confiscated food, and raped women (see Society and Culture: European Male Sexual Dominance Overseas), provoking the Hispaniola Arawak to war in 1495. With the advantage of horses and body armor, the Spaniards slaughtered tens of thousands of Arawak and forced the survivors to pay a heavy tax in gold, spun cotton, and food. Whoever failed to meet the quotas faced forced labor. Meanwhile, the cattle, pigs, and goats introduced by the settlers devoured the Arawak's food crops, causing deaths from famine and disease. A governor appointed by the Spanish crown in 1502 forced the Arawak on Hispaniola to become laborers under the control of Spanish settlers.

The actions of the Spanish in the Antilles reflected Spanish behavior during the wars against the Muslims in the previous centuries. They sought to serve God by defeating, controlling, and converting nonbelievers and to become rich in the process. Individual **conquistadors**° (conquerors) extended that pattern around the Caribbean. Some raided the Bahamas for gold and labor as both grew scarce on Hispaniola. Arawak from the Bahamas served as slaves on Hispaniola. Juan Ponce de León (1460–1521), a veteran of the conquest of Muslim Spain and the seizure of Hispaniola, conquered the island of Borinquen (Puerto Rico) in 1508 and in 1513 explored southeastern Florida.

An ambitious and ruthless nobleman, **Hernán Cortés**° (1485–1547), led the most audacious expedition to the mainland. Cortés left Cuba in 1519 with six hundred fighting men and most of the island's weapons to assault the Mexican mainland in search of slaves and trade. Learning of the rich Aztec Empire in central Mexico, Cortés expanded on the American mainland the exploitation and conquest carried out in the Greater Antilles.

Many of the Amerindians whom the Aztecs had subjugated during the previous century resented the tribute, forced labor, and the large-scale human sacrifices to Aztec gods their rulers imposed on them (see Chapter 10). Some gave the Spanish their support as allies against the Aztecs. Like the Caribbean people, the mainland Amerindians had no precedent by which to judge these strangers. Later accounts suggest that some believed Cortés to be the legendary ruler Quetzalcoatl°, whose return to earth had been prophesied, and treated him with great deference.

Another consequence of millennia of isolation proved even more fatal: the lack of acquired immunity to Old World diseases. Smallpox, the most deadly of the early epidemics, appeared for the first time on the island of Hispaniola late in 1518. An infected member of the Cortés expedition then transmitted smallpox to Mexico in 1519, where it spread with deadly efficiency.

---

conquistador (kon-KEY-stuh-dor)   Cortés (kor-TEZ)
Quetzalcoatl (ket-zahl-COH-ah-tal)

SOCIETY & CULTURE

European Male Sexual Dominance Overseas

European expansion and colonization involved mainly men. Missionaries chose celibacy; other men did not, as these two letters make clear. The first, dated 1495, is from Michele de Cuneo, an officer on Columbus's second voyage.

While I was in the boat I captured a very beautiful Carib woman, whom the said Lord Admiral [Columbus] gave to me, and with whom, having taken her into my cabin, she being naked according to their custom, I conceived desire to take pleasure. I wanted to put my desire into execution but she did not want it and treated me with her finger nails in such a manner that I wished I had never begun. But seeing that, (to tell you the end of it all), I took a rope and thrashed her well, for which she raised such unheard of screams that you would not have believed your ears. Finally we came to an agreement in such manner that I can tell you that she seemed to have been brought up in a school of harlots.

The second letter, dated 1550, is from an Italian Jesuit missionary in India to Ignatius Loyola, the founder of the Society of Jesus (the Jesuits), in Rome.

Your reverence must know that the sin of licentiousness is so widespread in these regions [India] that no check is placed upon it, which leads to great inconveniences, and to great disrespect of the sacraments. I say this of the Portuguese, who have adopted the vices and customs of the land without reserve, including the evil custom of buying droves of slaves, male and female, just as if they were sheep, large and small. There are countless men who buy droves of girls and sleep with all of them, and subsequently sell them. There are innumerable married settlers who have four, eight, or ten female slaves and sleep with them, as is common knowledge. This is carried to such excess that there was one man in Malacca who had twenty-four women of various races, all of whom were his slaves, and all of whom he enjoyed. I quote this city because it is a thing that everybody knows. Most men, as soon as they can afford to buy a female slave, almost invariably use her as a girl-friend (amiga), besides many other dishonesties, in my poor understanding.

What circumstances gave European men such power over indigenous women? How do the writers attribute some responsibility for these encounters to the sexual license of the women involved? Are such attributions credible?

Source: The first letter is reprinted from Samuel Eliot Morison, trans. and ed., *Journals and Other Documents in the Life and Voyages of Christopher Columbus* (New York: Heritage Press, 1963), 212. The second letter is from C. R. Boxer, *The Portuguese Seaborne Empire, 1415–1825* (New York: Knopf, 1969). Copyright © 1969 by C. R. Boxer. Reprinted by permission of Alfred A. Knopf, Inc.

The Aztec emperor **Moctezuma°** II (r. 1502–1520) sent messengers to greet Cortés and determine whether he was god or man, friend or foe. Cortés advanced steadily toward the capital, Tenochtitlan°, overcoming Aztec opposition with cavalry charges and steel swords and gaining the support of discontented tributary peoples. When the Spaniards drew near, the emperor went out in a great procession, dressed in all his finery, to welcome Cortés with gifts and flower garlands.

Despite Cortés's initial promise of friendship, Moctezuma quickly found himself a prisoner in his own palace. The Spaniards looted his treasury, melting down its gold. Soon full-scale battle broke out. The Aztecs and their supporters briefly gained the upper hand. They destroyed half the Spanish force and 4,000 of their Amerindian allies, sacrificing fifty-three Spanish prisoners and four horses to their gods and displaying their severed heads in

---

Moctezuma (mock-teh-ZOO-ma)
Tenochtitlan (teh-noch-TIT-lan)

Coronation of Emperor Moctezuma In this painting by an unnamed Aztec artist, Moctezuma, his nose pierced by a bone, receives the crown from a prince in the palace at Tenochtitlan. (Oronoz)

rows on pikes. Reinforcements from Cuba enabled Cortés to regain the advantage. Smallpox, which weakened and killed more of the city's defenders than died in the fighting, also assisted his capture of Tenochtitlan in 1520. One source remembered that the disease "spread over the people as a great destruction."

After the capital fell, the conquistadores took over other parts of Mexico. Then some Spaniards began eyeing the Inca Empire, stretching nearly 3,000 miles (5,000 kilometers) south from the equator and containing half of the population in South America. The Inca had conquered the inhabitants of the Andes Mountains and the Pacific coast of South America during the previous century, and their rule was not fully accepted by the subjugated peoples (see Chapter 10).

The Inca rulers administered a well-organized empire with highly productive agriculture, exquisite stone cities (such as the capital, Cuzco), and rich gold and silver mines. The power of the Inca emperor rested on the belief that he was descended from the Sun God and on an efficient system of roads and messengers that kept him informed about major events. Yet at the end of the 1520s, before the Spanish had even been heard of, smallpox claimed countless lives, perhaps including the Inca emperor in 1530.

An even more devastating threat loomed: **Francisco Pizarro°** (ca. 1478–1541) and his motley band of 180 men, 37 horses, and 2 cannon. With limited education and some military experience, Pizarro had come to the Americas in 1502 at the age of twenty-five to seek his fortune. He had participated in the conquest of Hispaniola and in Balboa's expedition across the isthmus of Panama. By 1520 a wealthy landowner and official in Panama, he nevertheless gambled his fortune on exploring the Pacific coast to a point south of the equator, where he learned of the riches of the Inca. With a license from the king of Spain, he set out from Panama in 1531 to conquer them.

In November 1532, Pizarro arranged to meet the new Inca emperor, **Atahualpa°** (r. 1531–1533), near the Andean city of Cajamarca°. With supreme boldness and brutality, Pizarro's small band grabbed Atahualpa from a rich litter borne by eighty nobles as it passed through an enclosed courtyard. Though surrounded by an Inca army of at least 40,000, the Spaniards used their cannon to create confusion while their swords sliced the emperor's lightly armed retainers and servants to pieces.

Noting the glee with which the Spaniards seized gold, silver, and emeralds, the captive Atahualpa offered them what he thought would satisfy even the greediest among them in exchange for his freedom: a roomful of gold and silver. But after receiving 13,400 pounds (6,000 kilograms) of gold and 26,000 pounds (12,000 kilograms) of silver, the Spaniards gave Atahualpa a choice: being burned at the stake as a heathen or being strangled after a Christian baptism. He chose the latter. His death and the Spanish occupation broke the unity of the Inca Empire.

In 1533, the Spaniards took Cuzco and from there set out to conquer and loot the rest of the empire. The defeat of a final rebellion in 1536 spelled the end of Inca rule. Five years later, Pizarro himself met a violent death at the hands of Spanish rivals, but the conquest of the mainland continued. Incited by the fabulous wealth of the Aztecs and Inca, conquistadores extended Spanish conquest and exploration in South and North America, dreaming of new treasuries to loot.

Pizarro (pih-ZAHR-oh) Atahualpa (ah-tuh-WAHL-puh)
Cajamarca (kah-hah-MAHR-kah)

Patterns of Dominance

Within fifty years of Columbus's first landing, the Spanish had located and occupied the major population centers of the Americas and penetrated many of the more thinly populated areas. Why did the peoples of the Americas suffer a fate so different from that of peoples in Africa and Asia? Why were the Spanish able to erect a vast land empire in the Americas so quickly?

First, unfamiliar illnesses devastated the Caribbean islands and then the mainland. Contemporaries estimated that between 25 and 50 percent of those infected with smallpox died. Repeated epidemics inhibited the Amerindians' ability to regain control. Estimates of the size of the population before Columbus's arrival, based on sparse evidence, vary widely. Yet historians agree that the Amerindian population fell sharply during the sixteenth century. The Americas became a "widowed land," open to resettlement from across the Atlantic.

A second factor was Spain's superior military technology. Steel swords, protective armor, and horses gave the Spaniards an advantage over their Amerindian opponents. Though few in number, muskets and cannon provided a psychological edge. However, the Spanish conquests depended heavily on large numbers of Amerindian allies armed with indigenous weapons. The most decisive military advantage may have been the no-holds-barred fighting techniques the Spaniards had developed during their wars at home.

The third factor in Spain's conquest was the precedent established by the reconquest of Granada in 1492: forced labor, forced conversion, and the incorporation of conquered lands into a new empire.

The same three factors help explain the different outcomes elsewhere. Centuries of contacts before 1500 meant that Europeans, Africans, and Asians shared the same Old World diseases. Only very isolated peoples in Africa and Asia suffered a demographic calamity. The Iberians enjoyed a military advantage at sea, but on land they had no decisive advantage against more numerous indigenous armies. Everywhere, Iberian religious zeal went hand in hand with a desire for riches. In Iberia and America, conquest itself brought wealth. But in Africa and Asia, existing trading networks made wealth dependent on commercial domination rather than conquest.

CONCLUSION

Historians consider the century between 1450 and 1550 a turning point in world history. Some assign names: the "Vasco da Gama epoch," the "Columbian era," the "age of Magellan," or simply the "modern period." During those years, European explorers opened new long-distance trade routes across the world's oceans, for the first time establishing regular contact among all the continents. By 1550, those who followed them had broadened trading contacts with sub-Saharan Africa, gained mastery of the Indian Ocean trade routes, and conquered a land empire in the Americas.

What gave this maritime revolution unprecedented importance had more to do with what happened after 1550 than with what happened earlier. European overseas empires would endure longer than the Mongols' and would continue to expand for three and a half centuries. Unlike the Chinese, the Europeans did not turn their backs on the world after an initial burst of exploration. Not content dominating the Indian Ocean, Europeans opened in the Atlantic a maritime network of comparable wealth. They also established regular trade across the Pacific. The maritime expansion begun between 1450 and 1550 marked the beginning of an age of growing global interaction.

■ Key Terms

Zheng He	Christopher Columbus
Arawak	Ferdinand Magellan
Henry the Navigator	conquistadors
caravel	Hernán Cortés
Gold Goast	Moctezuma
Bartolomeu Dias	Francisco Pizarro
Vasco da Gama	Atahualpa

■ Suggested Reading

The selections edited by Joseph R. Levenson, *European Expansion and the Counter Example of Asia, 1300–1600* (1967), describe Chinese expansion and Western impressions of China. Janet Abu-Lughod, *Before European Hegemony: The World System,* A.D. *1250–1350* (1989), affords a speculative reassessment of the Mongols and the Indian Ocean trade in creating the modern world system; she summarizes her thesis in the American Historical Association (AHA) booklet *The World System in the Thirteenth Century: Dead-End or Precursor?* (1993).

The Chinese account of Zheng He's voyages is Ma Huan, *Ying-yai Sheng-lan: "The Overall Survey of the Ocean's Shores"* [1433], edited and translated by J. V. G. Mills (1970). On Polynesian expansion, see Jesse D. Jennings, ed., *The Prehistory of Polynesia* (1979). In it, the chapter "Voyaging," by Ben R. Finney, encapsulates his *Voyage of Rediscovery: A Cultural Odyssey Through Polynesia* (1994). Felipe Fernandez-Armesto, *Before Columbus: Exploration and Colonization from the Mediterranean to the Atlantic, 1229–1492* (1987), summarizes the medieval background to European intercontinental voyages.

For the technologies of European expansion, see Carlo M. Cipolla, *Guns, Sails, and Empires: Technological Innovation and the Early Phases of European Expansion, 1400–1700* (1965; reprint, 1985), or the more advanced study by Roger C. Smith, *Vanguard of Empire: Ships of Exploration in the Age of Columbus* (1993).

Surveys of European explorations based on contemporary records include Boies Penrose, *Travel and Discovery in the Age of the Renaissance, 1420–1620* (1952); J. H. Parry, *The Age of Reconnaissance: Discovery, Exploration, and Settlement, 1450–1650* (1963); and G. V. Scammell, *The World Encompassed: The First European Maritime Empires, c. 800–1650* (1981).

C. R. Boxer, *The Portuguese Seaborne Empire, 1415–1825* (1969), gives a general account, with more detail to be found in Bailey W. Diffie and George D. Winius, *Foundations of the Portuguese Empire, 1415–1580* (1977); A. J. R. Russell-Wood, *The Portuguese Empire: A World on the Move* (1998); and Luc Cuyvers, *Into the Rising Sun: The Journey of Vasco da Gama and the Discovery of the Modern World* (1998). John William Blake, ed., *Europeans in West Africa, 1450–1560* (1942), excerpts contemporary Portuguese, Castilian, and English sources. Elaine Sanceau, *The Life of Prester John: A Chronicle of Portuguese Exploration* (1941), covers Portuguese relations with Ethiopia. *The Summa Oriental of Tomé Pires: An Account of the East, from the Red Sea to Japan, Written in Malacca and India in 1512–1515,* translated by Armando

Cortesão (1944), provides a firsthand account of the Portuguese in the Indian Ocean.

For Spanish expansion, see J. H. Parry, *The Spanish Seaborne Empire* (1967). Samuel Eliot Morison's excellent *Admiral of the Ocean Sea: A Life of Christopher Columbus* (1942) is available in an abridged version as *Christopher Columbus, Mariner* (1955). Tzvetan Todorov, *The Conquest of America,* translated by Richard Howard (1985), focuses on Spanish shortcomings. Marvin Lunenfeld, ed., *1492: Discovery, Invasion, Encounter* (1991), critically examines contemporary sources and interpretations. William D. Phillips and Carla Rhan Phillips, *The Worlds of Christopher Columbus* (1992), looks at the subject in terms of modern concerns. Peggy K. Liss, *Isabel the Queen: Life and Times* (1992), affords a sympathetic account. James Lockhart's *Men of Cajamarca: A Social and Biographical Study of the First Conquerors of Peru* (1972) contains biographies of Pizarro's men. A firsthand account of Magellan's expedition is *Antonio Pigafetta, Magellan's Voyage: A Narrative Account of the First Circumnavigation,* available in a two-volume edition (1969) that includes a facsimile reprint of the manuscript.

J. H. Elliott, *The Old World and the New, 1492–1650* (1970), describes the transatlantic encounters of Europe and the Americas. Alfred W. Crosby, *The Columbian Voyages, the Columbian Exchange, and Their Historians* (1987), available as an AHA booklet, surveys the first encounters and their long-term consequences. Mark A. Burkholder and Lyman L. Johnson, *Colonial Latin America,* 2d ed. (1994), give a balanced account of the Spanish conquest.

John Thornton, *Africa and Africans in the Making of the Atlantic World, 1400–1800,* 2d ed. (1998), examines encounters with Europeans, Africa in the Atlantic economy, and African impact in the New World. *The Broken Spears: The Aztec Account of the Conquest of Mexico,* edited by Miguel Leon-Portilla (1962), presents Amerindian chronicles, as does Nathan Wachtel, *The Vision of the Vanquished: The Spanish Conquest of Peru Through Indian Eyes* (1977). Anthony Reid, *Southeast Asia in the Age of Commerce, 1450–1680,* 2 vols. (1988, 1993), deals with that region.

■ Notes

1. Ma Huan, *Ying-yai Sheng-lan: "The Overall Survey of the Ocean's Shores,"* ed. Feng Ch'eng-Chün, trans. J. V. G. Mills (Cambridge, England: Cambridge University Press, 1970), 180.
2. Alvise da Cadamosto in *The Voyages of Cadamosto and Other Documents,* ed. and trans. G. R. Crone (London: Hakluyt Society, 1937), 2.

PART FIVE

THE GLOBE ENCOMPASSED, 1500–1800

European voyages of exploration greatly expanded global commercial, cultural, and biological exchanges between 1500 and 1750. Europeans built new commercial empires that grew stronger with each passing century. The Portuguese had begun the mastery of the seas by opening trade with sub-Saharan Africa and seizing control of maritime trading networks in the Indian Ocean. Then European colonization in the Americas stimulated the growth of a new Atlantic economy. From its colonial base in Mexico, Spain also pioneered new trade routes across the Pacific to the Philippines and China. In time, the Dutch, French, and English expanded these profitable maritime trading networks.

Commerce and colonization led to new interregional demographic and cultural exchanges. The introduction of unfamiliar diseases caused severe population losses in the Americas. To meet the resulting acute labor shortage, Europeans introduced enslaved Africans in ever-growing numbers. Europeans and Africans brought new languages, religious practices, music, and forms of personal adornment to the New World. Some Europeans who spent time overseas adopted new ways and developed new tastes that they later brought back with them when they returned to Europe.

In Asia and Africa, most important changes continued to come from internal causes rather than European expansion. The Islamic world saw the growth of regional empires in the Middle East, South Asia, and West Africa and continued its expansion into sub-Saharan Africa, southeastern Europe, and southern Asia. Secure from external penetration, China experienced military expansion and population growth, and the expansion of educational institutions reinforced traditional values among China's upper classes. In Japan, a strong new national government promoted economic development and stemmed foreign influence, and the development of an indigenous merchant class widened the gap between popular and elite cultures.

Some of the farthest-reaching cultural changes in this period occurred in Europe. Reformers challenged established religious and political institutions, and new scientific discoveries and humanist concerns raised questions about traditional Western values and beliefs.

Important ecological changes occurred in areas of rising population and economic activity. The spread of new plants and animals around the world enhanced food supplies and altered landscapes. Forests were cut down to meet the increasing need for farmland, lumber, and fuel. But the most significant environmental changes resulted from the growing mastery of the winds and currents that propelled European ships across the world's oceans. Europeans' leadership in navigational technology went hand in hand with their emerging dominance in military technology. Lacking an expanding economic base, the great Islamic empires and China fell behind the smaller European nations in military strength. After 1750, the consequences of this widening technological and economic gap were to become momentous.

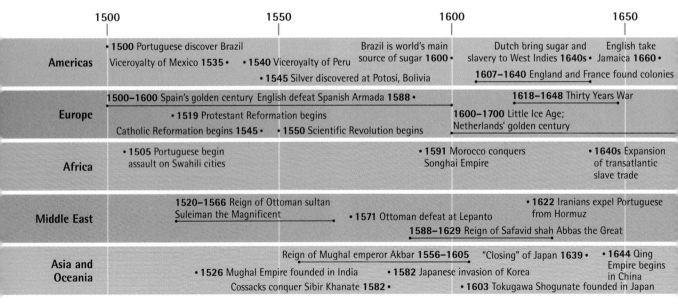

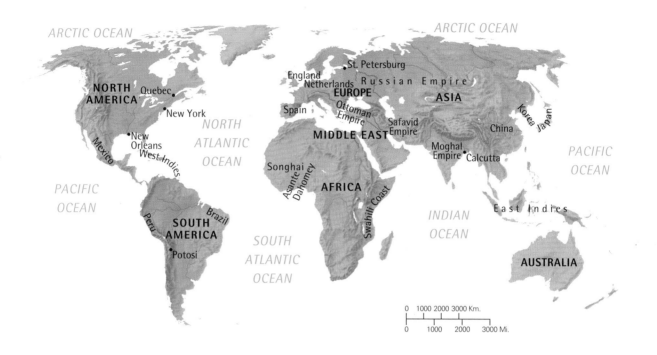

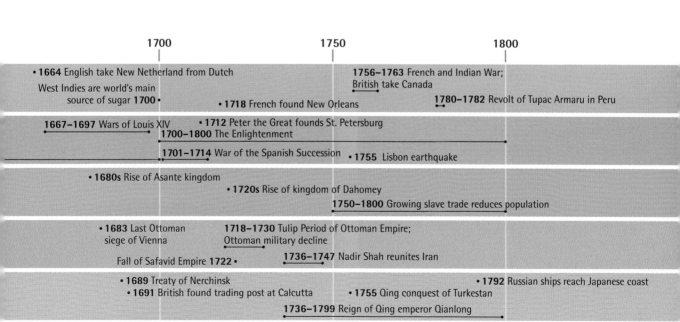

1700	1750	1800

• **1664** English take New Netherland from Dutch

West Indies are world's main source of sugar **1700** •

1756–1763 French and Indian War; British take Canada

• **1718** French found New Orleans

1780–1782 Revolt of Tupac Armaru in Peru

1667–1697 Wars of Louis XIV   • **1712** Peter the Great founds St. Petersburg

1700–1800 The Enlightenment

1701–1714 War of the Spanish Succession   • **1755** Lisbon earthquake

• **1680s** Rise of Asante kingdom

• **1720s** Rise of kingdom of Dahomey

1750–1800 Growing slave trade reduces population

• **1683** Last Ottoman siege of Vienna

1718–1730 Tulip Period of Ottoman Empire; Ottoman military decline

Fall of Safavid Empire **1722** •   **1736–1747** Nadir Shah reunites Iran

• **1689** Treaty of Nerchinsk

• **1691** British found trading post at Calcutta

• **1792** Russian ships reach Japanese coast

• **1755** Qing conquest of Turkestan

1736–1799 Reign of Qing emperor Qianlong

16

THE TRANSFORMATION OF EUROPE,

1500–1750

Religious and Political Innovations • Building State Power •
Urban Society and Commercial Technology • Rural Society and
the Environment • The Realm of Ideas
ENVIRONMENT AND TECHNOLOGY: Mapping the World

n the winter of 1697–1698, Tsar° Peter I, the young ruler of Russia, traveled in disguise through the Netherlands and England, eager to discover how western European societies were becoming so powerful and wealthy. A practical man, Peter paid special attention to ships and weapons. With great insight, he perceived that western European success owed as much to trade and toleration as to technology. Trade generated the money to spend on weapons, while toleration attracted talented persons fleeing persecution.

Upon his return to Russia, Peter resolved to "open a window onto Europe," to reform features of his vast empire that he believed were backward. He ended the servile status of women and personally trimmed his noblemen's long beards to conform to Western styles. Peter also put the skilled technical advisers he brought back with him to work on modernizing Russia's industry and military forces. He then turned to redesigning Russia's government on a German model and copied French rituals of absolute royal power.

As Peter's actions imply, by the end of the seventeenth century, western European achievements in state administration, warfare, business, and ideas were setting standards that others wished to imitate. Along with maritime expansion (examined in Chapter 15), these internal transformations promoted Western global ascendancy. Yet such achievements did not come smoothly. Warfare, poverty, persecution, and environmental degradation were also widespread in Europe between 1500 and 1750.

As you read this chapter, ask yourself the following questions:

tsar (zahr)

- Was Tsar Peter right in thinking that military, economic, and political changes were moving western Europe ahead of other parts of the world?

- What were the immediate and long-term consequences of those changes and others in European religious and scientific ideas?

- How did the many conflicts and rapid changes of this period affect ordinary men and women in Europe?

RELIGIOUS AND POLITICAL INNOVATIONS

Two bitter struggles in the early sixteenth century marked the end of Europe's medieval era and the beginning of the early modern period. One was the Reformation, a movement that introduced many religious reforms but shattered the ideal of Latin Christian unity. The other was an unsuccessful attempt to unite Christian Europe politically in order to block the inroads of the Muslim armies of the Ottoman Empire. Instead of achieving unity, early modern Europe was plagued by division and persistent warfare, yet such conflict promoted innovations that propelled western Europe forward.

Martin Luther   This detail of a painting by Lucas Cranach (1547) shows the Reformer preaching in his hometown church at Wittenberg.   (Church of St. Marien, Wittenberg, Germany/The Bridgeman Art Library, New York and London)

Religious Reformation

In 1500, the **papacy,** the central government of Latin Christianity, was simultaneously gaining stature and suffering from corruption and dissent. Economic prosperity produced larger donations and tax receipts, allowing popes to fund ambitious construction projects in Rome, their capital city. During the sixteenth century, Rome's new churches and other buildings showcased the artistic **Renaissance** then under way. However, the church's wealth and power also attracted some ambitious men whose personal lives became the source of scandal.

The personal life of Pope Leo X (r. 1513–1521) was free from scandal, but he was more a man of action than a spiritual leader. One technique that he used to raise funds for the church's building projects was to authorize an **indulgence**—a forgiveness of the punishment due for past sins, granted as a reward for a pious act such as making a pilgrimage, saying a particular prayer, or making a donation to a religious cause. In one German state, a young professor of sacred scripture, a monk named Martin Luther (1483–1546) was very upset by the indulgence preachers, who he thought emphasized the act of giving money more than the faith behind the act.

This theological dispute quickly escalated into a test of wills. When the papacy condemned Luther in 1519, the German monk burned the papal bull (document) of condemnation, rejected Pope Leo's authority, and began the movement known as the **Protestant Reformation.** Luther insisted that the only way to salvation was through faith in Jesus Christ, not "good works." He declared that Christian belief must be based on the word of God in the Bible and on Christian tradition, not on the authority of the pope. Eventually his conclusions led him to abandon his monastic vows and marry a former nun.

Inspired by Luther, others raised their voices to denounce the ostentation and corruption of church leaders. John Calvin (1509–1564), a Frenchman, became a highly influential Protestant leader. Calvin's teaching differed from that of Roman Catholics and Lutherans in two respects. First, while agreeing with Luther's emphasis on faith over works, Calvin denied that even human faith could merit salvation. Salvation, said Calvin, was God's free gift to those God "predestined" for it. Second, Calvin went further than Luther in curtailing the power of ordained clergymen and simplifying religious rituals.

The Reformers appealed to religious sentiments, but political and social agendas also inspired many who joined them. Lutheranism appealed to many Germans for nationalistic reasons. Peasants and urban laborers sometimes defied their masters by adopting a different faith. Neither tradition had a special attraction for women, since both Protestants and Roman Catholics believed in male dominance in the church and the family. Most Protestants, however, rejected the medieval tradition of celibate priests and nuns and advocated Christian marriage for all adults.

Shaken by the intensity of the Protestant Reformers' appeal, the Catholic Church undertook its own reforms. The Council of Trent issued decrees in 1563 reforming the education, discipline, and practices of the Roman Catholic clergy, reaffirmed the supremacy of the pope, and clarified Catholic beliefs (including those concerning indulgences) in light of Protestant challenges. Also important to this **Catholic Reformation** were the activities of a new religious order, the Society of Jesus. Well-educated Jesuits helped stem the Protestant tide and win back some adherents by their teaching and preaching (see Map 16.1).

Given the complexity of the issues and the intensity of the emotions that the Protestant Reforma-

tion stirred, it is not surprising that violence often flared up. Both sides persecuted and sometimes executed those of differing views. Bitter wars of religion, fought over a mixture of religious and secular issues, continued in parts of western Europe until 1648.

The Failure of Empire

Meanwhile, another great medieval institution, the **Holy Roman Empire,** was also in trouble (see Map 16.2). The threat that the Ottoman Turks posed to Europe stirred interest in a pan-European coalition to stop Muslim advances. A Latin Christian coalition led by Holy Roman Emperor Charles V eventually halted the Ottomans at the gates of Vienna in 1529, but Charles failed in his efforts to forge his several realms into Europe's strongest state. In the imperial Diet (assembly) many German princes, swayed partly by Luther's appeals to German nationalism, opposed Charles, a French-speaking emperor who defended the papacy. Some Lutheran princes enriched themselves by seizing the church's lands within their states in the name of reform.

After decades of bitter squabbles, Charles V gave up his efforts at unification. By the Peace of Augsburg (1555), he recognized the princes' right to choose whether Catholicism or Lutheranism would prevail in their particular states, and he allowed them to keep church lands they had seized before 1552.

Thus, two institutions that had symbolized Western unity during the Middle Ages, the papacy and the Holy Roman Empire, were seriously weakened by the mid-sixteenth century. Both continued to exist, but national kingdoms assumed much of the religious and political leadership in western Europe.

Building State Power

Talented rulers and their able ministers guided the rise of these European kingdoms. They worked to enhance royal authority by limiting the

CHRONOLOGY

	Politics and Culture	Environment and Technology	Warfare
1500	**1500s** Spain's golden century **1519** Protestant Reformation begins **1540s** Scientific Revolution begins **1545** Catholic Reformation begins		
		Mid-1500s Improved windmills and increasing land drainage in Holland	**1526–1571** Ottoman wars **1546–1555** German Wars of Religion **1562–1598** French Wars of Religion **1566–1648** Netherlands Revolt
	Late 1500s Witchhunts increase	**1590s** Little Ice Age begins	
1600	**1600s** Holland's golden century	**1600s** Depletion of forests growing **1609** Galileo's astronomical telescope	**1618–1648** Thirty Years War **1642–1648** English Civil War **1652–1678** Anglo-Dutch Wars **1667–1697** Wars of Louis XIV **1683–1697** Ottoman wars
		1682 Canal du Midi completed	
1700	**1700s** The Enlightenment begins		**1700–1721** Great Northern War **1701–1714** War of the Spanish Succession
		1755 Lisbon earthquake	

autonomy of the church and the nobility, while building the state's armed forces and economy.

Royal Centralization, 1500–1750

When the system of monarchical succession worked best, it brought to the throne a creative, energetic young person who gained experience and won loyalty over many decades. By good fortune, the leading states produced many such talented, hard-working, and long-lived rulers. Spain had only six rulers in the two centuries from 1556 to 1759, and France had but five between 1574 and 1774 (see Table 16.1). The long reigns of the Tudor monarchs Henry VIII and his Protestant daughter, Elizabeth I, helped stabilize sixteenth-century England, but their Stuart successors were twice overthrown by revolution during the next century.

Successful monarchs depended heavily on their chief advisers, who also eased the transition between rulers. Before 1650, advisers tended to be members of the clergy, but thereafter kings began to draw on the talents of successful businessmen. The prevalence of clerical advisers does not mean

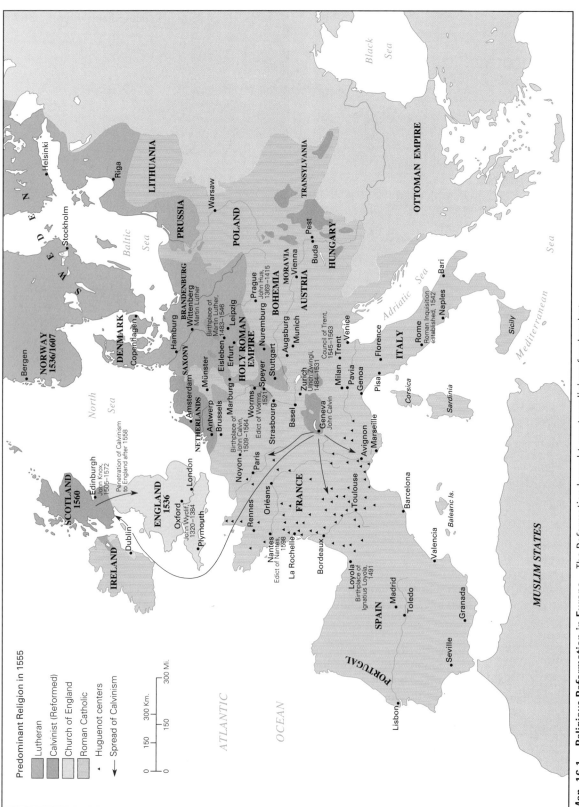

Map. 16.1 Religious Reformation in Europe The Reformation brought greater religious freedom but also led to religious conflict and persecution. In many places, the Reformation accelerated the trend toward state control of religion and added religious differences to the motives for wars among Europeans.

Predominant Religion in 1555

- Lutheran
- Calvinist (Reformed)
- Church of England
- Roman Catholic
- ▲ Huguenot centers
- → Spread of Calvinism

0   150   300 Km.
0   150   300 Mi.

NORWAY 1536/1607
Bergen
SWEDEN
Helsinki
Riga
LITHUANIA
Stockholm
Baltic Sea
PRUSSIA
Warsaw
POLAND
DENMARK
Copenhagen
Hamburg
BRANDENBURG
Wittenberg
Birthplace of Martin Luther, Martin Luther
Eisleben, 1483–1546
Leipzig
SAXONY
Münster
Erfurt
Prague
John Hus, 1369–1415
BOHEMIA
MORAVIA
Vienna
Buda
Pest
HUNGARY
TRANSLYVANIA
AUSTRIA
Nuremberg
HOLY ROMAN EMPIRE
Augsburg
Munich
Stuttgart
Speyer
Edict of Worms, 1521
Worms
Strasbourg
Zurich
Ulrich Zwingli, 1484–1531
Council of Trent, 1545–1563
Trent
Venice
Milan
Pavia
Genoa
ITALY
Florence
Pisa
Rome
Roman Inquisition established, 1542
Naples
Bari
NETHERLANDS
Amsterdam
Antwerp
Brussels
Birthplace of John Calvin, 1509–1564
Noyon
Paris
Geneva
John Calvin
Basel
Avignon
Marseille
FRANCE
Orléans
Rennes
Bordeaux
La Rochelle
Nantes
Edict of Nantes, 1598
Toulouse
Barcelona
Valencia
Balearic Is.
SPAIN
Madrid
Toledo
Loyola
Birthplace of Ignatius Loyola, 1491
Seville
Granada
PORTUGAL
Lisbon
ENGLAND 1536
London
Oxford
John Wyclif, 1320–1384
Plymouth
SCOTLAND 1560
Edinburgh
John Knox, 1505–1572
Penetration of Calvinism to England after 1558
IRELAND
Dublin
NORTH Sea
ATLANTIC OCEAN
Corsica
Sardinia
Sicily
Mediterranean Sea
Adriatic Sea
Black Sea
OTTOMAN EMPIRE
MUSLIM STATES

Map. 16.2   The European Empire of Charles V   Charles was Europe's most powerful ruler from 1519 to 1556, but he failed to unify the Christian West. In addition to being the elected head of the Holy Roman Empire, he was the hereditary ruler of the Spanish realms of Castile and Aragon and the possessions of the Austrian Habsburgs in Central Europe. The map does not show his extensive holdings in the Americas and Asia.

Table 16.1   **Rulers in Early Modern Western Europe**

Spain	France	England/Great Britain
Habsburg Dynasty	**Valois Dynasty**	**Tudor Dynasty**
Charles I (1516–1556) (Holy Roman-Emperor Charles V)	Francis I (1515–1547)	Henry VIII (1509–1547)
Philip II (1556–1598)	Henry II (1547–1559)	Edward VI (1547–1553)
	Francis II (1559–1560)	Mary I (1553–1558)
	Charles IX (1560–1574)	Elizabeth I (1558–1603)
	Henry III (1574–1589)	
	Bourbon Dynasty	**Stuart Dynasty**
Philip III (1598–1621)	Henry IV (1589–1610)[a]	James I (1603–1625)
Philip IV (1621–1665)	Louis XIII (1610–1643)	Charles I (1625–1649)[a, b]
Charles II (1665–1700)	Louis XIV (1643–1715)	(Puritan Republic, 1649–1660)
		Charles II (1660–1685)
		James II (1685–1688)[b]
		William III (1689–1702)
		and Mary II (1689–1694)
Bourbon Dynasty		Anne (1702–1714)
Philip V (1700–1746)		
		Hanoverian Dynasty
	Louis XV (1715–1774)	George I (1714–1727)
Ferdinand VI (1746–1759)		George II (1727–1760)

[a]Died a violent death.   [b]Was overthrown.

the clergy controlled the throne; rather, the opposite was the case. Well before the Reformation, rulers in Spain, Portugal, and France had gained control over church appointments and had used church revenues to enhance royal power.

This co-opting of the church by the state made religious uniformity a hot political issue. Following the pattern used by his predecessors to suppress Jewish and Muslim practices, King Philip II of Spain used an ecclesiastical court, the Spanish Inquisition, to bring into line those who resisted his authority. In France, Prince Henry of Navarre switched his faith from Calvinist to Catholic after gaining the military advantage in the French Wars of Religion (1562–1598), so that, as King Henry IV (the first of the Bourbon kings), he would share the faith of the majority of his subjects.

Elsewhere, the Protestant Reformation made it easier for monarchs to increase their control of the church. In England, the church lost its remaining autonomy after the pope turned down King Henry VIII's petition for an annulment of his marriage to Katharine of Aragon, and Henry ordered the English archbishop of Canterbury to annul the marriage. The breach with Rome was sealed in 1534 when Parliament made the English monarch head of the Church of England. Henry used his authority to disband monasteries and convents, giving some of their lands to his powerful allies and selling others to pay for his new navy. In other respects, religion changed little under Henry and his successors, despite growing pressures from English Calvinists known as Puritans to "purify" the Anglican church of Catholic practices and beliefs.

In addition to gaining control of the church, western European kings and queens enhanced their powers by promoting national institutions. In Spain, the Castilian dialect gained currency. In France, people increasingly imitated the speech of Paris. By 1750, uniform laws and administration were the pattern. Rulers also promoted common national languages. The Protestant emphasis on reading the Bible in vernacular languages (instead of in Latin) hastened the standardization of German and English.

Absolutism and Constitutionalism

The absence of any constitutional check on a ruler's power is called **absolutism.** Many seventeenth- and eighteenth-century European monarchs admired absolutism, but needed the approval of their representative assemblies to make war or levy new taxes.

In France, the strong Bourbon kings of the seventeenth and eighteenth centuries governed without summoning the Estates General that represented the clergy, the nobility, and the towns. By promoting economic development, collecting taxes more efficiently, and selling high offices, Louis XIV's astute ministers were able to bypass the Estates General's power to authorize new taxes, while permitting the king to wage a series of expensive wars and build a gigantic new palace at Versailles°. The palace was a sort of theme park of royal absolutism, where French nobles were diverted from the real politics of the kingdom through elaborate banquets and ceremonies centered on the king.

In England, King Charles I ruled for eleven years without summoning Parliament, his kingdom's representative body, by coercing "loans" from wealthy subjects and twisting tax laws to new uses. Then in 1640, a rebellion in Scotland forced him to summon the members of Parliament to approve new taxes to pay for an army. Before authorizing new taxes, Parliament insisted on strict guarantees that the king would never again ignore its traditional rights. King Charles refused to agree and in 1642 plunged the kingdom into civil war. When Charles refused to compromise even after being defeated on the battlefield, Parliament ordered him executed in 1649 and replaced the monarchy with a Puritan Republic under the Puritan general Oliver Cromwell.

The monarchy was restored in 1660, but when King James II refused to respect Parliament's rights, Parliament forced him into exile in the bloodless Glorious Revolution of 1688. The Bill of Rights of 1689 specified that Parliament had to be called "frequently" and had to consent to changes in laws and to the raising of an army in peacetime. By these steps, Parliament checked royal power and established **constitutionalism,** a system of government that subjects the ruler's power to limits specified by law and custom.

War and Diplomacy

Early modern European rulers, whether absolutist or constitutional, developed some of the world's most powerful armed forces. Warfare was almost constant (see the Chronology at the beginning of the chapter). Their struggles for dominance first produced a dramatic change in the size, skill, and weapons of armed forces and then an advance in diplomacy.

The number of men in arms increased steadily throughout the early modern period. French forces, for example, grew to 400,000 by the early eighteenth century. Only England did not maintain a standing army in peacetime because the Royal Navy could protect the island nation from invasion.

Large armies required better command structures. New signaling techniques improved control of battlefield maneuvers, and frequent marching drills instilled better discipline in the troops. To defend against these forces, cities built new fortifications able to withstand cannon bombardments. Battles between evenly matched armies often ended in stalemates, as in the Thirty Years War (1618–1648). Victory in war increasingly depended on naval superiority.

The rapid changes in naval warfare are evident in two fleets used by Philip II of Spain. In 1571, a combined Spanish and Italian fleet of 200 ships met an even larger Ottoman force off Lepanto on the Greek coast. Both fleets consisted principally of oar-powered galleys, which had only light armaments. To attack, one galley rammed another so that armed men could climb aboard for hand-to-hand combat. Four hours after the battle began, the remains of 200 Ottoman galleys littered the

---

Versailles (vuhr-SIGH)

Versailles, 1722   This painting by P.-D. Martin shows the east expanse of buildings and courtyards that make up the palace complex built by King Louis XIV.   (Giraudon/Art Resource, NY)

sea's surface, and the waters were red with the blood of 30,000 slain men.

A very different Spanish fleet, the Catholic Armada, sailed from Lisbon in 1588 hoping to repeat the Lepanto success over the Protestant enemies of the north. The complex mission of these 130 heavily armed ships was to replace the Protestant ruler of England, Queen Elizabeth, with a Roman Catholic, then put down the rebellion in the Netherlands, and finally intervene on the Catholic side in the French Wars of Religion. But history did not repeat itself. The English could fire more rapidly because of their new cannon carriages, and their smaller, quicker ships successfully evaded the ram-and-board technique, which the Spanish retained from their Mediterranean victory. Moreover, a chance storm,

celebrated by the English as a providential "Protestant wind," scattered and sank many Spanish ships that had survived the sea battles, thus dooming Philip's other plans for the armada.

The armada's defeat signaled the end of Spain's military dominance in Europe. By the early 1600s, France had recovered from its Wars of Religion to become Europe's most powerful state. With twice the population of Spain at their command, France's forceful kings of the Bourbon dynasty deployed Europe's largest armies to squelch domestic unrest, extend France's boundaries, and intervene in the affairs of neighboring states.

After emerging from its own civil conflicts in 1689, England became France's major rival. By then, England ruled a North American empire as well as Ireland, and in 1707 England merged with Scotland to become Great Britain. England's rise as a sea power had begun in the time of King Henry VIII, who spent heavily on ships and promoted a domestic iron-smelting industry to supply cannon. Queen Elizabeth's victorious fleet of 1588 was considerably improved by the copying of innovative ship designs from the Dutch in the second half of the seventeenth century. The Royal Navy grew in numbers, surpassing the French fleet by the early eighteenth century.

In a series of eighteenth-century wars, beginning with the War of the Spanish Succession (1701–1714), the combination of Britain's naval strength and the land armies of its Austrian and Prussian allies was able to block French expansionist efforts and prevent the Bourbons from uniting the thrones of France and Spain. This defeat of the French monarchy's empire-building efforts illustrated the principle of **balance of power** in international relations: the European powers formed temporary alliances to prevent any one state from becoming too powerful.

Nearly constant warfare had the unintended effect of enhancing diplomacy. During the next two centuries, though adhering to four different branches of Christianity, the great powers of Europe—Catholic France, Anglican Britain, Catholic Austria, Lutheran Prussia, and Orthodox Russia—maintained an effective balance of power in Europe by shifting their alliances for geopolitical rather than religious reasons.

Politics and the Economy

To pay for the heavy costs of their wars, European rulers had to increase their revenues. Dutch governments pioneered mutually beneficial alliances with rising commercial interests. Rulers in France and Britain were quick to follow. Both parties understood that trade thrived where government taxation and regulation were not excessive, where courts enforced contracts and collected debts, and where military power stood ready to protect overseas expansion by force when necessary.

Spain illustrates how the failure to promote economic development led sixteenth-century Europe's mightiest state into decline. For a time, vast imports of silver and gold bullion from the American colonies filled Spain's treasury and financed ambitious wars against the Ottomans, northern European Protestants, and rebellious Dutch subjects. But the treasury often ran dry, and loans raised on the promise of future treasure fleets could not always be paid. As a Spanish saying put it, American silver was like rain on the roof—it poured down and washed away. The bullion flowed out to pay creditors, purchase manufactured goods, and even buy food in the seventeenth century. Spanish rulers had not only failed to develop the economy; their intolerant religious policies had driven out of the kingdom commercially talented Jews and Protestants and exiled tens of thousands of skilled farmers and artisans because of their Muslim ancestry.

The rise of the Netherlands as an economic power teaches the opposite lesson. The Spanish crown had acquired these resource-poor but commercially successful provinces as part of Charles V's inheritance. But when King Philip II imposed Spain's ruinously heavy sales tax and enforced Catholic orthodoxy, he drove the Dutch to revolt. High taxes and intolerance would have discouraged business and driven away the Calvinists, Jews, and others who were essential to Dutch prosperity. The Dutch fought with skill and ingenuity, raising and training an army and a navy that were among the most effective in Europe. By 1609, Spain was forced to agree to a truce that recognized the autonomy of the northern part of the Netherlands. In 1648, the independence of these seven United Provinces of the Free Netherlands (to give their full name) became final.

Rather than being ruined by the long war, the United Netherlands emerged in the seventeenth century as the dominant commercial power in Europe and the world's greatest trading nation. During this golden century, the wealth of the Netherlands multiplied. Holland's many towns and cities were filled with skilled craftsmen. Factories and workshops turned out goods of exceptional quality at a moderate price and on a vast scale. The textile industry concentrated on the highly profitable finishing and printing of cloth, transforming the cloth spun and woven by low-paid workers into fine textiles. Other factories refined West Indian sugar, brewed beer from Baltic grain, cut Virginia

Port of Amsterdam   Ships, barges and boats of all types are visible in this busy seventeenth-century scene. The large building in the center is the Admiralty House, which housed the headquarters of the Dutch East India Company.   (Mansell Collection/Time Inc.)

tobacco, and made imitations of Chinese ceramics. Printers published books in many languages, free from the censorship imposed by political and religious authorities in neighboring countries. For a small province barely above sea level, lacking timber and other natural resources, this was a remarkable achievement.

Amsterdam, Holland's major city, was seventeenth-century Europe's financial center and major port. From there, Dutch ships dominated the sea trade of Europe, carrying over 80 percent of the trade to Spain from northern Europe, even while Spain and the Netherlands were at war. The Dutch dominance of Atlantic and Indian Ocean trade was such that by one estimate, they conducted more than half of all the oceangoing commercial shipping in the world (see Chapters 17 and 18).

URBAN SOCIETY AND COMMERCIAL TECHNOLOGY

Just as palaces were early modern Europe's centers of political power, cities were its economic power centers. The urban growth under way since the eleventh century was accelerating and spreading. In 1500, Paris was the only northern European city with over 100,000 inhabitants. By 1700, both Paris and London had populations over 500,000, Amsterdam had burgeoned from a fishing village to a metropolis of some 200,000, and twenty other European cities contained over 60,000 people apiece.

Urban Social Classes

The cities' growth depended primarily on the prosperous merchants who managed the great expansion of regional and overseas commerce, but wealth was unevenly distributed and social tension often ran high. The French called the well-off who dominated the cities **bourgeoisie°** (town dwellers).

Some bourgeoisie grew rich supplying the growing urban populations with grain, wine, and beer. Others imported exotic luxuries from the far corners of the earth: Caribbean and Brazilian sugar and rum, Mexican chocolate, Virginian tobacco, North American furs, East Indian cotton textiles and spices, and Chinese tea. The rise of the bourgeoisie was aided by mutually beneficial alliances with monarchs who saw economic growth as the best means of increasing state revenues. Unlike the old nobility, who shunned productive labor, members of the bourgeoisie devoted long hours to their businesses and poured their profits into new business ventures or other investments rather than spending them. Even so, they still had enough money to live comfortably in large houses with many servants.

Europe's cities were also home to craftworkers and many poor people. From 10 to 20 percent of the permanent city dwellers were so poor they were exempt from taxation. Cities also contained large numbers of temporary immigrants from impoverished rural areas, itinerant peddlers, beggars, and gangs of criminals.

In contrast to the arranged marriages common in much of the rest of the world, young men and women in early modern Europe generally chose their own spouses and after marriage set up their own households instead of living with their parents. The age of marriage was also later in Europe than elsewhere, so that young people could complete their education or apprenticeship to learn a trade and save enough money to live on their own. The late age of marriage in early modern Europe held down the birthrate and thus limited family size. Even so, about one-tenth of the births in a city were to unmarried women, often servants, who generally left their infants on the doorsteps of churches, convents, or rich families. Delayed marriage also had links to public brothels, where men satisfied their lust in cheap and impersonal encounters with unfortunate young women, often newly arrived from impoverished rural villages.

Commercial Techniques and Technology

The expansion of trade in early modern Europe prompted the development of new techniques to manage far-flung business enterprises and invest the profits they produced. As elsewhere in the world, most businesses ran on family funds or borrowed money. But a key change in Europe was the rise of large financial institutions to serve the interests of big business and big government. In the seventeenth century, private Dutch banks developed such a reputation for security that wealthy individuals and governments from all over western Europe entrusted them with their money. The banks invested these funds in real estate, local industries, loans to governments, and overseas trade.

Another commercial innovation was the **joint-stock company,** which sold shares to individuals. Often backed by a government charter, such companies offered a way to raise large sums for overseas enterprises while spreading the risks (and profits) among many investors (the operation of chartered joint-stock companies in the overseas trade is examined in Chapter 17). Investors could buy and sell shares in specialized financial markets called **stock exchanges.** The greatest stock market in the seventeenth and eighteenth centuries was the Amsterdam Exchange, founded in 1530.

Changes in technology also facilitated economic growth. Improvements in water transport expanded Europe's superb natural network of seas and navigable rivers for moving bulk items such as grain, wine, and timber. Governments financed the constructions of shipping canals with elaborate systems of locks to cross hills. The Canal du Midi in France, built between 1661 and 1682, linked the Atlantic and the Mediterranean.

The expansion of maritime trade led to new designs for merchant ships. Dutch ports built vast

---

bourgeoisie (boor-zwah-ZEE)

fleets of large-capacity cargo ships, including the heavily armed "East Indiaman" that helped the Dutch establish their supremacy in the Indian Ocean. The Dutch also excelled at mapmaking (see Environment and Technology: Mapping the World).

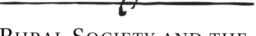

RURAL SOCIETY AND THE ENVIRONMENT

For all its new political, military, and commercial strengths, early modern Europe rested on a fragile agrarian base. Bad years brought famine; good ones provided only small surpluses. The circumstances of most rural Europeans probably worsened between 1500 and 1750.

The Struggle for Food and Fuel

Besides the devastation of warfare and other human-engineered ca-lamities, rural Europeans also felt the adverse effects of a century of relatively cool climate. During this **Little Ice Age,** average temperatures fell only a few degrees, but the effects were startling. Rivers and canals important to commerce froze solid from bank to bank. Crops ripened more slowly during cooler summers and were often damaged by frosts that came unexpect-edly late in spring or early in fall. When one cold year followed another, deaths due to malnutrition and cold increased sharply. The cold spell of 1694–1695 carried off between a quarter and a third of the population of Finland.

By 1700, new crops from the Americas were helping the rural poor avoid starvation. At first eaten only in desperate times, potatoes and maize (corn) became staples for the rural poor in the eighteenth century because they yielded more abundant food from small garden plots. Potatoes sustained life in northeastern and Central Europe and in Ireland. Peasants along the Mediterranean who could not af-ford to eat the wheat they raised for urban markets grew maize for their own consumption.

Another threat to rural life came from **defor-estation,** which emerged as a serious issue in the

seventeenth and eighteenth centuries. Early mod-ern Europeans cut down their great hardwood forests to provide timbers for ships; lumber for buildings, wagons, and barrels; fuel for heating and cooking; and charcoal for smelting ores and other industrial processes. Dependent on woodlands for abundant supplies of wild nuts and berries, free firewood and building materials, and wild game, the rural poor felt the depletion of the forests most strongly. Some flocked to the cities in hopes of finding better jobs, but most were disappointed.

Peasantry and Gentry

The bright side of rural life in western Europe was the remarkable per-sonal freedom of the peasantry in comparison with people of similar status in many other parts of the world. Serfdom, which bound men and women to land owned by a local lord, declined sharply after the great plague of the mid-fourteenth century. Most remaining serfs in western Europe gained their freedom by 1600. By that date, slavery had also come to an end.

Legal freedom in western Europe did little to make the peasants' lives safe and secure, however. Rising debts caused many to lose their land to large landowners who loaned them money. The desire of many successful members of the bourgeoisie to buy country estates and thus join the ranks of the gentry accelerated the transformation of rural ownership. These new owners of rural estates affected the lifestyle of the old aristocracy and sometimes re-ceived the aristocracy's exemption from taxation, but they did not have titles of nobility. The exemp-tion of the wealthy from taxation was a complaint frequently mentioned during the many rebellions that rural misery provoked in early modern Europe.

THE REALM OF IDEAS

New ideas and old beliefs pulled early modern Europeans in several different directions, even after the Reformation controversies subsided. The hold of biblical and traditional folk beliefs on the

Mapping the World

In 1602, the Jesuit missionary Matteo Ricci in China printed an elaborate map of the world. Working from maps produced in Europe and incorporating the latest knowledge gathered by European maritime explorers, Ricci introduced two changes to make the map more appealing to his Chinese hosts. He labeled it in Chinese characters, and he split his map down the middle of the Atlantic so that China lay in the center. This version pleased Chinese elites, who considered China the "Middle Kingdom" surrounded by lesser states. A copy of Ricci's map in six large panels adorned the emperor's Beijing palace.

The stunningly beautiful maps and globes of sixteenth-century Europe were the most complete, detailed, and useful representations of the earth that any society had ever produced. The best mapmaker of the century was Gerhard Kremer, who is remembered as Mercator (the merchant) because his maps were so useful to European ocean traders. By incorporating the latest discoveries and scientific measurements, Merca-

tor could depict the outlines of the major continents in painstaking detail, even if their interiors were still largely unknown to outsiders.

To represent the spherical globe on a flat map, Mercator drew the lines of longitude as parallel lines. Because such lines actually meet at the poles, Mercator's projection greatly exaggerated the size of every landmass and body of water distant from the equator. However, Mercator's rendering offered a practical advantage: sailors could plot their course by drawing a straight line between their point of departure and their destination. Because of this useful feature, the Mercator projection of the world remained in common use until quite recently. To some extent, its popularity came from the exaggerated size this projection gave to Europe. Like the Chinese, Europeans liked to think of themselves as at the center of things. Europeans also understood their true geographical position better than people in any other part of the world.

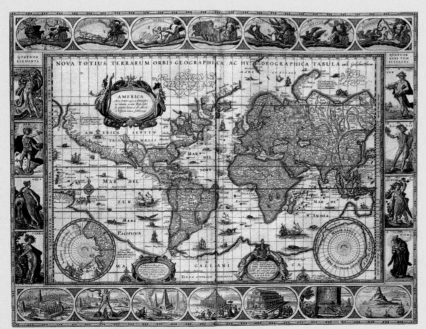

Dutch World Map, 1641
It is easy to see why the Chinese would not have liked to see their empire at the far right edge of this widely printed map. Besides the distortions caused by the Mercator projection, geographical ignorance exaggerates the size of North America and Antarctica. (Courtesy of the Trustees British Museum)

thinking of most people showed itself in widespread new fears about witches and the power of the devil. In education, writings from Greco-Roman antiquity popularized in the Renaissance remained most influential, but a few thinkers broke new scientific ground in deciphering the motion of the planets and constructing mathematical models of the force of gravitation. In time, the new laws of science encouraged some to reevaluate traditional social and political systems, with important implications for the future.

Traditional Thinking

In the minds of most Europeans, pre-Christian ideas of magic and folk spirits mixed with Christian teachings about miracles, saints, and devils. If crops failed or domestic animals died unexpectedly, many people blamed unseen spirits. When an earthquake destroyed much of Lisbon, Portugal's capital city, in November 1755, both educated and uneducated saw the event as a punishment sent by God to punish the city's residents for their sins.

Nowhere was the belief in unseen forces more evident than in the **witch-hunts** that swept across northern Europe in the late sixteenth and seventeenth centuries. It is estimated that secular and church authorities tried over 100,000 people—some three-fourths of them women—for practicing witchcraft. Some were acquitted, some recanted, but over half were executed. The trial records make it clear that both the accusers and the accused believed that evil magic and the power of the devil could cause people and domestic animals to sicken and die or crops to wither in the fields.

Modern historians believe that the fact that many accused of witchcraft were older women, especially widows, may reflect fears that women not directly under the control of fathers or husbands were likely to turn to evil. The Reformation had focused attention on the devil and may have helped revive older fears of witchcraft. Self-confessed "witches" may even have found release from the guilt they felt for wishing evil on their neighbors. No single reason can explain the rise in witchcraft accusations and fears in early modern Europe, but for both the accusers and the accused, there are plausible connections between the witch-hunts and rising social tensions, rural poverty, and environmental strains.

The Scientific Revolution

Among intellectuals, prevailing ideas about the natural world were based on the physics of Aristotle, the ancient Greek philosopher who taught that all matter was reducible to four elements. He held that the earth was composed of two heavy elements, earth and water, while the heavens were made of air and fire, which floated above the ground.

The prevailing conception of the universe was also influenced by the calculations of the ancient Greek mathematician Pythagoras, who proved the validity of the famous theorem that still bears his name: In a right triangle, the square of the hypotenuse is equal to the sum of the squares of the other two sides ($a^2 + b^2 = c^2$). Pythagoreans attributed to mystical properties the ability of simple mathematical equations to describe physical objects. They attached special significance to the simplest (to them perfect) geometrical shapes: the circle (a point rotated around another point) and the sphere (a circle rotated on its axis). They believed that celestial objects were perfect spheres orbiting the earth in perfectly circular orbits.

In the sixteenth century, however, the careful observations and mathematical calculations of some daring and imaginative European investigators began to challenge these prevailing conceptions of the physical world. These pioneers of the **Scientific Revolution** demonstrated that the workings of the universe could be explained by natural causes.

The first was a Polish monk and mathematician named Nicholas Copernicus (1473–1543). Copernicus did not challenge the idea that the sun, moon, and planets were light, perfect spheres, but his placement of the sun, not the earth, at the center of things began a revolution in understanding about the structure of the heavens and the central place of humans in the universe. To escape controversy, Copernicus delayed the publication of his heliocentric (sun-centered) theory until after his death.

Galileo in 1624   This engraving by Ottavio Leone shows the Italian scientist in full vigor at age sixty, before he was hounded by the Roman Inquisition.   (British Museum)

The most brilliant of those who improved on Copernicus's model was the Italian Galileo Galilei° (1564–1642). In 1609, Galileo built a telescope through which he saw that the moon had mountains and valleys, the sun had spots, and other planets had their own moons. In other words, the earth was not alone in being heavy and changeable.

At first, the Copernican universe found more critics than supporters. How, demanded Aristotle's defenders, could the heavy earth move without producing vibrations that would shake the planet apart? Is the Bible wrong, asked the theologians, when it says that, by God's command, "the sun stood still . . . a whole day" to give the ancient Israelites victory in their conquest of Palestine? Galileo's enemies had his ideas condemned by the Roman Inquisition in 1616.

Galileo Galilei (gal-uh-LAY-oh gal-uh-LAY-ee)

Despite official opposition, printed books spread the new scientific ideas among scholars across Europe. In England, members of the Royal Society were enthusiastic missionaries of mechanical science. One of them, Isaac Newton (1642–1727), formulated a set of mathematical laws demonstrating that the heavens and earth share a common physics. It was the force of gravity, not angels, that governed the elliptical orbits of heavenly bodies and caused cannonballs to fall back to earth. As president of the Royal Society from 1703 until his death, Newton used his prestige to promote the new science of physics that bears his name.

The Early Enlightenment

Advances in scientific thought had few practical applications until long after 1750, but they inspired governments and private groups in many countries to reexamine the reasonableness of everything from agricultural methods to laws, religion, and social hierarchies. The belief that human reason could discover the laws that governed social behavior and were just as scientific as the laws that governed physics energized a movement known as the **Enlightenment.** Like the Scientific Revolution, this movement was the work of a few individuals who often faced bitter opposition from the political, intellectual, and religious establishment. Leading Enlightenment thinkers became accustomed to having their books burned or banned, and many spent long periods in exile to escape being imprisoned for their ideas.

Influences besides the Scientific Revolution affected the Enlightenment. The partisan bickering and bloodshed of the Reformation era led some to doubt the superiority of any theological position and recommend toleration of all religions. The killing of suspected witches also shocked many thoughtful people. The leading French thinker Voltaire declared, "No opinion is worth burning your neighbor for."

Accounts of cultures in other parts of the world also led some European thinkers to question assumptions about the superiority of European political institutions, moral standards, and religious beliefs. Reports of Amerindian life, though romanticized, led some to conclude that those whom they had called savages were in many ways nobler than European Christians. Jesuit missionaries contrasted the lack of territorial ambition of the Chinese with the constant warfare in the West and attributed the difference to the fact that China was wisely ruled by educated men.

Another influence on the "enlightened" thinkers of the eighteenth century was the English political philosopher John Locke (1632–1704), who disputed the prevailing idea that government was sacred and kings ruled by divine right. He argued that absolute monarchy was incompatible with civil society and wrote that monarchs, like everyone else, were subject to the law that laid the basis for the compact that brought civil society into existence. If monarchs overstepped the law, Locke argued, citizens had not only the right but the duty to rebel. The consequences of this idea are considered in Chapter 20.

The Enlightenment was more a frame of mind than a coherent movement. Individuals who embraced it drew inspiration from different sources and promoted different agendas. By 1750, its proponents were clearer about what they disliked than about what new institutions should be created. Some "enlightened" thinkers thought society could be made to function with the mechanical orderliness of planets spinning in their orbits. Nearly all were optimistic that at least in the long run, human beliefs and institutions could be improved. This belief in progress would help foster political and social revolutions after 1750.

Despite the enthusiasm the Enlightenment aroused in some circles, Europe in 1750 was neither enlightened nor tolerant. Nevertheless, its political and religious divisions, growing literacy, and the printing press made possible the survival of the new ideas that would profoundly change life in future centuries.

CONCLUSION

Historians use the word *revolution* to describe many different changes that took place in Europe between 1500 and 1750. The inflation of the sixteenth century has been called a price revolution, the expansion of trade a commercial revolution, the reform of state spending a financial revolution, the changes in weapons and warfare a military revolution. We have also encountered a scientific revolution and the religious revolution of the Reformation.

These important changes in early modern European government, economy, society, and thought were parts of a dynamic process that began in the later Middle Ages and led to even bigger industrial and political revolutions before the eighteenth century was over. Yet the years from 1500 to 1750 were not simply—perhaps not even primarily—an age of progress for Europe. The conflicts of royal armies, religious beliefs, and contending ideas exacted a terrible price in death, destruction, and misery. The expanding economy benefited members of the emerging merchant elite and their political allies, but most Europeans became worse off as prices rose faster than wages. New scientific and enlightened ideas ignited new controversies long before they yielded any tangible benefits.

The historical significance of this period of European history is clearest when viewed in a global context. What stands out is the growing power and efficiency of European armies, economies, and governments. From a global perspective, the balance of political and economic power shifted slowly but inexorably in the Europeans' favor from 1500 to 1750. In 1500, the Ottomans threatened Europe. By 1750, as the remaining chapters of Part Five detail, Europeans had brought the world's seas and a growing part of its land and people under their control. No single group of Europeans accomplished this. The Dutch eclipsed the pioneering Portuguese and Spanish; then the English and French bested the Dutch. Competition, too, was a factor in the European success.

Other changes in Europe during this period had no great overseas significance yet. The full effects of the Scientific Revolution and the Enlightenment lay in the period after 1750.

■ Key Terms

papacy	bourgeoisie
Renaissance (Europe)	joint-stock company
indulgence	stock exchanges
Protestant Reformation	Little Ice Age
Catholic Reformation	deforestation
Holy Roman Empire	witch-hunt
absolutism	Scientific Revolution
constitutionalism	Enlightenment
balance of power	

■ Suggested Reading

Overviews of this period include Euan Cameron, *Early Modern Europe* (1999), and H. G. Koenigsberger, *Early Modern Europe: Fifteen Hundred to Seventeen Eighty-Nine* (1987). Global perspectives can be found in Fernand Braudel, *Civilization and Capitalism, 15th–18th Century*, trans. Siân Reynolds, 3 vols. (1979), and Immanuel Wallerstein, *The Modern World-System*, vol. 2, *Mercantilism and the Consolidation of the European World-Economy, 1600–1750* (1980).

Technological and environmental changes are the focus of Geoffrey Parker, *Military Revolution: Military Innovation and the Rise of the West, 1500–1800*, 2d ed. (1996); William H. McNeill, *The Pursuit of Power: Technology, Armed Force, and Society Since A.D. 1000* (1982); Robert Greenhalgh Albion, *Forests and Sea Power: The Timber Problem of the Royal Navy, 1652–1862* (1965); and Jean M. Grove, *The Little Ice Age* (1988).

Steven Stapin, *The Scientific Revolution* (1998), and Hugh Kearney, *Science and Change, 1500–1700* (1971), are accessible introductions. An excellent place to begin examining the complex subject of witchcraft is Brian Levack, *The Witch-Hunt in Early Modern Europe*, 2d ed. (1995).

Good single-country surveys are J. A. Sharpe, *Early Modern England: A Social History*, 2d ed. (1997); Emmanuel Le Roy Ladurie, *The Royal French State, 1460–1610* (1994) and *The Ancien Régime: A History of France, 1610–1774* (1998); Jonathan Israel, *The Dutch Republic: Its Rise, Greatness and Fall, 1477–1806* (1995); and James Casey, *Early Modern Spain: A Social History* (1999).

17

THE AMERICAS, THE ATLANTIC, AND AFRICA, 1530–1770

Spanish America and Brazil • English and French Colonies in North America • Colonial Expansion and Conflict • Plantations in the West Indies • Creating the Atlantic Economy • Africa and the Atlantic • The Columbian Exchange

SOCIETY AND CULTURE: Colonial Wealth and the Exploitation of Indigenous Peoples

ecause of their long isolation from other continents, the peoples of the New World lacked immunity to diseases introduced from the Old World. Smallpox arrived in the Caribbean in 1518, killing most of the native peoples there. In short order, smallpox killed 50 percent or more of the Amerindian population of Mexico and Central America. The disease then spread to North and South America with equally devastating effects. Other diseases added to the toll: measles in the 1530s, followed by diphtheria, typhus, influenza, and perhaps pulmonary plague. Between 1520 and 1521, influenza in combination with other ailments attacked the Cakchiquel of Guatemala. Their chronicle recalls:

> Great was the stench of the dead. After our fathers and grandfathers succumbed, half the people fled to the fields. The dogs and vultures devoured the bodies. . . . So it was that we became orphans, oh my sons! . . . We were born to die![1]

By the mid-seventeenth century, malaria and yellow fever were also present in tropical regions.

The development of English and French colonies in North America in the seventeenth century led to similar patterns of contagion and mortality. In 1616 and 1617, epidemics nearly exterminated many of New England's indigenous groups. French fur traders transmitted measles, smallpox, and other diseases as far as Hudson Bay and the Great Lakes.

Although there is very little evidence that Europeans consciously used disease as a tool of empire, the deadly results of contact clearly undermined the ability of native peoples to resist European settlement. Europeans and their African slaves occupied these depopulated lands. The

Americas were transformed biologically and culturally. They were subjected to Europeans' political and economic demands.

The colonies of the Americas were crucial pieces of a new **Atlantic system.** This network of trading links moved people and cultures as well as goods and wealth around the Atlantic. The Atlantic system also affected Africa, but less severely than the Americas. Despite the loss of millions of people to the slave trade, Africa did not suffer such severe population loss as the Americas. Most important, Africans remained in control of their lands.

Amerindians, Europeans, and Africans all contributed to the creation of new cultures in the Americas. The societies that arose reflected each colony's mix of native peoples, its connections to the slave trade, and the policies of its European rulers.

As you read this chapter, ask yourself the following questions:

- How different and how similar were the colonial societies and economies of the Americas?
- Why did forced labor and slavery become so important in many New World colonies?
- How did participation in the Atlantic system affect Europe, Africa, and the Americas?

SPANISH AMERICA AND BRAZIL

The frontiers of conquest and settlement expanded rapidly. Within one hundred years of Columbus's first voyage to the Western Hemisphere, the Spanish Empire in America included most of the islands of the Caribbean, Mexico, the American southwest, Central America, the Caribbean and Pacific coasts of South America, the Andean highlands, and the vast plains of the Río de la Plata region (a region that includes the modern nations of Argentina, Uruguay, and Paraguay). Portuguese settlement in the New World developed more slowly. But before the end of the sixteenth century, Portugal occupied most of the Brazilian coast.

Early settlers from Spain and Portugal sought to create colonial societies based on the institutions and customs of their homelands. They viewed society as a vertical arrangement of estates (classes of society), as uniformly Catholic, and as an arrangement of patriarchal extended-family networks. Despite the imposition of foreign institutions and the massive loss of life caused by epidemics, indigenous peoples still exercised a powerful influence on the development of colonial societies. Aztec and Inca elite families sought to protect their traditional privileges and rights through marriage or less formal alliances with the Spanish settlers. They also often used colonial courts to defend their claims to land. Nearly everywhere, Amerindian religious beliefs and practices survived beneath the surface of an imposed Christianity. Amerindian languages, cuisine, medical practices, and agricultural techniques also survived the conquest and influenced the development of Latin American culture.

The African slave trade added a third cultural stream to colonial Latin American society. By the end of the colonial era, Africans and their descendants were living throughout Latin America, enriching colonial societies with their traditional agricultural practices, music, religious beliefs, cuisine, and social customs.

State and Church   The Spanish crown moved quickly to curb the independent power of the conquistadors and establish royal authority over both the defeated native populations and the rising tide of European settlers. Created in 1524, the **Council of the Indies** in Spain supervised all government, ecclesiastical, and commercial activity in the Spanish colonies. Political and economic power was concentrated in Mexico City, capital of the Viceroyalty of New Spain, and in Lima, capital of the Viceroyalty of Peru. Each viceroyalty was divided into a number of judicial and administrative districts. Until the seventeenth century, almost all of the officials appointed to high positions in Spain's colonial bureaucracy were born in Spain. Later, local-born members of the colonial elite gained many offices.

In the sixteenth century, Portugal concentrated its resources and energies on Asia and Africa, because early settlers found neither mineral wealth nor rich native empires in Brazil. Finally, the king appointed a governor-general in 1549 and designated Salvador, in the northern province of Bahia, Brazil's capital. In 1720, the first viceroy of Brazil was named.

Just as these colonial bureaucracies imposed Iberian economic and political institutions, the Catholic Church became the primary agent for the introduction and transmission of Christian belief and European culture in South America. Spain and Portugal justified their American conquests by assuming an obligation to convert native populations to Christianity. In Mexico alone, hundreds of thousands of conversions and baptisms were achieved within a few years of the conquest.

The Catholic clergy sought to win over the Amerindians by first converting native elites. But these efforts were abandoned when church authorities discovered that many converts were secretly observing old beliefs and rituals. In the 1560s, Spanish clergy resorted to torture, executions, and the destruction of native manuscripts to eradicate traditional beliefs and rituals among the Maya. Repelled by these events, the church hierarchy ended both the violent repression of native religious practice and efforts to recruit an Amerindian clergy.

Despite its failures, the Catholic clergy did provide native peoples with some protections against the abuse and exploitation of Spanish settlers. The priest **Bartolomé de Las Casas** (1474–1566), who served as the most important advocate for native peoples, wrote a number of books that detailed their mistreatment by the Spanish. His most important achievement was the enactment of the New Laws of 1542, which outlawed the enslavement of Amerindians and limited other forms of forced labor.

Despite the disapproval of most European clergy and settlers, Amerindians blended Catholic Christian beliefs with important elements of traditional native cosmology and ritual. Most commonly, indigenous beliefs and rituals came to be embedded in the celebration of saints' days or Catholic rituals associated with the Virgin Mary. Instead, it was one component of the process of cultural borrowing and innovation that contributed to a distinct and original Latin American culture.

After 1600, the Catholic Church redirected most of its resources from the countryside to growing colonial cities and towns with large European populations. One important outcome of this altered mission was the founding of universities and secondary schools, which stimulated urban intellectual life.

Colonial Economies

The silver mines of Peru and Mexico and the sugar plantations of Brazil dominated the colonial economy and fueled the early development of European capitalism. Profits produced in these economic centers also promoted the growth of colonial cities, concentrated scarce investment capital and labor resources, and stimulated the development of livestock raising and agriculture in neighboring rural areas. Dependence on mineral and agricultural exports was an enduring theme in Latin America.

Although millions of pesos of gold were mined in Latin America, silver mines generated more wealth and exercised greater economic influence. In 1545, the single richest silver deposit in the Americas was discovered at **Potosí°,** in what is now Bolivia, and until 1680 the silver production of Bolivia and Peru dominated the Spanish colonial economy.

Silver mining also greatly altered the environment. Within a short time, wasteful use of forest resources for fuel destroyed forests near the mining centers. Faced with rising fuel costs, miners developed an efficient method of chemical extraction that relied on mixing mercury with the silver ore. But mercury is a poison, and its use contaminated

Potosí (poh-toh-SEE)

Chronology

	Latin America	North America	West Indies	Atlantic
1500	**1518** Smallpox arrives in Caribbean		**ca. 1500** Spanish settlers introduce sugar cane cultivation	
		1524–1554 French explore Newfoundland and Gulf of St. Lawrence		**1530** Amsterdam Exchange opens
	1535 Creation of Viceroyalty of New Spain			
	1540s Creation of Viceroyalty of Peru			
	1542 New Laws outlaw Amerindian enslavement			
	1545 Silver discovered at Potosí, Bolivia			
1600		**1607** Jamestown founded		
		1608 Quebec founded		
	By 1620 African slaves the majority of Brazilian plantation workers	**1620** Plymouth founded	**1620s and 1630s** English and French colonies in Caribbean	**1621** Dutch West India Company chartered
	1625 Population of Potosí reaches 120,000			
			1640s Dutch bring sugar plantation system from Brazil	**1638** Dutch take Elmina
			1655 English take Jamaica	
		1660 Slavery in Virginia begins to grow rapidly		**1660s** English Navigation Acts
		1664 English take New York from Dutch		
			1670s French occupy western half of Hispaniola	**1672** Royal African Company chartered
				1698 French *Exclusif*
1700		**1699** Louisiana founded	**1700** West Indies surpass Brazil in sugar production	**1700–1830** Slave trade at its peak
		1756–1763 French and Indian War		

the environment and sickened the Amerindian work force.

From the time of Columbus, indigenous populations had been compelled to provide labor for European settlers in the Americas. Until the 1540s in Spanish colonies, Amerindian peoples were divided among the settlers and were forced to provide them with labor or with textiles, food, or other goods. This form of forced labor was called the **encomienda°**. The discovery of silver in Peru led to a new form of compulsory labor called the mita°. Under this system, one-seventh of the adult male Amerindians were compelled to work for six months each year in mines or on farms or in textile factories. The most dangerous working conditions existed in the silver mines.

In the Spanish mita, few Amerindian workers could survive on their wages. Wives and children were commonly forced to join the work force to help meet expenses (see Society and Culture: Colonial Wealth and the Exploitation of Indigenous Peoples). Even those who remained behind in the village were forced to send food and cash to support mita workers.

The Portuguese, who had developed sugar plantations that depended on slave labor on the Atlantic islands of Madeira, the Azores, the Cape Verdes, and São Tomé, transferred this profitable form of agriculture to Brazil. By the seventeenth century, sugar dominated the Brazilian economy. At first, the Portuguese enslaved Amerindian men as field hands, but sugar planters eventually came to rely more on African slaves, who were more resistant to disease. Imports of African slaves rose from an average of 2,000 per year in the late sixteenth century to approximately 7,000 per year a century later, far outstripping the immigration of free Portuguese settlers.

The mining centers of Latin America exercised global economic influence. American silver increased the European money supply, promoting commercial expansion. Large amounts of silver also flowed across the Pacific, where it was exchanged for Asian spices, silks, and pottery. In the Americas, the rich mines stimulated urban population growth, as well as commercial links with agricultural and textile producers.

The sugar plantations of Brazil played a similar role in integrating the economy of the south Atlantic region. At the end of the seventeenth century, the discovery of gold in Brazil helped overcome this large region's currency shortage and promoted further economic integration.

Both Spain and Portugal attempted to control the trade of their American colonies, but the combination of monopoly commerce and convoy shipping slowed the flow of European goods to the colonies and kept prices high. Frustrated by these restraints, colonial populations established illegal commercial relations with the English, French, and Dutch. By the middle of the seventeenth century, a majority of European imports were arriving in Latin America illegally.

Society in Colonial Latin America

With the exception of a few early viceroys, few members of Spain's great noble families came to the New World. *Hidalgos°*—lesser nobles—were well represented, as were Spanish merchants, artisans, miners, priests, and lawyers. Small numbers of criminals, beggars, and prostitutes also found their way to the colonies. Spanish settlers, however, were always a tiny minority in a colonial society numerically dominated by Amerindians and rapidly growing populations of Africans, **creoles** (whites born in America to European parents), and people of mixed ancestry.

Conquistadors and early settlers who received from the Crown grants of labor and tribute goods (encomienda) from Amerindian communities as rewards for service to Spain dominated colonial society in early Spanish America. These *encomenderos* sought to create a hereditary social and political class comparable to the nobles of Europe. But their systematic abuse of Amerindian communities and the catastrophic loss of Amerindian life during the epidemics of the sixteenth century undermined their position, as did the growing power of colonial viceroys, judges, and bishops appointed by the king.

By the end of the sixteenth century, the elite of Spanish America included both European immigrants and creoles. Europeans dominated the

---

encomienda (in-co-mee-EN-dah)   mita (MEE-tah)

hidalgos (ee-DAHL-goes)

Colonial Wealth and the Exploitation of Indigenous Peoples

The conditions imposed on indigenous peoples in the Spanish colonies generated contentious debates from the early sixteenth century to the end of the colonial period. Two Spanish naval officers who accompanied a French scientific expedition to South America in the mid-eighteenth century wrote the following description.

Without having to assume anything that cannot be proved absolutely or exaggerating to stretch the truth, we can agree indisputably that all the wealth produced in the Indies [Spain's American colonies], even what is consumed there, stems from the toil of the Indians. From close observation one sees that Indians work the silver and gold mines, cultivate the fields, and raise the livestock. In a word, there is no heavy labor that the Indians do not perform. They are so badly recompensed for their work that if one wanted to find out what the Spaniards paid them, he would discover it to be nothing except consistently cruel punishment, worse than that meted out in the galleys. . . . The gold and silver which the Spaniards acquire at the expense of the natives' sweat and toil never falls into the hands of the Indians. [T]hose who contribute most are the ones who enjoy its fruits least and are the most poorly paid for the most arduous tasks. . . .

There are two ways to remedy the abuse perpetrated on the free and mita Indians [the mita was a forced labor system]. The most reasonable and just method would be to eliminate the mita entirely and have free labor work the haciendas, mines, obrajes [textile mills] and everything else. . . .

In the second place it would be fitting to prohibit completely all physical punishment of the Indians in the haciendas and obrajes under severe penalties.

How important were Amerindians to the economy of the Spanish Empire? How did these two visitors judge the treatment of Amerindian peoples? What remedies did these authors suggest?

Source: Jorge Juan and Antonio de Ulloa, *Discourse and Political Reflections on the Kingdom of Peru,* ed. John J. Tepaske and Besse A. Clement (Norman: University of Oklahoma Press, 1978), 126–148.

highest levels of the church and government, as well as commerce. Creoles commonly controlled colonial agriculture and mining. Although tensions between Spaniards and creoles were inevitable, most elite families had members from both groups.

Before the Europeans arrived in the Americas, the native peoples were members of a large number of distinct cultural and linguistic groups. Cultural diversity and class distinctions were present even in the highly centralized Aztec and Inca empires. The loss of life provoked by the European conquest undermined this rich social and cultural complexity, and the imposition of Catholic Christianity further eroded ethnic boundaries among native peoples. Colonial administrators and settlers broadly applied the racial label "Indian," which facilitated the imposition of special taxes and labor obligations while erasing long-standing class and ethnic differences.

Indigenous Amerindian elites survived only briefly in the Spanish colonies and Brazil. Some of the conquistadors and early settlers married or established less formal relations with elite Amerindian women, but fewer of these alliances occurred after European women began to arrive. Some

Painting of Castas   This is an example of a common genre of colonial Spanish American painting. In the eighteenth century, there was increased interest in ethnic mixing, and wealthy colonials, as well as some Europeans, commissioned sets of paintings that showed mixed families. Commonly, the paintings also indicated what the artist believed was an appropriate class setting. In this painting, a richly dressed Spaniard is depicted with his Amerindian wife dressed in European clothing. Notice that the painter has the mestiza daughter look to her European father for guidance. (Private Collection. Photographer: Camilo Garza/Fotocam, Monterrey, Mexico)

descendants of the powerful Amerindian families prospered in the colonial period as ranchers, muleteers, and merchants; many others lived in the same materially deprived conditions as Amerindian commoners.

Thousands of blacks participated in the conquest and settlement of Spanish America, and the opening of a direct slave trade with Africa added millions more. Settlers' views of African slaves' cultural differences as signs of inferiority ultimately served as a justification for slavery. By 1600, any-

one with black ancestry was barred from positions in church, government, and many skilled crafts. Even so, African languages, religious beliefs, and marriage customs mixed with European (and in some cases Amerindian) languages and beliefs to forge distinct local cultures. The rapid growth of an American-born slave population accelerated this process of cultural change.

African slaves became skilled artisans, musicians, servants, artists, cowboys, and even soldiers. However, the vast majority worked in agriculture. To escape harsh discipline, brutal punishments, and backbreaking labor, many slaves rebelled or ran away. Communities of runaways (called *quilombos*° in Brazil and *palenques*° in Spanish colonies) were common. The largest quilombo was Palmares, where thousands of slaves defended themselves against Brazilian authorities for sixty years until they were finally overrun in 1694.

ENGLISH AND FRENCH COLONIES IN NORTH AMERICA

The North American colonial empires of England and France and the colonies of Spain and Portugal had many characteristics in common. The governments of England and France hoped to find easily extracted forms of wealth or great indigenous empires like those of the Aztecs or Inca. Like the Spanish and Portuguese, English and French settlers responded to native peoples with a mixture of diplomacy and violence. African slaves proved crucial to the development of all four colonial economies.

There were also important differences. The English and French colonies were founded nearly a century after Cortés's conquest of Mexico and initial Portuguese settlement in Brazil. Distracted by ventures elsewhere, neither England nor France imitated the large and expensive colonial bureaucra-

---

quilombos (ley-LOM-bos)   *palenques* (pah-LEN-kays)

cies that Spain and Portugal established. Instead, private companies and individual proprietors pioneered the development of English and French colonies. This practice led to greater regional variety in economic activity, political institutions and culture, and social structure than was evident in Latin American colonies.

The South

London investors, organized as the privately funded Virginia Company, got off to a rocky start. Nearly 80 percent of the settlers at Jamestown in 1607 and 1608 soon died of disease or Amerindian attacks. After the English crown dissolved the Virginia Company in 1624 because of its mismanagement, colonists pushed deeper into the interior, developing a sustainable economy based on furs, timber, and, increasingly, tobacco. The profits from tobacco soon attracted new immigrants and new capital. Along the shoreline of Chesapeake Bay and the rivers that fed it, settlers spread out, developing plantations and farms.

Indentured servants eventually accounted for approximately 80 percent of all English immigrants to the Chesapeake Bay region. Young men and women unable to pay for their transportation to the New World accepted indentures (contracts) that bound them to a term ranging from four to seven years of labor in return for passage, a small parcel of land, and some tools and clothes. During the seventeenth century, approximately fifteen hundred indentured servants, mostly male, arrived each year. As life expectancy in the colony improved, planters began to purchase more slaves. They calculated that greater profits could be secured by paying the higher initial cost of slaves owned for life than by purchasing the contracts of indentured servants bound for short periods of time. As a result, Virginia's slave population grew rapidly from 950 in 1660 to 120,000 by 1756.

Ironically, this dramatic increase in the colony's slave population occurred along with the expansion in colonial liberties and political rights. At first, colonial government had been administered by a Crown-appointed governor and his council, as well as by representatives of towns meeting together as the **House of Burgesses.** When these representatives began to meet alone as a deliberative body, they initiated a form of democratic representation that distinguished the English colonies of North America from the colonies of other European powers. The intertwined evolution of freedom and slavery gave England's southern colonies a unique and conflicted political character.

Colonial South Carolina was the most hierarchical society in British North America. Planters controlled the economy and political life. The richest maintained households in both the countryside and Charleston, the largest city in the southern colonies. Small farmers, cattlemen, artisans, merchants, and fur traders held an intermediate but clearly subordinate social position. African slaves were present from the founding of Charleston. They were instrumental in introducing irrigated rice agriculture and in developing indigo (a plant that produced a blue dye) plantations. Native peoples remained influential participants in colonial society through commercial contacts and alliances, but they were increasingly marginalized.

New England

New England was colonized by two separate groups of Protestant dissenters. The **Pilgrims** established the colony of Plymouth on the coast of present-day Massachusetts in 1620. Although nearly half of the settlers died during the first winter, the colony survived. In 1691, Plymouth was absorbed into the larger Massachusetts Bay Colony of the **Puritans.** The Puritan leaders had received a royal charter to finance the Massachusetts Bay Colony. By 1643, more than 20,000 Puritans had settled in the Bay Colony.

Unlike the southern colonies, most newcomers to Massachusetts arrived with their families. A normal gender balance and a healthy climate resulted in a rapid natural increase in population. Massachusetts also was more homogeneous and less hierarchical than the southern colonies.

Political institutions evolved out of the terms of the royal charter. A governor was elected, along with a council of magistrates drawn from the board of directors of the Massachusetts Bay Company. Disagreements between this council and elected representatives of the towns led, by 1650, to the creation of a lower legislative house that selected its own speaker and began to develop procedures and rules similar to those of the House of Commons in England.

Economically, Massachusetts differed dramatically from the southern colonies. Agriculture met basic needs, but poor soils and harsh climate offered no opportunity to develop cash crops like tobacco or rice. To pay for imported tools, textiles, and other essentials, the colonists began to provide commercial and shipping services to the southern colonies, the smaller Caribbean islands, Africa, and Europe.

In contrast to Latin America's heavily capitalized monopolies, New England merchants' success rested on market intelligence, flexibility, and streamlined organization. With 16,000 inhabitants in 1740, Boston was the largest city in British North America.

Middle Atlantic Region

The rapid economic development and remarkable cultural diversity of the Middle Atlantic colonies added to the success of English-speaking North America. The **Iroquois Confederacy,** an alliance of several native peoples, established treaties and trading relationships with the Dutch. When confronted by an English military expedition in 1664, the Dutch surrendered their colony of New Netherland without a fight. Renamed New York, the colony's success was guaranteed in large measure by the development of New York City as a commercial and shipping center. Located at the mouth of the Hudson River, the city played an essential role in connecting the region's grain farmers to the booming markets of the Caribbean and southern Europe. By the early eighteenth century, New York Colony had a diverse population that included (in addition to English colonists) Dutch, German, and Swedish settlers, as well as a large slave community.

Pennsylvania began as a proprietary colony in 1682 and as a refuge for Quakers, a persecuted religious minority. The founder, William Penn, quickly lost control of the colony's political life, but the colony enjoyed remarkable success. By 1700, Pennsylvania had a population of more than 21,000, and Philadelphia, its capital, soon passed Boston to become the largest city in the British colonies. Healthy climate, excellent land, and relatively peaceful relations with native peoples attracted free workers, including a large number of German families. As a result, Pennsylvania's economic expansion in the late seventeenth century occurred without reproducing South Carolina's hierarchical and repressive social order. By the early eighteenth century, however, the prosperous city of Philadelphia included a large population of black slaves, servants, and skilled tradesmen.

French America

French settlement patterns more closely resembled those of Spain and Portugal than of England. The French were committed to missionary activity among Amerindian peoples and emphasized extracting resources—in this case, furs.

Coming to Canada after spending years in the West Indies, Samuel de Champlain founded the colony of **New France** at Quebec°, on the banks of the St. Lawrence River, in 1608. The European market for fur, especially beaver, fueled French settlement. Young Frenchmen were sent to live among native peoples to master their languages and customs. These men and their children by native women organized the fur trade and led French expansion to the west and south. Amerindians actively participated in this trade because they came to depend on the goods they received in exchange for furs: firearms, metal tools and utensils, textiles, and alcohol.

The Iroquois Confederacy responded to the increased military strength of France's Algonkian allies by forging commercial and military links with Dutch and later English settlements in the Hudson River Valley. Well armed by the Dutch and English, the Iroquois Confederacy nearly eradicated the Huron in 1649 and inflicted a series of humiliating defeats on the French. At the high point of their power in the early 1680s, Iroquois

---

Quebec (kwuh-BEC)

hunters and military forces gained control of much of the Great Lakes region and the Ohio River Valley. A large French military expedition and a relentless attack focused on Iroquois villages and agriculture finally checked Iroquois power in 1701.

Use of firearms in hunting and warfare moved west and south, reaching indigenous plains cultures that previously had adopted the horse introduced by the Spanish. This intersection of horse and gun frontiers in the early eighteenth century dramatically increased the military power and hunting efficiency of the Sioux, Comanche, Cheyenne, and other indigenous peoples and slowed the pace of European settlement in North America.

In French Canada, the Jesuits led the effort to convert native peoples to Christianity. Building on earlier evangelical efforts in Brazil and Paraguay, French Catholic missionaries mastered native languages, created boarding schools for young boys and girls, and set up model agricultural communities for converted Amerindians. The Jesuits' greatest successes coincided with a destructive wave of epidemics and renewed warfare among native peoples in the 1630s. Nevertheless, local cultures persisted.

Although the fur trade flourished, settlers were few. Founded at about the same time, Virginia had twenty times as many European residents as Canada by 1627. Canada's small settler population and the Amerindians' profitable fur trade allowed then to retain greater independence and more control over their encounters with new religious, technological, and market realities.

The French aggressively expanded. Louisiana, founded in 1699, depended on the fur trade with Amerindians. France's North American colonies were threatened by a series of wars with England and the neighboring English colonies. The "French and Indian War" (also known as the Seven Years War, 1756–1763) proved to be the final contest for North American empire (see Map 17.1). England committed a larger military force to the struggle and, despite early defeats, took the French capital of Quebec in 1759. The peace agreement forced France to yield Canada to the English and cede Louisiana to Spain. The French then concentrated their efforts on their sugar-producing colonies in the Caribbean.

PLANTATIONS IN THE WEST INDIES

The West Indies was the first place in the Americas that Columbus reached and the first part of the Americas where native populations collapsed. It took a long time to repopulate these islands from abroad and forge new economic links between them and other parts of the Atlantic. But after 1650, sugar plantations, African slaves, and European capital made these islands a major center of the Atlantic economy.

Spanish settlers had introduced sugar cane cultivation into the West Indies shortly after 1500, but these colonies soon fell into neglect as attention shifted to colonizing the American mainland. After 1600, the West Indies revived as a focus of colonization, this time by northern Europeans interested in growing tobacco and other crops. The islands' value mushroomed after the Dutch reintroduced sugar cultivation from Brazil in the 1640s and supplied the African slaves and European capital necessary to create a new economy.

Sugar and Slaves

The English colony of Barbados illustrates the dramatic transformation that sugar brought to the seventeenth-century Caribbean. In 1640, Barbados's economy depended largely on tobacco, mostly grown by European settlers, both free and indentured. By the 1680s, sugar had become the colony's principal crop, and enslaved Africans were three times as numerous as Europeans. Exporting up to 15,000 tons of sugar a year, Barbados had become the wealthiest and most populous of England's American colonies. By 1700, the West Indies had surpassed Brazil as the world's principal source of sugar.

The expansion of sugar plantations in the West Indies required a sharp increase in the volume of the slave trade from Africa. During the first half of the seventeenth century, about 10,000 slaves a year had arrived from Africa, most destined for Brazil

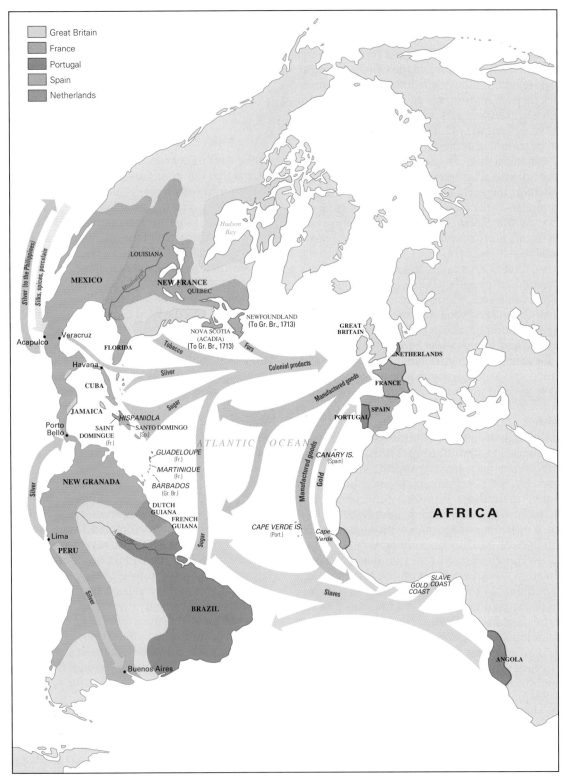

Map 17.1 The Atlantic World European colonization of the Americas and the opening up of trade to coastal Africa created a vast flow of goods and people that by 1750 rivaled the Indian Ocean basin in importance. A silver trade to East Asia gave birth to a Pacific Ocean economy.

and the mainland Spanish colonies. In the second half of the century, the trade averaged 20,000 slaves a year. More than half were intended for the English, French, and Dutch West Indies and most of the rest for Brazil. A century later, the volume of the Atlantic slave trade was three times larger.

What produced this shift in favor of African slaves? Recent scholarship has cast doubt on the once-common assertion that Africans were more suited than Europeans to field labor; in fact, both died in large numbers in the American tropics. The West Indian historian Eric Williams has also refuted the idea that the rise of African slave labor was primarily motivated by prejudice. Citing the West Indian colonies' prior use of enslaved Amerindians and indentured Europeans, along with European convicts and prisoners of war, he argued, "Slavery was not born of racism: rather, racism was the consequence of slavery."[2] Williams suggested the shift was due to the lower cost of African labor.

Yet slaves were far from cheap. Cash-short tobacco planters in the seventeenth century preferred indentured Europeans because they cost half as much as African slaves. Poor European men and women were willing to work for little in order to get to the Americas, where they could acquire their own land cheaply at the end of their term of service. However, as the cultivation of sugar spread after 1750, rich speculators drove the price of land in the West Indies up so high that end-of-term indentured servants could not afford to buy it. As a result, poor Europeans chose to indenture themselves in the mainland North American colonies, where cheap land was still available. Rather than raise wages to attract European laborers, Caribbean sugar planters switched to slaves.

Rising sugar prices helped the West Indian sugar planters afford the higher cost of African slaves. The planters could rely on the Dutch and other traders to supply them with enough new

Market in Rio de Janeiro   In many cities of colonial Latin America, female slaves and black free women dominated retail markets. In this scene from late colonial Brazil, Afro-Brazilian women sell a variety of foods and crafts.   (Sir Henry Chamberlain, *Views and Costumes of the City and Neighborhoods of Rio de Janeiro,* London, 1822)

slaves to meet the demands of the expanding plantations. Rising demand drove slave prices up steadily during the eighteenth century. These high labor costs were one more factor favoring large plantations over smaller operations.

To find more land for sugar plantations, France and England founded new Caribbean colonies. In 1655, the English had wrested the island of Jamaica from the Spanish (see Map 16.1). The French seized the western half of the large Spanish island of Hispaniola in the 1670s. During the eighteenth century, this new French colony of Saint Domingue° (present-day Haiti) became the greatest producer of sugar in the Atlantic world, while Jamaica surpassed Barbados as England's most important sugar colony.

Technology and Environment

What made the sugar plantation a complex investment was that it had to be a factory as well as a farm. Freshly cut canes needed to be crushed within a few hours to extract the sugary sap. Thus, for maximum efficiency, each plantation needed its own expensive crushing and processing equipment.

At the heart of the sugar works was the mill where canes were crushed between sets of heavy rollers. From the mill, lead-lined wooden troughs carried the cane juice to a series of large copper kettles in the boiling shed, where the excess water boiled off, leaving a thick syrup. Workers poured the syrup into conical molds in the drying shed. The sugar crystals that formed in the molds were packed in wooden barrels for shipment to Europe.

To make their operation more efficient and profitable, investors gradually increased the size of the typical West Indian plantation from around 100 acres (40 hectares) in the seventeenth century to at least twice that size in the eighteenth century. A plantation became a huge investment. One source estimated that a planter had to invest nearly £20,000 ($100,000) to acquire a Jamaican plantation of 600 acres (240 hectares) in 1774: a third for

land, a quarter for equipment, and £8,000 for 200 slaves. Jamaica specialized so heavily in sugar production that the island had to import most of its food. Saint Domingue was more diverse in its economy.

In some ways, the mature sugar plantation was environmentally responsible. The crushing mill was powered by water, wind, or animal power, not fossil fuels. The boilers were largely fueled by burning the crushed canes, and the fields were fertilized by cattle manure. In two respects, however, the plantation was very damaging to the environment: soil exhaustion and deforestation.

Instead of rotating sugar with other crops in order to restore the nutrients naturally, planters found it more profitable to clear new lands when yields declined too much in the old fields. When land close to the sea was exhausted, planters moved on to new islands. Many of the English who first settled Jamaica were from Barbados, and the pioneer planters on Saint Domingue came from older French sugar colonies. In the second half of the eighteenth century, Jamaican sugar production began to fall behind that of Saint Domingue, which still had access to virgin land. Thus, the plantations of this period were not a stable form of agriculture but one that gradually laid waste to the landscape.

Deforestation, the second form of environmental damage, continued a trend begun in the sixteenth century. By the end of the eighteenth century, only land in the interior of the islands retained dense forests.

The most tragic and dramatic transformation in the West Indies occurred in the human population. During the eighteenth century, West Indian plantation colonies were the world's most polarized societies. On most islands, 90 percent or more of the inhabitants became slaves. A small number of very rich men owned most of the slaves and most of the land as well. Between the slaves and the masters might be found only a few others: a few estate managers and government officials and, in the French islands, some small farmers, both white and black. The profitability of a Caribbean plantation depended on extracting as much work as possible from the slaves through the use of force and the threat of force.

Saint Domingue (san doh-MANGH)

Caribbean Sugar Mill   The windmill crushes sugar cane whose juice is boiled down in the smoking building next door.   (From William Clark, *Ten Views in the Islands of Antigua, 1823*. British Library)

On a typical Jamaican plantation, about 80 percent of the slaves actively engaged in productive tasks; the only exceptions were infants, the seriously ill, and the very old. The table also illustrates how slave labor was organized by age, sex, and ability. About 70 percent of the able-bodied slaves worked in the fields, generally in one of three labor gangs. Women formed the majority of the field laborers, even in the great gang. As the table shows, a little over half of the adult males were employed in nongang work, tending the livestock or serving as blacksmiths and carpenters. The most important artisan slave was the head boiler, who oversaw the delicate process of reducing the cane sap to crystallized sugar and molasses.

Skilled slaves received rewards of food and clothing or time off for good work, but the most common reason for working hard was to escape punishment. A slave gang was headed by a privileged male slave, appropriately called the **driver,** whose job was to ensure that the gang completed its work. Production quotas were high, and slaves toiled in the fields from sunup to sunset, except for meal breaks. Those who fell behind due to fatigue or illness soon felt the sting of the whip. Openly rebellious slaves who refused to work, disobeyed orders, or tried to escape were punished with flogging, confinement in irons, or mutilation.

The harsh conditions of plantation life played a major role in shortening slaves' lives, but the greatest killer was disease. The very young were carried off by dysentery caused by contaminated food and water. Slaves newly arrived from Africa went through a period of adjustment to the new environment known as **seasoning,** during which one-third on average died of unfamiliar diseases. Slaves also suffered from diseases they brought with them, including malaria. On one plantation, for example, more than half of the slaves incapacitated by illness had yaws, a painful and debilitating skin disease common in Africa.

Such high mortality greatly added to the volume of the Atlantic slave trade, since plantations had to purchase new slaves every year or two to re-

Punishment for Slaves   In addition to whipping and other cruel punishment, slave owners devised other ways to shame and intimidate slaves into obedience. This metal face mask prevented the wearer from eating or drinking.   (By permission of the Syndics of Cambridge University Library)

place those who had died. The additional imports of slaves to permit the expansion of the sugar plantations meant that the majority of slaves were Africans born on most West Indian plantations. As a result, African religious beliefs, patterns of speech, styles of dress and adornment, and music were prominent parts of West Indian life.

Given the harsh conditions of their lives, it is not surprising that slaves in the West Indies often sought to regain the freedom into which most had been born. Individual slaves often ran away, hoping to elude the men and dogs who would track them. Sometimes large groups of plantation slaves rose in rebellion against their bondage and abuse. For example, a large rebellion in Jamaica in 1760 was led by a slave named Tacky, who had been a chief on the Gold Coast of Africa. One night, his followers broke into a fort and armed themselves. Joined by slaves from nearby plantations, they stormed several plantations, setting them on fire and killing the planter families. Tacky died in the fighting that followed, and three other rebel lead-

ers stoically endured cruel deaths by torture that were meant to deter others from rebellion.

Because they believed rebellions were usually led by slaves with the strongest African heritage, European planters tried to curtail African cultural traditions. They required slaves to learn the colonial language and discouraged the use of African languages by deliberately mixing slaves from different parts of Africa. In French and Portuguese colonies, slaves were encouraged to adopt Catholic religious practices, though African deities and beliefs also survived. In the British West Indies, where only Quaker slave owners encouraged Christianity among their slaves before 1800, African herbal medicine remained strong, as did African beliefs concerning nature spirits and witchcraft.

As in Latin America, slavery provoked rebellion and flight. In the Caribbean, runaways were known as **maroons.** Maroon communities were especially numerous in the mountainous interiors of Jamaica and Hispaniola, as well as in the island parts of the Guianas°. The Jamaican maroons, after withstanding several attacks by the colony's militia, signed a treaty in 1739 that recognized their independence in return for their cooperation in stopping new runaways and suppressing slave revolts. Similar treaties with the large maroon population in the Dutch colony of Surinam (Dutch Guiana) recognized their possession of large inland regions.

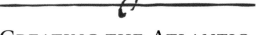

CREATING THE ATLANTIC ECONOMY

The West Indian plantation colonies were at once archaic in their cruel system of slavery and oddly modern in their specialization in a single product. Besides the plantation system itself, three other elements went into the creation of the new Atlantic economy: new economic institutions, new partnerships between private investors and

Guianas (guy-AHN-uhs)

governments in Europe, and new working relationships between European and African merchants. The new trading system is a prime example of how European capitalist relationships were reshaping the world.

Capitalism and Mercantilism

The Spanish and Portuguese voyages of exploration in the fifteenth and sixteenth centuries were government ventures, and both countries tried to keep their overseas trade and colonies royal monopolies. Monopoly control, however, proved both expensive and inefficient. The success of the Atlantic economy in the seventeenth and eighteenth centuries owed much to private enterprise, which made trading venues more efficient and profitable.

Two European innovations, capitalism and mercantilism, enabled private investors to fund the rapid growth of the Atlantic economy. **Capitalism** was a system of large financial institutions—banks, stock exchanges, and chartered trading companies—that enabled wealthy investors to reduce risks and increase profits. Early capitalism was buttressed by **mercantilism,** policies adopted by European states to promote their citizens' overseas trade and defend it, by armed force when necessary.

Chartered companies were one of the first examples of mercantilist capitalism. A charter issued by the government of the Netherlands in 1602 gave the Dutch East India Company a legal monopoly over all Dutch trade in the Indian Ocean. This privilege encouraged private investors to buy shares in the company. They were amply rewarded when the Dutch East India Company captured control of the long-distance trade routes in the Indian Ocean from the Portuguese (see Chapter 18). A sister firm, the **Dutch West India Company,** was chartered in 1621 to engage in the Atlantic trade and to seize sugar-producing areas in Brazil and African slaving ports from the Portuguese.

Such successes inspired other governments to set up their own chartered companies. In 1672, a royal charter placed all English trade with West Africa in the hands of the new **Royal African Company,** which established its headquarters at Cape

Coast Castle, just east of Elmina on the Gold Coast. The French government chartered East India and West India companies to reduce French colonies' dependence on Dutch and English traders.

French and English governments also used military force in pursuit of commercial dominance, especially to break the trading advantage of the Dutch in the Americas. Restrictions on Dutch access to French and English colonies provoked a series of wars with the Netherlands between 1652 and 1678, during which the larger English and French navies defeated the Dutch and drove the Dutch West India Company into bankruptcy.

With Dutch competition in the Atlantic reduced, the French and English governments moved to revoke the monopoly privileges of their chartered companies. England opened trade in Africa to any English subject in 1698 on the grounds that ending monopolies would be "highly beneficial and advantageous to this kingdom." It was hoped that such competition would also cut the cost of slaves to West Indian planters, though the demand for slaves soon drove the prices up again.

Such new mercantilist policies fostered competition among a nation's own citizens, while using high tariffs and restrictions to exclude foreigners. In the 1660s, England had passed a series of Navigation Acts that confined trade with its colonies to English ships and cargoes. The French called their mercantilist legislation, first codified in 1698, the *Exclusif°*, highlighting its exclusionary intentions. Other mercantilist laws defended manufacturing and processing interests in Europe against competition from colonies, imposing prohibitively high taxes on any manufactured goods and refined sugar imported from the colonies.

As a result of such mercantilist measures, the Atlantic became Britain, France, and Portugal's most important overseas trading area in the eighteenth century. Britain's imports from its West Indian colonies in this period accounted for over one-fifth of the value of total British imports. The French West Indian colonies played an even larger role in France's overseas trade. Only the Dutch, closed out of much of the American trade, found Asian trade of greater value. Profits from the Atlantic

---

Exclusif (ek-skloo-SEEF)

economy, in turn, promoted further economic expansion and increased the revenues of European governments.

The Great Circuit and the Middle Passage

At the heart of the Atlantic system was a great clockwise network of trade routes known as the **Great Circuit.** It began in Europe, ran south to Africa, turned west across the Atlantic Ocean to the Americas, and then swept back to Europe. Like Asian sailors in the Indian Ocean, Atlantic mariners depended on the prevailing winds and currents to propel their ships. What drove the ships as much as the winds and currents was the desire for the profits that each leg of the circuit was expected to produce.

The first leg, from Europe to Africa, carried European manufactures—notably metal bars, hardware, and guns—as well as great quantities of cotton textiles brought from India. Some of these goods were traded for West African gold, timber, and other products, which were taken back to Europe. More goods went to purchase slaves, who were transported across the Atlantic to the plantation colonies in the part of the Great Circuit known as the **Middle Passage.** On the third leg, plantation goods from the colonies returned to Europe. Each leg of the circuit carried goods from where they were abundant and relatively cheap to where they were scarce and therefore more valuable. Thus, in theory, each leg of the Great Circuit could earn much more than its costs, and a ship that completed all three legs could return a handsome profit to its owners. In practice, shipwrecks, deaths, piracy, and other risks could turn profit into loss.

The three-sided Great Circuit is only the simplest model of Atlantic trade. Many other trading voyages supplemented the basic circuit. Cargo ships made long voyages from Europe to the Indian Ocean, passed southward through the Atlantic with quantities of African gold and American silver, and returned with the cotton textiles necessary to the African trade. Other sea routes brought to the West Indies manufactured goods from Europe or foodstuffs and lumber from New England.

European interests dominated the Atlantic system. The manufacturers who supplied the trade goods and the investors who provided the capital were all based in Europe, as were the principal consumers of the plantation products. Before the seventeenth century, sugar had been rare and fairly expensive in western Europe. By 1700, annual consumption of sugar in England had risen to about 4 pounds (nearly 2 kilograms) per person. Rising western European prosperity and declining sugar prices promoted additional consumption, starting with the upper classes and working its way down the social ladder. People spooned sugar into popular new beverages imported from overseas—tea, coffee, and chocolate—to overcome the beverages' natural bitterness. By 1750, annual sugar consumption in Britain had doubled, and it doubled again to about 18 pounds (8 kilograms) per person by the early nineteenth century.

The flow of sugar to Europe depended on another key component of the Atlantic trading system: the flow of slaves from Africa. The rising volume of the Middle Passage also measures the Atlantic system's expansion. During the first 150 years after the European discovery of the Americas, some 800,000 Africans had begun the journey across the Atlantic. During the boom in sugar production between 1650 and 1800, the slave trade amounted to nearly 7.5 million. Of the survivors, over half landed in the West Indies and nearly a third in Brazil. Plantations in North America imported another 5 percent, and the rest went to other parts of Spanish America.

In these peak decades, the transportation of slaves from Africa was a highly specialized trade. Most slaves were carried in ships that had been specially built or modified for the slave trade by the construction between the ships' decks of additional platforms on which the human cargo was packed as tightly as possible.

Seventeenth-century mercantilist policies placed much of the Atlantic slave trade in the hands of chartered companies. During their existence, the Dutch West India Company and the English Royal African Company each carried about 100,000 slaves across the Atlantic. In the eighteenth century, private English traders from Liverpool and Bristol controlled about 40 percent of the slave trade. The French, operating out of Nantes and Bordeaux, handled about half as much, and the Dutch hung on to only 6 percent. The Portuguese, supplying

Brazil and other places, had nearly 30 percent of the Atlantic slave trade, in contrast to the 3 percent carried in North American ships.

To make a profit, European slave traders had to buy slaves in Africa for less than the cost of the goods they traded in return. Then they had to deliver as many healthy slaves as possible across the Atlantic for resale in the plantation colonies. The treacherous voyage to the Americas lasted from six to ten weeks. Some ships completed it with all of their slaves alive, but large, even catastrophic losses of life were common. On average between 1650 and 1800, about one slave in every six perished during the Middle Passage.

Some deaths resulted from the efforts of the captives to escape. To inhibit such attempts, African men were confined below deck during most of the voyage, and special netting was installed around the outside of the ship. Some slaves fell into deep psychological depression, known to contemporaries as "fixed melancholy," from which many perished. Others refused to eat, so forced feeding was used to keep slaves alive. When opportunities presented themselves (nearness to land, illness among the crew), some cargoes of enslaved Africans tried to overpower their captors. Such "mutinies" were rarely successful and were put down with brutality that occasioned further losses of life.

Other deaths during the Middle Passage were due to the ill treatment slaves received. Although it was in the interests of the captain and crew to deliver their slave cargo in good condition, whippings, beatings, and even executions were used to maintain order and force the captives to take nourishment. Moreover, the dangers and brutalities of the slave trade were so notorious that many ordinary seamen shunned such work. As a consequence, cruel and brutal characters abounded among the officers and crews on slave ships.

Although examples of unspeakable cruelties are common in the records, most deaths in the Middle Passage were the result of disease rather than abuse, just as on plantations. Dysentery spread by contaminated food and water caused many deaths. Others died of contagious diseases such as smallpox, carried by persons whose infections were not detected during the medical examinations of slaves prior to boarding. Such maladies spread quickly in the crowded and unsanitary confines of the ships, claiming the lives of many slaves already physically weakened and mentally traumatized by their ordeals.

Crew members who were in close contact with the slaves were equally exposed to the epidemics and regularly suffered heavy losses. Moreover, sailors often fell victim to tropical diseases, such as malaria, to which Africans had acquired resistance. It is a measure of the callousness of the age, as well as the cheapness of European labor, that over the course of a Great Circuit voyage the proportion of crew deaths could be as high as the slave deaths on the Middle Passage.

AFRICA AND THE ATLANTIC

The Atlantic system took a terrible toll in African lives both during the Middle Passage and under the harsh conditions of plantation slavery. Many other Africans died while being marched to African coastal ports for sale overseas. The overall effects on Africa of these losses and of other aspects of the slave trade have been the subject of considerable historical debate. It is clear that the trade's impact depended on the intensity and terms of different African regions' involvement.

Any assessment of the Atlantic system's effects in Africa must also take into consideration the fact that some Africans profited from the trade by capturing and selling slaves. They chained the slaves together or bound them to forked sticks for the march to the coast, then bartered them to the European slavers for trade goods. The effects on the enslaver were different from the effects on the enslaved.

The Gold Coast and the Slave Coast

The transition to slave trading was not sudden. Even as slaves were becoming Atlantic Africa's most valuable export, non-slave goods remained a significant part of the total trade. For example, during its eight decades of operation from 1672 to 1752, the English Royal African Company made 40 percent of its profits from dealings in gold, ivory, and forest products. In some parts of West Africa, such nonslave exports remained predominant even at the peak of the trade.

African merchants were very discriminating about what merchandise they received in return for slaves or other goods. A European ship that arrived with goods of low quality or unsuited to local tastes found it hard to purchase a cargo at a profitable price. Africans' greatest demands were for textiles, hardware, and guns. Of the goods the Royal African Company traded in West Africa in the 1680s, over 60 percent were Indian and European textiles and 30 percent hardware and weaponry. Beads and other jewelry formed 3 percent. The rest consisted of cowrie shells that were used as money. In the eighteenth century, tobacco and rum from the Americas became welcome imports.

Both Europeans and Africans naturally attempted to drive the best bargain for themselves and sometimes engaged in deceitful practices. The strength of the African bargaining position, however, may be inferred from the fact that as the demand for slaves rose, so too did their price in Africa. In the course of the eighteenth century, the goods needed to purchase a slave on the Gold Coast doubled and in some places tripled or quadrupled.

African governments on the Gold and Slave Coasts made Europeans observe African trading customs and prevented them from taking control of African territory. Rivalry among European nations, each of which established its own trading "castles" along the Gold Coast, also reduced Europeans' bargaining strength.

How did African kings and merchants obtain slaves for sale? Most accounts agree that prisoners taken in war were the greatest source of slaves for the Atlantic trade, but it is difficult to say how often capturing slaves for export was the main cause of warfare. An early-nineteenth-century king of Asante stated, "I cannot make war to catch slaves in the bush, like a thief. My ancestors never did so. But if I fight a king, and kill him when he is insolent, then certainly I must have his gold, and his slaves, and his people are mine too. Do not the white kings act like this?"[3] English rulers

had indeed sentenced seventeenth-century Scottish and Irish prisoners to forced labor in the West Indies.

The Bight of Biafra and Angola

In the eighteenth century, the slave trade expanded eastward to the Bight (bay) of Biafra. In contrast to the Gold and Slave Coasts, where strong kingdoms predominated, the densely populated interior of the Bight of Biafra contained no large states. Even so, the powerful merchant princes of the coastal ports still made European traders give them rich presents. Because of the absence of sizable states, there were no large-scale wars and consequently few prisoners of war. Instead, kidnapping was the major source of slaves.

As the volume of the Atlantic trade along the Bight of Biafra expanded in the late eighteenth century, some inland markets evolved into giant fairs, with different sections specializing in slaves and imported goods. An English ship's doctor reported that in the 1780s, slaves were "bought by the black traders at fairs, which are held for that purpose, at a distance of upwards of two hundred miles from the sea coast." He reported seeing from twelve hundred to fifteen hundred enslaved men and women arriving at the coast from a single fair.[4]

Angola, south of the Congo estuary, was the greatest source of slaves for the Atlantic trade. This was also the one place along the Atlantic coast where a single European nation, Portugal, controlled a significant amount of territory. Portuguese residents of the main coastal ports served as middlemen between caravans that arrived from the far interior and ships from Brazil.

Many of the slaves sold at Angolan markets were prisoners of war captured by expanding African states. As elsewhere in Africa, such prisoners seem to have been a by-product of African wars rather than the purpose for which the wars were fought.

Recent research has linked other enslavement with environmental crises in the hinterland of Angola. During the eighteenth century, these southern grasslands periodically suffered severe droughts, which drove famished refugees to areas with more plentiful water. In return for food and water, powerful African leaders gained control of many refugees and sold into the Atlantic trade the men, who were more likely than the women and children to escape or challenge the ruler's authority. The most successful of these inland Angolan leaders became heads of powerful new states that stabilized areas devastated by war and drought and repopulated them with the refugees and prisoners they retained. The slave frontier then moved farther inland. This cruel system worked to the benefit of a few African rulers and merchants at the expense of the many thousands of Africans who were sent to death or perpetual bondage in the Americas.

It is impossible to assess with precision the complex effects of the goods received in sub-Saharan Africa from these trades. Africans were very particular about what they received, so it is unlikely that they could have been consistently cheated. Some researchers have suggested that imports of textiles and metals undermined African weavers and metalworkers, but most economic historians calculate that on a per capita basis, the volume of these imports was too small to have idled many African artisans. Imports supplemented rather than replaced local production. The goods received in sub-Saharan Africa were intended for consumption and thus did not serve to develop the economy. Likewise, the sugar, tea, and chocolate Europeans consumed did little to promote economic development in Europe. However, both African and European merchants profited from trading these consumer goods. Because they directed the whole Atlantic system, Europeans gained far more wealth than Africans did.

Historians disagree in their assessment of how deeply European capitalism dominated Africa before 1800, but Europeans clearly had much less political and economic impact in Africa than in the West Indies or in other parts of the Americas. Still, it is significant that Western capitalism was expanding rapidly in the seventeenth century, while the Ottoman Empire, the dominant state of the Middle East, was entering a period of economic and political decline (see Chapter 21). The tide of influence in Africa was thus running in the Europeans' direction.

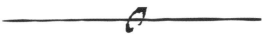

THE COLUMBIAN EXCHANGE

The term **Columbian Exchange** refers to the transfer of peoples, animals, plants, diseases, and technology between the New and Old Worlds that European trade in the Atlantic opened up. We have already seen how Old World diseases devastated Amerindian peoples and led to the resettlement of the Americas by Europeans and Africans. In addition, the domesticated livestock and major agricultural crops of the Old World had spread over much of the Americas, and Amerindians' staple crops had enriched the agricultures of Europe and Africa. This vast exchange of plants and animals radically altered diets and lifestyles around the Atlantic.

Transfers to the Americas

Within a century of Columbus's first voyage, new settlers in the Americas were growing all the staples of southern European agriculture—wheat, olives, grapes, and garden vegetables—along with African and Asian crops—rice, bananas, coconuts, breadfruit, and sugar cane. Native peoples remained loyal to their traditional staples but added many Old World plants to their diet. Citrus fruits, melons, figs, and sugar, as well as onions, radishes, and salad greens, all found a place in Amerindian cuisine.

By the eighteenth century, nearly all of the domesticated animals and cultivated plants in the Caribbean were ones that Europeans had introduced. The Spanish had brought cattle, pigs, and horses, all of which multiplied rapidly. They had also introduced new plants. Of these, bananas and plantain from the Canary Islands were a valuable addition to the food supply, and sugar and rice formed the basis of plantation agriculture, along with native tobacco. Other food crops arrived with the slaves from Africa, including okra, black-eyed peas, yams, grains such as millet and sorghum, and mangoes. Many of these new animals and plants were useful additions to the islands, but they crowded out indigenous species. The central importance of sugar cane in transforming Brazil and the Caribbean has already been noted.

The introduction of European livestock to the mainland had a dramatic impact. Faced with few natural predators, cattle, pigs, horses, and sheep, as well as pests like rats and rabbits, multiplied rapidly in the open spaces of the Americas. On the vast plains of present-day southern Brazil, Uruguay, and Argentina, herds of wild cattle and horses exceeded 50 million by 1700. Large herds of both animals also appeared in northern Mexico and what became the southwest of the United States.

Where Old World livestock spread most rapidly, environmental changes were most dramatic. Marauding livestock often had a destructive impact on Amerindian agriculturists. But on the plains of South America, northern Mexico, and Texas, cattle provided indigenous peoples with abundant supplies of meat and hides. In the present-day southwestern United States, the Navajo became sheepherders and expert weavers of woolen cloth. Individual Amerindians became muleteers, cowboys, and sheepherders.

No animal had a more striking effect on the cultures of native peoples than the horse, which increased the efficiency of hunters and the military capacity of warriors on the plains. The horse permitted the Apache, Sioux, Blackfoot, Comanche, Assiniboine, and others to hunt the vast herds of buffalo in North America more efficiently.

Cassava plant Both the leaves and the starchy root of the cassava plant could be eaten. (Engraving from André Thevet, *Les Singularitez de la Franc Antarctique*. Paris: Maurice de la Porte, 1557. Courtesy of the James Bell Library, University of Minnesota)

Transfers from the Americas

In return, the Americas offered the Old World an abundance of useful plants. The New World staples of maize and potatoes revolutionized agriculture and diet in parts of Europe, because they provided more calories per acre than any of the Old World staples except rice. Beans, squash, tomatoes, sweet potatoes, peanuts, chilis, and chocolate also gained widespread acceptance in Europe and other parts of the Old World. The New World also provided the Old with plants that provided dyes, medicines, and tobacco.

Maize and cassava (a Brazilian plant cultivated for its edible roots) moved across the Atlantic to Africa. The varieties of maize that spread to Africa were not modern high-bred sweet corn but starchier types found in white and yellow cornmeal. Cassava became the most important New World food in Africa. Truly a marvel, cassava had the highest yield of calories per acre of any staple food and thrived even in poor soils and during droughts. Both the leaves and the root could be eaten. Ground into meal, the root could be made into a bread that would keep for up to six months, or it could be fermented into a beverage.

Cassava and maize were probably introduced accidentally into Africa by Portuguese ships from Brazil that discarded leftover supplies after reaching Angola. It did not take long for local Africans to recognize the food value of these new crops, especially in drought-prone areas. By the eighteenth century, Central African rulers hundreds of miles from the Angolan coast were actively promoting the cultivation of maize and cassava on their royal estates in order to provide a more secure food supply. Some historians believe that in the inland areas, these Amerindian food crops provided the nutritional base for a population increase that partially offset losses due to the Atlantic slave trade.

CONCLUSION

The New World colonial empires of Spain, Portugal, France, and England had many characteristics in common. All subjugated Amerindian peoples and introduced large numbers of enslaved Africans. Within all four empires, forests were cut down, virgin soils were turned with the plow, and Old World animals and plants were introduced. Colonists in all four applied the technologies of the Old World to the resources of the New, producing wealth and exploiting the commercial possibilities of the emerging Atlantic market. Yet each of the New World empires also reflected the distinctive cultural and institutional heritages of its colonizing power.

Mineral wealth allowed Spain to develop the most centralized empire. Political and economic power was concentrated in the great capital cities of Mexico City and Lima. Portugal and France pursued similar objectives in their colonies. However, neither Brazil's agricultural economy nor France's Canadian fur trade produced the financial resources that made possible the centralized control achieved by Spain. Nevertheless, all three of these Catholic powers were able to impose and enforce significant levels of religious and cultural uniformity.

Greater cultural and religious diversity characterized British North America. Thus, colonists there were better able to respond to changing economic and political circumstances. Most important, the British colonies attracted many more European immigrants than did the other New World colonies. The new Atlantic trading system had great importance and momentous implications for world history. In the first phase of their expansion, Europeans had conquered and colonized the Americas and captured major Indian Ocean trade routes. The development of the Atlantic system showed Europeans' ability to move beyond the conquest and capture of existing systems to create a major new trading system that could transform a region almost beyond recognition.

The West Indies felt the transforming power of capitalism more profoundly than did any other place outside Europe in this period. The establishment of sugar plantation societies was not just a matter of replacing native vegetation with alien plants and native peoples with Europeans and Africans. More fundamentally, it made these once-isolated islands part of a dynamic trading system controlled from Europe. To be sure, the Caribbean was not the only place affected. Parts of northern Brazil were touched as deeply by the sugar revolution, and other parts of the Americas were yielding to the power of European colonization and capitalism.

Historians have seen the Atlantic system as a model of the kind of highly interactive economy that became global in later centuries. For that reason, the Atlantic system was a milestone in a much larger historical process, but not a monument to be admired. Its transformations were destructive as well as creative, producing victims as well as victors. Yet one cannot ignore that the system's awesome power came from its ability to create wealth. As the next chapter describes, southern Asia and the Indian Ocean basin were also beginning to feel the effects of Europeans' rising power.

■ Key Terms

Atlantic system	driver
Council of the Indies	seasoning
Bartolomé de Las Casas	maroons
Potosí	capitalism
encomienda	mercantilism
creoles	chartered companies
indentured servants	Dutch West India Company
House of Burgesses	Royal African Company
Pilgrims	Great Circuit
Puritans	Middle Passage
Iroquois Confederacy	Columbian Exchange
New France	

■ Suggested Reading

Alfred W. Crosby, Jr., is justifiably the best-known student of the Columbian Exchange. See his *The Columbian Exchange: Biological and Cultural Consequences of 1492* (1972) and *Ecological Imperialism* (1986). William H. McNeill, *Plagues and People* (1976), puts the discussion of the American exchange in a world history context. Elinor G. K. Melville, *A Plague of Sheep: Environmental Consequences of the Spanish Conquest of Mexico* (1994), is the most important recent contribution to this field.

Colonial Latin America, 2d ed. (1994), by Mark A. Burkholder and Lyman L. Johnson, provides a good introduction to colonial Latin American history. *Early Latin America* (1983) by James Lockhart and Stuart B. Schwartz and *Spain and Portugal in the New World, 1492–1700* (1984) by Lyle N. McAlister are both useful introductions as well.

Among the useful general studies of the British colonies are Charles M. Andrews, *The Colonial Period of American History: The Settlements,* 3 vols. (1934–1937); David Hackett Fischer, *Albion's Seed: Four British Folkways in America* (1989); and Gary B. Nash, *Red, White, and Black:*

The Peoples of Early America, 2d ed. (1982). For slavery, see David Brion Davis, *The Problem of Slavery in Western Culture* (1966).

On French North America, William J. Eccles, *France in America,* rev. ed. (1990), is an excellent overview; see also his *The Canadian Frontier, 1534–1760* (1969).

The global context of early modern capitalism is examined by Immanuel Wallerstein, *The Modern World-System,* 3 vols. (1974–1989), and by Fernand Braudel, *Civilization and Capitalism, 15th–18th Century,* 3 vols. (1982–1984). The best general introductions to the Atlantic system are Philip D. Curtin, *The Rise and Fall of the Plantation Complex* (1990), Herbert S. Klein, *The Atlantic Slave Trade* (1999), and David Ellis, *The Rise of African Slavery in the Americas* (2000). A useful collection of primary and secondary sources is David Northrup, ed., *The Atlantic Slave Trade,* 2d ed. (2001).

The cultural connections among African communities on both sides of the Atlantic are explored by John Thornton, *Africa and Africans in the Making of the Atlantic World, 1400–1800,* 2d ed. (1998). Herbert S. Klein's *African Slavery in Latin America and the Caribbean* (1986) is an exceptionally fine synthesis of research on New World slavery, including North American slave systems. For recent research on slavery and the African, Atlantic, and Muslim slave trades with Africa, see Paul Lovejoy, *Transformations in Slavery: A History of Slavery in Africa,* 2d ed. (2000).

■ Notes

1. Quoted in Alfred W. Crosby, Jr., *The Columbian Exchange: Biological and Cultural Consequences of 1492* (Westport, CT: Greenwood, 1972), 58.
2. Eric Williams, *Capitalism and Slavery* (Charlotte: University of North Carolina Press, 1944), 7.
3. King Osei Bonsu, quoted in David Northrup, ed., *The Atlantic Slave Trade,* 2d ed. (Boston: Houghton Mifflin, 2001), 176.
4. Alexander Falconbridge, *Account of the Slave Trade on the Coast of Africa* (London: J. Phillips, 1788), 12.

18

SOUTHWEST ASIA AND THE INDIAN OCEAN, 1500–1750

The Ottoman Empire • The Safavid Empire • The Mughal Empire •
Trade Empires in the Indian Ocean
ENVIRONMENT AND TECHNOLOGY: Metal Currency and Inflation

nthony Jenkinson, merchant-adventurer for the Muscovy Company, founded in 1555 to develop trade with Russia, was the first Englishman to set foot in Iran. Eight years after the first English ship dropped anchor at Archangel on the White Sea in Russia's frigid north, Jenkinson made his way through Russia, down the Volga River, and across the Caspian Sea. The local ruler he met when he disembarked in 1561 in northwestern Iran was an object of wonder, "richly apparelled with long garments of silk, and cloth of gold, embroidered with pearls of stone; upon his head was a *toli-pane* [headdress shaped like a tulip] with a sharp end pointing upwards half a yard long, of rich cloth of gold, wrapped about with a piece of India silk of twenty yards long, wrought in gold richly enameled, and set with precious stones; his earrings had pendants of gold a handful long, with two rubies of great value, set in the ends thereof."

Moving on to Qazvin°, Iran's capital, Jenkinson met the shah. After presenting a letter from Queen Elizabeth in Latin, English, Hebrew, and Italian but finding no one capable of reading it, he managed nevertheless to propose trade between England and Iran. The shah rejected the idea, since diverting Iranian silk from the markets of the Ottoman sultans, with whom he was negotiating a truce after a half-century of intermittent war, would have been undiplomatic.

Though Central Asia's bazaars were only meagerly supplied with goods, as Jenkinson and later merchants discovered, the idea of bypassing the Ottomans in the eastern Mediterranean and trading directly with Iran through Russia remained tempting. By the same token, the Ottomans were tempted by the idea of outflanking Safavid Iran. In 1569, an Ottoman army tried unsuccessfully to dig a 40-mile (64-kilometer)

Qazvin (kaz-VEEN)

canal between the Don River, which opened into the Black Sea, and the Volga, which flowed into the Caspian. Their objective was to enable Ottoman ships to reach the Caspian and attack Iran from the north.

The Ottomans' foe was Russia, then ruled by Tsar Ivan IV (r. 1533–1584), known as Ivan the Terrible or Awesome. Ivan transformed his principality from a second-rate power into the sultan's primary competitor in Central Asia. In the river-crossed steppe, where Turkic nomads had long enjoyed uncontested sway, Slavic Christian Cossacks from the region of the Don and Dnieper Rivers used armed wagon trains and river craft fitted with small cannon to push southward and establish a Russian presence.

A contest for trade with or control of Central Asia was natural after the centrality conferred on the region by three centuries of Mongol and Turkic conquest, highlighted by the campaigns of Genghis Khan and Timur. But as we shall see, changes in the organization of trade were sapping the vitality of the Silk Road. Wealth and power were shifting to European seaborne empires linking the Atlantic with the Indian Ocean. Though the Ottomans were a formidable naval power in the Mediterranean, neither they nor the Safavid shahs in Iran nor the Mughal emperors of India deployed more than a token navy in the southern seas.

As you read this chapter, ask yourself the following questions:

- What were the advantages and disadvantages of a land as opposed to a maritime empire?
- What role did religion play in political alliances and rivalries and in the formation of states?
- How did trading patterns change between 1500 and 1750?

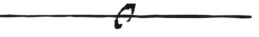

THE OTTOMAN EMPIRE

The most long-lived of the post-Mongol Muslim empires was the **Ottoman Empire,** founded around 1300 (see Map 18.1). By extending Islamic conquests into eastern Europe, starting in the late fourteenth century, and by taking Syria and Egypt from the Mamluk rulers in the early sixteenth, the Ottomans seemed to recreate the might of the original Islamic caliphate, the empire established by the Muslim Arab conquests in the seventh century. However, the empire was actually more like the new centralized monarchs of France and Spain (see Chapter 17) than any medieval model.

Enduring more than five centuries, until 1922, the Ottoman Empire survived several periods of wrenching change, some caused by internal problems, others by the growing power of European adversaries. These periods of change reveal the problems faced by huge land-based empires around the world.

Expansion and Frontiers

Established around 1300, the Ottoman Empire grew from a tiny state in northwestern Anatolia because of three factors: (1) the shrewdness of its founder, Osman (from which the name "Ottoman" comes), and his descendants, (2) control of a strategic link between Europe and Asia on the Dardanelles strait, and (3) the creation of an army that took advantage of the traditional skills of the Turkish cavalryman and the new military possibilities presented by gunpowder.

At first, Ottoman armies concentrated on Christian enemies in Greece and the Balkans, in 1389 conquering a strong Serbian kingdom at the Battle of Kosovo°. Much of southeastern Europe and Anatolia was under the control of the sultans by 1402. In 1453, Sultan Mehmed II, "the Conqueror," laid siege to Constantinople. His forces used enormous cannon to bash in the city's walls,

---

Kosovo (KO-so-vo)

CHRONOLOGY

	Ottoman Empire	Safavid Empire	Mughal Empire
1500		**1502–1524** Shah Ismail establishes Safavid rule in Iran	
	1514 Selim I conquers Egypt and Syria (1516–1517)	**1514** Defeat by Ottomans at Chaldiran limits Safavid growth	
	1520–1566 Reign of Suleiman the Magnificent; peak of Ottoman Empire		**1526** Babur defeats last sultan of Delhi at Panipat
	1529 First Ottoman siege of Vienna		**1556–1605** Akbar rules in Agra; peak of Mughal Empire
	1571 Ottoman naval defeat at Lepanto	**1587–1629** Reign of Shah Abbas the Great; peak of Safavid Empire	
1600	**1610** End of Anatolian revolts		
			1658–1707 Aurangzeb imposes conservative Islamic regime
1700	**1718–1730** Military decline apparent to Austria and Russia	**1722** Afghan invaders topple last Safavid shah	
		1736–1747 Nadir Shah temporarily reunites Iran; invades India (1739)	**1739** Iranians under Nadir Shah sack Delhi

dragged warships over a high hill from the Bosporus strait to the city's inner harbor to get around its sea defenses, and finally penetrated the city's land walls through a series of direct infantry assaults. The fall of Constantinople—henceforth commonly known as Istanbul—brought to an end over eleven hundred years of Byzantine rule and made the Ottomans seem invincible.

Selim° I, "the Inexorable," conquered Egypt and Syria in 1516 and 1517, making the Red Sea the Ottomans' southern frontier. His son, **Suleiman° the Magnificent** (r. 1520–1566), presided over the greatest Ottoman assault on Christian Europe.

Suleiman seemed unstoppable as he conquered Belgrade in 1521, expelled the Knights of the Hospital of St. John from the island of Rhodes the following year, and laid siege to Vienna in 1529. Vienna was saved by the need to retreat before the onset of winter more than by military action. In later centuries, Ottoman historians looked back on the reign of Suleiman as the period when the imperial system worked to perfection and spoke of it as the golden age of Ottoman greatness.

While Ottoman armies pressed deeper and deeper into eastern Europe, the sultans also sought to control the Mediterranean. Between 1453 and 1502, the Ottomans fought the opening rounds of a two-century war with Venice, the most powerful of

---

Selim (seh-LEEM) **Suleiman** (SOO-lay-man)

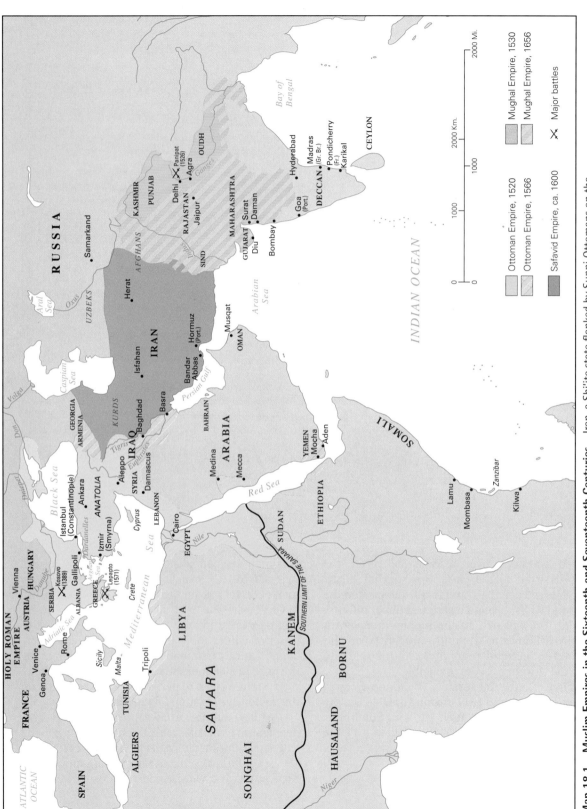

Map 18.1 Muslim Empires in the Sixteenth and Seventeenth Centuries Iran, a Shi'ite state flanked by Sunni Ottomans on the west and Sunni Mughals on the east, had the least exposure to European influences. Ottoman expansion across the southern Mediterranean Sea intensified European fears of Islam. The areas of strongest Mughal control dictated that Islam's spread into southeast Asia would be heavily influenced by merchants and religious figures from Gujarat instead of from eastern India.

Ottoman Empire, 1520
Ottoman Empire, 1566
Safavid Empire, ca. 1600
Mughal Empire, 1530
Mughal Empire, 1656
Major battles

Italy's commercial city-states. The initial fighting left Venice in control of its lucrative islands for another century. But it also left Venice a reduced military power compelled to pay tribute to the Ottomans.

It never occurred to the Ottomans that a sea empire held together by flimsy ships could truly rival a great land empire fielding an army of a hundred thousand men. In the early sixteenth century, merchants from southern India and Sumatra sent emissaries to Istanbul requesting naval support against the Portuguese. The Ottomans responded vigorously to Portuguese threats close to their territories, such as at Aden at the southern entrance to the Red Sea, but their efforts farther afield were insufficient to stifle growing Portuguese domination.

Eastern luxury products still flowed to Ottoman markets. Portuguese power was territorially limited to fortified coastal points, such as Hormuz at the entrance to the Persian Gulf, Goa in western India, and Malacca in Malaya. Why commit major resources to subduing an enemy whose main threat was a demand that merchant vessels, mostly belonging to non-Ottoman Muslims, buy protection from Portuguese attack? The Ottomans did send a small naval force to Indonesia, but they never formulated a consistent or aggressive policy with regard to political and economic developments in the Indian Ocean.

Ottoman Glassmakers on Parade   Celebrations of the circumcisions of the sultan's sons featured parades organized by the craft guilds of Istanbul. This float features glassmaking, a common craft in Islamic realms. The most elaborate glasswork included oil lamps for mosques and colored glass for the small stained-glass windows below mosque domes.   (Topkapi Saray Museum)

Central Institutions

By the 1520s, the Ottoman Empire was the most powerful and best-organized state in either Europe or the Islamic world. Its military was balanced between cavalry archers, primarily Turks, and **Janissaries°,** Christian prisoners of war induced to serve as military slaves.

Slave soldiery had a long history in Islamic lands, but the conquest of Christian territories in the Balkans in the late fourteenth century gave the Ottomans access to a new military resource. Converted to Islam, these "new troops," called *yeni cheri* in Turkish and *Janissary* in English, gave the

Ottomans unusual military flexibility. Since horseback riding and bowmanship were not part of their cultural backgrounds, they readily accepted the idea of fighting on foot and learning to use guns, which at that time were still too heavy and awkward for a horseman to load and fire. The Janissaries lived in barracks and trained all year round.

The process of selection for Janissary training changed early in the fifteenth century. The new system imposed a regular levy of male children on Christian villages in the Balkans and occasionally elsewhere. Recruited children were placed with Turkish families to learn their language and then were sent to the sultan's palace in Istanbul for an education that included instruction in Islam, military training, and, for the most talented, what we might call liberal arts. This regime, sophisticated for its time, produced not only the Janissary soldiers but also, from among the chosen few who received special training, senior military commanders and heads of government departments up to the rank of grand vizier.

Janissaries (JAN-nih-say-rees)

The cavalrymen were supported by land grants and administered most rural areas in Anatolia and the Balkans. They maintained order, collected taxes, and reported for each summer's campaign with their horses, retainers, and supplies, all paid for from the taxes they collected. When not campaigning, they stayed at home.

A galley-equipped navy was manned by Greek, Turkish, Algerian, and Tunisian sailors, usually under the command of an admiral from one of the North African ports. The balance of the Ottoman land forces brought success to Ottoman arms in recurrent wars with the Safavids, who were much slower to adopt firearms, and in the inexorable conquest of the Balkans. Expansion by sea was less dramatic. A major expedition against Malta in the western Mediterranean failed in 1565. Combined Christian forces also achieved a massive naval victory at the Battle of Lepanto, off Greece, in 1571. But the Ottomans' resources were so extensive that in a year's time, they had replaced all of the galleys sunk in that battle.

The Ottoman Empire became cosmopolitan in character. The sophisticated court language, Osmanli° (the Turkish form of *Ottoman*), shared basic grammar and vocabulary with Turkish, but Arabic and Persian elements made it distinct from the language spoken by Anatolia's nomads and villagers. Everyone who served in the military or the bureaucracy and conversed in Osmanli was considered to belong to the *askeri*°, or "military," class. Members of this class were exempt from taxes and owed their well-being to the sultan.

The Ottomans saw the sultan as providing justice for his "flock of sheep" (*raya*°) and the military protecting them. In return, the raya paid the taxes that supported both the sultan and the military. In reality, the sultan's government remained comparatively isolated from the lives of most subjects. As Islam gradually became the majority religion in Balkan regions, Islamic law (the Shari'a°) conditioned urban institutions and social life. Local customs prevailed among non-Muslims and in many rural areas; and non-Muslims looked to their own religious leaders for guidance in family and spiritual matters.

Crisis of the Military State, 1585–1650

As military technology evolved, cannon and lighter-weight firearms played an ever-larger role on the battlefield. Accordingly, the size of the Janissary corps—and its cost to the government—grew steadily, and the role of the Turkish cavalry diminished. To pay the Janissaries, the sultan started reducing the number of landholding cavalrymen. Revenues previously spent on their living expenses and military equipment went directly into the imperial treasury. Inflation caused by a flood of cheap silver from the New World (see Environment and Technology: Metal Currency and Inflation) bankrupted many of the remaining landholders restricted by law to collecting a fixed amount of taxes. Their land was returned to the state. Displaced cavalrymen, armed and unhappy, became a restive element in rural Anatolia.

This complicated situation resulted in revolts that devastated Anatolia between 1590 and 1610. Former landholding cavalrymen, short-term soldiers released at the end of the campaign season, peasants overburdened by emergency taxes, and even impoverished students of religion formed bands of marauders. Anatolia experienced the worst of the rebellions and suffered greatly from emigration and the loss of agricultural production. But an increase in banditry, made worse by the government's inability to stem the spread of muskets among the general public, beset other parts of the empire as well.

In the meantime, the Janissaries took advantage of their growing influence to gain relief from prohibitions on their marrying and engaging in business. Janissaries who involved themselves in commerce lessened the burden on the state budget, and married Janissaries who enrolled sons or relatives in the corps made it possible in the seventeenth century for the government to save state funds by abolishing forced recruitment. These savings, however, were more than offset by the increase in the total number of Janissaries and in

---

Osmanli (os-MAHN-lee)　*askeri* (AS-keh-ree)
raya (RAH-yah)　Shari'a (sha-REE-ah)

Metal Currency and Inflation

Inflation occurs when the quantity of goods and services available for purchase remains stable while the quantity of money in circulation increases. With more money in their pockets, people are willing to pay more to get what they want. Prices go up, and what people think of as the value of money goes down.

Today, with paper money and electronic banking, governments try to control inflation by regulating the printing of money or by other means. Prior to the nineteenth century, money consisted of silver and gold coins, and governments did not keep track of how much money was in circulation. As long as the annual production of gold and silver mines was quite small, inflation was not a worry. In the sixteenth and seventeenth centuries, however, precious metal poured into Spain from silver and gold mines in the New World, but there was no increase in the availability of goods and services. The resulting inflation triggered a "price revolution" in Europe—a general tripling of prices between 1500 and 1650. In Paris in 1650, the price of wheat and hay was fifteen times higher than the price had been in 1500.

This wave of inflation worked its way east, contributing to social disorder in the Ottoman Empire. European traders had more money available than Ottoman merchants and could outbid them for scarce commodities. Lacking silver and gold mines, the Ottoman government reduced the amount of precious metal in Ottoman coins. This made the problem worse. Hit hardest were people who had fixed incomes. Cavalrymen holding land grants worth a set amount each year were unable to equip themselves for military campaigns. Students living on fixed scholarships went begging.

Safavid Iran needed silver and gold to pay for imports from Mughal India, which imported few Iranian goods. Iranians sold silk to the Ottoman Empire for silver and gold, worsening the Ottoman situation, and then passed the precious metal on to India. Everyday life in Iran depended on barter or locally minted copper coinage, both more resistant to inflation. Copper for coins was sometimes imported from China.

Though no one then grasped the connection between silver production in Mexico and the trade balance between Iran and India, the world of the sixteenth and seventeenth centuries was becoming more closely linked economically than it had ever been before.

Set of Coin Dies   The lower die, called the anvil die, was set in a piece of wood. A blank disk of gold, silver, or copper was placed on top of it. The hammer die was placed on top of the blank and struck with a hammer to force the coin's image onto it.   (Courtesy, Israel Museum, Jerusalem)

their steady deterioration as a military force, which necessitated the hiring of more and more supplemental troops.

Economic Change and Growing Weakness

A very different Ottoman Empire emerged from this crisis. The sultan once had led armies. Now he mostly resided in his palace and had little experience of the real world, and the affairs of government were overseen more and more by the chief administrators—the grand viziers.

The Janissaries took advantage of their increased power to make membership in their corps hereditary. Their involvement in crafts and trading took a toll on their military skills, but they continued to be a powerful faction in urban politics. Land grants in return for military service also disappeared. Tax farming arose in their place. Tax farmers paid specific taxes, such as customs duties, in advance in return for the privilege of collecting a greater amount from the actual taxpayers.

Rural administration, already disrupted by the rebellions, suffered from the transition to tax farms. The former military landholders had kept order on their lands in order to maintain their incomes. Tax farmers were less likely to live on the land. The imperial government therefore faced greater administrative burdens and came to rely heavily on powerful provincial governors or on wealthy men who purchased lifelong tax collection rights and behaved more or less like private landowners.

Rural disorder and decline in administrative control sometimes opened the way for new economic opportunities. The Aegean port of Izmir° (ancient Smyrna) was able to transform itself between 1580 and 1650 from a small Muslim Turkish town into a multiethnic, multireligious, multilinguistic entrepôt because of the Ottoman government's inability to control trade and the slowly growing dominance of European traders in the Indian Ocean. Local farmers who previously had grown grain for subsistence shifted their plantings more and more to cotton and other cash crops sought by European traders at Izmir. After its introduction in the 1590s, tobacco quickly became popular in the Ottoman Empire despite government prohibitions. In this way, the agricultural economy of western Anatolia, the Balkans, and the Mediterranean coast—the Ottoman lands most accessible to Europe—became enmeshed in the seventeenth century in a growing European commercial network.

The Ottoman Empire lacked both the wealth and the inclination to match European economic advances. Overland trade from the east dwindled as political disorder in Safavid Iran cut deeply into Iranian silk production. Coffee, an Arabian product that rose from obscurity in the fifteenth century to become the rage first in the Ottoman Empire and then in Europe, was grown in the highlands of Yemen and exported by way of Egypt. By 1770, however, Muslim merchants trading in the Yemeni port of Mocha° (literally "the coffee place") were charged 15 percent in duties and fees. But European traders, benefiting from long-standing trade agreements with the Ottoman Empire, paid little more than 3 percent. Such trade agreements led to European domination of Ottoman import and export trade by sea.

To most people, the downward course of imperial power was not evident, much less the reasons behind it. Far from seeing Europe as the enemy that eventually would dismantle the weakening Ottoman Empire, the Istanbul elite experimented with European clothing and furniture styles and purchased printed books from the empire's first (and short-lived) press.

In 1730, however, a conservative Janissary revolt with strong religious overtones toppled Sultan Ahmed III. The rebellion confirmed the perceptions of a few that the Ottoman Empire was facing severe difficulties. But decay at the center spelled benefit elsewhere. In the provinces, ambitious and competent governors, wealthy landholders, urban notables, and nomad chieftains were well placed to take advantage of the central government's weakness.

By the middle of the eighteenth century, groups of Mamluks had regained a dominant position in Egypt, and Janissary commanders had become vir-

---

Izmir (IZ-meer)   **Mocha** (MOH-kuh)

tually independent rulers in Baghdad. Although no region declared full independence, the sultan's power was slipping away to the advantage of a broad array of lower officials and upstart chieftains in all parts of the empire, and the Ottoman economy was reorienting itself toward Europe.

THE SAFAVID EMPIRE

The **Safavid Empire** of Iran (see Map 18.1) resembled its long-time Ottoman foe in many ways: it initially relied militarily on cavalry paid through land grants; its population spoke several different languages; and it was oriented inward away from the sea. It also had distinct qualities that to this day set Iran off from its neighbors: it derived part of its legitimacy from the pre-Islamic dynasties of ancient Iran, and it adopted the Shi'ite form of Islam.

Safavid Society and Religion

The ultimate victor in a complicated struggle for power among Turkish chieftains west of the Ottoman Empire was Ismail°, a boy of Kurdish, Iranian, and Greek ancestry. In 1502, at the age of sixteen, Ismail proclaimed himself shah of Iran and declared that from that time forward, his realm would be devoted to **Shi'ite** Islam, which revered the family of Muhammad's son-in-law Ali. Although Ismail's reasons for compelling Iran's conversion to Shi'ism are unknown, the effect of this radical act was to create a deep chasm between Iran and its neighbors, all of which were Sunni. Iran became a truly separate country for the first time since its incorporation into the Islamic caliphate in the seventh century.

The imposition of Shi'ite belief made the split permanent, but differences between Iran and its neighbors had long been in the making. Persian, written in the Arabic script from the tenth century onward, had emerged as the second language of Is-

Ismail (IS-ma-eel)

lam. Iranian scholars and writers normally read Arabic as well as Persian and sprinkled their writings with Arabic phrases, but their Arab counterparts were much less inclined to learn Persian. After the Mongols destroyed Baghdad, the capital of the Islamic caliphate, in 1258, Iran developed largely on its own, having more extensive contacts with India—where Muslim rulers favored the Persian language—than with the Arabs.

In the post-Mongol period, artistic styles in the East also went their own way. Painted and molded tiles and tile mosaics, often in vivid turquoise blue, became the standard exterior decoration of mosques in Iran but never were used in Syria and Egypt. Persian poets raised verse to peaks of perfection that had no reflection in Arabic poetry, generally considered to be in a state of decline.

To be sure, Islam itself provided a tradition of belief, learning, and law that crossed ethnic and linguistic borders, but Shah Ismail's imposition of Shi'ism set Iran significantly apart. Shi'ite doctrine says that all temporal rulers, regardless of title, are temporary stand-ins for the **"Hidden Imam"**: the twelfth descendant of Ali, the prophet Muhammad's cousin and son-in-law who disappeared as a child in the ninth century. Some Shi'ite scholars concluded that the faithful should calmly accept the world as it was and wait quietly for the Hidden Imam's return. Others maintained that they themselves should play a stronger role in political affairs because they were best qualified to know the Hidden Imam's wishes. These two positions, which still play a role in Iranian Shi'ism, tended to enhance the self-image of religious scholars as independent of imperial authority and stood in the way of their becoming subordinate government functionaries, as happened in the Ottoman Empire.

Shi'ism also affected the psychological life of the people. Annual commemoration of the martyrdom of Imam Husayn (d. 680), Ali's son and the third Imam, regularized an emotional outpouring with no parallel in Sunni lands. Day after day for two weeks, preachers recited the woeful tale to crowds of weeping believers, and elaborate street processions, often organized by craft guilds, parade chanting and self-flagellating men past crowds of reverent onlookers. Of course, Shi'ites elsewhere observed rites of mourning for Imam

Safavid Shah with Attendants and Musicians This painting by Ali-Quli Jubbadar, a European convert working for the Safavid armory, reflects Western influences. Notice the use of light and shadow to model faces and the costume of the attendant to the shah's right. The shah's waterpipe indicates the spread of tobacco, a New World crop, to the Middle East.   (Courtesy of Oriental Institute, Academy of Sciences, Leningrad. Reproduced from *Album of Persian and Indian Miniatures* [Moscow, 1962], ill. no. 98)

Husayn, but the impact of these rites was especially great in Iran, where 90 percent of the population was Shi'ite. Over time, the subjects of the Safavid shahs came to feel more than ever a people apart.

Isfahan and Istanbul

Outwardly, the Ottoman capital of Istanbul looked quite different from Isfahan°, which became Iran's capital in 1598 by decree of **Shah Abbas I** (r. 1587–1629). Built on seven hills on the south side of the narrow Golden Horn inlet, Istanbul boasted a skyline punctuated by the gray stone domes and thin, pointed minarets of the great imperial mosques. The mosques surrounding the royal plaza in Isfahan, in contrast, had unobtrusive minarets and brightly tiled domes that rose to gentle peaks. High walls surrounded the sultan's palace in Istanbul. Shah Abbas in Isfahan focused his capital on the giant royal plaza, which was large enough for his army to play polo, and he used an airy palace overlooking the plaza to receive dignitaries and review his troops.

The harbor of Istanbul, the primary Ottoman seaport, teemed with sailing ships and smaller

craft, many of them belonging to a colony of European merchants perched on a hilltop on the north side of the Golden Horn. Isfahan, far from the sea, was only occasionally visited by Europeans. Most of its trade was in the hands of Jews, Hindus, and especially a colony of Armenian Christians brought in by Shah Abbas.

Beneath these superficial differences, the two capitals had much in common. Wheeled vehicles were scarce in hilly Istanbul and nonexistent in Isfahan. Both cities were built for walking and, aside from the royal plaza in Isfahan, lacked the open spaces common in contemporary European cities. Streets were narrow and irregular. Houses crowded against each other in dead-end lanes. Residents enjoyed their privacy in interior courtyards. Artisans and merchants organized themselves into guilds that had strong social and religious as well as economic bonds. The shops of each guild adjoined each other in the markets.

Women were seldom seen in public, even in Istanbul's mazelike covered market or in Isfahan's long, serpentine bazaar. At home, the women's quarters—called *anderun*°, or "interior," in Iran and *harem,* or "forbidden area," in Istanbul—were separate from the public rooms where the men of

---

Isfahan (is-fah-HAHN)   *anderun* (an-deh-ROON)

the family received visitors. In both areas, low cushions, charcoal braziers for warmth, carpets, and small tables constituted most of the furnishings.

The private side of family life has left few traces, but it is apparent that women's society—consisting of wives, children, female servants, and sometimes one or more eunuchs—was not entirely cut off from the outside world. Ottoman court records reveal that women, using male agents, were very active in the urban real estate market. Often they were selling inherited shares of their father's estate, but some both bought and sold real estate on a regular basis and even established religious endowments for pious purposes. The fact that Islamic law, unlike some European codes, permitted a wife to retain her property after marriage gave some women a stake in the general economy and a degree of independence from their spouses. Women also appeared in other types of court cases, where they often testified for themselves, for Islamic courts did not recognize the role of attorney. Although comparable Safavid court records do not survive, historians assume that a parallel situation prevailed in Iran.

European travelers commented on the veiling of women outside the home, but miniature paintings indicate that ordinary female garb consisted of a long, ample dress with a scarf or long shawl pulled tight over the forehead to conceal the hair. Lightweight trousers, either close-fitting or baggy, were often worn under the dress. This mode of dress was not far different from that of men. Poor men wore light trousers, a long shirt, a jacket, and a hat or turban. Wealthier men wore over their trousers ankle-length caftans, often closely fitted around the chest. The norm for both sexes was complete coverage of arms, legs, and hair.

Public life was almost entirely the domain of men. Poetry and art, both somewhat more elegantly developed in Isfahan than in Istanbul, were as likely to extol the charms of beardless boys as pretty women. Despite religious disapproval of homosexuality, attachments to adolescent boys were neither unusual nor hidden. Women who appeared in public—aside from non-Muslims, the aged, and the very poor—were likely to be slaves. Miniature paintings frequently depict female dancers, musicians, and even acrobats in attitudes and costumes that range from decorous to decidedly erotic.

Despite social similarities, the overall flavors of Isfahan and Istanbul were not the same. Isfahan had its prosperous Armenian quarter across the river from the city's center, but it was not a truly cosmopolitan capital, just as the peoples of the Safavid realm were not remarkably diverse. Like other rulers of extensive land empires, Shah Abbas located his capital toward the center of his domain within comparatively easy reach of any threatened frontier. Istanbul, in contrast, was a great seaport and crossroads located on the straits separating the sultan's European and Asian possessions. People of all sorts lived or spent time in Istanbul: Venetians, Genoese, Arabs, Turks, Greeks, Armenians, Albanians, Serbs, Jews, Bulgarians, and more. In this respect, Istanbul conveyed the cosmopolitan character of major seaports from London to Canton (Guangzhou) and belied the fact that its prosperity rested on the vast reach of the sultan's territories rather than on the voyages of its merchants.

Economic Crisis and Political Collapse

The silk fabrics of northern Iran were the mainstay of the Safavid Empire's foreign trade. However, the manufacture that eventually became most powerfully associated with Iran was the deep-pile carpet made by knotting colored yarns around stretched warp threads. Different cities produced distinctive carpet designs. Women and girls did much of the actual knotting work.

Overall, Iran's manufacturing sector was neither large nor notably productive. Most of the shah's subjects, whether Iranians, Turks, Kurds, or Arabs, lived by subsistence farming or herding. Neither area of activity recorded significant technological advances during the Safavid period.

The Safavids, like the Ottomans, had difficulty finding the money to pay troops armed with firearms. This crisis occurred somewhat later in Iran because of its greater distance from Europe. By the end of the sixteenth century, it was evident that a more systematic adoption of cannon and firearms in the Safavid Empire would be needed to hold off the Ottomans and the Uzbeks° (Turkish rulers who had succeeded the Timurids on Iran's Central Asian frontier; see Map 18.1). Like the Ottoman cavalry a century earlier, the warriors furnished by the nomad leaders were not inclined to trade in their bows for firearms. Shah Abbas responded by establishing a slave corps of year-round soldiers and arming them with guns. The Christian converts to Islam who initially provided the manpower for the new corps were mostly captives taken in raids on Georgia in the Caucasus°.

In the late sixteenth century, the inflation caused by cheap silver spread into Iran; then overland trade through Safavid territory declined because of mismanagement of the silk monopoly after Shah Abbas's death in 1629. As a result, the country faced the unsolvable problem of finding money to pay the army and bureaucracy. Trying to unseat the nomads from their lands to regain control of taxes was more difficult and more disruptive militarily than the piecemeal dismantlement of the land-grant system in the Ottoman Empire. The nomads were still a cohesive military force, and pressure from the center simply caused them to withdraw to their mountain pastures until the pressure subsided. By 1722, the government had become so weak and commanded so little support from the nomadic groups that an army of marauding Afghans was able to capture Isfahan and effectively end Safavid rule.

THE MUGHAL EMPIRE

What distinguished the Indian empire of the Mughal° sultans from the empires of the Ottomans and Safavids was the fact that India was a land of Hindus ruled by a Muslim minority. Muslim dominion in India was the result of repeated military campaigns from the early eleventh century onward, and the Mughals had to contend with the Hindus' long-standing resentment of the destruction of their culture by Muslims. Thus, the challenge facing the Mughals was not just conquering and organizing a large territorial state but also finding a formula for Hindu-Muslim coexistence.

Political Foundations

Babur° (1483–1530), the founder of the **Mughal Empire,** was a Muslim descendant of both Timur and Genghis Khan (*Mughal* is Persian for "Mongol"). Invading from Central Asia, Babur defeated the last Muslim sultan of Delhi in 1526. Babur's grandson **Akbar** (r. 1556–1605), a brilliant but mercurial man, established the central administration of the expanding state. Under him and his three successors—the last of whom died in 1707—all but the southern tip of India fell under Mughal rule, administered first from Agra and then from Delhi°.

Akbar granted land revenues to military officers and government officials in return for their service. Ranks, called *mansabs*°, some high and some low, entitled their holders to revenue assignments. As in the other Islamic empires, revenue grants were not considered hereditary, and the central government kept careful track of their issuance.

With a population of 100 million, a thriving trading economy based on cotton cloth, and a generally efficient administration, India under Akbar was probably the most prosperous empire of the sixteenth century. He and his successors faced few external threats and experienced generally peaceful conditions in their northern Indian heartland.

Foreign trade boomed at the port of Surat in the northwest, which also served as an embarkation point for pilgrims on their way to Mecca. Like the Safavids, the Mughals had no navy or merchant ships. The government saw the Europeans—after Akbar's time, primarily Dutch and English, the Portuguese having lost most of their Indian ports—less as enemies than as shipmasters whose naval support could be procured as needed in return for trading privileges.

Uzbeks (UHZ-bex) Caucasus (CAW-kuh-suhs)
Mughal (MOH-guhl)

Babur (BAH-bur) Delhi (DEL-ee) *mansabs* (MAN-sabz)

**New Year Celebration at the Court of Shah Jahan
(r. 1628–1658)**   The pre-Islamic Iranian tradition of
celebrating the New Year (in Persian *No Ruz*, "New Day") on
March 21, the vernal equinox, spread with Islamic rule. The
dancing girls are a characteristically Indian aspect of the
celebration.   (The Royal Collection © Her Majesty Queen
Elizabeth II)

Hindus and Muslims

The Mughal state inher-
ited traditions of unified
imperial rule from both
the Islamic caliphate and
the more recent examples of Genghis Khan and
Timur. Those traditions did not necessarily mean
religious intolerance. Seventy percent of the *mansabdars*° (officials holding land revenues) appointed under Akbar were Muslim soldiers born
outside India, but 15 percent were Hindus. Most of
the Hindu appointees were warriors from the

north called **Rajputs**°, one of whom rose to be a
powerful revenue minister.

Akbar, the most illustrious ruler of his dynasty,
differed from his Ottoman and Safavid counterparts—Suleiman the Magnificent and Shah Abbas
the Great—in his striving for social harmony and
not just for more territory and revenue. His marriage to a Rajput princess signaled his desire for
reconciliation and even intermarriage between
Muslims and Hindus. The birth of a son in 1569 ensured that future rulers would have both Muslim
and Hindu ancestry.

Akbar ruled that in legal disputes between two
Hindus, decisions would be made according to village custom or Hindu law as interpreted by local
Hindu scholars. Shari'a law was in force for Muslims. Akbar made himself the legal court of last
resort, creating an appeals process not usually present in Islamic jurisprudence.

Akbar also made himself the center of a new
"Divine Faith" incorporating Muslim, Hindu, Zoroastrian, Sikh°, and Christian beliefs. He was
strongly attracted by Sufi ideas, which permeated
the religious rituals he instituted at his court. To
promote serious consideration of his religious
principles, he oversaw, from a catwalk high above
the audience, debates among scholars of all religions assembled in his octagonal private audience
chamber. When courtiers uttered the Muslim exclamation "Allahu Akbar"—"God is great"—they
also understood it in its second grammatical
meaning: "God is Akbar."

Akbar's religious views did not survive him, but
the court culture he fostered, reflecting a mixture
of Muslim and Hindu traditions, flourished until
his zealous great-grandson Aurangzeb° (r. 1658–
1707) reinstituted many restrictions on Hindus.
Mughal and Rajput miniature paintings reveled in
precise portraits of political figures and depictions
of scantily clad women, even though they brought
frowns to the faces of pious Muslims, who deplored the representation of human beings. Most
of the leading painters were Hindus. In addition to
the florid style of Persian verse favored at court, a

mansabdars (man-sab-DAHRZ)

Rajputs (RAHJ-putz)   **Sikh** (sick)
Aurangzeb (ow-rang-ZEB)

new taste developed for poetry and prose in the popular language of the Delhi region. The modern descendant of this language is called *Urdu* in Pakistan and *Hindi* in India.

Central Decay and Regional Challenges

Mughal power did not long survive Aurangzeb's death in 1707. Some historians consider the land-grant system a central element in the rapid decline of imperial authority, but other factors were at play as well. Aurangzeb's additions to Mughal territory in southern India were not all well integrated into the imperial structure, and strong regional powers arose to challenge Mughal military supremacy. A climax came in 1739 when Nadir Shah, the warlord who had seized power in Iran after the fall of the Safavids, invaded the Mughal capital and carried off to Iran the "peacock throne," the priceless jewel-encrusted symbol of Mughal grandeur. Another throne was found for the later Mughals to sit on; but their empire, which survived in name to 1857, was finished.

In 1723, Nizam al-Mulk°, the powerful vizier of the Mughal sultan, gave up on the central government and established his own nearly independent state at Hyderabad in the eastern Deccan. Other officials bearing the title *nawab*° became similarly independent in Bengal and Oudh° in the northeast, as did the Marathas in the center. In the northwest, simultaneous Iranian and Mughal weakness allowed the Afghans to establish an independent kingdom.

Some of these regional powers, and the smaller princely states that arose on former Mughal territory, were prosperous and benefited from the removal of the sultan's heavy hand. Linguistic and religious communities, freed from the religious intolerance instituted during the reign of Aurangzeb, similarly enjoyed greater opportunity for political expression. However, this disintegration of central power favored the intrusion of European adventurers.

Joseph François Dupleix° took over the presidency of the French stronghold of Pondicherry° in 1741 and began a new phase of European involvement in India. He captured the English trading center of Madras and used his small contingent of European and European-trained Indian troops to become a power broker in southern India. Though offered the title *nawab,* Dupleix preferred to operate behind the scenes, using Indian princes as puppets. His career ended in 1754 when he was called home. Deeply involved in wars in Europe, the French government was unwilling to pursue further adventures in India. Dupleix's departure opened the way for the British, whose ventures in India are described in Chapter 22.

TRADE EMPIRES IN THE INDIAN OCEAN

Although the Ottomans, Safavids, and the Mughals did not seriously contest the growth of Portuguese and then Dutch, English, and French maritime power, the majority of non-European shipbuilders, captains, sailors, and traders were Muslim. Groups of Armenian, Jewish, and Hindu traders were also active, but they remained almost as aloof from the Europeans as the Muslims did. The presence in every port of Muslims following the same legal traditions and practicing their faith in similar ways cemented the Muslims' trading network. Islam, from its very outset in the life and preachings of Muhammad (570–632), was always congenial to trade and traders. Unlike Hinduism, it was a proselytizing religion, a factor that encouraged the growth of coastal Muslim communities as local non-Muslims were drawn into Muslim commercial activities, converted, and intermarried with Muslims from abroad.

Although European missionaries, particularly the Jesuits, tried to extend Christianity into Asia and Africa (see Chapters 15 and 17), most Europeans, the Portuguese excepted, were less inclined than the Muslims were to treat local converts or the

---

Nizam al-Mulk (nee-ZAHM al-MULK)   *nawab* (NAH-wab)
Oudh (OW-ad)

Dupleix (doo-PLAY)   Pondicherry (pon-dih-CHER-ree)

offspring of mixed marriages as full members of their communities. As a consequence, Islam spread extensively into East Africa and Southeast Asia during precisely the time of rapid European commercial expansion. Even without the support of the Muslim land empires, Islam became a source of resistance to growing European domination.

Muslims in the East Indies

Historians disagree about the chronology and manner of Islam's spread in Southeast Asia. Arab traders were well known in southern China as early as the eighth century, so Muslims probably reached the East Indies at a similarly early date. Nevertheless, the dominance of Indian cultural influences in the area for several centuries thereafter indicates that early Muslim visitors had little impact on local beliefs. Clearer indications of conversion and the formation of Muslim communities date from roughly the fourteenth century. The strongest overseas linkage is to the port of Cambay in India (see Map 18.2) rather than to the Arab world. Islam took root first in port cities and in some royal courts and spread inland slowly, possibly transmitted by itinerant Sufis.

Although appeals to the Ottoman sultan for support against the Europeans ultimately proved of little use, Islam as a political ideology strengthened resistance to Portuguese, Spanish, and Dutch intruders. When the Spaniards conquered the Philippines during the decades following the establishment of their first fort in 1565, they encountered Muslims on the southern island of Mindanao° and the nearby Sulu archipelago. They called them "Moros," the Spanish term for their old enemies, the Muslims of North Africa. In the ensuing Moro wars, the Spaniards portrayed the Moros as greedy pirates who raided non-Muslim territories for slaves. In fact, they were political, religious, and commercial competitors whose perseverance enabled them to establish the Sulu Empire based in the southern Philippines, one of the strongest states in Southeast Asia from 1768 to 1848.

Other local kingdoms that looked on Islam as a force to counter the aggressive Christianity of the Europeans included the actively proselytizing Brunei° Sultanate in northern Borneo and the **Acheh° Sultanate** in northern Sumatra. At its peak in the early seventeenth century, Acheh succeeded Malacca as the main center of Islamic expansion in Southeast Asia. It prospered from trade in pepper and cotton cloth from Gujarat in India. Acheh declined after the Dutch seized Malacca from Portugal in 1641.

How well Islam was understood in these Muslim kingdoms is open to question. In Acheh, for example, a series of women ruled between 1641 and 1699. This practice came to an end when local Muslim scholars obtained a ruling from scholars in Mecca and Medina that Islam did not approve of female rulers. This ruling became a turning point after which scholarly understandings of Islam gained greater prominence in the East Indies.

Historians have theorized that the first propagators of Islam in Southeast Asia were merchants, Sufi preachers, or both. The scholarly vision of Islam, however, took root in the sixteenth century by way of pilgrims returning from years of study in Mecca and Medina. Islam was the primary force in the dissemination of writing in the region. Some of the returning pilgrims wrote in Arabic, others in Malay or Javanese. As Islam continued to spread, *adat,* a form of Islam rooted in pre-Muslim religious and social practices, retained its preeminence in rural areas over practices centered on the Shari'a, the religious law. But the royal courts in the port cities began to heed the views of the pilgrim teachers, as in their condemnation of female rulers. Though different in many ways, both varieties of Islam provided believers with a firm basis of identification in the face of the growing European presence. Christian missionaries gained most of their converts in regions that had not yet converted to Islam, such as the northern Philippines.

Muslims in East Africa

The East African ports that the Portuguese began to visit in the fifteenth century were governed by Muslim rulers but were not linked politically

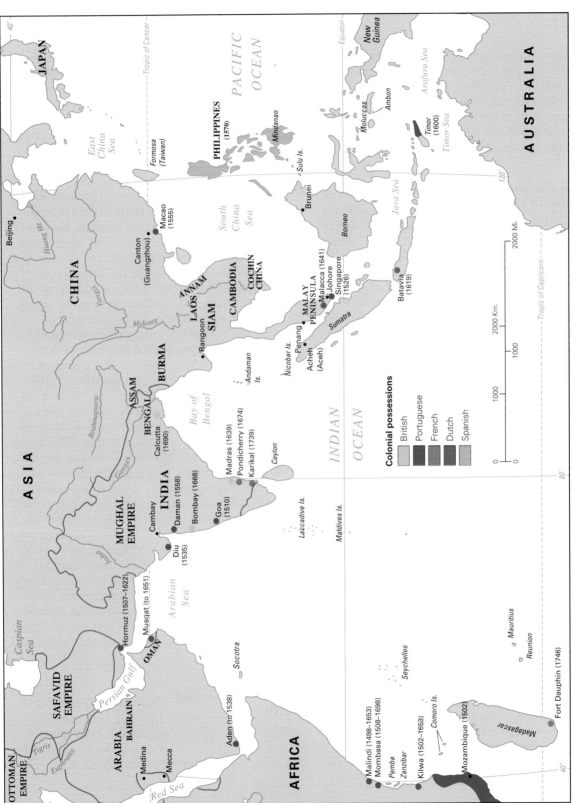

Map 18.2 European Colonization in the Indian Ocean to 1750 Since Portuguese explorers were the first Europeans to reach India by rounding Africa, Portugal gained a strong foothold in both areas. Rival Spain was barred from colonizing the region by the Treaty of Tordesillas in 1494, which limited Spanish efforts to lands west of a line drawn through the mid–Atlantic Ocean. The line carried around the globe provided justification of Spanish colonization in the Philippines. French, British, and Dutch colonies date from after 1600 when joint stock companies provided a new stimulus for overseas commerce.

(see Map 18.2). People living in the millet and rice lands of the Swahili Coast—from the Arabic *sawahil°* meaning "coasts"—had little contact with those in the dry hinterlands. Throughout this period, the East African lakes region and the highlands of Kenya witnessed unprecedented migration and relocation of peoples because of drought conditions that persisted from the late sixteenth through most of the seventeenth century.

Cooperation among the trading ports of Kilwa, Mombasa, and Malindi was hindered by the thick bush country that separated the cultivated tracts of coastal land and by the fact that the ports competed with one another in the export of ivory; ambergris° (a whale by-product used in perfumes); and forest products such as beeswax, copal tree resin, and wood (Kilwa also exported gold). In the eighteenth century, slave trading, primarily to Arabian ports but also to India, increased in importance. Because Europeans—the only peoples who kept consistent records of slave-trading activities—played a minor role in this slave trade, few records have survived to indicate its extent. Perhaps the best estimate is that 2.1 million slaves were exported between 1500 and 1890, a little over 12.5 percent of the total traffic in African slaves during that period (see Chapter 17).

The Portuguese conquered all of the coastal ports from Mozambique northward except Malindi, with whose ruler Portugal cooperated. A Portuguese description of the ruler indicates some of the cloth and metal goods that Malindi imported, as well as some local manufactures:

> The King wore a robe of damask trimmed with green satin and a rich [cap]. He was seated on two cushioned chairs of bronze, beneath a rough sunshade of crimson satin attached to a pole. An old man, who attended him as a page, carried a short sword in a silver sheath. There were many players on [horns], and two trumpets of ivory richly carved and of the size of a man, which were blown through a hole in the side, and made sweet harmony with the [horns].[1]

Initially, the Portuguese favored the port of Malindi, which caused the decline of Kilwa and Mombasa. Repeatedly plagued by local rebellion, Portuguese power suffered severe blows when the Arabs of **Oman** in southeastern Arabia captured their south Arabian stronghold at Musqat (1650) and then went on in support of African resistance to seize Mombasa (1698), which had become the Portuguese capital in East Africa. The Portuguese briefly retook Mombasa but lost control permanently in 1729. From then on, the Portuguese had to content themselves with Mozambique in Africa and a few remaining ports in India (Goa) and farther east (Macao and Timor).

The Omanis created a maritime empire of their own, but one that worked in greater cooperation with the African populations. The Bantu language of the coast, broadened by the absorption of Arabic, Persian, and Portuguese loan words, developed into **Swahili°,** which was spoken throughout the region. Arabs and other Muslims who settled in the region intermarried with local families, giving rise to a mixed population that played an important role in developing a distinctive Swahili culture.

Islam also spread in the southern Sudan in this period, particularly in the dry areas away from the Nile River. This growth coincided with a waning of Ethiopian power as a result of Portugal's stifling of trade in the Red Sea. Yet no significant contact developed between the emerging Muslim Swahili culture and that of the Muslims in the Sudan, to the north.

The Coming of the Dutch

The Dutch played a major role in driving the Portuguese from their possessions in the East Indies. They were better organized than the Portuguese through the Dutch East India Company (see Chapter 17). Just as the Portuguese had tried to dominate the trade in spices, so the Dutch concentrated at first on the spice-producing islands of Southeast Asia. The Portuguese had seized Malacca, a strategic town on the narrow strait at the end of the Malay Peninsula, from a local Malay ruler in 1511. The Dutch took it away from them in

---

sawahil (suh-WAH-hil) **ambergris** ((AM-ber-grees)

Swahili (swah-HEE-lee)

1641, leaving Portugal little foothold in the East Indies except the islands of Ambon° and Timor (see Map 18.2).

Although the United Netherlands was one of the least autocratic countries of Europe, the governors-general appointed by the Dutch East India Company deployed almost unlimited powers in their efforts to maintain their trade monopoly. They could even order the execution of their own employees for "smuggling"—that is, trading on their own. Under strong governors-general, the Dutch fought a series of wars against Acheh and other local kingdoms on Sumatra and Java. In 1628 and 1629, their new capital at **Batavia,** now the city of Jakarta on Java, was besieged by a fleet of fifty ships belonging to the sultan of Mataram°, a Javanese kingdom. The Dutch held out with difficulty and eventually prevailed when the sultan was unable to get effective help from the English.

Suppressing local rulers, however, was not enough to control the spice trade once other European countries adopted Dutch methods, became more knowledgeable about where goods might be acquired, and started to send more ships to Southeast Asia. In the course of the eighteenth century, therefore, the Dutch gradually turned from being a middleman for Southeast Asian producers and European buyers to being a producer of crops in areas they controlled, notably in Java. Javanese teak forests yielded high-quality lumber, and coffee, transplanted from Yemen, grew well in the hilly regions of western Java. In this new phase of colonial export production, Batavia developed from being the headquarters town of a far-flung enterprise to being the administrative capital of a conquered land.

Beyond the East Indies, the Dutch utilized their discovery of a band of powerful eastward-blowing winds (called the "Roaring Forties" because they blow throughout the year between 40 and 50 degrees south latitude) to reach Australia in 1606. In 1642 and 1643, Abel Tasman became the first European to set foot on Tasmania and New Zealand and to sail around Australia, signaling European involvement in that region.

CONCLUSION

It is no coincidence that the Mughal, Safavid, and Ottoman Empires declined simultaneously in the seventeenth and eighteenth centuries. The complex changes in military technology and in the world economy that were underway in smaller European countries either passed them by or affected them adversely. Despite their efforts on conquering more and more land, these land-based empires faced increasing difficulty in maintaining traditional military forces paid through land grants.

The opposite was true for seafaring countries intent on turning trade networks into maritime empires. Improvements in ship design, navigation accuracy, and the use of cannon gave an ever-increasing edge to European powers competing with local seafaring peoples. In contrast to the age-old Asian tradition that imperial wealth came from control of broad expanses of agricultural land, European countries promoted joint-stock companies and luxuriated in the prosperity gained from their ever increasing control of Indian Ocean commerce.

That a major shift in world economic and political alignments was well under way by the late seventeenth century was scarcely perceivable in those parts of Asia and Africa ruled by the Ottoman and Mughal sultans and the Safavid shahs. They relied mostly on land taxes, usually indirectly collected via holders of land grants or tax farmers, rather than on customs duties or control of markets to fill the government coffers. With ever-increasing military expenditures, these taxes fell short of the rulers' needs. Oblivious to the fundamental problem basic with the entire economic system, imperial courtiers pursued their luxurious ways, poetry and the arts continued to flourish, and the quality of manufacturing and craft production remained generally high. Eighteenth-century European observers marveled no less at the riches and industry of these eastern lands than at the fundamental weakness of their political and military systems.

Ambon (am-BOHN)   **Mataram** (MAH-ah-ram)

■ Key Terms

Ottoman Empire	Akbar
Suleiman the Magnificent	*mansabs*
Janissaries	Rajputs
Safavid Empire	Acheh Sultanate
Shi'ite	Oman
Hidden Imam	Swahili
Shah Abbas I	Batavia
Mughal Empire	

■ Suggested Reading

The best comprehensive and comparative account of the post-Mongol Islamic land empires, with an emphasis on social history, is Ira Lapidus, *A History of Islamic Societies* (1988). For a brief, general introduction to the relations between the Muslim land empires and the development of Indian Ocean trade, see Patricia Risso, *Merchants and Faith: Muslim Commerce and Culture in the Indian Ocean* (1995).

On the Ottoman Empire, the standard political history is Stanford J. Shaw, *History of the Ottoman Empire and Modern Turkey,* vol. 1, *Empire of the Ghazis: The Rise and Decline of the Ottoman Empire, 1280–1808* (1976). Jason Goodwin, *Lords of the Horizons: A History of the Ottoman Empire* (1999), offers a more readable and journalistic account.

The most comprehensive treatment of the history of Safavid Iran is in the articles in Peter Jackson and Laurence Lockhart, eds., *The Cambridge History of Iran,* vol. 6, *The Timurid and Safavid Periods* (1986). For the artistic side of Safavid history, abundantly illustrated, see Anthony Welch, *Shah Abbas and the Arts of Isfahan* (1973).

A highly readable work that situates the Mughal Empire within the overall history of the subcontinent is Stanley Wolpert, *A New History of India,* 4th ed. (1993). For a broad treatment of the entire development of Islamic society in India with emphasis on the Mughal period, see S. M. Ikram, *History of Muslim Civilization in India and Pakistan* (1989). Wheeler Thackston has made a lively translation of Babur's autobiography in *The Baburnama: Memoirs of Babur, Prince and Emperor* (1996). For a comprehensive history of the Mughals, see John F. Richards, *The Mughal Empire* (1993).

■ Note

1. Esmond Bradley Martin and Chryssee Perry Martin, *Cargoes of the East: The Ports, Trade and Culture of the Arabian Seas and Western Indian Ocean* (London: Elm Tree Books, 1978), 17.

19

EASTERN EURASIA,
1500–1800

New Relations in Eurasia • The Russian Empire • The Later Ming
and Early Qing Empires • Tokugawa Japan, to 1800
SOCIETY AND CULTURE: Style and Conversion: Christian Rivalries in Beijing

n the 1650s, two expanding empires battled for control of Siberia, the Amur° River basin, and the Pacific coast of northern Asia. Hardy Russian scouts, mostly Cossacks, came east across the tundra, hoping to stake an early claim to the great Amur waterway. They built wooden forts on its northern bank, but they were countered by Manchu agents of the Qing° Empire based in China, which hoped to secure the same stretch of Pacific coast the Russians sought. The Manchus built wooden forts on the southern bank of the Amur.

Neither empire sent large forces into the Amur territories, and the contest was mostly a struggle for the goodwill of the local Evenk and Dagur peoples. The Qing emperor emphasized the importance of treading lightly in the struggle and well understood the principles of espionage:

Upon reaching the lands of the Evenks and the Dagurs you will send to announce that you have come to hunt deer. Meanwhile, keep a careful record of the distance and go, while hunting, along the northern bank of the Amur until you come by the shortest route to the town of Russian settlement at Albazin. Thoroughly reconnoitre its location and situation. I don't think the Russians will take a chance on attacking you. If they offer you food, accept it and show your gratitude.[1]

That delicacy gives a false impression of the intensity of the struggle between these two great empires. The contest was partly for dominance in the new northeast Asian economy of furs, timber, and metals concentrated in Siberia, Manchuria, and Yakutsk. But even without the attraction of those specific resources, the Amur River would have been critical in the interplay of the two empires, because each had an overriding need to protect itself against the other. The kingdoms of Europe, and even Europe's emerging sea-based empires, were small in comparison

---

Amur (AH-moor)   **Qing** (ching)

with these titanic Eurasian empires. Where the Russian and Qing Empires faced each other—in Central Asia, in Mongolia, and in Northeast Asia—they had to expend great resources conquering and defending lands that in the long run yielded very little profit. But for either to have flinched would have meant disaster at the hands of the other.

In 1689, the Qing and Russian Empires formalized their stand-off with a treaty establishing a border and a set of customs regulations. Russia was denied access to the Pacific coast east of the Amur, but the Russians exploited a more northerly route to explore the North Pacific and colonize the northwestern coast of North America.

For the Russian and Qing Empires, size, agriculture, and infrastructure for overland communication and transport were of the greatest importance. When challenged by the new empires of Europe, the Russian and Qing Empires faced common problems and experienced similar outcomes. The response of Japan was spectacularly different. That small, relatively remote nation had been a minor player in Asian affairs but was able to withstand economic and political changes more effectively than Asia's greatest empires.

As you read this chapter, ask yourself the following questions:

- What did the Russian and Qing Empires have in common? How do their similarities explain the tensions between them?

- What were the Russian and Qing attitudes toward Europe in the times of Peter the Great and Emperor Kangxi? What were the long-term consequences of these attitudes?

- What explains the greater speed of Japanese economic and technological development in the 1700s?

New Relations in Eurasia

After 1500, no single power controlled all of Central Asia, and no unified economic policy protected and promoted trade. Large and ambitious empires based in the Middle East, in Russia, and in China competed for control of parts of Central Asia, and this competition deepened their conflicts with the remaining Mongol groups and further depressed both travel and profitable trade. As the 1500s passed, the transporting of many goods by caravan between East Asia and the Middle East was neither cheap nor reliable. Oasis cities that had been rich and cosmopolitan in the days when overland trade was vigorous became isolated. Their governors were often hostile to outside influences.

Along the southern and eastern coasts of Eurasia, merchants from Europe, the Middle East, and Asia were taking advantage of the new global trade connections. Seaborne trade was now cheaper, faster, and more reliable than overland trade.

Ancient Asian ports that had become rich from centuries of trade found new economic stimulation from the development of European commerce. China, and later Japan, were also beneficiaries of this new trade and sought means of cushioning the effects of globalization on their own economies and societies. Russia, in contrast, had to enter a period of renewed and more militant expansion or risk being left out of the Pacific trade.

The Land-Based Empires of Eurasia

The Portuguese, Spanish, and Dutch Empires relied on the sea for contact with their colonies. For the Ottoman, Russian, Mughal, and Ming Empires, things were very different. They were land-based empires and much larger than the sea-based empires of Europe. Their self-defense was extremely expensive. They had fewer choices than their smaller European contemporaries about where to expand and how to enrich themselves after they expanded.

Central Asia remained the strategic center of competition for the land-based Eurasian empires. Much of Central Asia, however, was arid steppes or desert, and its commercial importance had declined steeply by 1500. Maintaining garrisons in these regions was extremely expensive, for food, weapons, animals, and even building materials had to be brought in from far away. The best hope of eventually making these territories self-supporting lay in the development of agriculture and mining, which required the introduction of large-scale irrigation, crops able to thrive in cold and dry climates, extensive new roads, and large numbers of settlers or prisoners to serve as laborers. The Russian and Qing Empires achieved some success in agriculture and mining, but the costs were steep.

The challenge to make large, unprofitable areas in the land-based Eurasian empires self-supporting reinforced the emphasis on agriculture as the predominant source of wealth and government tax revenues. It also reinforced the tendency toward political centralization. If the herculean task of environmental transformation across Central Asia and parts of northern Asia was to be achieved, imperial governments had to be in full command of the massive resources necessary for development of the infrastructure. Forced labor by the domestic population persisted in the Russian and Qing Empires after it was abandoned in Europe; in Russia, serfdom became more brutal and widespread in the seventeenth and eighteenth centuries than ever before.

In the long run, these empires were at a disadvantage in the competition with the sea-based empires of Europe. The Europeans concentrated on the colonization of profitable areas, linked the development of commerce to the enrichment of their central governments, and enlisted the aid of joint-stock companies to acquire and develop territories. Between 1500 and about 1800, the land-based empires of Eurasia were the largest administrative and economic systems in the world, but they posed more of a danger to each other than they faced from any of the sea-based empires of Europe.

New Global Influences

The European entities that first challenged Russia and the Qing were not states. In the sixteenth and seventeenth centuries, the Society of Jesus and the East India companies created ties between Asia and Europe. One of the first **Jesuits,** Francis Xavier, went to India in the mid-sixteenth century looking for converts and later traveled throughout Southeast and East Asia. He spent two years in Japan and died in 1552 in China. Following Xavier, other Jesuits had a significant influence in China and presented Europeans with an intriguing picture of Asian life.

China reaped some material benefits from contact with the Jesuits. Chinese converts to Catholicism were important in introducing European techniques of crop production, irrigation, and engineering. The outstanding Jesuit of late Ming China, Matteo Ricci° (1552–1610), became expert in the Chinese language and an accomplished scholar of the Confucian classics. He and other Jesuits in China made a deep impression on the Ming elites at Beijing° and also in the wealthy, cosmopolitan cities of the Yangzi River delta and the southern China coast. The Society of Jesus was the most prominent transmitter of European science and technology to China and of Chinese philosophy and literature to Europe.

European merchant ships carried the Jesuits to East Asia. First came the Portuguese, who after 1500 dominated the spice trade of the Moluccas and Java and the trade routes around India. The Spanish also were interested in the trade and established a small base on the island of Taiwan, off the coast of southeast China. Soon after 1600, the Dutch dislodged the Portuguese and Spanish from Taiwan. To secure their influence in East Asia and to discredit their rivals, representatives of the Dutch East India Company (VOC) willingly complied with Chinese rituals by which foreigners were supposed to acknowledge the moral superiority of the emperor of China. The Dutch also got along well with the rulers of Japan and retained exclusive permission to live on an island off Nagasaki°, after other Europeans were banned from the country. Outside Japan, however, the VOC faced a strong

---

Matteo Ricci (ma-TAY-o REE-chee) **Beijing** (bay-JING)
Nagasaki (nah-gah-SAH-kee)

CHRONOLOGY

	Russia	China and Central Asia	Korea and Japan
1500			
	1547 Ivan IV tsar		
	1582 Cossacks conquer Khanate of Sibir		**1582** Japanese invasion of Korea
1600	**1613–1645** Rule of Mikhail, the first Romanov tsar	**1601** Matteo Ricci active in Ming China	**1600** Decisive battle begins Tokugawa Shogunate
		1644 Qing conquest of Beijing	**1649** Closing of Japan
		1662–1722 Rule of Emperor Kangxi	
	1689–1725 Rule of Peter the Great	**1689** Treaty of Nerchinsk with Russia	
		1691 Qing control of Inner Mongolia	
1700	**1712** St. Petersburg becomes Russia's capital	**1736–1795** Rule of Emperor Qianlong	
		1755 Qing conquest of Turkestan	
	1762–1796 Rule of Catherine the Great		
	1799 Alaska becomes a Russian colony		

rival in the East India Company of England, chartered by Queen Elizabeth I in 1600.

The European trading companies and the Jesuits are examples of the global organizations that became conduits between Asia and Europe. But in the 1700s, these organizations were viewed with suspicion by imperial authorities in Europe as well as in Asia.

selves on their southern border with Turkestan. Instead, they could turn their attention toward eastern Eurasia, including Mongolia and **Siberia,** and even to the Pacific coast. The expanding European empires diminished the need to maintain western and southern boundaries against the Ottoman Empire somewhat, because the Europeans held the line against further Ottoman expansion in the Balkans and began to challenge and distract the Ottomans in the eastern Mediterranean.

THE RUSSIAN EMPIRE

The shift toward the seas and away from inland Asia presented both challenges and opportunities to the rising Russian Empire. The fragmentation of political power in Central Asia lessened the pressure on the Russian rulers to defend them-

The Rise of Romanov Power

After the dissolution of Mongol power in Russia, the city of Moscow became the foundation for a new state, **Muscovy**°. By 1500, Muscovy dominated the lands that had been controlled by the

Muscovy (MUSS-koe-vee)

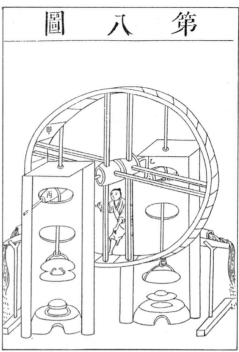

From the Jesuit Library at Beijing   Jesuits such as Matteo Ricci were willing to share books on technology and science with Chinese scholars. But without firsthand experience, it was impossible for Chinese translators to convey how the devices actually worked. Here, a man walking in a wheel drives a shaft that changes the pressure inside two pumps. In the Chinese translation of the drawing, the mechanisms were all lost.   (Left: From Zonca, *Trombe da Rota per Vavar Aqua* [1607]. Right: "Diagram Number Eight" from *Qi tushuo* [*Illustrations on Energy*] [1627]. Both courtesy of Joseph Needham, *Science and Civilization in China*, vol. 4)

Kievan state. By the mid-sixteenth century, Novgorod, which had been independent since the twelfth century, was absorbed. To mark the extension of Muscovy and of his personal power, the Muscovite ruler Ivan IV ("the Terrible") assumed the title **tsar** (from "caesar") in 1547. Within a few years, Ivan expanded Russia's borders far to the east through the conquest of the Khanates of Kazan and Astrakhan and the northern Caucasus region (see Map 19.1).

The westward extension of the territories ruled by Ivan IV and his successors did not progress much thereafter. Instead, Russia had to defend itself more strenuously on the European front. In the early seventeenth century, Swedish and Polish forces briefly occupied Moscow on separate occasions. In the midst of this "Time of Troubles," the old line of Muscovite rulers was finally deposed, and the Russian aristocracy—the *boyar*s°—allowed one of their own, **Mikhail Romanov°,** to become tsar (r. 1613–1645).

The early Romanov rulers realized that consolidation of their own authority and successful competition with neighboring powers went together. Options for Russian expansion were limited. The Ottoman Empire controlled the Balkans and Black Sea, the Safavid rulers of Iran dominated southern Central Asia, and Sweden controlled the Baltic Sea. The obvious direction for expansion was east.

---

boyar (BOY-ar)   **Romanov** (ROE-man-off or roe-MAN-off)

Map 19.1   The Expansion of Russia, 1500–1800   Sweden and Poland initially blocked Russian expansion in Europe, while the Ottoman Empire blocked the southwest. In the sixteenth century, Russia began to expand east, toward Siberia and the Pacific Ocean. By the end of the rule of Catherine the Great in 1796, Russia encompassed all of northern and northeastern Eurasia.

Russians and Turks

Under the Romanov dynasty, the divisions between Russians and Turks tended to be represented as conflicts between Christians and "infidels" or between the civilized and the "barbaric." Despite this rhetoric, it is important to understand that the interplay of Turkic (Central Asian) and Russian (Slavic) influences was what produced the Russian Empire. These cultural groups were defined not by blood ties but by the way in which they lived.

A revealing example is the **Cossacks.** Their name comes from a Turkic word for a warrior or mercenary and is related to the modern name *Kazakh.* The word *Cossack* in various forms seems to have first emerged in the Ukraine, where it referred to bands of people living on the steppes, herding or robbing for their livelihoods. But the Cossacks of the Ukraine were a diverse group. Many were escaped serfs from Muscovy or Lithuania; others were wandering Turks or Cumans, Poles, Hungarians, or Mongols. Who their ancestors were was irrelevant. What mattered was that they lived in close-knit bands, were superb riders and fighters, and were feared by both the villagers and the legal authorities.

The Muscovite and early Romanov rulers decided to take no chances with the Cossacks, but Russia also desired to exploit the Cossacks' extraordinary military spirit and skills. The empire reached an accommodation with them, enrolling them in special military regiments and allowing them to live in autonomous villages. In return, the Cossacks performed distinctive service for Russia, defending against Swedish and Ottoman incursions in the west and leading campaigns for exploration, conquest, and settlement in the east.

The Cossacks were an example of the ways in which Russia combined elements considered "Turk" with those considered "Russian." They displayed the military skills of Asian horsemen but were Russian speakers, Christians, and in most cases willing participants in the building of the Russian Empire.

Peter the Great

Peter the Great, who ruled Russia from 1689 to 1725, was determined to secure a warm-water port on the Black Sea. Peter described his wars with the Ottoman Empire as a new crusade to liberate Constantinople (now Istanbul) from the Muslim sultans. He also claimed the right to function as the legal protector of Orthodox Christians living in the Balkan territories under Ottoman rule. Peter's forces seized the port of Azov in 1696, but the fortress was lost again in 1713, and Russian expansion southward was blocked for the rest of Peter's reign.

Peter was more successful in his campaigns in the west. In the long and costly Great Northern War (1700–1721), his modernized armies broke Swedish control of the Baltic Sea, establishing direct contacts between Russia and Europe. Peter's victory forced the European powers to recognize Russia as a major power for the first time. Taking advantage of his new prestige in Europe, he built a new city, St. Petersburg, on land captured from Sweden. In 1712, the city became Russia's capital. Peter intended St. Petersburg to be a model to Russian elites seeking to absorb European culture and a demonstration to Europeans of Russian sophistication. Houses were to be built in the baroque style then fashionable in western Europe. Nobles were ordered to wear western styles and shave their beards. Peter attempted to end the traditional seclusion of upper-class Russian women by requiring officials, officers, and merchants to bring their wives to the social gatherings he organized in the capital.

There was also a political objective in building the new capital: Peter intended to break the power of the boyars by sharply reducing their traditional roles in government and the army. The old boyar council of Moscow was replaced by a group of advisers in St. Petersburg whom the tsar appointed. Members of the traditional nobility continued to serve as generals and admirals, but officers in Peter's modern, professional army and navy were promoted according to merit, not birth.

Peter admired European technology and culture, but he had no intention of following the movement of the Netherlands and Britain toward political liberalization. The goal of Westernization was to strengthen the Russian state and the institutions of personal power that the Russians called **autocracy.** A decree of 1716 proclaimed that the tsar "is not obliged to answer to anyone in the world for his doings, but possesses power and authority over his kingdom and land, to rule them at his will and pleasure as a Christian ruler." Under this expansive definition of his role, Peter brought the Russian Orthodox Church firmly under state control, built factories and iron and copper foundries to provide munitions and supplies for the military, and increased the burdens of taxes and forced labor on the serfs. **Serfs**—the great mass of Russian people, forced by law and custom to work the land of their overlords—could have been freed as part of Peter's reform. But there was no move to abolish serf status, because the Russian Empire was dependent on serfs for the production of basic foodstuffs.

The Russian Drive Eastward

Long before Peter's time, Russian rulers realized that the eastern frontier was wide open to Russian expansion because no other great empire controlled the northern tier of Asia. Russian exploration of Siberia began in the time of Ivan IV and was led by a Cossack, Yermak Timofeyovich°. By force of their rifles, Yermak's troops attacked the only political power in the region, the Khanate of Sibir in 1582. Yermak himself did not survive to return to Moscow, but Cossacks remained in the forefront of Russian campaigns to conquer and settle Siberia.

Siberian furs and timber were the first valued resources; after 1700, gold, coal, and iron also became important. By the 1650s, Cossack explorers had claimed the Amur Valley for the Russian Empire, and many villages along the Amur River were rendering tribute to Russian officials. Through the 1650s, clashes occurred between these soldiers and soldiers of the Qing Empire stationed near the river. To deprive the Russians of the goods rendered by the Amur villagers, the Qing Empire forcibly resettled native peoples westward in Qing territory.

By the late 1600s, the Russian and Qing rulers saw that their interests lay in a diplomatic agreement that would delineate their borders in Mongolia, Siberia, and the Amur River Valley, as well as fix trade and tariff regulations across their borders. The Treaty of Nerchinsk in 1689 was a strategic coup for both empires, and it was reinforced in the Treaty of Kiakhta in 1727.

The immediate results were two. First, Mongol groups lost the leverage they had gained by exploiting Russian and Qing competition. Thereafter, the Mongols steadily declined as a power, and the Qing Empire quickly consolidated its control over Mongolia and Central Asia. Second, with a fixed boundary and Siberia inside it, Russia could concentrate on further eastern expansion, all the way to the Pacific and into North America. When Catherine the Great (r. 1762–1796) died, Russian reach extended from Poland in the west to Alaska in the east and was still growing.

THE LATER MING AND EARLY QING EMPIRES

The economic and cultural achievements of the **Ming Empire** continued until 1600. An international market eager for Ming porcelain (called "china"), as well as for silk and lacquered furniture, stimulated the commercial development of East Asia, the Indian Ocean, and Europe.

The End of the Ming

This apparent golden age, however, was beset by serious problems that by the year 1600 left the Ming Empire economically exhausted, politically deteriorating, and technologically lagging behind both its East Asian neighbors and Europe. Some of these problems were the result of natural disasters associated with climate change. Average temperatures dropped, reached a low point about 1645, then remained low until the early 1700s. The resulting agricultural distress and famine fueled large uprisings that speeded the end of the Ming Empire. The devastation caused by these uprisings and the

---

Yermak Timofeyovich (YAIR-mak tih-mo-FAY-oh-vich)

Power and Youth   Emperor Kangxi (left) and Peter the Great (right) were contemporaries, great rulers, and rivals for control of Central and Northeast Asia. Both were child-emperors who outwitted their elders to achieve personal rule and then pursued all avenues of knowledge to strengthen their empires. But their youthful portraits show differences: Peter is depicted here while he was a student in Holland in 1697, learning engineering and shipbuilding. Kangxi, in a portrait from about 1690, preferred to be portrayed as a refined scholar.   (left: The Palace Museum, Beijing; right: Collection, Countess Bobrinskoy/Michael Holford)

spread of epidemic diseases resulted in steep declines in local populations.

Other kinds of global change also affected China. American silver flooded into China in exchange for goods sold to Europe. As the amount of silver in circulation rose, its relative value fell. Nevertheless, the Ming government maintained a strict ratio in price between silver coins and copper coins. As silver declined in value, more and more copper was needed to make purchases and pay taxes. In a time of worsening economic and population conditions, the consequent inflation hit the rural population especially hard.

Environmental and economic stress do not in themselves destroy societies. Indeed, both the eastern Mongols and the Manchus centralized their political systems and increased the territories under their control in the 1600s, all at the expense of the Ming Empire. The importance of global factors in the demise of the Ming must be placed in the context of the special factors operating on China.

For the entire later Ming period, the boundaries of the empire were critical to its health. The Mongols remained strong in the north. The **Manchus** grew stronger in the northeast. In the southwest, there were repeated uprisings among native peoples crowded by the immigration of Chinese farmers. Pirates based in Okinawa and in Taiwan frequently looted the southeastern coastal towns. Ming military resources, concentrated against the Mongols and the Manchus in the north, could not be deployed to defend the coasts. As a result, many southern Chinese migrated to Southeast Asia to profit from the sea trading networks of the Indian Ocean.

After decades of weakening control, the Ming ruler was deposed when rebellious forces captured Beijing. The imperial family left the city, but a Ming general entered into an agreement with Manchu leaders, inviting them to take Beijing from the rebels. The Manchu did so in the summer of 1644 but did not restore the Ming. They claimed China for their own and began a forty-year conquest of the rest of the Ming territories.

Power and Trade in the Early Qing

The new **Qing Empire** was ruled by a Manchu imperial family, and Manchus were the leaders of the military forces. But Manchus were a very small portion of the population, and from its beginnings, the empire was dependent on diverse peoples for its achievements. Though the Qing style of rule was multilingual and international, the overwhelming majority of officials, soldiers, merchants, and farmers were Chinese.

Before the year 1700, the Qing gained south China, and for the first time the island of Taiwan was incorporated into an empire based in China (see Map 19.2). The Qing Empire also conquered

Map 19.2   The Qing Empire, 1644–1783   The Qing Empire began in Manchuria and captured north China in 1644. Between 1644 and 1783, the Qing conquered all the former Ming territories and added Taiwan, the lower Amur River basin, Inner Mongolia, eastern Turkestan, and Tibet. The resulting state was more than twice the size of the Ming Empire.

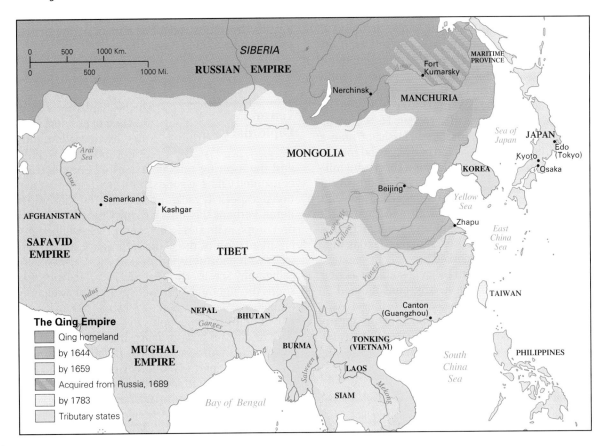

Mongolia and Central Asia. The seventeenth and eighteenth centuries in China—particularly the reigns of the Kangxi° (r. 1662–1722) and Qianlong° (r. 1736–1796) emperors—were a period of great economic, military, and cultural achievement.

The early Qing emperors wished to foster economic and demographic recovery in China. They repaired the roads and waterworks, lowered transit taxes, mandated comparatively low rents and interest rates, and helped resettle the areas devastated during the peasant rebellions of the late Ming period. Foreign trade was encouraged. Korea, Vietnam, Burma, and Nepal sent regular embassies to the Qing tribute court and carried the latest Chinese fashions back home. Overland routes of communication were revived.

Emperor Kangxi

The early Qing conquest of Beijing and north China was carried out under the leadership of a group of Manchu aristocrats who dominated the first Qing emperor based in China and were regents for his young son, who was declared emperor in 1662. This child-emperor, Kangxi, spent several years doing political battle with his regents, and in 1669 he gained real as well as formal control of the government by executing his chief regent. **Kangxi** was then sixteen. He was an intellectual prodigy who mastered classical Chinese, Manchu, and Mongolian at an early age and memorized the Chinese classics. He was a successful military commander who personally led troops in the great campaigns that brought Mongolia under Qing control by 1691. He battled with and then made peace with the Russian Empire and negotiated complex domestic political crises. His reign, lasting until his death in 1722, was marked not only by great expansion of the empire but by great stability as well.

As the Qing conquest was consolidated in north China, south China, and Northeast Asia, maps in the European style—reflecting the century of Jesuit influence at the Ming court—were created as practical guides to the newly conquered regions

and as symbols of Qing dominance. Kangxi considered introducing the European calendar, but protests were so strong that the plan was dropped. The emperor himself remained friendly with the Jesuits and frequently discussed scientific and philosophical issues with them (see Society and Culture: Style and Conversion: Christian Rivalries in Beijing). When he fell ill with malaria in the 1690s, he relied on Jesuit medical expertise (in this case, the use of quinine) for his recovery. He ordered the creation of illustrated books in Manchu detailing European anatomical and pharmaceutical knowledge.

The exchange of information between the Qing and the Europeans that Kangxi had fostered was never one-way. When the Jesuits informed the Qing court on matters of anatomy, for instance, the Qing were able to demonstrate to the Jesuits an early form of inoculation, called **variolation,** that had been used to stem the spread of smallpox after the Qing conquest of Beijing. Similarly, the enormous imperial factories that produced porcelain inspired the industrial management of practices of Josiah Wedgwood in England.

Tea and Diplomacy

The brilliant successes of the Qing in conquest and trade excited admiration in Europe. The wealthy and the aspiring middle classes of Europe avidly consumed Chinese goods, both genuine and imitations, especially silk, porcelain, and decorative items. Perhaps the most striking Chinese influence on European homes in this period was wallpaper—an adaptation of the Chinese practice of covering walls with enormous loose-hanging watercolors or calligraphy scrolls. By the mid-1700s, special workshops throughout China were producing wallpaper and other consumer items for export to Europe.

In political philosophy, too, the Europeans felt they had something to learn from the early Qing emperors. In the late 1770s, poems supposedly written by Emperor Qianlong were translated into French and disseminated through the intellectual circles of western Europe. These works depicted the Qing emperors as benevolent despots who

Kangxi (KAHNG-shee)   Qianlong (chee-YEN-loong)

Style and Conversion: Christian Rivalries in Beijing

The Treaty of Nerchinsk (1689) presented new opportunities for Russian missionaries in Beijing to continue their work of ministering to Russians in Beijing as well as spreading Orthodox Christianity in China. They failed to gain converts, largely because they did not learn Chinese. But they believed their failure was due to the interference of the Jesuits, who had arrived before them, knew Chinese, and made themselves indispensable in diplomatic communications between the Qing and Russian courts. In 1722, leaders of the Orthodox Church wrote the following comment to the new head of the Russian mission in Beijing.

It would be prudent if you kept your rank of bishop a secret, because your status might arouse opposition among our enemies—especially our main enemies, the Jesuits. They are constantly creating troubles between us and others, as well as strife among ourselves, in order to frustrate our good works. Of course it could not be otherwise, for remember that Jesus cried out to the Father, "Lord, have I not sown good seed? Where have these weeds come from?" And the Lord said, "The Devil has done this."

For their part, the Jesuits considered the Russian missionaries hopelessly unpersuasive, not only because of their limitations of language but also because of their poverty. Russians traveled overland, by caravan, to Beijing, which was very expensive. Once there, they lived on a very small allowance from the Qing court, and they were often short of food and fuel, not to mention new clothes. The relatively independent and wealthy Jesuits considered the Russian missionaries unprepared for international experience, as Matteo Ripa made clear in his report to the Vatican on the Russian mission in Beijing, probably in 1718.

I sent a present to the head of the mission, then visited him. His manners were courteous and dignified, and his dress remarkably neat. With me, he pretended to be a Roman Catholic (despite the fact he was obviously Orthodox), speaking just enough Latin to be understood. He told me that a priest who was ill and in bed could speak Latin, and so I went to visit him, but all I could get out of him was the word "intelligit, intelligit, [he understands, he understands]" over and over. The head of the mission told me that the congregation is limited to descendants of Russian prisoners of war. They cannot convert the Chinese because they don't speak Chinese, and besides they have so few priests that they have no time for any but their flock of Russians.

The truth is, their church services have no ceremony at all, and they allow men and women to worship together, which in China is considered abominable. And though the head of the mission looks elegant, the priests on his staff look very shabby. To make matters worse, the priests play in the streets in front of the mission. In China this is absolutely uncouth, and no respectable person would do it.

What do you think accounts for the tensions between the Jesuits and Russian Orthodox churchmen in China? What were they really competing for?

Source: Eric Widmer, The Russian Ecclesiastical Mission in Peking During the Eighteenth Century (Cambridge, MA: Harvard East Asian Research Center, 1976), 44, 63. © The President and Fellows of Harvard College 1976. Reproduced by permission of the Harvard University Asia Center.

campaigned against superstition and ignorance, curbed the excesses of the aristocracy, and patronized science and the arts. Voltaire proclaimed the Qing emperors model philosopher-kings and advocated such rulership as a protection against the growth of aristocratic privilege. Though Jesuit interest in China was in decline by this time, the works of the Jesuits stimulated interest in the languages and civilizations of East Asia.

The Qing were eager to expand China's economic influence but were determined to control the trade very strictly. Europeans were permitted to trade only at Canton. This system worked well enough for European traders until the late 1700s, when Britain became worried about its massive trade deficit with China. Because the Qing Empire rarely bought anything from Britain, British silver poured into China to pay for the imported tea and other products. In 1792, George Macartney was dispatched to China to open diplomatic relations with the Qing Empire and attempt to revise the trade system.

The **Macartney mission** to China, which extended into 1793, was a fiasco. Qing officials were not expecting Macartney and would not allow him to travel from Canton to Beijing. Moreover, they did not accept his credentials, and Macartney did not know how to make any headway through the Qing bureaucracy. There were prolonged disputes about rituals. The basic issues were unresolvable. Britain wished the Qing Empire to abandon its trade system and to open Chinese ports to a wide range of competing British firms to reverse the trade imbalance. The Qing, however, had no interest in changing the system that provided revenue to the imperial family and lessened serious piracy problems. Macartney left China humiliated by his inability to persuade the Qing to make changes.

Dutch, French, and Russian embassies soon attempted to achieve what Macartney had failed to do. When they failed also, European frustration with the Qing mounted. The great European admiration for China of the early 1700s faded, and China was considered despotic, self-satisfied, and unrealistic. Political solutions seemed impossible because the Qing court would not communicate with foreign envoys or observe the simplest rules of the diplomatic system familiar to Europeans.

Population and Social Stress

The early Qing population exploded from about 100 million under the Ming to between 350 million and 400 million by the end of the 1700s. Despite the efficiency of Chinese agriculture, population growth created economic and environmental decline. Whatever woodlands remained in China were rapidly diminishing. Even though his deforestation led to serious erosion and the danger of flooding grew, government corruption and general inefficiency limited efforts to prevent flooding or recover from its effects. Dams and dikes were not maintained, and silted-up river channels were not dredged. By the end of the eighteenth century, the Grand Canal was nearly unusable, and the towns that bordered it were starved for commerce.

The result was localized misery in many parts of interior China by the year 1800. Environmental deterioration and the decline of agriculture prompted many people to move. They sought seasonal jobs in better-off agricultural areas, or they worked in low-status jobs such as barge puller, charcoal burner, or nightsoil carrier. Many drifted to the cities to make their way by begging, prostitution, or theft. In central and southwestern China, where farmers had been impoverished by serious flooding, rebellions became endemic.

The Qing Empire was outgrowing the state's control. The Qing government employed about the same number of officials as the Ming even though the Qing Empire was twice the size of the Ming geographically and nearly four times its size in terms of population. To maintain local control, the Qing depended on working alliances with local elites, including gentry and aspiring official families. But this dependence undercut the government's ability to enforce tax regulations and to control standards for admission to government service, resulting in widespread corruption and shrinking government revenues.

In addition, the Qing fell victim to some of the basic characteristics of the land-based empires. To defend itself against Russia, it had conquered a huge stretch of territory, and the costs of maintaining it were enormous. Population growth and the need to transport food to nonagricultural areas stressed the food and grain systems. The need to invest in agriculture and in transport infrastructure limited investment in new industries and heightened government interest in taxing foreign trade. Russia was attempting to move out of that mode by turning toward European-style imperialism and industrialization. Japan, China's neighbor, was poised for an entirely different response.

Tokugawa Japan, to 1800

Like East Asia under the Qing rulers, Japan under the Tokugawa° shoguns moved from the intense militarization of the early 1600s to the comparative peace of the 1700s, while at the same time facing a decrease in state revenues and mounting European pressure. In nearly every respect, the Japanese reaction to these problems was more successful than the Qing response.

Shogunate and Economy

After the imperial collapse of the twelfth century, Japan was ruled by a series of decentralized military governments—the shogunates. Following a civil war during the later 1500s, a new shogun, Tokugawa Ieyasu°, declared victory. Though Japan was brought under a single military government, the structure of the **Tokugawa Shogunate** had a very important influence over the development of the Japanese economy in the early modern period.

The emperor of Japan had no political power; he remained at Kyoto°, the medieval capital. The Tokugawa shoguns built a new capital for themselves at Edo° (now Tokyo). A well-maintained road connected Kyoto and Edo, and trade and trading centers developed along this route.

Each regional lord maintained a castle town, a small bureaucracy, a population of warriors—*samurai*°—and military support personnel, and often an academy. Between these towns there was

Tokugawa (toe-koo-GAH-wah)   Ieyasu (ee-yeh-YAH-soo)
Kyoto (kee-YO-toe)   Edo (ED-doe)
samurai (SAH-moo-rie)

frequent traffic. Because Tokugawa shoguns required the lords to visit Edo frequently, good roads linked Edo to three of the four main islands of Japan.

The domestic peace of the Tokugawa era forced the warrior class to adapt itself to the growing bureaucratic needs of the state. As the samurai became better educated, more attuned to the tastes of the civil elite, and more interested in conspicuous consumption, merchants were well positioned to exploit the new opportunities. The state attempted—unsuccessfully—to curb the independence of the merchants when the economic well-being of the samurai was threatened, particularly when rice prices went too low or interest rates on loans were too high.

The 1600s and 1700s were centuries of high achievement in artisanship and commerce. Japanese skills in steel making, pottery, and lacquerware were joined by excellence in the production and decoration of porcelain, thanks in no small part to Korean experts brought back to Japan after the invasion of 1582. In the early 1600s, manufacturers and merchants amassed enormous family fortunes. Several of the most important industrial and financial companies had their origins in *sake*° or beer breweries of the early Tokugawa period, then branched out into manufacturing, finance, and transport.

Wealthy industrial families usually cultivated close alliances with their regional lords and, if possible, with the shogun himself. In this way, they could weaken the strict control of merchant activity that was an official part of Tokugawa policy. By the end of the 1700s, the industrial families of Tokugawa Japan held the key to modernization and the development of heavy industry, particularly in the prosperous provinces.

The "Closing" of Japan

Like China, Japan at the end of the 1500s was a target of missionary activity by the Jesuits. But converts to Catholic Christianity among the Japanese elite were comparatively few. Generally, Christianity was more successful among farmers in

sake (SAH-kay)

Silk Weaving by Japanese Women   Before the emergence of large factories, this sort of work could be done in the home or at a shared village site.   (From Hishikawa Mornobu, *Wakoku hyakujo* [1895]. Reproduced courtesy of the Harvard-Yenching Library)

the southern and eastern regions of Japan. But when these regions were the scenes of massive uprisings in the late 1630s by impoverished farmers, the rebellions were blamed on Christian influence. Hundreds of Japanese Christians were crucified as a warning to others; belief in Christianity was banned by law.

In 1649, the shogunate ordered the closing of the country, making it illegal and punishable by death for foreigners to come in or for Japanese to leave to prevent the spread of foreign influence in Japan. A few Europeans, primarily the Dutch, were permitted to reside on a small island near Nagasaki, and a few Japanese were licensed to supply their needs. The knowledge that these intermediaries acquired and eventually spread was known as "Dutch studies." It included information about European weapons, technology, shipbuilding, mathematics and astronomy, anatomy and medicine, and geography.

The closing of Japan was ignored by some of the regional lords whose fortunes depended on overseas trade with Korea, Okinawa°, Taiwan, China, and Southeast Asia. The "outer" lords at the northern and southern extremes of Japan tended to be under less control by the shoguns.

Okinawa (oh-kee-NAH-wah)

Elite Decline and Social Crisis

In the 1700s, population growth was putting a great strain on the well-developed lands of central Japan. In the remote provinces, where the lords had sponsored programs to settle and develop new agricultural lands, the rate of economic growth far outstripped the growth rate in centrally located domains. Also weakening the Tokugawa government in the 1700s was the shogunate's inability to halt the economic decline of the samurai, whose salaries paid in rice were being destabilized by the rice brokers. Laws designed to regulate the price of rice and the rate of interest had been passed early in the Tokugawa period, but these laws were not always enforced, sometimes because neither the lords nor the samurai wished them to be. By the early 1700s, members of both groups were dependent on the willingness of merchants to provide them credit.

The Tokugawa shoguns, like governments throughout East Asia, accepted the Confucian idea that agriculture should be the basis of state wealth and that merchants should occupy lowly positions in society because of their reputed lack of moral character. However, the Tokugawa government's decentralized system limited its ability to regulate merchant activities and actually stimulated the growth of commercial activities. Despite official disapproval, merchants and others involved in the growing economy enjoyed relative freedom and influence in eighteenth-century Japan. They produced a vivid culture of their own, fostering the development of *kabuki* theater, colorful woodblock prints and silkscreened fabrics, and restaurants.

The Tokugawa Shogunate put into place a political and economic system that fostered innovation, but the government itself could not exploit it. Thus, the government remained quite traditional during the Tokugawa period, while other segments of society developed new methods of productivity and management.

CONCLUSION

In the early eighteenth century, Eurasia was dominated by the enormous Russian and the Qing land-based empires. Both depended on large transportation systems and intense agricultural production, and they often competed for the same resources. At the center of their political structures were powerful emperors with the economic and legal resources to command armies. Each empire had its most brilliant period—under Peter the Great and Emperor Kangxi—when the throne was occupied by a talented, energetic, and far-sighted ruler.

There were also distinct differences between these empires. Although the Qing court was generally open to many kinds of foreign influences, distance and circumstance limited Qing contact with Europe. The European merchants did not make much of an impression. The Jesuits were influential in philosophy, mathematics, astronomy, and other issues of concern to them, but they were not an inexhaustible resource. From the Jesuits, the Kangxi emperor got very little insight into the emergence of European empires, their tactics, or their goals.

Russia's location and circumstances were different. St. Petersburg gave Peter the Great a "window" into Europe, and from that vantage point he gathered architecture, engineering, shipbuilding,

and military technologies of all kinds. He understood the meaning of the new European use of the sea, and set Russia on a path tending toward European practices of diplomacy and imperialism and away from the static values of the huge land empires.

These variations on an imperial pattern were not shared by Japan. Instead of pursuing centralization, standardization, and strengthening of the ruler, Japan was decentralized. Local lords had great incentive to develop their lands, and merchants worked with the regional lords to develop local enterprises, sustain local samurai, and outfit local soldiers. Many regions of Tokugawa Japan created innovative means of financing local industry and developed unique relationships with other countries, despite the official decision to limit Western contacts.

■ Key Terms

Jesuits	Ming Empire
Siberia	Manchus
Muscovy	Qing Empire
tsar	Kangxi
Mikhail Romanov	variolation
Cossacks	Macartney mission
Peter the Great	Tokugawa Shogunate
autocracy	*samurai*
serfs	

■ Suggested Reading

There is a great deal of literature focused on the Jesuits' history in various countries. For East Asia in the sixteenth and seventeenth centuries, see Michael Coopers, S.J., *Rodrigues the Interpreter: An Early Jesuit in Japan and China* (1974). For China, see David E. Mungello, *Curious Land: Jesuit Accommodation and the Origins of Sinology* (1985), and Jonathan D. Spence, *The Memory Palace of Matteo Ricci* (1984). For Japan, see C. R. Boxer, *The Christian Century in Japan, 1549–1650* (1951).

On early modern Russian history, see W. E. Brown, *A History of Eighteenth-Century Russia* (1980), and Robert O. Crummey, *Aristocrats and Servitors: The Boyar Elite in Russia, 1613–1689* (1983). Among the best-known books on Peter the Great are Matthew Smith Anderson, *Peter the Great* (1978); Robert K. Massie, *Peter the Great: His Life and World* (1980); and Lindsey Hughes, *Russia in the Age of Peter the Great: 1682–1725* (1998).

For China during the transition from the Ming to Qing periods, see James W. Tong, *Disorder Under Heaven: Collective Violence in the Ming Dynasty* (1991); Frederic Wakeman, *The Great Enterprise* (1985); and Lynn Struve, *Voices from the Ming-Qing Cataclysm: In Tiger's Jaws* (1993). On the history of the Manchus and of the Qing Empire, see Evelyn Sakakida Rawski, *The Last Emperors* (1999), and Pamela Kyle Crossley, *The Manchus* (1997).

There is a great deal published on the Macartney mission, much of it originating in the diaries and memoirs of the participants. See the exhaustively detailed Alain Peyrefitte, *The Immobile Empire*, trans. Jon Rothschild (1992). For a more theoretical discussion, see James L. Hevia, *Cherishing Men from Afar: Qing Guest Ritual and the Macartney Embassy of 1793* (1995).

On Japan in this period, see Chie Nakane and Shinzaburo Oishi *Tokugawa Japan: The Social and Economic Antecedents of Modern Japan,* trans. Conrad Totman (1990), and Tessa Morris-Suzuki, *The Technological Transformation of Japan from the Seventeenth to the Twenty-First Century* (1994).

■ Note

1. Adapted from G. V. Melikhov, "Manzhou Penetration into the Basin of the Upper Amur in the 1680s," in S. L. Tikhvinshii, ed., *Manzhou Rule in China* (Moscow: Progress Publishers, 1983).

PART SIX

REVOLUTIONS RESHAPE THE WORLD, 1750–1870

Between 1750 and 1870, dramatic political, economic, and social changes affected nearly every part of the world. In the West, the American, French, and Haitian Revolutions unleashed forces of nationalism and social reform. At this time, the Industrial Revolution introduced technologies and patterns of work that made industrial societies wealthier, more socially fluid, and militarily more powerful than nonindustrial, traditional societies. Even while Europe's colonial empires in the Western Hemisphere were being dismantled, the Industrial Revolution was fueling European economic expansion, which undermined traditional producers in distant places such as Asia and Africa. When this economic penetration was resisted, as it was in East Asia, the industrializing nations of the West used military force to open markets.

Great Britain expanded its empire by establishing colonial rule in distant Australia, New Zealand, and India. India alone had a population larger than the combined populations of all the colonies that Europe lost in the Americas. The Atlantic slave trade was ended by an international abolitionist movement and by Great Britain's use of diplomacy and naval power. European economic influence expanded in Africa.

Invigorated by this exchange, some African states created new institutions and introduced new economic sectors.

The Ottoman Empire, the Qing Empire, and Japan were deeply influenced by the expansion of Europe and the United States. Each society met the Western challenge with reform programs that preserved traditional structures while adopting elements of Western technology and organization. The Ottoman court introduced reforms in education, the military, and law and created the first constitution in an Islamic state. The Qing Empire survived the period of European expansion, but a series of military defeats and civil war seriously compromised China's centralization efforts. Japan experienced the most revolutionary change, abolishing its ancient political system and initiating radical top-down transformations.

The economic, political, and social revolutions that began in the mid-eighteenth century shook the foundations of European culture and led to the expansion of Western power across the globe. Societies throughout Asia, Africa, and Latin America responded to cross-cultural contacts. Some resisted foreign intrusion by using local culture and experience as a guide. Others adopted Western commercial policies, industrial technologies, and government institutions.

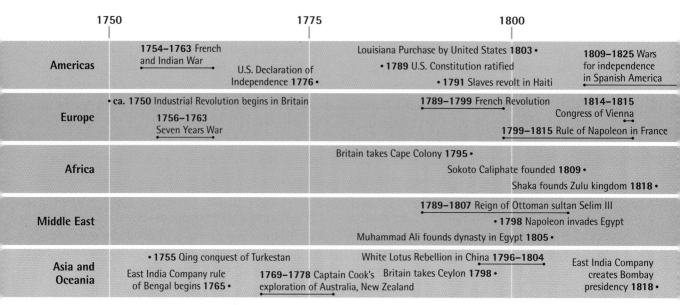

	1750	1775	1800
Americas	1754–1763 French and Indian War	U.S. Declaration of Independence 1776 •	Louisiana Purchase by United States 1803 • •1789 U.S. Constitution ratified •1791 Slaves revolt in Haiti	1809–1825 Wars for independence in Spanish America
Europe	•ca. 1750 Industrial Revolution begins in Britain 1756–1763 Seven Years War		1789–1799 French Revolution 1799–1815 Rule of Napoleon in France	1814–1815 Congress of Vienna
Africa		Britain takes Cape Colony 1795 • Sokoto Caliphate founded 1809 • Shaka founds Zulu kingdom 1818 •		
Middle East		1789–1807 Reign of Ottoman sultan Selim III •1798 Napoleon invades Egypt Muhammad Ali founds dynasty in Egypt 1805 •		
Asia and Oceania	•1755 Qing conquest of Turkestan East India Company rule of Bengal begins 1765 •	1769–1778 Captain Cook's exploration of Australia, New Zealand	White Lotus Rebellion in China 1796–1804 Britain takes Ceylon 1798 •	East India Company creates Bombay presidency 1818 •

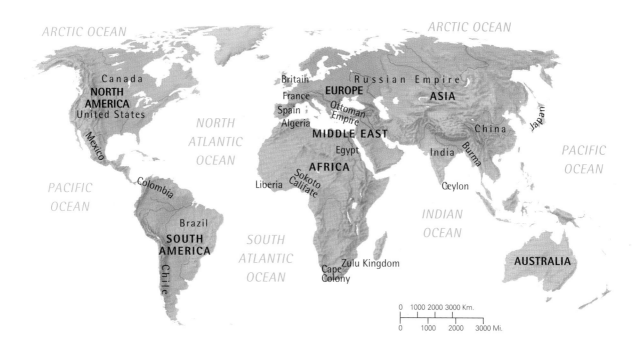

ARCTIC OCEAN   ARCTIC OCEAN

Canada
NORTH AMERICA
United States

NORTH ATLANTIC OCEAN

Mexico

PACIFIC OCEAN

Colombia

Brazil
SOUTH AMERICA

Chile

SOUTH ATLANTIC OCEAN

Britain
France
EUROPE
Spain
Algeria
Ottoman Empire
MIDDLE EAST
Egypt
AFRICA
Liberia
Sokoto Califate

Russian Empire

ASIA

China

Japan

India
Burma

Ceylon

PACIFIC OCEAN

INDIAN OCEAN

AUSTRALIA

Zulu Kingdom
Cape Colony

0   1000 2000 3000 Km.
0   1000   2000   3000 Mi.

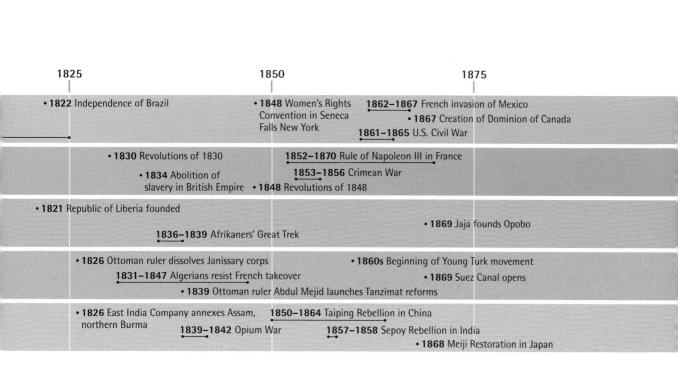

1825	1850	1875

• **1822** Independence of Brazil
1848 Women's Rights Convention in Seneca Falls New York
1862–1867 French invasion of Mexico
• **1867** Creation of Dominion of Canada
1861–1865 U.S. Civil War

• **1830** Revolutions of 1830
1852–1870 Rule of Napoleon III in France
• **1834** Abolition of slavery in British Empire
1853–1856 Crimean War
• **1848** Revolutions of 1848

• **1821** Republic of Liberia founded
• **1869** Jaja founds Opobo
1836–1839 Afrikaners' Great Trek

• **1826** Ottoman ruler dissolves Janissary corps
• **1860s** Beginning of Young Turk movement
1831–1847 Algerians resist French takeover
• **1869** Suez Canal opens
• **1839** Ottoman ruler Abdul Mejid launches Tanzimat reforms

• **1826** East India Company annexes Assam, northern Burma
1850–1864 Taiping Rebellion in China
1839–1842 Opium War
1857–1858 Sepoy Rebellion in India
• **1868** Meiji Restoration in Japan

20

REVOLUTIONARY CHANGES IN THE ATLANTIC WORLD, 1750–1850

Prelude to Revolution: War and the Enlightenment • The American Revolution • The French Revolution • Revolution in Haiti and Latin America • Economic and Social Liberation Movements
ENVIRONMENT AND TECHNOLOGY: The Pencil

On the evening of August 14, 1791, more than two hundred slaves and black freedmen met in secret in the plantation district of northern Saint Domingue° (present-day Haiti) to set the date for an armed uprising against local slave owners. Although the delegates agreed to delay the attack for a week, violence began almost immediately. During the following decade, the Haitian rebels abolished slavery, defeated military forces from Britain and France, and gained independence.

News and rumors about revolutionary events in France that had spread through the island incited the slave community and divided the island's white population between royalists (supporters of France's King Louis XVI) and republicans (supporters of democracy). The free mixed-race population initially gained some political rights from the French Assembly but was then forced to rebel when the slave-owning elite reacted violently.

Among those planning the insurrection was Toussaint L'Ouverture°, a black freedman. This remarkable revolutionary organized the rebels into a potent military force, negotiated with the island's royalist and republican factions and, with representatives of Great Britain and France, wrote his nation's first constitution. Throughout the Western Hemisphere, Toussaint became a towering symbol of resistance to oppression for slaves and a fiend for slave owners.

The Haitian slave rebellion was an important episode in the long and painful political and cultural transformation of the modern Western world. Economic expansion and the growth of trade were creating unprecedented wealth. Intellectuals were questioning the traditional place of monarchy and slavery in society. An emerging class of merchants, professionals, and manu-

---

Saint Domingue (san doe-MANG)

Toussaint L'Ouverture (too-SAN loo-ver-CHORE)

facturers began to press for a larger political role, and economies were increasingly opened to competition.

Imperial powers resisted the loss of colonies, and monarchs and nobles struggled to retain their ancient privileges. Revolutionary steps forward were often matched by reactionary steps backward. The liberal and nationalist ideals of the eighteenth-century revolutionary movements were only imperfectly realized in Europe and the Americas in the nineteenth century.

As you read this chapter, ask yourself the following questions:

- How did imperial wars among European powers provoke revolution?
- How did revolution in one country help to incite revolution elsewhere?
- Why were the revolutions in France and Haiti more violent than the American Revolution?
- How were political revolts linked to the abolition of slavery?

PRELUDE TO REVOLUTION: WAR AND THE ENLIGHTENMENT

In large measure, the cost of wars fought among Europe's major powers over colonies and trade precipitated the revolutionary era that began in 1775 with the American Revolution. The struggle of Britain, France, and Spain for political preeminence in western Europe and overseas produced many violent conflicts during the eighteenth century. In the Seven Years War (1756–1763), known as the French and Indian War in America, Britain gained dominance in North America and in India. All parties suffered from the enormous costs of these conflicts.

New Western ideas and political environments also made people much more critical of any effort to extend the power of a monarch or impose new taxes, and raised questions about the rights of individuals. As Chapter 16 recounted, the **Enlightenment** applied the methods and questions of the Scientific Revolution to the study of human society. Some thinkers challenged long-established religious and political institutions. They argued that if scientists could understand the laws of nature, then surely similar forms of disciplined investigation might reveal laws of human nature. Others wondered whether society and government might be better regulated and more productive if guided by reason rather than by hereditary rulers and the church.

These new perspectives and the intellectual optimism that fed them were to help guide the English political philosopher John Locke (1632–1704). Locke argued in 1690 that governments were created to protect life, liberty, and property and that the people had a right to rebel when a monarch violated these natural rights. In *The Social Contract,* published in 1762, the French-Swiss intellectual Jean-Jacques Rousseau° (1712–1778) asserted that the will of the people was sacred and that the legitimacy of the monarch depended on the consent of the people. Although both men believed that government rested on the will of the people rather than divine will, Locke emphasized the importance of individual rights, and Rousseau envisioned the people acting collectively because of their shared historical experience.

The Enlightenment is commonly associated with hostility toward monarchy, but Voltaire, one of the Enlightenment's most critical intellects, believed that Europe's monarchs were likely agents of political and economic reform, and he wrote favorably of China's Qing° emperors. Indeed, some sympathetic members of the nobility and reforming monarchs in Spain, Russia, Austria, and Prussia actively sponsored and promoted the dissemination of new ideas, providing patronage for many intellectuals. They recognized that elements of the Enlightenment critique of the ancien régime° buttressed their own efforts to expand royal authority at the expense of religious institutions, the nobility, and regional autonomy. Monarchs also understood that the era's passion for science and technology

---

Jean-Jacques Rousseau (zhahn-zhock roo-SOE)
Qing (ching)   *ancien régime* (ahn-see-EN ray-ZHEEM)

held the potential of fattening national treasuries and improving economic performance (see Environment and Technology: The Pencil).

The Western Hemisphere shared in the debates of Europe. In colonial societies where political rights were even more limited than in Europe, the idea that government authority ultimately rested on the consent of the governed was potentially explosive. The efforts of ordinary men and women to resist the growth of government power and the imposition of new cultural forms provide an important political undercurrent to much of the revolutionary agitation and conflict from 1750 to 1850. But spontaneous popular uprisings gained revolutionary potential only when they coincided with ideological divisions and conflicts within the governing class itself.

THE AMERICAN REVOLUTION

After defeating the French in the French and Indian War, the British government faced two related problems in its North American colonies. One was the likelihood of armed conflict with Amerindian peoples as settlers quickly pushed west of the Appalachian Mountains and across the Ohio River. Already burdened with war debts, Britain desperately wanted to avoid additional expenditures for frontier defense. The other problem was how to get the colonists to shoulder more of the costs of imperial defense and colonial administration. Every effort to impose new taxes or prevent the settlement of the trans-Appalachian frontier provoked angry protests in the colonies. The confrontational and impolitic way in which a succession of weak British governments responded made the situation politically explosive.

of already established farmers without effectively protecting Amerindian land. The Quebec Act of 1774 annexed disputed lands to the province of Quebec, thus denying eastern colonies the authority to distribute lands claimed as a result of original charters. Colonists saw the Quebec Act as punitive and tyrannical, and Amerindian peoples received no relief from the continuous assault on their land.

New commercial regulations that increased the cost of foreign molasses and endangered New England's profitable trade with Spanish and French Caribbean sugar colonies provoked widespread boycotts of British goods. The Stamp Act of 1765, which imposed a tax on all legal documents, newspapers, pamphlets, and other types of printed material, led to violent protest and more effective boycotts. Parliament imposed new taxes and duties soon after repealing the Stamp Act in 1766, even sending British troops to quell urban riots. Unable to control the streets of Boston, British authorities reacted by threatening traditional liberties, dissolving the colonial legislature of Massachusetts, and dispatching a warship and two regiments of soldiers to reestablish control. Support for a complete break with Britain grew when a British force fired on an angry Boston crowd on March 5, 1770, killing five civilians. This "Boston Massacre," which seemed to expose the naked force on which colonial rule rested, radicalized public opinion throughout the colonies.

Parliament attempted to calm public opinion by repealing some of the taxes and duties, then stumbled into another crisis by granting the British East India Company a monopoly for importing tea to the colonies, which raised anew the constitutional issue of Parliament's right to tax the colonies. It also offended wealthy colonial merchants, who were excluded from this profitable commerce. The crisis came to a head in the already politically overheated port of Boston when tea worth £10,000 was dumped into the harbor by protesters disguised as Amerindians.

Frontiers and Taxes

The British Proclamation of 1763, which sought to establish an effective western limit for settlement, threw into question the claims of thousands

The Course of the Revolution

As the crisis mounted, patriots created new governing bodies, effectively deposed many British governors and other officials, passed laws, appointed

CHRONOLOGY

	The Americas	Europe
1750		
	1756–1763 French and Indian War	**1756–1763** Seven Years War
1775	**1770** Boston Massacre **1776** American Declaration of Independence **1778** United States alliance with France **1783** Treaty of Paris ends American Revolution **1789** U.S. Constitution ratified **1791** Slaves revolt in Saint Domingue (Haiti)	**1789** Storming of Bastille begins French Revolution **1793–1794** Reign of Terror in France
1800	**1798** Toussaint L'Ouverture defeats British in Haiti **1804** Haitians defeat French invasion and declare independence **1808** Portuguese royal family arrives in Brazil **1808–1809** Revolutions for independence begin in Spanish South America	**1795–1799** The Directory rules France **1799** Napoleon overthrows the Directory **1804** Napoleon crowns himself emperor
1825	**1822** Brazil gains independence	**1814** Napoleon abdicates; Congress of Vienna opens **1830** Greece gains independence; revolution in France
1850	**1838** End of slavery in British Caribbean **1848** Women's Rights Convention in Seneca Falls, New York	**1848** Revolutions in France, Austria, Germany, Hungary, and Italy
1875	**1861–1865** American Civil War **1865** End of slavery in United States **1886** End of slavery in Cuba **1888** End of slavery in Brazil	

judges, and even took control of colonial militias. Simultaneously, radical leaders organized crowds to intimidate loyalists—people who were pro-British—and to enforce the boycott of British goods.

Events were propelling the colonies toward revolution. Elected representatives, meeting in Philadelphia as the Continental Congress in 1775, assumed the powers of government, creating a currency and organizing an army. **George Washington** (1732–1799), a Virginia planter who had served in the French and Indian War, was named commander. On July 4, 1776, Congress approved the Declaration of Independence, the document that proved to be the most enduring statement of the revolutionary era's ideology:

We hold these truths to be self evident: That all men are created equal; that they are endowed by their creator with certain unalienable rights; that among these are life, liberty and the pursuit of happiness; that, to secure these rights, governments are instituted among men, deriving their just powers from the consent of the governed.

This affirmation of popular sovereignty and individual rights influenced the language of revolution and popular protest around the world.

To shore up British authority, Great Britain sent more than 400 ships, 50,000 soldiers, and 30,000 German mercenaries. But this military commitment proved futile. Although British forces won most of the battles, Washington slowly built a competent Continental army and civilian support

The Pencil

From early times, Europeans had used sharp points, lead, and other implements to sketch, make marks, and write brief notes. At the end of the seventeenth century, a source of high-quality graphite was discovered at Borrowdale in northwestern England. Borrowdale graphite gained acceptance among artists, artisans, and merchants. At first, pure graphite was simply wrapped in string. By the eighteenth century, pieces of graphite were being encased in wooden sheaths and resembled modern pencils. Widespread use of this useful tool was retarded by the limited supply of high-quality graphite from the English mines.

The English crown periodically closed the Borrowdale mines or restricted production to keep prices high and maintain adequate supplies for future needs. As a result, artisans in other European nations developed alternatives that used lower-quality graphite or, most commonly, graphite mixed with sulfur and glues.

The major breakthrough occurred in 1793 in France when war with England ruptured trade links. The government of revolutionary France responded to the shortage of graphite by assigning a thirty-nine-year-old scientist, Nicolas-Jacques Conté, to find an alternative. Conté had earlier promoted the military use of balloons and conducted experiments with hydrogen. He also had had experience using graphite alloys in the development of crucibles for melting metal.

Within a short period, Conté produced a graphite that is the basis for most lead pencils today. He succeeded by mixing finely ground graphite with potter's clay and water. The resulting paste was dried in a long mold, sealed in a ceramic box, and fired in an oven. The graphite strips were then placed in a wooden case. Although some believed the Conté pencils were inferior to the pencils made from Borrowdale graphite, Conté

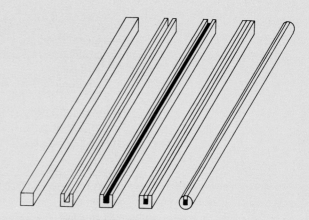

Pencils Wartime necessity led to invention of the modern pencil in France. (Drawing by Fred Avent for Henry Petroski. Reproduced by permission)

produced a very serviceable pencil that could be produced in uniform quality and unlimited amounts.

Henry Petroski, summarizing the achievement of Conté in his *The Pencil*, wrote: "The laboratory is really the modern workshop. And modern engineering results when the scientific method is united with experience with the tools and products of craftsmen. . . . Modern engineering, in spirit if not in name, would come to play a more and more active role in turning the craft tradition into modern technology, with its base of research and development."

Source: This discussion depends on Henry Petroski, *The Pencil: A History of Design and Circumstance* (New York: Knopf, 1990); the quotation is from pp. 50–78.

networks that provided supplies and financial resources. In the final decisive battle, fought at Yorktown, Virginia (see Map 20.1), an American army, supported by French soldiers, besieged a British army led by General Charles Cornwallis. With escape cut off by a French fleet, Cornwallis surrendered to Washington as the British military band played "The World Turned Upside-Down."

New Republican Institutions

Ignoring the British example of an unwritten constitution, representatives in each of the newly independent states drafted formal charters and submitted the results to voters for ratification. Europeans were fascinated by these written constitutions and by their formal ratification by the people. Here was the social contract of Locke and Rousseau made manifest. The state constitutions also placed severe limits on executive authority

Map 20.1   The American Revolutionary War   The British army won most of the major battles, and British troops held most of the major cities. Even so, the American revolutionaries eventually won a comprehensive military and political victory.

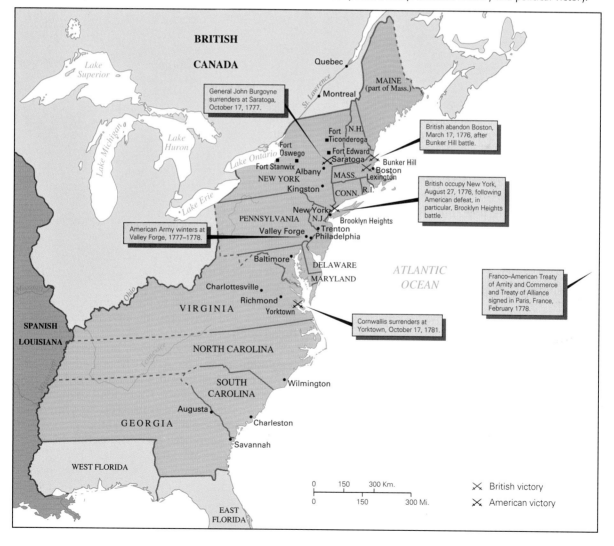

but granted legislatures greater powers than in colonial times. Many states also inserted in their constitutions a bill of rights to provide further protection against government tyranny.

An effective constitution for the new national government was developed more slowly and hesitantly. The Articles of Confederation—the first constitution of the United States—were not accepted by all the states until 1781. With the coming of peace in 1783, there was an effort to fashion a new constitution.

Debate at the **Constitutional Convention,** which began meeting in May 1787, focused on several issues: representation, electoral procedures, executive powers, and the relationship between the federal government and the states. The final compromise provided for a two-house legislature: the lower house (the House of Representatives) to be elected directly by voters and the upper house (the Senate) to be elected by state legislatures. The chief executive—the president—was to be elected indirectly by "electors" selected by ballot in the states (each state had a number of electors equal to the number of its representatives and senators).

Although the U.S. Constitution created the most democratic government of the era, only a minority of the adult population was given full rights. Southern leaders were able to protect the institution of slavery by counting three-fifths of the slave population in the calculations that determined their states' congressional representatives. Although women had led prewar boycotts and had organized relief and charitable organizations during the war, they were denied political rights in the new republic.

THE FRENCH REVOLUTION

The French Revolution confronted the entrenched privileges of an established church, monarchy, and aristocracy more directly than the American Revolution did. It also expanded mass participation in political life and radicalized the democratic tradition. But in the end, the passions unleashed in France by revolutionary events could not be sustained.

French Society and Fiscal Crisis

French society was divided into three groups. The clergy, the First Estate, numbered about 130,000 in a nation of 28 million. The Catholic Church owned about 10 percent of the nation's land and extracted substantial amounts of wealth from the economy in the form of tithes and ecclesiastical fees. Despite its substantial wealth, the church was exempted from nearly all taxes.

The 300,000 members of the nobility, the Second Estate, controlled about 30 percent of the land and retained ancient rights on much of the rest. Nobles held the vast majority of high administrative, judicial, military, and church positions. Though traditionally barred from some types of commercial activity, nobles were important participants in wholesale trade, banking, manufacturing, and mining.

The Third Estate included everyone else. There were three times as many members of the bourgeoisie°, in 1774, when Louis XVI took the throne, as there had been in 1715, at the end of Louis XIV's reign. Peasants accounted for 80 percent of the French population. They owned some property and lived decently when crops were good and prices stable. By 1780, poor harvests had decreased their incomes.

The nation's poor were a large, growing, and troublesome sector. Urban streets swarmed with beggars and prostitutes. Unable to afford decent housing, obtain steady employment, or protect their children, the poor periodically erupted in violent protest and rage. In the countryside, violence was often the reaction to increased dues and fees. In towns and cities, an increase in the price of bread often provided the spark.

These explosive episodes, however, were not revolutionary in character. The remedies sought were conventional and immediate rather than structural and long term. That was to change when the Crown tried to solve its fiscal crisis by imposing new taxes on the nobility and on other groups that in the past had enjoyed exemptions. But this effort failed in the face of widespread protest and the refusal of the Parlement of Paris, a court of appeal that heard appeals from local courts throughout

---

bourgeoisie (boor-zwah-ZEE)

France, to register the new tax. In 1768, frustrated authorities exiled the members of that Parlement and pushed through a series of unpopular fiscal measures. Despite the worsening fiscal crisis, the French took on the heavy burden of supporting the American Revolution, delaying collapse by borrowing enormous sums. By the end of the war with Britain, more than half of France's national budget was required to service the debt alone. In 1787, the desperate king called an Assembly of Notables to approve a radical and comprehensive reform of the economy and fiscal policy. Despite the fact that the members of this assembly were selected by the king's advisers from the high nobility, the judiciary, and the clergy, it proved unwilling to act as a rubber stamp for the proposed reforms or new taxes. Instead, these representatives of France's most privileged classes sought to protect their interests by questioning the competence of the king and his ministers to supervise the nation's affairs, thus creating the conditions for political revolution.

Protest Turns to Revolution

Unable to extract needed tax concessions from the notables, King Louis XVI was forced to call the **Estates General,** the French national legislature, which had not met since 1614. Traditionally, the three estates met separately, and a positive vote by two of the three was required for action. Tradition, however, was quickly overturned when the Third Estate refused to conduct business until the king ordered the other two estates to sit with it in a single body. During a six-week period of stalemate, many parish priests deserted the First Estate to meet with them.

When this expanded Third Estate declared itself the **National Assembly,** the king and his advisers recognized that the reformers intended to force them to accept a constitutional monarchy. Louis's agenda for fiscal reform was being displaced by the central ideas of the era: the people were sovereign, and the legitimacy of political institutions and individual rulers ultimately depended on their carrying out the people's will. Louis prepared for a confrontation with the National Assembly by moving military forces to Versailles. But before he could act, the people of Paris intervened.

A succession of bad harvests beginning in 1785 had propelled bread prices upward throughout France and provoked an economic depression. By the time the Estates General met, nearly a third of the Parisian work force was unemployed. Hunger and anger marched hand in hand through working-class neighborhoods.

When the people of Paris heard that the king was massing troops to arrest their representatives, crowds of common people began to seize arms and mobilize. On July 14, 1789, a crowd searching for military supplies attacked the Bastille°, a medieval fortress used as a prison. The futile defense of the Bastille cost ninety-eight lives before its garrison surrendered. Enraged, the attackers hacked the commander to death and then paraded through the city with his head and that of Paris's chief magistrate stuck on pikes.

These events coincided with uprisings in the country. Peasants sacked manor houses and destroyed documents that recorded their traditional obligations. They refused to pay taxes and dues to landowners and seized common lands. Forced to recognize the fury raging through rural areas, the National Assembly voted to end traditional obligations and to reform the tax system. Having forced acceptance of their narrow agenda, the peasants ceased their revolt.

These popular uprisings strengthened the hand of the National Assembly in its dealings with the king. One manifestation of this altered relationship was passage of the **Declaration of the Rights of Man.** The French declaration, however, was more sweeping in its language than the American Declaration of Independence. Among the enumerated natural rights were "liberty, property, security, and resistance to oppression." The Declaration of the Rights of Man also guaranteed free expression of ideas, equality before the law, and representative government.

While delegates debated political issues in Versailles, the economic crisis worsened in Paris. Because the working women of Paris faced high food prices every day as they struggled to feed their families, their anger had a hard edge. On October 5,

---

Bastille (bass-TEEL)

Parisian Stocking Mender The poor lived very difficult lives. This woman uses a discarded wine barrel as a shop where she mends socks. (Private collection)

The National Assembly achieved a radically restructured French society in the next two years. It passed a new constitution that dramatically limited monarchical power and abolished the nobility as a hereditary class. Economic reforms swept away monopolies and trade barriers within France. The Legislative Assembly created by the new constitution seized church lands to use as collateral for a new paper currency, and priests, who were to be elected, were put on the state payroll. When the government tried to force priests to take a loyalty oath, however, many Catholics joined a growing counterrevolutionary movement.

At first, many European monarchs had welcomed the weakening of the French king, but by 1791 Austria and Prussia threatened to intervene in support of the monarchy. The Legislative Assembly responded by declaring war. Although the war went badly at first for French forces, people across France responded patriotically to foreign invasions, forming huge new volunteer armies and mobilizing national resources to meet the challenge. By the end of 1792, French armies had gained the upper hand everywhere.

In this period of national crisis and foreign threat, the French Revolution entered its most radical phase. A failed effort by the king and queen to escape from Paris and find foreign allies cost the king any remaining popular support. As foreign armies crossed into France, his behavior was increasingly viewed as treasonous. In August 1792, the Legislative Assembly suspended the king, ordered his imprisonment, and called for the formation of a new National Convention to be elected by the vote of all men. Swept along by popular passion, the newly elected National Convention convicted Louis XVI of treason, sentencing him to death and proclaiming France a republic.

The guillotine ended the king's life in January 1793. Invented in the spirit of the era as a more humane way to execute the condemned, this machine was to become the bloody symbol of the revolution. During the period of repression called the Reign of Terror (1793–1794), approximately 40,000 people were executed or died in prison. This radical phase ended in July 1794 when the Terror's leaders were executed by guillotine.

market women organized a crowd of thousands to march the 12 miles (19 kilometers) to Versailles°. Once there, they forced their way into the National Assembly to demand action from the frightened representatives: "The point is that we want bread." The crowd then entered the royal apartments, killed some of the king's guards, and searched for Queen Marie Antoinette°, whom they loathed as a symbol of extravagance. Eventually, the crowd demanded that the royal family return to Paris. Preceded by the heads of two aristocrats carried on pikes and hauling away the palace's supply of flour, the triumphant crowd escorted the royal family to Paris.

Versailles (vuhr-SIGH) **Antoinette** (ann-twah-NET)

Parisian Women Marching on Versailles   When the market women of Paris marched to Versailles and forced the royal family to return to Paris with them, they altered the course of the French Revolution. In this drawing, the women are armed with pikes and swords and drag a cannon. Only the woman on the far left is clearly middle class, and she is pictured hesitating or turning away from the resolute actions of the poor women around her.   (Bibliothèque nationale de France)

Reaction and Dictatorship

Purged of the radicals, the National Convention—the new legislative assembly of the French republic—began to undo the radical reforms. It removed many of the emergency economic controls that had been holding down prices and protecting the working class. When the Paris working class rose in protest in 1795, the Convention approved the use of overwhelming military force. The Convention also permitted the Catholic Church to regain much of its former influence, but would not return the Church's confiscated wealth. Finally, it ratified a more conservative constitution, which protected property, established a voting process that reduced the power of the masses, and created a new executive authority, the Directory. Once installed in power, however, the Directory proved unable to end the foreign wars or solve domestic economic problems.

After losing the election of 1797, the Directory suspended the results. The republican phase of the Revolution was clearly dead. Legitimacy was now based on coercive power rather than on elections. Two years later, **Napoleon Bonaparte** (1769–1821), a brilliant young general in the French army, seized power. Just as the American and French Revolutions had been the start of the modern democratic tradition, the military intervention that brought Napoleon to power in 1799 marked the advent of another modern form of government: popular authoritarianism.

In contrast to the National Convention, Napoleon proved capable of realizing France's dream of dominating Europe and providing effective protection for persons and property at home. Negotiations with the Catholic Church led to the Concordat of 1801, which gave French Catholics the right to practice their religion freely. Napoleon's Civil Code of 1804 asserted two basic principles inherited from the moderate first stage of the French Revolution: equality in law and protection of property. Even some members of the nobility became supporters after Napoleon declared himself emperor and France an empire in 1804.

While providing personal security, the Napoleonic system denied or restricted many individual rights. Women were denied basic political rights. Free speech and free expression were limited. Criticism of the government, viewed as subversive, was proscribed, and most opposition newspapers disappeared.

Ultimately, the Napoleonic system depended on the success of French arms and French diplomacy (see Map 20.2). From Napoleon's assumption of power until his fall, no single European state could defeat the French military. Austria and Prussia were forced to become allies of France. Only Britain, protected by its powerful navy, remained able to thwart Napoleon's plans to dominate Europe. In June 1812, Napoleon made the fateful decision to invade Russia with the largest army ever assembled in Europe, approximately 600,000 men. Five weeks after occupying Moscow, he was forced to retreat. The brutal Russian winter and attacks by Russian forces destroyed his army. A broken and battered fragment of 30,000 men returned home to France.

After the debacle in Russia, Austria and Prussia deserted Napoleon and entered an alliance with Britain and Russia. Unable to defend Paris, Napoleon was forced to abdicate the French throne in April 1814. The allies exiled Napoleon to the island of Elba off the coast of Italy and restored the French monarchy.

Retrenchment, Reform, and Revolution

The French Revolution and Napoleon's imperial ambitions had threatened the very survival of the European old order. Ancient monarchies had been overturned and long-established political institutions tossed aside. The very existence of the nobility and church had been put at risk. Under the leadership of the Austrian foreign minister, Prince Klemens von Metternich° (1773–1859), Britain, Russia, Austria, and

Prussia worked together in Vienna to create a comprehensive peace settlement that they hoped would safeguard the conservative order. Because the participants in the **Congress of Vienna** believed that a strong and stable France was the best guarantee of future peace, the French monarchy was reestablished. Metternich sought to offset French strength with a balance of power.

Despite the power of the conservative monarchs, popular support for national self-determination and democratic reform grew throughout Europe. In 1821, Greek patriots launched a movement for independence from Ottoman control. In 1830, Russia, France, and Great Britain forced the Ottoman Empire to recognize Greek independence. That same year, the people of Paris rose up and forced King Charles X to abdicate. His successor, Louis Philippe° (r. 1830–1848), reestablished the constitution and extended voting privileges.

Despite limited political reform, conservatives continued to hold the upper hand in Europe. Finally, in 1848, the desire for democratic reform and national self-determination and the frustrations of urban workers led to upheavals across Europe. The **Revolutions of 1848** began in Paris, where members of the middle class and workers united to overthrow the regime of Louis Philippe and create the Second French Republic. Adult men were given voting rights, slavery was abolished in French colonies, the death penalty was ended, and a ten-hour workday was legislated for Paris. But Parisian workers' demand for programs to reduce unemployment and lower prices provoked conflicts with the middle class, which wanted to protect property rights. Desiring the reestablishment of order, the French elected Louis Napoleon, nephew of the former emperor, president in December 1848. Three years later, he overturned the constitution as a result of popular plebiscite and, after ruling briefly as dictator, became Emperor Napoleon III. He remained in power until 1871.

Despite their heroism on the barricades of Vienna, Rome, and Berlin, the revolutionaries of 1848 also failed to gain either their nationalist or their republican objectives. Metternich, the symbol of reaction, fled Vienna in disguise, but little lasting

---

Metternich (MET-uhr-nik)

Louis Philippe (loo-EE fee-LEEP)

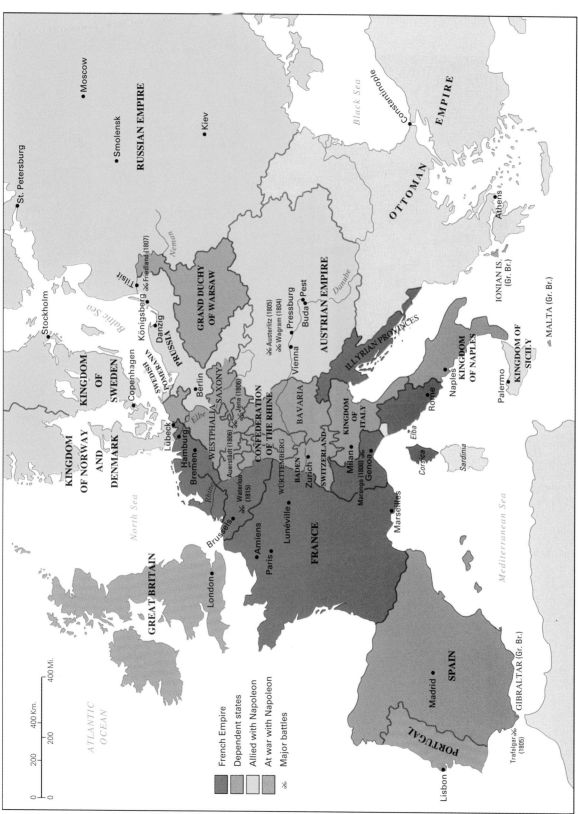

Map 20.2 Napoleon's Europe, 1810 By 1810, Great Britain was the only remaining European power at war with Napoleon. Because of the loss of the French fleet at the Battle of Trafalgar in 1805, Napoleon was unable to threaten Britain with invasion, and Britain was able to assist the resistance movements in Spain and Portugal, thereby helping to weaken French power.

French Empire
Dependent states
Allied with Napoleon
At war with Napoleon
Major battles

GREAT BRITAIN
London
ATLANTIC OCEAN
400 Mi.
400 Km.
200
200
0
0

KINGDOM OF NORWAY AND DENMARK
Stockholm
Copenhagen
KINGDOM OF SWEDEN
St. Petersburg
North Sea
Baltic Sea
SWEDISH POMERANIA

RUSSIAN EMPIRE
Moscow
Smolensk
Kiev

Neman
Tilsit
Friedland (1807)
Königsberg
Danzig
PRUSSIA
GRAND DUCHY OF WARSAW
Berlin
Lübeck
Hamburg
Bremen
WESTPHALIA
Auerstädt (1806)
Jena (1806)
SAXONY
Elbe
CONFEDERATION OF THE RHINE
WÜRTTEMBERG
BADEN
BAVARIA
Rhine
Waterloo (1815)
Brussels
Amiens
Paris
Lunéville
FRANCE
SWITZERLAND
Zurich
Marengo (1800)
Genoa
Milan
KINGDOM OF ITALY
Marseilles

Austerlitz (1805)
Wagram (1804)
Pressburg
Vienna
Buda
Pest
AUSTRIAN EMPIRE
Danube
ILLYRIAN PROVINCES

Black Sea
Constantinople
OTTOMAN EMPIRE
Athens

Corsica
Sardinia
Elba
Rome
Naples
KINGDOM OF NAPLES
Palermo
KINGDOM OF SICILY
Mediterranean Sea
IONIAN IS. (Gr. Br.)
MALTA (Gr. Br.)

SPAIN
Madrid
PORTUGAL
Lisbon
Trafalgar (1805)
GIBRALTAR (Gr. Br.)

The Revolution of 1830 in Belgium   After the 1830 uprising that overturned the restored monarchy in France, Belgians rose up to declare their independence from Holland. In Poland and Italy, similar uprisings, combining nationalism and a desire for self-governance, failed. This painting by Baron Gustaf Wappers romantically illustrates the popular nature of the Belgian uprising by bringing to the barricades men, women, and children drawn from both the middle and the working classes.   (Musées royaux des Beaux-Arts de Belgique, Brussels)

change occurred. Monarchs retained the support not only of aristocrats but also of professional militaries, largely recruited from among peasants who had little sympathy for urban workers.

REVOLUTION IN HAITI AND LATIN AMERICA

In the Americas, the revolutionary ideology of the American and French Revolutions was spreading and taking hold. On the island of Hispaniola, a revolution ended slavery and French rule in Saint Domingue. The same economic and political forces that had undermined British rule in the colonies that became the United States were present in Spanish America and Brazil.

The Haitian Revolution   The French colony of Saint Domingue produced two-thirds of France's tropical imports and generated nearly one-third of all French foreign trade. This impressive wealth depended on a brutal slave regime. Saint Domingue's harsh punishments and high mortality were notorious throughout the Caribbean.

In 1789, when news of the calling of France's Estates General arrived on the island, wealthy white planters sent a delegation to Paris charged with seeking more home rule and greater economic freedom. The ***gens de couleur*°** also sent representatives. Mostly small planters or urban merchants, these free mixed-race delegates focused on ending race discrimination and political inequality. They did not seek freedom for slaves, because the most prosperous gens de couleur were slave owners themselves.

The political turmoil in France weakened colonial authority, permitting rich planters, poor whites, gens de couleur, and slaves to pursue their narrow interests, in an increasingly bitter and confrontational struggle. By 1791, whites and the gens de couleur were engaged in open warfare. This breach between the two groups of slave owners gave the slaves an opening. Their rebellion began on the plantations of the north and spread throughout the colony. Plantations were destroyed, masters and overseers killed, and crops burned.

The rebellious slaves eventually gained the upper hand under the military leadership of **Toussaint L'Ouverture,** à former domestic slave. Politically strengthened in 1794 when the radical National Convention in Paris abolished slavery in all French possessions, Toussaint overcame his rivals in Saint Domingue, defeated a British expeditionary force in 1798, and then led an invasion of neighboring Santo Domingo, freeing the slaves there. Toussaint continued to assert his loyalty to France but gave the French government no effective role in local affairs.

In 1802, Napoleon sent a large military force to Saint Domingue to reestablish both French authority and slavery. At first, the French forces were successful. Toussaint was captured and sent to France, where he died in prison. Eventually, however, French losses to yellow fever and the resistance of the revolutionaries turned the tide. Few slave women had taken up arms during the early stages of the Haitian Revolution, but now they joined the armed resistance. In 1804, the free republic of Haiti joined the United States as the second independent nation in the Western Hemisphere. But independence and emancipation were achieved at a terrible price. Tens of thousands had died, and the economy was destroyed.

Latin American Revolutions

The great works of the Enlightenment as well as revolutionary documents like the Declaration of Independence and the Declaration of the Rights of Man circulated widely in Latin America. But it was Napoleon's decision to invade Portugal (1807) and Spain (1808), not revolutionary ideas, that ignited Latin America's struggle for independence.

In 1808, the royal family of Portugal fled to Brazil and maintained court there for over a decade. In Spain, in contrast, Napoleon forced King Ferdinand VII to abdicate and placed his own brother, Joseph Bonaparte, on the throne. When Spanish patriots fighting against the French created a new political body, the Junta° Central, and claimed the right to exercise the king's powers over Spain's colonies, a vocal minority of powerful colonists objected. In late 1808 and 1809, popular movements overthrew Spanish colonial officials in Venezuela, Mexico, and Bolivia and created local juntas. In each case, Spanish officials' harsh repression gave rise to a greater sense of a separate American nationality. By 1810, Spanish colonial authorities were facing a new round of revolutions more clearly focused on the achievement of independence.

In Caracas (the capital city of modern Venezuela), a revolutionary junta led by creoles (colonial-born whites) declared independence in 1811. Its leaders were large landowners who espoused popular sovereignty and representative democracy, defended slavery, and opposed full citizenship for the black and mixed-race majority. The junta's narrow agenda spurred loyalists in the colonial administration and church hierarchy to rally thousands of free blacks and slaves to defend the Spanish Empire. **Simón Bolívar°** (1783–1830) became the preeminent leader of the independence movement in Spanish South America.

Between 1813 and 1817, military advantage shifted back and forth between the patriots and loyalists, but by 1820, momentum swung irreversibly to the patriots. After liberating present-day Venezuela, Colombia, Ecuador, Peru, and Bolivia, Bolívar's army defeated the last Spanish armies in

---

gens de couleur (zhahn deh koo-LUHR)

Junta (HUN-tah)
Simón Bolívar (see-MOAN bow-LEE-varh)

1824. But Bolívar's attempt to draw the former Spanish colonies into a formal confederation failed (see Map 20.3).

Buenos Aires (the capital city of modern Argentina) was the second important center of revolutionary activity in Spanish South America. In the south, a coalition of militia commanders, merchants, and ranchers declared independence as the United Provinces of the Río de la Plata in 1816. Patriot leaders in Buenos Aires at first sought to retain control over the old Viceroyalty of Río de la Plata, but a separatist movement defeated these ambitions. A mixed force of Chileans and Argentines, led by José de San Martín° (1778–1850), liberated Chile in 1820. Simón Bolívar overcame final Spanish resistance in Peru in 1824.

The arrival of the Portuguese royal family in Brazil in 1808 had helped to maintain the loyalty of the colonial elite and to stimulate the local economy. But when King John VI returned to Portugal in 1821, Brazilians began to reevaluate Brazil's relationship with Portugal and to talk openly of independence.

Unwilling to return to Portugal and committed to maintaining his family's hold on Brazil, King John's son Pedro aligned himself with the rising tide of independence sentiment. In 1822, he declared Brazilian independence. Unlike its neighbors, which became constitutional republics, Brazil gained independence as a constitutional monarchy with Pedro I, heir to the throne of Portugal, as emperor. The monarchy lasted until 1889, when it was overthrown by republicans.

Mexico

In 1810, Mexico was Spain's richest and most populous colony. But the sharp distinctions among its creole, native, and Spanish populations made it ripe for revolution. The first stage of the revolution against Spain occurred in central Mexico, where wealthy ranchers and farmers had aggressively forced many Amerindian communities from their traditional agricultural lands. By the time news of Napoleon's invasion of Spain reached the region, crop failures and epidemics had further afflicted the poor.

On September 16, 1810, **Miguel Hidalgo y Costilla°**, parish priest of the small town of Dolores, rang the church bells, attracting thousands. In a fiery speech, he urged the crowd to rise up against the oppression of Spanish officials. Tens of thousands of the rural and urban poor joined his movement. They lacked military discipline and adequate weapons but knew who their oppressors were. At first sympathetic to Hidalgo's objectives, wealthy Mexicans eventually turned against Hidalgo, who was captured, tried, and executed in 1811.

Although insurgents continued to wage war against Spanish forces, colonial rule seemed secure in 1820. However, news of the military revolt in Spain unsettled the conservative groups and church officials who had defended Spanish rule against Hidalgo and Morelos. In 1821, Colonel Agustín de Iturbide° and other loyalist commanders forged an alliance with remaining insurgents and declared Mexico's independence. The conservative origins of Mexico's transition to independence were highlighted by the decision to create a monarchical form of government and crown Iturbide as emperor. In early 1823, however, the army overthrew Iturbide and Mexico became a republic.

ECONOMIC AND SOCIAL LIBERATION MOVEMENTS

During the nineteenth century, the newly independent nations of the Western Hemisphere struggled to realize the Enlightenment ideals of freedom and individual liberty. The persistence of slavery and women's inequality raised troubling questions about these ideals. By century's end, reform movements in many of the hemisphere's nations had made significant progress, but much remained to be done.

José de San Martín (hoe-SAY deh san mar-TEEN)

Miguel Hidalgo y Costilla (mee-GEHL ee-DAHL-go ee cos-TEA-ah)
Agustín de Iturbide (ah-goos-TEEN deh ee-tur-BEE-deh)

Map 20.3 Latin America by 1830 By 1830, patriot forces had overturned the Spanish and Portuguese Empires of the Western Hemisphere. Regional conflicts, local wars, and foreign interventions challenged the survival of many of these new nations following independence

Labels within the map:

OREGON COUNTRY (Joint U.S.-British occupation)

BRITISH NORTH AMERICA (Gr. Br.)

UNITED STATES

Mississippi

Colorado

Rio Grande

MEXICO 1821

San Antonio

ATLANTIC OCEAN

Gulf of Mexico

Mexico City • Veracruz

BAHAMA IS. (Gr. Br.)

Havana

CUBA (Spain)

HAITI 1804

PUERTO RICO (Spain)

BRITISH HONDURAS (Gr. Br.)

GUATEMALA
Guatemala

JAMAICA (Gr. Br.)

Caribbean Sea

UNITED PROVINCES OF CENTRAL AMERICA 1823—1839

Panama

Caracas

TRINIDAD (Gr. Br.)

VENEZUELA

BR. GUIANA (Gr. Br.)

DUTCH GUIANA (Neth.)

FRENCH GUIANA (France)

Socorro
Bogotá

Magdalena

GRAN COLOMBIA 1819—1830

Quito

ECUADOR

Galápagos Islands

Amazon

EMPIRE OF BRAZIL 1822

PERU 1824

Lima

PACIFIC OCEAN

Bahia

BOLIVIA 1825

La Paz

Sucre

Paraná

PARAGUAY 1811

São Paulo

Rio de Janeiro

CHILE 1817

UNITED PROVINCES OF THE RÍO DE LA PLATA 1816

Valparaíso
Santiago

ARGENTINA

Buenos Aires
Bahía Blanca

URUGUAY 1828

Montevideo

1811 Year independence gained

Colony

0   500   1000 Km.

0   500   1000 Mi.

PATAGONIA (Disputed between Argentina and Chile)

Islas Malvinas (Falkland Islands)

Benito Juárez's Triumph over the French   Benito Juárez overcame humble origins to lead the overthrow of French imperialism. He remains a powerful symbol of secularism and republican virtue in Mexico. In this 1948 mural by José Clemente Orozco, Juárez's face dominates a scene of struggle that pits Mexican patriots against the allied forces of the Catholic Church, Mexican conservatives, and foreign invaders.   (Museo Nacional de Historia/CENIDIAP-INBA)

The Abolition of Slavery

In both the United States and Latin America, strong antislavery sentiments were expressed during the struggles for independence. In nearly all the new nations of the Western Hemisphere, revolutionary leaders asserted universal ideals of freedom and citizenship that contrasted sharply with the reality of slavery. Men and women who wanted to outlaw slavery were called **abolitionists.** Despite the efforts of abolitionists, slavery survived in much of the hemisphere until the 1850s. In regions where the export of plantation products was most important—such as the United States, Brazil, and Cuba—the abolition of slavery was achieved with great difficulty.

In the United States, some northern states had abolished slavery after the revolution, and Congress banned the importation of new slaves in 1808. But this progress was stalled by the profitable expansion of cotton agriculture after the War of 1812. In Spanish America, tens of thousands of slaves gained freedom by joining revolutionary armies during the wars for independence. After independence, most Spanish American republics prohibited the slave trade. Counteracting that trend was the growing international demand for sugar and coffee, products traditionally produced on plantations by slaves. As prices rose for plantation products in the first half of the nineteenth century, Brazil and Cuba (a Spanish colony until 1899) increased their imports of slaves.

During the long struggle to end slavery in the United States, American abolitionists argued that slavery offended both morality and the universal rights asserted in the Declaration of Independence. Two groups denied full rights of citizenship under the Constitution, women and free African-Americans, played important roles in the abolition of slavery. Women served on the executive committee of the American Anti-Slavery Society and produced some of the most effective propaganda against slavery. Many women abolitionists advocated female suffrage as well. Frederick Douglass, a former slave, became one of the most effective abolitionist speakers and writers. More radical black leaders saw civil war or slave insurrection as necessary for ending slavery.

During the Civil War, pressure for emancipation rose as tens of thousands of black freemen and escaped slaves joined the Union army. Hundreds of thousands of other slaves fled their masters' plantations and farms for the protection of advancing northern armies. In 1863, in the midst of the Civil War, President Lincoln began the abolition of slavery by issuing the Emancipation Proclamation, which ended slavery in rebel states not occupied by the Union army. Final abolition was accomplished in 1865, by the Thirteenth Amendment to the Constitution.

After Britain ended its participation in the slave trade in 1807, it negotiated treaties with Spain, Brazil, and other importers of slaves to eliminate the slave trade to the Americas. But enforcement proved difficult. For example, Brazil, despite its treaty of 1830, illegally imported over a half-million more African slaves before the British navy finally forced compliance in the 1850s. The Brazilian parliament passed legislation abolishing slavery in 1888.

Slavery lasted longest in Cuba. Despite strong British pressure, the Spanish colony continued to import large numbers of African slaves until the 1860s. More important, however, was the growth of support for abolition in these colonies. Both Cuba and Puerto Rico had larger white and free colored populations than did the Caribbean colonies of Britain and France. As a result, there was less fear in Cuba and Puerto Rico that abolition would lead to the political ascendancy of former slaves (as had occurred in Haiti). In Puerto Rico, where slaves numbered approximately thirty thousand, local reformers sought and gained the abolition of slavery in 1873. Eventually, during a decade-long war to defeat forces seeking the independence of Cuba, the Spanish government moved toward gradual abolition. Finally, in 1886, slavery was abolished.

Equal Rights for Women and Blacks

The abolition of slavery in the Western Hemisphere did not end racial discrimination or provide full political rights for every citizen. Not only blacks but also women suffered political and economic discrimination during the nineteenth century.

In 1848, a group of women angered by their exclusion from an international antislavery meeting issued a call for a meeting to discuss women's rights. The **Women's Rights Convention** at Seneca Falls, New York, issued a statement that said in part, "We hold these truths to be self-evident: that all men and women are equal." While moderates focused on the issues of greater economic independence and full legal rights, increasing numbers of women demanded the right to vote. Others lobbied to provide better conditions for women working outside the home, especially in textile factories.

Progress toward equality between men and women was equally slow in Canada and Latin America. Canada's first women doctors received their training in the United States because no woman was able to receive a medical degree in Canada until 1895. Argentina and Uruguay were among the first Latin American nations to provide public education for women. Both nations introduced coeducation in the 1870s. Chilean women gained access to some careers in medicine and law in the 1870s. In Brazil, where many women were active in the abolitionist movement, four women graduated in medicine by 1882. Throughout the hemisphere, more rapid progress was achieved in lower-status careers that threatened male economic power less directly, and by the end of the century, women dominated elementary school teaching throughout the Western Hemisphere.

From Canada to Argentina and Chile, the majority of working-class women had no direct involvement in these reform movements, but in their daily lives, they succeeded in transforming gender relations. By the end of the nineteenth century, large numbers of poor women worked outside the home on farms, in markets, and, increasingly, in factories.

Throughout the hemisphere, there was little progress toward eliminating racial discrimination. Blacks were denied the vote throughout the southern United States and subjected to the indignity of segregation. Racial discrimination against men and women of African descent was also common in Latin America, though seldom spelled out in legal codes. Latin Americans tended to view racial identity across a continuum of physical characteristics rather than in the narrow terms of black and white that defined race relations in the United States.

CONCLUSION

The revolutions of the late eighteenth century hastened the transformation of Western society. Royal governments attempting to impose new taxes to pay war debts collided with ideas of elections and representative institutions. French officers who took part in the American Revolution helped ignite the French Revolution. Black freemen from Haiti traveled to France to seek their rights and returned to spread revolutionary passions. Napoleon's invasion of Portugal and Spain then helped initiate the movement toward independence in Latin America. The promises of universal citizenship were only partially achieved.

Each revolution had its own character. The revolutions in France and Haiti were more violent and destructive than the mainland American revolutions. In many places, monarchy, multinational empires, and the established church contested with liberal and nationalist sentiments well into the nineteenth century. Only a minority gained full political rights. Democratic institutions often failed. Slavery endured in the Americas past the mid-1800s.

■ Key Terms

Enlightenment
George Washington
Constitutional Convention
Estates General
National Assembly
Declaration of the
   Rights of Man
Napoleon Bonaparte
Congress of Vienna

Revolutions of 1848
gens de couleur
Toussaint L'Ouverture
Simón Bolívar
Miguel Hidalgo y Costilla
abolitionists
Women's Rights
   Convention

■ Suggested Reading

Eric Hobsbawm's *The Age of Revolution* (1962) provides a clear analysis of the class issues that appeared during this era. The American Revolution has received a great amount of attention from scholars. Colin Bonwick, *The American Revolution* (1991), and Edward Countryman, *The American Revolution* (1985), provide excellent introductions.

François Furet, *Interpreting the French Revolution* (1981), breaks with interpretations that emphasize class and ideological interpretations. Georges Lefebve, *The Coming of the French Revolution*, trans. R. R. Palmer (1947), presents the classic class-based analysis. George Rudé, *The Crowd in History: Popular Disturbances in France and England* (1981), remains the best introduction to the role of mass protest in the period. The recently published *The Women of Paris and Their French Revolution* (1998) by Dominique Godineau; Felix Markham, *Napoleon* (1963); and Robert B. Holtman, *The Napoleonic Revolution* (1967), provide reliable summaries of the period. For a brief survey of the revolutions of 1830 and 1848, see Arthur J. May, *The Age of Metternich, 1814–48*, rev. ed. (1963).

The classic study of the Haitian Revolution is C. L. R. James, *The Black Jacobins*, 2d ed. (1963). For the independence era in Latin America, see John Lynch, *The Spanish American Revolutions, 1808–1826*, 2d ed. (1986); Jay Kinsbruner, *Independence in Spanish America* (1994); and A. J. R. Russell-Wood, ed., *From Colony to Nation: Essays on the Independence of Brazil* (1976).

On the issue of slavery, see David Brion Davis, *Slavery and Human Progress* (1984); George M. Frederickson, *The Black Image in the White Mind: The Debate on Afro-American Character and Destiny, 1817–1914* (1971); and Benjamin Quarles, *Black Abolitionists* (1969). For abolition in Latin America and the Caribbean, see Rebecca Scott, *Slave Emancipation in Cuba: The Transition to Free Labor, 1860–1899* (1985); Robert Conrad, *The Destruction of Brazilian Slavery, 1850–1888* (1973); and William A. Green, *British Slave Emancipation: The Sugar Colonies and the Great Experiment, 1830–1865* (1976).

An excellent history of immigration is Walter Nagent, *Crossings: The Great Transatlantic Migrations, 1870–1914* (1992). For the women's rights movement see Ellen Carol DuBois, *Feminism and Suffrage: The Emergence of an Independent Women's Movement in America, 1848–1869* (1999).

21

THE EARLY INDUSTRIAL REVOLUTION, 1760–1851

Causes of the Industrial Revolution • The Technological
Revolution • The Impact of the Industrial Revolution • Responses
to Industrialization • The Effects of Industrialization in Russia
and the Ottoman Empire
SOCIETY AND CULTURE: Charles Babbage, Ada Lovelace,
and the "Analytical Engine"

n January 1840, a shipyard in Britain launched a radically new ship. The *Nemesis* had an iron hull, a flat bottom so it could navigate in shallow waters, and a steam engine to power it upriver and against the wind. The ship was heavily armed. In November, it arrived off the coast of China. Though ships from Europe had been sailing to China for three hundred years, the *Nemesis* was the first steam-powered iron gunboat seen in Asian waters. A Chinese observer noted: "Iron is employed to make it strong. The hull is painted black, weaver's shuttle fashion. On each side is a wheel, which by the use of coal fire is made to revolve as fast as a running horse. . . . At the vessel's head is a Marine God, and at the head, stern, and sides are cannon, which give it a terrific appearance. Steam vessels are a wonderful invention of for-eigners, and are calculated to offer delight to many."[1]

Instead of offering delight, the *Nemesis* and other steam-powered warships that soon joined it steamed up the Chinese rivers, bombarded forts and cities, and brought in troops and sup-plies. With this new weapon, Britain, a small is-land nation half a world away, was able to defeat the largest and most populated country in the world in its own heartland.

The *Nemesis* was no isolated invention. Its outstanding features—steam power and cheap iron—were part of a larger phenomenon, the **Industrial Revolution,** that involved dramatic innovations in manufacturing, mining, trans-portation, and communications and equally rapid changes in society and commerce. New technologies and new social and economic arrangements allowed the industrializing coun-tries—first Britain, followed by western Europe and the United States—to unleash massive in-creases in production and productivity, exploit the world's natural resources as never before, and transform the environment and human life in unprecedented ways.

The distribution of this power and wealth was very uneven within industrializing countries and around the world. The first countries to industrialize grew in wealth and power. China and other regions without industry were easily taken advantage of. Russia and eastern Europe managed their own industrial revolutions by the end of the nineteenth century. But in Egypt, India, and a few other non-Western countries, the economic and military power of the European countries soon stifled the tentative beginnings of industrialization.

As you read this chapter, ask yourself the following questions:

- What caused the Industrial Revolution?
- What were the key innovations that increased productivity and drove industrialization?
- What was the impact of these changes on the society and environment of the industrializing countries?
- How did the Industrial Revolution affect the relations between the industrialized and the nonindustrialized parts of the world?

CAUSES OF THE INDUSTRIAL REVOLUTION

What caused the Industrial Revolution, and why did it begin in England in the late eighteenth century? The basic precondition of this momentous event seems to have been economic development propelled by population growth, an agricultural revolution, the expansion of trade, and an openness to innovation.

Preconditions for Industrialization

The population of Europe rose in the eighteenth century—slowly at first, faster after 1780, then even faster in the early nineteenth century. The population of England and Wales rose unusually fast—from 5.5 million in 1688 to 18 million by 1851. Industrialization and the population boom reinforced each other. A high birthrate meant a large percentage of children, which explains both the vitality of the British people in that period and the widespread use of child labor.

This population explosion and urbanization could only have taken place alongside an **agricultural revolution** that provided food for city dwellers and forced poorer peasants off the land. Long before the eighteenth century, the introduction and acceptance of the potato and maize from the Americas had increased food supplies in Europe. In the cool and humid regions of Europe, from Ireland to Russia, potatoes yielded two or three times more food per acre than grain. Maize (American corn) was grown across Europe from southwestern France to the Balkans.

During the seventeenth century, rich English landowners began draining marshes, improving the soil, and introducing crop rotation using turnips, legumes, and clover that did not deplete the soil and could be fed to cattle. Additional manure from improved breeds of livestock fertilized the soil for other crops. Some also "enclosed" land—that is, consolidated their holdings, including commons that in the past had been open to all. This "enclosure movement" also turned tenants and sharecroppers into landless farm laborers. Many moved to the cities to seek work; others became homeless migrants and vagrants; still others emigrated.

The growth of the population and food supply was accompanied by the growth of trade. Most of it was local, but a growing share consisted of imports from other parts of the world like tea and sugar and simple goods that even middle-class people could afford, such as cotton textiles, iron hardware, and pottery.

Trade was accompanied by a growing interest in technology and innovation among educated people throughout Europe and eastern North

CHRONOLOGY

	Technology	Economy, Society, and Politics
1750		
	1759 Josiah Wedgwood opens pottery factory	
	1764 Spinning jenny	
	1769 Richard Arkwright's water frame; James Watt patents steam engine	**1776** Adam Smith's *Wealth of Nations*
		1776–1783 American Revolution
	1779 First iron bridge	
	1785 Boulton and Watt sell steam engines; Samuel Crompton's mule	**1789–1799** French Revolution
	1793 Eli Whitney's cotton gin	
1800	**1800** Alessandro Volta's battery	
	1807 Robert Fulton's *Clermont*	**1804–1815** Napoleonic Wars
	1820s Construction of Erie Canal	**1820s** U.S. cotton industry begins
	1829 *Rocket,* first steam-powered locomotive	
		1833 Factory Act in Britain
	1837 Wheatstone & Cooke's telegraph	**1834** German Zollverein; Robert Owen's Grand National Consolidated Trade Union
	1838 First ships steam across the Atlantic	
	1840 *Nemesis* sails to China	
	1843 Samuel Morse's Baltimore-to-Washington telegraph	**1846** Repeal of British Corn Laws
		1847–1848 Irish famine
		1848 Collapse of Chartist movement; revolutions in Europe
1850	**1851** Crystal Palace opens in London	**1853–1856** Crimean War

America. They read descriptions of new techniques and inventions in many publications, and some experimented on their own.

Britain's Advantages

These changes were widespread, but Britain in the eighteenth century had the fastest-growing population, food supply, and overseas trade. The British also put inventions into practice more quickly than other people. In the eighteenth century, Britain became the world's leading exporter of tools, guns, hardware, and other craft goods. Its mining and metal industries employed engineers willing to experiment with new ideas. It had the largest merchant marine and produced more ships, naval supplies, and navigation instruments than other countries.

Moreover, Britain had a more fluid society than the rest of Europe. Political power was not as centralized as on the European continent, and the government employed fewer bureaucrats and officials. Class lines eased as members of the gentry, and even some aristocrats, married into merchant families. Intermarriage among the families of petty merchants, yeoman farmers, and town craftsmen was common.

At a time when transportation by land was very costly, Great Britain had good water transportation, thanks to its indented coastline, navigable rivers, and growing network of canals (see Map 21.1). It had a unified internal market, with none of the duties and tolls that goods had to pay every few miles in France. This encouraged specialization and trade. More people there were involved in production for export and in trade and finance than in any other major country. It had financial and

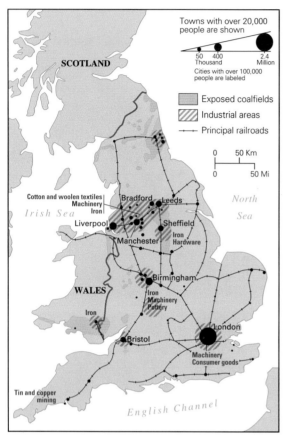

Map 21.1 The Industrial Revolution in Britain, ca. 1850 The first industries arose in northern and western England. These regions had abundant coal and iron-ore deposits for the iron industry and a moist climate and fast-flowing rivers, factors important for the cotton-textile industry.

insurance institutions able to support growing business enterprises and a patent system that offered inventors the hope of rich rewards.

By 1830, the political climate in western Europe was as favorable to business as Britain's had been a half-century earlier. Industrialization first took hold in Belgium and northern France, as their businessmen visited Britain to observe the changes and to spy out industrial secrets. In spite of British laws forbidding the emigration of skilled workers and the export of textile machinery, many slipped through, setting up machines, training workers in the new methods, and even starting their own businesses. European governments created technical schools; eliminated internal tariff barriers, tolls, and other hindrances to trade; and encouraged the formation of joint-stock companies and banks to channel private savings into industrial investments. On the European continent, as in Britain, cotton was the first industry to industrialize.

THE TECHNOLOGICAL REVOLUTION

Five revolutionary innovations spurred industrialization: (1) mass production through the division of labor, (2) new machines and mechanization, (3) a great increase in the supply of iron, (4) the steam engine and the changes it made possible in industry and transportation, and (5) the electric telegraph.

Mass Production and Mechanization

The pottery industry offers a good example of **mass production,** the making of many identical items by breaking the process into simple repetitive tasks. **Josiah Wedgwood** opened a pottery business in 1759 that was able to produce porcelain cheaply, by means of the **division of labor.** He subdivided the work into highly specialized and repetitive tasks, such as unloading the clay, mixing it, pressing flat pieces, dipping the pieces in glaze, putting handles on cups, packing kilns, and carrying things from one part of his plant to another. He substituted the use of molds for the potter's wheel wherever possible, a change that not only saved labor but created identical plates and bowls that could be stacked. These radical departures from the age-old methods of craftsmanship allowed Wedgwood to lower the cost of his products while improving their quality. As a result, his factory grew far larger than his competitors' factories and employed several hundred workers. His own salesmen traveled throughout England touting his goods.

Wedgwood's Potteries   In Staffordshire, England, Josiah Wedgwood established a factory to mass-produce beautiful and inexpensive china. The bottle-shape buildings are kilns in which thousands of pieces of china could be fired at one time. Kilns, factories, and housing were all mixed together in pottery towns, and smoke from burning coal filled the air.   (Mary Evans Picture Library)

Wedgwood was also interested in new technologies. He invested in toll roads and canals so that clay could be shipped economically from southwestern England to his factories in the Midlands. In 1782, to mix clay and grind flint, he purchased one of the first steam engines to be used in industry. Wedgwood's interest in applying technology to manufacturing was connected with his membership in the Birmingham Lunar Society, a group of manufacturers, scientists, and inventors who met when the moon was full so they could see their way home after dark. This critical mass of creative thinkers willing to exchange ideas and discoveries encouraged the atmosphere of experimentation and innovation that characterized late-eighteenth-century England. Similar societies

throughout Britain were creating a vogue for science and giving the word *progress* a new meaning: "change for the better" (see Society and Culture: Charles Babbage, Ada Lovelace, and the "Analytical Engine").

The cotton industry, the largest industry in this period, illustrates the role of **mechanization,** the use of machines to do work previously done by hand. The cotton plant did not grow in Europe, but the cloth was so much cooler, softer, and cleaner than wool that wealthy Europeans developed a liking for this costly import. When the powerful English woolen industry persuaded Parliament to forbid the import of cotton cloth into England, it stimulated attempts to import cotton fiber and make the cloth locally. Here was an opportunity for enterprising inventors to reduce costs with labor-saving machinery.

Beginning in the 1760s, a series of inventions—the spinning jenny, the water frame, and the mule—revolutionized the spinning of cotton thread and allowed British industry to undersell high-quality handmade cotton cloth from India. British cotton output increased tenfold between 1770 and 1790.

When the boom in thread production and the soaring demand for cloth created bottlenecks in weaving, inventors in England rose to the challenge with power looms, carding machines, chlorine bleach, and cylindrical printing presses. By the 1830s, large English textile mills powered by steam engines were turning raw cotton into printed cloth. This was a far cry from the cottage industries of the previous century.

Mechanization offered two advantages: (1) productivity for the manufacturer and (2) price for the consumer. Whereas in India it took 500 hours to spin a pound of cotton, the improved mule of 1830 required only 80 minutes. Cotton mills needed very few skilled workers, and managers often hired children to tend the spinning machines. Mechanization and cheap labor allowed the price of cloth to fall by 90 percent from 1782 to 1812, and it kept on dropping.

The industrialization of Britain made cotton into America's most valuable crop. In 1793, the American Eli Whitney patented his cotton gin, a simple device that separated the bolls from the fiber and made the growing of short-staple cotton

Charles Babbage, Ada Lovelace, and the "Analytical Engine"

In the early nineteenth century, many professions relied on tables of numbers such as logarithms, astronomical positions, and actuarial data. Calculated by hand, these tables were full of arithmetic and typographical errors. In 1820, while correcting such a table, the English mathematician Charles Babbage exclaimed: "I wish to God these calculations had been executed by steam." Babbage went on to devise a machine—he called it the "Difference Engine"—to perform calculations and print out the results as flawlessly as a power loom produced cloth. While a prototype was being built, he designed the "Analytical Engine," which could interpret instructions inserted on punched cards and could alter its calculations in response to the results of previous calculations.

One of Babbage's assistants, Ada, the countess of Lovelace, translated an article by the Italian military engineer L. F. Menabrea about the Analytical Engine for the magazine Taylor's Scientific Memoirs. *In his autobiography, published in 1864, Babbage recalled: "The late Countess of Lovelace informed me that she had translated the memoir of Menabrea. I asked why she had not herself written an original paper on a subject with which she was so intimately acquainted? To this Lady Lovelace replied that the thought had not occurred to her. I then suggested that she should add some notes to Menabrea's memoir; an idea which was immediately adopted. . . . The notes of the Countess of Lovelace extend to about three times the length of the original memoir. Their author has entered fully into almost all the very difficult and abstract questions concerned with the subject.*

In the notes that she added to Menabrea's article, Ada Lovelace wrote the following:

The distinctive characteristic of the Analytical Engine, and that which has rendered it possible to endow mechanism with such extensive faculties as bid fair to make this engine the executive right-hand of abstract algebra, is the introduction into it of the principle which Jacquard devised for regulating, by means of punched cards, the most complicated patterns in the fabrication of brocaded stuffs [fabrics]. . . .

The bounds of *arithmetic* were outstepped the moment the idea of applying the cards had occurred; and the Analytical Engine does not occupy common ground with mere "calculating machines." It holds a position wholly its own; and the considerations it suggests are most interesting in their nature. . . . A new, a vast, and a powerful language is developed for the future use of analysis, in which to wield its truths so that these may become of more speedy and accurate practical application for the purposes of mankind than the means hitherto in our possession have rendered possible. Thus not only the mental and the material, but the theoretical and the practical in the mathematical world, are brought into more intimate and effective connexion with each other. We are not aware of its being on record that anything partaking in the nature of what is so well designated the *Analytical Engine* has been hitherto proposed, or even thought of, as a practical possibility, any more than the idea of a thinking or of a reasoning machine.

In short, Babbage invented the computer.

The first working computers were not built until a hundred years later, but Babbage is honored as the first person to imagine such a machine. And the widely used programming language Ada is named after his friend, the countess of Lovelace.

Is "a thinking or . . . a reasoning machine" a good description of a computer? Because Babbage's Analytical Engine did not use electricity, can it really be called a computer?

Source: From Philip Morison and Emily Morison, eds., *Charles Babbage and His Calculating Engines: Selected Writings by Charles Babbage and Others* (New York: Dover, 1961), 68, 251–252. © Copyright 1961. Reprinted by permission of Dover Publications.

economical. This invention permitted the spread of cotton farming into Georgia, then into Alabama, Mississippi, and Louisiana, and finally as far west as Texas. By the late 1850s, the southern states were producing a million tons of cotton a year, five-sixths of the world's total.

With the help of British craftsmen who introduced jennies, mules, and power looms, Americans developed a cotton industry in the 1820s. By 1840, the United States had 1,200 cotton mills, two-thirds of them in New England, powered by water rather than steam. Americans so excelled at the use of interchangeable parts in mass-producing guns that Europeans called it the "American system of manufactures." In the next hundred years, the use of machinery to mass-produce consumer items was to become the hallmark of American industry.

Iron and Steam

Iron making also was transformed during the Industrial Revolution. Iron had been in use for thousands of years for tools, swords and other weapons, and household items such as knives, pots, hinges, and locks. Wherever it was produced, however, deforestation eventually drove up the cost of charcoal (used for smelting) and restricted output. Furthermore, iron had to be repeatedly heated and hammered to drive out impurities, a difficult and costly process. Then in 1709, Abraham Darby discovered that coke (coal from which the impurities have been cooked out) could be used in place of charcoal. The resulting metal was of lower quality than charcoal iron but much cheaper to produce, for coal was plentiful. Britain's iron production began rising fast, from 17,000 tons in 1740 to 3 million tons in 1844, as much as in the rest of the world put together.

Opening of the Saltash Bridge over the Tamar River in England in 1859   During the celebrations, a steam locomotive pulled a train over the bridge while a steam-powered paddle wheeler passed underneath.   (Elton Collection, Ironbridge Gorge Museum Trust)

Even more important than the mechanization of manufacturing was the invention of the **steam engine.** Thomas Newcomen developed a crude and inefficient steam engine between 1702 and 1712 for use in coal mines, where its voracious appetite for fuel mattered little. Then **James Watt,** an instrument maker at Glasgow University in Scotland, developed an improved version and patented his idea in 1769. Seven years later, he and Matthew Boulton began selling steam engines to manufacturers of iron, pottery, and cotton.

Watt's steam engine was the most celebrated invention of the eighteenth century. Because there seemed almost no limit to the amount of coal in the ground, steam-generated energy seemed an inexhaustible source of power, and steam engines could be used where animal, wind, and water power were lacking. Without the steam engine, industrialization would have been a limited phenomenon.

Inspired by the success of Watt's engine, inventors in France in 1783, in the United States in 1787, and in England in 1788 put steam engines on boats. The first commercially successful steamboat was Robert Fulton's *Clermont,* which steamed between New York City and Albany in 1807. The first steam engines used so much coal that no ship could carry more than a few days' worth, but engineers soon developed more efficient engines, and in 1838 two steamers, the *Great Western* and the *Sirius,* crossed the Atlantic on steam power alone.

On land as on water, the problem was not imagining uses for steam-powered vehicles but building ones that worked, for steam engines were too heavy and weak to pull any weight. After Watt's patent expired in 1800, inventors experimented with lighter, more powerful high-pressure engines and in the early 1800s built several steam-powered vehicles able to travel on roads or rails. Between 1830 and 1850, a railroad-building mania swept Britain. The first lines linked towns and mines with the nearest harbor or waterway. As passenger traffic soared, entrepreneurs built lines between the major cities and then to small towns as well. Railroads were far cheaper, faster, and more comfortable than stagecoaches, and millions of people got in the habit of traveling.

In the United States, entrepreneurs built railroads as fast and cheaply as possible. By the 1840s,

The *De Witt Clinton* Locomotive, 1835–1840 The *De Witt Clinton* was the first steam locomotive built in the United States. The high smokestack let the hot cinders cool so they would not set fire to nearby trees, an important consideration at a time when eastern North America was still covered with forests. The three passenger cars are clearly horse-carriages fitted with railroad wheels. (Corbis)

6,000 miles (10,000 kilometers) of track radiated westward from Boston, New York, Philadelphia, and Baltimore. The boom of the 1840s was dwarfed by the mania of the 1850s, when 21,000 miles (34,000 kilometers) of new track were laid, much of it westward across the Appalachians to Memphis, St. Louis, and Chicago. The trip from New York to Chicago, which once took three weeks by boat and on horseback, could be made in forty-eight hours. The railroads opened up the Midwest, turning the vast prairie into wheat fields and pasture for cattle to feed the industrial cities of the eastern United States.

Railways triggered the industrialization of Europe. Belgium, independent since 1830, quickly copied the British. State-planned and -supervised railroad construction in the mid-1840s in France and Prussia not only satisfied the long-standing need for transportation, but also stimulated the iron, machinery, and construction industries. In the 1850s and 1860s, the states of Germany also experienced an industrial boom.

Borsig Ironworks in Germany in the 1840s
This foundry was built to supply rails, locomotives, and other iron products to the German railroads, then under construction.
(Deutsches Technikmuseum Berlin. Photo: Hans-Joachim Bartsch. Bildarchiv Preussischer Kulturbesitz)

Communication over Wires

The advent of railroads coincided with the development of the **electric telegraph.** After the Italian scientist Alessandro Volta invented the battery in 1800, making it possible to produce an electric current, many inventors tried to apply electricity to communication. The first practical telegraphy systems were developed almost simultaneously in England and America. In England, Wheatstone and Cooke introduced a five-needle telegraph in 1837; it remained in use until the early twentieth century. That same year, the American Samuel Morse introduced a code of dots and dashes that could be transmitted with a single wire; in 1843, he erected a line between Washington and Baltimore.

By the late 1840s, telegraph wires were being strung throughout the eastern United States and western Europe. In 1851, the first submarine telegraph cable was laid across the English Channel from England to France; it was the beginning of a network that eventually enclosed the entire globe. The world was rapidly shrinking, to the applause of Europeans and Americans for whom speed was a clear measure of progress. No longer were communications limited to the speed of which a ship could sail or a horse could gallop.

THE IMPACT OF THE INDUSTRIAL REVOLUTION

Although inventions were the most visible aspect of the Industrial Revolution, many other changes in society, politics, and the economy took place. Early changes—smoky cities, slum neighborhoods, polluted water, child labor in mines and textile mills—were being alleviated by the mid-nineteenth century. But by then national or even international problems were replacing these local ones: business cycles, labor conflicts, and the transformation of entire regions into industrial landscapes.

New Industrial Cities

The most dramatic environmental changes brought about by industrialization occurred in the towns. Never before had towns grown so fast. London, one of the largest cities in Europe in 1700 with 500,000 inhabitants, grew to 959,000 by 1800 and to 2,363,000 by 1850, by then the largest city in the world. Smaller towns grew even faster. Manchester's population increased eightfold in a century. Liverpool grew sixfold in the first sixty years of the nineteenth century. New York City, already 100,000 strong in 1815, reached 600,000 (including Brooklyn) in 1850. In some areas, towns merged and formed megalopolises, such as Greater London, the English Midlands, central Belgium, and the Ruhr district of Germany.

People who prospered greatly from industrialization poured their new wealth into fine new homes, churches, museums, and theaters. Yet by all accounts, the industrial cities grew much too fast. As poor migrants streamed in from the countryside, developers built cheap, shoddy row houses for them to rent. These tenements were dangerously overcrowded. Often, several families had to live in one small room. Town dwellers recently arrived from the country brought country ways with them. People threw their sewage and trash out the windows to be washed down the gutters in the streets. The poor kept pigs and chickens, the rich kept horses, and pedestrians stepped into the street at their own risk. Air pollution from burning coal got steadily worse. People drank water drawn from wells and rivers contaminated by sewage and industrial runoff. The River Irwell, which ran through Manchester, was, in the words of one visitor, "considerably less a river than a flood of liquid manure."

To the long list of preindustrial urban diseases such as smallpox, dysentery, and tuberculosis, industrialization added new ailments. Rickets, a bone disease caused by lack of sunshine, became endemic in dark and smoky industrial cities. Steamships brought cholera from India, causing great epidemics that struck the poor neighborhoods especially hard. In the 1850s, when the average life expectancy in England was forty years, it was only twenty-four years in Manchester, and around seventeen years in Manchester's poorest neighborhoods, because of the high infant mortality. Shocking reports of slum life led to municipal reforms, such as garbage removal, water and sewage systems, and parks and schools. These measures began to alleviate the ills of urban life after the mid-nineteenth century.

Rural Environments

Long before the Industrial Revolution began, practically no wilderness areas were left in Britain and very few in western Europe. Human activity had turned almost every piece of land into fields, forests, pastures, or towns. The most serious problem was deforestation. People cut timber to build ships and houses, to heat homes, and to manufacture bricks, iron, glass, beer, bread, and many other items.

Americans transformed their environment even faster than Europeans did. Settlers viewed forests not as a valuable resource but as a hindrance to development. In their haste to "open up the West," pioneers felled trees and burned them, built houses and abandoned them when they moved on. The cultivation of cotton was especially harmful. Planters cut down forests, grew cotton for a few years until it depleted the soil, and then moved west, abandoning the land to scrub pines. The American idea of nature as an obstacle to be overcome and dominated persisted long after the entire continent was occupied.

To contemporaries, the new transportation systems brought the most obvious changes in rural life. Governments and private trusts built numerous roads. Canal building boomed in Britain, France, and the Low Countries in the late eighteenth century. Canals were marvels of construction, with deep cuts, tunnels, and even aqueducts that carried barges over rivers. They also were a sort of school where engineers learned skills they were able to apply to the next great transportation system: the railroads. They laid track across rolling country by cutting deeply into hillsides and erecting daringly long bridges of stone and iron across valleys. Soon, clanking trains pulled by puffing, smoke-belching locomotives were invading long-isolated districts.

Thus, in the century after industrialization began, the landscape of industrializing countries was transformed more rapidly than ever before. But the ecological changes, like the technological and economic changes that caused them, were only beginning.

The McCormick Reaper
In the nineteenth century, the machine age arrived in the countryside. The McCormick reaper increased productivity and also promoted the concentration of land in grain-producing regions of the United States. (Navistar International Harvester Archives)

Working Conditions

Most industrial jobs were unskilled, repetitive, and boring. Factory work did not vary with the seasons or the time of day but began and ended by the clock. Workdays were long, there were few breaks, and foremen watched constantly. Workers who performed one simple task over and over had little sense of achievement or connection to the final product. Industrial accidents were common and could ruin a family. Unlike even the poorest preindustrial farmer or artisan, factory workers had no control over their tools, jobs, or working hours.

Women workers were concentrated in textile mills, partly because of ancient traditions, partly because textile work required less strength than metalworking, construction, or hauling. On average, women earned one-third to one-half as much as men. Young unmarried women worked to support themselves or to save for marriage. Married women took factory jobs when their husbands were unable to support the family. Mothers of infants faced a hard choice: whether to leave their babies with wet nurses at great expense and danger or to bring them to the factory and keep them quiet with opiates. Rather than working together as family units, husbands and wives increasingly worked in different places.

Factory work was never the main occupation of working women. Most young women who sought paid employment in the early years of industrialization became domestic servants in spite of the low pay, drudgery, and risk of sexual abuse. Other women with small children tried hard to find work they could do at home, such as laundry, sewing, embroidery, millinery, or taking in lodgers.

Even with both parents working, poor families found it hard to make ends meet. As in preindustrial societies, parents thought children should contribute to their upkeep as soon as they were able to. The first generation of workers brought their children with them to the factories and mines as early as age five or six; they had little choice, since there were no public schools or day care centers. Employers encouraged the practice and even hired orphans. They preferred children because they were cheaper and more docile than adults and were better able to tie broken threads or crawl under machines to sweep the dust. Mine operators used children to pull coal carts along the low passageways from the coal face to the mine shaft. In the mid-nineteenth century, when the British government began restricting child labor, mill owners increasingly recruited Irish immigrants.

American industry began on a somewhat different note than the British. When Francis Cabot Lowell built a cotton mill in Massachusetts, he deliberately hired the unmarried daughters of New England farmers, promising decent wages and housing in dormitories under careful moral supervision. Other manufacturers eager to combine profits with morality followed his example. But soon the profit motive won out, and manufacturers imposed longer hours, harsher working conditions, and lower wages. When the young women went on strike, the factory owners replaced them with Irish immigrant women willing to accept lower pay and worse conditions.

The rising demand for cotton and the abolition of the African slave trade in the United States in 1808 caused an increase in the price of slaves. As the "Cotton Kingdom" expanded, the number of slaves rose through natural increase, from 700,000 in the 1790s to 3,200,000 slaves by 1850. Similarly, Europe's and North America's surging demand for tea and coffee prolonged slavery on sugar plantations in the West Indies and caused it to spread to the coffee-growing regions of southern Brazil. Slavery was part and parcel of the Industrial Revolution, just as much as child labor in Britain, the clothes that people wore, and the beverages they drank.

Changes in Society

Industrialization accentuated the polarization of society and disparities of income. In Britain, the worst-off were those who clung to an obsolete skill or craft, such as hand-loom weavers in a time of power looms. Even by working more hours, they could not escape destitution.

The wages and standard of living of factory workers did not decline steadily like those of hand-loom weavers; they fluctuated wildly with the cycles of economic growth and contraction. During the war years 1792 to 1815, the poor suffered hardship when the price of food rose faster than wages. Then, in the 1820s, real wages and public health began to improve, as industrial production grew at over 3 percent a year, pulling the rest of the economy along. Prices fell so that even the poor could afford comfortable, washable cotton clothes.

Overall, the benefits of industrialization—cheaper food, clothing, and utensils—did not improve workers' standard of living until the 1850s. The real beneficiaries of the early Industrial Revolution were the entrepreneurs whose money came from manufacturing. Most were the sons of middling shopkeepers, craftsmen, or farmers who had a little capital to start a cotton-spinning or machine-building business. Many tried and some succeeded, largely by plowing their profits back into the business. A generation later, in the nineteenth century, some newly rich industrialists bought their way into high society. With industrialization came a "cult of domesticity" that removed middle-class women from contact with the business world and left them responsible for the home, the servants, the education of children, and the family's social life.

RESPONSES TO INDUSTRIALIZATION

Changes as profound as the Industrial Revolution could not occur without political ferment and ideological conflict. So many other momentous events took place during those years—the American Revolution (1776–1783), the French Revolution (1789–1799), the Napoleonic Wars (1804–1815), the reactions and revolts that periodically swept over Europe after 1815—that we cannot neatly separate out the consequences of industrialization from the rest. But it is clear that the Industrial Revolution strengthened the ideas of laissez faire° and socialism and sparked workers' protests.

---

laissez faire (lay-say fair)

Laissez Faire

The most celebrated exponent of **laissez faire** ("let them do") was Adam Smith (1723–1790), a Scottish economist. In *The Wealth of Nations* (1776), Smith argued that if individuals were allowed to seek their personal gain, the effect, as though guided by an "invisible hand," would be to increase the general welfare. Except to protect private property, the government should refrain from interfering in business; it should even allow duty-free trade with foreign countries.

Although it was true that governments at the time were incompetent at regulating their national economies, it was becoming obvious that industrialization was not improving the general welfare but was for some causing great misery. Other thinkers blamed the workers' plight on the population boom, which outstripped the food supply and led to falling wages. The workers' poverty, they claimed, was as much a result of "natural law" as the wealth of successful businessmen, and the only way the working class could avoid mass famine was to delay marriage and practice self-restraint and sexual abstinence.

Laissez faire provided an ideological justification for a special kind of capitalism: banks, stock markets, and chartered companies allowed investors to obtain profits with reasonable risks but with much less government control and interference than in the past. But not everyone accepted the grim conclusions of the "dismal science," as economics was then known. Jeremy Bentham (1748–1832) believed that it was possible to maximize "the greatest happiness of the greatest number," if only a Parliament of enlightened reformers would study the social problems of the day and pass appropriate legislation; his philosophy became known as utilitarianism.

Positivism and Utopian Socialism

Some French social thinkers, moved by sincere concern for the poor, offered a more radically new vision of a just civilization. Espousing a philosophy called **positivism,** the count of Saint-Simon (1760–1825) argued that the scientific method could solve social as well as technical problems. He recommended that the poor, guided by scientists and artists, form workers' communities under the protection of benevolent business leaders. These ideas found no following among workers, but they attracted the enthusiastic support of bankers and entrepreneurs, inspired by visions of railroads, canals, and other symbols of progress.

Meanwhile, the **utopian° socialism** of Charles Fourier (1768–1837), who loathed capitalists, imagined an ideal society in which groups of sixteen hundred workers would live in dormitories and work together on the land and in workshops where music, wine, and pastries would soften the hardships of labor. For this idea, critics called him "utopian"—a dreamer.

The person who came closest to creating a utopian community was the Englishman Robert Owen (1771–1858), a successful cotton manufacturer who believed that industry could provide prosperity for all. Conscience-stricken by the appalling plight of the workers, Owen took over the management of New Lanark, a mill town south of Glasgow. He improved the housing and added schools, a church, and other amenities. He also testified before Parliament against child labor and for government inspection of working conditions, thereby angering his fellow industrialists.

Protests and Reforms

Workers benefited little from the ideas of these middle-class philosophers. Instead, they resisted the harsh working conditions in their own ways. They changed jobs frequently and were often absent, especially on Mondays. Periodically, workers rioted or went on strike. Such acts of resistance did nothing, however, to change the nature of industrial work. Not until workers learned to act together could they hope to have much influence.

Gradually, they formed benevolent societies and organizations to demand universal male suffrage and shorter workdays. In 1834, Robert Owen organized the Grand National Consolidated Trade Union to lobby for an eight-hour workday; it gained half a million members but failed a few months later in the face of government prosecution of trade union activities. The Chartist

---

utopian (you-TOE-pee-uhn)

movement had more success, gathering petitions by the thousands to present to Parliament. Although Chartism collapsed in 1848, it left a legacy of labor organizing. Eventually, mass movements persuaded political leaders to look into the abuses of industrial life, despite the prevailing laissez-faire philosophy.

In the 1820s and 1830s, the British Parliament began investigating conditions in the factories and mines. The Factory Act of 1833 prohibited the employment of children under age nine in textile mills and limited the working hours of children between the ages of nine and eighteen. The Mines Act of 1842 prohibited the employment of all women and of boys under age ten underground. Several decades passed before the government appointed enough inspectors to enforce the new laws.

The British learned to seek reform through accommodation. On the European continent, in contrast, the revolutions of 1848 (see Chapter 20) revealed widespread discontent with repressive governments but failed to soften the hardships of industrialization.

Emigration

Another response to growing population, rural crises, and business cycles was emigration. Many poor Irish emigrated to England in search of work in construction and factories. After the potato crop failed in Ireland in 1847–1848, one-quarter of the Irish population died in the resulting famine, and another quarter emigrated to England and America. On the European continent, the negative effects of economic downturns were tempered by the existence of small family farms to which urban workers could return when they were laid off, but vast numbers still left Europe in search of better opportunities in the Western Hemisphere.

The United States received approximately 600,000 European immigrants in the 1830s, 1.5 million in the 1840s, and then 2.5 million per decade until 1880. In the 1890s, an astonishing total of 5.2 million immigrants arrived. European immigration to Latin America also increased dramatically after 1880. Immigrants from Europe faced prejudice and discrimination from those who believed they threatened the well-being of na-

tive-born workers by accepting low wages, and they threatened national culture by resisting assimilation.

Asian immigration to the Western Hemisphere also increased after 1850. Between 1849 and 1875, approximately 570,000 Chinese immigrants arrived in the Americas, half in the United States. India also contributed more than a half-million immigrants to the Caribbean region. Asians faced more obstacles to immigration than did Europeans and were often victims of violence and more extreme forms of discrimination in the New World.

Despite discrimination, most immigrants were also motivated to assimilate. Many intellectuals and political leaders wondered if the evolving mix of culturally diverse populations could sustain a common citizenship. As a result, efforts were directed toward compelling immigrants to assimilate. They learned the language spoken in their adopted countries as fast as possible in order to improve their earning capacity.

Union movements and electoral politics in the hemisphere also felt the influence of new arrivals who aggressively sought to influence government and improve working conditions. Immigrants also introduced new languages, foods, and customs. Mutual benevolent societies and less formal ethnic associations pooled resources to help immigrants open businesses, aid the immigration of their relatives, or bury their family members, sometimes worsening the fears of the native-born that immigration posed a threat to national culture. They also established links with political movements, sometimes exchanging votes for favors.

THE EFFECTS OF INDUSTRIALIZATION IN RUSSIA AND THE OTTOMAN EMPIRE

For most places in the world, trade with the industrial countries of western Europe and North America meant exporting raw materials. In the few countries whose governments were tempted to imitate the West, cheap Western imports, backed by the power of Great Britain, thwarted the spread of industry for a century or more.

Two factors inhibited the spread of the industrial revolution. One was the active opposition of Great Britain and other industrial nations, whose tactics in Asia and Africa, ranging from military invasion to financial manipulation, are described in the chapters that follow. The other factor was that most parts of the world were ill prepared politically, socially, and/or economically to undertake industrial modernization. Russia and the Ottoman Empire illustrate how difficult it was to overcome both of these problems even in places that had long observed and copied changes underway in western Europe.

Russia

Eighteenth-century Russian tsars had actively promoted the Westernization of their giant land's armies and elite. Its aristocrats spoke French, its army was modeled on the armies of western Europe, and it participated in European wars and diplomacy. Yet Russia differed from western Europe in one important aspect: it had almost no middle class. Thus, industrialization there arose not from the initiative of local entrepreneurs but by government decree and through the work of foreign engineers.

Tsar Nicholas I (r. 1825–1855) built the first railroad in Russia from St. Petersburg, the capital, to his summer palace in 1837. A few years later, he insisted that the trunk line from St. Petersburg to Moscow run in a perfectly straight line. American engineers built locomotive workshops in Russia, and British engineers set up textile mills. These projects, though well publicized, were oddities in a society where most people were serfs tied to the estates of powerful noble landowners and towns were few and far apart.

Until the late nineteenth century, the Russian government's interest in industry was limited and hesitant. An industrial revolution, to be successful, required large numbers of educated and independent-minded artisans and entrepreneurs. Suspicious of Western ideas, especially anything smacking of liberalism, socialism, or revolution, the Russian government feared the spread of liter-

acy and of modern education beyond the minimum needed to train the officer corps and the bureaucracy. Rather than run the risk of allowing a middle class and a working class to arise that might challenge its control, the regime of Nicholas I kept the peasants in serfdom and preferred to import most industrial goods and pay for them with exports of grain and timber.

Russia aspired to Western-style economic development. But fear of political change caused the country to fall further behind western Europe, economically and technologically, than it had been a half-century before. When France and Britain went to war against Russia in 1854, they faced a Russian army equipped with obsolete weapons and bogged down for lack of transportation.

The Ottoman Empire

The Ottoman rulers were earlier than the rulers of other Eurasian empires to experiment with financial and military modernization. However, entrenched opposition kept the Ottoman government from putting most reforms into place until the mid-1800s. The reforms came too late to preserve the empire's independence from western Europe, but they added momentum for centralization, helped promote nationalism in the late nineteenth century, and created a practical base for the creation of a Turkish republic in the twentieth century.

When Sultan Selim° III (r. 1789–1807) introduced reforms at the end of the eighteenth century to strengthen the military and increase the control of the central government, a massive military uprising overthrew and executed him. In 1826, Selim's cousin Sultan Mahmud° II (r. 1808–1839) cautiously revived the reform movement. First he announced the creation of a new army corps. When the traditional military corps (the Janissaries) rose in revolt, he ordered loyal troops to attack the Janissary barracks and obliterate the force.

Mahmud also sought to secularize the state and reduce the political power of the Muslim religious elite. He brought education and law under the authority of the civil government and established

Selim (seh-LEEM)   Mahmud (MACH-mood)

a uniform code of civil law. One important proclamation called for public trials and equal protection under the law for all, whether Muslim, Christian, or Jew. No Islamic country had ever produced anything so nearly approaching a constitution, and the Ottoman Empire enjoyed a renewed reputation as a progressive influence in the Middle East.

In the 1830s, an Ottoman imperial school of military sciences was established at Istanbul. Instructors imported from western Europe taught chemistry, engineering, mathematics, and physics in addition to military history. In 1838, the first medical school was established, for army doctors and surgeons. Reforms in military education became the model for more general educational reforms. Urban elites in Istanbul, the capital, embraced European language and culture, as well as military professionalism and progressive political reform. Newspapers—most of them in French—were founded at Istanbul, and travel to Europe—particularly to England and France—by wealthy Turks became more common. European dress became the fashion for progressive men in the Ottoman cities of the later 1800s; traditional dress became a symbol of the religious, the rural, and the parochial.

Interest in importing European military, industrial, and communications technology remained strong through the 1800s, but the Ottoman rulers quickly learned that limited improvements in military technology had unforeseen cultural and social effects. The introduction of modern weapons and drill required a change in traditional military dress. Beards, deemed unhygienic and a fire hazard, were restricted, along with the wearing of loose trousers and turbans. The adoption of European military caps, which had leather bills on the front to protect against the glare of the sun, became controversial because they interfered with Muslim soldiers' touching their foreheads to the ground during daily prayers. The compromise was the brimless cap now called the *fez.*

The new public rights and political participation were explicitly restricted to men. Private life, including everything connected to marriage and divorce, was left within the sphere of religious law, and at no time was there a question of political participation or reformed education for women.

Indeed, the reforms actually decreased the influence of women.

The Crimean War, 1853–1856

Since the reign of Peter the Great (r. 1689–1725), the Russian Empire had been attempting to expand southward at the Ottomans' expense. By 1815, Russia had pried the Georgian region of the Caucasus away from the Ottomans, and the threat of Russian intervention in Serbia had prevented the Ottomans from crushing a Serbian independence effort (see Map 21.2).

Between 1853 and 1856, the **Crimean° War** raged on the Black Sea and its northern shore. Nominally a war between the Russian and Ottoman Empires about whether Russia could claim to protect Christians in the Ottoman domains, this extremely destructive conflict also involved in the dispute Austria, Britain, France, and the Italian kingdom of Sardinia-Piedmont, all of which sided—actively or passively—with the Ottoman Empire because they feared any expansion of Russia's power and influence.

During the prolonged sea conflict, Britain and France trapped the Russian fleet in the Black Sea. Russia's lack of railways hampered attempts to supply both its land and its sea forces. Tsar Alexander II (r. 1855–1881) abandoned the key fortress of Sevastopol in 1855 and sued for peace. The terms of peace blocked Russian expansion into eastern Europe and the Middle East but also gave the Ottoman Empire protection from western European imperialism, since Britain and France agreed that neither would take Ottoman territory for its exclusive use.

The Crimean War brought significant changes to all the combatants. The tsar and his government, already beset by demands for the reform of serfdom, education, and the military, plunged into reforms that slightly improved Russia's economy but profoundly destabilized its political system. The Ottoman rulers also continued their reform agendas after the war, but no reform could repair the chronic insolvency of the imperial government due to declining revenues from agricultural yields

---

Crimean (cry-ME-uhn)

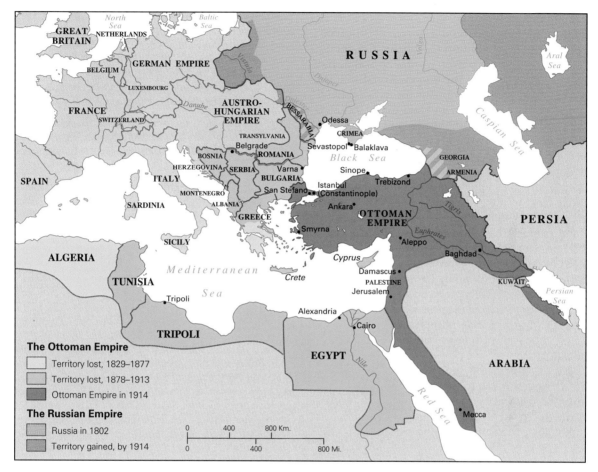

Map 21.2   Disintegration of the Ottoman Empire, 1829–1914   At its height, the Ottoman Empire controlled most of the perimeter of the Mediterranean Sea. But in the 1800s, Ottoman territory shrank as many countries gained their independence—frequently with the aid of France or Russia. The Black Sea, which left the Turkish coast vulnerable to assault by the Russian navy, was a weak spot that was intensely contested in the Crimean dispute.

and widespread corruption. From the conclusion of the Crimean War in 1856 on, the Ottoman government became heavily dependent on foreign loans and European imports.

Militarily, the Crimean War marked the transition from traditional to modern industrial warfare. Although all the combatant nations used cavalry in the Crimean War, the famous British "Light Brigade" and many other cavalry units were destroyed by the rapid and relatively accurate fire of new **breech-loading rifles.** Cavalry were not the only victims of the new speed of the guns. Many traditional infantry units came to grief attempting to use ranks of marching, brightly coated soldiers to overwhelm lines of rapidly firing riflemen.

CONCLUSION

In the period from 1760 to 1851, the new technologies of the Industrial Revolution greatly increased humans' power over nature. Goods could be manufactured in vast quantities at low cost. People and messages could travel at unprecedented speeds. In addition to utilizing the energy produced by muscle power, wind, and water, humans gained access to the energy stored in coal. Faster than ever before, humans turned woodland into farmland, dug canals and laid tracks, bridged rivers and cut through mountains, and covered the countryside with towns and cities.

This newfound power over nature, far from benefiting everyone, increased the disparities between individuals and societies. Some people acquired great wealth, while others lived in poverty and squalor. Middle-class women were restricted to the care of their homes and children. Many working-class women had to leave home to earn wages in factories or as domestic servants. These changes in work and family life provoked intense debates among intellectuals. Some defended the disparities in the name of laissez faire; others criticized the injustices that industrialization brought. Society was slow to bring these abuses under control.

By the 1850s, the Industrial Revolution had spread from Britain to western Europe and the United States, and its impact was being felt by Russia and the Ottoman Empire. Industrial Britain was on the move, as the next chapter recounts.

―――――――――――――――――――

■ Key Terms

Industrial Revolution	James Watt
agricultural revolution (eighteenth century)	electric telegraph
	laissez faire
mass production	positivism
Josiah Wedgwood	utopian socialism
division of labor	Crimean War
mechanization	breech-loading rifles
steam engine	

■ Suggested Reading

General works on the history of technology give pride of place to industrialization. For an optimistic overview, see

Joel Mokyr, *The Lever of Riches: Technological Creativity and Economic Progress* (1990). Other important recent works include James McClellan III and Harold Dorn, *Science and Technology in World History* (1999); David Landes, *The Wealth and Poverty of Nations* (1998); and Ian Inkster, *Technology and Industrialization: Historical Case Studies and International Perspectives* (1998).

There is a rich literature on the British industrial revolution, beginning with T. S. Ashton's classic *The Industrial Revolution, 1760–1830*, published in 1948 and often reprinted.

The impact of industrialization on workers is the theme of E. P. Thompson's classic work, *The Making of the English Working Class* (1963), but see also E. R. Pike, *"Hard Times": Human Documents of the Industrial Revolution* (1966). The role of women is most ably revealed in Lynn Y. Weiner, *From Working Girl to Working Mother: The Female Labor Force in the United States, 1820–1980* (1985), and in Louise Tilly and Joan Scott, *Women, Work, and Family* (1978).

European industrialization is the subject of J. Goodman and K. Honeyman, *Gainful Pursuits: The Making of Industrial Europe: 1600–1914* (1988); John Harris, *Industrial Espionage and Technology Transfer: Britain and France in the Eighteenth Century* (1998); and David Landes, *The Unbound Prometheus: Technological Change and Industrial Development in Western Europe from 1750 to the Present* (1972). On the beginnings of American industrialization, see David Jeremy, *Artisans, Entrepreneurs and Machines: Essays on the Early Anglo-American Textile Industry, 1770–1840* (1998).

On the environmental impact of industrialization, see Richard Wilkinson, *Poverty and Progress: An Ecological Perspective on Economic Development* (1973), and Richard Tucker and John Richards, *Global Deforestation in the Nineteenth-Century World Economy* (1983).

The first book to treat industrialization as a global phenomenon is Peter Stearns, *The Industrial Revolution in World History* (1993); see also Louise Tilly's important article "Connections," *American Historical Review* (February 1994). On the Ottoman Empire, see Huri Islamoglu-Inan, ed., *The Ottoman Empire and the World Economy* (1987). On Russia, see David Saunders, *Russia in the Age of Reaction and Reform, 1801–1881* (1993).

■ Note

1. *Nautilus Magazine* 12 (1843): 346.

22

AFRICA, INDIA, AND CHINA,
1750–1870

Changes and Exchanges in Africa • India Under British Rule •
The Qing Empire
ENVIRONMENT AND TECHNOLOGY: Whaling

n 1782, Tipu Sultan inherited the throne of Mysore°, which his father had made the most powerful state in south India. The ambitious and talented new ruler also inherited a healthy distrust of the British East India Company's territorial ambitions. Before the company could invade Mysore, Tipu Sultan launched his own attack in 1785. He then sent an embassy to France in 1788 seeking an alliance against Britain. Neither of these ventures was immediately successful.

Not until a decade later did the French agree to a loose alliance with Tipu Sultan to challenge Britain's colonial and commercial supremacy in the Indian Ocean. General Napoleon Bonaparte invaded Egypt in 1798 to threaten British trade routes to India and hoped to use the alliance with Tipu Sultan to drive the British out of India. The French invasion of Egypt went well enough

at first, but a British naval blockade and the ravages of disease crippled the French force. When the French withdrew, another military adventurer, Muhammad Ali, commander of the Ottoman army in Egypt, took advantage of the situation to revitalize Egypt and expand its rule.

Meanwhile, Tipu's alliance with France did not protect him from the East India Company, whose military victory in 1792 deprived him of most of his seacoast. Tipu lost his life in 1799 while defending his capital against another British assault. Mysore was divided between the British and their Indian allies.

As these events illustrate, talented local leaders and European powers were both vying to expand their influence in South Asia and Africa between 1750 and 1870. Midway through that period, it was by no means clear who would gain the upper hand. Britain and France were as likely to fight each other as they were to fight any Asian or African state. In 1800, the two nations were engaged in their third major war for

Mysore (my-SORE)

overseas supremacy since 1750. By 1870, however, Britain had gained a decisive advantage over France and had established commercial dominance in trade in Africa, the Indian Ocean, and East Asia. Moreover, Britain created a new colonial empire in the East.

As you read this chapter, ask yourself the following questions:

- Why were the British able to gain decisive advantages in distant lands?

- Why were Asians and Africans so divided, some choosing to cooperate with the Europeans while others resisted their advances?

- Why was even the Qing Empire unable to stop the European advance?

- How important an advantage were Britain's weapons, ships, and economic motives?

- How much of the outcome was the result of advance planning, and how much was due to particular individuals or to chance?

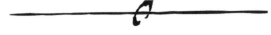

CHANGES AND EXCHANGES IN AFRICA

During the century before 1870, Africa underwent dynamic political changes and a great expansion of foreign trade. Indigenous African leaders as well as Middle Eastern and European imperialists built powerful new states or expanded old ones. As the continent's external slave trades to the Americas and to Islamic lands died slowly under British pressure, trade in goods such as palm oil, ivory, timber, and gold grew sharply. In return, Africans imported large quantities of machine-made textiles and firearms. These complex changes are best understood by looking at African regions separately.

New African States

Internal forces produced clusters of new states in two parts of sub-Saharan Africa in the early nineteenth century (see Map 22.1). In the fertile coastlands of southeastern Africa (in modern South Africa), a serious drought at the beginning of the nineteenth century led to conflict for grazing and farming lands among the small, independent chiefdoms of the region. An upstart named Shaka emerged in 1818 as head of a new **Zulu** kingdom, whose military discipline and courage soon made them the most powerful and most feared fighters in southern Africa. Shaka's regiments raided his African neighbors, seized their cattle, and captured their women and children. To protect themselves from the Zulu, some neighboring Africans created their own states.

Although Shaka ruled for little more than a decade, he successfully instilled a new national identity into his newly conquered subjects. He grouped all the young people into regiments that lived together and were taught Zulu customs and fighting methods. At public festivals, regiments of young men and women, paraded, danced, and pledged their loyalty to Shaka.

Meanwhile, Islamic reform movements were creating another powerful state in the savannas of West Africa. The reformers followed a classic Muslim pattern: a *jihad* (holy war) added new lands, spreading Islamic beliefs and laws among conquered people. The largest reform movement was led by Usuman dan Fodio° (1745–1817), whose armed supporters conquered and combined the older Hausa states into a new empire ruled by a caliph (sultan) in the city of Sokoto. The **Sokoto Caliphate** (1809–1906) was the largest state in West Africa since the fall of Songhai in the sixteenth century.

In addition to being a center of Islamic learning and reform, the Sokoto Caliphate became a center of slavery. Many captured in the wars were enslaved and put to work in the empire or sold away across the Sahara or the Atlantic.

Usuman dan Fodio (OO-soo-mahn dahn FOH-dee-oh)

CHRONOLOGY

	Africa	India	China
1750		**1756** Black Hole of Calcutta **1765** East India Company (EIC) rule of Bengal begins	
	1798 Napoleon invades Egypt	**1798** Britain annexes Ceylon **1799** EIC defeats Mysore	**1794–1804** White Lotus Rebellion
1800			
	1805 Muhammad Ali seizes Egypt **1806** Britain takes Cape Colony **1808** Britain outlaws slave trade and takes over Sierra Leone **1809** Sokoto Caliphate founded **1818** Shaka founds Zulu kingdom **1821** Foundation of Republic of Liberia; Egypt takes control of Sudan	**1818** EIC creates Bombay presidency **1826** EIC annexes Assam and northern Burma **1828** Brahmo Samaj founded	
	1831–1847 Algerians resist French takeover **1834** Britain abolishes slavery **1840** Omani sultan moves capital to Zanzibar		**1839–1842** Opium War
1850		**1857–1858** Sepoy Rebellion leads to end of EIC rule and Mughal rule	**1850–1864** Taiping Rebellion
	1867 End of Atlantic slave trade **1869** Jaja founds Opobo		**1860** Sack of Beijing
	1889 Menelik unites modern Ethiopia	**1877** Queen Victoria becomes empress of India **1885** First Indian National Congress	

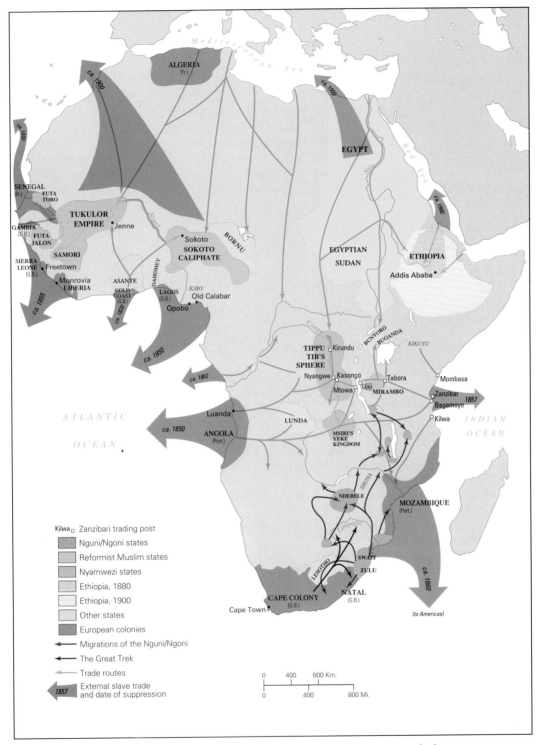

Map 22.1 Africa in the Nineteenth Century Expanding internal and overseas trade drew much of Africa into global networks, but foreign colonies in 1870 were largely confined to Algeria and southern Africa. Growing trade, Islamic reform movements, and other internal forces created important new states throughout the continent.

Modernization in Egypt and Ethiopia

In northeastern Africa, the ancient African states of Egypt and Ethiopia were undergoing a period of growth and **modernization.** Napoleon's invasion of Egypt ended in 1801, but the shock of this display of European strength and Egyptian weakness prompted **Muhammad Ali,** who eliminated his rivals and ruled Egypt from 1805 to 1848, to begin the political, social, and economic reforms.

Muhammad Ali's central aim was to give Egypt sufficient military strength to prevent another European conquest, but he was pragmatic enough to make use of European experts and techniques to achieve that goal. His reforms transformed Egyptian landholding, increased agricultural production, and created a modern administration and army. To pay for these ventures and for the European experts and equipment that he imported, he required Egyptian peasants to cultivate cotton and other crops for export.

By the end of Muhammad Ali's reign in 1848, the modernization of Egypt was well under way. The trade with Europe had expanded by almost 600 percent, and a new class of educated Egyptians had begun to replace the old ruling aristocracy. Egyptians were replacing many of the foreign experts, and the fledgling program of industrialization was providing the country with its own textiles, paper, weapons, and military uniforms. The demands on peasant families for labor and military service, however, were acutely disruptive.

Ali's grandson Ismail° (r. 1863–1879) placed even more emphasis on Westernizing Egypt. "My country is no longer in Africa," Ismail declared, "it is in Europe."[1] A huge increase in cotton exports during the American Civil War helped finance a network of new irrigation canals, 800 miles (1,300 kilometers) of railroads, a modern postal service, and the dazzling new capital city of Cairo.

State building and reform also were under way in the ancient Christian kingdom of Ethiopia. Beginning in the 1840s, Ethiopian rulers purchased modern weapons from European sources and created strong armies loyal to the ruler. Emperor Téwodros° II (r. 1833–1868) and his successor,

Yohannes° IV (r. 1872–1889), brought back under imperial rule large areas of ancient Ethiopia. When King Menelik of Shoa succeeded Yohannes as emperor in 1889, the merger of their separate realms created the modern boundaries of Ethiopia.

European Penetration

France's long and difficult war to conquer the North African country of Algeria from 1830 to 1848 was a rare example of European use of force in Africa before 1870. More typical was the peaceful penetration of European explorers, missionaries, and traders.

Small expeditions of adventurous explorers, using their own funds or financed by private geographical societies, were seeking to uncover the mysteries of inner Africa that had eluded earlier Europeans. Many of the explorers sought to map the course of Africa's great rivers: the Niger, the Nile, and the Congo.

In contrast to these heavily financed expeditions with hundreds of African porters, the Scottish missionary David Livingstone (1813–1873) organized modest treks through southern and Central Africa to scout out locations for Christian missions. His several expeditions in southern and equatorial Africa made him a celebrity. In 1871, he was met by the Welsh-American journalist Henry Morton Stanley (1841–1904) on a publicity-motivated search for the "lost" missionary doctor. On an expedition from 1874 to 1877, Stanley descended the Congo River to its mouth.

The most significant European influence in Africa between 1750 and 1870 was commercial. No sooner was the mouth of the Niger River discovered in 1830 than eager entrepreneurs began to send expeditions up the river to scout out its potential for trade. The value of trade between Africa and the other Atlantic continents more than doubled between the 1730s and the 1780s, then doubled again by 1870. Before about 1825, the slave trade accounted for most of that increase, but thereafter African exports of vegetable oils, gold, ivory, and other goods drove overseas trade to new heights.

Ismail (is-MAH-eel)   **Téwodros** (tay-WOH-druhs)

Yohannes (yoh-HAHN-nehs)

Téwodros's Mighty Cannon   Like other modernizers in the nineteenth century, Emperor Téwodros of Ethiopia sought to reform his military forces. In 1861, he forced resident European missionaries and craftsmen to build guns and cannon, including this 7-ton behemoth nicknamed "Sebastopol" after the Black Sea port that had been the center of the Crimean War. It took five hundred men to haul the cannon across Ethiopia's hilly terrain.   (From Hormuzd Rassam, *Narrative of the British Mission to Theodore, King of Abyssinia, II*, London 1869, John Murray)

As Chapter 20 recounted, the successful revolutions in the United States, France, Saint Domingue, and Latin America helped turn Western opinion against the slave trade and slavery. Once the world's greatest slave traders, the British became the most aggressive abolitionists. During the half-century after 1815, Britain spent some $60 million (£12 million) in its efforts to end the slave trade through naval patrols, a sum equal to the profits British slave traders had made in the fifty years before 1808. Although British patrols captured 1,635 slave ships and liberated over 160,000 enslaved Africans, continued demand for slaves in Cuba and Brazil kept the trade going until 1867.

The demand for slaves in the Americas claimed the lives and endangered the safety of untold numbers of Africans, but the exchanges also satisfied other Africans' desires for cloth, metals, and other goods. To continue their access to those imports, Africans expanded their **"legitimate" trade** (exports other than slaves). The most successful of the new exports from West Africa was palm oil, a vegetable oil used by British manufacturers for soap, candles, and lubricants. From the mid-1830s, the trading states of the Niger Delta emerged as the premier exporters of palm oil. Coastal Africans there grew rich and used their wealth to buy large numbers of male slaves to paddle the giant dugout canoes that transported palm oil from inland markets along the narrow delta creeks to the trading ports.

Another effect of the suppression of the slave trade was the spread of Western cultural influences in West Africa. To serve as a base for their anti–slave trade naval squadron, in 1808 the British had taken over the small colony of Sierra Leone°. Over the next several years, 130,000 men, women, and chil-

Sierra Leone (see-ER-uh lee-OWN)

King Jaja of Opobo This talented man rose from slavery in the Niger Delta port of Bonny to head one of the town's major palm oil trading firms, the Anna Pepple House, in 1863. Six years later, Jaja founded and ruled his own trading port of Opobo. (Reproduced from *West Africa: An Introduction to Its History,* by Michael Crowder, by courtesy of the publishers, Addison Wesley Longman)

dren taken from "captured" vessels were liberated in Sierra Leone. Christian missionaries helped settle these impoverished and dispirited **recaptives** in and around Freetown, the capital. In time, the mission churches and schools made many willing converts among such men and women.

Sierra Leone's schools also produced a number of distinguished graduates. For example, Samuel Adjai Crowther (1808–1891), freed as a youth from a slave ship in 1821 by the British squadron, became the first Anglican bishop in West Africa in 1864, administering a pioneering diocese along the lower Niger River. James Africanus Horton (1835–1882), the son of a slave liberated in Sierra Leone, became a doctor and the author of many studies of West Africa.

Other Western cultural influences came from people of African birth or descent returning to their ancestral homeland in this era. In 1821, to the south of Sierra Leone, free black Americans began a settlement that grew into the Republic of Liberia, a place of liberty at a time when slavery was illegal and flourishing in the United States. Free blacks from Brazil and Cuba chartered ships to return to their West African homelands, bringing with them Roman Catholicism, architectural motifs, and clothing fashions from the New World. Although the number of Africans exposed to Western culture in 1870 was still small, this influence grew rapidly.

Secondary Empires in Eastern Africa

When British patrols hampered the slave trade in West Africa, slavers moved southward and then around the tip of southern Africa to eastern Africa. There the Atlantic slave trade joined an existing trade in slaves to the Islamic world that also was expanding. Two-thirds of the 1.2 million slaves exported from eastern Africa in the nineteenth century went to markets in North Africa and the Middle East; the other third went to European plantations in the Americas and the Indian Ocean.

Slavery within eastern Africa also grew between 1800 and 1873, as Arab and Swahili owners purchased some 700,000 slaves from inland eastern Africa to do the labor-intensive work of harvesting cloves on plantations on Zanzibar Island and the neighboring coast. These territories belonged to the sultan of Oman, an Arabian kingdom on the Persian Gulf. The sultan moved his court to Zanzibar in 1840. Zanzibar also was an important market for ivory, most of which was shipped to India, where much of it was carved into decorative objects for middle-class Europeans.

Caravans led by African and Arab merchants brought ivory from hundreds of miles inland. Some of these merchants created large personal empires by using capital they had borrowed from Indian bankers and modern firearms they had bought from Europeans and Americans. These modern rifles felled countless elephants for their ivory tusks and inflicted widespread devastation and misery on the inland people.

One can blame the Zanzibari traders for the pillage and havoc in the once-peaceful center of Africa. However, the circle of responsibility was still broader. Europeans supplied the weapons used by the invaders and were major consumers of ivory and cloves. For this reason, histories have referred to the states carved out of eastern Africa as "secondary empires," in contrast to the empire that Britain was establishing directly. At the same time, Britain was working to bring the Indian Ocean slave trade to an end in eastern Africa. British officials pressured the sultan of Oman into halting the Indian Ocean slave trade from Zanzibar in 1857 and ending the import of slaves into Zanzibar in 1873.

C

INDIA UNDER BRITISH RULE

The people of South Asia felt the impact of European commercial, cultural, and colonial expansion more immediately and profoundly than did the people of Africa. While Europeans were laying claim to only small parts of Africa between 1750 and 1870, nearly all of India (with three times the population of all of Africa) came under Britain's direct or indirect rule. After the founding of East India Company in 1600, it took British interests 250 years to commandeer the colonies and trade of the Dutch, fight off French and Indian challenges, and pick up the pieces of the decaying Mughal° Empire. By 1763 the French were stymied, in 1795 the Dutch company was dissolved, and in 1858 the last

Mughal emperor was dethroned, leaving the vast subcontinent in British hands.

Company Men

As Mughal power weakened in the eighteenth century, British, Dutch, and French companies expanded into India (see Map 22.2). Such far-flung European trading companies were speculative and risky ventures. Their success depended on hard-drinking and ambitious young "Company Men," who used hard bargaining, and hard fighting when necessary, to persuade Indian rulers to allow them to establish trading posts at strategic points along the coast. To protect their fortified warehouses from attack by other Europeans or by native states, the companies hired and trained Indian troops known as **sepoys°**. In divided India, these private armies came to hold the balance of power.

In 1691, the East India Company (EIC) had convinced the **nawab°** (the term used for Mughal governors) of the large state of Bengal in northeast India to let the company establish a fortified outpost at the fishing port of Calcutta. A new nawab, pressing claims for additional tribute from the prospering port, overran the fort in 1756 and imprisoned a group of EIC men in a cell so small that many died of suffocation. To avenge their deaths in this "Black Hole of Calcutta," a large EIC force from Madras overthrew the nawab. The weak Mughal emperor was persuaded to acknowledge the EIC's right to rule Bengal in 1765. Fed by the tax revenues of Bengal as well as by profits from trade, the EIC was on its way. Calcutta grew into a city of 250,000 by 1788.

In southern India, EIC forces secured victory for the British Indian candidate for nawab of Arcot during the Seven Years War, thereby gaining an advantage over French traders who had supported the loser. The defeat of Tipu Sultan of Mysore at the end of the century (described at the start of the chapter) secured south India for the company and prevented a French resurgence.

Along with Calcutta and Madras, the third major center of British power in India was Bombay, on

---

Mughal (MOO-guhl)

sepoy (SEE-poy)   **nawab** (NAH-wab)

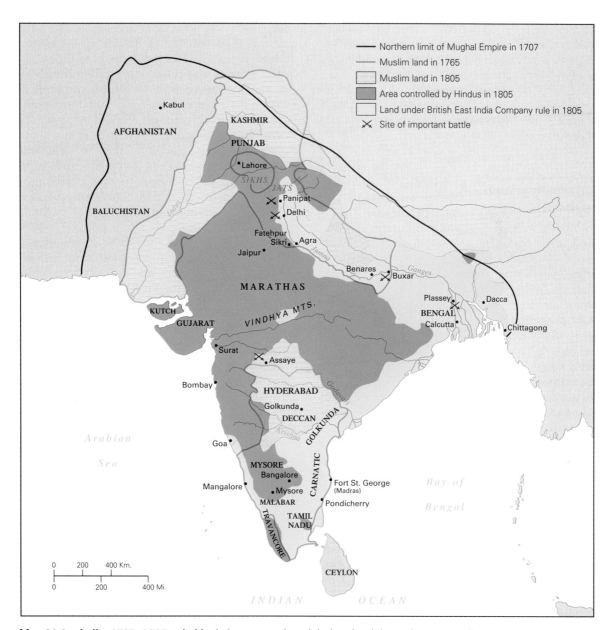

Map 22.2 India, 1707–1805 As Mughal power weakened during the eighteenth century, other Indian states and the British East India Company expanded their territories.

the western coast. There, after a long conflict with Indian rulers, the EIC gained a decisive advantage in 1818, annexing large territories to form the core of what was called the "Bombay Presidency." Some states were taken over completely, as Bengal had been, but very many others remained in the hands of local princes who accepted the political control of the company.

Raj and Rebellion, 1818–1857

In 1818, the EIC controlled an empire with more people than in all of western Europe and fifty times the population of the colonies the British had lost in North America. One thrust of **British raj** (reign) was to remake India on a British model through administrative and social reform, economic development, and the introduction of new technology. But at the same time, the Company Men—like the Mughals before them—had to temper their interference with Indian social and religious customs lest they provoke rebellion or lose the support of their Indian princely allies. For this reason and because of the complexity of the task of ruling such a vast empire, there were many inconsistencies in Britain's policies toward India.

The main policy was to create a powerful and efficient system of government. British rule before 1850 relied heavily on military power—170 sepoy regiments and 16 European regiments. Another policy was to disarm approximately 2 million warriors who had served India's many states and turn them to civilian tasks, mostly cultivation. A third policy gave freer rein to Christian missionaries eager to convert and uplift India's masses. Few converts were made, but the missionaries kept up steady pressure for social reforms.

Another key British policy was to turn India's complex and overlapping patterns of landholding into private property. In Bengal, this reform worked to the advantage of large landowners, but in Mysore, the peasantry gained. Private ownership made it easier for the state to collect the taxes that were needed to pay for the costs of administration, the army, and economic reform.

Such policies of "Westernization, Anglicization, and modernization," as they have been called, were only one side of British rule. The other side was the bolstering of "traditions"—both real and newly invented. In the name of tradition, the Indian princes who ruled nearly half of British India were permitted by their British overlords to expand their power, splendor, and tenure well beyond what their predecessors had ever had. The British rulers themselves invented many "traditions"—including elaborate parades and displays—half borrowed from European royal pomp, half freely improvised from Mughal ceremonies.

The British and Indian elites danced sometimes in close partnership, sometimes in apparent opposition. But the ordinary people of India—women of every status, members of subordinate Hindu castes, the "untouchables" and "tribals" outside the caste system, and the poor generally—found less benefit in the British reforms and much new oppression in the new taxes and "traditions."

The transformation of British India's economy was also doubled-edged. On the one hand, British raj created many new jobs as a result of the growth of internal and external trade and the expansion of agricultural production, such as in opium in Bengal—largely for export to China—coffee in Ceylon (an island off the tip of India), and tea in Assam (a state in northeastern India). On the other hand, competition from cheap cotton goods produced in Britain's industrial mills drove many Indians out of the handicraft textile industry. In the eighteenth century, India had been the world's greatest exporter of cotton textiles; in the nineteenth century, India increasingly shipped raw cotton fiber to Britain.

Even the beneficial economic changes introduced under British rule were disruptive, and there were no safety nets for the needy. Thus, local rebellions by displaced ruling elites, disgruntled religious traditionalists, and the economically dispossessed were almost constant during the first half of the nineteenth century. The greatest concern was over the continuing loyalty of Indian sepoys in the EIC's army.

Discontent was growing among Indian soldiers. In the early decades of EIC rule, most sepoys came from Bengal, one of the first states the company had annexed. The Bengali sepoys resented the active recruitment of other ethnic groups into the army after 1848, such as Sikhs° from Punjab and Gurkhas from Nepal. Many high-caste Hindus objected to a new law in 1856 requiring new recruits to be available for service overseas in the growing Indian Ocean empire, for their religion prohibited ocean travel. The replacement of the standard military musket by the far more accurate Enfield rifle in 1857 also caused problems. Soldiers were ordered to use their teeth to tear open the ammunition cartridges, which were greased with animal fat. Hindus were offended by this order if the fat came from cattle, which they considered sacred. Muslims were offended if the fat came from pigs, which they considered unclean.

Although the cartridge-opening procedure was quickly changed, the initial discontent grew into rebellion by Hindu sepoys in May 1857. British troubles mushroomed when Muslim sepoys, peasants, and discontented elites joined in. The rebels asserted old traditions to challenge British authority: sepoy officers in Delhi proclaimed their loyalty to the Mughal emperor; others rallied behind the Maratha leader Nana Sahib. The rebellion was put down by March 1858, but it shook this piecemeal empire to its core.

Historians have attached different names and meanings to the events of 1857 and 1858. Concentrating on the technical fact that the uprising was an unlawful action by soldiers, nineteenth-century British historians labeled it the **"Sepoy Rebellion"** or the "Mutiny," and these names are still commonly used. Seeing in these events the beginnings of the later movement for independence, some modern Indian historians have termed it the "Revolution of 1857." In reality, it was much more than a simple mutiny, because it involved more than soldiers, but it was not yet a nationalist revolution, for the rebels' sense of a common Indian national identity was weak.

Political Reform and Industrial Impact

Whatever it is called, the rebellion of 1857–1858 was a turning point in the history of modern India. In its wake, Indians

gained a new centralized government, entered a period of rapid economic growth, and began to develop a new national consciousness.

The changes in government were immediate. In 1858, Britain eliminated the last traces of Mughal and EIC rule. In their place, a new secretary of state for India in London oversaw Indian policy, and a new governor-general in Delhi acted as the British monarch's viceroy on the spot. A proclamation by Queen Victoria in November 1858 guaranteed all Indians equal protection of the law and the freedom to practice their religions and social customs; it also assured Indian princes that so long as they were loyal to the queen, British India would respect their control of territories and "their rights, dignity and honour."[2]

A powerful and efficient bureaucracy controlled the Indian masses. Members of the elite **Indian Civil Service** (ICS), mostly graduates of Oxford and Cambridge Universities, held the senior administrative and judicial posts. Only a thousand men at the end of the nineteenth century, they visited the villages in their districts, heard lawsuits and complaints, and passed judgments. Beneath them were a far greater number of Indian officials and employees. Recruitment into the ICS was by open examination given only in England and thus inaccessible to most Indians. In 1870, only one Indian was a member of the ICS. Subsequent reforms led to fifty-seven Indian appointments by 1887, but there the process stalled.

A second transformation of India after 1857 resulted from involvement with industrial Britain. The government invested millions of pounds sterling in harbors, cities, irrigation canals, and other public works. British interests felled forests to make way for tea plantations, persuaded Indian farmers to grow cotton and jute for export, and created great irrigation systems to alleviate the famines that periodically decimated whole provinces. As a result, India's trade expanded rapidly.

Most of the exports were agricultural commodities for processing elsewhere: cotton fiber, opium, tea, silk, and sugar. In return, India imported manufactured goods from Britain, including the flood of machine-made cotton textiles that severely undercut Indian hand-loom weavers. The effects on individual Indians varied enormously. Some women found new jobs, though at very low pay, on plantations or in the growing cities, where prostitution flourished. Others struggled to hold families together or ran away from abusive husbands. Everywhere in India, poverty remained the norm.

The Indian government also promoted the introduction of new technologies into India not long after their appearance in Britain. Earlier in the century, there were steamboats on the rivers and a massive program of canal building for irrigation. Beginning in the 1840s, a railroad boom (paid for out of government revenues) gave India its first national transportation network, followed shortly by telegraph lines. Indeed, in 1870, India had the greatest rail network in Asia and the fifth largest in the world.

The freer movement of Indians and rapid urban growth promoted the spread of cholera°, a disease transmitted through water contaminated by human feces. In 1867, officials demonstrated the close connection between cholera and pilgrims who bathed in and drank from sacred pools and rivers. The installation of a new sewerage system (1865) and a filtered water supply (1869) in Calcutta dramatically reduced cholera deaths there. Similar measures in Bombay and Madras also led to great reductions, but most Indians lived in small villages, where famine and lack of sanitation kept cholera deaths high. Only after 1900 did sanitary improvements lower the death rate from cholera.

Rising Indian Nationalism

Both the successes and the failures of British rule stimulated the development of Indian nationalism. The failure of the rebellion of 1857 led some thoughtful Indians to argue that the only way to regain control of their destiny was to reduce their country's social and ethnic divisions.

Individuals such as Rammohun Roy (1772–1833) had promoted pan-Indian nationalism a generation earlier. A Western-educated Bengali from a Brahmin family, Roy was a successful administrator for the EIC and a thoughtful student of comparative religion. His Brahmo Samaj° (Divine Society), founded in 1828, attracted Indians who sought to reconcile the values they found in the West with the ancient religious traditions of India. They backed the British outlawing of widow burning (*sati*°) in 1829 and of slavery in 1843 and sought to correct other abuses of women and female infanticide. Roy and his followers advocated reforming the caste system, and urged a return to the founding principles set out in the Upanishads, ancient sacred writings of Hinduism.

Although Brahmo Samaj remained an influential movement, a growing number of Indian intellectuals based their nationalism on the secular values they absorbed in Western schools. European and American missionaries played a prominent role in the spread of Western education. In 1870, there were 790,000 Indians in over 24,000 elementary and secondary schools, and India's three universities (established in 1857) awarded 345 degrees.

Many of the new nationalists came from the Indian middle class. Hoping to increase their influence and improve their employment opportunities in the Indian government, they convened the first **Indian National Congress** in 1885. The members sought a larger role for Indians in the civil service and called for more money to be spent on alleviating the poverty of the Indian masses. The Indian National Congress effectively voiced the opinions of elite, Western-educated Indians, but it would need the support of the masses to challenge British rule.

Colonies and Commerce

India was not only Britain's largest colony; it was also an increasingly important center of trade. British trade to India grew 350 percent between 1841 and 1870, while India's exports increased 400 percent. In addition to cotton fiber and indigo dye for Europe, India became a major producer of opium, largely destined for China. In the 1830s and 1840s, opium was 40 percent of India's exports.

---

cholera (KAHL-uhr-uh)

Brahmo Samaj (BRAH-moh suh-MAHJ)   *sati* (suh-TEE)

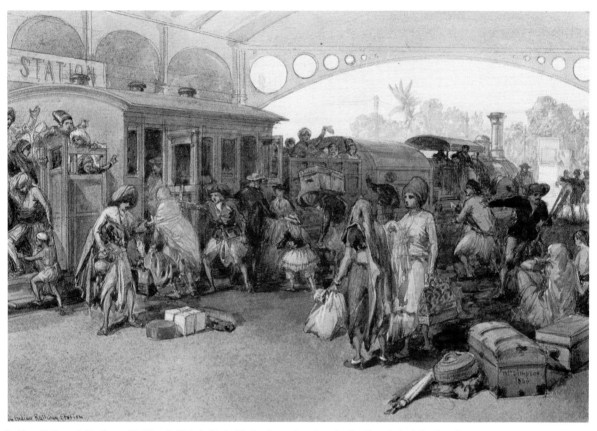

Indian Railroad Station, 1866   British India built the largest network of railroads in Asia. People of every social class traveled by train.   (Eyre and Hobbs House Art Gallery)

This new commercial expansion was closely tied to the needs of Britain's growing industrial economy and reflected a new philosophy of overseas trade. Rather than rebuilding the closed, mercantilist network of trade with its colonies, Britain sought to trade freely with all parts of the world, including the independent states of the Americas, Africa, and Asia.

To protect these valuable trade links, Britain acquired some new colonies. The Cape Colony at the tip of Africa was acquired from the Dutch in 1806 to serve ships on the long voyages from Europe to Asia. Other possessions were added in Southeast Asia. In 1824, the East India Company established a free port at Singapore, on the site of a small Malay fishing village with a superb harbor. Singapore soon became the center of trade and shipping between the Indian Ocean and China.

The shipbuilding revolution underway in the nineteenth century made global commerce easier. Merchant ships in the eighteenth century rarely exceeded 300 tons, but after 1850, swift **clipper ships** of 2,000 tons were commonplace in the British merchant fleet. Shipbuilders used iron to fasten American and tropical timbers together to make these larger vessels. The clippers' huge canvas sails and streamlined hulls cut voyage times between India and Europe from six months to three months, which lowered shipping costs and further stimulated maritime trade. Although the middle decades of the nineteenth century were the golden age of the sailing ship, industrial technology was also beginning to produce steam-powered iron vessels that found military uses in Britain's commercial penetration of China (see Environment and Technology: Whaling).

Whaling

The rapid expansion of whaling aptly illustrates the growing power of technology over nature in this period. Many contemporaries, like many people today, were sickened by the killing of the planet's largest living mammals. American novelist Herman Melville captured the conflicting sentiments in his epic whaling story, *Moby Dick* (1851). One of his characters enthusiastically explains why the grisly and dangerous business existed:

> But, though the world scorns us as whale hunters, yet does it unwittingly pay us the profoundest homage; yea, an all abounding adoration! for almost all the tapers, lamps, and candles that burn around the globe, burn, as before so many shrines, to our glory!

Melville's character overstates the degree to which whale oil dominated illumination and does not mention its many other industrial uses and the importance of whale meat for food in some countries. Whalebone

(baleen) was the plastic of its day. Whalebone was used for umbrella stays, carriage springs, fishing rods, suitcase frames, combs, and brushes, and its use in corsets allowed Western women to achieve the hourglass shape that fashion dictated.

New manufacturing technologies went hand in hand with new hunting technologies. The revolution in ship design enabled whalers from Europe and North America to extend the hunt into the southern oceans off New Zealand. By the nineteenth century, whaling ships were armed with guns that shot a steel harpoon armed with vicious barbs deep into the whale. In the 1840s, explosive charges on harpoon heads ensured the whale's immediate death. Yet as this depiction of Japanese whaling shows, simple tools and weapons remained part of the dangerous work.

Another century of extensive hunting devastated many whale species before international agreements finally limited the killing of these giant sea creatures.

Netting Whales   During the Tokugawa, whaling became an important new industry in parts of Japan.   (Courtesy Rizzoli)

THE QING EMPIRE

The Qing Empire, created by the Manchus, had distinguished itself in the 1600s for its adept maneuverings, both strategic and diplomatic, against Russia. The Qing rulers had earned the admiration of the Jesuits, who transmitted to Europe a very appealing image of the emperors in China as enlightened philosopher-kings. But the failure in 1793 of the British attempt to establish diplomatic and trade relations with the Qing—the Macartney mission (see Chapter 19)—turned European opinion against China, and in the very early 1800s few Europeans apart from traders based in Canton had much contact with or interest in China. For their part, the Qing rulers and bureaucrats were embroiled in serious domestic crises: rebellions by displaced indigenous peoples and the poor and protests against the injustice of the local magistrates. The Qing rulers of 1800 believed that Europe was remote and only casually interested in trade. Only slowly did officials learn that Britain was passionate about foreign trade and already had colonies in India, a major naval base at Singapore.

Economic and Social Disorder

The Qing conquest in the 1600s brought stability to central China, previously subjected to decades of rebellion and agricultural shortages. The result was a great expansion of the agricultural base, together with a doubling of the population between about 1650 and about 1800. By 1800, population strain on the land had caused serious environmental damage in some parts of central and western China. Deforestation, erosion, and soil exhaustion left swollen populations stranded on rapidly deteriorating land.

Many groups had serious grievances against the government. Minority peoples in central and southwestern China resented having been driven off their lands during the boom of the 1700s. Mongols resisted the appropriation of their grazing lands and the displacement of their traditional elites. Many people mistrusted the government, suspecting that all officials were corrupt. The growing presence of foreign merchants and missionaries in coastal cities added to their discontent.

As the nineteenth century opened, the White Lotus Rebellion (1794–1804)—partly inspired by a mystical ideology that predicted the restoration of the Chinese Ming dynasty and the coming of the Buddha—was raging across central China. The White Lotus was the first in a series of large internal conflicts that continued through the 1800s. Ignited by deepening social instabilities, these movements were sometimes intensified by local ethnic conflicts and by unapproved religions.

The Opium War, 1839–1842

For more than a century, British officials had been frustrated by the enormous trade deficit caused by the British demand for tea and the Qing refusal to facilitate the importation to China of any British product. In opium, British merchants discovered an extremely profitable trade. Despite a Qing law of 1729 making it illegal to import opium, European merchants and their Chinese partners were smuggling in growing quantities of the highly addictive drug that was grown in British India. By the 1830s, as many as 30,000 chests of opium were being imported. For a time, the Qing emperor and his officials debated whether to legalize and tax opium or to enforce the existing ban on the drug more strictly. They decided to root out the use and the importation of opium, and in 1839 they sent an official to Canton to deal with the matter.

Britain considered the Qing ban on the importation of opium an intolerable restraint of trade and a direct threat to Britain's economic health, and indirectly a cause for war. When British naval and marine forces arrived at the south China coast in late 1839 and negotiations broke down, the **Opium War** (1839–1842) broke out. The British kept most confrontations on the sea, where they had a distinct technological advantage. British ships landed marines who pillaged coastal cities and then returned to their ships and sailed to new destinations (see Map 22.3). The Qing had no

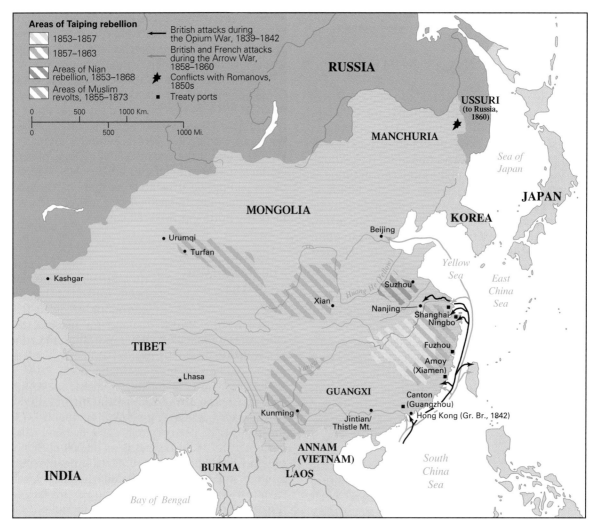

Map 22.3   Conflicts in the Qing Empire, 1839–1870   In the Opium War of 1839–1842 the seacoasts saw most of the action. Since the Qing had no imperial navy, the well-armed British ships encountered little resistance as they shelled the southern coasts. In inland conflicts, such as the Taiping Rebellion, the opposing armies were massive and slow moving. Battles on land were often prolonged attempts by one side to starve out the other side before making a major assault.

imperial navy, and even in the land engagements, the traditional, hereditary soldiers, the **Bannermen,** proved woefully inadequate. The British could quickly transport their forces by sea along the coast. Qing troops, in contrast, moved primarily on foot. Moving Qing reinforcements from central to eastern China took more than three months, and when the defense forces arrived, they were exhausted and basically without weapons.

Against the British invaders, the Bannermen used the few muskets the Qing had imported during the 1700s. Firing these obsolete weapons was slow and dangerous. A majority of the Bannermen, however, had no guns and fought with swords, knives, spears, and clubs. Soldiers under British command—many of them Indians—carried percussion-cap rifles, which were far quicker, safer, and more accurate than the matchlocks. In addition, the British deployed new gunboats able to proceed up the shallow water of the Yangzi River.

When the invaders approached Nanjing, the revered former Ming capital, the Qing decided to negotiate an end to the war. In 1842, the **Treaty of Nanking** (Nanjing) increased the number of **treaty ports**—cities opened to foreign residents—from one (Canton) to five, lowered tariffs to 5 percent, and made the island of Hong Kong a permanent British colony. British residents in China were granted the rights of extraterritoriality. The Qing government had to pay an indemnity of 21 million ounces of silver to Britain as a penalty for having started the war.

Later treaties expanded the privileges of foreign traders and missionaries in China. The number of treaty ports, where foreign merchants enjoyed the rights of extraterritoriality, grew to more than ninety by 1900. In Canton, Shanghai°, and other coastal cities, Europeans and Americans built comfortable housing in zones where Chinese were not permitted to live, and they entertained themselves in exclusive restaurants and bars. Some of the work of Christian missionaries was benevolent: hospitals, shelters, and soup kitchens. The missionaries themselves also undermined Confucian beliefs and condemned long-standing customs, such as footbinding. The foreigners and their privileges became a target of resentment.

The Taiping Rebellion, 1850–1864

The most startling demonstration of the inflammatory mixture of social unhappiness and foreign intrusion was the great civil war usually called the **Taiping Rebellion.** In Guangxi, where the Taiping movement originated, social problems had been generating disorders for half a century. Agriculture in the region was unstable, and many people made their living from arduous and despised trades such as disposing of human waste, making charcoal, and mining. Ethnic divisions complicated economic distress. A minority group, the Hakkas, were frequently found in the lowliest trades, and tensions between them and the majority were rising. Also, the area was close enough to Canton to feel the cultural and economic impact of the growing number of Europeans and Americans.

The founder of the movement, Hong Xiuquan°, came from a humble Hakka background. He saw himself as the younger brother of Jesus, commissioned by God to found a new kingdom on earth and drive the Manchu conquerors, the Qing, out of China. Hong called his new religious movement the "Heavenly Kingdom of Great Peace."

Hong quickly attracted a community of believers, primarily Hakkas like himself. When news of the heresy reached the government, Qing troops were sent to arrest the leaders. But after the Taipings soundly repelled the imperial troops, their numbers multiplied, and they began to enlarge their domain into eastern and northern China. Women participated fully in work, and military teams organized separately by sex.

Panic preceded the Taipings. Villagers feared being forced into Taiping units, and Confucian elites recoiled in horror from the bizarre ideology of foreign gods, totalitarian rule, and walking, working, warring women. But the huge numbers the Taipings were able to muster overwhelmed attempts at local defense. When the rebel army conquered Nanjing in 1853, the Taiping leaders decided to settle there and make it the capital of the new "Heavenly Kingdom of Great Peace."

By then, Qing military commanders were becoming more successful in halting the Taiping advances. The Qing court agreed to special taxes to fund the new armies and acknowledged the new combined leadership of the civilian and professional force. The new Qing armies surrounded Nanjing, hoping to starve out the rebels. The Taipings, however, mobilized enormous campaigns in nearby parts of eastern China, scavenging supplies, and Nanjing held out for more than a decade

In 1856, the British and French launched a series of swift, brutal coastal attacks—a second opium war, because the Qing had not observed the provisions of the treaties signed after the first Opium War. Their troops invaded Beijing, sacked

---

Shanghai (shahng-hie)

Hong Xiuquan (hoong shee-OH-chew-an)

Nanjing Encircled For a decade, the Taipings held the city of Nanjing as their capital. For years, Qing and international troops attempted to break the Taiping hold. By the summer of 1864, Qing forces had built tunnels leading to the foundations of Nanjing's city walls and had planted explosives. The detonation of explosives signaled the final Qing assault on the rebel capital. As shown here, the common people of the city, along with their starving livestock, were caught in the cross-fire. Many of the Taiping leaders escaped the debacle at Nanjing, but nearly all were hunted down and executed. (Roger-Viollet)

the Summer Palace in 1860, and imposed new treaties that punished the Qing for not enacting all the provisions of the Treaty of Nanking. Having secured their principal objective, the British and French forces now joined the Qing in the campaign against the Taipings. The injection of European weaponry and money aided in the quelling of the Taiping and other rebels during the 1860s.

The Taiping Rebellion ranks as the world's bloodiest civil war and the greatest armed conflict before the twentieth century. Estimates of deaths range from 20 million to 30 million. The loss of life was due primarily to starvation and disease, for most engagements consisted of surrounding the enemy holed up in fortified cities and waiting until they died, surrendered, or were so weakened that they could be easily defeated. Many of the most intensely cultivated regions of central and eastern China were depopulated and laid barren. Cities, too, were hard hit. Major cultural centers in eastern China lost masterpieces of art and architecture, imperial libraries were burned or their collections exposed to the weather, and the printing blocks used to make books were destroyed.

Decentralization at the End of the Qing Empire

The Qing government emerged from the 1850s with no hope of achieving solvency. The treasury had been bankrupted by decades of corruption, the indemnities demanded by Europeans after the Opium Wars, and the huge costs of the Taiping rebellion. To ensure that the Qing government began repaying its debt to Britain, Robert Hart was installed as inspector-general of a newly created Imperial Maritime Customs Service. The revenues he collected were split between Britain and the Qing. Britons and Americans put themselves in the employ of the Qing government as advisers and ambassadors, attempting to smooth communications between the Qing, Europe, and the United States while the imperial government started up the diplomatic machinery demanded by Europe in its latest treaties.

The real work of the recovery, however, was managed by the provincial governors who had come to the forefront in the struggle against the Taipings and who continued to levy their own taxes, raise their own troops, and run their own bureaucracies. Some became so powerful that they were managing Qing foreign policy as well as domestic affairs. From the 1860s forward, the Qing Empire disintegrated into a set of large power zones in which provincial governors handed over leadership to their protégés.

CONCLUSION

What is the global significance of these complex political and economic changes in Asia and Africa? One perspective stresses the continuing exploitation of the weak by the strong, of African, Asian, and Pacific peoples by aggressive Europeans. In this view, the emergence of Britain as the dominant imperial power continues the European expansion that the Portuguese and the Spanish pioneered and the Dutch continued. Yet even though the balance of power was shifting in the Europeans' favor between 1750 and 1870, Asian and African cultures were still vibrant, and most people were free of European control. Islamic reform movements and the rise of the Zulu nation had greater significance for their respective regions of Africa than did Western forces. Despite some ominous concessions to European power, the Chinese were still largely in control of their own destinies. Even in India, most people's lives and beliefs showed more continuity with the past than the change due to British rule.

From another perspective, what was most important about this period was not the political and military strength of the Europeans but their growing dominance of the world's commerce, especially through long-distance ocean shipping. In this view, like other Europeans, the British were drawn to Africa and southern Asia by a desire to obtain new materials. However, trade was similarly two-sided. Asians and Africans welcomed the industrial manufactures and other imports brought on European ships. The opium trade is a stark example of how harmful this trade could be, as are its effects on the weavers of India. But one should not overlook the beneficial side. Consumers found industrially produced goods far cheaper and sometimes better than the handicrafts these imports replaced or supplemented. Global trade also created larger markets for African and Asian goods, such as vegetable oil trade from West Africa, cotton from Egypt and India, and tea from China.

In short, it must not be imagined that Asians and Africans were powerless in dealing with European expansion. The Indian princes who extracted concessions from the British in return for their cooperation and the Indians who rebelled against the raj both forced the system to accommodate their needs. Moreover, some Asians and Africans were beginning to use European education, technology, and methods to transform their own societies. In 1870, no one could say how long and how difficult that learning process would be, but Africans and Asians would continue to shape their own futures.

Key Terms

Zulu	Sepoy Rebellion
Sokoto Caliphate	Indian Civil Service
modernization	Indian National Congress
Muhammad Ali	clipper ships
"legitimate" trade	Opium War
recaptives	Bannermen
sepoys	Treaty of Nanking
nawab	treaty ports
British raj	Taiping Rebellion

Suggested Reading

Volumes 2 and 3 of *The Oxford History of the British Empire,* edited by William Roger Louis, (1998, 1999), are the most up-to-date global surveys of this period. Less Anglo-centric in its interpretation is Immanuel Wallerstein's *The Modern World-System III: The Second Era of Great Expansion of the Capitalist World-Economy, 1730–1840s* (1989).

For more on African topics, see Roland Oliver and Anthony Atmore, *Africa Since 1800,* 4th ed. (1994); J. D. Omer-Cooper, *The Zulu Aftermath* (1966); Murray Last, *The Sokoto Caliphate* (1967); A. G. Hopkins, *An Economic History of West Africa* (1973); and Norman R. Bennett, *Arab Versus European: War and Diplomacy in Nineteenth Century East Central Africa* (1985).

Very readable introductions to India in this period are Sugata Bose and Ayeshia Jalal, *Modern South India* (1998); Burton Stein, *A History of India* (1998); and Stanley Wolpert, *A New History of India,* 6th ed. (1999). See also Daniel Headrick, *The Tentacles of Progress: Technology Transfer in the Age of Imperialism, 1850–1940* (1988).

On the later Qing Empire, see Pamela Kyle Crossley, *Orphan Warriors: Three Manchu Generations and the End of the Qing World* (1990); Peter Ward Fay, *The Opium War, 1840–1842: Barbarians in the Celestial Empire in the Early Part of the Nineteenth Century and the War by Which They Forced Her Gates Ajar* (1975); Christopher Hibbert, *The Dragon Wakes: China and the West, 1793–1911* (1970); and Jonathan D. Spence, *God's Chinese Son: The Taiping Heavenly Kingdom of Hong Xiuquan* (1996).

Notes

1. Quoted in P. J. Vatikiotis, *The History of Modern Egypt: From Muhammad Ali to Mubarak,* 4th ed. (Baltimore: Johns Hopkins University Press, 1991), 74.
2. Quoted by Bernard S. Cohn, "Representing Authority in Victorian England," in *The Invention of Tradition,* ed. Eric Hobsbawm and Terence Ranger (Cambridge: Cambridge University Press, 1983), 165.

PART SEVEN

GLOBAL DOMINANCE AND DIVERSITY,

1850–1949

etween 1850 and 1950, Europe, the United States, and Japan industrialized and became powerful. One cause of the power of Europe, the United States, and Japan was nationalism, a bond uniting people on the basis of a common culture or shared historical experiences. In some nations, public participation resulted in basic freedoms and strong parliamentary institutions. In others, authoritarian leaders used nationalist feelings to mobilize mass support.

Another cause of Western and Japanese power in this period was industrialization itself. New technologies and economic arrangements transformed the lives of people of all classes and profes-sions. Work increasingly took place in factories and offices, separating employment from home life, husbands from wives, children from parents. A growing proportion of married women became housewives, and compulsory education systems took over the care of children. Intensifying industrial activities transformed the natural environment. Pollution from manufacturing, long a local problem, began to affect entire regions.

Industrialization led to the creation of increasingly destructive weapons that enabled the Western powers to extend their commercial and political influence over Africa, most of Asia, and Latin America. By 1914, Britain, France, and the

United States dominated over half of the area and peoples of the world. By the time Germany and Japan entered the competition for overseas colonial empires, few unconquered territories remained.

Germany's desire to become a global power was a major cause of the First World War. The defeat of Germany did not restore the prewar equilibrium, as the victorious Allied nations had hoped. The Russian Revolution of 1917 led to the establishment of the world's first communist state. The collapse of the Ottoman Empire sparked changes in Middle Eastern societies, most dramatically in Turkey itself.

When the world economy collapsed in the 1930s, social disruption in Germany and Japan brought to power extremist politicians who sought to solve their countries' economic woes by seizing neighboring territories. Nationalism assumed its most hideous form in World War II. The war led to the massacre of millions of innocent people and the destruction of countless cities.

Domination by the great powers inspired a new generation of leaders to embrace the politics of national liberation. After decades of struggle, India achieved independence in 1947. Two years later, Communists led by Mao Zedong overthrew a Chinese government they denounced as too subservient to the West. In Latin America, leaders turned to nationalist economic and social politics.

The year 1945 marked the end of western European dominance. Only the United States and the Soviet Union remained to compete for global influence. Meanwhile, nationalism was rapidly spreading to the rest of the world, bringing with it the urge to acquire the benefits and power of industrial technology.

	1850	1870	1890
Americas	U.S. Civil War **1861–1865** Creation of Dominion of Canada **1867** •	British build railroads in Brazil and Argentina **1880s** •	• **1890** U.S. is leading steel producer Spanish-American War **1898** • **1880–1914** Immigration from southern & eastern Europe surges
Europe	• **1851** Majority of British population living in cities • **1856** Transformation of steel and chemical industries begins	**1870–1914** Era of the New Imperialism • **1871** Unification of Germany, Italy	**1894–1906** Dreyfus affair in France
Africa	**1853–1877** Livingstone, Stanley expeditions in central Africa End of transatlantic slave trade **1867** • Gold discovered in southern Africa **1884–1886**	• **1880s** West Africa conquered by France and Britain **1884–1885** Berlin Africa Conference	• **1896** Ethiopians defeat Italian army at Adowa Nigeria becomes British protectorate **1899** •
Middle East	**1863–1879** Ismail westernizes Egypt Suez Canal opens **1869** •	• **1882** British occupy Egypt • **1878** Ottoman Empire loses most of its European territories	• **1904** Young Turk reforms in Ottoman Empire
Asia and Oceania	Direct British rule in India **1858** • • **1862** French conquer Indochina Meiji Restoration in Japan **1868** •	First Indian National Congress **1885** • Russia conquers Central Asia **1884–1887**	Boxer Rebellion in China **1900** • Sino-Japanese War **1894** • **1904–1905** Russo-Japanese War

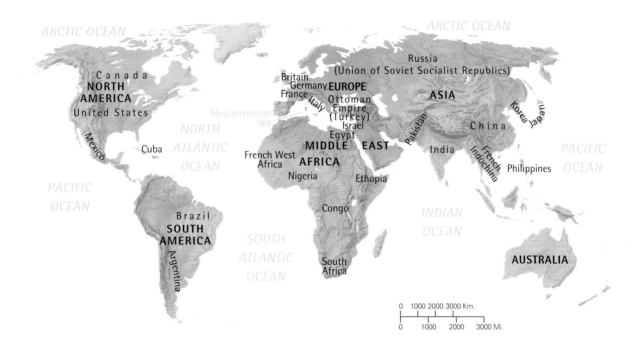

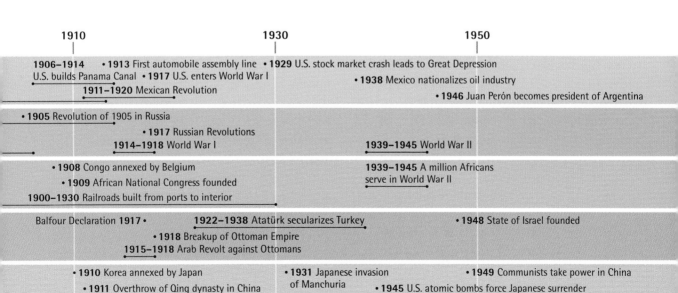

1910   1930   1950

1906–1914 • **1913** First automobile assembly line • **1929** U.S. stock market crash leads to Great Depression
U.S. builds Panama Canal • **1917** U.S. enters World War I   • **1938** Mexico nationalizes oil industry
     1911–1920 Mexican Revolution   • **1946** Juan Perón becomes president of Argentina

• **1905** Revolution of 1905 in Russia
         • **1917** Russian Revolutions
    1914–1918 World War I   **1939–1945** World War II

• **1908** Congo annexed by Belgium   **1939–1945** A million Africans
   • **1909** African National Congress founded   serve in World War II
1900–1930 Railroads built from ports to interior

Balfour Declaration **1917** •   **1922–1938** Atatürk secularizes Turkey   • **1948** State of Israel founded
         • **1918** Breakup of Ottoman Empire
    1915–1918 Arab Revolt against Ottomans

• **1910** Korea annexed by Japan   • **1931** Japanese invasion   • **1949** Communists take power in China
   • **1911** Overthrow of Qing dynasty in China   of Manchuria   • **1945** U.S. atomic bombs force Japanese surrender
                                       • **1947** India and Pakistan win independence

23

THE NEW POWER BALANCE,

1850–1900

New Technologies and the World Economy • Social Transformations • Nationalism and the Unification of Germany • The Great Powers of Europe, 1871–1900 • New Great Powers: The United States and Japan

SOCIETY AND CULTURE: Demonstrating for Women's Rights

On January 18, 1871, in the Hall of Mirrors of the palace of Versailles, King Wilhelm I of Prussia was proclaimed emperor of Germany before a crowd of officers and other German rulers. This ceremony marked the unification of many small German states into one nation. Off to one side stood Prussian chancellor Otto von Bismarck°, the man most responsible for the creation of a united Germany. A few years earlier, he had declared, "The great issues of the day will be decided not by speeches and votes of the majority—that was the great mistake of 1848 and 1849—but by iron and blood." Indeed it was "blood"—that is, victories on the battlefield—rather than popular participation that had led to the unification of Germany; among the dignitaries in the Hall of Mirrors that day, only two or three were civilians. As for "iron," it meant not only weapons but, more important, the industries required to produce weapons. Thus, after 1871, nationalism, once a dream of revolutionaries and romantics, became ever more closely associated with military force and with industry.

This chapter deals with a small group of countries—Germany, France, Britain, Russia, the United States, and Japan—that we call "great powers." In the next chapter, which deals with the era of the "New Imperialism" (1870–1914), we will see how these nations used their power to conquer colonial empires in Asia and Africa and to control Latin America. Together, Chapters 23 and 24 describe an era in which a handful of wealthy industrialized nations—all but one of them of European culture—imposed on the other peoples of the world a domination more powerful than any experienced before or since.

As you read this chapter, ask yourself the following questions:

Otto von Bismarck (UTT-oh fun BIS-mark)

- What new technologies and industries appeared between 1850 and 1900, and how did they affect the world economy?

- How did the societies of the industrial countries change during this period?

- Why do we call certain countries "great powers" but not others?

NEW TECHNOLOGIES AND THE WORLD ECONOMY

After 1850, industrialization took off in new directions. Germany and the United States surpassed Great Britain as the world's leading industrial powers by 1890. Small companies were overshadowed by large corporations owned by wealthy capitalists or (especially in Russia and Japan) by governments. New technologies based on advances in physics and chemistry revolutionized everyday life and transformed the world economy.

The Steel and Chemical Industries

Steel is a special form of iron, both hard and elastic. A series of inventions in the 1850s made steel the cheapest and most versatile metal ever known. As a result, world steel production rose from a half-million tons in 1870 to 28 million in 1900, of which the United States produced 10 million, Germany 8, and Britain 4.9. Steel became cheap and abundant enough to make rails, bridges, ships, and even "tin" cans meant to be used once and thrown away.

The new steel mills were hungry consumers of coal, iron ore, limestone, and other raw materials. They took up as much space as whole towns, belched smoke and particulate night and day, and left behind huge hills of slag and other waste products. Environmental degradation affected steel-producing regions such as the English Midlands, the German Ruhr, and parts of Pennsylvania.

The chemical industry followed a similar pattern. By the early nineteenth century, only soda, sulfuric acid, and chlorine bleach (used in the cotton industry) were manufactured on a large scale, especially in Britain. Then in 1856, the development of the first synthetic dye, aniline purple, from coal tar launched the mass production of organic chemicals—compounds containing carbon atoms. These bright, long-lasting colors delighted consumers but hurt tropical countries, such as India, that produced indigo, a blue vegetable dye.

Chemistry also made important advances in the manufacture of explosives. In 1866, the Swedish scientist Alfred Nobel found a way to turn nitroglycerin into a stable solid—dynamite. This and other new explosives were very useful in mining and the construction of railroads and canals. They also enabled the armies and navies of the great powers to arm themselves with increasingly accurate and powerful rifles and cannon.

The growing complexity of industrial chemistry made it one of the first fields where science and technology interacted on a daily basis. This development gave a great advantage to Germany, which had the most advanced engineering schools and scientific institutes of its time. By the end of the nineteenth century, Germany was the world's leading producer of dyes, drugs, synthetic fertilizers, ammonia, and nitrates used in making explosives.

Electricity

The third great innovation of the late nineteenth century was **electricity.** In the 1870s, inventors devised efficient generators that turned mechanical energy into electric current and opened the way to a host of new applications. Arc lamps lit up public squares, theaters, and stores. Then in 1879, **Thomas Edison** in the United States developed an incandescent lamp well suited to lighting small rooms and in 1882 created the world's first electrical distribution network, in New York City. By the turn of the century, electric lighting was rapidly replacing dim and smelly gas lamps in the cities of Europe and North America.

Other uses of electricity quickly appeared. Electric streetcars and, later, subways helped reduce the traffic jams that clogged large cities. Electric motors replaced steam engines and power belts, increasing productivity and improving workers' safety. As demand for electricity grew, engineers learned to use waterpower to produce electricity, and hydroelectric plants were built.

Electricity helped alleviate some environmental problems, since electric motors and lamps did not pollute the air. Power plants were built at a distance from cities. As electric trains and streetcars replaced horse-drawn trolleys and coal-burning locomotives, cities became noticeably cleaner and healthier. At the same time, electricity created a huge demand for copper, bringing Chile, Montana, and southern Africa into the world economy as never before.

Shipping and Telegraph Cables

At midcentury, a series of developments radically transformed ocean shipping. Iron and steel took the place of wood. Propellers replaced paddle wheels and sails. By the turn of the century, more efficient engines could convert the heat produced by burning a single sheet of paper into the power to move 1 ton over half a mile. The average size of freighters increased from 200 tons in 1850 to 7,500 tons in 1900. The Suez Canal, constructed in 1869, shortened the distance between Europe and Asia and triggered a massive switch from sail power to steam.

The world's fleet of merchant ships grew from 9 million to 35 million tons between 1850 and 1910, as passengers, mail, and perishable freight traveled on fast and reliable scheduled liners. To control their ships around the globe, shipping companies used a new medium of communications: **submarine telegraph cables** laid on the ocean floor linking the continents. Cables were laid across the Atlantic in 1866, and by the turn of the century, cables connected every country and almost every inhabited island.

Railroads

The fifty years after 1850 saw a tremendous expansion of the world's **railroad** networks. At the end of its Civil War in 1865, the United States already had 35,000 miles (over 56,000 kilometers) of track, three times as much as Britain, and still growing. Germany, France, Canada, Russia, and Japan also built large networks.

Railroads were not confined to industrialized nations, but were constructed around the world. The British built the fourth largest rail network in the world in India (see Chapter 22). Many old cities doubled in size to accommodate railroad stations, sidings, tracks, warehouses, and repair shops. In the countryside, railroads consumed vast amounts of land and timber for ties to hold the rails and for bridges. Throughout the world, they opened new land to agriculture, mining, and other uses.

World Trade and Finance

Thanks to the growing speed and falling cost of transportation between 1850 and 1913, world trade expanded tenfold, transforming the economies of different parts of the world in different ways. The capitalist economics of western Europe and North America grew more prosperous and diversified, despite deep depressions in which workers lost their jobs and investors their fortunes.

Long after German and American industries surpassed the British, Britain continued to dominate the flow of trade, finance, and information. In 1900, two-thirds of the world's submarine cables were British or passed through Britain. Over half of the world's shipping was British owned. Britain invested one-fourth of its national wealth overseas, much of it in the United States and Argentina.

Nonindustrial areas were more vulnerable to changes in price and demand than were the industrialized nations, for many of them produced raw materials that could be replaced by synthetic substitutes or alternative sources of supply. Nevertheless, until World War I, the value of exports from the tropical countries generally remained high.

SOCIAL TRANSFORMATIONS

The technological and economic changes of the late nineteenth century sparked profound social changes in the industrial nations. A fast-growing population swelled cities to unprecedented size, and millions of Europeans emigrated to the Americas. Workers spawned labor move-

CHRONOLOGY

	Europe	United States	East Asia
1850	**1851** Majority of British population living in cities **1856** Bessemer converter; first synthetic dye **1859** Charles Darwin, *On the Origin of Species* **1861** Emancipation of serfs (Russia) **1866** Alfred Nobel develops dynamite **1867** Karl Marx, *Das Kapital*		**1853** Commodore Perry "opens" Japan
		1865 Civil War ends; economic expansion begins **1865–1914** Surge of immigration from southern and eastern Europe	
	1871 Unification of Germany; unification of Italy		**1868** Meiji Restoration begins modernization drive in Japan
1875	**1875** Social Democratic Party founded in Germany **1882** Married Women's Property Act (Britain)	**1879** Thomas Edison develops incandescent lamp **1890** United States is the world's leading producer of steel **1890s** "Jim Crow" laws enforce segregation in southern states	**1894** Sino-Japanese War
1900	**1905** Revolution of 1905 (Russia)	**1899** United States acquires Puerto Rico and the Philippines	**1904–1905** Russo-Japanese War **1910** Japan annexes Korea

ments and new forms of radical policies, and women's lives were dramatically altered.

Population and Migrations

The population of Europe grew faster from 1850 to 1914 than ever before or since, almost doubling from 265 million to 468 million, despite mass migrations of Europeans to the United States, Canada, Australia, New Zealand, and Argentina. Between 1850 and 1900, on average, 400,000 Europeans migrated overseas every year; between 1900 and 1914, the flood rose to over 1 million a year. People of European ancestry rose from one-fifth to one-third in the world's population.

Much of the increase came from a drop in the death rate, as epidemics and starvation became less common. The Irish famine of 1847–1848 was the last peacetime famine in European history. North American wheat supplemented Europe's food. Year-round supplies of meat, fruit, vegetables, and oils improved the diet of European and North American city dwellers.

Urbanization and Social Structures

In 1851, Britain became the first nation to have a majority of its population living in towns and cities. By 1914, 80 percent of its population was urban, as were 60 percent of the German and 45 percent of the French populations. London grew from 2.7 million in 1850 to 6.6 million in 1900. New York

Urban Growth: Vienna in 1873 During the nineteenth century, European cities grew with unprecedented speed. This bird's-eye view of the Austro-Hungarian capital shows the transformation. The densely populated inner city surrounded the cathedral. In 1857, high walls that once had protected the old city from attack were torn down to make room for the Ringstrasse, a broad, tree-shaded boulevard lined with public buildings, museums, churches, and a university. Beyond the Ring, the newly wealthy bourgeoisie built new neighborhoods of large houses and apartment buildings. (Museen der Stadt, Vienna)

reached 3.4 million by 1900, a fifty-fold increase in the century. In the English Midlands, in the German Ruhr, and around Tokyo Bay, towns fused into one another, filling in the fields and woods that once had separated them.

In early industrial cities, the poor crowded together in unsanitary tenements. New urban technologies transformed city life for most residents. Pipes brought in clean water and carried away sewage. First gas and then electric lighting made cities safer and more pleasant at night. By the end of the century, municipal governments provided police and fire departments, schools, parks, and other amenities unheard of a century earlier.

As sanitation improved, urban death rates fell below birthrates for the first time. Confident that

their children would survive infancy, couples began to limit the number of children they had. To accommodate the growing population, planners laid out new cities, such as Chicago, on a rectangular grid, and middle-class families moved to new developments on the edges of cities. In Paris, older neighborhoods with narrow, crooked streets and rickety tenements were replaced with broad boulevards and modern apartment buildings. Brilliantly lit by gas and electricity, Paris became the "city of lights," a model for city planners from New Delhi to Buenos Aires. By 1900, electric streetcars and subways allowed working-class people to live miles from their workplaces.

In fast-growing cities such as London, New York, and Chicago, newcomers arrived so quickly that housing construction and municipal services could not keep up. Immigrants who saved their money to reunite their families could not afford costly municipal services. As a result, the poorest neighborhoods remained as overcrowded, unhealthy, and dangerous as they had been since the early decades of industrialization.

While urban environments improved in many ways, air quality worsened. Coal, burned to power steam engines and heat buildings, polluted the air, coating everything with a film of grimy dust. And the thousands of horses that pulled the carts and carriages covered the streets with their wastes, causing a terrible stench.

Labor Movements and Socialist Politics

Industrialization combined with the revolutionary ideas of the late eighteenth century to produce two kinds of movements—socialism and labor movements—calling for further changes. **Socialism** was an ideology developed by radical thinkers who questioned the sanctity of private property and argued in support of industrial workers against their employers. **Labor unions** were organizations formed by industrial workers to defend their interests in negotiations with employers. The socialist and labor movements were never identical. Most of the time they were allies; occasionally they were rivals.

Labor unions sought not only better wages but also improved working conditions and insurance against illness, accidents, disability, and old age. They grew slowly because strikes were illegal and hard to sustain. When laws were relaxed, British, German, and American labor grew rapidly.

By far the best-known socialist was **Karl Marx** (1818–1883), a German journalist who lived most of his life in England. The ideas he expressed succinctly in the *Communist Manifesto* (1848) and in great detail in *Das Kapital*° (1867) provided an intellectual framework for the growing dissatisfaction with raw industrial capitalism. He argued that the capitalists unfairly extracted the "surplus value" of workers' labor—that is, the difference between workers' wages and the value of the goods

Das Kapital (DUSS cop-ee-TALL)

they manufactured. The concentration of wealth in a few hands convinced Marx that class struggle between workers and owners was inevitable. But the International Working Man's Association Marx helped found in 1864 attracted more intellectuals than workers. Workers found other means of redressing their grievances, such as the vote and labor unions.

The nineteenth century saw a gradual extension of the right to vote throughout Europe and North America. Universal male suffrage became law in the United States in 1870, in France and Germany in 1871, in Britain in 1885, and in the rest of Europe soon after. With universal male suffrage, socialist politicians could expect to capture many seats in their nations' parliaments, because the newly enfranchised working class was so numerous. Democratic socialist parties sought to use voting power to gain concessions from government and eventually even to win elections.

Working-Class Women and Men

Working-class women led lives of toil and pain, considerably harder than the lives of their menfolk. Although the worst abuses of child labor had been banned in most European countries by 1850, parents expected girls as young as ten to contribute to the household. Many became domestic servants, commonly working sixteen or more hours a day, six and a half days a week, for little more than room and board. Their living quarters, usually in the attic or basement, contrasted with the luxurious quarters of their masters. Female servants were vulnerable to sexual abuse by their masters or their masters' sons.

Young women often preferred work in a factory to domestic service. Men worked in construction, iron and steel, heavy machinery, or on railroads; women worked in textiles and the clothing trades, two extensions of traditional women's household work. Most industrial countries passed legislation limiting the hours or forbidding the employment of women in the hardest and most dangerous occupations, such as mining and foundry work. Such legislation also reinforced gender divisions in industry, keeping women in low-paid, subordinate positions.

Married women with children were expected to stay home, even if their husbands did not make enough to support the family. In addition to the work of child rearing and housework, married women of the working class contributed to the family's income by taking in boarders, sewing, or weaving baskets. The hardest and worst-paid work was washing other people's clothes. Since electric lighting and indoor plumbing cost more than most working-class families could afford, even ordinary household duties like cooking and washing remained heavy burdens.

The poorest of the poor were orphans and single women with children. Unable to find jobs or support themselves at home, many turned to prostitution. The wealth of middle-class men made it easy for them to take advantage of the poverty of working-class women.

The Victorian Age and Women's "Separate Sphere"

In English-speaking countries, the period from about 1850 to 1914 is known as the **Victorian Age.** The expression refers not only to the reign of Queen Victoria of England (r. 1837–1901) but to rules of behavior and to an ideology surrounding the family and the relations between men and women. The Victorians contrasted the masculine ideals of strength and courage with the feminine virtues of beauty and kindness, and they idealized the home as a peaceful and loving refuge from the dog-eat-dog world of competitive capitalism.

Victorian morality claimed to be universal, yet it best fit the European upper- and middle-class family. Men and women were thought to belong in **"separate spheres."** Successful businessmen spent their time at work or relaxing in men's clubs. They put their wives in charge of rearing the children, running the household, and spending the family money to enhance the family's social status.

The most important duty of middle-class women was rearing children. Unlike the rich of previous eras, who handed their children over to wet nurses and tutors, Victorian mothers nursed their own babies and showered their children with love and attention. Even those who could afford nannies and governesses remained personally involved in their children's education. While boys were being prepared for the business world or the professions, girls were taught such skills as embroidery, drawing, and music, which offered no monetary reward or professional preparation but enhanced their social graces and marriage prospects.

Young women could work until they got married, but only in genteel occupations such as retail and office work. Jobs that required higher education, especially jobs in the professions, were closed to women. Until late in the century, few universities granted degrees to women. The first profession open to women was teaching, as more and more countries passed laws calling for universal compulsory education. Women were considered well suited to teaching young children and girls—an extension of the duties of Victorian mothers. Teaching, however, was judged suitable only for single women; married women were expected to stay home, taking care of their own children.

Governments enforced legal discrimination against women. Until the end of the century, most European countries considered women minors for life—that is, subject to their fathers before marriage and to their husbands after. Even Britain, among the most progressive countries, did not give women the right to control their own property until 1882, with passage of the Married Women's Property Act.

Some middle-class women organized to fight prostitution, alcohol, and child labor. By the turn of the century, a few were challenging male domination of politics and the law. By 1914, women had won the right to vote in twelve states of the United States. British women did not vote until 1918. (See Society and Culture: Demonstrating for Women's Rights.)

NATIONALISM AND THE UNIFICATION OF GERMANY

The most influential idea of the nineteenth century was **nationalism.** The French revolutionaries had defined people, previously considered the subjects of a sovereign, as the citizens

Demonstrating for Women's Rights

Before the First World War, no country allowed all women to vote. In Britain, women who demonstrated for voting rights were known as "suffragettes." When petitions to Parliament and peaceful demonstrations had no effect, Emmeline Pankhurst, the leader of the movement, concluded that more forceful measures were required. In the following passage, she describes the tactics she devised to call attention to the cause of women's suffrage.

Whatever preparations the police department were making to prevent the demonstration, they failed because, while as usual, we were able to calculate exactly what the police department were going to do, they were utterly unable to calculate what we were able to do. We had planned a demonstration for March 4th, and this one we announced. We planned another demonstration for March 1st, but this one we did not announce. Late on the afternoon of Friday, March 1st, I drove in a taxicab, accompanied by the Hon. Secretary of the Union, Mrs. Tuke and another of our members, to No. 10 Downing Street, the official residence of the Prime Minister. It was exactly half past five when we alighted from the cab and threw our stones, four of them, through the window panes. As we expected we were promptly arrested and taken to Cannon Row police station. The hour that followed will long be remembered in London. At intervals of fifteen minutes relays of women who had volunteered for the demonstration did their work. The first smashing of glass occurred in the Haymarket and Picadilly, and greatly startled and alarmed both pedestrians and po-

lice. A large number of women were arrested, and everybody thought that this ended the affair. But before the excited populace and the frustrated shop owners' first exclamation had died down, before the police had reached the station with their prisoners, the ominous crashing and splintering of plate glass began again, this time along both sides of Regent Street and the Strand. A furious rush of police and people toward the second scene of action ensued. While their attention was taken up with occurrences in this quarter, the third relay of women began breaking the windows in Oxford Circus and Bond Street. The demonstration ended for the day at half past six with the breaking of many windows in the Strand. . . .

The demonstration had taken place in the morning, when a hundred or more women had walked quietly into Knightsbridge and walking singly along the streets demolished nearly every pane of glass they passed. Taken by surprise the police arrested as many as they would reach, but most of the women escaped.

For that two days' work something like two hundred suffragettes were taken to the various police stations, and for days the long procession of women streamed through the courts.

If the goal was to obtain the right to vote, why did the demonstrators break store windows? And why did they do so at fifteen-minute intervals?

Source: Emmeline Pankhurst, *My Own Story* (London, 1914), pp. 211–219.

of a *nation*—a concept identified with a territory, the state that ruled it, and the culture of its people. Because the most widely spoken language in nineteenth-century Europe was German, the unification of most German-speaking people into a single state in 1871 had momentous consequences for the world.

National Identity Before 1871

The idea of redrawing the boundaries of states to accommodate linguistic, religious, or cultural differences was revolutionary. Language was usually the crucial element in creating a feeling of national unity, but language and citizenship seldom coincided. The fit between France and the French language was exceptional. The Italian- and German-speaking peoples were divided among many small states. Living in the Austrian Empire were peoples who spoke German, Czech, Slovak, Hungarian, Polish, and other languages. Even where people spoke a common language, they could be divided by religion or institutions. The Irish, though English speaking, were mostly Catholic, whereas the English were primarily Protestant.

Until the 1860s, nationalism was associated with **liberalism,** the revolutionary middle-class ideology that emerged from the French Revolution (see Chapter 20) and asserted the sovereignty of the people and demanded constitutional government, a national parliament, and freedom of expression. The most famous nationalist of the early nineteenth century, Giuseppe Mazzini° (1805–1872), led a failed liberal revolution of 1848 in Italy that sought to unify the Italian peninsula. Although the revolutions of 1848 failed except in France, their strength convinced conservative governments that they could not forever keep their citizens out of politics and that mass politics, if properly managed, could strengthen rather than weaken the state. A new generation of conservative political leaders learned how to preserve the social status quo through public education, universal military service, and colonial conquests, all of which built a sense of national unity.

Giuseppe Mazzini (jew-SEP-pay mat-SEE-nee)

The Unification of Germany

Some German nationalists wanted to unite all Germans under the Catholic Austrian throne. Others wanted to exclude Austria with its many non-Germanic peoples and unite all other German-speaking areas under Lutheran Prussia. The Prussian state had two advantages: (1) the newly developed industries of the Rhineland and (2) the first European army to make use of railroads, telegraphs, breechloading rifles, steel artillery, and other products of modern industry. The king of Prussia, Wilhelm I (r. 1861–1888), had entrusted the running of his government to his chancellor, the brilliant and authoritarian aristocrat **Otto von Bismarck** (1815–1898), who was determined to use Prussian military and German nationalism to advance the interests of the Prussian state.

In 1864, after a quick victory against Denmark, he set his sights on Austria, which surrendered in 1866. To everyone's surprise, Prussia took no Austrian territory. Instead, Prussia and some smaller states formed the North German Confederation, the nucleus of a future Germany. Then in 1870, Bismarck provoked a war with France. In this "Franco-Prussian War," German armies used their superior firepower and tactics to achieve a quick victory.

The spoils of victory included a large indemnity and two provinces of Alsace and Lorraine. To the Germans, this region was German because a majority of its inhabitants spoke German. To the French, it was French because it had been so when the nation of France was forged in the Revolution and because most of its inhabitants considered themselves French. These two conflicting definitions of nationalism kept enmity between France and Germany smoldering for decades.

Nationalism After 1871

The Franco-Prussian War changed the political climate of Europe. France became wholeheartedly liberal. The Italian peninsula became unified as the kingdom of Italy. Germany, Austria-Hungary (as the Austrian Empire had renamed itself in 1867), and Russia remained conservative.

All politicians tried to manipulate public opinion to bolster their governments. The spread of literacy allowed politicians and journalists to appeal to the emotions of the poor, diverting their anger from their employers to foreigners and their votes from socialist to nationalist parties.

In many countries, the dominant group used nationalism to justify the imposing of its language, religion, or customs on minority populations. The Russian Empire attempted to "Russify" its diverse ethnic populations. The Spanish government made the Spanish language compulsory in the schools, newspapers, and courts of its Basque- and Catalan-speaking provinces. Immigrants to the United States were expected to learn English.

Some people looked to science for support of political dominance. One of the most influential scientists of the century, and the one whose ideas were most widely cited and misinterpreted, was the English biologist **Charles Darwin** (1809–1882), who had spent years traveling through South America and the South Pacific studying plant and animal life. His famous book, *On the Origin of Species by Means of Natural Selection* (1859), argued that over hundreds of thousands of years, living beings had either evolved in the struggle for survival or become extinct. The philosopher Herbert Spencer (1820–1903) and others took up Darwin's ideas of "natural selection" and "survival of the fittest" and applied them to human society. Extreme Social Darwinists developed elaborate pseudo-scientific theories of racial differences, claiming that they were the result not of history but of biology.

THE GREAT POWERS OF EUROPE, 1871–1900

After 1871, politicians and journalists discovered how easily they could whip up popular frenzy against neighboring countries. Rivalries over colonial territories, ideological differences between liberal and conservative governments, and even minor border incidents or trade disagreements contributed to a growing atmosphere of international tension.

Germany at the Center of Europe

International relations revolved around a united Germany, because Germany was located in the center of Europe and had the most powerful army on the European continent. After creating a unified Germany in 1871, Bismarck worked to maintain peace in Europe. To isolate France, he forged a loose coalition with Austria-Hungary and Russia, which he was able to keep together for twenty years.

Bismarck proved equally adept at manipulating mass politics at home. To weaken the influence of middle-class liberals, he extended the vote to all adult men. By imposing high tariffs on manufactured goods and wheat, he gained the support of both the wealthy industrialists of the Rhineland and the great landowners of eastern Germany. He stole the thunder of the socialists by introducing social legislation—medical, unemployment, and disability insurance and old-age pensions—long before other industrial countries did. Under his leadership, the German people developed a strong sense of national unity and pride in their industrial and military power.

In 1888, Wilhelm I was succeeded by his grandson Wilhelm II (r. 1888–1918), who dismissed Chancellor Bismarck. Wilhelm II talked about his "global policy" and demanded that Germany, with the mightiest army and the largest industrial economy in Europe, have a colonial empire, "a place in the sun."

The Liberal Powers: France and Great Britain

France, once the dominant nation in Europe, had difficulty reconciling itself to being in second place. Its population and its army lagged far behind Germany's. French industry was growing much slower than Germany's, due to the loss of the iron and coal mines of Lorraine. The French people were deeply divided over the very nature of the state: some were monarchists and Catholics; a growing number held republican and anticlerical views. Despite these problems, a long tradition of popular participation in politics and a strong sense of nationhood, reinforced by a fine system of universal public education, gave the French people a deeper cohesion than appeared on the surface.

Great Britain was the only other country in Europe with a democratic tradition. The British government alternated smoothly between the Liberal and Conservative Parties, and the income gap between rich and poor gradually narrowed. Nevertheless, Britain had problems that grew more apparent as time went on.

One problem was Irish resentment of English rule as a foreign occupying force. Another problem was the British economy. Once the workshop of the world, Great Britain had fallen behind the United States and Germany in such important industries as iron and steel, chemicals, electricity, and textiles. Even in shipbuilding and shipping, Britain's traditional specialties, Germany was catching up. Britain was also preoccupied with its enormous and fast-growing empire. Though a source of wealth for investors and the envy of other imperialist nations, the empire was a constant drain on Britain's finances.

After the Crimean War of 1854–1856 (see Chapter 21), Britain turned its back on Europe and pursued a policy of "splendid isolation." Britain's preoccupation with India led British statesmen to exaggerate the Russian threat to the shipping routes through the Mediterranean and Central Asia.

The Conservative Powers: Russia and Austria-Hungary

The forces of nationalism weakened rather than strengthened Russia and Austria-Hungary. The reason for this effect was that their populations were far more divided, socially and ethnically, than were the German, French, or British peoples.

Nationalism was most divisive in the Austrian Empire. The decision to rename itself the Austro-Hungarian Empire in 1867 appeased its Hungarian critics but alienated its Slavic-speaking minorities. The Austro-Hungarian Empire still thought of itself as a great power and attempted to dominate the Balkans. This strategy irritated Russia, which thought of itself as the protector of Slavic peoples everywhere, and it eventually led to war.

Russia was the most misunderstood country in Europe. Its enormous size and population led many Europeans to exaggerate its military potential, but Russia was weakened by national and social divisions. All in all, only 45 percent of the peoples of the tsarist empire spoke Russian.

To strengthen the bonds between the monarchy and the Russian people and promote industrialization by enlarging the labor pool, the moderate conservative Tsar Alexander II (r. 1855–1881) emancipated the peasants from serfdom in 1861. That measure, however, did not create a modern society but only turned serfs into communal farmers with few skills and little capital. Though technically "emancipated," the great majority of Russians had little education, few legal rights, and no say in their government. After Alexander's assassination in 1881, his successors Alexander III (r. 1881–1894) and Nicholas II (r. 1894–1917) opposed all forms of social change. Industrialization consisted largely of state-sponsored projects, such as railroads, iron foundries, and armament factories, and led to social unrest among urban workers. Wealthy landowning aristocrats continued to dominate the Russian court and administration and succeeded in blocking most reforms.

The weaknesses in Russia's society and government became glaringly obvious after Russia's defeat in the Russo-Japanese War of 1904–1905 (see below). The shock of defeat caused a popular uprising, the Revolution of 1905, that forced Tsar Nicholas II to grant a constitution and an elected Duma (parliament). But as soon as he was able to rebuild the army and the police, he reverted to the traditional despotism of his forefathers. Small groups of radical intellectuals, angered by the contrast between the wealth of the elite and the poverty of the common people, began plotting the violent overthrow of the tsarist autocracy.

The Doss House   Late-nineteenth-century cities showed more physical than social improvements. This painting by Makovsky of a street in St. Petersburg contrasts the broad avenue and impressive buildings with the poverty of the crowd.   (The state Russian Museum/Smithsonian Institution Traveling Exhibit)

New Great Powers: The United States and Japan

Europeans had come to regard their continent as the center of the universe and their states as the only great powers in the world. The rest of the world was either ignored or used as bargaining chips in the game of power politics. The late nineteenth century marked the high point of European power and arrogance, yet at that very moment, two nations outside Europe were becoming great powers. One of them, the United States, was inhabited mainly by people of European origin, and its rise to great-power status had been predicted early in the nineteenth century by astute observers like the French statesman Alexis de Tocqueville. The other one, Japan, seemed so distant and exotic in 1850 that no European had guessed it would join the ranks of the great powers.

The United States, 1865–1900

After the Civil War ended in 1865, the United States entered a period of vigorous growth. Hundreds of thousands of immigrants arrived every year, mainly from Russia, Italy, and Central Europe, raising the population to 63 million in 1891. Although many settled on the newly opened lands west of the Mississippi (see Map 23.1), most of the migrants moved to the towns, which mushroomed

Emigrant Waiting Room   The opening of the western region of the United States attracted settlers from the east coast and from Europe. These migrants are waiting for a train to take them to the Black Hills of Dakota during one of the gold rushes of the late nineteenth century.   (Library of Congress)

into cities in a few years. In the process, the nation became an industrial giant. By 1900, the United States had overtaken Britain and Germany as the world's leading industrial power.

This explosive growth was accomplished with few government restrictions and much government help, such as free land for railroads and protective tariffs. In this atmosphere of unfettered free enterprise, the nation got rich fast, as did its upper and middle classes.

Expansion created many victims. First among them were the American Indians. When the railroads penetrated the west after the Civil War, they brought white colonists eager to start farming, ranching, or mining. The indigenous Indians whose lands they invaded fought back with great courage but were outnumbered and outgunned. In Canada, the government tried to protect the Indians from the whites. The United States Army, how-

ever, always sided with the settlers. The U.S. government had signed numerous treaties with the Indians but tore them up when settlers demanded land. After decades of warfare, massacres, and starvation, the government confined the remaining Indians to reservations on the poorest lands.

The U.S. government also abandoned African-Americans in 1877, after the end of Reconstruction, especially in the defeated southern states. Though freed from slavery in 1865, most of them became sharecroppers who were at the mercy of their landowners. In the 1890s, the southern states instituted "Jim Crow" laws segregating blacks in public transportation, jobs, and schools. Not only did southern judges apply harsh laws in a biased manner, but black Americans were also subject to the lawless violence of mobs, which lynched an average of fifty blacks a year until well into the twentieth century.

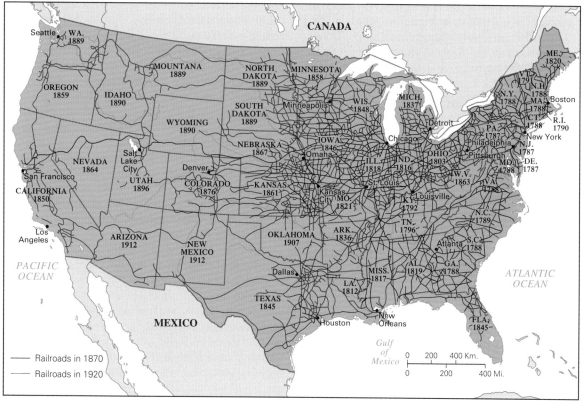

Map 23.1   The United States, 1850–1920   This map shows the expansion of the United States from the coasts into the interior of the continent. In the western half of the continent, only California and Texas were states in 1850; territories located farther from the coasts became states later. The economic development, shown by the railroad lines, followed much the same pattern, radiating west and south from the northeastern states and—to a lesser extent—eastward from California.

Racism also affected Asian immigrants, many of whom had come to the United States to build railroads in the western states. In 1882, the U.S. government barred the Chinese from immigrating by enacting the first of many racial exclusion laws.

Working-class whites benefited little from the booming economy. Economic depressions in 1873 and 1893 caused more distress in the United States than in Europe, because the United States had few labor laws and no unemployment compensation to soften the hardships. Police or the army repressed strikes and unions. The courts consistently supported employers against their employees, capital against labor, and business against government.

Working-class women bore the brunt of repressive labor practices because they earned less than men, had more responsibilities, and seldom were members of labor unions. As in Britain, activist middle-class women organized to demand female suffrage and to fight against alcohol, prostitution, and other social evils.

The booming economy and the waves of immigrants radically transformed the environment. Timber companies clear-cut large areas of Michigan, Wisconsin, and the Appalachian Mountains to provide lumber for railroad ties and frame houses, pulp for paper, and fuel for locomotives and iron foundries. Farmers cleared the forests and plowed the prairies. Buffalo, the dominant animals of the western territories, were massacred by the hundreds of thousands to starve out the Indians and clear the land for cattle. In the west, the government began massive irrigation projects. In the industrial northeast, iron foundries, steel mills, and steam engines caused severe local air pollution.

In spite of all the assaults, the North American continent was so huge that large parts of it remained unspoiled. A few especially beautiful areas were declared national parks, beginning with Yellowstone in Wyoming in 1872, thereby marking a new stage in Americans' attitude toward nature. Thanks to the efforts of naturalist John Muir and President Theodore Roosevelt (1901–1909), large parts of the western states were set aside as national forests.

Most citizens showed little interest in foreign affairs. Patriots tended to celebrate American freedom and democracy, the conquest of a huge continent, and the country's remarkable technological achievements. In this period, the inventor Thomas Edison was probably the most admired man in America.

The expansionism of the United States and its businesses did not stop at the borders but exerted a strong influence on Mexico and the Caribbean. Naval officers, bankers, and politicians urged active intervention in the Western Hemisphere. In 1899, the United States defeated Spain, annexed Puerto Rico and the Philippines, and turned Cuba into an American protectorate (see Chapter 24). Long recognized as the leading power in the Americas, the United States found itself involved in Asian affairs as well. Nevertheless, although their country was fast becoming a global power, most Americans still preferred George Washington's policy of "no European entanglements."

The Rise of Japan, 1850–1900

China and Japan both felt the influence of the Western powers as never before in the late nineteenth century, but their responses were completely opposite. As Chapter 22 explained, China resisted Western influence and became weaker. Japan transformed itself into a major industrial and military power (see Map 23.2).

In 1853, the arrival of a small U.S. fleet with demands for an opening of Japan to trade with the United States sparked a crisis in the Tokugawa Shogunate that governed Japan. Aware of China's humiliating defeats in the Opium Wars, officials signed a treaty in 1858. But the treaty sparked a political crisis in the country that led to the overthrow of the Shogunate in 1868 and proclaimed the "Meiji° Restoration." The new Japanese rulers, unlike the Chinese, were under no illusion that they could fend off the Westerners without changing their institutions or their society. In the Charter Oath issued in 1868, the young emperor included the prophetic phrase: "Knowledge shall be sought throughout the world and thus shall be strengthened the foundation of the imperial polity." It was to be the motto of a new Japan, which embraced all foreign ideas, institutions, and techniques that could strengthen the nation.

In the 1870s and 1880s, the government sent hundreds of students to Britain, Germany, and the United States and hired foreign experts to teach Japanese how to build railroads, organize a modern army and navy, and operate a bureaucracy. The Meiji leaders created a government structure similar to that of imperial Germany. They introduced Western-style posts and telegraphs, railroads and harbors, banking, clocks, and calendars. They modeled the new Japanese navy on the British and the army on the Prussian. They even encouraged foreign clothing styles and pastimes. In 1889, Japan promulgated a new and authoritarian constitution modeled on that of Germany, with a bicameral legislature and a cabinet led by a prime minister. But the army and navy remained free of civilian control, only wealthy men were allowed to vote, and important decisions were made without popular input or even knowledge.

The government was especially interested in Western technology. It opened vocational, technical, and agricultural schools and founded four imperial universities. It brought in foreign experts to advise on medicine, science, and engineering. The Japanese government also encouraged industrialization. It taxed farmers heavily to pay for the purchase of ships, machines, and other capital goods. It set up state-owned enterprises to manufacture cloth and inexpensive consumer goods for sale abroad. In 1881, to pay off its debts, the govern-

Meiji (MAY-gee)

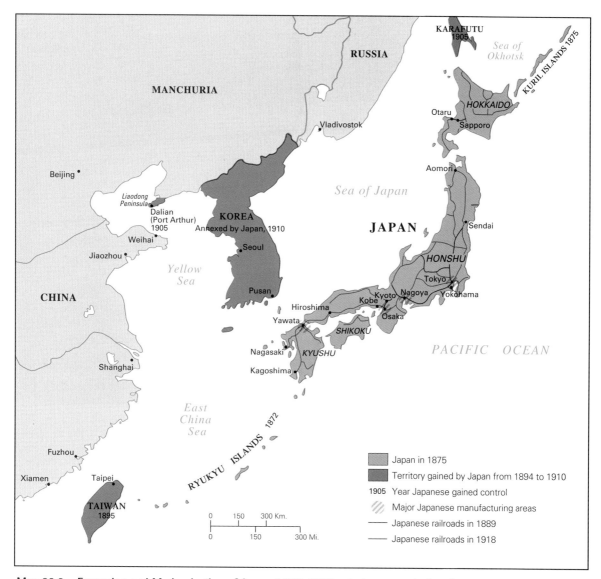

Map 23.2   Expansion and Modernization of Japan, 1868–1918   As Japan acquired modern industry, it followed the example of the European powers in seeking overseas colonies. Its colonial empire grew at the expense of its neighbors: Taiwan was taken from China in 1895, Karafutu (now Sakhalin) from Russia in 1905, and all of Korea became a colony in 1910.

Arrivals from the East In 1853, Commodore Matthew Perry's ships surprised the Tokugawa Shogunate by appearing not in Kyushu or southern Honshu, where European ships previously had been spotted, but at Uraga on the coast of eastern Honshu. The Japanese soon learned that Perry had come not from the south but across the Pacific from the east. The novelty of the threat unsettled the provincial leaders, who were largely responsible for their own defense. In this print done after the Meiji Restoration, the traditionally dressed local samurai go out to confront the mysterious "black ships."   (Courtesy of the Trustees of the British Museum)

ment sold these enterprises to private investors, mainly large *zaibatsu*°, or conglomerates.

Japan began to define its own "sphere of influence" that would include Korea, Manchuria, and part of China. In 1894, Japan went to war with China over Korea, defeating its much larger but weaker adversary in less than six months. China had to evacuate Korea, cede Taiwan and the Liaodong Peninsula, and pay a heavy indemnity. By 1900, Japan was sufficiently Westernized that the Western powers rescinded the unequal treaties

they had imposed forty years earlier, although they did make Japan return the Liaodong Peninsula to China.

Emboldened by China's obvious weakness, Japan and Russia competed for possession of the mineral-rich Chinese province of Manchuria. In 1905, Japan surprised the world by defeating Russia in the Russo-Japanese War. In spite of Western attempts to restrict it to the role of junior partner, Japan continued to increase its influence. It gained control of southern Manchuria, with its industries and railroads, and established a protectorate over Korea. In 1910, it finally annexed Korea, joining the ranks of the world's colonial powers.

zaibatsu (zye-BOT-soo)

CONCLUSION

After World War I broke out in 1914, many people, especially in Europe, looked back on the period from 1850 to 1914 as a golden age. For some, and in certain ways, it was. Industrialization was a powerful torrent changing Europe, North America, and East Asia. While other technologies like shipping and railroads increased their global reach, new ones—electricity, the steel and chemical industries, and the global telegraph network—contributed to the enrichment and empowerment of the industrial nations. Memories of the great scourges—famines, wars, and epidemics—faded. Clean water, electric lights, and railways began to improve the lives of city dwellers, even the poor. Goods from distant lands, even travel to other continents, came within the reach of millions.

European and American society seemed to be heading toward better organization and greater security. Municipal services made city life less dangerous and chaotic. Through labor unions, workers achieved some measure of recognition and security. By the turn of the century, liberal political reforms had taken hold in western Europe and the United States and seemed about to triumph in Russia as well. Morality and legislation aimed at providing security for women and families, though equality between the sexes was still beyond reach.

The framework for all these changes was the nation-state. The world economy, international politics, even cultural and social issues revolved around a handful of countries—the great powers—that believed themselves in control of the destiny of the world. These included the most powerful European nations of the previous century, as well as two newcomers—the United States and Japan—that were to play important roles in the future. Seldom in history had there been such a concentration of wealth, power, and self-confidence.

The success of the great powers rested on their ability to extract resources from nature and from other societies, especially in Asia, Africa, and Latin America. In a global context, the counterpart of the rise of the great powers is the story of imperialism and colonialism. To complete our understanding of the period before 1914, let us turn now to the relations between the great powers and the rest of the world.

■ Key Terms

steel	Karl Marx
electricity	Victorian Age
Thomas Edison	"separate spheres"
submarine telegraph cables	nationalism
railroads	liberalism
socialism	Otto von Bismarck
labor unions	Charles Darwin

■ Suggested Reading

Industrialization is the subject of Peter Stearns, *The Industrial Revolution in World History* (1993), and David Landes, *The Unbound Prometheus: Technological Change and Industrial Development in Western Europe from 1750 to the Present* (1969). Two interesting works on nationalism are E. J. Hobsbawm, *Nation and Nationalism Since 1780* (1990), and Benedict Anderson, *Imagined Communities: Reflections on the Origin and Spread of Nationalism* (1991).

Barrington Moore, *The Social Origins of Dictatorship and Democracy* (1966), is a classic essay on European society. On European women, see Renate Bridenthal, Claudia Koonz, and Susan Stuard, eds., *Becoming Visible: Women in European History* (1987); Patricia Branca, *Silent Sisterhood: Middle-Class Women in the Victorian Home* (1975); Louise Tilly and Joan Scott, *Women, Work, and Family* (1987); and Theresa McBride, *The Domestic Revolution: The Modernization of Household Service in England and France, 1820–1920* (1976). The history of family life is told in Beatrice Gottlieb, *The Family in the Western World from the Black Death to the Industrial Age* (1993). Albert Lindemann, *A History of European Socialism* (1983), covers the labor movements as well.

There are many excellent histories of individual countries. Germany in the late nineteenth century is well treated in Erich Eyck, *Bismarck and the German Empire* (1964). On Britain, see Donald Read, *The Age of Urban Democracy: England, 1868–1914* (1994), and David Thomson, *England in the Nineteenth Century, 1815–1914*

(1978). On France, Eugen Weber, *Peasants into Frenchmen* (1976), and Roger Price, *A Social History of Nineteenth-Century France* (1987), are especially recommended. A good introduction to Russian history is Hans Rogger, *Russia in the Age of Modernization and Revolution, 1881–1917* (1983).

Three very different aspects of American life are described in Carl Degler, *Out of Our Past: The Forces That Shaped Modern America* (1970); Thomas Hughes, *American Genesis: A Century of Invention and Technological Enthusiasm* (1989); and John Opie, *Nature's Nation: An Environmental History of the United States* (1998).

There are several interesting books on Japan, in particular Peter Duus, *The Rise of Modern Japan,* 2d ed. (1998), and Tessa Morris-Suzuki, *The Technological Transformation of Japan* (1994). Two fine books cover the history of modern China: John King Fairbank, *The Great Chinese Revolution, 1800–1985* (1987), and Jonathan D. Spence, *The Search for Modern China* (1990).

24

THE NEW IMPERIALISM,

1869–1914

A

The New Imperialism: Motives and Methods • The Scramble for Africa • Asia and Western Dominance • Imperialism in Latin America • The World Economy and the Global Environment

ENVIRONMENT AND TECHNOLOGY: Imperialism and Tropical Ecology

n November 1869, Empress Eugénie of France, Emperor Francis Joseph of Austria-Hungary, and sixteen hundred other dignitaries from the Middle East and Europe assembled at Port Said° in Egypt to celebrate the inauguration of the greatest construction project of the century: the **Suez Canal.** Ismail°, the khedive° (ruler) of Egypt, had invited all the Christian princes of Europe and all the Muslim princes of Asia and Africa, except the Ottoman sultan, his nominal overlord. He wanted to show that Egypt was not only independent but an equal of the great powers.

Ismail used this occasion to emphasize the harmony and cooperation between the peoples of Africa, Asia, and Europe. A French journalist wrote:

> This multitude, coming from all parts of the world, presented the most varied and singular spectacle. All races were represented. . . . We

saw, coming to attend this festival of civilization, men of the Orient wearing clothes of dazzling colors, chiefs of African tribes wrapped in their great coats, Circassians in war costumes, officers of the British army of India with their shakos [hats] wrapped in muslin, Hungarian magnates wearing their national costumes.[1]

To bless the inauguration, Ismail also had invited clergy of the Muslim, Orthodox, and Catholic faiths. A reporter noted: "The Khedive . . . wished to symbolize thereby the unity of men and their brotherhood before God, without distinction of religion; it was the first time that the Orient had seen such a meeting of faiths to celebrate and bless together a great event and a great work."[2]

The canal was a great success, but not in the way Ismail intended it to be. Ships using it could travel between Europe and India in less than two weeks—much less time than the month or longer consumed by sailing around Africa and into the Indian Ocean. By lowering freight costs, the canal stimulated shipping and the construction of steamships, giving an

---

Port Said (port sah-EED)   **Ismail** (is-mah-EEL)
khedive (kuh-DEEV)

Opening of the Suez Canal   When the canal opened in 1869, thousands of dignitaries and ordinary people gathered to watch the ships go by.   (Bildarchiv Preussischer Kulturbesitz)

advantage to nations that had heavy industry and a large maritime trade over land-based empires and countries that had few merchant ships. Great Britain, which long opposed construction of the canal for fear that it might fall into enemy hands, benefited more than any other nation. France, which provided half of the capital and most of the engineers, came in a distant second, for it had less trade with Asia than Britain did. Egypt, which contributed the other half of the money and most of the labor, was the loser in this affair. Instead of making Egypt powerful and independent, the Suez Canal provided

the excuse for a British invasion and occupation of Egypt. Far from inaugurating an era of harmony among the peoples of three continents and three faiths, the canal triggered a wave of European domination over Africa and Asia.

Between 1869 and 1914 Germany, France, Britain, Russia, and the United States used industrial technology to impose their will on the nonindustrial parts of the world. Historians use the expression **New Imperialism** to describe this exercise of power.

As you read this chapter, ask yourself the following questions:

CHRONOLOGY

	The Scramble for Africa	Asia and Western Dominance	Imperialism in Latin America
		1862–1895 French conquer Indochina **1865–1876** Russian forces advance into Central Asia	
1870	**1869** Opening of the Suez Canal **1874** British warfare against the Asante (Gold Coast) **1877–1879** British wars against the Xhosa and the the Zulu (South Africa) **1882** British forces occupy Egypt **1884–1885** Berlin Conference; Leopold II obtains Congo Free State	**1878** United States obtains Pago Pago Harbor (Samoa)	**1870–1910** Railroad building boom: British companies in Argentina and Brazil; U.S. companies in Mexico.
1890		**1885** Britain completes conquest of Burma **1887** United States obtains Pearl Harbor (Hawaii) **1894–1895** China defeated in Sino-Japanese War **1895** France completes conquest of Indochina	**1895–1898** Cubans revolt against Spanish rule
	1899–1902 South African War between Afrikaners and the British **1902** First Aswan Dam completed (Egypt)	**1898** United States annexes Hawaii and purchases Philippines from Spain **1899–1902** U.S. forces conquer and occupy Philippines **1903** Russia completes Trans-Siberian Railway **1904–1905** Russia defeated in Russo-Japanese War	**1898** Spanish-American War; United States annexes Puerto Rico and Guam **1903** United States backs secession of Panama from Colombia
1910	**1908** Belgium annexes Congo		**1904–1907, 1916** U.S. troops occupy Dominican Republic **1904–1914** United States builds Panama Canal **1912** U.S. troops occupy Nicaragua and Honduras

- What motivated the industrial nations to conquer new territories, and what means did they use?

- Which parts of the world were annexed to the new empires, and which ones became economic dependencies?

- How did the environment change in the lands subjected to the New Imperialism?

The New Imperialism: Motives and Methods

The New Imperialism was characterized by an explosion of territorial conquests. Between 1869 and 1914, Europeans seized territories in Africa and Central Asia, and both Europeans and Americans took territories in Southeast Asia and the Pacific. Approximately 10 million square miles (26 million square kilometers) and 150 million people fell under the rule of Europe and the United States in this period. The New Imperialism, however, was more than a land grab. The imperial powers used economic and technological means to reorganize dependent regions and bring Africa, Latin America, and other parts of the world into the world economy as suppliers of foodstuffs and raw materials and as consumers of industrial products.

What inspired Europeans and Americans to venture overseas and impose their will on other societies? There is no simple answer to this question. Economic, cultural, and political motives were involved in each case.

Political and Economic Motives

The great powers of the late nineteenth century, as well as less powerful countries like Italy, Portugal, and Belgium, were competitive and hypersensitive about their status. French leaders, humiliated by their defeat by Prussia in 1871 (see Chapter 23), sought to reestablish their nation's prestige through territorial acquisitions overseas. Great Britain, already in possession of the world's largest and richest empire, felt the need to protect India, its "jewel in the crown," by acquiring colonies in East Africa and Southeast Asia. Many Germans believed that a country as important as theirs required an impressive empire overseas.

Political motives were not limited to statesmen in the capital cities. Colonial governors, even officers posted to the farthest colonial outposts, practiced their own diplomacy. They often decided on their own to claim a piece of land before some rival got it. Armies fighting frontier wars found it easier to defeat their neighbors than to make peace with them. In response to border skirmishes with neighboring states, colonial agents were likely to send in troops, take over their neighbors' territories, and then inform their home governments. Governments felt obligated to back up their men-on-the-spot in order not to lose face. The great powers of Europe acquired much of West Africa, Southeast Asia, and the Pacific islands in this manner.

Industrialization had stimulated the demand for minerals, such as copper, tin, chrome, manganese, coal, and, most of all, gold and diamonds. The demand for such industrial crops as cotton and rubber and for stimulants such as sugar, coffee, tea, and tobacco also grew. These products were found in the tropics, but never in sufficient quantities. European merchants, manufacturers, and shippers secured sources of tropical raw materials and protected markets for their industries. Entrepreneurs and investors looked for profits from mines, plantations, and railroads in Asia, Africa, and Latin America.

Cultural Motives

The late nineteenth century saw a Christian revival in Europe and North America. Both Catholics and Protestants founded new missionary societies for purposes that were not just religious but more broadly cultural. They sought to export their own norms of "civilized" behavior. They were determined to abolish slavery in Africa and bring Western education, medicine, hygiene, and monogamous marriage to all the world's peoples.

The sense of moral duty and cultural superiority was not limited to missionaries. Many others,

Religion and Imperialism   European penetration into Africa was accompanied by enthusiastic efforts to convert the Africans to Christianity. European missionaries built schools and clinics as well as churches. Here, African schoolchildren are shown a picture of the Virgin Mary holding the baby Jesus, an image designed to replace traditional African religious objects. Mary and Jesus are represented as Europeans.   (USGP)

equating technological innovations with "progress" and "change for the better," believed that Western technology proved the superiority of Western ideas, customs, and culture. This attitude at least included the idea that non-Western peoples could achieve, through education, the same cultural level as Europeans and Americans. More harmful were racist ideas of Social Darwinists (see Chapter 23) that relegated non-Europeans to a status of permanent inferiority. Caucasians—whites—were always at the top of this ranking, which was often an excuse for permanent rule over Africans and Asians.

Imperialism soon attracted young men, finding few opportunities for adventure and glory at home in an era of peace. A few easy victories in the 1880s helped to overcome the indifference of the European public and parliaments. By the 1890s, imperialism was a popular cause, an overseas extension of European and American nationalism.

These motives alone do not explain the events of that time. What made it possible to conquer a piece of Africa, to convert the "heathen," or to start a plantation was the sudden increase in the power that industrial peoples could wield over nonindustrial peoples and over the forces of nature. Technological advances explain both the motives and the outcome of the New Imperialism.

The Tools of the Imperialists

The Industrial Revolution provided the means to achieve imperial objectives at a reasonable cost. More efficient steamships, the Suez Canal, and a global network of submarine telegraph cables became parts of a new technology of imperialism.

In 1854, a British doctor discovered that the drug quinine could prevent the deadly malaria that had hampered European penetration of tropical Africa. This and a few sanitary precautions sharply reduced European death rates in West Africa and opened the continent to more merchants, officials, and missionaries. The development of new and much deadlier firearms in the 1860s and 1870s shifted the balance of power on land between Westerners and other peoples. By the 1870s, armies in Europe and the United States had all switched to new breechloader rifles. Two more innovations appeared in the 1880s: smokeless powder, which did not foul the gun or reveal the soldier's position, and repeating rifles, which could shoot fifteen rounds in fifteen seconds. In the 1890s, European and American armies began using machine guns, which could fire eleven bullets per second. European-led forces of a few hundred could thereby defeat non-European armies of thousands.

Colonial Agents and Administration

Once colonial agents took over a territory, their home government expected them to cover their own costs and, if possible, return some profit to the home country. In some cases, such as along the West African coast or in Indochina, there was already a considerable trade that could be taxed. In other places, profits could come only from investments and a thorough reorganization of the indigenous societies.

The impact of colonial rule depended most on economic and social conditions. One important factor was the presence of European settlers. Where European settlers were numerous but still a minority of the population, as in Algeria and South Africa, settlers and the home country struggled for control over the indigenous population. In colonies with few white settlers, the European governors ruled autocratically.

Nowhere could colonialism operate without the cooperation of indigenous elites, because no colony was wealthy enough to pay the salaries of more than a handful of European officials. In most cases, the colonial governors exercised power through traditional rulers willing to cooperate, as in India (see Chapter 22). In addition, colonial governments educated a few local youths as clerks, nurses, policemen, customs inspectors, and the like.

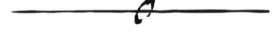

THE SCRAMBLE FOR AFRICA

Until the 1870s, African history was largely shaped by internal forces and local initiatives. Outside Algeria and southern Africa, European countries possessed only small enclaves on the coasts. Then within a decade, Africa was invaded and divided among the European powers in a movement often referred to as the **"scramble" for Africa** (see Map 24.1). This invasion affected all regions of the continent.

Egypt

Throughout the mid-nineteenth century, the khedives of Egypt had tried to modernize their armed forces; build canals, harbors, railroads, and other public works; and reorient agriculture toward export crops, especially cotton (see Chapter 22). Their interest in the Suez Canal was also part of this modernization policy. These ambitions cost vast sums of money, which the khedives borrowed from European creditors at high interest rates.

By 1876, interest payments on the large foreign debt consumed one-third of Egypt's foreign export earnings. To avoid bankruptcy, the Egyptian government sold its shares in the Suez Canal to Great Britain and accepted four foreign "commissioners of the debt" to oversee its finances. Still not satisfied, French and British bankers lobbied their governments to appoint a Frenchman as minister of public works and a Briton as minister of finance and, when high taxes caused hardship and popular discontent, to depose Ismail.

When this foreign intervention provoked a military uprising, the British sent an army into Egypt in 1882. In the name of defending the Suez Canal, this occupation lasted for seventy years, during which the British maintained the Egyptian government and the fiction of Egyptian sovereignty but retained real power in their own hands.

Eager to develop Egyptian cotton production, the British completed a dam across the Nile, at Aswan in upper Egypt in 1902, which doubled the effective acreage. This economic development enriched a small elite of landowners and merchants, many of them foreigners. Egyptian peasants got little relief from the heavy taxes collected to pay for their country's crushing foreign debt and the expenses of the British army of occupation. Muslim religious leaders objected to Western ways, such as the drinking of alcohol and the relative freedom of women. By the 1890s, Egyptian politicians and intellectuals were demanding that the British leave, but to no avail.

Western and Equatorial Africa

While the British were taking over Egypt, the French were planning to extend their empire into the interior of West Africa. In 1879, **King Leopold II** of Belgium used his personal fortune to lay claim to the giant Congo basin in equatorial Africa, while a French agent was laying claims to territory north of the river. These events sparked a flurry of diplomatic activity.

At the **Berlin Conference** on Africa in 1884 and 1885, the major powers agreed that henceforth,

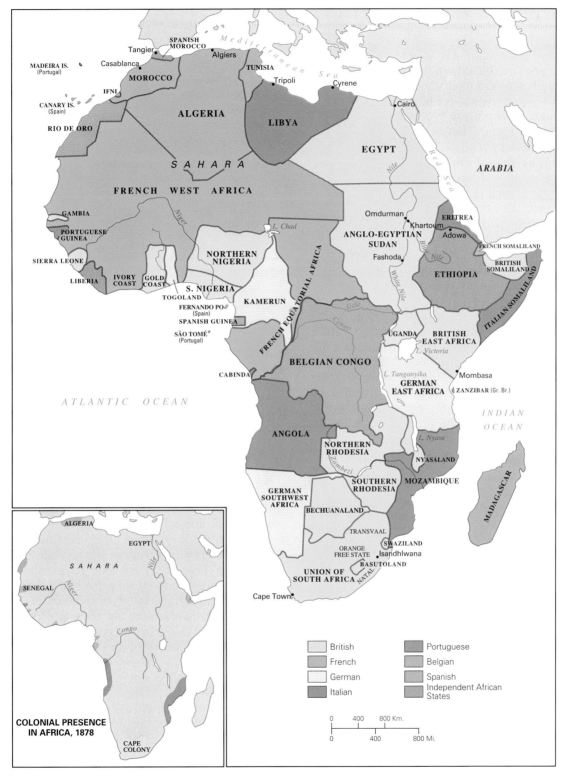

Map 24.1 Africa in 1878 and 1914 In 1878, the European colonial presence was limited to a few coastal enclaves, plus portions of Algeria and South Africa. By 1914, Europeans had taken over all of Africa except Ethiopia and Liberia.

"effective occupation" would replace the former trading relations between Africans and Europeans. Leopold II acquired a personal domain under the name "Congo Free State," while France and Portugal claimed most of the rest of equatorial Africa, at least on paper. "Effective occupation" required many more years of effort.

In West Africa, French troops encountered the determined opposition of Muslim leaders who resisted the French invasion for up to thirty years. The French advance encouraged the Germans to stake claims to parts of the region and the British to move north from their coastal enclaves, until all of West Africa was occupied by Britain, France, and Germany. West Africa had long had a flourishing trade. In the Gold Coast (now Ghana), British trading companies bought the cocoa grown by African farmers at low prices and resold it for large profits. Although French West Africa produced cotton, peanuts, and other crops, the difficulties of transportation limited its development before 1914.

Compared to West Africa, equatorial Africa had few inhabitants and little trade. Rather than try to govern these vast territories directly, authorities in the Congo Free State, the French Congo, and the Portuguese colonies of Angola and Mozambique farmed out huge pieces of land to private concession companies, offering them a monopoly on the natural resources and trade of their territories and the right to employ soldiers and tax the inhabitants. The inhabitants, however, had no cash crops that they could sell to raise the money they needed to pay their taxes.

Freed from outside supervision, the companies forced the African inhabitants at gunpoint to produce cash crops and carry them, on their heads or backs, to the nearest railroad or navigable river. The worst abuses took place in the Congo Free State, where a rubber boom lasting from 1895 to 1905 made it profitable for private companies to coerce Africans to collect latex from vines that grew in the forests. One Congolese refugee told the British consul Roger Casement, who investigated the atrocities:

> We begged the white men to leave us alone, saying we could get no more rubber, but the white men and their soldiers said: "Go. You are only beasts yourselves, you are only *nyama* (meat)."

> We tried, always going further into the forest, and when we failed and our rubber was short, the soldiers came to our towns and killed us. Many were shot, some had their ears cut off; others were tied up with ropes around their necks and bodies and taken away.[3]

After 1906, the British press began publicizing the horrors. The public outcry that followed, coinciding with the end of the rubber boom, convinced the Belgian government to take over Leopold's private empire in 1908.

Southern Africa

Southern Africa had long attracted European settlers because of its location on the sea route to India and because of its mild climate. By the 1850s, minorities of **Afrikaners** (descendants of early Dutch settlers), British settlers from the 1820s, and Indians brought by the British coexisted in four separate colonies with the indigenous African farmers and pastoralists. There were also independent African states, of which the Zulu kingdom was the most powerful (see Chapter 22).

The discovery of diamonds in 1868 and gold in 1886 lured thousands of new English-speaking white settlers as well as Africans looking for work. It also raised the region's importance to Great Britain, which fought a series of wars to subdue the independent Africans and the two Afrikaner republics. By 1879, Britain had annexed the diamond area around Kimberley as well as the separate territories of the Xhosa° people and had gone to war with the Zulu. Despite the superior weapons of the British, the Zulu scored a major victory at Isandhlwana° in the first battle of the war, but thereafter British might prevailed. King Cetshwayo° was captured and sent into exile, his kingdom was dismembered, and Zulu lands were given to white ranchers. Yet throughout those bitter times, the Zulu's sense of nationhood remained strong.

The British mining and railroad magnate **Cecil Rhodes** (1853–1902) led the political crusade to ex-

Xhosa (KOH-sah)   Cetshwayo (set-SHWAH-yo)
Isandhlwana (ee-sawn-dull-WAH-nah)

pand British influence in the region. He also led a concession company, the British South Africa Company, and founded two new colonies: Southern Rhodesia (now Zimbabwe) and Northern Rhodesia (now Zambia). When the Ndebele° and Shona people who inhabited the region resisted, British machine guns defeated them.

However, the gold mines lay firmly in Afrikaner territory. Efforts by Rhodes and the British government to annex the two Afrikaner republics, Transvaal° and Orange Free State, led to the South African War (1899–1902). At first, the well-armed Afrikaners had the upper hand, but Great Britain brought in 450,000 troops and crushed the Afrikaner armies. Nevertheless, Afrikaners emerged as the ruling element in the Union of South Africa, founded in 1910 by the four European settlers states. The clear loser was the African majority of this new state whose laws curtained their rights to land, the vote, and equal status with the white minority.

Political and Cultural Responses

Many African states and communities fought to preserve their independence, but only one succeeded in withstanding the power of European weaponry. By 1910, not only the Zulu and Ndebele, but the ancient kingdoms of **Asante°** and Benin and the newer Sokoto Caliphate and other new West Africa Muslim states (see Chapter 22) had met defeat. The one exception was **Emperor Menelik**'s newly enlarged kingdom of Ethiopia, whose well-armed and well-trained armies defeated a large Italian invasion in 1896.

Despite the imperialists' military victories, European control was weak in 1910, and most Africans continued living much as before. Gradually, they had to pay taxes by selling cash crops or migrate to places of employment. Such migrations were most disruptive in colonies that lost land to European settlers who took over African lands.

More Africans came into contact with missionaries than with any other Europeans. Missionaries, both men and women, opened schools to teach

reading, writing, and arithmetic to village children. Boys were taught crafts such as carpentry, while girls learned domestic skills such as cooking, laundry, and child care. Along with basic skills, the first generation of Africans educated in mission schools acquired Western ideas of justice and progress. Samuel Ajayi Crowther, a Yoruba rescued from slavery as a boy and educated in mission schools in Sierra Leone, went on to become an Anglican minister and, in 1864, the first African bishop.

Christianity proved successful in converting followers of traditional religions but made no inroads among Muslims. Instead, European colonialism unwittingly helped the diffusion of Islam, which spread along busier and safer trade routes. The number of Muslims in sub-Saharan Africa probably doubled between 1869 and 1914. In addition to new religious beliefs, colonial rule brought an end to fighting and slave raiding.

ASIA AND WESTERN DOMINANCE

During the period from 1869 to 1914, the pressure of the industrial powers was felt throughout Asia, the East Indies, and the Pacific islands. As trade with these regions grew in the late nineteenth century, so did their attractiveness to imperialists eager for economic benefits and national prestige (see Map 24.2).

Central Asia

Between 1865 and 1876, Russian forces with modern rifles and artillery advanced into Central Asia. Nomads like the Kazakhs, who lived east of the Caspian Sea, fought bravely but in vain. The fertile agricultural land of Kazakhstan attracted 200,000 Russian settlers. Despite government policies of not interfering in indigenous customs, by the end of the nineteenth century, the nomads were fenced out and reduced to starvation.

As the Qing Empire was losing control over Central Asia south of the Kazakh steppe land (see

Ndebele (en-duh-BELL-ay)   Transvaal (trans-VAHL)
Asante (uh-SAWN-tay)

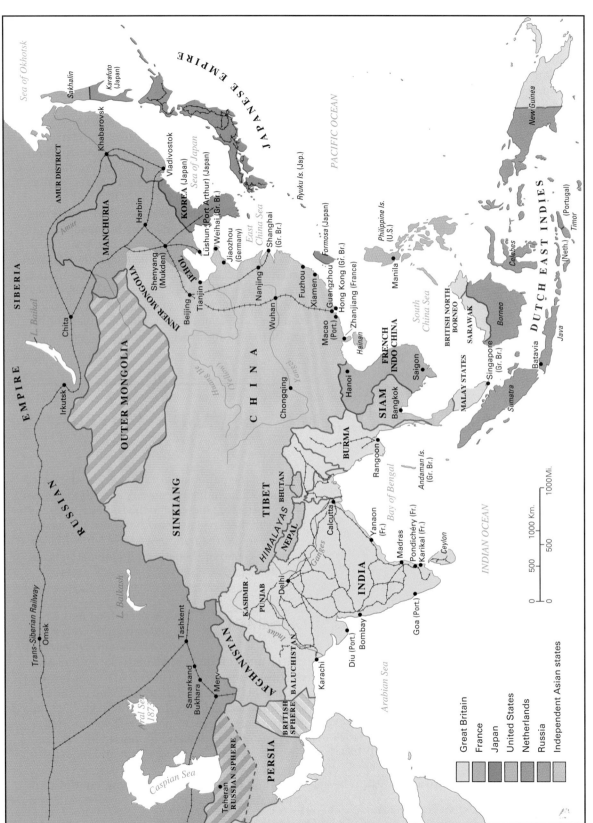

Map 24.2 Asia in 1914 By 1914, much of Asia was claimed by the colonial powers. The southern rim, from the Persian Gulf to the Pacific, was occupied by Great Britain, France, the Netherlands, and the United States. Central Asia had been incorporated into the Russian Empire. Japan, now industrialized, had joined the Western imperialist powers in expanding its territory and influence at the expense of China.

Chapter 22), Russia acquired land suitable for cotton, along with a large and growing Muslim population. Russian rule brought few benefits to the peoples of the Central Asian oases. The Russians abolished slavery, built railroads to link the region with Europe, and planted hundreds of thousands of acres of cotton. Unlike Europeans in Africa, they did not attempt to change the customs, languages, or religious beliefs of their subjects.

Southeast Asia and Indonesia

The peoples of the Southeast Asian peninsula and the Indonesian archipelago came under intense imperialist pressure during the nineteenth century. Burma (now Myanmar) and Malaya (now Malaysia) were gradually taken over by the British. Indochina fell piece by piece under French control. By the early 1900s, the Dutch had subdued northern Sumatra, the last part of the Dutch East Indies to be conquered. Only Siam (now Thailand) remained independent.

Despite their varied political histories, all of these regions had rich potential for agricultural cash crops, such as cinchona° (an antimalarial drug), natural rubber, sugar, tea, coffee, and palm oil (see Environment and Technology: Imperialism and Tropical Ecology). In exchange for these valuable exports, the inhabitants of the region received two benefits from colonial rule: peace and a reliable food supply. As a result, their numbers increased at an unprecedented rate.

Colonialism and the growth of population brought many social changes. The more numerous agricultural and commercial peoples gradually moved into mountainous and forest areas, displacing the earlier inhabitants who practiced hunting and gathering or shifting agriculture. The migrations of the Javanese to Borneo and Sumatra are but one example. Immigrants from China and India changed the ethnic composition and culture of every country in the region. Thus, the population of the Malay Peninsula became one-third Malay, one-third Chinese, and one-third Indian.

As in Africa, European missionaries attempted to spread Christianity under the colonial umbrella. Islam, however, was much more successful in gaining new converts, for it had been established in the region for centuries and people did not consider it a religion imposed on them by foreigners.

Hawaii and the Philippines, 1878–1902

By the 1890s, the United States had a fast-growing population and industries that produced more manufactured goods than they could sell at home. Merchants and bankers began to look for export markets. The political mood was also expansionist, and many echoed the feelings of naval strategist Alfred T. Mahan°: "Whether they will or no, Americans must now begin to look outward. The growing production of the country requires it."

Some Americans had been looking outward for quite some time, especially across the Pacific to China and Japan. In 1878, the United States obtained the harbor of Pago Pago in Samoa as a coaling and naval station, and in 1887 it secured the use of Pearl Harbor in Hawaii for the same purpose. Six years later, American settlers in Hawaii deposed Queen Liliuokalani (1838–1917) and offered the Hawaiian Islands to the United States. At the time, President Grover Cleveland (1893–1897) was opposed to annexation, and the settlers had to content themselves with an informal protectorate. By 1898, however, the United States under President William McKinley (1897–1901) had become openly imperialistic. It annexed Hawaii as a strategic steppingstone to Asia.

While large parts of Asia were falling under colonial domination, the people of the Philippines were chafing under their Spanish rulers. The movement for independence began among young Filipinos studying in Europe, but soon shifted to the Philippines, where **Emilio Aguinaldo,** leader of a secret society, rose in revolt and proclaimed a republic in 1898. The revolutionaries had a good chance of winning independence, for Spain had its hands full with a revolution in Cuba (see below).

---

cinchona (sin-CHO-nuh)

Mahan (muh-HAN)

ENVIRONMENT + TECHNOLOGY

Imperialism and Tropical Ecology

Like all conquerors before them, the European imperialists of the nineteenth century exacted taxes and rents from the peoples they conquered. But they also sent botanists and agricultural experts to their tropical colonies to increase the production of commercial crops. In doing so, they radically changed the landscapes of their tropical dependencies.

The most dramatic effects were brought about by the deliberate introduction of new crops—an acceleration of the Columbian Exchange that had begun in the fifteenth century. In the early nineteenth century, tea was transferred from China to India and Ceylon. In the 1850s, British and Dutch botanists smuggled seeds of the cinchona tree from the Andes in South America to India and Java. They had to operate in secret, because the South American republics, knowing the value of this crop, prohibited the export of seeds. With the seeds, the British and Dutch established cinchona plantations in Ceylon and Java, respectively, to produce quinine, which was essential as an antimalarial drug and a flavoring for tonic water. Similarly, in the 1870s, British agents stole seeds of the rubber tree from the Amazon rain forest and transferred them to Malaya and Sumatra.

Before these transfers, vast forests covered the highlands of India, Southeast Asia, and Indonesia, precisely the lands where the new plants grew best. So European planters had the forests cut down and replaced with thousands of acres of commercially profitable trees and bushes, all lined up in perfect rows and tended by thousands of indigenous laborers to satisfy the demands of customers in faraway lands. The crops that poured forth from the transformed environments brought great wealth to the European planters and the imperial powers. In 1909, the British botanist John Willis justified the transformation in these terms:

Whether planting in the tropics will always continue to be under European management is another question, but the northern powers will not permit that the rich and as yet comparatively undeveloped countries of the tropics should be entirely wasted by being devoted merely to the supply of the food

Unfortunately for Aguinaldo and his followers, the United States acquired the Philippines after the Spanish-American War lest the islands go to another imperialist power such as Japan or Germany. In 1899, Aguinaldo rose up again and proclaimed the independence of his country. In spite of protests by anti-imperialists in the United States, the U.S. government decided that its global interests outweighed the interests of the Filipino people. In rebel areas, a U.S. army of occupation tortured prisoners, burned villages and crops, and forced the inhabitants into "reconcentration camps." Many American soldiers tended to look on Filipinos with the same racial contempt with which Europeans viewed their colonial subjects. By the end of the insurrection in 1902, the war had cost the lives of 5,000 Americans and 200,000 Filipinos.

After the end of the insurrection, the United States attempted to soften its rule with public works and economic development projects. New buildings went up in the city of Manila; roads, harbors, and railroads were built; and the Philippine economy was tied ever more closely to that of the United States. In 1907, Filipinos were allowed to elect representatives to a legislative assembly; however, ultimate authority remained in the hands of a governor appointed by the president of the United States. In 1916, the Philippines were the first U.S. colony to be promised independence, a promise fulfilled thirty years later.

and clothing wants of their own people, when they can also supply the wants of the colder zones in so many indispensable products.

This quotation raises important questions about trade versus self-sufficiency. If a region's economy supplies the food and clothing wants of its own people, is its output "entirely wasted"? What is the advantage of trading the products of one region (such as the tropics) for those of another (such as the colder zones)? Is this trade an obligation? Should one part of the world (such as the "northern powers") let another refuse to develop and sell its "indispensable products"? Can you think of a case where a powerful country forced a weaker one to trade?

Source: The quotation is from John Christopher Willis, *Agriculture in the Tropics: An Elementary Treatise* (Cambridge: Cambridge University Press, 1909), 38–39.

Branch of a Cinchona Tree   The bark of the cinchona tree was the source of quinine, the only antimalarial drug known before 1940. Quinine made it much safer for Europeans to live in the tropics.   (From Bentley & Trimen's *Medicinal Plants*. Hunt Institute for Botanical Documentation, Carnegie Mellon University)

IMPERIALISM IN LATIN AMERICA

In the Western Hemisphere, therefore, the New Imperialism manifested itself not by a "scramble" for territories but in a form of economic dependence called **free-trade imperialism.** In the larger republics of South America, the pressure was mostly financial and economic. In Central America and the Caribbean, it also included military intervention by the United States.

Railroads and the Imperialism of Free Trade

Latin America's economic potential was huge, for the region could produce many agricultural and mineral products in demand in the industrial countries. What was needed was a means of opening the interior to development. Railroads seemed the perfect answer.

Starting in the 1870s, almost every country in Latin America acquired railroads, usually connecting mines or agricultural regions with the nearest port rather than linking up the different parts of the interior. Since Latin America did not have any steel or mechanical industries, all the equipment and building material came from Britain or the United States. So did the money to build the

Railroads Penetrate South America   The late nineteenth century saw the construction of several railroad networks in South America, often through rugged and dangerous terrain. This photograph shows the opening of a bridge on the Transandine Railroad in Peru. Flags were raised in honor of American construction and British ownership of the railroad.   (Tony Morrison/South American Pictures)

networks, the engineers who designed and maintained them, and the managers who ran them.

Argentina, a land of rich soil that produced wheat, beef, and hides, gained the longest and best-developed rail network south of the United States. By 1914, 86 percent of the railroads in Argentina were owned by British firms, 40 percent of the employees were British, and the official language of the railroads was not Spanish but English. The same was true of mining and industrial enterprises and public utilities throughout Latin America.

In many ways, the situation resembled that of India or Ireland, which also obtained a rail network in exchange for raw materials and agricultural prod-

ucts. The difference was that the Indians and Irish had little say in the matter because they were under British rule. But in Latin America, the political elites encouraged foreign companies with generous concessions as the most rapid way to modernize their countries and enrich the property owners.

American Expansionism and the Spanish-American War

After 1865, the European powers used their financial power to penetrate Latin America. But there was no need for territorial acquisitions, because the Latin American governments provided the political backing for the economic arrangements and Latin Americans had shown themselves capable of resisting invasions. In addition, by the Monroe Doctrine (1823), the United States closed the entire Western Hemisphere to all outside intervention—except its own.

The United States had long had interests in Cuba, the closest and richest of the Caribbean islands. American businesses invested great sums of money in the Spanish colony's sugar and tobacco industries. In 1895, the Cuban nationalist José Martí started a revolution against Spanish rule. American newspapers thrilled readers with lurid stories of Spanish atrocities, businessmen worried about their investments, and politicians demanded that the U.S. government help liberate Cuba.

On February 15, 1898, the U.S. battleship *Maine* accidentally blew up in Havana harbor, killing 266 American sailors. The U.S. government immediately blamed Spain and issued an ultimatum that the Spanish evacuate Cuba. Spain agreed to the ultimatum, but the American press and Congress were eager for war, and President McKinley did not restrain them.

The Spanish-American War was over quickly. On May 1, 1898, U.S. warships destroyed the Spanish fleet at Manila in the Philippines. Two months later, the United States Navy sank the Spanish Atlantic fleet off Santiago, Cuba. By mid-August, Spain was suing for peace. The United States purchased the Philippines from Spain and took over Puerto Rico and Guam as war booty. Cuba became an independent republic, subject, however, to American interference.

American Intervention in the Caribbean and Central America

The nations of the Caribbean and Central America were small and poor, and their governments were corrupt, unstable, and often bankrupt. They seemed to offer an open invitation to foreign interference. To ward off European intervention or for other reasons, the United States occupied Cuba, the Dominican Republic, Nicaragua, Honduras, and Haiti on one or more occasions before 1920. The United States was especially forceful in Panama, which was a province of Colombia. Here, the issue was not corruption or debts but a more vital interest: the construction of a canal across the isthmus of Panama to speed shipping between the east and west coasts of the United States. In 1878, the Frenchman Ferdinand de Lesseps, builder of the Suez Canal, had obtained a concession from Colombia to construct a canal across the isthmus, which lay in Colombian territory. Financial scandals and yellow fever, however, doomed his project.

When the United States acquired Hawaii and the Philippines, it recognized the strategic value of a canal that would allow warships to move quickly between the Atlantic and Pacific Oceans. The main obstacle was Colombia, whose senate refused to give the United States a piece of its territory. In 1903, the U.S. government supported a Panamanian rebellion against Colombia and quickly recognized the independence of Panama. In exchange, it obtained the right to build a canal and to occupy a zone 5 miles (8 kilometers) wide on either side of it. Work began in 1904, and the **Panama Canal** opened on August 15, 1914.

―――――――――― *Ɑ* ――――――――――

THE WORLD ECONOMY AND THE GLOBAL ENVIRONMENT

Although the New Imperialists' conquests were much larger that those of the Spanish conquistadors, their aim was not only to extend their power over new territories and peoples but to control both the natural world and indigenous societies and put them to work more efficiently than had ever been done before. They expressed their belief in progress and their good intentions in the clichés of the time: "the conquest of nature," "the annihilation of time and space," "the taming of the wilderness," and "our civilizing mission." The New Imperialism set in motion global environmental flows that were larger and more deliberate than the "Columbian Exchange" of that earlier imperial era.

Expansion of the World Economy

For centuries, spices, sugar, silk, and other exotic or tropical products had found a ready market in Europe. The Industrial Revolution vastly expanded this demand. Imports of foods and stimulants such as tea, coffee, and cocoa increased substantially during the nineteenth century. The trade in industrial raw materials grew even faster. Some were the products of agriculture, such as cotton, jute for bags, and palm oil for soap and lubricants. Others were minerals such as diamonds, gold, and copper. There also were wild forest products that only later came to be cultivated: timber for buildings and railroad ties, cinchona bark, rubber for rainwear and tires, and gutta-percha° to insulate electric cables.

The growing needs of the industrial world could not be met by the traditional methods of production and transportation of the nonindustrial world. When the U.S. Civil War interrupted the export of cotton to England in the 1860s, the British turned to India. But they found that Indian cotton was ruined by exposure to rain and dust during the long trip on open carts from the interior of the country to the harbors. To prevent the expansion of their industry from being stifled by the technological backwardness of their newly conquered territories, the imperialists made every effort to bring those territories into the mainstream of the world market.

One great change was in transportation. The Suez and Panama Canals cut travel time and lowered freight costs dramatically. Steamships became more numerous, and as their size increased, new, deeper harbors were needed. The Europeans also built railroads throughout the world; India alone had 37,000 miles (nearly 60,000 kilometers) of track by 1915, almost as much as Germany or Russia. Railroads reached into the interior of Latin America, Canada, China, and Australia. In 1903, the Russians completed the Trans-Siberian Railway from Moscow to Vladivostok on the Pacific. Visionaries even made plans for railroads from Europe to India and from Egypt to South Africa.

Transformation of the Global Environment

In addition to the vast exchange of natural products and manufactured goods that flowed through the speedy transportation networks of the industrial world, imperial botanists applied agricultural science to every promising plant species. In the nineteenth century, they founded botanical gardens in Java, India, Mauritius°, Ceylon, Jamaica, and other tropical colonies. These gardens not only collected local plants but also exchanged plants with other gardens. They were especially active in systematically transferring commercially valuable plant species from one tropical region to another. Cinchona, tobacco, sugar, and other crops were introduced, improved, and vastly expanded in the colonies of Southeast Asia and Indonesia (see Environment and Technology: Imperialism and Tropical Ecology). Cocoa and coffee growing spread over large areas of Brazil and Africa; oil-palm plantations were established in Nigeria and the Congo Basin. Rubber, used to make waterproof garments and bicycle tires, originally came from the latex of Hevea trees growing wild in the Brazilian rain forest. Then in the 1870s, British agents smuggled seedlings from Brazil to the Royal Botanic Gardens at Kew near London, and from there to the Botanic Garden of Singapore. These plants formed the nucleus of the enormous rubber economy of Southeast Asia.

Throughout the tropics, land once covered with forests or devoted to shifting slash-and-burn agriculture was transformed into permanent farms and plantations. Even in areas not developed to export crops, growing populations put pressure on the land. In Java and India, farmers felled trees to obtain arable land and firewood. They terraced hillsides, drained swamps, and dug wells.

Irrigation and water control transformed the dry parts of the tropics as well. In the 1830s, British engineers in India had restored ancient canals that had fallen into disrepair. Their success led them to build new irrigation canals, turning thousands of previously barren acres into well-watered, densely populated farmland. The migration of European experts spread the newest techniques of irrigation

---

gutta-percha (gut-tah–PER-cha)

Mauritius (maw-REE-shuss)

engineering around the world. By the turn of the century, irrigation projects were under way wherever rivers flowed through dry lands. In Egypt and Central Asia, irrigation brought more acres under cultivation in one forty-year span than in all previous history.

Railroads had voracious appetites for land and resources. They cut into mountains, spanned rivers and canyons with trestles, and covered as much land with their freight yards as whole cities had needed in previous centuries. They also consumed vast quantities of iron, timber for ties, and coal or wood for fuel. Most important of all, railroads brought people and their cities, farms, and industries to areas previously occupied by small, scattered populations.

Prospectors looking for valuable minerals opened the earth to reveal its riches: gold in South Africa, Australia, and Canada; tin in Nigeria, Malaya, and Bolivia; copper in Chile and Central Africa; iron ore in northern India; and much else. Where mines were dug deep inside the earth, the dirt and rocks brought up with the ores formed huge mounds near mine entrances. Open mines dug to obtain ores lying close to the surface created a landscape of lunar craters, and runoff from the minerals poisoned the water for miles around. Refineries that processed the ores fouled the environment with slag heaps and more toxic runoff.

The transformation of the land by human beings, a constant throughout history, accelerated sharply. Only the changes occurring since 1914 can compare with the transformation of the global environment that took place between 1869 and 1914.

CONCLUSION

The opening of the Suez Canal in 1869 was the symbolic beginning of the New Imperialism. It demonstrated the power of modern industry to subdue nature by carving the land. It stimulated shipping and trade between the industrial countries and the tropics. It deepened the involvement of Europeans in the affairs of the Middle East, Africa, and Asia. From that year until 1914, not only the great powers but smaller countries too—even,

in some cases, individual Europeans or Americans—had the power to decide the fate of whole countries. The motivation to conquer or control other lands surely helps explain the New Imperialism. But the means at the disposal of the imperialists—that is, the gap that opened between their technologies and forms of organization and those available to Asians, Africans, and Latin Americans—is equally important.

The new technological means and the enhanced motivations of the imperialists resulted in the most rapid conquest of territories in the history of the world. In less than half a century, almost all of Africa and large parts of Asia and Oceania were added to the colonial empires, while Latin America was turned into an economic colony of the industrial powers. In the process of developing the economic potential of their empires, the colonial powers transformed natural environments around the world.

The opening of the Panama Canal in August 1914 confirmed the new powers of the industrializing nations—but with a twist, for it was the United States, a latecomer to the game of imperialism, that created the canal. In that same month, the other imperialist nations turned their weapons against one another and began a life-or-death struggle for supremacy in Europe. That conflict is the subject of the next chapter.

■ Key Terms

Suez Canal	Cecil Rhodes
New Imperialism	Asante
"scramble" for Africa	Emperor Menelik
King Leopold II (Belgium)	Emilio Aguinaldo
Berlin Conference	free-trade imperialism
Afrikaners	Panama Canal

■ Suggested Reading

Two good introductions to imperialism are D. K. Fieldhouse, *Colonialism, 1870–1945* (1981), and Scott B. Cook, *Colonial Encounters in the Age of High Imperialism* (1996). The debate on the theories of imperialism is presented in Roger Owen and Robert Sutcliffe, *Studies in the Theory of Imperialism* (1972), and in Winfried Baumgart,

Imperialism (1982). The British Empire is the subject of Bernard Porter, *The Lion's Share: A Short History of British Imperialism, 1850–1970* (1976).

On Africa in this period, see Roland Oliver and Anthony Atmore, *Africa Since 1800*, new ed. (1994). Adam Hochschild's *King Leopold's Ghost: A Story of Greed, Terror, and Heroism in Colonial Africa* (1998) is a very readable account of imperialism in the Belgian Congo. The classic novel about the impact of colonial rule on African society is Chinua Achebe's *Things Fall Apart* (1958).

Imperial rivalries in Asia are the subject of Akira Iriye, *Across the Pacific: An Inner History of American–East Asian Relations*, rev. ed. (1992); David Gillard, *The Struggle for Asia, 1828–1914: A Study in British and Russian Imperialism* (1977); and Peter Hopkirk, *The Great Game: The Struggle for Empire in Central Asia* (1994). On other aspects of imperialism in Asia, see Clifford Geertz, *Agricultural Involution: The Process of Ecological Change in Indonesia* (1963), especially chapters 4 and 5, and Stanley Karnow, *In Our Image: America's Empire in the Philippines* (1989).

On Latin America in this period, see David Bushnell and Neill Macauley, *The Emergence of Latin America in the Nineteenth Century* (1994). Free-trade imperialism is the subject of D. C. M. Platt, *Latin America and British Trade, 1806–1914* (1973). On American expansionism, see David Healy, *Drive to Hegemony: The United States in the Caribbean, 1898–1917* (1989), and Walter LaFeber, *The Panama Canal*, rev. ed. (1990).

On race relations in the colonial world, see Robert Huttenback, *Racism and Empire: White Settlers and Colored Immigrants in the British Self-Governing Colonies, 1830–1910* (1976). Gender relations are the subject of Caroline Oliver, *Western Women in Colonial Africa* (1982), and Cheryl Walker, ed., *Women and Gender in Southern Africa to 1945* (1990). David Northrup's *Indentured Labor in the Age of Imperialism, 1834–1922* (1995), discusses migrations and labor.

The impact of technology on the New Imperialism is the subject of Daniel R. Headrick, *The Tools of Empire: Technology and European Imperialism in the Nineteenth Century* (1981) and *The Tentacles of Progress: Technology Transfer in the Age of Imperialism, 1850–1940* (1988), and Clarence B. Davis and Kenneth E. Wilburn, Jr., eds., *Railway Imperialism* (1991).

■ Notes

1. *Journal officiel* (November 29, 1869), quoted in Georges Douin, *Histoire du règne du khédive Ismaïl* (Rome: Real Societá di geografia d'Egritto, 1933), 453.
2. E. Desplaces in *Journal de l'Union des Deux Mers* (December 15, 1869), quoted ibid., 453.
3. "Correspondence and Report from His Majesty's Consul at Boma respecting the Administration of the Independent State of the Congo," *British Parliamentary Papers, Accounts and Papers*, 1904 (Cd. 1933), lxii, 357.

25

THE CRISIS OF THE IMPERIAL ORDER, 1900–1929

The Crisis in Europe and the Middle East • The "Great War" and the Russian Revolutions • Peace and Dislocation in Europe • China and Japan: Contrasting Destinies • The New Middle East • Science and Technology in the Industrialized World
SOCIETY AND CULTURE: The Experience of Battle

On June 28, 1914, Archduke Franz Ferdinand, heir to the throne of Austria-Hungary, was riding in an open carriage through Sarajevo, capital of the province of Bosnia-Herzegovina, which Austria had annexed six years before. When the carriage stopped momentarily, Gavrilo Princip, a member of a pro-Serbian conspiracy, fired his pistol twice, killing the archduke and his wife.

Those shots ignited a war that spread throughout Europe, then turned into a global war as the Ottoman Empire fought against Britain in the Middle East and Japan attacked German positions in China. France and Britain involved their empires in the war and brought Africans, Indians, Australians, and Canadians to Europe to fight and labor on the front lines. Finally, in 1917, the United States entered the fray.

The next three chapters tell a story of violence and hope. This chapter looks at the causes of war between the great powers; the consequences of that conflict in Europe, the Middle East, and Russia; and the upheavals in China and Japan. It also reviews the accelerating rate of technological change that made the first half of the twentieth century so violent and so hopeful. Entirely new technologies made war more dangerous yet allowed far more people to live healthier, more comfortable, and more interesting lives than ever before.

As you read this chapter, ask yourself the following questions:

- How did the First World War lead to revolution in Russia and the disintegration of other empires?

- What role did the war play in eroding European dominance in the world?

- Why did China and Japan follow such divergent paths in this period?

- How did European and North American society and technology change in the aftermath of the war?

THE CRISIS IN EUROPE AND THE MIDDLE EAST

When the twentieth century opened, the world seemed firmly under the control of the great powers. Its first decade saw peace and economic growth in most of the world. New technologies— airplanes, automobiles, radio, and cinema— aroused much excitement. With their colonial conquests over, the great powers seemed matched and likely to maintain peace. The only international war of the period, the Russo-Japanese War (1904–1905), ended quickly with a decisive Japanese victory.

However, two major changes were undermining the apparent stability of the world. In Europe, tensions mounted as Germany challenged Britain at sea and France in Morocco. As the Ottoman Empire grew weaker, the resulting chaos in the Balkans gradually drew the European powers into its hostilities.

The Ottoman Empire and the Balkans

By 1900, economic, technological, and military decline had made the once-great Ottoman Empire the "sick man of Europe," and it was losing its outlying provinces. Between 1902 and 1912, Macedonia rebelled, Austria-Hungary annexed Bosnia, Crete merged with Greece, Albania became independent, and Italy conquered Libya, the Ottomans' last foothold in Africa. In 1912–1913, Serbia, Bulgaria, Romania, and Greece chased the Turks out of the Balkans, except for a small enclave around Constantinople.

The European powers meddled in the internal affairs of the Ottoman Empire. Russia and Austria-Hungary competed to become the protector of the Slavic peoples of the Balkans. France and Britain, posing as protectors of Christian minorities, controlled Ottoman finances, taxes, railroads, mines, and public utilities.

In reaction, Turks began to assert themselves against rebellious minorities and meddling foreigners. In 1909, the group known as the Young Turks overthrew the sultan and replaced him with his brother. The new regime began to reform the police, the bureaucracy, and the education system and hired a German general to modernize Turkey's armed forces. At the same time, it cracked down on Greek and Armenian minorities.

Nationalism, Alliances, and Military Strategy

Nationalism was deeply rooted in European culture. It united the citizens of France, Britain, and Germany behind their respective governments and gave them tremendous cohesion and strength of purpose. But nationalism could also be a dividing rather than a unifying force. In the large but fragile multinational Russian, Austro-Hungarian, and Ottoman Empires, ethnic and religious minorities, repressed for centuries, were stirring. The easy victories in the wars of the New Imperialism led some in power to believe that only war could heal the divisions in their societies.

What turned assassination of the Archduke Franz Ferdinand in a small town in the Balkans into a conflict involving all the great powers was the system of alliances that had grown up over the previous decades. At the center of Europe stood Germany, the most heavily industrialized country in Europe and yearning to dominate. Its army was the best trained and equipped, and its heavily armed battleships were challenging Great Britain's naval supremacy. Germany joined Austria-Hungary and Italy in the Triple Alliance in 1882. When in 1907 Britain, France, and Russia formed an Entente° ("understanding"), Europe was divided into two blocs of roughly equal power (see Map 25.1).

The alliance system was cursed by inflexible military planning. In the years before World War I, military planners in France and Germany had worked out elaborate railroad timetables to mobilize their respective armies in a few days. Other countries were less well prepared. Russia, a large country with an underdeveloped rail system,

---

Entente (on-TONT)

CHRONOLOGY

	Europe and North America	Middle East	East Asia
1900			**1900** Boxer Rebellion in China
	1904 British-French Entente		**1904–1905** Russo-Japanese War
	1907 British-Russian Entente	**1909** Young Turks overthrow Sultan Abdul Hamid	
1910	**1912–1913** Balkan Wars		**1911** Chinese revolutionaries led by Sun Yat-sen overthrow Qing dynasty
	1914 Assassination of Archduke Franz Ferdinand sparks World War I		
	1916 Battles of Verdun and the Somme	**1916** Arab Revolt in Arabia	**1915** Japan presents Twenty-One Demands to China
	1917 Russian Revolutions; United States enters the war	**1917** Balfour Declaration	
	1918 Armistice ends World War I		
	1919 Treaty of Versailles	**1919–1922** War between Turkey and Greece	**1919** May Fourth Movement in China
1920	**1920** First commercial radio broadcast (United States)		
	1921 New Economic Policy in Russia		
		1922 Egypt nominally independent	
	1927 Charles Lindbergh flies alone across the Atlantic	**1923** Mustafa Kemal proclaims Turkey a republic	**1927** Guomindang forces occupy Shanghai and expel Communists

needed several weeks to mobilize its forces. Britain, with only a tiny volunteer army, had no mobilization plans. German generals, believing that the British would stay out of a future European war, made war plans to defeat France in a matter of days, then transport their entire army by train across Germany to the Russian border before Russia could fully mobilize.

On July 28, 1914, emboldened by the backing of Germany, Austria-Hungary declared war on Serbia, triggering the mobilization plans of Russia, France, and Germany. On July 29, the Russian government ordered general mobilization to force Austria to back down. On August 1, France honored its treaty obligation to Russia and ordered general mobilization. Minutes later, Germany did the same. Because of the rigid railroad timetables, war was now automatic.

The German General Staff expected France to capitulate before the British could get involved. But on August 3, when German troops entered Belgium, Britain demanded their withdrawal. When Germany refused, Britain declared war on Germany.

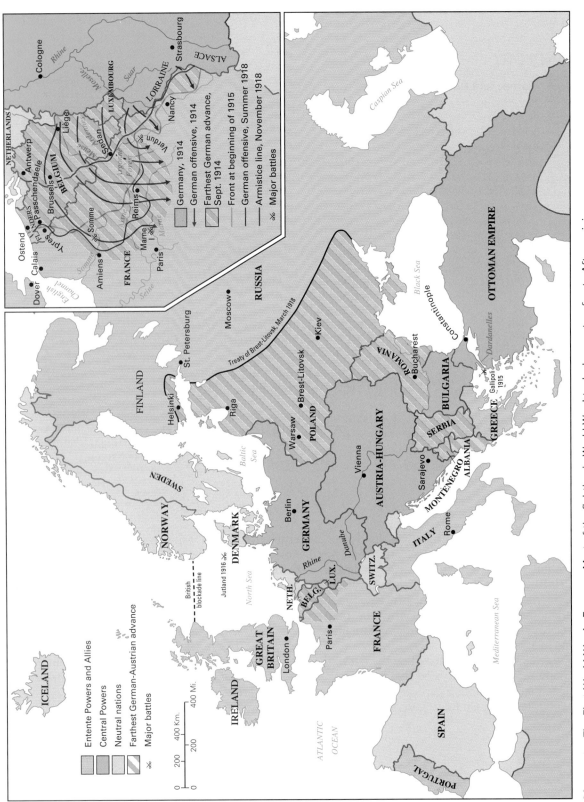

Map 25.1 The First World War in Europe Most of the fighting in World War I took place on two fronts. After an initial surge through Belgium into northern France, the German offensive bogged down for four years along the Western Front. To the east, the German armies conquered a large part of Russia during 1917 and early 1918. Despite spectacular victories in the east, Germany lost the war because its armies collapsed along the strategically important Western Front.

Map legend (main map):
- Entente Powers and Allies
- Central Powers
- Neutral nations
- Farthest German-Austrian advance
- ⚔ Major battles

0   200   400 Km.
0   200   400 Mi.

Inset legend:
- Germany, 1914
- German offensive, 1914
- Farthest German advance, Sept. 1914
- Front at beginning of 1915
- German offensive, Summer 1918
- Armistice line, November 1918
- ⚔ Major battles

THE "GREAT WAR" AND THE RUSSIAN REVOLUTIONS

Throughout Europe, people greeted the outbreak of war with parades and hopes for a quick victory. The German sociologist Max Weber wrote: "This war, with all its ghastliness, is nevertheless grand and wonderful. It is worth experiencing." Very few imagined that their side might not win, and no one foresaw that everyone would lose. The effect of the war was especially devastating in Russia, for it destroyed the old society, introduced a radical new political system, and put professional revolutionaries in charge of Russia's industrialization.

Stalemate, 1914–1917

In 1914, the generals' carefully drawn-up plans went awry from the start. Believing that a spirited attack would always prevail, French generals hurled their troops, dressed in bright blue-and-red uniforms, against the well-defended German border and suffered a crushing defeat. By early September, the German armies held Belgium and northern France and were fast approaching Paris.

German victory seemed assured. But when Russia attacked, German troops needed for the final push into France were shifted to the Russian front. A gap opened between two German armies along the Marne River, into which France's last reserves moved. At the Battle of the Marne, the Germans were thrown back several miles.

During the next month, both sides spread out until they formed an unbroken line extending over 300 miles (some 500 kilometers) from the North Sea to the border of Switzerland. All along this **Western Front,** machine guns provided an almost impenetrable defense against advancing infantry but were useless for the offensive because they were too heavy for one man to carry and took too much time to set up. To escape the deadly streams of bullets, soldiers dug holes for themselves in the ground, connected the holes to form shallow trenches, then dug communications trenches to the rear. Within weeks, the battlefields were scarred with lines of trenches several feet deep, their tops protected by sandbags and their floors covered with planks (see Society and Culture: The Experience of Battle).

For four years, generals on each side again and again ordered their troops to attack. In battle after battle, thousands of young men on one side climbed out of their trenches, raced across the open fields, and were mowed down by enemy machine-gun fire. Poison gas added to the horror of battle.

The year 1916 saw the bloodiest and most futile battles of the war. The Germans attacked French forts at Verdun, losing 281,000 men and causing 315,000 French casualties. In retaliation, the British attacked the Germans at the Somme River and suffered 420,000 casualties—60,000 on the first day alone—while the Germans lost 450,000 and the French 200,000.

This was not warfare as it had ever been waged before; it was mass slaughter. Neither side could win, for the armies were stalemated by trenches and machine guns. During four years of the bloodiest fighting the world had ever seen, the Western Front moved no more than a few miles one way or another.

At sea, the war was just as inconclusive. As soon as the war broke out, the British cut the German overseas telegraph cables, blockaded the coasts of Germany and Austria-Hungary, and set out to capture or sink all enemy ships still at sea. The German High Seas Fleet, built at enormous cost, seldom left port. Only once, in May 1916, did it confront the British Grand Fleet. At the Battle of Jutland, off the coast of Denmark, the two fleets lost roughly equal numbers of ships, and the Germans escaped back to their harbors.

In early 1915, in retaliation for the British naval blockade, Germany announced a blockade of Britain by submarines. German submarines attacked every vessel they could. One attack sank the British ocean liner *Lusitania,* killing 1,198 people, 139 of them Americans. When the United States protested, Germany ceased its submarine campaign, hoping to keep America neutral.

Trench Warfare in World War I   German and Allied soldiers on the Western Front faced each other from elaborate networks of trenches. Attacking meant jumping out of the trenches and racing across a no man's land of mud and barbed wire. Here we see Princess Patricia's Canadian Light Infantry repelling a German attack near Ypres, in northern France, in March 1915, using machine guns, rifles, and hand grenades.   (Courtesy, The Princess Patricia's Canadian Light Infantry, Regimental Museum and Archives)

The Home Front and the War Economy

The war economy transformed civilian life. In France and Britain, food rations were allocated according to need, improving nutrition among the poor. Unemployment vanished. Thousands of Africans, Indians, and Chinese were recruited for heavy labor in Europe. Employers hired women to fill jobs in steel mills, mines, and munitions plants vacated by men off to war. Women became streetcar drivers, mail carriers, and police or found work in government bureaucracies. Many joined auxiliary military services as doctors, nurses, mechanics, and ambulance drivers. These positions gave thousands of women a sense of participation and a taste of independence.

German civilians paid an especially high price because of the British naval blockade. The German chemical industry developed synthetic explosives and fuel, but synthetic food was not an option. Wheat flour disappeared, replaced first by rye, then by potatoes and turnips, then by acorns and chestnuts, and finally by sawdust. After the failure of the potato crop in 1916 came the "turnip winter," when people had to survive on 1,000 calories per day, half of the normal amount that an active adult needed. Women, children, and the elderly were especially hard hit.

During the war, the British and French overran German's African colonies except for German East Africa, which remained undefeated until the end of the war (see Map 24.1). The war brought hardships

The Experience of Battle

What is it like to be a soldier in the midst of a battle? Here is how the German writer Erich Maria Remarque, a veteran of World War I, described a battle from a soldier's point of view in his classic war novel, All Quiet on the Western Front *(1928).*

Night again. We are deadened by the strain—a deadly tension that scrapes along one's spine like a gapped knife. Our legs refuse to move, our hands tremble, our bodies are a thin skin stretched painfully over repressed madness, over an almost irresistible, bursting roar. We have neither flesh nor muscles any longer, we dare not look at one another for fear of some incalculable thing. So we shut our teeth—it will end—it will end—perhaps we will come through.

Suddenly the nearer explosions cease. The shelling continues but it has lifted and falls behind us, our trench is free. We seize the hand-grenades, pitch them out in front of the dug-out and jump after them. The bombardment has stopped and a heavy barrage now falls behind us. The attack has come.

No one would believe that in this howling waste there could still be men; but steel helmets now appear on all sides of the trench, and fifty yards from us a machine-gun is already in position and barking.

The wire entanglements are torn to pieces. Yet they offer some obstacle. We see the storm-troops coming.

Our artillery opens fire. Machine-guns rattle, rifles crack. The charge works its way across. Haie and Kropp begin with the hand-grenades. They throw as fast as they can, others pass them the handles with the strings already pulled. . . .

We recognize the smooth distorted faces, the helmets: they are French. They have already suffered heavily when they reach the remnants of the barbed wire entanglements. A whole line has gone down before our machine-guns; then we have a lot of stoppages and they come nearer.

I see one of them, his face upturned, fall into a wire cradle. His body collapses, his hands remain suspended as though he were praying. Then his body drops clean away and only his hands with the stumps of his arms, shot off, now hang in the wire.

How successful is Remarque in conveying a soldier's experiences to readers who have never been to war? How do you explain what makes men willing to fight such battles?

Source: Erich Maria Remarque, *All Quiet on the Western Front,* trans. A. W. Wheen (Boston: Little, Brown, 1958), 98–99. *Im Westen Nichts Neues,* copyright 1928 by Ullstein A. G. Copyright renewed © 1956, 1957, 1958 by Erich Maria Remarque. *All Quiet on the Western Front,* copyright © 1929, 1930 by Little, Brown and Company. All rights reserved.

---

to many African colonies, whose inhabitants faced heavy taxes, low prices for requisitioned export crops, and forced recruitment. Many Europeans stationed in Africa left to join the war, leaving large areas with little or no European presence. Over a million Africans served in the various armies, and perhaps three times that number were drafted as porters to carry army equipment. In some places, these impositions provoked African uprisings that lasted for years.

One country grew rich during the war: the United States, which for two and a half years stayed technically neutral while businesses engaging in war production did a roaring business supplying France and Britain. After the United States entered the war in 1917, civilians were exhorted to help the war effort by investing their savings in war bonds and growing food in backyard "victory gardens." Employment created by the war opened up jobs for hired women and African-Americans.

The Ottoman Empire at War

On August 2, 1914, the Turks signed a secret alliance with Germany. In November, they joined the fighting, hoping to gain land at Russia's expense. But the campaign in the Caucasus proved disastrous for both armies and for the civilian populations. Suspecting the Armenians of being pro-Russian, the Turks forced them to march from their homelands across the mountains in the winter. Hundreds of thousands of Armenians died of hunger and exposure, an omen of even ghastlier tragedies to come.

The Turks also closed the Dardanelles, the strait between the Mediterranean and Black Seas (see Map 25.1). When a British attempt to force open the Dardanelles failed, the British tried to subvert the Ottoman Empire from within by promising the emir (prince) of Mecca, Hussein ibn Ali, a kingdom of his own. In 1916, Hussein started an Arab revolt against the Turks. His son **Faisal**° led an Arab army in support of the British advance from Egypt into Palestine and Syria that contributed to the Ottoman defeat.

The British made promises to Chaim Weizmann°, leader of the British Zionists, that a Jewish homeland in Palestine would be carved out of the Ottoman Empire and placed under British protection. In November, as British armies were advancing on Jerusalem, Foreign Secretary Sir Arthur Balfour wrote that "His Majesty's Government view with favor the establishment in Palestine of a national home for the Jewish people and will use their best endeavours to facilitate the achievement of that object, it being clearly understood that nothing shall be done which may prejudice the civil and religious rights of existing non-Jewish communities in Palestine." The British did not foresee that this statement, known as the **Balfour Declaration,** would lead to conflicts between Palestinians and Jewish settlers.

Double Revolution in Russia, 1917

At the beginning of the war, Russia had the largest army in the world, but its generals were incompetent, supplies were lacking, and soldiers were poorly trained and equipped. In August 1914, two Russian armies invaded eastern Germany but were thrown back. Several times the Russians defeated the Austro-Hungarian army, only to be defeated by the Germans. In 1916, after a string of defeats, the Russian army ran out of ammunition and other essential supplies. Soldiers were ordered into battle unarmed and told to pick up the rifles of fallen comrades.

With so many men in the army, railroads broke down for lack of fuel and parts, and crops rotted in the fields. Civilians faced shortages and widespread hunger. In the cities, food and fuel became scarce. During the bitterly cold winter of 1916–1917, factory workers and housewives had to line up in front of grocery stores before dawn in order to get something to eat. The court of Tsar° Nicholas II, however, remained as extravagant and corrupt as ever.

When food ran out in Petrograd, the capital, in early March 1917, housewives and women factory workers staged mass demonstrations. Soldiers mutinied and joined striking workers to form soviets (councils) to take over factories and barracks. A few days later, the tsar abdicated, and leaders of the parliamentary parties formed a Provisional Government. Thus began what Russians called the "February Revolution" because their calendar was two weeks behind the one in use elsewhere.

Revolutionary groups came out of hiding. Most numerous were the Social Revolutionaries, who advocated the redistribution of land to the peasants. The Social Democrats, a Marxist party, were divided. The Mensheviks, who advocated electoral politics and reform in the tradition of European Socialists, had a large following among intellectuals and factory workers. The rival **Bolsheviks** were a small but tightly disciplined group dedicated to radical revolution. **Vladimir Lenin** (1870–1924), the Bolshevik leader, became a revolutionary in his teens when his older brother was executed for plotting to kill the tsar. His goal was to

---

Faisal (fie-SAHL)   Chaim Weizmann (hi-um VITES-mun)   tsar (zahr)

create a party that would lead the revolution rather than wait for it.

In early April 1917, the German government, hoping to destabilize Russia, allowed Lenin to travel from exile in Switzerland to Russia in a sealed railway car. As soon as he arrived in Petrograd, he announced his program: immediate peace, all power to the soviets, and transfers of land to the peasants and factories to the workers. This plan proved immensely popular among soldiers and workers exhausted by the war.

When the Provisional Government ordered another offensive against the Germans a few months later, Russian soldiers began to desert by the hundreds of thousands, throwing away their rifles and walking back to their villages. The Bolsheviks, meanwhile, were gaining support among the workers of Petrograd and the soldiers and sailors stationed there. On November 6, 1917 (October 24 in the Russian calendar), they rose up and took over the city. This "October Revolution" overthrew the Provisional Government and arrested Mensheviks, Social Revolutionaries, and other rivals.

The Bolsheviks nationalized all private land and ordered the peasants to hand over their crops without compensation. The peasants, having seized their landlords' estates, resisted. In the cities, the Bolsheviks took over the factories and drafted the workers into compulsory labor brigades. To enforce his rule, Lenin created the Cheka, a secret police force with powers to arrest and execute opponents. The Bolsheviks also sued for peace with Germany and Austria-Hungary. By the Treaty of Brest-Litovsk, signed on March 3, 1918, Russia lost territories containing a third of its population and wealth.

The End of the War in Western Europe, 1917–1918

Like many other Americans, President **Woodrow Wilson** wanted to stay out of the European conflict. For nearly three years, he kept the United States neutral and tried to persuade the belligerents to compromise. But in late 1916, German leaders decided to starve the British into submission by using submarines to sink merchant ships carrying food supplies to Great Britain. The Germans knew that unrestricted submarine warfare was likely to bring the United States into the war, but they were willing to gamble that Britain and France would collapse before the United States could send enough troops to help them.

The submarine campaign resumed on February 1, 1917, but the German gamble failed. The British organized their merchant ships into convoys protected by destroyers, and on April 6, President Wilson asked the United States Congress to declare war on Germany.

On the Western Front, the two sides were so evenly matched in 1917 that the war seemed unlikely to end until one side or the other ran out of young men. Losing hope of winning, soldiers began to mutiny. In May 1917, before the arrival of U.S. forces, fifty-four of one hundred French divisions along the Western Front refused to attack. During the summer, Italian troops also mutinied, panicked, or deserted.

Between March and August 1918, General Erich von Ludendorff launched a series of surprise attacks that broke through the front at several places and pushed to within 40 miles (64 kilometers) of Paris. But victory eluded him. Meanwhile, every month was bringing another 250,000 American troops to the front. In August, the Allies counterattacked, and the Germans began a retreat that could not be halted, for German soldiers, many of them sick with the flu, had lost the will to fight.

In late October, Ludendorff resigned, and sailors in the German fleet mutinied. Two weeks later, Kaiser Wilhelm fled to Holland as a new German government signed an armistice. On November 11 at 11 A.M., the guns on the Western Front went silent.

PEACE AND DISLOCATION IN EUROPE

The Great War lasted four years. It took almost twice as long for Europe to recover. Millions of people had died or been disabled, political tensions lingered, and national economies remained depressed until the mid-1920s. But the return of peace and prosperity soon proved illusory.

The Impact of the War

The war left more dead and wounded and more physical destruction than any previous conflict. It is estimated that between 8 million and 10 million people died, almost all of them young men. Perhaps twice that many returned home wounded, gassed, or shell-shocked, many of them injured for life. In addition, the war created millions of refugees.

Many refugees found shelter in France, which welcomed 1.5 million people, but the preferred destination was the United States. About 800,000 immigrants succeeded in reaching it before U.S. immigration laws passed in 1921 and 1924 closed the door to eastern and southern Europeans. Canada, Australia, and New Zealand adopted similar restrictions on immigration. The Latin American republics welcomed European refugees, but their poverty discouraged potential immigrants.

One unexpected by-product of the war was the great influenza epidemic of 1918–1919, which started among soldiers heading for the Western Front. This was no ordinary flu but a virulent strain that infected almost everyone on earth and killed one person in every forty. It caused the largest number of deaths in so short a time in the history of the world. Half a million Americans perished in the epidemic—five times as many as died in the war. Worldwide, some 30 million people died, 20 million in India alone.

The war also caused serious damage to the environment. No place on earth was ever so completely devastated as the scar across France and Belgium known as the Western Front. The fighting ravaged forests and demolished towns. The earth was gouged by trenches, pitted with craters, and littered with ammunition, broken weapons, chunks of concrete, and the bones of countless soldiers. After the war, it took a decade to clear away the debris and create military cemeteries with neat rows of crosses stretching for miles. The war also hastened the buildup of industry, with mines, factories, and railroad tracks.

The Peace Treaties

In early 1919, delegates of the victorious Allies met in Paris. The defeated powers were kept out until the treaties were ready for signing. Russia, in the throes of civil war, was not invited.

From the start, three men dominated the Paris Peace Conference: United States president Wilson, British prime minister David Lloyd George, and French premier Georges Clemenceau°. They ignored the Italians, who had joined the Allies in 1915, and paid even less attention to the delegates of smaller European nations. They rejected the Japanese proposal that all races be treated equally and ignored the call of the Pan-African Congress for attention to the concerns of African peoples around the world. They also ignored the ten thousand other delegates of various nationalities who did not represent sovereign states—the Arab leader Faisal, the Zionist Chaim Weizmann, and several Armenian delegations—who came to Paris to lobby for their causes.

Each man had his own agenda. Wilson wanted to apply the principle of self-determination, by which he meant creating nations that reflected European ethnic or linguistic divisions. He proposed a **League of Nations,** a world organization to safeguard the peace and foster international cooperation. His idealism clashed with the more hard-headed and self-serving nationalism of the Europeans. Lloyd George insisted that Germany pay a heavy indemnity. Clemenceau wanted Germany to give back Alsace and Lorraine, cede the industrial Saar region to France, and make the Rhineland a buffer state.

The result was a series of compromises that satisfied no one (see Map 25.2). The European powers formed a League of Nations, but the United States Congress, reflecting the isolationist feelings of the American people, refused to join. France recovered Alsace and Lorraine but was unable to detach the Rhineland and had to content itself with vague promises of British and American protection if Germany ever rebuilt its army. Britain acquired new territories in Africa and the Middle East but was greatly weakened by human losses and the disruption of its trade.

On June 28, 1919, the German delegates reluctantly signed the **Treaty of Versailles°.** Germany

---

Georges Clemenceau (zhorzh cluh-mon-SO)
Versailles (vuhr-SIGH)

Map 25.2   Territorial Changes in Europe After World War I   Although the heaviest fighting took place in western Europe, the territorial changes there were relatively minor; two provinces taken by Germany in 1871, Alsace and Lorraine, were returned to France. In eastern Europe, in contrast, the changes were enormous. The disintegration of the Austro-Hungarian Empire and the defeat of Russia allowed a belt of new countries to arise, stretching from Finland in the north to Yugoslavia in the south.

was forbidden to have an air force and was permitted only a token army and navy. It gave up large parts of its eastern territory to a newly reconstituted Poland. The Allies made Germany promise to pay reparations, but they did not set a figure or a period of time for payment. A "guilt clause," which was to rankle for years to come, obliged the Germans to accept "responsibility for causing all the loss and damage" of the war. The Treaty of Versailles left Germany humiliated but largely intact and potentially the most powerful nation in Europe. Establishing a peace neither of punishment nor of reconciliation, the treaty was one of the great failures in history.

In eastern Europe, the Allies created new national states in the lands lost by the old Russian, German, and Austro-Hungarian empires. Austria and Hungary became separate states; Poland was resurrected after over a century; Czechoslovakia and Yugoslavia were created from parts of Austria-Hungary. These small nations all contained disaffected minorities and were safe only as long as Germany and Russia remained weak.

Russian Civil War and the New Economic Policy

Fighting continued in Russia for another three years after the end of the Great War. The Bolshevik Revolution had provoked Allied intervention, and, in December 1918, civil war broke out in Russia. The Communists, as the Bolsheviks now called themselves, held central Russia, but all the surrounding provinces rose up against them. Counterrevolutionary armies led by former tsarist officers obtained weapons and supplies from the Allies. By 1921, the superior discipline of their Red Army, led by Leon Trotsky, gave the Communists victory over their enemies.

Gradually, the Communists reunited most of the rebellious provinces of the old Russian Empire. In 1920, Ukrainian Communists declared the independence of a Soviet republic of Ukraine; then in 1922, it merged with Russia to create the Union of Soviet Socialist Republics (USSR), or Soviet Union. In 1920–1921, the Red Army reconquered the oil-rich Caucasus and reestablished Soviet control of Central Asia. In 1922, the new Soviet republics of Georgia, Armenia, and Azerbaijan joined the USSR.

Years of warfare, revolution, and mismanagement had ruined the Russian economy. Factories and railroads had shut down. Farmland had been devastated and livestock killed, causing hunger in the cities. Lenin decided to release the economy from party and government control. In March 1921, he announced the **New Economic Policy** (N.E.P.), which allowed peasants to own land and sell their crops, private merchants to trade, and private workshops to produce goods and sell them on the free market. Only the biggest businesses, such as banks, railroads, and factories, remained under government ownership.

The relaxation of controls had an immediate effect. Production began to climb, and food and other goods became available. In the cities, food remained scarce because farmers used their crops to feed their livestock rather than sell them. But the N.E.P. reflected no change in the goal of the Communist Party to create a modern industrial economy without private property, under party guidance. It merely provided breathing space—what Lenin called "one step back to advance two steps forward." This meant investing in heavy industry and electrification, moving farmers to the new industries, while providing food for the urban workers. In other words, it meant making the peasants, the great majority of the Soviet people, pay for the industrialization of Russia.

When Lenin died in January 1924, his associates jockeyed for power. Leon Trotsky, commander of the Red Army, had the support of many "Old Bolsheviks" who had joined the party before the Revolution, but Joseph Stalin, general secretary of the Communist Party, got the support of the majority and filled the party bureaucracy with individuals loyal to himself. In January 1929, he forced Trotsky to flee the country. Then, as absolute master of the party, he prepared to industrialize the Soviet Union at breakneck speed.

An Ephemeral Peace

The decade after the end of the war can be divided into two distinct periods: five years of painful recovery and readjustment (1919–1923), followed by six years of growing peace and prosperity (1924–

1929). One of the big adjustments in many Western societies was granting political rights to women. Women in Norway were the first to obtain the vote in Europe, in 1915. Russian women followed in 1917 and Canadian and German women in 1918. Britain gave women over age thirty the vote in 1918 and later extended it to younger women. The Nineteenth Amendment to the U.S. Constitution granted suffrage to American women in 1920. To many people's surprise, the new women voters tended to vote just as their male relatives did.

Changes in international politics and economics were more upsetting. In the first period, the German government had printed money recklessly to fund reparations payments, causing the most severe inflation the world had ever seen. As Germany teetered on the brink of civil war, radical nationalists called for revenge and tried to overthrow the government. Finally, the German government issued a new currency and promised to resume reparations payments, and the French agreed to withdraw their troops from the Ruhr.

Then in 1924, the vexed issue of reparations vanished as Germany borrowed money from New York banks to make its payments to France and Britain, which used the money to repay their wartime loans from the United States. This triangular flow of money stimulated the rapid recovery of the European economies. France began rebuilding its war-torn northern zone, Germany recovered from its hyperinflation and joined the League of Nations, and in the United States a boom began that was to last over five years.

While their economies flourished, governments grew more cautious and businesslike. Yet neither Germany nor the Soviet Union accepted its borders with the small nations that had arisen between them. In 1922, they signed a secret pact allowing the German army to conduct maneuvers in Russia (in violation of the Versailles treaty) in exchange for German help in building up Russian industry.

For a time, the League of Nations proved adept at resolving issues pertaining to health, labor relations, and postal and telegraph communications. But without U.S. participation, sanctions against states that violated League rules carried little weight.

CHINA AND JAPAN: CONTRASTING DESTINIES

China and Japan took different directions in the early twentieth century. Still in need of deep internal reform, giant China went through a revolution but soon collapsed into chaos. Japan's reforms before 1900 had gained it industry and a powerful military, which it used to take advantage of China's weakness.

Revolution in China

China's population—about 400 million in 1900—was the largest of any other country in the world and growing fast, but China's society and government were falling behind. Most Chinese worked incessantly, survived on a diet of grain and vegetables, and spent their lives in fear of floods, bandits, and tax collectors. Peasant plots averaged half as large as they had been two generations earlier. Landowners lived off the rents of their tenants. Officials, chosen through an elaborate examination system, enriched themselves from taxes and the government's monopolies on salt, iron, and other products. Wealthy merchants handled China's growing import-export trade in collaboration with foreign companies. The contrast between the squalor in which most urban residents lived and the luxury of the foreigners' enclaves in the treaty ports sharpened the resentment of educated Chinese.

In 1900, China's **Empress Dowager Cixi°,** who had seized power in a palace coup two years earlier, encouraged a secret society, the Righteous Fists, or Boxers, to rise up and expel all the foreigners from China. When the Boxers threatened the foreign legation in Beijing, an international force from the Western powers and Japan captured the city and forced China to pay a huge indemnity. Shocked by these events, many Chinese students became convinced that China needed a revolution to get rid of the Qing dynasty and modernize their country.

Cixi (tsuh-shee)

Rice Paddies in China After irrigating all the level land, Chinese farmers turned to the hillsides. To grow rice even on the steepest slopes, they terraced the land and controlled the flow of water so that each field received the optimum amount that the rice shoots required. (Julia Waterlow/Eye Ubiquitous)

When Cixi died in 1908, the Revolutionary Alliance led by **Sun Yat-sen°** (Sun Zhongshan, 1867–1925) prepared to take over. Sun had spent much of his life in Japan, England, and the United States, plotting the overthrow of the Qing dynasty. His ideas, a mixture of nationalism, socialism, and Confucian philosophy, and his tenacious spirit attracted a large following. A revolutionary assembly elected Sun president of China in December 1911, and the last Qing ruler, the boy-emperor Puyi, abdicated the throne. But Sun had no military forces at his command. To avoid a clash with the army, he resigned after a few weeks, and a new national assembly elected **Yuan Shikai°,** the most powerful of the regional generals, president of the new Chinese republic.

Yuan was an able military leader, but he had no political program. When Sun reorganized his followers into a political party called **Guomindang°** (National People's Party), Yuan quashed every attempt at creating a Western-style government and harassed Sun's followers. Victory in the first round of the struggle to create a new China went to the military.

Japan and World War I

Japan's population reached 60 million in 1925 and was increasing by a million a year. The crash program of industrialization begun in 1868 by the Meiji oligarchs (see Chapter 23) accelerated during the First World War, when Japan exported textiles, consumer goods, and munitions. In the

---

Sun Yat-sen (soon yot-SEN) **Yuan Shikai** (you-AHN she-KIE)

Guomindang (gwo-min-dong)

war years, its economy grew four times as fast as western Europe's and eight times faster than China's. Blessed with a rainy climate and many fast-flowing rivers, Japan quickly expanded its hydroelectric capacity. By the mid-1930s, 89 percent of Japanese households had electric lights, compared with 44 percent of British households.

The main beneficiaries of prosperity were the *zaibatsu*°, four giant corporations—Mitsubishi, Sumitomo, Yasuda, and Mitsui—that controlled most of Japan's industry and commerce. Farmers, who constituted half of the population, remained poor; some, in desperation, sold their daughters to textile mills or into domestic service, where young women formed the bulk of the labor force. Labor unions were weak and repressed by the police.

The Japanese were quick to join the Allied side in World War I. They saw the war as a golden opportunity to advance their interests while the Europeans were occupied elsewhere. The war created an economic boom, as the Japanese suddenly found their products in greater demand than before.

The Japanese soon conquered the German colonies in the northern Pacific and on the coast of China, then turned their attention to the rest of China. In 1915, Japan presented China with Twenty-One Demands, which would have turned it into a virtual protectorate. Britain and the United States persuaded Japan to soften the demands but could not prevent it from keeping the German coastal enclaves and extracting railroad and mining concessions at China's expense. Thus began a bitter struggle between the two countries that was to last for thirty years.

China in the 1920s

To many educated Chinese, the great powers' decision at the Paris Peace Conference to go along with Japan's seizure of the German enclaves in China was a cruel insult. On May 4, 1919, students demonstrated in front of the Forbidden City of Beijing. Despite a government ban, the May Fourth Movement spread to other parts of China. A new generation was growing up to challenge the old officials, the regional generals, and the foreigners.

China's regional generals—the warlords—still supported their armies through plunder and arbitrary taxation. They frightened off trade and investment in railroads, industry, and agricultural improvement. While neglecting the dikes and canals on which the livelihood of Chinese farmers depended, they fought one another and protected the gangsters who ran the opium trade. During the warlord era, China grew poorer, and only the treaty ports prospered.

Sun Yat-sen tried to make a comeback in Canton (Guangzhou) in the early 1920s. Though not a Communist, he was impressed with the efficiency of Lenin's revolutionary tactics and let a Soviet adviser reorganize the Guomindang along Leninist lines. He also welcomed members of the newly created Chinese Communist Party into the Guomindang.

When Sun died in 1925, the leadership of his party passed to Chiang Kai-shek° (1887–1975). An officer and director of the military academy, Chiang trained several hundred young officers, who remained loyal to him thereafter. In 1927, he determined to crush the regional warlords. As his army moved north from its base in Canton, he briefly formed an alliance with the Communists. Once his troops had occupied Shanghai, however, he allied himself with local gangsters to crush the labor unions and decimate the Communists, whom he considered a threat. He then defeated or co-opted most of the other warlords and established a dictatorship.

Chiang's government issued ambitious plans to build railroads, develop agriculture and industry, and modernize China from the top down. However, his followers were neither competent administrators like the Japanese officials of the Meiji Restoration nor ruthless modernizers like the Russian Bolsheviks. Instead, the government attracted thousands of opportunists whose goal was to "become an official and get rich" by taxing and plundering businesses. In the countryside, tax collectors and landowners squeezed the peasants ever harder. What little money reached the government went

---

zaibatsu (zie-BOT-soo)

Chiang Kai-shek (chang kie-shek)

to the military. Twenty years after the fall of the Qing, China remained mired in poverty, subject to corrupt officials and the whims of nature.

THE NEW MIDDLE EAST

At the Paris Peace Conference, France, Britain, Italy, and Japan proposed to divide the territories of the Ottoman Empire among themselves, but their ambitions clashed with President Wilson's ideal of national self-determination. Turkish nationalists made modern Turkey a new independent country. The Arab-speaking territories of the old Ottoman Empire became part of the League of Nations' new **mandate system,** run by French and British administrations that were accountable to the League of Nations for "the material and moral well-being and the social progress of the inhabitants." In the midst of these territories, Zionists were encouraging Jewish immigration (see Map 25.3).

The Rise of Modern Turkey

At the end of the First World War, the Allied forces occupied the Ottoman Empire and made the sultan give up most of his lands. But they had to reckon with Mustafa Kemal, a war hero who had formed a nationalist government in central Anatolia with the backing of fellow army officers. His armies reconquered Anatolia and the area around Constantinople in 1922 and expelled hundreds of thousands of Greeks. In response, the Greek government expelled all Muslims from Greece.

As a war hero and proclaimed savior of his country, Kemal was able to impose wrenching changes on his people faster than any other reformer would have dared. An outspoken modernizer, he was eager to bring Turkey closer to Europe as quickly as possible. He abolished the sultanate, in 1923 declared Turkey a secular republic, and introduced European laws. In a radical break with Islamic tradition, he suppressed Muslim courts,

schools, and religious orders and replaced the Arabic alphabet with the Latin alphabet.

Kemal attempted to Westernize the traditional Turkish family. Women received civil equality, including the right to vote and be elected to the national assembly. Kemal forbade polygamy and instituted civil marriage and divorce. He even changed people's clothing, strongly discouraging women from veiling their faces and ordered Turkish men to wear European brimmed hats instead of the fez. He ordered everyone to take a family name, choosing the name Atatürk ("father of the Turks") for himself.

Arab Lands and the Question of Palestine

Among the Arab people, the thinly disguised colonialism of the mandate system set off protests and rebellions. Arabs viewed the European presence not as "liberation" from Ottoman "oppression" but as foreign occupation.

The British attempted to control the Middle East with a mixture of bribery and intimidation. They helped Faisal, leader of the Arab Revolt, become king of Syria. When the French ousted him, the British made him king of Iraq. They used bombers to quell rural insurrections in Iraq. In 1931, they reached an agreement with King Faisal's government: official independence for Iraq in exchange for the right to keep two air bases, a military alliance, and an assured flow of petroleum. France, meanwhile, sent thousands of troops to Syria and Lebanon to crush nationalist uprisings.

In Egypt as in Iraq, the British substituted a phony independence for official colonialism. They declared Egypt independent in 1922 but reserved the right to station troops along the Suez Canal to secure their link with India in the event of war. Despite nationalist opposition, Britain was successful in keeping Egypt in limbo—neither independent nor a colony—thanks to an alliance with King Farouk and conservative Egyptian politicians who feared both secular and religious radicalism.

As soon as Palestine became a British mandate in 1920, Jewish immigrants arrived, encouraged by the Balfour Declaration of 1917. Most settled in the cities, but some purchased land to establish *kib-*

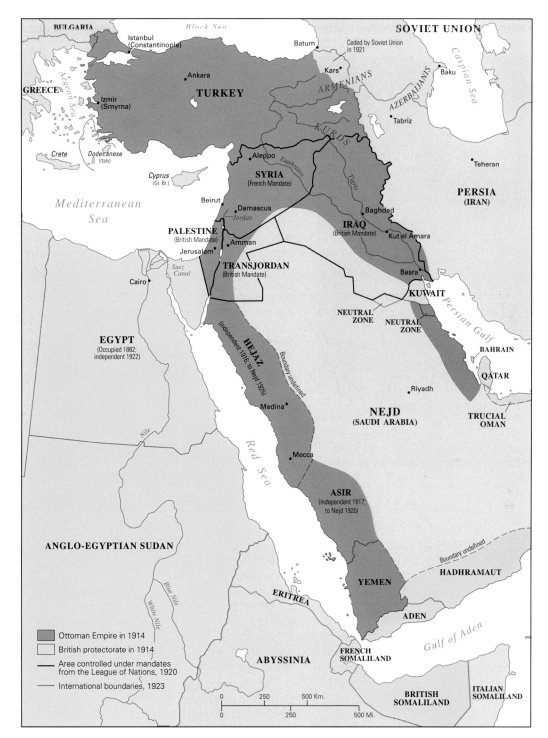

Map 25.3 Territorial Changes in the Middle East After World War I The defeat and dismemberment of the Ottoman Empire at the end of World War I resulted in an entirely new political map of the region. The Turkish Republic inherited Anatolia and a small piece of the Balkans, while the Ottoman Empire's Arab provinces were divided between France and Great Britain. The French acquired Syria and Lebanon and the British got Palestine (now Israel), Transjordan (now Jordan), and Iraq. Only Iran and Egypt remained as they had been.

Mustafa Kemal Atatürk After World War I, Mustafa Kemal was determined to modernize Turkey on the Western model. Here he is shown wearing a European-style suit and teaching the Latin alphabet. (Stock Montage)

butzim, communal farms. Their goals were to become self-sufficient and reestablish their ties to the land of their ancestors. The purchases of land by Jewish agencies angered the indigenous Palestinians, especially tenant farmers who had been evicted to make room for settlers. In 1920–1921, riots erupted between Jews and Arabs. When far more Jewish immigrants arrived than they had anticipated, the British tried to limit immigration, thereby alienating the Jews without mollifying the Arabs. Increasingly, Jews arrived without papers, smuggled in by militant Zionist organizations. In the 1930s, the country was torn by strikes and guerrilla warfare that the British could not control. In the process, Britain earned the hatred of both sides and of much of the Arab world as well.

SCIENCE AND TECHNOLOGY IN THE INDUSTRIALIZED WORLD

With the signing of the peace treaties, the countries that had fought for four years turned their efforts toward building a new future. Advances in science offered astonishing new insights into the mysteries of nature and the universe. New technologies, many of them pioneered in the United States, promised to change the daily lives of millions of people.

Revolution in the Sciences

For two hundred years, scientists, following in Isaac Newton's footsteps, had applied the same laws and equations to astronomical observations and to laboratory experiments. At the end of the nineteenth century, however, a revolution in physics undermined all the old certainties about nature. Physicists discovered that atoms, the building blocks of matter, are not indivisible but consist of far smaller subatomic particles. In 1900, the German physicist **Max Planck** (1858–1947) found that light and energy do not flow in a continuous stream but travel in small units, which he called *quanta.* These findings seemed strange enough, but what really undermined Newtonian physics was the general theory of relativity developed by **Albert Einstein** (1879–1955), another German physicist. In 1916, Einstein announced that not only is matter made of insubstantial particles, but time, space, and mass are not fixed but are relative to one another.

To nonscientists, it seemed as though theories expressed in arcane mathematical formulas were replacing truth and common sense. Far from being mere speculation, however, the new physics promised to unlock the secrets of matter and provide humans with plentiful—and potentially dangerous—new sources of energy.

The new social sciences were even more unsettling than the new physics, for they challenged Victorian morality, middle-class values, and notions of Western superiority. Sigmund Freud (1856–1939), a Viennese physician, developed a technique—psychoanalysis—to probe the minds of his patients. He found not only rationality but also hidden layers of emotion and desire repressed by social restraints. "The primitive, savage and evil impulses have not vanished from any individual, but continue their existence, although in a repressed state," he warned. Meanwhile, sociologists and anthropologists had begun the empirical study of societies, both Western and non-Western. Before the war, the French sociologist Emile Durkheim (1858–1917) had come to the then-shocking conclusion that "there are no religions that are false. All are true in their own fashion."

If the words *primitive* and *savage* applied to Europeans as well as to other peoples, and if religions were all equally "true," then what remained of the superiority of Western civilization? Cultural relativism, as the new approach to human societies was called, was as unnerving as relativity in physics.

Wartime experiences helped call into question the West's faith in reason and progress. Some people accepted the new ideas with enthusiasm. Others condemned and rejected them, clinging to the sense of order and faith in progress that had energized European and American culture before the war.

The New Technologies of Modernity

Some Europeans and Americans viewed the new sciences with mixed feelings, but new technologies aroused almost universal excitement. In North America, even working-class people could afford some of the new products of scientific research, inventors' ingenuity, and industrial production. Mass consumption lagged in Europe, but science and technology were just as advanced, and public fascination with the latest inventions—the cult of the modern—was just as strong.

No other innovation attracted public interest as much as airplanes. In 1903, two young American mechanics, Wilbur and Orville Wright, built the first aircraft that was heavier than air and could be maneuvered in flight. From that moment on, wherever they appeared, airplanes fascinated people. During the war, the exploits of air aces relieved the tedium of news from the front. In the 1920s, aviation became a sport and a form of entertainment, and flying daredevils achieved extraordinary fame by pushing their planes to the very limit—and often beyond. Among the most celebrated pilots were three Americans: Amelia Earhart, the first woman to fly across the Atlantic Ocean; Richard Byrd, the first to fly over the North Pole, in 1926; and Charles Lindbergh, the first person to fly alone across the Atlantic, in 1927. The heroic age of flight lasted until the late 1930s, when aviation became a means of transportation.

Electricity's impact on home life was more sweeping. The first home use of electricity was for lighting, thanks to the economical and long-lasting tungsten bulb. Then, having persuaded people to wire their homes, electrical utilities joined manufacturers in advertising electric irons, fans, washing machines, hot plates, radios, and other electric appliances. After the war, radio moved from the battlefield into the home. The first commercial station began broadcasting in Pittsburgh in 1920. By 1930, hundreds of stations were broadcasting news, sports, soap operas, and advertising to 12 million homes in North America. In Europe, radio spread more slowly because governments reserved the airwaves for cultural and official programs and taxed radio owners to pay for the service.

Another medium that spread explosively in the 1920s was film. Motion pictures had begun in France in 1895 and flourished in Europe. In the United States, filmmaking started at almost the same time, but American filmmakers saw the medium's potential to entertain audiences rather than preserve outstanding theatrical performances. After World War I, filmmaking took root and flourished in Japan, India, Turkey, Egypt, and a suburb of Los Angeles, California, called Hollywood. American and European movie studios were both successful in exporting films, since silent movies presented no language problems. In 1927, the United States had introduced the first "talking" motion picture, *The Jazz Singer*, which changed all the rules. The number of Americans who went to see their favorite stars in thrilling adventures and heart-breaking romances rose from 40 million in 1922 to 100 million in 1930, at a time when the population of the country was about 120 million. Europeans had the technology and the art but neither the wealth nor the huge market of the United States. Hollywood studios began the diffusion of American culture that has continued to this day.

Advances in medicine—some learned in the war—were another important—and life-saving—technology. Wounds were regularly disinfected, and x-ray machines helped diagnose fractures. After the war, cities built costly water supply and sewage treatment systems. By the 1920s, indoor plumbing and flush toilets were becoming common even in working-class neighborhoods. Interest in cleanliness altered private life. Soap and appliance manufacturers filled women's magazines with advertisements for products to help housewives keep their family's homes and clothing spotless and their meals fresh and wholesome. The decline in infant mortality and improvements in general health and life expectancy in this period owe as much to the cult of cleanliness as to advances in medicine.

Technology and the Environment

Two new technologies—the skyscraper and the automobile—transformed the urban environment even more radically than the railroad had done in the nineteenth century. At the end of the nineteenth century, architects had begun to design ever-higher buildings using load-bearing steel frames and passenger elevators. Major corporations in Chicago and New York competed to build the most daring buildings in the world, such as New York's 55-story Woolworth Building (1912) and Chicago's 34-story Tribune Tower (1923). A building boom in the late 1920s produced dozens of skyscrapers, culminating with the 86-story, 1,239-foot (377-meter) Empire State Building in New York City, completed in 1932.

European cities restricted the height of buildings to protect their architectural heritage; Paris forbade buildings over 56 feet (17 meters) high. In innovative designs, however, European architects led the way. In the 1920s, the Swiss architect known as Le Corbusier° outlined a new approach to architecture that featured simplicity of form, absence of surface ornamentation, easy manufacture, and inexpensive materials. Among his influential designs were the main buildings of Chandigarh, the new capital of the Indian state of Punjab. Other architects—including the Finn Eero Saarinen, the Germans Ludwig Mies van der Rohe° and Walter Gropius, and the American Frank Lloyd Wright—advanced his lines of thought and added their own to create what became known as the International Style.

While central business districts were reaching for the sky, outlying areas were spreading far out into the countryside, thanks to the automobile. The assembly line pioneered by Henry Ford mass-produced vehicles in ever-greater volume and at falling prices. By 1929, the United States had one car for every five people, five-sixths of the world's automobiles. Far from being blamed for their exhaust emissions, automobiles were praised as the solution to urban pollution. As cars replaced carts and carriages, horses disappeared from city streets, as did tons of manure.

The most important environmental effect of automobiles was suburban sprawl. Middle-class families could now live in single-family homes too spread apart to be served by public transportation. By the late 1920s, paved roads rivaled rail networks both in length and in the surface they occupied. As middle- and working-class families bought cars, cities acquired rings of automobile suburbs. Los Angeles, the first true automobile city, consisted of suburbs spread over hundreds of square miles and linked together by broad avenues. In those sections of the city where streetcar lines went out of business, the automobile, at first a plaything for the wealthy, became a necessity for commuters. Many Americans saw Los Angeles as the portent of a glorious future when everyone would have a car; only a few foresaw the congestion and pollution that would ensue.

Le Corbusier (luh cor-booz-YEH)
Ludwig Mies van der Rohe (LOOD-vig MEES fon der ROW-uh)

The Archetypal Automobile City   As Los Angeles grew from a modest town into a sprawling metropolis, broad avenues, parking lots, and garages were built to accommodate automobiles. By 1929, most families owned a car, and streetcar lines had closed for lack of passengers. This photograph shows a street in the downtown business district.   (Ralph Morris Archives/Los Angeles Public Library)

Farmers began buying cars and light trucks, using them to transport produce as well as passengers. Governments obliged by building new roads and paving old ones to make automobile travel smoother and safer. In 1915, Ford introduced a gasoline-powered tractor, and by the mid-1920s, these versatile machines began replacing horses. Tractors hastened the end of agriculture as a family enterprise.

CONCLUSION

The Great War caused a major realignment among the nations of the world. France and Britain, the two leading colonial powers, emerged economically weakened despite their victory. The war brought defeat and humiliation to Germany but did not reduce its military or industrial potential. It destroyed the old regime and the aristocracy of Russia, leading to civil war and revolution from which the victorious powers sought to isolate themselves. Two other old empires—the Austro-Hungarian and the Ottoman—were divided into many smaller and weaker nations. For a while, the Middle East seemed ripe for a new wave of imperialism. But there and throughout Asia, the war unleashed revolutionary nationalist movements that challenged European influence.

Only two countries benefited from the war. Japan took advantage of the European conflict to develop its industries and press its demands on a China weakened by domestic turmoil and social unrest. The United States emerged as the most prosperous and potentially most powerful nation, restrained only by the isolationist sentiments expressed by many Americans.

Modern technology and industrial organization had long been praised in the name of "progress" for their ability to reduce toil and disease and improve living standards. The war showed that they possessed an equally awesome destructive potential. In the late 1920s, it seemed as though the victors in the Great War might restore the prewar prosperity and European dominance of the globe. But the spirit of the 1920s was an illusion—not real peace but the eye of a hurricane. The prosperity of the late 1920s in most industrial states also proved illusory.

■ Key Terms

Western Front	New Economic Policy
Faisal	Cixi, Empress Dowager
Balfour Declaration	Sun Yat-sen
Bolsheviks	Yuan Shikai
Vladimir Lenin	Guomindang
Woodrow Wilson	mandate system
League of Nations	Max Planck
Treaty of Versailles	Albert Einstein

■ Suggested Reading

Bernadotte Schmitt and Harold C. Bedeler, *The World in the Crucible, 1914–1918* (1984), and John Keegan, *The First World War* (1999), are two engaging overviews of World War I. Imanuel Geiss, *July 1914: The Outbreak of the First World War* (1967), argues that Germany caused the conflict. Barbara Tuchman's *The Guns of August* (1962) and Alexander Solzhenitsyn's *August 1914* (1972) recount the first month of the war in detail. Keegan's *The Face of Battle* (1976) vividly describes the Battle of the Somme from the soldiers' perspective.

For the background to the Russian Revolution, read Theodore von Laue's *Why Lenin? Why Stalin?* 2d ed.

(1971); but see also Richard Pipes, *The Russian Revolution* (1990), and Orlando Figes, *A People's Tragedy: The Russian Revolution, 1891–1924* (1996). The classic eyewitness account of the Revolution is John Reed's *Ten Days That Shook the World* (1919).

John Maynard Keynes's *The Economic Consequences of the Peace* (1920) is a classic critique of the Paris Peace Conference. Arno Mayer's *Political Origins of the New Diplomacy, 1917–1918* (1959) analyzes the tensions and failures of great-power politics. The 1920s are discussed in Raymond Sontag's *A Broken World, 1919–1939* (1971).

The best recent book on Japan in the twentieth century is Daikichi Irokawa's *The Age of Hirohito: In Search of Modern Japan* (1995). See also Richard Storry, *A History of Modern Japan* (1982), and Tessa Morris-Suzuki, *The Technological Transformation of Japan* (1994). In the large and fast-growing literature on twentieth-century China, two general introductions are especially useful: John K. Fairbank, *The Great Chinese Revolution, 1800–1985* (1986), and Jonathan Spence, *The Search for Modern China* (1990).

On the war and its aftermath in the Middle East, see David Fromkin, *A Peace to End All Peace* (1989), and M. E. Yapp, *The Near East Since the First World War* (1991). Bernard Lewis, *The Emergence of Modern Turkey* (1968), is a good introduction.

The towering intellectuals of the era are the subject of Peter Gay, *Freud: A Life for Our Time* (1988), and Abraham Pais, *Subtle Is the Lord: The Science and Life of Albert Einstein* (1982). Three books capture the enthusiastic popular response to technological innovations: David E. Nye, *Electrifying America: Social Meanings of a New Technology* (1990); Peter Fritzsche, *A Nation of Fliers: German Aviation and the Popular Imagination* (1992); and the sweeping overview by Thomas Hughes, *American Genesis: A Century of Invention and Technological Enthusiasm, 1870–1970* (1989).

26

THE COLLAPSE OF THE OLD ORDER,

1929–1949

Stalin's Revolution • The Depression • The Rise of Fascism •
East Asia, 1931–1945 • The Second World War •
The Character of Warfare
ENVIRONMENT AND TECHNOLOGY: Biomedical Technologies

efore the First World War, the Italian futurist poets exalted violence as a noble and manly idea. Filippo Marinetti defined their creed in these words: "We want to glorify war, the world's only hygiene—militarism, deed, destroyer of anarchisms, the beautiful ideas that are death-bringing, and the subordination of women." His friend Gabriele d'Annunzio said: "If it is a crime to incite citizens to violence, I shall boast of this crime."

The war taught most survivors to abhor violence. During the 1920s, the world seemed to return to what United States president Warren Harding called "normalcy": prosperity in Europe and America, European colonialism in Asia and Africa, paternalistic U.S. domination of Latin America, and peace almost everywhere. But for a few, war and domination became a creed and a goal.

In 1929, the artificial normalcy of the 1920s began to come apart. The Great Depression caused governments to turn against one another in a desperate attempt to protect their people's livelihood. As the economic crisis spread around the world, businesses went bankrupt, prices fell, factories closed, and workers were laid off. Even wholly agricultural nations and colonies suffered as markets for their exports shriveled.

Some countries chose to solve their problems by violent means. When nations shut their doors to Japan's products, the Japanese military tried to save their country by conquering China. In Germany, the Depression reawakened resentments against the victors of the Great War; people who feared communism or blamed Jews for their troubles turned to Hitler and the Nazis, who promised to save their society by dominating others. In the Soviet Union, Stalin used energetic and murderous means to force his country into a communist version of the Industrial Revolution.

The result was war. The Second World War engulfed more lands and peoples and caused far more deaths and destruction than any previous conflict. At the end of it, much of Europe and East Asia lay in ruins, and millions of destitute refugees sought safety in other lands. The European colonial powers were either defeated or so weakened that they could no longer hold onto their empires when Asian and African peoples asserted their desire for independence.

As you read this chapter, ask yourself the following questions:

- How did the Soviet Union change under Stalin, and at what cost?
- What were the main causes of the Second World War?
- How was the war fought, and why did Japan and Germany lose?

STALIN'S REVOLUTION

After **Joseph Stalin** (1879–1953) achieved total mastery over the USSR in early 1929 (see Chapter 25), he led it through another revolution: an economic and social transformation that turned it into a great industrial and military power and intensified both admiration for and fear of communism throughout the world.

Five-Year Plans   Stalin's ambition to turn the USSR into an industrial nation was not intended initially to produce consumer goods for a mass market, much less enrich individuals as in Britain and the United States. Instead, his aim was to increase the power of the Communist Party domestically and the power of the Soviet Union in relation to other countries. By building up Russia's industry, Stalin was determined to prevent a repe-

tition of the humiliating defeat Russia had suffered at the hands of Germany in 1917.

Stalin encouraged rapid industrialization through a series of **Five-Year Plans,** a system of centralized control copied from the German experience of World War I. The goal of the first five-year plan was to quintuple the output of electricity and double that of heavy industry: iron, steel, coal, and machinery. Beginning in October 1928, the Communist government created whole industries and cities from scratch, then recruited millions of peasants and trained them to work in the new factories and mines and offices. In every way except actual fighting, Stalin's Russia resembled a nation at war.

Rapid industrialization hastened environmental changes. Hydroelectric dams turned rivers into strings of reservoirs. Roads, canals, and railroad tracks cut the landscape. Forests and grassland were turned into farmland. From an environmental perspective, the outcome of the Five-Year Plans resembled the transformation that had occurred in the United States and Canada a few decades earlier.

Collectivization of Agriculture   Since the Soviet Union was still a predominantly agrarian country, the only way to pay for these massive investments, provide the labor, and feed the millions of new industrial workers was to squeeze the peasantry. Stalin therefore proceeded with the most radical social experiment conceived up to that time: the collectivization of agriculture.

Collectivization meant consolidating small private farms into vast collectives and making the farmers work together in commonly owned fields. Each collective was expected to supply the government with a fixed amount of food and distribute what was left among its members. Collectives were to become outdoor factories through the use of machinery and techniques of mass production. Collectivization was expected to bring the peasants once and for all under government control so they never again could withhold food supplies as they had done during the period of Lenin's New Economic Policy (see Chapter 25).

The government mounted a massive propaganda campaign to enlist the farmers' support. At

CHRONOLOGY

	Europe and North Africa	Asia and the Pacific
1930	**1931** Great Depression reaches Europe **1933** Hitler comes to power in Germany	**1931** Japanese forces occupy Manchuria
1935	**1936** Hitler invades the Rhineland	
		1937 Japanese troops invade China, conquer coastal provinces; Chiang Kai-shek flees to Sichuan **1937–1938** Japanese troops take Nanjing
1940	**1939 (Sept. 1)** German forces invade Poland **1940 (March–April)** German forces conquer Denmark, Norway, the Netherlands, and Belgium **1940 (May–June)** German forces conquer France **1940 (June–Sept.)** Battle of Britain **1941 (June 21)** German forces invade USSR **1942–1943** Allies and Germany battle for control of North Africa; Soviet victory in Battle of Stalingrad (1943)	**1941 (Dec. 7)** Japanese aircraft bomb Pearl Harbor **1942 (Jan–March)** Japanese conquer Thailand, Philippines, Malaya **1942 (June)** United States Navy defeats Japan at Battle of Midway
	1943–1944 Red Army slowly pushes Wehrmacht back to Germany **1944 (June 6)** D-day: U.S., British, and Canadian troops land in Normandy	
1945	**1945 (May 7)** Germany surrenders	**1945 (Aug. 6)** United States drops atomic bomb on Hiroshima **1945 (Aug. 14)** Japan surrenders **1945–1949** Civil war in China **1949** Communists defeat Guomindang; Mao proclaims People's Republic (Oct. 1)

first, all seemed to go well, but soon *kulaks°* ("fists"), the better-off peasants, began to resist giving up all their property. When soldiers came to force them into collectives at gunpoint, the kulaks burned their own crops, smashed their own equipment, and slaughtered their own livestock. Within a few months, they slaughtered half of the Soviet Union's horses and cattle and two-thirds of its sheep and goats. In retaliation, Stalin ruthlessly ordered the "liquidation of kulaks as a class" and incited the poor peasants to attack their wealthier neighbors. Over 8 million kulaks were arrested. Many were executed. The rest were sent to slave labor camps, where most starved to death.

The peasants who were left had been the least successful before collectivization and proved to be the least competent after. Many were sent to work in factories. The rest were forbidden to leave their farms. With half of their draft animals gone, they could not plant or harvest enough to meet the swelling demands of the cities. Yet government agents took whatever they could find, leaving little or nothing for the farmers themselves. After bad harvests in 1933 and 1934, a famine swept through

kulaks (COO-lox)

the countryside, killing some 5 million people, about one in every twenty farmers.

Stalin's second Five-Year Plan, designed to run from 1933 to 1937, was originally intended to increase the output of consumer goods. But when the Nazis took over Germany in 1933 (see below), Stalin changed the plan to emphasize heavy industries that could produce armaments. Between 1927 and 1937, the Soviet output of metals and machines increased fourteen-fold while consumer goods became scarce and food was rationed. After a decade of Stalinism, the Soviet people were more poorly clothed, fed, and housed than they had been during the years of the New Economic Policy.

Terror and Opportunities

The 1930s brought both terror and new opportunities to the Soviet people. The forced pace of industrialization, the collectivization of agriculture, and the uprooting of millions of people could be accomplished only under duress. To prevent any possible resistance or rebellion, the NKVD, Stalin's secret police force, created a climate of suspicion and fear. The terror that pervaded the country was a reflection of Stalin's own paranoia, for he distrusted everyone and feared for his life.

First "Old Bolsheviks" and high officials were put on trial; then the terror spread steadily downward. The government regularly made demands on people that they could not meet, so everyone was guilty of breaking some regulation. People from all walks of life were arrested—sometimes on a mere suspicion or because of a false accusation by a jealous coworker or neighbor, sometimes for expressing a doubt or working too hard or not hard enough, sometimes for being related to someone previously arrested, sometimes for no reason at all. Millions of people were sentenced without a trial. At the height of the terror, some 8 million were sent to *gulags*° (labor camps), where perhaps a million died each year of exposure or malnutrition. To its victims, the terror seemed capricious and random.

Yet Stalin's regime received the support of many Soviet citizens. Suddenly, with so many people gone and new industries and cities being built everywhere, there were opportunities for those who remained, especially the poor and the young. Women entered careers and jobs previously closed to them, such as steelworkers, physicians, and office managers; but they retained their household and child-rearing duties, receiving little help from men. People who moved to the cities, worked enthusiastically, and asked no questions could hope to rise into the upper ranks of the Communist Party, the military, the government, or the professions, where the privileges and rewards were many.

Stalin's brutal methods helped the Soviet Union industrialize faster than any country had ever done. By the late 1930s, the USSR was the world's third largest industrial power, after the United States and Germany. To foreign observers, it seemed to be booming with construction projects, production increases, and labor shortages. Even anti-Communist observers admitted that only a planned economy subject to strict government control could avoid the Depression. To millions of Soviet citizens who took pride in the new strength of their country, and to many foreigners who contrasted conditions in the Soviet Union with the unemployment and despair in the West, Stalin's achievement seemed worth any price.

THE DEPRESSION

On October 24, 1929—"Black Thursday"—the New York stock market went into a dive. Within days, stocks lost half their value, and their value continued to fall for three years. Thousands of banks and businesses collapsed. Millions of workers lost their jobs. The stock-market crash started the deepest and most widespread depression in history.

Economic Crisis

As consumers reduced their purchases, businesses cut production. General Motors, for example, saw its sales drop by half between 1929 and 1931. Companies laid off thousands of workers, throwing them onto public charity. Business and government agencies re-

gulag (GOO-log)

placed their women workers with men, arguing that men had to support their families, whereas women worked only for "pin money." Jobless men deserted their families. As farm prices fell, small farmers went bankrupt and lost their land. By mid-1932, the American economy had fallen by half, and 25 percent of the work force was unemployed. Government spending on welfare and public works was unable to restore prosperity. Many observers thought the free-enterprise system would be replaced by bread lines, soup kitchens, men selling apples on street corners, and hoboes riding freight trains.

Frightened by the stock market collapse, the New York banks called in their loans to Germany and Austria. Without American money, Germany and Austria stopped paying reparations to France and Britain, which then could not repay their war loans to America. By 1931, the Depression had spread to Europe. Governments canceled both reparations payments and war loans, but it was too late to save the world economy.

In 1930, the U.S. government, hoping to protect domestic industries from foreign competition, imposed the highest import duty in American history. In retaliation, other countries raised their tariffs. As a result, global industrial production declined by 36 percent between 1929 and 1932, while world trade dropped by a breathtaking 62 percent.

Depression in Industrial Nations

This massive economic upheaval had profound political repercussions. In the United States, Franklin D. Roosevelt was elected president in 1932 on a "New Deal" platform of government programs to stimulate and revitalize the economy. British and French governments also intervened in their economies and escaped the worst of the Depression by making their colonial empires purchase their products. In the Soviet Union, the five-year plans continued to provide jobs and economic growth.

Nations that relied on exports to pay for imported food and fuel, in particular Japan and Germany, suffered much more. In Germany, unemployment reached 6 million by 1932, twice as high as in Britain. Half the German population lived in poverty. In Japan, the burden of the Depression fell on the farmers and fishermen, who saw their incomes drop sharply. Some, in desperation, revived the ancient practice of selling their daughters. As economic grievances worsened, radical politicians took over the governments in Germany and Japan, manipulated the economies, and turned their nations' military might to acquire empires large enough to support a self-sufficient economy.

Depression in Nonindustrial Regions

The Depression affected Asia, Africa, and Latin America in different ways. A wall of new import duties protected India's infant industries from foreign competition; living standards stagnated but did not drop. The Depression added little to China's problems, except in coastal regions.

Countries that depended on exports were hard hit by the Depression. When automobile production dropped by half in the United States and Europe, so did imports of rubber, devastating the economies of Southeast Asia. When the Depression hit, American tourists vanished from Cuba's beaches and bars, and with them went Cuba's prosperity. The industrialization of Argentina and Brazil was set back a decade or more by the loss of their export markets. In response, military officers seized power in several Latin American countries, consciously imitating dictatorships emerging in Europe.

Southern and central Africa recovered from the Depression quickly, because falling prices made their gold and other minerals more valuable. But this mining boom benefited only a small number of mine owners and investors. For Africans, it was at best a mixed blessing, for mining offered jobs and cash wages to men, while women had to manage without them in the villages.

THE RISE OF FASCISM

The Depression sharpened the polarization of European society that had been underway for decades. Many underpaid or unemployed workers saw in the seeming collapse of the capitalist economy an opportunity as well as temporary suffering. They urged the establishment of a socialist society through the ballot box and strikes instead of the violent revolution that had torn Russia apart.

Frightened investors and factory owners, along with conservative elements in society such as the church and the military, feared the consequences of this political shift to the left. In the democracies of western Europe and North America, middle-income voters kept politics in balance. But in some societies, the war and the Depression left people vulnerable to the appeals of ultranationalist politicians who became adept at using propaganda to appeal to people's fears. They promised to bring back full employment, stop the spread of communism, and achieve the territorial conquests that World War I had denied them.

Mussolini's Italy

The first country to seek radical answers was Italy. World War I, which had never been popular, left thousands of veterans who found neither pride in their victory nor jobs in the postwar economy. Unemployed veterans and violent youths banded together into *fasci di combattimento* (fighting units) to demand action and intimidate politicians. When socialist unions threatened to strike, factory and property owners hired gangs of these *fascisti* to defend them.

Benito Mussolini (1883–1945), a spellbinding orator, quickly became the leader of the **Fascist Party,** which glorified warfare and the Italian nation. By 1921, the party had 300,000 members, many of whom used violent methods to repress strikes, intimidate voters, and seize municipal governments. A year later, when the Fascists failed to win an election, Mussolini threatened to march on Rome if he was not appointed prime minister. The government gave in.

Mussolini proceeded to install Fascist Party members in all government jobs, crush all opposition parties, and jail anyone who criticized him. The party took over the press, public education, and youth activities and gave employers control over their workers. The Fascists lowered living standards but reduced unemployment and provided social security and public services. On the whole, they proved to be neither ruthless radicals nor competent administrators.

What Mussolini and the Fascist movement really excelled at was publicity: bombastic speeches, spectacular parades, news bulletins full of praise for *Il Duce*° ("the leader"), and signs everywhere proclaiming "Il Duce is always right!" Mussolini's genius was to apply the techniques of modern mass communications and advertisement to political life. Billboards, movie footage, and radio news bulletins galvanized the masses in ways never before seen in peacetime. Although his rhetoric was filled with words like *war, violence,* and *struggle,* his foreign policy was cautious. But his techniques of whipping up public enthusiasm were not lost on other radicals. By the 1930s, fascist movements had appeared in most European countries, as well as in Latin America, China, and Japan.

Hitler's Germany

Like Mussolini, **Adolf Hitler** (1889–1945) had served in World War I and looked back fondly on the clear lines of authority and the camaraderie he had experienced in battle. After the war, he too recreated that experience in a paramilitary group, the National Socialist German Workers' Party—**Nazis** for short. Hitler used his gifts as an orator to appeal to Germans disappointed at Germany's humiliation after the war and the hyperinflation of 1923. In 1924, he too led an uprising, but the attempted seizure of Munich was a failure. Germany was not yet ready to follow Italy's path.

The Depression changed that. While serving a jail sentence for the coup attempt, Hitler wrote *Mein Kampf*° (*My Struggle*), but when it was published in 1925, no one took the book or its author's extreme nationalist, racist, and anti-Jewish ideas seriously. Hitler believed that Germany should incorporate all German-speaking people, even those who lived in neighboring countries. He distinguished among a "master race" of Aryans (he meant Germans, Scandinavians, and Britons), a degenerate "Alpine" race of French and Italians,

---

Il Duce (eel DOO-chay)   *Mein Kampf* (mine compf)

Hitler the Orator   A masterful public speaker, Adolf Hitler often captivated mass audiences at Nazi Party rallies. (Roger Viollet)

owners frightened by the growing popularity of Communists. In March 1933, as leader of the largest party in Germany, Hitler became chancellor.

Once in office, he quickly assumed dictatorial power, just as Mussolini had done. He expelled the Communist Party from the Reichstag° (parliament), intimidated it to give him dictatorial powers, and then put Nazis in charge of all government agencies, educational institutions, and professional organizations. He banned all other political parties and threw their leaders into concentration camps. The Nazis deprived Jews of their citizenship and civil rights, prohibited them from marrying "Aryans," ousted them from the professions, and confiscated their property. In August 1934, Hitler proclaimed himself *Führer°* ("leader") and called Germany the "Third Reich" (empire)—the third after the Holy Roman Empire and the German Empire of 1871 to 1918.

The Nazis' economic and social policies were spectacularly effective. The government undertook massive public works projects. Businesses got contracts to manufacture weapons for the armed forces. Women, who had entered the work force during and after World War I, were urged to return to *"Kinder, Kirche, Küche"* (children, church, kitchen), releasing jobs for men. By 1936, business was booming, unemployment was at its lowest level since the 1920s, and living standards were rising. Hitler's popularity soared because most Germans believed their economic well-being outweighed the loss of liberty.

The Road to War, 1933–1939

Hitler sought not prosperity or popularity, but conquest. As soon as he came to office, he began to build up the armed forces with conquest in mind. Meanwhile, he tested the reactions of the other powers through a series of surprise moves followed by protestations of peaceful intent.

In 1933, Hitler withdrew Germany from the League of Nations. France and Britain hesitated to retaliate by blockading or invading Germany. Two

and an inferior race of Russian and eastern European Slavs, who, he believed, were fit only to be slaves of the master race. He reserved his most intense hatred for Jews, on whom he blamed every disaster that had befallen Germany, especially the defeat of 1918. He glorified violence, which would enable the "master race" to defeat and subjugate all others.

When the Depression hit, the Nazis gained supporters among the unemployed who believed Nazi promises of jobs for all and among property

---

Reichstag (RIKES-tog)   *Führer* (FEW-rer)

years later, he announced that Germany was going to introduce conscription, build up its army, and create an air force—in violation of the Versailles treaty. Instead of protesting, Britain signed a naval agreement with Germany. The message was clear: neither Britain nor France was willing to risk war by standing up to Germany. The United States, absorbed in its own domestic economic problems, had reverted to isolationism.

Emboldened by the weakness of the democracies, Italy in 1935 invaded Ethiopia, the last independent state in Africa and a member of the League of Nations. The League and the democracies protested but refused to close the Suez Canal to Italian ships or impose an oil embargo. The following year, when Hitler sent troops into the Rhineland on the borders of France and Belgium, the other powers merely protested.

By 1938, Hitler decided his rearmament plans were far enough advanced that he could escalate his demands. In March, Germany invaded and soon annexed Austria, with little protest from its German-speaking citizens. Then came the turn of Czechoslovakia. Hitler demanded autonomy for its German-speaking borderlands, then their annexation. At the Munich Conference of September 1938, the leaders of France, Britain, and Italy gave Hitler everything he wanted to keep him from starting a war. Once again, Hitler learned that aggression paid off and that the democracies always gave in.

The democracies' policy of "appeasement" ran counter to the European balance-of-power tradition for three reasons. The first was the deep-seated fear of war among all people who had lived through World War I. The second was fear of communism. The conservative politicians who ruled France and Britain were more afraid of Stalin than of Hitler, for Hitler claimed to respect Christianity and private property. Rather than revive the pre–World War I alliance of Britain, France, and Russia, they sold out the Czechs. The third cause was the very novelty of fascist tactics. Britain's prime minister, Neville Chamberlain, assumed that political leaders (other than the Bolsheviks) were honorable men and that an agreement was as valid as a business contract. Thus, when Hitler said he had "no further territorial demands," Chamberlain believed him.

After Munich, it was too late to stop Hitler, short of war. Germany and Italy were now united in an alliance called the Axis. In March 1939, Germany invaded what was left of Czechoslovakia. Belatedly realizing that Hitler could not be trusted, France and Britain sought Soviet help. Stalin, however, distrusted the "capitalists" as much as they distrusted him. Hitler, meanwhile, offered to divide Poland between Germany and the Soviet Union. On August 23, Stalin accepted. The Nazi-Soviet Pact freed Hitler from the fear of a two-front war and gave Stalin two more years of peace to build up his armies. One week later, on September 1, 1939, German forces swept into Poland across the Eastern Front. The war was on.

EAST ASIA, 1931–1945

When the Depression ruined Japan's export trade, ultranationalists, including young army officers, resented their country's dependence on foreign trade. If only Japan had a colonial empire, they thought, it would not be beholden to the rest of the world. But Europeans and Americans had already taken most potential colonies in Asia. Japan had only Korea, Taiwan, and a railroad in Manchuria. Japanese nationalists saw China, with its vast population and resources, as the solution to their country's problems.

The Manchurian Incident of 1931

Meanwhile, the Guomindang° was becoming stronger in China and preparing to challenge the Japanese presence in Manchuria, a province rich in coal and iron ore. Junior officers in the Japanese army guarding the South Manchurian Railway, frustrated by the caution of their superiors, determined to take action. In September 1931, an explosion on a railroad track, probably staged, gave them an excuse to conquer the entire

---

Guomindang (gwo-min-dong)

German Dive-Bomber over Eastern Europe   In this painting, a German ME-100 fighter plane attacks a Soviet troop convoy on the Eastern Front.   (AKG London)

province. In Tokyo, weak civilian ministers acquiesced to the attack to avoid losing face and shortly recognized the "independence" of Manchuria under the name "Manchukuo°."

The U.S. government condemned the Japanese conquest. The League of Nations refused to recognize Manchukuo and urged the Japanese to remove their troops from China. Persuaded that the Western powers would not fight, Japan resigned from the League.

During the next few years, the Japanese built railways and heavy industries in Manchuria and northeastern China and sped up their rearmament. The government grew more authoritarian, jailing thousands of dissidents. On several occasions, superpatriotic junior officers who mutinied

or assassinated leading political figures received mild punishments, and generals and admirals sympathetic to their views replaced more moderate civilian politicians.

The Chinese Communists and the Long March

Until the Japanese seized Manchuria, the Chinese government seemed to be consolidating its power and creating the conditions for a national recovery. The main challenge to the government of **Chiang Kai-shek°** came from the Chinese Communists, who were organizing industrial workers and who worked in alliance with the Nationalists until in 1927, when

---

Manchukuo (man-CHEW-coo-oh)

Chiang Kai-shek (chang kie-shek)

Chiang Kai-shek arrested and executed Communists and labor leaders alike.

The few Communists who escaped the mass arrests fled to the remote mountains of Jiangxi°, in southeastern China. Among them was **Mao Zedong**° (1893–1976), a farmer's son who had left home to study philosophy. In the early 1920s, Mao discovered the works of Karl Marx, joined the Communist Party, and soon became one of its leaders. In Jiangxi, Mao began studying conditions among the peasants, in whom Communists had previously shown no interest. He planned to redistribute land from the wealthier to the poorer peasants, thereby gaining adherents for the coming struggle with the Guomindang army.

Mao's reliance on the peasantry was a radical departure from Marxist-Leninist ideology, which stressed the backwardness of the peasants and pinned its hopes on industrial workers. Mao was also an advocate of women's equality. Before 1927, the Communists had organized the women who worked in Shanghai's textile mills, the most exploited of all Chinese workers. Later, in their mountain stronghold in Jiangxi, they organized women farmers, allowed divorce, and banned arranged marriages and footbinding.

The Guomindang army pursued the Communists into the mountains, building small forts throughout the countryside. Rather than risk direct confrontations, Mao responded with guerrilla warfare. Government troops often mistreated civilians, but Mao insisted that his soldiers help the peasants, pay a fair price for food and supplies, and treat women with respect. In spite of their good relations with the peasants of Jiangxi, the Communists decided to break out of the southern mountains and trek to Shaanxi°, an even more remote province in northwestern China. The so-called **Long March** took them 6,000 miles (nearly 9,700 kilometers) in one year, 17 miles (27 kilometers) a day over desolate mountains and through swamps and deserts, pursued by the army and bombed by Chiang's aircraft. Of the 100,000 Communists who left Jiangxi in October 1934, only 4,000 reached Shaanxi a year later.

Jiangxi (jang-she)   Mao Zedong (ma-oh zay-dong)
Shaanxi (SHAWN-she)

Mao on the Long March   In 1934–1935, Mao Zedong led his rag-tag army of guerrillas across the rugged mountains of southern and western China. In this romanticized painting, young Mao is speaking to a group of soldiers in spotless uniforms who look up at him with worshipful expressions.   (Library of Congress)

The Sino-Japanese War, 1937–1945

On July 7, 1937, Japanese troops attacked Chinese forces near Beijing. As in 1931, the junior officers who ordered the attack quickly obtained the support of their commanders and then, reluctantly, of the government. Within weeks, Japanese troops seized Beijing, Tianjin, Shanghai, and other coastal cities, and the Japanese navy blockaded the entire coast of China.

Once again, the United States and the League of Nations denounced the Japanese atrocities. Yet the Western powers were too preoccupied with events in Europe and with their own economic problems to risk a military confrontation in Asia. When the Japanese sank a U.S. gunboat and shelled a British ship on the Yangzi River, the U.S. and British governments responded only with righteous indignation and pious resolutions.

The large Chinese armies were poorly led and armed and lost every battle. Within a year, Japan controlled the coastal provinces of China and the lower Yangzi and Yellow River Valleys, China's richest and most populated regions, but the Chinese people continued to resist, either in the army or, increasingly, with the Communist guerrilla forces. Japan's periodic attempts to turn the tide by conquering one more piece of China only pushed Japan deeper into the quagmire.

Warfare between Chinese and Japanese was incredibly violent. In the winter of 1937–1938, Japanese troops took Nanjing, raped 20,000 women, killed 200,000 prisoners and civilians, and looted and burned the city. To slow them down, Chiang ordered the Yellow River dikes blasted open, causing a flood that destroyed 4,000 villages, killed 890,000 people, and made 12.5 million homeless. Two years later, when the Communists ordered a massive offensive, the Japanese retaliated with a "kill all, burn all, loot all" campaign, destroying hundreds of villages down to the last person, building, and farm animal.

The Chinese government, led by Chiang Kai-shek, escaped to the mountains of Sichuan in the center of the country. There he built up a huge army, not to fight Japan but to prepare for a future confrontation with the Communists. The army drafted over 3 million men, even though it had only a million rifles and could not provide food or clothing for all its soldiers. The Guomindang raised farmers' taxes, even when famine forced farmers to eat the bark of trees. Such taxes were not enough to support both a large army and the thousands of government officials and hangers-on who had fled to Sichuan. To avoid taxing its wealthy supporters, the government printed money, causing inflation, hoarding, and corruption.

From his capital of Yan'an in Shaanxi province, Mao also built up his army and formed a government. Unlike the Guomindang, the Communists listened to the grievances of the peasants, especially the poor, to whom they distributed land confiscated from wealthy landowners. Because they could present themselves as the only group in China that was serious about fighting the Japanese, the Communists obtained support and intelligence from farmers in Japanese-occupied territory.

THE SECOND WORLD WAR

The Second World War was much bigger and deadlier than the First in every way. It was fought around the world, from Norway to New Guinea, from Hawaii to Egypt, and on every ocean. It was a total war that showed how effectively industry, science, and nationalism could be channeled into mass destruction.

The War of Movement

Defensive maneuvers had dominated in World War I. In World War II, motorized weapons gave back the advantage to the offensive. Opposing forces moved fast, their victories hinging as much on the aggressive spirit of their commanders and the military intelligence they obtained as on numbers of troops or firepower.

The Wehrmacht°, or German armed forces, was the first to learn this lesson. It not only had tanks, trucks, and fighter planes but perfected their combined use in a tactic called *blitzkrieg*° (lightning war): fighter planes scattered enemy troops and disrupted communications, and tanks punctured the enemy's defenses and then, with the help of the infantry, encircled and captured enemy troops. At sea, the navies of both Japan and the United States had developed aircraft carriers that could launch planes against targets hundreds of miles away.

The very size and mobility of the opposing forces made the fighting far different from any the world had ever seen. Countries were conquered in a matter of days or weeks. The belligerents mobilized the economies of entire continents, squeezing them for every possible resource. They tried not only to defeat their enemies' armed forces

Wehrmacht (VAIR-mokt)   *blitzkrieg* (BLITS-creeg)

but—by means of blockades, submarine attacks on shipping, and bombing raids on industrial areas—to damage the economies that supported those armed forces. They thought of civilians not as innocent bystanders but as legitimate targets and, later, as vermin to be exterminated.

War in Europe and North Africa

It took less than a month for the Wehrmacht to conquer Poland. Britain and France declared war on Germany but took no military action. Meanwhile, the Soviet Union invaded eastern Poland and the Baltic republics of Lithuania, Latvia, and Estonia. Although the Poles fought bravely, the Polish infantry and cavalry were no match for German or Russian tanks. During the winter of 1939–1940, Germany and the Western democracies faced each other in what soldiers called a "phony war" and watched as the Soviet Union attacked Finland, which resisted for many months.

In March 1940, Hitler went on the offensive again, conquering Denmark, Norway, the Netherlands, and Belgium in less than two months. In May, he attacked France. Although the French army had as many soldiers, tanks, and aircraft as the Wehrmacht, its morale was low, and it quickly collapsed. By the end of June, Hitler was master of all of Europe between Russia and Spain.

Germany still had to face one enemy: Britain. The British had no army to speak of, but they had other assets: the English Channel, the Royal Navy and Air Force, and a tough new prime minister, Winston Churchill. The Germans knew they could invade Britain only by gaining control of the airspace over the Channel, so they launched a massive air attack—the Battle of Britain—lasting from June through September. They failed, however, because the Royal Air Force had better fighters and used radar and code breaking to detect approaching German planes.

Frustrated, Hitler turned his attention eastward against the Soviet Union. Within five months, the Wehrmacht conquered the Baltic states, Ukraine, and half of European Russia; captured a million prisoners of war; and stood at the very gates of Moscow and Leningrad (now St. Peters-

burg). The USSR seemed on the verge of collapse when suddenly the weather turned cold, machines froze, and the fighting came to a halt. Like Napoleon, Hitler had ignored the environment of Russia at his peril.

The next spring, the Wehrmacht renewed its offensive. It surrounded Leningrad in a siege that was to cost a million lives. Leaving Moscow aside, it turned toward the Caucasus and its oil wells. In August, the Germans attacked **Stalingrad** (now Volgagrad), the key to the Volga River and the supply of oil. For months, German and Soviet soldiers fought over every street and every house. When winter came, the Red Army counterattacked and encircled the city. In February 1943, the remnants of the German army in Stalingrad surrendered. Hitler had lost his greatest gamble (see Map 26.1).

From Europe, the war spread to Africa. During 1941, British forces conquered Italian East Africa and invaded Libya as well. The Italian rout in North Africa brought the Germans to their rescue. During 1942, the German army and the forces of the British Empire seesawed back and forth across the deserts of Libya and Egypt. Because the British could decode German messages and had more weapons and supplies, they were finally able to expel the Germans from Africa in May 1943.

War in Asia and the Pacific

The war presented Japan with the opportunity to take over European colonies in Southeast Asia, with their abundant oil, rubber, and other strategic materials. After Japanese forces occupied French Indochina in July 1941, the United States and Britain cut off shipments of steel, scrap iron, oil, and other products that Japan desperately needed. This left Japan with three alternatives: accept the shame and humiliation of giving up its conquests, as the Americans insisted; face economic ruin; or widen the war. Japan chose war.

On December 7, 1941, Japanese planes bombed the U.S. naval base at **Pearl Harbor,** Hawaii, sinking or damaging scores of warships. Then, between January and March 1942, the Japanese bombed Hong Kong and Singapore and in-

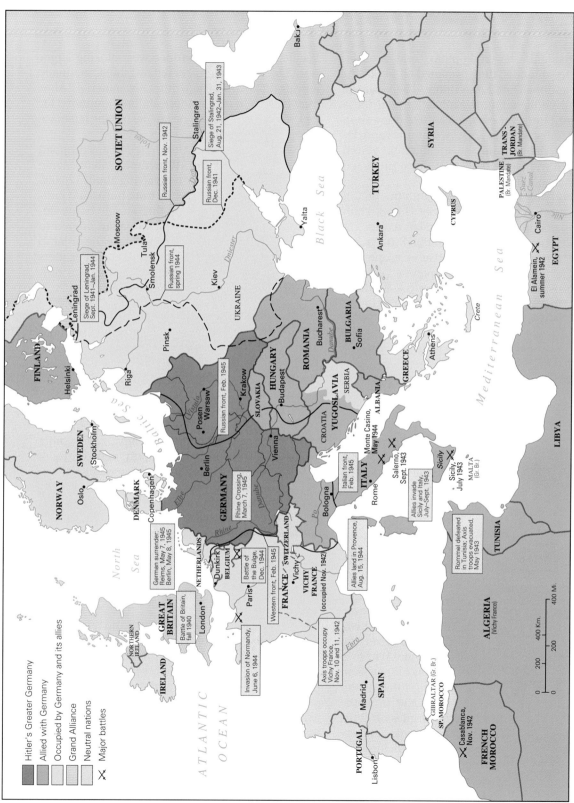

Map 26.1 World War II in Europe and North Africa   In a series of quick and decisive campaigns from September 1939 to December 1941, German forces overran much of Europe and North Africa. There followed three years of bitter fighting as the Allies slowly pushed the Germans back. This map shows the maximum extent of Germany's conquests and alliances, as well as the key battles and the front lines at various times.

Legend:
- Hitler's Greater Germany
- Allied with Germany
- Occupied by Germany and its allies
- Grand Alliance
- Neutral nations
- X Major battles

vaded Thailand, the Philippines, and Malaya. Within a few months, they occupied all of Southeast Asia and the Dutch East Indies. The Japanese claimed to be liberating the inhabitants of these lands from European colonialism. But they soon began to confiscate food and raw materials and demand heavy labor from the inhabitants, whom they treated with contempt. Those who protested were brutally punished.

The entry of the United States into the war, in alliance with Britain and the Soviet Union, challenged Japan's dream of an East Asian empire. In April 1942, American planes bombed Tokyo. In May, the United States Navy defeated a Japanese fleet in the Coral Sea, ending Japanese plans to conquer Australia. A month later, at the **Battle of Midway,** Japan lost four of its six largest aircraft carriers. Japan did not have enough industry to replace them, for its war production was only one-tenth that of the United States. In the vastness of the Pacific Ocean, aircraft carriers held the key to victory, and without them, Japan faced a long and hopeless war (see Map 26.2).

The End of the War

Its new American ally also helped the Soviet Union capitalize on the advantage it had won in the Battle of Stalingrad. Aided by a growing stream of supplies from factories in the United States, the Red Army began pushing the Wehrmacht back toward Germany.

The Western powers, meanwhile, staged two invasions of Europe. Beginning in July 1943, they captured Sicily and invaded Italy. Mussolini resigned, and Italy signed an armistice, but German troops held off the Allied advance for two years. Then on D-day (June 6, 1944), 156,000 British, American, and Canadian troops landed on the coast of Normandy in western France. Within a week, the Allies had more troops in France than Germany did. To meet this growing force, Hitler had to transfer part of the Wehrmacht from the Eastern Front. Despite advancing armies on three sides, Germany held out for almost a year. On May 7, 1945, a week after Hitler committed suicide, German military leaders surrendered.

By June 1944, U.S. bombers were also attacking Japan from newly captured island bases in the Pacific, and U.S. submarines were sinking larger numbers of Japanese merchant ships, gradually cutting off Japan's oil and other raw materials. After May 1945, with the Japanese air force grounded for lack of fuel, U.S. planes began destroying Japanese shipping, industries, and cities at will.

On August 6, 1945, the United States dropped an atomic bomb on **Hiroshima,** killing some 80,000 people in a flash and leaving about 120,000 more to die agonizing deaths from burns and radiation. Three days later, another atomic bomb destroyed Nagasaki. On August 14, Japan offered to surrender, and Emperor Hirohito gave the order to lay down arms. Two weeks later, Japanese leaders signed the terms of surrender. The war was officially over.

Chinese Civil War and Communist Victory

The Japanese surrender also meant the end of Japanese occupation of much of China, but instead of bringing peace, it marked an intensification of the contest between the Guomindang and the Communists. Guomindang forces started with many advantages: more troops and weapons, U.S. support, and control of China's cities. But their behavior eroded whatever popular support they had. They taxed the people they "liberated" more heavily than the Japanese had, looted businesses, confiscated supplies, and enriched themselves at the expense of the population. To pay its bills, Chiang's government printed money so fast that it soon lost all its value, ruining merchants and causing hoarding and shortages. In the countryside, the Guomindang's brutality alienated the peasants.

In contrast, the Communists' land reform programs had won them popular support, which was even more important than the heavy equipment brought by Guomindang soldiers, who began deserting by the thousands, and the Japanese equipment seized by the Soviets in the last weeks of the war. By 1949, the Guomindang armies were collapsing everywhere, defeated more by their own greed and ineptness than by the Communists. As the Communists advanced, high-ranking members of the Guomindang fled to Taiwan, protected from the mainland by the United States Navy. On

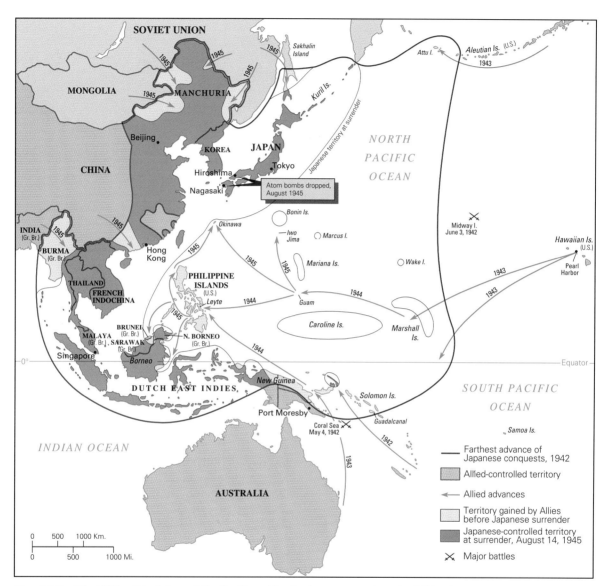

SOVIET UNION

MONGOLIA

MANCHURIA

Sakhalin Island

Kuril Is.

Aleutian Is. (U.S.)
1943

Attu I.

Japanese territory at surrender

Beijing

KOREA

JAPAN

NORTH PACIFIC OCEAN

CHINA

Tokyo

Hiroshima

Nagasaki

Atom bombs dropped, August 1945

INDIA (Gr. Br.)

Okinawa

Bonin Is.

Iwo Jima

Marcus I.

Midway I. June 3, 1942

Hawaiian Is. (U.S.)

Pearl Harbor

BURMA (Gr. Br.)

Hong Kong

Mariana Is.

Wake I.

1943

THAILAND

FRENCH INDOCHINA

PHILIPPINE ISLANDS (U.S.)

Leyte

1944

Guam

1944

1943

BRUNEI (Gr. Br.)

MALAYA (Gr. Br.) SARAWAK (Gr. Br.)

N. BORNEO (Gr. Br.)

Caroline Is.

Marshall Is.

Singapore

Borneo

DUTCH EAST INDIES

New Guinea

Port Moresby

Solomon Is.

Guadalcanal

SOUTH PACIFIC OCEAN

Samoa Is.

Coral Sea May 4, 1942

1942

0°   Equator

INDIAN OCEAN

1943

AUSTRALIA

0   500   1000 Km.

0   500   1000 Mi.

Farthest advance of Japanese conquests, 1942

Allied-controlled territory

Allied advances

Territory gained by Allies before Japanese surrender

Japanese-controlled territory at surrender, August 14, 1945

Major battles

Map 26.2   World War II in Asia and the Pacific   After having conquered much of China between 1937 and 1941, Japanese forces launched a sudden attack on Southeast Asia, Indonesia, and the Pacific in late 1941 and early 1942. American forces slowly reconquered the Pacific islands and the Philippines until August 1945, when the atomic bombing of Hiroshima and Nagasaki forced Japan's surrender.

Hiroshima After the Atomic Bomb   On August 6, 1945, an atomic bomb destroyed the city, killing over fifty thousand people. This photo shows the devastation of the city center, where only a few concrete buildings remained standing.   (Wide World Photos)

October 1, 1949, Mao Zedong announced the founding of the People's Republic of China.

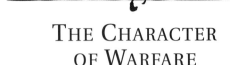

THE CHARACTER OF WARFARE

The war left an enormous death toll. Recent estimates place the figure at close to 60 million deaths, six to eight times more than in World War I. Over half of the dead were civilian victims of massacres, famines, or bombs. The Soviet Union lost between 20 million and 25 million people, more than any other country. China suffered 15 million deaths; Poland lost some 6 million, of whom half were Jewish; the Jewish people lost another 3 million outside Poland. Over 4 million Germans and over 2 million Japanese died. In much of the world, almost every family mourned one or more of its members. In contrast, Great Britain lost 400,000 people, the United States 300,000.

One reason for the terrible toll in human lives and suffering was a change in moral values, as belligerents identified not just soldiers but entire peoples as enemies. Another reason for the devastation was the appearance of new technologies that carried destruction deep into enemy territory far beyond the traditional battlefields.

The War of Science   Scientists made many contributions to the technology of warfare. Chemists found ways to make synthetic rubber from coal or oil. Physicists perfected radar, which warned of approaching enemy aircraft and submarines. Others broke enemy codes and developed antibiotics that saved the lives of countless wounded soldiers (see Environment and Technology: Biomedical Technologies).

Aircraft development was especially striking. As war approached, German, British, and Japanese aircraft manufacturers developed fast, maneuverable fighter planes. U.S. industry produced aircraft of every sort but was especially noted for its heavy bombers designed to fly in huge formations and drop tons of bombs on enemy cities. The Japanese developed the Mitsubishi "Zero" fighter plane—light, fast, and agile. Unable to produce heavy planes in large numbers, Germany responded with radically new designs, including the first jet fighters, low-flying buzz bombs, and fearful V-2 missiles.

In October 1939, President Roosevelt received a letter from physicist Albert Einstein, a Jewish refugee from Nazism, warning of the dangers of nuclear power. Fearing that Germany might develop a nuclear bomb first, Roosevelt placed the vast resources of the U.S. government at the disposal of physicists and engineers, both Americans and refugees from Europe. By 1945, they had built two atomic bombs, each one powerful enough to annihilate an entire city.

Bombing Raids

The Germans began the war from the air, but it was the British and Americans who excelled at large-scale urban bombardment. Since it was very hard to pinpoint individual buildings, especially at night, such raids were aimed at weakening the morale of the civilian population.

In May 1942, 1,000 British planes dropped incendiary bombs on Cologne, setting fire to most of the old city. Between July 24 and August 2, 1943, 3,330 British and Americans bombers set fire to Hamburg, killing 50,000 people. Later raids destroyed Berlin, Dresden, and other German cities. All in all, the bombing raids against Germany killed 600,000 people—more than half of them women and children—and injured 800,000. If the air strategists had hoped thereby to break the morale

of the German people, they failed. The only effective bombing raids were those directed against oil depots and synthetic fuel plants; by early 1945, they had almost brought the German war effort to a standstill.

American bombing raids on Japanese cities were even more devastating than the fire-bombing of German cities, for Japanese cities were built of wood. In March 1945, a large raid set Tokyo ablaze, killing 80,000 people and leaving a million homeless. Five months later, single atomic bombs did something similar.

The Holocaust

The Nazis killed defenseless civilians on an even larger scale. Their murders were not the by-products of some military goal but a calculated policy of extermination.

Their first targets were Jews. Soon after Hitler came to power, he deprived German Jews of their citizenship and legal rights. When eastern Europe fell under Nazi rule, the Nazis herded its large Jewish population into ghettos in the major cities, where many died of starvation and disease. Then, in early 1942, the Nazis decided to carry out Hitler's "final solution to the Jewish problem" by applying modern industrial methods to the slaughter of human beings. German companies built huge extermination camps in eastern Europe. Every day, trainloads of cattle cars arrived at the camps and disgorged thousands of captives and the corpses of those who had died of starvation or asphyxiation along the way. The strongest survivors were put to work and fed almost nothing until they died. Women, children, the elderly, and the sick were shoved into gas chambers and asphyxiated with poison gas. **Auschwitz,** the biggest camp, was a giant industrial complex designed to kill up to twelve thousand people a day. Most horrifying of all were the tortures inflicted on prisoners selected by Nazi doctors for "medical experiments." This mass extermination, now called the **Holocaust** ("burning"), claimed some 6 million Jewish lives.

Besides the Jews, the Nazis also killed 3 million Polish Catholics—especially professionals, army officers, and the educated—in an effort to reduce the Polish people to slavery. They also exterminated

Biomedical Technologies

Life expectancy at birth has nearly doubled in the past 150 years. Even in the poorest countries, life expectancy has risen from forty to sixty or seventy years. The cause of this remarkable change is threefold: clean water, immunizations, and antibiotics.

The realization that drinking water can spread disease came first to Dr. Charles Snow, who noticed the correlation between deaths from cholera and the water from a particular pump in London during an epidemic in 1854. Since then, public health officials have been very conscious of the quality of drinking water, although only wealthy cities can afford to purify and chlorinate water for all their inhabitants.

The practice of immunization goes back to the eighteenth century, when physicians in Turkey and in Europe applied infected pus from a person with smallpox (variolation) or an animal with cowpox (vaccination) to healthy persons to build up their resistance to smallpox. By the end of the nineteenth century, it became clear that immunity to many diseases could be conferred by injections of weakened bacteria. Immunizations offer the single most effective way to prevent childhood diseases and thereby increase life expectancy.

Antibiotics are more recent. In 1928, Dr. Alexander Fleming discovered that a certain mold, *Penicillin notatum,* could kill bacteria. Antibiotics were first used in large quantities in the Second World War. Along with two other innovations—synthetic antimalarial drugs and blood transfusions—antibiotics helped cut the fatality of battlefield wounds from 11 percent in World War I to 3 percent in World War II.

The remarkable success of these technologies has led people to consider good health their natural birthright. Unfortunately, the victory over disease is temporary at best. The abuse of antibiotics and of antibacterial products encourages the growth of new

Biotechnology in Action Campaigns to immunize children against diseases reached even remote villages, as here in Thailand. (Peter Charlesworth/Saba)

strains of old diseases, such as tuberculosis, which can resist all known antibiotics. And although bacterial diseases are no longer as prevalent as they once were, humans are still susceptible to viral afflictions such as influenza and AIDS.

homosexuals, Jehovah's Witnesses, Gypsies, the disabled, and the mentally ill—all in the interests of "racial purity." Whenever a German was killed in an occupied country, the Nazis retaliated by burning a village with all its inhabitants. After the invasion of Russia, the Wehrmacht was given orders to execute all captured communists, government employees, and officers. They also worked millions of prisoners of war to death or let them die of starvation.

The Home Front

Rapid military movements and air power carried the war to people's homes in China, Japan, Southeast Asia, and Europe. Armies swept through the land, confiscating food, fuel, and anything else of value. Bombers and heavy artillery pounded cities into rubble, leaving only the skeletons of buildings, while survivors cowered in cellars. Air-raid sirens awakened people throughout the night. Millions fled their homes in terror. Of all the major belligerents, only Americans escaped such nightmares, and war production ended the deprivations of the Depression years.

The war demanded an enormous production effort from civilians. In the face of advancing Germans in 1941, the Soviets dismantled over fifteen hundred factories and rebuilt them in the Ural Mountains and Siberia, where workers soon turned out more tanks and artillery than the Axis. American factories produced an unending supply of ships, aircraft, trucks, tanks, and other materiel for the Allied effort. The Axis Powers also could not compete.

With so many men mobilized for war, women were responsible for much of this production. For example, 6 million women entered the American labor force during the war, 2.5 million of them in manufacturing jobs previously considered "men's work." Soviet women took over half of all industrial and three-quarters of all agricultural jobs. In the other belligerent countries, women also played a major role in the war effort, replacing men in fields, factories, and offices. The Nazis, in contrast, believed that German women should stay home and bear children, and they imported 7 million "guest workers"—a euphemism for war prisoners and captured foreigners.

War and the Environment

As in World War I, battles scarred the landscape, leaving behind spent ammunition and damaged equipment. Retreating armies flooded large areas of China and the Netherlands. The bombing of cities left ruins that remained visible for a generation or more. The main cause of environmental stress, however, was not the fighting but the economic development that sustained it.

As war industries boomed—the United States increased its industrial production fourfold during the war—so did the demand for raw materials. Mining companies opened new mines and towns in Central Africa to supply strategic minerals. Brazil, Argentina, and other Latin American countries deprived of manufactured imports began building their own steel mills, factories, and shipyards. In India, China, and Europe, timber felling accelerated far beyond forest regrowth.

We must keep the environmental effects of the war in perspective. From the vantage point of the present, the environmental impact of the war seems quite modest in comparison with the damage inflicted on the earth by the long consumer boom that began in the post–World War II years.

CONCLUSION

Between 1929 and 1949, the old global order—conservative, colonialist, and dominated by Great Britain and France—was shattered by the Depression, the politics of violence, and the most devastating war in history. Stalin transformed the Soviet Union into an industrial giant at enormous human cost. Reacting to the Depression, which weakened the Western democracies, Hitler in Germany and military leaders in Japan prepared for a war of conquest. Though Germany and Japan achieved stunning victories at first, their forces soon faltered in the face of the greater industrial production of the United States and the Soviet Union.

The war was so destructive and spread to so much of the globe because rapidly advancing technology was readily converted from civilian to military production. Machines that had made cars could also manufacture bombers or tanks. Engineers could design factories to kill people with maximum efficiency. The accelerating technology of missiles and nuclear bombs made the entire planet vulnerable to human destruction for the first time in history.

Into the power vacuum left by the collapse of Germany and Japan stepped the two superpowers: the United States and the USSR. When the war ended, U.S. soldiers were stationed in Australia, Japan, and western Europe, and the Red Army occupied all of eastern Europe and parts of northern China. Within months of their victory, these one-time allies became ideological enemies.

The global impact of World War II was drastic and almost immediate, because the war weakened the European colonial powers and because so much of the fighting took place in North Africa, Southeast Asia, and other colonial areas. Within fifteen years of the end of the war, almost every European colonial empire had disappeared. As the long era of European domination receded, Asians and Africans began reclaiming their independence.

■ Key Terms

Joseph Stalin	Long March
Five-Year Plans	Stalingrad
Benito Mussolini	Pearl Harbor
Fascist Party	Battle of Midway
Adolf Hitler	Hiroshima
Nazis	Auschwitz
Chiang Kai-shek	Holocaust
Mao Zedong	

■ Suggested Reading

The literature on the period from 1929 to 1945 is enormous and growing fast. The following list is but a very summary introduction.

Charles Kindelberger's *The World in Depression, 1929–39* (1973) and Robert McElvaine's *The Great Depression: America, 1929–1941* (1984) provide a sophisticated economic analysis of the Depression. A. J. H. Latham's *The Depression and the Developing World, 1914–1939* (1981) gives a global perspective.

The best recent book on Japan in the twentieth century is Daikichi Irokawa's *The Age of Hirohito: In Search of Modern Japan* (1995). On Japanese expansion, see W. G. Beasley, *Japanese Imperialism, 1894–1945* (1987). The race to war is covered in Akira Iriye, *The Origins of the Second World War in Asia and the Pacific* (1987). Michael Barnhart, *Japan Prepares for Total War* (1987), is short and well written.

In the large and fast-growing literature on twentieth-century China, two general introductions are especially useful: John K. Fairbank, *The Great Chinese Revolution, 1800–1985* (1986), and Jonathan Spence, *The Search for Modern China* (1990). On the warlord and Guomindang periods, see Lucien Bianco, *Origins of the Chinese Revolution, 1915–1949* (1971). The Japanese invasion of China is the subject of Iris Chang, *The Rape of Nanking: The Forgotten Holocaust of World War II* (1997), and of James Hsiung and Steven Levine, eds., *China's Bitter Victory: The War with Japan, 1937–1945* (1992). Jung Chang, *Wild Swans: Three Daughters of China* (1991), is a fascinating account of women's experiences during the Revolution and the Mao era by the daughter of two Communist officials.

Among recent biographies of Stalin, see Dmitrii Volkogonov's *Stalin: Triumph and Tragedy* (1991) and Robert Tucker's *Stalin as Revolutionary, 1879–1929* (1973) and *Stalin in Power: The Revolution from Above, 1928–1941* (1990). On the transformation of the USSR, see Roy Medvedev's *Let History Judge: The Origins and Consequences of Stalinism* (1989) and Stephen Kotkin's *Magnetic Mountain: Stalinism as Civilization* (1995). Stalin's collectivization of agriculture is vividly portrayed in Robert Conquest's *Harvest of Sorrow* (1986); see also Sheila Fitzpatrick's *Stalin's Peasants: Resistance and Survival in the Russian Village After Collectivization* (1994). Conquest's *The Great Terror: A Reassessment* (1990) describes the purges of the 1930s. Alexander Solzhenitsyn, a veteran of Stalin's prisons, explores them in a detailed history, *The Gulag Archipelago, 1918–1956* (3 vols., 1974–1978), and in a short, brilliant novel, *One Day in the Life of Ivan Denisovich* (1978).

Alexander De Grand provides an excellent interpretation of fascism in *Italian Fascism: Its Origins and Development*, 2d ed. (1989). William Shirer's *The Rise and Fall of the Third Reich* (1960) is a long but very dramatic eyewitness description of Nazi Germany by a journalist. The dictators are the subject of two fine biographies: Denis Mack Smith's *Mussolini* (1982) and Alan Bullock's *Hitler: A Study in Tyranny* (1965). See also A. J. P. Taylor's controversial classic, *The Origins of the Second World War* (1966).

Two very detailed books on World War II are John Keegan, *The Second World War* (1990), and Gerhard Weinberg, *A World at Arms: A Global History of World War II* (1994). Particular aspects of the war in Europe are covered in Alexander Werth, *Russia at War, 1941–1945* (1965), and Conrad Crane, *Bombs, Cities, and Civilians* (1993). One of the most readable accounts of the war in Asia and the Pacific is Ronald Spector's *Eagle Against the Sun* (1988). Also see Akira Iriye, *Power and Culture: The Japanese-American War, 1941–1945* (1981), and James Hsiung and Steven Levine, eds., *China's Bitter Victory: The War with Japan, 1937–1945* (1992).

The terror of life under Nazi rule is the subject of two powerful memoirs: Anne Frank's *The Diary of a Young Girl* (1953) and Eli Wiesel's *Night* (1960). On the Holocaust, see Lucy Dawidowicz, *The War Against the Jews, 1933–1945,* 2d ed. (1986); Leni Yahil, *The Holocaust: The Fate of European Jewry* (1990); and a controversial book by Daniel Goldhagen, *Hitler's Willing Executioners: Ordinary Germans and the Holocaust* (1996).

Among the many books that capture the scientific side of warfare, two are especially recommended: Richard Rhodes's long but fascinating *The Making of the Atomic Bomb* (1986) and F. H. Hinsley and Alan Stripp, eds., *Code Breakers* (1993).

Among the many books on the home front in the United States, the most vivid is Studs Terkel, *"The Good War": An Oral History of World War Two* (1984). Margaret Higonnet et al., eds., *Behind the Lines: Gender and the Two World Wars* (1987), discusses the role of women in the war.

27

STRIVING FOR INDEPENDENCE: AFRICA, INDIA, AND LATIN AMERICA, 1900–1949

Sub-Saharan Africa, 1900–1945 • The Indian Independence
Movement, 1905–1947 • Latin America, 1900–1949
SOCIETY AND CULTURE: Self-Government in Africa

Emiliano Zapata°, leader of a peasant rebellion in the Mexican Revolution, liked to be photographed on horseback, carrying a sword and a rifle and draped with bandoliers of bullets. Mahatma Gandhi°, who led the independence movement in India, preferred to be seen sitting at a spinning wheel, dressed in a *dhoti*°, the simple loincloth worn by Indian farmers. The images they liked to project and the methods they used could not have been more opposed. Yet their goals were similar: each wanted social justice and a better life for the poor in a country free of foreign domination.

The previous two chapters focused on a world convulsed by war and revolution. The world wars involved Europe, East Asia, the Middle East, and the United States, and they sparked violent revolutions in Russia and China. They accelerated the development of aviation, electronics, nuclear power, and other technologies. Although these momentous events dominate the history of the first half of the twentieth century, parts of the world that were little touched by war also underwent profound changes in this period, partly for internal reasons and partly because of the influence of warfare and revolution in other parts of the world.

In this chapter, we examine the changes that took place in three regions: sub-Saharan Africa, India, and three major countries of Latin America—Mexico, Brazil, and Argentina. These three regions were very distinct culturally, yet they had much in common. Africa and India were colonies of Europe, both politically and economically. Though politically independent, the Latin American republics were dependent on Europe and the United States for the sale of raw

Zapata (zeh-PAH-teh)   Gandhi (GAHN-dee)
dhoti (DOE-tee)

materials and commodities and for imports of manufactured goods, technology, and capital. In all three regions, independence movements tried to wrest control from distant foreigners and improve the livelihood of their peoples. Their success was partial at best.

As you read this chapter, ask yourself the following questions:

- How did wars and revolutions in Europe and East Asia affect people in the tropics and farther south?

- Why did educated Indians and Africans want independence?

- How compatible were Latin American goals of social justice and economic development?

SUB-SAHARAN AFRICA, 1900–1945

Of all the continents, Africa was the last to be subject to European colonization (see Chapter 24). The first half of the twentieth century, when nationalist movements threatened European rule in Asia, was Africa's classic period of colonialism. After World War I, Britain, France, Belgium, and South Africa divided Germany's African colonies among themselves. In the 1930s, Italy invaded Ethiopia. The colonial empires reached their peak shortly before World War II.

Colonial Africa: Economic and Social Changes

Outside of Algeria, Kenya, and South Africa, few Europeans lived in Africa. In 1930, Nigeria, with a population of 20 million, was ruled by 386 British officials and 8,000 policemen and military, of whom 150 were European. Yet the presence of even a small number of Europeans stimulated deep changes.

From the turn of the century, the colonial powers built railroads from coastal cities to mines and plantations in the interior in order to provide raw materials to the industrial world. In many places, the economic boom of the interwar years benefited few Africans, because colonial governments sold or leased African communal lands to European companies or, in eastern and southern Africa, to white settlers. Where land was divided into small farms, some Africans benefited from the boom. Farmers in the Gold Coast (now Ghana°) profited from the high prices of cocoa, as did palm oil producers in Nigeria and coffee growers in East Africa.

In most of Africa, women played a major role in the retail trades, selling pots and pans and other hardware, toys, cloth, and food in the markets. Many maintained their economic independence and kept their household finances separate from those of their husbands, following a custom that predated the colonial period. However, they faced new competition from large European wholesalers and immigrant Indian, Greek, and Syrian retail traders.

For many Africans, economic development meant working in European-owned mines and plantations, often under compulsion. Eager to develop the resources of the territories under their control, colonial governments used their police powers to force Africans to work under harsh conditions for little or no pay. In the 1920s, when the government of French Equatorial Africa decided to build a railroad from Brazzaville to the Atlantic coast, a distance of 312 miles (502 kilometers), it drafted 127,000 men to carve a roadbed across mountains and through rain forests. For lack of food, clothing, and medical care, 20,000 of them died, an average of 64 deaths per mile of track.

Europeans prided themselves on bringing modern health care to Africa; yet before the 1930s, there was too little of it to help the majority of Africans, and other aspects of colonialism actually worsened public health. Migrants to cities, mines, and plantations and soldiers moving from post to post spread syphilis, gonorrhea, tuberculosis, and malaria. Sleeping sickness and smallpox epidemics raged throughout Central Africa. In

---

Ghana (GAH-nuh)

Diamond Mining in Southern Africa   The discovery of diamonds in the Transvaal in 1867 attracted prospectors to the area around Kimberley. The first wave of prospectors consisted of individual "diggers," including a few Africans. By the late 1870s, surface deposits had been exhausted, and further mining required complex and costly machinery. After 1889, one company, De Beers Consolidated, owned all the diamond mines. This photograph shows the entrance to a mine shaft and mine workers surrounded by heavy equipment.   (Royal Commonwealth Society. By permission of the Syndics of Cambridge University Library)

recruiting men to work, colonial governments depleted rural areas of farmers needed to plant and harvest crops. Forced requisitions of food taken to feed the workers left the remaining populations undernourished and vulnerable to diseases. Not until the 1930s did colonial governments realize the negative consequences of their labor policies and begin to invest in agricultural development and health care for Africans.

Africans migrated to cities because they offered the hope of jobs and excitement and, for a few, the chance to become wealthy. In 1900,

Ibadan° in Nigeria was the only city in sub-Saharan Africa with more than 100,000 inhabitants; fifty years later, dozens of cities had reached that size, including Nairobi° in Kenya, Johannesburg in South Africa, Lagos in Nigeria, Accra in Gold Coast, and Dakar in Senegal.

However, migrations damaged the family life of those involved, for almost all the migrants were men, leaving women in the countryside to farm and raise children. Cities built during the colonial period reflected the colonialists' attitudes with

---

Ibadan (ee-BAH-dahn)   **Nairobi** (nie-ROE-bee)

CHRONOLOGY

	Africa	India	Latin America
1900	**1900s** Railroads connect ports to the interior	**1905** Viceroy Curzon splits Bengal; mass demonstrations **1906** Muslims found All-India Muslim League	**1876–1910** Porfirio Díaz, dictator of Mexico **1911–1919** Mexican Revolution; Emiliano Zapata and Pancho Villa against the Constitutionalists **1917** New constitution proclaimed in Mexico
1920	**1920s** J. E. Casely Hayford organizes political movement in British West Africa	**1919** Amritsar Massacre **1929** Gandhi leads March to the Sea **1930s** Gandhi calls for independence; he is repeatedly arrested	**1928** Plutarco Elías Calles founds Mexico's National Revolutionary Party **1930–1945** Getulio Vargas, dictator of Brazil **1934–1940** Lázaro Cárdenas, president of Mexico **1938** Cárdenas nationalizes Mexican oil industry; Vargas proclaims Estado Novo in Brazil
1940		**1939** British bring India into World War II **1940** Muhammad Ali Jinnah demands a separate nation for Muslims **1947** Partition and independence of India and Pakistan	**1943** Juan Perón leads military coup in Argentina **1946** Perón elected president of Argentina

their racially segregated housing, clubs, restaurants, hospitals, and other institutions. Patterns of racial discrimination were most rigid in the white-settler colonies of eastern and southern Africa.

Religious and Political Changes

The dislocations caused by foreign rule, migration, and sudden economic change buffeted Africans' traditional beliefs. Many turned to one of the two universal religions, Christianity and Islam, for guidance. A major attraction of the Christian denominations was their mission schools, which provided access to employment as clerks, teachers, clergy, or shopkeepers. These schools educated a new elite, many of whom learned not only skills and literacy but Western political ideas as well.

Islam also emphasized literacy—in Arabic rather than in a European language—and was less disruptive of traditional African customs such as polygamy. Muslim traders spread Islam inland in East Africa and southward toward the West African coast.

The contrast between the liberal ideas imparted by Western education and the realities of racial discrimination under colonial rule contributed to the rise of nationalism among educated

Africans. These nationalist movements were also inspired by the ideas of pan-Africanists from America, who advocated the unity of African peoples around the world. These movements were small and had little influence until World War II (see Society and Culture: Self-Government in Africa). One of the most successful would be the **African National Congress,** which Western-educated lawyers and journalists founded in 1909 to defend the interests of Africans in South Africa.

The Second World War (1939–1945) had a profound effect on the peoples of Africa, even those far removed from the theaters of war. The war brought hardships, such as increased forced labor, inflation, and requisitions of raw materials. Yet it also brought hope. During the campaign to oust the Italians from Ethiopia, Emperor **Haile Selassie°** (r. 1930–1974) led his own troops into his capital, Addis Ababa, and reclaimed his title. Many Africans who served as soldiers and carriers in Burma, North Africa, and Europe listened to Allied propaganda in favor of European liberation movements and against Nazi racism. They returned to their countries with new and radical ideas.

THE INDIAN INDEPENDENCE MOVEMENT, 1905–1947

In British India, decades of economic transformations had already awakened nationalist ideas among the educated middle class. In response, the British gradually granted India a limited amount of political autonomy while maintaining overall control. But unresolved religious and communal tensions among the Indian peoples led to violent conflicts after the withdrawal of the British in 1947 (see Map 27.1).

The Land and the People

Economic development—what the British called the "moral and material progress of India"—hardly benefited the average Indian. To produce timber for construction and railroad ties and to clear land for tea and rubber plantations, government foresters cut down most of the tropical hardwood forests that had covered the subcontinent in the nineteenth century. In spite of deforestation and extensive irrigation, the amount of land available to peasant families shrank with each successive generation, because the Indian population grew from 250 million in 1900 to 389 million in 1941. Landless young men converged on the cities, exceeding the number of jobs available in the slowly expanding industries.

Indians were divided into many classes. Peasants, the great majority, paid rents to the landowner, interest to the village moneylender, and taxes to the government and had little left to improve their land or raise their standard of living. The government protected property owners, from village moneylenders all the way up to the princes and maharajahs°, who owned huge tracts of land. The cities were crowded with craftsmen, traders, and workers of all sorts, mostly very poor.

The peoples of India spoke many different languages. As a result of British rule and increasing trade and travel, English became, like Latin in medieval Europe, the common medium of communication of the Western-educated middle class. This new class of English-speaking government bureaucrats, professionals, and merchants was to play a leading role in the independence movement.

The majority of Indians practiced Hinduism and were subdivided into hundreds of castes, each affiliated with a particular occupation. Hinduism discouraged intermarriage and other social interactions among the castes and with people who were not Hindus. Muslims constituted one-quarter of the people of India but formed a majority in the northwest and in eastern Bengal. More reluctant than Hindus to learn English, Muslims felt discriminated against by both British and Hindus.

Haile Selassie (HI-lee seh-LASS-ee)

maharajah (mah-huh-RAH-juh)

SOCIETY & CULTURE

Self-Government in Africa

Colonialism rested on the presumption of European superiority. Nowhere was that presumption more evident than in Africa, where colonialists argued that Africans had not evolved politically and therefore would not be ready for self-rule for a long time. Here is an expression of such thinking from the pamphlet African Opportunity, by Lord Milverton, a former governor of Nigeria.

The African has had self-government. Until about fifty years ago he had had it for countless centuries, and all it brought him was blood-stained chaos, a brief, insecure life, haunted by fear, in which evil tradition and custom held him enslaved to superstition, hunger, disease, squalor and ruthless cruelty, even to his family and friends. For countless centuries, while all the pageant of history swept by, the African remained unmoved—in primitive savagery.

The Gold Coast nationalist J. E. Casely Hayford responded to that sort of attack by giving examples of progressive and beneficial government in precolonial Africa.

A people who could, indigenously, and without a literature, evolve the orderly representative government which obtained in Ashanti and the Gold Coast before the advent of the foreign interloper, are a people to be respected and shown consideration when they proceed to discuss questions of self-government.

How do these quotations illustrate the importance of history in an argument about the future?

Source: Quotations from Thomas Hodgkin, *Nationalism in Colonial Africa* (New York: New York University Press, 1957), 172–173.

British Rule and Indian Nationalism

Colonial India was ruled by a viceroy appointed by the British government; the country was administered by a few thousand members of the Indian Civil Service. These men, imbued with a sense of duty toward their subjects, formed one of the most honest (if not the most efficient) bureaucracies of all time. Drawn mostly from the English gentry, they liked to think of India as a land of lords and peasants. They considered it their duty to protect the Indian people from the dangers of industrialization and radical politics.

At the turn of the century, the majority of Indians—especially the peasants, landowners, and princes—accepted British rule. But the Europeans' racist attitude toward dark-skinned people increasingly offended those Indians who had learned English and absorbed English ideas of freedom and representative government and then discovered that thinly disguised racial quotas excluded them from the Indian Civil Service, the officer corps, and prestigious country clubs.

In 1885, a small group of English-speaking Hindu professionals had founded a political organization called the **Indian National Congress.** For twenty years, its members respectfully petitioned the government for access to the higher administrative positions and for a voice in official decisions, but they had little influence outside intellectual circles. Then, in 1905, Viceroy Lord Curzon divided the province of **Bengal** in two to improve the efficiency of its administration. This decision, made without consulting anyone, angered not only educated Indians, who saw it as a step taken to lessen their influence, but also millions of uneducated Hindu

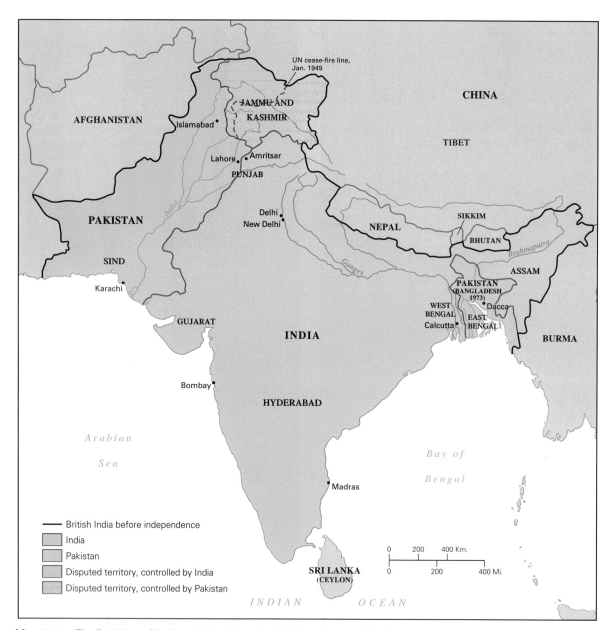

Map 27.1   The Partition of India, 1947   Before the British, India was divided among many states, ethnic groups, and religions. When the British left in 1947, the subcontinent split along religious lines. The predominantly Muslim regions of Sind and Punjab in the northwest and East Bengal in the east formed the new nation of Pakistan. The predominantly Hindu center became the Republic of India. Jammu and Kashmir remained disputed territories and poisoned relations between the two new countries.

Bengalis, who suddenly found themselves outnumbered by Muslims in East Bengal. Soon Bengal was the scene of demonstrations, boycotts of British goods, and even incidents of violence against the British. Meanwhile, fearful of Hindu dominance elsewhere in India, Muslims founded the **All-India Muslim League** in 1906. Politics, once primarily the concern of Westernized intellectuals, turned into two mass movements: one by Hindus and one by Muslims.

To maintain their commercial position and prevent social upheavals, the British resisted the idea that India could, or should, industrialize. Their geologists looked for minerals, such as coal or manganese, that British industry required. However, when the only Indian member of the Indian Geological Service, Pramatha Nath Bose, wanted to prospect for iron ore, he had to resign because the government wanted no part of an Indian steel industry that could compete with that of Britain. Bose joined forces with Jamsetji Tata, a Bombay textile magnate who decided to produce steel in spite of British opposition. With the help of German and American engineers and equipment, Tata's son Dorabji opened the first steel mill in India in 1911, in a town called Jamshedpur in honor of his father. Although it produced only a fraction of the steel that India required, Jamshedpur

Construction Site in Colonial India   British civil engineers were active throughout India building roads, railroads, and canals. Here, a British official supervises Indian workers building a bridge.   (The Billie Love Collection)

became a powerful symbol of Indian national pride. It prompted Indian nationalists to ask why did a country that could produce its own steel need foreigners to run its government.

During World War I, Indians supported Britain enthusiastically; 1.2 million men volunteered for the army, and millions more Indians voluntarily contributed money to the government. Many expected that the British would reward such loyalty with political concessions. Others organized to demand such concessions and began demanding a voice in the government. In 1917, in response to the agitation, the British government announced "the gradual development of self-governing institutions with a view to the progressive realization of responsible government in India as an integral part of the British Empire." This sounded like a promise of self-government, but the timetable was left so vague that nationalists denounced it as a devious maneuver to postpone India's independence.

The dreadful toll of the influenza epidemic of 1918 and 1919 increased the mounting political tensions. Leaders of the Indian National Congress declared that the British reform proposals were too little too late. On April 13, 1919, in the city of Amritsar in Punjab, General Reginald Dyer ordered his troops to fire into a peaceful crowd of some 10,000 demonstrators, killing at least 379 and wounding 1,200. As waves of angry demonstrations swept over India, the period of gradual accommodation between the British and the Indians came to a close.

Mahatma Gandhi and Militant Nonviolence

For the next twenty years, India teetered on the edge of violent uprisings and harsh repression, possibly even war. That it did not succumb was due to **Mohandas K. Gandhi** (1869–1948), a man known to his followers as "Mahatma," the "great soul."

Gandhi began life with every advantage. His family was wealthy enough to send him to England for his education. After his studies, he lived in southern Africa, where he practiced law for the small Indian community living there and developed his tactics of nonviolent protest. During World War I, he returned to India and joined the Indian National Congress.

Gandhi had some unusual political ideas. He denounced the popular ideals of violent struggle. Instead, inspired by both Hindu and Christian concepts, he preached the virtues of *ahimsa*° (nonviolence) and *satyagraha*° (the search for truth). He refused to countenance violence among his followers, and several times he called off demonstrations when they turned violent.

Gandhi had an affinity for the poor that was unusual even among socialist politicians. In 1921, he gave up the Western-style suits worn by lawyers and the fine raiment of wealthy Indians and henceforth wore simple peasant garb: a length of homespun cloth below his waist and a shawl. He attracted ever-larger numbers of followers among the poor and the illiterate, who soon began to revere him, and he transformed the cause of Indian independence from an elite movement of the educated into a mass movement with a quasi-religious aura.

Gandhi was a brilliant political tactician and a master of public relations gestures. In 1929, for instance, he led a few followers on an 80-mile (129-kilometer) walk, camped on a beach, and gathered salt from the sea in a blatant and well-publicized act of civil disregard for the government's monopoly of salt. But he discovered that unleashing the power of popular participation was one thing; controlling its direction was quite another. Within days of his "Walk to the Sea," demonstrations of support broke out all over India, in which the police killed 100 demonstrators and arrested over 60,000.

Many times during the 1930s, Gandhi threatened to fast "unto death," and several times he did come close to death, to protest the violence of both the police and his followers and to demand independence for India. He was repeatedly arrested and spent a total of six years in jail. But every arrest made him more popular. He became a cult figure not only in his own country but also in the Western media. He never won a battle or an election; instead, in the words of historian Percival Spear, he made the British "uncomfortable in their cherished field of moral rectitude," and he gave Indi-

---

ahimsa (uh-HIM-sah)   *satyagraha* (suh-TYAH-gruh-huh)

ans the feeling that theirs was the ethically superior cause.

India Moves Toward Independence

In the 1920s, slowly and reluctantly, the British began to give in to the pressure of the Indian National Congress and the Muslim League. They handed over to Indians control of "national" areas such as education, the economy, and public works. They also gradually admitted more Indians into the Civil Service and the officer corps.

Indian politicians obtained the right to erect high tariff barriers against imports in order to protect India's infant industries from foreign, even British, competition. Behind these barriers, Indian entrepreneurs built plants to manufacture iron and steel, cement, paper, cotton and jute textiles, sugar, and other products. Besides creating jobs, this early industrialization helped create a class of wealthy Indian businessmen who supported the Indian National Congress and its demands for independence. Though paying homage to Gandhi, they preferred his successor as leader of the Indian National Congress, **Jawaharlal Nehru°** (1889–1964). A highly educated nationalist and subtle thinker, Nehru, in contrast to Gandhi, looked forward to creating a modern industrial India.

When Viceroy Lord Linlithgow took India into World War II without consulting a single Indian, the Congress-dominated provincial governments resigned in protest and found that boycotting government office increased their popular support. Gandhi called Britain's offer of independence after the end of the war a "postdated cheque on a failing bank" and demanded full independence immediately. His "Quit India" campaign aroused popular demonstrations against the British and provoked a wave of arrests, including his own.

As in World War I, Indians contributed heavily to the Allied war effort, supplying 2 million soldiers and enormous amounts of resources, especially timber needed for emergency construction. The Second World War divided the Indian people. Most Indian soldiers felt they were fighting to defend their country rather than to support the British Empire. A small number of Indians, meanwhile, were so anti-British that they joined the Japanese side.

Partition and Independence

When the war ended, Britain's new Labour Party government prepared for Indian independence, but deep suspicions between Hindus and Muslims complicated the process. The break between the two communities had started in 1937, when the Indian National Congress won the provincial elections and refused to share power with the Muslim League. In 1940, the leader of the League, **Muhammad Ali Jinnah°** (1876–1948), demanded what many Muslims had been dreaming of for years: a country of their own, to be called Pakistan.

As independence approached, talks between Jinnah and Nehru broke down, and battle lines were drawn. Violent rioting between Hindus and Muslims broke out in Bengal and Bihar despite Gandhi's appeals for tolerance and cooperation. By early 1947, the Indian National Congress had accepted the idea of a partition of India into two states, one secular but dominated by Hindus, the other Muslim. In June, Lord Mountbatten, the last viceroy, decided that independence must come immediately. On August 15, British India gave way to a new India and Pakistan. The Indian National Congress, led by Nehru, formed the first government of India; Jinnah and the Muslim League established a government for the provinces that made up Pakistan.

The rejoicing over independence was marred by violent outbreaks between Muslims and Hindus. Throughout the land, Muslim and Hindu neighbors turned on one another, and armed members of one faith hunted down people of the other faith. Leaving all their possessions behind, Hindus fled from predominantly Muslim areas, and Muslims fled from Hindu areas, but trainloads of desperate refugees of one faith were attacked and massacred. Within a few months, some 12 million people had abandoned their ancestral homes

---

Nehru (NAY-roo)

Jinnah (jee-NAH)

and a half-million lay dead. In January 1948, Gandhi died too, gunned down by an angry Hindu refugee.

LATIN AMERICA, 1900–1949

Latin America achieved independence from Spain and Portugal but did not industrialize or resolve the huge gap between wealthy landowners and desperately poor peasants. Throughout the nineteenth century, ideological divisions, unstable governments, and violent upheavals were common, and Latin American states became economically dependent on the wealthier countries, especially the United States and Great Britain.

Three Latin American republics—Mexico, Brazil, and Argentina—contained well over half of Latin America's land, population, and wealth. Mexico underwent a traumatic social revolution, while Argentina and Brazil evolved more peaceably.

The Mexican Revolution, 1910–1920

Mexico gained its independence in 1821. At the beginning of the twentieth century, Mexican society was so deeply divided between rich and poor that only a revolution could move the country toward prosperity and democracy. A few very wealthy families of Spanish origin, less than 1 percent of the population, owned 85 percent of Mexico's land, mostly in huge haciendas (estates). Closely tied to this elite were the handful of American and British companies that controlled most of Mexico's railroads, silver mines, plantations, and other productive enterprises. At the other end of the social scale were Indians and mestizos°, people of mixed Indian and European ancestry. Most of them were peasants who worked on the haciendas or farmed small communal plots near their ancestral villages.

Despite many upheavals in Mexico in the nineteenth century, the government in 1910 seemed in control; no one expected a revolution. For thirty-four years, General Porfirio Díaz° (1830–1915) had ruled Mexico under the motto "Liberty, Order, Progress." To Díaz, "liberty" meant freedom for rich hacienda owners and foreign investors to acquire more land. The government imposed "order" through rigged elections and a policy of *pan o palo* (bread or the stick)—that is, bribes for Díaz's supporters and summary justice for those who opposed him. And "progress" meant mainly the importing of foreign capital, machinery, and technicians to take advantage of Mexico's labor, soil, and natural resources.

Though a mestizo himself, Díaz discriminated against the nonwhite majority of Mexicans. He and his supporters tried to eradicate what they saw as Mexico's embarrassingly rustic traditions. On many middle- and upper-class tables, French cuisine replaced traditional Mexican dishes. The wealthy replaced sombreros and ponchos with European garments, and they preferred horse racing and soccer to the traditional bullfighting and cockfighting. To the educated middle class—the only group with a strong sense of Mexican nationhood—this devaluation of Mexican culture became a symbol of the Díaz regime's failure to defend national interests against foreign influences.

When uprisings broke out in 1911, Días resigned and was replaced by a series of reform-minded governments. Unlike the independence movement in India, the Mexican Revolution was not the work of one party with a well-defined ideology. Instead, it developed haphazardly, led by a series of ambitious but limited leaders, each representing a different segment of Mexican society.

As early as 1911, **Emiliano Zapata** (1879–1919), an Indian farmer, had led a revolt against the haciendas in the mountains of Morelos, south of Mexico City (see Map 27.2). His soldiers were peasants, some of them women, mounted on horseback and armed with pistols and rifles. For several years, they periodically came down from the mountains, burned hacienda buildings, and returned land to the Indian villages.

---

mestizo (mess-TEE-zoh)

Díaz (DEE-as)

Emiliano Zapata   Zapata, the leader of a peasant rebellion in southern Mexico during the Mexican Revolution, stands in full revolutionary regalia: sword, rifles, bandoliers, boots, and sombrero.   (Brown Brothers)

dustrial workers. Calling themselves Constitutionalists, their leaders organized private armies and in 1914 succeeded in taking control of the government. By then, the revolution had spread to the countryside.

Zapata and Villa were part agrarian rebels, part social revolutionaries. They enjoyed tremendous popular support but could never rise above their regional and peasant origins and lead a national revolution. The Constitutionalists had fewer soldiers than Zapata and Villa; but they held the major cities, controlled the country's exports of oil, and used the proceeds of oil sales to buy modern weapons. Fighting continued for years, and gradually the Constitutionalists took over most of Mexico. In 1919, they defeated and killed Zapata; Villa was assassinated four years later. An estimated 2 million people lost their lives in the civil war, and much of Mexico lay in ruins.

During their struggle to win support against Zapata and Villa, the Constitutionalists adopted many of their rivals' agrarian reforms and also proposed social programs designed to appeal to workers and the middle class. The Constitution of 1917 promised universal suffrage and a one-term presidency; state-run education to free the poor from the hold of the Catholic Church; the end of debt peonage; restrictions on foreign ownership of property; and laws specifying minimum wages and maximum hours to protect laborers. Although these reforms were too costly to implement right away, they had important symbolic significance, for they enshrined the dignity of Mexicans and the equality of Indians, mestizos, and whites, as well as of peasants and city people.

Another leader appeared in Chihuahua, a northern state where seventeen individuals owned two-fifths of the land and 95 percent of the people had no land at all. Starting in 1913, **Francisco "Pancho" Villa** (1877–1923), a former ranch hand, mule driver, and bandit, organized an army of three thousand men, most of them cowboys. They too seized land from the large haciendas, not to rebuild traditional communities but to create family ranches.

The inequities of Mexican society and foreign intervention angered Mexico's middle class and in-

The Mexican Revolution Institutionalized, 1920–1940

In the early 1920s, after a decade of violence that exhausted all classes, the Mexican Revolution lost momentum. Only in Morelos did peasants receive land. Nevertheless, the revolution changed the social makeup of the governing class in important ways. For the first time in Mexico's history, representatives of rural communities, unionized workers, and public employees were admitted to the inner circle.

Map 27.2 The Mexican Revolution The Mexican Revolution began in two distinct regions of the country. One was the mountainous and densely populated area south of Mexico City, particularly Morelos, homeland of Emiliano Zapata. The other was the dry and thinly populated ranch country of the north, such as Chihuahua, home of Pancho Villa. The fighting that ensued crisscrossed the country along the main railroad lines, shown on the map.

In 1928, the establishment of the National Revolutionary Party, or PNR, gave the Mexican Revolution a second wind. **Lázaro Cárdenas°,** who became president in 1934, brought peasants' and workers' organizations into the party, renamed it the Mexican Revolutionary Party (PRM), and removed the generals from government positions. Then he set to work implementing the reforms promised in the Constitution of 1917. Cárdenas redistributed 44 million acres (17.6 million hectares) to peasant communes. He closed church-run schools, replacing them with government schools. He nationalized the railroads and numerous other businesses. Cárdenas's most dramatic move was

the expropriation of foreign-owned oil companies without provoking foreign intervention.

When Cárdenas's term ended in 1940, Mexico, like India, was still a land of poor farmers with a small industrial base. The revolution had brought great changes, however. The political system was free of both chaos and dictatorships. A small group of wealthy people no longer monopolized land and other resources. The military was tamed, the Catholic Church no longer controlled education, and the nationalization of oil had demonstrated Mexico's independence from foreign corporations and military intervention.

Lázaro Cárdenas (LAH-sah-roe KAHR-dih-nahs)

***The Agitator,* a Mural by Diego Rivera**   Diego Rivera (1886–1957) was politically committed to the Mexican Revolution and widely admired as an artist. This mural, painted at the National Agricultural School at Chapingo near Mexico City, shows a political agitator addressing peasants and workers. With one hand, the speaker points to miners laboring in a silver mine; with the other, to a hammer and sickle.   (Universidad Autonoma de Chapingo/CENIDIAP-INBA)

The Transformation of Argentina

At the end of the nineteenth century, railroads and refrigerator ships, which allowed the safe transportation of meat, changed not only the composition of Argentina's exports but also the way they were produced—in other words, the land itself. European consumers preferred the soft flesh of Lincoln sheep and Hereford cattle to the tough, sinewy meat of creole cattle and merino sheep. The valuable Lincolns and Herefords could not be allowed to roam and graze on the *pampas*° (grassy plains). To safeguard them, the pampas had to be divided, plowed, cultivated, and fenced with barbed wire to keep out predators and other unwelcome animals. Once fenced, the land could be used to produce wheat as well as beef and mutton. Within a few years, grasslands that had stretched to the horizon were transformed into farmland. Like the North American midwest, the pampas became one of the world's great producers of wheat and meat.

Argentina's government represented the interests of the *oligarquía*°, a very small group of wealthy landowners. Members of this elite controlled enormous haciendas where they grew rich raising cattle and sheep and growing wheat for export to Europe and the United States. Little interested in any business other than farming, they were content to let foreign companies, mainly British, build Argentina's railroads, processing plants, and public utilities. So important were British interests in the Argentinean economy that the language used on the railroads was not Spanish but English.

Brazil and Argentina, to 1929

Before the First World War, Brazil's elite produced most of the world's coffee and cacao, grown on vast estates, and natural rubber, gathered by Indians from rubber trees growing wild in the Amazon rain forest. Like their Argentinean counterparts, they had little interest in other forms of

---

pampas (POM-pus)

oligarquía (oh-lee gar-KEE-ah)

development; let British companies build rail-roads, harbors, and other infrastructure; and im-ported all manufactured goods. At the time, this situation seemed to offer a rational division of la-bor that allowed each country to do what it did best. If the British did not grow coffee, why should Brazil build locomotives?

Rubber exports collapsed after 1912, replaced by cheaper plantation rubber from Southeast Asia. The outbreak of war in 1914 put an end to imports from Europe. To a certain extent, the United States replaced the European countries as suppliers of machinery, but European immigrants in Argentina and Brazil also built factories to manufacture tex-tiles and household goods.

The disruption of the old trade patterns weak-ened the landowning class. In Argentina, the urban middle class obtained the secret ballot and univer-sal male suffrage in 1916 and elected a liberal politician, Hipólito Irigoyen°, as president. In Brazil, junior officers rebelled periodically against the government but accomplished little. In neither country did the urban middle class take power away from the wealthy landowners. Instead, the two classes shared power at the expense of both the landless peasants and the urban workers.

The 1920s were a period of peace and prosper-ity in South America, in contrast to Mexico. Trade with Europe resumed, prices received for agricul-tural exports remained high, and both Argentina and Brazil used profits accumulated during the war to industrialize and improve their transporta-tion systems and public utilities. Yet as they were moving forward, new technologies again left them dependent on the advanced industrial countries.

Right after the war, the major powers scram-bled to build powerful transmitters on every continent to compete with the telegraph cable companies and to take advantage of the boom in international business and news reporting. No Latin American country then possessed the knowl-edge or funds to build its own transmitters. So a cartel of British, French, German, and American communications companies set up a national ra-dio company in each Latin American republic, installing a prominent local politician as its presi-dent, but the cartel held all the stock and therefore received all the profits. Thus, even as Brazil and Ar-gentina were taking over their railroads and older industries, the major industrial countries con-trolled the diffusion of the newer aviation and ra-dio technologies.

The Depression and the Vargas Regime in Brazil

The Depression hit Latin America as hard as it hit Europe and the United States; in many ways, it marks a more important turning point for the region than either of the world wars. The sharp fall in the value of agricul-tural and mineral exports undermined the shaky political systems. Like European countries, Ar-gentina and Brazil veered toward authoritarian regimes that promised to solve their economic problems.

In 1930, **Getulio Vargas**° (1883–1953), a state governor, staged a coup and proclaimed himself president of Brazil. He proved to be a masterful politician. He wrote a new constitution that broad-ened the franchise and limited the president to one term. He raised import duties and promoted na-tional firms and state-owned enterprises, culmi-nating in the construction of the Volta Redonda steel mill in the 1930s. By 1936, industrial produc-tion had doubled, especially in textiles and small manufactures. Brazil was on its way to becom-ing an industrial country. Vargas's policy, called **import-substitution industrialization,** became a model for other Latin American countries as they attempted to break away from neocolonial de-pendency.

The industrialization of Brazil brought all the familiar environmental consequences. Powerful new machines allowed the reopening of old mines and the digging of new ones. Cities grew as poor peasants looking for work arrived from the coun-tryside. Around the older neighborhoods of Rio de Janeiro° and São Paulo°, the poor turned steep hill-sides and vacant lands into immense slums.

The countryside also was transformed. Scrub-land was turned into pasture, and new acreage was

---

Hipólito Irigoyen (ee-POH-lee-toe ee-ree-GO-yen)

Getulio Vargas (jay-TOO-lee-oh VAR-gus)
Rio de Janeiro (REE-oh day zhuh-NAIR-oh)
São Paulo (sow PAL-oh)

planted in wheat, corn, and sugar cane. Even the Amazon rain forest—half of the land area of Brazil—was affected. American industrialist Henry Ford invested $8 million to clear land for the world's largest rubber plantation. Although Brazilian opposition and rubber-tree diseases forced Ford to abandon the project, the project was a forerunner of the degradation that the Amazon forest would suffer later in the century.

Vargas instituted many reforms favorable to urban workers, such as labor unions, pension plans, and disability insurance, but he refused to take any measures that might help the millions of landless peasants or harm the interests of the great landowners. Because the benefits of Brazil's economic recovery were so unequally distributed, communist and fascist movements demanded even more radical changes.

In 1938, prohibited by his own constitution from being reelected, Vargas staged another coup, abolished the constitution, and instituted the Estado Novo°, or "New State," with himself as supreme leader. He abolished political parties, jailed opposition leaders, and turned Brazil into a fascist state. When the Second World War broke out, however, Vargas aligned Brazil with the United States and contributed troops and ships to the Allied war effort. Vargas was himself overthrown in 1945 by a military coup.

Argentina After 1930

Economically, the Depression hurt Argentina almost as badly as it hurt Brazil. Politically, it triggered a military overthrow of the popularly elected President Irigoyen in 1930. The new government represented the large landowners and big business interests. For thirteen years, the generals and the oligarquía ruled, doing nothing to lessen the poverty of the workers or the frustrations of the middle class. When World War II broke out, Argentina sympathized with the Axis but remained officially neutral.

In 1943, another military revolt, led by Colonel **Juan Perón**° (1895–1974), took place. Once in power, the officers took over the highest positions in government and business. Inspired by Nazi victories, their goal was nothing less than the conquest of South America. As the war turned against the Nazis, the officers saw their popularity collapse.

Perón, however, had other plans. Inspired by his charismatic wife **Eva Duarte Perón** (1919–1952), he appealed to the urban workers. Eva Perón became the champion of the *descamisados*°, or "shirtless ones," and campaigned tirelessly for social benefits and for the cause of women and children. With his wife's help, Perón won the presidency in 1946 and created a populist dictatorship in imitation of the Vargas regime in Brazil.

Like Brazil, Argentina industrialized rapidly under state sponsorship. Perón spent lavishly on social welfare projects as well as on the military, depleting the capital that Argentina had earned during the war. Though a skillful demagogue who played off the army against the navy and both against the labor unions, Perón could not create a stable government out of the chaos of coups and conspiracies. After Eva died in 1952, he lost his political skills (or perhaps they were hers), and soon Perón was overthrown in yet another military coup.

CONCLUSION

Sub-Saharan Africa, India, and Latin America lay outside the theaters of war that engulfed most of the Northern Hemisphere, but they were deeply affected by global events and by the demands of the industrial powers. Sub-Saharan Africa and India were still under colonial rule, and their political life revolved around the yearnings of their elites for political independence and their masses for social justice. Mexico, Argentina, and Brazil were politically independent, but economically they were also closely tied to the industrial nations with which they traded. Their deeply polarized societies and the stresses caused by their dependence on

---

Estado Novo (esh-TAH-doe NO-vo)
Juan Perón (hoo-AHN pair-OWN)

---

descamisados (des-cah-mee-SAH-dohs)

the industrial countries clashed with the expectations of ever larger numbers of their peoples.

In Mexico, these stresses brought about a long and violent revolution, out of which Mexicans forged a lasting sense of national identity. Argentina and Brazil moved toward greater economic independence, but at the price of militarism and dictatorship. In India, the conflict between growing expectations and the reality of colonial rule produced both a movement for independence and an ethnic split that tore the nation apart. In sub-Saharan Africa, demands for national self-determination and economic development were only beginning to be voiced by 1949.

Nationalism and the yearning for social justice were the two most powerful forces for change in the early twentieth century. These ideas originated in the industrialized countries but resonated in the independent countries of Latin America as well as in colonial regions such as the Indian subcontinent and sub-Saharan Africa. However, they did not always unite people against their colonial rulers or foreign oppressors; instead, they often divided them along social, ethnic, or religious lines. Western-educated elites looked to industrialization as a means of modernizing their country and ensuring their position in it, while peasants and urban workers supported nationalist and revolutionary movements in the hope of improving their lives. Often these goals were not compatible.

■ Key Terms

African National Congress

Haile Selassie

Indian National Congress

Bengal

All-India Muslim League

Mohandas K. (Mahatma) Gandhi

Jawaharlal Nehru

Muhammad Ali Jinnah

Emiliano Zapata

Francisco "Pancho" Villa

Lázaro Cárdenas

Getulio Vargas

import-substitution industrialization

Juan Perón

Eva Duarte Perón

■ Suggested Reading

Two excellent general introductions to Africa are Roland Oliver and Anthony Atmore, *Africa since 1800*, 4th ed. (1994), and A. E. Afigbo et al., *The Making of Modern Africa*, vol. 2, *The Twentieth Century* (1986). Outstanding novels about Africa in the colonial era include Chinua Achebe, *Arrow of God* (1964); Buchi Emecheta, *The Joys of Motherhood* (1980); and Peter Abraham, *Mine Boy* (1946).

For a general introduction to Indian history, see Sumit Sarkar, *Modern India, 1885–1947* (1983), and Percival Spear, *India: A Modern History*, rev. ed. (1972). On the influenza epidemic of 1918–1919, see Alfred W. Crosby, *America's Forgotten Pandemic: The Influenza of 1918* (1989). The Indian independence movement has received a great deal of attention. Judith M. Brown's most recent book on Gandhi is *Gandhi: Prisoner of Hope* (1989). *Gandhi's Truth: On the Origin of Militant Nonviolence* (1969), by noted psychoanalyst Erik Erikson, is also recommended. The environment is discussed in M. Gadgil and R. Guha, *This Fissured Land: An Ecological History of India* (1993).

Thomas Skidmore and Peter Smith, *Modern Latin America*, 3d ed. (1992), offer the best brief introduction. On the Mexican Revolution, two books are essential: Alan Knight, *The Mexican Revolution*, 2 vols. (1986), and John M. Hart, *Revolutionary Mexico: The Coming and Process of the Mexican Revolution* (1987). The standard work on Brazil is E. Bradford Burns, *A History of Brazil*, 3d ed. (1993). The history of modern Argentina is ably treated in David Rock, *Argentina, 1517–1987: From Spanish Colonization to Alfonsín* (1987). Mark Jefferson, *Peopling the Argentine Pampas* (1971), and Jeremy Adelman, *Frontier Development: Land, Labour and Capital on the Wheatlands of Argentina and Canada, 1890–1914* (1994), describe the transformation of the Argentinean environment.

PART EIGHT

THE PERILS AND PROMISES OF A GLOBAL COMMUNITY, 1945–2001

CHAPTER 28
THE COLD WAR AND DECOLONIZATION, 1945–1975

CHAPTER 29
CRISIS, REALIGNMENT, AND THE DAWN OF THE POST–COLD WAR WORLD, 1975–1991

CHAPTER 30
THE END OF A GLOBAL CENTURY, 1991–2001

The notion of a postwar era in which all the world's peoples could rejoice in the defeat of totalitarianism became increasingly hollow as the Cold War set in between the United States and the Soviet Union and more and more peoples engaged in struggles for national independence. From 1945 to 1991, conflicts between communist and noncommunist forces in emerging nations repeatedly involved the superpowers, sometimes as arms suppliers or allies, sometimes as combatants. The Korean War and the Vietnam War engaged American troops; the Soviet Union became bogged down in a war in Afghanistan. Leaders of the Third World, a group of states proclaiming nonalignment in the Cold War, tried to advance their state-building programs by playing off the United States against the Soviet Union and gaining favors from both sides.

A turning point of sorts arrived around 1975. Escalating oil prices, provoked by conflicts in the Middle East, shook the world's economic foundations. The major nuclear powers began to recognize the futility of the arms race. The countries of East Asia rapidly industrialized. And the attitudes of young people around the world increasingly clashed with those of the parental, World War II, generation.

In the relatively nonindustrialized parts of the world, population grew rapidly. Governments in Latin America, Africa, South Asia, China, and the Middle East faced serious problems in providing the necessities of life. The extension of agriculture and other pressures on resources sped the deterioration of the environment.

The dissemination of new technologies, ranging from "green revolution" agricultural practices to consumer electronics, transformed daily life. Regional cultures, many of them religiously based, felt threatened by the spread of Western consumer society and entertainment. The vision of a global culture excited some people while repelling others.

Formal relations among groups of states—the United Nations, Cold War alliances, and free trade agreements—brought the world's peoples closer together than ever before. With the emergence of a truly global community, peacekeeping, human rights, and gender equality became international issues.

The rapid collapse of the Soviet Empire beginning in 1989 also ended the overarching political and economic struggles of the Cold War. Global debates refocused variously on the global expansion of trade and high technology, on the widening gap between the rich nation of the North and the miserably poor South, and on growing degradation of the environment. Another perspective on globalization seized the world's attention on September 11, 2001, when Islamic terrorists attacked the symbols of America's global economic and political power. Was this another turning point? If so, only time would tell in what direction.

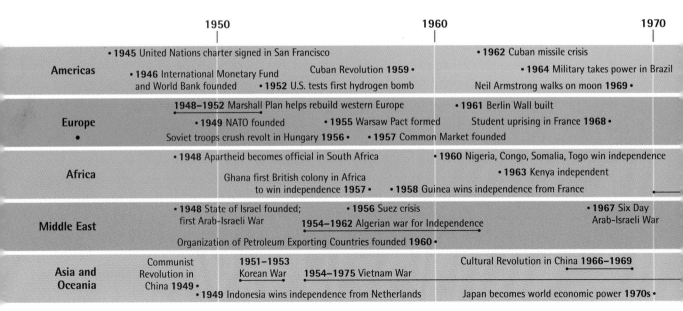

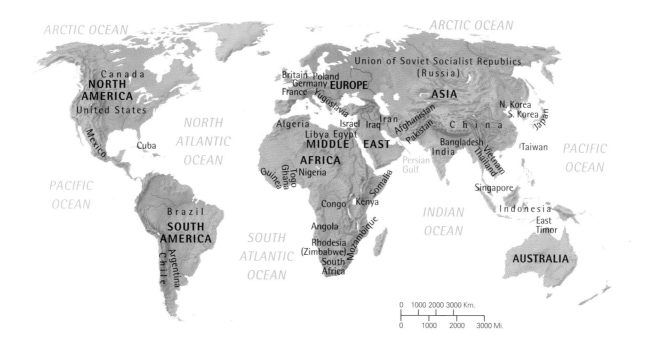

	1980	1990	2000

• **1973** Military coup overthrows Allende in Chile

       • **1976** Military takes
       power in Argentina

1983–1989 Democracy
restored in Brazil, Argentina, Chile

NAFTA agreement among
Canada, U.S., Mexico **1994** •

     1994 Maya uprising
     • in southern Mexico

Terrorists destroy
World Trade Center **2001** •

• **1975** Helsinki Accords

Solidarity union founded
in Poland **1980** •

Fall of communist regimes
in eastern Europe **1989** •

     End of USSR **1990** •

• **1990** Reunification of Germany

Introduction of euro **1999** •

1992–2000 Disintegration of Yugoslavia

• **1975** Angola and Mozambique win independence from Portugal

White domination of Rhodesia yields to
international pressure **1970–1980**

     • **1985** Africa equals Europe in population

1994–1999 Nelson Mandela
president of South Africa

• **1973** October Arab-Israeli War leads
to oil embargo, price hikes

     • **1979** Islamic Revolution overthrows shah of Iran

     1980–1988 Iran-Iraq War

• **1991** Persian Gulf War

U.S. invasion of
Afghanistan **2001** •

Average Japanese income exceeds average U.S. income **1986** •

     • **1980s** Taiwan, South Korea, Singapore industrialize

• **1971** Independence of Bangladesh

     • **1979** USSR enters war in Afghanistan

• **1989** Chinese troops suppress Tiananmen Square protest

East Timor independent from Indonesia **1999** •

Asian financial crisis starts in Thailand **1997** •

28

The Cold War and Decolonization,

1945–1975

Decolonization and Nation Building • The Cold War •
Beyond a Bipolar World
ENVIRONMENT AND TECHNOLOGY: The Green Revolution

n 1946, in a speech at Fulton, Missouri, Great Britain's wartime leader Winston Churchill declared that "an iron curtain has descended across the Continent [of Europe]. . . . I am convinced there is nothing they [the communists] so much admire as strength, and there is nothing for which they have less respect than weakness, especially military weakness." The phrase **"iron curtain"** became a watchword of the **Cold War,** the state of political tension and military rivalry that was then beginning between the United States and its allies and the Soviet Union and its allies.

In the early years of World War II, Churchill and President Franklin Roosevelt had looked forward to a postwar world of economic cooperation and restoration of sovereignty to peoples suffering Axis occupation and, above all, to a world where war and territorial conquest would not be tolerated. By the time Churchill delivered his "iron curtain" speech, however, Britain's electorate had voted him out of power, Harry S

Truman had succeeded to the presidency after Roosevelt's death, and the Soviet Union was dominating eastern Europe and supporting communist movements in China, Iran, Turkey, Greece, and Korea. Although Soviet diplomats sat with their former allies in the newly founded United Nations Organization, confrontation rather than cooperation was the hallmark of relations between East and West.

The intensity of the Cold War sometimes obscured a postwar phenomenon of even greater importance. Western domination of Asia, Africa, and Latin America was largely ended, and the colonial empires of the New Imperialism were gradually dismantled. A new generation of national leaders sometimes skillfully played Cold War antagonism to their own advantage. Their real business, however, was the difficult task of nation building.

Each land freeing itself from imperialism had its own specific history and conditions. After independence, some new nations sided openly with the United States and some with the Soviet Union. Others banded together in a posture of neutrality and spoke with one voice about their need for economic and technical assistance and the obligation of the wealthy nations to satisfy those needs.

The Cold War military rivalry stimulated extraordinary advances in weaponry and associated technologies, but many new nations struggled to educate their citizens, nurture industry, and escape the economic constraints imposed by their former imperialist masters. The environment suffered severe pressures, whether from oil exploration and transport to feed the growing economies of the wealthy nations or from deforestation in poor regions challenged by the need for cropland. Neither rich nor poor realized the costs associated with environmental change.

As you read this chapter, ask yourself the following questions:

• What impact did economic philosophy have on both the Cold War and the decolonization movement?

• How was a third world war averted?

• Was world domination by the superpowers good or bad for the rest of the world?

Decolonization and Nation Building

W hereas the losing countries in World War I were stripped of colonies, it was primarily countries on the winning side in World War II that ended up losing their colonies (see Map 28.1).

Circumstances differed profoundly from place to place. In some Asian countries, where colonial rule was of long standing, newly independent states found themselves in possession of viable industries, communications networks, and education systems. In other countries, notably in Africa, decolonization gave birth to nations facing dire economic problems and internal disunity. In Latin America, where political independence already had been achieved, the quest was for freedom from foreign economic domination, particularly by the United States.

New Nations in Southern Asia

Newly independent India and Pakistan were strikingly dissimilar. Muslim Pakistan defined itself according to religion and quickly fell under the control of military leaders. Though 90 percent Hindu, the much larger republic of India, led by Prime Minister Jawaharlal Nehru, was secular. It inherited most of the considerable industrial and educational resources the British had developed, along with the larger share of trained civil servants and military officers.

The decision of the Hindu ruler of the northwestern state of Jammu and Kashmir to join India without consulting his overwhelmingly Muslim subjects led to a war between India and Pakistan in 1947 that ended with an uneasy truce, only to resume briefly in 1965. Though Kashmir remains a flashpoint of patriotic feeling, the two countries managed to avoid further warfare.

Despite recurrent predictions that multilingual India might break up into a number of linguistically homogeneous states, most Indians recognized that unity benefited everyone; and the country pursued a generally democratic and socialist line of development. Pakistan, in contrast, did break up. In 1971, its Bengali-speaking eastern section seceded to become the independent country of Bangladesh.

Elsewhere in the region, nationalist movements won independence as well. Britain granted independence to Burma (now Myanmar°) in 1948 and established the Malay Federation that same year. (Singapore, once a member of the federation, became an independent city-state itself in 1965.)

Myanmar (myahn-MAH)

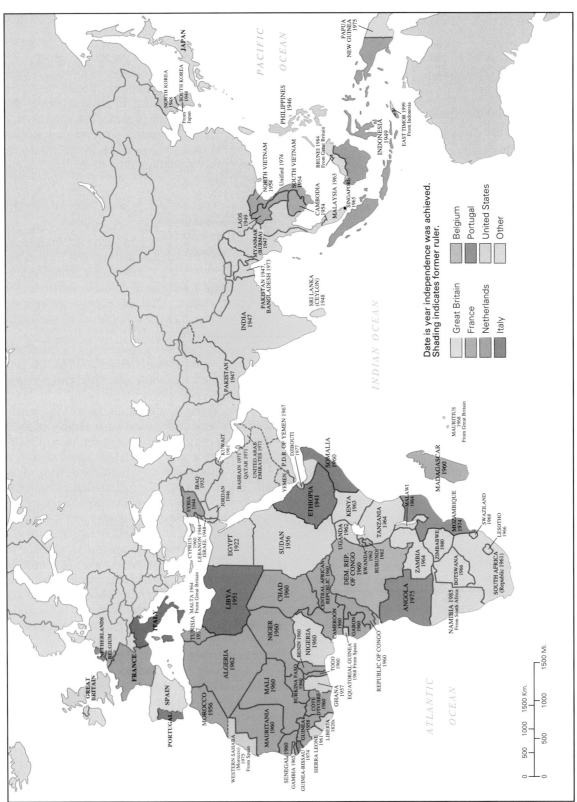

Map 28.1 Decolonization, 1947–1990 Notice that independence came a decade or so earlier in South and Southeast Asia than in Africa. Numerous countries that gained independence after World War II in the Caribbean, in South and Central America, and in the Pacific are not shown.

CHRONOLOGY

	Cold War	Decolonization
1945		
	1948–1949 Berlin airlift	**1947** Partition of India
	1949 NATO formed	**1949** Dutch withdraw from Indonesia
	1950–1953 Korean War	
	1952 United States detonates first hydrogen bomb	
		1954 CIA intervention in Guatemala; defeat at Dienbienphu ends French hold on Vietnam
1955	**1955** Warsaw Pact concluded	**1955** Bandung Conference
	1956 Soviet Union suppresses Hungarian revolt	
	1957 Soviet Union launches first artificial satellite into earth orbit	**1957** Ghana becomes first British colony in Africa to gain independence
		1959 Fidel Castro leads revolution in Cuba
		1960 Shootings in Sharpeville intensify South African struggle against apartheid; Nigeria becomes independent
	1961 East Germany builds Berlin Wall	
		1962 Algeria wins independence
1965		
		1971 Bangladesh secedes from Pakistan
1975	**1975** Helsinki Accords; end of Vietnam War	

In 1946, the United States kept its promise of postwar independence for the Philippine Islands but retained close economic ties and leases on military bases. In the Dutch East Indies, Sukarno (1901–1970) had cooperated with the Japanese occupation in hopes that the Dutch would never return. After a military confrontation, Dutch withdrawal was finally negotiated in 1949, and Sukarno went on to become the dictator of his resource-rich but underdeveloped nation of Indonesia.

In all these cases, communist insurgents plagued the departing colonial powers and the newly formed governments. The most important postwar communist movement arose in the part of Southeast Asia known as French Indochina. There, Ho Chi Minh° (1890–1969), who had spent several years in France during World War I, played the piv-

otal role. After training in Moscow, he returned to Vietnam to found the Indochina Communist Party in 1930.

Ho Chi Minh's nationalist coalition, then called the Viet Minh, fought the French with help from the People's Republic of China. After a brutal struggle, the French stronghold of Dienbienphu° fell in 1954, marking the doom of France's colonial enterprise. Ho's Viet Minh government took over in the north, and a noncommunist nationalist government ruled in the south. Fighting between North and South Vietnam eventually became a major Cold War conflict.

Ho Chi Minh (hoe chee min)

Dienbienphu (dyen-byen-phu)

The Struggle for Independence in Africa

In the quarter-century between 1955 and 1980, African nationalists succeeded in ending European colonial rule. Mostly they gained their independence peacefully, but where European settlers were numerous, violence became the norm.

Algeria rebelled in 1954. The French government was as determined to hold on to Algeria as it had been to keep Vietnam. Ten percent of the Algerian population was European, and Algeria's economy was strongly oriented toward France. Both sides pursued the revolt with great brutality. When the Algerians finally won independence in 1962, the flood of angry colonists returning to France undermined the Algerian economy because very few Arabs had received technical training or acquired management experience.

None of the independence movements in sub-Saharan Africa matched the Algerian struggle in scale. Some of the politicians who led the nationalist movements had devoted their lives to ridding their homelands of foreign occupation. An example is Kwame Nkrumah° (1909–1972), who in 1957 became prime minister of Ghana (formerly the Gold Coast), the first British colony in Africa to achieve independence. Only a few hundred Ghanaian children of Nkrumah's generation had graduated each year from the seven-year elementary schools, and he was one of only a handful who made it through teacher training college. After graduation, he spent a decade reading philosophy and theology in the United States and absorbing ideas about black pride and independence then being propounded by black leaders W. E. B. Du Bois and Marcus Garvey.

After a brief stay in Britain, Nkrumah returned in 1947 to the Gold Coast to work for independence. The time was right. Great Britain had already freed its Asian colonies, and Nkrumah quickly united the people of Ghana behind him. Independence thus came without war or protracted bloodshed. Nkrumah turned out to be more effective internationally as a spokesman for colonized peoples than he was at home as an ad-

French Soldiers on Patrol in Algeria   The Algerian war was one of the most savage struggles for independence in the era of decolonization. The French held out a more secular, Western-style view of life but did not hesitate to intrude into homes and residential areas in search of their enemies. At independence in 1961, most Algerian leaders spoke French more readily than Arabic.   (Marc Riboud/ Magnum Photos, Inc.)

ministrator. In 1966, a group of army officers ousted him.

Jomo Kenyatta (ca. 1894–1978) traveled a more difficult road in Kenya, where a substantial number of European coffee planters strengthened Britain's desire to retain control. A movement the settlers called Mau Mau, formed mostly by the Kikuyu° people, became active in 1952. As violence between settlers and movement fighters escalated, British troops hunted down the leaders and reset-

---

Kwame Nkrumah (KWAH-mee nn-KROO-muh)

Kikuyu (kih-KOO-you)

tled the Kikuyu. The British charged Kenyatta with being a Mau Mau leader and held him in prison and then in internal exile for eight years during a declared state of emergency. They released him in 1961, and negotiations with the British to write a constitution for an independent Kenya followed. In 1964, Kenyatta was elected the first president of the Republic of Kenya. He proved to be an effective, though autocratic, ruler.

In contrast, African leaders in the French colonies of sub-Saharan Africa were slow to call for independence. They visualized change in terms of promises of greater political and civil rights made in 1944 by the Free French movement of General Charles de Gaulle. This Brazzaville Conference also had promised to expand French education at the village level, to improve health services, and to open more lower-level administrative positions to Africans, but the word *independence* was never mentioned.

African politicians also realized that some French colonies—such as Ivory Coast with its coffee and cacao exports, fishing, and hardwood forests—had good economic prospects and others, such as land-locked, desert Niger, did not. As a Malagasy politician said in 1958, "When I let my heart talk, I am a partisan of total and immediate independence [for Madagascar]; when I make my reason speak, I realize that it is impossible." Ultimately, however, the heart prevailed everywhere. Guinea, under the dynamic leadership of Sékou Touré°, led the way in 1958. By the time Nigeria, the most populous West African state, achieved independence from Great Britain in 1960, the leaders of many former French colonies in West Africa could attend the celebrations as independent heads of state.

European settlers fought hard to hold on in southern Africa. The African struggle against Portuguese rule in Angola and Mozambique dragged on until frustrated Portuguese military commanders overthrew the government of Portugal in 1974 and granted the African colonies independence the following year. After a ten-year fight, European settlers in the British colony of Southern Rhodesia ceded power in 1980 to the African majority, who

renamed the country Zimbabwe. The change had been swift; a century after the "scramble" for Africa began, European colonial rule in Africa had ended.

Only South Africa and neighboring Southwest Africa remained in the hands of European minorities. After World War II, the white minority government had reconstructed South Africa along extreme racial separation, or *apartheid*°. The cities, the best jobs, and most of the land were reserved for Europeans. Africans and others classified as "nonwhites" were subjected to strict limitations on place of residence, right to travel, and access to jobs and public facilities.

The African National Congress (ANC), formed in 1912, led the fight against apartheid and in favor of a nonracial society. After police fired on demonstrators in the African town of Sharpeville in 1960, an African lawyer named Nelson Mandela (b. 1918) organized guerrilla resistance by the ANC. Mandela was sentenced to life in prison in 1964 (see in Chapter 30 Society and Culture: Nelson Mandela) and the government outlawed the ANC and other opposition organizations. For a time, things were quiet, but in 1976 young students reignited the bloody and prolonged struggle that would force an end to apartheid.

The Quest for Economic Freedom in Latin America

In Latin America, the postwar decades saw continuing struggles over foreign ownership and social inequality. American and European companies dominated Chile's copper, Cuba's sugar and resort hotels, Colombia's coffee, Guatemala's bananas, and the communications networks of several countries. Even in a country like Mexico, where the ruling Institutional Revolutionary Party, or PRI, was officially committed to revolutionary independence and economic development, a yawning gulf between rich and poor, urban and rural, persisted. According to one estimate from the mid-1960s, not more than 300 foreign and 800 Mexican companies dominated the country, and some 2,000 families made up the

Sékou Touré (SAY-koo too-RAY)

apartheid (uh-PART-hate)

industrial-financial elite. At the other end of the economic scale were peasants and the 14 percent of the population classified as Indian.

Jacobo Arbenz Guzmán, elected president of Guatemala in 1951, was typical of Latin American leaders who tried to confront the power of foreign interests. His expropriation of large estates angered the United Fruit Company, a U.S. corporation that dominated banana exports and held vast tracts of land in reserve. Reacting to reports that Arbenz was becoming friendly toward communism, the United States Central Intelligence Agency (CIA) prompted a takeover by the Guatemalan military in 1954. CIA intervention removed Arbenz from the scene; it also condemned Guatemala to decades of governmental instability and growing violence between leftist and rightist elements in society.

In Cuba, U.S. companies owned 40 percent of raw sugar production, 23 percent of nonsugar industry, 90 percent of telephone and electrical services, and 50 percent of public service railways. The needs of the U.S. economy largely determined Cuban foreign trade and held back development. Profits went north to the United States or to a small class of wealthy Cubans, many of foreign origin. Cuba's ruler during that period, Fulgencio Batista, became a symbol of corruption, repression, and foreign economic domination.

In 1959, a popular rebellion forced Batista to flee the country. Fidel Castro, the lawyer leader of the rebels, his brother Raoul Castro, and Ernesto "Che" Guevara°, who was the main theorist of communist revolution in Latin America, created a new regime. Within a year, Fidel Castro's government redistributed land, lowered urban rents, and raised wages, effectively transferring 15 percent of the national income from rich to poor. Within twenty-two months, the Castro government seized almost all U.S. property in Cuba and most Cuban corporations. This action resulted in a blockade by the United States, the flight of middle-class and technically trained Cubans, a drop in foreign investment, and the beginning of chronic food shortages.

Little evidence supports the view that Castro undertook his revolution to install a communist government. But at that time, the East-West rivalry of the Cold War was increasingly influencing international politics, and Castro soon turned to the Soviet Union for economic aid. In doing so, he unwittingly committed his nation to economic stagnation and dependence on a foreign power as damaging as the previous relationship with the United States had been.

In April 1961, some fifteen hundred Cuban exiles, whom the CIA had trained for a year in Guatemala, landed at the Bay of Pigs in an effort to overthrow Castro. The Cuban army defeated the attempted invasion in a matter of days, partly because the new U.S. president, John F. Kennedy, decided not to provide all the air support that the plan originally called for. The failure of the Bay of Pigs invasion tarnished the reputation of the United States and the CIA and provoked Castro into declaring that he and his revolution were and always had been Marxist-Leninist.

THE COLD WAR

As decolonization was altering one set of old relationships, relations among powerful nations were also changing. The wartime alliance between the United States, Great Britain, and the Soviet Union had been an uneasy one. American and British leaders committed to free markets and untrammeled capital investment had loathed socialism in its several forms for more than a century. After World War II, the iron curtain in Europe and communist insurgencies in China and elsewhere seemed to confirm the threat of worldwide revolution.

To protect themselves from the Soviet Union, which they perceived as the nerve center of world revolution and as a military power capable of launching a terrible new war, the United States and the countries of western Europe established the **North Atlantic Treaty Organization (NATO)** military alliance in 1949. But Soviet leaders felt themselves surrounded by hostile forces just when they

---

Che Guevara (chay guh-VAHR-uh)

were trying to recover from the terrible losses sustained in the war. The distrust and suspicion between the two sides played out on a worldwide stage.

The United Nations

In 1944, representatives from the United States, Great Britain, the Soviet Union, and China met and drafted specific charter proposals that finally bore fruit in the United Nations Charter, a treaty ratified on October 24, 1945. Like the League of Nations, the **United Nations** had two main bodies: the General Assembly, with representatives from all member states; and the Security Council, with five permanent members—China, France, Great Britain, the United States, and the Soviet Union—and seven rotating members. Various United Nations agencies focused on specialized international problems—for example, UNICEF (United Nations Children's Emergency Fund), FAO (Food and Agriculture Organization) and UNESCO (United Nations Educational, Scientific and Cultural Organization) (see Environment and Technology: The Green Revolution). The United Nations operated by majority vote, except that the five permanent members of the Security Council had veto power in that chamber.

All signatories to the United Nations Charter renounced war and territorial conquest. Nevertheless, peacekeeping, the sole preserve of the Security Council, became a vexing problem. The permanent members often exercised their veto to protect their friends and interests, though from time to time they authorized the United Nations to send observers or peacekeeping forces to monitor truces or agreements.

The decolonization of Africa and Asia greatly swelled the size of the General Assembly but not the Security Council. Many of the new nations looked to the United Nations for material assistance and access to a wider political world. While the vetoes of the Security Council's permanent members often stymied actions touching even indirectly on Cold War concerns, the General Assembly became an arena for expressing opinions on many issues involving decolonization, a movement that the Soviet Union strongly encouraged but the Western colonial powers resisted.

In the early years of the United Nations, General Assembly resolutions carried great weight. An example is a 1947 resolution that sought to divide Palestine into sovereign Jewish and Arab states. Gradually, though, the flood of new members produced a voting majority concerned more with poverty, racial discrimination, and the struggle against imperialism than with the Cold War. As a result, the Western powers increasingly disregarded the General Assembly, allowing the new nations of the world to have their say but not to act collectively.

Capitalism and Communism

In July 1944, with Allied victory a forgone conclusion, economic specialists representing over forty countries met at Bretton Woods, a New Hampshire resort, to devise a new international monetary system. The signatories eventually agreed to fix exchange rates. They also created the International Monetary Fund (IMF) to use currency reserves from member nations to finance temporary trade deficits and the **World Bank** to provide funds for reconstructing Europe and helping needy countries.

The Soviet Union attended the Bretton Woods Conference and signed the agreements, but by 1946, suspicion between the Soviet Union and the United States and Britain had deepened. While the rest of the world moved to a monetary system that relied for stability on most countries holding reserves of dollars and the United States holding reserves of gold, the Soviet Union established a closed monetary system for itself and the new communist regimes in eastern Europe. In the Western countries, supply and demand determined prices; in the Soviet command economy, government priorities and agencies allocated goods and set prices, irrespective of market forces.

Many leaders from the newly independent states preferred the Soviet Union's socialist example to the capitalism of their former colonizers. Thus, the relative success of economies patterned on Eastern or Western models became an element

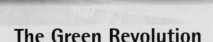

The Green Revolution

Concern about world food supplies grew directly out of the serious shortages that many nations faced because of the devastation and trade disruptions of World War II. The Food and Agriculture Organization of the United Nations, the Rockefeller Foundation, and the Ford Foundation took leading roles in fostering crop research and educating farmers about agricultural techniques. In 1966, the International Rice Research Institute (established in 1960–1962) began distributing seeds for an improved rice variety known as IR-8. Crop yields from this and other new varieties, along with improved farming techniques, were so impressive that the term *Green Revolution* was coined to describe a new era in agricultural history.

On the heels of the successful new rice strains came new varieties of corn and wheat. Building on twenty years of Rockefeller-funded research in Mexico, the Centro Internacional de Mejoramiento de Maiz y Trigo (International Center for the Improvement of Maize and Wheat) was established in 1966 under Norman Borlaug, who was awarded the Nobel Peace Prize four years later. This organization distributed around the world short, stiff-strawed varieties of wheat that were resistant to disease and responsive to fertilizer.

By 1970, other centers for research on tropical agriculture had been established in Ibadan, Nigeria, and Cali, Colombia. But the success of the Green Revolution and the growing need for its products called for a more comprehensive effort. The Consultative Group on International Agricultural Research brought together World Bank expertise, private foundations, international organizations, and national foreign aid agencies to undertake worldwide support of efforts to increase food productivity and improve natural resource management.

Miracle Rice New strains of so-called miracle rice made many nations in South and Southeast Asia self-sufficient in food production after decades of worry about the growth of population outstripping agricultural productivity.
(Victor Englebert)

in the Cold War rivalry. Each side trumpeted economic successes measured by such things as industrial output, changes in per capita income, and productivity gains as evidence of its superiority.

During World War II, increased military spending and the draft brought full employment and high wages to the United States. With peace, the United States enjoyed prosperity and an international competitive advantage, while European economies were still heavily damaged from the war. To support European reconstruction, the U.S. **Marshall Plan** provided $12.5 billion to friendly countries between 1948 and 1952. By 1963, a resurgent European economy had doubled 1940 output.

Western European governments generally increased their role in economic management during this period. In Great Britain, the Labour Party government of the 1950s nationalized coal, steel, railroads, and health care. The French government nationalized public utilities; the auto, banking, and insurance industries; and parts of the mining industry.

In 1948, European governments also promoted economic cooperation and integration with the creation of the Organization of European Economic Cooperation (OEEC). After cooperative policies on coal and steel proved successful, some OEEC countries were ready to begin lowering tariffs to encourage the movement of goods and capital. In 1957, France, West Germany, Italy, the Netherlands, Belgium, and Luxembourg signed a treaty creating the European Economic Community, also known as the Common Market. By the 1970s, the Common Market nations had nearly overtaken the United States in industrial production. The economic alliance expanded after 1970, as Great Britain, Denmark, Greece, Ireland, Spain, Portugal, Finland, Sweden, and Austria joined. The enlarged alliance called itself the **European Community (EC).**

Prosperity brought dramatic changes to European society. Average wages increased, unemployment fell, and social welfare benefits were expanded. Governments increased spending on health care, unemployment benefits, old age pensions, public housing, and grants to poor families with children. The combination of economic growth and income redistribution raised living standards and fueled demand for consumer goods.

The Soviet experience provided a dramatic contrast. The economy of the Soviet Union was just as devastated at the end of the Second World War as those of western Europe. However, with enormous natural resources, a large population, and abundant energy at its disposal, Soviet recovery was rapid at first. Moreover, Soviet planners had made large investments in technical and scientific education, and the Soviet state had developed heavy industry in the 1930s and during the war years. But as the postwar period progressed, bureaucratic control of the economy grew less efficient. In the 1970s, the gap with the West widened. The Soviet economy failed to meet domestic demand for clothing, housing, food, automobiles, and consumer electronics. Agricultural inefficiency forced the Soviet Union to rely on food imports.

The socialist nations of eastern Europe were compelled to follow the Soviet economic model, although some national differences appeared. Poland and Hungary, for example, implemented agricultural collectivization more slowly than did Czechoslovakia. Significant growth occurred among the socialist economies, but the inefficiencies and failures that plagued the Soviet economy troubled them as well.

The United States and the Soviet Union competed in providing loans and grants and in supplying arms (at bargain prices) to countries willing to align with them politically. Thus, the relative success or failure of capitalism and communism in Europe and the United States was not necessarily the strongest consideration in other parts of the world when the time came to construct new national economies.

West Versus East in Europe and Korea

For many countries, peace brought foreign military occupation and new governments installed and controlled by the occupiers. The Soviet Union's military occupation facilitated communist victories in eastern Europe. The United States occupied Japan. Korea and Germany were divided among the Allies.

For the United States, the shift from viewing the Soviet Union as an ally against Germany to seeing it as a worldwide enemy took two years. In the waning days of World War II, the United States had seemed amenable to the Soviet desire for freer access to the Mediterranean through Turkish straits. But in July 1947, the **Truman Doctrine** offered military aid to help both Turkey and Greece resist Soviet military pressure and subversion. In 1951, Greece and Turkey were admitted to NATO. NATO's Soviet counterpart, the **Warsaw Pact,** emerged in 1955 in response to the Western powers' decision to allow West Germany to rearm within limits set by NATO (see Map 28.2).

The Soviet Union tested Western resolve in 1948–1949 by blockading the areas of Berlin occupied by British, French, and American forces, which were surrounded by Soviet-controlled East Germany. Airlifts of food and fuel defeated the blockade. In 1961, the East German government accentuated Germany's political division by building the Berlin Wall, as much to prevent its citizens from fleeing to the noncommunist western part of that city as to keep Westerners from entering East German territory. The West tested the East, in turn, by encouraging a rift between the Soviet Union and Yugoslavia. Western aid and encouragement resulted in Yugoslavia's signing a defensive treaty with Greece and Turkey (but not with NATO) and deciding against joining the Warsaw Pact.

Soviet power set clear limits on how far any eastern European country might stray from Soviet domination. In 1956, Soviet troops crushed an anti-Soviet revolt in Hungary. Czechoslovakia suffered Hungary's fate in 1968. The West, a passive onlooker, had no recourse but to acknowledge that the Soviet Union had the right to intervene in the domestic affairs of any Soviet-bloc nation whenever it wished.

A more explosive crisis erupted in Korea, where the Second World War had left Soviet troops in control north of the thirty-eighth parallel and American troops in control to the south. When no agreement could be reached on holding country-wide elections, communist North Korea and noncommunist South Korea became independent states in 1948. Two years later, North Korea invaded South Korea. The United Nations Security Council, in the absence of the Soviet delegation, voted to condemn the invasion and called on members of the United Nations to come to the defense of South Korea. The United States was the primary ally of South Korea. The People's Republic of China supported North Korea. The **Korean War** lasted until 1953 when the two sides eventually agreed to a truce along the thirty-eighth parallel, but no peace treaty was concluded.

Japan benefited from the Korean War in an unexpected way. Massive purchases of supplies by the United States and spending by American servicemen on leave provided a financial stimulus to the Japanese economy similar to the stimulus that Europe received from the Marshall Plan.

U.S. Defeat in Vietnam

A shooting war also developed in Vietnam. In 1954, United States president Dwight D. Eisenhower (1953–1961) and his foreign policy advisers decided not to aid France in its effort to sustain colonial rule in Vietnam, perceiving that the days of the European colonial empires were numbered. After winning independence, however, communist North Vietnam supported a guerrilla movement— the Viet Cong—against the noncommunist government of South Vietnam.

When John F. Kennedy became president (1961–1963), he and his advisers decided to support the South Vietnamese government of President Ngo Dinh Diem°. They realized that the Diem government was corrupt and unpopular, but they feared that a communist victory would encourage communist movements throughout Southeast Asia and alter the Cold War balance of power. Kennedy steadily increased the number of American military advisers from 685 to almost 16,000 while secretly encouraging the overthrow and execution of Diem in hopes of seeing a more popular and honest government come to power.

Lyndon Johnson, who became president (1963–1969) after Kennedy was assassinated, gained support from Congress for unlimited expansion of U.S. military deployment. By the end of 1966, 365,000 U.S. troops were engaged in the

Diem (dee-EM)

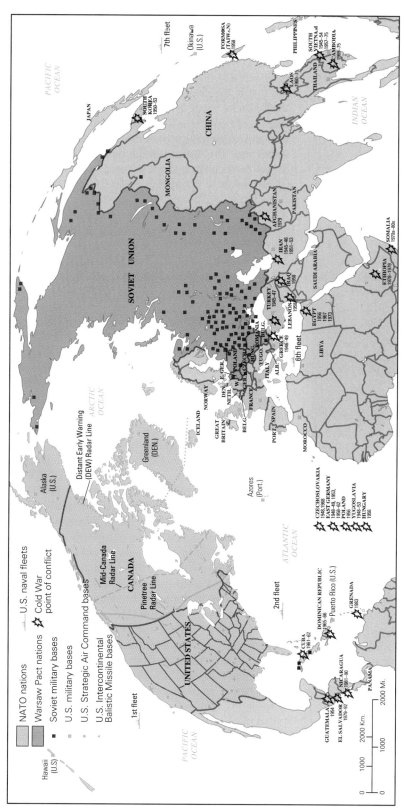

Map 28.2 Cold War Confrontation A polar projection is shown on this map because Soviet and U.S. strategists planned to attack one another by missile in the polar region, hence the Canadian–American radar lines. Military installations along the southern border of the Soviet Union were directed primarily at China.

The Vietnamese People at War   American and South Vietnamese troops burned many villages to deprive the enemy of civilian refuges. This policy undermined support for the South Vietnamese government in the countryside. (Dana Stone/ Black Star)

Vietnam War. Nothing the Americans tried, however, succeeded in stopping the Viet Cong guerrillas and their North Vietnamese allies. Diem's successors turned out to be just as corrupt and unpopular as he was, and the heroic nationalist image of North Vietnam's leader, Ho Chi Minh, evoked strong sympathies among many South Vietnamese.

In 1973, a treaty between North Vietnam and the United States ended U.S. involvement in the war and promised future elections. Two years later, in violation of the treaty, Viet Cong and North Vietnamese troops overran the South Vietnamese army and captured the southern capital of Saigon, re-

naming it Ho Chi Minh City. The two parts of Vietnam were reunited in a single state ruled from the north. The war was bloody and traumatic. The Vietnamese had over a million casualties. The deaths of fifty-eight thousand Americans overseas and the vigorous antiwar movement at home ensured that the United States would not easily be drawn into another shooting war.

The Race for Nuclear Supremacy

The devastation of Hiroshima and Nagasaki with atomic weapons had ushered in a new era. After the Soviet Union exploded its first nuclear device in 1949, fears of a worldwide holocaust grew and then became even greater when the United States exploded a far more powerful weapon, the hydrogen bomb, in 1952 and the Soviet Union followed suit less than a year later. The conviction that the nuclear superpowers were willing to use their terrible weapons if their vital interests were threatened spread despair around the world.

In 1954, President Eisenhower warned Soviet leaders against attacking western Europe. In response to such an attack, he said, the United States would reduce the Soviet Union to "a smoking, radiating ruin at the end of two hours." A few years later, the Soviet leader Nikita Khrushchev° offered an equally stark promise: "We will bury you." His reference was to economic competition, but the image produced in Americans was of literal burial.

Everyone's worst fears seemed about to be realized in the **Cuban missile crisis** of 1962. When the Soviet Union deployed nuclear-tipped missiles in Cuba in response to the U.S. installation of similar missiles in Turkey, the world held its breath. Confronted by unyielding diplomatic pressure and military threats from President Kennedy, Khrushchev backed down and pulled the missiles from Cuba. Subsequently, the United States removed its missiles from Turkey.

Arms limitation also saw progress. In 1963, Great Britain, the United States, and the Soviet Union agreed to ban the testing of nuclear

---

Khrushchev (KROOSH-chef)

weapons in the atmosphere, in space, and under water, thus reducing the environmental danger of radioactive fallout. In 1968, the United States and the Soviet Union together proposed a world treaty against further proliferation of nuclear weapons. It was signed by 137 countries. Not until 1972, however, did the two superpowers truly recognize the futility of squandering their wealth on ever-larger missile forces.

In Europe, the Soviet-American arms race outran the economic ability of atomic powers France and Britain to keep pace. Instead, the European states sought to relax tensions. Between 1972 and 1975, the Conference on Security and Cooperation in Europe (CSCE) brought delegates from thirty-seven European states, the United States, and Canada to Helsinki. The goal of the Soviet Union was to gain European acceptance of the political boundaries of the Warsaw Pact nations. The **Helsinki Accords** affirmed that no boundaries should be changed by military force. It also contained formal (but nonbinding) declarations calling for economic, social, and governmental contacts across the iron curtain, and for cooperation in humanitarian fields, a provision that paved the way for dialogue about human rights.

Space exploration was another offshoot of the nuclear arms race. The contest to build larger and more accurate missiles for delivery of warheads prompted the superpowers to prove their skills in rocketry by launching space satellites. The Soviet Union placed a small *Sputnik* satellite into orbit around the earth in October 1957. The United States responded with its own satellite three months later. The space race was on, a contest in which accomplishments in space were understood to signify equivalent achievements in the military sphere. *Sputnik* administered a deep shock to American pride and confidence, but in 1969 two Americans, Neil A. Armstrong and Edwin E. "Buzz" Aldrin, became the first humans to walk on the moon.

Despite rhetorical Cold War saber-rattling by Soviet and American leaders, the threat of nuclear war forced a measure of restraint on the superpower adversaries. Because fighting each other directly would have risked escalation to the level of nuclear exchange, they carefully avoided crises that might provoke such confrontations.

Beyond a Bipolar World

Although the East-West superpower rivalry dominated world affairs, newly independent states had concerns that were primarily domestic and regional. The challenge they faced was to find a way to pursue their ends within the bipolar structure of the Cold War—and possibly to take advantage of the East-West rivalry. In short, the superpowers dominated the world but did not control it. And as time progressed, they dominated it less and less.

The Third World

As one of the most successful leaders of the decolonization movement, Indonesia's President Sukarno was an appropriate figure to host a meeting in 1955 of twenty-nine African and Asian countries at Bandung, Indonesia. The conferees proclaimed solidarity among all peoples fighting against colonial rule. The Bandung Conference marked the beginning of an effort by the many new, poor, mostly non-European nations emerging from colonialism to gain more weight in world affairs by banding together. The terms **nonaligned nations** and **Third World,** which became commonplace in the following years, signaled these countries' collective stance toward the rival sides in the Cold War. If the West, led by the United States, and the East, led by the Soviet Union, represented two worlds locked in mortal struggle, the Third World consisted of everyone else.

Leaders of the so-called Third World countries preferred the label *nonaligned*, which signified freedom from membership on either side. However, because the Soviet Union supported national liberation movements and the nonaligned movement included communist countries such as China and Yugoslavia, many Western leaders did not take the term *nonaligned* seriously. They saw Sukarno, Nehru, Nkrumah, and Egypt's Gamal Abd al-Nasir° as stalking horses for a communist

Gamal Abd al-Nasir (gah-MAHL AHB-d al-NAH-suhr)

takeover of the world. This may also have been the hope of some Soviet leaders, who were quick to offer some of these countries military and financial aid.

For the movement's leaders, however, nonalignment was a means to extract money and support from one or both superpowers. By flirting with the Soviet Union, the United States, or the People's Republic of China, a country could get military and economic aid.

Some skillful nonaligned leaders were able to gain from both sides. Nasir, who ruled Egypt from 1952 to 1970, and his successor, Anwar al-Sadat°, played the game well. The United States offered to build a dam at Aswan°, on the Nile River, to increase Egypt's electrical generating and irrigation capacity. When Egypt turned to the Soviet Union for arms, the United States reneged on the dam project in 1956. The Soviet Union then picked it up and in the 1960s brought it to conclusion. In 1956, Israel, Great Britain, and France conspired to invade Egypt. Their objective was to overthrow Nasir, regain the Suez Canal (he had recently nationalized it), and secure Israel from any Egyptian threat. The invasion succeeded militarily, but both the United States and the Soviet Union pressured the invaders to withdraw, thus saving Nasir's government. In 1972, Sadat evicted his Soviet military advisers but a year later used his Soviet weapons to attack Israel. After he lost that war, he announced his faith in the power of the United States to solve Egypt's political and economic problems.

Numerous other countries adopted similar balancing strategies. In each case, local leaders were trying to develop their nation's economy and assert or preserve their nation's interests. Manipulating the superpowers was simply a means toward those ends and implied very little about true ideological orientation.

Japan and China

No other countries took better advantage of the opportunities presented by the superpowers' preoccupation than did Japan and China. Japan signed a peace treaty with most of its former enemies in 1951 and regained independence from American occupation the following year. Renouncing militarism and its imperialist past, Japan remained on the sidelines throughout the Korean War. Its new constitution, written under American supervision in 1946, allowed only a limited self-defense force, banned the deployment of Japanese troops abroad, and gave the vote to women.

The Japanese turned their talents and energies to rebuilding their industries and engaging in world commerce. By isolating Japan from most world political issues, the Cold War provided an exceptionally favorable environment for Japan to develop its economic strength.

Three industries that took advantage of government aid and the newest technologies paved the way for Japan's emergence as an economic superpower after 1975. Projects producing 60 million kilowatts of electricity were completed between 1951 and 1970, almost a third through dams on Japan's many rivers. Between 1960 and 1970, steel production more than quadrupled, reaching 15.7 percent of the total capacity of countries outside the Soviet bloc. The shipbuilding industry produced six times as much tonnage in 1970 as in 1960, almost half of the new tonnage produced outside the Soviet bloc.

While Japan benefited from being outside the Cold War, China was deeply involved in Cold War politics. When Mao Zedong° and the communists defeated the nationalists in 1949 and established the People's Republic of China (PRC), their main ally and source of arms was the Soviet Union. By 1956, however, the PRC and the Soviet Union were beginning to diverge politically, partly in reaction to the Soviet rejection of Stalinism and partly because of China's reluctance to be cast forever in the role of student. Mao had his own notions of communism, focusing strongly on the peasantry, whom the Soviets ignored in favor of the industrial working class.

Mao's Great Leap Forward in 1958 was supposed to vault China into the ranks of world industrial powers by maximizing the use of labor in small-scale, village-level industries. The policy failed but demonstrated Mao's willingness to carry

---

al-Sadat (al-seh-DAT)　**Aswan** (AS-wahn)

Mao Zedong (maow dzuh-dong)

out massive economic and social projects of his own devising.

In 1966, Mao instituted another radical nationwide program, the **Cultural Revolution.** He ordered the mass mobilization of Chinese youth into Red Guard units. His goal was to kindle revolutionary fervor in a new generation and to ward off the stagnation and bureaucratization he saw in the Soviet Union. Red Guard units criticized and purged teachers, party officials, and intellectuals for "bourgeois values." Internal party conflict continued until 1971, when Mao admitted that attacks on individuals had gotten out of hand. Meanwhile, small-scale industrialization resulted in record levels of agricultural and industrial production. The last years of the Cultural Revolution were dominated by radicals led by Mao's wife, Jiang Qing°, who focused on restrictions on artistic and intellectual activity.

In the meantime, the rift between the PRC and the Soviet Union had opened so wide that United States President Richard Nixon (1969–1974), by reputation a staunch anticommunist, dropped objections to the PRC's joining the United Nations. In 1971, the PRC occupied China's permanent seat on the Security Council, displacing the Chinese nationalist government on Taiwan. The following year, Nixon visited Beijing, making dramatically clear the new cooperation between the People's Republic of China and the United States.

The Middle East

Independence had come gradually to the Arab countries of the Middle East. Britain granted Syria and Lebanon independence after World War II. Other Arab countries— Iraq, Egypt, Jordan—enjoyed nominal independence during the interwar period but remained under indirect British control until the 1950s.

Overshadowing all Arab politics, however, was the struggle with the new state of Israel. British policy on Palestine between the wars oscillated between favoring Zionist Jewish immigrants and the indigenous Palestinian Arabs. After the war, under intense pressure to resettle European Jewish re-

fugees, Britain turned the Palestine problem over to the United Nations. In November 1947, the General Assembly voted in favor of partitioning Palestine into two states, one Jewish and one Arab. The Jewish community made plans to declare independence while the Palestinians, who felt the proposed land division was unfair, reacted in horror and took up arms. When Israel declared its independence in May 1948, neighboring Arab countries sent armies to help the Palestinians crush the newborn state.

Israel, however, prevailed on all fronts. Some 700,000 Palestinians became refugees. They found shelter in United Nations refugee camps in Jordan, Syria, Lebanon, and the Gaza Strip (a bit of coastal land on the Egyptian-Israeli border). The right of these refugees to return home remains a focal point of Arab politics. In 1967, Israel responded to threatening military moves by Egypt's Nasir by preemptively attacking Egyptian and Syrian air bases. In six days, Israel won a smashing victory. Israel won control of Jerusalem, previously split with Jordan, the West Bank, the Gaza Strip, the strategic Golan Heights in southern Syria, and the entire Sinai Peninsula. Acquiring all of Jerusalem satisfied Jews' deep longing to return to their holiest city, but Palestinians continued to regard Jerusalem as their destined capital, and Muslims in many countries protested Israeli control of the Dome of the Rock, a revered Islamic shrine located in the city. These acquisitions resulted in a new wave of Palestinian refugees.

The rival claims to Palestine continued to plague Middle Eastern politics. The Palestine Liberation Organization (PLO), headed by Yasir Arafat°, waged guerrilla war against Israel, frequently engaging in acts of terrorism. The militarized Israelis were able to blunt or absorb these attacks and launch counterstrikes that likewise involved assassinations and bombings. Though the United States proved a firm friend of Israel and the Soviet Union armed the Arab states, neither superpower saw the struggle between Zionism and Palestinian nationalism as a vital concern—until oil became a political issue.

Jiang Qing (jyahn ching)

Arafat (AR-uh-fat)

The phenomenal concentration of oil wealth in the Persian Gulf states—Iran, Iraq, Kuwait, Saudi Arabia, Qatar, Bahrain, and the United Arab Emirates—was not fully realized until after World War II when demand for oil rose sharply as civilian economies recovered. As a world oversupply diminished in the face of rising demand, oil-producing states in 1960 formed the **Organization of Petroleum Exporting Countries (OPEC)** to promote their collective interest in higher revenues.

Oil politics and the Arab-Israeli conflict intersected in October 1973. A surprise Egyptian attack across the Suez Canal threw the Israelis into temporary disarray. Within days, the war turned in Israel's favor, and an Egyptian army was trapped at the canal's southern end. The United States then arranged a cease-fire and the disengagement of forces. But before that could happen, the Arab oil-producing countries voted to embargo oil shipments to the United States and the Netherlands as punishment for their support of Israel.

The implications of oil as an economic weapon profoundly disturbed the worldwide oil industry. Prices rose—along with feelings of insecurity. In 1974, OPEC responded to the turmoil in the oil market by quadrupling prices, setting the stage for massive transfers of wealth to the producing countries and provoking a feeling of crisis throughout the consuming countries.

The Emergence of Environmental Concerns

Skyrocketing oil prices focused new attention on natural resource issues. Before the mid-1960s, only a few people noticed that untested technologies and all-out drives for industrial productivity were rapidly degrading the environment. The superpowers were particularly negligent of the environmental impact of pesticide and herbicide use, automobile exhaust, industrial waste disposal, and radiation hazards.

New youth activism focused awareness on environmental problems. In 1968, a wave of student unrest swept many parts of the world. Earth Day was first celebrated in 1970, the year in which the United States established its Environmental Protection Agency.

After 1974, making gasoline engines and home heating systems more efficient and lowering highway speed limits to conserve fuel became matters of national debate in the United States while

Oil Crisis at the Gas Station   Dislocations in the oil industry caused by OPEC price rises that began in 1974 produced long lines at gas pumps and local shortages. The crisis brought Middle East politics home to consumers and created a negative stereotype of "oil sheikhs."   (Keza/Liaison)

poorer countries struggled to find the money to import oil. A widely read 1972 study, *The Limits of Growth,* forecast a need to cut back on consumption of natural resources in the twenty-first century. Thus, as the most dangerous moments of the Cold War seemed to be passing, ecological and environmental problems of worldwide impact vied with the superpower rivalry and Third World nation building for public attention.

CONCLUSION

The Cold War and the decolonization movement seemed to arise as logical extensions of World War II. The question of who would control the parts of Europe and Asia liberated from Axis occupation led to Churchill's notion of an iron curtain dividing East and West. The war exhaustion of the European imperialist powers encouraged Asian and African peoples to seek independence and embark on building their own nations.

Intellectuals often framed their understanding of the period in terms of a philosophical struggle between capitalism and socialism dating back to the nineteenth century. But for leaders facing the challenge of governing new nations and creating viable economies, ideology became intertwined with questions of how to profit from the Cold War rivalry between the United States and the Soviet Union.

Historians do not all agree on the year 1975 as the end of the postwar era. The end of the Vietnam War, the beginning of the world oil crisis, and the signing of the Helsinki Accords that brought a measure of agreement among Europeans on both sides of the iron curtain were pivotal events for some countries. But the number of independent countries in the world had grown enormously, and each was in the process of working out its own particular problems. What marks the mid-1970s as the end of an era, therefore, is not a single event so much as the emergence of new concerns. Young people with no memories of World War II were less concerned with the Cold War and the specter of nuclear annihilation than with newly recognized threats to the world environment and with making their own way in the world. In the wealthier nations, this meant taking advantage of economic growth and increasing technological sophistication. In the developing world, it meant seeking the education and employment needed for playing active roles in the drama of nation building.

■ Key Terms

iron curtain	Warsaw Pact
Cold War	Korean War
North Atlantic Treaty Organization (NATO)	Vietnam War
United Nations	Cuban missile crisis
World Bank	Helsinki Accords
Marshall Plan	nonaligned nations
European Community (EC)	Third World
Truman Doctrine	Cultural Revolution (China)
	Organization of Petroleum Exporting Countries (OPEC)

■ Suggested Reading

The period since 1945 has been particularly rich in memoirs by government leaders. Some that are particularly relevant to the Cold War and decolonization are Dean Acheson (United States secretary of state under Truman), *Present at the Creation* (1969); Nikita Khrushchev, *Khrushchev Remembers* (1970); and Anthony Eden (British prime minister), *Full Circle* (1960).

Geoffrey Barraclough, *An Introduction to Contemporary History* (1964), is a remarkable early effort at understanding the broad sweep of history during this period.

Scholarship on the origins of the Cold War is extensive and includes Akira Iriye, *The Cold War in Asia: A Historical Introduction* (1974); Bruce Kuniholm, *The Origins of the Cold War in the Middle East* (1980); Madelaine Kalb, *The Congo Cables: The Cold War in Africa—From Eisenhower to Kennedy* (1982); and Michael J. Hogan, *A Cross of Iron: Harry S Truman and the Origins of the National Security State* (1998). For a recent reconsideration of earlier historical viewpoints, see Melvyn P. Leffler and David S. Painter (eds.), *Origins of the Cold War: An International History* (1994).

Good general histories of the Cold War include Martin Walker, *The Cold War: A History* (1993), and Walter Lafeber, *America, Russia, and the Cold War, 1945–1992* (1993). The latter puts emphasis on how the Cold War eroded American democratic values. For a look at the Cold War from the Soviet perspective, see William Taubman, *Stalin's America Policy* (1981); for the American perspective, see John Lewis Gaddis, *Strategies of Containment: A Critical Appraisal of Postwar American National Security Policy* (1982).

The nuclear arms race and the associated Soviet-U.S. competition in space are well covered by McGeorge Bundy, *Danger and Survival: Choices About the Bomb in the First Fifty Years* (1988), and Walter MacDougall, *The Heavens and the Earth: A Political History of the Space Age* (1985). Among the many novels illustrating the alarming impact of the arms race on the general public are Philip Wylie, *Tomorrow!* (1954), and Nevil Shute, *On the Beach* (1970). At a technical and philosophical level, Herman Kahn's *On Thermonuclear War* (1961) had a similar effect.

The end of the European empires is broadly treated by D. K. Fieldhouse, *The Colonial Empires* (1982); for the British Empire in particular, see Brian Lapping, *End of Empire* (1985). For a critical view of American policies toward the decolonized world, see Gabriel Kolko, *Confronting the Third World: United States Foreign Policy, 1945–1980* (1988).

For books on some of the specific episodes of decolonization treated in this chapter, see, on Algeria, Alistaire Horne, *A Savage War of Peace: Algeria, 1954–1962* (1987); on Cuba, Hugh Thomas, *Cuba: The Pursuit of Freedom* (1971); on the Suez crisis of 1956, Keith Kyle, *Suez 1956* (1991); on Britain's role in the Middle East over the period of the birth of Israel, William Roger Louis, *The British Empire in the Middle East, 1945–1951* (1984); on Vietnam, George Herring, *America's Longest War: The United States and Vietnam, 1950–1975* (1986), and Stanley Karnow, *Vietnam: A History* (1991); and on Latin America, Eric Wolf, *The Human Condition in Latin America* (1972).

The special cases of Japan and China in this period are covered by Takafusa Nakamura, *A History of Showa Japan, 1926–1989* (1998); Marius B. Jansen, *Japan and China: From War to Peace, 1894–1972* (1975); and Maurice Meisner, *Mao's China and After: A History of the People's Republic* (1986). John Merrill, *Korea: The Peninsular Origins of the War* (1989), presents the Korean War as a civil and revolutionary conflict as well as an episode of the Cold War. Among the hundreds of books on the Arab-Israeli conflict, Charles D. Smith, *Palestine and the Arab-Israel Conflict* (1992), and Trevor N. Dupuy, *Elusive Victory: The Arab-Israeli Wars, 1947–1974* (1978), stand out.

29

CRISIS, REALIGNMENT, AND THE DAWN OF THE POST– COLD WAR WORLD,

1975–1991

Postcolonial Crises and Asian Economic Expansion, 1975–1990 •
The End of the Bipolar World, 1989–1991 • **The Challenge of**
Population Growth • **Unequal Development and the Movement of**
Peoples • **Technological and Environmental Change**
SOCIETY AND CULTURE: China's Family–Planning Needs

*O*n Thursday, July 22, 1993, police officers in Rio de Janeiro's banking district attempted to arrest a young boy caught sniffing glue. In the resulting scuffle, one police officer was injured by stones thrown by a group of homeless children who lived in nearby streets and parks. Late the following night, hooded vigilantes in two cars fired hundreds of shots at a group of these children sleeping on the steps of a church. The attackers, later identified as off-duty police officers, killed five children there and two more in a park.

At that time, more than 350,000 abandoned children lived in Rio's streets and parks and resorted to begging, selling drugs, stealing, and prostitution to survive. In 1993 alone, death squads and drug dealers killed more than four hundred of them. Few people sympathized with the victims. One person living near the scene of the July shootings said, "Those street kids are bandits, and bandits have to die. They are a rotten branch that has to be pruned."[1]

At the end of the twentieth century, the brutality of those children's lives was an increasingly common feature of life in the developing world, where rapid population growth was outstripping economic resources. Similar problems of violence, poverty, and social breakdown could be found in most developing nations.

In wealthy industrialized nations as well, politicians and social reformers worried about the effects of unemployment, family breakdown, substance abuse, and homelessness. As had been true during the eighteenth-century Industrial Revolution (see Chapter 21), dramatic economic growth, increased global economic integration, and rapid technological progress in the post–World War II period coincided with growing social dislocation and inequality. Among the most important events of the period were the emergence of new industrial powers in Asia and the precipitous demise of the Soviet Union and its socialist allies.

New challenges also appeared in the form of world population growth and large-scale migrations. Population grew most rapidly in the world's poorest nations, worsening social and economic problems and undermining fragile political institutions. In the industrialized nations, the arrival of large numbers of culturally and linguistically distinct immigrants fueled economic growth but also led to the appearance of anti-immigrant political movements and, in some cases, violent ethnic conflict.

As you read this chapter, ask yourself the following questions:

- How did the Cold War affect politics in Latin America and the Middle East in the 1970s and 1980s?

- What forces led to the collapse of the Soviet Union?

- What is the relationship between the rate of population growth and the wealth of nations?

- How has technological change affected the global environment in the recent past?

POSTCOLONIAL CRISES AND ASIAN ECONOMIC EXPANSION, 1975–1989

Between 1975 and 1991, wars and revolutions provoked by a potent mix of ideology, nationalism, ethnic hatred, and religious fervor spread death and destruction through many of the world's least developed regions. Although often tied to earlier colonialism and foreign intervention, each conflict reflected a specific set of historical experiences. In many cases, conflicts provoked by local and regional causes tended to become more deadly and long lasting because the United States and the Soviet Union intervened. Conflicts in which the rival superpowers financed and armed competing factions or parties were called **proxy wars.**

Local and regional conflicts and proxy wars were not universal. During this same period, Japan gained a position among the world's leading industrial powers, while a small number of other Asian economies quickly entered the ranks of industrial and commercial powers. By the early 1990s, the collapse of the Soviet system in eastern Europe had ended the Cold War. As former socialist nations opened their markets to foreign investment and competition, economic transformation was often accompanied by wrenching social change. Other challenges facing the late twentieth century included growing inequalities among nations and within nations, rapid population expansion, and degradation of the environment.

Revolutions, Repression, and Democratic Reform in Latin America

After the Cuban Revolution, Fidel Castro sought to end the domination of the United States and uplift the Cuban masses by changing the economy in fundamental ways. Both objectives led to confrontation with the United States. The Cuban Revolution was the first revolution in the Western Hemisphere to nationalize foreign investment, redistribute the wealth of the elite, and forge an alliance with the Soviet Union. The fact that a communist government could come to power and thwart efforts by the United States to overthrow it energized the revolutionary left throughout Latin America (see Chapter 28). Unable to overthrow Castro and fearful that revolution would spread across Latin America, the United States mobilized its political and military allies in Latin America to defeat communism at all costs.

Brazil was the first to experience the full effects of the conservative reaction to the Cuban Revolution. Claiming that Brazil's civilian political leaders

CHRONOLOGY

	The Americas	Middle East	Asia	Eastern Europe
1970	**1964** Military takeover in Brazil **1970** Salvador Allende elected president of Chile **1973** Allende overthrown **1976** Military takeover in Argentina **1979** Sandinistas overthrow Anastasio Somoza in Nicaragua **1983–1990** Democracy returns in Argentina, Brazil, and Chile			
1980		**1979** Islamic Revolution overthrows shah of Iran **1980–1988** Iran-Iraq War	**1975** Vietnam war ends **1978** China opens its economy	**1978** USSR sends troops to Afghanistan
	1989 United States invades Panama		**1986** Average Japanese income overtakes income in United States **1989** Tiananmen Square confrontation	**1985** Mikhail Gorbachev becomes Soviet head of state **1989** USSR withdraws troops from Afghanistan; Berlin Wall falls **1989–1991** End of communism in eastern Europe
1990	**1990** Sandinistas defeated in elections in Nicaragua	**1990** Iraq invades Kuwait **1991** Persian Gulf War		**1990** Reunification of Germany

could not protect the nation from communist subversion, the army overthrew the democratically elected government in 1964. The military suspended the constitution, outlawed all existing political parties, and exiled former presidents and opposition leaders. Death squads—illegal paramilitary organizations sanctioned by the government—detained, tortured, and executed thousands of citizens. The dictatorship also undertook an ambitious economic program that promoted industrialization through import substitution, using tax and tariff policies to compel foreign-owned companies to increase investment in manufacturing.

Elements of this "Brazilian Solution" were imposed across much of Latin America in the 1970s and early 1980s. In 1970, Chile's new president, **Salvador Allende°**, undertook an ambitious program of socialist reforms to redistribute wealth from the elite and middle classes to the poor. He also nationalized most of Chile's heavy industry and

---

Salvador Allende (sal-vah-DOR ah-YEHN-day)

mines, including the American-owned copper companies that dominated the Chilean economy. From the beginning of Allende's presidency, the administration of United States President Richard Nixon (1969–1973) worked in Chile to organize opposition to Allende's reforms. After Chile's economy weakened, Allende was overthrown in 1973 by a military uprising led by General Augusto Pinochet° and supported by the United States. President Allende and thousands of Chileans died in this uprising, and thousands of others were illegally seized, tortured, and imprisoned without trial. Once in power, Pinochet rolled back Allende's reforms, reduced state participation in the economy, and encouraged foreign investment. In 1976, Argentina followed Brazil and Chile into military dictatorship. During the next seven years, the military fought what it called the **Dirty War** against terrorism. More than nine thousand Argentines lost their lives, and thousands of others endured arrest, terrible tortures, and the loss of property.

The flow of U.S. arms to regimes with the worst human rights records stopped during the four-year term of United States President Jimmy Carter (1977–1980). Carter championed human rights in the hemisphere and sought to placate Latin American resentment for past U.S. interventions by renegotiating the Panama Canal treaty, agreeing to the reestablishment of Panamanian sovereignty in the Canal Zone at the end of 1999. He also tried, but failed, to find some common ground with the **Sandinistas°,** a revolutionary movement in Nicaragua that overthrew the corrupt dictatorship of Anastasio Somoza in 1979. The Sandinistas received significant political and financial support from Cuba and, once in power, sought to imitate the command economies of Cuba and the Soviet Union. The Nicaraguan Revolution nationalized properties owned by members of the Nicaraguan elite and U.S. citizens.

In 1981, Ronald Reagan became president and replaced Carter's policy of conciliation with efforts at reversing the results of the Nicaraguan Revolution and defeat a revolutionary movement in neighboring El Salvador. His options, however, were limited by the U.S. Congress, which feared that Central America might become another Vietnam. The Reagan administration sought to roll back the Nicaraguan Revolution by the use of punitive economic measures and by supporting anti-Sandinista Contras (counterrevolutionaries), using both legal and illegal funds.

The Contras were unable to defeat the Sandinistas, but they did gain a bloody stalemate by the end of the 1980s. Confident that they were supported by the majority of Nicaraguans and assured that the U.S. Congress was close to cutting off aid to the Contras, the Sandinistas called for free elections in 1990. But they had miscalculated and lost the election. Exhausted by more than a decade of violence, a majority of Nicaraguan voters rejected the Sandinistas and elected a middle-of-the-road coalition led by Violeta Chamorro°.

The military dictatorships established in Brazil, Chile, and Argentina all came to an end between 1983 and 1990. In each case, reports of kidnappings, tortures, and corruption by military governments undermined public support. In Argentina, the military junta foolishly decided in 1982 to seize the Falkland Islands—the Argentines called them the "Malvinas." The Argentine junta had helped President Reagan support the Contras in Nicaragua and believed he would keep Britain's prime minister, Margaret Thatcher, from taking military action. When the Argentine garrison in the Falklands surrendered, military rule in Argentina itself collapsed.

In Chile and Brazil, the military dictatorships ended without the drama of foreign war. Despite significant economic growth under Pinochet, Chileans resented the violence and corruption of the military. In 1988, Pinochet called a plebiscite to extend his authority, but the majority vote went against him. Brazil's military initiated a gradual transition to civilian rule in 1985. By 1991, nearly 95 percent of Latin America's population lived under civilian rule.

Islamic Revolutions in Iran and Afghanistan

The Middle East was another region where the superpowers were involved in local revolutions. The United States was motivated to act in

---

Augusto Pinochet (ah-GOOS-toh pin-oh-CHET)
Sandinistas (sahn-din-EES-tahs)

Violeta Chamorro (vee-oh-LET-ah cha-MOR-roe)

The Nicaraguan Revolution Overturns Somoza   A revolutionary coalition that included Marxists drove the dictator Anastasio Somoza from power in 1979. The Somoza family had ruled Nicaragua since the 1930s and maintained a close relationship with the United States.   (Susan Meiselas/Magnum Photos, Inc.)

support of Israel and to protect access to petroleum from the region. The Soviet Union wished to prevent the spread of radical Islamic movements across the border into its own Muslim regions.

The Iranian Revolution of 1979 proved enormously frustrating to the United States. In 1953, covert intervention by the United States Central Intelligence Agency (CIA) helped Shah Muhammad Reza Pahlavi° retain his throne in the face of a movement to usurp royal power. Even when he finally nationalized the foreign-owned oil industry, the shah continued to enjoy special American support. As oil revenues increased following the price increases of the 1970s, the United States encouraged the shah to spend his nation's growing wealth on equipping the Iranian army with advanced

American weaponry. By the 1970s, there was mounting popular resentment against the shah's dependence on the United States, the ballooning wealth of the elite families that supported him, and the inefficiency, malfeasance, and corruption of his government, which led to mass opposition.

Ayatollah Ruhollah Khomeini°, a Shi'ite° philosopher-cleric who had spent most of his eighty-plus years in religious and academic pursuits, became the voice and symbolic leader of the opposition. Massive street demonstrations and crippling strikes forced the shah to flee Iran and ended the monarchy in 1979. In the Islamic Republic of Iran, which replaced the monarchy, Ayatollah Khomeini was supreme arbiter of disputes and

Reza Pahlavi (REH-zah PAH-lah-vee)

Ayatollah Ruhollah Khomeini (eye-uh-TOLL-uh ROOH-ol-LAH ko-MAY-nee)   **Shi'ite** (SHE-ite)

guarantor of religious legitimacy. Elections were held, but monarchists, communists, and other groups opposed to the idea of an Islamic Republic were barred from running for office. Shi'ite clerics with little training for government service emerged in many of the highest posts, and stringent measures were taken to replace Western styles and culture with Islamic norms. Universities were temporarily closed, and their faculties were purged of secularists and monarchists. Women were compelled to wear modest Islamic garments outside the house, and semi-official vigilante committees policed public morals.

The United States under President Carter had criticized the shah's repressive regime, but the overthrow of a long-standing ally and the creation of the Islamic Republic were blows to American prestige. Khomeini saw the United States as a "Great Satan" opposed to Islam, and he helped to foster Islamic revolutionary movements elsewhere, which threatened the interests of both the United States and Israel. In November 1979, Iranian radicals seized the U.S. embassy in Tehran and then held fifty-two diplomats hostage for 444 days. Americans felt humiliated by their inability to do anything, particularly after the failure of a military rescue attempt.

In the fall of 1980, shortly after negotiations for the release of the hostages began, **Saddam Husain°,** the ruler of neighboring Iraq, invaded Iran to topple the Islamic Republic. His own dictatorial rule rested on a secular Arab nationalist philosophy and long-standing friendship with the Soviet Union, which had provided him with advanced weaponry. He feared that the fervor of Iran's revolutionary Shi'ite leaders would infect his own country's Shi'ite majority and threaten his power. The war pitted American weapons in the hands of the Iranians against Soviet weapons in the hands of the Iraqis, but the superpowers avoided overt involvement during eight years of bloodshed. Covertly, however, the Reagan administration sent arms to Iran, hoping to gain the release of other American hostages held by radical Islamic groups in Lebanon and to help finance the Contra war against the Sandinista government of Nicaragua. When this deal came to the light in 1986, the result-

ing political scandal intensified American hostility toward Iran. Openly tilting toward Iraq, President Reagan sent the United States Navy to the Persian Gulf, ostensibly to protect nonbelligerent shipping. The move helped persuade Iran to accept a cease-fire in 1988.

While the United States faced anguish and frustration in Iran, the Soviet Union found itself facing even more serious problems in neighboring Afghanistan. Since World War II, the Soviet Union had succeeded in staying out of shooting wars by using proxies to challenge the United States. But in 1978, the Soviet Union sent its army to Afghanistan to support a fledgling communist regime against a hodgepodge of local, religiously inspired guerrilla bands that had taken control of much of the countryside.

With the United States, Saudi Arabia, and Pakistan paying, equipping, and training the Afghan rebels, the Soviet Union found itself in the same kind of unwinnable war the United States had stumbled into in Vietnam. Unable to justify the continuing drain on manpower, morale, and economic resources and facing widespread domestic discontent over the war, Soviet leaders finally withdrew their troops in 1989. The Afghan communists held on for another three years. But once rebel groups took control of the entire country, they began to fight among themselves over who should rule.

Asian Transformation

Japan has few mineral resources and is dependent on oil imports, but the Japanese economy weathered the oil price shocks of the 1970s better than did the economies of Europe and the United States. In fact, Japan experienced a faster rate of economic growth in the 1970s and 1980s than did any other major developed economy, growing at about 10 percent a year. Average income also increased rapidly, overtaking that of the United States in 1986.

There are some major differences between the Japanese industrial model and that of the United States. During the American occupation, Japanese industrial conglomerates, *zaibatsu* (see Chapter 25), were broken up. Although ownership of major

---

Saddam Husain (sah-DAHM who-SANE)

Muslim Women Mourning the Death of Ayatollah Khomeini in 1989 An Islamic revolution overthrew the shah of Iran in 1979. Ayatollah Khomeini sought to lead Iran away from the influences of Western culture and challenged the power of the United States in the Persian Gulf. (Alexandra Avakian/Woodfin Camp & Associates)

industries became less concentrated as a result, new industrial alliances appeared. There are now six major *keiretsu°* that each include firms in industry, commerce, construction, and a major bank tied together in an interlocking ownership structure. There are also minor keiretsu dominated by a major corporation, like Toyota, and including its major suppliers. These combinations of companies have close relationships with government. Government assistance in the form of tariffs and import regulations inhibiting foreign competition was crucial in the early stages of the development of Japan's automobile and semiconductor industries, among others.

Through the 1970s and 1980s, Japanese success at exporting manufactured goods produced huge trade surpluses with other nations, prompting the United States and the European Community to try to pry open the Japanese market through tough negotiating. These efforts had only limited success. In 1990, Japan enjoyed a trade surplus with the rest of the world that was twice as large as in 1985. Many experts assumed that the competitive advantages that Japan enjoyed in the 1980s would propel Japan past the United States as the world's preeminent industrial economy. But the Japanese economy began to stall at the end of the decade.

The Japanese model of close cooperation between government and industry was imitated by a small number of other Asian states. The most important of them was South Korea, which overcame the devastation of the Korean War in little more than a decade through a combination of inexpensive labor, strong technical education, and

keiretsu (kay-REHT-soo)

substantial domestic capital reserves. Despite large defense expenditures, South Korea developed heavy industries such as steel and shipbuilding, as well as consumer industries such as automobiles and consumer electronics. Japanese investment and technology transfers accelerated this process. Hyundai was typical of the four giant corporations that accounted for nearly half of South Korea's gross domestic product (GDP) in manufacturing products ranging from supertankers and cars to electronics and housing.

Taiwan, Hong Kong, and Singapore also developed modern industrial and commercial economies so rapidly that these three nations and South Korea were often referred to as the **Asian Tigers.** All shared many characteristics that helped explain their rapid industrialization. All had disciplined and hard-working labor forces, and all invested heavily in education. For example, as early as 1980, Korea had as many engineering graduates as Germany, Britain, and Sweden combined. All had high rates of personal saving that allowed them to fund investment in new technology generously. In 1987, the saving rates in Taiwan and South Korea were three times higher than in the United States. All emphasized outward-looking export strategies. And, like Japan, all of these dynamic Pacific Rim economies benefited from government sponsorship and protection. All were beneficiaries of the extraordinary expansion in world trade and international communication that permitted technology to be disseminated more rapidly than at any other time in the past. As a result, newly industrializing nations began with current technologies.

In China after Mao Zedong's death in 1976, the communist leadership introduced a comprehensive economic reform that allowed more individual initiative and permitted individuals to accumulate wealth. Beginning in 1978, the Communist Party in Sichuan province freed more than six thousand firms to compete for business outside the state planning process. The results were remarkable. Under China's leader, **Deng Xiaoping°**, these reforms were expanded across the nation. China also began to permit foreign investment for the first time since the communists came to power in 1949.

Between 1978 and the end of the 1990s, foreign investors committed more than $180 billion to the Chinese economy, and McDonald's, Coca-Cola, Airbus, and other foreign companies opened for business. But more than 100 million workers were still employed in state-owned enterprises, and most foreign-owned companies were segregated in special economic zones. The result was a dual industrial sector—one modern and efficient and connected to international markets, the other dominated by government and directed by political decisions.

In the countryside, Deng Xiaoping permitted the contracting of land to individuals and families, who were free to consume or sell whatever they produced. By 1984, 93 percent of China's agricultural land was in effect in private hands and producing for the market, tripling agricultural output.

Perhaps the best measure of the success of Deng's reforms is that between 1980 and 1993, China's per capita output more than doubled, averaging more than 8 percent growth per year in comparison with the world average of slightly more than 1 percent and Japan's average of 3.3 percent. This growth was overwhelmingly the result of exports to the developed nations of the West, especially the United States. Nevertheless, per capita measures of wealth indicated that China remained a poor nation. China's per capita GDP was roughly the same as Mexico's—about $3,600 per year. By comparison, Taiwan had a per capita GDP of $14,700.

Deng Xiaoping's strategy of balancing change and continuity helped China avoid some of the social costs and political consequences experienced by Russia and other European socialist countries that abruptly plunged into capitalism and democracy. As Chinese officials put it, China was "changing a big earthquake into a thousand tremors." The nation's leadership faced a major challenge in 1989. Responding to mass movements in favor of democracy across the globe and to inflation, Chinese students and intellectuals, many of whom had studied outside China, led a series of protests demanding more democracy and an end to inflation and corruption. This movement culminated in a massive occupation of **Tiananmen Square°** by

---

Deng Xiaoping (dung show-ping)

Tiananmen (tee-yehn-ahn-men)

protestors, in the heart of Beijing. After weeks of standoff, tanks pushed into the square, killing hundreds, perhaps thousands. Many more were arrested. Although the Communist party survived this challenge, it was not clear whether rapid economic growth, increasing inequality, high levels of unemployment, and massive migration from the countryside to the cities could occur without triggering a political transformation.

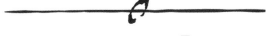

THE END OF THE BIPOLAR WORLD, 1989–1991

Few in 1980 predicted the startling collapse of the Soviet Union and the socialist nations of the Warsaw Pact. The once-independent nations and ethnic groups that had been brought within the Soviet Union and the eastern European nations seemed securely transformed by the experiences and institutions of communism. By 1990, however, nationalism was resurgent, and communism was nearly finished.

Crisis in the Soviet Union

Under United States President Ronald Reagan and the Soviet Union's General Secretary, Leonid Brezhnev°, the rhetoric of the Cold War remained intense. Massive new U.S. investments in armaments, including a space-based missile protection system that never became operational, placed heavy burdens on the Soviet economy, which was unable to absorb the cost of developing similar weapons. Soviet economic problems were systemic. Obsolete industrial plants and centralized planning stifled initiative and responsiveness to market demand. Government bureaucrats and Communist Party favorites received special privileges, including permission to shop in stores that stocked Western goods, but the average citizen faced long lines and waiting lists for goods. Soviet citizens contrasted their lot with the free and pros-

perous life of the West depicted in the increasingly accessible Western media. The arbitrariness of the bureaucracy, the cynical manipulation of information, and deprivations created a generalized crisis in morale.

Despite the unpopularity of the war in Afghanistan and growing discontent, Brezhnev refused to modify his rigid and unsuccessful policies. But he was unable to contain an underground current of protest. Self-published underground writings by critics of the regime circulated widely despite government efforts to suppress them. The physicist Andrei Sakharov and his wife, Yelena Bonner, protested the nuclear arms race and human rights violations and were condemned to banishment within the country. Some Jewish dissidents spoke out against anti-Semitism, but many more left for Israel or the United States.

By the time **Mikhail Gorbachev°** took up the reins of the Soviet government in 1985, war weariness, economic decay, and vocal protest had reached critical levels. Casting aside Brezhnev's hard line, Gorbachev authorized major reforms in an attempt to stave off total collapse. His policy of political openness (*glasnost*) permitted criticism of the government and the Communist Party. His policy of ***perestroika*°** ("restructuring") was an attempt to address long-suppressed economic problems by moving away from central state planning and toward a more open economic system. In 1989, he ended the war in Afghanistan, which had cost many lives and much money.

The Collapse of the Socialist Bloc

Events in eastern Europe were very important in forcing change on the Soviet Union. In 1980, protests by Polish shipyard workers in the city of Gdansk led to the formation of **Solidarity,** a labor union that soon enrolled 9 million members. The Roman Catholic Church in Poland, strengthened by the elevation of a Pole, Karol Wojtyla°, to the papacy as John Paul II in 1978, gave strong moral support to the protest movement. As Gorbachev

---

Leonid Brezhnev (leh-oh-NEED BREZ-nef)

Gorbachev (GORE-beh-CHOF)
perestroika (per-ih-STROY-kuh)
Karol Wojtyla (KAH-rol voy-TIL-ah)

loosened political controls in the Soviet Union after 1985, communist leaders elsewhere lost confidence in Soviet resolve, and critics and reformers in Poland and throughout the rest of eastern Europe were emboldened (see Map 29.1).

Beleaguered Warsaw Pact governments vacillated between relaxation of control and the suppression of dissent. As the Catholic clergy in Poland had supported Solidarity, Protestant and Orthodox religious leaders aided the rise of opposition groups elsewhere. This combination of nationalism and religion provided a powerful base for opponents of the communist regimes. Threatened

by these forces, communist governments sought to quiet the opposition by seeking solutions to their severe economic problems. They turned to the West for trade and financial assistance and opened their nations to travelers, ideas, styles, and money from Western countries, all of which accelerated the demand for change.

By the end of 1989, communist governments across eastern Europe had fallen. The dismantling of the Berlin Wall, the symbol of a divided Europe and the bipolar world, vividly represented this transformation. In Poland, Hungary, Czechoslovakia, and Bulgaria, communist leaders decided that

Map 29.1   The End of Soviet Domination in Eastern Europe   The creation of new countries out of Yugoslavia and Czechoslovakia and the reunification of Germany marked the most complicated changes of national borders since World War I. The Czech Republic and Slovakia separated peacefully, but Slovenia, Croatia, Macedonia, and Bosnia and Herzegovina achieved independence only after bitter fighting.

change was inevitable and initiated political reforms. When Romanian dictator Nicolae Ceausescu° refused to surrender power, he provoked a rebellion that ended with his arrest and execution. The comprehensiveness of these changes became clear in 1990, when Solidarity leader Lech Walesa° was elected president of Poland and dissident playwright Vaclav Havel° was elected president of Czechoslovakia. That same year, East and West Germany were reunited, and the eastern Baltic states of Lithuania, Estonia, and Latvia declared their independence of the Soviet Union.

The end of the Soviet Union came suddenly in 1991 (see Map 29.2). Gorbachev's efforts to transform the Soviet system could not keep up the tide of change sweeping through the region. After Communist hardliners botched a poorly conceived coup against Gorbachev, disgust with communism boiled over. Boris Yeltsin, the president of the Russian Republic and long-time member of the Communist Party, led popular resistance to the coup in Moscow and emerged as the most powerful leader in the country. Russia, the largest republic in the Soviet Union, was effectively taking the place of the disintegrating USSR. In September 1991, the Congress of People's Deputies voted to dissolve the union. Mikhail Gorbachev went into retirement.

The ethnic and religious passions that fueled the breakup of the Soviet Union soon challenged the survival of Yugoslavia and Czechoslovakia. The dismemberment of Yugoslavia began with declarations of independence in Slovenia and Croatia in 1991. A year later, Czechoslovakia peacefully divided into the Czech Republic and Slovakia.

The Persian Gulf War, 1990–1991

The breakup of the Soviet Union and the end of the Cold War did not bring an end to international conflict. The Persian Gulf War began when Iraq's ruler, Saddam Husain, invaded Kuwait in August 1991. Husain had failed to get Kuwait's royal family to reduce the size of Iraq's debt to the oil-rich nation. He was also eager to gain control of Kuwait's oil

fields. Husain believed that the smaller and militarily weaker nation could be quickly defeated and suspected, as a result of a conversation with an American diplomat, that the United States would not react.

Saudi Arabia, a key regional ally of the United States and a major oil producer, felt threatened by Iraq's action and helped draw the United States into the conflict. Soon the United States and its allies had concentrated an imposing military force of 500,000 in the region. With his intention to use force endorsed by the United Nations and with many Islamic nations supporting military action, President George Bush ordered an attack in early 1991. Iraq proved incapable of countering the sophisticated weaponry of the coalition. The missiles and bombs of the United States destroyed not only military targets but also "relegated [Iraq] to a pre-industrial age," reported the United Nations after the war. Although Iraq's military defeat was comprehensive, Husain remained in power, and the country was not occupied. Husain, in fact, crushed an uprising in the months following this defeat. In the wake of this event, the United States and its key allies imposed "no fly" zones that denied Iraq's military aircraft access to the northern and southern regions of the country.

In the United States, the results of the war were interpreted to mean that the U.S. military defeat in the Vietnam War could be forgotten and that U.S. military capability was unrivaled. Unable to deter military action by the U.S.-led coalition or to meaningfully influence the diplomacy that surrounded the war, Russia had been of little use to its former ally Iraq, and its impotence was clear.

THE CHALLENGE OF POPULATION GROWTH

For most of human history, population growth was viewed as beneficial, and human beings were seen as a source of wealth. Since the late eighteenth century, however, population growth has been viewed with increasing alarm. Some feared that food supplies could not keep up with population growth.

Nicolae Ceausescu (neh-koh-LIE chow-SHES-koo)
Lech Walesa (leck wah-LEN-suh)
Vaclav Havel (vah-SLAV hah-VEL)

Worker Unrest in Eastern Europe   After the collapse of the Soviet Union, workers such as these angry women surrounding plant managers in Minsk, capital of Belarus, demanded improvements in their working conditions.   (Yuri Ivanoff)

Others foresaw class and ethnic struggle as numbers overwhelmed resources. By the second half of the twentieth century, population growth was increasingly seen as a threat to the environment.

Demographic Transition

World population exploded in the twentieth century (see Table 29.1). At current rates of growth, world population increases by a number equal to the total population of the United States every three years. Unlike population growth in the eighteenth and nineteenth centuries, when much of the increase occurred in the wealthiest nations, population growth at the end of the twentieth century was overwhelmingly in the poorest nations. Fertility rates had dropped in most developing nations but remained much higher than rates in the industrialized nations. At the same time, improvements in hygiene and medical treatment caused mortality rates to fall. The result has been rapid population growth.

Educated Europeans of the nineteenth century had been ambivalent about the rapid increase in human population. Some saw it as a blessing that would promote economic well-being. Others warned that the seemingly relentless increase would bring disaster. Best known of these pessimists was the English cleric **Thomas Malthus,** who in 1798 argued convincingly that unchecked population growth would outstrip food production. When Malthus looked at Europe's future, he used a prejudiced image of China's huge population to terrify his European readers.

The generation that came of age in the years immediately following World War II inherited a world in which the views of Malthus were casually dismissed. Industrial and agricultural productivity had multiplied supplies of food and other necessities. Cultural changes associated with expanded fe-

Map 29.2   The End of the Soviet Union   When Communist hardliners failed to overthrow Gorbachev in 1991, popular anti-Communist sentiment swept the Soviet Union. Following Boris Yeltsin's lead in Russia, the republics that constituted the Soviet Union declared their independence.

male employment, older age at marriage, and more effective family planning had combined to slow the rate of population increase. And by the late 1960s, Europe and other industrial societies had made what was called the **demographic transition** to lower fertility rates (average number of births per woman) and reduce mortality. The number of births in the developed nations was just adequate for the maintenance of current population levels. Thus, many experts argued that the population growth then occurring in developing nations was a short-term phenomenon that would be ended by the combination of economic and social changes that had altered European patterns.

When the demographic transition failed to occur in the Third World by the late 1970s, the issue of population growth had become politicized.

The leaders of some developing nations actively promoted large families, arguing that larger populations would increase national power. Industrialized, mostly white, nations raised concerns about rapid population growth in Asia, Africa, and Latin America. Populist political leaders in those regions asked whether these concerns were not fundamentally racist.

However, once the economic shocks of the 1970s and 1980s revealed the vulnerability of developing economies, governments in the developing world jettisoned pronatalist policies. In the 1970s, Mexico's government had encouraged high fertility, and population growth in Mexico rose to 3 percent per year. By the 1980s, Mexico started to promote birth control, and the annual population growth rate fell to 2.3 percent.

Table 29.1   Population for World and Major Areas, 1750–2050

Population Size (Millions)

Major Area	1750	1800	1850	1900	1950	1998	2050
World	791	978	1,262	1,650	2,521	5,901	8,909
Africa	106	107	111	133	221	749	1,766
Asia	502	635	809	947	1,402	3,585	5,268
Europe	163	203	276	408	547	729	628
Latin America and the Caribbean	16	24	38	74	167	504	809
North America	2	7	26	82	172	305	392
Oceania	2	2	2	6	13	30	46

Percentage Distribution

Major Area	1750	1800	1850	1900	1950	1998	2050
World	100	100	100	100	100	100	100
Africa	13.4	10.9	8.8	8.1	8.8	12.7	19.8
Asia	63.5	64.9	64.1	57.4	55.6	60.8	59.1
Europe	20.6	20.8	21.9	24.7	21.7	12.4	7.0
Latin America and the Caribbean	2.0	2.5	3.0	4.5	6.6	8.5	9.1
North America	0.3	0.7	2.1	5.0	6.8	5.2	4.4
Oceania	0.3	0.2	0.2	0.4	0.5	0.5	0.5

Source: J. D. Durand, "Historical Estimates of World Population: An Evaluation" (Philadelphia: University of Pennsylvania, Population Studies Center, 1974, mimeographed); United Nations, *The Determinants and Consequences of Population Trends,* vol. 1 (New York: United Nations, 1973); United Nations, *World Population Prospects as Assessed in 1963* (New York: United Nations, 1966); United Nations, *World Population Prospects: The 1998 Revision* (New York: United Nations, 1999); United Nations Population Division, Department of Economic and Social Affairs, http://www.popin.org/pop1998/4.htm.

The Industrialized Nations

In much of Europe and Japan at the beginning of the twenty-first century, fertility levels are so low that population will fall unless immigration increases. In Japan, women have an average of 1.39 children; in Italy, the number is 1.2. Sweden provides cash payments, tax incentives, and job leaves to families with children, but the average number of births there fell to 1.4 in recent years. The low fertility found in mature industrial nations is tied to higher levels of female education and employment, the material values of consumer culture, and access to contraception and abortion. Educated women now defer marriage and child rearing until they are established in careers.

As fertility declined in the industrialized nations of western Europe, life expectancy has improved due to more abundant food, improved hygiene, and better medical care. Italy, for example, soon will have more than twenty adults fifty years old or over for each five-year-old child. Japan faces an even more drastic aging of its population. This demographic transformation presents a challenge very different from the one foreseen by Malthus. These nations generally offer a broad array of social services, including retirement income, medical services, and housing supplements for the elderly. As the number of retirees increases relative to the number of people who are employed, the costs of these services may become unsustainable.

In contrast, in Russia and some former socialist nations, life expectancy and birthrates have both fallen. Life expectancy for Russian men is now only fifty-seven years, down almost ten years since 1980. In the Czech Republic, Hungary, and Poland, life expectancy is improving in response to improved economic conditions, but in most of the rest of eastern Europe, the Russian pattern of declining life expectancy is found. High unemployment, low incomes, food shortages, and the dismantling of the social welfare system of the communist era have all contributed to this decline.

The Developing Nations

Population pyramids generated by demographers clearly illustrate the profound transformation in human reproductive patterns and life expectancy in the years since World War II. Figure 29.1 shows the 1985 age distributions in Pakistan, South Korea, and Sweden—nations at three different stages of economic development. Sweden is a mature industrial nation. South Korea is a rapidly industrializing nation that has surpassed many European nations in both industrial output and per capita wealth. Pakistan is a poor, traditional Muslim nation with rudimentary industrialization, low educational levels, and little effective family planning.

These demographic changes are transforming the global balance of population. At current rates, 95 percent of all future population growth will be in developing nations (see Table 29.1). A comparison between Europe and Africa illustrates these changes. In 1950, Europe had twice the population of Africa. By 1985, Africa had drawn even. According to projections, by 2025 Africa's population will be three times larger than Europe's. The populations of Latin America and Asia also were expanding dramatically, but at rates slower than those in sub-Saharan Africa and the Muslim world.

In Asia, the populations of India and China continued to grow despite government efforts to reduce family size (see Society and Culture: China's Family-Planning Needs). In China, efforts to enforce a limit of one child per family led to large-scale female infanticide as rural families sought to produce male heirs. India's policies of forced sterilization created widespread outrage and led to the electoral defeat of the ruling Congress Party. Yet both countries achieved some successes. Between 1960 and 1982, India's birthrate fell from 48 to 34 per thousand, while China's rate declined even more sharply—from 39 to 19. Still, by 2025, China and India will each have some 1.5 billion people.

UNEQUAL DEVELOPMENT AND THE MOVEMENT OF PEOPLES

Two characteristics of the postwar world should now be clear. First, despite decades of experimentation with state-directed economic development, most nations that were poor in 1960 were as poor or poorer at the end of the 1990s. The only exceptions were a few rapidly developing Asian industrial nations and an equally small number of

Figure 29.1   Age Structure Comparison: Islamic Nation (Pakistan), Non-Islamic Developing Nation (South Korea), and Developed Nation (Sweden), 1985   *Source:* Data from the World Bank.

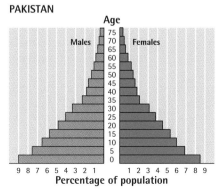

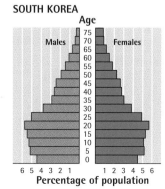

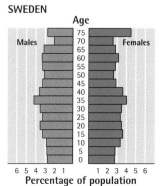

China's Family-Planning Needs

China has the world's largest population: over a billion people. Although China enjoyed rapid economic growth in the closing years of the twentieth century, population pressures continued to present severe problems. In 1993, the Chinese economy became the world's tenth largest. Nevertheless, China's per capita gross domestic product of $370 remained at Third World levels. Heavy pressure on families to have only one child resulted in the killing of female infants and the abandonment of children with disabilities. Peng Yu, vice minister of the State Family Planning Commission, explained the need for efforts at population control.

China is a developing country with a huge population but limited cultivated land, inadequate per capita resources and a weak economic foundation.... Despite continuous efforts in family planning, the huge base has created an annual net increase of around 14 million in recent years, equal to the total population of a medium-sized country. At present, per capita cultivated land in China has declined to less than 0.1 hectare, equivalent to only one-fourth the world average as are [its] per capita freshwater resources. . . . Although national income has been climbing by 25 percent annually, the increase has been eaten up by new population growth, resulting in reduced fund accumulation and also holding up the speed of economic construction. A fast-growing population has also created great difficulties in employment, education, housing, transportation, and health care. Confronted by such grim realities, to guarantee basic living conditions and constantly improve standards of living, China cannot follow the Western mode under which natural falling birth rates coincide with gradual economic growth.

The Chinese government's family-planning practices have been harshly criticized. Why has the Chinese government sought to control population growth? What effect has population growth had on the environment and economic development? What ethical questions are raised by the effort of any government to limit population growth?

oil-exporting nations. Second, world population increased to startlingly high levels, and most of the increase was in the poorest nations.

The combination of intractable poverty and growing population generated a surge in international immigration, both legal and illegal. Few other issues stirred more controversy. Even moderate voices sometimes framed the discussion of immigration as a competition among peoples. One commentator summarized his analysis this way: "As the better-off families of the northern hemisphere individually decide that having only one or at the most two children is sufficient, they may not recognize that they are in a small way vacating future space (that is, jobs, parts of inner cities, shares of population, shares of market preferences) to faster-growing ethnic groups both inside and outside their boundaries. But that, in fact, is what they are doing."[2]

The Problem of Growing Inequality

Since 1945, global economic productivity has expanded more rapidly than at any other time in the past. Faster, cheaper communications and transportation have combined with improvements in industrial and agricultural technologies to create levels of material abundance that would have amazed those who experienced the first Industrial Revolution (see Chapter 21). Despite this remarkable economic expansion and growing market integration, the majority of the world's population remains in poverty. The industrialized nations of the Northern Hemisphere now enjoy a larger share of the world's wealth than they did a century ago. As a result, the gap between rich and poor nations has grown much wider. The thousands of homeless street children who live among the gleaming glass and steel towers of Rio's banking district can be seen as a metaphor for the social consequences of postwar economic development.

Wealth inequality within nations also grew. In the United States, for example, the south and southwest grew richer in the past three decades relative to the older industrial regions of the midwest. Regional inequalities also appeared in developing nations. Generally, capital cities such as Buenos Aires, in Argentina, and Lagos, in Nigeria, attracted large numbers of migrants from rural areas because they offered more opportunities, even if those opportunities could not compare to the ones available in developed nations.

Even in the industrialized world, people were divided into haves and have-nots. During the presidency of Ronald Reagan (1981–1989), wealth inequality in the United States reached its highest level since the 1929 stock market crash. Some scholars estimated that the wealthiest 1 percent of households in the United States controlled more than 30 percent of the nation's total wealth. Even in Europe, where tax and inheritance laws redistributed wealth, unemployment, homelessness, and substandard housing were increasingly common.

Internal Migration: The Growth of Cities

Migration from rural areas to urban centers in developing nations increased threefold from 1925 to 1950. After that, the pace accelerated. Shantytowns sprawling

Garbage Dump in Manila, Philippines   Garbage pickers are a common feature of Third World urban development. Thousands of poor families in nearly every Third World city sort and sell bottles, aluminum cans, plastic, and newspapers to provide household income.   (Geoff Tompkinson/Aspect Picture Library Ltd.)

around major cities in developing nations are commonly seen as signs of social breakdown and economic failure. Nevertheless, city life was generally better than life in the countryside. A World Bank study estimated that three out of four migrants to cities made economic gains. Residents of cities in sub-Saharan Africa, for example, were six times more likely than rural residents to have safe water. An unskilled migrant from the depressed northeast of Brazil could triple his or her income by moving to Rio de Janeiro.

As the scale of rural-to-urban migration grew, these benefits proved more elusive, however. In many West African cities, basic services were crumbling under the pressure of rapid population growth. In 1990 in Mexico City, one of the world's largest cities, more than thirty thousand people lived in garbage dumps, where they scavenged for food and clothing. Worsening conditions and the threat of crime and political instability led many governments to try to slow migration to cities and, in some cases, to return people to the countryside. Indonesia, for example, has relocated more than half a million urban residents since 1969. Despite some successes with slowing the rate of internal migration, nearly every poor nation still faces the challenge of rapidly growing cities.

Global Migration

Each year, hundreds of thousands of men and women leave the developing world to emigrate to industrialized nations. After 1960, this movement increased in scale, and ethnic and racial tensions in the host nations worsened. By the 1990s, levels of immigration posed daunting social and cultural challenges for both host nations and immigrants.

Many European nations actively promoted guest worker programs and other inducements to immigration in the 1960s when an expanding European economy first confronted labor shortages. However, attitudes toward immigrants changed as the size of the immigrant population grew and as European economies slowed in the 1980s. Facing higher levels of unemployment, native-born workers saw immigrants as competitors willing to work for lower wages and less likely to support unions.

Because immigrants generally are young adults and commonly retain the positive attitudes toward early marriage and large families dominant in their native cultures, immigrant communities in Europe and the United States tended to have fertility rates higher than the rates of the host populations. In Germany in 1975, for example, immigrants made up about 7 percent of the population but accounted for nearly 15 percent of all births. Although the fertility of the Hispanic population in the United States is lower than the rates in Mexico and other Latin American nations, Hispanic groups will contribute well over 20 percent of all population growth in the United States during the next twenty-five years.

As the Muslim population in Europe and the Asian and Latin American populations in the United States expand in the twenty-first century, cultural conflicts will test definitions of citizenship and nationality. The United States will have some advantages in meeting these challenges because of long experience with immigration and relatively open access to citizenship. Yet in the 1990s, the United States was moving slowly in the direction of European efforts to restrict immigration and defend a culturally conservative definition of nationality.

TECHNOLOGICAL AND ENVIRONMENTAL CHANGE

Technological innovation powered the economic expansion that began after World War II by increasing productivity and disseminating human creativity. Because most of the economic benefits were concentrated in the advanced industrialized nations, technology increased the power of those nations relative to the developing world. Even within developed nations, postwar technological innovations did not benefit all classes, industries, and regions equally.

The multiplication of farms and factories intensified environmental threats. Loss of rain forest, soil erosion, global warming, pollution of air and water, and extinction of species imperiled human societies. Environmental protection measures, like the acquisition of new technology, progressed furthest in societies with the most economic resources.

New Technologies and the World Economy

Nuclear energy, jet engines, radar, and tape recording were among the many World War II developments that later had an impact on consumers' lives. When applied to industry, new technology increased productivity, reduced labor requirements, and improved the flow of information. As the Western economies recovered from the war and incomes rose, consumers purchased new products that reduced their workloads or provided entertainment.

Improvements in existing technologies accounted for much of the developed world's productivity increases during the 1950s and 1960s. Larger and faster trucks, trains, and airplanes cut transportation costs. Both capitalist and socialist governments expanded highway systems, improved railroad track, and constructed airports and nuclear power plants.

No other technology had greater significance in this period than the computer. Only large corporations, governments, and universities could afford the first computers. But by the mid-1980s, desktop computers had replaced typewriters in most of the developed world's offices, and technological advances continued. Each new generation of computers was faster and more powerful than the one before.

Computers also altered manufacturing. Small dedicated computers were used to control and monitor machinery in some industries. European and Japanese companies were the first to introduce such robots into the factory. The United States introduced robots more slowly because it enjoys lower labor costs.

The transnational corporation became the primary agent of these technological changes. In the post–World War II years, many companies with multinational ownership and management invested in and marketed products throughout the world. International trade agreements and open markets furthered the process.

As transnational manufacturers, agricultural conglomerates, and financial giants became wealthier and more powerful, they increasingly escaped the controls imposed by national governments. If labor costs were too high in Japan, antipollution measures too intrusive in the United States, or taxes too high in Great Britain, transnational companies relocated—or threatened to do so. Governments in the developing world were often hard-pressed to control the actions of these powerful enterprises. As a result, the worst abuses of labor or of the environment usually occurred in poor nations.

Conserving and Sharing Resources

In the 1960s, environmental activists and political leaders began warning about the devastating environmental consequences of population growth, industrialization, and the expansion of agriculture onto marginal lands. Assaults on rain forests and redwoods, the disappearance of species, and the poisoning of streams and rivers raised public consciousness. Environmental damage occurred in the advanced industrial economies and in the poorest of the developing nations. Perhaps the worst environmental record was achieved in the former Soviet Union, where industrial and nuclear wastes were often dumped with little concern for environmental consequences. The accumulated effect of scientific studies and public debate led to national and international efforts to slow, if not undo, damage to the environment.

The expanding global population required increasing quantities of food, housing, energy, and other resources as the twentieth century ended. In the developed world, the consumer-driven economic expansion of the post–World War II years became an obstacle to addressing environmental problems. How could the United States, Germany, or Japan change consumption patterns to protect the environment without endangering corporate profits, wages, and employment levels?

Many developing countries saw exploitation of their environmental resources and industrialization as the solution to their rapidly growing populations. The results were predictable: erosion and pollution.

Responding to Environmental Threats

Despite the gravity of environmental threats, there were many successful efforts to preserve and protect the environment. The Clean Air Act, the Clean Water Act, and the Endangered Species Act were passed in the United States in the 1970s as part of an environmental effort that included the nations of the European Community and Japan. Environmental awareness spread by means of the media and grassroots political movements, and most nations in the developed world enforced strict antipollution laws and sponsored massive recycling efforts. Many also encouraged resource conservation by rewarding energy-efficient factories and the manufacturers of fuel-efficient cars and by promoting the use of alternative energy sources such as solar and wind power.

These efforts produced significant results. In western Europe and the United States, air quality improved dramatically. In the United States, smog levels were down nearly a third from 1970 to 2000 even though the number of automobiles increased more than 80 percent. Emissions of lead and sulfur dioxide were down as well. The Great Lakes, Long Island Sound, and Chesapeake Bay were all much cleaner at the end of the century than they had been in 1970. The rivers of North America and Europe also improved. Still, more than thirty thousand deaths each year in the United States are attributed to exposure to pesticides and other chemicals.

New technologies made much of this improvement possible. Pollution controls on automobiles, planes, and factory smokestacks reduced harmful emissions. Similar progress was made in the chemical industry. Scientists identified the chemicals that threaten the ozone layer, and the phase-out of their use in new appliances and cars began.

Clearly the desire to preserve the natural environment was growing around the world. In the developed nations, continued political organization and enhanced awareness of environmental issues seemed likely to lead to step-by-step improvements in environmental policy. In the developing world and most of the former Soviet bloc, however, population pressures and weak governments were major obstacles to effective environmental policies. In China, for example, respiratory disease caused by pollution was the leading cause of death. Thus, it was likely that the industrialized nations would have to fund global improvements, and the cost was likely to be high.

CONCLUSION

The world was profoundly altered between 1975 and 1991. The Cold War dominated international relations to the end of the 1980s. Every conflict threatened to provoke a confrontation between the nuclear-armed superpowers, for both the United States and the Soviet Union feared that every conflict and every regime change represented a potential threat to their strategic interests. As a result, the superpowers were drawn into a succession of civil wars and revolutions. The costs in lives and property were terrible, the gains small. As defense costs escalated, the Soviet system crumbled. By 1991, the Soviet Union and the socialist Warsaw Pact had disappeared, transforming the international stage.

Latin America was pulled into the violence of the late Cold War period and paid a terrible price. The 1970s and 1980s witnessed a frontal assault on democratic institutions, a denial of human rights, and economic decline. This was the period of death squads and Dirty War. With the end of the Cold War, peace returned there, and democracy began to replace dictatorship.

In the Persian Gulf, the end of the Cold War did not lead to peace. Iran and Iraq have experienced deep cycles of political turmoil, war, and foreign threats since the late 1970s.

The world also was altered by economic growth and integration, by population growth and movement, and by technological and environmental change. Led by the postwar recovery of the industrial powers and the remarkable economic expansion of Japan and the Asian Tigers, the world economy grew dramatically. The development and application of new technology contributed significantly to this process. International markets were more open and integrated than at any other time. The new wealth and exciting technologies of the postwar era were not shared equally, however.

Population growth in the developing world was one reason for this divided experience. Unable to find adequate employment or, in many cases, bare subsistence, people in developing nations migrated across borders hoping to improve their lives. These movements often provided valuable labor in the factories and farms of the developed world, but they also provoked cultural, racial, and ethnic tension. Problems of inequality, population growth, and international migration would continue to challenge the global community in the coming decades.

Technology seemed to offer some hope for meeting these challenges. Engineering, financial services, education, and other professions developed an international character thanks to the communications revolution. Ambitious and talented people in the developing world could now fully participate in global intellectual and economic life. However, most people working in the developing world remained disconnected from this liberating technology by poverty. Technology also bolstered efforts to protect the environment, providing the means to clean auto and factory emissions, even while it helped produce much of the world's pollution. Technology has been intertwined with human culture since the beginning of human history. Our ability to control and direct its use will determine the future.

■ Key Terms

proxy wars	Asian Tigers
Salvador Allende	Deng Xiaoping
Dirty War	Tiananmen Square
Sandinistas	Mikhail Gorbachev
Ayatollah Ruhollah	*perestroika*
Khomeini	Solidarity
Saddam Husain	Thomas Malthus
keiretsu	demographic transition

■ Suggested Reading

Among the works devoted to postwar economic performance are W. L. M. Adriaasen and J. G. Waardensburg, eds., *A Dual World Economy: Forty Years of Development Experience* (1989); P. Krugman, *The Age of Diminished Expectations: U.S. Economic Policy in the 1990s* (1990); B. J. McCormick, *The World Economy: Patterns of Growth and Change* (1988); and H. van der Wee, *Prosperity and Upheaval: The World Economy, 1945–1980* (1986).

For Latin America, Thomas E. Skidmore and Peter H. Smith, *Modern Latin America*, 4th ed. (1996), provides an excellent general introduction to the period 1975 to 1991.

For the Pacific Rim, see Jonathan Spence, *The Search for Modern China* (1990); Edwin O. Reischauer, *The Japanese* (1988); H. Patrick and H. Rosovsky, *Asia's New Giant: How the Japanese Economy Works* (1976); and Staffan B. Linder, *Pacific Century: Economic and Political Consequences of Asian-Pacific Dynamism* (1986).

Focused examinations of the Soviet bloc are provided in K. Dawisha, *Eastern Europe, Gorbachev and Reform: The Great Challenge* (1988); Barbara Engel and Christine Worobec, eds., *Russia's Women: Accommodation, Resistance, Transformation* (1990); David Remnick, *Lenin's Tomb: The Last Days of the Soviet Empire* (1993); and Charles Maier, *Dissolution: The Crisis of Communism and the End of East Germany* (1997).

The story of the Iranian Revolution and the early days of the Islamic Republic of Iran is well told by Shaul Bakhash, *The Reign of the Ayatollahs: Iran and the Iranian Revolution* (1990). Barnet Rubin, *The Fragmentation of Afghanistan* (1995), provides excellent coverage of the struggle between Soviet forces and the Muslim resistance in that country.

A number of studies examine the special problems faced by women in the postwar period. See, for example, Elisabeth Croll, *Feminism and Socialism in China* (1978); J. Ginat, *Women in Muslim Rural Society: Status and Role in Family and Community* (1982); June Hahner, *Women in Latin America* (1976); P. Hudson, *Third World Women Speak Out* (1979); A. de Souza, *Women in Contemporary India and South Asia* (1980); and M. Wolf, *Revolution Postponed: Women in Contemporary China* (1985).

For general discussions of economic, demographic, and environmental problems facing the world, see R. N. Gwynne, *New Horizons? Third World Industrialization in an International Framework* (1990); P. R. Ehrlich and A. E. Ehrlich, *The Population Explosion* (1990); Paul M.

Kennedy, *Preparing for the Twenty-First Century* (1993); and J. L. Simon, *Population Matters: People, Resources, Environment and Immigration* (1990).

For issues associated with technological and environmental change, see M. Feshbach and A. Friendly, *Ecocide in the U.S.S.R.* (1992); John Bellamy Foster, *Economic History of the Environment* (1994); S. Hecht and A. Cockburn, *The Fate of the Forest: Developers, Destroyers, and Defenders of the Amazon* (1989); K. Marton, *Multinationals, Technology, and Industrialization: Implications and Impact in Third World Countries* (1986); S. P. Huntington, *The Third Wave: Demoralization in the Late Twentieth Century* (1993); L. Solomon, *Multinational Corporations and the Emerging World Order* (1978); and B. L. Turner II et al., eds., *The Earth as Transformed by Human Action: Global and Regional Changes in the Biosphere over the Past 300 Years* (1990).

■ Notes

1. *New York Times,* July 24, 1993, 1.
2. Paul Kennedy, *Preparing for the Twenty-First Century* (New York: Random House, 1993), 45.

30

THE END OF
A GLOBAL CENTURY,
1991–2001

A Fragmented World • Elements of a Global Culture

SOCIETY AND CULTURE: Nelson Mandela

s the year 1999 ended, *Time* magazine, in keeping with its long-standing tradition of choosing a "Person of the Year," decided to name the "Person of the Century." Instead of simply consulting among themselves or hiring a polling company to conduct a statistically sound survey, the editors conducted a poll over the Internet. Individuals with access to the Internet—well under half of the U.S. population—could vote for whomever they liked as many times as they wished. After deleting the names they considered frivolous, the editors came up with several lists of winners, ranging from revolutionaries to sports heroes. At the very top of the list was Albert Einstein; Franklin D. Roosevelt and Mahatma Gandhi were the first and second runners-up.

Time's winners encapsulated how many people viewed the world around them. Albert Einstein opened the door to the scientific wonders of the Atomic Age and inadvertently made possible the Cold War's "balance of terror."

Franklin D. Roosevelt led the military alliance that crushed fascism in World War II, leaving the United States the world's most powerful nation. Mahatma Gandhi pioneered nonviolence in the face of injustice as a technique for winning rights and in the process helped set in motion the wave of decolonization of the post–World War II decades. And the Internet, *Time*'s technological collaborator, symbolized a revolution in communication that promised to bring the peoples of the world into ever closer contact.

Despite these emblems of the twentieth century's achievements, the twenty-first century dawned on a world deeply concerned about ethnic conflicts, human rights violations, environmental problems, and economic uncertainties. While powerful economic and cultural forces pushed for greater globalization, peoples in many lands sought ways to preserve or achieve autonomy and identity and safeguard human rights. While affluent individuals in the most developed countries enjoyed unprecedented prosperity, growing disparities between rich and poor, both within and among countries, cast a shadow on the future.

As you read this chapter, ask yourself the following questions:

- How did technology contribute to the process of globalization in the late twentieth century?
- What are the main sources of conflict in the post–Cold War world?
- What role does the struggle for human rights play in the contemporary world?

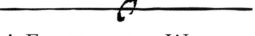

A FRAGMENTED WORLD

Religion, ethnicity, and race took stage center with the fading of the Cold War. In the era of decolonization, most governments in the newly independent states were too preoccupied with the problems of governance and economic development to put much effort into attempts to redraw boundaries, despite their lack of relationship to ethnic and linguistic realities. This generally conservative attitude toward change was reinforced by a number of violent episodes that aroused fears that the world order somehow might dissolve.

Challenges to the Nation-State

The modern idea of the world as a community of sovereign nation-states wielding absolute authority within recognized borders began with the Peace of Westphalia in 1648 that ended Europe's Wars of Religion. But international commitment to the concept of the sovereign nation-state did not erase the passions of groups within states who felt alienated from their rulers or their rulers' religion.

The conflicts were many, extending even to countries with only small religious minorities (see Map 30.1). The Tamil-speaking Hindu population in Sri Lanka fought a prolonged and merciless guer-

rilla struggle throughout the 1980s and 1990s against the dominant Singhalese-speaking Buddhists. Dissidents in mostly Catholic East Timor fought for separation from Muslim Indonesia from the moment Portuguese rule ended in 1975 down to 1999, when their goal was finally achieved by popular referendum. In East Africa, Eritrea fought for and won independence from religiously and linguistically different Ethiopia in 1993. The ethnic hatreds between the Hutu people and the Tutsi people that repeatedly wracked Rwanda and Burundi spilled over into Congo (then Zaire) in 1998, overturning the long-standing dictatorship of President Joseph Mobutu. Even constitutionally secular India saw instances of violence against Muslims and Christians in the name of Hindu nationalism.

In some instances, large-scale violence was avoided. Czechs and Slovaks agreed to divide postcommunist Czechoslovakia into the Czech Republic and the Republic of Slovakia in 1993. A brief uprising among the Maya population of southern Mexico in 1994 drew needed government attention and aid to that part of the country. And Malay-Chinese animosities in Malaysia and Indonesia were largely submerged in prosperity until economic calamity struck those countries in 1997. In Yugoslavia, a population that had seemed harmonious until 1991 dissolved into a morass of separatist and warring groups. Industrial and urban Slovenia and agricultural Croatia, the most northerly parts of Yugoslavia, were recognized as independent states in 1992 after brief struggles with federal Yugoslav forces.

The Yugoslavian province of Bosnia and Herzegovina faced greater difficulties. The people living there spoke Serbo-Croatian, but 40 percent were Muslims, 30 percent Eastern Orthodox Serbs, and 18 percent Croatian Catholics. The murderous three-sided fighting that broke out with the declaration of Bosnian national independence in 1992 gave rise to **ethnic cleansing,** an effort by one racial, ethnic, or religious group to eliminate the people and culture of a different group.

The Bosnia crisis challenged the international community to consider whether one country could rightly intervene in another nation's civil war when the intervening power had no national interests at stake. Since the territories that retained the

CHRONOLOGY

	Politics	Economics and Society
1991		**1991** CNN covers Persian Gulf War live from Baghdad
	1992 Yugoslavia disintegrates—Croatia and Slovenia become independent states	
	1992–1995 Bosnia crisis	
	1994 Maya uprising in southern Mexico	**1993** Nobel Peace Prize to Nelson Mandela
1995	**1995** Nerve gas released in Tokyo subway	**1995** World Trade Organization founded
		1997 Asian financial crisis
	1998 Terrorist bombings of U.S. embassies in Kenya and Tanzania; India and Pakistan test atomic bombs	
	1999 Kosovo crisis; East Timor secedes from Indonesia	**1999** Nobel Peace Prize to Doctors Without Borders
2000		
	2001 Terrorists attack World Trade Center and Pentagon; United States ousts Taliban government of Afghanistan	

name Yugoslavia—the southern regions centered on the heavily populated province of Serbia—were helping the Bosnian Serbs and independent Croatia was helping the Croatians of Bosnia, the question was whether anyone was going to come to the aid of the Muslims, Bosnia's largest ethnic group. No Muslim state had the capability to intervene in a major way. Finally, after much indecision—and extensive television coverage of atrocities and wanton destruction—the United States made a cautious intervention and eventually brokered a tentative settlement in 1995.

The shooting had hardly stopped in Bosnia when tension began to heighten in Kosovo, a southern province of Yugoslavia populated mostly by Albanian-speaking Muslims. The North Atlantic Treaty Organization (NATO) alliance repeatedly urged Serbia to stop mistreating the Kosovars (that is, the Albanian-speaking Muslims of Kosovo) and to permit them to participate in Yugoslavia's federal government as they had done before 1989, when Kosovo was an autonomous province within Yugoslavia. When NATO's warnings went unheeded, the United States, Britain, and France, acting under the NATO umbrella, launched an aerial war against Serbia in 1999.

In the aftermath of the air attacks, no one was certain whether new principles of international action had been established. Having nearly single-handedly won the Kosovo war without losing any American lives to enemy fire, the United States had again proven its might. But it was unclear when and where future U.S. or NATO interventions might occur.

Problems of the Global Economy

Issues of foreign intervention and national sovereignty also surfaced in the economic realm. World economic development after World War II at first favored industry in Europe and commodity production elsewhere. But unprecedented new avenues for the international flow of money helped once-poor East Asian countries such as Japan, Taiwan, and South Korea reach levels of industrial prosperity previously enjoyed only in Europe and North America.

Other factors similarly altered the world pattern of wealth distribution (see Map 30.2). During the decade of high oil prices starting in 1974, the oil-producing states became rich, but foreign debt

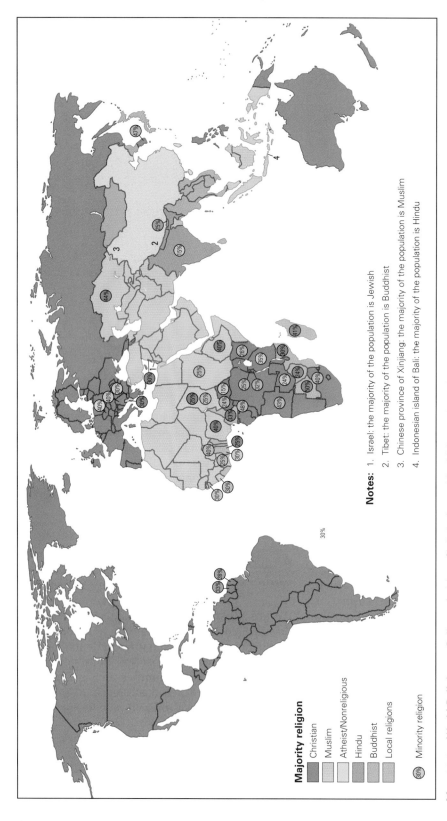

Map 30.1   World Religions   Believers in Islam, Christianity, and Buddhism make up large percentages of the population in many countries. Differing forms of these religions seldom coincide with national boundaries. As religion revives as a source of social identity or a rationale for political assertion or mass mobilization, the possibility of religious activism spreading across broad geographic regions becomes greater, as does the likelihood of domestic discord in multireligious states.

Majority religion

- Christian
- Muslim
- Atheist/Nonreligious
- Hindu
- Buddhist
- Local religions

⬤30% Minority religion

Notes: 1. Israel: the majority of the population is Jewish
2. Tibet: the majority of the population is Buddhist
3. Chinese province of Xinjiang: the majority of the population is Muslim
4. Indonesian island of Bali: the majority of the population is Hindu

became a major problem for some of the world's biggest countries, including Mexico and Brazil (see Chapter 29). After the collapse of the Soviet Union in 1991, the newly independent republics in eastern Europe required enormous investment to adapt their inefficient command economies to the global marketplace. By century's end, it was still unclear whether Russia's faltering economy would make a successful transition to capitalism.

At the same time, Southeast Asia boomed. Benefiting from investment and technical expertise from Japan and other industrial nations, Thailand, Malaysia, and Indonesia experienced rapid economic growth. Malaysia built the world's tallest skyscraper. Like other tropical countries, Indonesia cut down and sold its tropical hardwood trees on the world market. Groups concerned with protecting animal habitats and saving species from extinction protested these assaults, but quick profits and a national interest in economic development proved of greater weight.

The fevered pace of economic growth in Asia exploded in 1997. A financial crisis sent currency and stock values plummeting first in Thailand and then in neighboring countries, eventually triggering serious recession in Japan.

Such financial crises exemplified the tight interconnections within the global economy and raised the question of whether prosperous nations were obliged to rescue failing economies. A financial bailout for Mexico became a heated political issue in the United States in 1995, the year after the North American Free Trade Agreement (NAFTA), eliminating tariffs among the United States, Canada, and Mexico, went into effect. Arguing that Mexican prosperity was in the U.S. national interest, President Bill Clinton (1993–2001) pushed through a rescue plan that turned out to be successful. Other countries went to the International Monetary Fund and World Bank for assistance. These bodies made their assistance conditional on internal economic reforms that were often politically difficult, such as terminating government subsidies for basic foodstuffs and liberalizing investment.

Economic sanctions—embargoes, boycotts, freezing of assets, and restrictions on investment, all intended to harm another country's economy—became popular as a weapon, though one that only rich nations could wield. The United States, some-

times with the collaboration of its European allies, imposed severe sanctions on Iraq, Libya, Iran, Yugoslavia, and a number of other countries it had disputes with.

In 1995, in an effort to bring order to international trade, the world's major trading powers established the **World Trade Organization (WTO)** as the climax of a final round of negotiations under the rubric General Agreement on Tariffs and Trade (GATT). Charged with enforcing GATT agreements hammered out during periodic negotiating sessions over forty-seven years, the WTO seeks to reduce barriers to world trade. Despite a membership of 110 nations, however, the WTO is not without enemies, and its meetings have become the focus of protest demonstrations.

Old Threat, New Dangers

On September 11, 2001, the festering problems of the Middle East erupted in new danger for the United States and the rest of the world when nineteen terrorists hijacked four airliners and succeeded in crashing two of them into the twin skyscrapers of the World Trade Center in New York City and one into the Pentagon building in Washington, D.C. Over three thousand civilians perished. In response, the United States sent bombs and troops against a dictatorial and intolerant Islamic regime in Afghanistan, the Taliban. With the help of indigenous Afghan opposition groups, they overthrew that government. The Taliban had defiantly harbored and assisted the man accused of the suicide attacks, Usama bin Ladin°, a Saudi engineer from a wealthy family. He had volunteered to fight the Soviet Union in Afghanistan but subsequently transferred his animosity to the United States after the Saudi regime permitted American troops to be stationed on "sacred" Saudi soil during and after the Gulf War of 1991.

Bin Laden's attacks, beginning with the bombing of the American embassies in Kenya and Tanzania in 1998 and the destroyer *USS Cole* making a port call in Yemen in 2000, raised an old tactic to a new level. **Terrorism** rests on the belief that

---

Usama bin Ladin (oo-SAH-mah bin LAH-din)

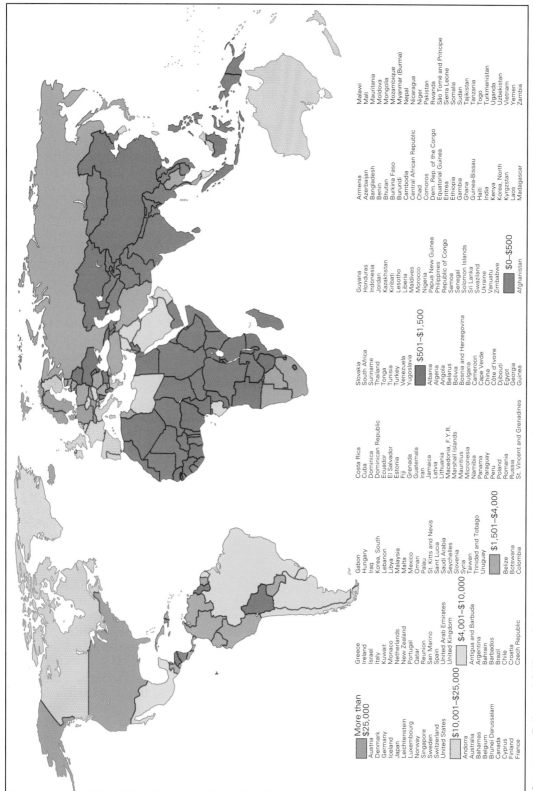

Map 30.2 **Estimated GNP per Capita, 1990s** Since World War II, wealth has increasingly been concentrated in a small number of industrialized nations in the Northern Hemisphere. The cost of developing and acquiring new technologies has widened the gap between rich and poor nations.

More than $25,000

Austria
Denmark
Germany
Iceland
Japan
Leichtenstein
Luxembourg
Norway
Singapore
Sweden
Switzerland
United Arab Emirates
United States

Greece
Ireland
Israel
Italy
Kuwait
Monaco
Netherlands
New Zealand
Portugal
Qatar
Reunion
San Marino
Spain
St. Kitts and Nevis
Saint Lucia
Saudi Arabia
Seychelles
Slovenia

$10,001–$25,000

Andorra
Antigua and Barbuda
Australia
Bahamas
Bahrain
Barbados
Belgium
Brunei Darussalam
Canada
Cyprus
Finland
France

Gabon
Hungary
Iraq
Korea, South
Lebanon
Libya
Malaysia
Malta
Mexico
Oman
Palau
Syria
Taiwan
Trinidad and Tobago
Uruguay

$4,001–$10,000

Belize
Botswana
Colombia

Costa Rica
Cuba
Dominica
Dominican Republic
Ecuador
El Salvador
Estonia
Fiji
Grenada
Guatemala
Iran
Jamaica
Latvia
Lithuania
Macedonia, F.Y.R.
Marshall Islands
Mauritius
Micronesia
Namibia
Panama
Paraguay
Peru
Poland
Romania
Russia
St. Vincent and Grenadines

$1,501–$4,000

Slovakia
South Africa
Suriname
Thailand
Tonga
Tunisia
Turkey
Venezuela
Yugoslavia

$501–$1,500

Albania
Algeria
Angola
Belarus
Bolivia
Bosnia and Herzegovina
Bulgaria
Cameroon
Cape Verde
China
Côte d'Ivoire
Djibouti
Egypt
Georgia
Guinea

Guyana
Honduras
Indonesia
Jordan
Kazakhstan
Kiribati
Lesotho
Liberia
Maldives
Morocco
Nigeria
Papua New Guinea
Philippines
Republic of Congo
Samoa
Senegal
Solomon Islands
Sri Lanka
Swaziland
Ukraine
Vanuatu
Zimbabwe

$0–$500

Afghanistan

Armenia
Azerbaijan
Bangladesh
Benin
Bhutan
Burkina Faso
Burundi
Cambodia
Central African Republic
Chad
Comoros
Dem. Rep. of the Congo
Equatorial Guinea
Eritrea
Ethiopia
Gambia
Ghana
Guinea-Bissau
Haiti
India
Kenya
Korea, North
Kyrgzstan
Laos
Madagascar

Malawi
Mali
Mauritania
Moldova
Mongolia
Mozambique
Myanmar (Burma)
Nepal
Nicaragua
Niger
Pakistan
Rwanda
São Tomé and Principe
Sierra Leone
Somalia
Sudan
Tajikistan
Tanzania
Togo
Turkmenistan
Uganda
Uzbekistan
Vietnam
Yemen
Zambia

Terrorist Attack on World Trade Center   The airline striking the tower ignited an intense fire that collapsed the entire building. The fire from a slightly earlier collision destroyed the twin tower. Over 300 fire fighters and police officers died evacuating the buildings before their collapse. A third hijacked airliner struck the Pentagon building in Washington D.C. A fourth crashed in Pennsylvania when passengers fought with the terrorists.   (Associated Press, AP)

horrendous acts of violence can provoke harsh reprisals or demonstrate such government incompetence that existing regimes will lose legitimacy and people will look to the terrorists for leadership. Global television broadcasts enhanced the impact of such attacks and made them more effective.

While anti-Israeli Palestinian groups set the tone for media-centered terrorism, hijacking airplanes in 1968 and killing Israeli athletes during the Munich Olympic Games of 1972, Bin Laden went beyond their short-range political objectives by urging Muslims throughout the world to see terrorist attacks as part of a jihad, or holy war, waged against non-Muslim enemies, the United States and Israel in particular. However, since the carefully planned and effective American counterstrike against Bin Laden's Taliban protectors took few civilian lives and the United States proclaimed its intent of assisting the Afghans in building a better government and at last repair the ravages of their struggle against the Soviet Union, Bin Laden's hope that Muslims would flock to his banner in response to American overreaction proved hollow.

With the declaration by President George W. Bush of a "war on terrorism," the future of this tactic, whether by Basque separatists in Spain, Tamil militants in Sri Lanka, or anti-Israeli Islamic extremists in the West Bank and Gaza Strip, became doubtful. Much seemed to hinge on the ability of the United States to identify and disrupt terrorist plans without generating intolerable levels of outrage in the Muslim world or unwarranted persecution of peaceful American citizens of Muslim faith. The challenge marked the end of a post–Cold War decade during which the United States had seemed uncertain of its role as the world's only superpower, and its foreign policy had garnered strong criticism—and not just in the Muslim world—for arrogance, selfishness, and failure to consult with allies.

Fear that nuclear devices might come into the possession of someone like Usama bin Laden reinvigorated the world community's determination to stem their spread. The sense of impending nuclear doom that had shadowed the world during the Cold War had quickly subsided after communism collapsed in Europe in 1991. Yet nuclear weapons remained, safeguards against their being sold or stolen seemed inadequate, and disposal of radioactive materials posed difficult technical problems.

In addition, a number of countries undertook nuclear programs in secret. The Cold War balance of nuclear forces between the United States and the Soviet Union had eventually proved an element of stability since neither side could have started a nuclear war without facing total annihilation. A small number of weapons in an unbalanced situation seemed more perilous. The difficulty of **nuclear nonproliferation**—prevention of countries with nuclear programs, like North Korea and Iraq, from deploying weapons—became evident when India and Pakistan openly tested nuclear bombs and missile delivery systems in 1998. Pakistan's program later evoked particular concern because of the sympathy of many Pakistanis for Usama bin Laden and the Taliban.

Chemical and biological weapons, which could kill massively and indiscriminately and be delivered in missile warheads, posed a similar threat.

But where nuclear weapons required advanced technology and large investments in factories and equipment, seemingly ordinary chemical and pharmaceutical plants using standard equipment could produce lethal chemicals and biological agents. United Nations inspections of Iraqi war-making potential (carried out as part of the settlement of the 1991 Persian Gulf War) uncovered and destroyed extensive stocks of chemical munitions and plants for producing nerve gas and lethal germs. In 1995, an apocalyptic Buddhist sect released nerve gas—ineffectively—in the Tokyo subway system; and after the 1991 attack on the World Trade Center and the Pentagon, an unknown terrorist sent letters through the U.S. mail containing spores of anthrax, a lethal disease. Assigning responsibility for terrorism raised worries of countries or religious groups being punished unfairly.

Human Rights

In addition to maintaining peaceful relations between states, the United Nations also aimed to protect the rights of individuals (see Society and Culture: Nelson Mandela). A General Assembly resolution passed on December 10, 1948, called the **Universal Declaration of Human Rights,** contained thirty articles that it proclaimed to be "a common standard of achievement for all peoples and nations."[1] It condemned slavery, torture, cruel and inhuman punishment, and arbitrary arrest, detention, or exile. It called for freedom of movement, assembly, and thought. It asserted rights to life, liberty, and security of person; to impartial public trials; and to education, employment, and leisure. The declaration ringingly asserted the principle of equality, most fully set forth in Article 2:

> Everyone is entitled to all the rights and freedoms set forth in this Declaration, without distinction of any kind, such as race, color, sex, language, religion, or political or other opinion, national or social origin, property, birth or other status.[2]

Religious tolerance had emerged from Europe's bloody religious wars of the sixteenth and seventeenth centuries. The idea of inalienable rights came from the U.S. Constitution (1788) and Bill of Rights (1791) and the French Declaration of

Nelson Mandela

The drama of decolonization in Africa climaxed in 1994 when Nelson Rolihlahla Mandela was elected president of South Africa in the first election open to citizens of all races. Born in 1918, Mandela became an active protester for civil rights as a college student in 1940. While working for a law degree, he helped found the Youth League of the African National Congress (ANC) in 1944.

After violent racial clashes in 1960 prompted the banning of the ANC, Mandela became its underground leader, challenging the apartheid regime (see Chapter 28) and calling for a new constitution based on democratic principles. Facing the full military mobilization of the apartheid state, he organized armed resistance and was arrested in 1962. While serving a life sentence, he refused several offers of freedom that would have required recognition of government racial policies.

In 1990, when it became evident that apartheid could not be maintained, Mandela was released and the next year elected president of the ANC. In 1993, he was awarded the Nobel Peace Prize, and in the following year he was elected president of South Africa. The following excerpt comes from his inauguration address.

Our daily deeds as ordinary South Africans must produce an actual South Africa that will reinforce humanity's belief in justice, strengthen its confidence in the nobility of the human soul and sustain all our hopes for a glorious life for all. . . .

To my compatriots, I have no hesitation in saying that each one of us is as intimately attached to the soil of this beautiful country as are the jacaranda trees of Pretoria and the mimosa trees of the bushveld. . . .

That spiritual and physical oneness we all share with this common homeland explains the depth of the pain we all carried in our hearts as we saw our country tear itself apart in a terrible conflict, and as we saw it spurned, outlawed and isolated by the peoples of the world, precisely because it had become the universal base of the pernicious ideology and practice of racism and racial oppression.

We, the people of South Africa, feel fulfilled that humanity has taken us back into its bosom, that we, who were outlaws not so long ago, have today been given the rare privilege to be host to the nations of the world on our own soil. . . .

The time for the healing of wounds has come.

The moment to bridge the chasms that divide us has come.

Why was Mandela's election considered a great victory for human rights? What is the significance of Mandela's use of the word compatriot?

Source: Inauguration Address of Nelson Mandela as State President of South Africa, May 10, 1994.

the Rights of Man (1789). The struggle against slavery and the woman suffrage movement in the nineteenth and twentieth centuries extended the concept of tolerance to all races and both sexes (see Chapters 25 and 28). The concept of social justice steadily advanced in Europe and America with the legalization of labor unions, the spread of universal education, and the establishment of government programs to care for the needy and ensure adequate standards of living for all citizens.

Although the ideological roots of the declaration lay mostly in European and American history, not all the countries that voted for the declaration in 1948 shared this heritage. Most countries later joining the United Nations willingly signed the declaration because it implicitly condemned the persistence of discriminatory European colonial regimes. Despite this apparent agreement, however, some people had philosophical reservations about the declaration's formulation of human rights.

Human rights activists, often working through international philanthropic bodies known as **nongovernmental organizations (NGOs),** focused their efforts on combating torture, imprisonment without trial, and summary execution by government death squads, as well as providing famine relief and refugee assistance. NGOs devoted to relieving hunger and oppression and bringing human rights abuses to world attention proliferated in the 1970s. Amnesty International, founded in 1961 and numbering a million members in 162 countries by the 1990s, concentrated on gaining freedom for people illegally imprisoned. Médecins Sans Frontières (Doctors Without Borders), founded in 1971, was awarded the Nobel Peace Prize in 1999 for the medical assistance it offered in scores of crisis situations. Even entertainers became involved in relieving suffering through Live Aid, a 1985 rock concert in London and Philadelphia that raised millions of dollars for famine assistance.

Such efforts raised the prominence of human rights as a global concern and put pressure on governments to consider human rights when making foreign policy decisions. Skeptics observed, however, that a Western country could prod a non-Western country to improve its human rights performance—for example, by barring the government from cutting off a thief's hand as stipulated by Islamic law—but reverse criticism of a Western country—for example, condemnation of persistent racial discrimination in the United States—often fell on deaf ears. Thus, the human rights movement was sometimes seen as another form of Western cultural imperialism, a club with which to beat former colonial societies into submission.

Women's Rights

No other issue exemplified this dichotomy of views so clearly as women's rights. Inspired by parallel efforts to combat racial discrimination and end the war in Vietnam, feminist activism revived in the United States in the 1960s and spread around the world. The movement focused on equal access to education and jobs and on quality-of-life matters such as ending sexual exploitation, gaining control of reproduction, and abandoning confining clothing styles. Ironically, the decades in which the feminist movement (followed by movements for gay and lesbian rights in North America and Europe) became a major force also saw sexuality become a more explicit and prominent aspect of commercial, artistic, and social life.

Feminists in the West decried the oppression of women in other parts of the world. At the same time, some non-Western women complained about the deterioration of morality and family life in the West and what they considered to be the feminists' misplaced concern with matters such as clothing. As with human rights, non-Western peoples disputed the West's definition of priorities. Western women and many secularized Muslim women protested Islam's requirement that a woman cover her head and wear loose-fitting garments to conceal the shape of her body, practices enforced by law in countries such as Iran and Saudi Arabia. Nevertheless, many outspoken Muslim women voluntarily donned concealing garments as expressions of personal belief, statements of resistance to secular dictatorship, or defenses against coarse male behavior. Some African women saw their real problems as deteriorating economic conditions, AIDS, and the customary practice of circumcising girls, a form of genital mutilation that could cause chronic infections or permanently impair sexual enjoyment.

Efforts to coordinate the struggle for women's rights internationally gained momentum in the 1970s with a series of highly publicized international conferences. The search for a universally accepted women's rights agenda proved elusive, but a rising global tide of women's education, access to employment, political participation, and control of fertility augured well for the eventual achievement of gender equality.

ELEMENTS OF A GLOBAL CULTURE

In many quarters, people voiced concerns about **cultural imperialism** that went beyond the issue

Beijing Women's Conference in 1995 This gathering of women, under United Nations auspices, from every part of the world illustrated the challenges posed by women's search for equality. The Chinese government, consistent with its policies of suppressing dissent and closely regulating social life, tried to limit press access to the conference. As in many other instances, these efforts to silence or control women's voices on issues like abortion and family planning proved ineffective. (Alesandra Boulat/Sipa Press)

of human rights. Critics complained that conglomerates were flooding the world with Western images, styles, and goods. In this view, global marketing was an especially insidious effort not only to overwhelm the world with a single Western outlook shaped by capitalist ideology, but also to suppress or devalue traditional cultures and alternative ideologies.

But in truth, technology, not ideology, played the central role in spreading Western culture. The idea that the United States was the primary culprit in cultural imperialism rested in part on the fact that Americans invented and developed much of the technology that formed and spread popular culture in the twentieth century. A close analysis of cultural trends reveals a diversity of voices that the case for cultural imperialism overlooks.

The Medium and the Message

With much of Europe's and Japan's industry in ruins after World War II, the United States became the world's main exporter of movies. Hollywood exported an image of the United States as a land of gangsters and cowboys, luxurious living, and—from the 1970s on—explicit sexuality. Although filmmakers in many other nations began to produce films of high artistic merit, they did not cut deeply into Hollywood's mass international audiences.

In contrast, the new medium of television outside the United States usually became a government monopoly, following the pattern of telegraph and postal service and radio broadcasting. However, many state broadcasters eventually turned to American and other foreign sources to meet the demand for shows because broadcasting American soap operas, adventure series, and situation comedies was cheaper than producing them locally. The United States, however, was not the only external source of programming.

American producers realized that satellite transmission provided an opening to an international market. Specializing in rock music videos aimed at a youth audience, MTV (Music Television) became an international enterprise offering special editions in different parts of the world. CNN (Cable News Network) became the most viewed and informative news source during the 1991 Persian Gulf War, when it broadcast live from Baghdad. Providing news around the clock, CNN began to supplant other commercial and government news programming as the best source of information about rapidly developing events.

At first, the computer industry, which mushroomed for defense and business purposes in the post–World War II decades, had little connection with television or movies. But as computers' electronic storage capacity and speed increased, their media uses expanded. In the 1990s, Japan introduced the first digital television broadcasting at about the time that disks containing digitized movies and computer programs with movie-like action became increasingly available.

More widespread was communication over the Internet, a linkage of academic, government, and business computer networks. Developed originally for U.S. defense research in the 1960s, the Internet became a major cultural phenomenon with the proliferation of personal computers in the 1980s. With the establishment of the World Wide Web as an easy-to-use graphic interface in the 1990s, the number of Internet users skyrocketed. Myriad new companies formed to explore "e-commerce," the commercial dimension of the Internet. By century's end, many American college students were spending less time studying conventional books and scholarly resources than they were spending to explore the Web for entertainment and to accomplish class assignments.

As in earlier eras, technological developments had unanticipated consequences. The new telecommunications and entertainment technologies derived disproportionately from American invention, industry, and cultural creativity. Thus, they could be seen as portents of Western, especially American, cultural domination. But the American input was rather uneven, and the more widespread the new technologies became, the greater the opportunities they afforded to people around the world to adapt them to their own purposes.

Japanese Adult Male Comic Book Comic magazines emerged after World War II as a major form of publication in Japan and a distinctive product of Japanese culture. Different series are directed to different age and gender groups. Issued weekly and running to some 300 pages in black and white, the most popular magazines sell as many copies as major news magazines do in the United States. (Private Collection)

The Spread of Popular Culture

The new technologies changed perceptions of culture. At the end of the nineteenth century, sophisticated Europeans and Americans, like earlier elite groups from imperial Rome to Ming China, valued most what they considered **high culture:** paintings, literature, and other works created to satisfy their tastes. They sneered at **popular culture** as localized entertainment for villagers and common folk—vigorous, picturesque, and quaint, but essentially vulgar. Influenced by the preferences of the European imperialist powers, modernizing elite groups around the world turned their backs on their own artistic traditions.

In fact, illustrious European composers and choreographers had been turning to folk tunes and dances for inspiration since the eighteenth century. And the search for fresh sounds and images intensified with the advent of modernism in Europe in the mid-nineteenth century. Some were captivated by the sounds and images of Europe's new industrial society; others drew inspiration from popular culture. Spanish artist Pablo Picasso (1881–1973), for example, borrowed the imagery of

African masks in some of his paintings, circuses and carnivals in others, and newspaper typography in still others.

The phonograph, invented by Thomas Edison in 1878, was the key that opened popular culture to global audiences. Phonograph records spread American popular music around the world. Jazz recordings and jazz musicians became popular in Europe in the 1920s. The driving force behind jazz was the creative skill of black musicians such as Duke Ellington, Louis Armstrong, Ella Fitzgerald, and Billie Holiday. Orchestral composers such as the Russian Igor Stravinsky and the Frenchman Maurice Ravel utilized jazz rhythms and themes. However, jazz remained the music of nightclubs and dance parties instead of concert halls. By World War II, black jazz musicians had become so much a part of the international image of the United States that Nazi propaganda frequently incorporated vile racial caricatures of them. Ironically, while jazz was widely perceived abroad as quintessential American popular culture, it remained largely the preserve of the African-American minority at home.

The international popularity of jazz derived from the appeal of its rhythms and naturalness—that is, from the music itself—not from its approval by a colonial ruling class. The same was true of rock 'n' roll, a dynamic, sensual, and audacious popular music that arose in the 1950s and became even more widespread than jazz. Rock grew out of black rhythm-and-blues and derived initially from innovative black American performers like Chuck Berry. The rise to international stardom in the 1960s of Britain's Beatles helped make rock 'n' roll a worldwide phenomenon. The core of rock remained American and British, but popular musicians from all over the world recorded in rock-influenced styles. Some achieved broad acclaim, as did Jamaica's Bob Marley with his Caribbean reggae style. Others gained strong local followings by blending rock with traditional forms, as happened with Malagasy music in Madagascar and Rai music in Algeria.

In the 1970s and 1980s, critics around the world identified the United States as the chief propagator of a worldwide consumer culture. This judgment seemed to be confirmed by the international cachet of American brand names like Levi's, Coca-Cola, Marlboro, Gillette, McDonald's, and Kentucky Fried Chicken. But names blazoned in neon atop the skyscrapers of Tokyo—Hitachi, Sony, Sanyo, and Mitsubishi—also commanded instant recognition, as did such European names as Nestlé, Mercedes, Pirelli, and Benetton. The concept of a globe-girdling American consumer culture had been overtaken by internationalization. Yet, on balance, the overall direction of change in popular culture and consumer taste during the decades following World War II was indeed toward the United States.

Some Marxist intellectuals interpreted the spread of American products as simply another form of imperialism, inevitably destroying local crafts, styles, and cultural traditions. But most young Turks, Nigerians, Taiwanese, and others who liked to wear Levis's jeans, drink Coke, smoke Camels, and listen to rock 'n' roll had little sense of being under the thumb of the imperialists. Although their nations' economies may have been in thrall to transnational business concerns, they themselves generally felt free to condemn American foreign policy and considered their personal style preferences simply a result of living within an increasingly global culture. Thus, the reality of cultural imperialism was far more ambiguous than European imperialism had been in the days of colonial viceroys and gunboat diplomacy.

Global Connections and Elite Culture

While the globalization of popular culture became a subject of dispute, cultural links across national and ethnic boundaries at a more elite level generated less controversy. The end of the Cold War reopened intellectual and cultural contacts between former adversaries, making possible such things as Russian-American collaboration on space missions and extensive business contacts among former rivals. Graduate education became increasingly global.

Spurred by American economic, political, and cultural eminence in the second half of the century, English spread as a global language even as the British Empire faded away. English became the most commonly taught second language in the world, and a number of technology-intensive industries, including air transportation and computers, used it extensively. In newly independent countries, even universities that took pride in teaching in the national language often had science faculties that operated in English.

Architectural design and engineering afford another example of globalization at the higher cultural level. The International Style pioneered by European architects in the 1920s (see Chapter 25) was the guiding aesthetic for the austere, ornament-free skyscrapers sheathed in glass that began to rise in world capitals in the 1960s.

The International Style was criticized, however, for neglecting local architectural traditions. In the United States, this criticism formed the foundation of **postmodernism,** a movement that called for abandoning the rigid rules of architectural modernism and showing greater sensitivity to history and local context and for allowing diverse voices, such as those of minorities, to be heard. Some architects, including a growing number from non-Western countries, responded to the postmodern critique. Conventional glass and steel skyscrapers continued to be built, but liberation from the International Style permitted architects in different countries to follow their own inclinations and experiment with a broad array of forms, surface decoration, and references to earlier architectural traditions.

Dance, music, literature, and cultural theory were all affected by postmodernist impulses, though the forms they took differed from one area to another. Common to much postmodernist thought was a sense that the modernist styles that composed the artistic avant-garde between 1850 and 1950 reflected the limited perspective of an elite, white, male European-American intelligentsia preoccupied with individualism and innovation. Against this background, postmodernism championed an aesthetic based on multiculturalism, social inclusion, historical continuity, and styles and forms from everyday life.

Postmodernism was not the only indicator of cultural change on a global scale. Among the ten winners of the Nobel Prize for literature between 1982 and 1991 were writers from Colombia, Nigeria, Egypt, Mexico, and the West Indies. By contrast, the previous decade's winners had included only one non-European. The prize committee thus helped the world recognize the growing strength of its cultural diversity.

The West, for good or ill, dominated the early postimperialist era because the web of international contact made possible by advanced technologies had yet to reach its full extent or become accessible to most people. According to one estimate, at the end of the century, half of the world's people had never spoken on a telephone. The cultural changes spurred by technology were only in midcourse, and technology seemed likely to offer a means of releasing profound creative energies in unexpected locales.

The Endurance of Cultural Diversity

Diverse cultural traditions persisted at the twentieth century's end despite globalization. Japan demonstrated that a country with a non-Western culture could perform at a high economic level. The efficiency, pride in workmanship, and group solidarity of Japanese workers, supported by closely coordinated government and corporate policies, played a major role in transforming Japan from a defeated nation with a demolished industrial base in 1945 to an economic power by the 1980s.

Japan's success in the modern industrial world called into question an assumption common in the immediate postwar era. Since industrialization was pioneered by Europeans and Americans, many Westerners thought that the spread of industrialization to different parts of the world would require the adoption of Western culture in every area of life. As awareness of the economic impact of Japanese culture and society began to spread, however, it became apparent that Taiwan and South Korea, along with Singapore and Hong Kong (a British colony before being reunited with China in 1997), were developing dynamic industrial economies of their own. Until the Asian financial crisis of 1997, Muslim Malaysia and Buddhist Thailand had appeared to be embarking on the same road to development. Had Japan been unique, or would cultural variety prove fully compatible with industrial growth and prosperity worldwide?

Clearly, the long-standing Western assumption of European and American exceptionalism—the belief that all of world history culminated in the exceptional convergence of political freedom, secularism, and industrialization in the West—needed to be abandoned. So, too, did the corollary that the twenty-first century would be as thoroughly dominated by Western culture and economic and political power as the previous two centuries had been.

Also coming into question was whether industrialization offered the only viable route to prosperity. As computer technology continued to change almost all aspects of life, perhaps countries could achieve prosperity in the twenty-first century primarily through their control of information and telecommunications.

The lesson to be drawn from the success of Japan and the other rising economic powers of Asia was not that Western technology pointed the way to universal well-being, but rather that human ingenuity and adaptability are endlessly fertile and creative. Human cultural achievement has historically followed unpredictable paths, reaching one sort of climax in one time and place and a different sort in another. In the same spirit, the future locus of spiritual and cultural achievement remained essentially unpredictable at the start of a new millennium.

CONCLUSION

The final decade of the twentieth century witnessed a burgeoning of computer and telecommunications technology that fostered the worldwide spread of popular culture while at the same time enabling businesses and financial markets to operate on a truly global scale. It also witnessed an intensification of world concerns for human rights as fears of international conflicts between great powers faded into the past. But in some respects, it was more strongly marked by things that came to an end than by things that had their start.

For nearly eight decades, from the outbreak of World War I to the dissolution of the Soviet Union, a world whose economic and political destiny had seemed firmly in the grip of European imperialism witnessed an increasingly lethal struggle between competing European ideologies. The outcome of the struggle, in which all the peoples of the world eventually became principals or pawns, was often in doubt. Each camp accused the other of leading humanity down the road to slavery—slavery to fascist or communist dictators according to one side, slavery to the insatiable greed of capitalist profiteers according to the other. Each camp similarly had a vision of how it would organize the world in the event of victory. Adolf Hitler visualized a "thousand year Reich [empire]" serving the desires of an Aryan superrace. Communists spoke of a "workers' paradise" of equality and brotherhood. Responding to these oppressive visions, Western leaders extolled the virtues of "freedom," a world order that would permit all peoples to elect their own governments and allow every individual to pursue his or her individual destiny in an open and competitive market environment.

Victory, when it came, proved far more complicated and puzzling than Western ideologues had anticipated. Though "democratization" and "economic liberalization" became watchwords of Western, and particularly American, foreign policy, many of the world's peoples proved less concerned with liberal ideology than with ethnic, linguistic, and religious quarrels or with simply maintaining life and hope in circumstances of increasing poverty and overpopulation. Developing countries and post-communist countries alike looked to the United States, Europe, and Japan for financial salvation, introducing democratic institutions and open markets only to the degree necessary to gain Western support.

The United States and the other major industrial countries recognized that they could not meet all of the world's demands, but they were reluctant to put too much trust in international bodies such as the United Nations, which had no financial resources beyond the dues paid by its member states. Thus, the end of the global contest among European ideologies did not produce a workable model of a world community. To the contrary, local conflicts and atrocities proliferated in the 1990s, and more and more countries debated whether to seek

Millennium Celebration in Sydney, Australia   Uncertainties about what lay ahead for the world in the twenty-first century took a backseat to exuberant festivities as the millennium ended. The sleek modern silhouette of Sidney's opera house and the neon signs of major corporations epitomized the hopes of many.   (Sydney Morning Herald/Sipa Press)

nuclear weapons or other weapons of mass destruction in anticipation of future confrontations.

Yet while world order seemed as unattainable as ever before, economic, technological, and cultural forces drew the world's peoples ever closer together. Since the victors in the world struggle had been the capitalists rather than the fascists or communists, private business and consumer economics expanded aggressively into every region of the globe, checked only by market conditions and rearguard efforts by authoritarian governments, such as that of China, to control the pace and direction of change.

For most of the world's population, the 1990s brought greater desire for and access to consumer goods, and a globalized culture became more and more a reality. But the logic of global economic growth, with its immense demands on clean water, clear air, and nonrenewable resources, made it clear that some of the world's greatest problems, including how to preserve the shared global environment for future generations of humanity, had no obvious solutions and had only begun to be addressed.

■ Key Terms

ethnic cleansing

economic sanctions

World Trade Organization (WTO)

terrorism

nuclear nonproliferation

Universal Declaration of Human Rights

nongovernmental organizations (NGOs)

cultural imperialism

high culture

popular culture

postmodernism

■ Suggested Reading

Many of the subjects in this chapter are covered by thematic essays in Richard W. Bulliet, ed., *The Columbia History of the Twentieth Century* (1998).

The Bosnian crisis is well covered in Susan L. Woodward, *Balkan Tragedy: Chaos and Dissolution After the Cold War* (1995). Other world crises involving international intervention are treated in William J. Durch, ed., *UN Peacekeeping, American Policy, and the Uncivil Wars of the 1990s* (1996). Terrorism is well covered by Bruce Hoffman, *Inside Terrorism* (1998). Gilles Kepel, *The Revenge of God: The Resurgence of Islam, Christianity, and Judaism in the Modern World* (1994), deals with recent religio-political movements. Human rights are well surveyed by Jack Donnelly, *International Human Rights*, 2d ed. (1998).

A seminal book in the awakening of the feminist movement in the 1970s is Betty Friedan, *The Feminine Mystique* (1974). For the revival of feminism in Europe, see Gisela Kaplan, *Contemporary Western European Feminism* (1992). For non-Western perspectives, see Phyllis Andors, *The Unfinished Liberation of Chinese Women, 1949–1980* (1983), and Chandra Talpade Mohanty, Ann Russo, and Lourdes Torres, eds., *Third World Women and the Politics of Feminism* (1991).

The interrelationships between high culture and popular culture during the twentieth century are treated from very different perspectives by Greil Marcus, *Lipstick Traces: A Secret History of the Twentieth Century* (1989), and Kurt Varnedoe, *High and Low: Modern Art and Popular Culture* (1991). The former concentrates on the avant-garde from dada to punk rock, the latter on images from popular culture used in art. Two very readable books by James B. Twitchell, *Carnival Culture: The Trashing of Taste in America* (1992) and *Adcult USA: The Triumph of Advertising in American Culture* (1996), detail the rise of popular culture in the United States and present various reactions to this phenomenon.

Many interpretations of and approaches to postmodernism are sampled in Thomas Docherty, ed., *Postmodernism: A Reader* (1993). These may be compared with a classic early statement of modernism: Amédée Ozenfant's *Foundations of Modern Art* (1931).

Thomas P. Hughes, *American Genesis: A Century of Invention and Technological Enthusiasm, 1870–1970* (1989), offers a far-ranging account of the American role in twentieth-century technological change by an outstanding historian of technology. Books on films and the film industry around the world are legion. A good place to start is Gerald Mast, *A Short History of the Movies* (1986). A similar survey of jazz music is available from Marshall W. Stearns, *The Story of Jazz* (1970). For the rock video phenomenon, see E. Ann Kaplan, *Rocking Around the Clock: Music Television, Postmodernism, and Consumer Culture* (1987).

Some noteworthy novels that have attempted to visualize the near future on the basis of current perceptions of technological change, environmental deterioration, and growth of transnational corporations are David Brin, *Earth* (1990), and Bruce Sterling, *Islands in the Net* (1988). See too William Gibson's "Sprawl" trilogy: *Neuromancer* (1984), *Count Zero* (1987), and *Mona Lisa Overdrive* (1988).

■ Notes

1. "Universal Declaration of Human Rights," in *Twenty-Five Human Rights Documents* (New York: Center for the Study of Human Rights, Columbia University, 1994), 6.
2. Ibid.

GLOSSARY

The glossary for *The Earth and Its Peoples,* 2/e Brief is for the complete text, Chapters 1 through 30.

Abbasid Caliphate Descendants of the Prophet Muhammad's uncle, al-Abbas, the Abbasids overthrew the **Umayyad Caliphate** and ruled an Islamic empire from their capital in Baghdad (founded 762) from 750 to 1258. (*p. 181*)

abolitionists Men and women who agitated for a complete end to slavery. British abolitionists achieved the abolition of the transatlantic slave trade in 1808 and slavery in 1834. American abolitionist activities were one factor leading to the Civil War (1861–1865). (*p. 460*)

absolutism The theory of unlimited royal power popular in France and other early modern European monarchies. (*p. 371*)

Acheh Sultanate Muslim kingdom in northern Sumatra. Main center of Islamic expansion in Southeast Asia in the early seventeenth century, it declined after the Dutch seized **Malacca** from Portugal in 1641. (*p. 419*)

Aden Port city in the modern south Arabian country of Yemen. A major center in Indian Ocean trade. (*p. 315*)

African National Congress An organization seeking equal voting and civil rights for black inhabitants of South Africa. Founded in 1912 as the South African Native National Congress, it changed its name in 1923. Though it was banned and its leaders were jailed, it helped bring majority rule to South Africa. (*p. 588*)

Afrikaners South Africans descended from Dutch and French settlers of the seventeenth century. Their Great Trek founded new colonies in the nineteenth century. A minority among South Africans, they held political power after 1910, imposing racial segregation (apartheid) after 1949. (*p. 530*)

Agricultural Revolution(s) (ancient) The change from food gathering to food production that occurred between ca. 8000 and 2000 B.C.E. Also known as the Neolithic Revolution. (*p. 8*)

Agricultural Revolution (eighteenth century) The transformation of farming resulting from the spread of new crops, improvements in cultivation and livestock breeding, and consolidation of small holdings into large farms from which tenants and sharecroppers were forcibly expelled. (*p. 464*)

Aguinaldo, Emilio (1869–1964) Leader of the Filipino independence movement against Spain (1895–1898). He proclaimed independence in 1899. His movement was crushed and he was captured by the United States Army in 1901. (*p. 533*)

Akbar (1542–1605) Most illustrious sultan of the Mughal Empire in India (r. 1556–1605). He expanded the empire and pursued a policy of conciliation with Hindus. (*p. 416*)

Akhenaten Egyptian pharaoh (r. 1353–1335 B.C.E.). He built a new capital at Amarna, fostered a new style of naturalistic art, and imposed worship of the sun-disk. The Amarna letters, largely from his reign, preserve official correspondence with subjects and neighbors. (*p. 47*)

Alexander (356–323 B.C.E.) King of Macedonia in northern Greece. Between 334 and 323 B.C.E. he conquered the Persian Empire, reached the Indus Valley, and founded many Greek-style cities. Later known as Alexander the Great. (*p. 105*)

Alexandria City on the Mediterranean coast of Egypt founded by Alexander. The capital of the Hellenistic kingdom of the **Ptolemies**, it contained the famous Library and the Museum—a center for science and literature. Its merchants traded in the Mediterranean and the Indian Ocean. (*p. 106*)

Allende, Salvador (1908–1973) Socialist politician elected president of Chile in 1970 and overthrown by the military in 1973. He died during the military attack. (*p. 625*)

All-India Muslim League Organization founded in India in 1906 to defend the interests of India's Muslim minority. Led by Muhammad Ali Jinnah, it negotiated with the **Indian National Congress.** In 1940, the League began demanding a separate state for Muslims, to be called Pakistan. (See also **Jinnah, Muhammad Ali.**) (*p. 591*)

amulet Charm meant to protect the bearer from evil. Amulets reflect the religious practices of the common people. (*p. 19*)

Anasazi Important culture of what is now the southwest of the United States (1000–1300 C.E.). Centered on Chaco Canyon in New Mexico and Mesa Verde in Colorado, the Anasazi culture built multistory residences and worshiped in subterranean buildings called kivas. (*p. 248*)

aqueduct A conduit, either elevated or under ground, using gravity to carry water from a source to a city. (*p. 134*)

Arawak Amerindian peoples who inhabited the Greater Antilles of the Caribbean at the time of Columbus. (*p. 345*)

Armenia Areas in eastern Anatolia and the western Caucasus occupied by speakers of the Armenian language. One of the earliest Christian kingdoms. (*p. 168*)

Asante African kingdom on the **Gold Coast** that expanded rapidly after 1680. Asante traded gold, slaves, and ivory and resisted British imperial ambitions for a quarter century before being absorbed into Britain's Gold Coast colony in 1902. (*p. 531*)

Ashikaga Shogunate (1336–1573) The second of Japan's military governments headed by a shogun (a military ruler). Sometimes called the Muromachi Shogunate. (*p. 298*)

Ashoka Third ruler of the **Mauryan Empire** in India (r. 270–232 B.C.E.). He converted to Buddhism and broadcast his precepts on inscribed stones and pillars, the earliest surviving Indian writing. (*p. 116*)

Ashur Chief deity of the Assyrians and bringer of victory in war. Also the name of an important Assyrian religious and political center. (*p. 70*)

Asian Tigers Collective name for South Korea, Taiwan, Hong Kong, and Singapore—nations that became economic powers in the 1970s and 1980s. (*p. 630*)

Atahualpa (1502?–1533) Last ruling Inca emperor of Peru. He was executed by the Spanish. (*p. 358*)

Atlantic system The trade network that after 1500 moved goods, people, and cultures around the Atlantic Ocean. (*p. 383*)

Augustus (63 B.C.E.–14 C.E.) Honorific name of Octavian, founder of the **Roman Principate,** the military dictatorship that replaced the failing rule of the **Roman Senate.** After defeating rivals, between 31 B.C.E. and 14 C.E. he laid the groundwork for stability and prosperity in the Roman Empire. (*p. 129*)

Auschwitz Nazi extermination camp in Poland, the largest center of mass murder during the **Holocaust.** Close to a million Jews, Gypsies, Communists, and others were killed there. (*p. 579*)

autocracy Strong, centralized rule, such as by the **tsar** in Russia or **Haile Selassie** in Ethiopia. Autocrats did not rely on the aristocracy or the clergy for legitimacy. (*p. 431*)

ayllu Andean lineage group or kin-based community. (*p. 250*)

Aztecs Also known as Mexica, the Aztecs created a powerful empire in central Mexico (1325–1521 C.E.). They forced defeated peoples to provide goods and labor as a tax. (*p. 245*)

Babylon The largest and most important city in Mesopotamia, the capital of the Amorite king **Hammurabi** in the eighteenth century B.C.E. and the Neo-Babylonian king Nebuchadnezzar in the sixth century B.C.E. (*p. 14*)

balance of power Political strategy by which, beginning in the eighteenth century, the European states acted together to prevent any from becoming too powerful. (*p. 373*)

Balfour Declaration Statement issued by Britain's Foreign Secretary Arthur Balfour in 1917 favoring the establishment of a Jewish national home in Palestine. (*p. 548*)

Bannermen Hereditary military servants of the **Qing Empire,** whose ancestors of various origins had fought for the founders of the empire. (*p. 496*)

Bantu Name of a large group of sub-Saharan African languages and of the peoples speaking them. (*p. 167*)

Batavia Fort established ca. 1619 as headquarters of Dutch East India Company operations in Indonesia; today the city of Jakarta. (*p. 422*)

Battle of Midway U.S. naval victory over the Japanese fleet in June 1942. The Japanese lost four of their best aircraft carriers, making it a turning point in World War II. (*p. 576*)

Beijing China's northern capital, first used as an imperial capital in 906 and now the capital of the People's Republic of China. (*p. 283*)

Bengal Region of northeastern India, the first to be conquered by the British in the eighteenth century. It remained the center of British India throughout the nineteenth century. The 1905 split of the province into predominantly Hindu West Bengal and predominantly Muslim East Bengal (now Bangladesh) sparked anti-British riots. (*p. 589*)

Berlin Conference (1884–1885) Conference that German chancellor Otto von Bismarck called to set rules for the partition of Africa. It led to the creation of the Congo Free State under King **Leopold II** of Belgium. (See also **Bismarck, Otto von.**) (*p. 528*)

Bhagavad-Gita The most important work of Indian sacred literature, a dialogue between the warrior Arjuna and the god Krishna on duty and the fate of the spirit. (*p. 117*)

Bismarck, Otto von (1815–1898) Chancellor (prime minister) of Prussia from 1862 until 1871, when he became chancellor of Germany. A conservative nationalist, he led Prussia to victory against Austria (1866) and France (1870) and was responsible for the creation of the German Empire in 1871. (*p. 512*)

Black Death An outbreak of **bubonic plague** that spread across Asia, North Africa, and Europe in the mid-fourteenth century, carrying off vast numbers of persons. (*p. 326*)

Bolívar, Simón (1783–1830) The most important military leader in the struggle for independence in South America. Born in Venezuela, he led military forces there and in Colombia, Ecuador, Peru, and Bolivia. (*p. 457*)

Bolsheviks Marxist party founded by Vladimir Lenin in 1903. Under Lenin's leadership, they seized power in November 1917 during the Russian Revolution. (See also **Lenin, Vladimir.**) (*p. 548*)

Bonaparte, Napoleon. See **Napoleon I.**

Borobodur A massive stone monument on the Indonesian island of Java, erected by the Sailendra kings around 800 C.E. (*p. 160*)

bourgeoisie In early modern Europe, the class of well-off town dwellers whose wealth came from manufacturing, finance, commerce, and allied professions. (*p. 375*)

breech-loading rifle Gun into which bullets were individually inserted at the end of the barrel above the trigger. Later guns had magazines, a compartment holding multiple bullets. (*p. 479*)

British raj The rule over much of South Asia between 1765 and 1947 by the East India Company and then by the British government. (*p. 490*)

bubonic plague A bacterial disease transmitted by flea bites to rodents and humans; humans in late stages of the illness can spread the bacteria by coughing. Highly lethal and hard to prevent, major plague epidemics have created crises in many parts of the world. (See also **Black Death.**) (*pp. 223, 268*)

Buddha (563–483 B.C.E.) An Indian prince named Siddhartha Gautama, who renounced his social position. After becoming "enlightened" (the meaning of *Buddha*) he enunciated the principles of Buddhism. (See also **Mahayana Buddhism; Theravada Buddhism.**) (*p. 112*)

Byzantine Empire Historians' name for the eastern portion of the Roman Empire from the fourth century onward, taken from "Byzantion," an early name for Constantinople, the Byzantine capital city. The empire fell to the Ottomans in 1453. (See also **Ottoman Empire.**) (*p. 196*)

caliphate Office established in succession to the Prophet Muhammad, to rule the Islamic empire; also the name of that empire. (See also **Abbasid Caliphate; Sokoto Caliphate; Umayyad Caliphate.**) (*p. 179*)

capitalism The economic system of investment in business in return for a share of the profits that first developed in early modern Europe. *Commercial capitalism,* the trading system of the early modern economy, is often distinguished from *industrial capitalism,* the system based on machine production. (*p. 397*)

caravel A small, highly maneuverable three-masted ship used by the Portuguese and Spanish in the exploration of the Atlantic. (*p. 348*)

Cárdenas, Lázaro (1895–1970) President of Mexico (1934–1940). He changed Mexican life by distributing land to the peasants, bringing representatives of workers and farmers into politics, and nationalizing the oil industry. (*p. 596*)

Carthage City located in present-day Tunisia, founded by **Phoenicians** ca. 800 B.C.E. It became a major commercial center and naval power in the western Mediterranean until defeated by Rome in the third century B.C.E. (*p. 81*)

Catholic Reformation Religious reform movement within the Latin Christian Church, begun in response to the **Protestant Reformation**. It clarified Catholic theology and reformed clerical training and discipline. (*p. 366*)

Celts Peoples sharing a common language and culture that originated in Central Europe in the first half of the first millennium B.C.E. After 500 B.C.E. they spread as far as Anatolia, Spain, and the British Isles. Later overtaken by Roman conquest and Germanic invasions, their descendants survive on the western fringe of Europe (Brittany, Wales, Scotland, Ireland). (*p. 68*)

Champa A state located in what is now southern Vietnam. It was hostile to Annam and was annexed by Annam and destroyed as an independent entity in 1500. (*p. 299*)

Champa rice Quick-maturing rice that yields two harvests in one growing season. Originally introduced into Champa from India, it was later sent to China as a tribute gift by the Champa state. (See also **tributary system.**) (*p. 235*)

Chang'an City in the Wei Valley in eastern China. It became the capital of the Zhou kingdom and the Qin and early Han Empires. (*p. 141*)

Charlemagne (742–814) King of the Franks (r. 768–814); emperor (r. 800–814). Through a series of military conquests he established the Carolingian Empire, which encompassed all of Gaul and parts of Germany and Italy. Though illiterate himself, he sponsored a brief intellectual revival. (*p. 195*)

chartered companies Groups of private investors who paid an annual fee to a European government in exchange for a monopoly over trade in a foreign area. (*p. 397*)

Chavín The first major urban civilization in South America (900–250 B.C.E.). Its capital, Chavín de Huántar, was located high in the Andes Mountains of Peru. Chavín became dominant in a densely populated region that included the Peruvian coastal plain and the Andean foothills. (*p. 67*)

Chiang Kai-shek (Jiang Jieshi; 1887–1975) General and leader of Nationalist China after 1925. Although he succeeded **Sun Yat-sen** as head of the **Guomindang,** he became a military dictator and enemy of the communist movement led by **Mao Zedong.** (*p. 571*)

chiefdom Form of political organization with rule by a hereditary leader exercising power over a collection of villages and towns. Less powerful than a kingdom or empire, a chiefdom was based on gift giving and commercial links. (*p. 249*)

Chimú Powerful Peruvian civilization based on conquest. Located in the region earlier dominated by **Moche.** Conquered by **Inca** in 1465. (*p. 252*)

chinampas Raised fields constructed along lake shores in Mesoamerica to increase agricultural yields. (*p. 240*)

city-state A small independent state consisting of an urban center and the surrounding agricultural territory. A characteristic political form in early Mesopotamia, Archaic and Classical Greece, Phoenicia, and early Italy. (See also **polis.**) (*p. 15*)

civilization An ambiguous term often used to denote complex societies but sometimes used by anthropologists to describe a group of people sharing a set of cultural traits. (*p. 5*)

Cixi, Empress Dowager (1835–1908) Empress of China and mother of Emperor Guangxi. She put her son under house arrest, supported antiforeign movements, and resisted reforms of the government and armed forces. (*p. 553*)

clipper ship Large, fast, streamlined sailing vessel, often American built, of the mid-to-late nineteenth century. (*p. 493*)

Cold War (1945–1991) The ideological struggle between communism (Soviet Union) and capitalism (United States) for world influence. The Soviet Union and the United States came to the brink of actual war during the **Cuban missile crisis** but never attacked one another. The Cold War came to an end when the Soviet Union dissolved in 1991. (See also **North Atlantic Treaty Organization; Warsaw Pact.**) (*p. 604*)

Columbian Exchange The exchange of plants, animals, diseases, and technologies between the Americas and the rest of the world following Columbus's voyage. (*p. 401*)

Columbus, Christopher (1451–1506) Genoese mariner who in the service of Spain led expeditions across the Atlantic, establishing contact between the Americas and the Old World and initiating Spanish conquest and colonization. (*p. 351*)

Confucius Western name for the Chinese philosopher Kongzi (551–479 B.C.E.). His doctrine of duty and public service influenced subsequent Chinese thought and served as a code of conduct for government officials. (*p. 43*)

Congress of Vienna (1814–1815) Meeting of representatives of European monarchs called to reestablish the old order after the defeat of **Napoleon I.** (*p. 454*)

conquistadors Early-sixteenth-century Spanish adventurers who conquered Mexico, Central America, and Peru. See **Cortés, Hernán; Pizarro, Francisco.**) (*p. 356*)

Constantine (285–337 C.E.) Roman emperor (r. 312–337). After reuniting the Roman Empire, he moved the capital to Constantinople and made Christianity a favored religion. (*p. 135*)

Constitutional Convention Meeting in 1787 of the elected representatives of the thirteen original states to write the Constitution of the United States. (*p. 450*)

constitutionalism The theory developed in early modern England and spread elsewhere that royal power should be subject to legal and legislative checks. (*p. 371*)

Cortés, Hernán (1485–1547) Spanish explorer and conquistador who led the conquest of Aztec Mexico in 1519–1521. (*p. 356*)

Cossacks Peoples of the Russian Empire who lived outside the farming villages, often as herders, mercenaries, or outlaws. Cossacks led the conquest of Siberia in the sixteenth and seventeenth centuries. (*p. 430*)

cottage industries Weaving, sewing, carving, and other small-scale industries that can be done in the home. (*p. 286*)

cotton The plant that produces fibers from which cotton textiles are woven. Native to India, cotton spread throughout Asia and then to the New World. It has been a major cash crop in various places, including early Islamic Iran, Yi Korea, and nineteenth-century Egypt and the United States. A related species was exploited for fiber in pre-Columbian America. (*p. 296*)

Council of the Indies The institution responsible for supervising Spain's colonies in the Americas from 1524 to the early eighteenth century, when it lost all but judicial responsibilities. (*p. 383*)

creoles In colonial Spanish America, term used to describe someone of European descent born in the New World. Elsewhere in the Americas, the term is used to describe all non-native peoples. (*p. 386*)

Crimean War (1853–1856) Conflict between the Russian and Ottoman Empires fought primarily in the Crimean Peninsula. To prevent Russian expansion, Britain and France sent troops to support the Ottomans. (*p. 478*)

Crusades (1096–1291) Armed pilgrimages to the Holy Land by Christians determined to recover Jerusalem from Muslim rule. The Crusades brought an end to western Europe's centuries of intellectual and cultural isolation. (*p. 210*)

Cuban missile crisis (1962) Brink-of-war confrontation between the United States and the Soviet Union over the latter's placement of nuclear-armed missiles in Cuba. (*p. 616*)

cultural imperialism Domination of one culture over another by a deliberate policy or by economic or technological superiority. (*p. 654*)

Cultural Revolution (China) (1966–1969) Campaign in China ordered by **Mao Zedong** to purge the Communist Party of his opponents and instill revolutionary values in the younger generation. (*p. 619*)

culture Socially transmitted patterns of action and expression. *Material culture* refers to physical objects, such as dwellings, clothing, tools, and crafts. Culture also includes arts, beliefs, knowledge, and technology. (*p. 5*)

cuneiform A Mesopotamian system of writing in which wedge-shaped symbols represented words or syllables. It was used initially for Sumerian and Akkadian but later was adapted to other languages of western Asia. (*p. 20*)

Cyrus (600–530 B.C.E.) Founder of the Achaemenid Persian Empire. Between 550 and 530 B.C.E. he conquered Media, Lydia, and Babylon. He employed Persians and Medes in his administration and respected the institutions and beliefs of subject peoples. (*p. 90*)

czar See **tsar.**

Daoism Chinese school of thought, originating in the Warring States Period with Laozi (604–531 B.C.E.). Daoism offered an alternative to the Confucian emphasis on hierarchy and duty. Daoists believe that the world is always changing and is devoid of absolute morality or meaning. They accept the world as they find it, avoid futile struggles, and deviate as little as possible from the *Dao,* or "path" of nature. (See also **Confucius.**) (*p. 44*)

Darius I (ca. 558–486 B.C.E.) Third ruler of the Persian Empire (r. 521–486 B.C.E.). He established a system of provinces and tribute, began construction of Persepolis, and expanded Persian control in the east (Pakistan) and west (northern Greece). (*p. 90*)

Darwin, Charles (1809–1882) English naturalist. He studied the plants and animals of South America and the Pacific islands, and in his book *On the Origin of Species by Means of Natural Selection* (1859) set forth his theory of **evolution.** (*p. 513*)

Declaration of the Rights of Man (1789) Statement of fundamental political rights adopted by the French **National Assembly** at the beginning of the French Revolution. (*p. 451*)

deforestation The removal of trees faster than forests can replace themselves. (*p. 376*)

Delhi Sultanate (1206–1526) Centralized Indian empire of varying extent, created by Muslim invaders. (*p. 306*)

democracy A system of government in which all "citizens" (however defined) have equal political and legal rights, privileges, and protections, as in the Greek city-state of Athens in the fifth and fourth centuries B.C.E. (*p. 98*)

demographic transition A change in the rates of population growth. Before the transition, both birth and death rates are high, resulting in a slowly growing population; then the death rate drops but the birth rate remains high, causing a population explosion; finally the birth rate drops and the population growth slows down. This transition took place in Europe in the late nineteenth and early twentieth centuries, in North America and East Asia in the mid-twentieth,

and, most recently, in Latin America and South Asia. (*p. 635*)

Deng Xiaoping (1904–1997) Communist Party leader who forced Chinese economic reforms after the death of **Mao Zedong.** (*p. 630*)

dhow Ship of small to moderate size used in the western Indian Ocean, traditionally with a triangular sail and a sewn timber hull. (*p. 313*)

Dias, Bartolomeu (1450?–1500) Portuguese explorer who in 1488 led the first expedition to sail around the southern tip of Africa and sight the Indian Ocean. (*p. 349*)

Diaspora A Greek word meaning "dispersal," used to describe the communities of a given ethnic group living outside their homeland. Jews, for example, spread from Israel to western Asia and Mediterranean lands in antiquity and today can be found throughout the world. (*p. 78*)

Dirty War War waged by the Argentine military (1976–1982) against leftist groups. Characterized by the use of illegal imprisonment, torture, and executions. (*p. 626*)

divination Techniques for ascertaining the future or the will of the gods by interpreting natural phenomena such as, in early China, the cracks on oracle bones or, in ancient Greece, the flight of birds. (*p. 42*)

division of labor The breaking down of a manufacturing process into a series of steps. The pottery shop of Josiah Wedgwood and other eighteenth-century factories divided labor into many simple and repetitive tasks that could be performed by unskilled laborers. This greatly increased the productivity of labor and lowered the cost of goods. (See also **Wedgwood, Josiah.**) (*p. 466*)

driver A privileged male slave whose job was to ensure that a slave gang did its work on a plantation. (*p. 395*)

Druids The class of religious experts who conducted rituals and preserved sacred lore among some ancient Celtic peoples. They provided education and mediated disputes until suppressed by the Romans as a potential focus of opposition. (See also **Celts.**) (*p. 68*)

Dutch West India Company (1621–1794) Company chartered by the Dutch government to trade in the Americas and Africa. (*p. 397*)

economic sanctions Boycotts, embargoes, and other economic measures that one country uses to pressure another country into changing its policies. (*p. 650*)

Edison, Thomas (1847–1931) American inventor of the electric light bulb, acoustic recording on wax cylinders, and motion pictures. (*p. 505*)

Einstein, Albert (1879–1955) German physicist who developed the theory of relativity, which states that time, space, and mass are relative to each other and not fixed. (*p. 558*)

electricity A form of energy used in telegraphy from the 1840s on and for lighting, industrial motors, and railroads beginning in the 1880s. (*p. 505*)

electric telegraph A device for transmission of information over an electric wire. It was introduced in England and North America in the 1830s and 1840s and replaced systems of visual signals such as semaphores. (See also **submarine telegraph cables.**) (*p. 470*)

encomienda A grant of authority over a population of Amerindians in the Spanish colonies. It provided the grant holder a supply of cheap labor and periodic payments of goods by the Amerindians. It obliged the grant holder to spread Christianity. (*p. 386*)

Enlightenment A philosophical movement in eighteenth-century Europe that fostered the belief that one could reform society by discovering rational laws that governed social behavior. (*pp. 379, 445*)

equites In ancient Italy, prosperous landowners second in status to the senatorial aristocracy. The Roman emperors allied with this group to counterbalance the old aristocracy and used them to staff the imperial civil service. (*p. 129*)

Estates General France's traditional national assembly with representatives of the three estates, or classes, in French society: the clergy, nobility, and commoners. The calling of the Estates General in 1789 led to the French Revolution. (*p. 451*)

Ethiopia East African highland nation lying east of the Nile River. (See also **Menelik II; Selassie, Haile.**) (*p. 168*)

ethnic cleansing Effort to eradicate a people and its culture by means of mass killing and the destruction of historical buildings and cultural materials. Ethnic cleansing was used by both sides in the conflicts that accompanied the disintegration of Yugoslavia in the 1990s. (*p. 646*)

European Community (EC) An organization promoting economic unity in Europe formed in 1967 by consolidation of earlier, more limited, agreements. Replaced by the European Union (EU) in 1993. (*p. 613*)

Faisal I (1885–1933) Arab prince, leader of the Arab Revolt in World War I. The British made him king of Iraq in 1921, and he reigned under British protection until 1933. (*p. 548*)

Fascist Party Italian political party created by Benito Mussolini during World War I. It emphasized aggressive nationalism and was Mussolini's instrument for the creation of a dictatorship in Italy from 1922 to 1943. (See also **Mussolini, Benito.**) (*p. 568*)

fief In medieval Europe, land granted in return for a sworn oath to provide specified military service. (*p. 202*)

First Temple A sanctuary built in Jerusalem by King Solomon in the tenth century B.C.E. to be the religious center for the Israelite god Yahweh. The First Temple was destroyed by the Babylonians in 587 B.C.E., rebuilt on a modest scale in the late sixth century B.C.E., and replaced by King Herod's Second Temple in the late first century B.C.E. (destroyed by the Romans in 70 C.E.) (*p. 76*)

Five-Year Plans Plans that Joseph Stalin introduced to industrialize the Soviet Union rapidly, beginning in 1928. They set goals for the output of steel, electricity, machinery, and most other products. Many countries followed this example after World War II. (See also **Stalin, Joseph.**) (*p. 564*)

foragers People who support themselves by hunting wild animals and gathering wild edible plants and insects. (*p. 7*)

Forbidden City The walled section of Beijing where emperors lived between 1121 and 1924. A portion is now a residence for leaders of the People's Republic of China. (*p. 289*)

free-trade imperialism Economic dominance of a weaker country by a more powerful one, while maintaining the legal independence of the weaker state. In the late nineteenth century, free-trade imperialism characterized the relations between the Latin American republics, on the one hand, and Great Britain and the United States, on the other. (*p. 535*)

fresco A technique of painting on walls covered with moist plaster. It was used to decorate Minoan and Mycenaean palaces and Roman villas, and became an important medium during the Italian Renaissance. (*p. 52*)

Funan An early complex society in Southeast Asia between the first and sixth centuries C.E. It was centered in southern Vietnam and controlled the passage of trade across the Malaysian isthmus. (*p. 158*)

Gama, Vasco da (1460?–1524) Portuguese explorer. In 1497–1498 he led the first naval expedition from Europe to India, opening an important commercial sea route. (*p. 349*)

Gandhi, Mohandas K. (Mahatma) (1869–1948) Leader of the Indian independence movement and advocate of nonviolent resistance. Educated as a lawyer in England, he returned to India and became leader of the **Indian National Congress** in 1920. He appealed to the poor and led nonviolent demonstrations against colonial rule. Soon after independence he was assassinated for attempting to stop Hindu-Muslim rioting. (*p. 592*)

Genghis Khan (ca. 1167–1227) The title of Temüjin when he ruled the Mongols (1206–1227). It means the "oceanic" or "universal" leader. Genghis Khan was the founder of the Mongol Empire. (*p. 262*)

gens de couleur Free men and women of color in Haiti. They sought greater political rights and later supported the Haitian Revolution. (See also **L'Ouverture, François Dominique Toussaint.**) (*p. 457*)

gentry In China, the class of prosperous families, next in wealth below the rural aristocrats, from which the emperors drew their administrative personnel. Respected for their education and expertise, these officials became a privileged group and made the government more efficient and responsive. The term also denotes the class of landholding families in England below the aristocracy. (*p. 141*)

Ghana First known kingdom in sub-Saharan West Africa between the sixth and thirteenth centuries C.E. Also the modern West African country once known as the Gold Coast. (*p. 164*)

Gold Coast (Africa) Region of the Atlantic coast of West Africa occupied by modern Ghana; named for its gold exports to Europe from the 1470s onward. (*p. 349*)

Golden Horde Mongol khanate founded by Genghis Khan's grandson Batu in southern Russia. It adopted the Turkic language and Islam. Also known as the Kipchak Horde. (*p. 269*)

Gorbachev, Mikhail (b. 1931) Head of the Soviet Union from 1985 to 1991. His liberalization effort improved relations with the West, but he lost power after his reforms led to the collapse of Communist governments in eastern Europe. (*p. 631*)

Gothic cathedrals Large churches originating in twelfth-century France; built in an architectural style featuring pointed arches, tall vaults and spires, flying buttresses, and large stained-glass windows. (*p. 333*)

Grand Canal The 1,100-mile (1,700-kilometer) waterway linking the Yellow and the Yangzi Rivers. It was begun in the **Han** period and completed during the Sui Empire. (*p. 219*)

Great Circuit The network of Atlantic Ocean trade routes between Europe, Africa, and the Americas that underlay the **Atlantic system.** (*p. 398*)

"great tradition" Historians' term for a literate, well-institutionalized complex of religious and social beliefs and practices adhered to by diverse societies over a broad geographical area. (See also **"small tradition."**) (*p. 165*)

Great Western Schism A division of the Latin (Western) Christian Church between 1378 and 1417, when rival claimants to the papacy existed in Rome and Avignon. (*p. 339*)

Great Zimbabwe City, now in ruins (in the modern African country of Zimbabwe), whose many stone structures were built between about 1250 and 1450, when it was a trading center and the capital of a large state. (*p. 314*)

guild In medieval Europe, an association of men (rarely women), such as merchants, artisans, or professors, who worked in a particular trade and banded together to promote their economic and political interests. Guilds were also important in other societies, such as the Ottoman and Safavid empires. (*p. 331*)

Gujarat Region of western India famous for trade and manufacturing; the inhabitants are called Gujarati. (*p. 312*)

gunpowder A mixture of saltpeter, sulfur, and charcoal, in various proportions. The formula, brought to China in the 400s or 500s, was first used to make fumigators to keep away insect pests and evil spirits. In later centuries it was used to make explosives and fire projectiles. (*p. 229*)

Guomindang Nationalist political party founded on democratic principles by **Sun Yat-sen** in 1912. After 1925, the party was headed by **Chiang Kai-shek**, who turned it into an increasingly authoritarian movement. (*p. 554*)

Gupta Empire (320–550 C.E.) A powerful Indian state based, like its Mauryan predecessor, on a capital at Pataliputra in the Ganges Valley. It controlled most of the Indian subcontinent through military force and the prestige of its sophisticated culture. (See also **theater-state.**) (*p. 117*)

hadith A tradition relating the words or deeds of the Prophet Muhammad; next to the **Quran,** the most important basis for Islamic law. (*p. 187*)

Hammurabi Amorite ruler of **Babylon** (r. 1792–1750 B.C.E.). He conquered many city-states in southern and northern Mesopotamia and is best known for a code of laws. (*p. 17*)

Han A term used to designate (1) the ethnic Chinese people who originated in the Yellow River Valley and spread throughout regions of China suitable for agriculture and (2) the dynasty of emperors who ruled from 206 B.C.E. to 220 C.E. (*p. 140*)

Hanseatic League An economic and defensive alliance of the free towns in northern Germany, founded about 1241 and most powerful in the fourteenth century. (*p. 329*)

Harappa Site in modern Pakistan of one of the great cities of the Indus Valley civilization of the third millennium B.C.E. (*p. 29*)

Hatshepsut Queen of Egypt (r. 1473–1458 B.C.E.). She dispatched a naval expedition down the Red Sea to Punt (possibly Somalia), the faraway source of myrrh. After her death her name and image were frequently defaced. (*p. 47*)

Hebrew Bible A collection of sacred books containing diverse materials concerning the origins, experiences, beliefs, and practices of the Israelites. Most of the extant text was compiled by members of the priestly class in the fifth century B.C.E. and reflects the concerns and view of this group. (*p. 74*)

Hellenistic Age Historians' term for the era, usually dated 323–30 B.C.E., in which Greek culture spread across western Asia and northeastern Africa after the conquests of **Alexander** the Great. The period ended with the fall of the last major Hellenistic kingdom to Rome, but Greek cultural influence persisted. (*p. 106*)

Helsinki Accords (1975) Political and human rights agreement signed in Helsinki, Finland, by the Soviet Union and western European countries. (*p. 617*)

Henry the Navigator (1394–1460) Portuguese prince who promoted the study of navigation and directed voyages of exploration down the western coast of Africa. (*p. 348*)

Herodotus (ca. 485–425 B.C.E.) Heir to the technique of *historia*—"investigation"—developed by Greeks in the late Archaic period. From a Greek community in Anatolia, he traveled extensively, collecting information in western Asia and the Mediterranean lands. He chronicled the **Persian Wars** between the Greek city-states and the Persian Empire. (*p. 100*)

Hidalgo y Costilla, Miguel (1753–1811) Mexican priest who led the first stage of the Mexican independence war in 1810. He was captured and executed in 1811. (*p. 458*)

Hidden Imam Last in a series of twelve descendants of Muhammad's son-in-law Ali, whom **Shi'ites** consider divinely appointed leaders of the Muslim community. In occlusion since ca. 873, he is expected to return as a messiah at the end of time. (*p. 413*)

hieroglyphics A system of writing in which pictorial symbols represented sounds, syllables, or concepts. It was used for official and monumental inscriptions in ancient Egypt. Cursive symbol-forms were developed for rapid composition on other media, such as **papyrus.** (*p. 24*)

high culture Canons of artistic and literary masterworks recognized by dominant economic classes. (*p. 656*)

Hinduism A general term for a wide variety of beliefs and ritual practices that have developed in the Indian subcontinent since antiquity. Hinduism has roots in ancient Vedic, Buddhist, and south Indian religious concepts and practices. It spread along the trade routes to Southeast Asia. (*p. 113*)

Hiroshima City in Japan, the first to be destroyed by an atomic bomb, on August 6, 1945. The bombing hastened the end of World War II. (*p. 576*)

history The study of past events and changes in the development, transmission, and transformation of cultural practices. (*p. 5*)

Hitler, Adolph (1889–1945) Born in Austria, Hitler became a radical German nationalist during World War I. He led the National Socialist German Workers' Party—the **Nazi Party**—in the 1920s and became dictator of Germany in 1933. He led Europe into World War II. (*p. 568*)

Hittites A people who established an empire in central Anatolia and Syria in the Late Bronze Age. The Hittites vied with New Kingdom Egypt for control of Syria-Palestine before falling to unidentified attackers ca. 1200 B.C.E. (See also **Ramesses II.**) (*p. 46*)

Holocaust Nazis' program during World War II to kill people they considered undesirable. Some 6 million Jews perished during the Holocaust, along with millions of Poles, Gypsies, Communists, Socialists, and others. (*p. 579*)

Holocene The geological era since the end of the Great Ice Age about 11,000 years ago. (*p. 11*)

Holy Roman Empire Loose federation of mostly German states and principalities, headed by an emperor elected by the princes. It lasted from 962 to 1806. (*p. 205*)

hoplite A heavily armored Greek infantryman of the Archaic and Classical periods who fought in the close-packed phalanx formation. Hoplite armies—militias composed of middle- and upper-class citizens supplying their own equipment—excelled contemporary military forces. (*p. 96*)

horse collar Harnessing method that increased the efficiency of horses by shifting the point of traction from the animal's throat to the shoulders; its adoption favors the spread of horse-drawn plows and vehicles. (*p. 212*)

House of Burgesses Elected assembly in colonial Virginia, created in 1618. (*p. 389*)

humanists (Renaissance) European scholars, writers, and teachers associated with the study of the humanities (grammar, rhetoric, poetry, history, languages, and moral philosophy), influential in the fifteenth century and later. (*p. 335*)

Hundred Years War (1337–1453) Series of campaigns over control of the throne of France, involving English and French royal families and French noble families. (*p. 339*)

Husain, Saddam (b. 1937) President of Iraq since 1979. Waged war on Iran in 1980–1988. In 1990 he ordered an invasion of Kuwait but was defeated by United States and its allies in the Gulf War (1991). (*p. 628*)

Ibn Battuta (1304–1369) Moroccan Muslim scholar, the most widely traveled individual of his time. He wrote a detailed account of his visits to Islamic lands from China to Spain and the western Sudan. (*p. 302*)

Ibn Khaldun (1332–1406) Arab historian. He developed an influential theory on the rise and fall of states. Born in Tunis, he spent his later years in Cairo as a teacher and judge. In 1400 he was sent to Damascus to negotiate the surrender of the city, where he met and exchanged views with **Timur.** (*p. 272*)

Il-khan A "secondary" or "peripheral" khan based in Persia. The Il-khans' khanate, founded by Hülegü, a grandson of **Genghis Khan,** was based at Tabriz in northwest Iran. (*p. 269*)

import-substitution industrialization An economic system aimed at building a country's industry by restricting foreign trade, forcing consumers to buy local manufactures instead of imports. (*p. 598*)

Inca Largest and most powerful Andean empire. Controlled the Pacific coast of South America from Ecuador to Chile from its capital of Cuzco. (*p. 254*)

indentured servant A migrant to British colonies in the Americas who paid for passage by agreeing to work for a set term ranging from four to seven years. (*p. 389*)

Indian Civil Service The elite professional class of officials who administered the government of British India. Originally composed exclusively of well-educated British men, it gradually added qualified Indians. (*p. 491*)

Indian National Congress A movement and political party founded in 1885 to demand greater Indian participation in government. Led after 1920 by Mohandas K. Gandhi, it appealed increasingly to the poor and organized mass protests demanding self-government and independence. (See also **Gandhi, Mohandas K.**) (*pp. 492, 589*)

Indian Ocean Maritime System in premodern times, a network of seaports, trade routes, and maritime culture linking countries on the rim of the Indian Ocean from Africa to Indonesia. (*p. 155*)

indulgence The forgiveness of the punishment due for sins, granted by the Catholic Church as a reward for a pious act. Martin Luther's protest against the sale of indulgences is often seen as touching off the **Protestant Reformation.** (*p. 365*)

Industrial Revolution The transformation of the economy, environment, and living conditions, occurring first in England in the eighteenth century, that resulted from the use of steam engines, the mechanization of manufacturing, and innovations in transportation (*p. 463*)

investiture controversy Dispute between the popes and the Holy Roman Emperors over who held ultimate authority over bishops in imperial lands. (*p. 205*)

Iron Age Historians' term for the period during which iron became the primary metal for tools and weapons. Iron technology began at different times in different regions. (*p. 63*)

iron curtain Winston Churchill's term for the Cold War division between the Soviet-dominated East and the U.S.-dominated West. (*p. 604*)

Iroquois Confederacy An alliance of five northeastern Amerindian peoples (after 1722 six) that made decisions on military and diplomatic issues through a council of representatives. Allied first with the Dutch and later with the English, the Confederacy dominated the area from western New England to the Great Lakes. (*p. 390*)

Islam Religion expounded by the Prophet Muhammad (570–632 C.E.) on the basis of divine revelations, which were collected after his death into the **Quran.** In the tradition of Judaism and Christianity, Islam calls on people to recognize one creator god—Allah—who rewards or punishes believers after death according to how they led their lives. (See also **hadith.**) (*p. 178*)

Israel In antiquity, the land between the eastern shore of the Mediterranean and the Jordan River, occupied by the Israelites from the early second millennium B.C.E. The modern state of Israel was founded in 1948. (*p. 74*)

Janissaries Infantry, originally of slave origin, armed with firearms and constituting the elite of the Ottoman army from the fifteenth century until the corps was abolished in 1826. (*p. 409*)

Jesuits Members of the Society of Jesus, a Roman Catholic order founded by Ignatius Loyola in 1534. They played an important part in the **Catholic Reformation** and helped create conduits of trade and knowledge between Asia and Europe. (*p. 439*)

Jesus (ca. 5 B.C.E.–34 C.E.) A Jew from Galilee in northern Israel who sought to reform Jewish beliefs and practices. He was executed as a revolutionary by the Romans. Hailed as the Messiah and son of God by his followers, he became the central figure in Christianity, a belief system that developed in the centuries after his death. (*p. 133*)

Jinnah, Muhammad Ali (1876–1948) Indian Muslim politician who founded the state of Pakistan. A lawyer by training, he joined the **All-India Muslim League** in 1913. As leader of the League from the 1920s on, he negotiated with the British and the **Indian National Congress** for Muslim participation in Indian politics. From 1940 on, he led the movement for the independence of India's Muslims in a separate state of Pakistan, founded in 1947. (*p. 593*)

joint-stock company A business, often backed by a government charter, that sold shares to individuals to raise money for its trading enterprises and to spread the risks (and profits) among many investors. (*p. 375*)

junk A very large flatbottom sailing ship produced in the **Tang** and **Song Empires,** specially designed for long-distance commercial travel. (*p. 228*)

Kamakura Shogunate The first of Japan's decentralized military governments. (1185–1333). (*p. 235*)

Kamikaze The "divine wind," which the Japanese credited with blowing Mongol invaders away from their shores in 1281. Term later used for suicide dive bombers in World War II. (*p. 298*)

Kangxi (1654–1722) Qing emperor (r. 1662–1722). He oversaw the greatest expansion of the **Qing Empire.** (*p. 434*)

karma In Indian tradition, the residue of deeds performed in past and present lives that adheres to a "spirit" and determines what form it will assume in its next life cycle. (*p. 111*)

keiretsu Alliances of corporations and banks that dominate the Japanese economy. (*p. 629*)

khipu System of knotted colored cords used by preliterate Andean peoples to transmit information. (*p. 250*)

Khomeini, Ayatollah Ruhollah (1900?–1989) Shi'ite philosopher and cleric who led the overthrow of the shah of Iran in 1979 and created an Islamic republic. (*p. 627*)

Khubilai Khan (1215–1294) Last of the Mongol Great Khans (r. 1260–1294) and founder of the **Yuan Empire.** (*p. 284*)

Kievan Russia State established at Kiev in Ukraine ca. 879 by Scandinavian adventurers asserting authority over a mostly Slavic farming population. (*p. 196*)

Korean War (1950–1953) Conflict that began with North Korea's invasion of South Korea and came to involve the United Nations (primarily the United States) allying with South Korea and the People's Republic of China allying with North Korea. (*p. 614*)

Koryo Korean kingdom founded in 918 and destroyed by a Mongol invasion in 1259. (*p. 234*)

Kush An Egyptian name for Nubia, the region alongside the Nile River south of Egypt, where an indigenous kingdom arose beginning in the early second millennium B.C.E. (*p. 50*)

labor union An organization of workers in a particular industry or trade, created to defend the interests of members through strikes or negotiations with employers. (*p. 509*)

laissez faire The idea that government should refrain from interfering in economic affairs. The classic exposition of laissez-faire principles is Adam Smith's *Wealth of Nations* (1776). (*p. 475*)

lama In Tibetan Buddhism, a teacher. (*p. 284*)

Las Casas, Bartolomé de (1474–1566) First bishop of Chiapas, in southern Mexico. He devoted most of his life to protecting Amerindian peoples from exploitation. His major achievement was the New Laws of 1542, which limited the ability of Spanish settlers to compel Amerindians to labor for them. (See also **encomienda.**) (*p. 384*)

Latin West Historians' name for the territories of Europe that adhered to the Latin rite of Christianity and used the Latin language for intellectual exchange in the period ca. 1000–1500. (*p. 323*)

League of Nations International organization founded in 1919 to promote world peace and cooperation but greatly weakened by the refusal of the United States to join. It was superseded by the **United Nations** in 1945. (*p. 550*)

Legalism In China, a political philosophy that emphasized the unruliness of human nature and justified state coercion and control. The **Qin** ruling class invoked it to validate the authoritarian nature of their regime. It was superseded in the **Han** era by a more benevolent Confucian doctrine of moderation. (*p. 43*)

"legitimate" trade Exports from Africa in the nineteenth century that did not include the newly outlawed slave trade. (*p. 486*)

Lenin, Vladimir (1870–1924) Leader of the Bolshevik (later Communist) Party. He lived in exile in Switzerland until 1917, then returned to Russia to lead the Bolsheviks to victory during the Russian Revolution and the civil war that followed. (*p. 548*)

Leopold II (1835–1909) King of Belgium (r. 1865–1909). He was active in encouraging the exploration of Central Africa and became the ruler of the Congo Free State (to 1908). (*p. 528*)

Li Shimin (599–649) One of the founders of the **Tang Empire** and its second emperor (r. 626–649). He led the expansion of the empire into Central Asia. (*p. 219*)

liberalism A political ideology that emphasizes the civil rights of citizens, representative government, and the protection of private property. This ideology, derived from the **Enlightenment,** was especially popular among the property-owning middle classes of Europe and North America. (*p. 512*)

Library of Ashurbanipal A large collection of writings drawn from the ancient literary, religious, and scientific traditions of Mesopotamia. It was assembled by the sixth century B.C.E. Assyrian ruler Ashurbanipal. (*p. 71*)

Linear B A set of syllabic symbols, derived from Linear A, the undeciphered writing system of **Minoan** Crete, used in the Mycenaean palaces of the Late Bronze Age to write an early form of Greek. It was used primarily for palace records. (*p. 53*)

Little Ice Age A century-long period of cool climate that began in the 1590s. Its ill effects on agriculture in northern Europe were notable. (*p. 376*)

llama A hoofed animal indigenous to the Andes Mountains in South America. It was the only domesticated beast of burden in the Americas before the arrival of Europeans. It provided meat and wool. (*p. 67*)

loess A fine, light silt deposited by wind and water. It constitutes the fertile soil of the Yellow River Valley in northern China. Because loess soil is not compacted, it can be worked with a simple digging stick. (*p. 38*)

Long March (1934–1935) The 6,000-mile (9,600-kilometer) flight of Chinese Communists from southeastern to northwestern China. The Communists, led by **Mao Zedong,** were pursued by the Chinese army under orders from **Chiang Kai-shek.** The four thousand survivors of the march formed the nucleus of a revived Communist movement that defeated the **Guomindang** after World War II. (*p. 572*)

L'Ouverture, François Dominique Toussaint (1743–1803) Leader of the Haitian Revolution. He freed the slaves and gained effective independence for Haiti despite military interventions by the British and French. (*p. 457*)

ma'at Egyptian concept of divinely created and maintained order in the universe. Reflecting the ancient Egyptians' belief in an essentially beneficent world, the divine ruler was the earthly guarantor of this order. (See also **pyramid.**) (*p. 24*)

Macartney mission (1792–1793) The unsuccessful attempt by the British Empire to establish diplomatic relations with the **Qing Empire.** (*p. 436*)

Magellan, Ferdinand (1480?–1521) Portuguese navigator who led the Spanish expedition of 1519–1522 that was the first to sail around the world. (*p. 352*)

Mahabharata Indian epic chronicling the events leading up to a war between related kinship groups. It includes the *Bhagavad-Gita*, an important work of Indian sacred literature. (*p. 116*)

Mahayana Buddhism "Great Vehicle" branch of Buddhism followed in China, Japan, and Central Asia. The focus is on reverence for **Buddha** and for bodhisattvas, enlightened persons who have postponed nirvana to help others attain enlightenment. (*p. 113*)

Malacca Port city in the modern Southeast Asian country of Malaysia, founded about 1400 as a trading center on the Strait of Malacca. Also spelled Melaka. (*p. 317*)

Malay peoples Peoples originating in south China and Southeast Asia who settled the Malay Peninsula, Indonesia, and the Philippines, then spread eastward across the islands of the Pacific Ocean and west to Madagascar. (*p. 158*)

Mali Empire created by indigenous Muslims in West Africa from the thirteenth to fifteenth century. It was famous for its role in the trans-Saharan gold trade. (See also **Timbuktu.**) (*p. 307*)

Malthus, Thomas (1766–1834) Eighteenth-century English intellectual who warned that population growth threatened future generations because population growth would always outstrip increases in agricultural production. (*p. 634*)

mamluks Under this Islamic system of military slavery, Turkic military slaves predominated in the armed forces of the **Abbasid Caliphate** of the ninth and tenth centuries. Mamluks eventually founded their own state, ruling Egypt and Syria (1250–1517). (*pp. 182, 278*)

Manchuria Region of Northeast Asia bounded by the Yau River on the south and the Amur River on the east and north. (*p. 288*)

Manchus Federation of Northeast Asian peoples who founded the **Qing Empire.** (*p. 432*)

Mandate of Heaven Chinese religious and political ideology developed by the **Zhou,** according to which it was the prerogative of Heaven, the chief deity, to grant power to the ruler of China and to take away that power if the ruler failed to conduct himself justly. (*p. 42*)

mandate system Allocation of former German colonies and Ottoman possessions to the victorious powers after World War I, to be administered under **League of Nations** supervision. (*p. 556*)

manor In medieval Europe, a large, self-sufficient landholding consisting of the lord's residence (manor house), outbuildings, peasant village, and surrounding land. (*p. 200*)

mansabs In India, grants of land given in return for service by rulers of the **Mughal Empire.** (*p. 536*)

Mansa Kankan Musa Ruler of **Mali** (r. 1312–1337). His pilgrimage through Egypt to **Mecca** in 1324–1325 established the empire's reputation for wealth in the Mediterranean world. (*p. 308*)

Mao Zedong (1892–1976) Leader of the Chinese Communist Party (1927–1976). He led the Communists on the **Long March** (1934–1935) and rebuilt the Communist Party and Red Army during the Japanese occupation of China (1937–1945). After World War II, he led the Communists to victory over the **Guomindang.** He ordered the **Cultural Revolution** in 1966. (*p. 572*)

maroon A slave who ran away from his or her master. Often a member of a community of runaway slaves in the West Indies and South America. (*p. 396*)

Marshall Plan U.S. program to support the reconstruction of western Europe after World War II. By 1961 more than $20 billion in economic aid had been dispersed. (*p. 613*)

Marx, Karl (1818–1883) German journalist and philosopher, founder of the Marxist branch of **socialism.** He is best known for two books: *The Communist Manifesto* (1840) and *Das Kapital* (Vols. I–III, 1867–1894). (*p. 509*)

mass deportation The forcible removal and relocation of large numbers of people or entire populations. (*p. 71*)

mass production The manufacture of many identical products by the **division of labor** into many small repetitive tasks. This method was introduced into the manufacture of pottery by Josiah Wedgwood and into the spinning of cotton thread by Richard Arkwright. (See also **Industrial Revolution; Wedgwood, Josiah.**) (*p. 466*)

Mauryan Empire The first state to unify most of the Indian subcontinent. It was founded by Chandragupta Maurya in 324 B.C.E. and survived until 187 B.C.E. (See also **Ashoka.**) (*p. 115*)

Maya Mesoamerican civilization concentrated in Mexico's Yucatán Peninsula and in Guatemala and Honduras but never unified into a single empire. (*p. 242*)

Mecca City in western Arabia; birthplace of the Prophet **Muhammad,** and ritual center of the Islamic religion. (*p. 176*)

mechanization The application of machinery on a large scale to manufacturing and other activities. Early undertakings include the spinning of cotton thread and the weaving of cloth in late-eighteenth- and early-nineteenth-century England. (*p. 467*)

medieval Literally "middle age," a term that historians of Europe use for the period ca. 500 to ca. 1500, signifying its intermediate point between Greco-Roman antiquity and the Renaissance. (*p. 195*)

Medina City in western Arabia to which the Prophet Muhammad and his followers emigrated in 622 to escape persecution in Mecca. (*p. 178*)

megaliths Structures and complexes of very large stones constructed for ceremonial and religious purposes in **Neolithic** times. (*p. 12*)

Memphis The capital of Old Kingdom Egypt, near the head of the Nile Delta. Early rulers were interred in the nearby **pyramids.** (*p. 24*)

Menelik II (1844–1911). Emperor of Ethiopia (r. 1889–1911). He enlarged Ethiopia to its present dimensions and defeated an Italian invasion at Adowa (1896). (*p. 531*)

mercantilism European government policies of the sixteenth, seventeenth, and eighteenth centuries designed to promote overseas trade between a country and its colonies and accumulate precious metals by requiring colonies to trade only with their motherland country. (*p. 397*)

Meroë Capital of a kingdom in southern Nubia from the fourth century B.C.E. to the fourth century C.E. In this period Nubian culture shows more independence from Egypt and the influence of sub-Saharan Africa. (*p. 51*)

Middle Passage The part of the **Great Circuit** involving the transportation of enslaved Africans across the Atlantic to the Americas. (*p. 398*)

Ming Empire (1368–1644) Empire based in China that Zhu Yuanzhang established after the overthrow of the **Yuan Empire**. The Ming emperor **Yongle** sponsored the building of the **Forbidden City** and the voyages of **Zheng He.** (*pp. 289, 431*)

Minoan Civilization on the Aegean island of Crete in the second millennium B.C.E. The Minoans engaged in far-flung commerce around the Mediterranean and influenced the early Greeks. (*p. 52*)

mit'a Andean labor system based on shared obligations to help kinsmen and work on behalf of the ruler and religious organizations. (*p. 250*)

Moche Civilization of north coast of Peru (200–700 C.E.) that built extensive irrigation networks as well as impressive urban centers dominated by brick temples. (*p. 251*)

Moctezuma II (1466?–1520) Last Aztec emperor, overthrown by the Spanish conquistador Hernán Cortés. (*p. 357*)

modernization The process of reforming political, military, economic, social, and cultural traditions in imitation of the early success of Western societies. (*p. 485*)

Mohenjo-Daro Largest of the cities of the Indus Valley civilization. It was centrally located in the extensive floodplain of the Indus River in contemporary Pakistan. The large scale of construction at Mohenjo-Daro, the orderly grid of streets, and the standardization of building materials are evidence of central planning. (*p. 29*)

moksha The Hindu concept of the spirit's "liberation" from the endless cycle of rebirths. Physical discipline, meditation, and acts of devotion to the gods can help the spirit distance itself from desire for the things of this world and merge with the divine force that animates the universe. (*p. 111*)

monasticism Living in a religious community apart from secular society and adhering to a rule stipulating chastity, obedience, and poverty. It was a prominent element of medieval Christianity and Buddhism. Monasteries were the primary centers of learning and literacy in medieval Europe. (*p. 206*)

Mongols A people of this name is mentioned as early as the records of the **Tang Empire,** living as nomads in northern Eurasia. After 1206 they established an enormous empire under **Genghis Khan,** linking western and eastern Eurasia. (*p. 262*)

monotheism Belief in the existence of a single divine entity. Some scholars cite the devotion of the Egyptian pharaoh **Akhenaten** to the Aten (sun-disk) and his suppression of traditional gods as the earliest instance. The Israelite worship of Yahweh developed into an exclusive belief in one god, and this concept passed into Christianity and Islam. (*p. 78*)

monsoon Seasonal winds in the Indian Ocean caused by the differences in temperature between the rapidly heating and cooling landmasses of Africa and Asia and the slowly changing ocean waters. These strong and predictable winds enable sailors to cross the open sea and also bring large amounts of rainfall to parts of India, Southeast Asia, and China. (*pp. 109, 303*)

movable type Type in which each individual character is cast as a separate piece of metal. It replaced woodblock printing, allowing for the arrangement of individual letters and other characters on a page, rather than requiring the carving of entire pages at a time. It may have been invented in Korea in the thirteenth century. (See also **printing press.**) (*p. 234*)

Mughal Empire Muslim state (1526–1857) exercising dominion over most of India in the sixteenth and seventeenth centuries. (*p. 416*)

Muhammad (570–632 C.E.) Arab prophet; founder of religion of Islam. (*p. 177*)

Muhammad Ali (1769–1849) Leader of Egyptian modernization in the early nineteenth century. He ruled Egypt as an Ottoman governor, but had imperial ambitions. His descendants ruled Egypt until overthrown in 1952. (*p. 485*)

mummy A body preserved by chemical processes or special natural circumstances, often in the belief that the deceased will need it again in the afterlife. In ancient Egypt the bodies of people who could afford mummification underwent a complex process of removing organs, filling body cavities, dehydrating the corpse with natron, and then wrapping the body with linen bandages and enclosing it in a wooden sarcophagus. (*p. 27*)

Muscovy Russian principality that emerged gradually during the era of Mongol domination. The Muscovite dynasty ruled from 1276 to 1598. (*p. 427*)

Muslim An adherent of the Islamic religion; a person who "submits" (in Arabic, *Islam* means "submission") to the will of God. (*p. 178*)

Mussolini, Benito (1883–1945) Fascist dictator of Italy (1922–1943). He led Italy to conquer Ethiopia (1935), joined Germany in the Axis pact (1936), and allied Italy with Germany in World War II. He was overthrown in 1943 when the Allies invaded Italy. (*p. 568*)

Mycenae A fortified palace complex in southern Greece that controlled a Late Bronze Age kingdom. In Homer's epic poems Mycenae was the base of King Agamemnon, who commanded the Greek's besieging Troy. Archaeologists call Greek society of the second millennium B.C.E. "Mycenaean." (*p. 53*)

Napoleon I (1769–1832) Overthrew French Directory in 1799 and became emperor of the French in 1804. Failed to defeat Great Britain and abdicated in 1814. Returned to power briefly in 1815 but was defeated and died in exile. (*p. 453*)

Nasir al-Din Tusi (1201–1274) Persian mathematician and cosmologist whose academy near Tabriz provided the model for the movement of the planets that helped to inspire the Copernican model of the solar system. (*p. 272*)

National Assembly French Revolutionary assembly (1789–1791). Called first as the **Estates General,** the three estates came together and demanded radical change. It passed the **Declaration of the Rights of Man** in 1789. (*p. 451*)

nationalism A political ideology that stresses people's membership in a nation—a community defined by a common culture and history as well as by territory. In the late eighteenth and early nineteenth centuries, nationalism was a force for unity in western Europe. In the late nineteenth century it hastened the disintegration of the Austro-Hungarian and Ottoman Empires. In the twentieth century it provided the ideological foundation for scores of independent countries emerging from **colonialism.** (*p. 510*)

nawab A Muslim prince allied to British India; technically, a semi-autonomous deputy of the Mughal emperor. (*p. 488*)

Nazi Party German political party joined by Adolf Hitler, emphasizing nationalism, racism, and war. When Hitler became chancellor of Germany in 1933, the Nazi Party became the only legal party and an instrument of Hitler's absolute rule. Its formal name was National Socialist German Workers' Party. (See also **Hitler, Adolf.**) (*p. 568*)

Nehru, Jawaharlal (1889–1964) Indian statesman. He succeeded Mohandas K. Gandhi as leader of the **Indian National Congress.** He negotiated the end of British colonial rule in India and became India's first prime minister (1947–1964). (*p. 593*)

Neo-Assyrian Empire An empire extending from western Iran to Syria-Palestine, conquered by the Assyrians of northern Mesopotamia between the tenth and seventh centuries B.C.E. (*p. 70*)

Neo-Babylonian kingdom Under the Chaldaeans (nomadic kinship groups that settled in southern Mesopotamia in the early first millennium B.C.E.), **Babylon** again became a major political and cultural center in the seventh and sixth centuries B.C.E. After participating in the destruction of Assyrian power, the monarchs Nabopolassar and Nebuchadnezzar took over the southern portion of the Assyrian domains. By destroying the **First Temple** in Jerusalem and deporting part of the population, they initiated the **diaspora** of the Jews. (*p. 84*)

Neolithic The period of the Stone Age associated with the ancient **Agricultural Revolution(s).** (*p. 7*)

Nevskii, Alexander (1220–1263) Prince of Novgorod (r. 1236–1263). He submitted to the invading Mongols in 1240 and received recognition as the leader of the Russian princes under the Golden Horde. (*p. 275*)

New Economic Policy Policy proclaimed by Vladimir Lenin in 1924 to encourage the revival of the Soviet economy by allowing small private enterprises. Joseph Stalin ended the N.E.P. in 1928 and replaced it with a series of **Five-Year Plans.** (See also **Lenin, Vladimir.**) (*p. 552*)

New France French colony in North America, with a capital in Quebec, founded 1608. New France fell to the British in 1763. (*p. 390*)

New Imperialism Historians' term for the late-nineteenth- and early-twentieth-century wave of conquests by European powers, the United States, and Japan, which were followed by the development and exploitation of the newly conquered territories for the benefit of the colonial powers. (*p. 524*)

new monarchies Historians' term for the monarchies in France, England, and Spain from 1450 to 1600. The centralization of royal power was increasing within more or less fixed territorial limits. (*p. 339*)

nomadism A way of life, forced by a scarcity of resources, in which groups of people continually migrate to find pastures and water. (*p. 264*)

nonaligned nations Developing countries that announced their neutrality in the **Cold War.** (*p. 617*)

nongovernmental organizations (NGOs) Nonprofit international organizations devoted to investigating human rights abuses and providing humanitarian relief. (*p. 694*)

North Atlantic Treaty Organization (NATO) Organization formed in 1949 as a military alliance of western European and North American states against the Soviet Union and its east European allies. (See also **Warsaw Pact.**) (*p. 610*)

nuclear nonproliferation Goal of international efforts to prevent countries other than the five declared nuclear powers (United States, Russia, Britain, France, and China) from obtaining nuclear weapons. The first Nuclear Non-Proliferation Treaty was signed in 1968. (*p. 652*)

Olmec The first Mesoamerican civilization. Between ca. 1200 and 400 B.C.E., the Olmec people of central Mexico created a civilization that included intensive agriculture, wide-ranging trade, ceremonial centers, and monumental construction. The Olmec had great cultural influence on later Mesoamerican societies. (*p. 64*)

Oman Arab state based in Musqat, the main port in the southeast region of the Arabian peninsula. Oman succeeded Portugal as a power in the western Indian Ocean in the eighteenth century. (*p. 421*)

Opium War (1839–1842) War between Britain and the **Qing Empire** that was, in the British view, occasioned by the Qing government's refusal to permit the importation of opium into its territories. The victorious British imposed the one-sided **Treaty of Nanking** on China. (*p. 495*)

Organization of Petroleum Exporting Countries (OPEC) Organization formed in 1960 by oil-producing states to promote their collective interest in generating revenue from oil (*p. 620*)

Ottoman Empire Islamic state founded by Osman in north-western Anatolia ca. 1300. After the fall of the **Byzantine Empire,** the Ottoman Empire was based at Istanbul (formerly Constantinople) from 1453 to 1922. It encompassed lands in the Middle East, North Africa, the Caucasus, and eastern Europe. (*pp. 277, 406*)

Paleolithic The period of the Stone Age associated with the earliest human societies. It predates the **Neolithic** period. (*p. 7*)

Panama Canal Ship canal cut across the isthmus of Panama by United States Army engineers; it opened in 1915. It greatly shortened the sea voyage between the east and west coasts of North America. The United States turned the canal over to Panama on January 1, 2000. (*p. 537*)

papacy The central administration of the Roman Catholic Church, of which the pope is the head. (*p. 203*)

papyrus A reed that grows along the banks of the Nile River in Egypt. From it was produced a coarse, paperlike writing medium used by the Egyptians and many other peoples in the ancient Mediterranean and Middle East. (*p. 25*)

Parthians Iranian ruling dynasty between ca. 250 B.C.E. and 226 C.E. (*p. 151*)

patron/client relationship In ancient Rome, a fundamental social relationship in which the patron—a wealthy and powerful individual—provided legal and economic protection and assistance to clients, men of lesser status and means, and in return the clients supported the political careers and economic interests of their patron. (*pp. 125–127*)

Paul (ca. 5–65 C.E.) A Jew from the Greek city of Tarsus in Anatolia, he initially persecuted the followers of Jesus but, after receiving a revelation on the road to Damascus, became a Christian. He traveled throughout Syria-Palestine, Anatolia, and Greece, preaching the new religion and establishing churches. Finding his greatest success among pagans ("gentiles"), he began the process by which Christianity separated from Judaism. (*p. 133*)

pax romana Literally, "Roman peace," it connoted the stability and prosperity that Roman rule brought to the lands of the Roman Empire in the first two centuries C.E. (*p. 132*)

Pearl Harbor Naval base in Hawaii attacked by Japanese aircraft on December 7, 1941. The sinking of much of the U.S. Pacific Fleet brought the United States into World War II. (*p. 574*)

Peloponnesian War A protracted (431–404 B.C.E.) and costly conflict between the Athenian and Spartan alliance systems. Possession of a naval empire allowed Athens to fight a war of attrition. Ultimately, Sparta prevailed because of Athenian errors and Persian financial support. (*p. 104*)

perestroika Policy of "openness" that was the centerpiece of Mikhail Gorbachev's efforts to liberalize communism in the Soviet Union. (See also **Gorbachev, Mikhail.**) (*p. 631*)

Pericles (ca. 495–429 B.C.E.) Aristocratic leader who guided the Athenian state through the transition to full participatory democracy for all male citizens, supervised construction of the Acropolis, and pursued a policy of imperial expansion that led to the **Peloponnesian War.** (*p. 101*)

Perón, Eva Duarte (1919–1952) Wife of **Juan Perón** and champion of the poor in Argentina. She was a gifted speaker and popular political leader who campaigned to improve the life of the urban poor by founding schools and hospitals and providing other social benefits. (*p. 899*)

Perón, Juan (1895–1974) President of Argentina (1946–1955, 1973–1974). As a military officer, he championed the rights of labor. He built up Argentinean industry, became very popular among the urban poor, but harmed the economy. (*p. 599*)

Persepolis A complex of palaces, reception halls, and treasury buildings erected by the Persian kings **Darius I**

and Xerxes in the Persian homeland. It is believed that the New Year's festival was celebrated here, as well as the coronations, weddings, and funerals of the Persian kings, who were buried in cliff-tombs nearby. (*p. 92*)

Persian Wars Conflicts between Greek city-states and the Persian Empire, ranging from the Ionian Revolt (499–494 B.C.E.) through Darius's punitive expedition that failed at Marathon (490 B.C.E.) and the defeat of Xerxes' invasion of Greece by the Spartan-led Hellenic League (480–479 B.C.E.). **Herodotus** chronicled these events in the first "history" in the Western tradition. (*p. 101*)

Peter the Great (1672–1725) Russian tsar (r. 1689–1725). He introduced Western languages and technologies to the Russian elite, moving the capital from Moscow to the new city of St. Petersburg. (*p. 430*)

pharaoh The central figure in the ancient Egyptian state. Believed to be an earthly manifestation of the gods, he wielded absolute power. (*p. 24*)

Phoenicians Semitic-speaking Canaanites living on the coast of modern Lebanon and Syria in the first millennium B.C.E. From Tyre and Sidon, Phoenician sailors explored the Mediterranean, engaged in widespread commerce, and founded **Carthage** and other colonies in the western Mediterranean. (*p. 79*)

pilgrimage Journey to a sacred shrine by Christians seeking to show their piety, fulfill vows, or gain absolution for sins. Other pilgrimage traditions include the Muslim pilgrimage to **Mecca** and the pilgrimages made by early Chinese Buddhists to India in search of sacred Buddhist writings. (*p. 214*)

Pilgrims Group of English Protestant dissenters who established Plymouth Colony in Massachusetts in 1620 to seek religious freedom after having lived briefly in the Netherlands. (*p. 389*)

Pizarro, Francisco (1475?–1541) Spanish explorer who led the conquest of the **Inca** Empire of Peru in 1531–1533. (*p. 358*)

Planck, Max (1858–1947) German physicist who developed quantum theory and was awarded the Nobel Prize for physics in 1918. (*p. 558*)

polis The Greek term for a **city-state**, an urban center and the agricultural territory under its control. It was the characteristic form of political organization in southern and central Greece in the Archaic and Classical periods. Of the hundreds of city-states settled by Greeks, some were oligarchic, others democratic, depending on the powers delegated to the Council and the Assembly. (*p. 96*)

popular culture Entertainment spread by mass communications and enjoying wide appeal. (*p. 656*)

positivism A philosophy developed by the French count of Saint-Simon. Positivists believed that social and economic problems could be solved by the application of the scientific method, leading to continuous progress. Their ideas became popular in France and Latin America in the nineteenth century. (*p. 475*)

postmodernism Post-World War II intellectual movement and cultural attitude focusing on cultural pluralism and release from the confines and ideology of Western high culture. (*p. 658*)

Potosí Located in Bolivia, one of the richest silver mining centers and most populous cities in colonial Spanish America. (*p. 384*)

printing press A mechanical device for transferring text or graphics from a woodblock or type to paper using ink. Presses using movable type first appeared in Europe in about 1450. See also **movable type.** (*p. 336*)

Protestant Reformation Religious reform movement within the Latin Christian Church beginning in 1519. It resulted in the "protesters" forming several new Christian denominations, including the Lutheran and Reformed Churches and the Church of England. (*p. 366*)

proxy wars During the **Cold War,** local or regional wars in which the superpowers armed, trained, and financed the combatants. (*p. 624*)

Ptolemies The Macedonian dynasty, descended from one of Alexander the Great's officers, that ruled Egypt for three centuries (323–30 B.C.E.). From their capital at Alexandria, the Ptolemies took over the governing system created by Egyptian pharaohs. (*p. 106*)

Puritans English Protestant dissenters who believed that God predestined souls to heaven or hell before birth. They founded Massachusetts Bay Colony in 1629. (*p. 389*)

pyramid A large, triangular stone monument, used in Egypt and Nubia as a burial place for the king. The largest pyramids, erected during the Old Kingdom near Memphis, reflect the Egyptian belief that the proper burial of the divine ruler would guarantee the continued prosperity of the land. (See also **ma'at.**) (*p. 24*)

Qin A people and state in the Wei Valley of eastern China that conquered rival states and created the first Chinese empire (221–206 B.C.E.). The Qin ruler, **Shi Huangdi,** standardized many features of Chinese society and ruthlessly marshalled subjects for military and construction projects, engendering hostility that led to the fall of his dynasty shortly after his death. The Qin framework was largely taken over by the succeeding **Han** Empire. (*p. 140*)

Qing Empire Empire established in China by Manchus who overthrew the **Ming Empire** in 1644. At various times the Qing also controlled Manchuria, Mongolia, Turkestan, and Tibet. The last Qing emperor was overthrown in 1911. (*p. 433*)

Quran Book composed of divine revelations made to the Prophet Muhammad between ca. 610 and his death in 632; the sacred text of the religion of **Islam.** (*p. 179*)

railroads Networks of iron (later steel) rails on which steam (later electric or diesel) locomotives pulled long trains at high speeds. The first railroads were built in England in the 1830s. Their success caused a railroad-building boom throughout the world that lasted well into the twentieth century. (*p. 506*)

Rajputs Members of a mainly Hindu warrior caste from northwest India. The Mughal emperors drew most of their Hindu officials from this caste, and **Akbar I** married a Rajput princess. (*p. 417*)

Ramesses II A long-lived ruler of New Kingdom Egypt (r. 1290–1224 B.C.E.). He reached an accommodation with the **Hittites** of Anatolia after a standoff in battle at Kadesh in Syria. (*p. 48*)

Rashid al-Din (d. 1318) Adviser to the **Il-khan** ruler Ghazan, who converted to Islam on Rashid's advice. (*p. 270*)

recaptives Africans rescued by Britain's Royal Navy from the illegal slave trade of the nineteenth century and restored to free status. (*p. 487*)

reconquest of Iberia Beginning in the eleventh century, military campaigns by various Iberian Christian states to recapture territory taken by Muslims. In 1492 the last Muslim ruler was defeated, and Spain and Portugal emerged as united kingdoms. (*p. 340*)

Renaissance (European) A period of intense artistic and intellectual activity, said to be a "rebirth" of Greco-Roman culture. Usually divided into an Italian Renaissance, from roughly the mid-fourteenth to mid-fifteenth century, and a Northern (trans-Alpine) Renaissance, from roughly the early fifteenth to early seventeenth century. (*pp. 334, 365*)

Revolutions of 1848 Democratic and nationalist revolutions in Europe. The monarchy in France was overthrown. In Germany, Austria, Italy, and Hungary the revolutions failed. (*p. 454*)

Rhodes, Cecil (1853–1902) British entrepreneur and politician involved in the expansion of the British Empire from South Africa into Central Africa. The colonies of Southern Rhodesia (now Zimbabwe) and Northern Rhodesia (now Zambia) were named after him. (*p. 530*)

Roman Principate A term characterizing Roman government in the first three centuries C.E., based on the ambiguous title *princeps* ("first citizen") adopted by **Augustus** to conceal his military dictatorship. (*p. 129*)

Roman Republic The period from 507 to 31 B.C.E., during which Rome was largely governed by the aristocratic **Roman Senate.** (*p. 124*)

Roman Senate A council whose members were the heads of wealthy, landowning families. Originally an advisory body to the early kings, in the era of the **Roman Republic** the Senate effectively governed the Roman state. Under Senate leadership, Rome conquered an empire in the lands surrounding the Mediterranean Sea. In the first century B.C.E. quarrels among powerful and ambitious senators and failure to

address social and economic problems led to civil wars and the emergence of the rule of the emperors. (*p. 124*)

Romanization The process by which the Latin language and Roman culture became dominant in the western provinces of the Roman Empire. The Roman government did not actively seek to Romanize the subject peoples, but indigenous peoples in the provinces often chose to Romanize for political and economic reasons. (*p. 133*)

Romanov, Mikhail (1590–1645) Russian tsar (r. 1613–1645). A member of the Russian aristocracy, he became tsar after the old line of Muscovite rulers was deposed. (*p. 428*)

Royal African Company A trading company chartered by the English government in 1672 to conduct its merchants' trade on the Atlantic coast of Africa. (*p. 397*)

sacrifice A gift given to a deity, often with the aim of creating a relationship, gaining favor, and obligating the god to provide some benefit to the sacrificer, sometimes in order to sustain the deity and thereby guarantee the continuing vitality of the natural world. The object devoted to the deity could be as simple as a cup of wine poured on the ground, a live animal slain on the altar, or, in the most extreme case, the ritual killing of a human being. (*p. 98*)

Safavid Empire Iranian kingdom (1502–1722) established by Ismail Safavi, who declared Iran a Shi'ite state. (*p. 413*)

Sahel Belt south of the Sahara; literally "coastland" in Arabic. (*p. 162*)

samurai Literally "those who serve," the hereditary military elite of the **Tokugawa Shogunate.** (*p. 437*)

Sandinistas Members of a leftist coalition that overthrew the Nicaraguan dictatorship of Anastasia Somoza in 1979 and attempted to install a socialist economy. The United States financed armed opposition by the Contras. The Sandinistas lost national elections in 1990. (*p. 626*)

Sasanid Empire Iranian empire, established ca. 226, with a capital in Ctesiphon, Mesopotamia. The Sasanid emperors established **Zoroastrianism** as the state religion. Muslim Arab armies overthrew the empire ca. 640. (*p. 173*)

satrap The governor of a province in the Achaemenid Persian Empire, often a relative of the king. (*p. 90*)

savanna Tropical or subtropical grassland, either treeless or with occasional clumps of trees. Most extensive in **sub-Saharan Africa** but also present in South America. (*p. 165*)

schism A formal split within a religious community. See **Great Western Schism.** (*p. 204*)

scholasticism A philosophical and theological system, associated with Thomas Aquinas, devised to reconcile Aristotelian philosophy and Roman Catholic theology in the thirteenth century. (*p. 334*)

Scientific Revolution The intellectual movement in Europe, initially associated with planetary motion and other aspects of physics, that by the seventeenth century had laid the groundwork for modern science. (*p. 378*)

"scramble" for Africa Sudden wave of conquests in Africa by European powers in the 1880s and 1890s. Britain obtained most of eastern Africa, France most of northwestern Africa. Other countries (Germany, Belgium, Portugal, Italy, and Spain) acquired lesser amounts. (*p. 528*)

scribe In many ancient societies, a professional position reserved for men who had undergone the lengthy training required to be able to read and write using **cuneiform, hieroglyphics,** or other early writing systems. (*p. 18*)

seasoning An often difficult period of adjustment to new climates, disease environments, and work routines, such as that experienced by slaves newly arrived in the Americas. (*p. 395*)

Selassie, Haile (1892–1975) Emperor of Ethiopia (r. 1930–1974) and symbol of African independence. He fought the Italian invasion of his country in 1935 and regained his throne during World War II, when British forces expelled the Italians. He ruled **Ethiopia** as a traditional **autocracy** until he was overthrown in 1974. (*p. 588*)

Semitic Family of related languages spoken across parts of western Asia and northern Africa. In antiquity these languages included Hebrew, Aramaic, and Phoenician. The most widespread modern language is Arabic. (*p. 15*)

"separate spheres" Nineteenth-century idea in Western societies that men and women, especially of the middle class, should have clearly differentiated roles in society: women as wives, mothers, and homemakers; men as breadwinners and participants in business and politics. (*p. 510*)

sepoy A soldier in South Asia, especially in the service of the British. (*p. 488*)

Sepoy Rebellion The revolt of Indian soldiers in 1857 against certain practices that violated religious customs; also known as the Sepoy Mutiny. (*p. 491*)

serf In medieval Europe, an agricultural laborer legally bound to a lord's property and obligated to perform set services for the lord. In Russia some serfs worked as artisans and in factories; serfdom was not abolished there until 1861. (*pp. 200, 431*)

shaft graves A term used for the burial sites of elite members of Mycenaean Greek society in the mid-second millennium B.C.E. At the bottom of deep shafts lined with stone slabs, the bodies were laid out along with gold and bronze jewelry, implements, weapons, and masks. (*p. 53*)

Shah Abbas I (1571–1629) Shah of Iran (r. 1587–1629). The most illustrious ruler of the **Safavid Empire,** he moved the imperial capital to Isfahan in 1598, where he erected many palaces, mosques, and public buildings. (*p. 414*)

Shamanism The practice of identifying special individuals (shamans) who will interact with spirits for the benefit of the community. Characteristic of the Korean kingdoms of the early medieval period and of early societies of Central Asia. (*p. 232*)

Shang The dominant people in the earliest Chinese dynasty for which we have written records (ca. 1750–1027 B.C.E.). Ancestor worship, divination by means of oracle bones, and the use of bronze vessels for ritual purposes were major elements of Shang culture. (*p. 40*)

Shi Huangdi Founder of the short-lived **Qin** dynasty and creator of the Chinese Empire (r. 221–210 B.C.E.). His tomb, with its army of life-size terracotta soldiers, has been partially excavated. (*p. 140*)

Shi'ites Muslims belonging to the branch of Islam believing that God vests leadership of the community in a descendant of Muhammad's son-in-law Ali. Shi'ism is the state religion of Iran. (See also **Sunnis.**) (*pp. 172, 413*)

Siberia The extreme northeastern sector of Asia, including the Kamchatka Peninsula and the present Russian coast of the Arctic Ocean, the Bering Strait, and the Sea of Okhotsk. (*p. 427*)

Silk Road Caravan routes connecting China and the Middle East across Central Asia and Iran. (*p. 151*)

"small tradition" Historians' term for a localized, usually non-literate, set of customs and beliefs adhered to by a single society, often in conjunction with a **"great tradition."** (*p. 165*)

socialism A political ideology that originated in Europe in the 1830s. Socialists advocated government protection of workers from exploitation by property owners and government ownership of industries. This ideology led to the founding of socialist or labor parties throughout Europe in the second half of the nineteenth century. (See also **Marx, Karl.**) (*p. 509*)

Socrates Athenian philosopher (ca. 470–399 B.C.E.) who shifted the emphasis of philosophical investigation from questions of natural science to ethics and human behavior. He attracted young disciples from elite families but made enemies by revealing the ignorance and pretensions of others, culminating in his trial and execution by the Athenian state. (*p. 103*)

Sokoto Caliphate A large Muslim state founded in 1809 in what is now northern Nigeria. (*p. 482*)

Solidarity Polish trade union created in 1980 to protest working conditions and political repression. It began the nationalist opposition to communist rule that led in 1989 to the fall of communism in eastern Europe. (*p. 631*)

Song Empire Empire in central and southern China (960–1126) while the Liao people controlled the north. Empire in southern China (1127–1279; the "Southern Song") while the Jin people controlled the north.

Distinguished for its advances in technology, medicine, astronomy, and mathematics. (*p. 226*)

Srivijaya A state based on the Indonesian island of Sumatra, between the seventh and eleventh centuries C.E. (See also **theater-state**.) (*p. 158*)

Stalin, Joseph (1879–1953) Bolshevik revolutionary, head of the Soviet Communist Party after 1924, and dictator of the Soviet Union from 1928 to 1953. Used **Five-Year Plans** to increase industrial production and terror to crush all opposition. (*p. 564*)

Stalingrad City in Russia, site of a Red Army victory over the German army in 1942–1943. The Battle of Stalingrad was the turning point in the war between Germany and the Soviet Union. Today Volgograd. (*p. 574*)

steam engine A machine that turns the energy released by burning fuel into motion. Thomas Newcomen built the first crude but workable steam engine in 1712. **James Watt** improved his device in the 1760s and 1770s. Steam power was later applied to moving machinery in factories and to powering ships and locomotives. (*p. 469*)

steel A form of iron that is both durable and flexible. It was first mass-produced in the 1860s and quickly became the most widely used metal in construction, machinery, and railroad equipment. (*p. 505*)

steppes Treeless plains, especially the high, flat expanses of northern Eurasia, which usually have little rain and are covered with coarse grass. Living on the steppes promoted the breeding of horses and the development of military skills that were essential to the rise of the Mongol Empire. (*pp. 165, 264*)

stirrup Device for securing a horseman's feet, enabling him to wield weapons more effectively. First evidence of the use of stirrups was among the Kushan people of northern Afghanistan in approximately the first century C.E. (*p. 155*)

stock exchange A place where shares in business enterprises are bought and sold. (*p. 375*)

Stone Age The historical period characterized by the production of tools from stone and other nonmetallic substances. It was followed in some places by the Bronze Age and more generally by the Iron Age. (*p. 7*)

submarine telegraph cables Insulated copper cables laid along the bottom of a sea or ocean for telegraphic communication. The first short cable was laid across the English Channel in 1851; the first successful transatlantic cable was laid in 1866. (See also **electric telegraph**.) (*p. 506*)

sub-Saharan Africa Portion of the African continent lying south of the Sahara. (*p. 164*)

Suez Canal Ship canal dug across the isthmus of Suez in Egypt, designed by Ferdinand de Lesseps. It opened to shipping in 1869 and shortened the sea voyage between Europe and Asia. Its strategic importance led to the British occupation of Egypt in 1882. (*p. 523*)

Suleiman the Magnificent (1494–1566) The most illustrious sultan of the **Ottoman Empire** (r. 1520–1566); also known as Suleiman Kanuni, "The Lawgiver." He significantly expanded the empire in the Balkans and eastern Mediterranean. (*p. 407*)

Sumerians The people who dominated southern Mesopotamia through the end of the third millennium B.C.E. They developed many fundamental elements of Mesopotamian culture—such as irrigation technology, **cuneiform,** and religious conceptions—taken over by their **Semitic** successors. (*p. 14*)

Sunnis Muslims belonging to branch of Islam believing that the community should select its own leadership. The majority religion in most Islamic countries. (See also **Shi'ites**.) (*p. 172*)

Sun Yat-sen (1867–1925) Chinese nationalist revolutionary, founder and leader of the **Guomindang** until his death. He attempted to create a liberal democratic political movement in China but was thwarted by military leaders. (*p. 554*)

Swahili Bantu language with Arabic loanwords spoken in coastal regions of East Africa. (*p. 421*)

Swahili Coast East African shores of the Indian Ocean between the Horn of Africa and the Zambezi River; from the Arabic *sawahil,* meaning "shores." (*p. 314*)

Taiping Rebellion (1853–1864) A Christian-inspired rural rebellion that threatened to topple the **Qing Empire**. (*p. 497*)

Tamil kingdoms The kingdoms of southern India, inhabited primarily by speakers of Dravidian languages, which developed in partial isolation, and somewhat differently, from the Aryan north. Elements of Tamil religious beliefs were merged into the Hindu synthesis. (*p. 117*)

Tang Empire Empire unifying China and part of Central Asia, founded 618 and ended 907. The Tang emperors ruled from their capital, Chang'an. (*p. 219*)

tax farming A government's use of private collectors to collect taxes. Individuals or corporations contract with the government to collect a fixed amount for the government and are permitted to keep as profit everything they collect over that amount. (*p. 271*)

technology transfer The communication of specific plans, designs, or educational programs necessary for the use of new technologies from one society or class to another. (*p. 293*)

Tenochtitlan Capital of the Aztec Empire, located on an island in Lake Texcoco. Its population was about 150,000 on the eve of Spanish conquest. Mexico City was constructed on its ruins. (*p. 245*)

Teotihuacan A powerful **city-state** in central Mexico (100–75 C.E.). Its population was about 150,000 at its peak in 600. (*p. 239*)

Terrorism Political belief that extreme and seemingly random violence will destabilize a government and permit the terrorists to gain political advantage. Though an old technique, terrorism gained prominence in the late twentieth century with the growth of worldwide mass media that, through their news coverage, amplified public fears of terrorist acts. (*p. 650*)

theater-state Historians' term for a state that acquires prestige and power by developing attractive cultural forms and staging elaborate public ceremonies (as well as redistributing valuable resources) to attract and bind subjects to the center. Examples include the **Gupta Empire** in India and **Srivijaya** in Southeast Asia. (*pp. 117, 160*)

Thebes Capital city of Egypt and home of the ruling dynasties during the Middle and New Kingdoms. Amon, patron deity of Thebes, became one of the chief gods of Egypt. Monarchs were buried across the river in the Valley of the Kings. (*p. 24*)

Theravada Buddhism "Way of the Elders" branch of Buddhism followed in Sri Lanka and much of Southeast Asia. Theravada remains close to the original principles set forth by the **Buddha;** it downplays the importance of gods and emphasizes austerity and the individual's search for enlightenment. (*p. 113*)

third-century crisis Historians' term for the political, military, and economic turmoil that beset the Roman Empire during much of the third century C.E.: frequent changes of ruler, civil wars, barbarian invasions, decline of urban centers, and near-destruction of long-distance commerce and the monetary economy. After 284 C.E. Diocletian restored order by making fundamental changes. (*p. 135*)

Third World Term applied to a group of developing countries who professed nonalignment during the **Cold War.** (*p. 617*)

three-field system A rotational system for agriculture in which one field grows grain, one grows legumes, and one lies fallow. It gradually replaced the two-field system in medieval Europe. (*p. 324*)

Tiananmen Square Site in Beijing where Chinese students and workers gathered to demand greater political openness in 1989. The demonstration was crushed by Chinese military with great loss of life. (*p. 630*)

Timbuktu City on the Niger River in the modern country of Mali. It was founded by the Tuareg as a seasonal camp sometime after 1000. As part of the **Mali** empire, Timbuktu became a major terminus of the trans-Saharan trade and a center of Islamic learning. (*p. 318*)

Timur (1336–1405) Member of a prominent family of the Mongols' Jagadai Khanate, Timur through conquest gained control over much of Central Asia and Iran. His descendants, the Timurids, maintained his empire for nearly a century and founded the **Mughal Empire** in India. (*p. 271*)

Tiwanaku Name of capital city and empire centered on the region near Lake Titicaca in modern Bolivia (375–1000 C.E.). (*p. 253*)

Tokugawa Shogunate (1600–1868) The last of the three shogunates of Japan. (*p. 437*)

Toltecs Powerful postclassic empire in central Mexico (900–1168 C.E.). It influenced much of Mesoamerica. Aztecs claimed ties to this earlier civilization. (*p. 244*)

tophet A cemetery containing burials of young children, possibly sacrificed to the gods in times of crisis, found at **Carthage** and other **Phoenician** settlements in the western Mediterranean. (*p. 83*)

trans-Saharan caravan routes Trading network linking North Africa with **sub-Saharan Africa** across the Sahara. (*p. 160*)

Treaty of Nanking (1842) The treaty that concluded the **Opium War**. It awarded Britain a large indemnity from the **Qing Empire,** denied the Qing government tariff control over some of its own borders, opened additional ports of residence to Britons, and ceded the island of Hong Kong to Britain. (*p. 497*)

Treaty of Versailles (1919) The treaty imposed on Germany by France, Great Britain, the United States, and other Allied Powers after World War I. It was resented by many Germans. (*p. 550*)

treaty ports Cities opened to foreign residents as a result of the forced treaties between the **Qing Empire** and foreign signatories. In the treaty ports, foreigners enjoyed extraterritoriality. (*p. 497*)

tributary system A system in which, from the time of the **Han** Empire, countries in East and Southeast Asia not under the direct control of empires based in China nevertheless enrolled as tributary states, acknowledging the superiority of the emperors in China in exchange for trading rights or strategic alliances. (*p. 222*)

tribute system A system in which defeated peoples were forced to pay a tax in the form of goods and labor. This forced transfer of food, cloth, and other goods subsidized the development of large cities. An important component of the Aztec and Inca economies. (*p. 246*)

trireme Greek and Phoenician warship of the fifth and fourth centuries B.C.E. It was sleek and light, powered by 170 oars arranged in three vertical tiers. Manned by skilled sailors, it was capable of short bursts of speed and complex maneuvers. (*p. 102*)

tropical rain forest High-precipitation forest zones of the Americas, Africa, and Asia lying between the Tropic of Cancer and the Tropic of Capricorn. (*p. 165*)

tropics Equatorial region between the Tropic of Cancer and the Tropic of Capricorn. It is characterized by generally warm or hot temperatures year-round, though much variation exists due to altitude and other factors. Temperate zones north and south of the tropics generally have a winter season. (*p. 303*)

Troy Site in northwest Anatolia, overlooking the Hellespont strait, where archaeologists have excavated a series of Bronze Age cities. One of these may have been destroyed by Greeks ca. 1200 B.C.E., as reported in Homer's epic poems. (*p. 53*)

Truman Doctrine Foreign policy initiated by U.S. president Harry Truman in 1947. It offered military aid to help Turkey and Greece resist Soviet military pressure and subversion. (*p. 614*)

tsar (czar) From Latin *caesar,* this Russian title for a monarch was first used in reference to a Russian ruler by Ivan III (r. 1462–1505). (*pp. 276, 428*)

tyrant Greek term used for someone who seized and held power in violation of normal procedures. Tyrants appeared in many Greek **city-states** in the seventh and sixth centuries B.C.E. (*p. 98*)

Uigurs A Turkic-speaking people who controlled their own centralized empire from 744 to 840 in Mongolia and Central Asia. (*p. 225*)

ulama Muslim religious scholars. From the ninth century onward, the primary interpreters of Islamic law and the social core of Muslim urban societies. (*p. 185*)

Umayyad Caliphate First hereditary dynasty of Muslim caliphs (661 to 750). From their capital at Damascus, the Umayyads ruled an empire that extended from Spain to India. Overthrown by the **Abbasid Caliphate.** (*p. 180*)

umma The community of all Muslims. A major innovation against the background of seventh-century Arabia, where traditionally kinship rather than faith had determined membership in a community. (*p. 178*)

United Nations International organization founded in 1945 to promote world peace and cooperation. It replaced the **League of Nations**. (*p. 611*)

Universal Declaration of Human Rights A 1948 United Nations covenant binding signatory nations to the observance of specified rights. (*p. 652*)

universities Degree-granting institutions of higher learning. Those that appeared in Latin West from about 1200 onward became the model of all modern universities. (*p. 334*)

Urdu A Persian-influenced literary form of Hindi written in Arabic characters and used as a literary language since the 1300s. (*p. 318*)

utopian socialism A philosophy introduced by the Frenchman Charles Fourier in the early nineteenth century. Utopian socialists hoped to create humane alternatives to industrial capitalism by building self-sustaining communities whose inhabitants would work cooperatively. (See also **socialism.**) (*p. 475*)

Vargas, Getulio (1883–1954) Dictator of Brazil from 1930 to 1945 and from 1951 to 1954. Defeated in the presidential election of 1930, he overthrew the government and created Estado Novo ("New State"), a dictatorship that emphasized industrialization and helped the urban poor but did little to alleviate the problems of the peasants. (*p. 598*)

variolation The technique of enhancing immunity by exposing patients to dried mucous taken from those already infected. (*p. 434*)

varna/jati Two categories of social identity in Indian history. *Varnas* are the four major social divisions: the *Brahmin* priest class, the *Ksatriya* warrior/administrator class, the *Vaishya* merchant/farmer class, and the *Shudra* laborer class. Within each *varna* are many *jatis,* regional groups of people who have a common occupational sphere, and who marry, eat, and generally interact with other members of their group. (*pp. 110–111*)

vassal In medieval Europe, a sworn supporter of a king or lord committed to rendering specified military service to that king or lord. (*p. 200*)

Vedas Early Indian sacred "knowledge"—the literal meaning of the term—long preserved and communicated orally by Brahmin priests and eventually written down. These religious texts, including the thousand poetic hymns to various deities contained in the Rig Veda, are our main source of information about the Vedic period (ca. 1500–500 B.C.E.). (*p. 110*)

Victorian Age The reign of Queen Victoria of Great Britain (r. 1837–1901). The term is also used to describe late-nineteenth-century society, with its rigid moral standards and sharply differentiated roles for men and women and for middle-class and working-class people. (See also **"separate spheres."**) (*p. 510*)

Vietnam War (1954–1975) Conflict pitting North Vietnam and South Vietnamese communist guerrillas against the South Vietnamese government, aided after 1961 by the United States. (*p. 616*)

Villa, Francisco "Pancho" (1878–1923) A popular leader during the Mexican Revolution. An outlaw in his youth, when the revolution started, he formed a cavalry army in the north of Mexico and fought for the rights of the landless in collaboration with **Emiliano Zapata.** He was assassinated in 1923. (See also **Zapata, Emiliano.**) (*p. 595*)

Wari Andean civilization culturally linked to **Tiwanaku,** perhaps beginning as colony of Tiwanaku. (*p. 252*)

Warsaw Pact The 1955 treaty binding the Soviet Union and countries of eastern Europe in an alliance against the **North Atlantic Treaty Organization.** (*p. 614*)

Washington, George (1732–1799) Military commander of the American Revolution. He was the first elected president of the United States (1789–1799). (*p. 447*)

water wheel A mechanism that harnesses the energy in flowing water to grind grain or to power machinery. It was used in many parts of the world but was especially common in Europe from 1200 to 1900. (*p. 328*)

Watt, James (1736–1819) Scot who invented the condenser and other improvements that made the **steam**

engine a practical source of power for industry and transportation. The watt, an electrical measurement, is named after him. (*p. 469*)

Wedgwood, Josiah (1730–1795) English industrialist whose pottery works were the first to produce fine-quality pottery by industrial methods. (*p. 466*)

Western Front A line of trenches and fortifications in World War I that stretched without a break from Switzerland to the North Sea. Scene of most of the fighting between Germany, on the one hand, and France and Britain, on the other. (*p. 545*)

Wilson, Woodrow (1856–1924) President of the United States (1913–1921) and the leading figure at the Paris Peace Conference of 1919. He was unable to persuade the U.S. Congress to ratify the **Treaty of Versailles** or join the **League of Nations.** (*p. 549*)

witch-hunt The pursuit of people suspected of witchcraft. (*p. 378*)

Women's Rights Convention An 1848 gathering of women angered by their exclusion from an international antislavery meeting. They met at Seneca Falls, New York, to discuss women's rights. (*p. 461*)

World Bank A specialized agency of the United Nations that makes loans to countries for economic development, trade promotion, and debt consolidation. Its former name is the International Bank for Reconstruction and Development. (*p. 611*)

World Trade Organization (WTO) An international body established in 1995 to foster and bring order to international trade. (*p. 650*)

Xiongnu A confederation of nomadic peoples living beyond the northwest frontier of ancient China. Chinese rulers tried a variety of defenses and stratagems to ward off these "barbarians," as they called them, and succeeded in dispersing the Xiongnu in the first century C.E. (*p. 143*)

Yi kingdom (1392–1910) The Yi dynasty ruled Korea from the fall of the **Koryo** kingdom to the colonization of Korea by Japan. (*p. 295*)

yin/yang In Chinese belief, complementary factors that help to maintain the equilibrium of the world. Yin is associated with masculine, light, and active qualities; yang with feminine, dark, and passive qualities. (*p. 45*)

Yongle Reign period of Zhu Di (1360–1424), the third emperor of the **Ming Empire** (r. 1403–1424). He sponsored the building of the **Forbidden City,** a huge encyclopedia project, the expeditions of **Zheng He,** and the reopening of China's borders to trade and travel. (*p. 289*)

Yuan Empire (1271–1368) Empire created in China and Siberia by **Khubilai Khan.** (*p. 283*)

Yuan Shikai (1859–1916) Chinese general and first president of the Chinese Republic (1912–1916). He stood in the way of the democratic movement led by **Sun Yat-sen.** (*p. 554*)

Zapata, Emiliano (1879–1919) Revolutionary and leader of peasants in the Mexican Revolution. He mobilized landless peasants in south-central Mexico to seize and divide the lands of the wealthy. Though successful for a time, he was ultimately defeated and assassinated. (*p. 594*)

Zen The Japanese word for a branch of **Mahayana Buddhism** based on highly disciplined meditation. It is known in Sanskrit as *dhyana,* in Chinese as *chan,* and in Korean as *son.* (*p. 229*)

Zheng He (1371–1433) An imperial eunuch and Muslim, entrusted by the Ming emperor **Yongle** with a series of state voyages that took his gigantic ships through the Indian Ocean, from Southeast Asia to Africa. (*p. 290*)

Zhou The people and dynasty that took over the dominant position in north China from the **Shang** and created the concept of the **Mandate of Heaven** to justify their rule. The Zhou era, particularly the vigorous early period (1027–771 B.C.E.), was remembered in Chinese tradition as a time of benevolent rule. In the later Zhou period (771–221 B.C.E.), centralized control broke down, and warfare among many small states became frequent. (*p. 42*)

ziggurat A massive pyramidal stepped tower made of mud-bricks. It is associated with religious complexes in ancient Mesopotamian cities, but its function is unknown. (*p. 19*)

Zoroastrianism A religion originating in ancient Iran with the prophet Zoroaster. It centered on a single benevolent deity—Ahuramazda. Emphasizing truthtelling, purity, and reverence for nature, the religion demanded that humans choose sides in the struggle between good and evil. The religion of the Achaemenid and Sasanid Persians, Zoroastrianism may have influenced Judaism, Christianity, and other faiths. (*p. 93*)

Zulu A people of modern South Africa whom King Shaka united beginning in 1818. (*p. 482*)

INDEX